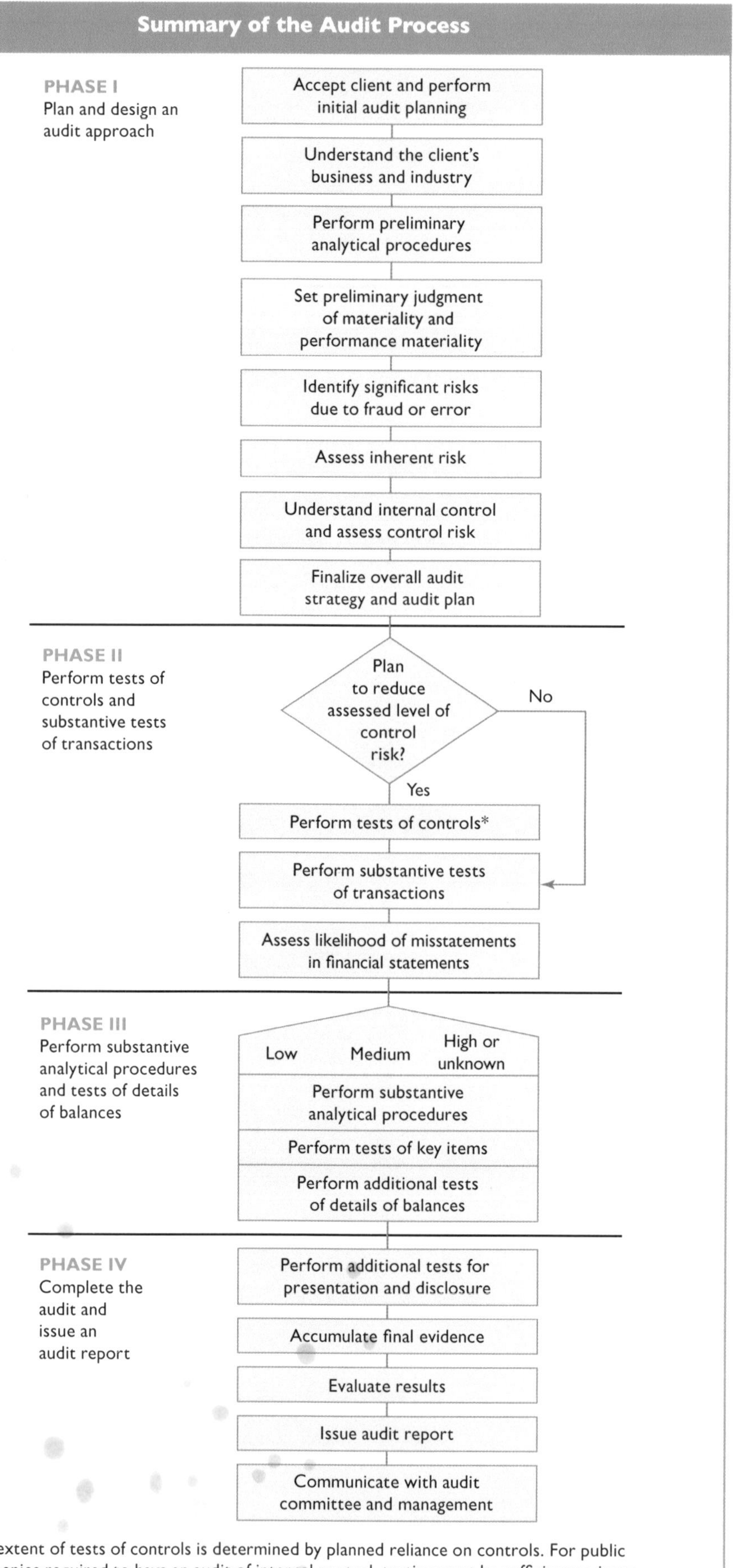
Summary of the Audit Process
PHASE I
Plan and design an audit approach
Accept client and perform initial audit planning
Understand the client's business and industry
Perform preliminary analytical procedures
Set preliminary judgment of materiality and performance materiality
Identify significant risks due to fraud or error
Assess inherent risk
Understand internal control and assess control risk
Finalize overall audit strategy and audit plan
PHASE II
Perform tests of controls and substantive tests of transactions
Plan to reduce assessed level of control risk?
No
Yes
Perform tests of controls*
Perform substantive tests of transactions
Assess likelihood of misstatements in financial statements
PHASE III
Perform substantive analytical procedures and tests of details of balances
Low
Medium
High or unknown
Perform substantive analytical procedures
Perform tests of key items
Perform additional tests of details of balances
PHASE IV
Complete the audit and issue an audit report
Perform additional tests for presentation and disclosure
Accumulate final evidence
Evaluate results
Issue audit report
Communicate with audit committee and management

* The extent of tests of controls is determined by planned reliance on controls. For public companies required to have an audit of internal control, testing must be sufficient to issue an opinion on internal control over financial reporting.

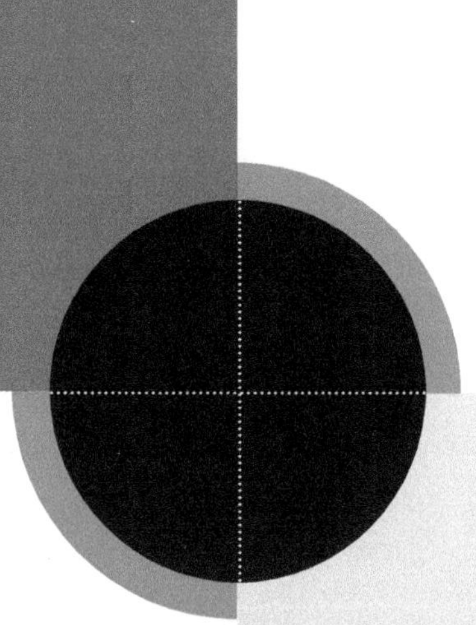

AUDITING AND ASSURANCE SERVICES

AN INTEGRATED APPROACH

SIXTEENTH EDITION

ALVIN A. ARENS
Former PricewaterhouseCoopers
Emeritus Professor
Michigan State University

RANDAL J. ELDER
Syracuse University
Professor

MARK S. BEASLEY
North Carolina State University
Deloitte Professor of Enterprise Risk Management

CHRIS E. HOGAN
Michigan State University
Professor

PEARSON

Boston Columbus Indianapolis New York San Francisco Amsterdam
Cape Town Dubai London Madrid Milan Munich Paris Montréal Toronto
Delhi Mexico City São Paulo Sydney Hong Kong Seoul Singapore Taipei Tokyo

Vice President, Business Publishing: Donna Battista
Editor-in-Chief: Adrienne D'Ambrosio
Acquisitions Editor: Ellen Geary
Editorial Assistant: Christine Donovan
Vice President, Product Marketing: Maggie Moylan
Director of Marketing, Digital Services and Products: Jeanette Koskinas
Executive Field Marketing Manager: Adam Goldstein
Field Marketing Manager: Natalie Wagner
Product Marketing Assistant: Jessica Quazza
Team Lead, Program Management: Ashley Santora
Program Manager: Daniel Petrino
Team Lead, Project Management: Jeff Holcomb
Project Manager: Roberta Sherman
Operations Specialist: Carol Melville
Creative Director: Blair Brown
Art Director: Jon Boylan
Vice President, Director of Digital Strategy and Assessment: Paul Gentile
Manager of Learning Applications: Paul DeLuca
Director, Digital Studio: Sacha Laustsen
Digital Studio Manager: Diane Lombardo
Digital Editor: Sarah Peterson
Digital Studio Project Manager: Andra Skaalrud
Digital Studio Project Manager: Alana Coles
Digital Studio Project Manager: Robin Lazrus
Digital Content Team Lead: Noel Lotz
Digital Content Project Lead: Martha LaChance
Full-Service Project Management and Composition: Integra Software Services
Interior Designer: Integra Software Services
Cover Designer: Lumina Datamatics
Cover Photo: © Rawpixel/Shutterstock
Printer/Binder: LSC Communications
Cover Printer: LSC Communications

Acknowledgments of third-party content appear on the appropriate page within the text and on p. 856 which constitutes an extension of this copyright page.

Library of Congress Cataloging-in-Publication Data

Arens, Alvin A.
Auditing and assurance services / Alvin A. Arens, Randal J. Elder, Mark S. Beasley, Chris Hogan. — 16 Edition.
pages cm
Revised edition of the authors' Auditing and assurance services, 2014.
ISBN 978-0-13-406736-0 — ISBN 0-13-406582-4
1. Auditing. I. Elder, Randal J. II. Beasley, Mark S. III. Arens, Alvin A. Auditing, an integrated approach. IV. Title.
HF5667.A69 2015
657'.45—dc23

2015030071

ISBN 10: 0-13-406582-4
ISBN 13: 978-0-13-406582-3

CONTINUING THE LEGACY OF ALVIN A. ARENS

November 24, 1935 – December 6, 2010

ALVIN A. ARENS: The author team of Randy Elder, Mark Beasley, and newest member of the author team, Chris Hogan, are pleased to continue the outstanding legacy of our book's founding author, Al Arens, in this 16th edition of *Auditing and Assurance Services: An Integrated Approach*. As was done for the 15th edition, we again dedicate this new edition to Al's memory.

Randy and Mark joined Al as coauthors on this textbook in the 8th edition, and have been honored to continue Al's leadership in helping shape classroom instruction and student learning about auditing concepts and their practical implementation around the world. Since the first edition was published, this textbook has impacted audit education for over 30 years in the U.S. and globally, including seven different language translations. Al's leadership at national and international levels and his commitment to expanding knowledge through the development of educational materials, including this textbook, continue to inspire us as we strive to advance his legacy for future generations of auditing professionals.

Al was the PricewaterhouseCoopers Auditing Professor and member of the Accounting & Information Systems faculty in the Eli Broad College of Business at Michigan State University from 1968 through 2007. Thus, we are especially pleased to have Chris Hogan, Professor at Michigan State University, join the author team on this edition, continuing the Michigan State connection started by Al.

Among his many honors, Al was selected as one of five national auditing educators to hold a Price Waterhouse Auditing professorship, was honored as AICPA Educator of the Year, served on the AICPA Auditing Standards Board, and was President of the American Accounting Association. Al taught accounting, mainly auditing, with a passion that is legendary. He had a heart for sharing his knowledge of auditing with students throughout his career.

This 16th edition continues his outstanding legacy in audit education.

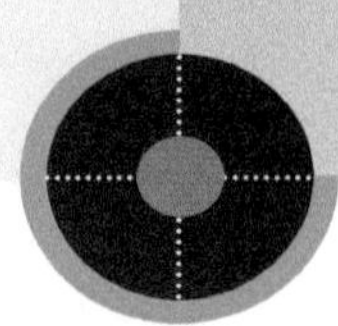

ABOUT THE AUTHORS

ALVIN A. ARENS

Al Arens, founding author of this textbook, was the PricewaterhouseCoopers Professor of Accounting Emeritus at Michigan State University. In addition to writing books on auditing, he was a coauthor of computerized accounting supplements and he was actively involved in the continuing education of practitioners with local and regional CPA firms. Al was a past president of the American Accounting Association and a former member of the AICPA Auditing Standards Board. He practiced public accounting with both a local CPA firm and the predecessor firm to Ernst & Young. He received many awards including the AAA Auditing Section Outstanding Educator award, the AICPA Outstanding Educator award, the national Beta Alpha Psi Professor of the Year award, and many teaching and other awards at Michigan State.

RANDAL J. ELDER

Randy Elder, who has served as a coauthor of this textbook since the 8th edition, is Professor of Accounting at Syracuse University. He teaches undergraduate and graduate auditing courses, and has received several teaching awards. His research focuses on audit quality and current audit firm practices and he served as the team leader for the American Accounting Association Auditing Section PCAOB research synthesis teams on audit confirmations and audit sampling. He has extensive public accounting experience with a large regional CPA firm, frequently teaches continuing education for a large international CPA firm, and is a member of the AICPA and Michigan Association of CPAs.

MARK S. BEASLEY

Mark Beasley, who has also served as a coauthor of this textbook since the 8th edition, is the Deloitte Professor of Enterprise Risk Management and Professor of Accounting at North Carolina State University. He has taught undergraduate and graduate auditing courses, and has received several teaching awards including membership in NC State's Academy of Outstanding Teachers. He has extensive professional audit experience with the predecessor firm to Ernst & Young and has extensive standards-setting experience working with the Auditing Standards Board as a Technical Manager in the Audit and Assurance Division of the AICPA. He served on the ASB Fraud Standard Task Force responsible for developing SAS 99, the ASB Antifraud Programs and Controls Task Force, and the Advisory Council overseeing the COSO Enterprise Risk Management—Integrated Framework project. He served over seven years as a member of the COSO Board, representing the AAA.

CHRIS E. HOGAN

We are pleased to have **Chris Hogan** join us as a coauthor for this 16th edition. Chris is a Professor of Accounting in the Eli Broad College of Business at Michigan State University. We are thrilled to continue the Michigan State connection started by Al Arens. Chris teaches graduate auditing and her research focuses on internal controls and integrated audits, audit firm client portfolios, and the impact of regulation on audit markets. Chris has auditing experience with Price Waterhouse, one of the predecessor firms to PricewaterhouseCoopers, LLP. She has served in multiple leadership roles within the American Accounting Association, including serving as President of the Auditing Section and on the Audit Committee of the AAA.

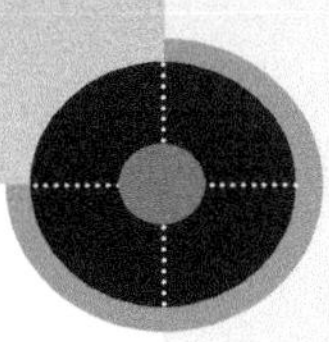

CONTENTS

*Multiple-Choice Questions Becker Professional Education

CHAPTER 3

AUDIT REPORTS

CHAPTER 4

PROFESSIONAL ETHICS

CHAPTER 5 LEGAL LIABILITY

PART 2 THE AUDIT PROCESS

CHAPTER 6 AUDIT RESPONSIBILITIES AND OBJECTIVES

CHAPTER 7

AUDIT EVIDENCE

CHAPTER 8

AUDIT PLANNING AND MATERIALITY

CHAPTER 9

ASSESSING THE RISK OF MATERIAL MISSTATEMENT

ASSESSING AND RESPONDING TO FRAUD RISKS

CHAPTER 10

INTERNAL CONTROL AND COSO FRAMEWORK

CHAPTER 11

PART 3 APPLICATION OF THE AUDIT PROCESS TO THE SALES AND COLLECTION CYCLE

CHAPTER 14 AUDIT OF THE SALES AND COLLECTION CYCLE: TESTS OF CONTROLS AND SUBSTANTIVE TESTS OF TRANSACTIONS

CHAPTER 15 AUDIT SAMPLING FOR TESTS OF CONTROLS AND SUBSTANTIVE TESTS OF TRANSACTIONS

PART 4 APPLICATION OF THE AUDIT PROCESS TO OTHER CYCLES

CHAPTER 18 AUDIT OF THE ACQUISITION AND PAYMENT CYCLE: TESTS OF CONTROLS, SUBSTANTIVE TESTS OF TRANSACTIONS, AND ACCOUNTS PAYABLE

CHAPTER 19 COMPLETING THE TESTS IN THE ACQUISITION AND PAYMENT CYCLE: VERIFICATION OF SELECTED ACCOUNTS

CHAPTER 22

AUDIT OF THE CAPITAL ACQUISITION AND REPAYMENT CYCLE

CHAPTER 23

AUDIT OF CASH AND FINANCIAL INSTRUMENTS

PART 5

COMPLETING THE AUDIT

CHAPTER 24

COMPLETING THE AUDIT

PART 6 OTHER ASSURANCE AND NONASSURANCE SERVICES

CHAPTER 25 OTHER ASSURANCE SERVICES

CHAPTER 26 INTERNAL AND GOVERNMENTAL FINANCIAL AUDITING AND OPERATIONAL AUDITING

PREFACE

INTEGRATED APPROACH FOR RISK ASSESSMENT AND AUDIT DECISION MAKING

Auditing and Assurance Services: An Integrated Approach is an introduction to auditing and other assurance services. It is intended for either a one-quarter or one-semester course at the undergraduate or graduate level. This book is also appropriate for introductory professional development courses for CPA firms, internal auditors, and government auditors.

The primary emphasis in this text is on the auditor's decision-making process in a financial statement audit, as well as an integrated audit of both financial statements and internal control over financial reporting required for accelerated filer public companies. We believe that the most fundamental concepts in auditing concern determining the nature and amount of evidence the auditor should gather after considering the unique circumstances of each engagement. If students of auditing understand the objectives to be accomplished in a given audit area, the risks related to the engagement, and the decisions to be made, they should be able to determine the appropriate evidence to gather and how to evaluate the evidence obtained.

Our objective is to provide up-to-date coverage of globally recognized auditing concepts with practical examples of the implementation of those concepts in real-world settings. The collective experience of the author team in the practice of auditing is extensive. We have all worked in the auditing profession involving both large international audit firms and regional firms. Members of our author team have taught extensively in continuing education for either large international or small CPA firms and have been involved in standards setting activities of the Auditing Standards Board and the PCAOB. One author served over seven years as one of the board members of the Committee of Sponsoring Organizations of the Treadway Commission (COSO). These experiences provide unique perspectives about the integration of auditing concepts in real-world settings.

As the title of this book reflects, our purpose is to integrate the most important internationally recognized concepts of auditing in a logical manner to assist students in understanding audit decision making and evidence accumulation in today's complex, global auditing environment. For example, developments related to issues affecting auditing in a global and economically volatile environment are described throughout the book and are emphasized in selected mid-chapter vignettes and homework problems. Key concepts related to risk assessment as emphasized in standards issued by the Auditing Standards Board (ASB) and the International Auditing and Assurance Standards Board (IAASB), including emphasis on significant risks, are integrated into all of the planning chapters, as well as each chapter dealing with a particular transaction cycle and related accounts. Our coverage of internal control is related to tests of controls and substantive tests of transactions that are performed in a financial statement audit and an integrated audit of financial statements and internal control over financial reporting, with an emphasis on the requirements of PCAOB Auditing Standards. Tests of controls and substantive tests of transactions are, in turn, related to the tests of details of financial statement balances for the area. Audit sampling is applied to the evaluation of audit evidence rather than treated as a separate topic. Risk assessment, technology, fraud, and auditing of internal control issues are integrated throughout the chapters.

WHAT'S NEW IN THIS EDITION

Current Coverage

New auditing standards are released without regard to textbook revision cycles. As auditing instructors, we appreciate how critical it is to have the most current content available. This edition includes complete coverage of the AICPA Clarity Project, including guidance in the recently issued SAS No. 130 *An Audit of Internal Control Over Financial Reporting That Is Integrated With an Audit of Financial Statements* and new PCAOB standards including Standard No. 18, *Related Parties.* We are committed to continually providing you with up-to-date content in this dynamic global auditing environment and will keep you updated with highlights posted on our Web site of major changes in new standards as they are issued.

AICPA Clarity Projects

As part of the effort to converge U.S. auditing standards with international standards, the AICPA Auditing Standards Board (ASB) recently completed its Clarity Project to redraft most of the existing GAAS standards to not only align them with the ISAs, but to also make them easier to read, understand, and apply. Chapter 2 provides an overview of the major implications of the clarified standards, including the new principles that provide the framework to help auditors fulfill the objectives of the audit of financial statements in accordance with AICPA auditing standards and the new Codification of Statements on Auditing Standards. Chapter 3 contains examples of the new standard auditor's report format updated by the Clarified SASs. All remaining chapters of the textbook reflect the various revisions resulting from the issuance of the Clarity standards.

The AICPA's Accounting and Review Services Committee (ARSC) has largely completed a similar Clarity Project affecting compilation and review standards with the issuance of SSARS No. 21, *Statement on Standards for Accounting and Review Services: Clarification and Recodification*. In redrafting SSARS, the ARSC used similar redrafting standards as those used by the Auditing Standards Board. Changes resulting from the redrafting of SSARS are addressed in Chapter 25. Additionally, that chapter also highlights forthcoming changes in Statements on Standards for Attestation Engagements (SSAEs) resulting from the AICPA's Clarity Project affecting attestation standards, which was recently voted for final issuance by the ASB.

Coverage of Revised AICPA *Code of Professional Conduct*

The AICPA recently restructured its *Code of Professional Conduct* to align it with international standards. The organization of the *Code* now presents the Principles as part of the Preface and then includes Rules for members in public practice separately from Rules for members in business and others. Chapter 4 has been substantially revised to provide an overview of the key elements of the revised *Code* based on this new structure.

Expanded Coverage of Professional Skepticism and Auditor Judgment

With the profession's continued focus on the importance of applying appropriate levels of professional skepticism, we have expanded coverage of this topic in Chapter 6, along with integrated coverage in later chapters, including Chapter 10, which addresses the auditor's responsibilities for detecting fraud. We discuss the importance of a questioning mindset and the need to critically evaluate audit evidence to strengthen student awareness of the elements of effective professional skepticism.

To assist auditors with maintaining an appropriate level of professional skepticism when making professional judgments during an audit, this edition features the Center for Audit Quality's *Professional Judgment Resource,* which outlines key elements of a process that auditors apply when making professional judgments. Chapter 6 illustrates an effective decision-making process that guides auditors' thinking to help them be aware of their own judgment tendencies, traps, and biases. We have added homework problems that expose students to this judgment framework and a number of the common traps and biases.

Expanded Coverage on Risk Assessment Procedures and Understanding Internal Control

The requirements of the Sarbanes–Oxley Act of 2002 and the PCAOB Auditing Standard 5 (AS 5) that impact accelerated filer public companies, and the risk assessment standards issued by the Auditing Standards Board are integrated throughout the text. Chapter 2 emphasizes the importance of understanding the client's business and its environment, including internal control. Chapter 3 highlights reporting on internal controls over financial reporting for auditors of accelerated filer public companies.

We have always emphasized understanding the client's business and industry in planning. For the 16th edition we reorganized Chapters 8–12 to include expanded coverage of the auditor's performance of risk assessment procedures, including the identification of significant risks. Chapter 9 addresses the performance of risk assessment procedures to address the risk of material misstatement, followed in Chapter 10 with discussion of assessing and responding to the risk of fraud.

Our coverage in Chapters 11 and 12 of internal controls, including coverage of IT general and application controls, has been restructured to reflect key elements of COSO's 2013 revision of its *Internal Control—Integrated Framework* and to better integrate the auditor's consideration of both manual and automated controls. Chapter 11 introduces students to important elements of effective internal controls, including those related to IT, while Chapter 12 outlines the auditor's responsibilities to understand the design and operating effectiveness of internal control, and also highlights auditor reports on internal control over financial reporting. Subsequent chapters that focus on the transaction cycles include extensive coverage of internal controls to help students understand how the auditor's consideration of internal controls is integrated for audits of the financial statements and internal controls over financial reporting.

Emphasis on International Issues

Chapter 1 introduces the importance of considering international auditing standards developments, followed by discussion in Chapter 2 about the role of the International Auditing and Assurance Standards Board (IAASB) in the issuance of international standards on auditing (ISAs) and the Auditing Standards Board's efforts to converge U.S. standards to international standards. Chapter 3 highlights implications for auditor reports on companies reporting under International Financial Reporting Standards (IFRS). Several chapters throughout the book include text or mid-chapter vignette coverage of international issues, and international issues are also addressed in homework problems.

Coverage of Financial Instruments

With the increasing volume and complexity of various types of financial instruments and challenges associated with fair value accounting, Chapter 23 addresses issues associated with auditing financial instruments and obtaining sufficient appropriate audit evidence for fair value account estimates. We believe this guidance will help strengthen student understanding of the challenges associated with auditing financial instruments.

Service Organization Controls (SOC) Reports

With more organizations taking advantage of cloud computing options and third party IT service providers, there is a greater need for information about the design and operating effectiveness of internal controls provided by these external service providers. This 16th edition contains expanded coverage of service organization control (SOC) reports issued by service center auditors. Both Chapters 12 and 25 reflect the new guidance for service auditors reporting on internal controls at service organizations, including coverage of the different types of reports provided in SOC 1, SOC 2, and SOC 3 engagements.

New Coverage of Preparation Service Engagements

The issuance of SSARS No. 21 introduced a new type of nonattest engagement service that allows nonissuers to engage a CPA to help management prepare monthly, quarterly, or annual financial statements without providing any assurance on the financial statements or issuing a report, even if the financial statements are expected to be used by, or provided to, a third party. Chapter 25 describes this new type of service and distinguishes it from compilation and review engagement requirements.

New Concept Checks

A new feature in the 16th edition is the inclusion of Concept Checks periodically within each chapter that highlight short-answer questions to help students recap content covered within different sections of the chapter. These short in-chapter review questions are intended to help call student attention to key concepts as they read the material in the chapter.

Expanded Homework Material

We are excited about the inclusion of a number of changes to the end-of-chapter homework material for all chapters. For the 16th edition, we have partnered with Becker CPA Review to include new multiple choice problems from their CPA exam preparation materials. These problems, which are included in all 26 chapters, are labeled with the Becker logo. Additionally, each chapter identifies new or revised Discussion Questions and Problems that instructors can use in class to generate discussion about important topics addressed in each chapter. These problems are highlighted by an "in-class" discussion icon in the margin next to the related homework problem. Each chapter also identifies homework problems that require students to research standards and other material using the Internet. While many of these research problems expose students to standards, such as those on the PCAOB Web site, other problems require students to examine recently issued financial statements or other corporate filings, or they expose students to best practices thought papers as part of the assignment. Sample problems, assignable in MyAccountingLab, provide an introduction to the CPA Exam format and an opportunity for early practice with CPA exam–style questions.

Data Analysis Problems

CPA firms expect auditors to analyze data using spreadsheets and audit software. A number of the problems in the text can be completed using Excel templates available on the text Web site. These problems are indicated by a spreadsheet icon in the margin next to the problem. CPA firms increasingly emphasize data analytics and increasingly use audit software to perform audit testing including tests for fraud. We have included selected problems using ACL in several chapters in the text. These problems are related to the topic of the chapter so that students can see how audit software is used to perform specific types of audit tests. Guidance for students on the use of ACL is included on the text Web site.

Hillsburg Hardware Annual Report

The annual report for the Hillsburg Hardware Company is included as an insert to the text. Financial statements and other information included in the annual report are used in examples throughout the text to illustrate chapter concepts. The annual report also includes management's report on internal control required by Section 404a and the auditor's report required by Section 404b, consistent with PCAOB Auditing Standard No. 5.

Pinnacle Manufacturing Integrated Case

The Pinnacle Manufacturing integrated case is based on a large, multi-division company. The case has been revised and expanded to now consist of seven parts included at the end of the chapter to which that part relates. Each part of the case is designed to give students hands-on experience, and the parts of the case are connected so that students will gain a better understanding of how the parts of the audit are integrated by the audit process.

ORGANIZATION

The text is divided into six parts. The chapters are relatively brief and designed to be easily read and comprehended by students.

Part 1, The Auditing Profession (Chapters 1–5) The book begins with an opening vignette featuring a Big 4 public accounting firm's assurance report contained in the Corporate Sustainability Report issued by United Parcel Service (UPS), to help students see the increasingly important role of auditors in providing assurance on a broad range of information important to key stakeholders. Chapter 1 introduces key provisions of the Sarbanes–Oxley Act, including the creation of the PCAOB and Section 404 internal control reporting requirements. Chapter 2 covers the CPA profession, with particular emphasis on the standards setting responsibilities of the International Auditing and Assurance Standards Board (IAASB) and the PCAOB and how those responsibilities differ from those of the AICPA Auditing Standards Board (ASB). Chapter 2 provides in-depth coverage of the AICPA Clarity Project and resulting changes to AICPA auditing standards. Chapter 3 provides a detailed discussion of audit reports issued under AICPA and PCAOB standards, including a separate section on the report on internal control over financial reporting for an accelerated filer public company. The chapter also emphasizes conditions affecting the type of report the auditor must issue and the type of audit report applicable to each condition under varying levels of materiality. Chapter 4 explains ethical dilemmas, professional ethics, and independence, and it features the newly revised AICPA *Code of Professional Conduct*. Chapter 5 ends this part with an investigation of auditors' legal liability.

Part 2, The Audit Process (Chapters 6–13) The first two of these chapters deal with auditor and management responsibilities, professional skepticism, a professional judgment framework for auditor decision making, audit objectives, general concepts of evidence accumulation, and audit documentation, including the management assertions and evidence concepts in the risk assessment standards. Chapter 8 deals with planning the engagement, including understanding the company's business and its industry as part of the auditor's risk assessment procedures, using analytical procedures as an audit tool, and making preliminary judgments about materiality. Chapter 9 provides expanded coverage of the auditor's performance of risk assessment procedures used to assess the risk of material misstatement due to fraud or error and how the auditor responds to risks of significant misstatement with further audit procedures. Fraud auditing is the focus of Chapter 10, which builds upon risk assessment concepts covered in the previous chapter to illustrate how risk assessment includes the assessment of fraud risk. The chapter also includes specific examples of fraud and discusses warning signs and procedures performed in response to heightened fraud risk. Chapter 11 outlines the key components of an effective system of internal controls over financial reporting, consistent with the 2013 revision of COSO's *Internal Control—Integrated Framework*. Because most internal control systems are heavily dependent on information technologies, this chapter integrates coverage of IT general controls and application controls. Chapter 12 shows how effective internal controls can reduce planned audit evidence in the audit of financial statements, and it outlines procedures auditors perform as tests of those controls to support a low control risk assessment. The chapter also describes how auditors of accelerated filer public companies integrate evidence to provide a basis for their report on the effectiveness of internal control over financial reporting with the assessment of control risk in the financial statement audit. Chapter 13 summarizes Chapters 6 through 12 and integrates them with the remainder of the text.

Part 3, Application of the Audit Process to the Sales and Collection Cycle (Chapters 14–17) These chapters apply the concepts from Part 2 to the audit of sales, cash receipts, and the related income statement and balance sheet accounts. The appropriate audit procedures for accounts in the sales and collection cycle are related to internal control and audit objectives for tests of controls, substantive tests of transactions, and tests of details of balances in the context of both the audit of financial statements and the audit of internal control over financial reporting.

Students also learn to apply audit sampling to the audit of sales, cash receipts, and accounts receivable. Chapter 15 begins with a general discussion of audit sampling for tests of controls and substantive tests of transactions. Similarly, Chapter 17 begins with general sampling concepts for tests of details of balances. The next topic in each chapter is extensive coverage of nonstatistical sampling. The last part of each chapter covers statistical sampling techniques.

Part 4, Application of the Audit Process to Other Cycles (Chapters 18–23) Each of these chapters deals with a specific transaction cycle or part of a transaction cycle in much the same manner as Chapters 14 through 17 cover the sales and collection cycle. Each chapter in Part 4 demonstrates the relationship of internal controls, tests of controls, and substantive tests of transactions for each broad category of transactions to the related balance sheet and income statement accounts. We integrate discussion of implications related to the audit of internal control throughout all these transaction cycle chapters. Cash and financial instruments are studied late in the text to demonstrate how the audit of cash and financial instrument balances is related to most other audit areas.

Part 5, Completing the Audit (Chapter 24) This part includes only one chapter, which deals with performing additional tests to address presentation and disclosure objectives, summarizing all audit tests, reviewing audit documentation, obtaining management representations in an integrated audit of financial statements and internal control, communicating with those charged with governance, and all other aspects of completing an audit.

Part 6, Other Assurance and Nonassurance Services (Chapters 25 and 26) The last two chapters deal with various types of engagements and reports, other than the audit of financial statements using generally accepted accounting principles. Topics covered include assurance services; review, compilation, and preparation services; agreed-upon procedures engagements; attestation engagements; other audit engagements; internal financial auditing; governmental financial auditing; and operational auditing. This edition also includes expanded coverage of service organization control (SOC) reports on internal controls at external service providers.

SUPPLEMENTS

Instructor's Resource Center www.pearsonhighered.com/arens This password-protected site is accessible from the catalog page for *Auditing and Assurance Services, 16th ed.*, and hosts the following resources:

Image Library The Image Library allows access to most of the images and illustrations featured in the text.

Instructor's Resource Manual Suggestions for each chapter include: Homework problems, how learning objectives correlate with chapter problem material, and visual aids that can be added to PowerPoint slides or used on document cameras or overhead projectors. Chapters have been designed so that their arrangement and selection provide maximum flexibility in course design. Sample syllabi and suggested term projects are provided.

Solutions Manual Included are detailed solutions to all the end-of-chapter exercises, problems, and cases. Guidelines for responses to review questions and discussion questions are offered.

Test Item File & TestGen The **Test Item File** includes multiple choice exercises, true/false responses, essay questions, and questions related to the chapter vignettes. To assist the instructor in selecting questions for use in examinations and quizzes, each question has been assigned one of three difficulty ratings—easy, medium, or challenging. In addition, questions that uniquely relate to the integrated audits of large public companies or to the provisions of the Sarbanes–Oxley Act and Section 404 have been separately labeled for easy identification by the professor. TestGen testing software is an easy-to-use computerized testing program. It can create exams as well as evaluate and track student results. All Test Item File questions are available in the TestGen format.

PowerPoint Slides PowerPoint presentations are available for each chapter of the text. Instructors have the flexibility to add slides and/or modify the existing slides to meet course needs.

Enhanced Companion Web Site Pearson's Learning on the Internet Partnership offers the most expansive Internet-based support available. Our Web site provides a wealth of resources for students and faculty. Periodically, faculty will be able to access electronic summaries and PowerPoint slides of the most recent changes to professional standards and summaries of major issues affecting the auditing profession. This will help instructors to stay informed of emerging issues.

***Auditing Cases, 6th ed.,* by Beasley/Buckless/Glover/Prawitt** This collection of 49 auditing cases addresses most major activities performed during the conduct of an audit, from client acceptance to issuance of an audit report. Several cases ask students to work with realistic audit evidence to prepare and evaluate audit schedules. The cases are available as part of Pearson Collections. For details, go to collections .pearsoned.com.

MyAccountingLab® MyAccountingLab is an online homework, tutorial, and assessment program designed to work with this text to engage students and improve results. Within its structured environment, students practice what they learn, test their understanding, and receive immediate feedback to help them better absorb course material and understand difficult concepts.

ACKNOWLEDGMENTS

We acknowledge the American Institute of Certified Public Accountants for permission to quote extensively from Statements on Auditing Standards, the *Code of Professional Conduct,* Uniform CPA Examinations, and other publications. The willingness of this major accounting organization to permit the use of its materials is a significant contribution to the book and audit education.

We gratefully acknowledge the contributions of the following reviewers for their suggestions and support in the 16th edition as well as previous editions:

Sherri Anderson, *Sonoma State University*
Stephen K. Asare, *University of Florida*
David Baglia, *Grove City College*
Brian Ballou, *Miami University*
William E. Bealing, Jr., *Bloomsburg University*
Stanley F. Biggs, *University of Connecticut*
Robert Braun, *Southeastern Louisiana University*
Joe Brazel, *North Carolina State University*
Billy Brewster, *University of Texas–Arlington*
Frank Buckless, *North Carolina State University*
Joseph V. Calmie, *Thomas Nelson Community College*
Eric Carlsen, *Kean College of New Jersey*
David Chan, *St. John's University*
Freddie Choo, *San Francisco State University*
Karl Dahlberg, *Rutgers University*
Frank Daroca, *Loyola Marymount University*
Stephen Del Vecchio, *University of Central Missouri*
Todd DeZoort, *University of Alabama–Tuscaloosa*
Magdy Farag, *California State Polytechnic University, Pomona*
William L. Felix, *University of Arizona*
Michele Flint, *Daemen College*
David S. Gelb, *Seton Hall University*
Stephanie Geter, *University of Cincinnati*
David Gilbertson, *Western Washington University*
John Giles, *North Carolina State University*
Lori Grady, *Bucks County Community College*
Charles L. Holley, *Virginia Commonwealth University*
Steve Hunt, *Western Illinois University*
Greg Jenkins, *Virginia Tech University*
James Jiambalvo, *University of Washington*
Ambrose Jones, III, *University of North Carolina–Greensboro*
David S. Kerr, *University of North Carolina at Charlotte*
William R. Kinney, Jr., *University of Texas at Austin*
W. Robert Knechel, *University of Florida*
Jason MacGregor, *Baylor University*
John Mason, *University of Alabama–Tuscaloosa*
Heidi H. Meier, *Cleveland State University*
Alfred R. Michenzi, *Loyola College in Maryland*
Charles R. (Tad) Miller, *California Polytechnic State University, San Luis Obispo*
Lawrence C. Mohrweis, *Northern Arizona University*
Norma Montague, *Wake Forest University*
Curtis Mullis, *University of Alabama*
Patricia M. Myers, *Brock University*
Kathy O'Donnell, *SUNY Buffalo*
Kristine N. Palmer, *Longwood College*
Vicki S. Peden, *California State Polytechnic University, Pomona*
Ron Reed, *University of Northern Colorado*
Pankaj Saksena, *Indiana University South Bend*
Cindy Seipel, *New Mexico State University*
Scott Showalter, *North Carolina State University*
Philip H. Siegel, *Troy University*
Robert R. Tucker, *Fordham University*
Barb Waddington, *Eastern Michigan University*
Karl Wang, *University of Mississippi*
Jeanne H. Yamamura, *University of Nevada, Reno*
Doug Ziegenfuss, *Old Dominion University*

We especially thank the Pearson book team for their hard work and dedication, including Ellen Geary, Acquisitions Editor; Daniel Petrino, Program Manager; Christine Donovan, Editorial Assistant; Donna Battista, Vice President of Business Publishing; Maggie Moylan, Vice President, Product Marketing; Natalie Wagner, Senior Field Marketer; Jessica Quazza, Product Marketing Assistant; Ashley Santora, Team Lead, Program Management; Roberta Sherman, Project Manager; and Jeff Holcomb, Team Lead, Project Management.

A. A. A.
R. J. E.
M. S. B.
C. E. H.

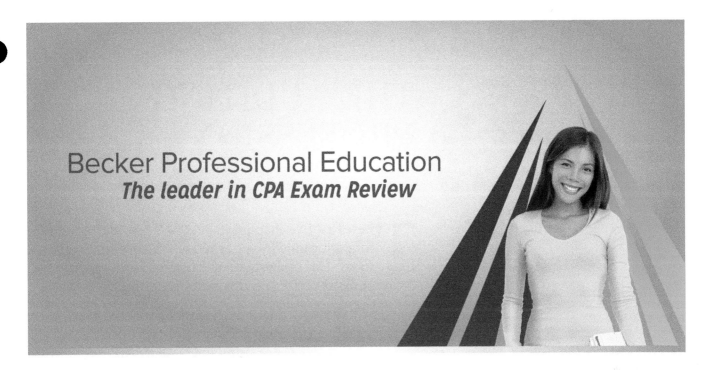

THE AUDITING PROFESSION

CHAPTERS 1–5

These first five chapters in **PART 1** provide background for performing financial audits, which is our primary focus. This background will help you understand why auditors perform audits the way they do.

- **Chapters 1 and 2** describe assurance services, including auditing and the role of certified public accounting (CPA) firms and other organizations in performing audits of financial statements and other information.
- **Chapter 3** provides a detailed discussion of audit reports, which are the final products of audits.
- **Chapters 4 and 5** emphasize the regulation and oversight of CPA firms through ethical standards and the legal responsibilities of auditors.

THE DEMAND FOR AUDIT AND OTHER ASSURANCE SERVICES

CHAPTER

1

LEARNING OBJECTIVES

After studying this chapter, you should be able to

1-1 Describe auditing.
1-2 Distinguish between auditing and accounting.
1-3 Explain the importance of auditing in reducing information risk.
1-4 List the causes of information risk, and explain how this risk can be reduced.
1-5 Describe assurance services and distinguish audit services from other assurance and nonassurance services provided by CPAs.
1-6 Differentiate the three main types of audits.
1-7 Identify the primary types of auditors.
1-8 Describe the requirements for becoming a CPA.

Brown Goes Green

United Parcel Service (UPS) is one of the largest shipment and logistics companies in the world, delivering more than 15 million packages a day in more than 220 countries. At the peak of the holiday season, UPS delivers 34 million packages daily. That's a lot of packages moved by planes and delivery trucks, and it obviously comes with a large carbon footprint. The UPS company nickname is "Brown" because of the company's brown delivery trucks and uniforms, but that does not capture the company's commitment to sustainability.

Recently, the company reduced its annual carbon emissions by 1.5 percent, even though delivery volume increased by 3.9 percent. One way the company reduces carbon emissions is through its proprietary On-Road Integrated Optimization and Navigation (ORION) IT system, which uses an advanced algorithm and customized map data to provide optimal route advice to drivers. The system reduced fuel usage by 1.5 million gallons in 2014, resulting in a reduction in annual CO_2 emissions of 14,000 metric tons. ORION is not only good for the environment, but it helps the bottom line. UPS estimates that a reduction of one mile driven per delivery driver per day will save the company up to $50 million per year.

The UPS Corporate Sustainability Report is prepared in accordance with the G4 framework established by the Global Reporting Initiative (GRI). The company received the "Materiality Matters" check from the GRI, indicating that it had fulfilled the necessary general standards of disclosures. The increase in sustainability reporting by companies such as UPS has also resulted in increased interest in the accuracy of the reported information, and the GRI recommends external assurance by accountants or other qualified experts to provide users with increased confidence in the accuracy of the information. The UPS Corporate Sustainability Report includes an assurance report from a Big 4 public accounting firm, including a separate assurance report on the company's global statement of greenhouse gas emissions. Many predict this form of assurance will be a frequent service performed by tomorrow's CPAs.

Sources: 1. UPS Corporate Sustainability Report (sustainability.ups.com); 2. *The External Assurance of Sustainability Reporting,* Global Reporting Initiative, Amsterdam 2013 (www.globalreporting.org).

Each chapter's opening story illustrates important auditing principles based on realistic situations. Some of these stories are based on public information about real companies, whereas others are fictitious. Any resemblance in the latter stories to real firms, companies, or individuals is unintended and purely coincidental.

The opening example involving the UPS Corporate Sustainability Report illustrates the increasingly important role of auditors in providing assurance on sustainability and other information of interest to a broad range of stakeholders. Of course, reporting on the financial statements of public companies, as well as private companies, government units, and nonprofit entities, remains a primary role of auditors. In addition, auditors provide assurance on internal control over financial reporting for larger public companies.

This chapter introduces auditing and other assurance services provided by auditors, as well as auditors' role in society. These services provide value by offering assurance on financial statements, the effectiveness of internal control, and many other types of information. There is also a discussion of the types of audits and auditors, including the requirements for becoming a certified public accountant (CPA).

NATURE OF AUDITING

OBJECTIVE 1-1

Describe auditing.

We have introduced the role of auditors in society and how auditors provide assurance on financial statements. Auditors also provide assurance on the effectiveness of internal control over financial reporting, as well as many other types of information such as corporate sustainability reports. We now examine auditing more specifically using the following definition:

> **Auditing** is the accumulation and evaluation of evidence about information to determine and report on the degree of correspondence between the information and established criteria. Auditing should be done by a competent, independent person.

The definition includes several key words and phrases. For ease of understanding, we'll discuss the terms in a different order than they occur in the description.

Information and Established Criteria

To do an audit, there must be information in a *verifiable form* and some standards (*criteria*) by which the auditor can evaluate the information. This information can take many forms. Auditors routinely perform audits of quantifiable information, including companies' financial statements and individuals' federal income tax returns. Auditors also audit more subjective information, such as the effectiveness of computer systems and the efficiency of manufacturing operations.

The criteria for evaluating information also vary depending on the information being audited. In the audit of historical financial statements by CPA firms, the criteria may be U.S. generally accepted accounting principles (GAAP) or International Financial Reporting Standards (IFRS). This means that in an audit of Apple's financial statements, the CPA firm will determine whether Apple's financial statements have been prepared in accordance with GAAP. For an audit of internal control over financial reporting, the criteria will be a recognized framework for establishing internal control, such as *Internal Control—Integrated Framework* issued by the Committee of Sponsoring Organizations of the Treadway Commission (widely known as COSO).

For the audit of tax returns by the Internal Revenue Service (IRS), the criteria are found in the Internal Revenue Code. In an IRS audit of Apple's corporate tax return, the internal revenue agent uses the Internal Revenue Code as the criteria for correctness, rather than GAAP.

For more subjective information, it is more difficult to establish criteria. Typically, auditors and the entities being audited agree on the criteria well before the audit starts. For example, in an audit of the effectiveness of specific aspects of computer operations, the criteria might include the allowable level of input or output errors.

Accumulating and Evaluating Evidence

Evidence is any information used by the auditor to determine whether the information being audited is stated in accordance with the established criteria. Evidence takes many different forms, including:

- Electronic and documentary data about transactions
- Written and electronic communication with outsiders

- Observations by the auditor
- Oral testimony of the auditee (client)

To satisfy the purpose of the audit, auditors must obtain a sufficient quality and quantity of evidence. Auditors must determine the types and amount of evidence necessary and evaluate whether the information corresponds to the established criteria. This is a critical part of every audit and the primary subject of this book.

Competent, Independent Person

The auditor must be qualified to understand the criteria used and must be *competent* to know the types and amount of evidence to accumulate in order to reach the proper conclusion after examining the evidence. The auditor must also have an *independent mental attitude.* The competence of those performing the audit is of little value if they are biased in the accumulation and evaluation of evidence.

Auditors strive to maintain a high level of independence to keep the confidence of users relying on their reports. Auditors reporting on company financial statements are often called **independent auditors**. Even though such auditors are paid fees by the company, they are normally sufficiently independent to conduct audits that can be relied on by users. Even internal auditors—those employed by the companies they audit—usually report directly to top management and the board of directors, keeping the auditors independent of the operating units they audit.

Reporting

The final stage in the auditing process is preparing the **audit report**, which communicates the auditor's findings to users. Reports differ in nature, but all must inform readers of the degree of correspondence between the information audited and established criteria. Reports also differ in form and can vary from the highly technical type usually associated with financial statement audits to a simple oral report in the case of an operational audit of a small department's effectiveness.

The key parts in the description of auditing are illustrated in Figure 1-1 using an IRS agent's audit of an individual's tax return as an example. To determine whether the tax return was prepared in a manner consistent with the requirements of the federal Internal Revenue Code, the agent examines supporting records provided by the taxpayer and from other sources, such as the taxpayer's employer. After completing the audit, the internal revenue agent issues a report to the taxpayer assessing additional taxes, advising that a refund is due, or stating that there is no change in the status of the tax return.

FIGURE 1-1 Audit of a Tax Return

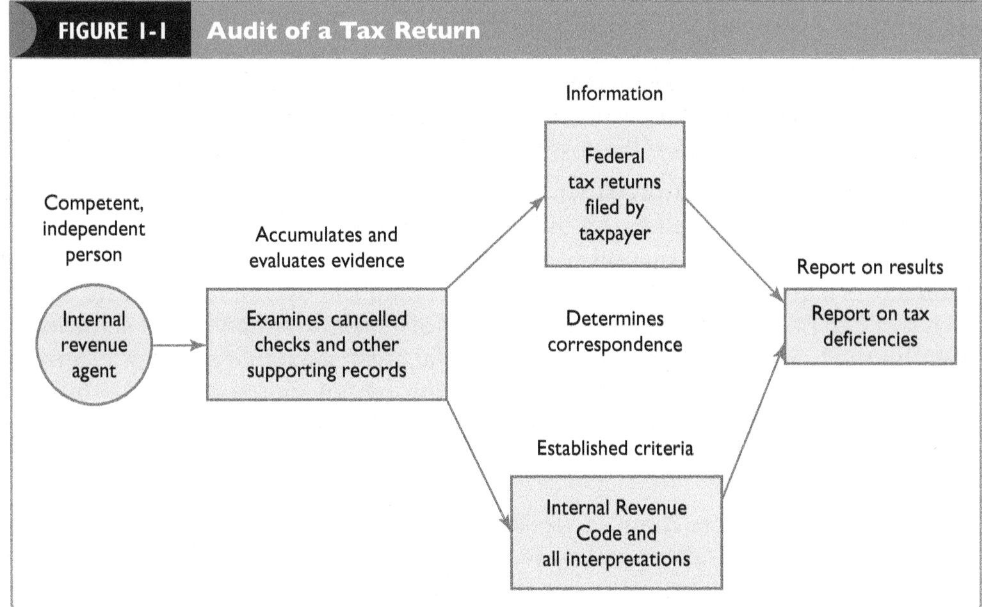

DISTINCTION BETWEEN AUDITING AND ACCOUNTING

OBJECTIVE 1-2

Distinguish between auditing and accounting.

Many financial statement users and the general public confuse auditing with accounting. The confusion results because most auditing is usually concerned with accounting information, and many auditors have considerable expertise in accounting matters. The confusion is increased by giving the title "certified public accountant" to many individuals who perform audits.

Accounting is the recording, classifying, and summarizing of economic events in a logical manner for the purpose of providing financial information for decision making. To provide relevant information, accountants must have a thorough understanding of the principles and rules that provide the basis for preparing the accounting information. In addition, accountants must develop a system to make sure that the entity's economic events are properly recorded on a timely basis and at a reasonable cost.

When auditing accounting data, auditors focus on determining whether recorded information properly reflects the economic events that occurred during the accounting period. Because U.S. or international accounting standards provide the criteria for evaluating whether the accounting information is properly recorded, auditors must thoroughly understand those accounting standards.

In addition to understanding accounting, the auditor must possess expertise in the accumulation and interpretation of audit evidence. It is this expertise that distinguishes auditors from accountants. Determining the proper audit procedures, deciding the number and types of items to test, and evaluating the results are unique to the auditor.

ECONOMIC DEMAND FOR AUDITING

OBJECTIVE 1-3

Explain the importance of auditing in reducing information risk.

To illustrate the need for auditing, consider the decision of a bank officer in making a loan to a business. This decision will be based on such factors as previous financial relationships with the business and the financial condition of the business as reflected by its financial statements. If the bank makes the loan, it will charge a rate of interest determined primarily by three factors:

1. *Risk-free interest rate.* This is approximately the rate the bank could earn by investing in U.S. treasury notes for the same length of time as the business loan.
2. *Business risk for the customer.* This risk reflects the possibility that the business will not be able to repay its loan because of economic or business conditions, such as a recession, poor management decisions, or unexpected competition in the industry.
3. *Information risk.* **Information risk** reflects the possibility that the information upon which the business risk decision was made was inaccurate. A likely cause of the information risk is the possibility of inaccurate financial statements.

Auditing has no effect on either the risk-free interest rate or business risk, but it can have a significant effect on information risk. If the bank officer is satisfied that there is minimal information risk because a borrower's financial statements are audited, the bank's risk is substantially reduced and the overall interest rate to the borrower can be reduced. The reduction of information risk can have a significant effect on the borrower's ability to obtain capital at a reasonable cost. For example, assume a large company has total interest-bearing debt of approximately $10 billion. If the interest rate on that debt is reduced by only 1 percent, the annual savings in interest is $100 million.

Causes of Information Risk

As society becomes more complex, decision makers are more likely to receive unreliable information. There are several reasons for this: remoteness of information, biases and motives of the provider, voluminous data, and the existence of complex exchange transactions.

Remoteness of Information In a global economy, it is nearly impossible for a decision maker to have much firsthand knowledge about the organization with which they do business. Information provided by others must be relied upon. When information is obtained from others, the likelihood of it being intentionally or unintentionally misstated increases.

OBJECTIVE 1-4

List the causes of information risk, and explain how this risk can be reduced.

Biases and Motives of the Provider If information is provided by someone whose goals are inconsistent with those of the decision maker, the information may be biased in favor of the provider. The reason can be honest optimism about future events or an intentional emphasis designed to influence users. In either case, the result is a misstatement of information. For example, when a borrower provides financial statements to a lender, there is considerable likelihood that the borrower will bias the statements to increase the chance of obtaining a loan. The misstatement could be incorrect dollar amounts or inadequate or incomplete disclosures of information.

Voluminous Data As organizations become larger, so does the volume of their exchange transactions. This increases the likelihood that improperly recorded information is included in the records—perhaps buried in a large amount of other information. For example, if a business overpays a vendor's invoice by $2,000, it is unlikely to be uncovered unless the company has instituted reasonably sophisticated procedures to find this type of misstatement. If many minor misstatements remain undiscovered, the combined total can be significant.

Complex Exchange Transactions In the past few decades, exchange transactions between organizations have become increasingly complex and therefore more difficult to record properly. The increasing complexity in transactions has also resulted in increasingly complex accounting standards. For example, the correct accounting treatment of the acquisition of one entity by another poses relatively difficult accounting problems, especially as it relates to fair value estimations. Other examples include properly combining and disclosing the results of operations of subsidiaries in different industries and properly valuing and disclosing derivative financial instruments.

Reducing Information Risk

After comparing costs and benefits, business managers and financial statement users may conclude that the best way to deal with information risk is simply to have it remain reasonably high. A small company may find it less expensive to pay higher interest costs than to incur the costs of reducing information risk.

For larger businesses, it is usually practical to incur costs to reduce information risk. There are three main ways to do so.

User Verifies Information The user may go to the business premises to examine records and obtain information about the reliability of the statements. Normally, this is impractical because of cost. In addition, it is economically inefficient for all users to verify the information individually. Nevertheless, some users perform their own verification. For example, the IRS does considerable verification of business and individual tax returns to determine whether the tax returns filed reflect the actual tax due the federal government. Similarly, if a business intends to purchase another business, it is common for the purchaser to use a special audit team to independently verify and evaluate key information of the prospective business.

User Shares Information Risk with Management There is considerable legal precedent indicating that management is responsible for providing reliable information to users. If users rely on inaccurate financial statements and as a result incur a financial loss, they may have a basis for a lawsuit against management. A difficulty with sharing information risk with management is that users may not be able to collect on losses. If a company is unable to repay a loan because of bankruptcy, it is unlikely that management will have sufficient funds to repay users.

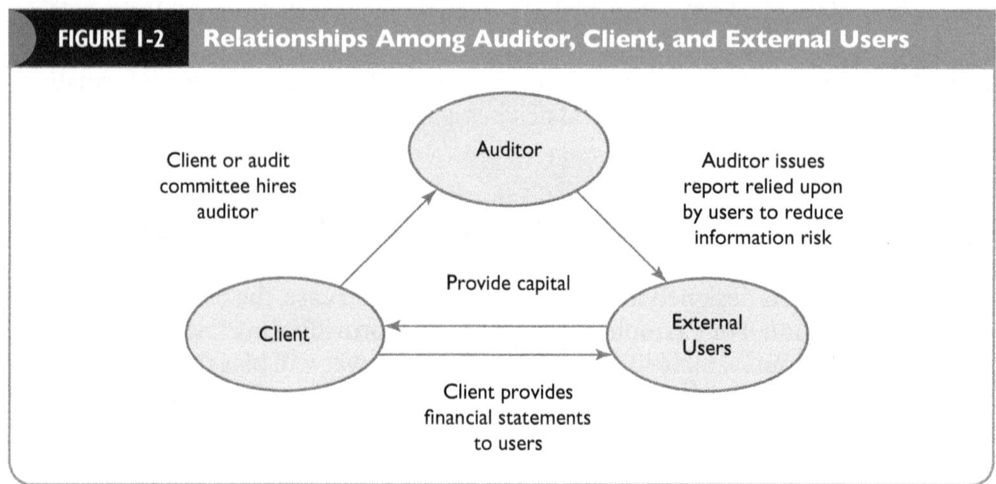
Auditor
Client or audit committee hires auditor
Auditor issues report relied upon by users to reduce information risk
Provide capital
Client
External Users
Client provides financial statements to users

FIGURE 1-2 Relationships Among Auditor, Client, and External Users

Audited Financial Statements Are Provided The most common way for users to obtain reliable information is to have an independent audit. Typically, management of a private company or the audit committee for a public company engages the auditor to provide assurances to users that the financial statements are reliable.

External users such as stockholders and lenders who rely on those financial statements to make business decisions look to the auditor's report as an indication of the statements' reliability. Decision makers can then use the audited information on the assumption that it is reasonably complete, accurate, and unbiased. They value the auditor's assurance because of the auditor's independence from the client and knowledge of financial statement reporting matters. Figure 1-2 illustrates the relationships among the auditor, client, and financial statement users.

CONCEPT CHECK

1. What is meant by determining the degree of correspondence between information and established criteria? What is the criteria for an audit of a company's financial statements?
2. What are the major causes of information risk? How can information risk be reduced?

ASSURANCE SERVICES

OBJECTIVE 1-5

Describe assurance services and distinguish audit services from other assurance and nonassurance services provided by CPAs.

An **assurance service** is an independent professional service that improves the quality of information for decision makers. Such services are valued because the assurance provider is independent and perceived as being unbiased with respect to the information examined. Individuals who are responsible for making business decisions seek assurance services to help improve the reliability and relevance of the information used as the basis for their decisions.

Assurance services can be done by CPAs or by a variety of other professionals. For example, Consumers Union, a nonprofit organization, tests a wide variety of products used by consumers and reports their evaluations of the quality of the products tested in *Consumer Reports*. The organization provides the information to help consumers make intelligent decisions about the products they buy. Many consumers consider the information in *Consumer Reports* more reliable than information provided by the product manufacturers because Consumers Union is independent of the manufacturers. Similarly, the Better Business Bureau (BBB) online reliability program, the BBB Accredited Business Seal, allows Web shoppers to check BBB information about a company and be assured the company will stand behind its service. Other assurance services provided by firms other than CPAs include the Nielsen television and Internet ratings and Arbitron radio ratings.

The need for assurance is not new. CPAs have provided many assurance services for years, particularly assurances about historical financial statement information. As a result of provisions in Section 404 of the **Sarbanes–Oxley Act**, CPA firms provide assurance on internal control over financial reporting for larger public companies. More recently, CPAs have expanded the types of assurance services they perform to include other information of interest to investors, customers, and other interested parties, such as reports on corporate social responsibility and sustainability reports. For example, businesses and consumers often seek assurances that companies with which they conduct business produce products and services in a socially responsible manner. The demand for assurance services continues to grow as shareholders and other stakeholders seek assurances about financial and nonfinancial information in addition to information in corporate financial reports.

Attestation Services

One category of assurance services provided by CPAs is attestation services. An **attestation service** is a type of assurance service in which the CPA firm issues a report about a subject matter or assertion that is made by another party. Primary categories of attestation services include:

- Audit of historical financial statements
- Audit of internal control over financial reporting
- Review of historical financial statements
- Other attestation services that may be applied to a broad range of subject matter

Audit of Historical Financial Statements In an **audit of historical financial statements**, management asserts that the financial statements are fairly stated in accordance with applicable U.S. or international accounting standards. An audit of these statements is a form of attestation service in which the auditor issues a written report expressing an opinion about whether the financial statements are fairly stated in accordance with the applicable accounting standards. These audits are the most common assurance service provided by CPA firms.

Audits are designed to provide reasonable assurance that the financial statements are free of material misstatements. Reasonable assurance is a high, but not absolute level of assurance. This level of assurance is usually sufficient to meet the information needs of financial statement users. Much of this book is about how auditors design tests to provide this level of assurance, considering the client's business and industry and risks of material misstatements in the financial statements.

Publicly traded companies in the United States are required to have audits under the federal securities acts. Auditor reports can be found in all public companies' annual financial reports. Most public companies' audited financial statements can be accessed over the Internet from the Securities and Exchange Commission (SEC) EDGAR database or directly from each company's Web site. Many privately held companies also have their annual financial statements audited to obtain financing from banks and other financial institutions. Government and not-for-profit entities often have audits to meet the requirements of lenders or funding sources.

Audit of Internal Control over Financial Reporting For an audit of **internal control over financial reporting**, management asserts that internal controls have been developed and implemented following well established criteria. Section 404 of the Sarbanes–Oxley Act requires public companies to report management's assessment of the effectiveness of internal control. The Act also requires auditors for larger public companies to attest to the effectiveness of internal control over financial reporting. This evaluation, which is integrated with the audit of the financial statements, increases user confidence about future financial reporting, because effective internal controls reduce the likelihood of future misstatements in the financial statements.

Review of Historical Financial Statements For a **review of historical financial statements**, management asserts that the statements are fairly stated in accordance with accounting standards, the same as for audits. The CPA provides a lower level of assurance for reviews of financial statements compared to a high level for audits, therefore less evidence is needed. A review is often adequate to meet financial statement users' needs. It can be provided by the CPA firm at a much lower fee than an audit because less evidence is needed. Many nonpublic companies use this attestation option to provide limited assurance on their financial statements without incurring the cost of an audit.

Other Attestation Services CPAs provide numerous other attestation services. Typically, the CPA is engaged to provide written assurance about the reliability of an assertion made by management. Many of these services are natural extensions of the audit of historical financial statements, as users seek independent assurances about other types of information. For example, when a bank loans money to a company, the loan agreement may require the company to engage a CPA to provide assurance about the company's compliance with the financial provisions of the loan. The company requesting the loan must assert the loan provisions to be attested to before the CPA can accumulate the evidence needed to issue the attestation report.

Another type of attestation involves internal controls at service organizations. Many companies use a third-party service provider to process some of their accounting activities, such as payroll, offsite at a separate IT service center or through cloud computing. The service provider often engages an auditor to provide an attestation report on the design and effectiveness of controls at the service organization. This report provides assurance to companies that use the service provider that payroll is accurately processed. Auditors of companies using the payroll service organization can also rely on the attestation report by the service company's auditor to reduce testing of payroll activities and accounts.

Other Assurance Services

CPAs also provide other assurance services that do not meet the definition of attestation services. These assurance services differ from attestation services in that the CPA is not required to issue a written report, and the assurance does not have to be about the reliability of another party's assertion about compliance with specified criteria. These other assurance service engagements focus on improving the quality of information for decision makers, just like attestation services.

CPA firms face a larger field of competitors in the market for other assurance services. Audits and some types of attestation services are limited by regulation to licensed CPAs, but the market for other forms of attestation and assurance is open to non-CPA competitors. For example, CPAs must compete with market research firms to assist clients in the preparation of customer surveys and in the evaluation of the reliability and relevance of survey information. However, CPA firms have the competitive advantage of their reputation for competence and independence.

The types of assurance services that CPAs can provide are almost limitless. A survey of large CPA firms identified more than 200 assurance services that are currently being provided. Table 1-1 lists some of the other assurance service opportunities for CPAs. Additional information on the performance of assurance and attestation services is included in Chapter 25.

"AND THE OSCAR GOES TO..."
"THERE SHE IS, MISS AMERICA..."
"WELCOME TO THE NEW YORK STATE LOTTERY..."

You probably recognize these statements from the Academy Awards, the Miss America Pageant, and the New York State Lottery drawing. What you may not recognize is what these well-known events have to do with assurance services. Each event is observed by CPAs from a major accounting firm to assure viewers that the contests were fairly conducted. So when you become a member of a CPA firm, you might not win an Oscar—but you could be on the Oscars!

CORPORATE RESPONSIBILITY REPORTING EXPANDS GLOBALLY

Companies report corporate responsibility under a number of terms, including corporate responsibility, corporate responsibility reporting, and sustainability reporting. Corporate responsibility reporting continues its tremendous growth, with rapid increases in reporting in emerging economies, and is now standard practice for many companies around the world. Over half of companies reporting globally include corporate responsibility information in their public annual financial reports. In contrast, only 20 percent of companies reported this information in 2011, and less than 10 percent reported it in 2008. The debate has changed from whether corporate responsibility reporting is worth the cost, to what information should be reported and how it should be presented. As a result, corporate responsibility has become an important element of companies' business strategies to create value for shareholders and other stakeholders.

Reporting using the Global Reporting Initiative (GRI) guidelines is increasingly standard, with 78 percent of reports issued by companies around the world prepared based on GRI guidelines. Assurance on corporate responsibility reporting is also becoming standard, with 59 percent of the Global Fortune 250 (G250) providing external assurance on their responsibility report. Major accounting firms were the choice for providing assurance for two-thirds of the G250 firms that issued responsibility reports with external assurance. These trends suggest providing assurance on corporate responsibility reporting will continue to be an area of significant growth for accounting firms.

Source: KPMG Survey of Corporate Responsibility Reporting 2013, KPMG International.

Nonassurance Services Provided by CPAs

CPA firms perform numerous other services that generally fall outside the scope of assurance services. Three specific examples are:

1. Accounting and bookkeeping services
2. Tax services
3. Management consulting services

Most accounting and bookkeeping services, tax services, and management consulting services fall outside the scope of assurance services, although there is similarity between some consulting and assurance services. While the primary purpose of an assurance service is to improve the quality of information, the primary

TABLE 1-1 Other Assurance Services Examples

Other Assurance Services	Service Activities
Controls over and risks related to investments, including policies related to derivatives	Assess the processes in a company's investment practices to identify risks and to determine the effectiveness of those processes
Mystery shopping	Perform anonymous shopping to assess sales personnel dealings with customers and procedures they follow
Assess risks of accumulation, distribution, and storage of digital information	Assess security risks and related controls over electronic data, including the adequacy of backup and off-site storage
Fraud and illegal acts risk assessment	Develop fraud risk profiles, and assess the adequacy of company systems and policies in preventing and detecting fraud and illegal acts
Organic ingredients	Provide assurance on the amount of organic ingredients included in a company's products
Compliance with entertainment royalty agreements	Assess whether royalties paid to artists, authors, and others comply with royalty agreements
ISO 9000 certifications	Certify a company's compliance with ISO 9000 quality control standards, which help ensure company products are of high quality
Corporate responsibility and sustainability	Report on whether the information in a company's corporate responsibility report is consistent with company information and established reporting criteria

purpose of a management consulting engagement is to generate a recommendation to management.

Although the quality of information is often an important criterion in management consulting, this goal is normally not the primary purpose. For example, a CPA may be engaged to design and install a new information technology system for a client as a consulting engagement. The purpose of that engagement is to install the new system, with the goal of improved information being a by-product of that engagement.

TYPES OF AUDITS

OBJECTIVE 1-6

Differentiate the three main types of audits.

CPAs perform three primary types of audits, as illustrated with examples in Table 1-2:

1. Operational audit
2. Compliance audit
3. Financial statement audit

Operational Audits

An **operational audit** evaluates the *efficiency* and *effectiveness* of any part of an organization's operating procedures and methods. At the completion of an operational audit, management normally expects recommendations for improving operations. For example, auditors might evaluate the efficiency and accuracy of processing payroll transactions in a newly installed computer system. Another example, where most accountants feel less qualified, is evaluating the efficiency, accuracy, and customer satisfaction in processing the distribution of letters and packages by a company such as Federal Express.

In operational auditing, the reviews are not limited to accounting. They can include the evaluation of organizational structure, computer operations, production methods, marketing, and any other area in which the auditor is qualified. Because of the many different areas in which operational effectiveness can be evaluated, it is impossible to characterize the conduct of a typical operational audit. In one organization, the auditor might evaluate the relevancy and sufficiency of the information used by management in making decisions to acquire new fixed assets. In a different organization, the auditor might evaluate the efficiency of the information flow in processing sales.

It is more difficult to objectively evaluate whether the efficiency and effectiveness of operations meets established criteria than it is for compliance and financial statement audits. Also, establishing criteria for evaluating the information in an operational audit is extremely subjective. In this sense, operational auditing is more like management consulting than what is usually considered auditing. Operational auditing is discussed in greater depth in Chapter 26.

TABLE 1-2 Examples of the Three Types of Audits

Type of Audit	Example	Information	Established Criteria	Available Evidence
Operational audit	Evaluate whether the computerized payroll processing for a Chinese subsidiary is operating efficiently and effectively	Number of payroll records processed in a month, costs of the department, and number of errors made	Company standards for efficiency and effectiveness in payroll department	Error reports, payroll records, and payroll processing costs
Compliance audit	Determine whether bank requirements for loan continuation have been met	Company records	Loan agreement provisions	Financial statements and calculations by the auditor
Financial statement audit	Annual audit of Apple's financial statements	Apple's financial statements	Generally accepted accounting principles	Documents, records, and outside sources of evidence

Compliance Audits

A **compliance audit** is conducted to determine whether the auditee is following specific procedures, rules, or regulations set by some higher authority. Following are examples of compliance audits for a private business.

- Determine whether accounting personnel are following the procedures prescribed by the company controller.
- Review wage rates for compliance with minimum wage laws.
- Examine contractual agreements with bankers and other lenders to be sure the company is complying with legal requirements.
- Determine whether a mortgage bank is in compliance with newly-enacted government regulations.

Governmental units, such as school districts, are subject to considerable compliance auditing because of extensive government regulation. Many private and not-for-profit organizations have prescribed policies, contractual agreements, and legal requirements that may require compliance auditing. Compliance audits for federally funded grant programs are often done by CPAs and are discussed in detail in Chapter 26.

Results of compliance audits are typically reported to management, rather than outside users, because management is the primary group concerned with the extent of compliance with prescribed procedures and regulations. Therefore, a significant portion of work of this type is often done by auditors employed by the organizational units. When an organization such as the IRS wants to determine whether individuals or organizations are complying with its requirements, the auditor is employed by the organization issuing the requirements.

Financial Statement Audits

A **financial statement audit** is conducted to determine whether the financial statements (the information being verified) are stated in accordance with specified criteria. Normally, the criteria are U.S. or international accounting standards, although auditors may conduct audits of financial statements prepared using the cash basis or some other basis of accounting appropriate for the organization. In determining whether financial statements are fairly stated in accordance with accounting standards, the auditor gathers evidence to determine whether the statements contain material errors or other misstatements. The primary focus of this book is on financial statement audits.

FRAUD EXAMINERS USE BIG DATA AND OTHER TOOLS TO FIGHT FINANCIAL FRAUD

According to the Association of Certified Fraud Examiners (ACFE), businesses lose an estimated $3.5 billion annually to fraud and financial crime. As a result, demand for forensic accountants continues to increase. The ACFE is the world's largest anti-fraud organization, with nearly 75,000 members. Certified Fraud Examiners (CFEs) have expertise in fraud prevention, detection, and deterrence, and are trained to identify the warning signs of fraud and increased fraud risk. CFEs have a unique skill set that combines knowledge of complex financial transactions with an understanding of methods, laws, and investigation of fraud allegations.

Because fraud is increasingly digital, data analytics is one of the best weapons in fraud detection. Cloud computing allows companies to consolidate data across locations and search for and detect unusual patterns in real time. For example, using Benford's Law (a formula for the expected frequency of digits in a list of numbers), one forensic team detected that several call center operators had issued fraudulent refunds to themselves, friends, and family members that totaled several hundred thousand dollars.

Fraud examiners perform a variety of forensic investigations such as examining books and records to detect and trace fraudulent transactions, interviewing suspects to obtain information and confessions, writing investigation reports, testifying at trials, and understanding factors that motivate individuals to commit fraud. Forensic accountants often work side-by-side with criminal justice and law enforcement personnel, as well as computer specialists, in conducting fraud examinations. Such examinations may relate to financial statement fraud, asset misappropriations, money laundering, bribery, or more recently, theft of information via computer hacking, and a long list of other fraudulent activities.

Sources: 1. The Association of Certified Fraud Examiners Web site (www.acfe.org); 2. Sarah Diamond, "How to Use Big Data to Fight Financial Fraud" (September 22, 2014) (www.forbes.com); 3. Jo Craven McGinty, "Accountants Increasingly Use Data Analysis to Catch Fraud" (December 5, 2014) (www.wsj.com).

As businesses increase in complexity, it is no longer sufficient for auditors to focus only on accounting transactions. An integrated approach to auditing considers both the risk of misstatements and operating controls intended to prevent misstatements. The auditor must also have a thorough understanding of the entity and its environment. This understanding includes knowledge of the client's industry and its regulatory and operating environment, including external relationships, such as with suppliers, customers, and creditors. The auditor also considers the client's business strategies and processes and critical success factors related to those strategies. This analysis helps the auditor identify business risks associated with the client's strategies that may affect whether the financial statements are fairly stated.

TYPES OF AUDITORS

OBJECTIVE 1-7

Identify the primary types of auditors.

Several types of auditors are in practice today. The most common are certified public accounting firms, government accountability office auditors, internal revenue agents, and internal auditors.

Certified Public Accounting Firms

Certified public accounting firms are responsible for auditing the historical financial statements of all publicly traded companies, most other reasonably large companies, and many smaller companies and noncommercial organizations. Because of the widespread use of audited financial statements in the U.S. economy, as well as businesspersons' and other users' familiarity with these statements, it is common to use the terms *auditor* and *CPA firm* synonymously, even though several different types of auditors exist. The title *certified public accounting firm* reflects the fact that auditors who express audit opinions on financial statements must be licensed as CPAs. CPA firms are often called *external auditors* or *independent auditors* to distinguish them from internal auditors.

Government Accountability Office Auditors

A **government accountability office auditor** is an auditor working for the U.S. Government Accountability Office (GAO), a nonpartisan agency in the legislative branch of the federal government. Headed by the Comptroller General, the GAO reports to and is responsible solely to Congress.

The GAO's primary responsibility is to perform the audit function for Congress, and it has many of the same audit responsibilities as a CPA firm. The GAO audits much of the financial information prepared by various federal government agencies before it is submitted to Congress. Because the authority for expenditures and receipts of governmental agencies is defined by law, there is considerable emphasis on compliance in these audits.

An increasing portion of the GAO's audit efforts are devoted to evaluating the operational efficiency and effectiveness of various federal programs. Also, because of the immense size of many federal agencies and the similarity of their operations, the GAO has made significant advances in developing better methods of auditing through the widespread use of highly sophisticated statistical sampling and computer risk assessment techniques.

In many states, experience as a GAO auditor fulfills the experience requirement for becoming a CPA. In those states, if an individual passes the CPA examination and fulfills the experience stipulations by becoming a GAO auditor, he or she may then obtain a CPA certificate.

As a result of their great responsibility for auditing the expenditures of the federal government, their use of advanced auditing concepts, their eligibility to be CPAs, and their opportunities for performing operational audits, GAO auditors are highly regarded in the auditing profession.

Internal Revenue Agents

The IRS, under the direction of the Commissioner of Internal Revenue, is responsible for enforcing the *federal tax laws* as they have been defined by Congress and interpreted by the courts. A major responsibility of the IRS is to audit taxpayers' returns to determine whether they have complied with the tax laws. These audits are solely compliance audits. The auditors who perform these examinations are called **internal revenue agents.**

It might seem that the audit of returns for compliance with the federal tax laws is a simple and straightforward problem, but nothing is farther from the truth. Tax laws are highly complicated, and there are hundreds of volumes of interpretations. The tax returns being audited vary from the simple returns of individuals who work for only one employer and take the standard tax deduction to the highly complex returns of multinational corporations. Taxation problems may involve individual income taxes, gift taxes, estate taxes, corporate taxes, trusts, and so on. An auditor involved in any of these areas must have considerable tax knowledge and auditing skills to conduct effective audits.

Internal Auditors

Internal auditors are employed by all types of organizations to audit for management with oversight by the board of directors, much as the GAO does for Congress. Internal auditors' responsibilities vary considerably, depending on the employer. Some internal audit staffs consist of only one or two employees doing routine compliance auditing. Other internal audit staffs may have more than 100 employees who have diverse responsibilities, including many outside the accounting area. Many internal auditors are involved in operational auditing or have expertise in evaluating computer systems.

To maintain independence from other business functions, the internal audit group typically reports directly to the president, another high executive officer, or the audit committee of the board of directors. However, internal auditors cannot be entirely independent of the entity as long as an employer–employee relationship exists. Users from outside the entity are unlikely to want to rely on information verified solely by internal auditors because of their lack of independence. This lack of independence is the major difference between internal auditors and CPA firms.

In many states, internal audit experience can be used to fulfill the experience requirement for becoming a CPA. Many internal auditors pursue certification as a certified internal auditor (CIA), and some internal auditors pursue both the CPA and CIA designations.

NEXT VERSION OF THE CPA EXAM TO LAUNCH IN 2017

The AICPA will announce the next version of the CPA Examination in 2016, and the new version will launch in 2017. The revision will be based on a comprehensive analysis and extensive research process that incorporates feedback and participation from relevant stakeholders to determine the knowledge and skills required of newly-licensed CPAs. CPA licensure requires the "three E's" of education, examination, and experience. However, only the CPA examination is uniform among the 55 jurisdictions (the 50 states; Washington, DC; Puerto Rico; the Virgin Islands; Guam; and the Commonwealth of the Northern Mariana Islands); the other requirements vary among the jurisdictions. The changes are designed to ensure that the CPA exam remains relevant and continues to effectively protect the public interest.

Input from focus groups has identified the following set of knowledge and skills:

- Critical thinking, problem solving, analytical ability, professional skepticism, and adaptability
- Strong understanding of the business environment and processes
- Effective communication skills
- Well-developed research skills
- Ability to analyze data
- Ethics and professional responsibilities

The current CPA examination consists of four sections, and is approximately 60 percent knowledge and 40 percent application. The changes being considered are designed to increase testing of higher-order skills through tasks such as writing, research, and calculations. Also under consideration is replacing the Business Environment and Concepts (BEC) section of the exam with an integrative section that would cover topics such as corporate governance, economics, financial management, information systems, strategic planning, and operations management, along with simulations that would draw on content from the other sections of the exam.

Source: Maintaining the Relevance of the Uniform CPA Examination (September 2, 2014) (www.aicpa.org).

CERTIFIED PUBLIC ACCOUNTANT

OBJECTIVE 1-8

Describe the requirements for becoming a CPA.

Use of the title **certified public accountant** (CPA) is regulated by state law through the licensing departments of each state. Within any state, the regulations usually differ for becoming a CPA and retaining a license to practice after the designation has been initially achieved. To become a CPA, three requirements must be met. These are summarized in Figure 1-3.

For a person planning to become a CPA, it is essential to know the requirements in the state where he or she plans to obtain and maintain the CPA designation. The best source of that information is the State Board of Accountancy for the state in which the person plans to be certified. The National Association of State Boards of Accountancy (NASBA) Web site (www.nasba.org) provides information on licensure requirements and links to the Web site of each state board. It is possible to transfer the CPA designation from one state to another, but additional requirements often must be met for formal education, practice experience, or continuing education.

Most young professionals who want to become CPAs start their careers working for a CPA firm. After they become CPAs, many leave the firm to work in industry, government, or education. These people may continue to be CPAs but often give up their right to practice as independent auditors. To maintain the right to practice as independent auditors in most states, CPAs must meet defined continuing education and licensing requirements. Therefore, it is common for accountants to be CPAs who do not practice as independent auditors.

Information about the CPA examination can be found in *The Uniform CPA Examination Candidate Bulletin* and the *Content and Skill Specifications for the Uniform CPA Examination,* both of which can be downloaded from the CPA Examination site found on the AICPA Web site (www.aicpa.org). The AICPA also publishes selected examination questions with unofficial answers indexed to the content specification outlines of the examination.

Some of the questions and problems at the end of the chapters in this book are based on past CPA examinations. They are designated as "based on AICPA questions."

FIGURE 1-3 Three Requirements for Becoming a CPA

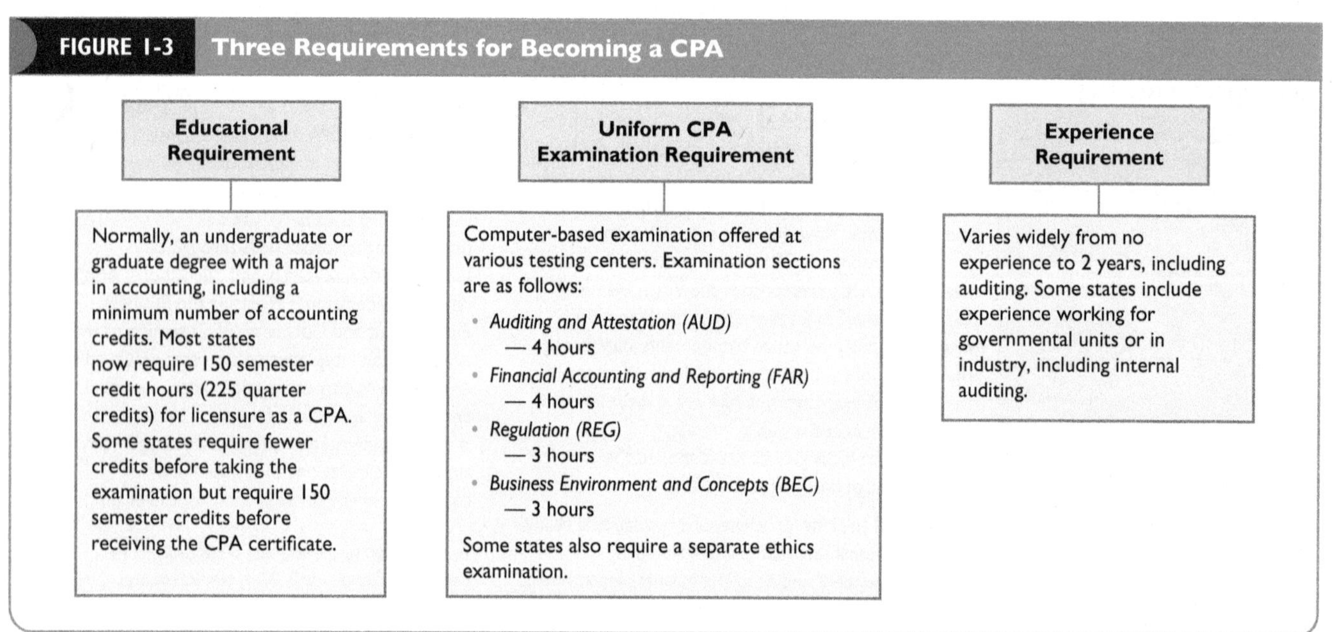

Educational Requirement
Normally, an undergraduate or graduate degree with a major in accounting, including a minimum number of accounting credits. Most states now require 150 semester credit hours (225 quarter credits) for licensure as a CPA. Some states require fewer credits before taking the examination but require 150 semester credits before receiving the CPA certificate.
Uniform CPA Examination Requirement
Computer-based examination offered at various testing centers. Examination sections are as follows:
• Auditing and Attestation (AUD) — 4 hours
• Financial Accounting and Reporting (FAR) — 4 hours
• Regulation (REG) — 3 hours
• Business Environment and Concepts (BEC) — 3 hours
Some states also require a separate ethics examination.
Experience Requirement
Varies widely from no experience to 2 years, including auditing. Some states include experience working for governmental units or in industry, including internal auditing.

CONCEPT CHECK

1. Indicate the three main types of audits. What are the similarities and differences among each type of audit?
2. What are the major differences in the scope of the audit responsibilities for CPAs, GAO auditors, IRS agents, and internal auditors?

SUMMARY

This chapter defined auditing and distinguished auditing from accounting. Audits are valuable because they reduce information risk, which lowers the cost of obtaining capital. The chapter also described attestation and assurance services, which include reports such as audits of historical financial statements and reports on the effectiveness of internal control over financial reporting. The chapter furthermore outlined different types of audits and auditors and requirements for becoming a CPA.

ESSENTIAL TERMS

Accounting—the recording, classifying, and summarizing of economic events in a logical manner for the purpose of providing financial information for decision making

Assurance service—an independent professional service that improves the quality of information for decision makers

Attestation service—a type of assurance service in which the CPA firm issues a report about a subject matter or assertion that is the responsibility of another party

Audit of historical financial statements—a form of attestation service in which the auditor issues a written report stating whether the financial statements are in material conformity with accounting standards

Audit report—the communication of audit findings to users

Auditing—the accumulation and evaluation of evidence about information to determine and report on the degree of correspondence between the information and established criteria

Certified public accountant—a person who has met state regulatory requirements, including passing the Uniform CPA Examination, and has thus been certified; a CPA may have as his or her primary responsibility the performance of the audit function on historical financial statements of commercial and noncommercial financial entities

Compliance audit—(1) a review of an organization's financial records performed to determine whether the organization is following specific procedures, rules, or regulations set by some higher authority; (2) an audit performed to determine whether an entity that receives financial assistance from the federal government has complied with specific laws and regulations

Evidence—any information used by the auditor to determine whether the information being audited is stated in accordance with established criteria

Financial statement audit—an audit conducted to determine whether the overall financial statements of an entity are stated in accordance with specified criteria (usually U.S. or international accounting standards)

Government accountability office auditor—an auditor working for the U.S. Government Accountability Office (GAO); the GAO reports to and is responsible solely to Congress

Independent auditors—certified public accountants or accounting firms that perform audits of commercial and noncommercial entities

Information risk—the risk that information upon which a business decision is made is inaccurate

Internal auditors—auditors employed by a company to audit for the company's board of directors and management

Internal control over financial reporting—an engagement in which the auditor reports on the effectiveness of internal control over financial reporting; such reports are required for accelerated filer public companies under Section 404 of the Sarbanes–Oxley Act

Internal revenue agents —auditors who work for the Internal Revenue Service (IRS) and conduct examinations of taxpayers' returns

Operational audit —a review of any part of an organization's operating procedures and methods for the purpose of evaluating efficiency and effectiveness

Review of historical financial statements—a form of attestation in which a CPA firm issues a written report that provides less assurance than an audit as to whether the financial statements are in material conformity with accounting standards

Sarbanes–Oxley Act—a federal securities law passed in 2002 that provides for additional regulation of public companies and their auditors; the Act established the Public Company Accounting Oversight Board and also requires auditors of larger public companies to audit the effectiveness of internal control over financial reporting

REVIEW QUESTIONS

1-1 (OBJECTIVE 1-1) What are the information and established criteria for the audit of Jones Company's tax return by an internal revenue agent? What are they for the audit of Jones Company's financial statements by a CPA firm?

1-2 (OBJECTIVE 1-2) In the conduct of audits of financial statements, it would be a serious breach of responsibility if the auditor did not thoroughly understand accounting. However, many competent accountants do not have an understanding of the auditing process. What causes this difference?

1-3 (OBJECTIVE 1-3) Discuss changes in accounting and business operations over the last decade that have increased the need for independent audits.

1-4 (OBJECTIVE 1-3) Distinguish among the following three factors impacting a loan interest rate: risk-free interest rate, business risk, and information risk. Which one or ones does the auditor reduce by performing an audit?

1-5 (OBJECTIVE 1-4) Identify the three main ways information risk can be reduced. What are the advantages and disadvantages of each?

1-6 (OBJECTIVE 1-4) Explain how the increased use of fair value accounting might increase information risk.

1-7 (OBJECTIVE 1-5) Explain audit services, attestation services, and assurance services, and give examples of each.

1-8 (OBJECTIVES 1-1, 1-7) Describe the nature of the evidence the internal revenue agent will use in the audit of Jones Company's tax return.

1-9 (OBJECTIVES 1-6, 1-7) List five examples of specific operational audits that can be conducted by an internal auditor in a manufacturing company.

1-10 (OBJECTIVES 1-5, 1-6) What knowledge does the auditor need about the client's business in an audit of historical financial statements? Explain how this knowledge may be useful in performing other assurance or consulting services for the client.

1-11 (OBJECTIVE 1-8) Identify the four parts of the Uniform CPA Examination.

MULTIPLE CHOICE QUESTIONS FROM CPA EXAMINATIONS

1-12 (OBJECTIVES 1-1, 1-3, 1-5) The following questions deal with audits by CPA firms. Choose the best response.

a. Which of the following best describes why an independent auditor is asked to express an opinion on the fair presentation of financial statements?
   (1) It is difficult to prepare financial statements that fairly present a company's financial position, operations, and cash flows without the expertise of an independent auditor.

(2) It is management's responsibility to seek available independent aid in the appraisal of the financial information shown in its financial statements.
(3) The opinion of an independent party is needed because a company may not be objective with respect to its own financial statements.
(4) It is a customary courtesy that all stockholders of a company receive an independent report on management's stewardship of the affairs of the business.

b. Which of the following professional services is an attestation engagement?
(1) A consulting service engagement to provide computer-processing advice to a client
(2) An engagement to report on compliance with statutory requirements
(3) An income tax engagement to prepare federal and state tax returns
(4) The preparation of financial statements from a client's financial records

c. Which of the following attributes is likely to be unique to the audit work of CPAs as compared to the work performed by practitioners of other professions?
(1) Independence
(2) Competence
(3) Due professional care
(4) Complex body of knowledge

1-13 **(OBJECTIVES 1-6, 1-7)** The following questions deal with types of audits and auditors. Choose the best response.

a. Operational audits generally have been conducted by internal auditors and governmental audit agencies but may be performed by certified public accountants. A primary purpose of an operational audit is to provide
(1) a means of assurance that internal accounting controls are functioning as planned.
(2) a measure of management performance in meeting organizational goals.
(3) the results of internal examinations of financial and accounting matters to a company's top-level management.
(4) aid to the independent auditor, who is conducting the audit of the financial statements.

b. Which of the following best describes the operational audit?
(1) It requires the constant review by internal auditors of the administrative controls as they relate to the operations of the company.
(2) It concentrates on implementing financial and accounting control in a newly organized company.
(3) It focuses on verifying the fair presentation of a company's results of operations.
(4) It concentrates on seeking aspects of operations in which waste could be reduced by the introduction of controls.

c. Compliance auditing often extends beyond audits leading to the expression of opinions on the fairness of financial presentation and includes audits of efficiency, economy, effectiveness, as well as
(1) accuracy.
(2) adherence to specific rules or procedures.
(3) evaluation.
(4) internal control.

MULTIPLE CHOICE QUESTIONS FROM BECKER CPA EXAM REVIEW

1-14 **(OBJECTIVES 1-5, 1-6)** The following questions deal with assurance services and types of audits. Choose the best response.

a. Which of the following is considered an assurance engagement?
(1) Bookkeeping
(2) Preparation
(3) Compilation
(4) Audit

b. Which of the following engagements is most likely to be considered an operational audit?
   (1) The auditor evaluates the organization's efficiency in processing payments.
   (2) The auditor examines information presented in an entity's financial statements to determine whether the financial statements are presented fairly in accordance with the applicable financial reporting framework.
   (3) The auditor determines whether the organization is following provisions of laws and regulations.
   (4) The auditor assists the client in preparation of financial statements.

c. In a financial statement audit, the auditor obtains a reasonable level of assurance about whether the financial statements are free of material misstatement in order to express an opinion. In order to obtain reasonable assurance, the auditor must
   (1) have prior experience in the industry in which the audit client operates.
   (2) examine all documents available that support the financial statements.
   (3) obtain sufficient audit evidence.
   (4) test controls around significant transaction cycles.

DISCUSSION QUESTIONS AND PROBLEMS

1-15 **(OBJECTIVE 1-5)** The list below indicates various audit, attestation, and other engagements involving auditors.

1. A report on the effectiveness of internal control over financial reporting as required by Section 404 of the Sarbanes–Oxley Act.
2. An auditor's report on whether the financial statements are fairly presented in accordance with International Financial Reporting Standards.
3. An engagement to help a company structure a merger transaction to minimize the taxes of the combined entities.
4. A report stating whether the company has complied with restrictive covenants related to officer compensation and payment of dividends contained in a bank loan agreement.
5. A report on the effectiveness of internal controls at a company that provides payroll processing for other companies.
6. An examination report stating whether a company's statement of greenhouse gas emissions is presented in conformity with standards issued by the World Business Council for Sustainable Development and the World Resources Institute.
7. Evaluating the voting process and certifying the outcome for *Rolling Stone Magazine*'s "Greatest Singer of All Time" poll.
8. A report indicating whether a governmental entity has complied with certain government regulations.
9. A review report that provides limited assurance about whether financial statements are fairly stated in accordance with U.S. GAAP.
10. A report about management's assertion on the effectiveness of controls over the availability, reliability, integrity, and maintainability of its accounting information system.
11. An evaluation of the effectiveness of key measures used to assess an entity's success in achieving specific targets linked to an entity's strategic plan and vision.

Required

a. Explain the relationships among audit services, attestation services, and other assurance and nonassurance services provided by CPAs.

b. For each of the services listed above, indicate the type of service from the list that follows.
   (1) An audit of historical financial statements.
   (2) An attestation service other than an audit service.
   (3) An assurance or nonassurance service that is not an attestation service.

1-16 **(OBJECTIVE 1-3)** Busch Corporation has an existing loan in the amount of $6 million with an annual interest rate of 6.0%. The company provides an internal company-prepared financial statement to the bank under the loan agreement. Two competing banks have offered to replace Busch Corporation's existing loan agreement with a new one. United National Bank has offered to loan Busch $6 million at a rate of 5.0% but requires Busch to provide financial statements that have been reviewed by a CPA firm. First City Bank has offered to loan Busch $6 million at a rate of 4.0% but requires Busch to provide financial statements that have been audited by a CPA firm. Busch Corporation's controller approached a CPA firm and was given an estimated cost of $35,000 to perform a review and $60,000 to perform an audit.

Required

a. Explain why the interest rate for the loan that requires a review report is lower than that for the loan that does not require a review. Explain why the interest rate for the loan that requires an audit report is lower than the interest rate for the other two loans.

b. Calculate Busch Corporation's annual costs under each loan agreement, including interest and costs for the CPA firm's services. Indicate whether Busch should keep its existing loan, accept the offer from United National Bank, or accept the offer from First City Bank.

c. Assume that United National Bank has offered the loan at a rate of 4.5% with a review, and the cost of the audit has increased to $80,000 due to new auditing standards requirements. Indicate whether Busch should keep its existing loan, accept the offer from United National Bank, or accept the offer from First City Bank.

d. Discuss why Busch may desire to have an audit, ignoring the potential reduction in interest costs.

e. Explain how a strategic understanding of the client's business may increase the value of the audit service.

1-17 **(OBJECTIVES 1-3, 1-4, 1-5)** Consumers Union is a nonprofit organization that provides information and counsel on consumer goods and services. A major part of its function is the testing of different brands of consumer products that are purchased on the open market and then the reporting of the results of the tests in *Consumer Reports*, a monthly publication. Examples of the types of products it tests are mid-sized automobiles, residential dehumidifiers, flat-screen TVs, and blue jeans.

Required

a. In what ways are the services provided by Consumers Union similar to assurance services provided by CPA firms?

b. Compare the concept of information risk introduced in this chapter with the information risk problem faced by a buyer of an automobile.

c. Compare the four causes of information risk faced by users of financial statements as discussed in this chapter with those faced by a buyer of an automobile.

d. Compare the three ways users of financial statements can reduce information risk with those available to a buyer of an automobile.

1-18 **(OBJECTIVE 1-1)** James Burrow is the loan officer for the National Bank of Dallas. National has a loan of $325,000 outstanding to Regional Delivery Service, a company specializing in delivering products of all types on behalf of smaller companies. National's collateral on the loan consists of 25 small delivery trucks with an average original cost of $24,000.

Burrow is concerned about the collectibility of the outstanding loan and whether the trucks still exist. He therefore engages Samantha Altman, CPA, to count the trucks, using registration information held by Burrow. She was engaged because she spends most of her time auditing used automobile and truck dealerships and has extensive specialized knowledge about used trucks. Burrow requests that Altman issue a report stating the following:

1. Which of the 25 trucks is parked in Regional's parking lot on the night of June 30, 2016.
2. Whether all of the trucks are owned by Regional Delivery Service.
3. The condition of each truck, using the guidelines of poor, good, and excellent.

4. The fair market value of each truck, using the current "blue book" for trucks, which states the approximate wholesale prices of all used truck models, and also using the poor, good, and excellent condition guidelines.

Required

a. For each of the following parts of the definition of auditing, state which part of the preceding narrative fits the definition:
   (1) Information
   (2) Established criteria
   (3) Accumulating and evaluating evidence
   (4) Competent, independent person
   (5) Reporting results
b. Identify the greatest difficulties Altman is likely to have doing this audit.

1-19 **(OBJECTIVE 1-7)** Five college seniors with majors in accounting are discussing alternative career plans. The first senior plans to become an internal revenue agent because his primary interest is income taxes. He believes the background in tax auditing will provide him with better exposure to income taxes than will any other available career choice. The second senior has decided to go to work for a CPA firm for at least 5 years, possibly as a permanent career. She believes the variety of experience in auditing and related fields offers a better alternative than any other available choice. The third senior has decided on a career in internal auditing with a large industrial company because of the many different aspects of the organization with which internal auditors become involved. The fourth senior plans to become an auditor for the GAO because she believes that this career will provide excellent experience in computer risk assessment techniques. The fifth senior would like to ultimately become a certified fraud examiner but is not sure where the best place is to begin his career so that he can achieve this long-term goal.

Required

a. What are the major advantages and disadvantages of each of the four types of auditing careers?
b. What do you think is the best early career choice for the senior interested in ultimately becoming a certified fraud examiner?
c. What other types of auditing careers are available to those who are qualified?

1-20 **(OBJECTIVES 1-6, 1-7)** In the normal course of performing their responsibilities, auditors often conduct audits or reviews of the following:

1. Federal income tax returns of an officer of the corporation to determine whether he or she has included all taxable income in his or her return.
2. Federal income tax returns of a corporation to determine whether the tax laws have been followed.
3. The computer operations of a large corporation to evaluate whether the internal controls are likely to prevent misstatements in accounting and operating data.
4. Financial statements for use by stockholders when there is an internal audit staff.
5. A bond indenture agreement to make sure a company is following all requirements of the contract.
6. Internal controls at a casino to ensure the casino is in compliance with federal and state regulations.
7. Computer operations of a corporation to evaluate whether the computer center is being operated as efficiently as possible.
8. Annual statements for the use of management.
9. Operations of the IRS to determine whether the internal revenue agents are using their time efficiently in conducting audits.
10. Statements for bankers and other creditors when the client is too small to have an audit staff.
11. Financial statements of a branch of the federal government to make sure that the statements present fairly the actual disbursements made during a period of time.

12. Disbursements of a branch of the federal government for a special research project to determine whether the expenditures were consistent with the legislative bill that authorized the project.

Required

a. For these 12 examples, state the most likely type of auditor (CPA, GAO, IRS, or internal) to perform each.
b. In each example, state the type of audit (financial statement audit, operational audit, or compliance audit).

1-21 **(OBJECTIVES 1-3, 1-5)** Dave Czarnecki is the managing partner of Czarnecki and Hogan, a medium-sized local CPA firm located outside of Chicago. Over lunch, he is surprised when his friend James Foley asks him, "Doesn't it bother you that your clients don't look forward to seeing their auditors each year?" Dave responds, "Well, auditing is only one of several services we provide. Most of our work for clients does not involve financial statement audits, and our audit clients seem to like interacting with us."

Required

a. Identify ways in which a financial statement audit adds value for clients.
b. List other services other than audits that Czarnecki and Hogan likely provides.
c. Assume Czarnecki and Hogan has hired you as a consultant to identify ways in which they can expand their practice. Identify at least one additional service that you believe the firm should provide and explain why you believe this represents a growth opportunity for CPA firms.

1-22 **(OBJECTIVE 1-5)** There are many types of information that require assurance. Individually or in groups, identify the following types of assurance services.

Required

a. Identify three or more assurance services that are likely to be provided only by public accounting firms.
b. Identify three or more assurance services that are likely to be provided by assurance providers other than public accounting firms.
c. Identify three or more assurance services that may be provided by public accounting firms or other assurance providers.

1-23 **(OBJECTIVE 1-5)** As discussed in the chapter opening vignette and on page 9, companies are increasingly issuing reports on corporate social responsibility. Visit the Global Reporting Initiative Web site (www.globalreporting.org) and answer the following questions.

Required

a. What is the vision and mission of the Global Reporting Initiative?
b. What is a sustainability report? Explain the use of sustainability reports in integrated reporting.
c. Explain the two "in accordance" GRI guideline reporting options. What is the GRI guidance on assurance for "in accordance" reports?

1-24 **(OBJECTIVE 1-8)** Individuals are licensed as CPAs by individual states. Information on the requirements for each state can be found on the National Association of State Boards of Accountancy (NASBA) Web site (www.nasba.org). The Uniform CPA Examination is administered by the American Institute of Certified Public Accountants (AICPA), and information on CPA examination requirements can be found on the AICPA Web site (www.aicpa.org).

Required

a. Identify the education requirements to be eligible to sit for the CPA exam in your state. Include any specific educational content requirements.
b. List the work experience requirements in your state. Is experience in industry as an accountant or an internal auditor sufficient to be eligible to become a CPA?
c. List any frequently asked questions (FAQ), if there are any, related to experience and education requirements for your state, along with a summary of the responses.
d. What are the Elijah Watts Sells awards?
e. What was the passing rate for each exam section in the most recent quarter?

CHAPTER

2

THE CPA PROFESSION

LEARNING OBJECTIVES

After studying this chapter, you should be able to

2-1 Describe the nature of CPA firms and what they do.

2-2 Describe the structure of CPA firms.

2-3 Understand the role of the Public Company Accounting Oversight Board and the effects of the Sarbanes–Oxley Act on the CPA profession.

2-4 Summarize the role of the Securities and Exchange Commission in accounting and auditing.

2-5 Describe the key functions performed by the AICPA.

2-6 Understand the role of international auditing standards and their relation to U.S. auditing standards.

2-7 Use U.S. auditing standards as a basis for further study.

2-8 Identify quality control standards and practices within the accounting profession.

Good Auditing Includes Good Client Service

"It had been a good week," thought Jeanine Wilson, as she drove out of the parking lot of Solberg Paints on Friday afternoon. Just a few months earlier, she graduated from State University and had already passed three parts of the CPA examination. Still, Jeanine did not think her transition to professional life had been all that smooth, and she was surprised at how much there still was to learn. But she had made great progress on the Solberg engagement.

John Hernandez was the audit senior on the Solberg Paints audit, and he had a reputation as a patient teacher and supervisor. Jeanine was not disappointed. At the start of the engagement, John told her, "Don't be afraid to ask questions. If you see anything that seems unusual, let's discuss it. And most importantly, if you have any ideas that will help the client, bring them up. The client expects us to deliver more than an audit report."

"I'd say I delivered," thought Jeanine. She found an error in the way the company had calculated LIFO inventory that was going to save the client a significant amount of taxes. But her biggest contribution almost did not happen. Jeanine read as much as she could about paint manufacturers and learned about some new production control methods that seemed like they could apply to Solberg. She was afraid to bring it up, thinking that she couldn't possibly know anything that the client didn't already know, but John encouraged her to discuss it with the client. The result was that the client wanted to meet further with Jeanine's firm to better understand how they could improve their production processes.

By Friday, the audit was basically completed, and the partner, Bill Marlow, was at the client's office to complete his review of the audit files. Jeanine was surprised to hear him say to her, "What are you doing on the 15th? We're going to meet with the client to discuss our audit findings. You've made a real contribution on this audit, and I'd like you to be there." Jeanine tried not to show her excitement too much, but she couldn't hide the smile on her face. "Yes, it had been a good week."

We learned in the first chapter that auditing plays an important role in society by reducing information risk and facilitating access to capital and that audit firms provide additional, value-added service to their clients. As the opening story to this chapter demonstrates, audit professionals at all experience levels serve as valued advisors to their clients. This chapter describes the organization of CPA firms and the types of services they provide. We also discuss the effects on auditing of the Sarbanes–Oxley Act and the Public Company Accounting Oversight Board (PCAOB), as well as other standards and regulatory agencies that influence auditor performance.

CERTIFIED PUBLIC ACCOUNTING FIRMS

OBJECTIVE 2-1

Describe the nature of CPA firms and what they do.

Except for certain governmental organizations, the audits of all general use financial statements in the United States are done by CPA firms. The legal right to perform audits is granted to CPA firms by regulation in each state. CPA firms also provide many other services to their clients, such as tax and advisory services.

Types of CPA Firms

It is estimated that more than 85,000 CPA firms exist in the United States. These firms range in size from 1 person to more than 50,000 partners and staff. Table 2-1 provides revenue and other data for some of the largest accounting firms in the United States. Three size categories are used to describe CPA firms: Big Four international firms, national and regional firms, and local firms.

- *Big Four international firms.* The four largest CPA firms in the United States are called the "Big Four" international CPA firms. They are the first four firms listed in Table 2-1. These four firms have offices throughout the United States

TABLE 2-1 Revenue and Other Data for the Largest CPA Firms in the United States

2014 Size by Revenue	Firm	Net Revenue—U.S. Only (in $ millions)	Partners	Professionals	U.S. Offices	Percentage of Total Revenue from Accounting and Auditing/Taxes/Management Consulting and Other
BIG FOUR						
1	Deloitte	$ 14,908.0	3,030	50,562	107	29/18/53
2	PwC	$ 11,724.0	2,691	33,024	72	41/28/31
3	Ernst & Young	$ 9,900.0	2,700	26,100	80	36/29/35
4	KPMG[1]	$ 6,870.0	1,813	20,113	101	34/28/38
NATIONAL/REGIONAL[2]						
5	McGladrey	$ 1,470.7	644	5,075	75	41/36/23
6	Grant Thornton	$ 1,382.5	529	4,692	57	41/28/31
7	BDO	$ 833.0	346	2,967	52	58/32/10
8	Crowe Horwath	$ 686.6	257	2,315	29	28/24/48
9	CBIZ/Mayer Hoffman McCann[3]	$ 600.0	429	1,832	103	30/35/35
10	CliftonLarsonAllen	$ 598.4	225	3,245	29	40/33/27
LOCAL						
50	Frank, Rimerman + Co.	$ 70.2	23	267	5	27/62/11
75	Freed Maxick CPAs	$ 45.5	35	240	4	38/38/24

(1) KPMG's office figure comprises business offices, rather than every physical location.
(2) Only the six largest national/regional firms are listed.
(3) Office figures are for CBIZ; MHM has 34 offices.
Source: Data from *Accounting Today* (www.accountingtoday.com).

and throughout the world. The Big Four firms audit nearly all of the largest companies both in the United States and worldwide and many smaller companies as well.

- *National/Regional firms.* National CPA firms in the United States have offices in most major cities while regional firms have several offices in a state or region and serve a large radius of clients. The six largest of the national/regional firms are listed in Table 2-1. These firms are large but considerably smaller than the Big Four. The national/regional firms perform the same services as the Big Four firms and compete directly with them for clients. Many of these firms are affiliated with firms in other countries and therefore have an international capability.
- *Local firms.* Some local firms have only one office and serve clients primarily within commuting distances while others may have several offices. The larger local firms compete for clients with other CPA firms, including national, regional, and Big Four firms. Many of the large local firms are affiliated with associations of CPA firms to share resources for such things as technical information and continuing education. Many of these firms also have international affiliations. Most small local CPA firms have fewer than 25 professionals in a single-office firm. They perform audits and related services primarily for smaller businesses and not-for-profit entities, although some have one or two clients with public ownership. Many small local firms do not perform audits and primarily provide accounting and tax services to their clients.

Activities of CPA Firms

As discussed in Chapter 1, CPA firms provide audit services, as well as other attestation and assurance services. Additional services commonly provided by CPA firms include accounting and bookkeeping services, tax services, and management consulting and risk advisory services. CPA firms continue to develop new products and services, such as financial planning, business valuation, forensic accounting, and information technology advisory services.

- *Accounting and bookkeeping services.* Many small clients with limited accounting staff rely on CPA firms to prepare their financial statements. Some small clients lack the personnel or expertise to use accounting software to maintain their own accounting records. Thus, CPA firms perform a variety of accounting and bookkeeping services to meet the needs of these clients. In some cases, the CPA firm is engaged by the client to help them prepare financial statements mostly for management's internal use. In many cases in which the financial statements are to be given to a third party, the client may engage the CPA to compile financial statements that are accompanied by a compilation report, which indicates the CPA assembled the statements but provides no assurance to third parties. In other situations, the client may engage the CPA to provide some assurance on those statements by performing a review or even an audit of the financial statements. As Table 2-1 (p. 25) shows, attestation services and accounting and bookkeeping services are a major source of revenue for most large CPA firms.
- *Tax services.* CPA firms prepare corporate and individual tax returns for both audit and nonaudit clients. Almost every CPA firm performs tax services, which may include estate tax, gift tax, tax planning, and other aspects of tax services. For many small firms, such services are far more important to their practice than auditing, as most of their revenue may be generated from tax services.
- *Management consulting and risk advisory services.* Most CPA firms provide certain services that enable their clients to operate their businesses more effectively.

These services are called management consulting, management advisory services, or risk advisory services. These services range from simple suggestions for improving the client's accounting system to advice in risk management, internal controls, information technology and e-commerce system design, mergers and acquisitions due diligence, business valuations, and actuarial benefit consulting. A number of organizations outsource or co-source their internal audit function to CPA firms. Many large CPA firms have departments involved exclusively in management consulting and risk advisory services with little interaction with the audit or tax staff.

Although the Sarbanes–Oxley Act and Securities and Exchange Commission (SEC) restrict auditors from providing many consulting services to public company audit clients, some services are allowed, and audit firms are not restricted from providing consulting to private companies and public companies that are not audit clients. Table 2-1 shows that management consulting and other risk advisory services are a significant source of revenue for most accounting firms.

STRUCTURE OF CPA FIRMS

OBJECTIVE 2-2

Describe the structure of CPA firms.

CPA firms vary in the nature and range of services offered, which affects the organization and structure of the firms. Three main factors influence the organizational structure of all firms:

1. *The need for independence from clients.* Independence permits auditors to remain unbiased in drawing conclusions about the financial statements.
2. *The importance of a structure to encourage competence.* Competence permits auditors to conduct audits and perform other services efficiently and effectively.
3. *The increased litigation risk faced by auditors.* Audit firms continue to experience increases in litigation-related costs. Some organizational structures afford a degree of protection to individual firm members.

Organizational Structures

Six organizational structures are available to CPA firms. Except for the proprietorship, each structure results in an entity separate from the CPA personally, which helps promote auditor independence. The last four organizational structures provide some protection from litigation loss.

Proprietorship Only firms with one owner can operate in this form. Traditionally, all one-owner firms were organized as proprietorships, but most have changed to organizational forms with more limited liability because of litigation risks.

General Partnership This form of organization is the same as a proprietorship, except that it applies to multiple owners. This organizational structure has also become less popular as other forms of ownership that offer some legal liability protection became authorized under state laws.

General Corporation The advantage of a corporation is that shareholders are liable only to the extent of their investment in the corporation. Most CPA firms do not organize as general corporations because they are prohibited by law from doing so in most states.

Professional Corporation A professional corporation (PC) provides professional services and is owned by one or more shareholders. PC laws in some states offer personal liability protection similar to that of general corporations, whereas the protection in other states is minimal. This variation makes it difficult for a CPA firm with clients in different states to operate as a PC.

TABLE 2-2	Staff Levels and Responsibilities	
Staff Level	**Average Experience**	**Typical Responsibilities**
Staff Assistant	0–2 years	Performs most of the detailed audit work.
Senior or in-charge auditor	2–5 years	Coordinates and is responsible for the performance of audit procedures, including supervising and reviewing staff work.
Manager and Senior Manager	5–10 years	Helps the in-charge plan and manage the audit, reviews the in-charge's work, and manages relations with the client. A manager may be responsible for more than one engagement at the same time.
Partner	10+ years	Reviews the overall audit work and is involved in significant audit decisions. A partner is an owner of the firm and therefore has the ultimate responsibility for conducting the audit and serving the client.

Limited Liability Company A limited liability company (LLC) combines the most favorable attributes of a general corporation and a general partnership. An LLC is typically structured and taxed like a general partnership, but its owners have limited personal liability similar to that of a general corporation. All of the states have LLC laws, and most also allow accounting firms to operate as LLCs.

Limited Liability Partnership A limited liability partnership (LLP) is owned by one or more partners. It is structured and taxed like a general partnership, but the personal liability protection of an LLP is less than that of a general corporation or an LLC. Partners of an LLP are personally liable for the partnership's debts and obligations, their own acts, and acts of others under their supervision. Partners are not personally liable for liabilities arising from negligent acts of other partners and employees not under their supervision. It is not surprising that all of the Big Four firms and many smaller firms now operate as LLPs.

Hierarchy of a Typical CPA Firm

The organizational hierarchy in a typical CPA firm includes partners or shareholders, managers, supervisors, seniors or in-charge auditors, and assistants. A new employee usually starts as an assistant and spends 2 or 3 years in each classification before achieving partner status. The titles of the positions vary from firm to firm, but the structure is similar in all. When we refer in this text to the auditor, we mean the person performing some aspect of an audit. It is common to have one or more auditors from each level on larger engagements.

Table 2-2 summarizes the experience and responsibilities of each classification level within CPA firms. Advancement in CPA firms is fairly rapid, with evolving duties and responsibilities. In addition, audit staff members usually gain diversity of experience across client engagements. Because of advances in computer and audit technology, as well as offshoring of more basic tasks, beginning assistants on the audit are rapidly given greater responsibility and challenges.

The hierarchical nature of CPA firms helps promote competence. Individuals at each level of the audit supervise and review the work of others at the level just below them in the organizational structure. A new staff assistant is supervised directly by the senior or in-charge auditor. The staff assistant's work is then reviewed by the in-charge as well as by the manager and partner.

CONCEPT CHECK

1. State the four major types of services CPAs perform, and explain each.
2. Identify the six organizational structures available to CPA firms. Why are most CPA firms not organized as general partnerships?

SARBANES–OXLEY ACT AND PUBLIC COMPANY ACCOUNTING OVERSIGHT BOARD

OBJECTIVE 2-3

Understand the role of the Public Company Accounting Oversight Board and the effects of the Sarbanes–Oxley Act on the CPA profession.

Triggered by the bankruptcies and alleged audit failures involving such companies as Enron and WorldCom, the Sarbanes–Oxley Act is considered by many to be the most important legislation affecting the auditing profession since the 1933 and 1934 Securities Acts. The provisions of the Act dramatically changed the relationship between publicly held companies and their audit firms.

The Sarbanes–Oxley Act established the **Public Company Accounting Oversight Board (PCAOB)**, appointed and overseen by the SEC. The PCAOB provides oversight for auditors of public companies; establishes auditing, attestation, and quality control standards for public company audits; and performs inspections of audit engagements as well as the quality controls at audit firms performing those audits. As a result of the 2010 Dodd-Frank financial reform legislation, auditors of brokers and dealers registered with the Securities and Exchange Commission are also required to register with the PCAOB, are subject to inspections, and must follow PCAOB auditing and attestation standards.

The PCAOB conducts inspections of registered accounting firms to assess their compliance with the rules of the PCAOB and SEC, professional standards, and each firm's own quality control policies. The PCAOB requires annual inspections of accounting firms that audit more than 100 issuers (public companies) and inspections of other registered firms at least once every three years. The largest eight firms listed in Table 2-1 (p. 25) are inspected annually. Any violations could result in disciplinary action by the PCAOB and be reported to the SEC and state accountancy boards.

DEVELOPING AUDIT QUALITY INDICATORS

Has audit quality improved since the passage and implementation of the Sarbanes–Oxley Act? This is a question that is of interest to regulators, audit firms, and users of financial statements. Audit partners at the largest firms believe that audit quality has improved, and many point to a decline in the frequency of financial statement restatements as evidence of improvement. However, PCAOB audit engagement inspection findings, which are publicly available, document an increase in audit deficiencies over the last decade. In addition, the PCAOB has publicly disclosed quality control deficiencies for all four of the large international audit firms.

One of the difficulties in answering whether audit quality has improved is that there is no agreed-upon definition, or measurement, of audit quality. The auditing profession's standards describe quality as a function of many aspects, including leadership within the firms ("tone at the top"), independence, integrity, objectivity, personnel management, client acceptance and continuation policies and procedures, engagement performance, and monitoring. In an effort to provide measures of audit quality, the PCAOB, the AICPA's Center for Audit Quality, and many of the large audit firms are developing sets of potential "Audit Quality Indicators," or AQIs, that may be informative about performance on individual audit engagements and at the firm level.

Proposals for use of AQIs include sharing the AQIs with the audit committee of the board of directors of an existing or potential audit engagement client and publicly disclosing the data at the firm level. The premise underlying such disclosure is that buyers of audit services—especially audit committees—will have new information to use as part of auditor hiring and retention decisions. Examples of potential AQIs include measures of engagement team experience and industry expertise; measures related to time spent on the audit engagement for each staffing level (e.g., partner, manager, staff) and the timing of those hours (e.g., hours spent on planning versus year-end audit procedures); workloads for individual staff, including average number of hours per week; and findings from the firm's internal monitoring process.

Regulators and professionals are optimistic about the potential benefits of measuring and disclosing AQIs. The process of measuring and disclosing these factors will focus the attention of the audit partner on important factors such as staff workloads and partner-staff hour ratios, which is likely to have an additional positive impact on audit quality.

Sources: 1. *CAQ Approach to Audit Quality Indicators*, Center for Audit Quality (www.thecaq.org); 2. Greg Jonas, PCAOB Office of Research and Analysis Director, "Update on Audit Quality Indicators" (December 10, 2013) (pcaobus.org); 3. Ken Tysiac, "SOX's Anniversary Marked with Congressional Debate on Benefits and Costs," *Journal of Accountancy* (July 26, 2012) (journalofaccountancy.com); 4. Ken Tysiac, "CAQ Proposes an Approach to Communicating Audit Quality Indicators," *Journal of Accountancy* (April 24, 2014) (journalofaccountancy.com).

SECURITIES AND EXCHANGE COMMISSION

OBJECTIVE 2-4

Summarize the role of the Securities and Exchange Commission in accounting and auditing.

The **Securities and Exchange Commission (SEC)**, an agency of the federal government, assists in providing investors with reliable information upon which to make investment decisions. The Securities Act of 1933 requires most companies planning to issue *new securities* to the public to submit a registration statement to the SEC for approval. The Securities Exchange Act of 1934 provides additional protection by requiring public companies and others to file detailed annual reports with the commission. The commission examines these statements for completeness and adequacy before permitting the company to sell its securities through the securities exchanges.

Although the SEC requires considerable information that is not of direct interest to CPAs, the securities acts of 1933 and 1934 require financial statements, accompanied by the opinion of an independent public accountant, as part of a registration statement and subsequent reports.

Of special interest to auditors are several specific reports that are subject to the reporting provisions of the securities acts. The most important of these are as follows:

- *Form S-1.* "S" forms apply to the Securities Act of 1933 and must be completed and registered with the SEC when a company plans to issue new securities to the public. The S-1 form is the general form used when there is no specifically prescribed form. The others are specialized forms. For example, S-11 is for registration of securities of certain real estate companies.
- *Form 8-K.* This report is filed to report significant events that are of interest to public investors. Such events include the acquisition or sale of a subsidiary, a change in officers or directors, an addition of a new product line, or a change in auditors.
- *Form 10-K.* This report must be filed annually within 60 to 90 days after the close of each fiscal year, depending on the size of the company. Extensive detailed financial information, including audited financial statements, is contained in this report.
- *Form 10-Q.* This report must be filed quarterly for all publicly held companies. It contains certain financial information and requires auditor reviews of the financial statements before filing with the commission.

Because large CPA firms usually have clients that must file one or more of these reports each year, and the rules and regulations affecting filings with the SEC are extremely complex, most CPA firms have specialists who spend a large portion of their time ensuring that their clients satisfy all SEC requirements.

The SEC has considerable influence in setting generally accepted accounting principles (GAAP) and disclosure requirements for financial statements as a result of its authority for specifying reporting requirements considered necessary for fair disclosure to investors, such as the requirement to file financial statement data in XBRL format. The SEC has power to establish rules for any CPA associated with audited financial statements submitted to the commission. The attitude of the SEC is generally considered in any major change proposed by the Financial Accounting Standards Board (FASB), the independent organization that establishes U.S. GAAP.

The SEC requirements of greatest interest to CPAs are set forth in the commission's Regulation S-X, Accounting Series Releases, and Accounting and Auditing Enforcement Releases. These publications constitute important regulations, as well as decisions and opinions on accounting and auditing issues affecting any CPA dealing with publicly held companies.

AMERICAN INSTITUTE OF CERTIFIED PUBLIC ACCOUNTANTS (AICPA)

OBJECTIVE 2-5

Describe the key functions performed by the AICPA.

CPAs are licensed by the state in which they practice, but a significant influence on CPAs is exerted by their national professional organization, the **American Institute of Certified Public Accountants (AICPA)**. Membership in the AICPA is restricted to CPAs, but not all members are practicing as independent auditors. Many members formerly worked for CPA firms but are currently working in government, industry, and education. AICPA membership is voluntary, so not all CPAs join. With over 400,000 CPAs, the AICPA is the largest professional association for CPAs in the United States.

The AICPA sets professional requirements for CPAs, conducts research, and publishes materials on many different subjects related to accounting, auditing, attestation and assurance services, management consulting services, and taxes. The AICPA also promotes the accounting profession through organizing national advertising campaigns, promoting new assurance services, and developing specialist certifications to help market and ensure the quality of services in specialized practice areas. For example, the association currently offers specialty designations in business valuation, financial planning, information technology, financial forensics, and global management accounting.

Establishing Standards and Rules

The AICPA sets standards and rules that all members and other practicing CPAs must follow. Four major areas in which the AICPA has authority to set standards and make rules are as follows:

1. *Auditing standards.* The Auditing Standards Board (ASB) of the AICPA is responsible for issuing pronouncements on auditing matters in the U.S. for all entities other than publicly traded companies and broker-dealers registered with the SEC. ASB pronouncements are called **Statements on Auditing Standards (SASs)**. They are further discussed later in this chapter and throughout the text.
2. *Compilation and review standards.* The Accounting and Review Services Committee is responsible for issuing pronouncements of the CPA's responsibilities when a CPA is associated with financial statements of privately owned companies that are not audited. They are called Statements on Standards for Accounting and Review Services (SSARS), and they provide guidance for performing preparation, compilation, and review services. In both a preparation service and a compilation service, the accountant helps the client prepare financial statements without providing any assurance. When a client engages a CPA to perform a compilation service, the CPA issues a compilation report; however, in a preparation service no report is issued by the CPA, but the face of the financial statements must include a statement that "no assurance is provided." In a review service, the accountant performs inquiry and analytical procedures that provide a reasonable basis for expressing limited assurance on the financial statements.
3. *Other attestation standards.* Statements on Standards for Attestation Engagements are standards that may be used to provide assurance on nonfinancial information, and are also used to develop standards for specific attestation services. For example, detailed standards have been developed for reports on prospective financial information in forecasts and projections. Attestation standards are studied in Chapter 25.
4. *Code of Professional Conduct.* The AICPA Professional Ethics Executive Committee sets rules of conduct that CPAs are required to meet. The rules and their relationships to ethical conduct are the subject of Chapter 4.

Other AICPA Functions

In addition to writing and grading the CPA examination, the AICPA performs many educational and other functions for CPAs. The association supports research by its own research staff and provides grants to others. It also publishes a variety of materials, including journals such as the *Journal of Accountancy*, industry audit guides for several industries, periodic updates of the *Codification of Statements on Auditing Standards*, and the *Code of Professional Conduct*.

CPAs must meet continuing education requirements to maintain their licenses to practice and to stay current on the extensive and ever-changing body of knowledge in accounting, auditing, attestation and assurance services, management consulting and risk advisory services, and taxes. The AICPA provides a considerable number of seminars and educational aids in a variety of subjects, such as online continuing education opportunities and reference materials in its *CPExpress* online learning library and its daily email alert about emerging professional issues through its *CPA Letter Daily*.

INTERNATIONAL AND U.S. AUDITING STANDARDS

OBJECTIVE 2-6

Understand the role of international auditing standards and their relation to U.S. auditing standards.

Auditing standards provide requirements and application and other explanatory material to aid auditors in fulfilling their professional responsibilities in the audit of historical financial statements. They include consideration of professional qualities such as competence and independence, reporting requirements, and evidence. The three main sets of auditing standards are International Standards on Auditing, AICPA auditing standards for entities other than public companies, and PCAOB Auditing Standards.

International Standards on Auditing

International Standards on Auditing (ISAs) are issued by the International Auditing and Assurance Standards Board (IAASB) of the International Federation of Accountants (IFAC). IFAC is the worldwide organization for the accountancy profession, with over 175 member organizations in 130 countries, representing more than 2.5 million accountants throughout the world. The IAASB works to improve the uniformity of auditing practices and related services throughout the world by issuing pronouncements on a variety of audit and attest functions and by promoting their acceptance worldwide.

ISAs do not override a country's regulations governing the audit of financial or other information, as each country's own regulations generally govern audit practices. These regulations may be either government statutes or statements issued by regulatory or professional bodies, such as the Australian Auditing & Assurance Standards Board or Spain's Instituto de Contabilidad y Auditoría de Cuentas. Most countries, including the United States, base their auditing standards on ISAs, modified as appropriate for each country's regulatory environment and statutory requirements.

The Auditing Standards Board in the U.S. has revised its audit standards to converge with the international standards. In addition, the PCAOB considers existing international standards in developing its standards. As a result, U.S. standards are mostly consistent with international standards, except for certain requirements that reflect unique characteristics of the U.S. environment, such as legal and regulatory requirements. For example, PCAOB Standard 5 (AS 5) addresses audits of internal control over financial reporting required by the Sarbanes–Oxley Act.

AICPA Auditing Standards

Auditing standards for private companies and other entities in the United States are established by the Auditing Standards Board (ASB) of the AICPA. These standards are referred to as Statements on Auditing Standards (SASs). Because the ASB has harmonized its agenda with the IAASB, the AICPA auditing standards are similar to the ISAs, although there are some differences. When developing a new SAS, the ASB uses the ISA as the base standard and then modifies that base standard only when modifications are appropriate for the U.S. environment. If an auditor in the United States is auditing historical financial statements in accordance with ISAs, the auditor must meet any ISA requirements that extend beyond the requirements in the AICPA standards.

Prior to passage of the Sarbanes–Oxley Act, the ASB established auditing standards in the U.S. for private and public companies. The PCAOB now has responsibility for auditing standards for U.S. public companies and broker-dealers registered with the SEC, while the ASB continues to provide auditing standards for private companies and other entities. The AICPA auditing standards are also referred to as U.S. **generally accepted auditing standards (GAAS)**.

CONVERGENCE AND CLARITY PROJECT COMPLETION IMPACTS AUDITING STANDARDS

CPAs in the U.S. need to be familiar with international standards on auditing and attest services (ISAs) as these standards become accepted worldwide and are more common in cross-border operations and financing. To address this need, the AICPA Auditing Standards Board (ASB) embarked on its Clarity Project to redraft existing AICPA auditing standards to align them with the ISAs and to make them easier to read, understand, and apply. The ASB completed this project for auditing standards in 2014.

The ASB concluded that it should move its standard-setting process to be more formally aligned with international standards on auditing and the international standard-setting process. The ASB redrafted existing AICPA auditing standards to align them with the respective ISAs and in the future will develop new SASs in conjunction with the IAASB as it develops new ISAs. When developing a new AICPA auditing standard, the ASB uses the new ISA as the base standard and modifies that base when appropriate for the U.S. environment.

Simultaneously with the move toward international convergence, the ASB Clarity Project was intended to make the U.S. auditing standards easier to read, understand, and apply. As the ASB redrafted existing guidance, each modified SAS now:

- Briefly introduces the standard and its context within the audit of financial statements;
- Establishes objectives for each of the standards and aligns those objectives with the overall objective of an audit of financial statements and the overall objective of the auditor in conducting the audit;
- Includes a definition section, where relevant, in each standard;
- Separates requirements from applications or other explanatory material;
- Uses formatting techniques, such as bulleted lists, to enhance readability; and
- Includes special considerations in the audits of smaller, less complex entities and governmental audits.

The overall objective of the ASB Clarity Project is to clarify and converge AICPA audit, attest, and quality control standards with the standards of the IAASB. With the completion of the Clarity Project for auditing standards, the ASB has now begun clarifying the Statements on Standards for Attestation Engagements

Sources: 1. "Financial Reporting Whitepaper: The AICPA's Guide to Clarified and Converged Standards for Auditing and Quality Control" (www.aicpa.org); 2. "Clarified Statements on Auditing Standards" (www.aicpa.org); 3. "Attestation Clarity Project" (www.aicpa.org).

PCAOB Auditing Standards

The PCAOB initially adopted existing auditing standards established by the ASB as interim audit standards. In addition, the PCAOB considers international auditing standards when developing new standards. As a result, auditing standards for U.S. public and private companies are mostly similar. Standards issued by the PCAOB apply only to the audits of U.S. public companies and other SEC registrants including brokers and dealers, and are referred to as "the standards of the Public Company Accounting Oversight Board (United States)" in the audit reports of public companies. When referenced in this text, we refer to these standards as PCAOB Auditing Standards.

Figure 2-1 summarizes the relations among international auditing standards, AICPA auditing standards, and PCAOB auditing standards. International auditing standards as adopted by standard-setting bodies in individual countries apply to

FIGURE 2-1 Relation of U.S. and International Auditing Standards

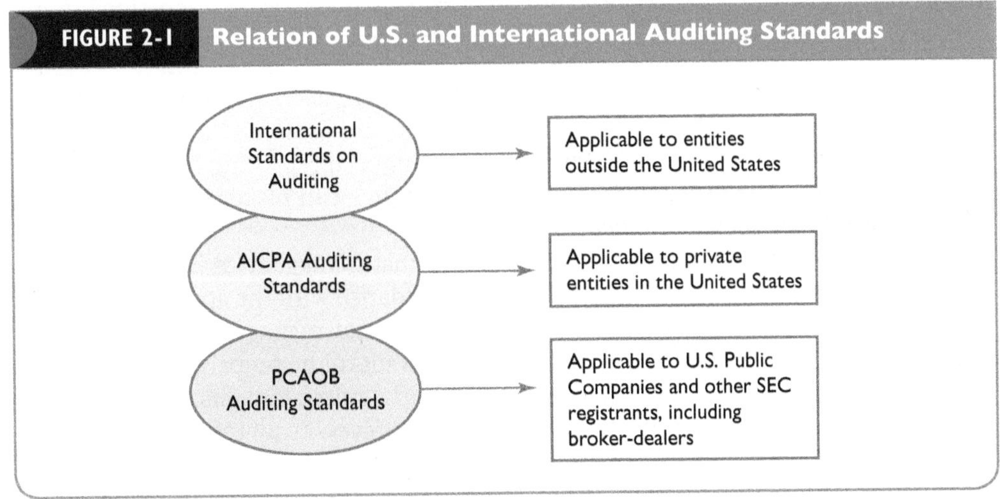

audits of entities outside the United States. AICPA auditing standards are similar to international auditing standards and apply to the audits of private companies and other entities in the United States. PCAOB auditing standards apply to audits of U.S. public companies and other SEC registrants.

The overlapping ovals illustrate that there are more similarities than differences in the three sets of standards. The auditing concepts illustrated throughout this book are generally applicable to all audits. When we refer to "auditing standards," the term applies to all audits unless otherwise noted.

ORGANIZATION OF U.S. AUDITING STANDARDS

OBJECTIVE 2-7

Use U.S. auditing standards as a basis for further study.

As part of its Clarity Project, the ASB issued a Preface to the Codification of Auditing Standards that contains the "Principles Underlying an Audit in Accordance with Generally Accepted Auditing Standards" (referred to as the principles). The **principles underlying an audit** provide a framework to help auditors fulfill the following two objectives when conducting an audit of financial statements:

1. Obtain reasonable assurance about whether the financial statements as a whole are free from material misstatement, whether due to fraud or error, thereby enabling the auditor to express an opinion on whether the financial statements are presented fairly, in all material respects, in accordance with an applicable financial reporting framework; and
2. Report on the financial statements, and communicate as required by GAAS, in accordance with the auditor's findings.

While the principles are not requirements and do not carry any authority, they are used as a framework to provide the structure for the clarified Codification. This structure is organized around the following principles, which are summarized in Figure 2-2:

- Purpose of an audit (Purpose)
- Personal responsibilities of the auditor (Responsibilities)
- Auditor actions in performing the audit (Performance)
- Reporting (Reporting)

When the PCAOB initially adopted ASB standards as interim standards, they adopted the framework existing at that time. This framework was referred to as the 10 generally accepted auditing standards (GAAS), classified into three categories: general standards, standards of field work, and reporting standards. These 10 GAAS standards generally address the same concepts as the principles. The PCAOB is reorganizing their standards using a topical framework, which would eliminate the 10 GAAS standards from the PCAOB standards. We use the ASB principles as a basis for discussing the content of U.S. auditing standards since this framework is relevant to all auditing standards.

Purpose

The purpose of an audit is to provide financial statement users with an opinion issued by the auditor on whether the financial statements are presented fairly, in all material respects, in accordance with the applicable financial reporting framework. That opinion enhances the users' degree of confidence they can place in the information presented in the financial statements.

An audit is conducted based on the premise that management is responsible for the preparation of the financial statements in accordance with the applicable financial reporting framework selected by management and that management has designed, implemented, and maintained internal control relevant to the preparation and presentation of financial statements that are free of material misstatements. An auditor also presumes that management will provide the auditor access to all information relevant to the preparation and presentation of financial statements, including unrestricted access to persons within the entity from whom the auditor may obtain audit evidence.

FIGURE 2-2 AICPA Principles Underlying an Audit

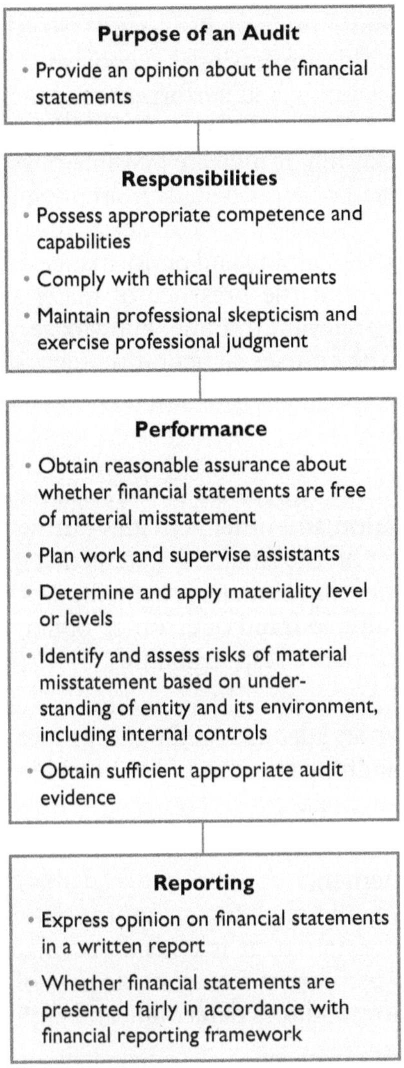

Purpose of an Audit
- Provide an opinion about the financial statements

Responsibilities
- Possess appropriate competence and capabilities
- Comply with ethical requirements
- Maintain professional skepticism and exercise professional judgment

Performance
- Obtain reasonable assurance about whether financial statements are free of material misstatement
- Plan work and supervise assistants
- Determine and apply materiality level or levels
- Identify and assess risks of material misstatement based on understanding of entity and its environment, including internal controls
- Obtain sufficient appropriate audit evidence

Reporting
- Express opinion on financial statements in a written report
- Whether financial statements are presented fairly in accordance with financial reporting framework

Responsibilities

Principles related to the auditor's responsibilities in the audit stress important personal qualities that the auditor should possess.

Appropriate Competence and Capabilities Auditors are responsible for having appropriate competence and capabilities to perform the audit. This is normally interpreted as requiring the auditor to have formal education in auditing and accounting, adequate practical experience for the work being performed, and continuing professional education. Court cases clearly demonstrate that auditors must be technically qualified and experienced in those industries in which their clients are engaged.

In any case in which the CPA or the CPA's assistants are not qualified to perform the work, a professional obligation exists to acquire the requisite knowledge and skills, suggest someone else who is qualified to perform the work, or decline the engagement.

Comply with Relevant Ethical Requirements The AICPA *Code of Professional Conduct* outlines the ethical requirements for CPAs who practice in accounting firms or work in organizations as part of management. The Code and auditing standards stress the need for independence in an audit engagement. Of particular importance are requirements for CPA firms to follow several practices to increase the likelihood of independence of all personnel. For example, there are established procedures on larger audits when there is a dispute between management and the auditors. Specific methods to ensure that auditors maintain their independence and comply with other relevant ethical requirements are studied in Chapter 4.

Maintain Professional Skepticism and Exercise Professional Judgment Auditors are responsible for maintaining professional skepticism and exercising professional judgment throughout the planning and performance of the audit. Auditing standards describe professional skepticism as an attitude that includes a questioning mind, being alert to conditions that might indicate possible misstatements due to fraud or error, and a critical assessment of audit evidence. Simply stated, auditors are to remain alert for the possibility of the presence of material misstatements whether due to fraud or error throughout the planning and performance of an audit.

In making judgments about the presence of material misstatements, auditors are responsible for applying relevant training, knowledge, and experience in making informed decisions about the courses of action that are appropriate in the circumstances of the audit engagement. Auditors are responsible for fulfilling their duties diligently and carefully.

Performance

Responsibilities related to the performance of the audit relate to auditor actions concerning evidence accumulation and other activities during the actual conduct of the audit. To express an opinion on the financial statements, the auditor obtains reasonable assurance about whether the financial statements as a whole are free from material misstatement, whether due to fraud or error. To obtain reasonable assurance, the auditor fulfills several performance responsibilities.

Adequate Planning and Supervision The auditor is responsible for sufficiently planning an audit to ensure an adequate audit and proper supervision of assistants. Supervision is essential in auditing because a considerable portion of the audit is done by less experienced staff members.

Determine and Apply Materiality Levels Because the auditor's opinion is about whether the financial statements contain material misstatements, the auditor is responsible for determining and applying an appropriate materiality level or levels throughout the audit. A misstatement is considered material if knowledge of the misstatement will affect a decision of a reasonable user of the financial statements. Chapters 3 and 8 discuss how auditors determine and apply materiality levels.

Assess Risks of Material Misstatement To adequately perform the audit, the auditor is responsible for assessing the risks that the financial statements contain material misstatements and then performing further audit procedures in response to those risks to determine if material misstatements exist. To adequately assess the risk of material misstatements, the auditor must have an understanding of the client's business and industry. This understanding helps the auditor identify significant client business risks that impact the risk of significant misstatements in the financial statements. For example, to audit a bank, an auditor must understand the nature of the bank's operations, federal and state regulations applicable to banks, and risks affecting significant accounts such as loan loss reserves.

One of the most widely accepted concepts in the theory and practice of auditing is the importance of the client's system of internal control for mitigating client business risks, safeguarding assets and records, and generating reliable financial information. If the auditor is convinced that the client has an excellent system of internal control, one that includes adequate internal controls for providing reliable data, the amount of audit evidence to be accumulated can be significantly less than when controls are not adequate. In some instances, internal control may be so inadequate as to preclude conducting an effective audit.

Sufficient Appropriate Evidence The auditor is responsible for obtaining sufficient appropriate audit evidence about whether material misstatements exist by designing and implementing appropriate responses to the assessed risks. Decisions about how much and what types of evidence to accumulate for a given set of circumstances require professional judgment. A major portion of this book is concerned with the study of evidence accumulation and the circumstances affecting the amount and types needed.

Reporting

The principles related to reporting note that the auditor is responsible for expressing an opinion in the form of a written report about whether the financial statements are presented fairly, in all material respects, in accordance with the applicable financial reporting framework. This opinion is based on the evaluation of audit evidence obtained and the auditor's findings. If an opinion cannot be expressed, the auditor's report should state that conclusion.

Principles versus Auditing Standards

The principles underlying auditing standards are too general to provide meaningful guidance, so auditors turn to the SASs issued by the AICPA and the PCAOB auditing standards (ASs) for more specific guidance. In this book, we refer to these pronouncements as auditing standards, and we distinguish between AICPA and PCAOB standards only when there are substantive differences. Auditing standards are regarded as *authoritative* literature, and every member who performs audits of historical financial statements is required to follow them under the AICPA *Code of Professional Conduct*. The AICPA and the PCAOB issue new statements when an auditing problem arises of sufficient importance to warrant an official interpretation. At this writing, SAS 129 and AS18 were the last ones issued by the AICPA and PCAOB, respectively, and incorporated into the text materials, but readers should be alert to subsequent standards that influence auditing requirements.

Classification of Auditing Standards

All SASs issued by the AICPA are given two classification numbers: an SAS and an AU-C number that indicates its location in the *Codification of Auditing Standards*. Both classification systems are used in practice. For example, the Statement on Auditing Standards, *Substantive Changes Related to Using the Work of Internal Auditors*, is SAS No. 128 and AU-C 610. The SAS number identifies the order in which it was issued in relation to other SASs; the AU-C number identifies its location in the AICPA Codification of all SASs. The AU-C section numbering is equivalent to the ISA numbers. The letter "C" is used to distinguish clarified standards from earlier standards issued by the AICPA.

Auditing Standards issued by the PCAOB are also numbered consecutively (e.g., AS1, AS2). The AICPA standards adopted by the PCAOB as interim standards retained the original AU classification that was used for those standards. The PCAOB is proposing a numerical reorganization of their standards by topical area. This would avoid confusion with the AICPA AU-C section numbering, but also facilitate comparison of the two sets of auditing standards.

Standards of Performance

Although the auditing standards are authoritative guidance for members of the profession, they provide less direction to auditors than might be assumed. A limited number of specific audit procedures are required by the standards, and there are no specific requirements for auditors' decisions, such as determining sample size, selecting sample items from the population for testing, or evaluating results. Many practitioners believe that the standards should provide more clearly defined guidelines for determining the extent of evidence to be accumulated. Such specificity would eliminate some difficult audit decisions and provide a line of defense for a CPA firm charged with conducting an inadequate audit. However, highly specific requirements could turn auditing into mechanistic evidence gathering, devoid of professional judgment. From the point of view of both the profession and the users of auditing services, there is probably greater harm in defining authoritative guidelines too specifically than too broadly.

The AICPA principles and the auditing standards should be viewed by practitioners as *minimum standards* of performance rather than as maximum standards or ideals. At the

AUDIT QUALITY AROUND THE WORLD

Global audit quality is of interest to U.S. investors, as many multinational companies are listed on a U.S. stock exchange. Non-U.S. audit firms of foreign companies listed on a U.S. stock exchange are required to register with the PCAOB and are subject to inspections, similar to U.S. audit firms. Currently, there are over 900 foreign audit firms registered with the PCAOB. However, the PCAOB has been unable to conduct inspections of audit firms in certain countries, including several European Union countries, China, and Hong Kong, primarily because the PCAOB has been denied access under local laws. U.S. investors must then rely on audit regulators in those countries to provide oversight of these audit firms. The list of audit firms that have not yet been inspected by the PCAOB is publicly available so that investors have knowledge and can "invest at their own risk."

Audit regulators from around the world are collaborating through the International Federation of Independent Audit Regulators (IFIAR) to share knowledge with a goal of improving audit quality. The membership of IFIAR has grown in recent years as more independent audit regulatory bodies are established and now consists of independent audit regulators from 51 jurisdictions, including the U.S. As one example of their knowledge-sharing efforts, IFIAR conducts surveys related to inspection findings. Their recent survey from year 2014 inspection findings identified similar deficiencies in audit engagements of publicly traded companies around the world. The most common themes in the inspection findings for the 29 countries participating in the survey relate to deficiencies in auditing fair value measurements, internal control testing, and revenue recognition. These findings are consistent with the prior year's IFIAR survey results, as well as with audit deficiencies identified in the PCAOB inspection process in the U.S., suggesting audit firms around the world face similar challenges.

IFIAR encourages audit firms to use the survey evidence and individual inspection findings to identify the root causes of the audit deficiencies as well as actions to improve quality. Collectively, the regulators and audit firms hope to work together to reduce the number of audit deficiencies and improve audit quality.

Sources: 1. International Federation of Independent Audit Regulators Report on 2014 Survey of Inspection Findings (March 3, 2015) (www.ifiar.org); 2. PCAOB International Inspections (www.pcaobus.org/international).

same time, the existence of auditing standards does not mean the auditor must always follow them blindly. If an auditor believes that the requirement of a standard is impractical or impossible to perform, the auditor is justified in following an alternative course of action, provided that sufficient appropriate evidence is obtained. Similarly, if the issue in question is immaterial in amount, it is also unnecessary to follow the standard. However, the burden of justifying departures from the standards falls on the auditor.

When auditors desire more specific guidelines, they must turn to less authoritative sources, including textbooks, journals, and technical publications. Materials published by the AICPA, such as the *Journal of Accountancy* and industry audit guides, furnish assistance on specific questions. We provide further study of the standards and make frequent reference to specific standards throughout the text.

CONCEPT CHECK

1. What is the role of the Public Company Accounting Oversight Board?
2. What roles are played by the American Institute of Certified Public Accountants for its members?
3. Describe the relations among international auditing standards, AICPA auditing standards, and PCAOB auditing standards.

QUALITY CONTROL

OBJECTIVE 2-8

Identify quality control standards and practices within the accounting profession.

For a CPA firm, **quality control** comprises the methods used to ensure that the firm meets its professional responsibilities to clients and others. These methods include the organizational structure of the CPA firm and the procedures the firm establishes. For example, a CPA firm might have an organizational structure that ensures the technical review of every engagement by a partner who has expertise in the client's industry. Auditing standards require each CPA firm to establish quality control policies and procedures. The standards recognize that a quality control system can provide only reasonable assurance, not a guarantee, that auditing standards are followed.

Quality control is closely related to but distinct from auditing standards. To ensure that the principles in auditing standards are followed on every audit, a CPA firm follows specific quality control procedures that help it meet those standards consistently on every engagement. Quality controls are therefore established for the entire CPA firm, whereas auditing standards are applicable to individual engagements.

Elements of Quality Control

Each firm should document its quality control policies and procedures. Procedures should depend on such things as the size of the firm, the number of practice offices, and the nature of the practice. The quality control procedures of a 150-office international firm with many complex, multinational clients should differ considerably from those of a five-person firm specializing in small audits in one or two industries.

The system of quality control should include policies and procedures that address six elements. These are listed in Table 2-3 with brief descriptions and procedural examples that firms might use to satisfy the requirement.

Peer Review

It should be noted that public accounting firms must be enrolled in an AICPA-approved practice-monitoring program for members in the firm to be eligible for membership in the AICPA. Practice-monitoring, also known as **peer review**, is the review, by CPAs, of another CPA firm's compliance with its quality control system. The purpose of a peer review is to determine and report whether the CPA firm being reviewed has developed adequate quality control policies and procedures and follows them in practice. Unless a firm has a peer review, all members of the CPA firm lose their eligibility for AICPA membership.

The AICPA Peer Review Program is administered by the state CPA societies under the overall direction of the AICPA peer review board. Reviews are conducted every

TABLE 2-3 Elements of Quality Control

Element	Summary of Requirements	Example of a Procedure
Leadership responsibilities for quality within the firm ("tone at the top")	The firm should promote a culture that quality is essential in performing engagements and should establish policies and procedures that support that culture.	The firm's training programs emphasize the importance of quality work, and this is reinforced in performance evaluation and compensation decisions.
Relevant ethical requirements	All personnel on engagements should maintain independence in mind and in appearance, perform all professional responsibilities with integrity, and maintain objectivity in performing their professional responsibilities.	Each partner and employee must answer an "independence questionnaire" annually, dealing with such things as stock ownership and membership on boards of directors.
Acceptance and continuation of client relationships and specific engagements	Policies and procedures should be established for deciding whether to accept or continue a client relationship or specific engagement. These policies and procedures should minimize the risk of associating with a client whose management lacks integrity. The firm should also only undertake engagements that can be completed with professional competence.	A client evaluation form, dealing with such matters as predecessor auditor comments and evaluation of management, must be prepared for every new client before acceptance.
Human resources	Policies and procedures should be established to provide the firm with reasonable assurance that • All new personnel should be qualified to perform their work competently. • Work is assigned to personnel who have adequate technical training and proficiency. • All personnel should participate in continuing professional education and professional development activities that enable them to fulfill their assigned responsibilities. • Personnel selected for advancement have the qualifications necessary for the fulfillment of their assigned responsibilities.	Each professional must be evaluated on every engagement using the firm's individual engagement evaluation report.
Engagement performance	Policies and procedures should exist to ensure that the work performed by engagement personnel meets applicable professional standards, legal and regulatory requirements, and the firm's standards of quality.	The firm's director of accounting and auditing is available for consultation and must approve all engagements before their completion.
Monitoring	Policies and procedures should exist to ensure that the other quality control elements are being effectively applied.	The quality control partner must test the quality control procedures at least annually to ensure the firm is in compliance.

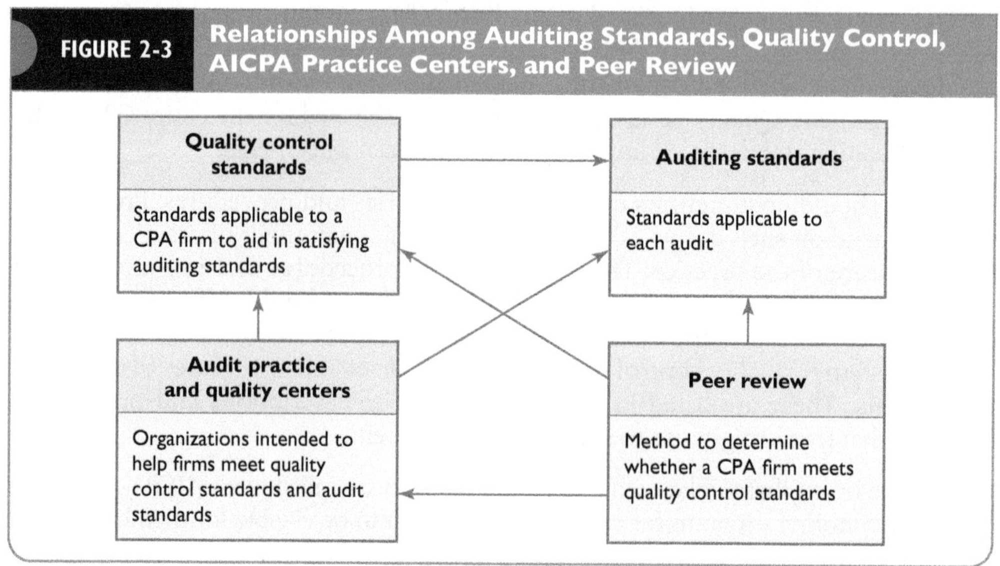

three years, and are normally performed by a CPA firm selected by the firm being reviewed, although the firm can request that it be assigned a reviewer through the administering state society. Firms required to be registered with and inspected by the PCAOB must be reviewed by the AICPA National Peer Review Committee to evaluate the non-SEC portion of the firm's accounting and auditing practice that is not inspected by the PCAOB. After the review is completed, the reviewers issue a report stating their conclusions and recommendations. Results of the peer review are included in a public file by the AICPA.

Peer review benefits individual firms by helping them meet quality control standards, which, in turn, benefits the profession through improved practitioner performance and higher-quality audits. A firm having a peer review can further benefit if the review improves the firm's practice, thereby enhancing its reputation and effectiveness and reducing the likelihood of lawsuits. Of course, peer reviews are expensive to conduct, so the benefits come at a cost.

Audit Practice and Quality Centers

The AICPA has established audit practice and quality centers as resource centers to improve audit practice quality. The **Center for Audit Quality (CAQ)** is a public policy organization affiliated with the AICPA serving investors, public company auditors, and the capital markets. The Center's mission is to foster confidence in the audit process and to make public company audits even more reliable and relevant for investors. The Private Companies Practice Section (PCPS) provides practice management information to firms of all sizes.

In addition to these firm resources, the AICPA has established audit quality centers for governmental audits and employee benefit plan audits. Figure 2-3 summarizes the relationships among auditing standards, quality control, the audit practice and quality centers, and peer review in ensuring audit quality.

SUMMARY

This chapter discussed the nature of the CPA profession and the activities of CPA firms. Because CPA firms play an important social role, several organizations, including the PCAOB, SEC, and AICPA, provide oversight to increase the likelihood of appropriate audit quality and professional conduct. These are summarized in Figure 2-4. Shaded circles in the figure indicate items discussed in this or the last chapter. The AICPA *Code of Professional Conduct* provides a standard of conduct for practitioners and is discussed in Chapter 4. The potential for legal liability is also a significant influence on auditor conduct and is discussed in Chapter 5.

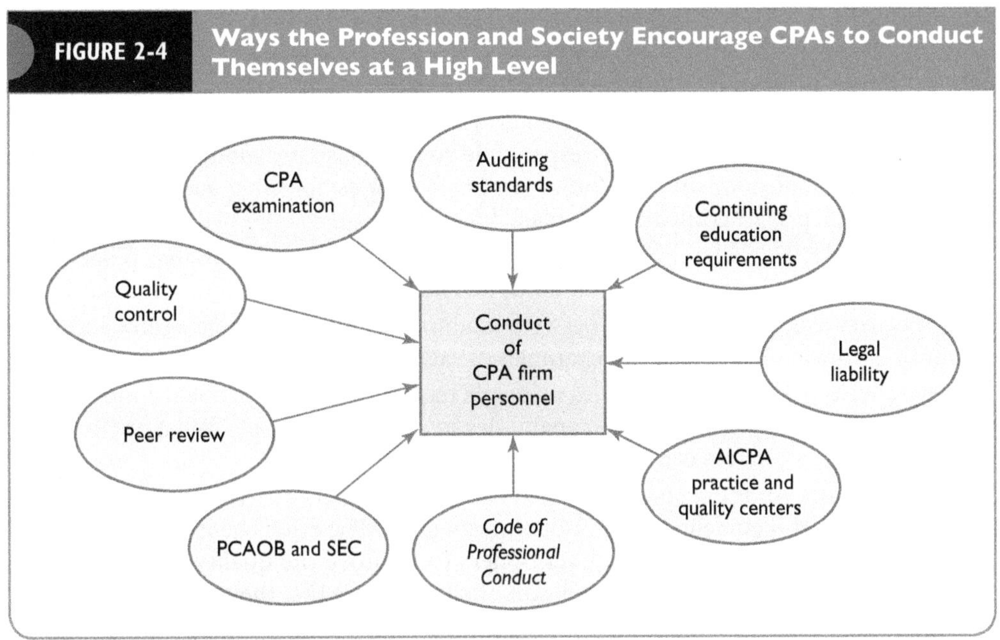

FIGURE 2-4 Ways the Profession and Society Encourage CPAs to Conduct Themselves at a High Level

ESSENTIAL TERMS

American Institute of Certified Public Accountants (AICPA)—a voluntary organization of CPAs that sets professional requirements, conducts research, and publishes materials relevant to accounting, auditing, advisory services, and taxes

Center for Audit Quality (CAQ)—a public policy organization with a mission to foster confidence in the audit process and to make public company audits even more reliable and relevant for investors

Generally accepted auditing standards (GAAS)—refers to AICPA auditing standards developed and issued in the form of Statements on Auditing Standards (SASs) and codified in AU-C sections in the *Codification of Auditing Standards*

International Standards on Auditing (ISAs)—statements issued by the International Auditing and Assurance Standards Board of the International Federation of Accountants to promote international acceptance of auditing standards

Peer review—the review by CPAs of a CPA firm's compliance with its quality control system

Principles underlying an audit—framework helpful in understanding and explaining an audit; provide a structure for the *Codification of Statements on Auditing Standards*

Public Company Accounting Oversight Board (PCAOB)—board created by the Sarbanes–Oxley Act; oversees auditors of public companies and broker-dealers, including establishing auditing, attestation, and quality control standards and performing inspections of registered accounting firms

Quality control—methods used by a CPA firm to ensure that the firm meets its professional responsibilities to clients and others

Securities and Exchange Commission (SEC)—a federal agency that oversees the orderly conduct of the securities markets; the SEC assists in providing investors in public corporations with reliable information upon which to make investment decisions

Statements on Auditing Standards (SASs)—pronouncements issued by the Auditing Standards Board of the AICPA applicable to audits of entities other than public issuers

REVIEW QUESTIONS

2-1 **(OBJECTIVES 2-1, 2-2, 2-8)** What major characteristics of the organization and conduct of CPA firms permit them to fulfill their social function competently and independently?

2-2 **(OBJECTIVE 2-3)** What events led to the creation of the Public Company Accounting Oversight Board and what is their role in the oversight of audit firms?

2-3 **(OBJECTIVE 2-4)** Describe the role of the SEC in society and discuss its relationship with and influence on the practice of auditing.

2-4 **(OBJECTIVE 2-5)** What are the purposes of the AICPA *Statements on Standards for Attestation Engagements?*

2-5 **(OBJECTIVES 2-3, 2-5, 2-6)** Who is responsible for establishing auditing standards for audits of U.S. public companies? Who is responsible for establishing auditing standards for audits of U.S. private companies? Explain.

2-6 **(OBJECTIVE 2-6)** Describe the role of International Standards on Auditing. What is the relationship between International Standards on Auditing and U.S. auditing standards?

2-7 **(OBJECTIVES 2-4, 2-7)** Distinguish between auditing standards and generally accepted accounting principles, and give two examples of each.

2-8 **(OBJECTIVE 2-7)** The Responsibilities principle requires that auditors be responsible for having appropriate competence and capabilities to perform the audit. What are the various ways in which auditors can fulfill this principle?

2-9 **(OBJECTIVE 2-7)** Auditing standards have been criticized by different sources for failing to provide useful guidelines for conducting an audit. The critics believe the standards should be more specific to enable practitioners to improve the quality of their performance. As the standards are now stated, some critics believe that they provide little more than an excuse to conduct inadequate audits. Evaluate this criticism of auditing standards.

2-10 **(OBJECTIVE 2-8)** What is meant by the term *quality control* as it relates to a CPA firm?

2-11 **(OBJECTIVE 2-8)** The following is an example of a CPA firm's quality control procedure requirement: "Any person being considered for employment by the firm must have completed a basic auditing course and have been interviewed and approved by an audit partner of the firm before he or she can be hired for the audit staff." Which element of quality control does this procedure affect and what is the purpose of the requirement?

2-12 **(OBJECTIVE 2-8)** State what is meant by the term *peer review*. What are the implications of peer review for the profession?

MULTIPLE CHOICE QUESTIONS FROM CPA EXAMINATIONS

2-13 **(OBJECTIVE 2-7)** The following questions deal with auditing standards. Choose the best response.

a. Which of the following best describes what is meant by U.S. auditing standards?
   (1) Acts to be performed by the auditor
   (2) Measures of the quality of the auditor's performance
   (3) Procedures to be used to gather evidence to support financial statements
   (4) Audit objectives generally determined on audit engagements

b. The Responsibilities principle underlying AICPA auditing standards includes a requirement that
   (1) the audit be adequately planned and supervised.
   (2) the auditor's report state whether or not the financial statements conform to generally accepted accounting principles.
   (3) professional judgment be exercised by the auditor.
   (4) informative disclosures in the financial statements be reasonably adequate.

c. What is the general character of the responsibilities characterized by the Performance principles?
   (1) The competence, independence, and professional care of persons performing the audit
   (2) Criteria for the content of the auditor's report on financial statements and related footnote disclosures
   (3) The criteria of audit planning and evidence gathering
   (4) The need to maintain an independence in mental attitude in all matters pertaining to the audit

2-14 **(OBJECTIVE 2-8)** The following questions concern quality control standards. Choose the best response.

a. The nature and extent of a CPA firm's quality control policies and procedures depend on

	The CPA Firm's Size	The Nature of the CPA Firm's Practice	Cost-benefit Considerations
(1)	Yes	Yes	Yes
(2)	Yes	Yes	No
(3)	Yes	No	Yes
(4)	No	Yes	Yes

b. Which of the following are elements of a CPA firm's quality control that should be considered in establishing its quality control policies and procedures?

	Human Resources	Monitoring	Engagement Performance
(1)	Yes	Yes	No
(2)	Yes	Yes	Yes
(3)	No	Yes	Yes
(4)	Yes	No	Yes

c. One of a CPA firm's basic objectives is to provide professional services that conform with professional standards. Reasonable assurance of achieving this objective is provided through
   (1) a system of quality control.
   (2) a system of peer review.
   (3) continuing professional education.
   (4) compliance with generally accepted reporting standards.

MULTIPLE CHOICE QUESTIONS FROM BECKER CPA EXAM REVIEW

2-15 **(OBJECTIVES 2-3, 2-4, 2-6, 2-7)** The following questions address CPA firms and entities that regulate them. Choose the best response.

a. An auditor of an entity subject to the rules of the SEC must conduct the financial statement audit in accordance with
   (1) PCAOB standards.
   (2) Statements on Standards for Accounting and Review Services.
   (3) International Auditing Standards.
   (4) Generally Accepted Government Auditing Standards.

b. Which of the following provides authoritative guidance for the auditor of a nonpublic company?
   (1) An article in the *Journal of Accountancy* that discusses new audit requirements
   (2) Information obtained from continuing professional education programs
   (3) Publication from state CPA societies that provides questions and answers on frequently asked audit questions
   (4) Statements on Auditing Standards

c. The Public Company Accounting Oversight Board (PCAOB) has the duty to
   (1) select the public accounting firm for the issuer's annual audit.
   (2) establish rules related to the preparation of audit reports for nonissuers.
   (3) conduct investigations concerning registered public accounting firms.
   (4) conduct disciplinary proceedings for nonpublic accounting firms.

DISCUSSION QUESTIONS AND PROBLEMS

2-16 **(OBJECTIVE 2-7)** Sarah O'Hann enjoyed taking her first auditing course as part of her undergraduate accounting program. While at home during her semester break, she and her father discussed the class, and it was clear that he didn't really understand the nature of the audit process as he asked the following questions:

a. What is the main objective of the audit of an entity's financial statements?
b. The audit represents the CPA firm's guarantee about the accuracy of the financial statements, right?
c. Isn't the auditor's primary responsibility to detect all kinds of fraud at the client?
d. Given the CPA firm is auditing financial statements, why would they need to understand anything about the client's business?
e. What does the auditor do in an audit other than verify the mathematical accuracy of the numbers in the financial statements?

Required If you were Sarah, how would you respond to each question?

2-17 **(OBJECTIVE 2-8)** For each of the following procedures taken from the quality control manual of a CPA firm, identify the applicable element of quality control from Table 2-3 on page 39.

a. Appropriate accounting and auditing research requires adequate technical reference materials. Each firm professional has online password access through the firm's Web site to electronic reference materials on accounting, auditing, tax, SEC, and other technical information, including industry data.
b. The partners accept responsibility for leading and promoting a quality assurance culture within the firm and for providing and maintaining a quality assurance manual and all other necessary practical aids and guidance to support engagement quality.
c. Each office of the firm shall be visited at least annually by review persons selected by the director of accounting and auditing. Procedures to be undertaken by the reviewers are illustrated by the office review program.
d. Audit engagement team members enter their electronic signatures in the firm's engagement management software to indicate the completion of specific audit program steps. At the end of the audit engagement, the engagement management software will not allow archiving of the engagement file until all audit program steps have been electronically signed.
e. At all stages of any engagement, an effort is made to involve professional staff at appropriate levels in the accounting and auditing decisions. Various approvals of the manager or senior accountant are obtained throughout the audit.
f. No employee will have any direct or indirect financial interest, association, or relationship (for example, a close relative serving a client in a decision-making capacity) not otherwise disclosed that might be adverse to the firm's best interest.
g. Individual partners submit the nominations of those persons whom they wish to be considered for partner. To become a partner, an individual must have exhibited a high degree of technical competence; must possess integrity, motivation, and judgment; and must have a desire to help the firm progress through the efficient dispatch of the job responsibilities to which he or she is assigned.
h. Through our continuing employee evaluation and counseling program and through the quality control review procedures as established by the firm, educational needs are reviewed and formal staff training programs modified to accommodate changing needs. At the conclusion of practice office reviews, apparent accounting and auditing deficiencies are summarized and reported to the firm's director of personnel.
i. All potential new clients are reviewed before acceptance. The review includes consultation with predecessor auditors, and background checks. All new clients are approved by the firm management committee, including assessing whether the firm has the technical competence to complete the engagement.
j. Each audit engagement must include a concurring partner review of critical audit decisions.

2-18 **(OBJECTIVES 2-6, 2-7)** You have been asked to make a presentation in your International Business class about how globalization is impacting the auditing profession. In preparation, you met with your auditing professor and discussed these questions:

a. What organizations are responsible for establishing U.S. auditing standards used by CPA firms when auditing financial statements prepared by organizations based in the U.S.?
b. What organization is responsible for establishing auditing standards internationally?
c. To what extent are AICPA auditing standards and international auditing standards similar?
d. What is the process the AICPA Auditing Standards Board (ASB) uses to develop AICPA auditing standards?
e. To what extent are PCAOB auditing standards impacted by international standards?
f. What auditing standards should an audit firm follow when they audit a client located in a foreign country that is listed on both a foreign stock exchange and a U.S. stock exchange?

Required

Briefly outline key points that you would make in your presentation to address these questions.

2-19 **(OBJECTIVE 2-6)** For each engagement described below, indicate whether the engagement is likely to be conducted under international auditing standards, AICPA auditing standards, or PCAOB auditing standards.

a. An audit of a U.S. private company with no public equity or debt.
b. An audit of a German private company with public debt in Germany.
c. An audit of a U.S. broker-dealer registered with the SEC.
d. An audit of a United Kingdom public company that is listed in the United States and whose financial statements will be filed with the SEC.
e. An audit of a U.S. not-for-profit organization.
f. An audit of a U.S. private company to be used for a loan from a publicly traded bank.
g. An audit of a U.S. public company.
h. An audit of a U.S. public company that is a subsidiary of a Japanese company that will be used for reporting by the parent company in Japan.

2-20 **(OBJECTIVE 2-7)** Ray, the owner of a small company, asked Holmes, a CPA, to conduct an audit of the company's records. Ray told Holmes that an audit was to be completed in time to submit audited financial statements to a bank as part of a loan application. Holmes immediately accepted the engagement and agreed to provide an auditor's report within three weeks. Ray agreed to pay Holmes a fixed fee plus a bonus if the loan was granted.

Holmes hired two accounting students to conduct the audit and spent several hours telling them exactly what to do. Holmes told the students not to spend time reviewing internal controls but instead to concentrate on proving the mathematical accuracy of the ledger accounts and summarizing the data in the accounting records that supported Ray's financial statements. The students followed Holmes's instructions and after two weeks gave Holmes the financial statements, which did not include footnotes. Holmes reviewed the statements and prepared an unmodified auditor's report. The report did not refer to generally accepted accounting principles or to the consistent application of such principles.

Required

Briefly describe each of the principles underlying AICPA auditing standards and indicate how the action(s) of Holmes resulted in a failure to comply with each principle.

Organize your answer as follows:*

Brief Description of Principle	Holmes' Actions Resulting in Failure to Comply with the Principle

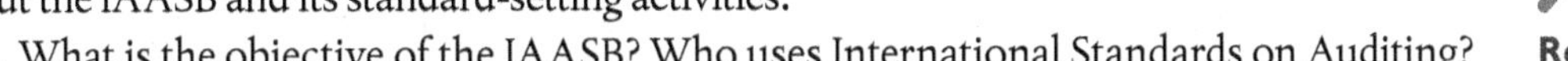

2-21 **(OBJECTIVE 2-6)** International Standards on Auditing (ISAs) are issued by the International Auditing and Assurance Standards Board (IAASB). Use the IAASB Web site to learn more about the IAASB and its standard-setting activities.[1]

Required

a. What is the objective of the IAASB? Who uses International Standards on Auditing?
b. Summarize the due process followed by the IAASB in setting standards.
c. How is the IAASB committed to transparency in the standard-setting process?

* Based on AICPA question paper, American Institute of Certified Public Accountants.

[1] The IAASB Web site can be accessed at www.iaasb.org.

CHAPTER

3

AUDIT REPORTS

LEARNING OBJECTIVES

After studying this chapter, you should be able to

3-1 Describe the parts of the standard unmodified opinion audit report for nonpublic entities under AICPA auditing standards.

3-2 Specify the conditions required to issue the standard unmodified opinion audit report.

3-3 Understand reporting on financial statements and internal control under PCAOB auditing standards.

3-4 Describe the five circumstances when an emphasis-of-matter explanatory paragraph or nonstandard wording is appropriate to include in an unmodified opinion audit report.

3-5 Identify the types of audit reports that can be issued when an unmodified opinion is not justified.

3-6 Explain how materiality affects audit reporting decisions.

3-7 Draft appropriately modified opinion audit reports under a variety of circumstances.

3-8 Determine the appropriate audit report for a given audit situation.

3-9 Understand use of international accounting and auditing standards by U.S. companies.

The Audit Report Was Timely, But at What Cost?

Halvorson & Co., CPAs, was hired as the auditor for Machinetron, Inc., a company that manufactured high-precision, computer-operated lathes. The owner, Al Trent, hired Halvorson to conduct the upcoming audit and assist with an initial public offering registration with the SEC.

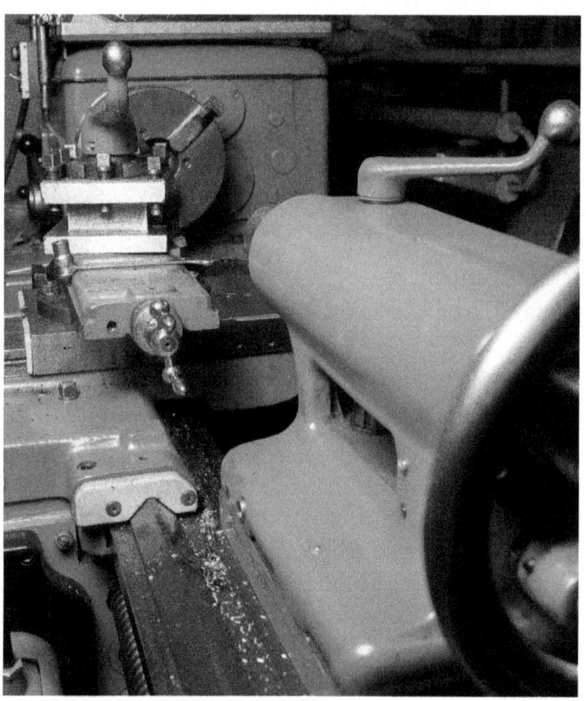

Because Machinetron's machines were large and complex, they were expensive. Each sale was negotiated individually by Trent, and the sales often transpired over several months. Improper recording of one or two machines could represent a material misstatement of the financial statements.

The engagement partner in charge of the Machinetron audit was Bob Lehman, who had significant experience auditing manufacturing companies. He recognized the risk for improper recording of sales, and he insisted that his staff confirm all receivables at year-end directly with customers. Lehman conducted his review of the Machinetron audit files the same day that Trent wanted to file the company's registration statement for the initial public stock offering with the SEC. Lehman saw that a receivable for a major sale at year-end was supported by a fax, rather than the usual written confirmation reply. Apparently, relations with this customer were "touchy," and Trent had discouraged the audit staff from communicating with the customer.

At the end of the day, there was a meeting attended by Lehman, Trent, the underwriter of the stock offering, and the company's attorney. Lehman indicated that a better form of confirmation would be required to support the receivable. After hearing this, Trent blew his stack. Machinetron's attorney offered to write a letter to Halvorson & Co. stating that in his opinion, a fax had legal substance as a valid confirmation reply. Lehman, feeling tremendous pressure, accepted this proposal and signed off on an unmodified audit opinion.

Six months after the stock offering, Machinetron announced that its revenues for the prior year were overstated as a result of improperly recorded sales, including the sale supported by the fax confirmation. The subsequent SEC investigation uncovered that the fax was returned to the audit firm by Trent, not the customer. Halvorson & Co. recalled their audit report, but this was too late to prevent the harm done to investors. Halvorson & Co. was forced to pay substantial damages, and Bob Lehman was forbidden to practice before the SEC. He subsequently left public accounting.

Reports are essential to audit and assurance engagements because they communicate the auditor's findings. Users of financial statements rely on the auditor's report to provide assurance on the company's financial statements. As the story at the beginning of this chapter illustrates, the auditor will likely be held responsible if an incorrect audit report is issued.

The audit report is the final step in the entire audit process. The reason for studying it now is to permit reference to different audit reports as we study the accumulation of audit evidence throughout this text. These evidence concepts are more meaningful after you understand the form and content of the final product of the audit. We begin by describing the content of the standard auditor's report.

As discussed in Chapter 2, the AICPA Auditing Standard Board (ASB) sets standards for nonpublic entities, and the PCAOB sets auditing standards for public companies. Because the PCAOB adopted the existing AICPA standards as interim standards, auditing standards, including those related to audit reporting, were similar for public companies and nonpublic entities. However, as part of the AICPA Clarity Project, the ASB modified audit reporting for nonpublic entities to be similar to reporting under international auditing standards. As a result, the formats of audit reports for public and nonpublic entities currently differ, although the overall substance of the content in the report is similar under both AICPA and PCAOB auditing standards.

STANDARD UNMODIFIED OPINION AUDIT REPORT FOR NONPUBLIC ENTITIES

OBJECTIVE 3-1

Describe the parts of the standard unmodified opinion audit report for nonpublic entities under AICPA auditing standards.

To allow users to understand audit reports, AICPA auditing standards provide uniform wording for the auditor's report, as illustrated in the auditor's standard unmodified opinion audit report in Figure 3-1 (p. 48). The reference to "standard" refers to the uniform wording typically used in audit reports, while "unmodified opinion" refers to the fact that the auditor's opinion about the financial statements contains no material exceptions or qualifications. Different auditors may alter the wording or presentation slightly, but the meaning will be the same.

Parts of Standard Unmodified Opinion Audit Report

The auditor's **standard unmodified opinion audit report** contains eight distinct parts, and these are labeled in bold letters in the margin beside Figure 3-1.

1. *Report title.* Auditing standards require that the report be titled and that the title include the word *independent.* For example, appropriate titles include "independent auditor's report," "report of independent auditor," or "independent accountant's opinion." The requirement that the title include the word *independent* conveys to users that the audit was unbiased in all aspects.
2. *Audit report address.* The report is usually addressed to those for whom the report is prepared, including the company, its stockholders, or the board of directors. In recent years, it has become customary to address the report to the board of directors and stockholders to indicate that the auditor is independent of the company.
3. *Introductory paragraph.* The first paragraph of the report indicates that the CPA firm has performed an audit, which distinguishes the report from a compilation or review report. The first paragraph also lists the financial statements that were audited, including the notes to the financial statements as well as the balance sheet dates and the accounting periods covered in the income statement and statement of cash flows. The wording of the financial statements in the report should be identical to the titles used by management on the financial statements. Notice that the report in Figure 3-1 is on comparative financial statements. Therefore, a report on both years' statements is needed.
4. *Management's responsibility.* The report must include the heading "Management's Responsibility for the Financial Statements" and a paragraph that describes management's responsibility for the financial statements. This responsibility includes selecting the appropriate accounting principles and maintaining internal control over financial

FIGURE 3-1 Standard Unmodified Opinion Audit Report on Comparative Statements for a U.S. Nonpublic Company—AICPA Auditing Standards

	ANDERSON and ZINDER, P.C. **Certified Public Accountants** **Park Plaza East – Suite 100** **Denver, Colorado 80110** **303/359-0800**
Report Title	**INDEPENDENT AUDITOR'S REPORT**
Audit Report Address	To the Board of Directors and Stockholders General Ring Corporation
Introductory Paragraph	We have audited the accompanying balance sheets of General Ring Corporation as of December 31, 2016 and 2015, and the related statements of income, changes in stockholders' equity, and cash flows for the years then ended, and the related notes to the financial statements.
Management's Responsibility	**Management's Responsibility for the Financial Statements** Management is responsible for the preparation and fair presentation of the financial statements in accordance with accounting principles generally accepted in the United States of America; this includes the design, implementation, and maintenance of internal control relevant to the preparation and fair presentation of financial statements that are free from material misstatement, whether due to fraud or error.
Auditor's Responsibility	**Auditor's Responsibility** Our responsibility is to express an opinion on these financial statements based on our audits. We conducted our audits in accordance with auditing standards generally accepted in the United States of America. Those standards require that we plan and perform the audit to obtain reasonable assurance about whether the financial statements are free of material misstatement.
Scope paragraph	An audit involves performing procedures to obtain audit evidence about the amounts and disclosures in the financial statements. The procedures selected depend on the auditor's judgment, including the assessment of the risks of material misstatement of the financial statements, whether due to fraud or error. In making those risk assessments, the auditor considers internal control relevant to the entity's preparation and fair presentation of the financial statements in order to design audit procedures that are appropriate in the circumstances, but not for the purpose of expressing an opinion on the effectiveness of the entity's internal control. Accordingly, we express no such opinion. An audit also includes evaluating the appropriateness of accounting policies used and the reasonableness of significant accounting estimates made by management, as well as evaluating the overall presentation of the financial statements. We believe that the audit evidence we have obtained is sufficient and appropriate to provide a basis for our audit opinion.
Auditor's Opinion	**Opinion** In our opinion, the financial statements referred to above present fairly, in all material respects, the financial position of General Ring Corporation as of December 31, 2016 and 2015, and the results of their operations and cash flows for the years then ended in accordance with accounting principles generally accepted in the United States of America.
Signature and Address of CPA Firm	*Anderson and Zinder, P.C., CPAs* Denver, Colorado
Audit Report Date (Date Auditor Has Obtained Sufficient Appropriate Evidence	February 15, 2017

reporting sufficient for preparation of financial statements that are free of material misstatements due to fraud or error.

5. *Auditor's responsibility.* This section must include the heading "Auditor's Responsibility" followed by three paragraphs that describe the auditor's responsibility.

The first paragraph states that the auditor's responsibility is to express an opinion on the financial statements and that the audit was conducted in accordance with auditing standards generally accepted in the United States of America. This paragraph also notes that the audit is designed to obtain *reasonable assurance* about whether the financial statements are free of **material misstatement**. The inclusion of the word *material* conveys that auditors are only responsible to search for significant misstatements, not minor misstatements that do not affect users' decisions. The use of the term *reasonable assurance* is intended to indicate that an audit cannot be expected to completely eliminate the possibility that a material misstatement will exist in the financial statements. In other words, an audit provides a high level of assurance, but it is not a guarantee.

The second paragraph describes the scope of the audit and the evidence accumulated about the amounts and disclosures in the financial statements. This paragraph indicates that the procedures depend on the auditor's judgment and includes an assessment of the risk of material misstatements in the financial statements. It also indicates that the auditor considers internal control relevant to the preparation and fair presentation of the financial statements in designing the audit procedures performed, but this assessment of internal control is not for the purpose of and is not sufficient to express an opinion on the effectiveness of the entity's internal control. The last sentence of this paragraph indicates that the audit includes evaluating the appropriateness of accounting policies selected, the reasonableness of accounting estimates, and the overall financial statement presentation.

The third paragraph indicates the auditor believes that sufficient appropriate evidence has been obtained to support the auditor's opinion.

6. *Opinion paragraph.* This section must include the heading "Opinion" preceding the final paragraph in the standard report, which states the auditor's conclusions based on the results of the audit. This part of the report is so important that often the entire audit report is referred to simply as the *auditor's opinion.* The opinion paragraph is stated as an opinion rather than as a statement of absolute fact or a guarantee. The intent is to indicate that the conclusions are based on professional judgment. The phrase *in our opinion* indicates that there may be some information risk associated with the financial statements, even though the statements have been audited.

A controversial part of the auditor's report is the meaning of the term *present fairly.* Does this mean that if generally accepted accounting principles are followed, the financial statements are presented fairly, or something more? Occasionally, the courts have concluded that auditors are responsible for looking beyond generally accepted accounting principles to determine whether users might be misled, even if those principles are followed. Most auditors believe that financial statements are "presented fairly" when the statements are in accordance with generally accepted accounting principles, but that it is also necessary to examine the substance of transactions and balances for possible misinformation.

7. *Signature and address of CPA firm.* The signature identifies the CPA firm or practitioner who performed the audit. Typically, the firm's name is used because the entire CPA firm has the legal and professional responsibility to ensure that the quality of the audit meets professional standards. The city and state of the audit firm should also be indicated.

8. *Audit report date.* The appropriate date for the report is the one on which the auditor completed the auditing procedures needed to obtain sufficient appropriate audit evidence. This date is important to users because it indicates the last day of the auditor's responsibility for the review of significant events that occurred after the date of the

financial statements. In the audit report in Figure 3-1 (p. 48), the balance sheet is dated December 31, 2016, and the audit report is dated February 15, 2017. This indicates that the auditor searched for material unrecorded transactions and events that occurred up to February 15, 2017.

CONDITIONS FOR STANDARD UNMODIFIED OPINION AUDIT REPORT

OBJECTIVE 3-2

Specify the conditions required to issue the standard unmodified opinion audit report.

The standard unmodified opinion audit report is issued when the following conditions have been met:

1. All statements—balance sheet, income statement, statement of changes in stockholders' equity, and statement of cash flows—are included in the financial statements.
2. Sufficient appropriate evidence has been accumulated, and the auditor has conducted the engagement in a manner that enables him or her to conclude that the audit was performed in accordance with auditing standards.
3. The financial statements are presented fairly in all material respects in accordance with U.S. generally accepted accounting principles or other appropriate accounting framework. This also means that adequate disclosures have been included in the footnotes and other parts of the financial statements.
4. There are no circumstances requiring the addition of an emphasis-of-matter paragraph or modification of the wording or auditor's opinion in the report.

When these conditions are met, the standard unmodified opinion audit report for an audit of a nonpublic company, as shown in Figure 3-1, is issued. The standard unmodified opinion audit report is sometimes called a clean opinion because there are no circumstances requiring a modification of the auditor's opinion. The standard unmodified opinion audit report is the most common audit opinion. Sometimes circumstances beyond the client's or auditor's control prevent the issuance of an unmodified ("clean") opinion. However, in most cases, companies make the appropriate changes to their accounting records to avoid a qualification or modification by the auditor.

If any of the requirements for the standard unmodified opinion audit report are not met, the standard unmodified opinion audit report cannot be issued. Figure 3-2 indicates the categories of audit reports that can be issued by the auditor. The departures from a standard unmodified opinion audit report are considered increasingly severe as one moves down the figure. Financial statement users are normally much more concerned about a disclaimer or adverse opinion than an unmodified opinion audit report that contains an additional emphasis-of-matter or other matters paragraph. These other categories of audit reports are discussed in the following sections.

STANDARD AUDIT REPORT AND REPORT ON INTERNAL CONTROL OVER FINANCIAL REPORTING UNDER PCAOB AUDITING STANDARDS

OBJECTIVE 3-3

Understand reporting on financial statements and internal control under PCAOB auditing standards.

There are two significant audit reporting differences for public companies. First, the standard unmodified opinion audit report is different for audits of financial statements of public companies. Second, auditors of larger public companies must also issue an opinion on internal control over financial reporting.

FIGURE 3-2 Categories of Audit Reports

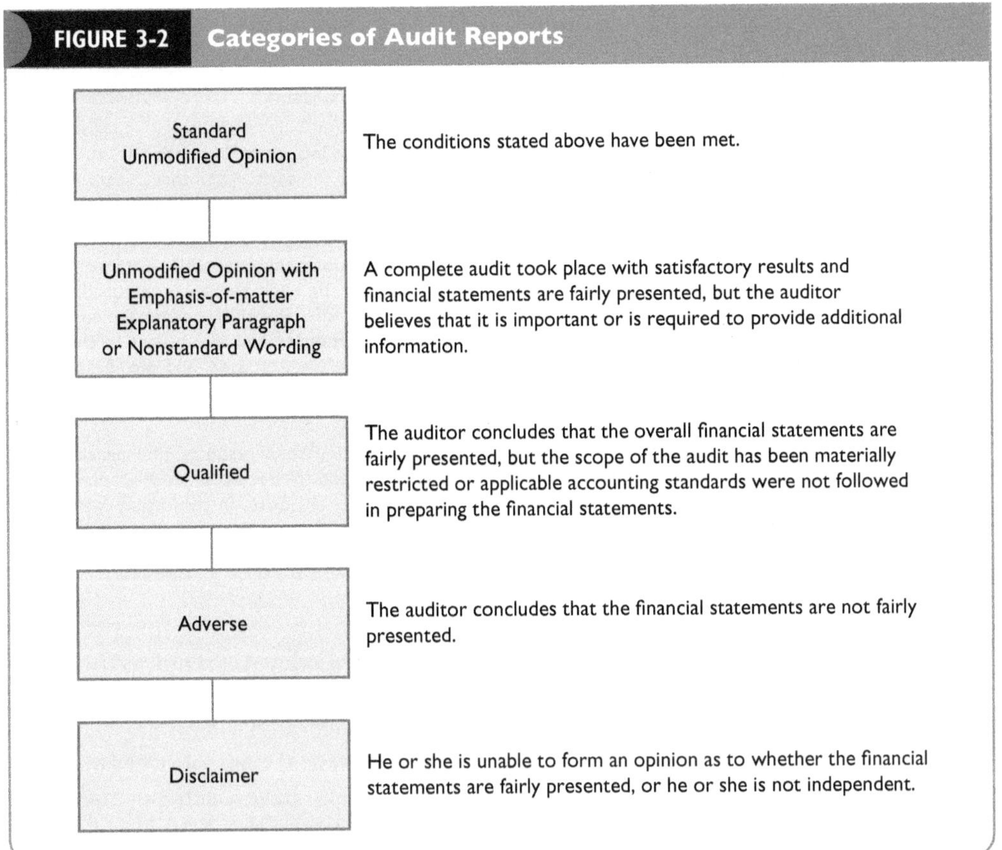

Standard Unmodified Opinion
The conditions stated above have been met.
Unmodified Opinion with Emphasis-of-matter Explanatory Paragraph or Nonstandard Wording
A complete audit took place with satisfactory results and financial statements are fairly presented, but the auditor believes that it is important or is required to provide additional information.
Qualified
The auditor concludes that the overall financial statements are fairly presented, but the scope of the audit has been materially restricted or applicable accounting standards were not followed in preparing the financial statements.
Adverse
The auditor concludes that the financial statements are not fairly presented.
Disclaimer
He or she is unable to form an opinion as to whether the financial statements are fairly presented, or he or she is not independent.

Standard Unmodified Opinion Audit Report for Public Companies

PCAOB standards refer to the standard unmodified opinion audit report as an "unqualified opinion" audit report. Throughout this book, we use the term "unmodified opinion" to represent the term "unqualified opinion" unless the setting is clearly applicable only to a public company, where we use the term "unqualified opinion" as in PCAOB auditing standards. The standard unmodified opinion audit report for public companies includes three paragraphs as illustrated in Figure 3-3 (p. 52). The report title, address, CPA firm name, and audit report date are similar for public companies and nonpublic entities and are not included in Figure 3-3. The report is quite similar to the audit report for nonpublic entities in Figure 3-1, with some differences in wording.

The first paragraph is the *introductory paragraph* and indicates that an audit was performed and the financial statements that were audited. The introductory paragraph also indicates that the financial statements are the responsibility of management and that the auditor's responsibility is to express an opinion on the financial statements. Note that this information is similar to the first three paragraphs in the standard unmodified opinion audit report for nonpublic entities in Figure 3-1.

The *scope paragraph* is similar to the second paragraph under the auditor's responsibilities in Figure 3-1, and indicates that an audit is designed to provide reasonable assurance that the financial statements are free of material misstatement. The scope paragraph notes that auditing is done on a test basis.

The third paragraph is the *opinion paragraph* and is similar to the opinion paragraph included in Figure 3-1. If the auditor also issues a separate report on internal control over financial reporting, a fourth paragraph would follow the opinion paragraph and reference the audit report on internal control.

FIGURE 3-3 **Standard Unmodified Opinion Audit Report on Comparative Statements for a U.S. Public Company—PCAOB Auditing Standards**

Introductory Paragraph	We have audited the accompanying balance sheets of Westbrook Company, Inc., as of December 31, 2016 and 2015, and the related statements of operations, equity, and cash flows for each of the three years in the period ended December 31, 2016. These financial statements are the responsibility of the Company's management. Our responsibility is to express an opinion on the financial statements based on our audits.
Scope Paragraph	We conducted our audits in accordance with the standards of the Public Company Accounting Oversight Board (United States). Those standards require that we plan and perform the audit to obtain reasonable assurance about whether the financial statements are free of material misstatement. An audit includes examining, on a test basis, evidence supporting the amounts and disclosures in the financial statements. An audit also includes assessing the accounting principles used and significant estimates made by management, as well as evaluating the overall financial statement presentation. We believe that our audits provide a reasonable basis for our opinion.
Opinion Paragraph	In our opinion, the financial statements referred to above present fairly, in all material respects, the financial position of Westbrook Company, Inc., as of December 31, 2016 and 2015, and the results of its operations and cash flows for each of the three years in the period ended December 31, 2016, in conformity with accounting principles generally accepted in the United States of America.

Reports on Internal Control Over Financial Reporting

As discussed in Chapter 1, Section 404(b) of the Sarbanes–Oxley Act requires the auditor of a public company to report on the effectiveness of internal control over financial reporting. Larger public companies (known as accelerated filers) are required by the SEC to annually obtain an auditor's report on internal control over financial reporting. As noted in Chapter 1, non-accelerated filers have been permanently exempted from this requirement by the passage by Congress of the 2010 Dodd-Frank financial reform legislation.

PCAOB Auditing Standard 5 requires the audit of internal control to be integrated with the audit of the financial statements. However, the auditor may choose to issue separate reports, such as the **separate report on internal control over financial reporting** shown in Figure 3-4, or in a combined report. The **combined report on financial statements and internal control over financial reporting** addresses both the financial statements and management's report on internal control over financial reporting. While the combined report is permitted, the separate report on internal control over financial reporting is more common and includes these elements:

- A title that includes the word "independent."
- The introductory, scope, and opinion paragraphs describe that the scope of the auditor's work and opinion is on internal control over financial reporting, and the introductory paragraph highlights management's responsibility for and its separate report that contains management's assessment of internal control over financial reporting.
- The introductory and opinion paragraphs also refer to the framework used to evaluate internal control and that the audit was conducted in accordance with PCAOB standards.
- The report includes a paragraph after the scope paragraph defining internal control over financial reporting.
- The report also includes an additional paragraph before the opinion that addresses the inherent limitations of internal control.
- Although the audit opinion on the financial statements addresses multiple reporting periods, the auditor's opinion about the effectiveness of internal control is as of the end of the most recent fiscal year.

- The last paragraph of the report includes a cross-reference to the auditor's separate report on the financial statements.

The separate report in Figure 3-4 is an unmodified opinion on the effectiveness of internal control over financial reporting prepared in accordance with PCAOB Auditing Standard 5. The auditor may issue a qualified opinion, adverse opinion, or disclaimer of opinion on the operating effectiveness of internal control over financial reporting. Conditions that require the auditor to issue a report other than an unmodified opinion on the operating effectiveness of internal control are discussed in Chapter 12, along with the effects of these conditions on the wording of the auditor's report on internal control over financial reporting.

Auditor reporting on internal controls for private companies is covered in Chapter 25.

FIGURE 3-4 Separate Report on Internal Control over Financial Reporting for a U.S. Public Company

REPORT OF INDEPENDENT REGISTERED PUBLIC ACCOUNTING FIRM	
To the Board of Directors and Shareholders of Westbrook Company, Inc.:	
We have audited Westbrook Company, Inc.'s internal control over financial reporting as of December 31, 2016, based on criteria established in *Internal Control–Integrated Framework* issued by the Committee of Sponsoring Organizations of the Treadway Commission (the COSO criteria). Westbrook Company, Inc.'s management is responsible for maintaining effective internal control over financial reporting and for its assessment of the effectiveness of internal control over financial reporting included in the accompanying Management Report on Internal Control Over Financial Reporting. Our responsibility is to express an opinion on the company's internal control over financial reporting based on our audit.	**Introductory Paragraph**
We conducted our audit in accordance with the standards of the Public Company Accounting Oversight Board (United States). Those standards require that we plan and perform the audit to obtain reasonable assurance about whether effective internal control over financial reporting was maintained in all material respects. Our audit included obtaining an understanding of internal control over financial reporting, assessing the risk that a material weakness exists, testing and evaluating the design and operating effectiveness of internal control based on the assessed risk, and performing such other procedures as we considered necessary in the circumstances. We believe that our audit provides a reasonable basis for our opinion.	**Scope Paragraph**
A company's internal control over financial reporting is a process designed to provide reasonable assurance regarding the reliability of financial reporting and the preparation of financial statements for external purposes in accordance with generally accepted accounting principles. A company's internal control over financial reporting includes those policies and procedures that (1) pertain to the maintenance of records that, in reasonable detail, accurately and fairly reflect the transactions and dispositions of the assets of the company; (2) provide reasonable assurance that transactions are recorded as necessary to permit preparation of financial statements in accordance with generally accepted accounting principles, and that receipts and expenditures of the company are being made only in accordance with authorizations of management and directors of the company; and (3) provide reasonable assurance regarding prevention or timely detection of unauthorized acquisition, use, or disposition of the company's assets that could have a material effect on the financial statements.	**Definition Paragraph**
Because of its inherent limitations, internal control over financial reporting may not prevent or detect misstatements. Also, projections of any evaluation of effectiveness to future periods are subject to the risk that controls may become inadequate because of changes in conditions, or that the degree of compliance with the policies or procedures may deteriorate.	**Inherent Limitations Paragraph**
In our opinion, Westbrook Company, Inc., maintained, in all material respects, effective internal control over financial reporting as of December 31, 2016, based on the COSO criteria.	**Opinion Paragraph**
We also have audited, in accordance with the standards of the Public Company Accounting Oversight Board (United States), the consolidated balance sheets of Westbrook Company, Inc., as of December 31, 2016 and 2015, and the related consolidated statements of income, shareholders' equity, and cash flows for each of the three years in the period ended December 31, 2016, of Westbrook Company, Inc., and our report dated February 11, 2017, expressed an unqualified opinion thereon.	**Cross Reference Paragraph**

PCAOB CONSIDERING CHANGES TO THE AUDIT REPORT

The PCAOB has proposed changes to the audit report for audits of financial statements of public companies. In its August 2013 exposure draft, the PCAOB included a number of proposed revisions to the wording in the standard audit report, while retaining the pass/fail model whereby auditors provide their opinion on whether or not the financial statements are in conformity with GAAP.

The most notable proposed change is the requirement to communicate in the audit report "critical audit matters," which represent matters the auditor addressed during the audit of the financial statements that involved the most difficult, subjective, or complex auditor judgments or that posed the most difficulty to the auditor in obtaining sufficient appropriate evidence for forming an opinion. The PCAOB believes the communication of critical audit matters would be helpful to investors and other financial statement users who would be interested in understanding challenging issues identified in the audit.

The PCAOB's proposal has been met with resistance. A number of well-known companies, including Apple, Chevron, and FedEx Corporation, along with the U.S. Chamber of Commerce, have voiced opposition in comment letters to the PCAOB. They argue that the financial statements are the responsibility of management and that the proper source of information about such matters resides with management, not the auditor. They also note that disclosure of critical audit matters may publicize aspects of the audit process that may not be useful to investors.

The PCAOB is evaluating these and other comments received about its exposure draft and will likely issue either a revised exposure draft or a new standard by 2016.

Sources: 1. "The Auditor's Report on an Audit of Financial Statements When the Auditor Expresses an Unqualified Opinion," PCAOB Release No. 2013-005, August 13, 2013, PCAOB Rulemaking Docket Matter No. 34 (www.pcaobus.org); 2. "Preparers Oppose PCAOB's Plan for More Auditor Disclosures," K. Tysiac, *Journal of Accountancy*, January 3, 2014 (www.journalofaccountancy.com).

UNMODIFIED OPINION AUDIT REPORT WITH EMPHASIS-OF-MATTER EXPLANATORY PARAGRAPH OR NONSTANDARD REPORT WORDING

OBJECTIVE 3-4

Describe the five circumstances when an emphasis-of-matter explanatory paragraph or nonstandard wording is appropriate to include in an unmodified opinion audit report.

The remainder of this chapter deals with reports other than standard unmodified opinion audit reports. In certain situations, an unmodified opinion audit report on the financial statements is issued, but the report deviates from the standard wording. The **unmodified opinion audit report with emphasis-of-matter paragraph or nonstandard report wording** meets the criteria of a complete audit with satisfactory results and financial statements that are fairly presented, but the auditor believes it is important to draw the reader's attention to certain matters or the auditor is required to provide additional information. In a qualified, adverse, or disclaimer report, the auditor either has not been able to perform a satisfactory audit, is not satisfied that the financial statements are fairly presented, or is not independent.

The following are the most important causes of the addition of an emphasis-of-matter paragraph or a modification in the wording of the standard unmodified opinion audit report under both AICPA and PCAOB audit standards:

- Lack of consistent application of generally accepted accounting principles
- Substantial doubt about going concern
- Auditor agrees with a departure from promulgated accounting principles
- Emphasis of other matters
- Reports involving other auditors

The first four reports all require the addition of an explanatory paragraph. In each case, the standard report paragraphs, including the opinion paragraph, are presented without changes in wording, and a separate explanatory paragraph follows the opinion paragraph. Only reports involving other auditors use different wording in the introductory, scope, and opinion paragraphs.

The term "explanatory paragraph" was replaced in the AICPA auditing standards with "emphasis-of-matter" or "other-matter" paragraphs. "Emphasis-of-matter" paragraphs are used to draw the reader's attention to information presented or disclosed in the financial statements, such as a footnote disclosure. "Other-matter" paragraphs refer to a matter that is not presented or disclosed in the financial statements, such as an explanation by the auditor of responsibilities related to a law or regulation. If reporting on a nonpublic entity under AICPA auditing standards, the explanatory paragraph should be preceded by the header "Emphasis of a Matter" for the first three types of explanatory paragraphs. When the auditor wishes to emphasize other matters, the report should include the heading "Other Matters." These paragraphs continue to be referred to as explanatory paragraphs under PCAOB auditing standards. We refer to explanatory paragraphs in this chapter to include both emphasis-of-matter and other-matter paragraphs.

Lack of Consistent Application of GAAP

Auditing standards require the auditor to call attention to circumstances in which accounting principles have not been consistently observed in the current period in relation to the preceding period. Generally accepted accounting principles require that changes in accounting principles or their method of application be to a preferable principle and that the nature and impact of the change be adequately disclosed. When a material change occurs, the auditor should add an explanatory paragraph after the opinion paragraph that discusses the nature of the change and points the reader to the footnote that discusses the change. The materiality of a change is evaluated based on the current year effect of the change. An explanatory paragraph is required for both voluntary changes and required changes due to a new accounting pronouncement. Figure 3-5 presents such an explanatory paragraph.

It is implicit in the explanatory paragraph in Figure 3-5 that the auditor concurs with the appropriateness of the change in accounting principles. If the auditor does not concur, the change is a violation of generally accepted accounting principles and the auditor's opinion must be qualified.

Consistency Versus Comparability The auditor must be able to distinguish between changes that affect consistency and those that may affect comparability but do not affect consistency. The following are examples of changes that affect consistency and therefore require an explanatory paragraph if they are material:

1. Changes in accounting principles, such as a change from FIFO to LIFO inventory valuation
2. Changes in reporting entities, such as the inclusion of an additional company in combined financial statements
3. Corrections of errors involving principles, by changing from an accounting principle that is not generally acceptable to one that is generally acceptable, including correction of the resulting error

Changes that affect comparability but not consistency and therefore need not be included in the audit report include the following:

1. Changes in an estimate, such as a decrease in the life of an asset for depreciation purposes
2. Error corrections not involving principles, such as a previous year's mathematical error

FIGURE 3-5 Explanatory Paragraph Because of Change in Accounting Principle

INDEPENDENT AUDITOR'S REPORT	
(Same paragraphs as the standard report)	
As discussed in Note 8 to the financial statements, the Company changed its method of computing depreciation in 2016. Our opinion is not modified with respect to this matter.	**Added Explanatory Paragraph**

3. Variations in format and presentation of financial information
4. Changes because of substantially different transactions or events, such as new endeavors in research and development or the sale of a subsidiary

Items that materially affect the comparability of financial statements generally require disclosure in the footnotes. A qualified audit report for inadequate disclosure may be required if the client refuses to properly disclose the items.

Substantial Doubt About Going Concern

Even though the purpose of an audit is not to evaluate the financial health of the business, the auditor has a responsibility under auditing standards to evaluate whether the company is likely to continue as a going concern. For example, the existence of one or more of the following factors causes uncertainty about the ability of a company to continue as a going concern:

1. Significant recurring operating losses or working capital deficiencies
2. Inability of the company to pay its obligations as they come due
3. Loss of major customers, the occurrence of uninsured catastrophes such as an earthquake or flood, or unusual labor difficulties
4. Legal proceedings, legislation, or similar matters that have occurred that might jeopardize the entity's ability to operate

The auditor's concern in such situations is the possibility that the client may not be able to continue its operations or meet its obligations for a reasonable period. The Financial Accounting Standards Board (FASB) recently clarified that management should consider the ability of the entity to continue its operations for a reasonable period not to exceed 1 year from the date the financial statements are issued. Thus, when the entity financial statements are based on FASB standards, the auditor's evaluation of the time horizon would be the same as that considered by management.

When the auditor concludes that there is substantial doubt about the entity's ability to continue as a going concern, an unmodified opinion audit report with an explanatory paragraph is required, regardless of the disclosures in the financial statements. Figure 3-6 provides an example in which there is substantial doubt about going concern.

Auditing standards permit but do not require a disclaimer of opinion when there is substantial doubt about going concern. The criteria for issuing a disclaimer of opinion instead of adding an explanatory paragraph are not stated in the standards, and this type of opinion is rarely issued in practice. An example for which a disclaimer might be issued is when a regulatory agency, such as the Environmental Protection Agency, is considering a severe sanction against a company and, if the proceedings result in an unfavorable outcome, the company will be forced to liquidate.

Auditor Agrees with a Departure from a Promulgated Principle

The AICPA *Code of Professional Conduct* states that in unusual situations, a departure from a generally accepted accounting principle may not require a qualified or adverse opinion. However, to justify an unmodified opinion, the auditor must be satisfied and

FIGURE 3-6 Explanatory Paragraph Because of Substantial Doubt About Going Concern

INDEPENDENT AUDITOR'S REPORT

(Same paragraphs as the standard report)

Added Explanatory Paragraph

The accompanying financial statements have been prepared assuming that Fairfax Company will continue as a going concern. As discussed in Note 11 to the financial statements, Fairfax Company has suffered recurring losses from operations and has a net capital deficiency that raise substantial doubt about the company's ability to continue as a going concern. Management's plans in regard to these matters are also described in Note 11. The financial statements do not include any adjustments that might result from the outcome of this uncertainty.

must state and explain, in a separate paragraph or paragraphs in the audit report, that adhering to the principle would produce a misleading result in that situation.

Emphasis of Other Matters

Under certain circumstances, the CPA may want to emphasize specific matters regarding the financial statements, even though he or she intends to express an unmodified opinion. Normally, such explanatory information should be included in a separate paragraph in the report. Examples of explanatory information the auditor may report as an emphasis of a matter include the following:

- The existence of material related party transactions
- Important events occurring subsequent to the balance sheet date
- The description of accounting matters affecting the comparability of the financial statements with those of the preceding year
- Material uncertainties disclosed in the footnotes such as unusually important litigation or regulatory action
- A major catastrophe that has had or continues to have a significant effect on the entity's financial position

Reports Involving Other Auditors

CPAs often rely on a different CPA firm to perform part of the audit when the client has widespread operations. The primary auditor issuing the opinion on the financial statements is called the *principal auditor* under PCAOB auditing standards and the *group engagement partner* under AICPA auditing standards. The other auditor who performs work on the financial information of a component is called the *component auditor* under AICPA auditing standards. We use the PCAOB terminology to reference the different auditor responsibilities. When the CPA relies on a different CPA firm to perform part of the audit, the principal CPA firm has three alternatives. Only the second is an unmodified opinion audit report with modified wording.

1. Make No Reference in the Audit Report When no reference is made to the other auditor, a standard unmodified opinion is given unless other circumstances require a departure. This approach is typically followed when the other auditor audited an immaterial portion of the statements, the other auditor is well known or closely supervised by the principal auditor, or the principal auditor has thoroughly reviewed the other auditor's work. The other auditor is still responsible for his or her own report and work in the event of a lawsuit or SEC action.

2. Make Reference in the Report This type of report is called a shared opinion or report. A shared unmodified opinion audit report is appropriate when the portion of the financial statements audited by the other CPA is material in relation to the whole. An example of an audit report that includes an unmodified opinion but makes reference to the report of another auditor for a nonpublic company is shown in Figure 3-7 (p. 58). Notice that the report does not include a separate paragraph that discusses the shared responsibility, but does so in the auditor's responsibility and opinion paragraphs. The portions of the financial statements audited by the other auditor can be stated as percentages or absolute amounts.

3. Qualify the Opinion A qualified opinion or disclaimer, depending on materiality, is required if the principal auditor is not willing to assume any responsibility for the work of the other auditor. The principal auditor may also decide that a qualification is required in the overall report if the other auditor qualified his or her portion of the audit. Qualified opinions and disclaimers are discussed in a later section of this chapter.

CONCEPT CHECK

1. What are the eight parts of a standard unmodified opinion audit report for a nonpublic entity and what is the main content provided in each part?
2. When should the auditor include an explanatory paragraph in an unmodified opinion audit report?

FIGURE 3-7 Unmodified Opinion Shared Report—AICPA Auditing Standards

INDEPENDENT AUDITOR'S REPORT

(Same introductory and management's responsibility paragraphs as the standard report)

Auditor's Responsibility

Our responsibility is to express an opinion on these financial statements based on our audits. We did not audit the financial statements of Stewart Pane and Lighting, a wholly-owned subsidiary, which statements reflect total assets constituting 20 percent and 22 percent, respectively, of consolidated total assets at December 31, 2016 and 2015, and total revenues constituting 18 percent and 20 percent, respectively, of consolidated total revenues for the years then ended. Those statements were audited by other auditors whose report has been furnished to us, and our opinion, insofar as it relates to the amounts included for Stewart Pane and Lighting, is based solely on the report of the other auditors. We conducted our audits in accordance with auditing standards generally accepted in the United States of America. Those standards require that we plan and perform the audit to obtain reasonable assurance about whether the financial statements are free of material misstatement.

(Same scope paragraph under auditor's responsibility as the standard report)

We believe that the audit evidence we have obtained is sufficient and appropriate to provide a basis for our audit opinion.

Opinion

In our opinion, based on our audit and the report of the other auditors, the financial statements referred to above present fairly, in all material respects, the financial position of Washington Felp Corporation as of December 31, 2016 and 2015, and the results of their operations and cash flows for the years then ended in accordance with accounting principles generally accepted in the United States of America.

MODIFICATIONS TO THE OPINION IN THE AUDIT REPORT

OBJECTIVE 3-5

Identify the types of audit reports that can be issued when an unmodified opinion is not justified.

It is essential that auditors and readers of audit reports understand the circumstances when an unmodified opinion in the audit report is inappropriate and the type of audit report issued in each circumstance. In the study of audit reports that depart from an unmodified opinion, there are three closely related topics: the conditions requiring a modification to the opinion, the types of opinions other than unmodified, and materiality.

First, the three conditions requiring a modification to the opinion are briefly summarized. Each is discussed in greater depth later in the chapter.

1. The Scope of the Audit Has Been Restricted (Scope Limitation) When the auditor has not accumulated sufficient appropriate evidence to conclude whether financial statements are stated in accordance with the appropriate financial reporting framework, a scope restriction exists. There are two major causes of scope restrictions: restrictions imposed by the client and those caused by circumstances beyond either the client's or auditor's control. An example of a client restriction is management's refusal to permit the auditor to confirm material receivables or to physically examine inventory. An example of a restriction caused by circumstances is when the auditor is not appointed until after the client's year-end. It may not be possible to physically observe inventories, confirm receivables, or perform other important procedures after the balance sheet date.

2. The Financial Statements Have Not Been Prepared in Accordance with Generally Accepted Accounting Principles (GAAP Departure) For example, if the client insists on using replacement costs for fixed assets or values inventory at selling price rather than historical cost as required by generally accepted accounting principles, a departure from the unmodified opinion audit report is required. When U.S. generally accepted accounting principles or international financial reporting standards (IFRS) are referred to in this context, consideration of the adequacy of all informative disclosures, including footnotes, is especially important. While most U.S. companies prepare their financial statements in accordance with GAAP, some entities might use other financial reporting frameworks, such as IFRS. References to GAAP in this chapter also apply to situations where the client has selected another appropriate financial reporting framework.

3. The Auditor Is Not Independent Independence ordinarily is determined by the AICPA *Code of Professional Conduct*. Auditor independence requirements and the AICPA *Code* are further discussed in Chapter 4.

When any of the three conditions requiring a departure from an unmodified opinion exists and is material, the opinion in the audit report must be modified. Three main types of audit reports are issued under these conditions: qualified opinion, adverse opinion, and disclaimer of opinion.

Qualified Opinion

A **qualified opinion** report can result from a limitation on the scope of the audit or failure to follow generally accepted accounting principles. A qualified opinion report can be used *only when the auditor concludes that the overall financial statements are fairly stated*. A disclaimer or an adverse report must be used if the auditor believes that the condition being reported on is highly material to the financial statements as a whole. Therefore, the qualified opinion is considered the least severe type of departure from an unmodified opinion audit report.

A qualified report can take the form of a *qualification of both the scope and the opinion* or of the *opinion alone*. A scope and opinion qualification can be issued only when the auditor has been unable to accumulate all of the evidence sufficient to support an opinion on the financial statements. Therefore, this type of qualification is used when the auditor's scope has been restricted by the client or when circumstances exist that prevent the auditor from conducting a complete audit. The use of a qualification of the opinion alone is restricted to situations in which the financial statements are not stated in accordance with GAAP.

When an auditor issues a qualified report, he or she must use the term *except for* in the opinion paragraph. The implication is that the auditor is satisfied that the overall financial statements are correctly stated "except for" a specific aspect of them. Examples of this qualification are given later in this chapter. It is unacceptable to use the phrase *except for* with any other type of audit opinion.

Adverse Opinion

An **adverse opinion** is used only when the auditor believes that the overall financial statements are so *materially misstated or misleading* that they do not present fairly the financial position or results of operations and cash flows in conformity with GAAP. The adverse opinion report can arise only when the auditor has knowledge, after an adequate investigation, of the absence of conformity. This is uncommon and thus the adverse opinion is rarely used.

Disclaimer of Opinion

A **disclaimer of opinion** is issued when the auditor has been *unable to satisfy himself or herself* that the overall financial statements are fairly presented. The necessity for disclaiming an opinion may arise because of a *severe limitation on the scope* of the audit or a *nonindependent relationship* under the AICPA *Code of Professional Conduct* between the auditor and the client. Either of these situations prevents the auditor from expressing an opinion on the financial statements as a whole. The auditor also has the option to issue a disclaimer of opinion for a going concern problem.

The disclaimer is distinguished from an adverse opinion in that a disclaimer can arise only from a *lack of knowledge* by the auditor, whereas to express an adverse opinion, the auditor must have knowledge that the financial statements are not fairly stated. Both disclaimers and adverse opinions are used only when the condition is highly material.

MATERIALITY

OBJECTIVE 3-6

Explain how materiality affects audit reporting decisions.

Materiality is an essential consideration in determining the appropriate type of report for a given set of circumstances. For example, if a misstatement is immaterial relative to the financial statements of the entity for the current period, it is appropriate to issue an unmodified opinion audit report. A common instance is the immediate expensing of office supplies rather than carrying the unused portion in inventory because the amount is insignificant.

The situation is totally different when the amounts are of such significance that the financial statements are materially affected as a whole. In these circumstances, it is necessary to issue a disclaimer of opinion or an adverse opinion, depending on whether a scope limitation or GAAP departure is involved. In situations of lesser materiality, a qualified opinion is appropriate.

Levels of Materiality

The common definition of materiality as it applies to accounting and therefore to audit reporting is as follows:

> A misstatement in the financial statements can be considered material if knowledge of the misstatement will affect a decision of a reasonable user of the statements.

In applying this definition, three levels of materiality are used for determining the type of opinion to issue.

Amounts Are Immaterial When a misstatement in the financial statements exists but is unlikely to affect the decisions of a reasonable user, it is considered to be immaterial. An unmodified opinion is therefore appropriate. For example, assume that management recorded prepaid insurance as an asset in the previous year and decides to expense it in the current year to reduce record-keeping costs. Management has failed to follow GAAP, but if the amounts are small, the misstatement is immaterial and a standard unmodified opinion audit report is appropriate.

Amounts Are Material but Do Not Overshadow the Financial Statements as a Whole The second level of materiality exists when a misstatement in the financial statements would affect a user's decision, but the overall statements are still fairly stated and therefore useful. For example, knowledge of a large misstatement in fixed assets might affect a user's willingness to loan money to a company if the assets were the collateral. A misstatement of inventory does not mean that cash, accounts receivable, and other elements of the financial statements, or the financial statements as a whole, are materially incorrect.

To make materiality decisions when a condition requiring a departure from an unmodified opinion audit report exists, the auditor must evaluate all effects on the financial statements. Assume that the auditor is unable to satisfy himself or herself whether inventory is fairly stated in deciding on the appropriate type of opinion. Because of the effect of a misstatement in inventory on other accounts and on totals in the statements, the auditor needs to consider the materiality of the combined effect on inventory, total current assets, total working capital, total assets, income taxes, income taxes payable, total current liabilities, cost of goods sold, net income before taxes, and net income after taxes.

When the auditor concludes that a misstatement is material but does not overshadow the financial statements as a whole, a qualified opinion (using "except for") is appropriate.

Amounts Are So Material or So Pervasive That Overall Fairness of the Statements Is in Question The highest level of materiality exists when users are likely to make incorrect decisions if they rely on the overall financial statements. To return to the previous example, if inventory is the largest balance on the financial statements, a large misstatement would probably be so material that the auditor's report should indicate the financial statements taken as a whole cannot be considered fairly stated. When the highest level of materiality exists, the auditor must issue either a disclaimer of opinion or an adverse opinion, depending on which conditions exist.

When determining whether an exception is highly material, the extent to which the exception affects different parts of the financial statements must be considered. This is called pervasiveness. A misclassification between cash and accounts receivable affects only those two accounts and is therefore not pervasive. On the other hand, failure to record a material sale is highly pervasive because it affects sales, accounts receivable, income tax expense, accrued income taxes, and retained earnings, which in turn affect current assets, total assets, current liabilities, total liabilities, owners' equity, gross margin, and operating income.

As misstatements become more pervasive, the likelihood of issuing an adverse opinion rather than a qualified opinion increases. For example, suppose the auditor decides a misclassification between cash and accounts receivable should result in a qualified opinion because it is material; the failure to record a sale of the same dollar amount may result in an adverse opinion because of pervasiveness.

Regardless of the amount involved, a disclaimer of opinion must be issued if the auditor is deemed to lack independence under the rules of the AICPA *Code of Professional Conduct*. This strict requirement reflects the importance of independence to auditors. Any deviation from the independence rule is therefore considered highly material. Table 3-1 summarizes the relationship between materiality and the type of opinion to be issued.

Materiality Decisions

In concept, the effect of materiality on the type of opinion to issue is straightforward. In application, deciding on actual materiality in a given situation is a difficult judgment. There are no simple, well-defined guidelines that enable auditors to decide when something is immaterial, material, or highly material. The evaluation of materiality also depends on whether the situation involves a failure to follow GAAP or a scope limitation.

Materiality Decisions—Non-GAAP Condition When a client has failed to follow GAAP, the audit report will contain an unmodified opinion, a qualified opinion only, or an adverse opinion, depending on the materiality of the departure. Several aspects of materiality must be considered.

Dollar Amounts Compared with a Benchmark The primary concern in measuring materiality when a client has failed to follow GAAP is usually the total dollar misstatement in the accounts involved, compared with some benchmark or base. A $10,000 misstatement might be material for a small company but not for a larger one. Therefore, misstatements must be compared with some measurement base before a decision can be made about the materiality of the failure to follow GAAP. Common bases include net income, total assets, current assets, and working capital.

TABLE 3-1 Relationship of Materiality to Type of Opinion

Materiality Level	Significance in Terms of Reasonable Users' Decisions	Type of Opinion
Immaterial	Users' decisions are unlikely to be affected.	Unmodified
Material	Users' decisions are likely to be affected only if the information in question is important to the specific decisions being made. The effect of the misstatement(s) is not pervasive to the financial statements and the overall financial statements are presented fairly.	Qualified
Highly material	Most or all users' decisions based on the financial statements are likely to be significantly affected. The effect of the misstatement(s) is pervasive to the financial statements.	Disclaimer or Adverse

Note: Lack of independence requires a disclaimer regardless of materiality.

For example, assume that the auditor believes there is a $100,000 overstatement of inventory because of the client's failure to follow GAAP. Also assume recorded inventory of $1 million, current assets of $3 million, and net income before taxes of $2 million. In this case, the auditor must evaluate the materiality of a misstatement of inventory of 10 percent, current assets of 3.3 percent, and net income before taxes of 5 percent.

To evaluate overall materiality, the auditor must also combine all unadjusted misstatements and judge whether there may be individually immaterial misstatements that, when combined, significantly affect the statements. In the inventory example just given, assume the auditor believes there is also an overstatement of $150,000 in accounts receivable. The total effect on current assets is now 8.3 percent ($250,000 divided by $3,000,000) and 12.5 percent on net income before taxes ($250,000 divided by $2,000,000).

When comparing potential misstatements with a base, the auditor must carefully consider all accounts affected by a misstatement (pervasiveness). For example, it is important not to overlook the effect of an understatement of inventory on cost of goods sold, income before taxes, income tax expense, and accrued income taxes payable.

Measurability The dollar amount of some misstatements cannot be accurately measured. For example, a client's unwillingness to disclose an existing lawsuit or the acquisition of a new company subsequent to the balance sheet date is difficult if not impossible to measure in terms of dollar amounts. The materiality question the auditor must evaluate in such situations is the effect on statement users of the failure to make the disclosure.

Nature of the Item The decision of a user may also be affected by the kind of misstatement. The following may affect a user's decision and therefore the auditor's opinion in a different way than most misstatements:

1. Transactions are illegal or fraudulent.
2. An item may materially affect some future period, even though it is immaterial when only the current period is considered.
3. An item has a "psychological" effect (for example, the item changes a small loss to a small profit, maintains a trend of increasing earnings, or allows earnings to exceed analysts' expectations).
4. An item may be important in terms of possible consequences arising from contractual obligations (for example, the effect of failure to comply with a debt restriction may result in a material loan being called).

Materiality Decisions—Scope Limitations Condition When there is a scope limitation in an audit, the audit report will be a standard unmodified opinion report, a report with a qualified scope and opinion, or a disclaimer report, depending on the materiality of the scope limitation. The auditor will consider the same three factors included in the previous discussion about materiality decisions for failure to follow GAAP, but they will be considered differently. The size of *potential* misstatements, rather than known misstatements, is important in determining whether an unmodified opinion report, a qualified scope and opinion report, or a disclaimer of opinion is appropriate for a scope limitation. For example, if recorded accounts payable of $400,000 was not audited, the auditor must evaluate the potential misstatement in accounts payable and decide how materially the financial statements could be affected. The pervasiveness of these potential misstatements must also be considered.

It is typically more difficult to evaluate the materiality of potential misstatements resulting from a scope limitation than for failure to follow GAAP. Misstatements resulting from failure to follow GAAP are known. Those resulting from scope limitations must usually be subjectively measured in terms of potential or likely misstatements. For example, a recorded accounts payable of $400,000 might be understated by more than $1 million, which may affect several totals, including gross margin, net earnings, and total assets.

DISCUSSION OF CONDITIONS REQUIRING A MODIFICATION OF OPINION

OBJECTIVE 3-7

Draft appropriately modified opinion audit reports under a variety of circumstances.

You should now understand the relationships among the conditions requiring a departure from an unmodified opinion audit report, the major types of reports other than the standard unmodified opinion report, and the three levels of materiality. This part of the chapter examines the conditions requiring modification of the opinion in greater detail and shows examples of reports under AICPA auditing standards. The wording of the opinion and the nature of the paragraph explaining the reason for a modified opinion are similar under PCAOB auditing standards.

Auditor's Scope Has Been Restricted

Two major categories of scope restrictions exist: those caused by a client and those caused by conditions beyond the control of either the client or the auditor. The effect on the auditor's report is the same for either, but the interpretation of materiality is likely to be different. When there is a scope restriction, the appropriate response is to issue a report with an unmodified opinion, a report with a qualification of scope and opinion, or a report with a disclaimer of opinion, depending on materiality.

For client-imposed restrictions, the auditor should be concerned about the possibility that management is trying to prevent discovery of misstated information. In such cases, PCAOB auditing standards encourage a disclaimer of opinion, while the AICPA auditing standards actually require a disclaimer of opinion or withdrawal from the engagement if the auditor is unable to perform alternative procedures to obtain sufficient appropriate evidence. When restrictions result from conditions beyond the client's control, a qualification of scope and opinion is more likely.

Two restrictions occasionally imposed by clients on the auditor's scope relate to the observation of physical inventory and the confirmation of accounts receivable, but other restrictions may also occur. Reasons for client imposed scope restrictions may be a desire to save audit fees and, in the case of confirming receivables, to prevent possible conflicts between the client and customer when amounts differ.

The most common case in which conditions beyond the client's and auditor's control cause a scope restriction is when the auditor is appointed after the client's balance sheet date. The confirmation of accounts receivable, physical examination of inventory, and other important procedures may be impossible under those circumstances. When the auditor cannot perform procedures he or she considers desirable but can be satisfied with alternative procedures that the information being verified is fairly stated, a standard unmodified opinion report is appropriate. If alternative procedures cannot be performed, a qualified scope and opinion or disclaimer of opinion is necessary, depending on materiality.

A restriction on the scope of the auditor's examination requires a qualifying paragraph preceding the opinion paragraph to describe the restriction. AICPA auditing standards require the auditor to include a heading such as "Basis for Qualified Opinion" preceding that qualifying paragraph, and those standards also require a heading before the opinion paragraph. For example, the report in Figure 3-8 (p. 64) is appropriate for an audit of a nonpublic entity in which the amounts were material but not pervasive and the auditor could not obtain audited financial statements supporting an investment in a foreign affiliate and could not satisfy himself or herself by alternate procedures. Notice the headings preceding each paragraph.

When the amounts are so material and pervasive that a disclaimer of opinion rather than a qualified opinion is required, the first (introductory) paragraph is modified slightly to say "We were engaged to audit…." The first paragraph of the auditor's responsibility is modified to indicate that the auditor was not able to obtain sufficient appropriate evidence to express an audit opinion. The last two paragraphs under auditor's responsibility included in the standard unmodified opinion audit report

FIGURE 3-8 Qualified Report Due to Scope Restriction—AICPA Auditing Standards

INDEPENDENT AUDITOR'S REPORT

(Same introductory paragraph, management's responsibility paragraph, and first two auditor's responsibility paragraphs as the standard report)

We believe that the audit evidence we have obtained is sufficient and appropriate to provide a basis for our qualified audit opinion.

Basis for Qualified Opinion

Laughlin Corporation's investment in XYZ Company, a foreign affiliate acquired during the year and accounted for under the equity method, is carried at $2,475,000 on the balance sheet at December 31, 2016, and Laughlin's share of XYZ Company's net income of $365,000 is included in Laughlin Corporation's net income for the year then ended. We were unable to obtain sufficient appropriate evidence about the carrying amount of Laughlin Corporation's investment in XYZ Company as of December 31, 2016, and Laughlin's share of XYZ Company's net income for the year then ended because we were denied access to the financial information, management, and the auditors of XYZ Company. Consequently, we were unable to determine whether any adjustments to these amounts were necessary.

Qualified Opinion

In our opinion, except for the effects of the matter described in the Basis for Qualified Opinion paragraph, the financial statements referred to above present fairly, in all material respects, the financial position of Laughlin Corporation as of December 31, 2016, and the results of its operations and its cash flows for the year then ended in conformity with accounting principles generally accepted in the United States of America.

are eliminated to avoid stating anything that might lead readers to believe that other parts of the financial statements were audited and therefore might be fairly stated. Figure 3-9 shows the audit report assuming the auditor had concluded that the facts in Figure 3-8 required a disclaimer rather than a qualified opinion.

Statements Are Not in Conformity with GAAP

When the auditor knows that the financial statements may be misleading because they were not prepared in conformity with GAAP, and the client is unable or unwilling to correct the misstatement, he or she must issue a qualified or an adverse opinion, depending on the materiality of the item in question. The opinion must clearly state the nature of the departure from accepted principles and the amount of the misstatement, if it is known. Figure 3-10 shows an example of a qualified opinion when a client did not capitalize leases as required by GAAP.

FIGURE 3-9 Disclaimer of Opinion Due to Scope Restriction—AICPA Auditing Standards

INDEPENDENT AUDITOR'S REPORT

We were engaged to audit . . . *(remainder is the same as the introductory paragraph in the standard report)*

(Same management's responsibility paragraph as the standard report)

Auditor's Responsibility

Our responsibility is to express an opinion on these financial statements based on conducting the audit in accordance with auditing standards generally accepted in the United States of America. Because of the matter described in the Basis for Disclaimer of Opinion paragraph, however, we were not able to obtain sufficient appropriate evidence to provide a basis for an audit opinion.

Basis for Disclaimer of Opinion

(Same wording as the Basis for Qualified Opinion paragraph in Figure 3-8)

Disclaimer of Opinion

Because of the significance of the matter described in the Basis for Disclaimer of Opinion paragraph, we have not been able to obtain sufficient appropriate evidence to provide a basis for an audit opinion. Accordingly, we do not express an opinion on these financial statements.

FIGURE 3-10 **Qualified Opinion Report Due to Non-GAAP—AICPA Auditing Standards**

INDEPENDENT AUDITOR'S REPORT

(Same introductory, management's responsibility, and auditor's responsibility paragraphs as the standard report. Only the last sentence of the auditor's responsibility paragraph would be modified as shown next.)

We believe that the audit evidence we have obtained is sufficient and appropriate to provide a basis for our qualified audit opinion.

Basis for Qualified Opinion

The Company has excluded from property and debt in the accompanying balance sheet certain lease obligations that, in our opinion, should be capitalized to conform with accounting principles generally accepted in the United States of America. If these lease obligations were capitalized, property would be increased by $4,600,000, long-term debt by $4,200,000, and retained earnings by $400,000 as of December 31, 2016, and net income and earnings per share would be increased by $400,000 and $1.75, respectively, for the year then ended.

Qualified Opinion

In our opinion, except for the effects of the matter described in the Basis for Qualified Opinion paragraph, the financial statements referred to above present fairly, in all material respects, the financial position of Ajax Company as of December 31, 2016, and the results of its operations and its cash flows for the year then ended in conformity with accounting principles generally accepted in the United States of America.

When the amounts are so material or pervasive that an adverse opinion is required, the scope is still unlimited and the qualifying paragraph can remain the same, but the opinion paragraph might be as shown in Figure 3-11.

When the client fails to include information that is necessary for the fair presentation of financial statements in the body of the statements or in the related footnotes, it is the auditor's responsibility to present the information in the audit report and to issue a qualified or an adverse opinion. It is common to put this type of qualification in an added paragraph preceding the opinion and to refer to the added paragraph in the opinion paragraph. Again, AICPA auditing standards require appropriate headings before the added paragraph and the opinion paragraph.

Justified Departure from GAAP Determining whether statements are in accordance with GAAP can be difficult. The Accounting Principles Rule in the AICPA *Code of Professional Conduct* permits a departure from generally accepted accounting principles when the auditor believes that adherence to these would result in misleading financial statements, although this circumstance is rare.

When the auditor decides that adherence to GAAP would result in misleading statements, there should be a complete explanation in an added paragraph.

FIGURE 3-11 **Adverse Opinion Due to Non-GAAP—AICPA Auditing Standards**

INDEPENDENT AUDITOR'S REPORT

(Same introductory, management's responsibility, and auditor's responsibility paragraphs as the standard report. Only the last sentence of the auditor's responsibility paragraph wold be modified as shown next.)

We believe that the audit evidence we have obtained is sufficient and appropriate to provide a basis for our adverse audit opinion.

Basis for Adverse Opinion

(Same wording as the Basis for Qualified Opinion paragraph in Figure 3-10)

Adverse Opinion

In our opinion, because of the significance of the matter described in the Basis for Adverse Opinion paragraph, the financial statements referred to above do not present fairly the financial position of Ajax Company as of December 31, 2016, or the results of its operations and its cash flows for the year then ended.

FIGURE 3-12 Disclaimer Due to Lack of Independence

> We are not independent with respect to Home Decors.com, Inc., and the accompanying balance sheet as of December 31, 2016, and the related statements of income, retained earnings, and cash flows for the year then ended were not audited by us. Accordingly, we do not express an opinion on them.

Note: When the auditor lacks independence, no report title is included.

The paragraph should fully explain the departure and why GAAP would result in misleading statements. The opinion paragraph should then be unmodified except for the reference to the added explanatory paragraph. As discussed earlier in the chapter, this is called an unmodified opinion audit report with an emphasis-of-matter explanatory paragraph.

Auditor Is Not Independent

If the auditor is not independent as specified by the AICPA *Code of Professional Conduct*, a disclaimer of opinion is required even though all the audit procedures considered necessary in the circumstances were performed. The wording in Figure 3-12 is recommended when the auditor is not independent.

The lack of independence overrides any other scope limitations. Therefore, no other reason for disclaiming an opinion should be cited. There should be no mention in the report of the performance of any audit procedures.

AUDITOR'S DECISION PROCESS FOR AUDIT REPORTS

OBJECTIVE 3-8

Determine the appropriate audit report for a given audit situation.

Auditors use a well-defined process for deciding the appropriate audit report in a given set of circumstances. The auditor must first assess whether any conditions exist requiring a departure from a standard unmodified opinion audit report. If any conditions exist, the auditor must then assess the materiality of the condition and determine the appropriate type of report.

Determine Whether Any Condition Exists Requiring a Departure from a Standard Unmodified Opinion Report The most important conditions are identified in Table 3-2. Auditors identify these conditions as they perform the audit and include information about any condition in the audit files as discussion items for audit reporting. If none of these conditions exist, which is the case in most audits, the auditor issues a standard unmodified opinion audit report.

Decide the Materiality for Each Condition When a condition requiring a departure from a standard unmodified opinion exists, the auditor evaluates the potential effect on the financial statements. For departures from GAAP or scope restrictions, the auditor must decide among immaterial, material, and highly material. All other conditions, except for lack of auditor independence, require only a distinction between immaterial and material. The materiality decision is a difficult one, requiring considerable judgment. For example, assume that there is a scope limitation in auditing inventory. It is difficult to assess the potential misstatement of an account that the auditor does not audit.

Decide the Appropriate Type of Report for the Condition, Given the Materiality Level After making the first two decisions, it is easy to decide the appropriate type of opinion by using a decision aid. An example of such an aid is Table 3-2. For example, assume that the auditor concludes that there is a departure from GAAP and it is material, but not highly material. Table 3-2 shows that the appropriate audit report is a qualified opinion with an additional paragraph discussing the departure. The other report paragraphs will be included using standard wording.

TABLE 3-2 Audit Report for Each Condition Requiring a Departure from a Standard Unmodified Opinion Report at Different Levels of Materiality

Condition Requiring an Unmodified Opinion Report with Nonstandard Wording or Explanatory Paragraph	Level of Materiality: Immaterial	Level of Materiality: Material
Accounting principles not consistently applied*	Standard unmodified opinion	Unmodified opinion with explanatory paragraph
Substantial doubt about going concern†	Standard unmodified opinion	Unmodified opinion with explanatory paragraph
Justified departure from GAAP or other accounting principle	Standard unmodified opinion	Unmodified opinion with explanatory paragraph
Emphasis of other matters	Standard unmodified opinion	Unmodified opinion with explanatory paragraph
Use of another auditor	Standard unmodified opinion	Unmodified opinion with revised wording in other report paragraphs

Condition Requiring a Departure from Unmodified Opinion Audit Report	Level of Materiality: Immaterial	Material, But Not Pervasive to the Financial Statements as a Whole	So Material That Overall Fairness Is in Question
Scope restricted by client or other conditions	Standard unmodified opinion	Additional paragraph, and qualified opinion (except for)	Disclaimer
Financial statements not prepared in accordance with GAAP‡	Standard unmodified opinion	Additional paragraph and qualified opinion (except for)	Adverse
Auditor is not independent		Disclaimer, regardless of materiality	

* If the auditor does not concur with the appropriateness of the change, the condition is considered a violation of GAAP.
† The auditor has the option of issuing a disclaimer of opinion.
‡ If the auditor can demonstrate that GAAP would be misleading, an unmodified opinion audit report with an explanatory paragraph is appropriate.

Write the Audit Report Most CPA firms have computer templates that include precise wording for different circumstances to help the auditor write the audit report. Also, one or more partners in most CPA firms have special expertise in writing audit reports. These partners typically write or review all audit reports before they are issued.

More Than One Condition Requiring a Departure or Modification

Auditors may encounter situations involving more than one of the conditions requiring a departure from an unmodified opinion audit report or revisions to the standard report wording. In these circumstances, the auditor should modify his or her opinion for each condition unless one has the effect of neutralizing the others. For example, if there is a scope limitation and a situation in which the auditor is not independent, the scope limitation should not be revealed. The following situations are examples when more than one modification should be included in the report:

- The auditor is not independent and the auditor knows that the company has not followed generally accepted accounting principles.
- There is a scope limitation and there is substantial doubt about the company's ability to continue as a going concern.
- There is a substantial doubt about the company's ability to continue as a going concern and information about the causes of the uncertainties is not adequately disclosed in a footnote.
- There is a deviation in the statements' preparation in accordance with GAAP and another accounting principle was applied on a basis that was not consistent with that of the preceding year.

INTERNATIONAL DEVELOPMENTS RELATED TO THE AUDITOR'S REPORT

A number of initiatives related to the auditor's report have been underway around the globe. The International Auditing and Assurance Standards Board (IAASB) released its new audit report standards in January 2015 that revise the audit reporting requirements in International Standards on Auditing (ISAs). Similar to the PCAOB's proposal to require the auditor to communicate "critical audit matters" in the auditor's report, the new IAASB standards require auditors to communicate "Key Audit Matters" in the auditor's report. Key audit matters represent those matters that the auditor views as most significant. The standard requires not only disclosure about such matters, but also explanation of how they were addressed in the audit.

The financial crisis in 2008 led to audit report changes that became effective in 2012 in the United Kingdom, which are widely known as the "extended auditor's report." Audit reports of companies subject to the UK Corporate Governance Code must now include the following within their report:

a. A description of those assessed risks of material misstatement that were identified by the auditor and that had the greatest effect on the overall audit strategy, the allocation of resources in the audit, and directing the efforts of the engagement team;
b. An explanation of how the auditor applied the concept of materiality; and
c. A summary of the audit scope, including an explanation of how the scope was responsive to the assessed risks of material misstatement and the concept of materiality.

Similar issues motivated the European Commission to issue a new statutory audit framework in 2014 effective June 2016. Among other changes, the new audit framework contains specific requirements for the auditor's report, and it also allows member states in the EU to establish additional requirements to the auditor's report.

Sources: 1. "IAASB Issues Final Standards to Improve Auditor's Reports," International Federation of Accountants, January 15, 2015 (www.ifac.org); 2. "Extended Auditor's Reports: A Review of Experience in the First Year," Financial Reporting Council, March 2015 (www.frc.org.uk); and 3. "Directive 2014/56/EU of the European Parliament and of the Council," European Parliament and the Council of the European Union, April 16, 2014 (www.europarl.europa.eu).

INTERNATIONAL ACCOUNTING AND AUDITING STANDARDS

OBJECTIVE 3-9

Understand use of international accounting and auditing standards by U.S. companies.

The increasing globalization of the world's capital markets and the expanding presence of business operations in multiple countries are leading to calls for the establishment of a single set of accounting standards to be used around the world. IFRS is increasingly accepted worldwide as the basis of accounting used to prepare financial statements in other countries.

Currently, U.S. public companies are required to prepare financial statements that are filed with the Securities and Exchange Commission (SEC) in accordance with generally accepted accounting principles in the United States. The SEC has been working on a plan to determine whether to incorporate IFRS into the U.S. financial reporting system. While the SEC's 2010–2015 strategic plan seemed to suggest that U.S. public companies may be able to use IFRS as early as 2015, more recent developments suggest the SEC may be slowing down its efforts towards embracing IFRS any time soon.

An auditor may be engaged to report on financial statements prepared in accordance with IFRS. When the auditor reports on financial statements prepared in conformity with IFRS, the auditor refers to those standards rather than U.S. generally accepted accounting principles as follows:

> In our opinion, the financial statements referred to above present fairly, in all material respects, the financial position of Carlos Incorporated as of December 31, 2016 and 2015, and the results of its operations, comprehensive income, changes in equity, and its cash flows for the years then ended in conformity with International Financial Reporting Standards as issued by the International Accounting Standards Board.

As discussed in Chapter 2, the International Auditing and Assurance Standards Board (IAASB) issues International Standards on Auditing (ISAs). Auditing standards in the United States now allow an auditor to perform an audit of financial statements of a nonpublic U.S. entity in accordance with both generally accepted auditing standards in the U.S. and the ISAs. The auditor's scope paragraph is modified to indicate that the audit was conducted in accordance with auditing standards generally accepted in the United States of America and in accordance with International Standards on Auditing.

CONCEPT CHECK

1. What are the three conditions that require a departure from an unmodified opinion audit report? Give an example of each.
2. What are the three alternative opinions that may be appropriate when the client's financial statements are not in accordance with GAAP? Under what circumstance is each appropriate?

SUMMARY

This chapter described the auditor's standard unmodified opinion audit report under AICPA and PCAOB standards, as well as reports on internal control over financial reporting under Section 404 of the Sarbanes–Oxley Act. The four categories of audit reports and the auditor's decision process in choosing the appropriate audit report to issue were then discussed. In some circumstances, an explanatory paragraph or nonstandard wording of the unmodified opinion audit report is required. When there is a material departure from GAAP or a material limitation on the scope of the audit, the audit opinion must be modified. The appropriate report to issue in these circumstances depends on whether the situation involves a GAAP departure or a scope limitation, as well as the level of materiality.

ESSENTIAL TERMS

Adverse opinion—a report issued when the auditor believes the financial statements are so materially misstated or misleading as a whole that they do not present fairly the entity's financial position or the results of its operations and cash flows in conformity with GAAP

Combined report on financial statements and internal control over financial reporting—audit report on the financial statements and the effectiveness of internal control over financial reporting required for larger public companies under Section 404 of the Sarbanes–Oxley Act

Disclaimer of opinion—a report issued when the auditor is not able to become satisfied that the overall financial statements are fairly presented or the auditor is not independent

Material misstatement—a misstatement in the financial statements, knowledge of which would affect a decision of a reasonable user of the statements

Qualified opinion—a report issued when the auditor believes that the overall financial statements are fairly stated but that either the scope of the audit was limited or the financial data indicated a failure to follow GAAP

Separate report on internal control over financial reporting—audit report on the effectiveness of internal control over financial reporting required for larger public companies under Section 404 of the Sarbanes–Oxley Act that cross-references the separate audit report on the financial statements

Standard unmodified opinion audit report—the report a CPA issues when all auditing conditions have been met, no significant misstatements have been discovered and left uncorrected, and it is the auditor's opinion that the financial statements are fairly stated in accordance with the applicable financial reporting framework

Unmodified opinion audit report with emphasis-of-matter paragraph or nonstandard report wording—an unmodified opinion audit report in which the financial statements are fairly presented, but the auditor believes it is important, or is required, to provide additional information or the wording of other paragraphs of the report require revision

REVIEW QUESTIONS

3-1 **(OBJECTIVE 3-1)** Explain why auditors' reports are important to users of financial statements and why it is desirable to have standard wording.

3-2 **(OBJECTIVE 3-1)** What are the purposes of the scope paragraph under the auditor's responsibility in the auditor's report? Identify the most important information included in the scope paragraph.

3-3 **(OBJECTIVE 3-1)** What are the purposes of the opinion paragraph in the auditor's report? Identify the most important information included in the opinion paragraph.

3-4 **(OBJECTIVE 3-1)** On February 17, 2017, a CPA completed all the evidence gathering procedures on the audit of the financial statements for the Buckheizer Technology Corporation for the year ended December 31, 2016. The audit is satisfactory in all respects except for the existence of a change in accounting principles from FIFO to LIFO inventory valuation, which results in an explanatory paragraph on consistency. On February 26, the auditor completed the tax return and the draft of the audit report. The final audit report was completed, attached to the financial statements, and delivered to the client on March 7. What is the appropriate date on the auditor's report?

3-5 **(OBJECTIVE 3-2)** What four circumstances are required for a standard unmodified opinion audit report to be issued?

3-6 **(OBJECTIVE 3-3)** Describe the information included in the introductory, scope, and opinion paragraphs in a separate audit report on the effectiveness of internal control over financial reporting. What is the nature of the additional paragraphs in the audit report?

3-7 **(OBJECTIVES 3-1, 3-3)** Compare the wording in the standard unmodified opinion audit report for a nonpublic entity under AICPA auditing standards in Figure 3-1 (p. 48) with the wording for a public company audit under PCAOB auditing standards in Figure 3-3 (p. 52). How are the reports similar? How are they different?

3-8 **(OBJECTIVES 3-4, 3-5)** Distinguish between an unmodified opinion audit report that contains an emphasis-of-matter explanatory paragraph and a qualified report.

3-9 **(OBJECTIVE 3-4)** Describe what is meant by reports involving the use of other auditors. What are the three options available to the primary auditor responsible for the opinion, and when should each be used?

3-10 **(OBJECTIVE 3-4)** The client changed from FIFO to LIFO inventory valuation in the current year and reflected this change in their financial statements. How should this be reflected in the auditor's report?

3-11 **(OBJECTIVE 3-4)** Distinguish between changes that affect consistency and those that may affect comparability but not consistency. Give an example of each.

3-12 **(OBJECTIVE 3-5)** How do the eight parts of a standard unmodified opinion audit report for nonpublic companies differ from those found in a qualified opinion report?

3-13 **(OBJECTIVE 3-5)** Distinguish between a qualified opinion, an adverse opinion, and a disclaimer of opinion, and explain the circumstances under which each is appropriate.

3-14 **(OBJECTIVE 3-5)** Distinguish between a report qualified due to a GAAP departure and one qualified due to a scope limitation.

3-15 **(OBJECTIVE 3-6)** Define materiality as it is used in audit reporting. What conditions will affect the auditor's determination of materiality?

3-16 **(OBJECTIVE 3-6)** Explain how materiality differs for failure to follow GAAP and for lack of independence.

3-17 **(OBJECTIVE 3-7)** How does the auditor's opinion differ between scope limitations caused by client restrictions and limitations resulting from conditions beyond the client's control? Under which of these two will the auditor be most likely to issue a disclaimer of opinion? Explain.

3-18 **(OBJECTIVE 3-8)** When an auditor discovers more than one condition that requires departure from or modification of the standard unmodified opinion audit report, what should the auditor's report include?

3-19 **(OBJECTIVE 3-9)** Discuss why the adoption of international accounting and auditing standards might be beneficial to investors and auditors.

MULTIPLE CHOICE QUESTIONS FROM CPA EXAMINATIONS

3-20 **(OBJECTIVES 3-1, 3-2, 3-3, 3-4, 3-8)** The following questions concern unmodified opinion audit reports. Choose the best response.

a. Which of the following is not a required element of a standard unmodified opinion audit report issued in accordance with AICPA auditing standards?
   (1) A title that emphasizes the report is from an independent auditor
   (2) The city and state of the audit firm issuing the report
   (3) A statement explaining management's responsibilities for the financial statements
   (4) The signature of the engagement partner

b. The date of the CPA's opinion on the financial statements of the client should be the date of the
   (1) completion of all important audit procedures.
   (2) closing of the client's books.
   (3) finalization of the terms of the audit engagement.
   (4) submission of the report to the client.

c. If a principal auditor decides to refer in his or her report to the audit of another auditor, he or she is required to disclose the
   (1) name of the other auditor.
   (2) nature of the inquiry into the other auditor's professional standing and extent of the review of the other auditor's work.
   (3) reasons for being unwilling to assume responsibility for the other auditor's work.
   (4) portion of the financial statements audited by the other auditor.

3-21 **(OBJECTIVES 3-4, 3-8)** The following questions concern unmodified opinion audit reports with an emphasis-of-matter explanatory paragraph or nonstandard wording in report paragraphs. Choose the best response.

a. An entity changed from the straight-line method to the declining-balance method of depreciation for all newly acquired assets. This change has no material effect on the current year's financial statements but is reasonably certain to have a substantial effect in later years. If the change is disclosed in the notes to the financial statements, the auditor should issue a report with a(n)
   (1) unmodified opinion.
   (2) qualified opinion.
   (3) unmodified opinion with explanatory paragraph.
   (4) qualified opinion with explanatory paragraph regarding consistency.

b. When the financial statements are fairly stated but the auditor concludes there is substantial doubt whether the client can continue in existence, the auditor should issue a(n)
   (1) adverse opinion.
   (2) qualified opinion only.
   (3) unmodified opinion.
   (4) unmodified opinion with explanatory paragraph.

c. The auditor's report contains the following: "We did not audit the financial statements of EZ, Inc., a wholly owned subsidiary, which statements reflect total assets and revenues constituting 27 percent and 29 percent, respectively, of the consolidated totals. Those statements were audited by other auditors whose report has been furnished to us, and our opinion, insofar as it relates to the amounts included for EZ, Inc., is based solely on the report of the other auditors." These sentences
   (1) assume responsibility for the other auditor.
   (2) indicate a division of responsibility.
   (3) require a departure from an unmodified opinion.
   (4) are an improper form of reporting.

MULTIPLE CHOICE QUESTIONS FROM BECKER CPA EXAM REVIEW

3-22 **(OBJECTIVES 3-5, 3-7, 3-8)** The following questions concern audit reports other than unmodified opinion audit reports with standard wording. Choose the best response.

a. As compared to an unmodified opinion, an opinion qualified due to a material departure from generally accepted accounting principles would
   (1) include an extra paragraph, following the opinion paragraph.
   (2) indicate that, except for the problem noted, the financial statements are presented fairly.
   (3) include a slight modification to the introductory paragraph.
   (4) include a slight modification to the auditor's responsibility paragraph.

b. An auditor who qualified an opinion because of an insufficiency of audit evidence should refer to the scope limitation in the

	Auditor's Responsibility Paragraph	Opinion Paragraph	Note to the Financial Statements
(1)	Yes	No	Yes
(2)	No	Yes	No
(3)	Yes	Yes	No
(4)	Yes	Yes	Yes

c. An adverse opinion and a disclaimer of opinion
   (1) may be used interchangeably.
   (2) both require modification of the introductory paragraph.
   (3) result in the auditor's withdrawal from the engagement.
   (4) indicate situations in which there are material departures from the standards.

DISCUSSION QUESTIONS AND PROBLEMS

3-23 **(OBJECTIVE 3-1)** A careful reading of an unmodified opinion audit report indicates several important phrases. Explain why each of the following phrases or clauses is used rather than the alternative provided:

a. "The financial statements referred to above present fairly, in all material respects, the financial position" rather than "The financial statements mentioned above are correctly stated."
b. "In conformity with accounting principles generally accepted in the United States of America" rather than "are properly stated to represent the true economic conditions."
c. "In our opinion, the financial statements present fairly" rather than "The financial statements present fairly."
d. "Brown & Phillips, CPAs (firm name)," rather than "James E. Brown, CPA (individual partner's name)."
e. "We conducted our audit in accordance with auditing standards generally accepted in the United States of America" rather than "Our audit was performed to detect material misstatements in the financial statements."

3-24 **(OBJECTIVES 3-1, 3-2, 3-4, 3-6, 3-7)** Patel, CPA, has completed the audit of the financial statements of Bellamy Corporation as of and for the year ended December 31, 2016. Patel also audited and reported on the Bellamy financial statements for the prior year. Patel drafted the following report for 2016.

We have audited the balance sheet and statements of income and retained earnings of Bellamy Corporation as of December 31, 2016. We conducted our audit in accordance with generally accepted accounting standards. Those standards require that we plan and perform the audit to obtain reasonable assurance about whether the financial statements are free of misstatement.

We believe that our audits provide a reasonable basis for our opinion.

In our opinion, the financial statements referred to above present fairly the financial position of Bellamy Corporation as of December 31, 2016, and the results of its operations for the year then ended in conformity with generally accepted auditing standards, applied on a basis consistent with those of the preceding year.

Patel, CPA
(Signed)

Other Information

- Bellamy is a private corporation and is presenting comparative financial statements.
- During 2016, Bellamy acquired Stockard Inc. and the effects of that transaction are reflected in the current year financial statements. Information about this transaction is disclosed in footnote 12.
- Patel was unable to perform normal accounts receivable confirmation procedures for accounts that are material, but not pervasive, to the financial statements. Unfortunately, Patel was not able to perform alternative procedures to support the existence of the receivables.
- Bellamy Corporation is the defendant in litigation where there is a reasonable possibility that Bellamy may be required to pay a substantial amount of cash, which might require the sale of certain fixed assets. Because management does not want to provide any information that the plaintiff might use against Bellamy, the case is not discussed in the financial statements.
- Bellamy issued debentures on January 31, 2015, in the amount of $10 million. The funds obtained from the issuance were used to finance the expansion of plant facilities. The debenture agreement restricts the payment of future cash dividends to earnings after December 31, 2020. Bellamy has disclosed this in the footnotes to the financial statements.

Required

a. Identify and explain any items included in "Other Information" that need not be part of the auditor's report.
b. Explain the deficiencies in Patel's report as drafted.*

3-25 **(OBJECTIVES 3-4, 3-5, 3-6, 3-7, 3-8)** For the following independent situations, assume that you are the audit partner on the engagement:

1. Auto Delivery Company has a fleet of several delivery trucks. In the past, Auto Delivery had followed the policy of purchasing all equipment. In the current year, they decided to lease the trucks. The method of accounting for the trucks is therefore changed to lease capitalization. This change in policy is fully disclosed in footnotes.
2. You are auditing Deep Clean Services for the first time. Deep Clean has been in business for several years but over the last two years has struggled to stay afloat given the economic conditions. Based on your audit work, you have substantial doubt that Deep Clean will be in business by the end of its next fiscal year.
3. One of your audit clients has a material investment in a privately held biosciences company. Your audit firm engaged a business valuation specialist to assist in evaluating the client's estimation of the investment's fair value. You conclude that the valuation specialist's work provides sufficient appropriate audit evidence.
4. Four weeks after the year-end date, a major customer of Prince Construction Co. declared bankruptcy. Because the customer had confirmed the balance due to Prince

* Based on AICPA question paper, American Institute of Certified Public Accountants.

at the balance sheet date, management refuses to charge off the account or otherwise disclose the information. The receivable represents approximately 10% of accounts receivable and 20% of net earnings before taxes.

5. During your audit of Raceway.com, Inc., you conclude that there is a possibility that inventory is materially overstated. The client refuses to allow you to expand the scope of your audit sufficiently to verify whether the balance is actually misstated.
6. You complete the audit of Munich Department Store, and in your opinion, the financial statements are fairly presented. On the last day of the audit, you discover that one of your supervisors assigned to the audit has a material investment in Munich.

Required For each situation, do the following:

a. Identify which of the conditions requiring a deviation from a standard unmodified opinion audit report is applicable, if any.
b. State the level of materiality as immaterial, material, or highly material. If you cannot decide the level of materiality, state the additional information needed to make a decision.
c. Given your answers in parts a. and b., state the type of audit report that should be issued. If you have not decided on one level of materiality in part b., state the appropriate report for each alternative materiality level.

3-26 **(OBJECTIVES 3-4, 3-5, 3-6, 3-7, 3-8)** For the following independent situations, assume that you are the audit partner on the engagement:

1. A number of frozen yogurt stores have opened in the last few years and your client, YogurtLand, has experienced a noticeable decline in customer traffic over the past several months that has caused you to have substantial doubt about YogurtLand's ability to continue as a going concern.
2. Intelligis Electronics is a manufacturer of advanced electrical components. During the year, changes in the market resulted in a significant decrease in the demand for their products, which are now being sold significantly below cost. Management refuses to write-off the products or to increase the reserve for obsolescence.
3. In the last 3 months of the current year, Oil Refining Company decided to change direction and go significantly into the oil drilling business. Management recognizes that this business is exceptionally risky and could jeopardize the success of its existing refining business, but there are significant potential rewards. During the short period of operation in drilling, the company has had three dry wells and no successes. The facts are adequately disclosed in footnotes.
4. Your client, Harrison Automotive, has changed from straight-line to sum-of-the-years' digits depreciation. The effect on this year's income is immaterial, but the effect in future years may be highly material. The change is not disclosed in the footnotes.
5. Marseilles Fragrance, Inc., is based in New York but has operations throughout Europe. Because users of the audited financial statement are international, your audit firm was engaged to conduct the audit in accordance with U.S. auditing standards and International Standards on Auditing (ISAs).
6. Circumstances prevent you from being able to observe the counting of inventory at Brentwood Industries. The inventory amount is material in relation to Brentwood Industries' financial statements. But, you were able to perform alternative procedures to support the existence and valuation of the inventory at year-end.
7. Approximately 20% of the audit of Lumberton Farms, Inc., was performed by a different CPA firm, selected by you. You have reviewed their audit files and believe they did an excellent job on their portion of the audit. Nevertheless, you are unwilling to take complete responsibility for their work.

Required For each situation, do the following:

a. Identify which of the conditions requiring a deviation from a standard unmodified opinion audit report is applicable, if any.
b. State the level of materiality as immaterial, material, or highly material. If you cannot decide the level of materiality, state the additional information needed to make a decision.

c. Given your answers in parts a. and b., state the appropriate audit report from the following alternatives (if you have not decided on one level of materiality in part b., state the appropriate report for each alternative materiality level):

(1) Unmodified opinion—standard wording
(2) Unmodified opinion—explanatory paragraph
(3) Unmodified opinion—nonstandard report wording
(4) Qualified opinion only—GAAP departure
(5) Qualified opinion—scope limitation
(6) Disclaimer
(7) Adverse*

3-27 **(OBJECTIVES 3-4, 3-5, 3-6, 3-7, 3-8)** The following are independent situations for which you will recommend an appropriate audit report:

1. Subsequent to the date of the financial statements as part of his post-balance sheet date audit procedures, a CPA learned that a recent fire caused heavy damage to one of a client's two plants; the loss will not be reimbursed by insurance. The newspapers described the event in detail. The financial statements and footnotes as prepared by the client did not disclose the loss caused by the fire.
2. During the course of his audit of the financial statements of a corporation for the purpose of expressing an opinion on the statements, a CPA is refused permission to inspect the minutes of board of director meetings that document significant decisions of the board. The corporation secretary instead offers to give the CPA a certified copy of all resolutions and actions involving accounting matters.
3. A CPA is engaged in the audit of the financial statements of a large manufacturing company with branch offices in many widely separated cities. The CPA was not able to count the substantial undeposited cash receipts at the close of business on the last day of the fiscal year at all branch offices.

   As an alternative to this auditing procedure used to verify the accurate cutoff of cash receipts, the CPA observed that deposits in transit as shown on the year-end bank reconciliation appeared as credits on the bank statement on the first business day of the new year. He was satisfied as to the cutoff of cash receipts by the use of the alternative procedure.
4. On January 2, 2017, the Retail Auto Parts Company received a notice from its primary supplier that effective immediately, all wholesale prices will be increased 10%. On the basis of the notice, Retail Auto Parts revalued its December 31, 2016, inventory to reflect the higher costs. The inventory constituted a material proportion of total assets; however, the effect of the revaluation was material to current assets but not to total assets or net income. The increase in valuation is adequately disclosed in the footnotes.
5. A CPA has completed her audit of the financial statements of a bus company for the year ended December 31, 2016. Prior to 2016, the company depreciated its buses over a 10-year period. During 2016, the company determined that a more realistic estimated life for its buses was 12 years and computed the 2016 depreciation on the basis of the revised estimate. The CPA has satisfied herself that the 12-year life is reasonable.

   The company has adequately disclosed the change in estimated useful lives of its buses and the effect of the change on 2016 income in a note to the financial statements.
6. E-Lotions.com, Inc., is an online retailer of body lotions and other bath and body supplies. The company records revenues at the time customer orders are placed on the Web site, rather than when the goods are shipped, which is usually 2 days after the order is placed. The auditor determined that the amount of orders placed but not shipped as of the balance sheet date is not material.
7. For the past 5 years, a CPA has audited the financial statements of a manufacturing company. During this period, the audit scope was limited by the client as to the observation of the annual physical inventory. Because the CPA considered the inventories to be material and he was not able to satisfy himself by other auditing procedures, he was unable to express an unmodified opinion on the financial statements in each of the 5 years.

* Based on AICPA question paper, American Institute of Certified Public Accountants.

The CPA was allowed to observe physical inventories for the current year ended December 31, 2016, because the client's banker would no longer accept the audit reports. However, to minimize audit fees, the client requested that the CPA not extend his audit procedures to the inventory as of the beginning of the year, January 1, 2016.

Required For each situation, do the following:

a. Identify which of the conditions requiring a deviation from a standard unmodified opinion audit report is applicable, if any.
b. State the level of materiality as immaterial, material, or highly material. If you cannot decide the level of materiality, state the additional information needed to make a decision.
c. Given your answers in parts a. and b., state the appropriate audit report from the following alternatives (if you have not decided on one level of materiality in part b., state the appropriate report for each alternative materiality level):

(1) Unmodified opinion—standard wording
(2) Unmodified opinion—explanatory paragraph
(3) Unmodified opinion—nonstandard report wording
(4) Qualified opinion—GAAP departure
(5) Qualified opinion—scope limitation
(6) Disclaimer
(7) Adverse*

3-28 **(OBJECTIVES 3-3, 3-9)** The PCAOB has proposed changes to the auditor's report for public companies that include requirements for the auditor to communicate "critical audit matters." Critical audit matters include those matters during the audit that involved difficult, subjective, or complex auditor judgments or that posed difficulty to the auditor in obtaining sufficient appropriate evidence or in forming the opinion on the financial statements. Similarly, the International Auditing and Assurance Standards Board (IAASB) recently revised the auditor's report in the International Standards on Auditing (ISAs) to require auditors to communicate "key audit matters." Key audit matters include communication of similar kinds of information as proposed by the PCAOB such as areas of higher assessed risk of material misstatement and the effects of significant events or transactions that occurred during the period.

Required

a. Describe how users of the financial statements may benefit from communications about these matters in an audit report.
b. Describe how communication of these matters may not be beneficial to users of the financial statements.
c. What difficulties, if any, may auditors face in communicating about these matters?

3-29 **(OBJECTIVES 3-1, 3-3, 3-7, 3-9)** The International Auditing and Assurance Standards Board (IAASB) recently revised its standards related to audit reporting. ISA 700 (Revised), *Forming an Opinion and Reporting on Financial Statements*, requires the auditor's report to include the following paragraphs under the headings "Basis for Opinion" and "Auditor's Responsibilities for the Audit of the Financial Statements":

Basis for Opinion

We conducted our audit in accordance with International Standards on Auditing (ISAs). Our responsibilities under those standards are further described in the Auditor's Responsibilities for the Audit of the Financial Statements section of our report. We are independent of the Company in accordance with the International Ethics Standards Board for Accountants' Code of Ethics for Professional Accountants (IESBA Code) together with the ethical requirements that are relevant to our audit of the financial statements in [the home country] and we have fulfilled our other ethical responsibilities in accordance with these requirements and the IESBA Code. We believe that the audit evidence we have obtained is sufficient and appropriate to provide a basis for our opinion.

* Based on AICPA question paper, American Institute of Certified Public Accountants.

Auditor's Responsibilities for the Audit of the Financial Statements

Our objectives are to obtain reasonable assurance about whether the financial statements as a whole are free from material misstatement, whether due to fraud or error, and to issue an auditor's report that includes our opinion. Reasonable assurance is a high level of assurance, but is not a guarantee that an audit conducted in accordance with ISAs will always detect a material misstatement when it exists. Misstatements can arise from fraud or error and are considered material if, individually or in the aggregate, they could reasonably be expected to influence the economic decisions of users taken on the basis of these financial statements.

Read the preceding paragraphs to answer the following:

Required

a. How does the information in the preceding paragraphs compare to the information in the paragraphs under the "Auditor's Responsibility" heading in the standard unmodified opinion audit report example for a nonpublic company shown in Figure 3-1 (p. 48)?
b. How does the information in the preceding paragraphs compare to the information in the scope paragraph in the standard unmodified opinion audit report example for a public company shown in Figure 3-3 (p. 52)?
c. Discuss whether you believe these paragraphs in the ISA audit report improve auditor communications to users of the financial statements.

3-30 (OBJECTIVES 3-3, 3-4) Publicly traded companies must electronically file a variety of forms or reports with the U.S. Securities and Exchange Commission (SEC), including the Form 10-K, which includes the audited annual financial statements. The SEC makes most of these electronic documents available on the Internet via EDGAR, which stands for Electronic Data Gathering, Analysis, and Retrieval system. The primary purpose for EDGAR is to increase the efficiency and fairness of the securities market for the benefit of investors, corporations, and the economy by accelerating the receipt, acceptance, dissemination, and analysis of time-sensitive corporate information filed with the agency.

Required

a. Visit the SEC Web site (www.sec.gov) and use the link to "Company Filings Search" (under "Filings") to locate the Form 10-K filing for Google, Inc., for the year ended December 31, 2015, to answer the following questions:
   1. Who was Google's auditor?
   2. Did the audit firm issue a combined or separate report(s) on the financial statements and on internal controls over financial reporting?
   3. What type of audit opinion did the auditor provide for the financial statements?
   4. What was the auditor's opinion about internal controls over financial reporting?
   5. What was the report date for the audit report?
b. Visit the PCAOB's Web site (www.pcaob.org) and use the link to "Auditing" under the heading for "Standards" to locate the PCAOB's Auditing Standards. Search the links to the Auditing Standards to answer the following questions:
   1. Where would the auditor locate guidance about changes to the auditor's report if Google makes a change in accounting principle that is considered material? Identify the appropriate section in the Auditing Standards and identify the relevant paragraph(s) within that section that would be applicable to this situation. Assume that Google properly reports the change in the financial statements.
   2. Where would the auditor locate guidance to determine the effect on the auditor's report if he or she has substantial doubt about Google's ability to continue as a going concern? Identify the appropriate section and the relevant paragraph(s) within that section that would be applicable to this situation.
   3. Google's Form 10-K contains information that is in addition to the financial statements and related footnotes. Where would the auditor locate guidance that addresses his or her responsibility for this other information and what is the auditor's obligation related to that information? Identify the appropriate section and the relevant paragraph(s) within that section that would be applicable to this situation.

CHAPTER

4

PROFESSIONAL ETHICS

LEARNING OBJECTIVES

After studying this chapter, you should be able to

4-1 Distinguish ethical from unethical behavior in personal and professional contexts.

4-2 Resolve ethical dilemmas using an ethical framework.

4-3 Explain the importance of ethical conduct for the accounting profession.

4-4 Describe the purpose and content of the AICPA *Code of Professional Conduct.*

4-5 Apply the AICPA *Code* rules and interpretations on independence and explain their importance.

4-6 Understand Sarbanes–Oxley Act and other SEC and PCAOB independence requirements and additional factors that influence auditor independence.

4-7 Understand the requirements of other rules under the AICPA *Code.*

4-8 Describe the enforcement mechanisms for CPA conduct.

Big 4 Partner Convicted of Insider Trading for Disclosing Confidential Information

Auditors frequently receive access to confidential client information, such as earnings information before the earnings announcement or information about planned mergers and acquisitions. The AICPA *Code of Professional Conduct* prohibits members in public practice from disclosing any confidential information without the consent of the client. Trading in publicly traded companies on such inside information before it becomes public is also often a violation of federal securities laws on insider trading.

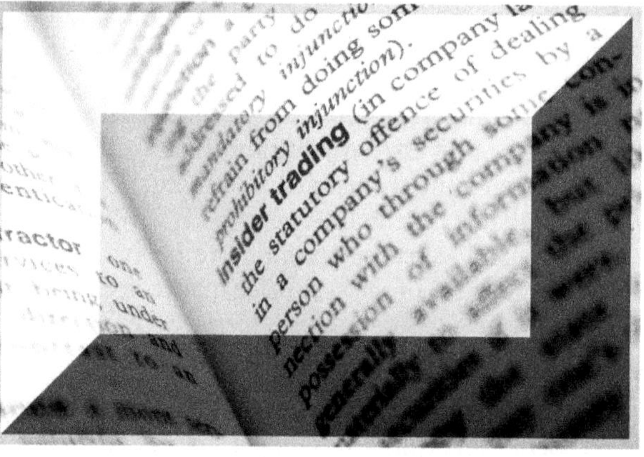

As a senior partner in the Los Angeles office of KPMG, Scott London had access to client information such as company earnings reports and planned acquisitions. Although he did not personally trade using this information, he passed the information on to Bryan Shaw, a friend who was in the jewelry business. Over the course of several years, Shaw used the tips to make trades that resulted in profits of over $1 million. In exchange for the information, Shaw would arrange to meet London on a street near his business and give him bags containing $100 bills wrapped in $10,000 bundles. In court documents, Shaw also stated he gave London a $12,000 Rolex watch, jewelry, and concert tickets.

London's defense team argued that London began providing the tips because he wanted to help Mr. Shaw, whose jewelry business was struggling, and that he went down a "slippery slope." Although the judge noted that the $70,000 that London received was a "drop in the bucket" compared to his annual salary of over $900,000, he also noted that by the 14th time London engaged in this activity, "it wasn't inadvertent." London was sentenced to 14 months in prison and fined $100,000. Although KPMG was unaware of London's actions, they were forced to resign from clients Herbalife and Skechers because London was the lead partner on these audit engagements.

Sources: 1. Stuart Pfeifer, "Former KPMG Partner Scott London Pleads Guilty to Insider Trading," *The Los Angeles Times* (July 1, 2013) (articles.latimes.com); 2. Tamara Audi, "Former KPMG Partner Scott London Gets 14 Months for Insider Trading," *The Wall Street Journal* (April 24, 2014) (www.wsj.com).

In preceding chapters, audit reports and the demand for audit and other assurance services were discussed. The value of the audit report and the demand for audit services depend on public confidence in the independence and integrity of CPAs. This chapter discusses ethics and the independence and other ethical requirements for CPAs, including the AICPA *Code of Professional Conduct*, PCAOB standards, and international ethics standards. We begin the chapter with a discussion of general ethical principles and their application to the CPA profession.

WHAT ARE ETHICS?

OBJECTIVE 4-1

Distinguish ethical from unethical behavior in personal and professional contexts.

Ethics can be defined broadly as a set of moral principles or values. Each of us has such a set of values, although we may or may not have considered them explicitly. Philosophers, religious organizations, and other groups have defined in various ways ideal sets of moral principles or values. Examples of prescribed sets of moral principles or values include laws and regulations, church doctrine, codes of business ethics for professional groups such as CPAs, and codes of conduct within organizations.

An example of a prescribed set of principles is included in Figure 4-1. These principles were developed by the Josephson Institute of Ethics, a nonprofit membership organization for the improvement of the ethical quality of society.

It is common for people to differ in their moral principles and values and the relative importance they attach to these principles. These differences reflect life experiences, successes and failures, as well as the influences of parents, teachers, and friends.

Need for Ethics

Ethical behavior is necessary for a society to function in an orderly manner. It can be argued that ethics is the glue that holds a society together. Imagine, for example, what would happen if we couldn't depend on the people we deal with to be honest. If parents, teachers, employers, siblings, coworkers, and friends all consistently lied, it would be almost impossible to have effective communication.

The need for ethics in society is sufficiently important that many commonly held ethical values are incorporated into laws. However, many of the ethical values found in Figure 4-1, such as caring, cannot be incorporated into laws because they cannot be defined well enough to be enforced. That does not imply, however, that the principles are less important for an orderly society.

Why People Act Unethically

Most people define *unethical behavior* as conduct that differs from what they believe is appropriate given the circumstances. Each of us decides for ourselves what we consider unethical behavior, both for ourselves and others. It is important to understand what causes people to act in a manner that we decide is unethical.

FIGURE 4-1 Illustrative Prescribed Ethical Principles

The following are the six core ethical values that the Josephson Institute associates with ethical behavior:

Trustworthiness includes honesty, integrity, reliability, and loyalty. Honesty requires a good faith intent to convey the truth. Integrity means that the person acts according to conscience, regardless of the situation. Reliability means making all reasonable efforts to fulfill commitments. Loyalty is a responsibility to promote and protect the interests of certain people and organizations.

Respect includes notions such as civility, courtesy, decency, dignity, autonomy, tolerance, and acceptance. A respectful person treats others with consideration and accepts individual differences and beliefs without prejudice.

Responsibility means being accountable for one's actions and exercising restraint. Responsibility also means pursuing excellence, self-restraint, and leading by example, including perseverance and engaging in continuous improvement.

Fairness and justice include issues of equality, impartiality, proportionality, openness, and due process. Fair treatment means that similar situations are handled consistently.

Caring means being genuinely concerned for the welfare of others and includes acting altruistically and showing benevolence.

Citizenship includes obeying laws and performing one's fair share to make society work, including such activities as voting, serving on juries, conserving resources, and giving more than one takes.

There are two primary reasons why people act unethically: The person's ethical standards are different from those of society as a whole, or the person chooses to act selfishly. Frequently, both reasons exist.

Person's Ethical Standards Differ from General Society's Extreme examples of people whose behavior violates almost everyone's ethical standards are drug dealers, bank robbers, and larcenists. Most people who commit such acts feel no remorse when they are apprehended because their ethical standards differ from those of society as a whole.

There are also many far less extreme examples when others violate our ethical values. When people cheat on their tax returns, treat other people with hostility, lie on resumes and employment applications, or perform below their competence level as employees, most of us regard that as unethical behavior. If the other person has decided that this behavior is ethical and acceptable, there is a conflict of ethical values that is unlikely to be resolved.

The Person Chooses to Act Selfishly The following example illustrates the difference between ethical standards that differ from general society's and acting selfishly. Person A finds a briefcase in an airport containing important papers and $1,000. He tosses the briefcase and keeps the money. He brags to his family and friends about his good fortune. Person A's values probably differ from most of society's. Person B faces the same situation but responds differently. He keeps the money but leaves the briefcase in a conspicuous place. He tells nobody and spends the money on a new wardrobe. It is likely that Person B has violated his own ethical standards, but he decided that the money was too important to pass up. He has chosen to act selfishly.

A considerable portion of unethical behavior results from selfish behavior. Political scandals result from the desire for political power; cheating on tax returns and expense reports is motivated by financial greed; performing below one's competence and cheating on tests typically arise from laziness. In each case, the person knows that the behavior is inappropriate but chooses to do it anyway because of the personal sacrifice needed to act ethically.

ETHICAL DILEMMAS

OBJECTIVE 4-2

Resolve ethical dilemmas using an ethical framework.

An **ethical dilemma** is a situation a person faces in which a decision must be made about the appropriate behavior. A simple example of an ethical dilemma is finding a diamond ring, which necessitates deciding whether to attempt to find the owner or to keep it. A far more difficult ethical dilemma to resolve is the following example. It is the type of case that might be used in an ethics course.

- A man was near death from a rare blood disease. There was one experimental drug that the doctors thought might save him, but the man was not admitted into the free experimental trial. The drug had recently been developed by a start-up pharmaceutical company. The drug was expensive to make, but the company was charging twenty times what it cost to make and develop. The sick man's wife went to everyone she knew to borrow the money to pay for the drug, but she could only get together about $10,000, which is half of what it cost. She told the company that her husband was dying and asked that they sell the drug for a lower price or let her pay later. But the company said: "We discovered the drug and need to make money for our shareholders who have invested in its development." The wife became desperate and broke into the treatment center to steal the drug for her husband. What do you think about the wife's actions?

Auditors, accountants, and other businesspeople face many ethical dilemmas in their business careers. Dealing with a client who threatens to seek a new auditor unless an unmodified opinion is issued presents an ethical dilemma if an unmodified opinion is inappropriate. Deciding whether to confront a supervisor who has materially overstated departmental revenues as a means of receiving a larger bonus is an ethical dilemma. Continuing to be a part of the management of a company that harasses and mistreats employees or treats customers dishonestly is an ethical dilemma, especially if the person has a family to support and the job market is tight.

Rationalizing Unethical Behavior

There are alternative ways to resolve ethical dilemmas, but care must be taken to avoid methods that are rationalizations of unethical behavior. The following are rationalization methods commonly employed that can easily result in unethical conduct:

Everybody Does It The argument that it is acceptable behavior to falsify tax returns, cheat on exams, or sell defective products is commonly based on the rationalization that everyone else is doing it and therefore it is acceptable.

If It's Legal, It's Ethical Using the argument that all legal behavior is ethical relies heavily on the perfection of laws. Under this philosophy, one would have no obligation to return a lost object unless the other person could prove that it was his or hers.

Likelihood of Discovery and Consequences This philosophy relies on evaluating the likelihood that someone else will discover the behavior. Typically, the person also assesses the severity of the penalty (consequences) if there is a discovery. An example is deciding whether to correct an unintentional overbilling to a customer when the customer has already paid the full amount. If the seller believes that the customer will detect the error and respond by not buying in the future, the seller will inform the customer now; otherwise, the seller will wait to see if the customer complains.

Resolving Ethical Dilemmas

Formal frameworks have been developed to help people resolve ethical dilemmas. The purpose of such a framework is to help identify the ethical issues and decide an appropriate course of action using the person's own values. The six-step approach that follows is intended to be a relatively simple approach to resolving ethical dilemmas:

1. Obtain the relevant facts.
2. Identify the ethical issues from the facts.
3. Determine who is affected by the outcome of the dilemma and how each person or group is affected.
4. Identify the alternatives available to the person who must resolve the dilemma.
5. Identify the likely consequence of each alternative.
6. Decide the appropriate action.

An illustration is used to demonstrate how a person might use this six-step approach to resolve an ethical dilemma.

Ethical Dilemma

Bryan Longview has been working six months as a staff assistant for Barton & Barton, CPAs. Currently he is assigned to the audit of Reyon Manufacturing Company under the supervision of Charles Dickerson, an experienced audit senior. There are three auditors assigned to the audit, including Bryan, Charles, and a more experienced assistant, Martha Mills. During lunch on the first day, Charles says, "It will be necessary for us to work a few extra hours on our own time to make sure we come in on budget. This audit isn't very profitable anyway, and we don't want to hurt our firm by going over budget. We can accomplish this easily by coming in a half hour early, taking a short lunch break, and working an hour or so after normal quitting time. We just won't enter that time on our time report." Bryan recalls reading the firm's policy that working hours and not charging for them on the time report is a violation of Barton & Barton's employment policy. He also knows that seniors are paid bonuses, instead of overtime, whereas staff are paid for overtime but get no bonuses. Later, when discussing the issue with Martha, she says, "Charles does this on all of his jobs. He is likely to be our firm's next audit manager. The partners think he's great because his jobs always come in under budget. He rewards us by giving us good engagement evaluations, especially under the cooperative attitude category. Several of the other audit seniors follow the same practice."

Resolving the Ethical Dilemma Using the Six-Step Approach

Relevant Facts There are three key facts in this situation that deal with the ethical issue and how the issue will likely be resolved:

1. The staff person has been informed that he will work hours without recording them as hours worked.
2. Firm policy prohibits this practice.
3. Another staff person has stated that this is common practice in the firm.

Ethical Issue The ethical issue in this situation is not difficult to identify.

- Is it ethical for Bryan to work hours and not record them as hours worked in this situation?

Who Is Affected and How Is Each Affected? There are typically more people affected in situations in which ethical dilemmas occur than might be expected. The following are the key persons involved in this situation:

Who	How Affected
Bryan	Being asked to violate firm policy. Hours of work will be affected. Pay will be affected. Performance evaluations may be affected. Attitude about firm may be affected.
Martha	Same as Bryan.
Charles	Success on engagement and in firm may be affected. Hours of work will be affected.
Barton & Barton	Stated firm policy is being violated. May result in underbilling clients in the current and future engagements. May affect firm's ability to realistically budget engagements and bill clients. May affect the firm's ability to motivate and retain employees.
Staff assigned to Reyon Manufacturing in the future	May result in unrealistic time budgets. May result in unfavorable time performance evaluations. May result in pressures to continue practice of not charging for hours worked.
Other staff in firm	Following the practice on this engagement may motivate others to follow the same practice on other engagements.

Bryan's Available Alternatives

- Refuse to work the additional hours.
- Perform in the manner requested.
- Inform Charles that he will not work the additional hours or will charge the additional hours to the engagement.
- Talk to a manager or partner about Charles's request.
- Refuse to work on the engagement.
- Quit working for the firm.

Each of these options includes a potential consequence, including possible termination by the firm.

Consequences of Each Alternative In deciding the consequences of each alternative, it is essential to evaluate both the short- and long-term effects. There is a natural tendency to emphasize the short term because those consequences will occur quickly, even when the long-term consequences may be more important. For example, consider the potential consequences if Bryan decides to work the additional hours and not report them. In the short term, he will likely get good evaluations for cooperation and perhaps a salary increase. In the longer term, what will be the effect of not reporting the hours this time when other ethical conflicts arise? Consider the following similar ethical dilemmas Bryan might face in his career as he advances:

- A supervisor asks Bryan to work three unreported hours daily and 15 unreported hours each weekend.
- A supervisor asks Bryan to initial certain audit procedures as having been performed when they were not.
- Bryan concludes that he cannot be promoted to manager unless he persuades assistants to work hours that they do not record.
- Management informs Bryan, who is now a partner, that either the company gets an unmodified opinion for a $40,000 audit fee or the company will change auditors.
- Management informs Bryan that the audit fee will be increased $25,000 if Bryan can find a plausible way to increase earnings by $1 million.

Appropriate Action Only Bryan can decide the appropriate option to select in the circumstances after considering his ethical values and the likely consequences of each option. At one extreme, Bryan can decide that the only relevant consequence is the potential impact on his career. Most of us would believe that Bryan is an unethical person if he follows that course. At the other extreme, Bryan can decide to refuse to work for a firm that permits even one supervisor to violate firm policies. Many people would consider such an extreme reaction naive. Most CPA firms have policies such as an anonymous hotline to report unethical behavior and provide employees with mentors and other more formal methods of communication to help staff resolve ethical questions.

SPECIAL NEED FOR ETHICAL CONDUCT IN PROFESSIONS

OBJECTIVE 4-3

Explain the importance of ethical conduct for the accounting profession.

Our society has attached a special meaning to the term *professional*. Professionals are expected to conduct themselves at a higher level than most other members of society. For example, when the press reports that a physician, clergyperson, U.S. senator, or CPA has been indicted for a crime, most people feel more disappointment than when the same thing happens to people who are not labeled as professionals.

The term *professional* means a responsibility for conduct that extends beyond satisfying individual responsibilities and beyond the requirements of our society's laws and regulations. A CPA, as a professional, recognizes a responsibility to the public, to the client, and to fellow practitioners, including honorable behavior, even if that means personal sacrifice.

The reason for an expectation of a high level of professional conduct by any profession is the need for *public confidence* in the quality of service by the profession, regardless of the individual providing it. For the CPA, it is essential that the client and external financial statement users have confidence in the quality of audits and other services. If users of services do not have confidence in physicians, judges, or CPAs, the ability of those professionals to serve clients and the public effectively is diminished.

It is not practical for most customers to evaluate the quality of the performance of professional services because of their *complexity*. A patient cannot be expected to evaluate whether an operation was properly performed. A financial statement user cannot be expected to evaluate audit performance. Most users have neither the competence nor the time for such an evaluation. Public confidence in the quality of professional services is enhanced when the profession encourages high standards of performance and conduct on the part of all practitioners.

Difference Between CPA Firms and Other Professionals

CPA firms have a different relationship with users of financial statements than most other professionals have with their customers. Attorneys, for example, are typically engaged and paid by a client and have primary responsibility to be an advocate for that client. CPA firms are usually engaged by management for private companies and the audit committee for public companies, and are paid by the company issuing the financial statements, but the primary beneficiaries of the audit are financial statement users. Often, the auditor does not know or have contact with the financial statement users but has frequent meetings and ongoing relationships with client personnel.

It is essential that users regard CPA firms as competent and unbiased. If users believe that CPA firms do not perform a valuable service (reduce information risk), the value of CPA firms' audit and other attestation reports is reduced and the demand for these services will thereby also be reduced. Therefore, there is considerable incentive for CPA firms to conduct themselves at a high professional level.

Ways CPAs Are Encouraged to Conduct Themselves Professionally

Figure 4-2 summarizes the most important ways in which CPAs can conduct themselves appropriately and perform high-quality audits and related services. In Chapter 2 we discussed auditing standards and their interpretations, the CPA examination, quality control, peer review requirements, the PCAOB and SEC, AICPA audit practice and quality centers, and continuing education. The legal liability of CPA firms also exerts considerable influence on the way in which practitioners conduct themselves and audits, and this topic is examined in Chapter 5.

In the United States, the two most influential factors—shown shaded in Figure 4-2—are the AICPA *Code of Professional Conduct* and the PCAOB and SEC. The *Code of Professional Conduct* is meant to provide a standard of conduct for all members of the AICPA. The PCAOB is authorized to establish ethics and independence standards for auditors of public companies, and the SEC also plays a significant role in establishing independence standards for auditors of public companies.

At the international level, the International Ethics Standards Board for Accountants (IESBA), an independent standards-setting body within the International Federation of Accountants (IFAC), establishes ethical standards and guidance and fosters international debate on ethical issues faced by accountants through its *Code of Ethics for Professional Accountants*. As a member body of IFAC, the AICPA agrees to have ethics standards that are at least as stringent as the IESBA ethics standards. While CPAs in the United States must follow the AICPA *Code*, the AICPA Professional Ethics

FIGURE 4-2 Ways the Profession and Society Encourage CPAs to Conduct Themselves at a High Level

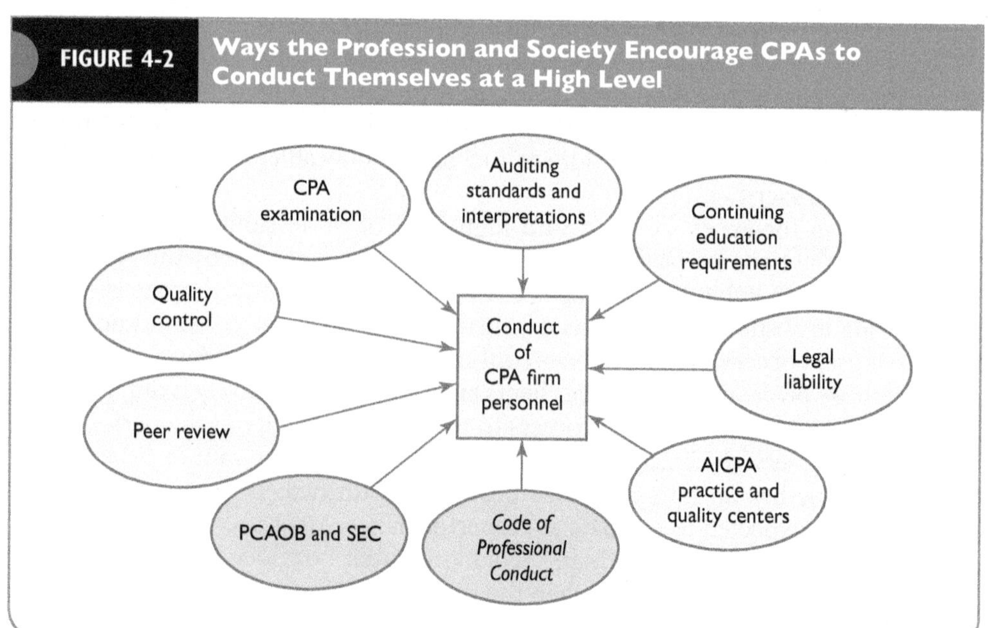

Executive Committee closely monitors IESBA activities to converge the U.S. guidance, where appropriate, to guidance in the IESBA *Code*. The remainder of this chapter addresses the AICPA *Code* and related PCAOB and SEC requirements.

CONCEPT CHECK

1. Suppose that you share a ride to a client with another audit staff member. Your colleague proposes that you both submit mileage reimbursement requests for each day of the audit even though you share rides. Explain the six-step approach to resolving an ethical dilemma and apply it to this situation.
2. Why is there a special need for professional conduct by CPAs? How does this differ from the need for special conduct in other professions?

CODE OF PROFESSIONAL CONDUCT

OBJECTIVE 4-4

Describe the purpose and content of the AICPA *Code of Professional Conduct.*

Members of the AICPA agree to follow the AICPA *Code of Professional Conduct.* As noted in Chapter 2, many CPAs no longer practice in an accounting firm, but work in business or in government or nonprofit organizations. As a result, the *Code* has been restructured to provide separate guidance for members in public practice, those in business, and other AICPA members, such as members who are retired or no longer working. Table 4-1 summarizes the organization of the *Code of Professional Conduct.*

The *Code* consists of principles and rules, in addition to interpretations. The principles provide the framework for the rules that govern the CPA's performance of professional responsibilities. AICPA bylaws require that members comply with the rules of the *Code.* Interpretations of the rules address circumstances members may face that are threats to compliance with the rules of conduct. Part 1 of the *Code* includes rules for members in public practice, while Part 2 includes rules for members in business. Part 3 includes rules for all other members.

Because only members in public practice can audit financial statements, we focus on the rules and related interpretations for members in public practice in Part 1, as well as the Principles of Professional Conduct that are applicable to all members. The revised *Code* also provides a conceptual framework to provide guidance for members in situations where an interpretation of the rules does not exist.

A few definitions from the AICPA *Code* are presented to help you understand and interpret the rules.

- *Client.* Any person or entity, other than the member's employer, that engages a member or a member's firm to perform professional services.
- *Firm.* A form of organization permitted by law or regulation whose characteristics conform to resolutions of the Council of the American Institute of Certified Public Accountants that is engaged in public practice. A firm includes the individual partners thereof, except for purposes of applying the rule on independence.
- *Institute.* The American Institute of Certified Public Accountants.

TABLE 4-1 Organization of AICPA Code of *Professional Conduct*

Section	Applicability	Primary Contents
Preface	All members	Principles of Professional Conduct
Part 1	Members in public practice	Conceptual Framework Rules and Interpretations
Part 2	Members in business	Conceptual Framework Rules and Interpretations
Part 3	Other members	Rules and Interpretations

- *Member.* A member, associate member, or international associate of the American Institute of Certified Public Accountants.
- *Public Practice.* Consists of the performance of professional services for a client by a member or a member's firm.

Principles of Professional Conduct

The section of the AICPA *Code* dealing with principles of professional conduct includes a general discussion of characteristics required of a CPA. The principles section consists of two main parts: a list of six ethical principles and a discussion of those principles. The ethical principles are listed in Table 4-2. The principles indicate the profession's responsibilities to the public, clients, and professional colleagues. The principles are designed to guide members in the performance of their professional responsibilities and in meeting the basic requirements of ethical and professional conduct. They call for an unwavering commitment to honorable behavior that overrides personal advantage. Discussions throughout this chapter include ideas taken from the principles section.

Conceptual Framework for Rules of Conduct

Although interpretations of the rules address many of the situations that may threaten compliance with the rules, they cannot address all such circumstances. To assist members in such circumstances, the *Code* includes the following conceptual framework approach for the member to evaluate threats to compliance with the *Code.*

1. *Identify threats.* When a member encounters a relationship or circumstance that is not specifically addressed by a rule or interpretation, the member should evaluate whether the relationship or circumstance creates a threat to following the rule.
2. *Evaluate the significance of the threat.* In evaluating the significance of a threat, the member should determine whether the threat is at an acceptable level. A threat is at an acceptable level when a reasonable and informed third party who is aware of the relevant information would be expected to conclude that the threat would not compromise the member's compliance with the rules.
3. *Identify and apply safeguards.* If the member concludes that the threat is not at an acceptable level, the member should apply safeguards to eliminate the threat or reduce it to an acceptable level.

Threats to Compliance Threats to compliance with the rules fall into seven broad categories: adverse interest, advocacy, familiarity, management participation, self-interest, self-review, and undue influence. Table 4-3 provides a definition of each threat, along with a specific example of a threat to compliance with the rules. For example, suppose the parent of a staff member at the firm works as a controller at an audit client. This may represent a threat to independence. The firm should evaluate

TABLE 4-2 Principles of Professional Conduct

Principle	Description
Responsibilities	In carrying out their responsibilities as professionals, members should exercise sensitive professional and moral judgments in all their activities.
The Public Interest	Members should accept the obligation to act in a way that will serve the public interest, honor the public trust, and demonstrate a commitment to professionalism.
Integrity	To maintain and broaden public confidence, members should perform all professional responsibilities with the highest sense of integrity.
Objectivity and Independence	A member should maintain objectivity and be free of conflicts of interest in discharging professional responsibilities. A member in public practice should be independent in fact and appearance when providing auditing and other attestation services.
Due Care	A member should observe the profession's technical and ethical standards, strive continually to improve competence and quality of services, and discharge professional responsibility to the best of the member's ability.
Scope and Nature of Services	A member in public practice should observe the principles of the *Code of Professional Conduct* in determining the scope and nature of services to be provided.

TABLE 4-3	Threats to Compliance with Rules Under the AICPA *Code of Professional Conduct*	
Threat	**Definition**	**Example of a Threat**
Adverse interest	The threat that a member will not act with objectivity because the member's interests are opposed to the client's interests.	An officer, director, or significant shareholder participates in litigation against the firm.
Advocacy	The threat that a member will promote a client's interest or position to the point that his or her objectivity or independence is compromised.	A member endorses a client's services or products.
Familiarity	The threat that, due to a long or close relationship with a client, a member will become too sympathetic to the client's interest or too accepting of the client's work or product.	A member's close friend is employed by the client.
Management participation	The threat that a member will take on the role of client management or otherwise assume management responsibilities, such as may occur during an engagement to provide nonattest services.	Due to a loss of client personnel, the client asks a member firm to assist with accounting activities, including the authorization of transactions.
Self-interest	The threat that a member could benefit, financially or otherwise, from an interest in, or relationship with, a client or persons associated with the client.	The member has a financial interest in a client, and the outcome of a professional services engagement may affect the fair value of the financial interest.
Self-review	The threat that a member will not appropriately evaluate the results of a previous judgment or service performed or supervised by the member or an individual in the member's firm and that the member will rely on that service in forming a judgment as part of another service.	The member performs bookkeeping services for the client and then performs an audit of those financial statements.
Undue influence	The threat that a member will subordinate his or her judgment to an individual associated with a client or any relevant third party due to that individual's reputation or expertise, aggressive or dominant personality, or attempts to coerce or exercise excessive influence over the member.	The client indicates that it will not award additional engagements to the firm if the firm continues to disagree with the client on an accounting or tax matter.

the significance of this threat and whether safeguards can reduce this threat to an acceptable level in deciding whether to accept or continue with the client.

Safeguards After evaluating the significance of a threat, if the member concludes that the threat is not at an acceptable level, the member should identify safeguards that eliminate the threat or reduce it to an acceptable level. Depending on the severity of the threat and the nature and effectiveness of the safeguards, more than one safeguard may be necessary. In other cases, the member may conclude that the threat is so severe that no safeguards can eliminate the threat or reduce it to an acceptable level. In such cases, providing the professional service would compromise the member's compliance with the rules. The member should determine whether to decline or discontinue the professional services engagement, or resign from the engagement.

Safeguards fall into three broad categories:

1. Safeguards created by the profession, legislation, or regulation.
2. Safeguards implemented by the client.
3. Safeguards implemented by the firm, including policies and procedures to implement professional and regulatory requirements.

For example, excessive reliance on revenue from a single client could pose a threat to objectivity and independence. The firm may implement policies to monitor the firm's or a partner's excessive reliance on revenue from a single client, and if necessary, take actions to reduce this excessive reliance. Although safeguards may be applied from one or more than one category, it is not possible to rely on safeguards implemented by the client alone to eliminate or reduce significant threats to an acceptable level.

Rules of Conduct

This part of the *Code* includes the explicit rules that must be followed by every member.[1] Because the rules of conduct are enforceable, they are stated in more

[1]The AICPA *Code of Professional Conduct* is applicable to every CPA who is a member of the AICPA. Each state also has rules of conduct that are required for licensing by the state. Many states follow the AICPA rules, but some have somewhat different requirements.

FIGURE 4-3 Standards of Conduct

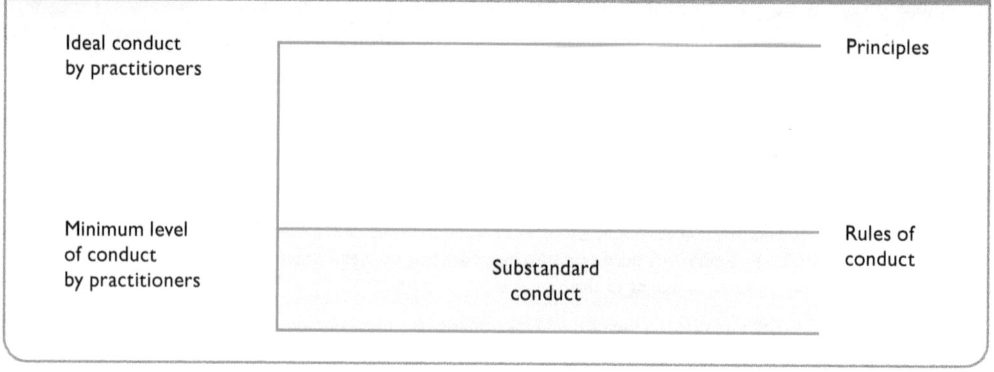

precise language than the section on principles. Because of their enforceability, many practitioners refer to the rules as the AICPA *Code of Professional Conduct.*

The difference between the standards of conduct set by the *principles* and those set by the *rules of conduct* is shown in Figure 4-3. When practitioners conduct themselves at the minimum level in Figure 4-3, this does not imply unsatisfactory conduct. The profession has presumably set the standards sufficiently high to make the minimum conduct satisfactory.

At what level do practitioners conduct themselves in practice? As in any profession, the level varies among practitioners. Most practitioners conduct themselves at a high level. Unfortunately, a few conduct themselves below the minimum level set by the profession. The activities designed to encourage CPAs to conduct themselves at a high level, described in Figure 4-2 (p. 84), help minimize any substandard practice.

Interpretations of Rules of Conduct

The need for interpretations of the rules of conduct arises when there are frequent questions from practitioners about a specific rule. The Professional Ethics Executive Committee of the AICPA prepares each interpretation based on a consensus of a committee made up principally of public accounting practitioners. Before interpretations are finalized, they are issued as exposure drafts to the profession and others for comment. Interpretations provide guidelines about the scope and application of the rules, and members must justify any departure in a disciplinary hearing. The most important interpretations are discussed as a part of each section of the rules.

Applicability of the Rules of Conduct

While most rules apply to members in business, requirements such as independence do not. The rules for members in public practice apply to attestation services and, *unless stated otherwise,* apply to all services provided by CPA firms such as taxes and management services. The most notable exception is the Independence Rule, which requires independence only when the AICPA has established independence requirements through its rule-setting bodies, such as the Auditing Standards Board. The AICPA requires independence only for attestation engagements. For example, a CPA firm can perform management services for a company in which the partner owns stock. Of course, if the CPA firm also performs an audit, that violates the independence requirements for attestation services.

It is a violation of the rules if someone does something on behalf of a member that is a violation if the member does it. An example is a banker who puts in a newsletter that Johnson and Able CPA firm has the best tax department in the state and consistently gets large refunds for its tax clients. That is likely to create false or unjustified expectations and is a violation of the rule on advertising. A member is also responsible for compliance with the rules by employees, partners, and shareholders. The remainder of this chapter highlights these rules, which are summarized in Table 4-4 later in this chapter (p. 104).

IESBA CODE OF ETHICS FOR PROFESSIONAL CONDUCT

The International Ethics Standard Board for Accountants (IESBA) *Code of Ethics for Professional Accountants* is also a principles-based framework consisting of three parts. Part A establishes the five fundamental principles related to integrity, objectivity, professional competence and due care, confidentiality, and professional behavior. Part A also provides a conceptual framework that accountants can apply to identify threats to compliance with the fundamental principles, evaluate the significance of identified threats, and apply safeguards, when necessary, to eliminate the threat or reduce the threat to an acceptable level. Parts B and C of the IESBA *Code* describe how the conceptual framework applies in certain situations, including examples of safeguards and descriptions of situations where safeguards are not available to address threats. Part B applies to professional accountants in public practice while Part C applies to professional accountants in business. As you can see, the general organizational structure of the IESBA *Code* and the AICPA *Code* are similar. This is because the AICPA Professional Ethics Executive Committee (PEEC) has sought to align or "converge" the AICPA *Code* with the *Code of Ethics for Professional Accountants* issued by the International Ethics Standards Board for Accountants (IESBA).

Source: Based on International Ethics Standards Board for Accountants, *Code of Ethics for Professional Accountants* (www.ifac.org).

CONCEPT CHECK

1. What is the purpose of the Principles of Professional Conduct? Identify the six principles.
2. Explain the conceptual framework for the Rules of Conduct and how it should be applied.

INDEPENDENCE RULE

OBJECTIVE 4-5

Apply the AICPA *Code* rules and interpretations on independence and explain their importance.

The value of auditing depends heavily on the public's perception of the independence of auditors. The reason that many diverse users are willing to rely on CPA reports is the users' expectation of an unbiased viewpoint. The AICPA *Code of Professional Conduct* and the IESBA *Code of Ethics for Professional Conduct* both define independence as consisting of two components: independence of mind and independence in appearance. **Independence of mind** reflects the auditor's state of mind that permits the audit to be performed with an unbiased attitude. Independence of mind is often referred to as being **independent in fact. Independence in appearance** is the result of others' interpretations of this independence. If auditors are independent in fact but users believe them to be advocates for the client, most of the value of the audit function is lost.

Because of the importance of auditor independence, the AICPA Independence Rule under the AICPA *Code* and related interpretations is the first rule of conduct we discuss. We then discuss SEC and related PCAOB independence rules, including those required by the Sarbanes–Oxley Act. Organizations and standards other than the AICPA *Code* that influence auditor independence are also described.

Independence Rule A member in public practice shall be independent in the performance of professional services as required by standards promulgated by bodies designated by Council.

CPA firms are required to be independent for certain services that they provide, but not for others. The last phrase in the Independence Rule, "as required by standards promulgated by bodies designated by Council," is a convenient way for the AICPA to include or exclude independence requirements for different types of services. For example, the Auditing Standards Board requires that auditors of historical financial statements be independent. The Independence Rule therefore applies to audits. Independence is also required for other types of attestations, such as review services and audits of prospective financial statements. However, a CPA firm can do tax returns and provide management services without being independent. The Independence Rule does not apply to those types of services.

Because it is impossible to address all of the possible relationships or circumstances in which the appearance of independence may be questioned, the AICPA *Code* provides a conceptual framework for independence that is similar to the general conceptual framework that was discussed earlier. There are also more interpretations for independence than for any of the other rules of conduct. Some of the more significant issues and interpretations involving independence are discussed in the following sections.

Financial Interests

The AICPA *Code* prohibits covered members from owning *any stock or other direct investment* in audit clients regardless of materiality because it is potentially damaging to actual audit independence (independence of mind), and it certainly is likely to affect users' perceptions of the auditors' independence (independence in appearance). *Indirect investments*, such as ownership of stock in a client's company by an auditor's grandparent, are also prohibited, but *only if the amount is material* to the auditor. The ownership of stock rule is more complex than it appears at first glance. A more detailed examination of that requirement is included to aid in understanding and to show the complexity of one of the rules. There are three important distinctions in the rules as they relate to independence and stock ownership.

Covered Members The prohibition on direct financial interests applies to covered members in a position to influence an attest engagement. Covered members include the following:

1. Individuals on the attest engagement team
2. An individual in a position to influence the attest engagement, such as individuals who supervise or evaluate the engagement partner
3. A partner or manager who provides more than 10 hours of nonattest services to the client in a fiscal year
4. A partner in the office of the partner responsible for the attest engagement
5. The firm and its employee benefit plans
6. An entity that can be controlled by any of the covered members listed above or by two or more of the covered individuals or entities operating together

For example, a staff member in a national CPA firm could own stock in a client corporation and not violate the Independence Rule if the staff member is not involved in the engagement. However, if the staff member is assigned to the engagement or becomes a partner in the office of the partner responsible for the attest engagement, he or she would have to dispose of the stock or the CPA firm would no longer be independent of that client.

These independence rules also generally apply to the covered member's immediate family. Immediate family members are a spouse, spousal equivalent, or dependent. Some CPA firms do not permit any ownership by staff of a client's stock regardless of which office serves the client. These firms have decided to have stricter requirements than the minimums set by the rules of conduct.

Direct Versus Indirect Financial Interest The ownership of stock or other equity shares and debt securities by members or their immediate family is called a **direct financial interest**. For example, if either a partner in the office in which an audit is conducted or the partner's spouse has a financial interest in a company, the CPA firm is prohibited from expressing an opinion on the financial statements of that company.

An **indirect financial interest** exists when there is a close, but not a direct, ownership relationship between the auditor and the client. An example of an indirect ownership interest is the covered member's ownership of a mutual fund that has an investment in a client.

Material or Immaterial *Materiality* affects whether ownership is a violation of independence only for *indirect* ownership. Materiality must be considered in relation to the member person's wealth and income. For example, if a covered member has a significant amount of his or her personal wealth invested in a mutual fund and that fund has a large ownership position in a client company, a violation of the *Code* may exist.

Financial Interests of Close Relatives As previously noted, the financial interests of immediate family members, defined as a spouse, spousal equivalent, or dependent, are ordinarily treated as if they were the financial interest of the covered member. Ownership interests of close family members, defined as a parent, sibling, or nondependent child, do not normally impair independence unless the member knows or has reason to believe the ownership interest is material to the close relative or enables the close relative to exercise significant influence over the attest client. Similar rules apply to other individuals in a position to influence the audit engagement or partners in the audit-engagement office. Immaterial ownership interests of close family members do not normally impair independence.

Related Financial Interest Issues

Several interpretations of the Independence Rule deal with specific aspects of financial and other relationships between CPA firm personnel and clients. Some of the more common issues faced by members are summarized in this section.

Normal Lending Procedures Generally, loans between a CPA firm or covered members and an audit client are prohibited because it is a financial relationship. There are several exceptions to the rule, however, including automobile loans, loans fully collateralized by cash deposits at the same financial institution, and unpaid credit card balances not exceeding $10,000 in total. These are permissible only if the loans are made under the lending institution's normal lending terms, procedures, and requirements. It is also permissible to accept a financial institution as a client, even if covered members of the CPA firm have existing home mortgages, other fully collateralized secured loans, and immaterial loans with the institution. No new loans are permitted, however. Both the restrictions and exceptions are reasonable ones, considering the trade-off between independence and the need to permit CPAs to function as businesspeople and individuals.

Employment of Immediate and Close Family Members Imagine the potential difficulty in maintaining independence and objectivity if the firm is asked to audit a client where the parent of the audit partner is chief executive officer. Independence is impaired if individuals on the engagement team, individuals in a position to influence the engagement, or partners in the office of the lead attest engagement partner have an immediate or close family member in a key position with the client. An individual is in a key position if he or she has primary responsibility for preparation of the financial statements or significant accounting functions that support material components of the financial statements, or has ability to exercise influence over the contents of the financial statements.

Joint Closely Held Investments with a Client Assume, for example, that a CPA owns stock in a nonaudit client, Jackson Company. Frank Company, which is an audit client, also owns stock in Jackson Company. This may be a violation of independence. A joint closely held investment is an investment by the member and the client that enables them to control the entity or property. A covered member's independence is considered to be impaired if the joint closely held investment is material to the covered member.

Director, Officer, Management, or Employee of a Company If a CPA is a member of the board of directors or an officer of a client company, his or her ability to make independent evaluations of the fair presentation of financial statements is affected. Even if holding one of these positions did not actually affect the auditor's independence, the frequent involvement with management and the decisions it makes is likely to affect how statement users perceive the CPA's independence. To eliminate this possibility, interpretations prohibit covered members, partners, and professional staff in the office of the partner responsible for the attest engagement from being a director or officer of an audit client company. Similarly, the auditor cannot be an underwriter, voting trustee, promoter, or trustee of a client's pension fund; or act in any other capacity of management; or be an employee of the company.

Independence can also be impaired when a former partner or member of the audit firm leaves the firm and is employed by the client in a key position, unless certain conditions are met. For example, the audit engagement team may need to modify audit procedures to reduce the risk that the former employee has knowledge of the audit plan, and the firm will need to evaluate whether members of the engagement team can maintain an effective level of professional skepticism when evaluating audit information and other representations provided by the former firm member. Independence can also be impaired when a member of the audit team discusses potential employment or receives an offer of employment from the audit client. In those situations, independence can be preserved if the individual promptly reports the offer to appropriate firm personnel and is removed from the engagement until the offer is accepted or rejected.

Interpretations permit CPAs to do audits and be *honorary* directors or trustees for not-for-profit organizations, such as charitable and religious organizations, as long as the position is purely honorary. To illustrate, it is common for a partner of the CPA firm doing the audit of a city's United Way drive to also be an honorary director, along with many other civic leaders. The CPA cannot vote or participate in any management functions.

Consulting, Bookkeeping, and Other Nonattest Services

CPA firms offer many other services to attest clients that may potentially impair independence. Such activities are permissible as long as the member does not perform management functions or make management decisions. For example, a CPA firm may assist in the installation of a client's information system as long as the client makes necessary management decisions about the design of the system. Subject to some restrictions, CPA firms may also provide internal auditing and other extended auditing services to their clients as long as management maintains responsibility for the direction and oversight of the internal audit function.

The CPA firm must assess the client's willingness and ability to perform all management functions related to the engagement and must document the understanding with the client. The understanding should include a description of the services, the engagement objectives, any limitations on the engagement, the member's responsibilities, and the client's agreement to accept its responsibilities.

If a CPA records transactions in the journals for the client, posts monthly totals to the general ledger, makes adjusting entries, and subsequently does an audit, there is some question as to whether the CPA can be independent in the audit role. The interpretations permit a CPA firm to do both bookkeeping and auditing for a private company audit client. The client must be responsible for authorizing all transactions, including preparation and authorization of source documents. For example, a member can process an attest client's payroll using payroll records that the client has prepared and approved. The CPA, in making an audit of financial statements prepared from books and records that the CPA has maintained completely or in part, must conform to auditing standards. The fact that the CPA has processed or maintained certain records does not eliminate the need to make sufficient audit tests.

The AICPA independence rules require members to adhere to more restrictive independence rules of other regulatory bodies, such as the SEC. For example, the Sarbanes–Oxley Act and SEC rules prohibit auditors of public companies from providing bookkeeping services to their public company audit clients. As a result, it is not permissible for an audit firm to provide bookkeeping services to a public company audit client under both SEC rules and the AICPA rules on independence.

Litigation Between CPA Firm and Client

When there is a lawsuit or intent to start a lawsuit between a CPA firm and its client, the ability of the CPA firm and client to remain objective is questionable, and the threat to the auditor's independence may not be at an acceptable level. In situations where management sues a CPA firm claiming a deficiency in the previous audit, the CPA firm is not considered independent for the current year's audit. Similarly, if the CPA firm sues management for fraudulent financial reporting or deceit, the audit firm is no longer independent. The CPA firm and client company or management may be defendants in a suit brought by a third party, such as in a securities class action. This litigation in itself does not affect independence. However, independence may be affected if cross-claims between the auditor and client are filed that have a significant risk of a material loss to the CPA firm or client.

Litigation by the client related to tax or other nonaudit services for an amount that is immaterial, or litigation against both the client and the CPA firm by another party, does not usually impair independence. The key consideration in all such suits is the likely effect on the ability of client, management, and CPA firm personnel to remain objective and comment freely.

Unpaid Fees

Interpretations indicate that independence is considered impaired if billed or unbilled fees remain unpaid for professional services provided more than one year before the date of the report. Such unpaid fees are considered a loan from the auditor to the client and are therefore a violation of independence. Unpaid fees from a client in bankruptcy do not violate independence.

Network of Firms

Audit firms frequently join larger groups or associations of other firms to enhance their capabilities to provide professional services. When they share certain characteristics, such as a common brand name, common control, common business strategy, or common quality control procedures, or they share in profits, costs, or professional resources, the network firm is required to be independent of audit and review clients of other network firms. For other attest clients, the covered member should apply the conceptual framework to assess whether the threat to independence is at an acceptable level.

SARBANES–OXLEY AND RELATED INDEPENDENCE REQUIREMENTS

OBJECTIVE 4-6

Understand Sarbanes–Oxley Act and other SEC and PCAOB independence requirements and additional factors that influence auditor independence.

Auditors of public companies must comply with independence requirements of the Sarbanes–Oxley Act, as well as requirements of the PCAOB and SEC. We review some of the most important of these requirements in this section.

Sarbanes–Oxley Act and SEC Provisions Addressing Auditor Independence

The SEC adopted rules strengthening auditor independence that are consistent with the requirements of the Sarbanes–Oxley Act. The SEC rules further restrict the provision of nonaudit services to audit clients, and they also include restrictions on employment of former audit firm employees by the client and provide for audit partner rotation to enhance independence. The PCAOB has also issued additional independence rules related to the provision of certain tax services.

Nonaudit Services The Sarbanes–Oxley Act and SEC rules restrict, but do not completely eliminate, the types of nonaudit services that can be provided to publicly held audit clients. The following nine services are prohibited:

1. Bookkeeping and other accounting services
2. Financial information systems design and implementation
3. Appraisal or valuation services
4. Actuarial services
5. Internal audit outsourcing
6. Management or human resource functions
7. Broker, dealer, investment adviser, or investment banker services
8. Legal and expert services unrelated to the audit
9. Any other service that the PCAOB determines by regulation is impermissible

CPA firms are not prohibited from performing these services for private companies and for public companies that are not audit clients. In addition, CPA firms may still provide other services that are not prohibited for public company audit clients. For example, SEC and PCAOB rules allow CPAs to provide tax services for audit clients, except for tax services for company executives who oversee financial reporting, and tax avoidance planning services. Nonaudit services that are not prohibited by the Sarbanes–Oxley Act and the SEC rules must be preapproved by the company's audit committee. In addition, a CPA firm is not independent if an audit partner receives compensation for selling services to the client other than audit, review, and attest services.

Companies are required to disclose in their proxy statement or annual filings with the SEC the total amount of audit and nonaudit fees paid to the CPA firm for the two most recent years. Four categories of fees must be reported: (1) audit fees, (2) audit-related fees, (3) tax fees, and (4) all other fees. Audit-related fees are for services such as comfort letters and reviews of SEC filings that can only be provided by CPA firms. Companies are also required to provide further breakdown of the "other fees" category and to provide qualitative information on the nature of the services provided.

Audit Committees An **audit committee** is a selected number of members of a company's board of directors whose responsibilities include helping auditors remain independent of management. Most audit committees are made up of three to five, or sometimes as many as seven, directors who are not a part of company management. In response to the Sarbanes–Oxley Act requirement that all members of the audit committee be independent, the national stock exchanges amended their listing rules to reflect the provision. Now, with very limited exceptions, public company audit committees should be comprised solely of independent members, and companies must disclose whether or not the audit committee includes at least one member who is a financial expert.

The Sarbanes–Oxley Act further requires the audit committee of a public company to be responsible for the appointment, compensation, and oversight of the work

INCREASE IN CONSULTING BRINGS CALLS FOR LIMITS

In the period immediately preceding the passage of the Sarbanes–Oxley Act (SOX), three of the Big 4 firms sold or spun off their consulting practices. Prior to SOX, consulting and advisory services were the largest source of revenue for the Big 4 firms. However, after the dispositions of these consulting practices, auditing again became the major source of revenue for the Big 4—but not for long. In the years since the passage of SOX, the Big 4 firms have rebuilt their consulting practices. Advisory services are once again the largest source of revenue for the Big 4, and these services are growing much faster than auditing revenues. Although SOX restricts firms from providing many nonaudit services to public company audit clients, the firms have developed new services, and increasingly provide services to companies that are not public audit clients. The rise of consulting has once again raised concerns by regulators.

PCAOB Board Member Steven Harris describes four potential threats from the increased advisory services:

- *Distraction by the audit firm away from audit and its core values.* As consulting revenue grows in importance, the audit practice may lose influence, and values at the core of the audit practice may decrease in importance.
- *Use of inappropriate performance measurements.* As advisory and consulting services grow, performance measures for partners may emphasize revenue growth and profitability over audit quality.
- *Potential independence impairment.* The growth of advisory services may result in insufficient monitoring of services provided to audit clients, and provision of allowed tax consulting services that could affect auditor independence.
- *Rise of internal conflicts.* The expanding consulting practice could result in conflict between audit and advisory services in the firm. These conflicts could arise because of the differing nature of each line of business, and because advisory practices are not allowed to provide many services to public company audit clients.

There are currently no proposals to further restrict consulting and advisory services beyond the restriction in the Sarbanes–Oxley Act. However, in the European Union, recently enacted rules on audit firm rotation would also limit the amount of nonaudit fees that can be earned from public clients to 70 percent of the audit fee.

Sources: 1. Steven B. Harris, "The Rise of Advisory Services in Audit Firms," speech given at the Practicing Law Institute 12th Annual Directors Institute on Corporate Governance, New York, NY (November 24, 2014) (www.pcaobus.org); 2. Vincent Huck, "EU Settles on 10 Years Mandatory Audit Rotation" (December 17, 2013) (www.theaccountant-online.com).

of the auditor. The audit committee must preapprove all audit and nonaudit services, and is responsible for oversight of the work of the auditor, including resolution of disagreements involving financial reporting between management and the auditor. Auditors are responsible for communicating all significant matters identified during the audit to the audit committee.

For public companies, PCAOB rules require a CPA firm, before its selection as the company's auditor, to describe in writing and document its discussions with the audit committee about all relationships between the firm and the company, including executives in financial reporting positions, to determine whether there is any impairment of the CPA firm's independence. If selected as the auditor, these communications are to be made at least annually.

Collectively, these provisions increase the independence and role of the audit committee and enhance auditor independence by effectively making the audit committee the client for public companies, rather than management.

Conflicts Arising from Employment Relationships The employment of former audit team members with an audit client raises independence concerns. Consistent with the requirements of the Sarbanes–Oxley Act, the SEC added a one-year "cooling off" period before a member of the audit engagement team can work for the client in certain key management positions. This has important implications for an auditor working for a CPA firm who receives an employment offer from a publicly held client for a position as a chief executive officer, controller, chief financial officer, chief accounting officer, or equivalent position. The CPA firm cannot continue to audit that client if the auditor accepts the position and has participated in any capacity in the audit for one year preceding the start of the audit. This has no effect on the CPA firm's ability to continue the audit if the former auditor accepts a position such as assistant controller or accountant without primary accounting responsibilities.

Under SEC rules existing before the Sarbanes–Oxley Act and continuing, a CPA firm is not independent with respect to an audit client if a former partner, principal, shareholder, or professional employee of the firm accepts employment with a client if he or she has a continuing financial interest in the CPA firm or is in a position to influence the CPA firm's operations or financial policies.

Partner Rotation As required by the Sarbanes–Oxley Act, the SEC independence rules require the lead and concurring audit partner to rotate off the audit engagement after five years. (The concurring partner is not involved with the actual performance of the audit and reviews the work at the completion of the audit.) Although not addressed in the Sarbanes–Oxley Act, the SEC requires a five-year "time-out" for the lead and concurring partners after rotation before they can return to that audit client. Additional audit partners with significant involvement on the audit must rotate after seven years and are subject to a two-year time-out period.

Ownership Interests SEC rules on financial relationships take an engagement perspective and prohibit ownership in audit clients by those persons who can influence the audit. The rules prohibit any ownership by covered persons and their immediate family, including (a) members of the audit engagement team, (b) those in a position to influence the audit engagement in the firm chain of command, (c) partners and managers who provide more than 10 hours of nonaudit services to the client, and (d) partners in the office of the partner primarily responsible for the audit engagement. These rules are designed to provide workable rules that still safeguard independence.

Shopping for Accounting Principles

Both management and representatives of management, such as investment bankers, often consult with other accountants on the application of accounting principles. Although consultation with other accountants is appropriate, it can lead to a loss of independence in certain circumstances. For example, suppose one CPA firm replaces the existing auditors on the strength of accounting advice offered but later finds facts

AUDIT FIRM ROTATION IN THE EUROPEAN UNION

Current U.S. rules require rotation of the audit engagement *partner* on a regular basis, but many clients have retained the same audit firm for decades, creating a question as to whether the audit firm is truly independent. Proponents of audit *firm* rotation argue that rotation will increase audit quality by increasing auditor independence and professional skepticism. Opponents of mandatory audit firm rotation argue that rotation would increase fees and could result in lower audit quality due to the significant learning curve that takes place when an audit firm begins a relationship with a new client. Opponents also argue that there are already sufficient deterrents to impairment of independence, such as legal liability, PCAOB inspections and enforcement actions, and the threat of being sanctioned for violations of the *Code of Professional Conduct.* After issuing a concept release on auditor independence and auditor rotation, the PCAOB received over 650 comment letters on the concept release, many of them opposed to audit firm rotation, and the PCAOB indicates this subject is not currently on its agenda.

However, the European Commission (EC) has approved rules that will bring mandatory rotation to the European Union beginning in 2016. As initially proposed, the EC would have required public interest entities, which include public companies, banks, and insurance companies, to change auditors after six years. The rule as adopted requires audit firm rotation after 10 years. This period can be extended to 20 years if the audit is put out to bid, and 24 years in the case of a joint audit in which more than one firm conducts the audit.

Sources: 1. Ken Tysiac, "Mandatory Audit Firm Rotation Rules Published in EU," *Journal of Accountancy* (May 28, 2014) (www.journalofaccountancy.com); 2. PCAOB Release No. 2011-016, "Concept Release on Auditor Independence and Audit Firm Rotation," August 16, 2011 (www.pcaobus.org).

and circumstances that require the CPA firm to change its stance. It may be difficult for the new CPA firm to remain independent in such a situation. Auditing standards set forth requirements that must be followed when a CPA firm is requested to provide a written or oral opinion on the application of accounting principles or the type of audit opinion that would be issued for a specific or hypothetical transaction of an audit client of another CPA firm. The purpose of the requirement is to minimize the likelihood of management following the practice commonly called "opinion shopping" and to minimize the potential threat to independence of the kind described. Primary among the requirements is that the consulted CPA firm should communicate with the entity's existing auditors to ascertain all the available facts relevant to forming a professional judgment on the matters on which the firm has been requested to report.

Engagement and Payment of Audit Fees by Management

Can an auditor be truly independent in fact and appearance if the payment of the audit fees is dependent on the entity's management? There is probably no satisfactory answer to this question, but it does demonstrate the difficulty of assuring that auditors are independent. The alternative to engagement of the CPA firm by the audit committee and payment of audit fees by management is probably the use of either government or quasi-government auditors. All things considered, it is questionable whether the audit function would be performed better or more cheaply by the public sector.

CONCEPT CHECK

1. Distinguish between independence of mind and independence in appearance. Identify an activity that may not affect independence of mind but is likely to affect independence in appearance.
2. Explain the role of the audit committee in enhancing auditor independence.

OTHER RULES OF CONDUCT

OBJECTIVE 4-7

Understand the requirements of other rules under the AICPA *Code.*

Although independence is critical to public confidence in CPAs, it is also important that auditors adhere to the other rules of conduct listed in Table 4-4 (p. 104). We discuss the rules and interpretations in a slightly different order than they are presented in the AICPA *Code.* We begin by discussing the rules for integrity and objectivity.

Integrity and Objectivity

Integrity means impartiality in performing all services. The Integrity and Objectivity Rule is presented below:

> **Integrity and Objectivity Rule** In the performance of any professional service, a member shall maintain objectivity and integrity, shall be free of conflicts of interest, and shall not knowingly misrepresent facts or subordinate his or her judgment to others.

To illustrate the meaning of integrity and objectivity, assume the auditor believes that accounts receivable may not be collectible but accepts management's opinion without an independent evaluation of collectibility. The auditor has subordinated his or her judgment and thereby lacks objectivity. Now assume a CPA is preparing the tax return for a client and, as a client advocate, encourages the client to take a deduction on the return that the CPA believes is valid, but for which there is some but not complete support. This is not a violation of either objectivity or integrity, because it is acceptable for the CPA to be a client advocate in tax and management services. If the CPA encourages the client to take a deduction for which there is no support but has little chance of discovery by the IRS, a violation has occurred. That is a misrepresentation of the facts; therefore, the CPA's integrity has been impaired.

Audit staff members should not subordinate their judgment to supervisors on the audit. Staff auditors are responsible for their own judgments documented in the audit files and should not change those conclusions at the request of supervisors on the engagement unless the staff auditor agrees with the supervisor's conclusion. Firm procedures should allow assistants to document situations where they disagree with a conclusion involving a significant matter.

Freedom from conflicts of interest means the absence of relationships that might interfere with objectivity or integrity. For example, it is inappropriate for an auditor who is also an attorney to represent a client in legal matters. The attorney is an advocate for the client, whereas the auditor must be impartial.

Apparent conflicts of interest may not be a violation of the rules of conduct if the information is disclosed to the member's client or employer. For example, if a partner of a CPA firm recommends that a client have the security of its Web site evaluated by a technology consulting firm that is owned by the partner's spouse, a conflict of interest may appear to exist. No violation of the Integrity and Objectivity Rule occurs if the partner informs the client's management of the relationship and management proceeds with the evaluation with that knowledge. The interpretation of the rule makes it clear that the independence requirements cannot be eliminated by these disclosures. The Integrity and Objectivity Rule also applies to members in business. For example, a CPA who, as an employee of an entity, makes false or misleading entries or representations in financial statements is in violation of the rules on integrity and objectivity.

Technical Standards

Three *Code* rules relate to the auditor's adherence with the requirements of technical standards. The primary purpose of the requirements is to provide support for the ASB, PCAOB, FASB, IASB, and other technical standards-setting bodies. The following are the requirements of the technical standards:

> **General Standards Rule** A member shall comply with the following standards and with any interpretations thereof by bodies designated by Council.
>
> A. *Professional competence.* Undertake only those professional services that the member or the member's firm can reasonably expect to be completed with professional competence.
>
> B. *Due professional care.* Exercise due professional care in the performance of professional services.
>
> C. *Planning and supervision.* Adequately plan and supervise the performance of professional services.
>
> D. *Sufficient relevant data.* Obtain sufficient relevant data to afford a reasonable basis for conclusions or recommendations in relation to any professional services performed.

Compliance with Standards Rule A member who performs auditing, review, compilation, management consulting, tax, or other professional services shall comply with standards promulgated by bodies designated by Council.

Accounting Principles Rule A member shall not (1) express an opinion or state affirmatively that the financial statements or other financial data of any entity are presented in conformity with generally accepted accounting principles or (2) state that he or she is not aware of any material modifications that should be made to such statements or data in order for them to be in conformity with generally accepted accounting principles, if such statements or data contain any departure from an accounting principle promulgated by bodies designated by Council to establish such principles that has a material effect on the statements or data taken as a whole. If, however, the statements or data contain such a departure and the member can demonstrate that due to unusual circumstances the financial statements or data would otherwise have been misleading, the member can comply with the rule by describing the departure, its approximate effects, if practicable, and the reasons why compliance with the principle would result in a misleading statement.

Confidentiality

It is essential that practitioners not disclose **confidential client information** obtained in any type of engagement without the consent of the client. The specific requirements of the rule on confidential client information are shown in the box below.

Confidential Client Information Rule A member in public practice shall not disclose any confidential client information without the specific consent of the client.

This rule shall not be construed (1) to relieve a member of his or her professional obligations under the Compliance with Standards Rule or the Accounting Principles Rule, (2) to affect in any way the member's obligation to comply with a validly issued and enforceable subpoena or summons, or to prohibit a member's compliance with applicable laws and government regulations, (3) to prohibit review of a member's professional practice under AICPA or state CPA society or Board of Accountancy authorization, or (4) to preclude a member from initiating a complaint with, or responding to any inquiry made by, the professional ethics division or trial board of the Institute or a duly constituted investigative or disciplinary body of a state CPA society or Board of Accountancy.

Members of any of the bodies identified in (4) above and members involved with professional practice reviews identified in (3) above shall not use to their own advantage or disclose any member's confidential client information that comes to their attention in carrying out those activities. This prohibition shall not restrict members' exchange of information in connection with the investigative or disciplinary proceedings described in (4) above or the professional practice reviews described in (3) above.

Need for Confidentiality During audits and most other types of engagements, practitioners obtain considerable confidential information, including officers' salaries, product pricing and advertising plans, and product cost data. If auditors divulge this information to outsiders or to client employees who have been denied access to the information, their relationship with management can be seriously strained and, in extreme cases, the client can be harmed. The confidentiality requirement applies to all services provided by CPA firms, including tax and management services.

Ordinarily, the CPA's audit files can be made available to someone else only with the express permission of the client. This is the case even if a CPA sells the practice to another CPA firm or is willing to permit a successor auditor to examine the audit documentation prepared for a former client.

Exceptions to Confidentiality As stated in the second paragraph of the Confidential Client Information Rule, there are four exceptions to the confidentiality requirements.

All four exceptions concern responsibilities that are more important than maintaining confidential relations with the client.

1. *Obligations related to technical standards.* Suppose that three months after an unmodified opinion audit report was issued, the auditor discovers that the financial statements were materially misstated. When the chief executive officer is confronted, he responds that even though he agrees that the financial statements are misstated, confidentiality prevents the CPA from informing anyone. The rule makes it clear that the auditor's responsibility to discharge professional standards is greater than that for confidentiality. In such a case, a revised, correct audit report must be issued. Note, however, that the conflict seldom occurs.
2. *Subpoena or summons and compliance with laws and regulations.* Legally, information is called **privileged information** if legal proceedings cannot require a person to provide the information, even if there is a subpoena. Information communicated by a client to an attorney or by a patient to a physician is privileged. *Information obtained by a CPA from a client generally is not privileged.* The second exception to the rule is needed to allow CPA firms to comply with laws and regulations.
3. *Peer review.* When a CPA or CPA firm conducts a peer review of the quality controls of another CPA firm, it is normal practice to examine several sets of audit files. If the peer review is authorized by the AICPA, state CPA society, or state Board of Accountancy, client permission to examine the audit documentation is not needed. Requiring permission from each client may restrict access of the peer reviewers and would be a time burden on all concerned. Naturally, the peer reviewers must keep the information obtained confidential and cannot use the information for other purposes. Note that access to files for PCAOB inspections is also allowed to comply with the requirements of the Sarbanes–Oxley Act.
4. *Response to ethics division.* If a practitioner is charged with inadequate technical performance by the AICPA Ethics Division trial board under any of the technical standards rules, board members are likely to want to examine audit documentation. The fourth exception prevents a CPA firm from denying the inquirers access to audit documentation by saying that it is confidential information. Similarly, a CPA firm that observes substandard audit documentation of another CPA firm cannot use confidentiality as the reason for not initiating a complaint of substandard performance against the firm.

Contingent Fees

To help CPAs maintain objectivity in conducting audits or other attestation services, basing fees on the outcome of engagements is prohibited. The requirements related to contingent fees are shown below.

Contingent Fees Rule A member in public practice shall not

(1) Perform for a contingent fee any professional services for, or receive such a fee from, a client for whom the member or member's firm performs:

  (a) an audit or review of a financial statement; or

  (b) a compilation of a financial statement when the member expects, or reasonably might expect, that a third party will use the financial statement and the member's compilation report does not disclose a lack of independence; or

  (c) an examination of prospective financial information;

or

(2) Prepare an original or amended tax return or claim for a tax refund for a contingent fee for any client.

The prohibition in (1) above applies during the period in which the member or the member's firm is engaged to perform any of the services listed above and the period covered by any historical financial statements involved in any such listed services.

> Except as stated in the next sentence, a contingent fee is a fee established for the performance of any service pursuant to an arrangement in which no fee will be charged unless a specified finding or result is attained, or in which the amount of the fee is otherwise dependent upon the finding or result of such service. Solely for purposes of this rule, fees are not regarded as being contingent if fixed by courts or other public authorities, or, in tax matters, if determined based on the results of judicial proceedings or the findings of governmental agencies.
>
> A member's fees may vary depending, for example, on the complexity of services rendered.

To illustrate the need for a rule on contingent fees, suppose a CPA firm was permitted to charge a fee of $50,000 if an unmodified opinion was provided but only $25,000 if the opinion was modified. Such an agreement may tempt a practitioner to issue the wrong opinion and is a violation of the rule on contingent fees.

CPA firms are permitted to charge contingent fees *for nonattestation services, unless the CPA firm is also performing attestation services* for the same client. For example, it is *not* a violation for a CPA to charge fees as an expert witness determined by the amount awarded to the plaintiff or to base consulting fees on a percentage of a bond issue *if the CPA firm does not also do an audit or other attestation for the same client.*

Prohibiting contingent fees for attestation services and tax return preparation is important because of the importance of independence and objectivity. Because CPAs compete when providing other services with other professions who do not have contingent fee restrictions, it would be unfair to prohibit CPAs from providing these services on the same basis. When these nonattestation services are provided for a client receiving attestation services, the need for independence and objectivity prevails and the auditor is not allowed to provide the services on a contingent fee basis.

Commissions and Referral Fees

Commissions are compensation paid for recommending or referring a third party's product or service to a client or recommending or referring a client's product or service to a third party. Restrictions on commissions are similar to the rules on contingent fees. CPAs are prohibited from receiving commissions for a client who is receiving attestation services from the CPA firm. Commissions are permissible for other clients, but they must be disclosed. Referral fees for recommending or referring the services of another CPA are not considered commissions and are not restricted. However, any referral fees for CPA services must also be disclosed.

> **Commissions and Referral Fees Rule** A member in public practice shall not for a commission recommend or refer to a client any product or service, or for a commission recommend or refer any product or service to be supplied by a client, or receive a commission, when the member or the member's firm also performs for that client:
>
> (a) an audit or review of a financial statement; or
> (b) a compilation of a financial statement when the member expects, or reasonably might expect, that a third party will use the financial statement and the member's compilation report does not disclose a lack of independence; or
> (c) an examination of prospective financial information.
>
> This prohibition applies during the period in which the member is engaged to perform any of the services listed above and the period covered by any historical financial statements involved in such listed services.
>
> A member in public practice who is not prohibited by this rule from performing services for or receiving a commission and who is paid or expects to be paid a commission shall disclose that fact to any person or entity to whom the member recommends or refers a product or service to which the commission relates. Any member who accepts a referral fee for recommending or referring any service of a CPA to any person or entity or who pays a referral fee to obtain a client shall disclose such acceptance or payment to the client.

The rule for commissions and referral fees means that a CPA firm does not violate AICPA rules of conduct if it sells such things as real estate, securities, and entire firms on a commission basis if the transaction does not involve a client who is receiving attestation services from the same CPA firm. This rule enables CPA firms to profit by providing many services to nonattestation services clients that were previously prohibited.

The reason for the AICPA continuing to prohibit commissions for any attestation service client is the need to ensure that the CPA firm is independent. This requirement and the reasons for it are the same as those discussed under contingent fees.

Advertising and Solicitation

To encourage CPAs to conduct themselves professionally, the rules also prohibit advertising or solicitation that is false, misleading, or deceptive.

> **Advertising and Other Forms of Solicitation Rule** A member in public practice shall not seek to obtain clients by advertising or other forms of solicitation in a manner that is false, misleading, or deceptive. Solicitation by the use of coercion, overreaching, or harassing conduct is prohibited.

Solicitation consists of the various means that CPA firms use to engage new clients other than accepting new clients who approach the firm. Examples include taking prospective clients to lunch to explain the CPA's services, offering seminars on current tax law changes to potential clients, and advertising on an Internet site. The last example is advertising, which is only one form of solicitation.

Many CPA firms have developed sophisticated advertising for national journals read by businesspeople and for local newspapers. It is common for CPA firms to identify potential clients being serviced by other CPA firms and make formal and informal presentations to convince management to change CPA firms. Price bidding for audits and other services is common and often highly competitive. Some companies now change auditors more often than previously to reduce audit cost.

Is the quality of audits endangered by these activities? Although there have been several high-profile cases in the past involving apparent audit failures, the existing legal exposure of CPAs, peer review requirements, PCAOB inspections, and the potential for interference by the SEC and government has kept audit quality high.

Form of Organization and Name

The organizational structure of CPA firms was first discussed in Chapter 2. The rules of conduct restrict the permissible forms of organization and prohibit a member from practicing under a firm name that is misleading. Practitioners are allowed to organize in any of six forms, as long as they are permitted by state law: proprietorship, general partnership, general corporation, professional corporation (PC), limited liability company (LLC), or limited liability partnership (LLP). Each of these forms of organization was discussed in Chapter 2 (pp. 27–28).

> **Form of Organization and Name Rule** A member may practice public accounting only in a form of organization permitted by state law or regulation whose characteristics conform to resolutions of Council.
>
> A member shall not practice public accounting under a firm name that is misleading. Names of one or more past owners may be included in the firm name of a successor organization.
>
> A firm may not designate itself as "Members of the American Institute of Certified Public Accountants" unless all of its CPA owners are members of the Institute.

Non-CPAs are allowed to have ownership interests in the firm. However, CPAs must own a majority of the firm's financial interests and voting rights. A CPA must also have ultimate responsibility for all financial statement attest, compilation, and other services provided by the firm that are governed by Statements on Auditing Standards or Statements on Standards for Accounting and Review Services.

A fairly recent development has been the use of alternative practice structures in which a firm that provides attest services is closely aligned with another public or private organization that performs other professional services. These alternative practice structures are permissible, but an AICPA Council resolution makes it clear that to protect the public interest, CPAs remain responsible for the conduct of their attest work as they are in traditional practice structures.

A CPA firm may use any name as long as it is not misleading. Most firms use the name of one or more of the owners. It is not unusual for a firm name to include the names of five or more owners. A CPA firm can use a trade name, although this is unusual in practice. Names such as Marshall Audit Co. or Chicago Tax Specialists are permissible if they are not misleading.

Discreditable Acts

Because of the special need for CPAs to conduct themselves in a professional manner, the *Code* has a specific rule prohibiting acts discreditable to the profession. Note in Table 4-4 (p. 104) that the rule on discreditable acts applies to all members, including members in business and other members. Although a discreditable act is not well defined in the rules or interpretations, some of the requirements are discussed below.

> **Acts Discreditable Rule** A member shall not commit an act discreditable to the profession.

Do excessive drinking, rowdy behavior, or other acts that many people consider unprofessional constitute a discreditable act? Probably not. Determining what constitutes professional behavior continues to be the responsibility of each professional.

For guidance as to what constitutes a discreditable act, the AICPA bylaws provide clearer guidelines than the AICPA *Code*. The bylaws state that membership in the AICPA can be terminated without a hearing for judgment of conviction for any of the following four crimes: (1) a crime punishable by imprisonment for more than one year; (2) the willful failure to file any income tax return that the CPA, as an individual taxpayer, is required by law to file; (3) the filing of a false or fraudulent income tax return on the CPA's or client's behalf; or (4) the willful aiding in the preparation and presentation of a false and fraudulent income tax return of a client. Observe that three of these deal with income tax matters of the member or a client.

Interpretations of the Acts Discreditable Rule identify several acts that are considered to be discreditable. For example, it is discreditable to retain a client's records after a demand is made for them or whenever a member is found to have violated any federal, state, or local antidiscrimination laws. In addition, auditors conducting audits of governmental entities must comply with standards for government audits. Similarly, when a member accepts an engagement that involves reporting to a regulatory agency such as the SEC, the member must follow the additional requirements of the regulatory agency. The solicitation or disclosure of Uniform CPA examination questions and answers without permission of the AICPA is also not permitted.

A member in business is considered to have committed an act discreditable if by his or her negligence others are made or permitted or directed to make materially false and misleading entries in the financial statements and records of an entity; the member fails to correct financial statements that are materially false and misleading; or the member signs or permits or directs another to sign a document containing materially false and misleading information. Also, if a member prepares financial statements or related information for reporting to governmental bodies, commissions, or regulatory agencies, the member should follow the requirements of such organizations in addition to requirements of accounting standards.

Code Classification System

The numbering system for the revised AICPA *Code* is "ET section X.XXX.XXX." The single digit at the beginning of the citation identifies the part of the *Code*. Material from the preface begins with 0, and content from part 1, part 2, and part 3 begin with the numbers 1, 2, and 3, respectively. The next two sets of digits represent the section and subsection, respectively. For example, section 1.200 is the section on auditor independence, and the citation ET section 1.295.105 is section 295 on nonattest services under the section on independence, and 105 is the subsection on advisory services. When a section appears in two or more parts of the *Code* because it applies to members who are not in public practice, the same number is used. For example, the Acts Discreditable Rule appears in all three parts of the *Code*, and the citations are 1.400.001, 2.400.001, and 3.400.001, respectively

A summary of the rules of conduct is included in Table 4-4.

CONCEPT CHECK

1. Identify the circumstances under which a CPA can disclose confidential information without client permission.
2. Explain the rule on contingent fees. Why is this rule necessary?

ENFORCEMENT

OBJECTIVE 4-8

Describe the enforcement mechanisms for CPA conduct.

Failure to follow the rules of conduct can result in *expulsion* from the AICPA. This by itself does not prevent a CPA from practicing public accounting, but it is an important social sanction. In addition to the rules of conduct, the AICPA bylaws provide for automatic suspension or expulsion from the AICPA for conviction of a crime punishable by imprisonment for more than one year and for various tax-related crimes.

Action by AICPA Professional Ethics Division

The AICPA Professional Ethics Division is responsible for investigating violations of the *Code* and deciding disciplinary action. The division's investigations result from information obtained primarily from complaints of practitioners or other individuals, state societies of CPAs, or governmental agencies. A member can be automatically sanctioned without an investigation if the member has been disciplined by governmental agencies or other organizations that have been granted the authority to regulate accountants, such as the SEC and PCAOB.

There are two primary levels of disciplinary action. For less serious, and probably unintentional, violations, the division limits the discipline to a requirement of remedial or corrective action. An example is the unintentional failure to make sure that a small audit client included all disclosures in its financial statements, which violates the Accounting Principles Rule of the rules of conduct. The division is likely to require the member to attend a specified number of hours of continuing education courses to improve technical competence. The second level of disciplinary action is action before the Joint Trial Board. This board has authority to *suspend or expel members from the AICPA* for various violations of professional ethics. Actions taken by the board, including automatic sanctions, are reported in the Disciplinary Actions sections of the AICPA Web site, including the name and location of the person suspended or expelled and reasons for the action.

Action by a State Board of Accountancy

Even more important than expulsion from the AICPA are the rules of conduct, similar to those of the AICPA, that have been enacted by the Board of Accountancy of each of the 50 states. Because each state grants the individual practitioner a license to practice as a CPA, a significant breach of a state Board of Accountancy's code of conduct can result in the *loss of the CPA certificate and the license to practice.* Although it rarely happens, the loss removes the practitioner from public accounting. Most states adopt the AICPA rules of conduct, but several have more restrictive codes. For example, some states have retained restrictions on advertising and other forms of solicitation.

PCAOB Enforcement Actions

In addition to enforcement actions by the AICPA and state boards of accountancy, auditors of public companies are subject to PCAOB sanctions. The PCAOB has authority to investigate and discipline registered public accounting firms and

TABLE 4-4 Summary of Rules of Conduct

Rules of Conduct		Applicability			Summary of Rule
Section Number	Topic	Members in Public Practice	Members in Business	Other Members	
100	Integrity and objectivity	X	X		In the performance of any professional service, a member shall maintain objectivity and integrity, shall be free of conflicts of interest, and shall not knowingly misrepresent facts or subordinate his or her judgment to others.
200	Independence	X			A member in public practice shall be independent in the performance of professional services as required by standards promulgated by bodies designated by Council.
300	General standards	X	X		A member shall comply with the following standards and with any interpretations thereof by bodies designated by Council: (1) undertake only those professional services that the member or member's firm can reasonably expect to be completed with professional competence, (2) exercise due professional care, (3) adequately plan and supervise all engagements, and (4) obtain sufficient relevant data to afford a reasonable basis for all conclusions or recommendations.
310	Compliance with standards	X	X		A member who performs auditing, review, compilation, management consulting, tax, or other professional services shall comply with standards promulgated by bodies designated by Council.
320	Accounting principles	X	X		A member shall follow the professional audit reporting standards promulgated by bodies designated by Council in issuing reports about entities' compliance with generally accepted accounting principles.
400	Acts discreditable	X	X	X	A member shall not commit an act discreditable to the profession.
510	Contingent fees	X			A member in public practice shall not perform for a contingent fee any professional service if the member also performs for the client an audit, review, or certain compilations of financial statements, or an examination of prospective financial statements. A member in public practice shall also not prepare an original or amended tax return or claim for a tax refund for a contingent fee for any client.
520	Commissions and referral fees	X			A member in public practice shall not receive or pay a commission or referral fee for any client if the member also performs for the client an audit, review, or certain compilations of financial statements, or an examination of prospective financial statements. For nonprohibited commissions or referral fees, a member must disclose the existence of such fees to the client.
600	Advertising and other forms of solicitation	X			A member in public practice shall not seek to obtain clients by advertising or other forms of solicitation in a manner that is false, misleading, or deceptive. Solicitation by the use of coercion, overreaching, or harassing conduct is prohibited.
700	Confidential client information	X			A member in public practice shall not disclose any confidential client information without the specific consent of the client, except for the four specific situations included in the rule.
800	Form of organization and name	X			A member may practice public accounting only in a form of organization permitted by state law or regulation whose characteristics conform to resolutions of Council and shall not practice public accounting under a firm name that is misleading.

persons associated with those firms for noncompliance with the Sarbanes–Oxley Act of 2002, as well as the rules of the PCAOB and the Securities and Exchange Commission governing the audits of public companies. When violations are found, the PCAOB can impose appropriate sanctions, including suspension or revocation of a firm's registration, suspension or barring of an individual from associating with a registered public accounting firm, and monetary penalties. The PCAOB may also require improvements in the firm's quality control, additional training, or other remedial measures.

SUMMARY

The demand for audit and other assurance services provided by CPA firms depends on public confidence in the profession. This chapter discussed the role of ethics in society and the unique ethical responsibilities of CPAs.

The professional activities of CPAs are governed by the AICPA *Code of Professional Conduct,* and auditors of public companies are also subject to oversight by the PCAOB and SEC. Foremost of all ethical responsibilities of CPAs is the need for independence. The rules of conduct and interpretations provide guidance on permissible financial and other interests to help CPAs maintain independence. Other rules of conduct are also designed to maintain public confidence in the profession. The ethical responsibilities of CPAs are enforced by the AICPA for members and by state boards of accountancy for licensed CPAs.

ESSENTIAL TERMS

Audit committee—selected members of a client's board of directors whose responsibilities include helping auditors to remain independent of management

Confidential client information—client information that may not be disclosed without the specific consent of the client except under authoritative professional or legal investigation

Direct financial interest—the ownership of stock or other equity shares by members or their immediate family

Ethical dilemma—a situation in which a decision must be made about the appropriate behavior

Ethics—a set of moral principles or values

Independence in appearance—the auditor's ability to maintain an unbiased viewpoint *in the eyes of others*

Independence of mind—the auditor's state of mind that enables an unbiased viewpoint in the performance of professional services; also described as "independent in fact"

Independent in fact—see "independence of mind"

Indirect financial interest—a close, but not direct, ownership relationship between the auditor and the client; an example is the ownership of stock by a member's grandparent

Privileged information—client information that the professional cannot be legally required to provide; information that an accountant obtains from a client is confidential but not privileged

REVIEW QUESTIONS

4-1 **(OBJECTIVE 4-1)** What are the six core ethical values described by the Josephson Institute? What are some other sources of ethical values?

4-2 **(OBJECTIVE 4-2)** Describe an ethical dilemma. How does a person resolve an ethical dilemma?

4-3 **(OBJECTIVE 4-3)** Identify some of the most important ways that the profession and society encourage CPAs to conduct themselves at a high level.

4-4 **(OBJECTIVE 4-4)** What are the three categories of members under the AICPA *Code of Professional Conduct*?

4-5 **(OBJECTIVE 4-4)** What organization is responsible for developing ethics standards at the international level? What are the fundamental principles of the international ethics standards?

4-6 **(OBJECTIVE 4-5)** Why is an auditor's independence so essential?

4-7 **(OBJECTIVE 4-5)** Explain how the rules concerning stock ownership apply to partners and professional staff. Give an example of when stock ownership would be prohibited for each.

4-8 **(OBJECTIVE 4-6)** What consulting or nonaudit services are prohibited for auditors of public companies? What other restrictions and requirements apply to auditors when providing nonaudit services to public companies?

4-9 **(OBJECTIVE 4-6)** Many people believe that a CPA cannot be truly independent when payment of fees is dependent on the management of the client. Explain two approaches that could reduce this appearance of lack of independence.

4-10 **(OBJECTIVE 4-7)** After accepting an engagement, a CPA discovers that the client's industry is more technical than he realized and that he is not competent in certain areas of the operation. What are the CPA's options?

4-11 **(OBJECTIVE 4-7)** Assume that an auditor makes an agreement with a client that the audit fee will be contingent upon the number of days required to complete the engagement. Is this a violation of the AICPA *Code of Professional Conduct*? What is the essence of the rule of professional conduct dealing with contingent fees, and what are the reasons for the rule?

4-12 **(OBJECTIVE 4-7)** Identify and explain factors that should keep the quality of audits high even though advertising and competitive bidding are allowed.

4-13 **(OBJECTIVE 4-7)** Identify two examples of acts or behavior by CPAs that would be considered acts discreditable to the profession.

4-14 **(OBJECTIVE 4-7)** What is the purpose of the AICPA *Code of Professional Conduct* restriction on commissions?

4-15 **(OBJECTIVE 4-7)** State the allowable forms of organization a CPA firm may assume.

4-16 **(OBJECTIVE 4-8)** What types of disciplinary action may be taken if a member has violated the AICPA *Code of Professional Conduct*?

MULTIPLE CHOICE QUESTIONS FROM CPA EXAMINATIONS

4-17 **(OBJECTIVES 4-5, 4-6)** The following questions concern auditor independence. Choose the best response.

a. What is the meaning of the rule that requires the auditor be independent?
   (1) The auditor must be without bias with respect to the client under audit.
   (2) The auditor must adopt a critical attitude during the audit.
   (3) The auditor's sole obligation is to third parties.
   (4) The auditor may have a direct ownership interest in the client's business if it is not material.

b. Which of the following services can be offered to public company audit clients under SEC requirements and the Sarbanes–Oxley Act?
   (1) Tax services for executives involved in financial reporting
   (2) Internal audit outsourcing
   (3) Tax planning not involving tax shelters
   (4) Bookkeeping and other accounting services

c. An auditor strives to achieve independence in appearance to
   (1) comply with auditing standards related to audit performance.
   (2) become independent in fact.
   (3) maintain public confidence in the profession.
   (4) maintain an unbiased mental attitude.

4-18 **(OBJECTIVE 4-7)** The following questions concern possible violations of the AICPA *Code of Professional Conduct*. Choose the best response.

a. In which one of the following situations would a CPA be in violation of the AICPA *Code of Professional Conduct* in determining the audit fee?
   (1) A fee based on whether the CPA's report on the client's financial statements results in the approval of a bank loan.
   (2) A fee based on the outcome of a bankruptcy proceeding.
   (3) A fee based on the nature of the service rendered and the CPA's expertise instead of the actual time spent on the engagement.
   (4) A fee based on the fee charged by the prior auditor.

b. The AICPA *Code of Professional Conduct* states that a CPA shall not disclose any confidential client information obtained in the course of a professional engagement except with the consent of the client. In which one of the following situations would disclosure by a CPA be in violation of the *Code*?
   (1) Disclosing confidential information to another accountant interested in purchasing the CPA's practice.
   (2) Disclosing confidential information in compliance with a subpoena issued by a court.
   (3) Disclosing confidential information in order to properly discharge the CPA's responsibilities in accordance with the profession's standards.
   (4) Disclosing confidential information during an AICPA-authorized peer review.

c. A CPA's retention of client records as a means of enforcing payment of an overdue audit fee is an action that is
   (1) not addressed by the AICPA *Code of Professional Conduct*.
   (2) acceptable if sanctioned by the state laws.
   (3) prohibited under the AICPA rules of conduct.
   (4) a violation of generally accepted auditing standards.

MULTIPLE CHOICE QUESTIONS FROM BECKER CPA REVIEW

4-19 **(OBJECTIVES 4-5, 4-6, 4-7)** The following questions concern auditor professional responsibilities. Choose the best response.

a. The concept of materiality would be least important to an auditor when considering the
   (1) adequacy of disclosure of a client's illegal act.
   (2) discovery of weaknesses in a client's internal control structure.
   (3) effects of a direct financial interest in the client on the CPA's independence.
   (4) types of evidence to use in testing accounts receivable.

b. According to the profession's ethical standards, which of the following events may justify a departure from GAAP?
   I. New legislation.
   II. Conflicting industry practices.
   III. Evolution of a new form of business transaction.
      (1) I and II
      (2) II and III
      (3) I and III
      (4) I, II, and III

c. Which of the following is not a provision of the Sarbanes–Oxley Act of 2002?
   (1) The auditor of an issuer may not provide internal audit outsourcing services for the issuer.
   (2) Audit documentation must be maintained for five years.
   (3) The lead and reviewing partners must rotate off the audit after five years.
   (4) Tax services must be preapproved by the audit committee.

DISCUSSION QUESTIONS AND PROBLEMS

4-20 **(OBJECTIVES 4-1, 4-2)** Newspaper headlines frequently highlight instances where business professionals, politicians, and others are accused of engaging in unethical behavior. In response, there have been numerous attempts to reduce their occurrence. For example, some have argued for universities to include more courses in ethics.

Required

a. Describe what constitutes "ethics" and highlight the challenges of developing a set of rules and guidance to increase ethical behavior in society.
b. Why is ethics important to the conduct of business in a market-based economy?
c. Why do individuals act unethically?
d. What are common rationalizations individuals use to justify their unethical behavior?
e. Discuss whether ethics should be taught, for example, in university courses.

4-21 **(OBJECTIVES 4-5, 4-6)** The following situations involve the provision of nonaudit services. Indicate whether providing the service is a violation of AICPA rules or SEC rules including Sarbanes–Oxley requirements on independence. Explain your answer as necessary.

a. Providing bookkeeping services to a public company. The services were preapproved by the audit committee of the company.
b. Providing internal audit services to a public company audit client with the preapproval of the audit committee.
c. Providing advice to a private company client on accounting for a merger with another private company.
d. Providing bookkeeping services to a private company. The source documents were prepared and authorized by the client.
e. Providing internal audit services to a public company that is not an audit client.
f. Implementing a financial information system designed by management for a private company.
g. Recommending a tax shelter to a client that is publicly held. The services were preapproved by the audit committee.

4-22 **(OBJECTIVES 4-5, 4-7)** Each of the following situations involves a possible violation of the AICPA *Code of Professional Conduct*. For each situation, state the applicable rule of conduct and whether it is a violation.

a. Emrich, CPA, provides tax services, management advisory services, and bookkeeping services and also conducts audits for the same nonpublic client. Because the firm is small, the same person often provides all the services.
b. Steve Custer, CPA, set up a casualty and fire insurance agency to complement his auditing and tax services. He does not use his own name on anything pertaining to the insurance agency and has a highly competent manager, Jack Long, who runs it. Custer often requests Long to review the adequacy of a client's insurance with management if it seems underinsured. He believes that he provides a valuable service to clients by informing them when they are underinsured.
c. Seven small Seattle CPA firms have become involved in an information project by taking part in an interfirm working paper review program. Under the program, each firm designates two partners to review the audit files, including the tax returns and the financial statements, of another CPA firm taking part in the program. At the end of each review, the auditors who prepared the working papers and the reviewers have

a conference to discuss the strengths and weaknesses of the audit. They do not obtain authorization from the audit client before the review takes place.

d. Franz Marteens is a CPA, but not a partner, with three years of professional experience with Roberts and Batchelor, CPAs. He owns 25 shares of stock in an audit client of the firm, but he does not take part in the audit of the client, and the amount of stock is not material in relation to his total wealth.

e. A nonaudit client requests assistance of M. Wilkenson, CPA, in the installation of a local area network. Wilkenson has no experience in this type of work and no knowledge of the client's computer system, so he obtains assistance from a computer consultant. The consultant is not in the practice of public accounting, but Wilkenson is confident of his professional skills. Because of the highly technical nature of the work, Wilkenson is not able to review the consultant's work.

f. In preparing the personal tax returns for a client, Sarah Milsaps, CPA, observed that the deductions for contributions and interest were unusually large. When she asked the client for backup information to support the deductions, she was told, "Ask me no questions, and I will tell you no lies." Milsaps completed the return on the basis of the information acquired from the client.

g. Roberta Hernandez, CPA, serves as controller of a U.S.-based company that has a significant portion of its operations in several South American countries. Certain government provisions in selected countries require the company to file financial statements based on international standards. Roberta oversees the issuance of the company's financial statements and asserts that the statements are based on international financial accounting standards; however, the standards she uses are not those issued by the International Accounting Standards Board.

h. Archer Ressner, CPA, stayed longer than he should have at the annual holiday party of Ressner and Associates, CPAs. On his way home he drove through a red light and was stopped by a police officer, who observed that he was intoxicated. In a jury trial, Ressner was found guilty of driving under the influence of alcohol. Because this was not his first offense, he was sentenced to 30 days in jail and his driver's license was revoked for one year.

4-23 **(OBJECTIVES 4-5, 4-7)** Each of the following situations involves possible violations of the AICPA *Code of Professional Conduct*. For each situation, state whether it is a violation of the *Code*. In those cases in which it is a violation, explain the nature of the violation and the rationale for the existing rule.

a. The audit firm of Miller and Yancy, CPAs, has joined an association of other CPA firms across the country to enhance the types of professional services the firm can provide. Miller and Yancy share resources with other firms in the association, including audit methodologies, audit manuals, and common IT systems for billing and time reporting. One of the partners in Miller and Yancy has a direct financial interest in the audit client of another firm in the association.

b. Connor Bradley is the partner in charge of the audit of Southern Pinnacle Bank. Bradley is in the process of purchasing a beach condo and has obtained mortgage financing from Southern Pinnacle.

c. Jennifer Crowe's audit client has a material investment in Polex, Inc. Crowe's nondependent parents also own shares in Polex, and Polex is not an attest client of Crowe's firm. The amount of her parent's ownership in Polex is not significant to Crowe's net worth.

d. Joe Stokely is a former partner in Bass and Sims, CPAs. Recently, he left the firm to become the chief operating officer of Lacy Foods, Inc., which is an audit client of Bass and Sims. In his new role, Stokely has no responsibilities for financial reporting. Bass and Sims made significant changes to the audit plan for the upcoming audit.

e. Odonnel Incorporated has struggled financially and has been unable to pay the audit fee to its auditor, Seale and Seale, CPAs, for the 2014 and 2015 audits. Seale and Seale is currently planning the 2016 audit.

f. Jessica Alma has been serving as the senior auditor on the audit of Carolina BioHealth, Inc. Because of her outstanding work, the head of internal audit at Carolina BioHealth extended her an offer of employment to join the internal audit department as an audit manager. When the discussions with Carolina BioHealth began, Jessica informed her office's managing partner and was removed from the audit engagement.

g. Morris and Williams, a regional CPA firm, is providing information systems consulting to one of their publicly traded audit clients. They are assisting in the implementation of a new financial reporting system selected by management.

h. Audrey Glover is a financial analyst in the financial reporting department of Technologies International, a privately held corporation. Audrey was asked to prepare several journal entries for Technologies International related to transactions that have not yet occurred. The entries are reflected in financial statements that the company recently provided to the bank in connection with a loan outstanding due to the bank.

i. Austin and Houston, CPAs, is performing consulting services to help management of McAlister Global Services streamline its production operations. Austin and Houston structured the fee for this engagement to be a fixed percentage of costs savings that result once the new processes are implemented. Austin and Houston perform no other services for McAlister Global.

4-24 **(OBJECTIVE 4-5)** Marie Janes encounters the following situations in doing the audit of a large auto dealership. Janes is not a partner.

1. The sales manager tells her that there is a sale (at a substantial discount) on new cars that is limited to long-established customers of the dealership. Because her firm has been doing the audit for several years, the sales manager has decided that Janes should also be eligible for the discount.
2. The auto dealership has an executive lunchroom that is available free to employees above a certain level. The controller informs Janes that she can also eat there any time.
3. Janes is invited to and attends the company's annual holiday party. When presents are handed out, she is surprised to find her name included. The present has a value of approximately $200.

Required Use the three-step process in the AICPA conceptual framework to assess whether Janes' independence has been impaired.

a. Describe how each of the situations might threaten Janes' independence from the auto dealership.
b. Identify a safeguard that Janes' firm could impose that would eliminate or mitigate the threat of each situation to Janes' independence.
c. Assuming no safeguards are in place and Janes accepts the offer or gift in each situation, discuss whether she has violated the rules of conduct.
d. Discuss what Janes should do in each situation.

4-25 **(OBJECTIVE 4-6)** The U.S. national stock exchanges require listed companies to have an independent audit committee.

Required

a. Describe an audit committee.
b. What does it mean for the audit committee members to be "independent"?
c. What are the typical functions performed by an audit committee?
d. Explain how an audit committee can help an auditor be more independent.
e. Describe the nature of the audit firm's communications with the audit committee regarding independence issues.
f. Some critics of audit committees believe that they bias companies in favor of larger and perhaps more expensive CPA firms. These critics contend that a primary concern of audit committee members is to reduce their exposure to legal liability. The committees will therefore recommend larger, more prestigious CPA firms, even if the cost is somewhat higher, to minimize the potential criticism of selecting an unqualified firm. Evaluate these comments.

4-26 **(OBJECTIVES 4-5, 4-6)** The following relate to auditors' independence:

Required

a. Why is independence so essential for auditors?
b. Compare the importance of independence of CPAs with that of other professionals, such as attorneys.
c. Explain the difference between independence in appearance and independence of mind.
d. Assume that a partner of a CPA firm owns two shares of stock of a large audit client on which he serves as the engagement partner. The ownership is an insignificant part of his total wealth.
   (1) Has he violated the AICPA *Code of Professional Conduct?*
   (2) Explain whether the ownership is likely to affect the partner's independence of mind.
   (3) Explain the reason for the strict requirements about stock ownership in the rules of conduct.
e. Discuss how each of the following could affect independence of mind and independence in appearance, and evaluate the social consequence of prohibiting auditors from doing each one:
   (1) Owning stock in a client company.
   (2) Having bookkeeping services for an audit client performed by the same person who does the audit.
   (3) Having a spouse who is the chief financial officer of a client company.
   (4) Having the annual audit performed by the same CPA firm for 10 years in a row.
   (5) Having management select the CPA firm.
   (6) Recommending adjusting entries to the client's financial statements and preparing financial statements, including footnotes, for the client.
   (7) Providing valuation services on complex financial instruments for an audit client performed by individuals in a department that is separate from the audit department.
f. Which of (1) through (7) are prohibited by the AICPA *Code of Professional Conduct?* Which are prohibited by the Sarbanes–Oxley Act or the SEC?

4-27 **(OBJECTIVES 4-5, 4-7)** The following questions relate to the AICPA *Code of Professional Conduct,* which can be viewed online or downloaded in pdf format at www.aicpa.org:

Required

a. When should a member apply the conceptual framework for members in public practice? Which rule or rules have their own conceptual framework?
b. Covered members are not allowed to have a direct financial interest in a client. What should covered members do if they become aware they are to receive an unsolicited financial interest in an attest client as a result of a bequest? Be sure to note where you can find the applicable guidance in the *Code.*
c. The Accounting Principles Rule indicates that members can justify a departure from generally accepted accounting principles only in unusual circumstances. What are examples of unusual circumstances discussed in the *Code?*
d. The AICPA provides for a number of specialist designations. How should a member use the designation? When may a firm include a specialty designation on firm letterhead? Where would you find the applicable guidance in the *Code?*

CASES

4-28 **(OBJECTIVES 4-5, 4-7)** The following are situations that may violate the AICPA *Code of Professional Conduct.* Assume, in each case, that the CPA is a partner, unless stated otherwise.

1. Elbert is a staff accountant at a CPA firm. Elbert's wife works in human resources at one of the clients audited by Elbert's firm, although Elbert is not on the audit engagement. As part of an employee stock ownership program at her company, Elbert's wife receives shares of stock in her company.

2. Contel, CPA, advertises in the local paper that his firm does the audit of 14 of the 36 largest community banks in the state. The advertisement also states that the average audit fee, as a percentage of total assets for the banks he audits, is lower than any other CPA firm's in the state.
3. Baker, CPA, approaches a new audit client and tells the president that he has an idea that could result in a substantial tax refund in the prior year's tax return by application of a technical provision in the tax law that the client had overlooked. Baker adds that the fee will be 50% of the tax refund after it has been resolved by the Internal Revenue Service. The client agrees to the proposal.
4. Jon Davis is a former partner at Davis, Harrison, Smith. He left the firm to work for an audit client of DHS. Since Davis was the only expert in the firm on not-for-profit clients, DHS pays him as a consultant when they have questions related to their not-for-profit audit engagements.
5. Able, CPA, owns a substantial limited partnership interest in an apartment building. Frederick Marshall is a 100% owner in Marshall Marine Co. Marshall also owns a substantial interest in the same limited partnership as Able. Able does the audit of Marshall Marine Co.
6. Finigan, CPA, does the audit, tax return, bookkeeping, and management services work for Gilligan Construction Company. Mildred Gilligan follows the practice of calling Finigan before she makes any major business decision to determine the effect on her company's taxes and the financial statements. Finigan attends continuing education courses in the construction industry to make sure that she is technically competent and knowledgeable about the industry. Finigan normally attends board of directors meetings and accompanies Gilligan when she is seeking loans. Mildred Gilligan often jokingly introduces Finigan with this statement, "I have my three business partners—my banker, the government, and my CPA, but Finny's the only one that is on my side."

Required Discuss whether the facts in any of the situations indicate violations of the AICPA *Code of Professional Conduct.* If so, identify the nature of the violation(s).

4-29 **(OBJECTIVES 4-2, 4-7)** Barbara Whitley had great expectations about her future as she sat in her graduation ceremony in May 2015. She was about to receive her Master of Accounting degree, and next week she would begin her career on the audit staff of Green, Thresher & Co., CPAs.

Things looked a little different to Barbara in February 2016. She was working on the audit of Delancey Fabrics, a textile manufacturer with a calendar year-end. The pressure was enormous. Everyone on the audit team was putting in 70-hour weeks, and it still looked as if the audit wouldn't be done on time. Barbara was doing work in the property area, vouching additions for the year. The audit program indicated that a sample of all items over $20,000 should be selected, plus a judgmental sample of smaller items. When Barbara went to take the sample, Jack Bean, the senior, had left the client's office and couldn't answer her questions about the appropriate size of the judgmental sample. Barbara forged ahead with her own judgment and selected 50 smaller items. Her basis for doing this was that there were about 250 such items, so 50 was a reasonably good proportion of such additions.

Barbara audited the additions with the following results: The items over $20,000 contained no misstatements; however, the 50 small items contained a large number of misstatements. In fact, when Barbara projected them to all such additions, the amount seemed quite significant.

A couple of days later, Jack Bean returned to the client's office. Barbara brought her work to Jack in order to apprise him of the problems she found and got the following response:

> "Gosh, Barbara, why did you do this? You were only supposed to look at the items over $20,000 plus 5 or 10 little ones. You've wasted a whole day on that work, and we can't afford to spend any more time on it. I want you to throw away the schedules where you tested the last 40 small items and forget you ever did them."

When Barbara asked about the possible audit adjustment regarding the small items, none of which arose from the first 10 items, Jack responded, "Don't worry, it's not material anyway. You just forget it; it's my concern, not yours."

Required

a. In what way is this an ethical dilemma for Barbara?
b. Use the six-step approach discussed in this chapter to resolve the ethical dilemma.

4-30 **(OBJECTIVE 4-2)** Ann Donnelly is a senior audit manager in an East Coast office of a public accounting firm. Her prospects for promotion to partner are excellent if she continues to perform at the same high-quality level as in the past. Ann was recently married, and she and her husband bought a large home in a prestigious neighborhood.

Ann just returned from a vacation and was immediately called into an audit partner's office for a discussion related to one of her publicly traded audit clients. This audit engagement, which had been completed with an audit report issued several months prior, had been selected for a PCAOB inspection and the partner is concerned. PCAOB inspections can be stressful for the primary engagement partner and often result in the identification of audit deficiencies by the PCAOB, which are then discussed with the audit firm. The partner is concerned he will look bad and may even face penalties from the firm if there are serious deficiencies identified.

Under PCAOB auditing standards, all working paper documentation for an audit of a publicly traded client should be completed within 45 days of the audit report release date. Any working papers added to the file after that date should be dated accordingly, be signed by the preparer, and include a note as to the purpose of the added working paper. The audit engagement team is not allowed to modify or delete original documentation included in the working papers.

In the current meeting between Ann and the partner, the partner on the audit engagement feels they need to provide further support for one of the judgmental audit areas on the audit engagement in order to avoid scrutiny from the PCAOB, and that they also need to go through the working papers and ensure that all work was appropriately signed off by the manager and partner. The partner suggests to Ann that she include an additional memo to support their conclusion on the judgmental audit area in question, that she date this memo as if she had completed it at the time she and the staff originally did the work, and that she ensure all required signatures are in the working papers. Ann reminds the partner this is in violation of the PCAOB auditing standards; however, the partner assures Ann that no one will know and they can avoid possible penalties that would result if they do not ensure that their audit engagement will pass inspection. "After all," the engagement partner reminds Ann, "you will soon be considered for promotion to partner and you would not want a negative inspection outcome on a prior engagement to stand in your way of making partner."

Required

Use the six-step approach discussed in this chapter to resolve the ethical dilemma.

CHAPTER

5

LEGAL LIABILITY

LEARNING OBJECTIVES

After studying this chapter, you should be able to

5-1 Understand the litigious environment in which CPAs practice.

5-2 Explain why the failure of financial statement users to differentiate among business failure, audit failure, and audit risk has resulted in lawsuits.

5-3 Use the primary legal concepts and terms concerning accountants' liability as a basis for studying legal liability of auditors.

5-4 Describe accountants' liability to clients and related defenses.

5-5 Describe accountants' liability to third parties under common law and related defenses.

5-6 Describe accountants' civil liability under the federal securities laws and related defenses.

5-7 Specify what constitutes criminal liability for accountants.

5-8 Describe how the profession and individual CPAs can reduce the threat of litigation.

It Takes the Net Profit from Many Audits to Offset The Cost of One Lawsuit

Orange & Rankle, a CPA firm in San Jose, audited a small high-tech client that developed software. A significant portion of the client's capital was provided by a syndicate of 40 limited partners. The owners of these interests, including several lawyers, were knowledgeable business and professional people.

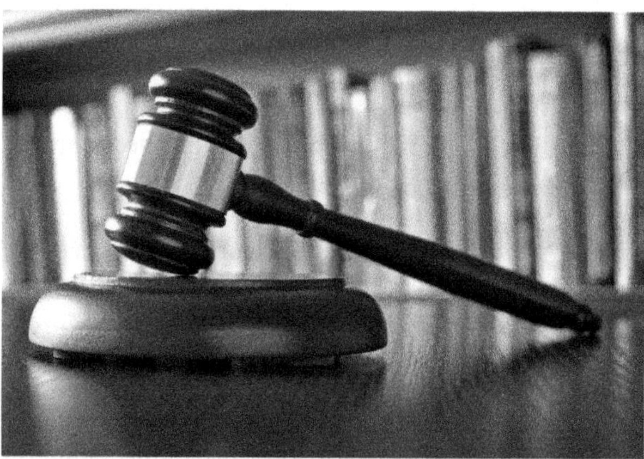

Orange & Rankle audited the company for four consecutive years, from its inception, for an average annual fee of approximately $66,000. The audits were well done by competent auditors. It was clear to the firm and to others who subsequently reviewed the audits that they complied with auditing standards in every way.

In the middle of the fifth year of the company's existence, it became apparent that the marketing plan it had developed was overly optimistic and the company was going to require additional capital or a significant strategy change. The limited partners were polled and refused to provide the capital. The company folded its tent and filed bankruptcy. The limited partners lost their investment in the company. They subsequently filed a lawsuit against all parties involved in the enterprise, including the auditors.

Over the next several years, the auditors proceeded through the process of preparing to defend themselves in the lawsuit. They went through complete discovery, hired an expert witness on auditing-related issues, filed motions, and so forth. They attempted a settlement at various times, but the plaintiffs would not agree to a reasonable amount. Finally, during the second day of trial, the plaintiffs settled for a nominal amount.

It was clear that the plaintiffs knew the auditors bore no fault but kept them in the suit anyway. The total out-of-pocket cost to the audit firm was $5 million, not to mention personnel time, possible damage to their reputation, and general stress and strain. Thus, the cost of this suit, in which the auditors were completely innocent, was more than 75 times the average annual audit fee earned from this client.

As the auditors at Orange & Rankle learned the hard way, legal liability and its consequences are significant. Although firms have insurance to help alleviate the impact of assessed damages, the premiums are high and the policies available to the firms require large deductibles. The amount of these deductibles is such that large firms are essentially self-insured for losses of many millions of dollars.

This chapter on legal liability and the preceding one on professional ethics highlight the environment in which CPAs operate. These chapters provide an overview of the importance of protecting the profession's reputation of high ethical standards, highlight consequences accountants face when others believe they have failed to live up to those standards, and show how CPAs can be held legally liable for the professional services they provide.

In this chapter we focus on legal liability for CPAs both on a conceptual level and in terms of specific legal suits that have been filed against CPAs. We also discuss actions available to the profession and individual practitioners to minimize liability while, at the same time, maintaining high ethical and professional standards and meeting the needs of society.

CHANGED LEGAL ENVIRONMENT

OBJECTIVE 5-1

Understand the litigious environment in which CPAs practice.

Professionals have always been required to provide a reasonable level of care while performing work for those they serve. Under common law, audit professionals have a responsibility to fulfill implied or expressed contracts with clients. Should auditors fail to provide the services or not exercise due care in their performance, they are liable to their clients for negligence and/or breach of contract, and, in certain circumstances, to parties other than their clients.

Although the criteria for legal actions against auditors by third parties vary by state, the auditor generally owes a duty of care to third parties who are part of a limited group of persons whose reliance is "foreseen" by the auditor. In addition to common law liability, auditors may be held liable to third parties under statutory law. The Securities Act of 1933, the Securities Exchange Act of 1934, and the Sarbanes–Oxley Act contain provisions that serve as a basis for legal action against auditors. In rare cases, auditors have even been held liable for criminal acts. A criminal conviction against an auditor can result when plaintiffs demonstrate that the auditor intended to deceive or harm others.

Despite efforts by the profession to address legal liability of CPAs, both the number of lawsuits and sizes of awards to plaintiffs remain high, including suits involving third parties under both common law and the federal securities acts. No simple reasons explain this trend, but the following factors are major contributors:

- Growing awareness of the responsibilities of public accountants by users of financial statements
- An increased consciousness on the part of the Securities and Exchange Commission (SEC) for its responsibility for protecting investors' interests
- The complexity of auditing and accounting functions caused by the increasing size of businesses, the globalization of business, and the complexities of business operations and financing transactions
- The tendency of society to accept lawsuits by injured parties against anyone who might be able to provide compensation, regardless of who was at fault, coupled with the joint and several liability doctrine (often called the deep-pocket concept of liability)
- Global recession and tough economic times resulting in business failures, which prompt stakeholders to seek restitution from others, including external auditors
- Large civil court judgments against CPA firms awarded in a few cases, encouraging attorneys to provide legal services on a contingent-fee basis, which offers the injured party a potential gain when the suit is successful, but minimal losses when it is not
- Many CPA firms being willing to settle legal problems out of court in an attempt to avoid costly legal fees and adverse publicity, rather than pursuing resolution through the judicial process

- The difficulty judges and jurors have understanding and interpreting technical accounting and auditing matters

Litigation costs for accountants are a concern because they are borne by all members of society. In recent years, legislative efforts have attempted to control litigation costs by discouraging nonmeritorious lawsuits and by bringing damages more in line with relative fault. Nevertheless, accountants' liability remains burdensome and is a major consideration in the conduct of a CPA firm's professional practice.

DISTINGUISHING BUSINESS FAILURE, AUDIT FAILURE, AND AUDIT RISK

OBJECTIVE 5-2

Explain why the failure of financial statement users to differentiate among business failure, audit failure, and audit risk has resulted in lawsuits.

Many accounting and legal professionals believe that a major cause of lawsuits against CPA firms is financial statement users' lack of understanding of two concepts:

1. The difference between a business failure and an audit failure
2. The difference between an audit failure and audit risk

A **business failure** occurs when a business is unable to repay its lenders or meet the expectations of its investors because of economic or business conditions, such as a recession, poor management decisions, or unexpected competition in the industry. **Audit failure** occurs when the auditor issues an incorrect audit opinion because it failed to comply with the requirements of auditing standards. An example is a firm assigning unqualified assistants to perform certain audit tasks where they failed to notice material misstatements in the client's records that a qualified auditor would have found. **Audit risk** represents the possibility that the auditor concludes after conducting an adequate audit that the financial statements were fairly stated when, in fact, they were materially misstated. Audit risk is unavoidable, because auditors gather evidence only on a test basis and because well-concealed frauds are extremely difficult to detect. An auditor may fully comply with auditing standards and still fail to uncover a material misstatement due to fraud.

Accounting professionals tend to agree that in most cases, when an audit has failed to uncover material misstatements and the wrong type of audit opinion is issued, it is appropriate to question whether the auditor exercised due care in performing the audit. In cases of audit failure, the law often allows parties who suffered losses to recover some or all of the losses caused by the audit failure. In practice, because of the complexity of auditing, it is difficult to determine when the auditor has failed to use due care. Also, legal precedent makes it difficult to determine who has the right to expect the benefit of an audit and recover losses in the event of an audit failure. Nevertheless, an auditor's failure to follow due care often results in liability and, when appropriate, damages against the CPA firm.

As highlighted by the lawsuit against Orange & Rankle in the opening story, difficulties often arise when a business failure, not an audit failure, occurs. For example, when a company files for bankruptcy protection or cannot pay its debts, statement users commonly claim that an audit failure has occurred, especially when the most recently issued auditor's report indicates that the financial statements were fairly stated. Even worse, if a business failure happens and the financial statements are later determined to have been misstated, users may claim the auditor was negligent even if the audit was conducted in accordance with auditing standards. This conflict between statement users and auditors often arises because of an "expectation gap" between users and auditors. Most auditors believe that the conduct of the audit in accordance with auditing standards is all that can be expected of auditors. However, many users believe that auditors guarantee the accuracy of financial statements, and some users even believe that the auditor guarantees the financial viability of the business. Fortunately for the profession, courts continue to support the auditor's view.

BIG FOUR SUED FOR NOT PAYING OVERTIME COMPENSATION

Auditors are subject to lawsuits filed by clients or third parties based on work performed, but they are also subject to lawsuits related to other issues, such as fair labor laws. Recently, all four of the largest international audit firms were named as defendants in class action lawsuits filed by their own audit associates related to overtime pay. The audit associates argue they should be compensated for the overtime hours they work as low-level employees. The Fair Labor Standards Act (FLSA) states that low-level employees must be compensated for overtime work; however, the Act provides an exemption for executive, administrative, and professional employees who are compensated on a salary basis. In one of the class action lawsuits filed, KPMG audit associates claim the audit firm unlawfully misclassified them as administrative or professional employees, which meant the audit firm was not required to provide overtime compensation under the provisions of the FLSA. A federal court ruled in KPMG's favor, claiming the audit associates exercised a level of professional discretion in performing their duties and had a level of specialized knowledge sufficient to meet the overtime exemption requirements in FLSA. In a similar complaint, audit assistants and seniors at Deloitte allege the firm misclassified their duties as administrative or professional despite the duties being low-level. In the case against Deloitte, the assistants and seniors allege their duties do not require them to hold a CPA license, and their work is required to be reviewed by higher-level employees, which suggests the "professional" and "administrative" exemptions should not apply. These cases, as well as similar cases filed against PwC and EY, have implications for other professional service firms who do not provide overtime compensation, as a ruling in favor of the assistants could encourage additional lawsuits.

Sources: 1. *Pippins* v. *KPMG LLP*, No. 11 Civ. 00377; 2. Lawrence Buckfire, "Deloitte Auditors Work Toward Overtime Settlement" (March 10, 2015) (overtimepaylaws.org); 3. Michael Cohn, "Audit Firms Slapped with Overtime Lawsuits" (January 11, 2012) (accountingtoday.com).

Nonetheless, the expectation gap often results in unwarranted lawsuits, which ultimately result in millions of dollars spent in defense. The profession must continue to educate statement users about the role of auditors and the differences among business failure, audit failure, and audit risk. However, auditors must recognize that, in part, the claims of audit failure result from the hope of those who suffer a business loss to recover from any source, regardless of who is at fault.

LEGAL CONCEPTS AFFECTING LIABILITY

OBJECTIVE 5-3

Use the primary legal concepts and terms concerning accountants' liability as a basis for studying legal liability of auditors.

A CPA is responsible for every aspect of his or her public accounting work, including auditing, taxes, management advisory services, and accounting and bookkeeping services. If a CPA failed to correctly prepare and file a client's tax return, the CPA can be held liable for any penalties and interest that the client was required to pay plus the tax preparation fee charged. In some states, the court can also assess punitive damages.

Most of the major lawsuits against CPA firms have dealt with audited or unaudited financial statements. The discussion in this chapter is restricted primarily to those two aspects of public accounting. First, we examine several legal concepts pertinent to lawsuits involving CPAs.

Prudent Person Concept

There is agreement within the profession and the courts that the auditor is not a guarantor or insurer of financial statements. The auditor is expected only to conduct the audit with due care, and is not expected to be perfect. This standard of due care is often called the **prudent person concept**. It is expressed in *Cooley on Torts* as follows:

- Every man who offers his service to another and is employed assumes the duty to exercise in the employment such skill as he possesses with reasonable care and diligence. In all these employments where peculiar skill is prerequisite, if one offers his service, he is understood as holding himself out to the public as possessing the degree of skill commonly possessed by others in the same employment, and, if his pretensions are unfounded, he commits a species of fraud upon every man who employs him in reliance on his public profession. But no man, whether skilled or unskilled, undertakes that the task he assumes shall be performed successfully, and without fault or error. *He undertakes for good faith and integrity, but not for infallibility*, and he is liable to his employer for negligence, bad faith, or dishonesty, but not for losses consequent upon pure errors of judgment.

Liability for the Acts of Others

Generally, the partners, or shareholders in the case of a professional corporation, are jointly liable for the civil actions against any owner. It is different, however, if the firm operates as a limited liability partnership (LLP), a limited liability company (LLC), a general corporation, or a professional corporation with limited liability. Under these business structures, the liability for one owner's actions does not extend to another owner's *personal assets,* unless the other owner was directly involved in the actions of the owner causing the liability. Of course, the firm's assets are all subject to the damages that arise.

The partners may also be liable for the work of others on whom they rely under the laws of agency. The three groups an auditor is most likely to rely on are *employees, other CPA firms* engaged to do part of the work, and *specialists* called upon to provide technical information. If an employee performs improperly in doing an audit, the partners can be held liable for the employee's performance.

Lack of Privileged Communication

Under common law, CPAs do not have the right to withhold information from the courts on the grounds that the information is privileged. Confidential discussions between the client and auditor cannot be withheld from the courts. (See page 99 in Chapter 4 on how auditor's documentation can be subpoenaed by a court.)

Several states have statutes that permit privileged communication between the client and auditor. Even then, the intent at the time of the communication must have been for the communication to remain confidential. A CPA can refuse to testify in a state with privileged communications statutes. However, that privilege does not extend to federal courts.

Legal Terms Affecting CPAs' Liability

Before proceeding in the discussion of legal liability, we examine several common legal terms that affect CPAs' liability. These terms are defined in Table 5-1. Take a moment to review these definitions. When the auditor has failed to conduct an adequate audit, liability may depend on the level of negligence, which can range from ordinary negligence to fraud. Also note the distinction between joint and several liability and separate and proportionate liability, because the amounts assessed will likely vary greatly between these two approaches when courts assess damages. Generally, these damage approaches only apply in cases of liability to third parties under common law and under the federal securities laws. When lawsuits are filed in state court, state laws determine which approach to damages applies. When lawsuits are brought under the federal securities laws, the separate and proportionate approach applies, except where it can be shown that the CPA defendant had actual knowledge of fraud or has participated in fraud, in which case joint and several liability applies. Under the federal statutes, the amount of damages under separate and proportionate liability can be increased to 150 percent of the amount determined to be proportionate to the CPA's degree of fault when the main defendant is insolvent.

Sources of Legal Liability

The remainder of this chapter addresses the four sources of auditors' **legal liability**:

1. Liability to clients
2. Liability to third parties under common law
3. Civil liability under the federal securities laws
4. Criminal liability

Figure 5-1 (p. 120) provides examples of each of these classifications of liability. We examine each of these liability classifications in more detail.

CONCEPT CHECK

1. State several factors that have affected the incidence of lawsuits against CPAs in recent years.
2. Distinguish between business failure and audit risk. Why is business failure a concern to auditors?
3. Distinguish between fraud and constructive fraud.

TABLE 5-1	Legal Terms Affecting CPAs' Liability
Legal Term	**Description**
Terms Related to Negligence and Fraud	
Ordinary negligence	Absence of reasonable care that can be expected of a person in a set of circumstances. For auditors, it is in terms of what other competent auditors would have done in the same situation.
Gross negligence	Lack of even slight care, tantamount to reckless behavior, that can be expected of a person. Some states do not distinguish between ordinary and gross negligence.
Constructive fraud	Existence of extreme or unusual negligence even though there was no intent to deceive or do harm. Constructive fraud is also termed *recklessness*. Recklessness in the case of an audit is present if the auditor knew an adequate audit was not done but still issued an opinion, even though there was no intention of deceiving statement users.
Fraud	Occurs when a misstatement is made and there is both the knowledge of its falsity and the intent to deceive.
Terms Related to Contract Law	
Breach of contract	Failure of one or both parties in a contract to fulfill the requirements of the contract. An example is the failure of a CPA firm to deliver a tax return on the agreed-upon date. Parties who have a relationship that is established by a contract are said to have privity of contract.
Third-party beneficiary	A third party who does not have privity of contract but is known to the contracting parties and is intended to have certain rights and benefits under the contract. A common example is a bank that has a large loan outstanding at the balance sheet date and requires an audit as a part of its loan agreement. While the contract for the audit engagement is between the client and the audit firm, both parties are aware the bank will be relying on the audited financial statements.
Other Terms	
Common law	Laws that have been developed through court decisions rather than through government statutes.
Statutory law	Laws that have been passed by the U.S. Congress and other governmental units. The Securities Acts of 1933 and 1934 and Sarbanes–Oxley Act of 2002 are important statutory laws affecting auditors.
Joint and several liability	The assessment against a defendant of the full loss suffered by a plaintiff, regardless of the extent to which other parties shared in the wrongdoing. For example, if management intentionally misstates financial statements, an auditor can be assessed the entire loss to shareholders if the company is bankrupt and management is unable to pay.
Separate and proportionate liability	The assessment against a defendant of that portion of the damage caused by the defendant's negligence. For example, if the courts determine that an auditor's negligence in conducting an audit was the cause of 30% of a loss to a defendant, only 30% of the aggregate damage will be assessed to the CPA firm.

LIABILITY TO CLIENTS

OBJECTIVE 5-4

Describe accountants' liability to clients and related defenses.

The most common source of lawsuits against CPAs is from clients. The suits vary widely, including such claims as failure to complete a nonaudit engagement on the agreed-upon date, inappropriate withdrawal from an audit, failure to discover an embezzlement (theft of assets), and breach of the confidentiality requirements of CPAs. Typically, the amount of these lawsuits is relatively small, and they do not receive the publicity often given to suits involving third parties.

A typical lawsuit brought by a client involves a claim that the auditor did not discover an employee theft as a result of negligence in the conduct of the audit. The lawsuit can be for breach of contract, a tort action for negligence, or both. Tort actions are more common because the amounts recoverable under them are normally larger than under breach of contract. Tort actions can be based on ordinary negligence, gross negligence, or fraud. Refer to Table 5-1 for distinctions among these three levels of negligent actions.

The principal issue in cases involving alleged negligence is usually the level of care required. Although it is generally agreed that no one is perfect, not even a professional, in most instances, any significant error or mistake in judgment creates at least a presumption of negligence that the professional will have to rebut. In audits, failure to meet auditing standards is often conclusive evidence of negligence. Let's examine a typical case that raised the question of negligent performance by a CPA

FIGURE 5-1 Four Major Sources of Auditors' Legal Liability

Source of Liability	Example of Potential Claim
Liability to clients	Client sues auditor for not discovering a material fraud during the audit.
Liability to third parties under common law	Bank sues auditor for not discovering that a borrower's financial statements are materially misstated.
Civil liability under federal securities laws	Combined group of stockholders sues auditor for not discovering materially misstated financial statements.
Criminal liability	Federal government prosecutes auditor for knowingly issuing an incorrect audit report.

firm: *Cenco Incorporated* v. *Seidman & Seidman*. The case, which is described in more detail in Figure 5-2, involved alleged negligence by the auditor in failing to find fraud. In the legal suit by Cenco's management, the auditor was able to successfully argue that it was not negligent and that the previous management team's deceitful actions prevented the auditor from uncovering the fraud.

The question of level of care becomes more difficult in the environment of a review or a compilation of financial statements in which there are fewer accepted standards to evaluate performance. Figure 5-3 summarizes a widely known example of a lawsuit dealing with the failure to uncover fraud in unaudited financial statements. Although the CPA was never engaged to conduct an audit for the 1136 Tenants Corporation, the CPA was found liable for failing to detect an embezzlement scheme conducted by one of the client's managers. One of the reasons for this outcome was the lack of a clear understanding between the client and the CPA as to the exact nature of the services to be performed by the CPA. As noted in Figure 5-3, *engagement letters* between the client and the CPA firm developed as a result of this case. Now, CPA firms and clients typically sign engagement letters, which are required for audits, to formalize their agreements about the services to be provided, fees, and timing. Privity of contract (see breach of contract in Table 5-1 on p. 119) can exist without a written agreement, but an engagement letter defines the contract more clearly.

Auditor's Defenses Against Client Suits

The CPA firm normally uses one or a combination of four defenses when there are legal claims by clients: lack of duty to perform the service, nonnegligent performance, contributory negligence, and absence of causal connection.

FIGURE 5-2 ***Cenco Incorporated* v. *Seidman & Seidman* (1982)— Liability to Clients**

Between 1970 and 1975 Cenco's managerial employees, ultimately including top management, were involved in a massive fraud to inflate the value of the company's inventory. This in turn enabled the company to borrow money at a lower interest rate and to obtain higher fire insurance settlements than were proper. After the fraud was discovered by an employee of Cenco and reported to the SEC, a class action suit was filed by stockholders against Cenco, its management, and its auditors. The CPA firm settled out of court on the class action suit by paying $3.5 million.

By now, new management was operating Cenco. They brought a second suit against the CPA firm on behalf of Cenco for breach of contract, professional negligence, and fraud. The primary defense used by the CPA firm was that a diligent attempt was made on the part of the auditors to follow up any indications of fraud, but the combined efforts of a large number of Cenco's management prevented them from uncovering the fraud. The CPA firm argued that the wrongdoings of management were a valid defense against the charges.

The Seventh Circuit Court of Appeals concluded that the CPA firm was not responsible in this case. The wrongdoings of Cenco's management were considered an appropriate defense against the charges of breach of contract, negligence, and fraud, even though the management no longer worked for the company. Considering management's involvement, the CPA firm was not deemed negligent.

Source: Cenco, Inc., v. *Seidman & Seidman*, 686 F. 2nd 449 (1982).

FIGURE 5-3 *1136 Tenants v. Max Rothenberg and Company (1967)*—Liability to Clients

The *1136 Tenants* case was a civil case concerning a CPA's failure to uncover fraud as a part of unaudited financial statements. The tenants recovered approximately $235,000.

A CPA firm was engaged by a real estate management agent for $600 per year to prepare financial statements, a tax return, and a schedule showing the apportionment of real estate taxes for the 1136 Tenants Corporation, a cooperative apartment house. The statements were sent periodically to the tenants. The statements included the words *unaudited*, and there was a cover letter stating that "the statement was prepared from the books and records of the cooperative and no independent verifications were taken thereon."

During the period of the engagement, from 1963 to 1965, the manager of the management firm embezzled significant funds from the tenants of the cooperative. The tenants sued the CPA firm for negligence and breach of contract for failure to find the fraud.

There were two central issues in the case. Was the CPA firm engaged to do an audit instead of only accounting, and was there negligence on the part of the CPA firm? The court answered yes on both counts. The reasoning for the court's conclusion that an audit had taken place was the performance of "some audit procedures" by the CPA firm, including the preparation of a worksheet entitled "missing invoices." Had the CPA followed up on these, the fraud would likely have been uncovered. Most important, the court concluded that even if the engagement had not been considered an audit, the CPA had a duty to follow up on any potential significant exceptions uncovered during an engagement.

Two developments resulted from the *1136 Tenants* case and similar lawsuits concerning unaudited financial statements:

- Engagement letters between the CPA and client were strongly recommended for all engagements, but especially for unaudited engagements. The letter should clearly define the intent of the engagement, the CPA's responsibilities, and any restrictions imposed on the CPA.
- The Accounting and Review Services Committee (ARSC) was formed as a major committee of the AICPA to set forth guidelines for unaudited financial statements of nonpublic companies. The role of the ARSC and services other than audits are included in Chapter 25.

Source: 1136 Tenants Corporation v. Max Rothenberg & Company, 227 New York Supp., 2nd 996 (1967).

Lack of Duty The **lack of duty to perform** the service means that the CPA firm claims that there was no implied or expressed contract. For example, the CPA firm might claim that misstatements were not uncovered because the firm did a review service, not an audit. The CPA's use of an engagement letter provides a basis to demonstrate a lack of duty to perform. Many litigation experts believe that a well-written engagement letter significantly reduces the likelihood of adverse legal actions. Engagement letters are further discussed in Chapter 8.

Nonnegligent Performance For **nonnegligent performance** in an audit, the CPA firm claims that the audit was performed in accordance with auditing standards. Even if there were undiscovered misstatements, the auditor is not responsible if the audit was conducted properly. The prudent person concept (discussed on page 117) establishes in law that the CPA firm is not expected to be infallible. Similarly, auditing standards make it clear that an audit is subject to limitations and cannot be relied on for complete assurance that all misstatements will be found. Requiring auditors to discover all material misstatements would, in essence, make them insurers or guarantors of the accuracy of the financial statements. The courts do not require that.

Contributory Negligence A defense of **contributory negligence** exists when the auditor claims the client's own actions either resulted in the loss that is the basis for damages or interfered with the conduct of the audit in such a way that prevented the auditor from discovering the cause of the loss. Suppose a client claims that a CPA firm was negligent in not uncovering an employee's theft of cash. If the CPA firm had notified the client (preferably in writing) of a deficiency in internal control that would have prevented the theft but management did not correct it, the CPA firm would have a defense of contributory negligence. Or, suppose a CPA firm failed to determine that certain accounts receivable were uncollectible and, in reviewing collectibility, the auditors were lied to and given false documents by the credit manager. In this circumstance, assuming the audit of accounts receivable was done in accordance with auditing standards, the auditor can claim a defense of contributory negligence.

Absence of Causal Connection To succeed in an action against the auditor, the client must be able to show that there is a close causal connection between the auditor's failure to follow auditing standards and the damages suffered by the client. Assume that an auditor failed to complete an audit on the agreed-upon date. The client alleges that this caused a bank not to renew an outstanding loan, which caused damages. A potential auditor defense is that the bank refused to renew the loan for other reasons, such as the weakening financial condition of the client. This defense is called an **absence of causal connection**.

LIABILITY TO THIRD PARTIES UNDER COMMON LAW

OBJECTIVE 5-5

Describe accountants' liability to third parties under common law and related defenses.

In addition to being sued by clients, CPAs may be liable to third parties under common law. Third parties include actual and potential stockholders, vendors, bankers and other creditors, employees, and customers. A CPA firm may be liable to third parties if a loss was incurred by the claimant due to reliance on misleading financial statements. A typical suit occurs when a bank is unable to collect a major loan from an insolvent customer and the bank then claims that misleading audited financial statements were relied on in making the loan and that the CPA firm should be held responsible because it failed to perform the audit with due care.

Ultramares Doctrine

The leading precedent-setting auditing case in third-party liability was *Ultramares Corporation* v. *Touche* (1931), which established the ***Ultramares* doctrine**. Take a moment to read the summary of the case in Figure 5-4.

In this case, the court held that although the accountants were negligent, they were not liable to the creditors because the creditors were not a *primary beneficiary*. In this context, a primary beneficiary is one about whom the auditor was informed before conducting the audit (*a known third party*). This case established a precedent, commonly called the *Ultramares* doctrine, that ordinary negligence is insufficient for liability to third parties because of the lack of *privity of contract* between the third party and the auditor, unless the third party is a *primary beneficiary*. However, in a subsequent trial of the *Ultramares* case, the court pointed out that had there been fraud or gross negligence on the part of the auditor, the auditor could be held liable to third parties who are not primary beneficiaries.

Foreseen Users

In subsequent decisions, courts have broadened the *Ultramares* doctrine to allow recovery by third parties in more circumstances by introducing the concept of **foreseen users**, who are members of a limited class of users that the auditor knows will rely on the financial statements. For example, a bank that has loans outstanding to a client at the balance sheet date may be a foreseen user. Under this concept, a foreseen user is treated the same as a known third party.

FIGURE 5-4 ***Ultramares Corporation v. Touche* (1931)—Liability to Third Parties**

The creditors of an insolvent corporation (Ultramares) relied on the audited financials and subsequently sued the accountants, alleging that they were guilty of negligence and fraudulent misrepresentation. The accounts receivable had been falsified by adding to approximately $650,000 in accounts receivable another item of over $700,000. The creditors alleged that careful investigation would have shown the $700,000 to be fraudulent. The accounts payable contained similar discrepancies.

The court held that the accountants had been negligent but ruled that accountants would not be liable to third parties for honest blunders beyond the bounds of the original contract unless they were primary beneficiaries. The court held that only one who enters into a contract with an accountant for services can sue if those services are rendered negligently.

Source: Ultramares v. *Touche*, 174 N.E. 441 (N.Y. 1931).

FIGURE 5-5 ***Rusch Factors* v. *Levin* (1968)—Liability to Third Parties**

The plaintiff, Rusch Factors, a lender, asked the defendant auditor to audit the financial statements of a company seeking a loan. The auditor, Levin, issued an unqualified opinion on the financial statements, indicating that the company was solvent when, in fact, it was insolvent. The plaintiff loaned the company money, suffered a subsequent loss, and sued the auditor for recovery.

The auditor's defense in the case was based on the absence of privity on the part of Rusch Factors. The court found in favor of this plaintiff. Although the court could have found in favor of Rusch Factors under *Ultramares* in that it was a primary beneficiary, it chose to rely on the *Restatement of Torts*, stating that the auditor should be liable for ordinary negligence in audits where the financial statements are relied on by *actually foreseen and limited classes of persons.*

Source: Rusch Factors, Inc., v. *Levin*, 284 F. Supp. 85 (D.C.R.I. 1968).

Although the concept of foreseen users may appear straightforward, courts have generated several different interpretations. At present, the three leading approaches taken by the courts that have emerged are described as follows:

Credit Alliance In *Credit Alliance* v. *Arthur Andersen & Co.* (1986) in New York, a lender brought suit against the auditor of one of its borrowers, claiming that it relied on the financial statements of the borrower, who was in default, in granting the loan. The New York State Court of Appeals upheld the basic concept of privity established by *Ultramares* and stated that to be liable, (1) an auditor must know and intend that the work product would be used by the third party for a specific purpose, and (2) the knowledge and intent must be evidenced by the auditor's conduct.

Restatement of Torts The approach followed by most states is to apply the rule cited in the *Restatement of Torts*, an authoritative set of legal principles. The *Restatement Rule* is that foreseen users must be members of a *reasonably limited and identifiable group of users* who have relied on the CPA's work, such as creditors, even though those persons were not specifically known to the CPA at the time the work was done. A leading case supporting the application of this rule is *Rusch Factors* v. *Levin*, as presented in Figure 5-5.

Foreseeable User The broadest interpretation of the rights of third-party beneficiaries is to use the concept of **foreseeable users**. Under this concept, any users who the auditor should have reasonably been able to foresee as likely users of the client's financial statements have the same rights as those with privity of contract. These users are often called an unlimited class. Although a significant number of states followed this approach in the past, it is now used in only a minority of states.

Table 5-2 summarizes the three approaches to third-party liability taken by the courts under common law. There is confusion caused by these differing views of liability to third parties under common law, but the movement is clearly away from the

TABLE 5-2 **Approaches Courts Take to Assign Third-Party Liability Under Common Law**

Interpretation	Approaches by Courts and Example Cases	Definition of Third-Party User	Example
Narrow	Primary beneficiary/identified user *Ultramares Corporation* v. *Touche* (1931) *Credit Alliance* v. *Arthur Andersen* (1986)	Auditor knows and intends that user will use audit report.	Auditor is aware of bank loan agreement that requires audited financial statements.
↕	Foreseen user *Rusch Factors* v. *Levin* (1968)	Reasonably limited and identifiable group of users who have relied on the auditor's work.	Bank or trade creditors when the auditor is aware that the client has provided audited financial statements to such users.
Broad	Foreseeable user *Rosenblum, Inc.,* v. *Adler* (1983)	An unlimited class of users that the auditor should have reasonably been able to foresee as being likely users of the financial statements.	A trade creditor that has not previously conducted business with the client. That client has not furnished financial statements to trade creditors in the past.

foreseeable user approach, and thus toward the first two approaches. For example, in *Bily* v. *Arthur Young* (1992), the California Supreme Court reversed a lower court decision against Arthur Young, clearly upholding the *Restatement* doctrine. In its decision, the court stated that "an auditor owes no general duty of care regarding the conduct of an audit to persons other than the client" and reasoned that the potential liability to auditors under the foreseeable user doctrine would be distinctly out of proportion to any fault.

Auditor Defenses Against Third-Party Suits

Three of the four defenses available to auditors in suits by clients are also available in third-party lawsuits: lack of duty to perform the service, nonnegligent performance, and absence of causal connection. Contributory negligence is ordinarily not available because a third party is not in a position to contribute to misstated financial statements.

A lack of duty defense in third-party suits contends lack of privity of contract. The extent to which privity of contract is an appropriate defense and the nature of the defense depend heavily on the approach to foreseen users in the state and the judicial jurisdiction of the case.

If the auditor is unsuccessful in using the lack of duty defense to have a case dismissed, the preferred defense in third-party suits is nonnegligent performance. If the auditor conducted the audit in accordance with auditing standards, that eliminates the need for the other defenses. Unfortunately, nonnegligent performance can be difficult to demonstrate to a court, especially in jury trials when laypeople with no accounting experience make up the jury.

Absence of causal connection in third-party suits often means nonreliance on the financial statements by the user. Assume that the auditor can demonstrate that a lender relied on an ongoing banking relationship with a customer, rather than the financial statements, in making a loan. In that situation, auditor negligence in the conduct of the audit is not relevant. Of course, it is difficult to prove nonreliance on the financial statements. Absence of causal connection can be difficult to establish because users may claim reliance on the statements even when investment or loan decisions were made without considering the company's financial condition.

CIVIL LIABILITY UNDER THE FEDERAL SECURITIES LAWS

OBJECTIVE 5-6

Describe accountants' civil liability under the federal securities laws and related defenses.

Although there has been some growth in actions brought against accountants by clients and third parties under common law, the greatest growth in CPA liability litigation has been under the federal securities laws. Litigants commonly seek federal remedies because of the availability of class-action litigation and the ability to obtain significant damages from defendants.

Other factors also make federal courts attractive to litigants. For example, several sections of the securities laws impose strict liability standards on CPAs, and federal courts are often likely to favor plaintiffs in lawsuits when there are strict standards. However, fairly recent tort reform legislation may result in a reduction of negative outcomes for CPA firms in federal courts.

Securities Act of 1933

The **Securities Act of 1933** deals only with the reporting requirements for companies issuing new securities, including the information in registration statements and prospectuses. The only parties who can recover from auditors under the 1933 act are the original purchasers of securities. The amount of the potential recovery equals the original purchase price less the value of the securities at the time of the suit. (If the securities have been sold, users can recover the amount of the loss incurred.)

The Securities Act of 1933 imposes an unusual burden on the auditor. Section 11 of the 1933 act defines the rights of third parties and auditors, which are summarized as follows:

- Any third party who purchased securities described in the registration statement may sue the auditor for material misrepresentations or omissions in audited financial statements included in the registration statement.

- Third-party users do not have the burden of proof that they relied on the financial statements or that the auditor was negligent or fraudulent in doing the audit. Users must only prove that the audited financial statements contained a material misrepresentation or omission.
- The auditor has the burden of demonstrating as a defense that (1) an adequate audit was conducted or (2) all or a portion of the plaintiff's loss was caused by factors other than the misleading financial statements. The 1933 act is the only common or statutory law where the burden of proof is on the defendant.

Furthermore, the auditor is responsible for making sure that the financial statements are fairly stated beyond the date of issuance, up to the date the registration statement becomes effective, which can be several months later. Assume that the audit report date for December 31, 2015, financial statements is February 10, 2016, but the registration statement is dated November 1, 2016. In a typical audit, the auditor must review transactions through the audit report date, February 10, 2016. In statements filed under the 1933 act, the auditor is responsible for reviewing transactions—for almost nine additional months—through the registration statement date, November 1, 2016.

While the threshold to file a case against auditors is relatively low, comparatively few cases are tried under the 1933 act, with cases often dismissed or resolved outside of court. One of the most significant cases tried under the 1933 act is *Escott et al.* v. *BarChris Construction Corporation* (1968). As noted in Figure 5-6, the CPA firm was held liable for a lack of due diligence required under the 1933 act when performing its review of events occurring subsequent to the balance sheet date. This case brought about two noteworthy consequences:

1. Auditing standards were changed to require greater emphasis on procedures that the auditor must perform for events subsequent to the balance sheet date.
2. A greater emphasis began to be placed on the importance of the audit staff understanding the client's business and industry.

Securities Exchange Act of 1934

The liability of auditors under the **Securities Exchange Act of 1934** often centers on the audited financial statements issued to the public in annual reports submitted to the SEC as a part of annual Form 10-K reports. Every company with securities traded on national and over-the-counter exchanges is required to submit audited statements

FIGURE 5-6 ***Escott et al. v. BarChris Construction Corporation* (1968)—Securities Act of 1933**

BarChris filed an S-1 registration statement with the SEC in 1961 for the issuance of convertible subordinated debentures, thereby subjecting the company to the Securities Act of 1933. Approximately 17 months later, BarChris filed for bankruptcy. The purchasers of the debentures filed suit against the CPA firm under the 1933 act.

The most significant issue of the case, especially to audit staff personnel, was the matter of the review for events subsequent to the balance sheet, called an S-1 review for registration statements. The courts concluded that the CPA firm's written audit program was in conformity with auditing standards in existence at that time. However, they were highly critical of the auditor conducting the review, who was inexperienced in audits of construction companies, for the failure to appropriately follow up on answers by management. The following is an important part of the court's opinion in the case:

- Accountants should not be held to a higher standard than that recognized in their profession. I do not do so here. Richard's review did not come up to that written standard. He did not take the steps which the CPA firm's written program prescribed. He did not spend an adequate amount of time on a task of this magnitude. *Most important of all, he was too easily satisfied with glib answers to his inquiries.* This is not to say that he should have made a complete audit. But there were enough danger signals in the materials which he did examine to require some further investigation on his part.... It is not always sufficient merely to ask questions. (Italics were added and the name used in the case was changed.)

The CPA firm was found liable in the case on the grounds that they had not established due diligence required under the 1933 securities act.

Source: Escott v. BarChris Construction Corporation, 283 F. Supp. 643 (1968).

annually. Obviously, a much larger number of statements fall under the 1934 act than under the 1933 act.

Auditors also face potential legal exposure for quarterly information (Form 10-Q) or other reporting information filed with the SEC, such as an unusual event filed in a Form 8-K. The auditor must perform a review of the Form 10-Q before it is filed with the SEC, and the auditor is frequently involved in reviewing the information in other reports, and, therefore, may be legally responsible. However, few cases have involved auditors for reports other than reports on annual audits.

Rule 10b-5 of the Securities Exchange Act of 1934

The principal focus on CPA liability litigation under the 1934 act is Rule 10b-5. Section 10 and Rule 10b-5 are often called the antifraud provisions of the 1934 act, as they prohibit any fraudulent activities involving the purchase or sale of any security. Numerous federal court decisions have clarified that Rule 10b-5 applies not only to direct sellers but also to accountants, underwriters, and others. Generally, accountants can be held liable under Section 10 and Rule 10b-5 if they intentionally or recklessly misrepresent information intended for third-party use.

In 1976, in *Hochfelder* v. *Ernst & Ernst*, known both as a leading securities law case and as a CPA liabilities case, the U.S. Supreme Court ruled that **scienter**, which is knowledge and intent to deceive, is required before CPAs can be held liable for violation of Rule 10b-5. A summary of *Hochfelder* is included in Figure 5-7.

Many auditors believed the knowledge and intent to deceive requirement established in the *Hochfelder* case would significantly reduce auditors' exposure to liability. However, subsequent cases were brought arguing the knowledge and deceit standard

FIGURE 5-7 ***Hochfelder* v. *Ernst & Ernst* (1976)—Securities Exchange Act of 1934**

The case involved the auditor's responsibility for detecting fraud perpetrated by the president of the client firm. Lestor Nay, the president of First Securities Co. of Chicago, fraudulently convinced certain customers to invest funds in escrow accounts that he represented would yield a high return. There were no escrow accounts. Nay converted the customers' funds to his own use.

The transactions were not in the usual form of dealings between First Securities and its customers. First, all correspondence with customers was made solely with Nay. Second, checks of the customers were drawn payable to Nay and because of a *mail rule* that Nay imposed, such mail was opened only by him. Third, the escrow accounts were not reflected on the books of First Securities, or in filings with the SEC, or in connection with customers' other investment accounts. The fraud was uncovered at the time of Nay's suicide.

Respondent customers originally sued in district court for damages against the auditors, Ernst & Ernst, as aiders and abettors under Section 10b-5. They alleged that Ernst & Ernst failed to conduct a proper audit that should have led them to discover the "mail rule" and the fraud. No allegations were made as to Ernst & Ernst's fraudulent and intentional conduct. The action was based solely on a claim that Ernst & Ernst failed to conduct a proper audit. The district court dismissed the action but did not resolve the issue of whether a cause of action could be based merely on allegations of negligence.

The court of appeals reversed the district court. The appeals court held that one who breaches a duty of inquiry and disclosure owed another is liable in damages for aiding and abetting a third party's violation of Rule 10b-5 if the fraud would have been discovered or prevented had the breach not occurred. The court reasoned that Ernst & Ernst had a common-law and statutory duty of inquiry into the adequacy of First Securities' internal control because it had contracted to audit First Securities and to prepare for filing with the commission the annual report of its financial condition.

The U.S. Supreme Court reversed the court of appeals, concluding that the interpretation of Rule 10b-5 required the "intent to deceive, manipulate or defraud." Justice Powell wrote in the Court's opinion that

- When a statute speaks so specifically in terms of manipulation and deception, and of implementing devices and contrivances—the commonly understood terminology of intentional wrongdoing—and when its history reflects no more expansive intent, we are quite unwilling to extend the scope of the statute to negligent conduct.

The Court pointed out that in certain areas of the law, recklessness is considered to be a form of intentional conduct for purposes of imposing liability. This left open the possibility that reckless behavior may be sufficient for liability under Rule 10b-5.

Source: Hochfelder v. *Ernst & Ernst*, 503 F. 2nd 1100 (1974).

FIGURE 5-8 ***Howard Sirota v. Solitron Devices, Inc.* (1982)—Securities Exchange Act of 1934**

Solitron was a manufacturer of electronic devices, with its stock issued on the American Stock Exchange. It was involved in government contracts that subjected it to assessments on excess profits as determined by the Renegotiations Board. When the board determined that profits were excessive, management admitted that profits had been intentionally overstated to aid in acquiring new companies. It was subsequently shown in court, through an audit by another CPA firm, that earnings had been materially overstated by more than 30 percent in two different years, by overstating inventory.

A jury trial found the auditor responsible for reckless behavior in the conduct of the audit. The trial judge overturned the jury verdict on the grounds that the CPA firm could not be held liable for damages under Rule 10b-5 unless there was proof that the CPA firm *had actual knowledge* of the misstatement. Reckless behavior was not sufficient for damages.

On appeal, the Second Circuit Court of Appeals concluded that there had been sufficient evidence for the jury to conclude that the CPA firm had knowledge of the fraud. It therefore overturned the trial judge's findings and affirmed the original jury's guilty verdict.

The court of appeals also stated that proof of recklessness may meet the requirement of intent in Rule 10b-5, but that it need not address whether there was sufficient recklessness in this case because the CPA firm had knowledge of the misstatement.

Source: Sirota v. Solitron Devices, Inc., 673 F. 2nd 566 (1982).

was met in cases in which the auditor knew all the relevant facts but made poor judgments. In such situations, the courts emphasized that the CPAs had requisite knowledge. The *Solitron Devices* case, described in Figure 5-8, is an example of that reasoning. In that case, the court of appeals ruled that reckless behavior on the part of the auditor was sufficient to hold the auditor liable for violation of Rule 10b-5. However, in subsequent suits under Rule 10b-5, *Worlds of Wonder* (1994) and *Software Toolworks* (1994), two key Ninth Circuit court decisions stated that poor judgment is not proof of fraud. This view appears now to be winning favor in the courts.

Recent rulings by the Supreme Court make it more difficult to hold secondary defendants, such as auditors, liable for fraudulent statements made by the primary defendant responsible for making the false statement or omission. In prior cases, auditors and other third parties have been held liable as "aiders or abettors" of fraud. However, in the *Central Bank of Denver* (1994) case, the Supreme Court ruled that liability under Rule 10b-5 did not extend to aiders or abettors who participated in financial statement misstatements but were not the primary defendants. Subsequently, in the Supreme Court's ruling on the *Janus Capital Group, Inc.* (2011) case, they further clarified that a defendant in a case brought forth under Rule 10b-5 can only be held liable if they are the "maker" of a misstatement. The implication of these rulings for audit firms is that an audit firm can be held liable for misstatements made in their audit report, but not for aiding or abetting management's financial statement misstatements. In order to prove intent to deceive in an audit report, a plaintiff would have to prove that the audit firm either did not believe their own opinion, or had no basis for such opinion. Although Rule 10b-5 continues to be a basis for lawsuits against auditors, *Hochfelder* and subsequent court decisions have limited the liability somewhat.

Auditor Defenses—1934 Act

The same three defenses available to auditors in common-law suits by third parties are also available for suits under the 1934 act: nonnegligent performance, lack of duty, and absence of causal connection.

As we just discussed, the use of the lack of duty defense in response to actions under Rule 10b-5 has had varying degrees of success, depending on the jurisdiction. In the *Hochfelder* case, the court ruled that knowledge and intent to deceive were necessary for the auditor to be found liable. In other cases, gross negligence or reckless behavior was sufficient for the auditor to be found liable. Continued court interpretations are likely to clarify this unresolved issue.

SEC and PCAOB Sanctions

Closely related to auditors' liability is the SEC and PCAOB authority to sanction. The SEC and the PCAOB have the power in certain circumstances to sanction or suspend practitioners from doing audits for SEC companies. The SEC *Rules of Practice* and the PCAOB *Rules of the Board* permit them to temporarily or permanently deny a CPA or CPA firm from being associated with financial statements of public companies, either because of a lack of appropriate qualifications or having engaged in unethical or improper professional conduct.

In recent years, the SEC has temporarily suspended a number of individual CPAs from doing any audits of SEC clients. It has similarly prohibited a number of CPA firms from accepting any new SEC clients for a period, such as six months. In some cases, the SEC has required an extensive review of a major CPA firm's practices by another CPA firm, or made CPA firms make changes in their practices. Individual CPAs and their firms have also been required to participate in continuing education programs. Sanctions such as these are published by the SEC and are often reported in the business press, making them a significant embarrassment to those involved.

Foreign Corrupt Practices Act of 1977

Another significant congressional action affecting both CPA firms and their clients was the passage of the **Foreign Corrupt Practices Act of 1977**. The act makes it illegal to offer a bribe to an official of a foreign country for the purpose of exerting influence and obtaining or retaining business. The prohibition against payments to foreign officials is applicable to all U.S. domestic firms, regardless of whether they are publicly or privately held, and to all foreign companies filing with the SEC.

The law also requires SEC registrants under the Securities Exchange Act of 1934 to meet additional requirements of reasonably complete and accurate records, plus an adequate system of internal control. The law significantly affected all SEC companies, and potentially affected auditors because of their responsibility to review and evaluate systems of internal control as a part of the audit. Although the provisions of the Foreign Corrupt Practices Act remain in effect, the provisions related to accounting records and internal control are largely superseded by the more stringent requirements of the Sarbanes–Oxley Act of 2002.

Sarbanes–Oxley Act of 2002

The Sarbanes–Oxley Act greatly increases the responsibilities of public companies and their auditors. The Act requires the CEO and CFO to certify the annual and quarterly financial statements filed with the SEC. In addition, as discussed in Chapter 3, management must report its assessment of the effectiveness of internal control over financial reporting, and for accelerated filers, the auditor must provide an opinion on the effectiveness of internal control over financial reporting. As a result, auditors may be exposed to legal liability related to their opinions on internal control. The PCAOB also has the authority to sanction registered CPA firms for any violations of the Act.

Table 5-3 summarizes the sources of liability to clients and others for breach of contract under common law, liability to third parties under common law, and liability

FOREIGN CORRUPT PRACTICES ACT CHARGES AGAINST WAL-MART

For a period of time, there was little focus on enforcement of the Foreign Corrupt Practices Act; however, that has changed sharply in recent years. In 2004 only five cases were settled, compared to 33 cases in 2010 and 21 cases in 2014. The April 2012 news of a massive alleged bribery scheme involving Wal-Mart added significant attention to the Act, with members of Congress announcing an investigation into allegations that Wal-Mart's Mexican subsidiary, Walmex, paid bribes to local government officials prior to 2006 to speed permits to open new stores in Mexico. Walmex opened 95 new stores in Mexico in 2005 and by 2011 it had opened an additional 365 new outlets. News of these allegations caused Wal-Mart shares to drop 4.7 percent, erasing over $10 billion in market value. In other significant FCPA cases settled in 2014, Alcoa World Alumina pled guilty to bribery charges and agreed to pay $223 million in fines, and Avon Products also pled guilty to bribery charges and will pay a total of $135 million in criminal and regulatory penalties. The Wal-Mart case is ongoing but Wal-Mart reported investigation and compliance costs of $439 million and counting in their fiscal 2014 10-K.

Sources: 1. Andrew Ackerman and Amy Guthrie, "Wal-Mart Shares Hit by Probe," *The Wall Street Journal* (April 23, 2012) (www.wsj.com); 2. Charles Savage, "With Wal-Mart Claims, Greater Attention on a Law," *The New York Times* (April 25, 2012) (www.nytimes.com); 3. United States Department of Justice (www.justice.gov/criminal/fraud/fcpa).

TABLE 5-3 Summary of Auditor Liability

Alleged Auditor Action	Liability to Client	Liability to Third Parties Under Common Law	Liability to Third Parties Under 1933 Securities Act	Liability to Third Parties Under 1934 Securities Act
Breach of contract	Yes	N/A	N/A	N/A
Negligence	Yes	Primary Beneficiary — Yes Other third parties — depends on jurisdiction	N/A[1]	No
Gross Negligence	Yes	Yes	N/A	Yes — likely
Constructive fraud/Recklessness	Yes	Yes	N/A	Yes — likely
Fraud	Yes	Yes	N/A	Yes — likely

"Yes" indicates that the auditor could be held liable to a client or third party for the alleged auditor action.
"No" means the auditor would not be liable for the alleged action.
"N/A" means that the alleged auditor action is not an available basis to seek liability from the auditor under common law or the securities acts.

[1]Material error or omission is required for liability under the 1933 act.

to third parties under the 1933 and 1934 Securities acts. The table illustrates the strict burden on auditors to defend themselves under the 1933 act. Liability to third parties under common law and the 1934 act depends on the degree of negligence. Liability to third parties under common law also depends upon the jurisdiction and whether the third party is a primary beneficiary or known user of the financial statements.

The defenses available to the auditor are summarized in Table 5-4. If the auditor is unable to prove a lack of duty to perform the service, the preferred defense is generally nonnegligent performance.

CONCEPT CHECK

1. What are the four major sources of auditors' legal liability?
2. Compare and contrast traditional auditors' legal responsibilities to clients and third-party users under common law. How has that law changed in recent years?
3. What are the auditor's possible defenses against lawsuits filed under the Securities Exchange Act of 1934?

TABLE 5-4 Auditor Defenses Against Suits by Client, Third Parties Under Common Law, and Under the 1933 and 1934 Securities Acts

Available Auditor Defenses	Client Suits	Third Parties Common Law	1933 Securities Act	1934 Securities Act
Lack of duty to perform service	X	X	N/A	X
Nonnegligent performance (audit in accordance with audit standards)	X	X	X[1]	X
Contributory negligence by client or third party	X	N/A	N/A	N/A
Absence of causal connection (no reliance on financial statements)	X	X	N/A[2]	X

"X" indicates the auditor defense would be available.
"N/A" indicates the defense generally would not be applicable.

[1]Under the 1933 Securities Act, the auditor must prove due diligence in the performance of the audit.
[2]Auditor may prove that the loss was not attributable to the misleading financial statements.

CRIMINAL LIABILITY

OBJECTIVE 5-7

Specify what constitutes criminal liability for accountants.

A fourth way CPAs can be held liable is under **criminal liability for accountants**. CPAs can be found guilty for criminal action under both federal and state laws. Under state law, the most likely statutes to be enforced are the Uniform Securities Acts, which are similar to parts of the SEC rules. The more relevant federal laws affecting auditors are the 1933 and 1934 securities acts, as well as the Federal Mail Fraud Statute and the Federal False Statements Statute. All make it a criminal offense to defraud another person through *knowingly being involved* with false financial statements. In addition, the Sarbanes–Oxley Act of 2002 made it a felony to destroy or create documents to impede or obstruct a federal investigation. Under Sarbanes–Oxley, a person may face fines and imprisonment of up to 20 years for altering or destroying documents. These provisions were adopted following the *United States* v. *Andersen* (2002) case described in Figure 5-9, in which the government charged Andersen with obstruction of justice for the destruction and alteration of documents related to its audit of Enron.

Unfortunately, a few notorious criminal cases have involved CPAs. Historically, one of the leading cases of criminal action against CPAs is *United States* v. *Simon*, which occurred in 1969. In this case, three auditors were prosecuted for filing false financial statements of a client with the government, and all three were held criminally liable. Three major criminal cases followed *Simon*:

- In *United States* v. *Natelli* (1975), two auditors were convicted of criminal liability under the 1934 act for certifying financial statements of National Student Marketing Corporation that contained inadequate disclosures.
- In *United States* v. *Weiner* (1975), three auditors were convicted of securities fraud in connection with their audit of Equity Funding Corporation of America. The fraud was so extensive and the audit work so poor that the court concluded that the auditors must have been aware of the fraud and were therefore guilty of knowing complicity.
- In *ESM Government Securities* v. *Alexander Grant & Co.* (1986), management revealed to the partner in charge of the audit of ESM that the previous year's audited financial statements contained a material misstatement. Rather than complying with professional and firm standards, the partner agreed to say nothing in the hope that management would work its way out of the problem during the current year. The partner was convicted of criminal charges for his role in sustaining the fraud.

These cases teach several critical lessons:

- An investigation of the integrity of management is an important part of deciding on the acceptability of clients and the extent of work to perform. Auditing guidance for auditors in investigating new clients will be discussed in Chapter 8.

FIGURE 5-9 ***United States* v. *Andersen* (2002)—Criminal Liability**

In this case, the government charged Andersen with destruction of documents related to the firm's audit of Enron. During the period between October 19, 2001, when Enron alerted Andersen that the SEC had begun an inquiry into Enron's accounting for certain special purpose entities, and November 8, 2001, when the SEC served Andersen with a subpoena in connection with its work for Enron, Andersen personnel shredded extensive amounts of physical documentation and deleted computer files related to Enron.

The firm was ultimately convicted of one count of obstruction of justice. The conviction was not based on the document shredding, but it was based on the alteration of a memo related to Enron's characterization of charges as nonrecurring in its third quarter 2001 earnings release, in which the company announced a loss of $618 million.

As a result of the conviction, Andersen was no longer able to audit publicly traded U.S. companies. The conviction was overturned by the U.S. Supreme Court in 2005 because the instructions provided the jury were too broad. The victory was largely symbolic since the firm effectively ceased operations after the original conviction.

Source: United States v. *Arthur Andersen, LLP*, 374 F. 3d 281 (2002).

- As discussed in Chapter 4, independence by all individuals on the engagement is essential, especially in a defense involving criminal actions.
- Transactions with related parties require special scrutiny because of the potential for misstatement. Auditing requirements for related-party transactions are discussed in Chapter 8.
- Accounting principles cannot be relied on exclusively in deciding whether financial statements are fairly presented. The substance of the statements, considering all facts, is required.
- The potential consequences of the auditor knowingly committing a wrongful act are so severe that it is unlikely that the potential benefits can ever justify the actions.

THE PROFESSION'S RESPONSE TO LEGAL LIABILITY

OBJECTIVE 5-8

Describe how the profession and individual CPAs can reduce the threat of litigation.

The AICPA and the profession as a whole can do a number of things to reduce practitioners' exposure to lawsuits:

1. Seek protection from nonmeritorious litigation
2. Improve auditing to better meet users' needs
3. Educate users about the limits of auditing

Let's discuss some specific activities briefly:

- *Standard and rule setting.* The IAASB, AICPA, and PCAOB must constantly set standards and revise them to meet the changing needs of auditing. For example, changes in auditing standards on the auditor's responsibility to detect fraud were issued to address users' needs and expectations as to auditor performance.
- *Oppose lawsuits.* CPA firms must continue to oppose unwarranted lawsuits even if, in the short run, the costs of winning are greater than the costs of settling.
- *Education of users.* The AICPA, leaders of CPA firms, and educators should educate investors and others who read financial statements as to the meaning of an auditor's opinion and to the extent and nature of the auditor's work. In addition, users need to understand that auditors do not guarantee the accuracy of the financial records or the future prosperity of an audited company. People outside of the profession need to understand that accounting and auditing are arts, not sciences. Perfection and precision are simply not achievable.
- *Sanction members for improper conduct and performance.* A profession must police its own membership. The AICPA and the PCAOB have made progress in dealing with the problems of inadequate CPA performance, but more rigorous review of alleged failures is still needed.
- *Lobby for changes in laws.* Since the 1990s several changes in state and federal laws have favorably impacted the legal environment for the profession. Most states have revised their laws to allow accounting firms to practice in different organizational forms, including limited liability organizations that provide some protection from litigation. The passage of the **Private Securities Litigation Reform Act of 1995** (the Reform Act) and the Securities Litigation Uniform Standards Act of 1998 significantly reduced potential damages in federal securities-related litigation by providing for proportionate liability in most instances. The profession continues to pursue litigation reform at the state level, including application of a strict privity standard for liability to nonclients and proportionate liability in all cases not involving fraud.

Protecting Individual CPAs from Legal Liability

Practicing auditors may also take specific action to minimize their liability. Some of the more common actions are as follows:

- *Deal only with clients possessing integrity.* There is an increased likelihood of having legal problems when a client lacks integrity in dealing with customers, employees,

units of government, and others. A CPA firm needs procedures to evaluate the integrity of clients and should dissociate itself from clients found lacking integrity.
- *Maintain independence.* Independence is more than merely financial. Independence requires an attitude of responsibility separate from the client's interest. Much litigation has arisen from auditors' too willing acceptance of client representations or from client pressure. The auditor must maintain an attitude of *healthy professional skepticism.*
- *Understand the client's business.* In several cases, the lack of knowledge of industry practices and client operations has been a major factor in auditors failing to uncover misstatements.
- *Perform quality audits.* Quality audits require that auditors obtain appropriate evidence and make appropriate judgments about the evidence. It is essential, for example, that the auditor understands the client's internal controls and modifies the evidence to reflect the findings. Improved auditing reduces the likelihood of failing to detect misstatements and the likelihood of lawsuits.
- *Document the work properly.* The preparation of good audit documentation helps the auditor perform quality audits. Quality audit documentation is essential if an auditor has to defend an audit in court, including an *engagement letter* and a *representation letter* that define the respective obligations of the client and the auditor.
- *Exercise professional skepticism.* Auditors are often liable when they are presented with information indicating a problem that they fail to recognize. Auditors need to strive to maintain a healthy level of skepticism, one that keeps them alert to potential misstatements, so that they can recognize misstatements when they exist.

It is also important for CPAs to carry adequate insurance and choose a form of organization that provides some form of legal liability protection to owners. In the event of actual or threatened litigation, an auditor should consult with experienced legal counsel.

SUMMARY

This chapter provides insight into the environment in which CPAs operate by highlighting the significance of the legal liability facing the CPA profession. No reasonable CPA wants to eliminate the profession's legal responsibility for fraudulent or incompetent performance. It is certainly in the profession's best interest to maintain public trust in the competent performance of the auditing profession, while avoiding liability for cases involving strictly business failure and not audit failure. To more effectively avoid legal liability, CPAs need to have an understanding of how they can be held liable to their clients or third parties. Knowledge about how CPAs are liable to clients under common law, to third parties under common law, to third parties under federal securities laws, and for criminal liability, provides auditors an awareness of issues that may subject them to greater liability. CPAs can protect themselves from legal liability in numerous ways, and the profession has worked diligently to identify ways to help CPAs reduce the profession's potential exposure. It is necessary for the profession and society to determine a reasonable trade-off between the degree of responsibility the auditor should take for the financial statements and the audit cost to society. CPAs, Congress, the SEC, and the courts will all continue to have a major influence in shaping the final solution.

ESSENTIAL TERMS

Absence of causal connection—an auditor's legal defense under which the auditor contends that the damages claimed by the client were not brought about by any act of the auditor

Audit failure—a situation in which the auditor issues an incorrect audit opinion as the result of an underlying failure to comply with the requirements of auditing standards

Audit risk—the risk that the auditor will conclude after conducting an adequate audit that the financial statements are fairly stated and an unmodified opinion can therefore be issued when, in fact, they are materially misstated

Business failure—the situation when a business is unable to repay its lenders or meet the expectations of its investors because of economic or business conditions

Contributory negligence—an auditor's legal defense under which the auditor claims that the client failed to perform certain obligations and that it is the client's failure to perform those obligations that brought about the claimed damages

Criminal liability for accountants—defrauding a person through knowing involvement with false financial statements

Foreign Corrupt Practices Act of 1977—a federal statute that makes it illegal to offer a bribe to an official of a foreign country for the purpose of exerting influence and obtaining or retaining business and that requires U.S. companies to maintain reasonably complete and accurate records and an adequate system of internal control

Foreseeable users—an unlimited class of users that the auditor should have reasonably been able to foresee as being likely users of financial statements

Foreseen users—members of a limited class of users who the auditor is aware will rely on the financial statements

Lack of duty to perform—an auditor's legal defense under which the auditor claims that no contract existed with the client; therefore, no duty existed to perform the disputed service

Legal liability—the professional's obligation under the law to provide a reasonable level of care while performing work for those served

Nonnegligent performance—an auditor's legal defense under which the auditor claims that the audit was performed in accordance with auditing standards

Private Securities Litigation Reform Act of 1995—a federal law passed in 1995 that significantly reduced potential damages in securities-related litigation

Prudent person concept—the legal concept that a person has a duty to exercise reasonable care and diligence in the performance of obligations to another

Scienter—commission of an act with knowledge or intent to deceive

Securities Act of 1933—a federal statute dealing with companies that register and sell securities to the public; under the statute, third parties who are original purchasers of securities may recover damages from the auditor if the financial statements are misstated, unless the auditor proves that the audit was adequate or that the third party's loss was caused by factors other than misleading financial statements

Securities Exchange Act of 1934—a federal statute dealing with companies that trade securities on national and over-the-counter exchanges; auditors are involved because the annual reporting requirements include audited financial statements

***Ultramares* doctrine**—a common-law approach to third-party liability, established in 1931 in the case of *Ultramares Corporation* v. *Touche*, in which ordinary negligence is insufficient for liability to third parties because of the lack of *privity of contract* between the third party and the auditor, unless the third party is a *primary beneficiary*

REVIEW QUESTIONS

5-1 **(OBJECTIVE 5-1)** Lawsuits against CPA firms continue to increase. State your opinion of the positive and negative effects of the increased litigation on CPAs and on society as a whole.

5-2 **(OBJECTIVE 5-2)** Distinguish between audit risk and audit failure. Why is there at least some level of audit risk on every audit engagement?

5-3 **(OBJECTIVE 5-3)** How does the prudent person concept affect the liability of the auditor?

5-4 **(OBJECTIVES 5-1, 5-8)** Discuss why many CPA firms have willingly settled lawsuits out of court. What are the implications to the profession?

5-5 **(OBJECTIVES 5-3, 5-4)** What is meant by contributory negligence? Under what conditions will this likely be a successful defense?

5-6 **(OBJECTIVE 5-4)** A common type of lawsuit against CPAs is for the failure to detect a fraud. State the auditor's responsibility for such discovery. Give authoritative support for your answer.

5-7 **(OBJECTIVE 5-4)** Explain how an engagement letter might affect an auditor's liability to clients under common law.

5-8 **(OBJECTIVE 5-5)** Is the auditor's liability under common law affected if the third party was unknown rather than known? Explain.

5-9 **(OBJECTIVE 5-6)** Contrast the auditor's liability under the Securities Act of 1933 with that under the Securities Exchange Act of 1934.

5-10 **(OBJECTIVES 5-4, 5-5, 5-6, 5-7)** Distinguish among the auditor's potential liability to the client, liability to third parties under common law, civil liability under the securities laws, and criminal liability. Describe one situation for each type of liability in which the auditor can be held legally responsible.

5-11 **(OBJECTIVE 5-6)** What potential sanctions does the SEC have against a CPA firm?

5-12 **(OBJECTIVE 5-7)** How did the Sarbanes–Oxley Act of 2002 increase criminal liability for auditors?

5-13 **(OBJECTIVE 5-8)** In what ways can the profession positively respond to and reduce liability in auditing?

MULTIPLE CHOICE QUESTIONS FROM CPA EXAMINATIONS

5-14 **(OBJECTIVES 5-4, 5-5)** The following questions concern CPA firms' liability under common law. Choose the best response.

a. In a common law action against an accountant, lack of privity is a viable defense if the plaintiff
   (1) is the client's creditor who sues the accountant for negligence.
   (2) can prove the presence of gross negligence that amounts to a reckless disregard for the truth.
   (3) is the accountant's client.
   (4) bases the action upon fraud.

b. The *1136 Tenants* case was important chiefly because of its emphasis on the legal liability of the CPA when associated with
   (1) an SEC engagement.
   (2) an audit resulting in a disclaimer of opinion.
   (3) letters for underwriters.
   (4) unaudited financial statements.

c. DMO Enterprises, Inc., engaged the accounting firm of Martin, Seals, & Anderson to perform its annual audit. The firm performed the audit in a competent, nonnegligent manner and billed DMO for $48,000, the agreed fee. Shortly after delivery of the audited financial statements, Hightower, the assistant controller, disappeared, taking with him $82,000 of DMO's funds. It was then discovered that Hightower had been engaged in a highly sophisticated, novel defalcation scheme during the past year. He had previously embezzled $105,000 of DMO funds. DMO has refused to pay the accounting firm's fee and is seeking to recover the $187,000 that was stolen by Hightower. Which of the following is most likely true?
   (1) The accountants cannot recover their fee and are liable for $187,000.
   (2) DMO is entitled to rescind the audit contract and thus is not liable for the $48,000 fee, but it cannot recover damages.
   (3) The accountants are entitled to collect their fee and are not liable for $187,000.
   (4) DMO is entitled to recover the $82,000 defalcation and is not liable for the $48,000 fee.

5-15 **(OBJECTIVE 5-6)** The following questions deal with liability under the 1933 and 1934 securities acts. Choose the best response.

a. Major, Major & Sharpe, CPAs, are the auditors of MacLain Technologies. In connection with the public offering of $10 million of MacLain securities, Major expressed an unmodified opinion as to the financial statements. Subsequent to the offering, certain misstatements were revealed. Major has been sued by the purchasers of the stock offered pursuant to the registration statement that included the financial statements audited by Major. In the ensuing lawsuit by the MacLain investors, Major will be able to avoid liability if

(1) the misstatements were caused primarily by MacLain.
(2) it can be shown that at least some of the investors did *not* actually read the audited financial statements.
(3) it can prove due diligence in the audit of the financial statements of MacLain.
(4) MacLain had expressly assumed any liability in connection with the public offering.

b. Donalds & Company, CPAs, audited the financial statements included in the annual report submitted by Markum Securities, Inc., to the SEC. The audit was improper in several respects. Markum is now insolvent and unable to satisfy the claims of its customers. The customers have instituted legal action against Donalds based on Section 10b and Rule 10b-5 of the Securities Exchange Act of 1934. Which of the following is likely to be Donalds' best defense?

(1) Section 10b does *not* apply to them.
(2) They did *not* intentionally certify false financial statements.
(3) They were *not* in privity of contract with the creditors.
(4) Their engagement letter specifically disclaimed any liability to any party that resulted from Markum's fraudulent conduct.

c. Which is the true statement concerning an auditor's statutory legal liability?

(1) The Securities Act of 1933 broadened the auditor's liability relative to common law and the Securities Exchange Act of 1934 narrowed it.
(2) Criminal liability only arises under state law.
(3) The auditor may limit exposure to liability by destroying documents that might suggest an improper act.
(4) The auditor has a greater burden of defense under the Securities Act of 1933 than the Securities Exchange Act of 1934.

MULTIPLE CHOICE QUESTIONS FROM BECKER CPA EXAM REVIEW

5-16 (OBJECTIVES 5-3, 5-5, 5-6) The following questions concern CPA firms' liability under common law or statutory law. Choose the best response.

a. Which of the following elements is required to be proven by the plaintiff to hold an accountant liable for gross negligence but not for actual fraud?

(1) Misrepresentation of a material fact
(2) Intention to deceive
(3) Intention to induce client's reliance on the misrepresentation
(4) Reckless action

b. One of the elements that a plaintiff must prove to hold a CPA who signs off on financial statements in a registration statement liable for misstatements in the financial statements under Section 11 of the 1933 Act is that the

(1) plaintiff relied on the misrepresentation.
(2) CPA intended to deceive.
(3) plaintiff suffered a loss.
(4) CPA was negligent.

c. Under the *Ultramares* rule, an accountant that negligently prepares a client's financial report will be liable to

(1) clients and any person or limited foreseeable class of persons who the CPA knows will be relying on the CPA's work.
(2) persons in privity of contract with the CPA and intended third parties.
(3) clients and any third party that foreseeably relied on the accountant's report.
(4) the client only.

DISCUSSION QUESTIONS AND PROBLEMS

5-17 **(OBJECTIVES 5-2, 5-3)** The following are five independent situations.

1. Joanie Brogan is a partner in an audit firm that operates as a limited liability partnership (LLP). The firm has been sued for an alleged audit failure related to an audit engagement handled by a different partner in the firm. While Brogan had no involvement in the engagement, she is concerned that the plaintiff may successfully sue her seeking restitution from her personal assets.
2. A lawsuit has been filed against Carter Hockaday, CPA, charging him with constructive fraud in the audit of Broughton Company's financial statements. Hockaday has examined all the audit documentation in his files and reviewed all relevant auditing standards. He is convinced that his audit fully complies with standards of the profession but is uncertain what he should use as his primary defense tactic.
3. West Camera Co. filed for bankruptcy in January 2015. A recent blog suggested that West's external auditors should be sued for failing to include a going concern explanatory paragraph in the firm's opinion on the financial statements issued before the bankruptcy, even though the fair presentation of the financial statements is not being disputed.
4. The audit firm Weaver and Jones, LLP, received a subpoena for its documentation related to the audit of Westbrook Corporation's financial statements. The firm has refused to respond, alleging that the documentation is considered privileged communication between the firm and its client.
5. Spencer Cullen, CPA, is a defendant in a lawsuit alleging that Cullen should be held legally liable for gross negligence for a fraud involving the valuation of securities included in the financial statements of one of his clients. Cullen was uncertain how to establish a correct valuation for the securities and decided to rely on the price estimation supplied by management.

Required Analyze each situation and provide your assessment of the potential resolution of each scenario, including potential liability for the auditor or audit firm involved.

5-18 **(OBJECTIVES 5-3, 5-4, 5-5, 5-6)** Following are eight statements with missing terms involving auditor legal liability.

1. A third party lacking privity will often be successful in bringing a claim against the auditor if they can demonstrate _______ or _______.
2. Under the *Ultramares* doctrine, an auditor is generally not liable for _______ to third parties lacking _______.
3. The auditor will use a defense of _______ in a suit brought under the 1933 Securities Act.
4. Under the 1933 Act, plaintiffs do not have to demonstrate _______, but need merely demonstrate the existence of a(n) _______.
5. After passage of the Private Securities Litigation Reform Act, auditors generally have _______ liability in federal securities cases.
6. The broadest class of third parties under common law is known as _______.
7. Based on the ruling in *Hochfelder* v. *Ernst & Ernst*, an auditor generally must have knowledge and _______ to be found guilty of a violation of Rule 10b-5 of the 1934 Act.
8. _______ is generally only available as a defense in suits brought by clients.

Terms

a. Due diligence
b. Reliance on the financial statements
c. Fraud
d. Ordinary negligence
e. Separate and proportionate
f. Contributory negligence
g. Intent to deceive
h. Privity of contract
i. Gross negligence
j. Foreseen users
k. Material error or omission

Required For each of the 11 blanks in statements 1 through 8, identify the most appropriate term. No term can be used more than once.

5-19 **(OBJECTIVES 5-3, 5-7)** The following independent scenarios describe auditor behavior on an audit engagement.

1. Chad Lewis is the lead audit partner on the audit engagement of a publicly traded company. Chad followed auditing standards on the audit engagement and issued an unmodified opinion. It was subsequently discovered that the financial statements contained a material misstatement that had been undetected by the management of the company and by the audit team.
2. Maria Marquez, CPA, is a sole proprietor. She recently accepted a new audit client who was applying for a bank loan and needed to present audited financial statements to the bank. Maria was not able to complete the audit engagement by herself, so she hired several college students to assist her. The students completed the audit procedures without much guidance, and Maria issued an unmodified opinion on the client's financial statements.
3. On a recent audit engagement, the client firm neglected to inform the audit firm that a significant percentage of inventory was stored at an outside warehouse. As a result, the auditors did not observe the physical inventory count for that inventory, which represented 20% of the client's inventory balance. The auditors were able to satisfy themselves that the inventory existed through alternative procedures, and issued an unmodified opinion on the financial statements as a whole.
4. The audit engagement partner, Marc Johnson, recently received a subpoena for workpapers related to an audit engagement on which his audit firm has been named as a defendant. Marc asked the staff auditor to remove and discard two memos from the workpaper files documenting communication between the engagement partner and the CFO regarding the goodwill impairment analysis.
5. Melissa Louis is the lead engagement partner on a publicly traded company. The company's CEO recently approached Melissa and informed her that they had identified a material misstatement in the prior year's financial statements, which had been audited by Melissa's firm and submitted to the SEC. The CEO suggested they correct the misstatement by recording a journal entry in the current year for half of the amount of the misstatement, and in the following year for the remaining half. Melissa agreed to this plan to avoid a public announcement of a restatement and a potential lawsuit, since the amount of the journal entries recorded in the current and subsequent years would be considered immaterial to the financial statements.

Required

For each of the scenarios listed above, discuss whether the auditor's behavior would be considered nonnegligence, ordinary negligence, gross negligence, constructive fraud, fraud, or criminal behavior.

5-20 **(OBJECTIVES 5-4, 5-5)** Lauren Yost & Co., a medium-sized CPA firm, was engaged to audit Stuart Supply Company. Several staff were involved in the audit, all of whom had attended the firm's in-house training program on effective auditing methods. Throughout the audit, Yost spent most of her time in the field planning the audit, supervising the staff, and reviewing their work.

A significant part of the audit entailed verifying the physical count, cost, and summarization of inventory. Inventory was highly significant to the financial statements, and Yost knew the inventory was pledged as collateral for a large loan to First City National Bank. In reviewing Stuart's inventory count procedures, Yost told the president she believed the method of counting inventory at different locations on different days was highly undesirable. The president stated that it was impractical to count all inventory on the same day because of personnel shortages and customer preference. After considerable discussion, Yost agreed to permit the practice if the president signed a statement that no other method was practical. The CPA firm had at least one person at each site to audit the inventory count procedures and actual count. There were more than 40 locations.

Eighteen months later, Yost found out that the worst had happened. Management below the president's level had conspired to materially overstate inventory as a means of covering up obsolete inventory and inventory losses resulting from mismanagement. The misstatement occurred by physically transporting inventory at night to other locations after it had been counted in a given location. The accounting records were inadequate to uncover these illegal transfers.

Both Stuart Supply Company and First City National Bank sued Lauren Yost & Co.

Required Answer the following questions, setting forth reasons for any conclusions stated:

a. What defense should Lauren Yost & Co. use in the suit by Stuart?
b. What defense should Lauren Yost & Co. use in the suit by First City National Bank?
c. Is Yost likely to be successful in her defenses?
d. Would the issues or outcome be significantly different if the suit was brought under the Securities Exchange Act of 1934?

5-21 (OBJECTIVE 5-5) The CPA firm of Bigelow, Barton, and Brown was expanding rapidly. Consequently, it hired several junior accountants, including a man named Small. The partners of the firm eventually became dissatisfied with Small's productivity and warned him they would be forced to discharge him unless his output increased significantly.

At that time, Small was engaged in audits of several clients. He decided that to avoid being fired, he would reduce or omit some of the standard auditing procedures listed in audit programs prepared by the partners. One of the CPA firm's clients, Newell Corporation, was in serious financial difficulty and had adjusted several of the accounts being audited by Small to appear financially sound. Small prepared fictitious audit documentation in his home at night to support purported completion of auditing procedures assigned to him, although he in fact did not examine the adjusting entries. The CPA firm rendered an unmodified opinion on Newell's financial statements, which were grossly misstated. Several creditors, relying on the audited financial statements, subsequently extended large sums of money to Newell Corporation.

Required Will the CPA firm be liable to the creditors who extended the money because of their reliance on the erroneous financial statements if Newell Corporation should fail to pay them? Explain.*

5-22 (OBJECTIVES 5-3, 5-5) Doyle and Jensen, CPAs, audited the accounts of Regal Jewelry, Inc., a corporation that imports and deals in fine jewelry. Upon completion of the audit, the auditors supplied Regal Jewelry with 20 copies of the audited financial statements. The firm knew in a general way that Regal Jewelry wanted that number of copies of the auditor's report to furnish to banks and other potential lenders.

The balance sheet in question was misstated by approximately $800,000. Instead of having a $600,000 net worth, the corporation was insolvent. The management of Regal Jewelry had doctored the books to avoid bankruptcy. The assets had been overstated by $500,000 of fictitious and nonexisting accounts receivable and $300,000 of nonexisting jewelry listed as inventory when in fact Regal Jewelry had only empty boxes. The audit failed to detect these fraudulent entries. Thompson, relying on the audited financial statements, loaned Regal Jewelry $200,000. She seeks to recover her loss from Doyle and Jensen.

Required State whether each of the following is true or false and give your reasons:

a. If Thompson alleges and proves negligence on the part of Doyle and Jensen, she will be able to recover her loss.
b. If Thompson alleges and proves constructive fraud (that is, gross negligence on the part of Doyle and Jensen), she will be able to recover her loss.
c. Thompson does not have a contract with Doyle and Jensen.
d. Unless actual fraud on the part of Doyle and Jensen can be shown, Thompson cannot recover her loss.
e. Thompson is a third-party beneficiary of the contract Doyle and Jensen made with Regal Jewelry.*

5-23 (OBJECTIVES 5-5, 5-6) In order to expand its operations, Barton Corp. raised $5 million in a public offering of common stock, and also negotiated a $2 million loan from First National Bank. In connection with this financing, Barton engaged Hanover & Co., CPAs, to audit Barton's financial statements. Hanover knew that the sole purpose of the audit was so that Barton would have audited financial statements to provide to First National Bank and the purchasers of the common stock. Although Hanover conducted the audit in conformity with its audit program, Hanover failed to detect material acts of embezzlement committed by Barton Corp.'s president. Hanover did not detect the embezzlement because of its inadvertent failure to exercise due care in designing the audit program for this engagement.

*Based on AICPA question paper, American Institute of Certified Public Accountants.

After completing the engagement, Hanover issued an unmodified opinion on Barton's financial statements. The financial statements were relied upon by the purchasers of the common stock in deciding to purchase the shares. In addition, First National Bank approved the loan to Barton based on the audited financial statements. Within sixty days after the sale of the common stock and the issuance of the loan, Barton was involuntarily petitioned into bankruptcy. Because of the president's embezzlement, Barton became insolvent and defaulted on the loan from the bank. Its common stock became virtually worthless. Actions have been brought against Hanover by:

- The purchasers of the common stock, who have asserted that Hanover is liable for damages under Section 10(b) and Rule 10b-5 of the Securities Exchange Act of 1934.
- First National Bank, based upon Hanover's negligence.
- Trade creditors who extended credit to Barton based upon Hanover's negligence.

Required

a. Discuss whether you believe Hanover will be found liable to the purchasers of common stock.
b. Indicate whether you believe First National Bank will be successful in its claim against Hanover.
c. Indicate whether you believe the trade creditors will be successful in their claim against Hanover.*

5-24 **(OBJECTIVE 5-6)** Under Section 11 of the Securities Act of 1933 and Section 10(b), Rule 10b-5, of the Securities Exchange Act of 1934, a CPA may be sued by a purchaser of registered securities. The following items relate to what a plaintiff who purchased securities must prove in a civil liability suit against a CPA.

The plaintiff security purchaser must allege or prove:

1. Material misstatements were included in a filed document.
2. A monetary loss occurred.
3. Lack of due diligence by the CPA.
4. Privity with the CPA.
5. Reliance on the financial statements.
6. The CPA had scienter (knowledge and intent to deceive).

Required

For each of the items 1 through 6 listed above, indicate whether the statement must be proven under

a. Section 11 of the Securities Act of 1933 only.
b. Section 10(b) of the Securities Exchange Act of 1934 only.
c. Both Section 11 of the Securities Act of 1933 and Section 10(b) of the Securities Exchange Act of 1934.
d. Neither Section 11 of the Securities Act of 1933 nor Section 10(b) of the Securities Exchange Act of 1934.*

5-25 **(OBJECTIVE 5-5)** Sarah Robertson, CPA, had been the auditor of Majestic Co. for several years. As she and her staff prepared for the audit for the year ended December 31, 2015, Herb Majestic told her that he needed a large bank loan to "tide him over" until sales picked up as expected in late 2016.

In the course of the audit, Robertson discovered that the financial situation at Majestic Co. was worse than Majestic had revealed and that the company was technically bankrupt. She discussed the situation with Majestic, who pointed out that the bank loan would "be his solution"—he was sure he would get it as long as the financial statements didn't look too bad.

Robertson stated that she believed the statements would have to include a going concern explanatory paragraph. Majestic said that this wouldn't be needed because the bank loan was so certain and that inclusion of the going concern paragraph would certainly cause the management of the bank to change its mind about the loan.

Robertson finally acquiesced and the audited statements were issued without a going concern paragraph. The company received the loan, but things did not improve as Majestic thought they would and the company filed for bankruptcy in August 2016.

The bank sued Sarah Robertson for fraud.

Required

Indicate whether or not you think the bank will succeed. Support your answer.

*Based on AICPA question paper, American Institute of Certified Public Accountants.

5-26 **(OBJECTIVE 5-6)** The SEC Enforcement Division investigates possible violations of securities laws, recommends SEC action when appropriate, either in a federal court or before an administrative law judge, and negotiates settlements. Litigation Releases, which are descriptions of SEC civil and selected criminal suits in the federal courts, are posted on the SEC Web site (www.sec.gov/litigation/litreleases.shtml). Find Litigation Release No. 22902, dated January 9, 2014.

Required

a. What is the nature of the complaint underlying LR No. 22902?
b. What sections of the federal securities laws are the individuals involved accused of violating?
c. What is the role of the independent auditor in this fraud? What possible defense(s) could the auditors use if they were also accused of violating federal securities laws in this case?

CASE

5-27 **(OBJECTIVES 5-5, 5-6)** *Part 1.* Whitlow & Company is a brokerage firm registered under the Securities Exchange Act of 1934. The act requires such a brokerage firm to file audited financial statements with the SEC annually. Mitchell & Moss, Whitlow's CPAs, performed the annual audit for the year ended December 31, 2016, and rendered an unqualified opinion, which was filed with the SEC along with Whitlow's financial statements. During 2016, Charles, the president of Whitlow & Company, engaged in a huge embezzlement scheme that eventually bankrupted the firm. As a result, substantial losses were suffered by customers and shareholders of Whitlow & Company, including Thaxton, who had recently purchased several shares of stock of Whitlow & Company after reviewing the company's 2016 audit report. Mitchell & Moss's audit was deficient; if they had complied with auditing standards, the embezzlement would have been discovered. However, Mitchell & Moss had no knowledge of the embezzlement, nor can their conduct be categorized as reckless.

Required

Answer the following questions, setting forth reasons for any conclusions stated:

a. What liability to Thaxton, if any, does Mitchell & Moss have under the Securities Exchange Act of 1934?
b. What theory or theories of liability, if any, are available to Whitlow & Company's customers and shareholders under common law?

Part 2. Jackson is a sophisticated investor. As such, she was initially a member of a small group that was going to participate in a private placement of $1 million of common stock of Clarion Corporation. Numerous meetings were held between management and the investor group. Detailed financial and other information was supplied to the participants. Upon the eve of completion of the placement, it was aborted when one major investor withdrew. Clarion then decided to offer $2.5 million of Clarion common stock to the public pursuant to the registration requirements of the Securities Act of 1933. Jackson subscribed to $300,000 of the Clarion public stock offering. Nine months later, Clarion's earnings dropped significantly, and as a result, the stock dropped 20% beneath the offering price. In addition, the Dow Jones Industrial Average was down 10% from the time of the offering.

Jackson sold her shares at a loss of $60,000 and seeks to hold all parties liable who participated in the public offering, including Clarion's CPA firm of Allen, Dunn, and Rose. Although the audit was performed in conformity with auditing standards, there were some relatively minor misstatements. The financial statements of Clarion Corporation, which were part of the registration statement, also contained minor misleading facts. It is believed by Clarion and Allen, Dunn, and Rose that Jackson's asserted claim is without merit.

Required

Answer the following questions, setting forth reasons for any conclusions stated:

a. If Jackson sues under the Securities Act of 1933, what will be the basis of her claim?
b. What are the probable defenses that might be asserted by Allen, Dunn, and Rose in light of these facts?*

*Based on AICPA question paper, American Institute of Certified Public Accountants.

THE AUDIT PROCESS

CHAPTERS 6–13

PART 2 presents the audit process in a manner that will enable you to apply the concepts developed in these chapters to any audit area. Because the planning concepts covered in these chapters will be used extensively throughout the rest of the book, it is essential for you to master this material and fully understand the importance of audit planning.

- **Chapters 6 and 7** deal with auditors' and managements' responsibilities, management assertions and audit objectives, and general audit evidence concepts.
- **Chapters 8 through 12** study various aspects of audit planning in depth, including risk assessment, understanding internal control, and auditors' responsibility for detecting fraud.
- **Chapter 13** summarizes and integrates audit planning and audit evidence.

Throughout the remainder of the book, many of the concepts are illustrated with examples based on the Hillsburg Hardware Company. The financial statements and other information from the company's annual report are included in the glossy insert material to the textbook.

CHAPTER

6

AUDIT RESPONSIBILITIES AND OBJECTIVES

LEARNING OBJECTIVES

After studying this chapter, you should be able to

6-1 Explain the objective of conducting an audit of financial statements and an audit of internal controls.

6-2 Distinguish management's responsibility for the financial statements from the auditor's responsibility for verifying those statements.

6-3 Explain the auditor's responsibility for discovering material misstatements due to fraud or error.

6-4 Describe the need to maintain professional skepticism when conducting an audit.

6-5 Describe the key elements of an effective professional judgment process.

6-6 Identify the benefits of a cycle approach to segmenting the audit.

6-7 Describe why the auditor obtains assurance by auditing transactions and ending balances, including presentation and disclosure.

6-8 Distinguish among the management assertions about financial information.

6-9 Link transaction-related audit objectives to management assertions for classes of transactions.

6-10 Link balance-related and presentation and disclosure-related audit objectives to management assertions.

6-11 Explain the relationship between audit objectives and the accumulation of audit evidence.

Riding the Tiger: Indian Computer Company Engages in Billion-Dollar Fraud

During the period 2003 to 2008, Satyam Computer Services Limited, an information technology services company based in Hyderabad, India, that serviced more than a third of the Fortune 500 companies, roiled Indian stock markets when it announced it deceived investors by engaging in a massive fraud. Company chairman Ramalinga Raju resigned after announcing that 50.4 billion rupees ($1.04 billion) of the 53.6 billion rupees the company listed as assets in its financial statements for the second quarter ending in September 2008 did not exist.

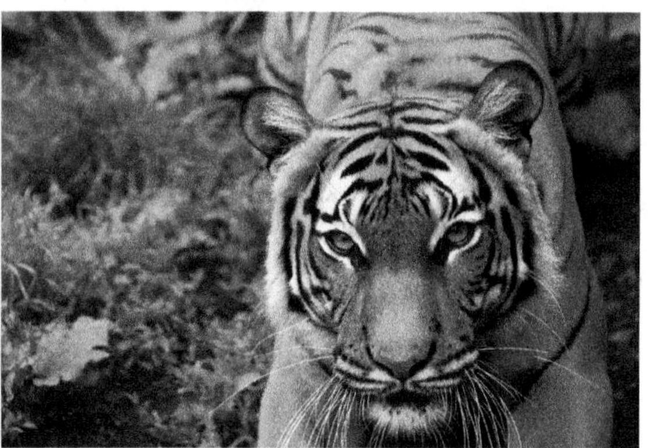

During the period of the fraud, senior management manufactured over 6,000 fictitious invoices representing over $1 billion in revenue for services that were never provided, in some cases for customers that did not exist. Management also created false bank statements to reflect payments on the false invoices and support the fictitious cash balances. Satyam provided certain employees with an administrative "super user" login identification and password that allowed them to access the invoice management system to record the false invoices. This process allowed those invoices to be included in revenue, but concealed their existence from the heads of Satyam's business units, who would recognize that the services had not been provided.

Satyam's auditors sent confirmations to verify the existence of the bank balances. However, they did not maintain control over the confirmations as required by auditing standards. The audit engagement team relied on Satyam management to mail out the confirmation requests to the banks, and to return the confirmation responses to the engagement team, instead of directly contacting the banks as required by auditing standards.

Raju admitted that he intentionally maintained the inflated revenues and profits because public knowledge of the company's poor performance would likely lead to a takeover of the company, thereby exposing the fraud. Raju indicated, "It was like riding a tiger, not knowing how to get off without being eaten." On January 7, 2009, the New York Stock Exchange suspended trading of the company's American Depository Shares (ADS). When trading resumed on January 12, 2009, Satyam's ADS price declined nearly 85 percent to close at $1.46. The Government of India assumed control of the company by dissolving Satyam's Board of Directors and then selected a strategic investor to run the company.

Sources: 1. "SEC Charges Satyam Computer Services with Financial Fraud," April 5, 2011 (www.sec.gov); 2. SEC Litigation Release 21915, April 5, 2011 (www.sec.gov); 3. PCAOB Release No. 105-2011-002, April 5, 2011 (pcaobus.org/Enforcement).

The Satyam story illustrates failure by the auditors to achieve the objectives of the audit of the company's financial statements. This chapter describes the overall objectives of the audit, the auditor's responsibilities in conducting the audit, and the specific objectives the auditor tries to accomplish. Without an understanding of these topics, planning and accumulating audit evidence during the audit has no relevance. Figure 6-1 summarizes the five topics that provide keys to understanding evidence accumulation. These are the steps used to develop specific audit objectives.

OBJECTIVE OF CONDUCTING AN AUDIT OF FINANCIAL STATEMENTS

OBJECTIVE 6-1

Explain the objective of conducting an audit of financial statements and an audit of internal controls.

The preface to the clarified AICPA auditing standards indicates

> The purpose of an audit is to provide financial statement users with an opinion by the auditor on whether the financial statements are presented fairly, in all material respects, in accordance with the applicable financial accounting framework. An auditor's opinion enhances the degree of confidence that intended users can place in the financial statements.

Source: AICPA Professional Standards, U.S. Auditing Standards AICPA (Clarified), 2015.

Our primary focus is the section that emphasizes issuing an opinion on *financial statements*. For larger public companies, the auditor also issues a report on internal control over financial reporting as required by Section 404 of the Sarbanes–Oxley Act. Auditors accumulate evidence in order to reach conclusions about whether the financial statements are fairly stated and to determine the effectiveness of internal control, after which they issue the appropriate audit report.

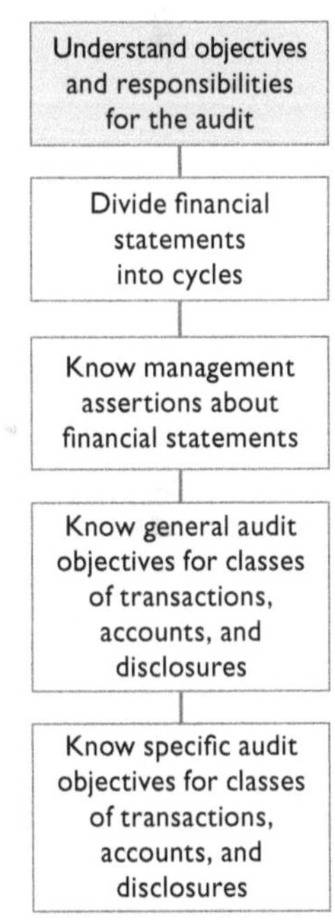
Understand objectives and responsibilities for the audit
Divide financial statements into cycles
Know management assertions about financial statements
Know general audit objectives for classes of transactions, accounts, and disclosures
Know specific audit objectives for classes of transactions, accounts, and disclosures

If the auditor believes that the statements are not fairly presented or is unable to reach a conclusion because of insufficient evidence, the auditor has the responsibility of notifying users through the auditor's report. Subsequent to their issuance, if facts indicate that the statements were not fairly presented, as in the Satyam case, the auditor will probably have to demonstrate to the courts or regulatory agencies that the audit was conducted in a proper manner and the auditor reached reasonable conclusions.

FIGURE 6-1 Steps to Develop Audit Objectives

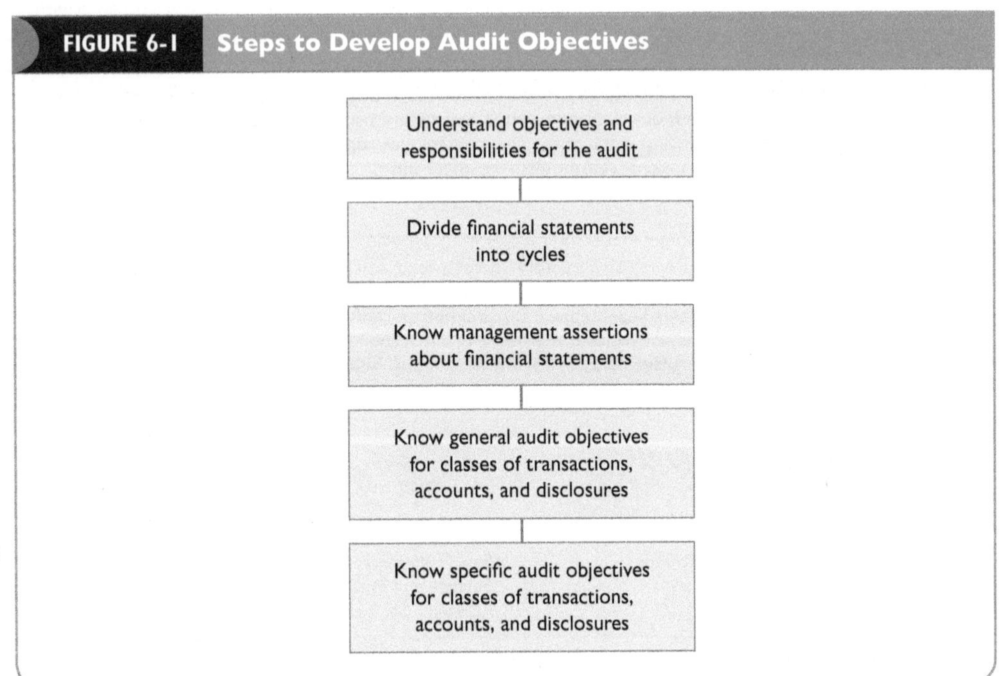
Understand objectives and responsibilities for the audit
Divide financial statements into cycles
Know management assertions about financial statements
Know general audit objectives for classes of transactions, accounts, and disclosures
Know specific audit objectives for classes of transactions, accounts, and disclosures

MANAGEMENT'S RESPONSIBILITIES

OBJECTIVE 6-2

Distinguish management's responsibility for the financial statements from the auditor's responsibility for verifying those statements.

The responsibility for adopting sound accounting policies, maintaining adequate internal control, and making fair representations in the financial statements *rests with management* rather than with the auditor. Because they operate the business daily, a company's management knows more about the company's transactions and related assets, liabilities, and equity than the auditor. In contrast, the auditor's knowledge of these matters and internal control is limited to that acquired during the audit.

The annual reports of many public companies include a statement about management's responsibilities and relationship with the CPA firm. Figure 6-2 presents selected sections of the report of management for International Business Machines (IBM) Corporation as a part of its annual report. Read the report carefully to determine what management states about its responsibilities.

Management's responsibility for the integrity and fairness of the representations (assertions) in the financial statements carries with it the privilege of determining which presentations and disclosures it considers necessary. If management insists on financial statement disclosure that the auditor finds unacceptable, the auditor can either issue an adverse or qualified opinion or withdraw from the engagement.

The Sarbanes–Oxley Act requires the chief executive officer (CEO) and the chief financial officer (CFO) of public companies to certify the quarterly and annual financial statements submitted to the SEC. In signing those statements, management certifies that the financial statements fully comply with the requirements of the Securities Exchange Act of 1934 and that the information contained in the financial statements fairly presents, in all material respects, the financial condition and results of operations. The Sarbanes–Oxley Act provides for criminal penalties, including significant monetary fines or imprisonment up to 20 years, for anyone who knowingly falsely certifies those statements.

FIGURE 6-2 International Business Machines Corporation's Report of Management

REPORT OF MANAGEMENT

International Business Machines Corporation and Subsidiary Companies

Management Responsibility for Financial Information

Responsibility for the integrity and objectivity of the financial information presented in this Annual Report rests with IBM management. The accompanying financial statements have been prepared in accordance with accounting principles generally accepted in the United States of America, applying certain estimates and judgments as required.

IBM maintains an effective internal control structure. It consists, in part, of organizational arrangements with clearly defined lines of responsibility and delegation of authority, and comprehensive systems and control procedures. An important element of the control environment is an ongoing internal audit program. Our system also contains self-monitoring mechanisms, and actions are taken to correct deficiencies as they are identified.

[third paragraph omitted]

The Audit Committee of the Board of Directors is composed solely of independent, non-management directors, and is responsible for recommending to the Board the independent registered public accounting firm to be retained for the coming year, subject to stockholder ratification. The Audit Committee meets periodically and privately with the independent registered public accounting firm, with the company's internal auditors, as well as with IBM management, to review accounting, auditing, internal control structure, and financial reporting matters.

Virginia M. Rometty
President and Chief Executive Officer
February 24, 2015

Martin J. Schroeter
Senior Vice President and Chief Financial Officer, Finance and Enterprise Transformation
February 24, 2015

Source: IBM 2007 Annual Report: Report of Management.

AUDITOR'S RESPONSIBILITIES

OBJECTIVE 6-3

Explain the auditor's responsibility for discovering material misstatements due to fraud or error.

AICPA auditing standards state

> The overall objectives of the auditor, in conducting an audit of financial statements, are to:
>
> (a) obtain reasonable assurance about whether the financial statements as a whole are free from material misstatement, whether due to fraud or error, thereby enabling the auditor to express an opinion on whether the financial statements are presented fairly, in all material respects, in accordance with an applicable financial reporting framework; and
>
> (b) report on the financial statements, and communicate as required by auditing standards, in accordance with the auditor's findings.

Source: AICPA Professional Standards, U.S. Auditing Standards AICPA (Clarified), "Overall Objectives of the Independent Auditor (AU-C 200)," 2015.

This paragraph discusses the auditor's responsibility for detecting material misstatements in the financial statements. When the auditor also reports on the effectiveness of internal control over financial reporting, the auditor is also responsible for identifying material weaknesses in internal control over financial reporting. The auditor's responsibilities for audits of internal control are discussed in Chapters 11 and 12.

This paragraph and the related discussion in the standards about the auditor's responsibility to detect material misstatements include several important terms and phrases.

Material Versus Immaterial Misstatements Misstatements are usually considered material if the combined uncorrected errors and fraud in the financial statements would likely have changed or influenced the decisions of a reasonable person using the statements. Although it is difficult to quantify a measure of materiality, auditors are responsible for obtaining reasonable assurance that this materiality threshold has been satisfied. It would be extremely costly (and probably impossible) for auditors to have responsibility for finding all immaterial errors and fraud.

Reasonable Assurance Assurance is a measure of the level of certainty that the auditor has obtained at the completion of the audit. Auditing standards indicate reasonable assurance is a high, but not absolute, level of assurance that the financial statements are free of material misstatements. The concept of reasonable, but not absolute, assurance indicates that the auditor is not an insurer or guarantor of the correctness of the financial statements. Thus, an audit that is conducted in accordance with auditing standards may fail to detect a material misstatement.

The auditor is responsible for reasonable, but not absolute, assurance for several reasons:

1. Most audit evidence results from testing a sample of a population such as accounts receivable or inventory. Sampling inevitably includes some risk of not uncovering a material misstatement. Also, the areas to be tested; the type, extent, and timing of those tests; and the evaluation of test results require significant auditor judgment. Even with good faith and integrity, auditors can make mistakes and errors in judgment.
2. Accounting presentations contain complex estimates, which inherently involve uncertainty and can be affected by future events. As a result, the auditor has to rely on evidence that is persuasive, but not convincing.
3. Fraudulently prepared financial statements are often extremely difficult, if not impossible, for the auditor to detect, especially when there is collusion among management.

If auditors were responsible for making certain that all the assertions in the statements were correct, the types and amounts of evidence required and the resulting cost of the audit function would increase to such an extent that audits would not be economically practical. Even then, auditors would be unlikely to uncover all material misstatements in every audit. The auditor's best defense when material misstatements are not uncovered is to have conducted the audit in accordance with auditing standards.

CABLE MOGULS ARRESTED FOR CORPORATE LOOTING

Sometimes, misappropriation of assets involves significant amounts and occurs at the very top of the organization. In 2002 the SEC charged former Adelphia CEO John Rigas and other Rigas family members with "rampant self dealing" at Adelphia Communications Corp. in what has been called one of the most extensive financial frauds ever to take place at a public company. According to the SEC complaint, the Rigas family used Adelphia funds to finance open market purchases of stock, pay off margin loans and other family debts, purchase timber rights, construct a golf club, and purchase luxury condominiums in Colorado, Mexico, and New York City.

In the criminal complaint, prosecutors charged that the Rigas family "looted Adelphia on a massive scale, using the company as the Rigas family's personal piggy bank, at the expense of public investors and creditors." After details of the misappropriations and fraudulent reporting in the company's financial statements became public, Adelphia filed for bankruptcy, and its stock collapsed from a price of $20 per share to less than $1 per share. John Rigas was convicted and sentenced to 15 years in prison; his son Timothy, the company's former CFO, was sentenced to 20 years in prison.

Sources: 1. "Adelphia founder sentenced to 15 years" (June 20, 2005) (money.cnn.com); 2. SEC press release 2002-110 (www.sec.gov).

Errors Versus Fraud Auditing standards distinguish between two types of misstatements: errors and fraud. Either type of misstatement can be material or immaterial. An **error** is an *unintentional* misstatement of the financial statements, whereas **fraud** is *intentional*. Two examples of errors are: a mistake in extending price times quantity on a sales invoice and overlooking older raw materials in determining the lower of cost or market for inventory.

For fraud, there is a distinction between **misappropriation of assets**, often called defalcation or employee fraud, and **fraudulent financial reporting**, often called management fraud. An example of misappropriation of assets is a clerk taking cash at the time a sale is made and not entering the sale in the cash register. An example of fraudulent financial reporting is the intentional overstatement of sales near the balance sheet date to increase reported earnings.

Auditor's Responsibilities for Detecting Material Errors

Auditors spend a great portion of their time planning and performing audits to detect unintentional mistakes made by management and employees. Auditors find a variety of errors resulting from such things as mistakes in calculations, omissions, misunderstanding and misapplication of accounting standards, and incorrect summarizations and descriptions.

Auditor's Responsibilities for Detecting Material Fraud

Auditing standards make no distinction between the auditor's responsibilities for searching for errors and fraud. In either case, the auditor must obtain reasonable assurance about whether the statements are free of material misstatements. Throughout the rest of this book, we consider how the auditor plans and performs audits for detecting both errors and fraud. The standards recognize that fraud is often more difficult to detect because management or the employees perpetrating the fraud *attempt to conceal the fraud*, similar to the Satyam case. Still, the difficulty of detection does not change the auditor's responsibility to properly plan and perform the audit to detect material misstatements, whether caused by fraud or error.

Fraud Resulting from Fraudulent Financial Reporting Versus Misappropriation of Assets Both fraudulent financial reporting and misappropriation of assets are potentially harmful to financial statement users, but there is an important difference between them. Fraudulent financial reporting harms users by providing them incorrect financial statement information for their decision making. When assets are misappropriated, stockholders, creditors, and others are harmed because assets are no longer available to their rightful owners.

Typically, fraudulent financial reporting is committed by management, sometimes without the knowledge of employees. Management is in a position to make accounting and reporting decisions without employees' knowledge. An example is the decision to omit an important footnote disclosure about pending litigation.

Usually, but not always, theft of assets is perpetrated by employees and not by management, and the amounts are often immaterial. However, there are well-known examples of extremely material misappropriation of assets by employees and management, similar to the Adelphia fraud described in the vignette box on the previous page.

There is an important distinction between the theft of assets and misstatements arising from the theft of assets. Consider the following three situations:

1. Assets were taken and the theft was covered by misstating assets. For example, cash collected from a customer was stolen before it was recorded as a cash receipt, and the account receivable for the customer's account was not credited. The misstatement has not been discovered.
2. Assets were taken and the theft was covered by understating revenues or overstating expenses. For example, cash from a cash sale was stolen, and the transaction was not recorded. Or, an unauthorized disbursement to an employee was recorded as a miscellaneous expense. The misstatement has not been discovered.
3. Assets were taken, but the misappropriation was discovered. The income statement and related footnotes clearly describe the misappropriation.

In all three situations, there has been a misappropriation of assets, but the financial statements are misstated only in situations 1 and 2. In situation 1, the balance sheet is misstated, whereas in situation 2, revenues or expenses are misstated.

Auditor's Responsibility to Consider Laws and Regulations

In obtaining reasonable assurance that the financial statements are free of material misstatement, the auditor takes into account applicable legal and regulatory frameworks relevant to the client. For example, when auditing the financial statements of a bank, the auditor would need to consider requirements of banking regulators such as the FDIC, Federal Reserve, or state banking commission, among others. The auditor's ability to detect material misstatements arising from failure to comply with laws and regulations is impacted by the following factors:

- Many laws and regulations primarily relate to operating aspects of the business and typically do not affect the financial statements and are not captured by the client's information systems related to financial reporting.
- Noncompliance may involve actions to conceal it, such as collusion, forgery, deliberate failure to record transactions, management override of controls, or intentional misrepresentations made to the auditor.
- Whether an act constitutes noncompliance is a matter for legal determination, such as by a court of law.

One of the difficulties for the auditor is determining how laws and regulations impact financial statement amounts and disclosures. As the impact from noncompliance is further removed from affecting financial statements, the less likely the auditor is to become aware of or recognize noncompliance when auditing the financial statements. The auditor's responsibilities regarding **noncompliance with laws and regulations** (frequently referred to as illegal acts) depend on whether the laws or regulations are expected to have a direct effect on the amounts and disclosures in the financial statements.

Laws and Regulations with a Direct Effect on the Financial Statements The provisions of certain laws and regulations, such as tax and pension laws and regulations, are generally recognized to have a direct effect on the amounts and disclosures in the financial statements. For example, a violation of federal tax laws directly affects income tax expense and income taxes payable. The auditor should obtain sufficient appropriate evidence regarding material amounts and disclosures that are directly affected by laws and regulations. For example, in auditing income tax expense, to identify whether there have been any material violations of federal or state tax laws, the auditor might hold discussions with client personnel and examine reports issued by the Internal Revenue Service after completion of an examination of the client's tax return.

Laws and Regulations That Do Not Have a Direct Effect on the Financial Statements The provisions of many laws and regulations are unlikely to have a direct effect on the financial statements. However, compliance with those laws and regulations is often fundamental to operation of the business and necessary to avoid material penalties. Examples include complying with the terms of an operating license, federal employee safety requirements, and environmental regulations.

The auditor should perform the following procedures to identify instances of noncompliance with other laws and regulations that may have a material effect on the financial statements:

- Inquire of management and those charged with governance about whether the entity is in compliance with such laws and regulations.
- Inspect correspondence, if any, with the relevant licensing or regulatory authorities.

During the audit, other audit procedures may bring instances of suspected noncompliance to the auditor's attention. However, in the absence of identified or suspected noncompliance, the auditor is not required to perform audit procedures beyond those previously discussed.

Audit Procedures When Noncompliance Is Identified or Suspected If the auditor becomes aware of information concerning an instance of noncompliance or suspected noncompliance with laws and regulations, the auditor should obtain an understanding of the nature and circumstances of the act. Additional information should be obtained to evaluate the possible effects on the financial statements.

The auditor should discuss the matter with management at a level above those involved with the suspected noncompliance and, when appropriate, those charged with governance. If management or those charged with governance are unable to provide sufficient information that supports that the entity is in compliance with the laws and regulations, and the auditor believes the effect of the noncompliance may be material to the financial statements, the auditor should consider the need to obtain legal advice. The auditor should also evaluate the effects of the noncompliance on other aspects of the audit, including the auditor's risk assessment and the reliability of other representations from management.

Reporting of Identified or Suspected Noncompliance Unless the matters involved are inconsequential, the auditor should communicate with those charged with governance matters involving noncompliance with laws and regulations that came to the auditor's attention during the course of the audit. If the matter involved is believed to be intentional and material, it should be communicated to those charged with governance, such as the board of directors, as soon as practicable. The auditor should also identify whether a responsibility exists to report the identified or suspected noncompliance to parties outside the entity, such as regulatory authorities.

If the noncompliance has a material effect and has not been adequately reflected in the financial statements, the auditor should express a qualified or adverse opinion on the financial statements. If the auditor is precluded by management or those charged with governance from obtaining sufficient appropriate evidence to evaluate whether noncompliance that may be material to the financial statements has occurred or is likely to have occurred, the auditor should express a qualified opinion or disclaim an opinion on the financial statements on the basis of the scope limitation.

PROFESSIONAL SKEPTICISM

OBJECTIVE 6-4

Describe the need to maintain professional skepticism when conducting an audit.

Auditing standards require that an audit be designed to provide reasonable assurance of detecting *both* material errors and fraud in the financial statements. To accomplish this, the audit must be planned and performed with an *attitude of professional skepticism* in all aspects of the engagement, recognizing the possibility that a material misstatement could exist regardless of the auditor's prior experience with the integrity and honesty of client management and those charged with governance.

Aspects of Professional Skepticism **Professional skepticism** consists of two primary components: a questioning mind and a critical assessment of the audit evidence. While auditors would like to believe that the organizations they accept as clients have integrity and are honest, maintaining a questioning mind helps auditors offset the natural bias to want to trust the client. A questioning mindset means the auditor approaches the audit with a "trust but verify" mental outlook. Similarly, as they obtain and evaluate evidence supporting financial statement amounts and disclosures, professional skepticism also involves a critical assessment of the evidence that includes asking probing questions and paying attention to inconsistencies. When auditors embrace the responsibility to maintain a questioning mind and to critically evaluate evidence, they significantly reduce the likelihood of audit failure throughout the audit.

Elements of Professional Skepticism While the concept of professional skepticism has been a foundational element of auditing standards for years, it continues to be difficult to implement in practice. Unfortunately, auditors are human and thus are subject to natural biases to trust individuals they know and with whom they interact on a regular basis. In an audit environment, auditors sometimes convince themselves that they only accept clients they can trust and who have high integrity. Thus, it is often difficult for auditors to embrace the possibility that even their clients may lack competence or may try to deceive them throughout the entire audit process. Despite these limitations, auditors need to work to overcome these judgment biases and they need to be continually reminded of the importance of maintaining appropriate professional skepticism, and recognize that the risk of material misstatements is present in all audits.

Academic research on the topic of professional skepticism suggests there are six characteristics of skepticism:[1]

1. Questioning mindset—a disposition to inquiry with some sense of doubt
2. Suspension of judgment—withholding judgment until appropriate evidence is obtained
3. Search for knowledge—a desire to investigate beyond the obvious, with a desire to corroborate
4. Interpersonal understanding—recognition that people's motivations and perceptions can lead them to provide biased or misleading information

PCAOB STAFF ALERT ON PROFESSIONAL SKEPTICISM

The PCAOB publishes Staff Audit Practice Alerts to highlight new, emerging, or otherwise noteworthy circumstances that may affect how auditors conduct audits under the existing requirements of the PCAOB standards. In December 2012, the PCAOB issued Staff Audit Practice Alert No. 10, *Maintaining and Applying Professional Skepticism in Audits*, emphasizing that professional skepticism is essential to the performance of effective audits, and it is to be applied throughout the audit by each individual auditor on the engagement team. It is especially important in those areas of the audit that involve significant management judgments or transactions outside the normal course of business, and it is important in the consideration of fraud.

The Alert describes important impediments to professional skepticism, noting that auditors are often challenged in maintaining a questioning mindset and critical assessment of audit evidence as a result of subconscious human biases and other circumstances. These can cause auditors to gather, evaluate, rationalize, and recall information in a manner that is consistent with expectations and pressures of the client rather than external users. Incentives and pressures exist that interfere with the application of professional skepticism, allowing subconscious biases to prevail. Fee pressures, scheduling, or workload demands may lead auditors to accept information too quickly. And, over time, auditors may be lured into placing too much trust in management, which causes them to avoid negative encounters with members of management.

Source: PCAOB Staff Practice Alert No. 10, *Maintaining and Applying Professional Skepticism in Audits*, December 4, 2012 (pcaobus.org).

[1] Based on "Development of a Scale to Measure Professional Skepticism," by R. Kathy Hurtt, *Auditing: A Journal of Practice & Theory*, May 2010.

5. Autonomy—the self-direction, moral independence, and conviction to decide for oneself, rather than accepting the claims of others
6. Self-esteem—the self-confidence to resist persuasion and to challenge assumptions or conclusions

Awareness of these six elements throughout the engagement can help auditors fulfill their responsibility to maintain an appropriate level of professional skepticism. Asking the right questions and probing further with follow-up questions until the auditor is satisfied with the responses, while being alert to unusual behaviors from respondents as they answer questions, can make the difference between detecting and failing to detect a material misstatement in the financial statements.

PROFESSIONAL JUDGMENT

OBJECTIVE 6-5

Describe the key elements of an effective professional judgment process.

To assist auditors with maintaining an appropriate level of professional skepticism when professional judgments are made during an audit, the profession has developed professional judgment frameworks that illustrate an effective decision-making process and that guide auditors' thinking to help them be aware of their own judgment tendencies, traps, and biases.

Elements of the Judgment Process The Center for Audit Quality's *Professional Judgment Resource* outlines five key elements of a professional judgment process, as illustrated in Figure 6-3, that auditors apply when making professional judgments.

Identify and Define the Issue The starting point to an effective professional judgment begins with identifying and defining the issue by carefully analyzing the situation and its potential effect on the audit. Failure to identify the correct issue often leads to an incorrect analysis and an inappropriate judgment. Taking time to identify the primary issue to be addressed and incorporating perspectives on other important considerations that need to be evaluated are both part of the initial step in developing an appropriate conclusion. As part of this step, the auditor considers the impact of the

FIGURE 6-3 Elements of an Effective Judgment Process

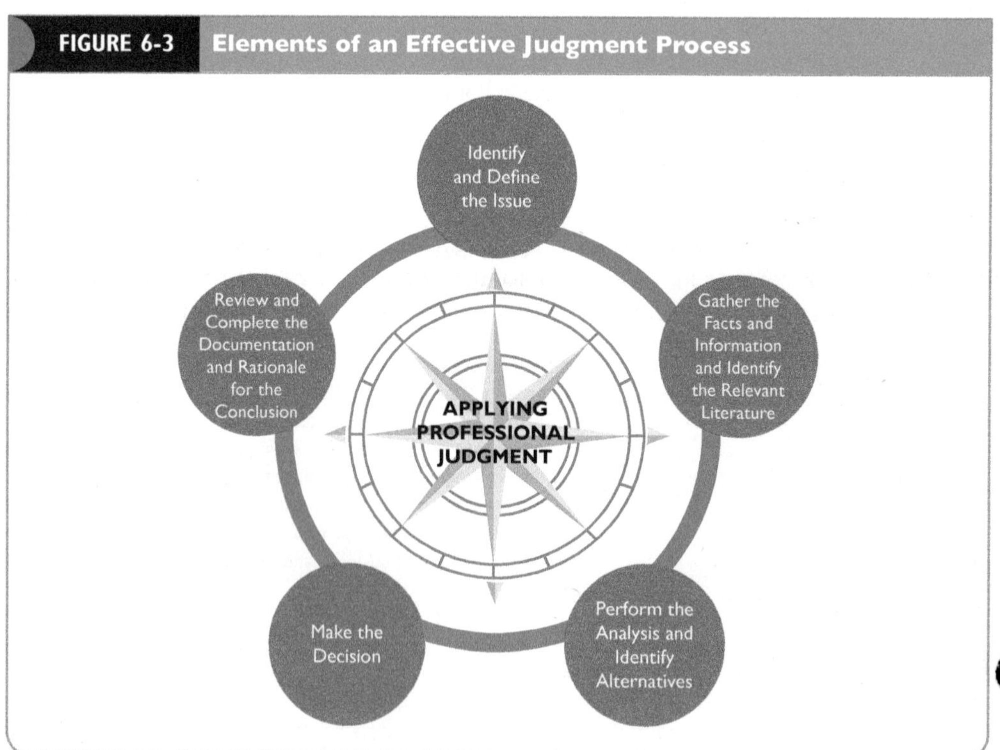

Identify and Define the Issue
Gather the Facts and Information and Identify the Relevant Literature
Perform the Analysis and Identify Alternatives
Make the Decision
Review and Complete the Documentation and Rationale for the Conclusion
APPLYING PROFESSIONAL JUDGMENT

Source: Professional Judgment Resource, Provided courtesy of the Center for Audit Quality (2014).

issue on the financial statements, the level of complexity and uncertainty surrounding the issue, whether there are any related issues that should be considered, and the impact of the issue on planned audit procedures. For example, an entity may have recorded an unusual sales transaction that involves terms different from the normal course of business. The auditor may benefit from first thinking about the important issues associated with this transaction, such as whether the terms of the transaction support its inclusion as revenue in the financial statements, whether there are unique valuation concerns associated with related receivables, and whether any unique disclosures should be made in light of its unusual nature.

Gather the Facts and Information and Identify the Relevant Literature With the problem defined, the auditor seeks to understand the relevant facts and available information concerning the issue. This might include obtaining facts and information about key inputs and assumptions to a transaction, event, or situation through discussions with client personnel who are knowledgeable of the situation. When gathering facts and information, the auditor should be alert for other information that either confirms or contradicts facts and information, in addition to evaluating the sources of that information. To evaluate the effect of the issue on the audit of the financial statements, the auditor should consider the accounting and auditing standards and rules relevant to the issue. As more is learned about the facts and circumstances surrounding the issue, the auditor may determine that subject-matter experts are needed to make the judgment. For example, the auditor may need to gather contracts related to the unusual sales transaction in addition to other documentation evidencing delivery of products or services associated with the sale, and the auditor may want to discuss the transaction with management, including those in sales functions, to better understand the business rationale underlying the transaction so that the auditor is aware of those facts when evaluating the appropriateness of the revenue recognition in light of GAAP requirements.

Perform the Analysis and Identify Potential Alternatives The next element of the professional judgment process involves analyzing the issue based on the facts and information gathered and the relevant authoritative literature identified. As part of that analysis, the auditor considers a number of factors such as whether he or she understands the form and substance of the transaction or event, whether the relevant authoritative literature has been applied consistently by the client to similar situations, whether the auditor has been able to corroborate the facts and assumptions that are important to the analysis, and whether the auditor has identified any discrepancies or inconsistencies in the facts and information obtained. For example, the auditor would determine if the facts and information associated with the unusual sales transaction satisfy the accounting criteria for revenue recognition and related financial statement disclosure. The auditor would consider whether there is any information that is incomplete or contradictory with the information used by the entity to justify the inclusion of that revenue in the financial statements and would obtain other information to resolve any inconsistencies.

Make the Decision Once the analysis of the facts and information has been completed, the auditor applies judgment to make a decision. The analysis may identify only one appropriate response to the issue, or it may conclude that there are multiple responses that could reasonably be made in the circumstances, requiring the auditor to identify which alternative best addresses the issue. After making the decision, the auditor should step back and evaluate the judgment process to determine that all of the key activities in the judgment process have been appropriately performed. In light of all the information obtained for the unusual sales transaction, the auditor would determine whether the inclusion of the transaction is in accordance with accounting standards.

Review and Complete the Documentation and Rationale for the Conclusion As the auditor articulates in written form the rationale of his or her judgment, the auditor may find that the reasoning appears faulty or incomplete and therefore is not persuasive. This should direct the auditor to evaluate which aspects of the analysis and judgment process

TABLE 6-1	Strategies to Mitigate Common Judgment Tendencies
Judgment Tendency	**Strategy to Avoid or Mitigate Tendency**
Confirmation: The tendency to put more weight on information that is consistent with initial beliefs or preferences	Make the opposing case and consider alternative explanations Consider potentially disconfirming or conflicting information
Overconfidence: The tendency to overestimate one's own abilities to perform tasks or to make accurate assessments of risks or other judgments and decisions	Challenge opinions and experts Challenge underlying assumptions
Anchoring: The tendency to make assessments by starting from an initial value and then adjusting insufficiently away from that initial value	Solicit input from others Consider management bias, including the potential for fraud or material misstatements
Availability: The tendency to consider information that is easily retrievable or what's easily accessible as being more likely or more relevant	Consider why something comes to mind Obtain and consider objective data Consult with others and make the opposing case

Source: Professional Judgment Resource, Provided courtesy of the Center for Audit Quality (2014).

may warrant further consideration. The process of documenting helps the auditor to be more objective and complete in assessing the reasoning used in reaching a judgment decision. For example, the auditor's documentation of the facts and information associated with the unusual sales transaction and the auditor's rationale for concluding the transaction was recorded in accordance with standards and may help the auditor identify for further consideration any aspects that might not be clear or persuasive before reaching a final conclusion about the appropriateness of the accounting treatment.

The judgment process illustrated by Figure 6-3 (p. 150) is often iterative and may require some steps to be combined, repeated, or evaluated in a different order.

Potential Judgment Tendencies, Traps, and Biases Auditors should be alert for potential judgment tendencies, traps, and biases that may impact the decision-making process. All people are subject to common pitfalls that affect their ability to make sound judgments. A number of research studies have identified common judgment tendencies along with a number of strategies that can be employed to mitigate their effects. Table 6-1 includes four common judgment tendencies and related strategies to avoid them and mitigate bias.

Awareness of these and other potential traps helps the auditor take steps to mitigate their effects and strengthen professional skepticism. There are a number of other techniques auditors can employ to avoid potential traps, such as reassessing how the decision or judgment was reached, explaining the judgment rationale to others, and engaging in self-reflection that includes assessing whether time pressures, self-interest, and biases might have influenced the auditor's decision-making process.

CONCEPT CHECK

1. Distinguish between management's and the auditor's responsibility for the financial statements being audited.
2. Explain the concept of professional skepticism and identify its two elements.

FINANCIAL STATEMENT CYCLES

OBJECTIVE 6-6

Identify the benefits of a cycle approach to segmenting the audit.

Audits are performed by dividing the financial statements into smaller segments or components. The division makes the audit more manageable and aids in the assignment of tasks to different members of the audit team. For example, most auditors treat fixed assets and notes payable as different segments. Each segment is audited separately but not on a completely independent basis. (For example, the audit of fixed assets may reveal an unrecorded note payable.) After the audit of each segment is completed, including interrelationships with other segments, the results are combined. A conclusion can then be reached about the financial statements taken as a whole.

There are different ways of segmenting an audit. One approach is to treat every account balance on the statements as a separate segment. Segmenting that way is usually inefficient. It would result in the independent audit of such closely related accounts as inventory and cost of goods sold.

Cycle Approach to Segmenting an Audit

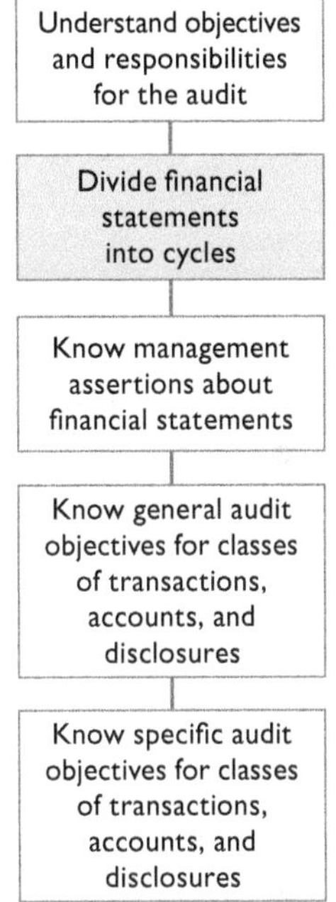

A common way to divide an audit is to keep closely related types (or classes) of transactions and account balances in the same segment. This is called the **cycle approach**. For example, sales, sales returns, cash receipts, and charge-offs of uncollectible accounts are the four classes of transactions that cause accounts receivable to increase and decrease. Therefore, they are all parts of the sales and collection cycle. Similarly, payroll transactions and accrued payroll are parts of the payroll and personnel cycle.

The logic of using the cycle approach is that it ties to the way transactions are recorded in journals and summarized in the general ledger and financial statements. Figure 6-4 shows that flow. To the extent that it is practical, the cycle approach combines transactions recorded in different journals with the general ledger balances that result from those transactions.

The cycles used in this text are listed below and are then explained in detail. Note that each of these cycles is so important that one or more later chapters address the audit of each cycle:

- Sales and collection cycle
- Acquisition and payment cycle
- Payroll and personnel cycle
- Inventory and warehousing cycle
- Capital acquisition and repayment cycle

Figure 6-5 (p. 154) illustrates the application of cycles to audits using the December 31, 2016, trial balance for Hillsburg Hardware Company. (The financial statements prepared from this trial balance are included in the glossy insert to the textbook.) A trial balance is used to prepare financial statements and is a primary focus of every audit. Prior-year account balances are usually included for comparative purposes, but are excluded from Figure 6-5 in order to focus on transaction cycles. The letter representing a cycle is shown for each account in the left column beside the account name. Observe that each account has at least one cycle associated with it, and only cash and inventory are a part of two or more cycles.

FIGURE 6-4 Transaction Flow from Journals to Financial Statements

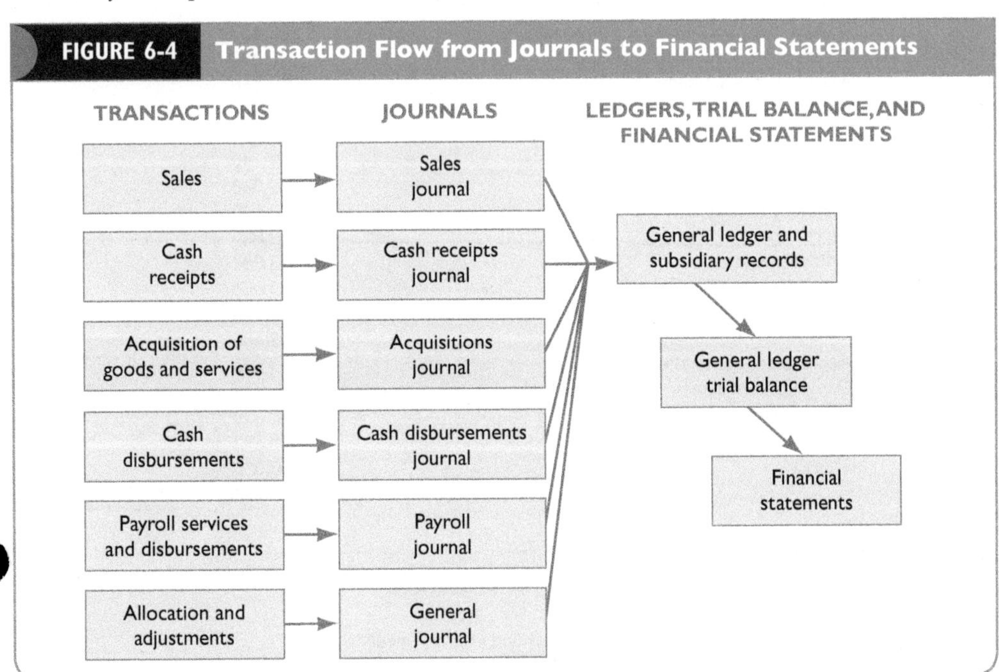

FIGURE 6-5 Hillsburg Hardware Co. Adjusted Trial Balance

HILLSBURG HARDWARE CO.
TRIAL BALANCE
December 31, 2016

		Debit	Credit
S,A,P,C	Cash in bank	$ 827,568	
S	Trade accounts receivable	20,196,800	
S	Allowance for uncollectible accounts		$ 1,240,000
S	Other accounts receivable	945,020	
A,I	Inventories	29,864,621	
A	Prepaid expenses	431,558	
A	Land	3,456,420	
A	Buildings	32,500,000	
A	Computer and other equipment	3,758,347	
A	Furniture and fixtures	2,546,421	
A	Accumulated depreciation		31,920,126
A	Trade accounts payable		4,719,989
C	Notes payable		4,179,620
P	Accrued payroll		1,349,800
P	Accrued payroll taxes		119,663
C	Accrued interest		149,560
C	Dividends payable		1,900,000
A	Accrued income tax		795,442
C	Long-term notes payable		24,120,000
A	Deferred tax		738,240
A	Other accrued payables		829,989
C	Capital stock		5,000,000
C	Capital in excess of par value		3,500,000
C	Retained earnings		11,929,075
S	Sales		144,327,789
S	Sales returns and allowances	1,241,663	
I	Cost of goods sold	103,240,768	
P	Salaries and commissions	7,738,900	
P	Sales payroll taxes	1,422,100	
A	Travel and entertainment—selling	1,110,347	
A	Advertising	2,611,263	
A	Sales and promotional expense	321,620	
A	Sales meetings and training	924,480	
A	Miscellaneous sales expense	681,041	
P	Executive and office salaries	5,523,960	
P	Administrative payroll taxes	682,315	
A	Travel and entertainment—administrative	561,680	
A	Computer maintenance and supplies	860,260	
A	Stationery and supplies	762,568	
A	Postage	244,420	
A	Telecommunications	722,315	
A	Rent	312,140	
A	Legal fees and retainers	383,060	
A	Auditing and related services	302,840	
A	Depreciation	1,452,080	
S	Bad debt expense	3,323,084	
A	Insurance	722,684	
A	Office repairs and maintenance	843,926	
A	Miscellaneous office expense	643,680	
A	Miscellaneous general expense	323,842	
A	Gain on sale of assets		719,740
A	Income taxes	1,746,600	
C	Interest expense	2,408,642	
C	Dividends	1,900,000	
		$237,539,033	$237,539,033

Note: Letters in the left-hand column refer to the following transaction cycles:

S = Sales and collection
I = Inventory and warehousing
A = Acquisition and payment
C = Capital acquisition and repayment
P = Payroll and personnel

The accounts for Hillsburg Hardware Co. are summarized in Table 6-2 by cycle, and include the related journals and financial statements in which the accounts appear. The following observations expand on the information contained in Table 6-2.

- All general ledger accounts and journals for Hillsburg Hardware Co. are included at least once. For a different company, the number and titles of journals and general ledger accounts will differ, but all will be included.
- Some journals and general ledger accounts are included in more than one cycle. When that occurs, it means that the journal is used to record transactions from more than one cycle and indicates a tie-in between the cycles. The most important general ledger account included in and affecting several cycles is general cash (cash in bank). General cash connects most cycles.

TABLE 6-2 Cycles Applied to Hillsburg Hardware Co.

		General Ledger Accounts Included in the Cycle (See Figure 6-5)	
Cycle	**Journals Included in the Cycle (See Figure 6-4, p. 153)**	**Balance Sheet**	**Income Statement**
Sales and collection	Sales journal Cash receipts journal General journal	Cash in bank Trade accounts receivable Other accounts receivable Allowance for uncollectible accounts	Sales Sales returns and allowances Bad debt expense
Acquisition and payment	Acquisitions journal Cash disbursements journal General journal	Cash in bank Inventories Prepaid expenses Land Buildings Computer and other equipment Furniture and fixtures Accumulated depreciation Trade accounts payable Other accrued payables Accrued income tax Deferred tax	Advertising[S] Travel and entertainment[S] Sales meetings and training[S] Sales and promotional expense[S] Miscellaneous sales expense[S] Travel and entertainment[A] Stationery and supplies[A] Postage[A] Telecommunications[A] Computer maintenance and supplies[A] Depreciation[A] Rent[A] Legal fees and retainers[A] Auditing and related services[A] Insurance[A] Office repairs and maintenance expense[A] Miscellaneous office expense[A] Miscellaneous general expense[A] Gain on sale of assets Income taxes
Payroll and personnel	Payroll journal General journal	Cash in bank Accrued payroll Accrued payroll taxes	Salaries and commissions[S] Sales payroll taxes[S] Executive and office salaries[A] Administrative payroll taxes[A]
Inventory and warehousing	Acquisitions journal Sales journal General journal	Inventories	Cost of goods sold
Capital acquisition and repayment	Acquisitions journal Cash disbursements journal General journal	Cash in bank Notes payable Long-term notes payable Accrued interest Capital stock Capital in excess of par value Retained earnings Dividends Dividends payable	Interest expense

S = Selling expense; A = general and administrative expense.

- The sales and collection cycle is the first cycle listed and is a primary focus on most audits. Collections on trade accounts receivable in the cash receipts journal is the primary operating inflow to cash in the bank.
- The capital acquisition and repayment cycle is closely related to the acquisition and payment cycle. Transactions in the acquisition and payment cycle include the purchase of inventory, supplies, and other goods and services related to operations. Transactions in the capital acquisition and repayment cycle are related to financing the business, such as issuing stock or debt, paying dividends, and repaying debt.

Although the same journals are used for transactions in the acquisition and payment and the capital acquisition and repayment cycles, it is useful to separate capital acquisition and repayment cycle transactions into a separate transaction cycle. First, capital acquisitions and repayments relate to financing the business, rather than operations. Second, most capital acquisition and repayment cycle accounts involve few transactions, but each is often highly material and therefore should be audited extensively. Considering both reasons, it is more convenient to separate the two cycles.

- The inventory and warehousing cycle is closely related to all other cycles, especially for a manufacturing company. The cost of inventory includes raw materials (acquisition and payment cycle), direct labor (payroll and personnel cycle), and manufacturing overhead (acquisition and payment cycle and payroll and personnel cycle). The sale of finished goods involves the sales and collection cycle. Because inventory is material for most manufacturing companies, it is common to borrow money using inventory as security. In those cases, the capital acquisition and repayment cycle is also related to inventory and warehousing. Inventory is included as a separate cycle both because it is related to other cycles and because for most manufacturing and retail companies, inventory is usually highly material, there are unique systems and controls for inventory, and inventory is often complex to audit.

Relationships Among Cycles

Figure 6-6 illustrates the relationships of the five cycles and general cash. Note that cycles have no beginning or end except at the origin and final disposition of a company. A company begins by obtaining capital, usually in the form of cash. In a manufacturing company, cash is used to acquire raw materials, fixed assets, and related goods and services to produce inventory (acquisition and payment cycle). Cash is also used to acquire labor for the same reason (payroll and personnel cycle). Acquisition and payment and payroll and personnel are similar in nature, but the functions are sufficiently different to justify separate cycles. The combined result of these two cycles is inventory (inventory and warehousing cycle). At a subsequent point, the inventory is sold and billings and collections result (sales and collection cycle). The cash generated is used to pay dividends and interest or finance capital expansion and to start the

FIGURE 6-6 Relationships Among Transaction Cycles

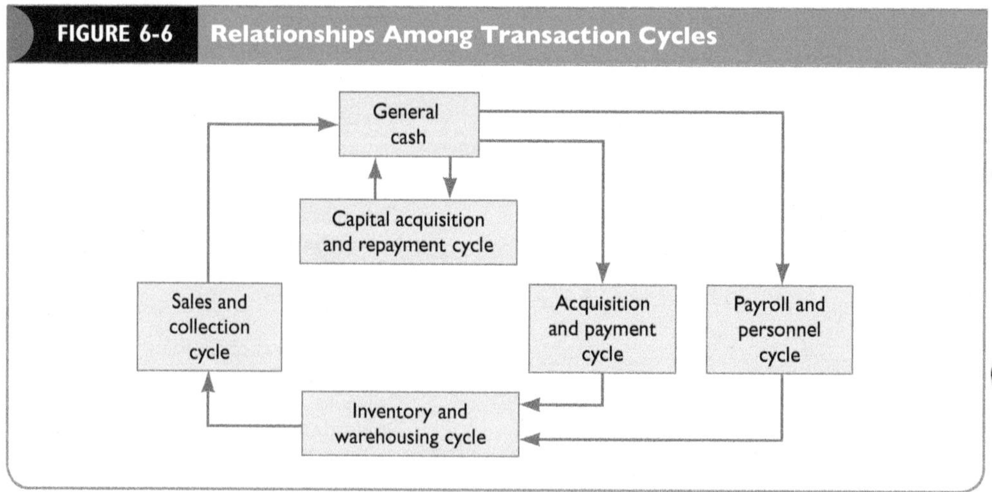

cycles again. The cycles interrelate in much the same way in a service company, where there will be billings and collections, although there will be no inventory.

Transaction cycles are an important way to organize audits. For the most part, auditors treat each cycle separately during the audit. Although auditors need to consider the interrelationships between cycles, they typically treat cycles independently to the extent practical to manage complex audits effectively.

SETTING AUDIT OBJECTIVES

OBJECTIVE 6-7

Describe why the auditor obtains assurance by auditing transactions and ending balances, including presentation and disclosure.

Auditors conduct financial statement audits using the cycle approach by performing audit tests of the transactions making up ending balances and also by performing audit tests of the account balances and related disclosures. Figure 6-7 illustrates this concept by showing the four classes of transactions that determine the ending balance in accounts receivable for Hillsburg Hardware Co. Assume that the beginning balance of $17,521 (thousand) was audited in the prior year and is therefore considered fairly stated. If the auditor could be completely sure that each of the four classes of transactions is correctly stated, the auditor could also be sure that the ending balance of $20,197 (thousand) is correctly stated. But it is almost always impractical for the auditor to obtain complete assurance about the correctness of each class of transactions, resulting in less than complete assurance about the ending balance in accounts receivable. In almost all audits, overall assurance can be increased by also auditing the ending balance of accounts receivable. Auditors have found that, generally, the most efficient and effective way to conduct audits is to *obtain some combination of assurance for each class of transactions and for the ending balance in the related accounts.*

For any given class of transactions, several audit objectives must be met before the auditor can conclude that the transactions are properly recorded. These are called **transaction-related audit objectives** in the remainder of this book. For example, there are specific sales transaction-related audit objectives and specific sales returns and allowances transaction-related audit objectives.

Similarly, several audit objectives must be met for each account balance. These are called **balance-related audit objectives.** For example, there are specific accounts receivable balance-related audit objectives and specific accounts payable balance-related audit objectives. We show later in this chapter that the transaction-related and balance-related audit objectives are somewhat different but closely related.

The third category of audit objectives relates to the presentation and disclosure of information in the financial statements. These are called **presentation and disclosure-related audit objectives.** For example, there are specific presentation and disclosure-related audit objectives for accounts receivable and notes payable.

FIGURE 6-7 Balances and Transactions Affecting Those Balances for Accounts Receivable

Accounts Receivable (in thousands)

	Debit	Credit	
Beginning balance	$ 17,521		
Sales	$144,328	$137,087	Cash receipts
		$ 1,242	Sales returns and allowances
		$ 3,323	Charge-off of uncollectible accounts
Ending balance	$ 20,197		

Throughout this text, the term *audit objectives* refers to transaction-related, balance-related, and presentation and disclosure-related audit objectives. Before examining audit objectives in more detail, we first deal with management assertions.

MANAGEMENT ASSERTIONS

OBJECTIVE 6-8

Distinguish among the management assertions about financial information.

Management assertions are implied or expressed representations by management about classes of transactions and the related accounts and disclosures in the financial statements. In most cases they are implied. Examine Figure 6-5 on page 154. Management of Hillsburg Hardware Co. asserts that cash of $827,568 was present in the company's bank accounts as of the balance sheet date. Unless otherwise disclosed in the financial statements, management also asserts that the cash was unrestricted and available for normal use. Management further asserts that all required disclosures related to cash are accurate and are understandable. Similar assertions exist for each asset, liability, owners' equity, revenue, and expense item in the financial statements. These assertions apply to classes of transactions, account balances, and presentation and disclosures.

Management assertions are directly related to the financial reporting framework used by the company (usually U.S. GAAP or IFRS), as they are part of the *criteria that management uses to record and disclose accounting information in financial statements.* The definition of auditing in Chapter 1, in part, states that auditing is a comparison of information (financial statements) to established criteria (assertions established according to accounting standards). Auditors must therefore understand the assertions to do adequate audits.

PCAOB Assertions

PCAOB auditing standards note that management implicitly or explicitly makes assertions regarding the recognition, measurement, presentation, and disclosure of the various elements of the financial statements and related disclosures. The PCAOB describes five categories of management assertions:

- Existence or occurrence—Assets or liabilities of the public company exist at a given date, and recorded transactions have occurred during the period.
- Completeness—All transactions and accounts that should be presented in the financial statements are so included.
- Valuation or allocation—Assets, liability, equity, revenue, and expense components have been included in the financial statements at appropriate amounts.
- Rights and obligations—The public company holds or controls rights to the assets, and liabilities are obligations of the company at a given date.
- Presentation and disclosure—The components of the financial statements are properly classified, described, and disclosed.

These assertions are similar to the assertions in international and AICPA auditing standards, as described next.

International and AICPA Assertions

PCAOB standards provide for one set of assertions that apply to all financial statement information. International auditing standards and AICPA auditing standards further divide management assertions into three categories:

1. Assertions about classes of transactions and events for the period under audit
2. Assertions about account balances at period end
3. Assertions about presentation and disclosure

The mapping of PCAOB assertions to the assertions in international auditing standards and AICPA auditing standards is shown in Table 6-3. The first three PCAOB assertions are applicable to account balances and classes of transactions. Presentation and disclosure is treated as a single assertion. Not only do the international auditing

TABLE 6-3 Management Assertions for Each Category of Assertions

PCAOB Auditing Standards Assertions	International Auditing Standards and AICPA Auditing Standards Assertions		
Assertions About Transactions, Balances, and Presentation and Disclosure	**Assertions About Classes of Transactions and Events**	**Assertions About Account Balances**	**Assertions About Presentation and Disclosure**
Existence or occurrence—Assets or liabilities exist at a given date, and recorded transactions have occurred during the period.	*Occurrence*—Transactions and events that have been recorded have occurred and pertain to the entity.	*Existence*—Assets, liabilities, and equity interests exist.	*Occurrence and rights and obligations*—Disclosed events and transactions have occurred and pertain to the entity.
Completeness—All transactions and accounts that should be presented in the financial statements are so included.	*Completeness*—All transactions and events that should have been recorded have been recorded.	*Completeness*—All assets, liabilities, and equity interests that should have been recorded have been recorded.	*Completeness*—All disclosures that should have been included in the financial statements have been included.
Valuation or allocation—Assets, liability, equity, revenue, and expense components have been included in the financial statements at appropriate amounts.	*Accuracy*—Amounts and other data relating to recorded transactions and events have been recorded appropriately.	*Valuation and allocation*—Assets, liabilities, and equity interests are included in the financial statements at appropriate amounts and any resulting valuation adjustments are appropriately recorded.	*Accuracy and valuation*—Financial and other information is disclosed appropriately and at appropriate amounts.
	Classification—Transactions and events have been recorded in the proper accounts.		*Classification and understandability*—Financial and other information is appropriately presented and described and disclosures are clearly expressed.
	Cutoff—Transactions and events have been recorded in the correct accounting period.		
Rights and obligations—The company holds or controls rights to the assets, and liabilities are obligations of the company at a given date.		*Rights and obligations*—The entity holds or controls the rights to assets, and liabilities are the obligation of the entity.	
Presentation and disclosure—The components of the financial statements are properly classified, described, and disclosed.	(See the international and AICPA assertions for presentation and disclosure.)	(See the international and AICPA assertions for presentation and disclosure.)	(See above assertions.)

standards and AICPA auditing standards separate the assertions related to transactions from the assertions related to account balances and presentation and disclosure, they also provide additional assertions related to the PCAOB valuation or allocation assertion, as shown in Table 6-3. The international auditing standards and AICPA auditing standards assertions are grouped so that assertions related across categories are included on the same table row.

Assertions About Classes of Transactions and Events Management makes several assertions about transactions. These assertions also apply to other events that are reflected in the accounting records, such as recording depreciation and recognizing pension obligations. As illustrated in Table 6-3, international auditing standards and AICPA auditing standards include three specific assertions that relate to the valuation or allocation assertion in the PCAOB auditing standards. The accuracy assertion addresses whether the transactions have been recorded at correct amounts. The classification assertion addresses whether transactions have been recorded in the appropriate accounts. The cutoff assertion addresses whether transactions have been recorded in the proper accounting period.

Assertions About Account Balances International auditing standards and AICPA auditing standards include four assertions related to account balances, as shown in Table 6-3 (p. 159). These address existence, completeness, valuation and allocation, and rights and obligations for account balances at year-end. They map directly to four of the five PCAOB auditing standards assertions.

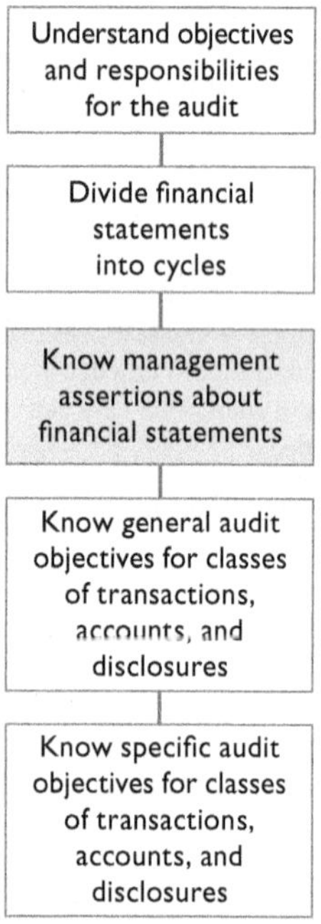

Understand objectives and responsibilities for the audit
Divide financial statements into cycles
Know management assertions about financial statements
Know general audit objectives for classes of transactions, accounts, and disclosures
Know specific audit objectives for classes of transactions, accounts, and disclosures

Assertions About Presentation and Disclosure With increases in the complexity of transactions and the need for expanded disclosures about these transactions, assertions about presentation and disclosure have increased in importance. While the PCAOB auditing standards include an overall assertion related to presentation and disclosure, international auditing standards and AICPA auditing standards provide four specific assertions that address occurrence and rights and obligations, completeness, accuracy and valuation, and classification and understandability.

The occurrence and rights and obligations assertion addresses whether disclosed events have occurred and are the rights and obligations of the entity. For example, if the client discloses that it has acquired another company, it asserts that the transaction has been completed. The completeness assertion deals with whether all required disclosures have been included in the financial statements. As an example, management asserts that all material transactions with related parties have been disclosed in the financial statements. The accuracy and valuation assertion deals with whether financial information is disclosed fairly and at appropriate amounts. Management's disclosure of the amount of unfunded pension obligations and the assumptions underlying these amounts is an example of this assertion. Finally, the classification and understandability assertion relates to whether amounts are appropriately classified in the financial statements and footnotes, and whether the balance descriptions and related disclosures are understandable. For example, management asserts that the classification of inventories as finished goods, work-in-process, and raw materials is appropriate, and the disclosures of the methods used to value inventories are understandable.

Assertions Lead to Audit Objectives

Auditors may use different terms to express the management assertions as long as all the aspects included in Table 6-3 are addressed. The auditor should consider the relevance of each assertion for each significant class of transactions, account balance, and presentation and disclosure. **Relevant assertions** have a meaningful bearing on whether the account is fairly stated and are used to assess the risk of material misstatement and the design and performance of audit procedures. For example, valuation is likely to be a relevant assertion for accounts receivable, but not for cash.

After the relevant assertions have been identified, the auditor can then develop audit objectives for each category of assertions. The auditor's audit objectives follow and are closely related to management assertions. That is not surprising because the auditor's primary responsibility is to determine whether management assertions about financial statements are justified. The reason for using audit objectives, rather than the assertions, is to provide a framework to help the auditor accumulate sufficient appropriate evidence and decide the proper evidence to accumulate given the circumstances of the engagement. The objectives remain the same from audit to audit, but the evidence varies depending on the circumstances.

Developing audit objectives for classes of transactions, account balances, and presentation and disclosure helps the auditor design audit procedures to accumulate sufficient appropriate evidence about each aspect of the assertions. For example, developing an audit objective specific to the accuracy of transactions helps the auditor design and perform audit procedures to obtain evidence about the accuracy of transactions, while developing an audit objective for the classification of transactions helps the auditor design and perform audit procedures to obtain evidence about whether the transactions are recorded in the appropriate accounts. The remainder of this book focuses on audit objectives related to transactions, audit objectives related to account balances, and audit objectives related to presentation and disclosure.

TRANSACTION-RELATED AUDIT OBJECTIVES

OBJECTIVE 6-9

Link transaction-related audit objectives to management assertions for classes of transactions.

The auditor's transaction-related audit objectives follow and are closely related to management's assertions about classes of transactions. There is a difference between general transaction-related audit objectives and specific transaction-related audit objectives for each class of transactions. The six general transaction-related audit objectives discussed here are applicable to every class of transactions and are stated in broad terms. Specific transaction-related audit objectives are also applied to each class of transactions but are stated in terms tailored to a specific class of transactions, such as sales transactions. Once the auditor establishes general transaction-related audit objectives, they can be used to develop specific transaction-related audit objectives for each class of transactions being audited.

General Transaction-Related Audit Objectives

Occurrence—Recorded Transactions Exist This objective deals with whether recorded transactions have actually occurred. Inclusion of a sale in the sales journal when no sale occurred violates the occurrence objective. This objective is the auditor's counterpart to the management assertion of occurrence for classes of transactions.

Completeness—Existing Transactions Are Recorded This objective deals with whether all transactions that should be included in the journals have actually been included. Failure to include a sale in the sales journal and general ledger when a sale occurred violates the completeness objective. This objective is the counterpart to the management assertion of completeness for classes of transactions.

The occurrence and completeness objectives emphasize opposite audit concerns. Occurrence deals with potential overstatement; completeness deals with unrecorded transactions (understatement).

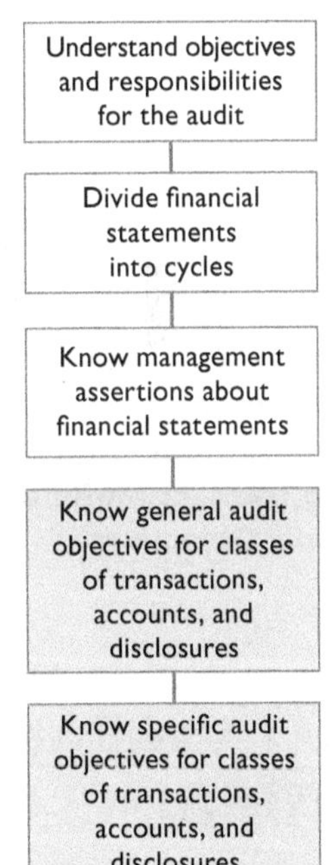

Understand objectives and responsibilities for the audit
Divide financial statements into cycles
Know management assertions about financial statements
Know general audit objectives for classes of transactions, accounts, and disclosures
Know specific audit objectives for classes of transactions, accounts, and disclosures

Accuracy—Recorded Transactions Are Stated at the Correct Amounts This objective addresses the accuracy of information for accounting transactions and is one part of the accuracy assertion for classes of transactions. For sales transactions, this objective is violated if the quantity of goods shipped was different from the quantity billed, the wrong selling price was used for billing, extension or adding errors occurred in billing, or the wrong amount was included in the sales journal.

It is important to distinguish between accuracy and occurrence or completeness. For example, if a recorded sales transaction should not have been recorded because the shipment was on consignment, the occurrence objective has been violated, even if the amount of the invoice was accurately calculated. If the recorded sale was for a valid shipment but the amount was calculated incorrectly, there is a violation of the accuracy objective but not of the occurrence objective. The same relationship exists between completeness and accuracy.

Posting and Summarization—Recorded Transactions Are Properly Included in the Master Files and Are Correctly Summarized This objective deals with the accuracy of the transfer of information from recorded transactions in journals to subsidiary records and the general ledger. It is part of the accuracy assertion for classes of transactions. For example, if a sales transaction is recorded in the wrong customer's record or at the wrong amount in the master file or the sum of all sales transactions posted from the sales journal to the general ledger is inaccurate, this objective is violated. Because the posting of transactions from journals to subsidiary records, the general ledger, and other related master files is typically accomplished automatically by computerized accounting systems, the risk of random human error in posting is minimal. Once the auditor can establish that the computer is functioning properly, there is a reduced concern about posting process errors.

Classification—Transactions Included in the Client's Journals Are Properly Classified As the auditor's counterpart to management's classification assertion for classes of transaction, this objective addresses whether transactions are included in

TABLE 6-4 Hillsburg Hardware Co.: Management Assertions and Transaction-Related Audit Objectives Applied to Sales Transactions

Management Assertions About Classes of Transactions and Events	General Transaction-Related Audit Objectives	Specific Sales Transaction-Related Audit Objectives
Occurrence	Occurrence	Recorded sales are for shipments made to nonfictitious customers.
Completeness	Completeness	Existing sales transactions are recorded.
Accuracy	Accuracy	Recorded sales are for the amount of goods shipped and are correctly billed and recorded.
	Posting and summarization	Sales transactions are properly included in the master file and are correctly summarized.
Classification	Classification	Sales transactions are properly classified.
Cutoff	Timing	Sales transactions are recorded on the correct dates.

the appropriate accounts. Examples of misclassifications for sales are: including cash sales as credit sales, recording a sale of operating fixed assets as revenue, and misclassifying commercial sales as residential sales.

Timing—Transactions Are Recorded on the Correct Dates The timing objective for transactions is the auditor's counterpart to management's cutoff assertion. A timing error occurs if a transaction is not recorded on the day it took place. A sales transaction, for example, should be recorded on the date of shipment.

Specific Transaction-Related Audit Objectives

After the general transaction-related audit objectives are determined, specific transaction-related audit objectives for each material class of transactions can be developed. Such classes of transactions typically include sales, cash receipts, acquisitions of goods and services, payroll, and so on. At least one specific transaction-related audit objective should be included for each general transaction-related audit objective unless the auditor believes that the general transaction-related audit objective is not relevant or is unimportant in the circumstances.

Relationships Among Management Assertions and Transaction-Related Audit Objectives

Table 6-4 illustrates the relationships among management assertions, the general transaction-related audit objectives, and specific transaction-related audit objectives as applied to sales for Hillsburg Hardware Co. Notice that there is a one-to-one relationship between assertions and objectives, except for the accuracy assertion. The accuracy assertion has two objectives because of the need to provide auditors with guidance in testing transaction accuracy.

BALANCE-RELATED AND PRESENTATION AND DISCLOSURE-RELATED AUDIT OBJECTIVES

OBJECTIVE 6-10

Link balance-related and presentation and disclosure-related audit objectives to management assertions.

Balance-related audit objectives are similar to the transaction-related audit objectives just discussed. They also follow from management assertions and they provide a framework to help the auditor accumulate sufficient appropriate evidence related to account balances. Presentation and disclosure-related audit objectives are similar to both transaction-related and balance-related audit objectives, except that they focus on presentation of the financial statements and on the footnote disclosure information that accompanies those statements. There are also both general and specific balance-related and presentation and disclosure-related audit objectives.

There are two differences between balance-related and transaction-related audit objectives. First, as the terms imply, balance-related audit objectives are applied to account balances such as accounts receivable and inventory rather than classes of transactions such as sales transactions and purchases of inventory. Second, there are eight balance-related audit objectives compared to six transaction-related audit objectives.

Because of the way audits are performed, balance-related audit objectives are almost *always* applied to the ending balance in balance sheet accounts, such as accounts receivable, inventory, and notes payable. However, some balance-related audit objectives are applied to certain income statement accounts. These usually involve nonroutine transactions and unpredictable expenses, such as legal expense or repairs and maintenance. Other income statement accounts are closely related to balance sheet accounts and are tested simultaneously, such as depreciation expense with accumulated depreciation and interest expense with notes payable.

When using the balance-related audit objectives to audit account balances, the auditor accumulates evidence to verify detail that supports the account balance, rather than verifying the account balance itself. For example, in auditing accounts receivable, the auditor obtains a listing of the accounts receivable master file that agrees to the general ledger balance (see p. 532 for an illustration). The accounts receivable balance-related audit objectives are applied to the customer accounts in that listing.

There are four presentation and disclosure-related audit objectives that focus mostly on information included in the footnotes to the financial statements, including its accuracy and understandability. The presentation and disclosure-related audit objectives are similar to the transaction-related and balance-related audit objectives, except that they focus on the presentation of information in the form of financial statements and the related footnote disclosures.

General Balance-Related Audit Objectives

Throughout the following discussion of the eight balance-related audit objectives, we make references to a supporting schedule, by which we mean a client-provided schedule or electronic file, such as the list of accounts receivable just discussed.

Existence—Amounts Included Exist This objective deals with whether the amounts included in the financial statements should actually be included. For example, inclusion of an account receivable from a customer in the accounts receivable trial balance when there is no receivable from that customer violates the existence objective. This objective is the auditor's counterpart to the management assertion of existence for account balances.

Completeness—Existing Amounts Are Included This objective deals with whether all amounts that should be included have actually been included. Failure to include an account receivable from a customer in the accounts receivable trial balance when a receivable exists violates the completeness objective. This objective is the counterpart to the management assertion of completeness for account balances.

The existence and completeness objectives emphasize opposite audit concerns. Existence deals with potential overstatement; completeness deals with unrecorded amounts (understatement).

Accuracy—Amounts Included Are Stated at the Correct Amounts The accuracy objective refers to amounts being included at the correct amount. An inventory item on a client's inventory listing can be wrong because the number of units of inventory on hand was misstated, the unit price was wrong, or the total was incorrectly extended. Each of these violates the accuracy objective. Accuracy is one part of the valuation and allocation assertion for account balances.

Classification—Amounts Included in the Client's Listing Are Properly Classified Classification involves determining whether items included on a client's listing are included in the correct general ledger accounts. For example, on the accounts receivable listing, receivables must be separated into short-term and long-term, and amounts due from affiliates, officers, and directors must be classified separately from amounts due from customers. Classification is also part of the valuation and allocation assertion. The classification balance-related audit objective is closely related to the presentation and disclosure-related audit objectives, but relates to how balances are classified in general ledger accounts so they can be appropriately presented and disclosed in the financial statements.

Cutoff—Transactions Near the Balance Sheet Date Are Recorded in the Proper Period In testing for cutoff of account balances, the auditor's objective is to determine whether transactions are recorded and included in account balances in the proper period. An account balance will be misstated if transactions near the end of the accounting period are not properly recorded. For an annual audit, the end of the accounting period is the balance sheet date. Cutoff tests can be thought of as a part of verifying either the balance sheet accounts or the related transactions, but for convenience, auditors usually perform them as a part of auditing balance sheet accounts. For this reason, we also include cutoff as a balance-related audit objective related to the valuation and allocation assertion for account balances. The timing objective for transactions deals with the proper timing of recording transactions throughout the year, whereas the cutoff objective for balance-related audit objectives relates only to transactions near year-end. For example, in a December 31 year-end audit, a sales transaction recorded in March for a February shipment is a transaction-related audit objective error, but not a balance-related audit objective error.

Understand objectives and responsibilities for the audit

Divide financial statements into cycles

Know management assertions about financial statements

Know general audit objectives for classes of transactions, accounts, and disclosures

Know specific audit objectives for classes of transactions, accounts, and disclosures

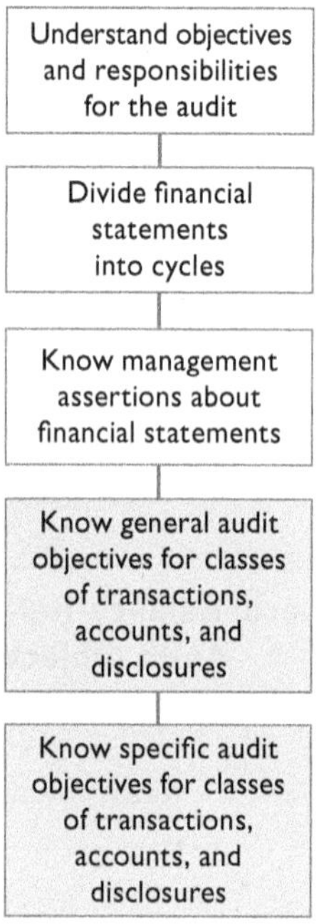

Detail Tie-In—Details in the Account Balance Agree with Related Master File Amounts, Foot to the Total in the Account Balance, and Agree with the Total in the General Ledger Account balances on financial statements are supported by details in master files and schedules prepared by clients. The detail tie-in objective is concerned that the details on lists are accurately prepared, correctly added, and agree with the general ledger. For example, individual accounts receivable on a listing of accounts receivable should be the same in the accounts receivable master file, and the total should equal the general ledger control account. Detail tie-in is also a part of the valuation and allocation assertion for account balances.

Realizable Value—Assets Are Included at the Amounts Estimated to Be Realized This objective concerns whether an account balance has been reduced for declines from historical cost to net realizable value or when accounting standards require fair market value accounting treatment. Examples when the objective applies are considering the adequacy of the allowance for uncollectible accounts receivable and write-downs of inventory for obsolescence. The objective generally applies only to asset accounts, although some liabilities are recorded at fair value, and is also a part of the valuation and allocation assertion for account balances.

Rights and Obligations In addition to existing, most assets must be owned before it is acceptable to include them in the financial statements. Similarly, liabilities must belong to the entity. Rights are always associated with assets and obligations with liabilities. This objective is the auditor's counterpart to the management assertion of rights and obligations for account balances.

Specific Balance-Related Audit Objectives

The same as for transaction-related audit objectives, after the general balance-related audit objectives are determined, specific balance-related audit objectives for each account balance on the financial statements can be developed. At least one specific balance-related audit objective should be included for each general balance-related audit objective unless the auditor believes that the general balance-related audit objective is not relevant or is unimportant for the account balance being considered. There may be more than one specific balance-related audit objective for a general balance-related audit objective. For example, specific balance-related audit objectives for rights and obligations of the inventory of Hillsburg Hardware Co. could include (1) the company has title to all inventory items listed and (2) inventory is not pledged as collateral for a loan unless it is disclosed.

TABLE 6-5 **Hillsburg Hardware Co.: Management Assertions and Balance-Related Audit Objectives Applied to Inventory**

Management Assertions About Account Balances	General Balance-Related Audit Objectives	Specific Balance-Related Audit Objectives Applied to Inventory
Existence	Existence	All recorded inventory exists at the balance sheet date.
Completeness	Completeness	All existing inventory has been counted and included in the inventory summary.
Valuation and allocation	Accuracy	Inventory quantities on the client's perpetual records agree with items physically on hand. Prices used to value inventories are materially correct. Extensions of price times quantity are correct and details are correctly added.
	Classification	Inventory items are properly classified as to raw materials, work in process, and finished goods.
	Cutoff	Purchase cutoff at year-end is proper. Sales cutoff at year-end is proper.
	Detail tie-in	Total of inventory items agrees with general ledger.
	Realizable value	Inventories have been written down where net realizable value is impaired.
Rights and obligations	Rights and obligations	The company has title to all inventory items listed. Inventories are not pledged as collateral.

Relationships Among Management Assertions and Balance-Related Audit Objectives

Table 6-5 illustrates the relationships among management assertions, the general balance-related audit objectives, and specific balance-related audit objectives as applied to inventory for Hillsburg Hardware Co. Notice that there is a one-to-one relationship between assertions and objectives, except for the valuation and allocation assertion. The valuation and allocation assertion has multiple objectives because of the complexity of valuation issues and the need to provide auditors with additional guidance for testing valuation.

Presentation and Disclosure-Related Audit Objectives

The presentation and disclosure-related audit objectives are identical to the management assertions for presentation and disclosure discussed previously. The same concepts that apply to balance-related audit objectives apply equally to presentation and disclosure audit objectives. Table 6-6 includes the management assertions about presentation and disclosure, related general presentation and disclosure-related audit objectives, and specific audit objectives for notes payable for Hillsburg Hardware Co.

TABLE 6-6 **Hillsburg Hardware Co.: Management Assertions and Presentation and Disclosure-Related Audit Objectives Applied to Notes Payable**

Management Assertions About Presentation and Disclosure	General Presentation and Disclosure-Related Audit Objectives	Specific Presentation and Disclosure-Related Audit Objectives Applied to Notes Payable
Occurrence and rights and obligations	Occurrence and rights and obligations	Notes payable as described in the footnotes exist and are obligations of the company.
Completeness	Completeness	All required disclosures related to notes payable are included in the financial statement footnotes.
Accuracy and valuation	Accuracy and valuation	Footnote disclosures related to notes payable are accurate.
Classification and understandability	Classification and understandability	Notes payable are appropriately classified as to short-term and long-term obligations, and related financial statement disclosures are understandable.

HOW AUDIT OBJECTIVES ARE MET

OBJECTIVE 6-11

Explain the relationship between audit objectives and the accumulation of audit evidence.

The auditor must obtain sufficient appropriate audit evidence to support all management assertions in the financial statements. This is done by accumulating evidence in support of some appropriate combination of transaction-related audit objectives and balance-related audit objectives. A comparison of Tables 6-4 (p. 162) and 6-5 (p. 165) illustrates the significant overlap between the transaction-related and balance-related audit objectives. Rights and obligations is the only balance-related assertion without a similar transaction-related assertion. Presentation and disclosure-related audit objectives are closely related to the balance-related audit objectives. Auditors often consider presentation and disclosure audit objectives when addressing the balance-related audit objectives.

The auditor must decide the appropriate audit objectives and the evidence to accumulate to meet those objectives on every audit. To do this, auditors follow an audit process, which is a well-defined methodology for organizing an audit to ensure that the evidence gathered is both sufficient and appropriate and that all required audit objectives are both specified and met. If the client is an accelerated filer public company, the auditor must also plan to meet the objectives associated with reporting on the effectiveness of internal control over financial reporting. PCAOB Auditing Standard 5 requires that the audit of the effectiveness of internal control be integrated with the audit of the financial statements. The audit process, as described in this text, has four specific phases, as shown in Figure 6-8. The rest of this chapter provides a brief introduction to each of the four **phases of the audit process**.

Plan and Design an Audit Approach (Phase I)

For any given audit, there are many ways in which an auditor can accumulate evidence to meet the overall audit objective of providing an opinion on the financial statements. Two overriding considerations affect the approach the auditor selects:

1. Sufficient appropriate evidence must be accumulated to meet the auditor's professional responsibility.
2. The cost of accumulating the evidence should be minimized.

The first consideration is the most important, but cost minimization is necessary if CPA firms are to be competitive and profitable. If there were no concern for controlling costs, evidence decision making would be easy. Auditors would keep adding evidence, without concern for efficiency, until they were sufficiently certain that there were no material misstatements.

Concern for sufficient appropriate evidence and cost control necessitates planning the engagement. The plan should result in an effective audit approach at a reasonable cost. The auditor performs procedures to assess the risk that material misstatements in the financial

FIGURE 6-8 Four Phases of a Financial Statement Audit

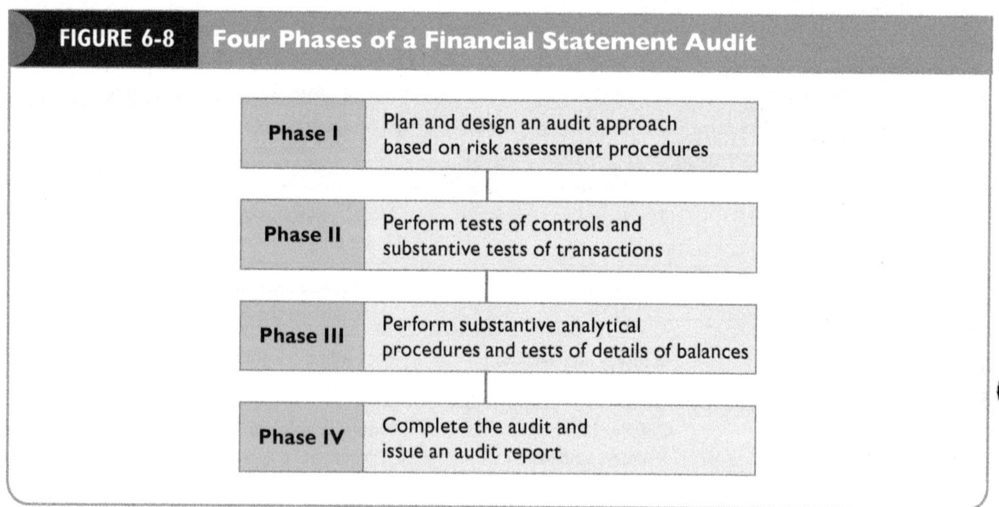
Phase I
Plan and design an audit approach based on risk assessment procedures
Phase II
Perform tests of controls and substantive tests of transactions
Phase III
Perform substantive analytical procedures and tests of details of balances
Phase IV
Complete the audit and issue an audit report

statements may be present. Those **risk assessment procedures** are a critical component to planning and designing an audit approach, which can be broken down into several parts. Three key aspects are introduced here and are discussed in subsequent chapters.

Obtain an Understanding of the Entity and Its Environment To adequately assess the risk of misstatements in the financial statements and to interpret information obtained throughout the audit, the auditor must have a thorough understanding of the client's business and related environment, including knowledge of strategies and processes. The auditor should study the client's business model, perform analytical procedures, and make comparisons to competitors. The auditor must also understand any unique accounting requirements of the client's industry. For example, when auditing an insurance company, the auditor must understand how loss reserves are calculated.

Understand Internal Control and Assess Control Risk The risk of misstatement in the financial statements is reduced if the client has effective controls over computer operations and transaction processing. In Chapter 2, we discussed how the ability of the client's internal controls to generate reliable financial information and safeguard assets and records is one of the most important and widely accepted concepts in the theory and practice of auditing. The auditor identifies internal controls and evaluates their effectiveness, a process called *assessing control risk*. If internal controls are considered effective, planned assessed control risk can be reduced and the amount of audit evidence to be accumulated can be significantly less than when internal controls are not adequate.

Assess Risk of Material Misstatement The auditor uses the understanding of the client's industry and business strategies, as well as the effectiveness of controls, to assess the risk of misstatements in the financial statements. This assessment will then impact the audit plan and the nature, timing, and extent of audit procedures. For example, if the client is expanding sales by taking on new customers with poor credit ratings, the auditor will assess a higher risk of misstatement for net realizable value of accounts receivable and plan to expand testing in this area.

Perform Tests of Controls and Substantive Tests of Transactions (Phase II)

Before auditors can justify reducing planned assessed control risk when internal controls are believed to be effective, they must first test the effectiveness of the controls. The procedures for this type of testing are commonly referred to as **tests of controls**. For example, assume a client's internal controls require computer matching of all relevant terms on the customer sales order, shipping document, and sales invoice before sales invoices are transmitted to customers. This control is directly related to the occurrence and accuracy transaction-related audit objectives for sales. The auditor might test the effectiveness of this control by comparing a sample of sales invoices to related shipping documents and customer sales orders, or by performing tests of the computerized controls related to this process.

Auditors also evaluate the client's recording of transactions by verifying the monetary amounts of transactions, a process called **substantive tests of transactions**. For example, the auditor might use computer software to compare the unit selling price on duplicate sales invoices with an electronic file of approved prices as a test of the accuracy objective for sales transactions. Like the test of control in the preceding paragraph, this test satisfies the accuracy transaction-related audit objective for sales. For the sake of efficiency, auditors often perform tests of controls and substantive tests of transactions at the same time.

Perform Substantive Analytical Procedures and Tests of Details of Balances (Phase III)

There are two general categories of phase III procedures. **Analytical procedures** consist of evaluations of financial information through analysis of plausible relationships among financial and nonfinancial data. When analytical procedures are used as evidence to provide assurance about an account balance, they are referred to as **substantive analytical procedures**. For example, to provide some assurance for the accuracy objective for both sales transactions (transaction-related audit objective) and accounts receivable (balance-related audit objective), the auditor might examine sales transactions in the sales journal for unusually large amounts and also compare total monthly sales with prior years. If a company is consistently using incorrect sales prices or improperly recording sales, significant differences are likely.

Tests of details of balances are specific procedures intended to test for monetary misstatements in the balances in the financial statements. An example related to the existence objective for accounts receivable (balance-related audit objective) is direct, written communication with the client's customers to identify whether the receivable exists. Tests of details of ending balances are essential to the conduct of the audit because much of the evidence is obtained from third-party sources and therefore is considered to be of high quality.

Complete the Audit and Issue an Audit Report (Phase IV)

After the auditor has completed all procedures for each audit objective and for each financial statement account and related disclosures, it is necessary to combine the information obtained to reach an *overall conclusion* as to whether the financial statements are fairly presented. This highly subjective process relies heavily on the auditor's professional judgment. When the audit is completed, the CPA must issue an audit report to accompany the client's published financial statements. These reports were discussed in Chapter 3.

CONCEPT CHECK

1. Describe what is meant by the cycle approach to auditing. What are the advantages of dividing the audit into different cycles?
2. Define what is meant by a management assertion about financial statements. Describe how PCAOB assertions and assertions in international and AICPA auditing standards are similar and different.

SUMMARY

This chapter described management's responsibility for the financial statements and internal control and the auditor's responsibility to audit the financial statements and the effectiveness of internal control over financial reporting. This chapter emphasized the critical importance of maintaining an attitude of professional skepticism and highlighted a professional judgment process to help auditor decision making. This chapter also discussed management assertions and the related objectives of the audit and the way the auditor subdivides an audit to result in specific audit objectives. The auditor then accumulates evidence to obtain assurance that each audit objective has been satisfied. The illustration for sales transactions and accounts receivable shows that the auditor can obtain assurance by accumulating evidence using tests of controls, substantive tests of transactions, substantive analytical procedures, and tests of details of balances. In some audits, there is more emphasis on certain tests such as substantive analytical procedures and tests of controls, whereas in others, there is emphasis on substantive tests of transactions and tests of details of balances.

ESSENTIAL TERMS

Analytical procedures—evaluations of financial information through analysis of plausible relationships among financial and nonfinancial data

Balance-related audit objectives—eight audit objectives that must be met before the auditor can conclude that any given account balance is fairly stated; the general balance-related audit objectives are existence, completeness, accuracy, classification, cutoff, detail tie-in, realizable value, and rights and obligations

Cycle approach—a method of dividing an audit by keeping closely related types of transactions and account balances in the same segment

Error—an unintentional misstatement of the financial statements

Fraud—an intentional misstatement of the financial statements

Fraudulent financial reporting—intentional misstatements or omissions of amounts or disclosures in financial statements to deceive users; often called management fraud

Management assertions—implied or expressed representations by management about classes of transactions, related account balances, and presentation and disclosures in the financial statements

Misappropriation of assets—a fraud involving the theft of an entity's assets; often called defalcation

Noncompliance with laws and regulations—failure to comply with applicable laws and regulations; often referred to as illegal acts

Phases of the audit process—the four aspects of a complete audit: (1) plan and design an audit approach, (2) perform tests of controls and substantive tests of transactions, (3) perform substantive analytical procedures and tests of details of balances, and (4) complete the audit and issue an audit report

Presentation and disclosure-related audit objectives—four audit objectives that must be met before the auditor can conclude that presentation and disclosures are fairly stated; the four presentation and disclosure-related audit objectives are occurrence and rights and obligations, completeness, accuracy and valuation, and classification and understandability

Professional skepticism—an attitude of the auditor that includes a questioning mind that is alert to conditions that may indicate possible misstatement due to fraud or error, and a critical assessment of audit evidence

Relevant assertions—assertions that have a meaningful bearing on whether an account is fairly stated and used to assess the risk of material misstatement and the design and performance of audit procedures

Risk assessment procedures—audit procedures performed to obtain an understanding of the entity and its environment, including the entity's internal control, to identify and assess the risks of material misstatement

Substantive analytical procedure—an analytical procedure in which the auditor develops an expectation of recorded amounts or ratios to provide evidence supporting an account balance

Substantive tests of transactions—audit procedures testing for monetary misstatements to determine whether the six transaction-related audit objectives have been satisfied for each class of transactions

Tests of controls—audit procedures to test the effectiveness of controls in support of a reduced assessed control risk

Tests of details of balances—audit procedures testing for monetary misstatements to determine whether the eight balance-related audit objectives have been satisfied for each significant account balance

Transaction-related audit objectives—six audit objectives that must be met before the auditor can conclude that the total for any given class of transactions is fairly stated; the general transaction-related audit objectives are occurrence, completeness, accuracy, classification, timing, and posting and summarization

REVIEW QUESTIONS

6-1 (OBJECTIVE 6-1) State the objective of the audit of financial statements. In general terms, how do auditors meet that objective?

6-2 (OBJECTIVE 6-3) Distinguish between the terms *errors* and *fraud*. What is the auditor's responsibility for finding each?

6-3 (OBJECTIVE 6-3) Distinguish between fraudulent financial reporting and misappropriation of assets. Discuss the likely difference between these two types of fraud on the fair presentation of financial statements.

6-4 (OBJECTIVE 6-3) List two major characteristics that are useful in predicting the likelihood of fraudulent financial reporting in an audit. For each of the characteristics, state two things that the auditor can do to evaluate its significance in the engagement.

6-5 (OBJECTIVE 6-3) Explain the auditor's responsibility to consider compliance with laws and regulations. How does this responsibility differ for laws and regulations that have a direct effect on the financial statements compared to other laws and regulations that do not have a direct effect?

6-6 **(OBJECTIVE 6-3)** What is the auditor's responsibility when noncompliance with laws or regulations is identified or suspected?

6-7 **(OBJECTIVE 6-4)** What are the six elements of professional skepticism? Describe two of those six elements.

6-8 **(OBJECTIVE 6-5)** What are the five elements of an effective professional judgment process?

6-9 **(OBJECTIVE 6-5)** Describe two of the more common judgment traps and biases.

6-10 **(OBJECTIVE 6-6)** Identify the cycle to which each of the following general ledger accounts will ordinarily be assigned: sales, accounts payable, retained earnings, accounts receivable, inventory, and repairs and maintenance.

6-11 **(OBJECTIVES 6-6, 6-7)** Why are sales, sales returns and allowances, bad debts, cash discounts, accounts receivable, and allowance for uncollectible accounts all included in the same cycle?

6-12 **(OBJECTIVE 6-8)** Identify the three broad categories of management assertions.

6-13 **(OBJECTIVES 6-7, 6-8)** Distinguish between the general audit objectives and management assertions. Why are the general audit objectives more useful to auditors?

6-14 **(OBJECTIVE 6-9)** An acquisition of a fixed-asset repair by a construction company is recorded on the wrong date. Which transaction-related audit objective has been violated? Which transaction-related audit objective has been violated if the acquisition had been capitalized as a fixed asset rather than expensed?

6-15 **(OBJECTIVE 6-10)** Distinguish between the existence and completeness balance-related audit objectives. State the effect on the financial statements (overstatement or understatement) of a violation of each in the audit of accounts receivable.

6-16 **(OBJECTIVES 6-9, 6-10)** What are specific audit objectives? Explain their relationship to the general audit objectives.

6-17 **(OBJECTIVES 6-8, 6-10)** Identify the management assertion and general balance-related audit objective for the specific balance-related audit objective: All recorded fixed assets exist at the balance sheet date.

6-18 **(OBJECTIVES 6-8, 6-10)** Identify the management assertion and presentation and disclosure-related audit objective for the specific presentation and disclosure-related audit objective: Read the fixed asset footnote disclosure to determine that the types of fixed assets, depreciation methods, and useful lives are clearly disclosed.

6-19 **(OBJECTIVE 6-11)** Identify the four phases of the audit. What is the relationship of the four phases to the objective of the audit of financial statements?

MULTIPLE CHOICE QUESTIONS FROM CPA EXAMINATIONS

6-20 **(OBJECTIVE 6-1)** The following questions concern the reasons auditors do audits. Choose the best response.

a. Which of the following best describes the reason why an independent auditor reports on financial statements?
   (1) A misappropriation of assets may exist, and it is more likely to be detected by independent auditors.
   (2) Different interests may exist between the company preparing the statements and the persons using the statements.
   (3) A misstatement of account balances may exist and is generally corrected as the result of the independent auditor's work.
   (4) Poorly designed internal controls may be in existence.

b. Because of the risk of material misstatement, an audit should be planned and performed with an attitude of
   (1) objective judgment.
   (2) independent integrity.
   (3) professional skepticism.
   (4) impartial conservatism.

c. The major reason an independent auditor gathers audit evidence is to
   (1) form an opinion on the financial statements.
   (2) detect fraud.
   (3) evaluate management.
   (4) assess control risk.

6-21 **(OBJECTIVE 6-3)** The following questions deal with errors and fraud. Choose the best response.

a. An independent auditor has the responsibility to design the audit to provide reasonable assurance of detecting errors and fraud that might have a material effect on the financial statements. Which of the following, if material, is a fraud as defined in auditing standards?
   (1) Misappropriation of an asset or groups of assets
   (2) Clerical mistakes in the accounting data underlying the financial statements
   (3) Mistakes in the application of accounting principles
   (4) Misinterpretation of facts that existed when the financial statements were prepared

b. What assurance does the auditor provide that errors and fraud that are material to the financial statements will be detected?

Errors	Fraud
(1) Limited	Negative
(2) Reasonable	Reasonable
(3) Limited	Limited
(4) Reasonable	Limited

c. Which of the following statements describes why a properly designed and executed audit may not detect a material misstatement in the financial statements resulting from fraud?
   (1) Audit procedures that are effective for detecting unintentional misstatements may be ineffective for an intentional misstatement that is concealed through collusion.
   (2) An audit is designed to provide reasonable assurance of detecting material errors, but there is no similar responsibility concerning fraud.
   (3) The factors considered in assessing control risk indicated an increased risk of intentional misstatements, but only a low risk of unintentional misstatements.
   (4) The auditor did not consider factors influencing audit risk for account balances that have effects pervasive to the financial statements taken as a whole.

6-22 **(OBJECTIVE 6-8)** The following questions deal with management assertions. Choose the best response.

a. An auditor reviews aged accounts receivable to assess likelihood of collection to support management's assertion about account balances of
   (1) existence.
   (2) completeness.
   (3) valuation and allocation.
   (4) rights and obligations.

b. An auditor will most likely review an entity's periodic accounting for the numerical sequence of shipping documents to ensure all documents are included to support management's assertion about classes of transactions of
   (1) occurrence.
   (2) completeness.
   (3) accuracy.
   (4) classification.

c. In the audit of accounts payable, an auditor's procedures will most likely focus primarily on management's assertion about account balances of
   (1) existence.
   (2) completeness.
   (3) valuation and allocation.
   (4) classification and understandability.

MULTIPLE CHOICE QUESTIONS FROM BECKER CPA EXAM REVIEW

6-23 **(OBJECTIVES 6-3, 6-11)** The following questions concern auditor responsibilities in an audit of financial statements. Choose the best response.

a. The auditor's responsibility regarding material misstatements caused by *fraud* is
   (1) less than the auditor's responsibility regarding material misstatements caused by *error*.
   (2) greater than the auditor's responsibility regarding material misstatements caused by *error*.
   (3) the same as the auditor's responsibility regarding material misstatements caused by *error*.
   (4) either less than or greater than the auditor's responsibility regarding material misstatements caused by *error*, depending on the circumstances.

b. When determining the auditor's or management's responsibility for compliance with laws and regulations during an audit, which of the following statements below would be incorrect?
   (1) The auditor is not responsible for preventing noncompliance with laws and regulations.
   (2) Management and those charged with governance are responsible for ensuring that the company's operations are conducted in accordance with all applicable laws and regulations.
   (3) The auditor provides reasonable assurance that the financial statements are free of material misstatement due to noncompliance with laws and regulations.
   (4) The auditor is expected to detect the client's noncompliance with all laws and regulations affecting transaction cycles under review during the audit itself.

c. While auditing a client's accounting estimates used for their specific elements and accounts, the auditor has certain responsibilities. Which of the following is not a required audit procedure that the auditor would perform when evaluating a client's accounting estimate?
   (1) Verify that all material accounting estimates have been developed.
   (2) Ensure that the accounting estimates used are properly disclosed in accordance with GAAP.
   (3) Determine if the accounting estimates used are consistent with those of the client's primary competitors.
   (4) Evaluate the degree of uncertainty that is associated with the client's accounting estimates.

DISCUSSION QUESTIONS AND PROBLEMS

6-24 **(OBJECTIVE 6-1)** This problem requires you to access authoritative standards to compare the objective of an audit as defined by AICPA auditing standards (see p. 145) and International Standards on Auditing (ISA 200) (www.iaasb.org) and the objective of an

audit of internal control over financial reporting as defined by PCAOB auditing standards (AS 5) (www.pcaobus.org).

Required

a. Compare the objective of an audit under AICPA Auditing Standards and International Standards on Auditing. Are there substantive differences in the objective of an audit as defined by these two sets of standards?
b. What is the objective of an audit of internal control over financial reporting according to PCAOB auditing standards?
c. What defines whether financial statements are fairly stated, and what defines whether internal control is considered effective? Are they related?

6-25 **(OBJECTIVES 6-2, 6-3)** The following are selected portions of the report of management from a published annual report.

Report of Management

Management's Report on Internal Control over Financial Reporting

The Company's management is responsible for establishing and maintaining adequate internal control over financial reporting. The Company's internal control over financial reporting is a process designed under the supervision of its President and Chief Executive Officer and Chief Financial Officer to provide reasonable assurance regarding the reliability of financial reporting and the preparation of the Company's financial statements for external reporting in accordance with accounting principles generally accepted in the United States of America. Management evaluates the effectiveness of the Company's internal control over financial reporting using the criteria set forth by the Committee of Sponsoring Organizations of the Treadway Commission (COSO) in *Internal Control–Integrated Framework*. Management, under the supervision and with the participation of the Company's President and Chief Executive Officer and Chief Financial Officer assessed the effectiveness of the Company's internal control over financial reporting as of December 31, 2016, and concluded it is effective.

Management's Responsibility for Consolidated Financial Statements

Management is also responsible for the preparation and content of the accompanying consolidated financial statements as well as all other related information contained in this annual report. These financial statements have been prepared in conformity with accounting principles generally accepted in the United States, and necessarily include amounts which are based on management's best estimates and judgments.

Required

a. What are the purposes of the two parts of the report of management?
b. What is the auditor's responsibility related to the report of management?

6-26 **(OBJECTIVES 6-1, 6-3)** Auditors provide "reasonable assurance" that the financial statements are "fairly stated, in all material respects." Questions are often raised as to the responsibility of the auditor to detect material misstatements, including misappropriation of assets and fraudulent financial reporting.

Required

a. Discuss the concept of "reasonable assurance" and the degree of confidence that financial statement users should have in the financial statements.
b. What are the responsibilities of the independent auditor in the audit of financial statements? Discuss fully, but in this part do not include fraud in the discussion.
c. What are the responsibilities of the independent auditor for the detection of fraud involving misappropriation of assets and fraudulent financial reporting? Discuss fully, including your assessment of whether the auditor's responsibility for the detection of fraud is appropriate.

6-27 **(OBJECTIVE 6-4)** The following information was obtained from several accounting and auditing enforcement releases issued by the Securities and Exchange

Commission (SEC) after its investigation of fraudulent financial reporting involving Just for Feet, Inc.:

> **Just for Feet, Inc.**, was a national retailer of athletic and outdoor footwear and apparel based in Birmingham, AL. The company incurred large amounts of advertising expenses and most vendors offered financial assistance through unwritten agreements with Just for Feet to help pay for these advertising expenses. If Just for Feet promoted a particular vendor's products in one of its advertisements, that vendor typically would consider agreeing to provide an "advertising co-op credit" to the Company to share the costs of the advertisement. Just for Feet offset this co-op revenue against advertising expense on its income statement, thereby increasing its net earnings. Although every vendor agreement was somewhat different, Just for Feet's receipt of advertising co-op revenue was contingent upon subsequent approval by the vendor. If the vendor approved the advertisement, it would usually issue the co-op payment to Just for Feet in the form of a credit memo offsetting expenses on Just for Feet's merchandise purchases from that vendor. The company's CFO, controller, and VP of Operations directed the company's accounting department to book co-op receivables and related revenues that they knew were not owed by certain vendors, including Asics, New Balance, Nike, and Reebok. These fraudulent practices resulted in over $19 million in fictitious pretax earnings being reported, out of total pretax income of approximately $43 million. The SEC ultimately brought charges against a number of senior executives at Just for Feet and some vendor representatives.

Required

a. What does it mean to approach an audit with an attitude of professional skepticism?
b. What circumstances related to the accounting treatment of the vendor allowances should increase an auditor's professional skepticism?
c. What factors might have caused the auditor to inappropriately accept the assertions by management that the vendor allowances should be reflected in the financial statements?
d. Develop three probing questions related to the vendor allowances that the auditor should have asked in the audit of Just for Feet's financial statements.

6-28 **(OBJECTIVE 6-5)** The following independent scenarios describe auditor decisions made during an audit engagement.

1. Chen Li worked on the audit of American Healthcare Associations (AHA), which operates hospitals and outpatient centers in Texas and Oklahoma. Chen was assigned responsibility to audit the allowance for patient receivables. For the past several years, AHA's accounting policy required that the recorded allowance for patient receivables be set to equal the total amount of receivables over 180 days past due. Prior audit testing of the allowance in previous years has found that the subsequent write-offs of patient receivables has closely approximated the amount included in the allowance. During the current year audit, Chen examined the amount recorded in the general ledger allowance account and reconciled that amount to the amount shown in AHA's consolidated aged trial balance in the 180 days past due amount. Given that the dollar amounts agreed, Chen concluded that the allowance was in accordance with AHA accounting policy and fairly stated. While media reports and other industry publications suggested that recent regulatory changes in healthcare insurance were affecting patients' ability to pay, Chen concluded that AHA's allowance was fairly stated given the amounts complied with AHA's policy.

2. Sherry Zipersky was assigned responsibility for evaluating the goodwill impairment testing process at Georgia Metals, Inc. Because Georgia Metals' growth strategy was based mostly on acquisitions, the company had experience in performing annual impairment tests of goodwill. The client provided Sherry extensive information along with detailed schedules that documented management's testing approaches, and it provided her support for key assumptions made by management. Sherry reviewed the schedules in detail and tested the key calculations. While Sherry's firm has a

number of valuation specialists as part of its staff, Sherry decided not to request their assistance in making an independent assessment of goodwill impairment given that the client's documentation was extensive and it would take too much time to have the firm's valuation specialists complete an independent assessment.

3. Jason Jackson was responsible for auditing the occurrence of sales transactions in the audit of Asheville Manufacturing. As part of his testing, he reviewed the contracts signed between Asheville Manufacturing and its customers to determine that the transaction terms justified the recording of sales for the year under audit. In addition, he examined documentation related to the sales transactions, including the customers' purchase orders, shipping documents, and invoices generated by Asheville. That evidence examined supported the correct recording of sales in the current year. However, Jason also noticed in the customer files copies of email exchanges between Asheville Manufacturing sales agents and the customers suggesting that some of the terms of the sales agreements could be waived at the customers' discretion. Jason decided to rely on the contracts and sales transactions documentation to conclude that the sales were properly stated, given that the other information was only included in emails.
4. Allison Garrett works on a number of audits of technology equipment manufacturers and has developed extensive knowledge and experience in the industry. On the recent audit engagement of financial statements for Zurich Technologies, Allison was responsible for auditing the valuation of inventories, including the reserve for obsolescence. Given her familiarity with the industry, Allison decided to conduct a quick substantive analytical procedure regarding the days in inventory and determined that the reserve was fairly stated, given it was in line with reserves established by some of her other clients. She determined that additional evidence was not necessary to obtain because of her experience with other clients.

For each of the scenarios listed above, describe the most likely judgment trap that ultimately biased the auditor's decision making in the audit. **Required**

6-29 **(OBJECTIVE 6-5)** The following general ledger accounts are included in the trial balance for an audit client, Jones Wholesale Stationery Store.

Accounts payable
Accounts receivable
Accrued interest expense
Accrued sales salaries
Accumulated depreciation—furniture and equipment
Advertising expense
Allowance for doubtful accounts
Bad debt expense
Cash
Common stock
Depreciation expense—furniture and equipment
Furniture and equipment
Income tax expense
Income tax payable
Insurance expense
Interest expense
Inventory
Loans payable
Notes payable
Notes receivable—trade
Prepaid insurance
Property tax expense
Property tax payable
Purchases
Rent expense
Retained earnings
Salaries, office and general
Sales
Sales salaries expense
Telecommunications expense

a. Identify the accounts in the trial balance that are likely to be included in each transaction cycle. Some accounts will be included in more than one cycle. Use the format that follows. **Required**

Cycle	Balance Sheet Accounts	Income Statement Accounts
Sales and collection		
Acquisition and payment		
Payroll and personnel		
Inventory and warehousing		
Capital acquisition and repayment		

b. How will the general ledger accounts in the trial balance most likely differ if the company were a retail store rather than a wholesale company? How will they differ for a hospital or a government unit?

6-30 **(OBJECTIVE 6-8)** The following are various management assertions (a. through m.) related to sales and accounts receivable.

Management Assertion

a. Receivables are appropriately classified as to trade and other receivables in the financial statements and are clearly described.
b. Sales transactions have been recorded in the proper period.
c. Accounts receivable are recorded at the correct amounts.
d. Sales transactions have been recorded in the appropriate accounts.
e. All required disclosures about sales and receivables have been made.
f. All accounts receivable have been recorded.
g. Disclosures related to receivables are at the correct amounts.
h. Sales transactions have been recorded at the correct amounts.
i. Recorded accounts receivable exist.
j. Disclosures related to sales and receivables relate to the entity.
k. Recorded sales transactions have occurred.
l. There are no liens or other restrictions on accounts receivable.
m. All sales transactions have been recorded.

Required

a. Explain the differences among management assertions about classes of transactions and events, management assertions about account balances, and management assertions about presentation and disclosure.
b. For each assertion, indicate whether it is an assertion about classes of transactions and events, an assertion about account balances, or an assertion about presentation and disclosure.
c. Indicate the name of the assertion made by management. (*Hint:* See Table 6-3 on p. 159.)

6-31 **(OBJECTIVES 6-8, 6-10)** The following are specific balance-related audit objectives applied to the audit of accounts receivable (a. through h.) and management assertions about account balances (1 through 4). The list referred to in the specific balance-related audit objectives is the list of the accounts receivable from each customer at the balance sheet date.

Specific Balance-Related Audit Objective

a. There are no unrecorded receivables.
b. Uncollectible accounts have been provided for.
c. Receivables that have become uncollectible have been written off.
d. All accounts on the list are expected to be collected within one year.
e. The total of the amounts on the accounts receivable listing agrees with the general ledger balance for accounts receivable.
f. All accounts on the list arose from the normal course of business and are not due from related parties.
g. Sales cutoff at year-end is proper.
h. Receivables have not been sold or discounted.

Management Assertion About Account Balances

1. Existence
2. Completeness
3. Valuation and allocation
4. Rights and obligations

Required

For each specific balance-related audit objective, identify the appropriate management assertion. (*Hint:* See Table 6-5 on p. 165.)

6-32 **(OBJECTIVES 6-8, 6-9)** The following are specific transaction-related audit objectives applied to the audit of cash disbursement transactions (a. through f.), management assertions about classes of transactions (1 through 5), and general transaction-related audit objectives (6 through 11).

Specific Transaction-Related Audit Objective

a. Existing cash disbursement transactions are recorded.
b. Recorded cash disbursement transactions are for the amount of goods or services received and are correctly recorded.
c. Cash disbursement transactions are properly included in the accounts payable master file and are correctly summarized.
d. Recorded cash disbursements are for goods and services actually received.
e. Cash disbursement transactions are properly classified.
f. Cash disbursement transactions are recorded on the correct dates.

Management Assertion About Classes of Transactions	General Transaction-Related Audit Objective
1. Occurrence	6. Occurrence
2. Completeness	7. Completeness
3. Accuracy	8. Accuracy
4. Classification	9. Posting and summarization
5. Cutoff	10. Classification
	11. Timing

Required

a. Explain the differences among management assertions about classes of transactions and events, general transaction-related audit objectives, and specific transaction-related audit objectives and their relationships to each other.
b. For each specific transaction-related audit objective, identify the appropriate management assertion.
c. For each specific transaction-related audit objective, identify the appropriate general transaction-related audit objective.

6-33 **(OBJECTIVE 6-10)** The following (1 through 18) are the balance-related, transaction-related, and presentation and disclosure-related audit objectives.

Balance-Related Audit Objectives	Transaction-Related Audit Objectives	Presentation and Disclosure Audit Objectives
1. Existence	9. Occurrence	15. Occurrence and rights
2. Completeness	10. Completeness	16. Completeness
3. Accuracy	11. Accuracy	17. Accuracy and valuation
4. Classification	12. Classification	18. Classification and understandability
5. Cutoff	13. Timing	
6. Detail tie-in	14. Posting and summarization	
7. Realizable value		
8. Rights and obligations		

Required

Identify the specific audit objective (1 through 18) that each of the following specific audit procedures (a. through l.) satisfies in the audit of sales, accounts receivable, and cash receipts for fiscal year ended December 31, 2016.

a. Examine a sample of duplicate sales invoices to determine whether each one has a shipping document attached.
b. Add all customer balances in the accounts receivable trial balance and agree the amount to the general ledger.
c. For a sample of sales transactions selected from the sales journal, verify that the amount of the transaction has been recorded in the correct customer account in the accounts receivable subledger.
d. Inquire of the client whether any accounts receivable balances have been pledged as collateral on long-term debt and determine whether all required information is included in the footnote description for long-term debt.
e. For a sample of shipping documents selected from shipping records, trace each shipping document to a transaction recorded in the sales journal.

f. Discuss with credit department personnel the likelihood of collection of all accounts as of December 31, 2016, with a balance greater than $100,000 and greater than 90 days old as of year end.
g. Examine sales invoices for the last five sales transactions recorded in the sales journal in 2016 and examine shipping documents to determine they are recorded in the correct period.
h. For a sample of customer accounts receivable balances at December 31, 2016, examine subsequent cash receipts in January 2017 to determine whether the customer paid the balance due.
i. Determine whether all risks related to accounts receivable are adequately disclosed.
j. Foot the sales journal for the month of July and trace postings to the general ledger.
k. Send letters to a sample of accounts receivable customers to verify whether they have an outstanding balance at December 31, 2016.
l. Determine whether long-term receivables and related party receivables are reported separately in the financial statements.

6-34 (OBJECTIVE 6-11) Following are seven audit activities.

a. Examine invoices supporting recorded fixed asset additions.
b. Review industry databases to assess the risk of material misstatement in the financial statements.
c. Summarize misstatements identified during testing to assess whether the overall financial statements are fairly stated.
d. Test computerized controls over credit approval for sales transactions.
e. Send letters to customers confirming outstanding accounts receivable balances.
f. Perform analytical procedures comparing the client with similar companies in the industry to gain an understanding of the client's business and strategies.
g. Compare information on purchases invoices recorded in the acquisitions journal with information on receiving reports.

Required For each activity listed above, indicate in which phase of the audit the procedure was likely performed.

a. Plan and design an audit approach based on risk assessment procedures (Phase I)
b. Perform tests of controls and substantive tests of transactions (Phase II)
c. Perform substantive analytical procedures and tests of details of balances (Phase III)
d. Complete the audit and issue an audit report (Phase IV)

AUDIT EVIDENCE

CHAPTER

7

LEARNING OBJECTIVES

After studying this chapter, you should be able to

7-1 Contrast audit evidence with evidence used by other professions.
7-2 Identify the four audit evidence decisions that are needed to create an audit program.
7-3 Specify the characteristics that determine the persuasiveness of evidence.
7-4 Identify and apply the eight types of evidence used in auditing.
7-5 Know the types of analytical procedures and their purposes.
7-6 Compute common financial ratios.
7-7 Understand the purposes of audit documentation.
7-8 Prepare organized audit documentation.

CEO Confesses to Falsifying Documents to Hide Fraud for Over Twenty Years

Nine days after his surprise Las Vegas wedding, Russell Wasendorf, Chief Executive Officer of Peregrine Financial Group, was found unconscious in his car with a tube running from the exhaust pipe into the vehicle. By week's end, regulators had discovered that approximately $215 million in customer money was missing, the futures trading firm had filed for Chapter 7 liquidating bankruptcy, and its fancy offices were closed. A suicide note was found inside the car that admitted the CEO had committed fraud for over 20 years.

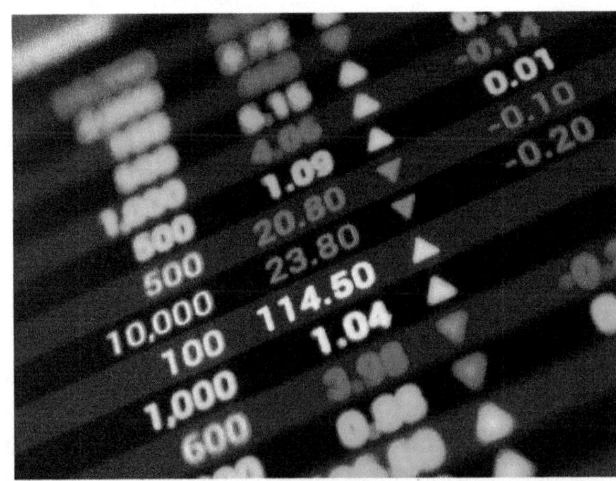

The fraud was exposed when the National Futures Association (NFA) sent an audit team to review Peregrine's books and pressure Peregrine into participating in a new online system for verifying accounts, which would have likely made it impossible for Wasendorf to continue the fraud. Wasendorf had fooled the NFA a year earlier after the regulator received a report on a Friday that Peregrine's account for customer balances had less than $10 million. The following Monday, the NFA received a fax purportedly from the bank indicating the account held more than $200 million; investigation revealed that the fax had been sent by Wasendorf.

In the signed note found in his car, Mr. Wasendorf admitted to using basic computer software programs to make "very convincing forgeries" of bank statements and official correspondence from the bank. To prevent other Peregrine employees from learning about the real bank balances, Wasendorf insisted that only he could open mail from the bank. Auditors typically confirm bank balances directly with the bank. However, Wasendorf supplied the auditor with the address for a post office box that he controlled for the mailing of the confirmations.

Although Wasendorf's son was Peregrine's president, Wasendorf claims that he was the sole perpetrator of the fraud. He indicated that the scheme began out of financial desperation as he was unable to obtain capital. He admits to taking less than half of the $215 million investigators claim is missing, and investigators continue to track the missing funds. Some called for leniency because of Wasendorf's support for charities, but the judge imposed the maximum 50-year sentence.

Sources: 1. P.J. Huffstutter, "Peregrine Boss Wasendorf Gets 50 Years Jail for Fraud," Reuters (January 30, 2013) (www.reuters.com); 2. Jacob Bunge, Scott Patterson, and Julie Steinberg, "Peregrine CEO's Dramatic Confession," *The Wall Street Journal* (July 14-15, 2012) (www.wsj.com); 3. Jacob Bunge, "Peregrine CEO Arrested," *The Wall Street Journal* (July 13, 2012) (www.wsj.com); 4. Azam Ahmed and Peter Lattman, "At Peregrine Financial, Signs of Trouble Seemingly Missed for Years," *The New York Times* (July 13, 2012) (www.nytimes.com).

The foundation of any audit is the evidence obtained and evaluated by the auditor. The auditor must have the knowledge and skill to accumulate sufficient appropriate evidence on every audit to meet the standards of the profession. As described in this opening story, new technologies can improve the quality of audit evidence, but can also create new opportunities for evidence to be compromised. This chapter deals with the types of evidence decisions auditors make, the evidence available to auditors, and the use of that evidence in performing audits and documenting the results.

NATURE OF EVIDENCE

OBJECTIVE 7-1

Contrast audit evidence with evidence used by other professions.

Evidence was defined in Chapter 1 as any *information used by the auditor* to determine whether the information being audited is stated in accordance with the established criteria. The information varies greatly in the extent to which it persuades the auditor whether financial statements are fairly stated. Evidence includes information that is highly persuasive, such as the auditor's count of marketable securities, and less persuasive information, such as responses to questions of client employees.

Audit Evidence Contrasted with Legal and Scientific Evidence

The use of evidence is not unique to auditors. Evidence is also used extensively by scientists, lawyers, and historians. For example, most people are familiar with legal dramas on television in which evidence is collected and used to argue for the guilt or innocence of a party charged with a crime. In legal cases, there are well-defined rules of evidence enforced by the judge for the protection of the innocent. In scientific experiments, researchers obtain evidence to test hypotheses using controlled experiments, such as a drug trial to test the effectiveness of a new medical treatment. Similarly, gathering evidence is a large part of what auditors do. Although these professionals rely on different types of evidence, and use evidence in different settings and in different ways, lawyers, scientists, and auditors all use evidence to help them draw conclusions.

Table 7-1 illustrates six key characteristics of evidence from the perspectives of a scientist doing an experiment, an attorney prosecuting an accused thief, and an auditor of financial statements. There are six bases of comparison. Notice the similarities and differences among these three professions.

TABLE 7-1 Characteristics of Evidence for a Scientific Experiment, Legal Case, and Audit of Financial Statements

Basis of Comparison	Scientific Experiment Involving Testing a Medicine	Legal Case Involving an Accused Thief	Audit of Financial Statements
Use of the evidence	Determine effects of using the medicine	Decide guilt or innocence of accused	Determine whether statements are fairly presented
Nature of evidence used	Results of repeated experiments	Direct evidence and testimony by witnesses and parties involved	Various types of audit evidence generated by the auditor, third parties, and the client
Party or parties evaluating evidence	Scientist	Jury and judge	Auditor
Certainty of conclusions from evidence	Vary from uncertain to near certainty	Requires guilt beyond a reasonable doubt	High level of assurance
Nature of conclusions	Recommend or not recommend use of medicine	Innocence or guilt of party	Issue one of several alternative types of audit reports
Typical consequences of incorrect conclusions from evidence	Society uses ineffective or harmful medicine	Guilty party is not penalized or innocent party is found guilty	Statement users make incorrect decisions and auditor may be sued

AUDIT EVIDENCE DECISIONS

OBJECTIVE 7-2

Identify the four audit evidence decisions that are needed to create an audit program.

A major decision facing every auditor is determining the *appropriate types and amounts* of evidence needed to be satisfied that the client's financial statements are fairly stated. There are four *decisions* about what evidence to gather and how much of it to accumulate:

1. Which audit procedures to use
2. What sample size to select for a given procedure
3. Which items to select from the population
4. When to perform the procedures

Audit Procedures

An **audit procedure** is the detailed instruction that explains the audit evidence to be obtained during the audit. It is common to spell out these procedures in sufficiently specific terms so an auditor may follow these instructions during the audit. For example, the following is an audit procedure for the verification of cash disbursements:

- Examine the cash disbursements journal in the accounting system and compare the payee, name, amount, and date with online information provided by the bank about checks and electronic transfers processed for the account.

Sample Size

Once an audit procedure is selected, auditors can vary the sample size from one to all the items in the population being tested. In an audit procedure to verify cash disbursements, suppose 6,600 checks and electronic transfers are recorded in the cash disbursements journal. The auditor might select a sample size of 50 disbursements for comparison with the cash disbursements journal. The decision of how many items to test must be made by the auditor for each audit procedure. The sample size for any given procedure is likely to vary from audit to audit, depending on client characteristics such as the extent of automated controls and the required level of assurance from the procedure.

Items to Select

After determining the sample size for an audit procedure, the auditor must decide which items in the population to test. If the auditor decides, for example, to select 50 disbursements from a population of 6,600 for comparison with the cash disbursements journal, several different methods can be used to select the specific items to be examined. The auditor can (1) select a week and examine the first 50 transactions, (2) select the 50 disbursements with the largest amounts, (3) select the items randomly, or (4) select those transactions that the auditor thinks are most likely to be in error. Or, a combination of these methods can be used.

Timing

An audit of financial statements usually covers a period such as a year. Normally, an audit is not completed until several weeks or months after the end of the period. The timing of audit procedures can therefore vary from early in the accounting period to long after it has ended. In part, the timing decision is affected by when the client needs the audit to be completed. In the audit of financial statements, the client normally wants the audit completed one to three months after year-end. The SEC currently requires that all public companies file audited financial statements with the SEC within 60 to 90 days of the company's fiscal year-end, depending on the company's size. However, timing is also influenced by when the auditor believes the audit evidence will be most effective and when audit staff is available. For example, auditors often prefer to do counts of inventory as close to the balance sheet date as possible.

Audit procedures often incorporate sample size, items to select, and timing into the procedure. The following is a modification of the audit procedure previously used to include all four audit evidence decisions. (Italics identify the timing, items to select, and sample size decisions.)

- Obtain the *October* cash disbursements journal and compare the payee name, amount, and date on the cancelled check or electronic transfer information with the cash disbursements journal for a *randomly selected sample of* 40 disbursements.

Audit Program

The list of audit procedures for an audit area or an entire audit is called an **audit program**. The audit program always includes a list of the audit procedures, and it usually includes sample sizes, items to select, and the timing of the tests. Audit engagement software assists the auditor in selecting the procedures to be performed and other evidence decisions, based on identified risks and other audit planning decisions. Normally, there is an audit program, including several audit procedures, for each component of the audit. Therefore, there will be an audit program for accounts receivable, one for sales, and so on. (To see an example of an audit program that includes audit procedures, sample size, items to select, and timing, turn to page 427 and see Table 13-4. The right side of the audit program also includes the balance-related audit objectives for each procedure, which were discussed in Chapter 6.)

PERSUASIVENESS OF EVIDENCE

OBJECTIVE 7-3

Specify the characteristics that determine the persuasiveness of evidence.

Audit standards require the auditor to accumulate *sufficient appropriate evidence to support the opinion issued.* Because of the nature of audit evidence and the cost considerations of doing an audit, it is unlikely that the auditor will be completely convinced that the opinion is correct. However, the auditor must be persuaded that the opinion is correct with a high level of assurance. By combining all evidence from the entire audit, the auditor is able to decide when he or she is persuaded to issue an audit report. The two determinants of the **persuasiveness of evidence** are *appropriateness* and *sufficiency.*

Appropriateness

Appropriateness of evidence is a measure of the quality of evidence, meaning its relevance and reliability in meeting audit objectives for classes of transactions, account balances, and related disclosures. If evidence is considered highly appropriate, it is a great help in persuading the auditor that financial statements are fairly stated.

Note that appropriateness of evidence deals only with the audit procedures selected. Appropriateness cannot be improved by selecting a larger sample size or different population items. It can be improved only by selecting audit procedures that are more relevant or provide more reliable evidence.

Relevance of Evidence Evidence must *pertain to or be relevant to the audit objective* that the auditor is testing before it can be appropriate. For example, assume that the auditor is concerned that a client is failing to bill customers for shipments (completeness transaction objective). If the auditor selects a sample of duplicate sales invoices and traces each to related shipping documents, the evidence is *not relevant* for the completeness objective and therefore is not appropriate evidence for that objective. A relevant procedure is to trace a sample of shipping documents to related duplicate sales invoices to determine whether each shipment was billed. The second audit procedure is relevant because the shipment of goods is the normal criterion used for determining whether a sale has occurred and should have been billed. By tracing from shipping documents to duplicate sales invoices, the auditor can determine whether shipments have been billed to customers. In the first procedure, when the auditor traces from duplicate sales invoices to shipping documents, it is impossible to find unbilled shipments.

Relevance can be considered only in terms of specific audit objectives, because evidence may be relevant for one audit objective but not for a different one. In the previous shipping example, when the auditor traced from the duplicate sales invoices to related shipping documents, the evidence was relevant for the occurrence transaction objective. Most evidence is relevant for more than one, but not all, audit objectives.

Reliability of Evidence **Reliability of evidence** refers to the degree to which evidence can be believable or worthy of trust. Like relevance, if evidence is considered reliable it is a great help in persuading the auditor that financial statements are fairly stated. For example, if an auditor counts inventory, that evidence is more reliable than if management gives the auditor its own count amounts.

Reliability, and therefore appropriateness, depends on the following six characteristics of reliable evidence:

1. *Independence of provider.* Evidence obtained from a source outside the entity is more reliable than that obtained from within. Communications from banks, attorneys, or customers is generally considered more reliable than answers obtained from inquiries of the client. Similarly, documents that originate from outside the client's organization, such as an insurance policy, are considered more reliable than are those that originate within the company and have never left the client's organization, such as a purchase requisition.
2. *Effectiveness of client's internal controls.* When a client's internal controls are effective, evidence obtained is more reliable than when they are not effective. For example, if internal controls over sales and billing are effective, the auditor can obtain more reliable evidence from sales invoices and shipping documents than if the controls were inadequate.
3. *Auditor's direct knowledge.* Evidence obtained directly by the auditor through physical examination, observation, recalculation, and inspection is more reliable than information obtained indirectly. For example, if the auditor calculates the gross margin as a percentage of sales and compares it with previous periods, the evidence is more reliable than if the auditor relies on the calculations of the controller.
4. *Qualifications of individuals providing the information.* Although the source of information is independent, the evidence will not be reliable unless the individual providing it is qualified to do so. Therefore, communications from attorneys and bank confirmations are typically more highly regarded than accounts receivable confirmations from persons not familiar with the business world. Also, evidence obtained directly by the auditor may not be reliable if the auditor lacks the qualifications to evaluate the evidence. For example, examining an inventory of diamonds by an auditor not trained to distinguish between diamonds and cubic zirconia is not reliable evidence for the existence of diamonds.
5. *Degree of objectivity.* Objective evidence is more reliable than evidence that requires considerable judgment to determine whether it is correct. Examples of objective evidence include confirmation of accounts receivable and bank balances, the physical count of securities and cash, and adding (footing) a list of accounts payable to determine whether it agrees with the balance in the general ledger. Examples of subjective evidence include a letter written by a client's attorney discussing the likely outcome of outstanding lawsuits against the client, observation of obsolescence of inventory during physical examination, and inquiries of the credit manager about the collectibility of noncurrent accounts receivable.
6. *Timeliness.* The timeliness of audit evidence can refer either to when it is accumulated or to the period covered by the audit. Evidence is usually more reliable for balance sheet accounts when it is obtained as close to the balance sheet date as possible. For example, the auditor's count of marketable securities on the balance sheet date is more reliable than a count two months earlier. For income statement accounts, evidence is more reliable if there is a sample from the entire period under audit, such as a random sample of sales transactions for the entire year, rather than from only a part of the period, such as a sample limited to only the first six months.

Sufficiency

The *quantity* of evidence obtained determines its sufficiency. For some audit objectives, **sufficiency of evidence** is measured primarily by the sample size the auditor selects. For a given audit procedure, the evidence obtained from a sample of 100 is ordinarily more sufficient than from a sample of 50. For other objectives, sufficiency is determined primarily by the number and quality of procedures performed to meet the audit objective.

Several factors determine the appropriate sample size in audits. The two most important ones are the auditor's expectation of misstatements and the effectiveness of the client's internal controls. To illustrate, assume in the audit of Jones Computer Parts Co. that the auditor concludes that there is a high likelihood of obsolete inventory because of the nature of the client's industry. The auditor will sample more inventory items for obsolescence in this audit than one where the likelihood of obsolescence is low. Similarly, if the auditor concludes that a client has effective rather than ineffective internal controls over recording fixed assets, a smaller sample size in the audit of acquisitions of fixed assets may be warranted.

In addition to sample size, the individual items tested affect the sufficiency of evidence. Samples containing population items with large dollar values, items with a high likelihood of misstatement, and items that are representative of the population are usually considered sufficient. In contrast, most auditors usually consider samples insufficient that contain only the largest dollar items from the population, unless these items make up a large portion of the total population amount.

Combined Effect

The persuasiveness of evidence can be evaluated only after considering the combination of appropriateness and sufficiency, including the effects of the factors influencing appropriateness and sufficiency. A large sample of evidence provided by an independent party is not persuasive unless it is relevant to the audit objective being tested. A large sample of evidence that is relevant but not objective is also not persuasive. Similarly, a small sample of only one or two pieces of highly appropriate evidence also typically lacks persuasiveness. When determining the persuasiveness of evidence, the auditor must evaluate the degree to which both appropriateness and sufficiency, including all factors influencing them, have been met.

Direct relationships among the four evidence decisions and the two qualities that determine the persuasiveness of evidence are shown in Table 7-2. To illustrate these relationships, assume an auditor is verifying inventory that is a major item in the financial statements. Auditing standards require that the auditor be reasonably persuaded that inventory is not materially misstated. The auditor must therefore obtain a sufficient amount of relevant and reliable evidence about inventory. This means deciding which procedures to use for auditing inventory, as well as determining the sample size and items to select from the population to satisfy the sufficiency requirement. The combination of these four evidence decisions must result in sufficiently persuasive evidence to satisfy the auditor that inventory is materially correct.

Persuasiveness and Cost

In making decisions about evidence for a given audit, both persuasiveness and cost must be considered. It is rare when only one type of evidence is available for verifying information. The persuasiveness and cost of all alternatives should be considered before selecting the best type or types of evidence. The auditor's goal is to obtain a

TABLE 7-2 Relationships Among Evidence Decisions and Persuasiveness

Audit Evidence Decisions	Qualities Affecting Persuasiveness of Evidence

Audit procedures and timing	Appropriateness
	  Relevance
	  Reliability
	    Independence of provider
	    Effectiveness of internal controls
	    Auditor's direct knowledge
	    Qualifications of provider
	    Objectivity of evidence
	  Timeliness
	    When procedures are performed
	    Portion of period being audited

Sample size and items to select	Sufficiency
	  Adequate sample size
	  Selection of proper population items

sufficient amount of appropriate evidence at the lowest possible total cost. However, cost is never an adequate justification for omitting a necessary procedure or not gathering an adequate sample size.

TYPES OF AUDIT EVIDENCE

OBJECTIVE 7-4

Identify and apply the eight types of evidence used in auditing.

In deciding which audit procedures to use, the auditor can choose from eight broad categories of evidence, which are called *types of evidence*. Every audit procedure obtains one or more of the following types of evidence:

1. Physical examination
2. Confirmation
3. Inspection
4. Analytical procedures
5. Inquiries of the client
6. Recalculation
7. Reperformance
8. Observation

Figure 7-1 shows the relationships among auditing standards, types of evidence, and the four evidence decisions. Auditing standards provide general guidance in three categories, including evidence accumulation. The types of evidence are broad categories of the evidence that can be accumulated. Audit procedures include the four evidence decisions and provide specific instructions for the accumulation of evidence.

FIGURE 7-1 Relationships Among Auditing Standards, Types of Evidence, and the Four Audit Evidence Decisions

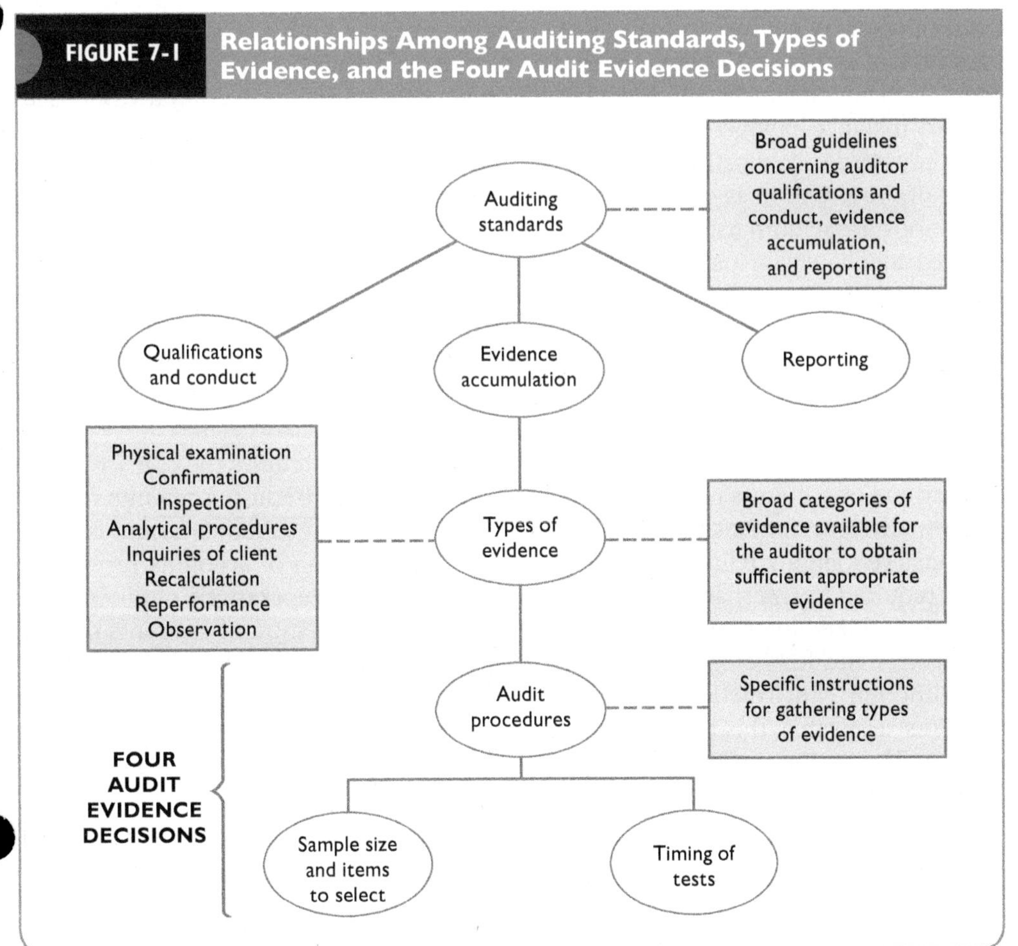

Physical Examination

Physical examination is the inspection or count by the auditor of a *tangible asset.* This type of evidence is most often associated with inventory and cash, but it is also applicable to the verification of securities, notes receivable, and tangible fixed assets. There is a distinction in auditing between the inspection or physical examination of assets, such as marketable securities and cash, and the inspection of documents, such as cancelled checks and sales documents. If the object being examined, such as a sales invoice, has no inherent value, the evidence being inspected is called documentation. While AICPA auditing standards and PCAOB auditing standards refer to inspection of physical assets and inspection of documents as one type of evidence, we separate them into physical examination of assets and inspection of documents in this text to help auditors distinguish the nature of these types of evidence.

Physical examination is a direct means of verifying that an asset actually exists (existence objective), and is considered one of the most reliable and useful types of audit evidence. Generally, physical examination is an objective means of ascertaining both the quantity and the description of the asset. In some cases, it is also a useful method for evaluating an asset's condition or quality. However, physical examination is not sufficient evidence to verify that existing assets are owned by the client (rights and obligations objective), and proper valuation for financial statement purposes usually cannot be determined by physical examination (accuracy and realizable value objectives).

Confirmation

Confirmation describes the *receipt* of a *direct written response* from a *third party* verifying the accuracy of information that was *requested by the auditor.* The response may be in paper form or electronic or other medium, such as the auditor's direct access to information held by the third party. The request is made to the client, and the client asks the third party to respond directly to the auditor. Because confirmations come from third-party sources instead of the client, they are a highly regarded and often-used type of evidence. However, confirmations are relatively costly to obtain and may cause some inconvenience to those asked to supply them. Therefore, they are not used in every instance in which they are applicable.

Auditors decide whether or not to use confirmations depending on the reliability needs of the situation as well as the alternative evidence available. For example, confirmations are seldom used in the audit of fixed asset additions because these can be verified adequately by inspection and physical examination. Similarly, confirmations are ordinarily not used to verify individual transactions between organizations, such as sales transactions, because the auditor can use documents for that purpose. Naturally, there are exceptions. Assume the auditor determines that there are two extraordinarily large sales transactions recorded three days before year-end. Confirmation of these two transactions may be appropriate.

When practical and reasonable, U.S. auditing standards require the confirmation of a sample of accounts receivable. This requirement exists because accounts receivable usually represent a significant balance on the financial statements, and confirmations are a highly reliable type of evidence. Confirmation of accounts receivable is not required by international auditing standards, and is one example of differences between U.S. and international auditing standards. Confirmation of accounts receivable is discussed further in Chapter 16.

Although confirmation is currently not required for any account other than accounts receivable, this type of evidence is useful in verifying many types of information. The major types of information that are often confirmed, along with the source of the confirmation, are indicated in Table 7-3.

Inspection

Inspection is the auditor's examination of the *client's documents and records* to substantiate the information that is, or should be, included in the financial statements. The documents examined by the auditor are the records used by the client to provide

TABLE 7-3 Information Often Confirmed

Information	Source
Assets	
Cash in bank	Bank
Marketable securities	Investment custodian
Accounts receivable	Customer
Notes receivable	Maker
Owned inventory out on consignment	Consignee
Inventory held in public warehouses	Public warehouse
Cash surrender value of life insurance	Insurance company
Liabilities	
Accounts payable	Creditor
Notes payable	Lender
Advances from customers	Customer
Mortgages payable	Mortgagor
Bonds payable	Bondholder
Owners' Equity	
Shares outstanding	Registrar and transfer agent
Other Information	
Insurance coverage	Insurance company
Contingent liabilities	Bank, lender, and client's legal counsel
Bond indenture agreements	Bondholder
Collateral held by creditors	Creditor

information for conducting its business in an organized manner, and may be in paper form, electronic form, or other media. Because each transaction in the client's organization is normally supported by at least one document, a large volume of this type of evidence is usually available. For example, the client often retains a customer order, a shipping document, and a duplicate sales invoice for each sales transaction. These same documents are useful evidence for the auditor to verify the accuracy of the client's records for sales transactions. Documentation is widely used as evidence in audits because it is usually readily available at a relatively low cost. Sometimes, it is the only reasonable type of evidence available.

Documents can be conveniently classified as internal and external. An **internal document** has been prepared and used within the client's organization and is retained without ever going to an outside party. Internal documents include duplicate sales invoices, employees' time reports, and inventory receiving reports.

ELECTRONIC CONFIRMATIONS

Confirmations have traditionally been mailed in paper form, but several factors have helped promote the use of electronic confirmations of bank balances and other information. An interpretation of an earlier confirmation standard indicated that confirmation requests may be transmitted and received electronically. After a fraud at Parmalat involving a fraudulent bank confirmation, Bank of America announced that it would only respond to bank confirmation requests submitted electronically through a designated third-party service provider. The third party provides a secure environment for transmitting the confirmation to authenticated confirmation respondents, reducing the risk of interception and response time.

The clarified confirmation standard indicates that direct access to information held by the third party (the confirming party) may meet the definition of an external confirmation if the electronic access codes or information necessary to access a secure Web site is provided to the auditor by the confirming party or third-party service provider. However, if the access information is provided to the auditor by management, the evidence obtained from accessing the information does not meet the definition of an external confirmation.

Sources: 1. AU-C Section 505, *External Confirmations*; 2. *Guidance for Dealing with Electronic Confirmations*, November 13, 2008 (www.journalofaccountancy.com).

An **external document** has been handled by someone outside the client's organization who is a party to the transaction being documented, but that is either currently held by the client or readily accessible. In some cases, external documents originate outside the client's organization and end up in the hands of the client. Examples of external documents include vendors' invoices, cancelled notes payable, and insurance policies. Some documents, such as cancelled checks, originate with the client, go to an outsider, and are finally returned to the client.

The primary determinant of the auditor's willingness to accept a document as reliable evidence is whether it is internal or external and, when internal, whether it was created and processed under conditions of effective internal control. Internal documents created and processed under conditions of deficient internal control may not constitute reliable evidence. Documentary evidence in either paper or electronic form is more reliable than the same evidence obtained orally, and original documents are more reliable than photocopies or documents that have been digitized. Although auditors should consider the reliability of documentation, they rarely verify the authenticity of documentation. Auditors are not expected to be trained or be experts in document authentication.

Because external documents have been in the hands of both the client and another party to the transaction, there is some indication that both members are in agreement about the information and the conditions stated on the document. Therefore, external documents are considered more reliable evidence than internal ones. Some external documents, such as title to land, insurance policies, indenture agreements, and contracts, have exceptional reliability because they are almost always prepared with considerable care and often have been reviewed by attorneys or other qualified experts.

When auditors use documentation to support recorded transactions or amounts, the process is often called **vouching**. To vouch recorded acquisition transactions, the auditor might, for example, verify entries in the acquisitions journal by examining supporting vendors' invoices and receiving reports and thereby satisfy the occurrence objective. If the auditor traces from receiving reports to the acquisitions journal to satisfy the completeness objective, this latter process is called **tracing**.

Analytical Procedures

Analytical procedures are defined by auditing standards as *evaluations of financial information through analysis of plausible relationships among financial and nonfinancial data.* For example, an auditor may compare the gross margin percent in the current year with the preceding year's gross margin. Analytical procedures are used extensively in practice, and are *required during the planning and completion phases on all audits.* We first introduce the purposes of analytical procedures and then discuss the different types of analytical procedures more extensively.

Understand the Client's Industry and Business Auditors must obtain knowledge about a client's industry and business as a part of planning an audit. By conducting analytical procedures in which the current year's unaudited information is compared with prior years' audited information or industry data, changes are highlighted. These changes can represent important trends or specific events, all of which will influence audit planning. For example, a decline in gross margin percentages over time may indicate increasing competition in the company's market area and the need to consider inventory pricing more carefully during the audit. Similarly, an increase in the balance in fixed assets may indicate a significant acquisition that must be reviewed.

Assess the Entity's Ability to Continue as a Going Concern Analytical procedures are often a useful indicator for determining whether the client company has financial problems. Certain analytical procedures can help the auditor assess the likelihood of failure. For example, if a higher-than-normal ratio of long-term debt to net worth is combined with a lower-than-average ratio of profits to total assets, a relatively high risk of financial failure may be indicated. Not only will such conditions affect the audit plan, they may indicate that substantial doubt exists about the entity's ability to continue as a going concern, which, as discussed in Chapter 3, requires an emphasis-of-matter explanatory paragraph in the audit report.

Indicate the Presence of Possible Misstatements in the Financial Statements Significant unexpected differences between the current year's unaudited financial data and other data used in comparisons are commonly called **unusual fluctuations.** Unusual fluctuations occur when significant differences are not expected but do exist, or when significant differences are expected but do not exist. In either case, the presence of an accounting misstatement is one possible reason for the unusual fluctuation. If the unusual fluctuation is large, the auditor must determine the reason and be satisfied that the cause is a valid economic event and not a misstatement. For example, in comparing the ratio of the allowance for uncollectible accounts receivable to gross accounts receivable with that of the previous year, suppose that the ratio has decreased while, at the same time, accounts receivable turnover also decreased. The combination of these two pieces of information indicates a possible understatement of the allowance. This aspect of analytical procedures is often called "attention directing" because it results in more detailed procedures in the specific audit areas where misstatements might be found.

Provide Evidence Supporting an Account Balance In many cases, an analytical procedure can be used to provide evidence supporting recorded account balances. When a predictable relationship exists and the analytical procedure is based on reliable inputs, **substantive analytical procedures** may be performed, although they are not required. In such cases, the analytical procedure constitutes substantive evidence in support of the related account balances. Depending on the significance of the account, the predictability of the relationship, and the reliability of the underlying data, the substantive analytical procedure may eliminate the need to perform detailed tests of the account balance. In other cases, detailed tests will still be performed, but sample sizes can be reduced, or the timing of the procedures can be moved farther away from the balance sheet date.

Inquiries of the Client

Inquiry is the obtaining of *written* or *oral* information from the client in response to questions from the auditor. Although considerable evidence is obtained from the client through inquiry, it usually cannot be regarded as conclusive because it is not from an independent source and may be biased in the client's favor. Therefore, when the auditor obtains evidence through inquiry, it is normally necessary to obtain corroborating evidence through other procedures. (Corroborating evidence is additional evidence to support the original evidence.) As an illustration, when the auditor wants to obtain information about the client's method of recording and controlling accounting transactions, the auditor usually begins by asking the client how the internal controls operate. Later, the auditor performs audit tests using inspection and observation to determine whether the transactions are recorded (completeness objective) and authorized (occurrence objective) in the manner stated.

Recalculation

Recalculation involves rechecking a sample of calculations made by the client. Rechecking client calculations consists of testing the client's arithmetical accuracy and includes such procedures as extending sales invoices and inventory, adding journals and subsidiary records, and checking the calculation of depreciation expense and prepaid expenses. A considerable portion of auditors' recalculation is done using spreadsheet or audit software.

Reperformance

Reperformance is the auditor's independent tests of client accounting procedures or controls that were originally done as part of the entity's accounting and internal control system. Whereas recalculation involves rechecking a computation, reperformance involves checking other procedures. For example, the auditor may compare the price on an invoice to an approved price list, or may reperform the aging of accounts receivable. Another type of reperformance is for the auditor to recheck transfers of information by tracing information included in more than one place to verify that it is recorded at the same amount each time. For example, the auditor normally makes limited tests to ascertain that the information in the sales journal has been included for the proper customer and at the correct amount in the subsidiary accounts receivable records and is accurately summarized in the general ledger.

Observation

Observation consists of looking at a process or procedure being performed by others. The auditor may tour the plant to obtain a general impression of the client's facilities, or watch individuals perform accounting tasks to determine whether the person assigned a responsibility is performing it properly. Observation provides evidence about the performance of a process or procedure but is limited to the point in time at which the observation takes place. Observation is rarely sufficient by itself because of the risk of client personnel changing their behavior because of the auditor's presence. They may perform their responsibilities in accordance with company policy but resume normal activities once the auditor is not in sight. Therefore, it is necessary to follow up initial impressions with other kinds of corroborative evidence. Observation is particularly useful in evaluating the effectiveness of client procedures in counting inventory, as well as in many other parts of the audit.

Appropriateness of Types of Evidence

As discussed earlier in this chapter, the characteristics for determining the appropriateness of evidence are relevance and reliability. Table 7-4 includes the eight types of evidence related to five of the six criteria that determine the reliability of evidence. Note that two of the characteristics that determine the appropriateness of evidence—relevance and timeliness—are not included in Table 7-4. Each of the eight types of evidence included in the table has the potential to be both relevant and timely, depending on its source and when the evidence is obtained. Several other observations are apparent from studying Table 7-4.

- First, the effectiveness of a client's internal controls has significant influence on the reliability of most types of evidence. Obviously, internal documentation from a company with effective internal control is more reliable because the

TABLE 7-4 Appropriateness of Types of Evidence

	Criteria to Determine Appropriateness				
Type of Evidence	**Independence of Provider**	**Effectiveness of Client's Internal Controls**	**Auditor's Direct Knowledge**	**Qualifications of Provider**	**Objectivity of Evidence**
Physical examination	High (auditor does)	Varies	High	Normally high (auditor does)	High
Confirmation	High	Not applicable	Low	Varies—usually high	High
Inspection	Varies—external documents more independent than internal documents	Varies	Low	Varies	High
Analytical procedures	High/low (auditor does/client responds)	Varies	Low	Normally high (auditor does/client responds)	Varies—depends on reliability of data
Inquiries of client	Low (client provides)	Not applicable	Low	Varies	Varies—low to high
Recalculation	High (auditor does)	Varies	High	High (auditor does)	High
Reperformance	High (auditor does)	Varies	High	High (auditor does)	High
Observation	High (auditor does)	Varies	High	Normally high (auditor does)	Medium

documents are more likely to be accurate. Conversely, analytical procedures will not be reliable evidence if the controls that produced the data provide inaccurate information.

- Second, both physical examination and recalculation are likely to be highly reliable if the internal controls are effective, but their use differs considerably. This effectively illustrates that two completely different types of evidence can be equally reliable.
- Third, inquiry alone is usually not sufficient to provide appropriate evidence to satisfy any audit objective.

Cost of Types of Evidence

The two most expensive types of evidence are physical examination and confirmation. Physical examination (auditing standards refer to this as "inspection of tangible assets") is costly because it normally requires the auditor's presence when the client is counting the asset, often on the balance sheet date. For example, physical examination of inventory can result in several auditors traveling to scattered geographical locations. Confirmation is costly because the auditor must follow careful procedures in the confirmation preparation, transmittal, receipt, and in the follow-up of nonresponses and exceptions.

Inspection, analytical procedures, and reperformance are moderately costly. If client personnel provide documents and electronic files for the auditor and organize them for convenient use, inspection usually has a fairly low cost. When auditors must find those documents themselves, however, inspection can be extremely costly. Even under ideal circumstances, information and data on documents are sometimes complex and require interpretation and analysis. It is usually time-consuming for an auditor to read and evaluate a client's contracts, lease agreements, and minutes of the board of directors meetings. Because analytical procedures are considerably less expensive than confirmations and physical examination, most auditors prefer to replace tests of details with analytical procedures when possible. For example, it may be far less expensive to calculate and review sales and accounts receivable ratios than to confirm accounts receivable. If it is possible to reduce the use of confirmations by performing analytical procedures, considerable cost savings can be achieved. But analytical procedures require the auditor to decide which analytical procedures to use, make the calculations, and evaluate the results. Doing so often takes considerable time. The cost of reperformance tests depends on the nature of the procedure being tested. Comparatively simple tests such as reperforming the comparison of invoices to price lists are likely to take minimal time. However, reperforming procedures such as the client's bank reconciliation are likely to take considerable time.

The three least-expensive types of evidence are observation, inquiries of the client, and recalculation. Observation is normally done concurrently with other audit procedures. Auditors can easily observe whether client personnel are following appropriate inventory counting procedures at the same time they count a sample of inventory (physical examination). Inquiries of clients are done extensively on every audit and normally have a low cost, although certain inquiries may be costly, such as obtaining written statements from the client documenting discussions throughout the audit. Recalculation is usually low cost because it involves simple calculations and tracing that can be done at the auditor's convenience. Often, computer software is used to perform many of these tests.

Terms Used in Audit Procedures

As stated earlier, audit procedures are the detailed steps, usually written in the form of instructions, for the accumulation of the eight types of audit evidence. They should be sufficiently clear to enable all members of the audit team to understand what is to be done.

Several terms commonly used to describe audit procedures are defined in Table 7-5. To illustrate each term, an audit procedure and associated type of evidence are also shown.

TABLE 7-5 Terms, Audit Procedures, and Types of Evidence

Term and Definition	Illustrative Audit Procedure	Type of Evidence
Examine—A reasonably detailed study of a document or record to determine specific facts about it.	*Examine* a sample of vendors' invoices to determine whether the goods or services received are reasonable and of the type normally used by the client's business.	Inspection
Scan—A less-detailed examination of a document or record to determine whether there is something unusual warranting further investigation.	*Scan* the sales journal, looking for large and unusual transactions.	Analytical procedures
Read—An examination of written information to determine facts pertinent to the audit.	*Read* the minutes of a board of directors meeting and summarize all information that is pertinent to the financial statements in an audit file.	Inspection
Compute—A calculation done by the auditor independent of the client.	*Compute* inventory turnover ratios and compare with those of previous years as a test of inventory obsolescence.	Analytical procedures
Recompute—A calculation done to determine whether a client's calculation is correct.	*Recompute* the unit sales price times the number of units for a sample of duplicate sales invoices and compare the totals with the calculations.	Recalculation
Foot—Addition of a column of numbers to determine whether the total is the same as the client's.	*Foot* the sales journal for a one-month period and compare all totals with the general ledger.	Recalculation
Trace—An instruction normally associated with inspection or reperformance. The instruction should state what the auditor is tracing and where it is being traced from and to. Often, an audit procedure that includes the term *trace* will also include a second instruction, such as *compare* or *recalculate*.	*Trace* a sample of sales transactions from sales invoices to the sales journal, and *compare* customer name, date, and the total dollar value of the sale. *Trace* postings from the sales journal to the general ledger accounts.	Inspection Reperformance
Compare—A comparison of information in two different locations. The instruction should state which information is being compared in as much detail as practical.	Select a sample of sales invoices and *compare* the unit selling price as stated on the invoice to the list of unit selling prices authorized by management.	Inspection
Count—A determination of assets on hand at a given time. This term should be associated only with the type of evidence defined as physical examination.	*Count* a sample of 100 inventory items and compare quantity and description to client's counts.	Physical examination
Observe—The act of observation should be associated with the type of evidence defined as observation.	*Observe* whether the two inventory count teams independently count and record inventory counts.	Observation
Inquire—The act of inquiry should be associated with the type of evidence defined as inquiry.	*Inquire* of management whether there is any obsolete inventory on hand at the balance sheet date.	Inquiries of client
Vouch—The use of documents to verify recorded transactions or amounts.	*Vouch* a sample of recorded acquisition transactions to vendors' invoices and receiving reports.	Inspection

CONCEPT CHECK

1. Identify the six characteristics that determine the reliability of evidence. For each characteristic, provide one example of a type of evidence that is likely to be reliable.
2. List the eight types of audit evidence included in this chapter and give two examples of each.

ANALYTICAL PROCEDURES

OBJECTIVE 7-5

Know the types of analytical procedures and their purposes.

Analytical procedures are one of the eight types of evidence introduced earlier in the chapter. Because of the increased emphasis on the use of analytical procedures throughout the audit, this section provides additional discussion of the uses of analytical procedures, including examples of each type.

Analytical procedures may be performed at any of three times during an engagement:

2016 Annual Report

HILLSBURG HARDWARE Co.

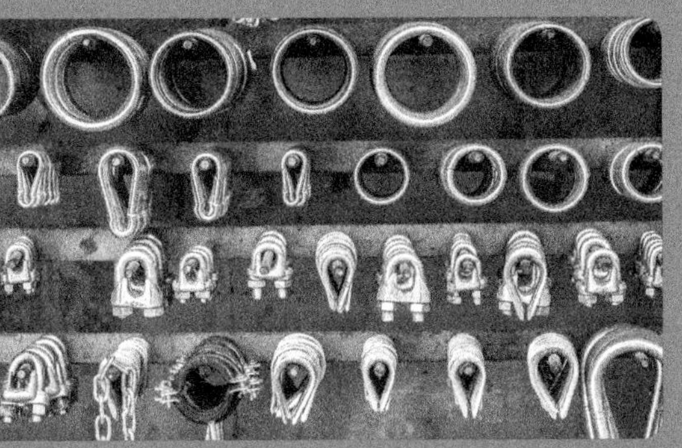

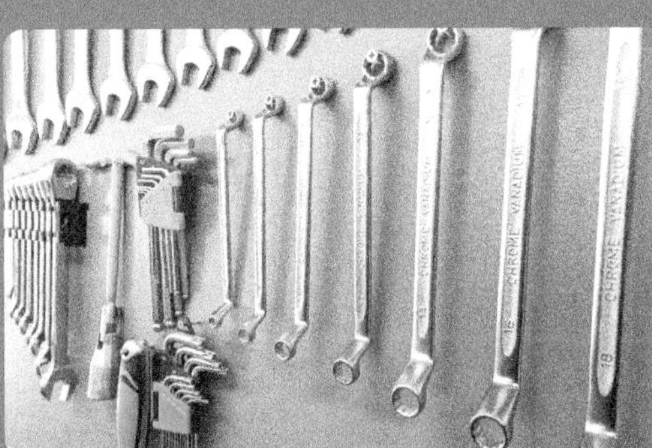

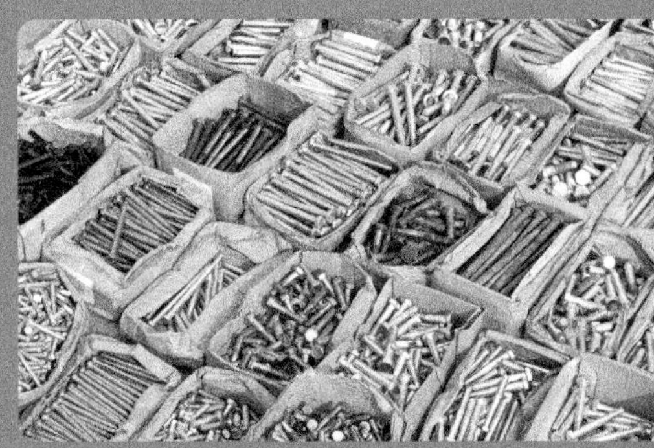

CONTENTS

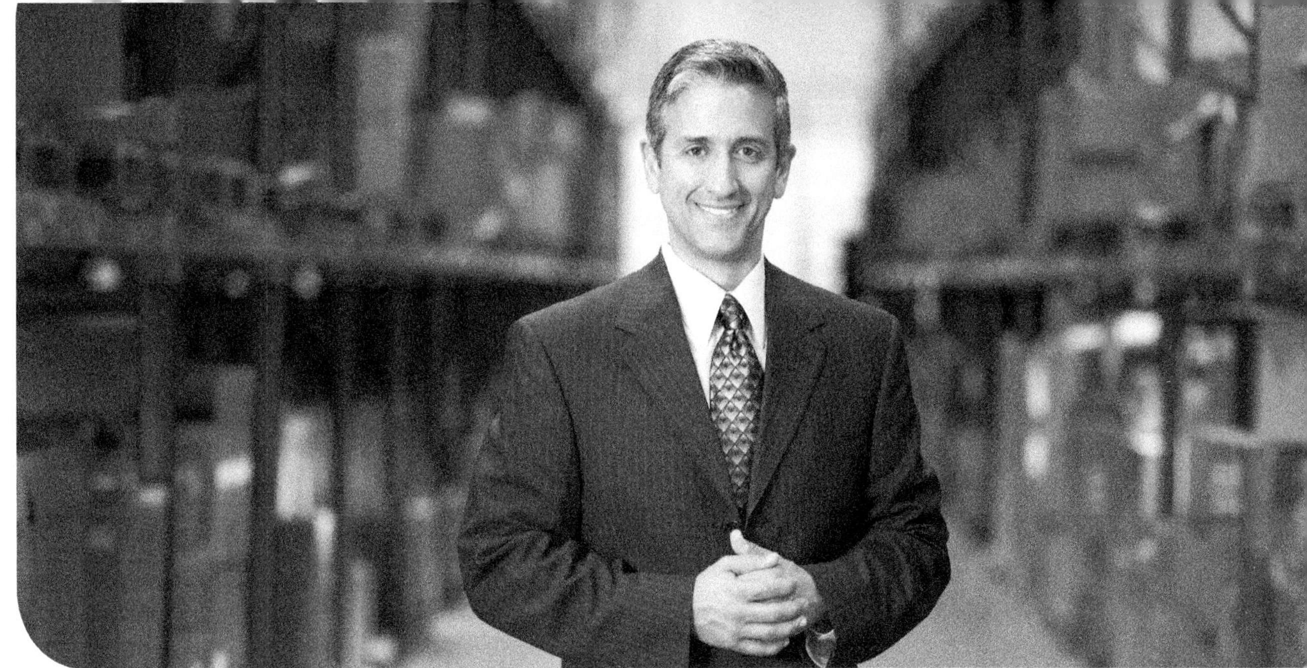

Rick Chulick, President and Chief Operating Officer

DEAR SHAREHOLDERS

March 29, 2017

We are proud to announce another year of noticeable improvement.

In last year's letter we stated, "We are committed to increasing the efficiency and effectiveness of operations through cost savings and productivity improvements, in light of current economic conditions. In addition, we intend to maintain and further develop our customer base through recently implemented post-sale service programs." The operating results in this report demonstrate that our objectives have been achieved, resulting in a net income increase of $740,000 from 2015 to 2016. This amounts to 15 cents per share, a 23.2% increase from last year. Our goal in the current year is to further improve the results of operations and create value for shareholders. In doing so, we will focus primarily on the following three strategic components of our business plan:

1. Post-sale service arrangements designed to further develop and maintain our customer base.
2. Aggressive advertising campaigns that allow us to penetrate markets dominated by national wholesale hardware store chains.
3. Implementation of new warehouse technology designed to increase productivity and reduce stocking and distribution costs.

We will report our progress throughout the year.

Christopher J. Kurran
Chief Executive Officer

Rick Chulick
President and Chief Operating Officer

   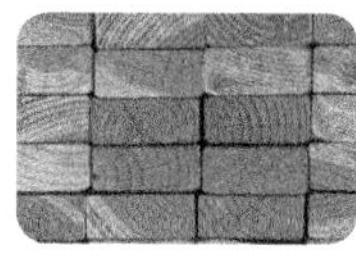

History

Hillsburg Stores Inc. began operations in 1987 in Gary, Indiana, as a retail hardware store chain. On September 25, 1993, Hillsburg merged with Handy Hardware and Lumber Company, which established the concept of selling high-quality hardware through wholesale distribution outlets, to form Handy-Hillsburg, Inc., a Washington corporation. On June 5, 1997, after spinning off all of its lumber-related assets to Handy Corporation, the company changed its name to Hillsburg Hardware, Inc. On October 22, 1999, the company reincorporated from Washington to Delaware and changed its name to Hillsburg Hardware Company (hereafter referred to as "the Company"), which trades on the NASDAQ under the symbol "HLSB."

Overview

Hillsburg Hardware Company is a wholesale distributor of hardware equipment to a variety of independent, high-quality hardware stores in the midwestern part of the United States. The primary products are power and hand tools, landscaping equipment, electrical equipment, residential and commercial construction equipment, and a wide selection of paint products.

More than 90% of the Company's products are purchased from manufacturers and shipped either directly to customers or to the main warehouse in Gary, Indiana, where shipments are combined to minimize the costs of freight and handling.

Hardware retailers, now more than ever, find it advantageous to purchase from us rather than directly from manufacturers. We make it possible for smaller, independent retailers to purchase on an as-needed basis, rather than in bulk. Moreover, we offer our customers a range of high-quality products that cannot be found at most national chains.

We also offer far more post-sale services to customers than are offered by manufacturers and other national distributors. We simplify the purchasing process by assigning each customer a permanent salesperson. Each salesperson becomes involved in the sales process, and also acts as a liaison between the customer and post-sale service areas. For example, when customers experience technical problems with recently purchased hardware, their salesperson has the responsibility to coordinate both exchanges and warranty repairs with the manufacturer. This process adds value for customers and makes post-sales service more efficient and less problematic. Low turnover and extensive training of our salespeople enhance this service.

To further encourage customer loyalty, each customer is given access to our internal database system—ONHAND (Online Niche-Hardware Availability Notification Database). The ONHAND system lets customers check the availability of hard-to-find products instantly over the Internet. Moreover, the system includes data such as expected restock dates for items that are currently sold out and expected availability dates for items that will soon be introduced to the market.

Because of the two aforementioned processes, we have managed to maintain a repeat-customer base. Nearly 75% of all first-time customers make at least one additional purchase within one year of their first purchase.

Recently, there have been major consolidations in the wholesale hardware industry. We believe this consolidation trend is advantageous to our operations as a distributor of hard-to-find, high-quality hardware equipment. The recent consolidation of Builder's Plus Hardware, Inc., one of the top ten largest national hardware store chains, is a case in point. One month after the consolidation, Builder's Plus decided not to carry high-end construction and landscaping equipment in order to focus on what it called the "typical hardware customer."

Products

To more effectively manage inventory, we carefully monitor the composition of net sales by category of items sold. The following chart indicates the percentage of net sales by class of merchandise sold during the years 2016, 2015, and 2014:

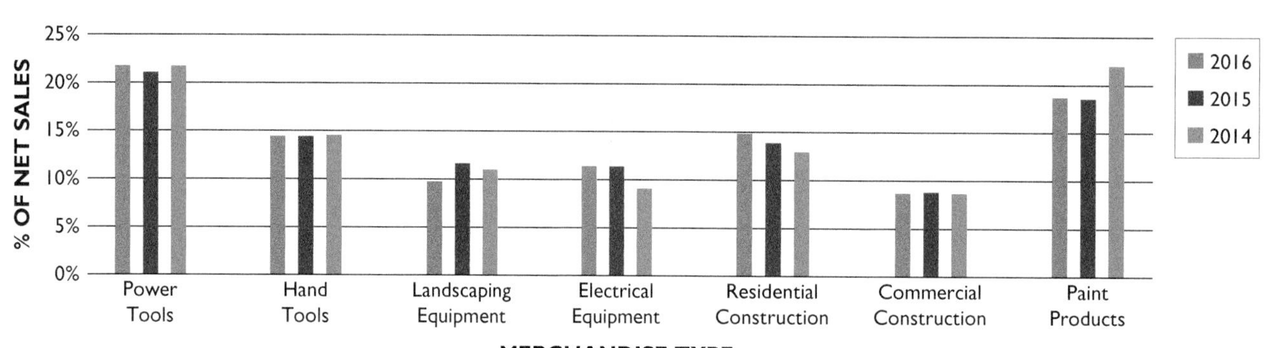

Competitors

There are other regional wholesale hardware distributors that compete with the Company, but national wholesale hardware store chains dominate the industry. Most of our competitors are not only larger, but have greater financial resources than our company. Ten national chains exist in the geographic area in which Hillsburg Hardware Co. operates. Of the ten national chains, Hardware Bros., Tools & Paint, and Construction City account for a significant portion of the wholesale hardware market share and also carry the hard-to-find and high-quality items we provide. The success of our business depends on our ability to keep distribution costs to a minimum and our customers satisfied through superior customer service.

The chart below is a breakdown of market share in the wholesale hardware market by competitor category, including the 2% market share held by the Company. The chart illustrates that we have considerable opportunity for sales growth.

Marketing Program

This year, the Company made a significant investment in a new advertising campaign. Various Internet, radio, newspaper, magazine, and television advertisements were purchased at the local and regional levels using the Company's new catchphrase, "Hardware for Hard Workers." The new jingle has been partially responsible for the fiscal 2016 increase in sales of 9%.

Customers

The majority of our customers are located in Illinois, Michigan, Wisconsin, Ohio, and Missouri. Our current customer base consists of more than 400 independently owned hardware stores. Approximately 25% of our customers make up more than 80% of total sales revenue. To promote long-standing relationships with customers, we offer an array of incentive and customer appreciation programs. Since these programs were implemented in 2007, customer satisfaction ratings have improved steadily in each subsequent year.

Suppliers

We purchase hardware and other products from more than 300 manufacturers in the United States. No single vendor accounted for more than 5% of our purchases during fiscal 2016, but our 25 largest vendors accounted for nearly 35%. We currently have long-term supply agreements with two vendors: Mechanical Tools and Painter's Paradise. These agreements are in effect until the end of fiscal year 2017. The combined dollar amount of each contract is not expected to exceed 5% of total purchases for the year.

Employees

Hillsburg Hardware currently employs 319 individuals. The majority of our employees are involved in day-to-day sales. Because of our marketing and customer relations strategy, we make significant investments in ongoing training and professional development activities. Each year employees are required to attend 75 hours of professional training. Each employee receives a performance evaluation at least four times per year, usually once each quarter. Our turnover is among the lowest in the industry because of our compensation, training, and evaluation programs. We regard our employees as our most valuable asset.

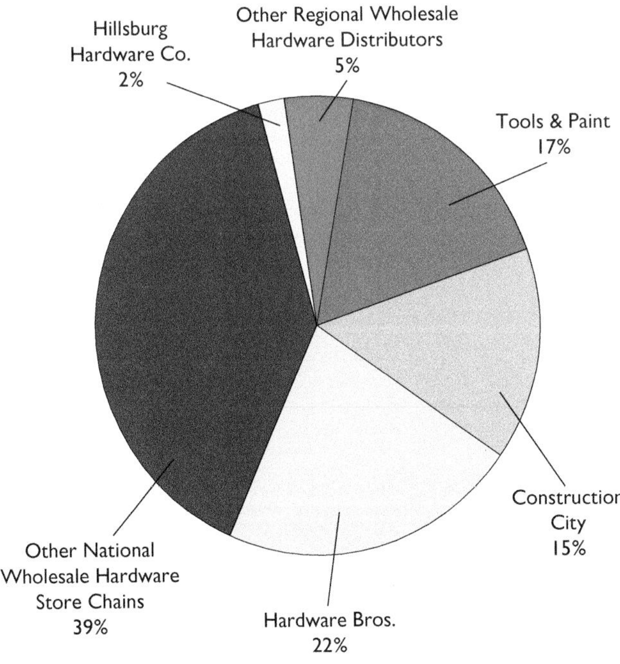

Properties

The Company owns and operates its main warehouse and an administrative office. The main warehouse and administrative office are in the same 475,000 square-foot building. We also rent a second warehouse for which rental fees are $312,000 annually. The building, located in Detroit, Michigan, serves as an off-site storage facility.

Legal Proceedings

On September 3, 2015, a suit was filed in the Circuit Court in Gary, Indiana, against the Company. The product liability suit, *"Don Richards v. Hillsburg Hardware Co."* is related to injuries that resulted from an alleged defective design of a tractor manufactured by Silo-Tractor, a U.S. corporation. The suit is currently in pretrial proceedings. In the opinion of our legal counsel the suit is without merit. We intend to vigorously defend our position.

The Company does not believe any other legal issues materially affect its finances.

Executive Officers

The following list provides names, ages, and present positions of the Company's officers:

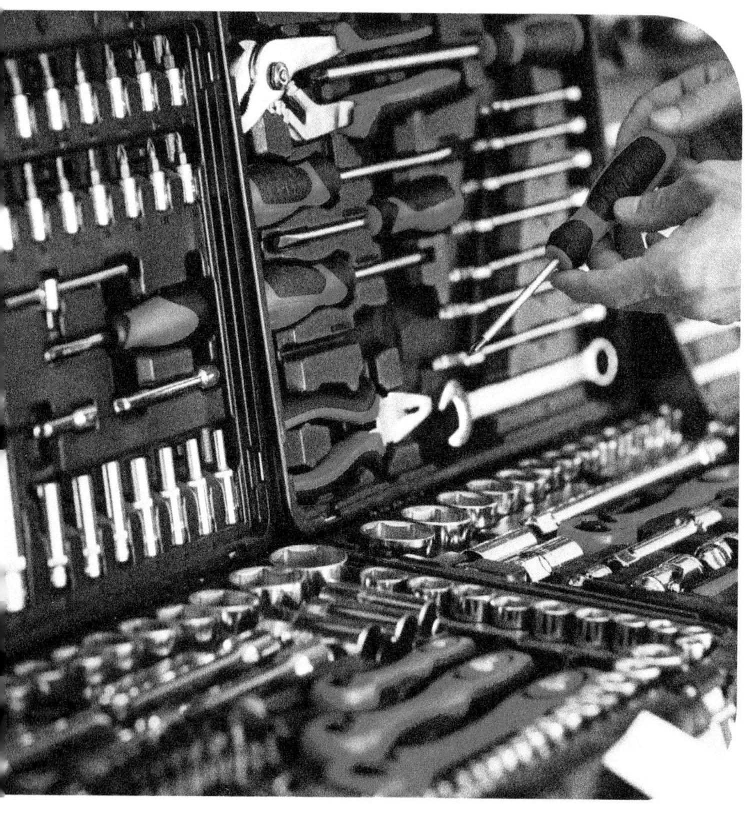

NAME	AGE	POSITION
John P. Higgins	55	Chairman of the Board
Christopher J. Kurran	47	Chief Executive Officer (b)
Rick Chulick	48	President and Chief Operating Officer (a)
Avis A. Zomer	44	Chief Financial Officer
Brandon S. Mack	51	Vice President Sales and Marketing
Mary R. Moses	36	Vice President Merchandising
Vanessa M. Namie	53	Vice President Operations (c)
Joseph A. Akins	64	Vice President Quality Assurance (d)

(a) Mr. Chulick has been President and Chief Operating Officer of the Company since November 2006.

(b) Mr. Kurran has been Chief Executive Officer of the Company since September 2006. Prior to his role as CEO, Mr. Kurran was employed from 1997–2005 by Trini Enterprises, an industrial distributor.

(c) Ms. Namie has been employed by the company since its inception in 1999. She has held her current position since 2005 and served as an operations manager from 1999–2005.

(d) Mr. Akins was Chief Operating Officer and President of Hardware Bros., one of the ten largest wholesale hardware chains in the nation, from 2003–2008.

> "We offer our customers a range of high-quality products that cannot be found at most national chains."

Controls and Procedures

Pursuant to Section 404 of the Sarbanes–Oxley Act of 2002 and related Exchange Act Rules, we have carefully evaluated the design and operating effectiveness of our internal control over financial reporting. After careful review of all key controls over financial reporting, our Chief Executive Officer and Chief Financial Officer implemented new controls to strengthen processes surrounding revenue recognition. In compliance with Section 404 and related Exchange requirements, management has issued its report that internal controls over financial reporting are operating effectively as of December 31, 2016 based on criteria established in the COSO *Internal Control-Integrated Framework.*

Information Regarding Common Equity

Hillsburg Hardware Company's common stock currently trades on the NASDAQ under the symbol "HLSB." The following chart shows the high and low prices of the Company's common stock by quarter for the years 2016 and 2015:

	2016		2015	
	HIGH	LOW	HIGH	LOW
Quarter 1	22.50	19.05	23.30	20.00
Quarter 2	22.55	20.10	22.75	20.25
Quarter 3	22.30	20.99	24.10	19.75
Quarter 4	22.40	17.95	21.50	18.20

On March 23, 2017, there were 1,250 shareholders of our common stock.

Dividend Policy

Dividend payments on common stock are authorized annually by the Board of Directors. For 2016, dividend payments totaled $1.9 million, which is $.38 per share.

REPORT OF INDEPENDENT REGISTERED ACCOUNTING FIRM

Board of Directors and Stockholders
Hillsburg Hardware Company

We have audited the accompanying balance sheets of Hillsburg Hardware Company as of December 31, 2016 and 2015, and the related statements of income, stockholders' equity and comprehensive income, and cash flows for each of the years in the three-year period ended December 31, 2016. We have also audited Hillsburg Hardware Company, Inc.'s internal control over financial reporting as of December 31, 2016, based on criteria established in Internal Control-Integrated Framework issued by the Committee of Sponsoring Organizations of the Treadway Commission (COSO). Hillsburg Hardware Company's management is responsible for these financial statements, for maintaining effective internal control over financial reporting, and for its assessment of the effectiveness of internal control over financial reporting, included in the accompanying report, Management's Responsibility for the Financial Statements. Our responsibility is to express an opinion on these financial statements and an opinion on the company's internal control over financial reporting based on our audits.

We conducted our audits in accordance with the standards of the Public Company Accounting Oversight Board (United States). Those standards require that we plan and perform the audits to obtain reasonable assurance about whether the financial statements are free of material misstatement and whether effective internal control over financial reporting was maintained in all material respects. Our audit of financial statements included examining, on a test basis, evidence supporting the amounts and disclosures in the financial statements, assessing the accounting principles used and significant estimates made by management, and evaluating the overall financial statement presentation. Our audit of internal control over financial reporting included obtaining an understanding of internal control over financial reporting, assessing the risk that a material weakness exists, and testing and evaluating the design and operating effectiveness of internal control based on the assessed risk. Our audits also included performing such other procedures as we considered necessary in the circumstances. We believe that our audits provide a reasonable basis for our opinions.

A company's internal control over financial reporting is a process designed to provide reasonable assurance regarding the reliability of financial reporting and the preparation of financial statements for external purposes in accordance with generally accepted accounting principles. A company's internal control over financial reporting includes those policies and procedures that (1) pertain to the maintenance of records that, in reasonable detail, accurately and fairly reflect the transactions and dispositions of the assets of the company; (2) provide reasonable assurance that transactions are recorded as necessary to permit preparation of financial statements in accordance with generally accepted accounting principles, and that receipts and expenditures of the company are being made only in accordance with authorizations of management and directors of the company; and (3) provide reasonable assurance regarding the prevention or timely detection of unauthorized acquisition, use, or disposition of the company's assets that could have a material effect on the financial statements.

Because of its inherent limitations, internal control over financial reporting may not prevent or detect misstatements. Also, projections of any evaluation of effectiveness to future periods are subject to the risk that controls may become inadequate because of changes in conditions, or that the degree of compliance with the policies or procedures may deteriorate.

In our opinion, the financial statements referred to above present fairly, in all material respects, the financial position of Hillsburg Hardware Company, Inc. as of December 31, 2016 and 2015, and the results of its operations and its cash flows for each of the years in the three-year period ended December 31, 2016, in conformity with accounting principles generally accepted in the United States of America. Also in our opinion, Hillsburg Hardware Company maintained, in all material respects, effective internal control over financial reporting as of December 31, 2016, based on criteria established in Internal Control-Integrated Framework issued by the Committee of Sponsoring Organizations of the Treadway Commission (COSO).

Berger & Anthony, LLP

Berger and Anthony, LLP
Gary, Indiana
March 21, 2017

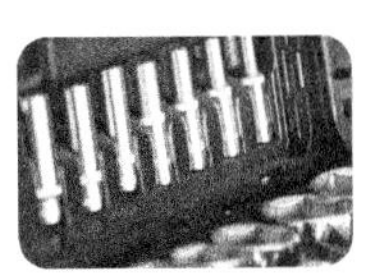
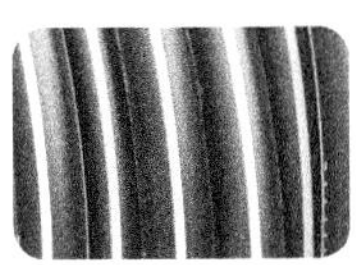

Management's Responsibility for the Financial Statements

To Our Shareholders:

The accompanying financial statements of Hillsburg Hardware Company have been prepared by management, which is responsible for their integrity and objectivity. The statements have been prepared in conformity with accounting principles generally accepted in the United States of America and include amounts based on management's best estimates and judgments. Management has also prepared information elsewhere in this Annual Report that is consistent with data in the financial statements. The Company's financial statements have been audited by Berger and Anthony, independent Certified Public Accountants. Our auditors were given unrestricted access to all financial records and related data, including minutes of the meetings of the Board of Directors. We believe all representations made to Berger and Anthony were legitimate and appropriate.

The management of Hillsburg Hardware Company is responsible for establishing and maintaining adequate internal control over financial reporting. Hillsburg Hardware Company's internal control system was designed to provide reasonable assurance to the company's management and board of directors regarding the preparation and fair presentation of published financial statements.

Hillsburg Hardware Company management assessed the effectiveness of the company's internal control over financial reporting as of December 31, 2016. In making this assessment, it used the criteria set forth by the Committee of Sponsoring Organizations of the Treadway Commission (COSO) in *Internal Control-Integrated Framework*. Based on our assessment we believe that, as of December 31, 2016, the company's internal control over financial reporting is effective based on those criteria.

Hillsburg Hardware Company's independent auditors have issued an audit report on our financial statements and internal control over financial reporting. This report appears on the preceding page.

John P. Higgins
Chairman of the Board

Christopher J. Kurran
Chief Executive Officer

Avis A. Zomer
Chief Financial Officer

Hillsburg Hardware Company
Balance Sheets (in thousands)

	December 31	
ASSETS	**2016**	**2015**
Current assets		
Cash and cash equivalents	$ 828	$ 743
Trade receivables (net of allowances of $1,240 and $1,311)	18,957	16,210
Other receivables	945	915
Merchandise inventory	29,865	31,600
Prepaid expenses	432	427
Total current assets	51,027	49,895
Property and equipment		
Land	3,456	3,456
Buildings	32,500	32,000
Equipment, furniture, and fixtures	6,304	8,660
Less: accumulated depreciation	(31,920)	(33,220)
Total property and equipment (net)	10,340	10,896
Total assets	**$ 61,367**	**$ 60,791**
LIABILITIES AND STOCKHOLDERS' EQUITY		
Current liabilities		
Trade accounts payable	$ 4,720	$ 4,432
Notes payable	4,180	4,589
Accrued payroll	1,350	715
Accrued payroll tax	120	116
Accrued interest and dividends payable	2,050	1,975
Accrued income tax	796	523
Total current liabilities	13,216	12,350
Long-term notes payable	24,120	26,520
Deferred income taxes	738	722
Other long-term payables	830	770
STOCKHOLDERS' EQUITY		
Capital stock ($1 par value; 5,000,000 shares issued)	5,000	5,000
Capital in excess of par value	3,500	3,500
Retained earnings	13,963	11,929
Total stockholders' equity:	**22,463**	**20,429**
Total liabilities and stockholders' equity	**$ 61,367**	**$ 60,791**

See Notes to Financial Statements.

Hillsburg Hardware Company
Statement of Operations (in thousands)

	Year Ended December 31		
	2016	**2015**	**2014**
Net sales	$ 143,086	$ 131,226	$ 122,685
Cost of sales	103,241	94,876	88,724
Gross profit	39,845	36,350	33,961
Selling, general and administrative expenses	32,475	29,656	28,437
Operating income	7,370	6,694	5,524
Other income and expense			
Interest expense	2,409	2,035	2,173
Gain on sale of assets	(720)	—	—
Total other income/expense (net)	1,689	2,035	2,173
Earnings before income taxes	5,681	4,659	3,351
Provision for income taxes	1,747	1,465	1,072
Net income	$ 3,934	$ 3,194	$ 2,279
Earnings per share	$ 0.79	$ 0.64	$ 0.46

See Notes to Financial Statements.

Statement of Operations

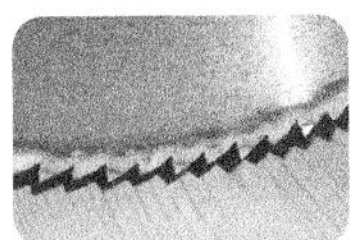

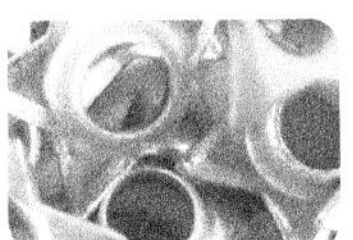
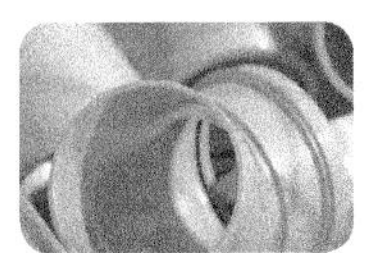

Hillsburg Hardware Company
Statement of Stockholders' Equity (in thousands)

	Common Stock		Paid-in	Retained	Total
	Shares	Par value	Capital	Earnings	Stockholders' Equity
Balance as of December 31, 2013	**5,000**	**$ 5,000**	**$ 3,500**	**$ 10,256**	**$ 18,756**
Net income				2,279	2,279
Dividends paid				(1,900)	(1,900)
Balance as of December 31, 2014	**5,000**	**$ 5,000**	**$ 3,500**	**$ 10,635**	**$ 19,135**
Net income				3,194	3,194
Dividends paid				(1,900)	(1,900)
Balance as of December 31, 2015	**5,000**	**$ 5,000**	**$ 3,500**	**$ 11,929**	**$ 20,429**
Net income				3,934	3,934
Dividends paid				(1,900)	(1,900)
Balance as of December 31, 2016	**5,000**	**$ 5,000**	**$ 3,500**	**$ 13,963**	**$ 22,463**

See Notes to Financial Statements.

Stockholders' Equity

Hillsburg Hardware Company
Statement of Cash Flows (in thousands)

	Year Ended December 31		
OPERATING ACTIVITIES	**2016**	**2015**	**2014**
Net income	$ 3,934	$ 3,194	$ 2,279
Adjustments to reconcile net income to net cash provided by (used in) operating activities:			
Depreciation and amortization	1,452	1,443	1,505
(Gain) or Loss on sale of assets	(720)	–	–
Deferred income taxes increase (decrease)	16	(8)	43
Changes in assets and liabilities:			
Trade and other receivables	(2,777)	(393)	(918)
Merchandise inventory	1,735	(295)	(430)
Prepaid expenses	(5)	(27)	(55)
Accounts payable	288	132	76
Accrued liabilities	714	77	142
Income taxes payable	273	23	13
Net cash provided by operating activities	4,910	4,146	2,655
INVESTING ACTIVITIES			
Capital expenditures	(10,500)	(1,800)	(2,292)
Sale of equipment	10,324	–	–
Net cash used in investing activities	(176)	(1,800)	(2,292)
FINANCING ACTIVITIES			
Dividend payment	(1,900)	(1,900)	(1,900)
Proceeds (repayments) from borrowings (net)	(2,749)	(423)	1,602
Net cash used in financing activities	(4,649)	(2,323)	(298)
Net increase in cash and cash equivalents	85	23	65
Cash and cash equivalents at beginning of year	743	720	655
Cash and cash equivalents at end of year	$ 828	$ 743	$ 720

See Notes to Financial Statements.

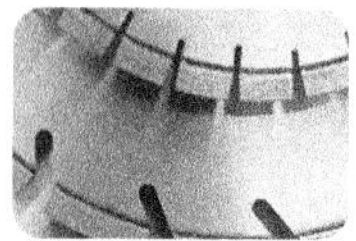
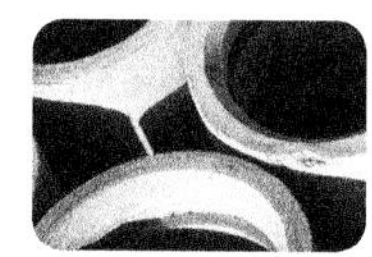

1. Description of Significant Accounting Policies and Business

Hillsburg Hardware is a wholesale distributor of high-quality power tools, hand tools, electrical equipment, landscaping equipment, residential and commercial construction equipment, and paint products. The majority of customers are smaller, independent hardware stores located in Illinois, Michigan, Wisconsin, Ohio, and Missouri.

Allowance for Doubtful Accounts: The allowance for doubtful accounts is maintained to account for expected credit losses. Estimates of bad debts are based on individual customer risks and historical collection trends. Allowances are evaluated and updated when conditions occur that give rise to collection issues.

Merchandise Inventory: Merchandise inventory is presented at the lower of average cost or market. To present accurately the estimated net realizable value of the accounts, inventory balances are adjusted when current and expected future market conditions, as well as recent and historical turnover trends, indicate adjustments are necessary.

Property, Plant and Equipment: Land, buildings, computers and other equipment, and furniture and fixtures are stated at historical cost. Depreciation is calculated on a straight-line basis over estimated useful lives of the assets. Estimated useful lives are 20 to 35 years for buildings and 2 to 10 years for equipment and furniture and fixtures.

Revenue Recognition: Revenues are recognized when goods are shipped, title has passed, the sales price is fixed, and collectibility is reasonably assured. A sales returns and allowance account is maintained to reflect estimated future returns and allowances. Adjustments to the sales returns and allowance account are made in the same period as the related sales are recorded and are based on historical trends, as well as analyses of other relevant factors. Sales are recorded net of returns and allowances in the statements referred to in this report.

Income Taxes: The deferred income tax account includes temporary differences between book (financial accounting) income and taxable income (for IRS reporting purposes). The account consists largely of temporary differences related to (1) the valuation of inventory, (2) depreciation, and (3) other accruals.

2. Other Receivables

The other receivables balance consists largely of vendor allowances and vendor rebates. When vendor allowances and vendor rebates are recognized (all activities required by the supplier are completed, the amount is determinable, and collectibility is reasonably certain), they are recorded as reductions of costs of goods sold.

3. Notes Payable

Notes payable for the year ended December 31, 2016, consists of three notes payable to the bank. Each note carries a fixed interest rate of 8.5%. One note for $4,180,000 matures in June 2017 and the other two mature on December 31, 2019. During 2016, there was an additional note outstanding in the amount of $4,400,000, which was paid off during October 2016.

4. Commitments

The Company is currently committed to an operating lease that expires in 2020. Rental payments for the remainder of the contract are set at $312,000 per annum.

5. Segment Reporting

The Company operates in one segment. The breakdown of revenues (in thousands) from different products is listed in the chart below:

SEGMENT REPORTING

	2016	2015	2014
Power Tools	$ 31,479	$ 27,557	$ 26,991
Hand Tools	21,463	19,684	18,403
Landscaping Equipment	14,309	15,645	13,494
Electrical Goods	17,170	15,849	11,042
Residential Construction Equipment	21,463	18,372	15,949
Commercial Construction Equipment	11,447	10,498	9,815
Paint Products	25,755	23,621	26,991
	$143,086	**$131,226**	**$122,685**

6. Earnings Per Share

Earnings per share calculations for 2016, 2015, and 2014 were computed as follows:

Numerators
(net income in thousands): $3,934, $3,194, and $2,279

Denominators
(shares of common stock): 5,000,000 (unchanged for all years)

Diluted earnings per share was the same as basic earnings per share for all years.

Management's Discussion and Analysis of Financial Condition and Results of Operations

The following discussion and analysis of the results of our operations and our financial condition are based on the financial statements and related notes included in this report. When preparing the financial statements, we are frequently required to use our best estimates and judgments. These estimates and judgments affect certain asset, liability, revenue, and expense account balances. Therefore, estimates are evaluated constantly based on our analyses of historical trends and our understanding of the general business environment in which we operate. There are times, however, when different circumstances and assumptions cause actual results to differ from those expected when judgments were originally made. The accounting policies referred to in Note 1 to the financial statements, in our opinion, influence the judgments and estimates we use to prepare our financial statements.

Results of Operations

For the year ended December 31, 2016, gross profit increased by 9.6% or $3,495,000 from 2015. This increase in gross profit more than offsets the increase in operating expenses from 2015 to 2016 of $2,819,000 or 9.5%. The increase in gross margin largely explains the operating income increase of $676,000.

For the year ended December 31, 2015, gross profit increased by $2,389,000 or 7% from 2014. Total operating expenses increased by $1,219,000 or approximately 4.3% from 2014. The increase in gross profit offset the total operating expense increase, and the net result was a $1,170,000 increase in operating income.

Net Sales: From 2015 to 2016 net sales increased by $11,860,000 or 9%. The increase in net sales can be explained largely by an aggressive advertising campaign that the Company organized during the second half of 2016. Net sales for 2015 increased by $8,541,000 or 7.0% from 2014, which is consistent with industrywide average revenue growth of 7% from 2014 to 2015.

Gross Profit: Gross profit as a percentage of net sales stayed relatively stable at 27.68% and 27.70% in 2014 and 2015, respectively, but increased to 27.85% in 2016. The 2016 increase is mostly due to improved vendor incentive programs, our focus on cost containment, and increases in the resale values of certain commodities such as PVC piping material and certain types of metal wiring. While gross profit percentages in the industry have declined somewhat, our position as a niche provider in the overall hardware market allows us to charge premium prices without losing customers.

Selling, General, and Administrative Expenses: Selling expenses increased by $1,911,000 or 14.8% from 2015 to 2016 and by $805,000 or 6.7% from 2014 to 2015. As a percentage of net sales, selling expenses increased by 0.52% since 2015 and decreased by 0.03% from 2014 to 2015. The increase in selling expenses as a percentage of net sales from 2015 to 2016 is due to our new advertising campaign and increased expenditures on sales meetings and training.

General and administrative expenses increased by $908,000 or 5.4% from 2015 to 2016 and by $414,000 or 2.5% from 2014 to 2015. As a percentage of net sales, general and administrative expenses decreased by 0.42% since 2015 and decreased by 0.55% from 2014 to 2015. The overall increase from 2015 to 2016 was caused mostly by unexpected repairs needed to reattach and replace damaged shelving units in our main warehouse building.

Interest Expense: In 2016, interest expense increased by $374,000, or approximately 18.4%, compared to 2015. The increase was due to an overall interest rate increase and the restructuring of debt covenants that are less restrictive but demand higher interest rates. In 2015 interest expense decreased by $138,000 or 6.4% compared to 2014. The 2015 decrease was mainly due to the Company's decision to decrease the level of long-term debt. The average interest rates on short- and long-term debt during 2016 were approximately 10.5% and 8.5% respectively.

Liquidity

During 2016, our working capital requirements were primarily financed through our line of credit, under which we are permitted to borrow up to the lesser of $7,000,000 or 75% of accounts receivable outstanding less than 30 days. The average interest rate on these short-term borrowings in 2016 was approximately 10.5%

Cash provided by operating activities for 2016 and 2015 was $4,910,000 and $4,146,000 respectively. The change from 2015 to 2016 is primarily due to the increase in net income. Increases in receivables were largely offset by decreases in inventories and increases in payables and other current liabilities. The increase in cash provided from operating activities of $1,491,000 from 2014 to 2015 is largely the result of the increase in net income and smaller increases in receivables and merchandise inventory in 2015 compared to 2014. We believe that cash flow from operations and the available short-term line of credit will continue to allow us to finance operations throughout the current year.

Statement of Condition

Merchandise inventory and trade accounts receivable together accounted for over 95% of current assets in both 2016 and 2015. Merchandise inventory turned over approximately 3.4 times in 2016 and 3.0 times in 2015. Average days to sell inventory were 108.6 and 120.9 in 2016 and 2015 respectively. Net trade receivables turned over approximately 7.6 times in 2016 and in 2015. Days to collect accounts receivable computations were 48.1 and 48.0 in 2016 and 2015 respectively. Both inventory and accounts receivable turnover are lower than industry averages. We plan for this difference to satisfy the market in which we operate. Our market consists of smaller, independent hardware stores that need more favorable receivable collection terms and immediate delivery of inventory. Because we hold large amounts of inventory, we are able to fill orders quicker than most of our competitors even during the busiest times of the year.

Outlook

During 2016 we experienced another year of noticeable improvement, despite the economic environment. The Company's financial performance can largely be attributed to (1) a continued focus on cost containment, (2) productivity improvements, (3) aggressive advertising, and (4) the implementation of programs designed to enhance customer satisfaction.

During 2017, we will continue to apply the same strategic efforts that improved 2016 performance. We are also implementing a new warehouse information system designed to increase productivity and reduce stocking and distribution costs. Management believes that earnings growth will be primarily driven by (1) continued focus on customer satisfaction, (2) penetration into markets currently dominated by national wholesale hardware store chains, and (3) the use of technology to attract additional customers and promote more efficient operations.

Information Concerning Forward-Looking Statements

This report contains certain forward-looking statements (referenced by such terms as "expects" or "believes") that are subject to the effects of various factors including (1) changes in wholesale hardware prices, (2) changes in the general business environment, (3) the intensity of the competitive arena, (4) new national wholesale hardware chain openings, and (5) certain other matters influencing the Company's ability to react to changing market conditions. Therefore, management wishes to make readers aware that the aforementioned factors could cause the actual results of our operations to differ considerably from those indicated by any forward-looking statements included in this report.

Hillsburg Hardware Company
Five-Year Financial Summary (in thousands)

BALANCE SHEET DATA:	2016	2015	2014	2013	2012
Current assets	$ 51,027	$ 49,895	$ 49,157	$ 47,689	$ 46,504
Total assets	61,367	60,791	59,696	57,441	51,580
Current liabilities	13,216	12,350	12,173	12,166	9,628
Long-term notes payable	24,120	26,520	26,938	25,432	25,223
Total stockholders' equity	22,463	20,429	19,135	18,756	15,764
INCOME STATEMENT DATA:					
Net sales	$ 143,086	$ 131,226	$ 122,685	$ 120,221	$ 117,115
Cost of sales	103,241	94,876	88,724	88,112	85,663
Gross profit	39,845	36,350	33,961	32,109	31,452
Earnings before income taxes	5,681	4,659	3,351	3,124	1,450
Net income	3,934	3,194	2,279	2,142	994
Cash provided by operating activities	4,910	4,146	2,655	1,811	1,232
Per common share data:					
Net income	$ 0.79	$ 0.64	$ 0.46	$ 0.43	$ 0.22
Cash dividends per share	$ 0.38	$ 0.38	$ 0.38	$ —	$ —
Common shares outstanding	5,000	5,000	5,000	5,000	4,500
KEY OPERATING RESULTS AND FINANCIAL POSITION RATIOS:					
Gross profit (%)	27.85%	27.70%	27.68%	26.71%	26.86%
Return on assets (%)	9.30%	7.73%	5.72%	5.73%	2.86%
Return on common equity (%)	26.49%	23.55%	17.69%	18.10%	9.50%

HILLSBURG
HARDWARE Co.

Purposes of Analytical Procedures During the Audit Engagement

1. Analytical procedures are *required* in the *planning phase* as part of risk assessment procedures to understand the client's business and industry and to assist in determining the nature, extent, and timing of audit procedures. This helps the auditor identify significant matters requiring special consideration later in the engagement. For example, the calculation of inventory turnover before inventory price tests are done may indicate the need for special care during those tests. The sophistication, extent, and timing of the analytical procedures vary among clients, and analytical procedures done in the planning phase typically use data aggregated at a high level, such as using overall financial statement balances. For some clients, the comparison of prior-year and current-year account balances using the unaudited trial balance may be sufficient.
2. Analytical procedures are often done *during the testing phase* of the audit as a substantive test in support of account balances. These substantive analytical procedures are often done in conjunction with other audit procedures. For example, the prepaid portion of each insurance policy might be compared with the same policy for the previous year as a part of doing tests of prepaid insurance. The assurance provided by analytical procedures depends on the predictability of the relationship, as well as the precision of the auditor's expectation of the account balance and the reliability of the data used to develop the expectation. When substantive analytical procedures are used during the testing phase of the audit, auditing standards require the auditor to document in the working papers the auditor's expectation and factors considered in its development. The auditor is also required to evaluate the reliability of the data used to develop the expectation, including the source of the data and controls over the data's preparation.
3. Analytical procedures are also *required during the completion phase* of the audit. Such tests serve as a final review for material misstatements or financial problems and help the auditor take a final "objective look" at the audited financial statements. Typically, a senior partner with extensive knowledge of the client's business conducts the analytical procedures during the final review of the audit files and financial statements to identify possible oversights in the audit.

As this discussion illustrates, the purposes of analytical procedures and their nature depend on when they are used during the audit. Analytical procedures performed during audit planning generally use aggregate data to help understand the client's business and identify areas where misstatements are more likely. In contrast, substantive analytical procedures used to provide audit evidence require more reliable evidence, often using disaggregated data for the auditor to develop an expectation of the account balance being tested.

Types of Analytical Procedures

The usefulness of analytical procedures as audit evidence depends significantly on appropriate comparison data. The auditor typically compares the client's balances and ratios with expected balances and ratios using one or more of the following types of analytical procedures. In each case, auditors compare client data with:

1. Industry data
2. Similar prior-period data
3. Client-determined expected results
4. Auditor-determined expected results

Compare Client and Industry Data

Suppose that you are doing an audit and obtain the following information about the client and the average company in the client's industry:

	Client		Industry	
	2016	**2015**	**2016**	**2015**
Inventory turnover	3.4	3.5	3.9	3.4
Gross margin percent	26.3%	26.4%	27.3%	26.2%

If we look only at client information for the two ratios shown, the company appears to be stable with no apparent indication of difficulties. However, if we use industry data to develop expectations about the two ratios for 2016, we should expect both ratios for the client to increase. Although these two ratios by themselves may not indicate significant problems, these data illustrate how using industry data may provide useful information about the client's performance and potential misstatements. Perhaps the company has lost market share, its pricing has not been competitive, it has incurred abnormal costs, or perhaps it has obsolete items in inventory or made errors in recording purchases. The auditor needs to determine if either of the last two occurred to have reasonable assurance that the financial statements are not misstated.

Dun & Bradstreet, Standard and Poor's, and other analysts accumulate financial information for thousands of companies and compile the data for different lines of business. Many CPA firms purchase this industry information for use as a basis for developing expectations about financial ratios in their audits. The most important benefits of industry comparisons are to aid in understanding the client's business and as an indication of the likelihood of financial failure. They can also be helpful in identifying potential misstatements. However, a major weakness in using industry ratios for auditing is the difference between the nature of the client's financial information and that of the firms making up the industry totals. Because the industry data are broad averages, the comparisons may not be meaningful. Often, the client's line of business is not the same as the industry standards. In addition, different companies follow different accounting methods, and this affects the comparability of data. For example, if most companies in the industry use FIFO inventory valuation and straight-line depreciation and the audit client uses LIFO and double-declining-balance depreciation, comparisons may not be meaningful. This does not mean that industry comparisons should be avoided. Rather, it is an indication of the need for care in using industry data to develop expectations about financial relationships and in interpreting the results. One approach to overcome the limitations of industry averages is to compare the client to one or more benchmark firms in the industry.

Compare Client Data with Similar Prior-Period Data

Suppose that the gross margin percentage for a company has been between 26 and 27 percent for each of the past four years but has dropped to 23 percent in the current year. This decline in gross margin should be a concern to the auditor if a decline is not expected. The cause of the decline could be a change in economic conditions. But, it could also be caused by misstatements in the financial statements, such as sales or purchase cutoff errors, unrecorded sales, overstated accounts payable, or inventory costing errors. The decline in gross margin is likely to result in an increase in evidence in one or more of the accounts that affect gross margin. The auditor needs to determine the cause of the decline to be confident that the financial statements are not materially misstated.

A wide variety of analytical procedures allow auditors to compare client data with similar data from one or more prior periods. Here are some common examples:

Compare the Current Year's Balance with that of the Preceding Year One of the easiest ways to perform this test is to include the preceding year's adjusted trial balance results in a separate column of the current year's trial balance spreadsheet. The auditor can easily compare the current year's balance and the previous year's balance to decide, early in the audit, whether an account should receive more than the normal amount of attention because of a significant change in the balance. For example, if the auditor observes a substantial increase in supplies expense, the auditor should determine whether the cause was an increased use of supplies, an error in the account due to a misclassification, or a misstatement of supplies inventory.

Compare the Detail of a Total Balance with Similar Detail for the Preceding Year If there have been no significant changes in the client's operations in the current year, much of the detail making up the totals in the financial statements should also remain unchanged. By briefly comparing the detail of the current period with similar

TABLE 7-6 Internal Comparisons and Relationships	
Ratio or Comparison	**Possible Misstatement**
Raw material turnover for a manufacturing company	Misstatement of inventory or cost of goods sold or obsolescence of raw material inventory
Sales commissions divided by net sales	Misstatement of sales commissions
Sales returns and allowances divided by gross sales	Misclassified sales returns and allowances or unrecorded returns or allowances subsequent to year-end
Bad debt expense divided by net sales	Misstatement in the allowance for bad debts
Each of the individual manufacturing expenses as a percent of total manufacturing expense	Significant misstatement of individual expenses within a total

detail of the preceding period, auditors often isolate information that needs further examination. Comparison of details may take the form of details over time, such as comparing the monthly totals for the current year and preceding year for sales, repairs, and other accounts, or details at a point in time, such as comparing the details of loans payable at the end of the current year with the detail at the end of the preceding year.

Compute Ratios and Percent Relationships for Comparison with Previous Years Comparing totals or details with previous years has two shortcomings. First, it fails to consider growth or decline in business activity. Second, relationships of data to other data, such as sales to cost of goods sold, are ignored. Ratio and percent relationships overcome both shortcomings. For example, the gross margin is a common percent relationship used by auditors.

Table 7-6 includes a few ratios and internal comparisons to show the widespread use of ratio analysis. In all these cases, the comparisons should be made with calculations made in previous years for the same client. Many of the ratios and percents used for comparison with previous years are the same ones used for comparison with industry data. For example, auditors often compare current year gross margin with industry averages, as well as margins for previous years.

Compare Client Data with Client-Determined Expected Results

Most companies prepare **budgets** for various aspects of their operations and financial results. Because budgets represent the client's expectations for the period, auditors should investigate the most significant differences between budgeted and actual results, as these areas may contain potential misstatements. The absence of differences may indicate that misstatements are unlikely. For example, audits of local, state, and federal governmental units commonly use this type of analytical procedure.

When client data are compared with budgets, there are two special concerns. First, the auditor must evaluate whether the budgets were realistic plans. In some organizations, budgets are prepared with little thought or care and therefore are not helpful in developing auditor expectations. A discussion of budget procedures with client personnel can provide insights about this concern. The second concern is the possibility that current financial information was changed by client personnel to conform to the budget. If that has occurred, the auditor will find no differences in comparing actual data with budgeted data, even if there are misstatements in the financial statements. Assessing control risk and performing detailed audit tests of actual data are usually done to minimize this concern.

Compare Client Data with Auditor-Determined Expected Results

Another common comparison of client data with expected results occurs when the *auditor calculates the expected balance for comparison with the actual balance*. In this type of substantive analytical procedure, the auditor develops an expectation of what an account balance should be by relating it to some other balance sheet or income statement account or accounts or by making a projection based on nonfinancial data or some historical trend.

Suppose that you are auditing a hotel. You may develop an expectation for total revenue from rooms by multiplying the number of rooms, the average daily rate for each room, and the average occupancy rate. You can then compare your estimate with recorded revenue as a test of the reasonableness of recorded revenue. The same approach can be applied to create estimates in other situations, such as tuition revenue at universities (average tuition multiplied by enrollment), factory payroll (total hours worked times the wage rate), and cost of materials sold (units sold times materials cost per unit).

Figure 7-2 illustrates how the auditor may make an independent calculation of interest expense on notes payable by multiplying the average ending balances and interest rates for both short-term and long-term notes payable as a substantive test of the reasonableness of recorded interest expense. Notice how the auditor's substantive analytical procedure begins with the development of the auditor's expectation of interest expense for short-term notes payable and combines that with the auditor's calculation of an estimated interest expense for long-term notes payable to arrive at the expected amount of total interest expense of $2,399,315. Because of the fluctuating nature of the short-term notes payable balance from month to month, the auditor's calculation of a twelve-month average balance and average interest rate generates a more precise estimate of expected interest expense. Less precision is needed for long-term notes payable given the constant rate of interest across the year and the stable nature of the balance outstanding. This working paper also effectively documents the auditor's expectation that is required by auditing standards for substantive analytical procedures.

COMMON FINANCIAL RATIOS

OBJECTIVE 7-6

Compute common financial ratios.

Auditors' analytical procedures often include the use of general financial ratios during planning and final review of the audited financial statements. These are useful for understanding recent events and the financial status of the business and for viewing the statements from the perspective of a user. The general financial analysis may be effective for identifying possible problem areas, where the auditor may do additional analysis and audit testing, as well as business problem areas in which the auditor can provide other assistance. When using these ratios, auditors must be sure to make appropriate comparisons. The most important comparisons are to those of previous years for the company and to industry averages or similar companies for the same year.

Ratios and other analytical procedures are normally calculated using spreadsheets and other types of audit software, in which several years of client and industry data can be maintained for comparative purposes. Ratios can be linked to the trial balance so that calculations are automatically updated as adjusting entries are made to the client's statements. For example, an adjustment to inventory and cost of goods sold affects a large number of ratios, including inventory turnover, the current ratio, gross margin, and other profitability measures.

We next examine some widely used financial ratios. The following computations are based on the 2016 financial statements of Hillsburg Hardware Co., which appear in the glossy insert to the textbook. These ratios were prepared from the trial balance in Figure 6-5 on page 154.

Short-term Debt-Paying Ability

$$\text{Cash ratio} = \frac{\text{cash + marketable securities}}{\text{current liabilities}} \quad \frac{828}{13{,}216} = 0.06$$

$$\text{Quick ratio} = \frac{\text{cash + marketable securities + net accounts receivable}}{\text{current liabilities}} \quad \frac{828 + 18{,}957 + 945}{13{,}216} = 1.57$$

$$\text{Current ratio} = \frac{\text{current assets}}{\text{current liabilities}} \quad \frac{51{,}027}{13{,}216} = 3.86$$

FIGURE 7-2 Hillsburg Hardware Overall Test of Interest Expense December 31, 2016

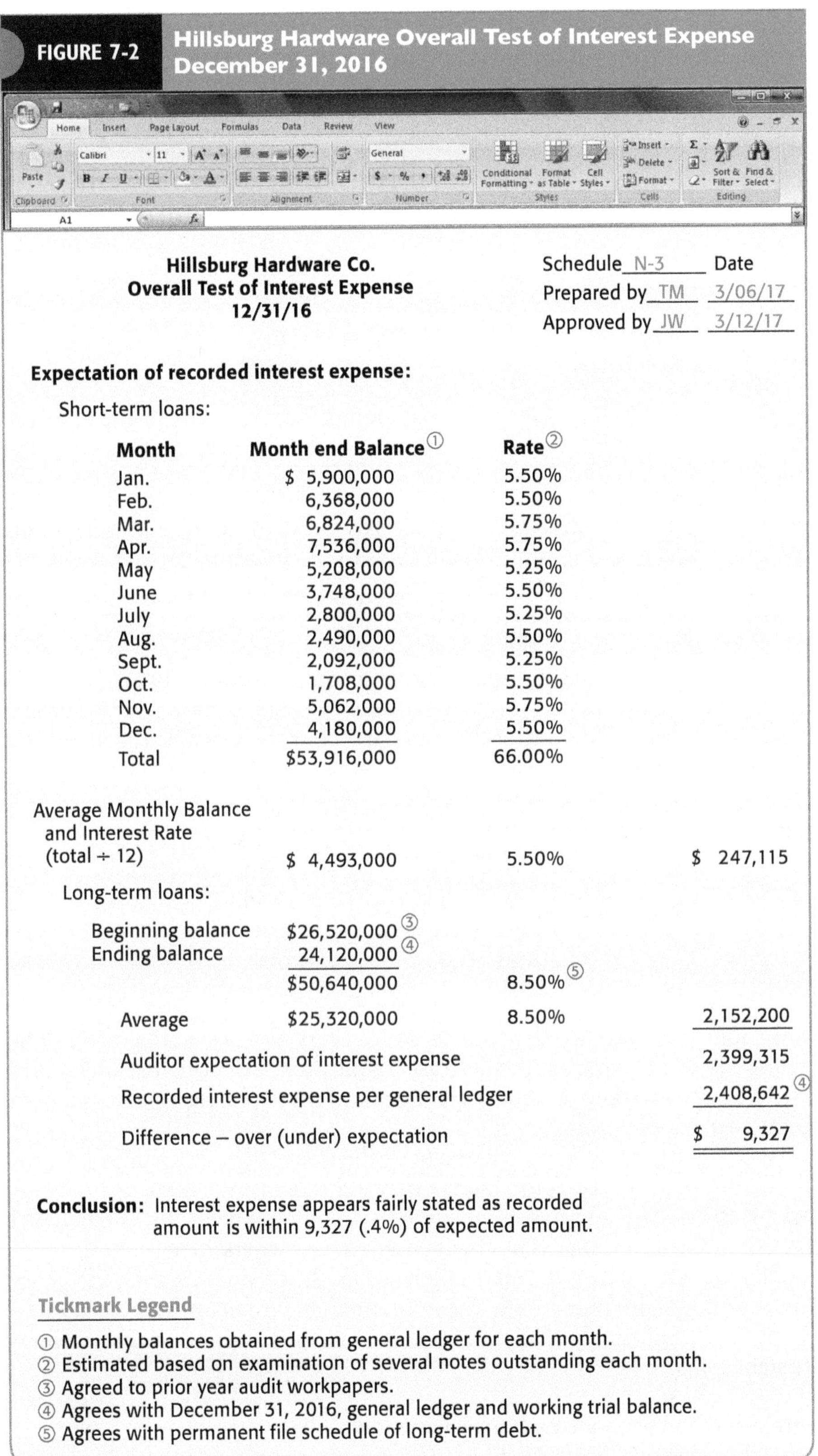

Hillsburg Hardware Co.
Overall Test of Interest Expense
12/31/16

Schedule N-3 Date
Prepared by TM 3/06/17
Approved by JW 3/12/17

Expectation of recorded interest expense:

Short-term loans:

Month	Month end Balance ①	Rate ②	
Jan.	$ 5,900,000	5.50%	
Feb.	6,368,000	5.50%	
Mar.	6,824,000	5.75%	
Apr.	7,536,000	5.75%	
May	5,208,000	5.25%	
June	3,748,000	5.50%	
July	2,800,000	5.25%	
Aug.	2,490,000	5.50%	
Sept.	2,092,000	5.25%	
Oct.	1,708,000	5.50%	
Nov.	5,062,000	5.75%	
Dec.	4,180,000	5.50%	
Total	$53,916,000	66.00%	
Average Monthly Balance and Interest Rate (total ÷ 12)	$ 4,493,000	5.50%	$ 247,115
Long-term loans:			
Beginning balance	$26,520,000 ③		
Ending balance	24,120,000 ④		
	$50,640,000	8.50% ⑤	
Average	$25,320,000	8.50%	2,152,200
Auditor expectation of interest expense			2,399,315
Recorded interest expense per general ledger			2,408,642 ④
Difference – over (under) expectation			$ 9,327

Conclusion: Interest expense appears fairly stated as recorded amount is within 9,327 (.4%) of expected amount.

Tickmark Legend

① Monthly balances obtained from general ledger for each month.
② Estimated based on examination of several notes outstanding each month.
③ Agreed to prior year audit workpapers.
④ Agrees with December 31, 2016, general ledger and working trial balance.
⑤ Agrees with permanent file schedule of long-term debt.

Companies need a reasonable level of liquidity to pay their debts as they come due, and these three ratios measure liquidity. It is apparent by examining the three ratios that the cash ratio may be useful to evaluate the ability to pay debts immediately, whereas the current ratio requires the conversion of assets such as inventory and accounts receivable to cash before debts can be paid. The most important difference between the quick and current ratios is the inclusion of inventory in current assets for the current ratio.

Liquidity Activity Ratios

$$\text{Accounts receivable turnover} = \frac{\text{net sales}}{\text{average gross receivables}} \qquad \frac{143{,}086}{((18{,}957 + 1{,}240) + (16{,}210 + 1{,}311))/2} = 7.59$$

$$\text{Days to collect receivables} = \frac{365 \text{ days}}{\text{accounts receivable turnover}} \qquad \frac{365 \text{ days}}{7.59} = 48.09 \text{ days}$$

$$\text{Inventory turnover} = \frac{\text{cost of goods sold}}{\text{average inventory}} \qquad \frac{103{,}241}{(29{,}865 + 31{,}600)/2} = 3.36$$

$$\text{Days to sell inventory} = \frac{365 \text{ days}}{\text{inventory turnover}} \qquad \frac{365 \text{ days}}{3.36} = 108.63 \text{ days}$$

If a company does not have sufficient cash and cash-like items to meet its obligations, the key to its debt-paying ability is the time it takes the company to convert less-liquid current assets into cash. This is measured by the liquidity activity ratios.

The activity ratios for accounts receivable and inventory are especially useful to auditors, who often use trends in the accounts receivable turnover ratio to assess the reasonableness of the allowance for uncollectible accounts. Auditors use trends in the inventory turnover ratio to identify potential inventory obsolescence. Average days to collect is a different way of looking at the average accounts receivable turnover data. The same is true of average days to sell compared to average inventory turnover.

Ability to Meet Long-term Debt Obligations

$$\text{Debt to equity} = \frac{\text{total liabilities}}{\text{total equity}} \qquad \frac{13{,}216 + 25{,}688}{22{,}463} = 1.73$$

$$\text{Times interest earned} = \frac{\text{operating income}}{\text{interest expense}} \qquad \frac{7{,}370}{2{,}409} = 3.06$$

A company's long-run solvency depends on the success of its operations and on its ability to raise capital for expansion, as well as its ability to make principal and interest payments. Two ratios are key measures creditors and investors use to assess a company's ability to pay its debts.

The debt-to-equity ratio shows the extent of the use of debt in financing a company. If the debt-to-equity ratio is too high, it may indicate that the company has used up its borrowing capacity and has no cushion for additional debt. If it is too low, it may mean that available leverage is not being used to the owners' benefit.

The ability to make interest payments depends on the company's ability to generate positive cash flow from operations. The times interest earned ratio shows whether the company can comfortably make its interest payments, assuming that earnings trends are stable.

Profitability Ratios

A company's ability to generate cash for payment of obligations, expansion, and dividends is heavily dependent on profitability. The most widely used profitability ratio is earnings per share. Auditors calculate additional ratios to provide further insights into operations.

Gross profit percent shows the portion of sales available to cover all expenses and profit after deducting the cost of the product. Auditors find this ratio especially useful for assessing misstatements in sales, cost of goods sold, accounts receivable, and inventory.

Profit margin is similar to gross profit margin but subtracts both cost of goods sold and operating expenses in making the calculations. This ratio enables auditors to assess potential misstatements in operating expenses and related balance sheet accounts.

$$\text{Earnings per share} = \frac{\text{net income}}{\text{average common shares outstanding}} \quad \frac{3{,}934}{5{,}000} = 0.79$$

$$\text{Gross profit percent} = \frac{\text{net sales} - \text{cost of goods sold}}{\text{net sales}} \quad \frac{143{,}086 - 103{,}241}{143{,}086} = 27.85\%$$

$$\text{Profit margin} = \frac{\text{operating income}}{\text{net sales}} \quad \frac{7{,}370}{143{,}086} = 0.05$$

$$\text{Return on assets} = \frac{\text{income before taxes}}{\text{average total assets}} \quad \frac{5{,}681}{(61{,}367 + 60{,}791)/2} = 0.09$$

$$\text{Return on common equity} = \frac{\text{income before taxes} - \text{preferred dividends}}{\text{average stockholders' equity}} \quad \frac{5{,}681 - 0}{(22{,}463 + 20{,}429)/2} = 0.26$$

Return on assets and return on common equity are measures of overall profitability of a company. These ratios show a company's ability to generate profit for each dollar of assets and equity.

CONCEPT CHECK

1. When are analytical procedures required on an audit? What is the primary purpose of analytical procedures during each phase of the audit?
2. Name the four categories of financial ratios and give an example of a ratio in each category. What is the primary information provided by each financial ratio category?

AUDIT DOCUMENTATION

OBJECTIVE 7-7

Understand the purposes of audit documentation.

Auditing standards state that **audit documentation** is the *record of the audit procedures performed, relevant audit evidence, and conclusions the auditor reached.* Audit documentation should include all the information the auditor considers necessary to adequately conduct the audit and to provide support for the audit report. Audit documentation may also be referred to as working papers or workpapers, although audit documentation is usually maintained in computerized files.

Purposes of Audit Documentation

The overall objective of audit documentation is to aid the auditor in providing reasonable assurance that an adequate audit was conducted in accordance with auditing standards. More specifically, audit documentation provides:

A Basis for Planning the Audit If the auditor is to plan an audit adequately, the necessary reference information must be available in the audit files. The files may include such diverse planning information as descriptive information about internal control, a time budget for individual audit areas, the audit program, and the results of the preceding year's audit.

A Record of the Evidence Accumulated and the Results of the Tests Audit documentation is the primary means of documenting that an adequate audit was conducted in accordance with auditing standards. If the need arises, the auditor must be able to demonstrate to regulatory agencies and courts that the audit was well planned and adequately supervised; the evidence accumulated was appropriate and sufficient; and the audit report was proper, considering the results of the audit.

Audit documentation should identify the items tested, any significant audit findings or issues, actions taken to address them, and the basis for the conclusions reached. For example, the auditor should document specific transactions at year-end to determine whether transactions were recorded in the proper period. If misstatements are detected during these cutoff tests, the auditor should document the additional procedures performed to determine the extent of cutoff misstatements, the conclusion as to whether the account balances affected are fairly stated, and whether any audit adjustments should be proposed.

Data for Determining the Proper Type of Audit Report Audit documentation provides an important source of information to assist the auditor in deciding whether sufficient appropriate evidence was accumulated to justify the audit report in a given set of circumstances. The data in the files are equally useful for evaluating whether the financial statements are fairly stated, given the audit evidence.

A Basis for Review by Supervisors and Partners The audit files are the primary frame of reference used by supervisory personnel to review the work of assistants. The careful review by supervisors also provides evidence that the audit was properly supervised. Audit documentation should indicate who performed the audit work, the date the work was performed, who reviewed the work, and the date of that review.

In addition to the purposes directly related to the audit report, the audit files often serve as the basis for preparing tax returns, filings with the SEC, and other reports. They are also a source of information for issuing communications to management and those charged with governance, such as the audit committee, concerning various matters such as internal control deficiencies or operational recommendations. Audit files are also a useful frame of reference for training personnel and as an aid in planning and coordinating subsequent audits.

Ownership of Audit Files

Audit documentation prepared during the engagement, including schedules prepared by the client for the auditor, is the *property of the auditor.* The only time anyone else, including the client, has a legal right to examine the files is when they are subpoenaed by a court as legal evidence or when they are examined by approved peer reviewers or regulatory inspectors. At the completion of the engagement, audit files are retained on the CPA's premises for future reference and to comply with auditing standards related to document retention.

Confidentiality of Audit Files

The need to maintain a confidential relationship with the client is expressed in the AICPA *Code of Professional Conduct,* which states

- A member in public practice shall not disclose any confidential client information without the specific consent of the client.[1]

During the course of the audit, auditors obtain a considerable amount of information of a confidential nature, including officers' salaries, product pricing and advertising plans, and product cost data. If auditors divulged this information to outsiders or to client employees who have been denied access, their relationship with management would be seriously strained. Furthermore, having access to the audit files would give employees an opportunity to alter the files. For these reasons, care must be taken to safeguard the audit files at all times.

Requirements for Retention of Audit Documentation

Auditing standards require that records for audits of private companies be retained for a minimum of five years. The Sarbanes–Oxley Act requires auditors of public companies to prepare and maintain audit files and other information related to any audit report in sufficient detail to support the auditor's conclusions, for a period of not less than seven years. The law makes the knowing and willful destruction of audit documentation within the seven-year period a criminal offense subject to financial fines and imprisonment up to ten years.

[1] *Source:* Copyright American Institute of CPAs. All rights reserved. Used with permission.

FIGURE 7-3 Audit File Contents and Organization

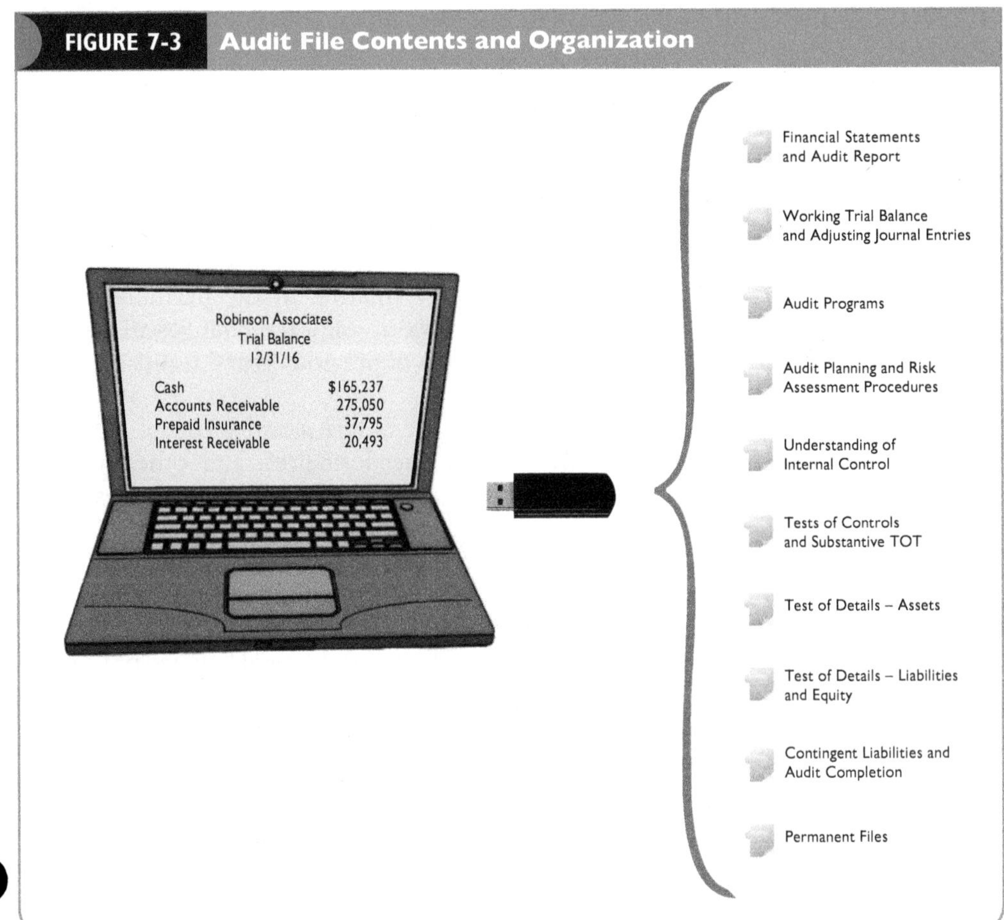

SEC rules require public company auditors to maintain the following documentation:

- Working papers or other documents that form the basis for the audit of the company's annual financial statements or review of the company's quarterly financial statements
- Memos, correspondence, communications, other documents and records, including electronic records, related to the audit or review

These rules significantly increase the audit documentation that must be retained for audits of public companies. For example, auditors of public companies are required to retain e-mail correspondence that contains information meeting the preceding criteria.

Contents and Organization

OBJECTIVE 7-8

Prepare organized audit documentation.

Each CPA firm establishes its own approach to preparing and organizing audit files, and the beginning auditor must adopt the firm's approach. This text emphasizes general concepts common to all audit documentation.

Figure 7-3 illustrates the contents and organization of a typical set of audit files. They contain virtually everything involved in the audit. There is logic to the type of audit documentation prepared for an audit and the way it is arranged in the files, though different firms may follow somewhat different approaches. In the figure, the audit files include general information, such as corporate data in the permanent files, in addition to current files that contain documentation of the auditor's tests, the financial statements, and audit report.

Permanent Files

Permanent files contain data of a *historical or continuing nature* pertinent to the current audit. These files provide a convenient source of information about the audit that is of continuing interest from year to year. The permanent files typically include the following:

- *Extracts or copies of such company documents of continuing importance as the articles of incorporation, bylaws, bond indentures, and contracts.* The contracts may include pension plans, leases, stock options, and so on. Each of these documents is significant to the auditor for as many years as it is in effect.
- *Analyses from previous years of accounts that have continuing importance to the auditor.* These include accounts such as long-term debt, stockholders' equity accounts, goodwill, and fixed assets. Having this information in the permanent files enables the auditor to concentrate on analyzing only the changes in the current year's balance while retaining the results of previous years' audits in a form accessible for review.
- *Information related to understanding internal control and assessing control risk.* This includes organization charts, flowcharts, questionnaires, and other internal control information, including identification of controls and deficiencies in the system. These records are used as a starting point for documenting the auditor's understanding of the control system, since aspects of the system are often unchanged from year to year.
- *The results of analytical procedures from previous years' audits.* Among these data are ratios and percentages computed by the auditor and the total balance or the balance by month for selected accounts. This information is useful in helping the auditor decide whether there are unusual changes in the current year's account balances that should be investigated more extensively.

Documenting analytical procedures, understanding of internal control, and assessing control risk are included in the current period audit files rather than in the permanent file by many CPA firms.

Current Files

The **current files** include all audit documentation applicable to the year under audit. There is one set of permanent files for the client and a set of current files for each year's audit. The following are types of information often included in the current file:

Audit Program Auditing standards require a written audit program for every audit. The audit program is often maintained in a separate file to improve the coordination and integration of all parts of the audit, although some firms also include a copy of the audit program with each audit section's audit documentation. As the audit progresses, each auditor initials or electronically signs the program for the audit procedures performed and indicates the date of completion. The inclusion in the audit files of a well-designed audit program completed in a conscientious manner is evidence of a high-quality audit.

Working Trial Balance Because the basis for preparing the financial statements is the general ledger, the amounts included in that record are the focal point of the audit. As early as possible after the balance sheet date, the auditor obtains or prepares a listing of the general ledger accounts and their year-end balances. This schedule is the **working trial balance**. Software programs enable the auditor to download the client's ending general ledger balances into a working trial balance file.

The technique used by many firms is to have the auditor's working trial balance in the same format as the financial statements. Each line item on the trial balance is supported by a **lead schedule**, containing the detailed accounts from the general ledger making up the line item total. Each detailed account on the lead schedule is, in turn, supported by proper schedules supporting the audit work performed and the conclusions reached. For example, the relationship between cash as it is stated on the financial statements, the working trial balance, the lead schedule for cash, and the supporting audit documentation is presented in Figure 7-4. As indicated, cash on the financial statements is the same as on the working trial balance and the total of the detail on the cash lead schedule. Initially,

FIGURE 7-4 Relationship of Audit Documentation to Financial Statements

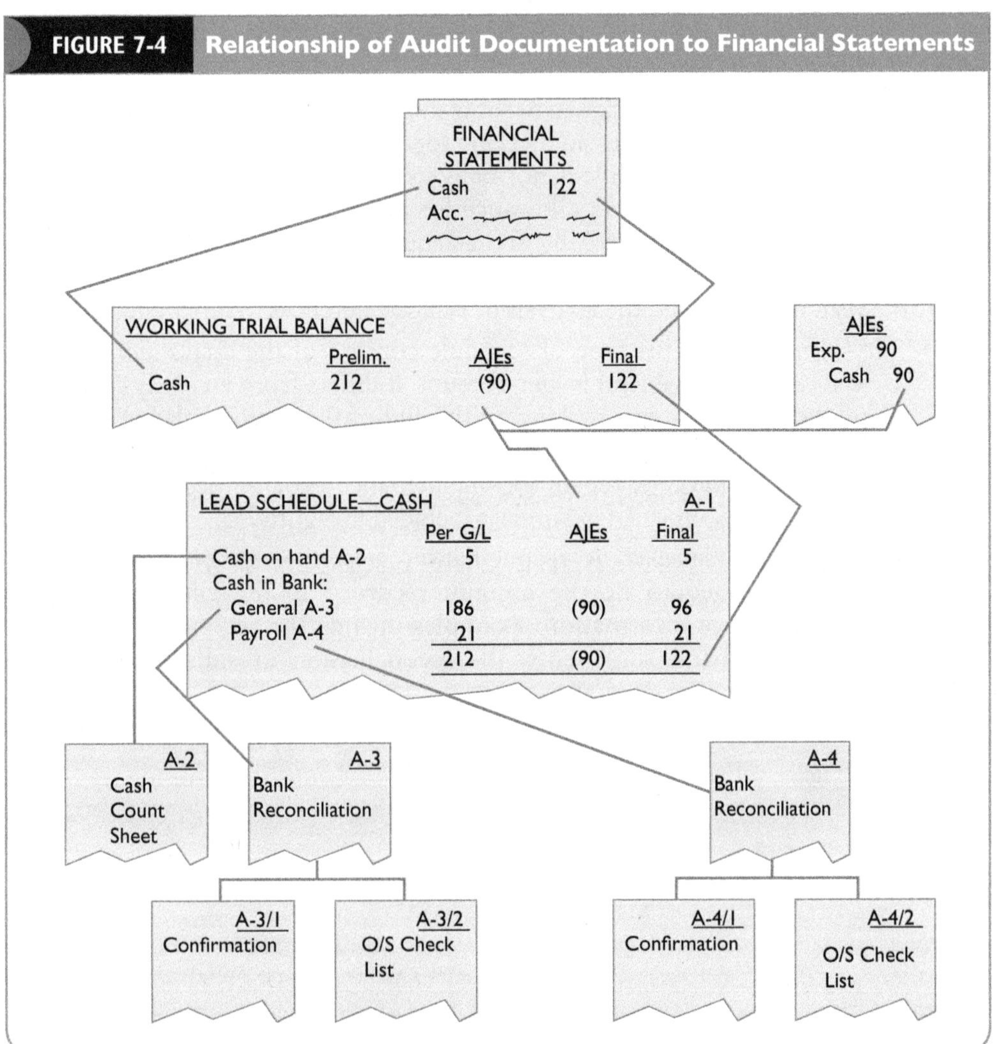

amounts for the lead schedule were taken from the general ledger. The audit work performed resulted in an adjustment to cash that will be shown in the detail schedules and is reflected on the lead schedule, the working trial balance, and the financial statements.

Adjusting Entries When the auditor discovers material misstatements in the accounting records, the financial statements must be corrected. For example, if the client failed to properly reduce inventory for obsolete raw materials, the auditor can propose an adjusting entry to reflect the realizable value of the inventory. Even though adjusting entries discovered in the audit are often prepared by the auditor, they must be approved by the client because management has primary responsibility for the fair presentation of the statements. Figure 7-4 illustrates an adjustment of the general cash account for $90 (thousand).

Only those adjusting entries that significantly affect the fair presentation of financial statements must be recorded. Auditors decide when a misstatement should be adjusted based on materiality. At the same time, auditors must keep in mind that several immaterial misstatements that are not adjusted could, when combined, result in a material overall misstatement. It is common for auditors to summarize all entries that have not been recorded in a separate audit schedule as a means of assessing their cumulative effect.

Supporting Schedules The largest portion of audit documentation includes the detailed **supporting schedules** prepared by the client or the auditors in support of specific amounts on the financial statements. Auditors must choose the proper type of schedule for a given aspect of the audit in order to document the adequacy of the audit and to fulfill the other objectives of audit documentation. Here are the major types of supporting schedules:

- *Analysis.* An analysis is designed to show the *activity in a general ledger* account during the entire period under audit, tying together the beginning and ending balances. This type of schedule is normally used for accounts such as marketable securities; notes receivable; allowance for doubtful accounts; property, plant, and equipment; long-term debt; and all equity accounts. The common characteristic of these accounts is the significance of the activity in the account during the year. In most cases, the analysis has cross-references to other audit files.
- *Trial balance or list.* This type of schedule consists of the *details that make up a year-end balance* of a general ledger account. It differs from an analysis in that it includes only those items making up the end-of-the-period balance. Common examples include trial balances or lists in support of trade accounts receivable, trade accounts payable, repair and maintenance expense, legal expense, and miscellaneous income. An example is included in Figure 7-5.
- *Reconciliation of amounts.* A reconciliation *supports a specific amount* and is normally expected to tie the amount recorded in the client's records to another source of information. Examples include the reconciliation of cash balances with bank statements, the reconciliation of subsidiary accounts

FIGURE 7-5 Common Characteristics of Proper Audit Documentation

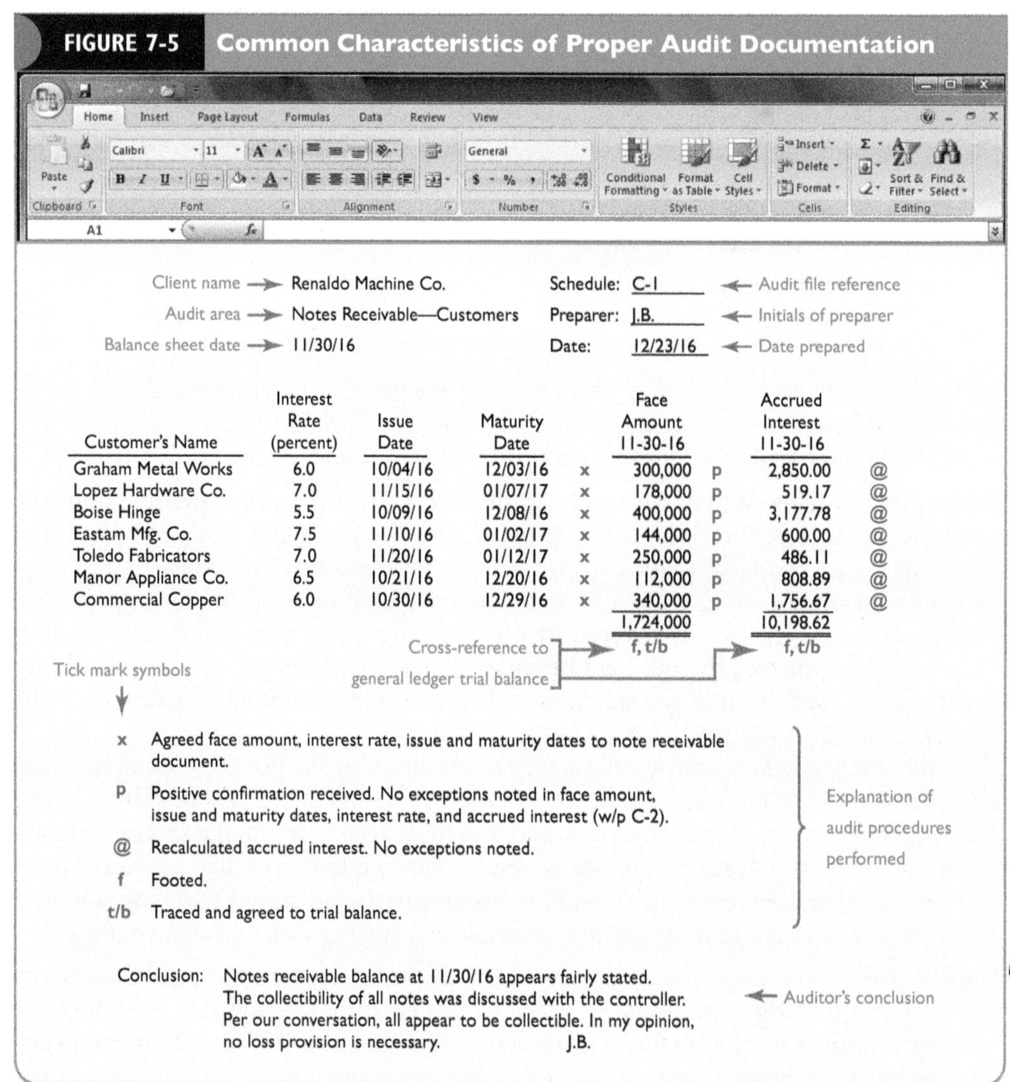

Client name → Renaldo Machine Co. | Schedule: C-1 ← Audit file reference

Audit area → Notes Receivable—Customers | Preparer: J.B. ← Initials of preparer

Balance sheet date → 11/30/16 | Date: 12/23/16 ← Date prepared

Customer's Name	Interest Rate (percent)	Issue Date	Maturity Date		Face Amount 11-30-16		Accrued Interest 11-30-16	
Graham Metal Works	6.0	10/04/16	12/03/16	x	300,000	p	2,850.00	@
Lopez Hardware Co.	7.0	11/15/16	01/07/17	x	178,000	p	519.17	@
Boise Hinge	5.5	10/09/16	12/08/16	x	400,000	p	3,177.78	@
Eastam Mfg. Co.	7.5	11/10/16	01/02/17	x	144,000	p	600.00	@
Toledo Fabricators	7.0	11/20/16	01/12/17	x	250,000	p	486.11	@
Manor Appliance Co.	6.5	10/21/16	12/20/16	x	112,000	p	808.89	@
Commercial Copper	6.0	10/30/16	12/29/16	x	340,000	p	1,756.67	@
					1,724,000		10,198.62	
					f, t/b		f, t/b	

Cross-reference to general ledger trial balance

Tick mark symbols

x Agreed face amount, interest rate, issue and maturity dates to note receivable document.

p Positive confirmation received. No exceptions noted in face amount, issue and maturity dates, interest rate, and accrued interest (w/p C-2).

@ Recalculated accrued interest. No exceptions noted.

f Footed.

t/b Traced and agreed to trial balance.

} Explanation of audit procedures performed

Conclusion: Notes receivable balance at 11/30/16 appears fairly stated. The collectibility of all notes was discussed with the controller. Per our conversation, all appear to be collectible. In my opinion, no loss provision is necessary. J.B. ← Auditor's conclusion

WILL IT STAND UP IN COURT?

Rhonda McMillan had been the in-charge auditor on the audit of Blaine Construction Company in 2011. Now she is sitting here, in 2017, in a room full of attorneys who are asking her questions about the 2011 audit. Blaine was sold to another company in 2012 at a purchase price that was based primarily on the 2011 audited financial statements. Several of the large construction contracts showed a profit in 2011 using the percentage of completion method, but they ultimately resulted in large losses for the buyer. Because Rhonda's firm audited the 2011 financial statements, the buyer is trying to make the case that Rhonda's firm failed in their audit of contract costs and revenues.

The buyer's attorney is taking Rhonda's deposition and is asking her about the audit work she did on contracts. Referring to the audit files, his examination goes something like this:

ATTORNEY Do you recognize this exhibit, and if you do, would you please identify it for us?

RHONDA Yes, this is the summary of contracts in progress at the end of 2011.

ATTORNEY Did you prepare this schedule?

RHONDA I believe the client prepared it, but I audited it. My initials are right here in the upper right-hand corner.

ATTORNEY When did you do this audit work?

RHONDA I'm not sure, I forgot to date this one. But it must have been about the second week in March, because that's when we did the audit testing.

ATTORNEY Now I'd like to turn your attention to this tick mark next to the Baldwin contract. You see where it shows Baldwin, and then the red sort of cross-like mark?

RHONDA Yes.

ATTORNEY In the explanation for that tick mark it says: "Discussed status of job with Elton Burgess. Job is going according to schedule, and he believes that the expected profit will be earned." Now my question is, Ms. McMillan, what exactly was the nature and content of your discussion with Mr. Burgess?

RHONDA Other than what is in the explanation to this tick mark, I have no idea. I mean, this all took place over five years ago. I only worked on the engagement that one year, and I can hardly even remember that.

Rhonda's work was not adequately documented, and what was there indicated that her testing relied almost exclusively on management inquiry without any required corroboration. Her audit firm was required to pay a significant settlement for damages to the buyer.

receivable balances with confirmations from customers, and the reconciliation of accounts payable balances with vendors' statements. See the bank reconciliation example on page 743.

- *Substantive analytical procedures.* Substantive analytical procedures, discussed earlier in the chapter, include evidence documenting the auditor's expectation of the balance in an account, as illustrated in Figure 7-2 on page 197.
- *Summary of procedures.* Another type of schedule *summarizes the results* of a specific audit procedure. A summary schedule documents the extent of testing, the misstatements found, and the auditor's conclusion based on the testing. Examples are the summary of the results of accounts receivable confirmations and the summary of inventory observations.
- *Examination of supporting documents.* A number of special-purpose schedules are designed to *show detailed tests performed*, such as documents examined during tests of controls and substantive tests of transactions. These schedules show no totals, and they do not tie in to the general ledger because their purpose is to document the tests performed and the results found. However, the schedules must state a positive or negative conclusion about the objective of the test.
- *Informational.* This type of schedule contains information as opposed to audit evidence. These schedules include information for tax returns and SEC Form 10-K and data such as time budgets and the client's working hours, which are helpful in administration of the engagement.
- *Outside documentation.* Some of the content of the audit files consists of outside documentation gathered by auditors, such as confirmation replies and copies of client agreements. Although not "schedules" in the usual sense, they are indexed and filed. Audit procedures are indicated on them in the same manner as on other schedules.

Preparation of Audit Documentation

Read the story on the preceding page about Rhonda McMillan and imagine yourself in her position several years after completing an audit. The proper preparation of schedules to document the audit evidence accumulated, the results found, and the conclusions reached is an important part of the audit. The documentation should be prepared in sufficient detail to provide an experienced auditor with no connection to the audit a clear understanding of the work performed, the evidence obtained and its source, and the conclusions reached. Although the design depends on the objectives involved, audit documentation should possess certain characteristics:

- Each audit file should be properly identified with such information as the client's name, the period covered, a description of the contents, the initials of the preparer, the date of preparation, and an index code.
- Audit documentation should be indexed and cross-referenced to aid in organizing and filing. One type of indexing is illustrated in Figure 7-4 (p. 203). The lead schedule for cash has been indexed as A-1, and the individual general ledger accounts making up the total cash on the financial statements are indexed as A-2 through A-4. The final indexing is for the schedules supporting A-3 and A-4.
- Completed audit documentation must clearly indicate the audit work performed. This is accomplished in three ways: by a written statement in the form of a memorandum, by initialing the audit procedures in the audit program, and by notations directly on the schedules. Notations on schedules are accomplished by the use of **tick marks**, which are symbols adjacent to the detail on the body of the schedule. These notations must be clearly explained at the bottom of the schedule.
- Audit documentation should include sufficient information to fulfill the objectives for which it was designed. To properly prepare audit documentation, the auditor must know his or her goals. For example, if a schedule is designed to list the detail and show the verification of support of a balance sheet account, such as prepaid insurance, it is essential that the detail on the schedule reconciles with the trial balance.
- The conclusions that were reached about the segment of the audit under consideration should be plainly stated.

The common characteristics of proper audit documentation preparation are indicated in Figure 7-5 (p. 204).

Auditors often use audit engagement management software to organize and analyze audit documentation. Using audit management software, an auditor can prepare a trial balance, lead schedules, supporting audit documentation, and financial statements, as well as perform ratio analysis. The software also facilitates tracking audit progress by indicating the performance and review status of each audit area. Tick marks and other explanations, such as reviewer notes, can be entered directly into computerized files. In addition, data can be imported and exported to other applications, so auditors may download a client's general ledger or export tax information to a commercial tax preparation package. Auditors also use local area networks and groupshare software programs to access audit documentation simultaneously from remote locations.

CONCEPT CHECK

1. List the purposes of audit documentation and explain why each purpose is important.
2. Explain why it is important for audit documentation to include each of the following: identification of the name of the client, period covered, description of the contents, initials of the preparer and the reviewer, dates of the preparation and review, and an index code.

SUMMARY

An important part of every audit is determining the proper types and amounts of audit evidence to gather. Auditors use eight types of evidence in an audit. The persuasiveness of the evidence depends on both its appropriateness and sufficiency. The appropriateness of audit evidence is determined by its relevance in meeting audit objectives and its reliability.

Analytical procedures are the evaluation of recorded accounting information by computing ratios and developing other plausible relationships for comparison to expectations developed by the auditor. These analytical procedures are used in planning to understand the client's business and industry and also used throughout the audit to identify possible misstatements, reduce detailed tests, and assess going-concern issues. The use of analytical procedures has increased because of their effectiveness at identifying possible misstatements at a low cost, and they are required in the planning and completion phases of the audit.

Audit documentation is an essential part of every audit for effectively planning the audit, providing a record of the evidence accumulated and the results of the tests, deciding the proper type of audit report, and reviewing the work of assistants. CPA firms establish their own policies and approaches to audit documentation to make sure that these objectives are met. High-quality CPA firms make sure that audit documentation is properly prepared and is sufficient for the circumstances in the audit.

ESSENTIAL TERMS

Analytical procedures—evaluations of financial information through analysis of plausible relationships among financial and nonfinancial data

Appropriateness of evidence—a measure of the quality of evidence; appropriate evidence is relevant and reliable in meeting audit objectives for classes of transactions, account balances, and related disclosures

Audit documentation—record of the audit procedures performed, relevant audit evidence, and conclusions the auditor reached

Audit procedure—detailed instruction for the collection of a type of audit evidence

Audit program—list of audit procedures for an audit area or an entire audit; the audit program always includes audit procedures and may also include sample sizes, items to select, and timing of the tests

Budgets—written records of the client's expectations for the period; a comparison of budgets with actual results may indicate whether or not misstatements are likely

Confirmation—the auditor's receipt of a direct written or electronic response from a third party verifying the accuracy of information requested

Current files—all audit files applicable to the year under audit

External document—a document, such as a vendor's invoice, that has been used by an outside party to the transaction being documented and that the client now has or can easily obtain

Inquiry—the obtaining of written or oral information from the client in response to specific questions during the audit

Inspection—the auditor's examination of the client's documents and records to substantiate the information that is or should be included in the financial statements

Internal document—a document, such as an employee time report, that is prepared and used within the client's organization

Lead schedule—an audit schedule that contains the detailed accounts from the general ledger making up a line item total in the working trial balance

Observation—looking at a process or procedure being performed by others

Permanent files—auditors' files that contain data of a *historical or continuing nature* pertinent to the current audit such as copies of articles of incorporation, bylaws, bond indentures, and contracts

Persuasiveness of evidence—the degree to which the auditor is convinced that the evidence supports the audit opinion; the two determinants of persuasiveness are the appropriateness and sufficiency of the evidence

Physical examination—the auditor's inspection or count of a tangible asset

Recalculation—the rechecking of a sample of the computations made by the client, including mathematical accuracy of individual transactions and amounts and the adding of journals and subsidiary records

Reliability of evidence—the extent to which evidence is believable or worthy of trust; evidence is reliable when it is obtained (1) from an independent provider, (2) from a client with effective internal controls, (3) from the auditor's direct knowledge, (4) from qualified providers such as law firms and banks, (5) from objective sources, and (6) in a timely manner

Reperformance—the auditor's independent tests of client accounting procedures or controls that were originally done as part of the entity's accounting and internal control system

Substantive analytical procedure—an analytical procedure in which the auditor develops an expectation of recorded amounts or ratios to provide evidence supporting an account balance

Sufficiency of evidence—the quantity of evidence; proper sample size

Supporting schedules—detailed schedules prepared by the client or the auditor in support of specific amounts on the financial statements

Tick marks—symbols used on an audit schedule that provide additional information or details of audit procedures performed

Tracing—the use of documentation to determine if transactions or amounts are included in the accounting records

Unusual fluctuations—significant unexpected differences indicated by analytical procedures between the current year's unaudited financial data and other data used in comparisons

Vouching—the use of documentation to support recorded transactions or amounts

Working trial balance—a listing of the general ledger accounts and their year-end balances

REVIEW QUESTIONS

7-1 **(OBJECTIVE 7-1)** Discuss the similarities and differences between evidence in a legal case and evidence in an audit of financial statements.

7-2 **(OBJECTIVE 7-2)** List the four major evidence decisions that must be made on every audit.

7-3 **(OBJECTIVE 7-2)** Describe what is meant by an audit procedure. Why is it important for audit procedures to be carefully worded?

7-4 **(OBJECTIVE 7-2)** Describe what is meant by an audit program for accounts receivable. What four things should be included in an audit program?

7-5 **(OBJECTIVE 7-3)** Explain why the auditor can be persuaded only with a reasonable level of assurance, rather than convinced, that the financial statements are correct.

7-6 **(OBJECTIVE 7-3)** Identify the two factors that determine the persuasiveness of evidence. How are these two factors related to audit procedures, sample size, items to select, and timing?

7-7 **(OBJECTIVE 7-4)** What are the characteristics of a confirmation? Distinguish between a confirmation and external documentation.

7-8 **(OBJECTIVE 7-4)** Distinguish between internal documentation and external documentation as audit evidence and give three examples of each.

7-9 **(OBJECTIVE 7-4)** Identify the most important reasons for performing analytical procedures.

7-10 **(OBJECTIVE 7-5)** What is the primary purpose of analytical procedures performed during the completion phase of the audit?

7-11 **(OBJECTIVE 7-5)** Distinguish between attention-directing analytical procedures and those intended to eliminate or reduce detailed substantive procedures.

7-12 **(OBJECTIVE 7-5)** At the completion of every audit, Roger Morris, CPA, calculates a large number of ratios and trends for comparison with industry averages and prior-year calculations. He believes the calculations are worth the relatively small cost of doing them because they provide him with an excellent overview of the client's operations. If the ratios are out of line, Morris discusses the reasons with the client and often makes suggestions on how to bring the ratio back in line in the future. In some cases, these discussions with management have been the basis for management consulting engagements. Discuss the major strengths and shortcomings in Morris's use of ratio and trend analysis.

7-13 **(OBJECTIVE 7-6)** Describe the liquidity activity ratios and explain why these ratios are useful to auditors.

7-14 **(OBJECTIVE 7-7)** Who owns the audit files? Under what circumstances can they be used by other people?

7-15 **(OBJECTIVE 7-7)** For how long does the Sarbanes–Oxley Act require auditors of public companies to retain audit documentation?

7-16 **(OBJECTIVE 7-8)** Define what is meant by a permanent file, and list several types of information typically included. Why does the auditor not include the contents of the permanent file with the current year's audit file?

7-17 **(OBJECTIVE 7-8)** Distinguish among the following types of current period supporting schedules and state the purpose of each: analysis, trial balance, and substantive analytical procedures.

7-18 **(OBJECTIVE 7-8)** Why is it essential that the auditor not leave questions or exceptions in the audit documentation without an adequate explanation?

7-19 **(OBJECTIVE 7-8)** Define what is meant by a tick mark. What is its purpose?

7-20 **(OBJECTIVE 7-8)** Explain the purposes and benefits of audit engagement management software.

MULTIPLE CHOICE QUESTIONS FROM CPA EXAMINATIONS

7-21 **(OBJECTIVES 7-3, 7-4)** The following questions concern persuasiveness of evidence. Choose the best response.

a. Which of the following types of documentary evidence should the auditor consider to be the most reliable?
   (1) A sales invoice issued by the client and supported by a delivery receipt from an outside trucker
   (2) Confirmation of an account payable balance mailed by and returned directly to the auditor
   (3) A check, issued by the company and bearing the payee's endorsement, that is included with the bank statements mailed directly to the auditor
   (4) An audit schedule prepared by the client's controller and reviewed by the client's treasurer

b. Audit evidence can come in different forms with different degrees of persuasiveness. Which of the following is the least persuasive type of evidence?
   (1) Vendor's invoice
   (2) Bank statement obtained from the client
   (3) Computations made by the auditor
   (4) Prenumbered sales invoices

c. Which of the following presumptions is correct about the reliability of audit evidence?
   (1) Information obtained indirectly from outside sources is the most reliable audit evidence.
   (2) To be reliable, audit evidence should be convincing rather than merely persuasive.
   (3) Reliability of audit evidence refers to the amount of corroborative evidence obtained.
   (4) Effective internal control provides more assurance about the reliability of audit evidence.

7-22 **(OBJECTIVES 7-5, 7-6)** The following questions concern the use of analytical procedures during an audit. Select the best response.

a. For all audits of financial statements made in accordance with auditing standards, the use of analytical procedures is required to some extent

	In the Planning Stage	As a Substantive Test	In the Completion Stage
(1)	Yes	No	Yes
(2)	No	Yes	No
(3)	No	Yes	Yes
(4)	Yes	No	No

b. Which of the following situations has the best chance of being detected when a CPA compares 2016 revenues and expenses with the prior year and investigates all changes exceeding a fixed percent?
   (1) An increase in property tax rates has not been recognized in the company's 2016 accrual.
   (2) The cashier began lapping accounts receivable in 2016.
   (3) Because of worsening economic conditions, the 2016 provision for uncollectible accounts was inadequate.
   (4) The company changed its capitalization policy for small tools in 2016.

c. Which of the following would *not* be considered to be an analytical procedure?
   (1) Estimating payroll expense by multiplying the number of employees by the average hourly wage rate and the total hours worked.
   (2) Projecting the error rate by comparing the results of a statistical sample with the actual population characteristics.
   (3) Computing accounts receivable turnover by dividing credit sales by the average net receivables.
   (4) Developing the expected current year sales based on the sales trend of the prior five years.

7-23 **(OBJECTIVES 7-7, 7-8)** The following questions concern audit documentation. Choose the best response.

a. Which of the following is *not* a primary purpose of audit documentation?
   (1) To coordinate the audit
   (2) To assist in preparation of the audit report
   (3) To support the financial statements
   (4) To provide evidence of the audit work performed

b. During an audit engagement, pertinent data are compiled and included in the audit files. The audit files primarily are considered to be
   (1) a client-owned record of conclusions reached by the auditors who performed the engagement.
   (2) evidence supporting financial statements.
   (3) support for the auditor's representations as to compliance with auditing standards.
   (4) a record to be used as a basis for the following year's engagement.

c. Although the quantity, type, and content of audit documentation will vary with the circumstances, audit documentation generally will include the
   (1) copies of those client records examined by the auditor during the course of the engagement.
   (2) evaluation of the efficiency and competence of the audit staff assistants by the partner responsible for the audit.
   (3) auditor's comments concerning the efficiency and competence of client management personnel.
   (4) auditing procedures followed and the testing performed in obtaining audit evidence.

MULTIPLE CHOICE QUESTIONS FROM BECKER CPA EXAM REVIEW

7-24 **(OBJECTIVES 7-3, 7-5, 7-7)** The following questions concern audit evidence and audit documentation. Choose the best response.

a. According to PCAOB audit standards, audit documentation must be retained for
   (1) one year.
   (2) three years.
   (3) five years.
   (4) seven years.

b. Which of the following types of audit evidence is generally the most reliable?
   (1) A bank statement
   (2) A bank confirmation
   (3) Analytical procedures
   (4) Inquiries made of the audit committee

c. An auditor most likely would apply analytical procedures in the overall review stage of an audit to
   (1) identify unusual or unexpected balances that were not previously identified.
   (2) obtain an understanding of high-risk areas.
   (3) evaluate the design and implementation of internal control.
   (4) identify related party transactions that may not have been previously identified.

DISCUSSION QUESTIONS AND PROBLEMS

7-25 **(OBJECTIVE 7-4)** The following are examples of documentation typically obtained by auditors:

1. Duplicate sales invoices
2. Subsidiary accounts receivable records
3. Vendors' invoices
4. General ledgers
5. Title insurance policies for real estate
6. Notes receivable
7. Bank statements
8. Cancelled payroll checks
9. Cancelled notes payable
10. Payroll time cards
11. Purchase requisitions
12. Articles of incorporation
13. Receiving reports (documents prepared when merchandise is received)
14. Minutes of the board of directors
15. Signed W-4s (Employee's Withholding Exemption Certificates)
16. Remittance advices
17. Signed lease agreements
18. Duplicate copies of bills of lading

Required

a. Classify each of the preceding items according to type of documentation: (1) internal or (2) external.
b. Explain why external evidence is more reliable than internal evidence.

7-26 **(OBJECTIVE 7-4)** The following are examples of audit procedures:

1. Calculate the ratio of sales commission expense to sales as a test of sales commissions.
2. Review the accounts receivable with the credit manager to evaluate their collectibility.

3. Compare a duplicate sales invoice with the sales journal for customer name and amount.
4. Obtain a written statement from a bank stating that the client has $15,671 on deposit and liabilities of $500,000 on a demand note.
5. Add the sales journal entries to determine whether they were correctly totaled.
6. Count a sample of inventory items and record the amount in the audit files.
7. Obtain a letter from the client's attorney addressed to the CPA firm stating that the attorney is not aware of any existing lawsuits.
8. Extend the cost of inventory times the quantity on an inventory listing to test whether it is accurate.
9. Obtain a letter from an insurance company to the CPA firm stating the amount of the fire insurance coverage on buildings and equipment.
10. Examine an insurance policy stating the amount of the fire insurance coverage on buildings and equipment.
11. Calculate the ratio of cost of goods sold to sales as a test of overall reasonableness of gross margin relative to the preceding year.
12. Obtain information about internal control by requesting the client to fill out a questionnaire.
13. Trace the total in the cash disbursements journal to the general ledger.
14. Watch employees count inventory to determine whether company procedures are being followed.
15. Examine a piece of equipment to make sure that a major acquisition was actually received and is in operation.
16. Examine corporate minutes to determine the authorization of the issue of bonds.
17. Obtain a letter from management stating that there are no unrecorded liabilities.
18. Review the total of repairs and maintenance for each month to determine whether any month's total was unusually large.

Required Classify each of the preceding items according to the eight types of audit evidence: (1) physical examination, (2) confirmation, (3) inspection, (4) analytical procedures, (5) inquiries of the client, (6) recalculation, (7) reperformance, and (8) observation.

7-27 **(OBJECTIVE 7-4)** As auditor of the Star Manufacturing Company, you have obtained a trial balance taken from the books of Star one month before year-end:

	Dr. (Cr.)		Dr. (Cr.)
Cash in bank	$ 87,000	Mortgages payable	(400,000)
Trade accounts receivable	345,000	Capital stock	(300,000)
		Retained earnings	(510,000)
Notes receivable	125,000	Sales	(3,130,000)
Inventories	317,000	Cost of sales	2,300,000
Land	66,000	General and administrative expenses	622,000
Buildings, net	350,000		
Furniture, fixtures, and equipment, net	325,000	Legal and professional fees	3,000
		Interest expense	35,000
Trade accounts payable	(235,000)		

There are no inventories consigned either in or out.
All notes receivable are due from outsiders and held by Star.

Required Which accounts should be confirmed with outside sources? Briefly describe from whom they should be confirmed and the information that should be confirmed. Organize your answer in the following format*:

Account Name	From Whom Confirmed	Information to Be Confirmed

*Based on AICPA question paper, American Institute of Certified Public Accountants.

7-28 (OBJECTIVE 7-4) The following are various audit procedures performed to satisfy specific transaction-related audit objectives as discussed in Chapter 6. The general transaction-related audit objectives from Chapter 6 are also included.

Audit Procedures

1. Trace from receiving reports to vendors' invoices and entries in the acquisitions journal.
2. Add the sales journal for the month of July and trace amounts to the general ledger.
3. Examine expense voucher packages and related vendors' invoices for approval of expense account classification.
4. Observe opening of cash receipts to determine that cash receipts are promptly deposited and recorded.
5. Ask the accounts payable clerk about procedures for verifying prices, quantities, and extensions on vendors' invoices.
6. Vouch entries in sales journal to sales invoices and related shipping documents.

General Transaction-Related Audit Objectives

Occurrence	Posting and summarization
Completeness	Classification
Accuracy	Timing

Required

a. Identify the type of audit evidence used for each audit procedure.
b. Identify the general transaction-related audit objective or objectives satisfied by each audit procedure.

7-29 (OBJECTIVE 7-4) The following audit procedures were performed in the audit of inventory to satisfy specific balance-related audit objectives as discussed in Chapter 6. The audit procedures assume that the auditor has obtained the inventory count sheets that list the client's inventory. The general balance-related audit objectives from Chapter 6 are also included.

Audit Procedures

1. Select a sample of inventory items in the factory warehouse and trace each item to the inventory count sheets to determine if it has been included and if the quantity and description are correct.
2. Trace selected quantities from the inventory list to the physical inventory to make sure that it exists and the quantities are the same.
3. Compare the quantities on hand and unit prices on this year's inventory count sheets with those in the preceding year as a test for large differences.
4. Test the extension of unit prices times quantity on the inventory list for a sample of inventory items, test foot the list, and compare the total to the general ledger.
5. Send letters directly to third parties who hold the client's inventory, and request that they respond directly to the auditors.
6. Examine sales invoices and contracts with customers to determine whether any goods are out on consignment with customers. Similarly, examine vendors' invoices and contracts with vendors to determine whether any goods on the inventory listing are owned by vendors.
7. Question operating personnel about the possibility of obsolete or slow-moving inventory.

General Balance-Related Audit Objectives

Existence	Cutoff
Completeness	Detail tie-in
Accuracy	Realizable value
Classification	Rights and obligations

Required

a. Identify the type of audit evidence used for each audit procedure.
b. Identify the general balance-related audit objective or objectives satisfied by each audit procedure.

7-30 **(OBJECTIVES 7-3, 7-4)** The following are nine situations, each containing two means of accumulating evidence:

1. Confirm receivables with consumers versus confirming accounts receivable with business organizations.
2. Physically examine 3-inch steel plates versus examining electronic parts.
3. Examine duplicate sales invoices when several competent people are checking each other's work versus examining documents prepared by a competent person on a one-person staff.
4. Physically examine inventory of parts for the number of units on hand versus examining them for the likelihood of inventory being obsolete.
5. Discuss the likelihood and amount of loss in a lawsuit against the client with client's in-house legal counsel versus discussion with the CPA firm's own legal counsel.
6. Confirm the oil and gas reserves with a geologist specializing in oil and gas versus confirming a bank balance.
7. Confirm a bank balance versus examining the client's bank statements.
8. Physically count the client's inventory held by an independent party versus confirming the count with an independent party.
9. Obtain a physical inventory count from the company president versus physically counting the client's inventory.

Required

a. Identify the six factors that determine the reliability of evidence.
b. For each of the nine situations, state whether the first or second type of evidence is more reliable.
c. For each situation, state which of the six factors affected the reliability of the evidence.

7-31 **(OBJECTIVE 7-4)** Following are 10 audit procedures with words missing and a list of several terms commonly used in audit procedures.

Audit Procedures

1. ______ the unit selling price times quantity on the duplicate sales invoice and compare the total to the amount on the duplicate sales invoice.
2. ______ whether the accounts receivable bookkeeper is prohibited from handling cash.
3. ______ the ratio of cost of goods sold to sales and compare the ratio to previous years.
4. ______ the sales journal and ______ the total to the general ledger.
5. ______ the sales journal, looking for large and unusual transactions requiring investigation.
6. ______ of management whether all accounting employees are required to take annual vacations.
7. ______ all marketable securities as of the balance sheet date to determine whether they equal the total on the client's list.
8. ______ the balance in the bank account directly with the East State Bank.
9. ______ a sample of duplicate sales invoices to determine if the controller's approval is included and ______ each duplicate sales invoice to the sales journal for agreement of name and amount.
10. ______ the agreement between Johnson Wholesale Company and the client to determine whether the shipment is a sale or a consignment.

Terms

a. Examine	e. Recompute	i. Count
b. Scan	f. Foot	j. Observe
c. Read	g. Trace	k. Inquire
d. Compute	h. Compare	l. Confirm

Required

a. For each of the 12 blanks in procedures 1 through 10, identify the most appropriate term. No term can be used more than once.
b. For each of the procedures 1 through 10, identify the type of evidence that is being used.

7-32 **(OBJECTIVES 7-4, 7-5)** Analytical procedures consist of evaluations of financial information made by a study of plausible relationships among both financial and nonfinancial data. They range from simple comparisons to the use of complex models involving many relationships and elements of data. They involve comparisons of recorded amounts, or ratios developed from recorded amounts, to expectations developed by the auditors.

Required

a. Describe the broad purposes of analytical procedures.
b. When are analytical procedures required during an audit? Explain why auditors use analytical procedures extensively in all parts of the audit.
c. Describe the factors that influence the extent to which an auditor will use the results of analytical procedures to reduce detailed tests in meeting audit objectives.*

7-33 **(OBJECTIVES 7-4, 7-5)** Analytical procedures are an important part of the audit process and consist of the evaluation of financial information by the study of plausible relationships among financial and nonfinancial data. Analytical procedures may be done during planning, as a substantive test, or as a part of the overall review of an audit.

The following are various statements regarding the use of analytical procedures:

1. Should focus on enhancing the auditor's understanding of the client's business and the transactions and events that have occurred since the last audit date
2. Should focus on identifying areas that may represent specific risks relevant to the audit
3. Require documentation in the working papers of the auditor's expectation of the ratio or account balance
4. Do not result in detection of misstatements
5. Designed to obtain evidential matter about particular assertions related to account balances or classes of transactions
6. Generally use data aggregated at a lower level than the other stages
7. Should include reading the financial statements and notes to consider the adequacy of evidence gathered
8. Not required during this stage
9. Involve reconciliation of confirmation replies with recorded book amounts
10. Use the preliminary or unadjusted working trial balance as a source of data

Required

For each of the 10 statements listed above, select the stage of the audit for which the statement is most accurate using the following responses:

a. Planning the audit
b. Substantive testing
c. Overall review
d. Statement is not correct concerning analytical procedures.*

7-34 **(OBJECTIVE 7-5, 7-6)** Following are the auditor's calculations of several key ratios for Cragston Star Products. The primary purpose of this information is to understand the client's business and assess the risk of financial failure, but any other relevant conclusions are also desirable.

Required

Ratio	2016	2015	2014	2013	2012
1. Current ratio	2.08	2.26	2.51	2.43	2.50
2. Quick ratio	.97	1.34	1.82	1.76	1.64
3. Times interest earned	3.50	3.20	4.10	5.30	7.10
4. Accounts receivable turnover	4.20	5.50	4.10	5.40	5.60
5. Days to collect receivables	86.90	66.36	89.02	67.59	65.18
6. Inventory turnover	2.03	1.84	2.68	3.34	3.36
7. Days to sell inventory	179.80	198.37	136.19	109.28	108.63

*Based on AICPA question paper, American Institute of Certified Public Accountants.

Ratio	2016	2015	2014	2013	2012
8. Net sales divided by tangible assets	.68	.64	.73	.69	.67
9. Profit margin	.13	.14	.16	.15	.14
10. Return on assets	.09	.09	.12	.10	.09
11. Return on equity	.05	.06	.10	.10	.11
12. Earnings per share	$4.30	$4.26	$4.49	$4.26	$4.14

Required

a. What major conclusions can be drawn from this information about the company's future?
b. What additional information would be helpful in your assessment of this company's financial condition?
c. Based on the preceding ratios, which aspects of the company do you believe should receive special emphasis in the audit?

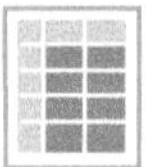

7-35 **(OBJECTIVE 7-5)** You are auditing payroll for the Morehead Technologies company for the year ended October 31, 2016. Included next are amounts from the client's trial balance, along with comparative audited information for the prior year.

	Audited Balance 10/31/2015	Preliminary Balance 10/31/2016
Sales	$ 51,316,234	$ 57,474,182
Executive salaries	546,940	615,970
Factory hourly payroll	10,038,877	11,476,319
Factory supervisors' salaries	785,825	810,588
Office salaries	1,990,296	2,055,302
Sales commissions	2,018,149	2,367,962

You have obtained the following information to help you perform preliminary analytical procedures for the payroll account balances.

1. There has been a significant increase in the demand for Morehead's products. The increase in sales was due to both an increase in the average selling price of four percent and an increase in units sold that resulted from the increased demand and an increased marketing effort.
2. Even though sales volume increased, there was no addition of executives, factory supervisors, or office personnel.
3. All employees including executives, but excluding commission salespeople, received a three percent salary increase starting November 1, 2015. Commission salespeople receive their increased compensation through the increase in sales.
4. The increased number of factory hourly employees was accomplished by recalling employees that had been laid off. They receive the same wage rate as existing employees. Morehead does not permit overtime.
5. Commission salespeople receive a five percent commission on all sales on which a commission is given. Approximately 75 percent of sales earn sales commission. The other 25 percent are "call-ins," for which no commission is given. Commissions are paid in the month following the month they are earned.

Required

a. Use the final balances for the prior year included above and the information in items 1 through 5 to develop an expected value for each account, except sales.
b. Calculate the difference between your expectation and the client's recorded amount as a percentage using the formula (expected value−recorded amount)/expected value.

7-36 **(OBJECTIVES 7-4, 7-7)** Use AICPA (www.aicpa.org) and PCAOB (pcaobus.org) auditing standards to answer the following questions about audit evidence and audit documentation.

Required

a. According to PCAOB Auditing Standard 3 on audit documentation, the complete audit documentation must be assembled by 45 days after the report release date. What does this standard say about whether documentation can be deleted after the document completion date or whether documentation can be added after the document completion date?

b. According to AU-C 230.08, what are the requirements for the form, content, and extent of audit documentation?

c. AU-C 500, *Audit Evidence,* in the AICPA auditing standards refers to information produced by the entity. What must the auditor do to evaluate whether information provided by the client is sufficiently reliable?

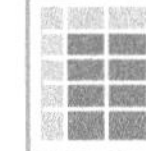

7-37 **(OBJECTIVES 7-7, 7-8)** You are the in-charge auditor on the audit of Vandervoort Company and are to review the audit schedule shown below.

Required

a. List the deficiencies in the audit schedule.

b. For each deficiency, state how the audit schedule could be improved.

c. Prepare an improved audit schedule, using an electronic spreadsheet software program. Include an indication of the audit work done as well as the analysis of the client data (instructor's option).

Vandervoort Company
A/C # 110—Notes Receivable
12-31-16

Schedule	**N-1**	**Date**
Prepared by	**JD**	**1-21-17**
Approved by	**PP**	**2-15-17**

	APEX CO.	AJAX, INC.	J.J. CO.	P. SMITH	MARTIN-PETERSON	TENT CO.	TOTALS
Date made	6/15/15	11/21/15	11/1/15	7/26/16	5/12/15	9/3/16	
Date due	6/15/17	Demand	$200/mo.	$1,000/mo.	Demand	$400/mo.	
Paid to date	None	Paid	12/31/16	9/30/16	Paid	11/30/16	
Face amount	$5,000 x	$3,591 x	$ 13,180 x	$ 25,000 x	$2,100 x	$ 12,000 x	
Interest rate	5%	5%	5%	5%	5%	6%	
Value of security	None	None	$ 24,000	$ 50,000	None	$ 10,000	
Note Receivable:							
12/31/15 bal.	$4,000 py	$ 3,591 py	$ 12,780 py	$ 0	$2,100 py	$ 0	
Additions				25,000		12,000	
Payments	(1,000) x	$(3,591) x	(2,400) x	(5,000) x	(2,100) x	(1,600) x	
12/31/16 bal.	$3,000	$ 0	$ 10,380	$ 20,000	$ 0	$ 10,400	TOTALS
Current	$3,000	–	$ 2,400	$ 12,000	–	$ 4,800	$22,200 tb
Long-term	–	–	7,980	8,000	–	5,600	21,580 tb
Total end. bal.	$3,000 @	$ 0	$ 10,380 @	$ 20,000 @	$ 0	$ 10,400 @	$43,780 tb
Interest Receivable:							
12/31/15 bal.	$ 104 py	$ 0 py	$ 24 py	$ 0	$ 0 py	$ 0	$ 128
Interest earned	175 x	102 x	577 x	468 x	105 x	162 x	1,589 #
Interest received	0	(102) x	(601) x	(200) x	(105) x	(108) x	(1,116)
12/31/16 bal.	$ 279	$ 0	$ 0	$ 268	$ 0	$ 54	$ 601 a/r

x = Tested
py = Agrees with prior year's audit schedules.
tb = Agrees with working trial balance.
# = Agrees with miscellaneous income analysis in operations w/p.
a/r = Agrees with A/R lead schedule.

CASE

7-38 (OBJECTIVE 7-4) Grande Stores is a large discount catalog department store chain. The company has recently expanded from six to 43 stores by borrowing from several large financial institutions and from a public offering of common stock. A recent investigation has disclosed that Grande materially overstated net income. This was accomplished by understating accounts payable and recording fictitious supplier credits that further reduced accounts payable. An SEC investigation was critical of the evidence gathered by Grande's audit firm, Montgomery & Ross, in testing accounts payable and the supplier credits.

The following is a description of some of the fictitious supplier credits and unrecorded amounts in accounts payable, as well as the audit procedures.

1. McClure Advertising Credits—Grande had arrangements with some vendors to share the cost of advertising the vendor's product. The arrangements were usually agreed to in advance by the vendor and supported by evidence of the placing of the ad. Grande created a 114-page list of approximately 1,100 vendors, supporting advertising credits of $300,000. Grande's auditors selected a sample of 4 of the 1,100 items for direct confirmation. One item was confirmed by telephone, one traced to cash receipts, one to a vendor credit memo for part of the amount and cash receipts for the rest, and one to a vendor credit memo. Two of the amounts confirmed differed from the amount on the list, but the auditors did not seek an explanation for the differences because the amounts were not material.

   The rest of the credits were tested by selecting 20 items (one or two from each page of the list). Twelve of the items were supported by examining the ads placed, and eight were supported by Grande debit memos charging the vendors for the promotional allowances.

2. Springbrook Credits—Grande created 28 fictitious credit memos totaling $257,000 from Springbrook Distributors, the main supplier of health and beauty aids to Grande. Grande's controller initially told the auditor that the credits were for returned goods, then said they were a volume discount, and finally stated they were a payment so that Grande would continue to use Springbrook as a supplier. One of the Montgomery & Ross staff auditors concluded that a $257,000 payment to retain Grande's business was too large to make economic sense.

   The credit memos indicated that the credits were for damaged merchandise, volume rebates, and advertising allowances. The audit firm requested a confirmation of the credits. In response, Jon Steiner, the president of Grande Stores, placed a call to Mort Seagal, the president of Springbrook, and handed the phone to the staff auditor. In fact, the call had been placed to an officer of Grande. The Grande officer, posing as Seagal, orally confirmed the credits. Grande refused to allow Montgomery & Ross to obtain written confirmations supporting the credits. Although the staff auditor doubted the validity of the credits, the audit partner, Mark Franklin, accepted the credits based on the credit memoranda, telephone confirmation of the credits, and oral representations of Grande officers.

3. Ridolfi Credits—$130,000 in credits based on 35 credit memoranda from Ridolfi, Inc., were purportedly for the return of overstocked goods from several Grande stores. A Montgomery & Ross staff auditor noted the size of the credit and that the credit memos were dated subsequent to year-end. He further noticed that a sentence on the credit memos from Ridolfi had been obliterated by a felt-tip marker. When held to the light, the accountant could read that the marked-out sentence read, "Do not post until merchandise received." The staff auditor thereafter called Harold Ridolfi, treasurer of Ridolfi, Inc., and was informed that the $130,000 in goods had not been returned and the money was not owed to Grande by Ridolfi. Steiner advised Franklin, the audit partner, that he had talked to Harold Ridolfi, who claimed he had been misunderstood by the staff auditor. Steiner told Franklin not to have anyone call Ridolfi to verify the amount because of pending litigation between Grande and Ridolfi, Inc.

4. Accounts Payable Accrual—Montgomery & Ross assigned a senior with experience in the retail area to audit accounts payable. Although Grande had poor internal control, Montgomery & Ross selected a sample of 50 for confirmation of the several thousand vendors who did business with Grande. Twenty-seven responses were received, and 21 were reconciled to Grande's records. These tests indicated an unrecorded liability of approximately $290,000 when projected to the population of accounts payable. However, the investigation disclosed that Grande's president made telephone calls to some suppliers who had received confirmation requests from Montgomery & Ross and told them how to respond to the request.

   Montgomery & Ross also performed a purchases cutoff test by vouching accounts payable invoices received for nine weeks after year-end. The purpose of this test was to identify invoices received after year-end that should have been recorded in accounts payable. Thirty percent of the sample ($160,000) was found to relate to the prior year, indicating a potential unrecorded liability of approximately $500,000. The audit firm and Grande eventually agreed on an adjustment to increase accounts payable by $260,000.

Required

Identify deficiencies in the sufficiency and appropriateness of the evidence gathered in the audit of accounts payable of Grande Stores.

ACL PROBLEM

7-39 **(OBJECTIVE 7-4)** This problem requires the use of ACL software, which can be accessed through the textbook Web site. Information about downloading and using ACL and the commands used in this problem can also be found on the textbook Web site. You should read all of the reference material preceding the instructions about "Quick Sort" before locating the appropriate command to answer parts a. through f. For this problem, use the file labeled "Payroll_details" in the "Payroll" subfolder in the ACL_Rockwood project. The suggested command or other source of information needed to solve the problem requirement is included at the end of each question.

Required

a. Determine the number of payroll transactions in the file. (Read the bottom of the Payroll_detail file screen.)
b. Determine the largest and smallest payroll transaction (gross pay) for all pay periods combined. (Quick Sort)
c. Determine total gross pay for all pay periods. (Total)
d. Determine and print gross pay by pay period. (Summarize)
e. Recalculate net pay for each payroll transaction for all pay periods and compare it to the amount included in the file. (Filter)
f. Determine if there are any gaps in the pay period sequence. If you were to identify gaps in the sequence, what would be your concern? (Gaps)
g. For parts a. through f. above, identify the type of audit evidence used for each procedure. How might the auditor use this evidence in testing of payroll expense?

CHAPTER

8

AUDIT PLANNING AND MATERIALITY

LEARNING OBJECTIVES

After studying this chapter, you should be able to

8-1 Discuss why adequate audit planning is essential.

8-2 Make client acceptance decisions and perform initial audit planning.

8-3 Gain an understanding of the client's business and industry.

8-4 Perform preliminary analytical procedures.

8-5 Apply the concept of materiality to the audit.

8-6 Make a preliminary judgment about what amounts to consider material.

8-7 Determine performance materiality during audit planning.

8-8 Use materiality to evaluate audit findings.

The Fall of Enron: Did Anyone Understand Their Business?

The bankruptcy of Enron Corporation, at one time the nation's largest energy wholesaling company, represents one of the biggest corporate collapses in American history. Despite being listed as No. 7 on the Fortune 500 list with a market capitalization of $75 billion before its collapse, Enron's meltdown was rapid. The fall began in October 2001, when Enron officials reported a shocking $618 million quarterly loss related to allegedly mysterious and hidden related party partnerships with company insiders. Then, in early November 2001, company officials were forced to admit that they had falsely claimed almost $600 million in earnings dating back to 1997, requiring the restatement of four years of audited financial statements. By the end of 2001, the company was in bankruptcy.

Enron was created in 1985 out of a merger of two gas pipelines, and was a pioneer in trading natural gas and electricity in the newly deregulated utilities markets. In its earlier years, Enron made its money from hard assets like pipelines. Enron built new markets, such as trading of weather securities, and by the end of the 1990s, 80% of Enron's earnings came from a more vague business known as "wholesale energy operations and services." In early 2001, speculation about Enron's business dealings began to surface. One highly regarded investment banker publicly stated that no one could explain how Enron actually made money.

In the wake of the collapse, many wondered how these issues could have gone undetected for so long. Many pointed to Enron's incredibly complicated business structure and related vague and confusing financial statements. "What we are looking at here is an example of superbly complex financial reports. They didn't have to lie. All they had to do was to obfuscate it with sheer complexity," noted John Dingell, U.S. Congressman from Michigan. Others alleged that the individuals running the company never even understood their business concept because it was too complicated.

Apparently, the complexity and uncertainty surrounding Enron's business and financial statements fooled their auditors, too. Enron's auditors faced a flurry of attacks, class action lawsuits, and a criminal indictment that ultimately led to the firm's demise. In December 2001 congressional testimony, the audit firm's CEO admitted that the firm's professional judgment "turned out to be wrong" and that they mistakenly let Enron keep the related entities separate when they should have been consolidated.

The Enron disaster continues to provide many lessons for the auditing profession. One to be underscored for auditors is the paramount importance of understanding the company's business and industry to identify significant business risks that increase the risk of material misstatements in the financial statements. Without that understanding, it will be almost impossible to identify the next Enron.

Source: Based on Bethany McLean, "Why Enron Went Bust," *Fortune* (December 24, 2001), pp. 58–68.

As the chapter story illustrates, Enron's complex and confusing business structure helped disguise material misstatements in Enron's financial statements for several years. Gaining an understanding of the client's business and industry is one of the most important steps in audit planning. This chapter explains audit planning in detail, including gaining an understanding of the client's business and industry, developing an overall audit plan and strategy, and making a preliminary judgment about materiality.

PLANNING

OBJECTIVE 8-1

Discuss why adequate audit planning is essential.

Principles underlying AICPA auditing standards indicate:

> The auditor must plan the work and properly supervise any assistants.

There are three main reasons why the auditor should properly plan engagements: to enable the auditor to obtain sufficient appropriate evidence for the circumstances, to help keep audit costs reasonable, and to avoid misunderstandings with the client. Obtaining sufficient appropriate evidence is essential if the CPA firm is to minimize legal liability and maintain a good reputation in the business community. Keeping costs reasonable helps the firm remain competitive. Avoiding misunderstandings with the client is necessary for good client relations and for facilitating high-quality work at reasonable cost. Suppose that the auditor informs the client that the audit will be completed before June 30 but is unable to finish it until August because of inadequate scheduling of staff. The client is likely to be upset with the CPA firm and may even sue for breach of contract.

Figure 8-1 presents the eight major parts of audit planning. Each of the first seven parts is intended to help the auditor develop the last part, an effective and efficient overall audit plan and audit program. The first four parts of the planning phase of an audit are studied in this chapter. The last four are studied separately in later chapters.

FIGURE 8-1 Planning an Audit and Designing an Audit Approach

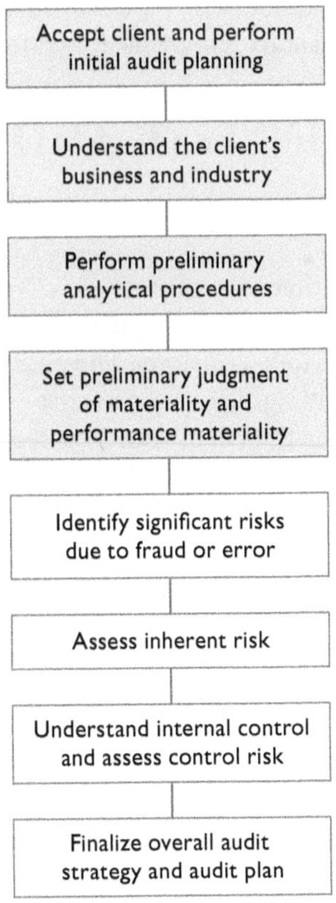

Accept client and perform initial audit planning
↓
Understand the client's business and industry
↓
Perform preliminary analytical procedures
↓
Set preliminary judgment of materiality and performance materiality
↓
Identify significant risks due to fraud or error
↓
Assess inherent risk
↓
Understand internal control and assess control risk
↓
Finalize overall audit strategy and audit plan

Before beginning our discussion, we briefly introduce three risk terms: *acceptable audit risk, client business risk,* and *risk of material misstatement.* These risks significantly influence the conduct and cost of audits. Much of the early planning of audits deals with obtaining information to help auditors assess these risks.

Acceptable audit risk is a measure of how willing the auditor is to accept that the financial statements may be materially misstated after the audit is completed and an unmodified opinion has been issued. When the auditor decides on a lower acceptable audit risk, it means that the auditor wants to be more certain that the financial statements are *not* materially misstated. Zero risk is certainty, and a 100 percent risk is complete uncertainty.

Client business risk is the risk that the entity fails to achieve its objectives or execute its strategies. Business risk can arise from factors such as significant changes in industry conditions or events such as regulatory changes, or from the setting of inappropriate objectives or strategies. For example, the auditor may identify declines in economic conditions that adversely affect sales and the collectibility of accounts receivable.

The **risk of material misstatement** is the risk that the financial statements contain a material misstatement due to fraud or error prior to the audit. The risk of material misstatement is a function of the susceptibility of the financial statements (as a whole or in individual accounts) to misstatement, and the effectiveness of the client's controls in preventing or detecting and correcting the misstatements. Continuing with the previous example, declining economic conditions may increase the likelihood that the company may take inappropriate actions to meet sales targets or understate the allowance for doubtful accounts, especially if the client does not have adequate controls over sales and collection of accounts receivable.

Assessing acceptable audit risk, client business risk, and risk of material misstatement is an important part of audit planning because it helps determine the audit procedures and amount of evidence that will need to be accumulated, as well as the experience level of staff needed for the engagement. For example, if the auditor identifies a risk of material misstatement for inventory valuation because of complex valuation issues, additional evidence will be accumulated in the audit of inventory valuation and more experienced staff will be assigned to perform testing in this area.

ACCEPT CLIENT AND PERFORM INITIAL AUDIT PLANNING

OBJECTIVE 8-2

Make client acceptance decisions and perform initial audit planning.

Initial audit planning involves four things, all of which should be done early in the audit:

1. The auditor decides whether to accept a new client or continue serving an existing one. This determination is typically made by an experienced auditor who is in a position to make important decisions. The auditor wants to make this decision early, before incurring any significant costs that cannot be recovered.
2. The auditor identifies why the client wants or needs an audit. This information is likely to affect the remaining parts of the planning process.
3. To avoid misunderstandings, the auditor obtains an understanding with the client about the terms of the engagement.
4. The auditor develops the overall strategy for the audit, including engagement staffing and any required audit specialists.

Client Acceptance and Continuance

Even though obtaining and retaining clients is not easy in a competitive profession such as public accounting, a CPA firm must use care in deciding which clients are acceptable. The firm's legal and professional responsibilities are such that clients who lack integrity or argue constantly about the proper conduct of the audit and fees can cause more problems than they are worth. Some CPA firms refuse clients in certain high-risk industries, such as software technology companies or subprime lenders, and may even discontinue auditing existing clients in those industries. Some smaller

CPA firms will not do audits of publicly held clients because of the risk of litigation or because of costs associated with registering the audit firm with the PCAOB. An auditor is unlikely to accept a new client or continue serving an existing client if the risk associated with the client is greater than the risk the firm is willing to accept.

New Client Investigation Before accepting a new client, most CPA firms investigate the company to determine its acceptability. They do this by examining, to the extent possible, the prospective client's standing in the business community, financial stability, and relations with its previous CPA firm. For example, many CPA firms use considerable caution in accepting new clients in newly formed, rapidly growing businesses. Many of these businesses fail financially and expose the CPA firm to significant potential liability. The CPA firm must also determine that it has the competency, such as industry knowledge, to accept the engagement and that the firm can satisfy all independence requirements.

For prospective clients that have previously been audited by another CPA firm, the new (successor) auditor is *required* by auditing standards *to communicate with the predecessor auditor*. The purpose of the requirement is to help the successor auditor evaluate whether to accept the engagement. The communication may, for example, inform the successor auditor that the client lacks integrity or that there have been disputes over accounting principles, audit procedures, or fees.

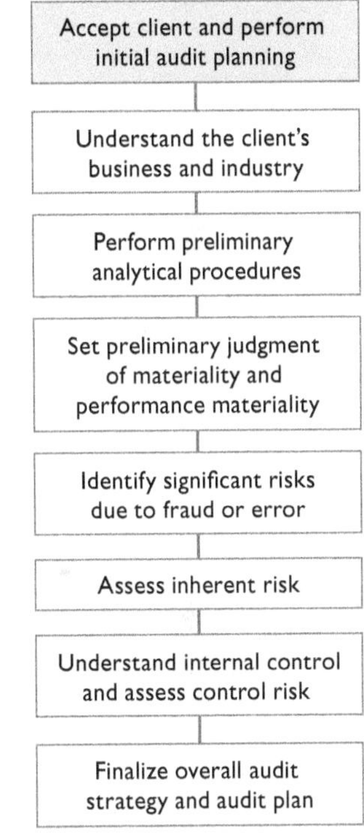
Accept client and perform initial audit planning
Understand the client's business and industry
Perform preliminary analytical procedures
Set preliminary judgment of materiality and performance materiality
Identify significant risks due to fraud or error
Assess inherent risk
Understand internal control and assess control risk
Finalize overall audit strategy and audit plan

The burden of initiating the communication rests with the successor auditor, but the predecessor auditor is required to respond to the request for information. However, the confidentiality requirement in the *Code of Professional Conduct* requires that the predecessor auditor obtain permission from the client before the communication can be made. In the event of unusual circumstances such as legal problems or disputes between the client and the predecessor, the predecessor's response can be limited to stating that no information will be provided. If a client will not permit the communication or the predecessor will not provide a comprehensive response, the successor should seriously consider the desirability of accepting a prospective engagement, without considerable other investigation.

Even when a prospective client has been audited by another CPA firm, a successor may make other investigations by gathering information from local attorneys, other CPAs, banks, and other businesses. In some cases, the auditor may even hire a professional investigator to obtain information about the reputation and background of key members of management. Such extensive investigation is appropriate when there has been no previous auditor, when a predecessor auditor will not provide the desired information, or if any indication of problems arises from the communication.

AICPA auditing standards also require that the auditor determine whether the financial reporting framework to be used by management to prepare the financial statements is appropriate. Without an appropriate financial reporting framework, the auditor does not have suitable criteria for auditing the financial statements. In making that determination, the auditor considers the nature of the entity, the purpose and nature of the financial statements, and whether laws or regulations prescribe a particular framework. Common financial reporting frameworks include U.S. generally accepted accounting principles and international financial reporting standards (IFRS).

Continuing Clients Many CPA firms evaluate existing clients annually to determine whether there are reasons for not continuing to do the audit. Previous conflicts over the appropriate scope of the audit, the type of opinion to issue, unpaid fees, or other matters may cause the auditor to discontinue association. The auditor may also drop a client after determining the client lacks integrity.

Even if none of the previously discussed conditions exist, the CPA firm may decide not to continue doing audits for a client because of excessive risk. For example, a CPA firm might decide that considerable risk of a regulatory conflict exists between a governmental agency and a client, which could result in financial failure of the client and ultimately lawsuits against the CPA firm. Even if the engagement is profitable, the long-term risk may exceed the short-term benefits of doing the audit.

Investigating new clients and reevaluating existing ones is an essential part of deciding acceptable audit risk. For example, assume that a potential client operates in a reasonably risky industry, that its management has a reputation of integrity, but that it is also known to take aggressive financial risks. If the CPA firm decides that acceptable audit risk is extremely low, it may choose not to accept the engagement. If the CPA firm concludes that acceptable audit risk is low but the client is still acceptable, the firm may accept the engagement but increase the fee proposed to the client. Audits with a low acceptable audit risk will normally result in higher audit costs, which should be reflected in higher audit fees.

Identify Client's Reasons for Audit

Two major factors affecting acceptable audit risk are the likely statement users and their intended uses of the statements. The auditor is likely to accumulate more evidence when the statements are to be used extensively, as is often the case for publicly held companies, those with extensive indebtedness, and companies that are to be sold in the near future.

The most likely uses of the statements can be determined from previous experience with the client and discussions with management. Throughout the engagement, the auditor may get additional information about why the client is having an audit and the likely uses of the financial statements. This information may affect the auditor's acceptable audit risk.

Obtain an Understanding with the Client

A clear understanding of the terms of the engagement should exist between the client and the CPA firm. Auditing standards require that auditors obtain an understanding with the client in an **engagement letter**, including the engagement's objectives, the responsibilities of the auditor and management, identification of the financial reporting framework used by management, reference to the expected form and content of the audit report, and the engagement's limitations. For public companies, the audit committee is responsible for hiring the auditor as required by the Sarbanes–Oxley Act. The engagement letter is typically signed by management for private companies. An example of an engagement letter for the audit of a private company is provided in Figure 8-2.

The engagement letter may also include an agreement to provide other services such as tax returns or management consulting allowed under the *Code of Professional Conduct* and regulatory requirements. It should also state any restrictions to be imposed on the auditor's work, deadlines for completing the audit, assistance to be provided by the client's personnel in obtaining records and documents, and schedules to be prepared for the auditor. It often includes an agreement on fees. The engagement letter also serves the purpose of informing the client that the auditor cannot guarantee that all acts of fraud will be discovered.

Engagement letter information is important in planning the audit principally because it affects the timing of the tests and the total amount of time the audit and other services will take. For example, if the deadline for submitting the audit report is soon after the balance sheet date, a significant portion of the audit must be done before the end of the year. If unexpected circumstances arise or if client assistance is not available, arrangements must be made to extend the amount of time for the engagement. Client-imposed restrictions on the audit can affect the procedures performed and possibly even the type of audit opinion issued.

Develop Overall Audit Strategy

After understanding the client's reasons for the audit, the auditor should develop and document a preliminary **audit strategy** that sets the scope, timing, and direction of the audit and that guides the development of the audit plan. This strategy considers the nature of the client's business and industry, including areas where there is greater risk of significant misstatements. The auditor also considers other factors such as the

FIGURE 8-2 Engagement Letter

HILYER AND RIDDLE, CPAs
Macon, Georgia 31212

June 14, 2016

Mr. Chuck Milsaps, President
Babb Clothing Co.
4604 Oakley St.
Macon, Georgia 31212

Dear Mr. Milsaps:

You have requested that we audit the financial statements of Babb Clothing Co., which comprise the balance sheet as of December 31, 2016, and the related statements of income, changes in stockholders' equlity, and cash flows for the year then ended, and the related notes to the financial statements. We are pleased to confirm our acceptance and our understanding of this audit engagement by means of this letter. Our audit will be conducted with the objective of our expressing an opinion on the financial statements.

We will conduct our audit in accordance with auditing standards generally accepted in the United States of America (GAAS). Those standards require that we plan and perform the audit to obtain reasonable assurance about whether the financial statements are free from material misstatement. An audit involves performing procedures to obtain audit evidence about the amounts and disclosures in the financial statements. The procedures selected depend on the auditor's judgment, including the assessment of the risks of material misstatement of the financial statements, whether due to fraud or error. An audit also includes evaluating the appropriateness of accounting policies used and the reasonableness of significant accounting estimates made by management, as well as evaluating the overall presentation of the financial statements.

Because of the inherent limitations of an audit, together with the inherent limitations of internal control, an unavoidable risk that some material misstatements may not be detected exists, even though the audit is properly planned and performed in accordance with GAAS.

In making our risk assessments, we consider internal control relevant to the entity's preparation and fair presentation of the financial statements in order to design audit procedures that are appropriate in the circumstances but not for the purpose of expressing an opinion on the effectiveness of the entity's internal control. However, we will communicate to you in writing concerning any significant deficiencies or material weaknesses in internal control relevant to the audit of the financial statements that we have identified during the audit.

Our audit will be conducted on the basis that management acknowledges and understands that they have responsibility

a. for the preparation and fair presentation of the financial statements in accordance with accounting principles generally accepted in the United States of America;
b. for the design, implementation, and maintenance of internal control relevant to the preparation and fair presentation of financial statements that are free of material misstatement, whether due to fraud or error; and
c. to provide us with
    i. access to all information of which management is aware that is relevant to the preparation and fair presentation of the financial statements such as records, documentation, and other matters;
    ii. additional information that we may request from management for the purpose of the audit; and
    iii. unrestricted access to persons within the entity from whom we determine it necessary to obtain audit evidence.

As part of our audit process, we will request from management written confirmation concerning representations made to us in connection with the audit.

As part of our engagement for the year ending December 31, 2016, we will also prepare the federal and state income tax returns for Babb Clothing Co.

Our fees will be billed as work progresses and are based on the amount of time required at various levels of responsibility, plus actual out-of-pocket expenses. Invoices are payable upon presentation. We will notify you immediately of any circumstances we encounter that could significantly affect our initial estimate of total fees of $135,000.

We will issue a written report upon completion of our audit of Babb Clothing Co.'s financial statements. Our report will be addressed to the board of directors of Babb Clothing Co. We cannot provide assurance that an unmodified opinion will be expressed. Circumstances may arise in which it is necessary for us to modify our opinion, add an emphasis-of-matter or other-matter paragraph(s), or withdraw from the engagement.

Please sign and return the attached copy of this letter to indicate your acknowledgement of, and agreement with, the arrangements for our audit of the financial statements including our respective responsibilities.

Yours very truly:

Alan Hilyer

Alan Hilyer
Partner

Accepted:

By: *Chuck Milsaps*
Date: 6-21-16

number of client locations and the past effectiveness of client controls in developing a preliminary approach to the audit. The planned strategy helps the auditor determine the resources required for the engagement, including engagement staffing.

Select Staff for Engagement The auditor must assign the appropriate staff to the engagement to comply with auditing standards and to promote audit efficiency. One of the underlying principles in auditing standards is that:

> Auditors are responsible for having appropriate competence and capabilities to perform the audit.

Staff must therefore be assigned with that requirement in mind, and those assigned to the engagement must be knowledgeable about the client's industry. Larger audit engagements are likely to require one or more partners and staff at several experience levels. Individuals in multiple offices of the firm may be involved, including offices outside the United States, if the client has operations in numerous locations around the world. Specialists in such technical areas as statistical sampling, business valuation, and information technology risk assessment may also be assigned. On smaller audits, only one or two staff members may be needed.

A major consideration of staffing is the need for continuity from year to year. Continuity helps the CPA firm maintain familiarity with the technical requirements and closer interpersonal relations with client personnel. An inexperienced staff assistant is likely to become the most experienced nonpartner on the engagement within a few years.

Consider a computer manufacturing client with extensive inventory of computers and computer parts where risk of material misstatement for inventory has been assessed as high. It is essential for the staff person doing the inventory portion of the audit to be experienced in auditing inventory. The auditor should also have a good understanding of the computer manufacturing industry. The CPA firm may decide to engage a specialist if no one within the firm is qualified to evaluate whether the inventory is obsolete.

Evaluate Need for Outside Specialists If the audit requires specialized knowledge, it may be necessary to consult a specialist. Auditing standards establish the requirements for selecting specialists and reviewing their work. Examples include using a diamond expert in evaluating the replacement cost of diamonds and an actuary for determining the appropriateness of the recorded value of insurance loss reserves. Another common use of specialists is consulting with attorneys on the legal interpretation of contracts and titles or business valuation experts on fair value accounting treatments.

The auditor must have a sufficient understanding of the client's business to recognize whether a specialist is needed. The auditor needs to evaluate the specialist's professional qualifications and understand the objectives and scope of the specialist's work. The auditor should also consider the specialist's relationship to the client, including circumstances that might impair the specialist's objectivity. The use of a specialist does not affect the auditor's responsibility for the audit, and the audit report should not refer to the specialist unless the specialist's report results in a modification of the audit opinion.

UNDERSTAND THE CLIENT'S BUSINESS AND INDUSTRY

OBJECTIVE 8-3

Gain an understanding of the client's business and industry.

A thorough understanding of the client's business and industry and knowledge about the company's operations are essential for the auditor to conduct an adequate audit. Another of the underlying principles in auditing standards states:

The auditor identifies and assesses risks of material misstatement, whether due to fraud or error, based on an understanding of the entity and its environment, including the entity's internal control.

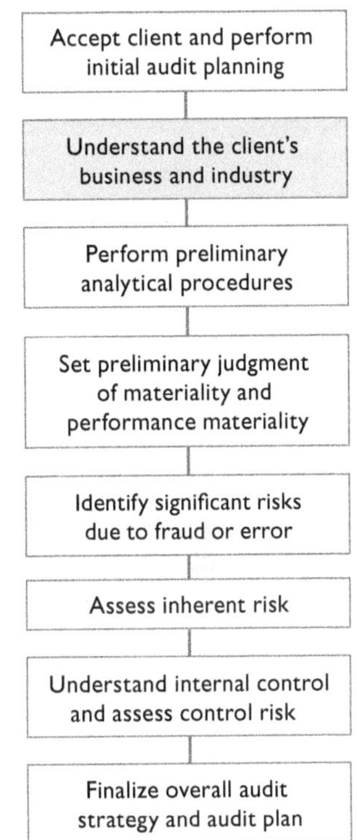

Accept client and perform initial audit planning
Understand the client's business and industry
Perform preliminary analytical procedures
Set preliminary judgment of materiality and performance materiality
Identify significant risks due to fraud or error
Assess inherent risk
Understand internal control and assess control risk
Finalize overall audit strategy and audit plan

Auditing standards require the auditor to perform **risk assessment procedures** to obtain an understanding of the client's business and its environment to assess the risk of material misstatements in the financial statements, including inquiries of management and analytical procedures. The auditor uses this information to assess client business risk and the risk of material misstatement. Several factors have increased the importance of understanding the client's business and industry:

- Recent significant declines in economic conditions around the world are likely to significantly increase a client's business risks. Auditors need to understand the nature of the client's business to understand the impact of major economic downturns on the client's financial statements and ability to continue as a going concern.
- Information technology connects client companies with major customers and suppliers. As a result, auditors need greater knowledge about major customers and suppliers and related risks. That connectivity also exposes the client to potential cyber risks that the auditor should consider.
- Clients have expanded operations globally, often through joint ventures or strategic alliances.
- Information technology affects internal client processes, improving the quality and timeliness of accounting information.
- The increased importance of human capital and other intangible assets has increased accounting complexity and the importance of management judgments and estimates.
- Many clients may have invested in complex financial instruments, such as collateralized debt obligations or mortgage backed securities, which may have declined in value, require complex accounting treatments, and often involve unknown counterparties who may create unexpected financial risks for the client.

Figure 8-3 provides an overview of the strategic approach to understanding the client's business and industry. Next, we will discuss several aspects of this approach.

FIGURE 8-3 Strategic Understanding of the Client's Business and Industry

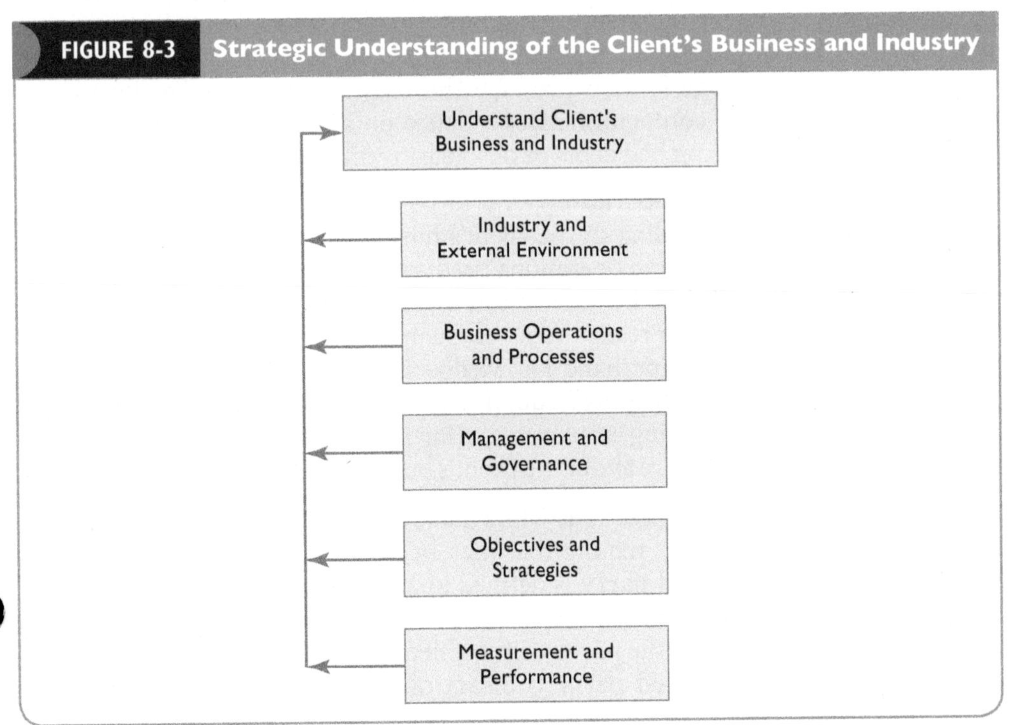

Understand Client's Business and Industry
Industry and External Environment
Business Operations and Processes
Management and Governance
Objectives and Strategies
Measurement and Performance

Industry and External Environment

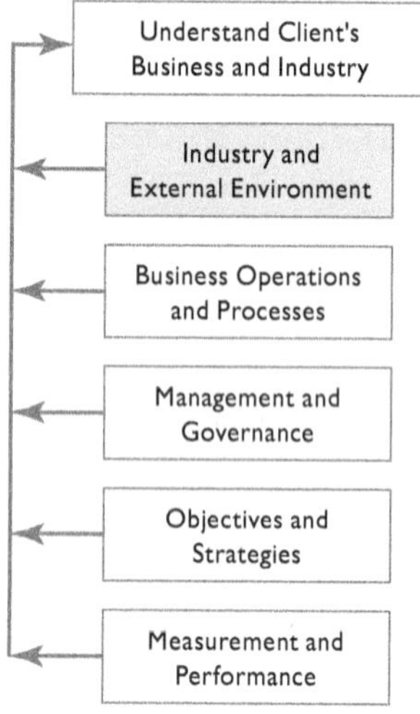

The three primary reasons for obtaining a good understanding of the client's industry and external environment are:

1. Risks associated with specific industries may affect the auditor's assessment of client business risk and acceptable audit risk—and may even influence auditors against accepting engagements in riskier industries, such as the financial services and health insurance industries.
2. Many risks are common to all clients in certain industries. Familiarity with those risks aids the auditor in determining their relevance to the client when assessing client business risk and risk of material misstatement. Examples include potential inventory obsolescence in the fashion clothing industry, accounts receivable collection risk in the consumer loan industry, and loss reserve risk in the casualty insurance industry.
3. Many industries have unique accounting requirements that the auditor must understand to evaluate whether the client's financial statements are in accordance with accounting standards. For example, if the auditor is doing an audit of a city government, the auditor must understand governmental accounting and auditing requirements. Unique accounting requirements exist for construction companies, railroads, not-for-profit organizations, financial institutions, and many other organizations.

Many auditor litigation cases (like those described in Chapter 5) result from the auditor's failure to fully understand the nature of transactions in the client's industry, similar to what occurred in the Enron case discussed in the opening vignette to this chapter. The auditor must also understand the client's external environment, including such things as wide volatility in economic conditions, extent of competition, and regulatory requirements. For example, auditors of utility companies need more than an understanding of the industry's unique regulatory accounting requirements. They must also know how deregulation in this industry has increased competition and how fluctuations in energy prices impact firm operations. To develop effective audit plans, auditors of all companies must have the expertise to assess external environment risks.

Business Operations and Processes

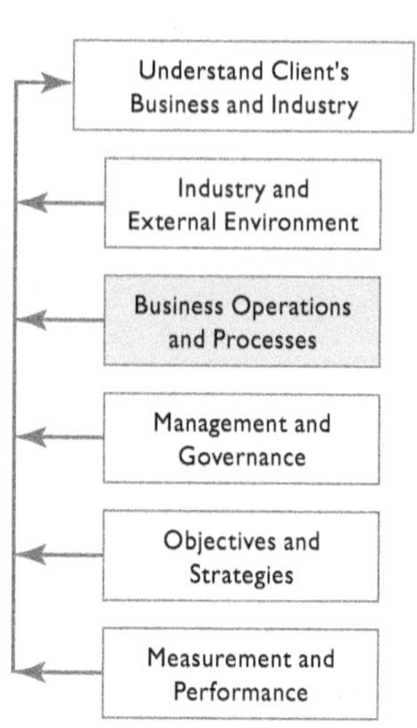

The auditor should understand factors such as major sources of revenue, key customers and suppliers, sources of financing, and information about related parties that may indicate areas of increased client business risk. For example, many technology firms are dependent on one or a few products that may become obsolete due to new technologies or stronger competitors. Dependence on a few major customers may result in material losses from bad debts or obsolete inventory.

Tour Client Facilities and Operations A tour of the client's facilities is helpful in obtaining a better understanding of the client's business operations because it provides an opportunity to observe operations firsthand and to meet key personnel. By viewing the physical facilities, the auditor can assess physical safeguards over assets and interpret accounting data related to assets such as inventory in process and factory equipment. With such first-hand knowledge, the auditor is better able to identify risks from factors such as unused equipment or potentially unsalable inventory. Discussions with nonaccounting employees during the tour and throughout the audit also help the auditor learn more about the client's business to aid in assessing risk.

Identify Related Parties Transactions with related parties are important to auditors because accounting standards require that they be *disclosed in the financial statements* if they are material. A **related party** is defined in auditing standards as an affiliated company, a principal owner of the client company, or any other party with which the client deals, where one of the parties can influence the management or operating policies of the other. A **related party transaction** is any transaction between the client and a related party. Common examples include sales or purchase transactions between a parent company and its subsidiary, exchanges of equipment between two companies owned by the same person, and loans to officers. A less common example is the exercise of significant management influence on an audit client by its most important customer.

A transaction with a related party is not an arm's-length transaction. Therefore, there is a risk that they may not be valued at the same amount as a transaction with an independent third party. For example, a company may be able to purchase inventory from a related company at more favorable terms than from an outside vendor. Most auditors assess risk of material misstatement as high for related parties and related party transactions, because of the accounting disclosure requirements, the lack of independence between the parties involved in the transactions, and the opportunities they may provide to engage in fraudulent financial reporting.

Because material related party transactions must be disclosed, all related parties need to be *identified and included in the auditor's permanent files* early in the engagement. (The disclosure requirements include the nature of the related party relationship; a description of transactions, including dollar amounts; and amounts due from and to related parties.) Having all related parties included in the permanent audit files, and making sure all auditors on the team know who the related parties are, helps auditors identify undisclosed related party transactions as they do the audit. Auditing standards require the auditor to ask management to identify the entity's related parties and inquire as to whether the entity has entered into any transactions with these related parties and, if so, the type and purpose of the transaction. Those standards also require the auditor to inquire of management and perform other procedures to obtain an understanding of controls that management has established to identify, authorize, and approve related party transactions. Auditors may also learn about related parties by reviewing SEC filings and examining stockholders' listings to identify principal stockholders.

Because of the lack of independence between related parties, the Sarbanes–Oxley Act prohibits related party transactions that involve personal loans to any director or executive officer of a public company. Banks and other financial institutions, however, are permitted to make normal loans, such as residential mortgages, to their directors and officers using market rates.

Management and Governance

Because management establishes a company's strategies and business processes, an auditor should assess management's philosophy and operating style and its ability to identify and respond to risk, as these significantly influence the risk of material misstatements in the financial statements. Research commissioned by the Committee of Sponsoring Organizations of the Treadway Commission (COSO), *Fraudulent Financial Reporting 1998–2007*, found that in over 340 instances of fraudulent financial

FAILURE TO ADDRESS RELATED PARTY TRANSACTIONS LEADS TO SEC CHARGES AGAINST AUDIT PARTNER

Joseph Sofo was the audit partner for Kurcias, Jaffe & Co. LLP on the audit of North American Globex Fund (Globex) from 2001 through 2009. Globex was a hedge fund that purportedly maintained most of its assets in a related entity, North American Globex Group, Inc. (Group). The Globex Fund intentionally overstated its assets held with Globex Group, and kept the Group bank and brokerage statements hidden from the auditors. For example, in 2007 Globex Fund claimed it held $14,564,461 with the Globex Group, but Globex Group only held $8,000 in assets.

Before accepting the Globex engagement, Kurcias Jaffe did not have any expertise in auditing hedge funds, and the Globex Fund was its only hedge fund client. Although Sofo knew that Globex Fund and Globex Group were related parties and the related party relationship had been identified as a fraud risk, he relied on confirmations to Globex Group to support the assets allegedly held at Globex Group. The SEC charged that these confirmations had almost no value from an audit perspective because they were sent to a related party. Auditing standards require that confirmations be sent to a third party. Sofo was charged with failing to exercise due professional care, lack of professional skepticism, and failure to obtain sufficient appropriate evidence.

Source: Accounting and Auditing Enforcement Release No. 3303 (July 14, 2011) (www.sec.gov).

reporting investigated by the SEC, the chief executive officer (CEO) or chief financial officer (CFO) was named as being involved in perpetrating the fraud, representing almost 90 percent of the cases.

A firm's governance includes its organizational structure, as well as the activities of the board of directors and the audit committee. An effective board of directors helps ensure that the company takes only appropriate risks, while the audit committee, through oversight of financial reporting, can reduce the likelihood of overly aggressive accounting. To gain an understanding of the client's governance system, the auditor should understand how the board and audit committee exercise oversight, including consideration of the company's code of ethics and evaluation of the corporate minutes.

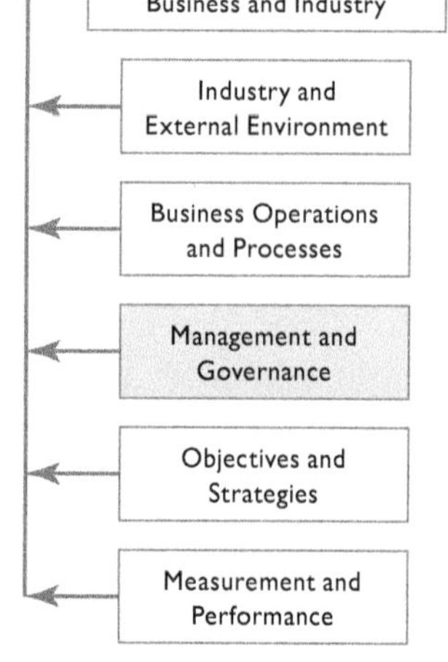

Code of Ethics Companies frequently communicate the entity's values and ethical standards through policy statements and codes of conduct. In response to requirements in the Sarbanes–Oxley Act, the SEC requires each public company to disclose whether it has adopted a code of ethics that applies to senior management, including the CEO, CFO, and principal accounting officer or controller. A company that has not adopted such a code must disclose this fact and explain why it has not done so. The SEC also requires companies to promptly disclose amendments and waivers to the code of ethics for any of those officers. Auditors should gain knowledge of the company's code of ethics and examine any changes and waivers of the code of conduct that have implications about the governance system and related integrity and ethical values of senior management.

Minutes of Meetings The **corporate minutes** are the official record of the meetings of the board of directors and stockholders. They include key authorizations and summaries of the most important topics discussed at these meetings and the decisions made by the directors and stockholders. Common authorizations in the minutes include compensation of officers, new contracts and agreements, acquisitions of property, loans, and dividend payments. Examples of other information relevant to the audit include discussions about litigation, a pending issuance of stock, or a potential merger.

The auditor should read the minutes to obtain authorizations and other information that is relevant to performing the audit. This information should be included in the audit files with significant portions highlighted. Before the audit is completed, the auditor must follow up on this information to be sure that management has complied with actions taken by the stockholders and the board of directors. For example, the auditor should compare the authorizations of loans with notes payable to make certain that these liabilities are recorded and key terms disclosed. Litigation, pending stock issuances, and merger information may need to be included in footnotes. Auditors often supplement their review of minutes with inquiries of the audit committee or full board about their awareness of events that might affect financial reporting.

Client Objectives and Strategies

Strategies are approaches followed by the entity to achieve organizational objectives. Auditors should understand client objectives related to:

1. Reliability of financial reporting
2. Effectiveness and efficiency of operations
3. Compliance with laws and regulations

Despite management's best efforts, business risks arise that threaten management's ability to achieve its objectives. As a result, knowledge of client objectives and strategies helps the auditor to assess client business risk and risk of misstatements in the financial statements. For example, product quality can have a significant impact on the financial statements through lost sales and through warranty and product liability claims. Toyota, Inc., suffered significant losses arising from business risks when production problems involving gas pedals and brakes in several of its most popular vehicles triggered significant declines in sales and stockholder value.

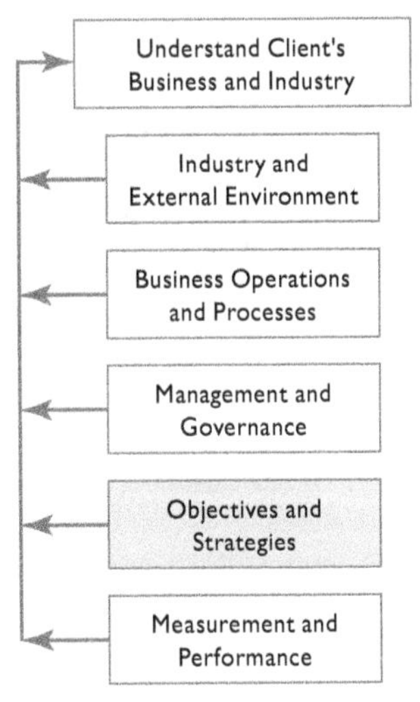

As part of understanding the client's objectives related to compliance with laws and regulations, the auditor should become familiar with the terms of client contracts and other legal obligations. These can include such diverse items as long-term notes and bonds payable, stock options, pension plans, contracts with vendors for future delivery of supplies, government contracts for completion and delivery of manufactured products, royalty agreements, union contracts, and leases. Most contracts are of primary interest in individual parts of the audit and, in practice, receive special attention during the different phases of the detailed tests. For example, the provisions of a pension plan will receive substantial emphasis as a part of the audit of the unfunded liability for pensions. The auditor should review and abstract the documents early in the engagement to gain a better perspective of the organization and to better assess risk. Later, these documents can be examined more carefully as a part of the tests of individual audit areas.

Measurement and Performance

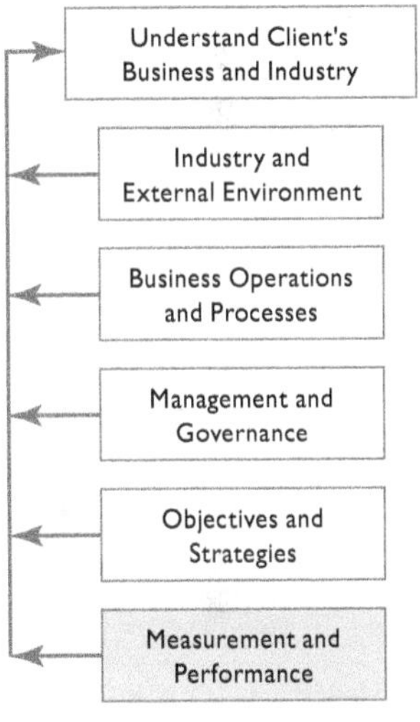

A client's performance measurement system includes key performance indicators that management uses to measure progress toward its objectives. These indicators go beyond financial statement figures, such as sales and net income, to include measures tailored to the client and its objectives. Such key performance indicators may include market share, sales per employee, unit sales growth, unique visitors to a Web site, same-store sales, sales by country, and sales per square foot for a retailer.

Inherent risk of financial statement misstatements may be increased if the client has set unreasonable objectives or if the performance measurement system encourages aggressive accounting. For example, a company's objective may be to obtain the leading market share of industry sales. If management and salespeople are compensated based on achieving this goal, there is increased incentive to record sales before they have been earned or record sales for nonexistent transactions. In such a situation, the auditor is likely to increase assessed inherent risk and the extent of testing for the occurrence transaction-related audit objective for sales.

Performance measurement includes ratio analysis and benchmarking against key competitors. As part of understanding the client's business, the auditor should perform ratio analysis or review the client's calculations of key performance ratios. Performing preliminary analytical procedures is the third step in the planning process and is discussed next.

PERFORM PRELIMINARY ANALYTICAL PROCEDURES

OBJECTIVE 8-4

Perform preliminary analytical procedures.

As first introduced in Chapter 7, auditors are required to perform preliminary analytical procedures as part of risk assessment procedures to better understand the client's business and industry, and to assess client business risk. One such procedure compares client ratios to industry or competitor benchmarks to provide an indication of the company's performance. Such preliminary tests can reveal unusual changes in ratios compared to prior years, or to industry averages, and help the auditor identify areas with increased risk of misstatements that require further attention during the audit.

The Hillsburg Hardware Co. example is used to illustrate the use of preliminary analytical procedures as part of audit planning. Table 8-1 presents key financial ratios for Hillsburg Hardware Co., along with comparative industry information that auditors might consider during audit planning. These ratios are based on the Hillsburg Hardware Co. financial statements. (See the glossy insert in this textbook.) Hillsburg's Annual Report to Shareholders described the company as a wholesale distributor of hardware equipment to independent, high-quality hardware stores in the midwestern United States. The company is a niche provider in the overall hardware industry, which is dominated by national chains like Home Depot and Lowe's. Hillsburg's

TABLE 8-1 Examples of Planning Analytical Procedures

Selected Ratios	Hillsburg 12/31/16	Industry 12/31/16	Hillsburg 12/31/15	Industry 12/31/15
Short-Term Debt-Paying Ability				
Cash ratio	0.06	0.22	0.06	0.20
Quick ratio	1.57	3.10	1.45	3.00
Current ratio	3.86	5.20	4.04	5.10
Liquidity Activity Ratios				
Accounts receivable turnover	7.59	12.15	7.61	12.25
Days to collect accounts receivable	48.09	30.04	47.96	29.80
Inventory turnover	3.36	5.20	3.02	4.90
Days to sell inventory	108.63	70.19	120.86	74.49
Ability to Meet Long-Term Obligations				
Debt to equity	1.73	2.51	1.98	2.53
Times interest earned	3.06	5.50	3.29	5.60
Profitability Ratios				
Gross profit percent	27.85	31.00	27.70	32.00
Profit margin	0.05	0.07	0.05	0.08
Return on assets	0.09	0.09	0.08	0.09
Return on common equity	0.26	0.37	0.24	0.35

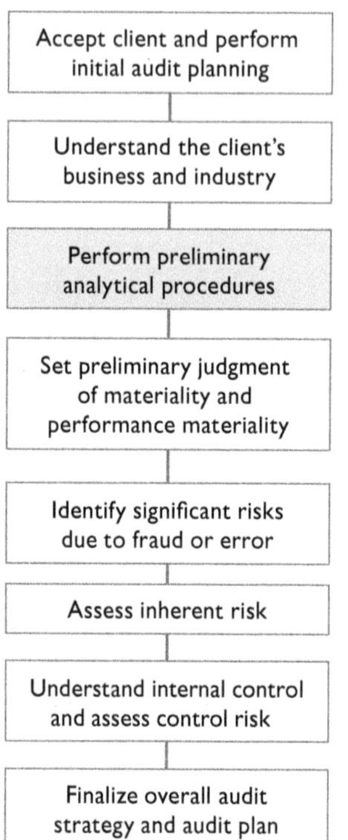
Accept client and perform initial audit planning
Understand the client's business and industry
Perform preliminary analytical procedures
Set preliminary judgment of materiality and performance materiality
Identify significant risks due to fraud or error
Assess inherent risk
Understand internal control and assess control risk
Finalize overall audit strategy and audit plan

auditors identified potential increased competition from national chains as a specific client business risk. Hillsburg's market consists of smaller, independent hardware stores. Increased competition could affect the sales and profitability of these customers, likely affecting Hillsburg's sales and the value of assets such as accounts receivable and inventory. An auditor might use ratio information to identify areas where Hillsburg faces increased risk of material misstatements.

The profitability measures indicate that Hillsburg is performing fairly well, despite the increased competition from larger national chains. Although lower than the industry averages, the liquidity measures indicate that the company is in good financial condition, and the leverage ratios indicate additional borrowing capacity. Because Hillsburg's market consists of smaller, independent hardware stores, the company holds more inventory and takes longer to collect receivables than the industry average.

In identifying areas of specific risk, the auditor is likely to focus on the liquidity activity ratios. Inventory turnover has improved but is still lower than the industry average. Accounts receivable turnover has declined slightly and is lower than the industry average. The collectibility of accounts receivable and inventory obsolescence are likely to be assessed as having higher risk of material misstatement and will therefore likely warrant additional attention in the current year's audit. These areas likely received additional attention during the prior year's audit as well.

Numerous potential comparisons of current- and prior-period data extend beyond those normally available from industry data. For example, the percent of each expense category to total sales can be compared with that of previous years. Similarly, in a multiunit operation such as a retail chain, internal data comparisons for each unit can be made with previous periods.

Auditors often prepare *common-size* financial statements for one or more years that display all items as a percent of a common base, such as sales. Common-size financial statements allow for comparison between companies or for the same company over different time periods, revealing trends and providing insight into how different companies compare. Common-size income statement data for the past three years for Hillsburg Hardware are included in Figure 8-4. The auditor

FIGURE 8-4 Hillsburg Hardware Common-Size Income Statement

HILLSBURG HARDWARE CO.
COMMON-SIZE INCOME STATEMENT
Three Years Ending December 31, 2016

	2016		2015		2014	
	(000) Preliminary	% of Net Sales	(000) Audited	% of Net Sales	(000) Audited	% of Net Sales
Sales	$144,328	100.87	$132,421	100.91	$123,737	100.86
Less: Returns and allowances	1,242	0.87	1,195	0.91	1,052	0.86
Net sales	143,086	100.00	131,226	100.00	122,685	100.00
Cost of goods sold	103,241	72.15	94,876	72.30	88,724	72.32
Gross profit	39,845	27.85	36,350	27.70	33,961	27.68
Selling expense						
Salaries and commissions	7,739	5.41	7,044	5.37	6,598	5.38
Sales payroll taxes	1,422	0.99	1,298	0.99	1,198	0.98
Travel and entertainment	1,110	0.78	925	0.70	797	0.65
Advertising	2,611	1.82	1,920	1.46	1,790	1.46
Sales and promotional literature	322	0.22	425	0.32	488	0.40
Sales meetings and training	925	0.65	781	0.60	767	0.62
Miscellaneous sales expense	681	0.48	506	0.39	456	0.37
Total selling expense	14,810	10.35	12,899	9.83	12,094	9.86
Administration expense						
Executive and office salaries	5,524	3.86	5,221	3.98	5,103	4.16
Administrative payroll taxes	682	0.48	655	0.50	633	0.52
Travel and entertainment	562	0.39	595	0.45	542	0.44
Computer maintenance and supplies	860	0.60	832	0.63	799	0.65
Stationery and supplies	763	0.53	658	0.50	695	0.57
Postage	244	0.17	251	0.19	236	0.19
Telephone and fax	722	0.51	626	0.48	637	0.52
Rent	312	0.22	312	0.24	312	0.25
Legal fees and retainers	383	0.27	321	0.25	283	0.23
Auditing and related services	303	0.21	288	0.22	265	0.22
Depreciation	1,452	1.01	1,443	1.10	1,505	1.23
Bad debt expense	3,323	2.32	3,394	2.59	3,162	2.58
Insurance	723	0.51	760	0.58	785	0.64
Office repairs and maintenance	844	0.59	538	0.41	458	0.37
Miscellaneous office expense	644	0.45	621	0.47	653	0.53
Miscellaneous general expense	324	0.23	242	0.18	275	0.22
Total administrative expenses	17,665	12.35	16,757	12.77	16,343	13.32
Total selling and administrative expenses	32,475	22.70	29,656	22.60	28,437	23.18
Earnings from operations	7,370	5.15	6,694	5.10	5,524	4.50
Other income and expense						
Interest expense	2,409	1.68	2,035	1.55	2,173	1.77
Gain on sale of assets	(720)	(0.50)	0	0.00	0	0.00
Earnings before income taxes	5,681	3.97	4,659	3.55	3,351	2.73
Income taxes	1,747	1.22	1,465	1.12	1,072	0.87
Net income	$ 3,934	2.75	$ 3,194	2.43	$ 2,279	1.86

should calculate income statement account balances as a percent of sales when the level of sales has changed from the prior year—a likely occurrence in many businesses. Hillsburg's sales have increased significantly over the prior year. Note that accounts such as cost of goods sold, as well as sales salaries and commissions, have also increased significantly but are fairly consistent as a percent of sales, which we expect for these accounts.

The auditor is likely to require further explanation and corroborating evidence for the changes in advertising, bad debt expense, and office repairs and maintenance.

- Note that advertising expense has increased as a percent of sales. One possible explanation is the development of a new advertising campaign.
- The dollar amount of bad debt expense has not changed significantly but has decreased as a percent of sales. The auditor needs to gather additional evidence to determine whether bad debt expense and the allowance for doubtful accounts are understated.
- Repairs and maintenance expense has also increased. Fluctuations in this account are not unusual if the client has incurred unexpected repairs. The auditor should investigate major expenditures in this account to determine whether they include any amounts that should be capitalized as a fixed asset.

CONCEPT CHECK

1. Identify the eight major steps in planning audits.
2. What factors should an auditor consider prior to accepting an engagement?
3. Explain the five elements that are part of a strategic understanding of the client's business.

MATERIALITY

OBJECTIVE 8-5

Apply the concept of materiality to the audit.

After performing preliminary analytical procedures, the fourth step in the audit planning process is to make a preliminary judgment about materiality for the audit of the financial statements. Materiality is a major consideration in determining the appropriate audit report to issue, and the materiality concepts discussed in this chapter are directly related to those we introduced in Chapter 3. Auditing standards define **materiality** as the magnitude of misstatements that individually, or when aggregated with other misstatements, could reasonably be expected to influence the economic decisions of users made on the basis of the financial statements.

Because auditors are responsible for determining whether financial statements are materially misstated, they must, upon discovering a material misstatement, bring it to the client's attention so that a correction can be made. If the client refuses to correct the statements, the auditor must issue a qualified or an adverse opinion, depending on the materiality of the misstatement. To make such determinations, auditors depend on a thorough knowledge of the application of materiality.

Because materiality depends on the decisions of users who rely on the statements to make decisions, auditors must have knowledge of the likely users of the client's statements and the decisions that are being made. For example, if an auditor knows that financial statements will be relied on in a buy-sell agreement for the entire business, the amount that the auditor considers material may be smaller than that for an otherwise similar audit. In practice, of course, auditors may not know who all the users are or what decisions they may make based on the financial statements. As a result, applying materiality in practice is a difficult professional judgment.

Auditors follow five closely related steps in applying materiality, as shown in Figure 8-5. The auditor first determines materiality for the financial statements as a whole. Second, the auditor determines **performance materiality**, which is materiality for segments of the audit (classes of transactions, account balances, or disclosures) as shown in the first bracket of the figure. These two steps, which are part of planning, are our primary focus for the discussion of materiality in this chapter. Step 3 occurs throughout the engagement, when auditors estimate the amount of misstatements in each segment as they evaluate audit evidence. Near the end of the audit, during the engagement completion phase, auditors proceed through the final two steps. These latter three steps, as shown in the second bracket in Figure 8-5, are part of evaluating the results of audit tests.

MATERIALITY FOR FINANCIAL STATEMENTS AS A WHOLE

OBJECTIVE 8-6

Make a preliminary judgment about what amounts to consider material.

Auditing standards require auditors to decide on the combined amount of misstatements in the financial statements that they would consider material early in the audit as they are developing the overall strategy for the audit. We refer to this as the **preliminary judgment about materiality**. It is called a preliminary judgment about materiality because, although a professional opinion, it may change during the engagement. This judgment must be documented in the audit files.

The preliminary judgment about materiality for the financial statements as a whole (step 1 in Figure 8-5) is the maximum amount by which the auditor believes the statements could be misstated and still *not* affect the decisions of reasonable users. This judgment is one of the most important decisions the auditor makes, and it requires considerable professional wisdom.

Auditors set a preliminary judgment about materiality to help plan the appropriate evidence to accumulate. The lower the dollar amount of the preliminary judgment, the more evidence required. Examine the financial statements of Hillsburg Hardware

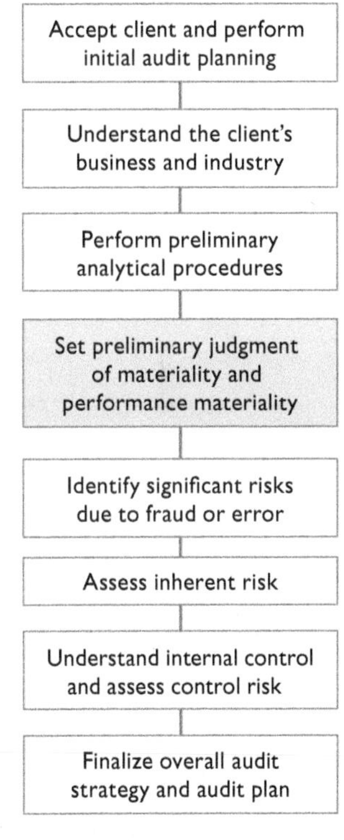

Accept client and perform initial audit planning
Understand the client's business and industry
Perform preliminary analytical procedures
Set preliminary judgment of materiality and performance materiality
Identify significant risks due to fraud or error
Assess inherent risk
Understand internal control and assess control risk
Finalize overall audit strategy and audit plan

FIGURE 8-5 Steps in Applying Materiality

Step	Description	Phase
Step 1	Set materiality for the financial statements as a whole	Planning extent of tests
Step 2	Determine performance materiality	Planning extent of tests
Step 3	Estimate total misstatement in segment	Evaluating results
Step 4	Estimate the combined misstatement	Evaluating results
Step 5	Compare combined estimate with preliminary or revised judgment about materiality	Evaluating results

Co., in the glossy insert to the textbook. What combined amount of misstatements will affect decisions of reasonable users? Do you believe that a $100 misstatement will affect users' decisions? If so, the amount of evidence required for the audit is likely to be beyond that for which the management of Hillsburg Hardware is willing to pay. Do you believe that a $10 million misstatement will be material? Most experienced auditors believe that amount is far too large as a combined materiality amount in these circumstances.

During the audit, auditors may change the preliminary judgment about materiality. We refer to this as the **revised judgment about materiality**. Auditors are likely to make the revision because of changes in one of the factors used to determine the preliminary judgment; that is, the auditor decides that the preliminary judgment was too large or too small. For example, a preliminary judgment about materiality is often determined before year-end and is based on prior years' financial statements or annualized interim financial statement information. The judgment may be reevaluated after current financial statements are available. Or, client circumstances may have changed due to qualitative events such as the issuance of debt, which created a new class of financial statement users.

Factors Affecting Preliminary Materiality Judgment

Several factors affect the auditor's preliminary judgment about materiality for a given set of financial statements. The most important of these are:

Materiality Is a Relative Rather Than an Absolute Concept A misstatement of a given magnitude might be material for a small company, whereas the same dollar misstatement could be immaterial for a large one. This makes it impossible to establish dollar-value guidelines for a preliminary judgment about materiality that are applicable to all audit clients. For example, a total misstatement of $10 million would be extremely material for Hillsburg Hardware Co. because, as shown in their financial statements, total assets are about $61 million and net income before taxes is less than $6 million. A misstatement of the same amount is almost certainly immaterial for a company such as IBM, which has over $100 billion in total assets and net income of several billion dollars.

Benchmarks Are Needed for Evaluating Materiality Because materiality is relative, it is necessary to have benchmarks for establishing whether misstatements are material. *Net income before taxes* is often the primary benchmark for deciding what is material for profit-oriented businesses because it is regarded as a critical item of information for users. Some firms use a different primary benchmark, because net income often fluctuates considerably from year to year and therefore does not provide a stable benchmark, or when the entity is a not-for-profit organization. Other primary benchmarks include net sales, gross profit, and total or net assets. After establishing a primary benchmark, auditors should also decide whether the misstatements could materially affect the reasonableness of other benchmarks such as current assets, total assets, current liabilities, and owners' equity. Auditing standards require the auditor to document in the audit files the preliminary judgment about materiality and the basis used to determine it.

Assume that for a given company, an auditor decides that a misstatement of income before taxes of $100,000 or more would be material, but that a misstatement would need to be $250,000 or more to be material for current assets. It is not appropriate for the auditor to use a preliminary judgment about materiality of $250,000 for both income before taxes and current assets. Instead, the auditor must plan to find all misstatements affecting income before taxes that exceed the preliminary judgment about materiality of $100,000. Because almost all misstatements affect both the income statement and balance sheet, the auditor uses a primary preliminary materiality level of $100,000 for most tests. The only other misstatements that will affect current assets are misclassifications within balance sheet accounts, such as misclassifying a long-term asset as a current one. So, in addition to the primary preliminary judgment about materiality of $100,000, the auditor will also need to plan the audit with the $250,000 preliminary judgment about materiality for misclassifications of current assets.

Qualitative Factors Also Affect Materiality Certain types of misstatements are likely to be more important to users than others, even if the dollar amounts are the same. For example:

- Amounts involving fraud are usually considered more important than unintentional errors of equal dollar amounts because fraud reflects on the honesty and reliability of the management or other personnel involved. For example, most users consider an intentional misstatement of inventory more important than clerical errors in inventory of the same dollar amount.
- Misstatements that are otherwise minor may be material if there are possible consequences arising from contractual obligations. Say that net working capital included in the financial statements is only a few hundred dollars more than the required minimum in a loan agreement. If the correct net working capital were less than the required minimum, putting the loan in default, the current and noncurrent liability classifications would be materially affected.
- Misstatements that are otherwise immaterial may be material if they affect a trend in earnings. For example, if reported income has increased three percent annually for the past five years but income for the current year has declined one percent, that change may be material. Similarly, a misstatement that would cause a loss to be reported as a profit may be of concern.

Illustrative Guidelines

Accounting and auditing standards do not provide specific materiality guidelines to practitioners. The concern is that such guidelines might be applied without considering all the complexities that should affect the auditor's final decision. However, in this chapter, we do provide guidelines to illustrate the application of materiality. These are intended only to help you better understand the concept of applying materiality in practice. The guidelines are stated in Figure 8-6 (p. 238) in the form of policy guidelines of a CPA firm. Notice that the guidelines are formulas using one or more benchmarks and a range of percentages. The application of guidelines, such as the ones we present here, requires considerable professional judgment.

Application to Hillsburg Hardware

Using the illustrative guidelines in Figure 8-6, let's examine a preliminary judgment about materiality for Hillsburg Hardware Co. The guidelines are as follows:

	Preliminary Judgment About Materiality (Rounded, in Thousands)			
	Minimum		Maximum	
	Percentage	Dollar Amount	Percentage	Dollar Amount
Earnings from operations	3	$221	6	$442
Current assets	3	1,531	6	3,062
Total assets	1	614	3	1,841
Current liabilities	3	396	6	793

If the auditor for Hillsburg Hardware decides that the general guidelines are reasonable, the first step is to evaluate whether any qualitative factors significantly affect the materiality judgment. Assuming no qualitative factors exist, if the auditor concludes at the end of the audit that combined misstatements of operating income before taxes are less than $221,000, the statements will be considered fairly stated. If the combined misstatements exceed $442,000, the statements will not be considered

FIGURE 8-6 Illustrative Materiality Guidelines

BERGER AND ANTHONY, CPAs
Gary, Indiana 46405

POLICY STATEMENT
No. 32IC
Title: Materiality Guidelines

Charles G. Berger
Joe Anthony

Professional judgment is to be used at all times in setting and applying materiality guidelines. As a general guideline, the following policies are to be applied:

1. The combined total of misstatements in the financial statements exceeding 6 percent is normally considered material. A combined total of less than 3 percent is presumed to be immaterial in the absence of qualitative factors. Combined misstatements between 3 percent and 6 percent require the greatest amount of professional judgment to determine their materiality.
2. The 3 percent to 6 percent must be measured in relation to the appropriate benchmark. Many times there is more than one benchmark to which misstatements should be compared. The following guides are recommended in selecting the appropriate benchmark:
   a. *Income statement.* Combined misstatements in the income statement should ordinarily be measured at 3 percent to 6 percent of operating income before taxes. A guideline of 3 percent to 6 percent may be inappropriate in a year in which income is unusually large or small. When operating income in a given year is not considered representative, it is desirable to substitute as a benchmark a more representative income measure. For example, average operating income for a 3-year period may be used as the benchmark.
   b. *Balance sheet.* Combined misstatements in the balance sheet should originally be evaluated for current assets, current liabilities, and total assets. For current assets and current liabilities, the guidelines should be between 3 percent and 6 percent, applied in the same way as for the income statement. For total assets, the guidelines should be between 1 percent and 3 percent, applied in the same way as for the income statement.
3. Qualitative factors should be carefully evaluated on all audits. In many instances, they are more important than the guidelines applied to the income statement and balance sheet. The intended uses of the financial statements and the nature of the information in the statements, including footnotes, must be carefully evaluated.

fairly stated. If the misstatements are between $221,000 and $442,000, a more careful consideration of all facts will be required. The auditor then applies the same process to the other three bases.

DETERMINE PERFORMANCE MATERIALITY

OBJECTIVE 8-7

Determine performance materiality during audit planning.

Performance materiality is defined as the amount(s) set by the auditor at less than materiality for the financial statements as a whole to reduce to an appropriately low level the probability that the aggregate of uncorrected and undetected misstatements exceeds materiality for the financial statements as a whole. Determining performance materiality (step 2 in Figure 8-5 on p. 235) is necessary because auditors accumulate evidence by segments rather than for the financial statements as a whole, and the level of performance materiality helps them decide the appropriate audit evidence to accumulate. Performance materiality is inversely related to the amount of evidence an auditor will accumulate. For an accounts receivable balance of $1,000,000, for example, the auditor should accumulate more evidence if a misstatement of $50,000 is considered material than if $300,000 were considered material. However, if auditors assigned the same level of materiality to each segment of the audit that was assigned for the overall financial statements, there would likely be unidentified misstatements that exceed materiality for the financial statements as a whole.

Many auditors set performance materiality for most tests as a standard percentage of the preliminary judgment about materiality for the financial statements as a whole. Performance materiality is commonly set at 50–75% of overall materiality. However, performance materiality can vary for different classes of transactions, account balances, or disclosures, especially if there is a focus on a particular area. For example, users of financial statements might expect disclosures of related party transactions involving the CEO or the purchase price of a newly acquired subsidiary to be more precise, and therefore auditors might set a lower materiality level in these audit areas. In addition, overall audit assurance and the cost of audit evidence can be considered when determining performance materiality, as discussed further below.

We refer to the process of determining performance materiality as the **allocation of the preliminary judgment about materiality** to segments in our discussion that follows. If auditors do not use a standard percentage and consider audit assurance and the cost of audit evidence in determining performance materiality, most practitioners allocate materiality to balance sheet rather than income statement accounts, because most income statement misstatements have an equal effect on the balance sheet due to the nature of double-entry accounting. For example, a $20,000 overstatement of accounts receivable is also a $20,000 overstatement of sales. Because most audit procedures focus on balance sheet accounts, materiality is usually allocated only to balance sheet accounts.

The determination of performance materiality is based on professional judgment and reflects the amount of misstatement an auditor is willing to accept in a particular segment. For example, if an auditor decides to allocate $100,000 of a total preliminary judgment about materiality of $200,000 to accounts receivable, this means the auditor is willing to consider accounts receivable fairly stated if it is misstated by $100,000 or less. PCAOB auditing standards refer to this amount as **tolerable misstatement**, whereas AICPA standards define tolerable misstatement as the application of performance materiality to a particular sampling procedure. We use the term performance materiality rather than tolerable misstatement throughout this chapter to be consistent with AICPA and IAASB standards.

Auditors face three major difficulties in allocating materiality to balance sheet accounts:

1. Auditors expect certain accounts to have more misstatements than others.
2. Both overstatements and understatements must be considered.
3. Relative audit costs affect the allocation.

All three of these difficulties are considered in the allocation in Figure 8-7 (p. 240). It is worth keeping in mind that at the end of the audit, the auditor must combine all actual and estimated misstatements and compare them to the preliminary judgment about materiality. In determining performance materiality levels, the auditor is attempting to do the audit as efficiently as possible.

Allocation Illustrated

Figure 8-7 illustrates the allocation approach used to establish different performance materiality levels across segments of the financial statements for the audit of Hillsburg Hardware Co. It summarizes the balance sheet, combining certain accounts, and shows the allocation of total materiality of $442,000 (six percent of earnings from operations). The allocation approach uses judgment in the allocation, subject to the following two arbitrary requirements established by Berger and Anthony, CPAs:

- Performance materiality for any account cannot exceed 60 percent of the preliminary judgment (60 percent of $442,000 = $265,000, rounded).
- The sum of all performance materiality levels cannot exceed twice the preliminary judgment about materiality (2 × $442,000 = $884,000).

The first requirement keeps the auditor from allocating all of preliminary materiality to one account. If, for example, all of the preliminary judgment of $442,000 is allocated to trade accounts receivable, a $442,000 misstatement in that account will be acceptable. However, it may not be acceptable to have such a large misstatement in one account, and even if it is acceptable, it does not allow for any misstatements in other accounts.

FIGURE 8-7 Performance Materiality Levels for Hillsburg Hardware Co.

	Balance 12-31-16 (in Thousands)	Performance Materiality (in Thousands)	
Cash	$ 828	$ 6 (a)	
Trade accounts receivable (net)	18,957	265 (b)	
Inventories	29,865	265 (b)	
Other current assets	1,377	60 (c)	
Property, plant, and equipment	10,340	48 (d)	
Total assets	$61,367		
Trade accounts payable	$ 4,720	90 (e)	
Notes payable—total	28,300	6 (a)	
Accrued payroll and payroll tax	1,470	60 (c)	
Accrued interest and dividends payable	2,050	6 (a)	
Other liabilities	2,364	72 (c)	
Capital stock and capital in excess of par	8,500	6 (a)	
Retained earnings	13,963	NA (f)	
Total liabilities and equity	$61,367	$884	(2 × $442)

NA = Not applicable.
(a) Small performance materiality because account can be completely audited at low cost and no misstatements are expected.
(b) Large performance materiality because account is large and requires extensive sampling to audit the account.
(c) Large performance materiality as a percent of account because account can be verified at extremely low cost, probably with substantive analytical procedures.
(d) Small performance materiality as a percent of account balance because most of the balance is in land and buildings, which is unchanged from the prior year and need not be audited further this year.
(e) Moderately large performance materiality because a relatively large number of misstatements are expected.
(f) Not applicable—retained earnings is a residual account that is affected by the net amount of the misstatements in the other accounts.

There are two reasons for the second requirement, permitting the sum of performance materiality to exceed overall materiality:

- It is unlikely that all accounts will be misstated by the full amount of performance materiality. If, for example, other current assets have a performance materiality of $100,000 but no misstatements are found in auditing those accounts, it means that the auditor, after the fact, could have allocated zero or a small performance materiality to other current assets. It is common for auditors to find fewer misstatements than performance materiality.
- Some accounts are likely to be overstated, whereas others are likely to be understated, resulting in a net amount that is likely to be less than the preliminary judgment.

Notice in the allocation that the auditor is concerned about the combined effect on operating income of the misstatement of each balance sheet account. An overstatement of an asset account will therefore have the same effect on the income statement as an understatement of a liability account. In contrast, a misclassification in the balance sheet, such as a classification of a note payable as an account payable, will have no effect on operating income. Therefore, the materiality of items not affecting the income statement must be considered separately.

Figure 8-7 also includes the rationale followed in deciding performance materiality for each account. For example, a small amount of performance materiality was assigned to notes payable, even though it is as large as inventories. If $132,500 had been assigned to each of those two accounts, more evidence would have been required in inventories, but the confirmation of the balance in notes payable would still have been necessary. It was therefore more efficient to allocate $265,000 to inventories and a small amount to notes payable. Similarly, $60,000 was assigned to other current assets and to accrued payroll and payroll tax, both of which are large compared with the recorded account balance. This was done because these accounts can be verified within $60,000 by using only substantive analytical procedures, which are lower cost. If performance materiality were set lower, more costly audit procedures such as inspection and confirmation would be necessary.

In practice, it is often difficult to predict in advance which accounts are most likely to be misstated and whether misstatements are likely to be overstatements or understatements. Similarly, the relative costs of auditing different account balances often cannot be determined. It is therefore a difficult professional judgment to allocate the preliminary judgment about materiality to accounts. Accordingly, many accounting firms have developed rigorous guidelines and sophisticated methods for doing so. These guidelines also help ensure the auditor appropriately documents the overall materiality level and performance materiality levels and the factors considered in determining those amounts in the audit files.

To summarize, the purpose of allocating the preliminary judgment about materiality to balance sheet accounts is to help the auditor decide the appropriate evidence to accumulate for each account on both the balance sheet and income statement. An aim of the allocation is to minimize audit costs without sacrificing audit quality. Regardless of how the allocation is done, when the audit is completed, the auditor must be confident that the combined misstatements in all accounts are less than or equal to the preliminary (or revised) judgment about materiality.

ESTIMATE MISSTATEMENT AND COMPARE WITH PRELIMINARY JUDGMENT

OBJECTIVE 8-8

Use materiality to evaluate audit findings.

The first two steps in applying materiality involve planning (see Figure 8-5 on p. 235) and are our primary concern in this chapter. The last three steps result from performing audit tests. These steps are introduced here and discussed in more detail in subsequent chapters.

When auditors perform audit procedures for each segment of the audit, they document all misstatements found. Misstatements in an account can be of two types: known misstatements and likely misstatements. **Known misstatements** are those where the auditor can determine the amount of the misstatement in the account. For example, when auditing property, plant, and equipment, the auditor may identify capitalized leased equipment that should be expensed because it is an operating lease. There are two types of **likely misstatements**. The first are misstatements that arise from differences between management's and the auditor's judgment about estimates of account balances. Examples are differences in the estimate for the allowance for uncollectible accounts or for warranty liabilities. The second are projections of misstatements based on the auditor's tests of a sample from a population. For example, assume the auditor finds six client misstatements in a sample of 200 in testing inventory costs. The auditor uses these misstatements to estimate the *total* likely misstatements in inventory (step 3). The total is called an estimate or a "projection" or "extrapolation" because only a sample, rather than the entire population, was audited. The projected misstatement amounts for each account are combined on the worksheet (step 4), and then the combined likely misstatement is compared with materiality (step 5).

Table 8-2 illustrates the last three steps in applying materiality. For simplicity, only three accounts are included. The misstatement in cash of $2,000 is a known misstatement related to unrecorded bank service charges detected by the auditor. Unlike for cash, the misstatements for accounts receivable and inventory are based on samples. The auditor calculates likely misstatements for accounts receivable and inventory using known misstatements detected in those samples. To illustrate the calculation, assume that in auditing inventory the auditor found $3,500 of net overstatement amounts in a sample of $50,000 of the total population of $450,000. The $3,500 identified misstatement is a known misstatement. To calculate the estimate of the likely misstatements for the total population of $450,000, the auditor makes a direct projection of the known misstatement from the sample to the population and adds an estimated allowance for sampling risk. The calculation of the direct projection estimate of misstatement is:

$$\frac{\text{Net misstatements in the sample (\$3,500)}}{\text{Total sampled (\$50,000)}} \times \begin{matrix}\text{Total recorded}\\ \text{population value}\\ \text{(\$450,000)}\end{matrix} = \begin{matrix}\text{Direct projection}\\ \text{estimate of}\\ \text{misstatement}\\ \text{(\$31,500)}\end{matrix}$$

(Note that the direct projection of likely misstatement for accounts receivable of $12,000 is not illustrated.)

The allowance for **sampling risk** results because the auditor has sampled only a portion of the population and there is a risk that the sample does not accurately represent the population. (We'll discuss this in more detail in Chapters 15 and 17.) In this simplified example, we'll assume the estimated allowance for sampling risk is 50 percent of the direct projection of the misstatement amounts for the accounts where sampling was used (accounts receivable and inventory). There is no allowance for sampling risk for cash because the total amount of misstatement is known, not estimated.

In combining the misstatements in Table 8-2, we can observe that the known misstatements and direct projection of likely misstatements for the three accounts adds to $45,500. However, the total allowance for sampling risk is less than the sum of the individual sampling risk amounts. This is because the allowance for sampling risk represents the maximum misstatement in account details not audited. It is unlikely that this maximum misstatement amount exists in all accounts subjected to sampling.

Table 8-2 shows that total estimated likely misstatement of $62,300 exceeds the preliminary judgment about materiality of $50,000. The major area of difficulty is inventory, where estimated misstatement including allowance for sampling risk of $47,250 is significantly greater than performance materiality of $36,000. Because the estimated combined misstatement exceeds the preliminary judgment, the financial statements are not acceptable. The auditor can either determine whether the estimated likely misstatement actually exceeds $50,000 by performing additional audit

TABLE 8-2 Illustration of Comparison of Estimated Total Misstatement to Preliminary Judgment About Materiality

Account	Performance Materiality	Known Misstatement and Direct Projection	Allowance for Sampling Risk	Total
Cash	$ 4,000	$ 2,000	$ NA	$ 2,000
Accounts receivable	20,000	12,000	6,000	18,000
Inventory	36,000	31,500	15,750	47,250
Total estimated misstatement amount		$45,500	$16,800	$62,300
Preliminary judgment about materiality	$50,000			

NA = Not applicable.
Cash audited 100 percent.

procedures or require the client to make an adjustment for estimated misstatements. If the auditor decides to perform additional audit procedures, they will be concentrated in the inventory area.

If the estimated net overstatement amount for inventory had been $28,000 ($18,000 plus $10,000 allowance for sampling risk), the auditor probably would not have needed to expand audit tests because it would have met both the tests of performance materiality ($36,000) and the preliminary judgment about materiality ($2,000 + $18,000 + $28,000 = $48,000 < $50,000). In fact, the auditor would have had some leeway with that amount because the results of cash and accounts receivable procedures indicate that those accounts are within their performance materiality limits. If the auditor approaches the audit of the accounts in a sequential manner, the findings of the audit of accounts audited earlier can be used to revise the performance materiality established for accounts audited later. In the illustration, if the auditor had audited cash and accounts receivable before inventories, performance materiality for inventories could have been increased.

CONCEPT CHECK

1. What is meant by setting a preliminary judgment about materiality? Identify the most important factors affecting the preliminary judgment.
2. Distinguish between the terms *performance materiality* and *preliminary judgment about materiality*. How are they related to each other?
3. Explain the difference between known and likely misstatements. Assume the auditor tests a sample of $100,000 of inventory and finds misstatements totaling $5,000. What is the likely misstatement if the account balance is $500,000?

SUMMARY

A major purpose of audit planning is to gain an understanding of the client's business and industry, which is used to assess acceptable audit risk, client business risk, and the risk of material misstatements in the financial statements. Figure 8-8 (p. 244) summarizes the four major parts of audit planning discussed in this chapter and the key components of each part, with a brief illustration of how a CPA firm applied each component to a continuing client, Hillsburg Hardware Co.

There are four additional parts of audit planning that are discussed in subsequent chapters. The four subsequent parts are:

- Identify significant risks due to fraud or error (Chapters 9 and 10)
- Assess inherent risk (Chapter 9)
- Understand internal control and assess control risk (Chapters 11 and 12)
- Finalize the overall audit plan and audit program (Chapter 13)

ESSENTIAL TERMS

Acceptable audit risk—a measure of how willing the auditor is to accept that the financial statements may be materially misstated after the audit is completed and an unmodified opinion has been issued

Allocation of the preliminary judgment about materiality—the process of assigning to each balance sheet account the misstatement amount considered to be material for that account based on the auditor's preliminary judgment

Audit strategy—overall approach to the audit that considers the nature of the client, risk of significant misstatements, and other factors such as the number of client locations and past effectiveness of client controls

Client business risk—the risk that the client will fail to achieve its objectives related to (1) reliability of financial reporting, (2) effectiveness and efficiency of operations, and (3) compliance with laws and regulations

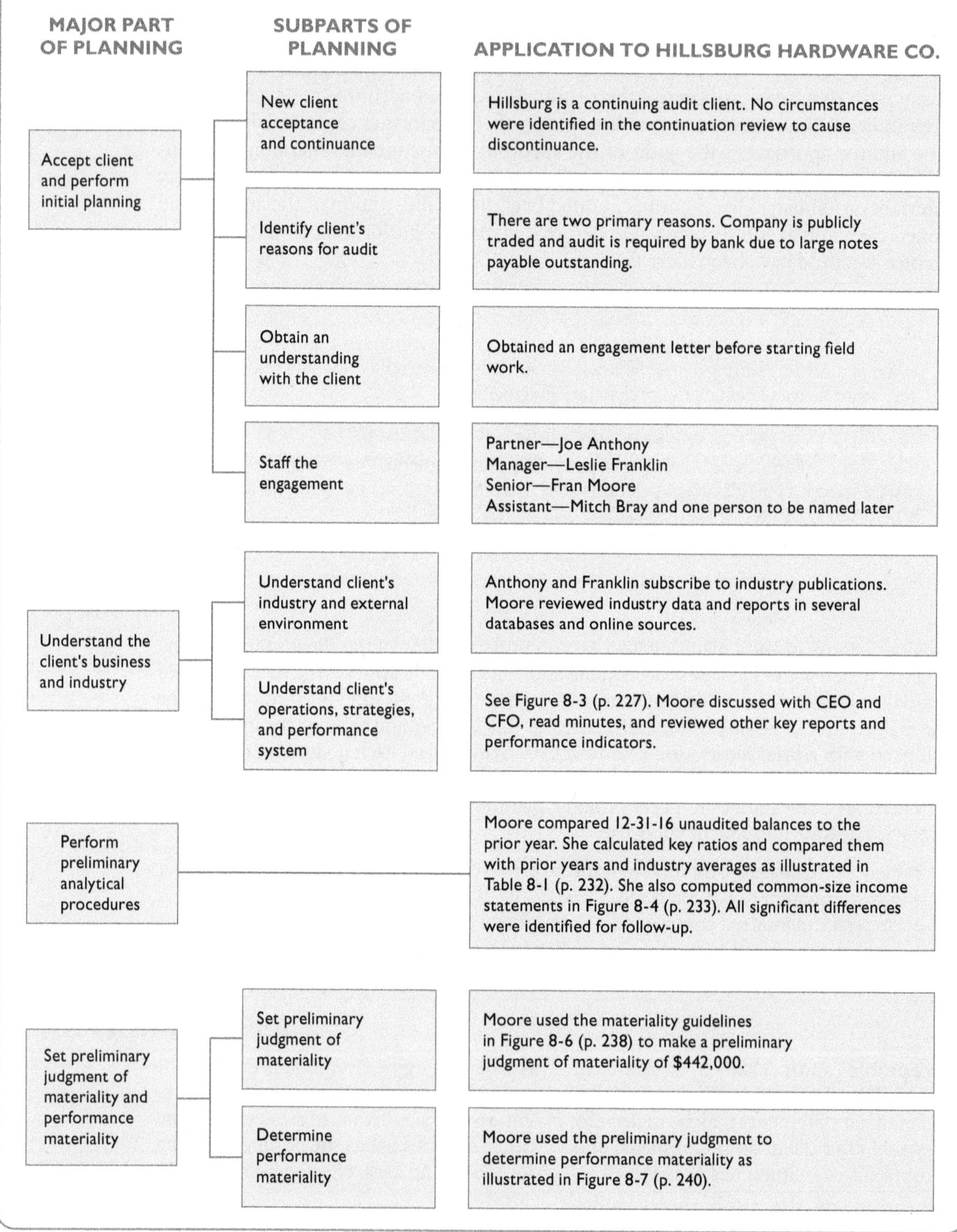

MAJOR PART OF PLANNING
SUBPARTS OF PLANNING
APPLICATION TO HILLSBURG HARDWARE CO.
Accept client and perform initial planning
New client acceptance and continuance
Hillsburg is a continuing audit client. No circumstances were identified in the continuation review to cause discontinuance.
Identify client's reasons for audit
There are two primary reasons. Company is publicly traded and audit is required by bank due to large notes payable outstanding.
Obtain an understanding with the client
Obtained an engagement letter before starting field work.
Staff the engagement
Partner—Joe Anthony
Manager—Leslie Franklin
Senior—Fran Moore
Assistant—Mitch Bray and one person to be named later
Understand the client's business and industry
Understand client's industry and external environment
Anthony and Franklin subscribe to industry publications. Moore reviewed industry data and reports in several databases and online sources.
Understand client's operations, strategies, and performance system
See Figure 8-3 (p. 227). Moore discussed with CEO and CFO, read minutes, and reviewed other key reports and performance indicators.
Perform preliminary analytical procedures
Moore compared 12-31-16 unaudited balances to the prior year. She calculated key ratios and compared them with prior years and industry averages as illustrated in Table 8-1 (p. 232). She also computed common-size income statements in Figure 8-4 (p. 233). All significant differences were identified for follow-up.
Set preliminary judgment of materiality and performance materiality
Set preliminary judgment of materiality
Moore used the materiality guidelines in Figure 8-6 (p. 238) to make a preliminary judgment of materiality of $442,000.
Determine performance materiality
Moore used the preliminary judgment to determine performance materiality as illustrated in Figure 8-7 (p. 240).

FIGURE 8-8 Key Parts of Planning: Accept Client and Perform Initial Planning, Understand the Client's Business and Industry, Perform Preliminary Analytical Procedures, and Set Preliminary Judgment About Materiality and Performance Materiality Applied to Hillsburg Hardware Co.

Corporate minutes—the official record of the meetings of a corporation's board of directors and stockholders, in which corporate issues such as the declaration of dividends and the approval of contracts are documented

Engagement letter—an agreement between the CPA firm and the client as to the terms of the engagement for the conduct of the audit and related services

Initial audit planning—involves deciding whether to accept or continue doing the audit for the client, identifying the client's reasons for the audit, obtaining an engagement letter, and developing an audit strategy

Known misstatements—specific misstatements in a class of transactions or account balance identified during the audit

Likely misstatements—misstatements that arise either from differences between management's and the auditor's judgment about estimates of account balances or from projections of misstatements based on the auditor's test of a sample from a population

Materiality—the magnitude of an omission or misstatement of accounting information that, in the light of surrounding circumstances, makes it *probable* that the judgment of a reasonable person relying on the information would have been changed or influenced by the omission or misstatement

Performance materiality—the materiality amount(s) for segments of the audit, set by the auditor at less than materiality for the financial statements as a whole

Preliminary judgment about materiality—the maximum amount by which the auditor believes that the statements could be misstated and still *not* affect the decisions of reasonable users; used in audit planning

Related party—affiliated company, principal owner of the client company, or any other party with which the client deals, where one of the parties can influence the management or operating policies of the other

Related party transaction—any transaction between the client and a related party

Revised judgment about materiality—a change in the auditor's preliminary judgment made when the auditor determines that the preliminary judgment was too large or too small

Risk assessment procedures—audit procedures performed to obtain an understanding of the entity and its environment, including the entity's internal control, to identify and assess the risks of material misstatement

Risk of material misstatement—the risk that the financial statements are materially misstated prior to the audit

Sampling risk—results because the auditor has sampled only a portion of the population

Tolerable misstatement—the application of performance materiality to a sampling procedure (AICPA standards) or the materiality allocated to any given account balance (PCAOB standards)

REVIEW QUESTIONS

8-1 **(OBJECTIVE 8-1)** What are the benefits derived from planning audits?

8-2 **(OBJECTIVE 8-2)** What are the responsibilities of the successor and predecessor auditors when a company is changing auditors?

8-3 **(OBJECTIVE 8-2)** What is the purpose of an engagement letter? What subjects should be covered in such a letter?

8-4 **(OBJECTIVE 8-2)** Who is considered the client when auditing public companies?

8-5 **(OBJECTIVE 8-3)** Explain why auditors need an understanding of the client's industry. What information sources are commonly used by auditors to learn about the client's industry?

8-6 **(OBJECTIVE 8-3)** When a CPA has accepted an engagement from a new client who is a manufacturer, it is customary for the CPA to tour the client's plant facilities. Discuss the ways in which the CPA's observations made during the course of the plant tour will be of help in planning and conducting the audit.

8-7 **(OBJECTIVE 8-3)** An auditor often tries to acquire background knowledge of the client's industry as an aid to audit work. How does the acquisition of this knowledge aid the auditor in distinguishing between obsolete and current inventory?

8-8 **(OBJECTIVE 8-3)** Define what is meant by a related party. What are the auditor's responsibilities for related parties and related party transactions?

8-9 **(OBJECTIVE 8-3)** Which types of loans to executives are permitted by the Sarbanes–Oxley Act?

8-10 **(OBJECTIVE 8-3)** In recent years the global economy experienced recession levels unprecedented since the Great Depression, and the instability of the Euro continues to cause volatility in stock and bond markets. Why might it be important for you to consider current economic events as part of planning an audit?

8-11 **(OBJECTIVE 8-3)** For the audit of Radline Manufacturing Company, the audit partner asks you to carefully read the new mortgage contract with the First National Bank and abstract all pertinent information. List the information in a mortgage that is likely to be relevant to the auditor.

8-12 **(OBJECTIVE 8-3)** Identify two types of information in the client's minutes of the board of directors meetings that are likely to be relevant to the auditor. Explain why it is important to read the minutes early in the engagement.

8-13 **(OBJECTIVE 8-3)** Identify the three categories of client objectives. Indicate how each objective may affect the auditor's assessment of risk of material misstatement and need for evidence accumulation.

8-14 **(OBJECTIVE 8-3)** What is the purpose of the client's performance measurement system? How might that system be useful to the auditor? Give examples of key performance indicators for the following businesses: (1) a chain of retail clothing stores; (2) an Internet portal; (3) a hotel chain.

8-15 **(OBJECTIVE 8-4)** Gale Gordon, CPA, has found ratio and trend analysis relatively useless as a tool in conducting audits. For several engagements, he computed the industry ratios included in publications by Standard and Poor's and compared them with industry standards. For most engagements, the client's business was significantly different from the industry data in the publication, and the client automatically explained away any discrepancies by attributing them to the unique nature of its operations. In cases in which the client had more than one branch in different industries, Gordon found the ratio analysis to be no help at all. How can Gordon improve the quality of his analytical procedures?

8-16 **(OBJECTIVE 8-4)** Your client, Harper Company, has a contractual commitment as a part of a bond indenture to maintain a current ratio of 2.0. If the ratio falls below that level on the balance sheet date, the entire bond becomes payable immediately. In the current year, the client's financial statements show that the ratio has dropped from 2.6 to 2.05 over the past year. How should this situation affect your audit plan?

8-17 **(OBJECTIVE 8-5)** Define the meaning of the term *materiality* as it is used in accounting and auditing. What is the relationship between materiality and the phrase *obtain reasonable assurance* used in the auditor's report?

8-18 **(OBJECTIVES 8-5, 8-6)** Explain why materiality is important but difficult to apply in practice.

8-19 **(OBJECTIVE 8-6)** What is meant by using benchmarks for setting a preliminary judgment about materiality? How will those benchmarks differ for the audit of a manufacturing company and a government unit such as a school district?

8-20 **(OBJECTIVE 8-6)** Assume that Rosanne Madden, CPA, is using 5% of net income before taxes, current assets, or current liabilities as her major guidelines for evaluating materiality. What qualitative factors should she also consider in deciding whether misstatements may be material?

8-21 **(OBJECTIVE 8-6)** How will the conduct of an audit of a medium-sized company be affected by the company's being a small part of a large conglomerate as compared with it being a separate entity?

8-22 **(OBJECTIVE 8-7)** Assume a company with the following balance sheet accounts:

You are concerned only about overstatements of owner's equity. Set performance materiality for the three relevant accounts such that the preliminary judgment about materiality does not exceed $5,000. Justify your answer.

Account	Amount	Account	Amount
Cash	$10,000	Long-term loans	$30,000
Fixed assets	60,000	M. Johnson, proprietor	40,000
	$70,000		$70,000

8-23 **(OBJECTIVE 8-7)** Provide two examples of when an auditor might set a lower level of performance materiality for a particular class of transactions, account balance, or disclosure.

8-24 **(OBJECTIVE 8-8)** Assume materiality for the financial statements as a whole is $100,000 and performance materiality for accounts receivable is set at $40,000. If the auditor finds one receivable that is overstated by $55,000, what should the auditor do?

MULTIPLE CHOICE QUESTIONS FROM CPA EXAMINATIONS

8-25 **(OBJECTIVES 8-1, 8-3, 8-4)** The following questions concern the planning of the engagement. Select the best response.

a. Which of the following will most likely indicate the existence of related parties?
   (1) Writing down obsolete inventory prior to year end
   (2) Failing to correct deficiencies in the client's internal control
   (3) An unexplained increase in gross margin
   (4) Borrowing money at a rate significantly below the market rate

b. Which of the following is least likely to be included in the auditor's engagement letter?
   (1) Details about the preliminary audit strategy
   (2) Overview of the objectives of the engagement
   (3) Statement that management is responsible for the financial statements
   (4) Description of the level of assurance obtained when conducting the audit

c. Analytical procedures used in planning an audit should focus on identifying
   (1) material weaknesses in internal control.
   (2) the predictability of financial data from individual transactions.
   (3) the various assertions that are embodied in the financial statements.
   (4) areas that may represent specific risks relevant to the audit.

8-26 **(OBJECTIVE 8-2)** The following questions pertain to client acceptance. Choose the best response.

a. When approached to perform an audit for the first time, the CPA should make inquiries of the predecessor auditor. This is a necessary procedure because the predecessor may be able to provide the successor with information that will assist the successor in determining whether
   (1) the predecessor's work should be used.
   (2) the company follows the policy of rotating its auditors.
   (3) in the predecessor's opinion, internal control of the company has been satisfactory.
   (4) the engagement should be accepted.

b. A successor would most likely make specific inquiries of the predecessor auditor regarding
   (1) specialized accounting principles of the client's industry.
   (2) the competency of the client's internal audit staff.
   (3) the uncertainty inherent in applying sampling procedures.
   (4) disagreements with management as to auditing procedures.

c. Which of the following circumstances would most likely pose the greatest risk in accepting a new audit engagement?
   (1) Staff will need to be rescheduled to cover this new client.
   (2) There will be a client-imposed scope limitation.

(3) The firm will have to hire a specialist in one audit area.
(4) The client's financial reporting system has been in place for 10 years.

8-27 **(OBJECTIVES 8-5, 8-6)** The following questions deal with materiality. Choose the best response.

a. Which one of the following statements is correct concerning the concept of materiality?
 (1) Materiality is determined by reference to guidelines established by the AICPA.
 (2) Materiality depends only on the dollar amount of an item relative to other items in the financial statements.
 (3) Materiality depends on the nature of an item rather than the dollar amount.
 (4) Materiality is a matter of professional judgment.

b. In considering materiality for planning purposes, an auditor believes that misstatements aggregating \$10,000 will have a material effect on an entity's income statement, but that misstatements will have to aggregate \$20,000 to materially affect the balance sheet. Ordinarily, it is appropriate to design audit procedures that are expected to detect misstatements that aggregate
 (1) \$10,000.
 (2) \$15,000.
 (3) \$20,000.
 (4) \$30,000.

c. A client decides not to record an auditor's proposed adjustments that collectively are not material and wants the auditor to issue the report based on the unadjusted numbers. Which of the following statements is correct regarding the financial statement presentation?
 (1) The financial statements are free from material misstatement, and no disclosure is required in the notes to the financial statements.
 (2) The financial statements do not conform with generally accepted accounting principles (GAAP).
 (3) The financial statements contain unadjusted misstatements that should result in a qualified opinion.
 (4) The financial statements are free from material misstatement, but disclosure of the proposed adjustment is required in the notes to the financial statements.

MULTIPLE CHOICE QUESTIONS FROM BECKER CPA EXAM REVIEW

8-28 **(OBJECTIVES 8-1, 8-2, 8-6)** The following questions deal with client acceptance, audit planning, and materiality. Choose the best response.

a. Which of the following procedures would a CPA *least likely* perform during the planning stage of the audit?
 (1) Determine the timing of testing
 (2) Take a tour of the client's facilities
 (3) Perform inquiries of outside legal counsel regarding pending litigation
 (4) Determine the effect of information technology on the audit

b. A successor auditor's inquiries of the predecessor auditor should include questions regarding
 (1) the number of engagement personnel the predecessor assigned to the engagement.
 (2) the assessment of the objectivity of the client's internal audit function.
 (3) communications to management and those charged with governance regarding significant deficiencies in internal control.
 (4) the response rate for confirmations of accounts receivable.

c. In which of the following circumstances would an auditor of an issuer be *least likely* to reevaluate established materiality levels?
   (1) The materiality level was established based on preliminary financial statement amounts that differ significantly from actual amounts.
   (2) The client disposed of a major portion of the client's business.
   (3) The client released third-quarter results before the SEC-prescribed deadline.
   (4) Significant new contractual arrangements draw attention to a particular aspect of a client's business that is separately disclosed in the financial statements.

DISCUSSION QUESTIONS AND PROBLEMS

8-29 **(OBJECTIVES 8-2, 8-3, 8-4, 8-5)** The following are various activities an auditor does during audit planning.

1. Review accounting principles unique to the client's industry
2. Determine the likely users of the financial statements
3. Evaluate the appropriate financial statement measures for determining amounts likely to be considered material by users of the financial statements
4. Identify whether any specialists are required for the engagement
5. Send an engagement letter to the client
6. Tour the client's plant and offices
7. Specify materiality levels to be used in testing of accounts receivable
8. Compare key ratios for the company to those for industry competitors
9. Review management's risk management controls and procedures
10. Identify potential related parties that may require disclosure

Required

For each procedure, indicate which of the first four parts of audit planning the procedure primarily relates to: (1) accept client and perform initial audit planning; (2) understand the client's business and industry; (3) perform preliminary analytical procedures; (4) set preliminary judgment about materiality and performance materiality.

8-30 **(OBJECTIVE 8-3)** In your audit of Canyon Outdoor Provision Company's financial statements, the following transactions came to your attention:

1. Canyon Outdoor's operating lease for its main store is with York Properties, which is a real estate investment firm owned by Travis Smedes. Mr. Smedes is a member of Canyon Outdoor's board of directors.
2. One of Canyon Outdoor's main suppliers for kayaks is Hessel Boating Company. Canyon Outdoor has purchased kayaks and canoes from Hessel for the last 25 years under a long-term contract arrangement.
3. Short-term financing lines of credit are provided by Cameron Bank and Trust. Suzanne Strayhorn is the lending officer assigned to the Canyon Outdoor account. Suzanne is the wife of the largest investor of Canyon Outdoor.
4. Hillsborough Travel partners with Canyon Outdoor to provide hiking and rafting adventure vacations. The owner of Hillsborough Travel lives in the same neighborhood as the CEO of Canyon Outdoor. They are acquaintances, but not close friends.
5. The board of directors consists of several individuals who own stock in Canyon Outdoor. At a recent board meeting, the board approved its annual dividend payable to shareholders effective June 1.

Required

a. Define what constitutes a "related party."
b. Which of the preceding transactions would most likely be considered a related party transaction?
c. What financial statement implications, if any, would each of the above transactions have for Canyon Outdoor?
d. What procedures might auditors consider to help them identify potential related party transactions for clients like Canyon Outdoor?

8-31 **(OBJECTIVE 8-3)** The minutes of the board of directors of the Tetonic Metals Company for the year ended December 31, 2016, were provided to you.

Meeting of March 5, 2016

The meeting of the board of directors of Tetonic Metals was called to order by James Cook, the chairman of the board, at 8:30 am. The following directors were in attendance:

Irene Arnold	James Cook	Brian McDonald
Robert Beardsley	Larry Holden	Tony Williams
Mary Beth Cape	Heather Jackson	

The board approved the minutes from the November 22, 2015, meeting.

The board reviewed the financial statements for the most recent fiscal year that ended December 31, 2015. Due to strong operating results, the board declared an increase in the annual dividend to common shareholders from $0.32 to $0.36 per common share payable on May 10, 2016, to shareholders of record on April 25, 2016.

Tony Williams, CEO, led a discussion of the seven core strategic initiatives in the 2016–2018 strategic plan. The most immediate initiative is the expansion of Tetonic operations into the Pacific Northwest. The board approved an increased budget for 2016 administrative expenses of $1 million to open offices in the Portland, Oregon, area.

Mr. Williams also led a discussion of a proposed acquisition of one of Tetonic's smaller competitors. The board discussed synergies that might be possible if the operations of the acquired company could be successfully integrated with the operations of Tetonic. The board granted Williams and the management team approval to continue negotiations with the other company's board and management.

The board continued its discussion from prior meetings about the October 2015 report from the Environmental Protection Agency (EPA) regarding dust impact at Tetonic's zinc refineries. Legal counsel for Tetonic updated the board on the status of negotiations with the EPA regarding findings contained in the report. The board asked management to include an update on the status of any resolutions for its next meeting. The board also asked management to schedule a conference call, if necessary, for the board if issues need to be resolved before the next meeting.

Officer bonuses for the year ended December 31, 2015, were approved for payment on April 14, 2016, as follows:

Tony Williams—Chief Executive Officer	$275,000
Mary Beth Cape—Chief Operating Officer	$150,000
Bob Browning—Chief Financial Officer	$125,000

The Audit Committee and the Compensation Committee provided an update of issues discussed at each of their respective meetings.

The meeting adjourned 5:30 pm.

Meeting of October 21, 2016

The meeting of the board of directors of Tetonic Metals was called to order by James Cook, the chairman of the board, at 8:30 am. The following directors were in attendance:

Irene Arnold	James Cook	Brian McDonald
Robert Beardsley	Larry Holden	Tony Williams
Mary Beth Cape	Heather Jackson	

The board approved the minutes from the March 5, 2016, meeting.

Tony Williams, CEO, provided an overview of financial performance and operating results for the nine months ended September 30, 2016. Given the volatility in the economy, Tetonic sales have fallen by over 8% compared to the same period in 2015. To address the drop in revenues, Tetonic has scaled back mining operations by a similar percentage to reduce labor and shipping costs.

Bob Browning, CFO, updated the board on discussions with banks that will be financing the acquisition of the Tetonic competitor. The terms of the $7 million financing include a floating interest rate that is 2% above prime over the ten-year life of the loan. Payments will be made quarterly and Tetonic will have to maintain compliance with certain loan covenant restrictions that are tied to financial performance. The board approved the acquisition and related loan transaction and scheduled a closing date for the financing to be November 1, 2016.

To prepare for the proposed acquisition, the board approved an increase in the capital expenditures budget of $1.5 million to cover costs of expanding computer operations, including new servers. The new equipment is needed to successfully integrate IT operations at Tetonic and the acquired company. The equipment will be installed in December 2016. Existing equipment that was purchased in 2014 will no longer be used in the IT operations at Tetonic.

The board discussed the creation of an incentive stock option plan for senior executives as a way to better align management and shareholder incentives. Consultants from a compensation advisory firm and tax attorneys from a national accounting firm led a discussion of the components of the proposed plan, including discussion of the related tax implications. The board asked the consultants to revise the plan based on comments received at the meeting for presentation at the board's next meeting.

Tetonic's external auditor provided an update of its interim work related to tests of the operating effectiveness of internal controls over financial reporting. The audit partner presented a written report that provided information about three deficiencies in internal control considered to be significant by the auditor.

Legal counsel for Tetonic updated the board on final resolution of the EPA report findings. The final settlement requires Tetonic to modify some of the air handling equipment at its zinc refineries, which is expected to cost about $400,000. No other penalties were imposed by the EPA.

The Audit Committee and the Compensation Committee provided an update of issues discussed at each of their respective meetings.

Required

a. How do you, as the auditor, know that all minutes have been made available to you?

b. Read the minutes of the meetings of March 5 and October 21. Use the following format to list and explain information that is relevant for the 2016 audit:

	Information Relevant to 2016 Audit	Audit Action Required
1.		
2.		

c. Read the minutes of the meeting of March 5, 2016. Did any of that information pertain to the December 31, 2015, audit? Explain what the auditor should have done during the December 31, 2015, audit with respect to 2016 minutes.

8-32 **(OBJECTIVE 8-4)** Your comparison of the gross margin percent for Jones Drugs for the years 2013 through 2016 indicates a significant decline. This is shown by the following information:

	2016	2015	2014	2013
Sales (thousands)	$ 14,211	$ 12,916	$ 11,462	$ 10,351
CGS (thousands)	9,223	8,266	7,313	6,573
Gross margin	$ 4,988	$ 4,650	$ 4,149	$ 3,778
Percent	35.1	36.0	36.2	36.5

A discussion with Marilyn Adams, the controller, brings to light two possible explanations. She informs you that the industry gross profit percent in the retail drug industry declined fairly steadily for three years, which accounts for part of the decline. A second factor was the declining percent of the total volume resulting from the pharmacy part of the business. The pharmacy sales represent the most profitable portion of the business, yet the competition from discount drugstores prevents it from expanding as fast as the nondrug items such as magazines, candy, and many other items sold. Adams feels strongly that these two factors are the cause of the decline.

The following additional information is obtained from independent sources and the client's records as a means of investigating the controller's explanations:

	Jones Drugs ($ in thousands)				Industry Gross Profit Percent for Retailers of Drugs and Related Products
	Drug Sales	Nondrug Sales	Drug Cost of Goods Sold	Nondrug Cost of Goods Sold	
2016	$5,126	$9,085	$3,045	$6,178	32.7
2015	5,051	7,865	2,919	5,347	32.9
2014	4,821	6,641	2,791	4,522	33.0
2013	4,619	5,732	2,665	3,908	33.2

Required

a. Evaluate the explanation provided by Adams. Show calculations to support your conclusions.

b. Which specific aspects of the client's financial statements require intensive investigation in this audit?

8-33 **(OBJECTIVE 8-4)** You have performed preliminary analytical procedures on one of your audit engagements and observed the following independent situations:

1. The allowance for obsolete inventory increased from the prior year, but the allowance as a percentage of inventory decreased from the prior year.
2. Long-term debt increased from the prior year, but total interest expense decreased as a percentage of long-term debt.
3. The dollar amount of operating income is consistent with the prior year, although the entity was more profitable on a net income basis.
4. The quick ratio decreased from the prior year, although the amount of cash and net accounts receivable is almost the same as the prior year.

Required Below are possible explanations for each of the observed changes in the financial statement amounts and ratios. For each observed change, select the most likely explanation(s) from the list below. Note: There may be more than one explanation for a given observed change, and an explanation can be used more than once.

a. Shipments of inventory sold prior to year end were included in the client's inventory counts as of the balance sheet date.
b. Selling and general administrative expenses were lower this year relative to last year.
c. Sales have decreased compared to the prior year, and the client is maintaining less inventory as a result.
d. Portions of existing long-term debt were refinanced at lower interest rates.
e. The effective tax rate decreased, as compared to the prior year.
f. The client purchased a large block of inventory on account close to year end.
g. Sales increased at a greater percentage than cost of goods sold, as compared to the prior year.
h. Client inventory items are off-site on consignment at retailers and are thus excluded from the year-end inventory counts.
i. Short-term borrowings were refinanced on a long-term basis at lower interest rates.

8-34 **(OBJECTIVE 8-4)** In the audit of the Worldwide Wholesale Company, you did extensive ratio and trend analysis as part of preliminary audit planning. Your analytical procedures identified the following:

1. Commission expense as a percent of sales was constant for several years but has increased significantly in the current year. Commission rates have not changed.
2. The rate of inventory turnover has steadily decreased for three years.
3. Inventory as a percent of current assets has steadily increased for four years.
4. The number of days' sales in accounts receivable has steadily increased for three years.
5. Allowance for uncollectible accounts as a percent of accounts receivable has steadily decreased for three years.
6. The absolute amounts of depreciation expense and depreciation expense as a percent of gross fixed assets are significantly smaller than in the preceding year.

Required

a. Evaluate the potential significance of each of the changes in ratios or trends identified in your analysis on the fair presentation of financial statements.
b. State the follow-up procedures you would perform for each fluctuation to determine whether a material misstatement exists.

8-35 **(OBJECTIVES 8-3, 8-4)** Target and Kohl's are chains of stores that cater to customers who desire name-brand goods at lower prices. The Securities and Exchange Commission (SEC) Form 10-K filing rules require management of U.S. public companies to include background information about the business, as well as the most recent financial condition and results of operations. Access each company's most recent Form 10-K. These can be obtained through the SEC Web site (www.sec.gov), or directly from the investor relations section of the Target (www.target.com) and Kohl's (www.kohls.com) Web sites.

Required

a. Read the description of each company's business in Part I, Item 1 of Form 10-K. Evaluate the similarity of each company as a basis for making financial comparisons.
b. Each company follows what is called a 52/53 week year in which the fiscal year ends on the Saturday nearest January 31. Given the nature of these companies, does a January 31 year-end make sense? Note that most public companies have a December 31 year-end.
c. Use the financial statements included in Part II, Item 8 to calculate the gross margin percentage and inventory turnover ratio for each company for the most recent year. Which company has the higher gross margin percentage? Which company has the higher inventory turnover?
d. Evaluate whether the relation between the gross margin percentage and inventory turnover makes sense given the description of each company's business.

8-36 **(OBJECTIVES 8-5, 8-8)** You are evaluating audit results for assets in the audit of Roberts Manufacturing. You set the preliminary judgment about materiality at $50,000. The account balances, performance materiality, and estimated overstatements in the accounts are shown next.

Account	Account Balance	Performance Materiality	Estimate of Total Overstatements
Cash	$ 50,000	$ 5,000	$ 1,000
Accounts receivable	1,200,000	30,000	20,000
Inventory	2,500,000	50,000	?
Other assets	250,000	15,000	12,000
Total	$4,000,000	$100,000	?

Required

a. Assume you tested inventory amounts totaling $1,000,000 and found $10,000 in overstatements. Ignoring sampling risk, what is your estimate of the total misstatement in inventory?
b. Based on the audit of the assets accounts and ignoring other accounts, are the overall financial statements acceptable? Explain.
c. What do you believe the auditor should do in the circumstances?

8-37 **(OBJECTIVE 8-7)** Ling, an audit manager, is planning the audit of Modern Technologies, Inc. (MT, Inc.), a manufacturer of electronic components. This is the first year that Ling's audit firm has performed the audit for MT, Inc. Ling set the preliminary judgment about materiality for the financial statements as a whole at $66,000 and is now in the process of setting performance materiality for asset accounts. Asset balances for the current year (unaudited) and prior year (audited) are listed below, as well as Ling's initial determination of performance materiality for each account. Based on preliminary discussions with management, a tour of the production facility, and background reading about the electronic components industry, Ling determines that MT, Inc., has strong credit policies, and most customers pay their full balance on time. Competition in the electronic components industry is high and inventory can become obsolete quickly due to rapid technology changes (inventory turnover is a measure that analysts focus on when assessing performance for electronic component manufacturers). Production equipment is relatively specialized and additional investment is required when new electronic components are introduced.

	Current Year (unaudited)	Performance Materiality	Prior Year (audited)
Cash	$ 397,565	$10,000	$ 356,122
Accounts receivable, net of allowance	2,583,991	25,000	2,166,787
Inventory	1,953,845	15,000	1,555,782
Total current assets	4,935,401		4,078,691
Property, plant, and equipment, net	1,556,342	20,000	1,458,963
Other assets	153,000	20,000	149,828
Total assets	$6,644,743		$5,687,482

Required

a. What factors should Ling consider in setting performance materiality for the asset accounts?
b. Explain why Ling set performance materiality for cash at the lowest amount.
c. Explain why Ling set performance materiality for inventory at a lower amount as compared to accounts receivable, PP&E, and other assets.
d. Explain why Ling set performance materiality for accounts receivable at the highest amount.
e. Does setting materiality at a lower level result in collecting more or less audit evidence (as compared to setting materiality at a higher level)?

8-38 **(OBJECTIVES 8-6, 8-7, 8-8)** Following are statements of earnings and financial position for Wexler Industries.

Consolidated Statements of Earnings
Wexler Industries (in Thousands)

	For the Year Ended		
	March 31, 2016	March 31, 2015	March 31, 2014
Revenue			
Net sales	$ 8,351,149	$ 6,601,255	$ 5,959,587
Other income	59,675	43,186	52,418
	8,410,824	6,644,441	6,012,005
Costs and expenses			
Cost of sales	5,197,375	4,005,548	3,675,369
Marketing, general, and administrative expenses	2,590,080	2,119,590	1,828,169
Provision for loss on restructured operations	64,100	—	—
Interest expense	141,662	46,737	38,546
	7,993,217	6,171,875	5,542,084

	March 31, 2016	For the Year Ended March 31, 2015	March 31, 2014
Earnings from continuing operations before income taxes	417,607	472,566	469,921
Income taxes	(196,700)	(217,200)	(214,100)
Earnings from continuing operations	220,907	255,366	255,821
Provision for loss on discontinued operations, net of income taxes	(20,700)	—	—
Net earnings	$ 200,207	$ 255,366	$ 255,821

Consolidated Statements of Financial Position
Wexler Industries (in Thousands)

Assets	March 31, 2016	March 31, 2015
Current assets		
Cash	$ 39,683	$ 37,566
Temporary investments, including time deposits of $65,361 in 2016 and $181,589 in 2015 (at cost, which approximates market)	123,421	271,639
Receivables, less allowances of $16,808 in 2016 and $17,616 in 2015	899,752	759,001
Inventories		
Finished product	680,974	550,407
Raw materials and supplies	443,175	353,795
	1,124,149	904,202
Deferred income tax benefits	9,633	10,468
Prepaid expenses	57,468	35,911
Current assets	2,254,106	2,018,787
Land, buildings, and equipment, at cost, less accumulated depreciation	1,393,902	1,004,455
Investments in affiliated companies and sundry assets	112,938	83,455
Goodwill and other intangible assets	99,791	23,145
Total	$3,860,737	$3,129,842

Liabilities and Stockholders' Equity	March 31, 2016	March 31, 2015
Current liabilities		
Notes payable	$ 280,238	$ 113,411
Current portion of long-term debt	64,594	12,336
Accounts and drafts payable	359,511	380,395
Accrued salaries, wages, and vacations	112,200	63,557
Accrued income taxes	76,479	89,151
Other accrued liabilities	321,871	269,672
Current liabilities	1,214,893	928,522
Long-term debt	730,987	390,687
Other noncurrent liabilities	146,687	80,586
Deferred income taxes	142,344	119,715
Stockholders' equity		
Common stock issued, 51,017,755 shares in 2016 and 50,992,410 in 2015	51,018	50,992
Additional paid-in capital	149,177	148,584
Cumulative foreign currency translation adjustment	(76,572)	—
Retained earnings	1,554,170	1,462,723
Common stock held in treasury, at cost, 1,566,598 shares	(51,967)	(51,967)
Stockholders' equity	1,625,826	1,610,332
Total	$3,860,737	$3,129,842

Required

a. Use professional judgment in deciding on the preliminary judgment about materiality for earnings, current assets, current liabilities, and total assets. Your conclusions should be stated in terms of percents and dollars.
b. Assume that you define materiality for the financial statements as a whole as a combined misstatement of earnings from continuing operations before income taxes of 5%. Also assume that you believe there is an equal likelihood of a misstatement of every account in the financial statements, and each misstatement is likely to result in an overstatement of earnings. Allocate materiality to these financial statements as you consider appropriate.
c. As discussed in part b., net earnings from continuing operations *before* income taxes was used as a base for calculating materiality for the Wexler Industries audit. Discuss why most auditors use *before*-tax net earnings instead of *after*-tax net earnings when calculating materiality based on the income statement.
d. Now assume that you have decided to allocate 75% of your preliminary judgment to accounts receivable, inventories, and accounts payable because you believe all other accounts have a low risk of material misstatement. How does this affect evidence accumulation on the audit?
e. Assume that you complete the audit and conclude that your preliminary judgment about materiality for current assets, current liabilities, and total assets has been met. The actual estimate of misstatements in earnings exceeds your preliminary judgment. What should you do?

CASE

8-39 (OBJECTIVES 8-2, 8-3)

Winston Black was an audit partner in the firm of Henson, Davis & Company. He was in the process of reviewing the audit files for the audit of a new client, McMullan Resources. McMullan was in the business of heavy construction. Black was conducting his first review after the audit was substantially complete. Normally, he would have done an initial review during the planning phase as required by his firm's policies; however, he had been overwhelmed by an emergency with his largest and most important client. He rationalized not reviewing audit planning information because (1) the audit was being overseen by Sarah Beale, a manager in whom he had confidence, and (2) he could "recover" from any problems during his end-of-audit review.

Now Black found that he was confronted with a couple of problems. First, he found that the firm may have accepted McMullan without complying with its new-client acceptance procedures. McMullan came to Henson, Davis & Company on a recommendation from a friend of Black's. Black got "credit" for the new business, which was important to him because it would affect his compensation from the firm. Because Black was busy, he told Beale to conduct a new-client acceptance review and let him know if there were any problems. He never heard from Beale and assumed everything was okay. In reviewing Beale's preaudit planning documentation, he saw a check mark in the box "Contact prior auditors" but found no details indicating what was done. When he asked Beale about this, she responded with the following:

> "I called Gardner Smith [the responsible partner with McMullan's prior audit firm] and left a voicemail message for him. He never returned my call. I talked to Ted McMullan about the change, and he told me that he informed Gardner about the change and that Gardner said, 'Fine, I'll help in any way I can.' Ted said Gardner sent over copies of analyses of fixed assets and equity accounts, which Ted gave to me. I asked Ted why they replaced Gardner's firm, and he told me it was over the tax contingency issue and the size of their fee. Other than that, Ted said the relationship was fine."

The tax contingency issue that Beale referred to was a situation in which McMullan had entered into litigation with a bank from which it had received a loan. The result of the litigation was that the bank forgave several hundred thousand dollars in debt. This was a windfall to McMullan, and they recorded it as a gain, taking the position that it was nontaxable. The prior auditors disputed this position and insisted that a contingent tax liability existed that required disclosure. This upset McMullan, but the company agreed in order to receive an unmodified opinion. Before hiring Henson, Davis & Company as their new auditors, McMullan requested that the firm review the situation. Henson, Davis & Company believed the contingency was remote and agreed to the elimination of the disclosure.

The second problem involved a long-term contract with a customer in Montreal. Under accounting standards, McMullan was required to recognize income on this contract using the percentage-of-completion method. The contract was partially completed as of year-end and had a material effect on the financial statements. When Black went to review the copy of the contract in the audit files, he found three things. First, there was a contract summary that set out its major features. Second, there was a copy of the contract written in French. Third, there was a signed confirmation confirming the terms and status of the contract. The space requesting information about any contract disputes was left blank, indicating no such problems.

Black's concern about the contract was that to recognize income in accordance with accounting standards, the contract had to be enforceable. Often, contracts contain a cancellation clause that might mitigate enforceability. Because he was not able to read French, Black couldn't tell whether the contract contained such a clause. When he asked Beale about this, she responded that she had asked the company's vice president for the Canadian division about the contract and he told her that it was their standard contract. The company's standard contract did have a cancellation clause in it, but it required mutual agreement and could not be cancelled unilaterally by the buyer.

Required

a. Evaluate and discuss whether Henson, Davis & Company complied with auditing standards in their acceptance of McMullan Resources as a new client. What can they do at this point in the engagement to resolve deficiencies if they exist?
b. Evaluate and discuss whether sufficient audit work has been done with regard to McMullan's Montreal contract. If not, what more should be done?
c. Evaluate and discuss whether Black and Beale conducted themselves in accordance with auditing standards.

INTEGRATED CASE APPLICATION—PINNACLE MANUFACTURING: PART I

8-40 (OBJECTIVES 8-3, 8-4)

Introduction

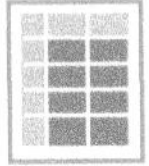

This case study is presented in seven parts. Each part deals largely with the material in the chapter to which that part relates. However, the parts are connected in such a way that in completing all seven, you will gain a better understanding of how the parts of the audit are interrelated and integrated by the audit process. The parts of this case appear in the following textbook chapters:

- Part I—Perform analytical procedures for different phases of the audit, **Chapter 8.**
- Part II—Understand factors influencing risks and the relationship of risks to audit evidence, **Chapter 9.**
- Part III—Conduct fraud brainstorming and assess fraud risks, **Chapter 10.**
- Part IV—Understand internal control and assess control risk for the acquisition and payment cycle, **Chapter 12.**
- Part V—Design tests of controls and substantive tests of transactions, **Chapter 14.**
- Part VI—Determine sample sizes using audit sampling and evaluate results, **Chapter 15.**
- Part VII—Design, perform, and evaluate results for tests of details of balances, **Chapter 16.**

Background Information

Your audit firm has recently been engaged as the new auditor for Pinnacle Manufacturing, effective for the audit of the financial statements for the year ended December 31, 2016. Pinnacle is a medium-sized corporation, with its headquarters located in Detroit, Michigan. The company is made up of three divisions. The first division, Welburn, has been in existence for 35 years and creates powerful diesel engines for boats, trucks, and commercial farming equipment. The second division, Solar-Electro, was recently acquired from a high-tech manufacturing firm based out of Dallas, Texas. Solar-Electro produces state-of-the-art, solar-powered engines. The solar-powered engine market is relatively new, and Pinnacle's top management believes that the Solar-Electro division will be extremely profitable in the future as the focus on global climate change continues and when highly anticipated EPA regulations make solar-powered engines mandatory for certain public transportation vehicles. Finally, the third division, Machine-Tech, engages in a wide variety of machine service and repair operations. This division, also new to Pinnacle, is currently in its second year of operations. Pinnacle's board of directors has recently considered selling the Machine-Tech division in order to focus more on core operations—engine manufacturing. However, before any sale will be made, the board has agreed to evaluate this year's operating results. Excellent operating results may have the effect of keeping the division as part of Pinnacle for the next few years. The vice president for Machine-Tech is committed to making it profitable.

PART I

The purpose of Part I is to perform preliminary analytical procedures as part of the audit planning process. You have been asked to focus your attention on two purposes of analytical procedures: obtaining an understanding about the client's business and indicating where there is an increased likelihood of misstatements.

Required

a. Refer to the financial statement data in Figure 8-9 for the current year and prior two years. Analyze the year-to-year change in account balance for at least five financial statement line items. Document the trend analysis in a format similar to the following:

Account Balance	% Change 2015–2016	% Change 2014–2015
Net sales		

b. Calculate at least five common ratios shown in Chapter 7 on pages 196–199 and document them in a format similar to the following:

Ratio	2016	2015	2014
Current ratio			

c. Based on the analytical procedures calculated in parts a. and b., summarize your observations about Pinnacle's business, including your assessment of the client's business risk.

d. Go to the Pinnacle link on the textbook Web site (www.pearsonhighered.com/arens) and open the Pinnacle income statement, which is located in the Pinnacle Income Statement worksheet of the Pinnacle_Financials Excel file. Use the income statement information to prepare a common-size income statement for all three years. See Figure 8-4 (p. 233) for an example. Use the information to identify accounts for which you believe there is a concern about material misstatements. Use a format similar to the following:

Account Balance	Estimate of $ Amount of Potential Misstatement

FIGURE 8-9 Pinnacle Manufacturing Financial Statements

Pinnacle Manufacturing Company
Income Statement
For the Year Ended December 31

	2016	2015	2014
Net sales	$ 150,737,628	$ 148,586,037	$ 144,686,413
Cost of goods sold	109,284,780	106,255,499	101,988,165
Gross profit	41,452,848	42,330,538	42,698,248
Operating expenses	37,177,738	38,133,969	37,241,108
Income from operations	4,275,110	4,196,569	5,457,140
Other revenues and gains	—	—	—
Other expenses and losses	2,181,948	2,299,217	2,397,953
Income before income tax	2,093,162	1,897,352	3,059,187
Income tax	883,437	858,941	1,341,536
Net income for the year	1,209,725	1,038,411	1,717,651
Earnings per share	$1.21	$1.04	$1.72

Pinnacle Manufacturing Company
Balance Sheet
As of December 31

	2016	2015	2014
Assets			
Current assets			
Cash and cash equivalents	$ 7,721,279	$ 7,324,846	$ 8,066,545
Net receivables	13,042,165	8,619,857	7,936,409
Inventory	32,236,021	25,537,198	25,271,503
Other current assets	172,278	143,206	131,742
Total current assets	53,171,743	41,625,107	41,406,199
Property, plant, and equipment	62,263,047	61,635,530	58,268,732
Total assets	$ 115,434,790	$ 103,260,637	$ 99,674,931
Liabilities			
Current liabilities			
Accounts payable	$ 12,969,686	$ 9,460,776	$ 7,586,374
Short/current long-term debt	15,375,819	10,298,668	9,672,670
Other current liabilities	2,067,643	1,767,360	1,682,551
Total current liabilities	30,413,148	21,526,804	18,941,595
Long-term debt	24,420,090	22,342,006	22,379,920
Total liabilities	54,833,238	43,868,810	41,321,515
Stockholders' equity			
Common stock	1,000,000	1,000,000	1,000,000
Additional paid-in capital	15,717,645	15,717,645	15,717,645
Retained earnings	43,883,907	42,674,182	41,635,771
Total stockholders' equity	60,601,552	59,391,827	58,353,416
Total liabilities & stockholders' equity	$ 115,434,790	$ 103,260,637	$ 99,674,931

e. Use the three divisional income statements in the Pinnacle_Financials Excel file on the Web site to prepare a common-size income statement for each of the three divisions for all three years. Each division's income statement is in a separate worksheet in the Excel file. Use the information to identify accounts for which you believe there is a concern about material misstatements. Use a format similar to the one in requirement d.

f. Explain whether you believe the information in requirement d. or e. provides the most useful data for evaluating the potential for misstatements. Explain why.

g. Analyze the account balances for accounts receivable, inventory, and short/current long-term debt. Describe any observations about those accounts and discuss additional information you want to consider during the current year audit.

h. Based on your calculations, assess the likelihood (high, medium, or low) that Pinnacle is likely to fail financially in the next 12 months.

ACL PROBLEM

8-41 **(OBJECTIVE 8-4)** This problem requires the use of ACL software, which can be accessed through the textbook Web site. Information about downloading and using ACL and the commands used in this problem can also be found on the textbook Web site. You should read all of the reference material preceding the instructions about "Quick Sort" before locating the appropriate command to answer questions a. through c. For this problem, use the "Invoices" file in the "Sales and Collection" subfolder under tables in the ACL_Rockwood project. This file contains information on sales invoices generated during calendar year 2014, including those that have been paid versus those still outstanding. The suggested command or other source of information needed to solve the problem requirement is included at the end of each question.

Required

a. Obtain and print statistical information for Invoice Amount. What is the total amount of invoices generated during the year? Do any invoices have a negative value? (Statistics)

b. What is the total amount of invoices still outstanding (not yet paid) at the end of the year? Note the file includes a default payment date for unpaid invoices that will be updated once payment is received. (Summarize)

c. From the summary created in part b. above, click on the "Outstanding" invoices to examine the details of those still outstanding. Sort the "invoice_date" column in ascending order. What concerns do you have, if any, about the collectibility of the invoice amounts? (Quick Sort)

d. How might the evidence obtained in parts a. through c. above help the auditor in testing accounts receivable?

ASSESSING THE RISK OF MATERIAL MISSTATEMENT

CHAPTER

9

LEARNING OBJECTIVES

After studying this chapter, you should be able to

9-1 Define risk in auditing.

9-2 Distinguish the different types of risk assessment procedures.

9-3 Understand important auditor considerations related to the risk of material misstatement due to fraud.

9-4 Describe the auditor's responsibility to identify significant risks.

9-5 Describe the audit risk model and its components.

9-6 Assess acceptable audit risk.

9-7 Consider the impact of several factors on the assessment of inherent risk.

9-8 Discuss the relationship of risks to audit evidence.

9-9 Discuss how materiality and risk are related and integrated into the audit process.

What's the Big Deal About Risk?

With the explosion of the Internet over the past decade, new advertising approaches have been launched to market products and services to consumers. A California-based company, WebXU, emerged in 2010 as a performance media company generating revenues from advertisers interested in finding sales leads from engaged consumers. Advertisers bid in a real-time auction on a cost-per-lead or cost-per-auction basis for access to consumers expressing interest in a particular product.

On December 5, 2011, the Las Vegas–based accounting firm of L.L. Bradford & Company, LLC, was engaged to audit WebXU's financial statements for the year ended December 31, 2011. WebXU filed its 2011 annual financial statements with the Securities and Exchange Commission (SEC) on April 9, 2012, which included L.L. Bradford & Company's opinion that WebXU's financial statements were presented fairly, in all material respects, in accordance with U.S. GAAP. Three short years later, the SEC revoked the registration of the securities of WebXU, an action prompted by WebXU's failure to file any periodic reports with the SEC since it had filed its Form 10-K for the year ended December 31, 2012.

The PCAOB alleged that the partner had failed to properly assess the risk of material misstatement with respect to WebXU's 2011 financial statements and had failed to develop an audit plan that included planned risk assessment procedures and responses to the risk of material misstatement. According to the PCAOB, the firm's "risk assessment was performed at a level of aggregation above that permitted by PCAOB standards." For example, the auditor assessed the risk on all assets and all liabilities collectively. "As a result, cash carried the same risk assessment as goodwill." At the time, goodwill recorded in connection with a recent acquisition was the largest item on WebXU's balance sheet and constituted nearly two-thirds of reported assets. Less than nine months later, WebXU wrote off the full value of that goodwill.

Disciplinary proceedings issued by the PCAOB in April 2015 against the engagement partner imposed sanctions that censured and suspended him for one year from the date of the order and also prevented him from being an associated person with a PCAOB-registered firm. In addition to the one-year suspension, the engagement partner was also ordered to not serve as or supervise another person in the role of engagement partner or engagement quality reviewer for one additional year.

Sources: 1. PCAOB Release No. 105-2015-007, April 1, 2015 (pcaobus.org); 2. SEC Release No. 73869, December 18, 2014 (www.sec.gov).

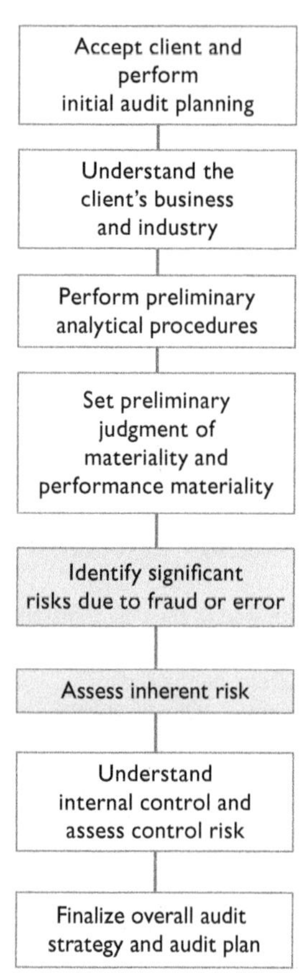
Accept client and perform initial audit planning
Understand the client's business and industry
Perform preliminary analytical procedures
Set preliminary judgment of materiality and performance materiality
Identify significant risks due to fraud or error
Assess inherent risk
Understand internal control and assess control risk
Finalize overall audit strategy and audit plan

The auditor's responsibility section in an audit report includes two important phrases (italicized below) that are directly related to materiality and risk.

- We conducted our audits in accordance with auditing standards generally accepted in the United States of America. Those standards require that we plan and perform the audit to *obtain reasonable assurance* about whether the financial statements are *free of material misstatement.*

The phrase *obtain reasonable assurance* is intended to inform users that auditors do not guarantee or ensure the fair presentation of the financial statements. Some risk that the financial statements are not fairly stated exists, even when the opinion is unmodified.

The phrase *free of material misstatement* is intended to inform users that the auditor's responsibility is limited to material financial information. Materiality is important because it is impractical for auditors to provide assurances on immaterial amounts.

Chapter 8 described the auditor's consideration of materiality as part of audit planning. This chapter focuses on the risk assessment process that is fundamental to planning the audit and designing an audit approach. In this chapter, we will show how these concepts fit into the planning phase of the audit. Note that the topic of this chapter is closely related to earlier discussions of auditor's responsibilities, transaction cycles, audit objectives (Chapter 6), along with materiality and planning the audit (Chapter 8).

In this chapter, we apply the assessment of the risk of material misstatements to the concepts studied in Chapter 6. We introduce the fifth and sixth steps in planning the audit, as shown in the shaded boxes in the figure in the margin, which build on the first four steps that were covered in Chapter 8. These steps relate to the auditor's assessment of the risks of material misstatement, including significant risks and inherent risks. When auditors assess risks, they use a considerable amount of the information acquired and documented during the first four parts of audit planning. As noted in the opening vignette about WebXU's auditor, failure to assess the risk of material misstatement can be hugely detrimental.

AUDIT RISK

OBJECTIVE 9-1

Define risk in auditing.

Auditing standards require the auditor to obtain an understanding of the entity and its environment, including its internal control, to assess the risk of material misstatements in the client's financial statements. Chapter 8 described how the auditor gains an understanding of the client's business and industry to assess client business risk and the risk of material misstatements.

Auditors accept some level of **risk** or uncertainty in performing the audit function. The auditor recognizes, for example, the inherent uncertainty about the appropriateness of evidence, uncertainty about the effectiveness of a client's internal controls, and uncertainty about whether the financial statements are fairly stated when the audit is completed. An effective auditor recognizes that risks exist and deals with those risks in an appropriate manner. Most risks auditors encounter are difficult to measure and require careful consideration before the auditor can respond appropriately. Because the assessment of risks is a matter of professional judgment, rather than a precise measurement, responding to these risks properly is critical to achieving a high-quality audit.

As discussed in Chapter 8, the risk of material misstatement is the risk that the financial statements contain a material misstatement due to fraud or error prior to the audit. The risk of material misstatement is a function of the susceptibility of the financial statements as a whole or individual accounts to misstatement, including the risk that the client's controls may not be effective in preventing or detecting and correcting the misstatements. The risk of material misstatement exists at two levels: the overall financial statement level and at the assertion level for classes of transactions, account balances, and presentation and disclosures. Auditing standards require the auditor to assess the risk of material misstatement at each of these levels and to plan the audit in response to those assessed risks.

Risk of Material Misstatement at the Overall Financial Statement Level

The risk of material misstatement at the overall financial statement level refers to risks that relate pervasively to the financial statements as a whole and potentially affect a number of different transactions and accounts. It is important for the auditor to consider risks at the overall financial statement level, given those risks may increase the likelihood of risks of material misstatement across a number of accounts and assertions for those accounts.

A number of overarching factors may increase the risks of material misstatement at the overall financial statement level. For example, deficiencies in management's integrity or competence, ineffective oversight by the board of directors, or inadequate accounting systems and records increase the likelihood that material misstatements may be present in a number of assertions affecting several classes of transactions, account balances, or financial statement disclosures. Similarly, declining economic conditions or significant changes in the industry may increase the risk of material misstatement at the overall financial statement level.

Risk of Material Misstatement at the Assertion Level

Auditing standards require the auditor to assess the risk of material misstatement at the assertion level for classes of transactions, account balances, and presentation and disclosure in order to determine the nature, timing, and extent of further audit procedures. As discussed in Chapter 6, auditors develop audit objectives for each of the assertions and perform audit procedures to obtain persuasive audit evidence that each of those audit objectives is achieved. As a result, auditors typically assess the risk that audit objectives related to assertions for classes of transactions, account balances, and presentation and disclosure are not achieved.

The risk of material misstatement at the assertion level consists of two components: inherent risk and control risk. Inherent risk represents the auditor's assessment of the susceptibility of an assertion to material misstatement, before considering the effectiveness of the client's internal controls. For example, inherent risk may be higher for accounts whose valuations are dependent on complex calculations or accounting estimates subject to significant estimation judgment. Control risk represents the auditor's assessment of the risk that a material misstatement could occur in an assertion and not be prevented or detected on a timely basis by the client's internal controls. For example, control risk may be higher if the client's internal control procedures fail to include independent review and verification by other client personnel of complex calculations used or significant estimates developed to determine the valuation of an account balance recorded in the client's financial statements. Inherent risk and control risk are the client's risks and they exist independent of the audit of the financial statements. We will discuss both inherent risk and control risk later in this chapter.

RISK ASSESSMENT PROCEDURES

OBJECTIVE 9-2

Distinguish the different types of risk assessment procedures.

As first discussed in Chapter 8, to obtain an understanding of the entity and its environment, including the entity's internal controls, the auditor performs risk assessment procedures to identify and assess the risk of material misstatement, whether due to fraud or error. Risk assessment procedures include the following:

1. Inquiries of management and others within the entity
2. Analytical procedures
3. Observation and inspection
4. Discussion among engagement team members
5. Other risk assessment procedures

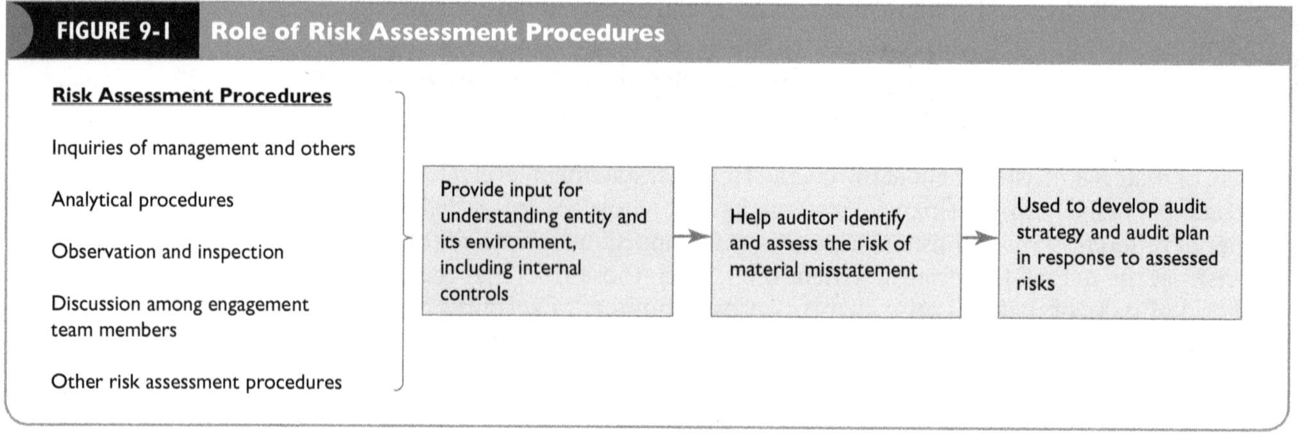
Risk Assessment Procedures
Inquiries of management and others
Analytical procedures
Observation and inspection
Discussion among engagement team members
Other risk assessment procedures
Provide input for understanding entity and its environment, including internal controls
Help auditor identify and assess the risk of material misstatement
Used to develop audit strategy and audit plan in response to assessed risks
FIGURE 9-1 Role of Risk Assessment Procedures

Collectively, the performance of risk assessment procedures is designed to help the auditor obtain an understanding of the entity and its environment, including internal controls, for purposes of assessing the risk of material misstatement when planning the audit, as illustrated in Figure 9-1; however, risk assessment procedures do not provide sufficient appropriate audit evidence to form an audit opinion on the financial statements.

Inquiries of Management and Others Within the Entity

Management and others within the entity may have important information to assist the auditor in identifying the risks of material misstatement. Auditors will frequently interact with members of management and others with financial reporting responsibilities to understand the entity and its environment and to learn about the design and operation of internal controls. In addition to making inquiries of those individuals, auditing standards emphasize the benefits and importance of obtaining information or different perspectives through inquiries of others within the entity and other employees with different levels of authority.

Inquiries of those charged with governance, such as the board of directors or audit committee, may provide information about the overall competitive environment and strategy of the business that may provide important insights about overall client business risks. Those charged with governance are often involved in significant strategic and operational decisions, such as the pursuit of acquisitions or new lines of business. As a result, they may have insider knowledge that may help the auditor identify heightened risks of material misstatements. Additionally, inquiries of those charged with governance provide the auditor with important insights about the overall governance oversight provided by the board of directors and others, which is an importance aspect of internal control. While AICPA auditing standards suggest that inquiries of those charged with governance may be informative to the auditor, PCAOB auditing standards require the auditor to inquire of the audit committee or its equivalent about risks of material misstatement.

Similarly, because internal auditors typically have exposure to all aspects of the client's business and operations, they may have important information about risks at the overall financial statement level or assertion level. Most internal audit functions develop their internal audit scope based on a risk assessment process that considers risks to design their audit strategies. Inquiries of internal audit personnel may provide important information about key risks to the business affecting not only financial reporting, but also operations and compliance with laws and regulations that may increase the likelihood of material misstatements. Because a primary focus of most internal audit functions is evaluating the effectiveness of the entity's internal processes related to financial reporting, operations, and compliance, inquiries of internal audit personnel may provide valuable information about the design and operating effectiveness of internal controls. Similar to inquiries related to those charged with governance, AICPA auditing standards suggest making inquiries of internal audit personnel, while PCAOB auditing standards require inquiry of internal audit personnel.

Auditors may also benefit from making inquiries of others within the entity who are involved in different roles and who are at different levels within the client's operations. For example, individuals who help manage legal affairs or regulatory compliance for the entity may have knowledge relevant to the auditor's assessment of the risk of material misstatements, especially the impact of noncompliance on financial reporting. Other personnel, such as those involved in marketing or sales or those involved with complex or unusual transactions, may provide insights about risks related to revenue recognition or issues involving valuation of receivables.

Analytical Procedures

As described in Chapter 8, auditors are required to perform preliminary analytical procedures as part of audit planning in every audit to better understand the entity and to assess client business risks. The performance of analytical procedures may help the auditor identify unusual amounts, ratios, or trends that might identify unusual transactions or events having audit implications. Analytical procedures performed as part of the auditor's risk assessment procedures may include both financial and nonfinancial information, and they often use data aggregated at a high level. As a result, they may only provide a broad indication about whether a material misstatement exists. Auditors should consider information obtained by performing other risk assessment procedures in combination with the results from preliminary analytical procedures. The preliminary analytical procedures applied to Hillsburg Hardware illustrated in Table 8-1 (p. 232) of Chapter 8 provide an example of how they are effective in helping the auditor assess the risks of material misstatement as part of audit planning.

Observation and Inspection

The types of evidence described in Chapter 7 include both observation and inspection. Recall the evidence obtained through observation generally involves the auditor looking at a process or procedure being performed by others. For example, observation of the entity's operations, such as the manufacturing and shipping of products to customers, and tours of the entity's facilities may increase the auditor's understanding of the entity and its environment. Additionally, the inspection of documents such as the organization's strategic plan, business model, and its organizational structure increases the auditor's understanding of how the business is structured and how it organizes key business functions and leaders in the oversight of day-to-day operations.

In addition to learning about the business and its environment, auditors also observe client personnel performing important processes related to financial reporting to help them understand the design of internal controls related to the financial statements as a whole and to specific audit objectives related to classes of transactions, account balances, and presentation and disclosure. They often combine observation of processes with the inspection of documents and records, such as purchase orders, invoices, and receiving reports related to disbursements, that are part of those processes to gain an understanding of the design effectiveness of internal controls related to financial reporting. Together, observation and inspection provide the auditor with a basis for understanding internal controls, which is an important input for the assessment of the risk of material misstatement. Understanding internal control is discussed further in Chapter 12.

Discussions Among Engagement Team Members

Auditing standards require the engagement partner and other key engagement team members to discuss the susceptibility of the client's financial statements to material misstatement. Those standards explicitly require that this discussion specifically considers the susceptibility of the client's financial statements to fraud, in addition to their susceptibility of material misstatement due to errors.

Discussion among the engagement partner and other key members of the engagement team provides an opportunity for more experienced team members, including the engagement partner, to share their insights about the entity and its environment, including their understanding of internal controls, with other members of the engagement team. The discussion should include an exchange of ideas or brainstorming among the engagement team members about business risks and how and where the financial statements might be susceptible to material misstatement, whether due to fraud or error. By including key members of the engagement team in discussions with the engagement partner, all members of the engagement team become better informed about the potential for material misstatement of the financial statements in specific areas of the audit assigned to them, and it helps them gain an appreciation for how the results of audit procedures performed by them affect other areas of the audit.

While auditing standards specifically require a discussion among the key engagement team members, including the engagement partner, about how and where the entity's financial statements may be susceptible to material misstatement due to fraud, this can be held concurrently with the discussion about the susceptibility of financial statements to material misstatement due to error. It may not be practical for all members of the engagement team to be included in a single discussion. For example, on large global audit engagements with team members located in multiple cities around the globe, it may not be feasible for all of them to participate in a single discussion. The engagement partner may choose to discuss matters with members of the engagement team who are responsible for audits of components of the financial statement, such as the Asia Pacific region of a multinational company, while delegating discussion with others to other members of the engagement team leadership. Regardless, the engagement partner is responsible for determining which matters should be communicated to engagement team members not involved in the discussion. For large, complex engagements, the engagement partner may create a communication plan to ensure that these critical discussions occur appropriately.

Other Risk Assessment Procedures

Other procedures may be performed to assist in the auditor's assessment of the risk of material misstatement. For example, information obtained during the client acceptance or continuance evaluation process, such as discussions with predecessor

ITEM 1.A RISK FACTOR DISCLOSURES

Publicly traded companies must file an annual report in a Form 10-K each year with the Securities and Exchange Commission (SEC). The Form 10-K can be a rich source of information about a company's business, the risks it faces, and the operating and financial results of the fiscal year. SEC guidelines specify the content that must be reported in the Form 10-K.

Among the required elements, the company must provide information as part of Item 1—"Business"—that describes the company's business, including its main products and services, subsidiaries it owns, and markets where it operates. Disclosures in Item 1 might also include information about recent events, competition, regulations, and other factors that might help investors better understand how the company operates and the environment it faces.

Item 1.A—"Risk Factors"—includes information about the most significant risks that apply to the company. Typically, companies list those risks in order of importance. In this section, management must include a description of those risks, which might include macroeconomic risks that broadly affect a number of entities or risks affecting the industry or geographic regions. Other risks might be company specific.

Both Item 1 and Item 1.A may provide helpful information to the auditor when assessing the risk of material misstatement. In particular, auditors might find it helpful to review not only Item 1.A risk factors included in the most recently filed Form 10-K for the company being audited, but also the Item 1.A disclosures reported by the company's key competitors to understand the entity and the environment in which it operates.

Source: "How to Read a 10-K," Securities and Exchange Commission (www.sec.gov).

auditors or insights obtained from background checks for new client engagements, may heighten the auditor's awareness of the risks of material misstatement. Similarly, evidence obtained during the performance of other engagements for the client, such as a tax-related engagement, may provide important knowledge about unique or nonroutine transactions that indicate a heightened risk of material misstatement. Information obtained from external sources, such as analyst or credit agency reports, trade and economic journals, and regulatory publications, may strengthen the auditor's understanding of the entity and its environment to assess the risk of material misstatement. For example, the auditor may learn about new regulatory requirements that impact the accounting for certain types of transactions within an industry.

CONSIDERING FRAUD RISK

OBJECTIVE 9-3

Understand important auditor considerations related to the risk of material misstatement due to fraud.

While auditors perform risk assessment procedures to assess the risk of material misstatement due to fraud or error, the risk of not detecting a material misstatement due to fraud is higher than the risk of not detecting a misstatement due to error. Fraud often involves complex and sophisticated schemes designed by perpetrators to conceal it, such as forgery of approvals and authorizations for unusual cash disbursement transactions or intentional efforts to not record a transaction in the accounting records. And, individuals engaged in conducting a fraud often intentionally misrepresent information to the auditor, and they may try to conceal the transaction through collusion with others. As a result, identifying material misstatements due to fraud is difficult.

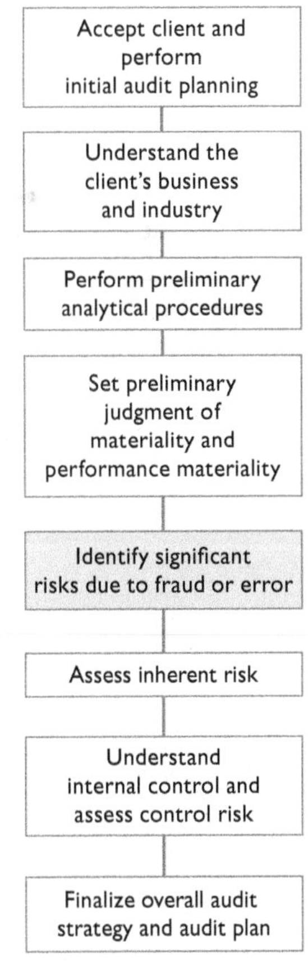

Accept client and perform initial audit planning
Understand the client's business and industry
Perform preliminary analytical procedures
Set preliminary judgment of materiality and performance materiality
Identify significant risks due to fraud or error
Assess inherent risk
Understand internal control and assess control risk
Finalize overall audit strategy and audit plan

As discussed in Chapter 6, the audit must be planned and performed with an attitude of professional skepticism in all aspects of the engagement, recognizing the possibility that a material misstatement could exist regardless of the auditor's prior experience with the integrity and honesty of client management and those charged with governance. The application of professional skepticism consists of two primary components: a questioning mind and a critical assessment of the audit evidence.

To assist the auditor in assessing the risk of material misstatement due to fraud, auditing standards outline procedures the auditor should perform to obtain information from management about their consideration of fraud. For example, the auditor should inquire of management about their assessment of the risk that the financial statements may be materially misstated due to fraud. As part of those inquiries, the auditor should ask management to describe the frequency of management's assessments and the extent of their consideration of risks due to fraud, including discussion about management's processes that are designed to identify, respond to, and monitor the risks of fraud in the organization. Auditing standards require the auditor to make inquiries of management and others within the entity about their knowledge of any actual, suspected, or alleged fraud affecting the client and whether management has communicated any information about fraud risks to those charged with governance.

The auditor's consideration of the risk of material misstatement due to fraud is made at both the financial statement level and at the assertion level for classes of transactions, account balances, and presentation and disclosures. The auditor's risk assessment should be ongoing throughout the audit, given the auditor may obtain knowledge and information from the performance of audit procedures that suggest fraud may be present. Because a number of high-profile instances of fraudulent financial reporting have involved misstatements in revenue recognition, auditing standards require the auditor to presume that risks of fraud exist in revenue recognition. As a result, risks related to audit objectives for revenue transactions and their related account balances and presentation and disclosure are presumed to be significant risks in most audits. If the auditor determines that the presumption is not applicable to a particular audit engagement, the auditor must document his or her conclusions in the working papers. We will discuss the auditor's consideration and response to fraud risk in Chapter 10.

IDENTIFICATION OF SIGNIFICANT RISKS

OBJECTIVE 9-4

Describe the auditor's responsibility to identify significant risks.

As part of the auditor's assessment of the risk of material misstatement, whether due to fraud or error, auditing standards require the auditor to determine whether any of the risks identified are, in the auditor's professional judgment, a significant risk. A **significant risk** represents an identified and assessed risk of material misstatement that, in the auditor's professional judgment, requires special audit consideration. As illustrated by the first shaded rectangle in the figure in the margin on page 262, the identification of significant risks due to fraud and error is a core element of effective audit planning. Auditing standards require the auditor to obtain an understanding of the entity's controls relevant to significant risks to evaluate the design and implementation of those controls, and the auditor must perform substantive tests related to assertions deemed to have significant risks. This will be discussed more extensively in Chapters 12 and 13.

Nonroutine Transactions

Significant risks often relate to **nonroutine transactions**, which represent transactions that are unusual, either due to size or nature, and that are infrequent in occurrence. For example, a retail client that normally sells its products through company-owned stores across the country may decide to sell to a competitor a large block of inventory located in a distribution center. The terms of that transaction may be based on significant negotiations that include various buy-back provisions and warranties that increase risks of material misstatement related to revenue recognition and receivables collection.

Nonroutine transactions may increase the risk of material misstatement because they often involve a greater extent of management intervention, including more reliance on manual versus automated data collection and processing, and they can involve complex calculations or unusual accounting principles not subject to effective internal controls due to their infrequent nature. Related party transactions often reflect these characteristics, thereby increasing the likelihood they are considered significant risks.

Matters That Require Significant Judgment

Significant risks also relate to matters that require significant judgment because they include the development of accounting estimates for which significant measurement uncertainty exists. For example, a client may engage in a new type of hedging transaction that management has not done in the past, thereby increasing the potential that the client's lack of experience and expertise in the underlying accounting treatment and estimation process will increase the risks of material misstatement.

Classes of transactions or account balances that are based on the development of accounting estimates often require significant judgment that is subjective or complex because it is based on assumptions about future events. As a result, those types of transactions or balances frequently are identified as significant risks. For example, fair value accounting related to unique and material hedging transactions would likely be considered a significant risk.

Fraud Risk

Because fraud generally involves concealment, detecting material misstatements due to fraud is difficult. As a result, when auditors identify a potential risk of material misstatement due to fraud, auditing standards require the auditor to consider that risk a significant risk, which triggers required responses to those risks. We will discuss those responses further in Chapter 10.

CONCEPT CHECK

1. At what two levels does the auditor assess the risk of material misstatement?
2. Describe the types of procedures that constitute risk assessment procedures.

AUDIT RISK MODEL

OBJECTIVE 9-5

Describe the audit risk model and its components.

We discussed earlier how the auditor's assessment of the risk of material misstatement at the assertion level consists of two components: inherent risk and control risk. Auditors consider these risks in planning procedures to obtain audit evidence primarily by applying the **audit risk model**. The model is introduced here and discussed in greater detail later in the chapter. You will need a thorough understanding of the model to conduct effective audit planning and to master the content presented in the remaining chapters of this book.

Audit Risk Model for Planning

The audit risk model helps auditors decide how much and what types of evidence to accumulate for each relevant audit objective. It is usually stated as follows:

$$PDR = \frac{AAR}{IR \times CR}$$

where:

PDR = planned detection risk

AAR = acceptable audit risk

IR = inherent risk

CR = control risk

Figure 9-2 shows the relationship between the audit risk model and the understanding of the client's business and industry discussed in Chapter 8. Auditors use the audit risk model to further identify the potential for misstatements in the overall financial statements and at the audit objective level for specific account balances, classes of transactions, and disclosures where misstatements are most likely to occur.

Illustration Concerning Risks and Evidence

Before we discuss the audit risk model components, review the illustration for a hypothetical company in Table 9-1 (p. 270). The auditor assesses risks at the overall financial

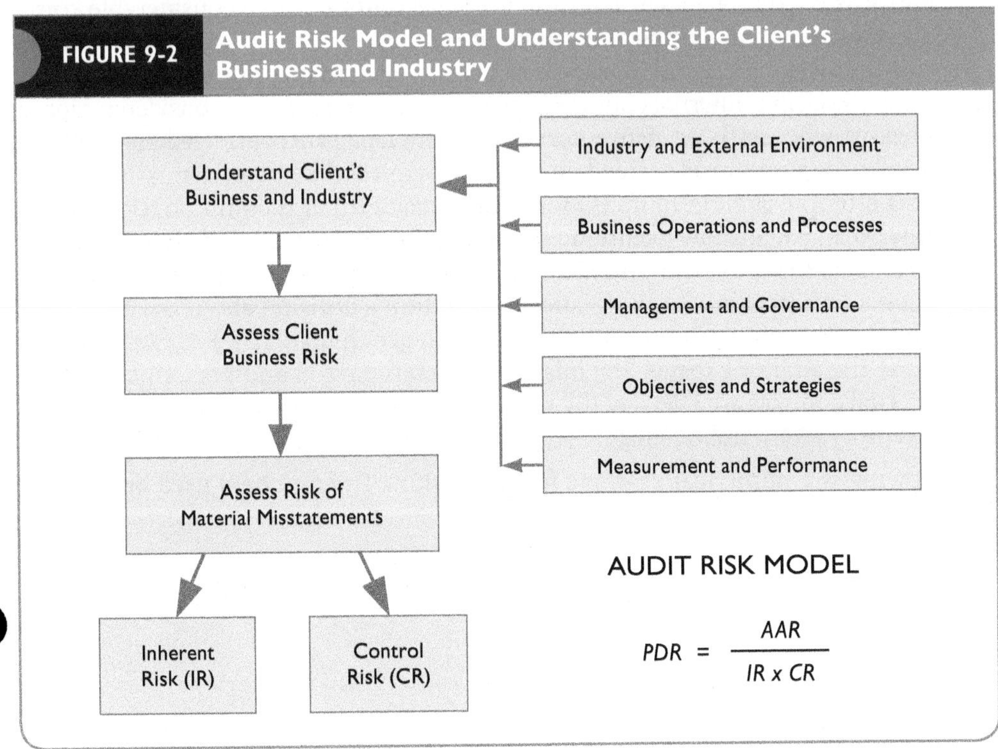

TABLE 9-1 Illustration of Differing Evidence Among Cycles

		Sales and Collection Cycle	Acquisition and Payment Cycle	Payroll and Personnel Cycle	Inventory and Warehousing Cycle	Capital Acquisition and Repayment Cycle
A	Auditor's assessment of expectation of material misstatement before considering internal control (inherent risk)	Expect some misstatements (medium)	Expect many misstatements (high)	Expect few misstatements (low)	Expect many misstatements (high)	Expect few misstatements (low)
B	Auditor's assessment of effectiveness of internal controls to prevent or detect material misstatements (control risk)	Medium effectiveness (medium)	High effectiveness (low)	High effectiveness (low)	Low effectiveness (high)	Medium effectiveness (medium)
C	Auditor's willingness to permit material misstatements to exist after completing the audit (acceptable audit risk)	Low willingness (low)	Low willingness (low)	Low willingness (low)	Low willingness (low)	Low willingness (low)
D	Extent of evidence the auditor plans to accumulate (planned detection risk)	Medium level (medium)	Medium level (medium)	Low level (high)	High level (low)	Medium level (medium)

statement level and at the audit objective level. Table 9-1 illustrates how the auditor might begin by considering risks at the transaction (cycle) level. The auditor will also consider differences in risk levels across various audit objectives within an individual class of transactions. For example, risks related to the occurrence of sales may be greater than risks related to accuracy of sales. Let's walk through the illustration point by point:

- The first row in the table shows the differences among cycles in the frequency and size of expected misstatements (A). Almost no misstatements are expected in payroll and personnel, but many are expected in inventory and warehousing. It is possible that the payroll transactions are routine, while considerable complexities exist in recording and valuing inventory.
- Similarly, internal control is believed to differ in effectiveness among the five cycles (B). For example, internal controls in payroll and personnel are considered highly effective, whereas those in inventory and warehousing are considered ineffective.
- Finally, the auditor has decided on a low willingness that material misstatements exist after the audit is complete for all five cycles (C). It is common for auditors to want an equally low likelihood of misstatements for each cycle after the audit is finished to permit the issuance of an unmodified opinion audit report.
- These considerations (A, B, C) affect the auditor's decision about the appropriate nature, timing, and extent of evidence to accumulate (D). For example, because the auditor expects few misstatements in payroll and personnel (A) and internal controls are effective (B), the auditor plans for less evidence (D) than for inventory and warehousing.

Following is a numerical example for discussion. The numbers used are for the inventory and warehousing cycle in Table 9-1.

$$IR = 100\%$$

$$CR = 100\%$$

$$AAR = 5\%$$

$$PDR = \frac{.05}{1.0 \times 1.0} = .05 \text{ or } 5\%$$

Note that the assessments in Table 9-1 are not in numerical form. Although risk model assessments may be quantitative or nonquantitative, most firms prefer nonquantitative assessments of risk (such as low, moderate, and high) due to the difficulty in precisely quantifying measures of risk.

Each of the four risks in the audit risk model is sufficiently important to merit detailed discussion. This section briefly discusses all four to provide an overview of the risks. Acceptable audit risk and inherent risk are discussed in greater detail later in this chapter. Control risk is examined more fully in Chapter 12.

Planned Detection Risk

Planned detection risk is the risk that audit evidence for an audit objective will fail to detect misstatements exceeding performance materiality. There are two key points to know about planned detection risk.

Planned detection risk is dependent on the other three factors in the model. It will change only if the auditor changes one of the other risk model factors.

Planned detection risk determines the amount of substantive evidence that the auditor plans to accumulate, inversely with the size of planned detection risk. If planned detection risk is reduced, the auditor needs to accumulate more evidence to achieve the reduced planned risk. For example, in Table 9-1, planned detection risk (D) is low for inventory and warehousing, which causes planned evidence to be high. The opposite is true for payroll and personnel.

In the preceding numerical example, the planned detection risk (PDR) of .05 means the auditor plans to accumulate evidence until the risk of misstatements exceeding performance materiality is reduced to 5 percent. If control risk (CR) were .50 instead of 1.0, planned detection risk (PDR) would be .10, and planned evidence could therefore be reduced.

Inherent Risk

Inherent risk measures the auditor's assessment of the susceptibility of an assertion to material misstatement, before considering the effectiveness of related internal controls. If the auditor concludes that a high likelihood of misstatement exists, the auditor will conclude that inherent risk is high. Internal controls are ignored in setting inherent risk because they are considered separately in the audit risk model as control risk. In Table 9-1, inherent risk (A) was assessed high for acquisitions and payments and inventory and warehousing and lower for payroll and personnel and capital acquisition and repayment. Such assessments are typically based on discussions with management, knowledge of the company, and results in audits of previous years.

Inherent risk is inversely related to planned detection risk and directly related to evidence. Inherent risk for inventory and warehousing in Table 9-1 is high, which results in a lower planned detection risk and more planned evidence than if inherent risk were lower. We'll examine this in greater detail later in the chapter.

In addition to increasing audit evidence for a higher inherent risk in a given audit area, auditors commonly assign more experienced staff to that area and review the completed audit tests more thoroughly. For example, if inherent risk for inventory obsolescence is extremely high, it makes sense for the CPA firm to assign an experienced staff person to perform more extensive tests for inventory obsolescence and to more carefully review the audit results.

Control Risk

Control risk measures the auditor's assessment of the risk that a material misstatement could occur in an assertion and not be prevented or detected on a timely basis by the client's internal controls. Assume that the auditor concludes that internal controls are completely ineffective to prevent or detect misstatements. That is the likely conclusion for inventory and warehousing (B) in Table 9-1. The auditor will therefore assign a high, perhaps 100 percent, risk factor to control risk. The more effective the internal controls, the lower the risk factor that can be assigned to control risk.

The audit risk model shows the close relationship between inherent and control risks. For example, an inherent risk of 40 percent and a control risk of 60 percent affect planned detection risk and planned evidence the same as an inherent risk of 60 percent and a control risk of 40 percent. In both cases, multiplying *IR* by *CR* results in a denominator in the audit risk model of 24 percent. The risk of material misstatement reflects the combined effect of inherent risk and control risk. The auditor may make a combined assessment of the risk of material misstatements or the auditor can separately assess inherent risk and control risk. (Remember, inherent risk is the expectation of misstatements *before* considering the effect of internal control.)

As with inherent risk, the relationship between control risk and planned detection risk is inverse, whereas the relationship between control risk and substantive evidence is direct. If the auditor concludes that internal controls are effective, planned detection risk can be increased and evidence therefore decreased. The auditor can increase planned detection risk when controls are effective because effective internal controls reduce the likelihood of misstatements in the financial statements.

Before auditors can set control risk less than 100 percent, they must obtain an understanding of internal control, evaluate how well it should function based on the understanding, and test the internal controls for effectiveness. Obtaining an understanding of internal control is required for all audits. The latter two are assessment of control risk steps that are required only when the auditor assesses control risk below maximum.

Auditors of larger public companies choose to rely extensively on controls because they must test the effectiveness of internal control over financial reporting to satisfy Sarbanes–Oxley Act requirements. Auditors of other companies and other types of entities are also likely to rely on controls that are effective, especially when day-to-day transaction processing involves highly automated procedures. When controls are likely to be ineffective and inherent risk is high, the use of the audit risk model causes the auditor to decrease planned detection risk and thereby increase planned evidence. We devote Chapters 11 and 12 to understanding internal control, assessing control risk, and evaluating their impact on evidence requirements.

Acceptable Audit Risk

Acceptable audit risk is a measure of how willing the auditor is to accept that the financial statements may be materially misstated after the audit is completed and an unmodified opinion has been issued. When auditors decide on a lower acceptable audit risk, they want to be more certain that the financial statements are *not* materially misstated. Zero risk is certainty, and a 100 percent risk is complete uncertainty. Complete assurance (zero risk) of the accuracy of the financial statements is not economically practical. Moreover, as we discussed in Chapter 6, the auditor cannot guarantee the complete absence of material misstatements.

Often, auditors refer to the term **audit assurance** (also called *overall assurance* or *level of assurance*) instead of acceptable audit risk. Audit assurance or any of the equivalent terms is the complement of acceptable audit risk, that is, one minus acceptable audit risk. In other words, acceptable audit risk of 2 percent is the same as audit assurance of 98 percent.

The concept of acceptable audit risk can be more easily understood by thinking in terms of a large number of audits, say, 10,000. What portion of these audits can include material misstatements without having an adverse effect on society? Certainly, the portion is below 10 percent. It is probably much closer to 1 percent or less. If an auditor believes that the appropriate percentage is 1 percent, then acceptable audit risk should be set at 1 percent, or perhaps lower, based on the specific circumstances.

When employing the audit risk model, there is a direct relationship between acceptable audit risk and planned detection risk, and an inverse relationship between acceptable audit risk and planned evidence. If the auditor decides to reduce acceptable audit risk, planned detection risk is thereby reduced, and planned evidence must be increased. For a client with lower acceptable audit risk, auditors also often assign more experienced staff or review the audit files more extensively.

Distinction Among Risks in the Audit Risk Model

There are important distinctions in how the auditor assesses the four risk factors in the audit risk model. For acceptable audit risk, the auditor decides the risk the CPA firm is willing to take that the financial statements are misstated after the audit is completed, based on certain client-related factors. An example of a client where the auditor will accept very little risk (low acceptable audit risk) is for an initial public offering. We will discuss factors affecting acceptable audit risk shortly. Inherent risk and control risk are based on auditors' expectations or predictions of client conditions. An example of a high inherent risk is inventory that has not been sold for two years. An example of a low control risk is adequate separation of duties between asset custody and accounting. The auditor cannot change these client conditions, but can only make a likelihood assessment. Inherent risk factors are discussed later in the chapter and control risk is covered more fully in Chapter 12. Detection risk is dependent completely on the other three risks. It can be determined only after the auditor assesses the other three risks.

ASSESSING ACCEPTABLE AUDIT RISK

OBJECTIVE 9-6

Assess acceptable audit risk.

Auditors must decide the appropriate acceptable audit risk for an audit, preferably during audit planning. First, auditors decide engagement risk and then use engagement risk to modify acceptable audit risk.

Impact of Engagement Risk on Acceptable Audit Risk

Engagement risk is the risk that the auditor or audit firm will suffer harm after the audit is finished, even though the audit report was correct. Engagement risk is closely related to client business risk, which was discussed in Chapter 8. For example, if a client declares bankruptcy after an audit is complete, the likelihood of a lawsuit against the CPA firm is reasonably high, even if the quality of the audit was high.

It is worth noting that auditors disagree about whether engagement risk should be considered in planning the audit. Opponents of modifying evidence for engagement risk contend that auditors do not provide audit opinions for different levels of assurance and therefore should not provide more or less assurance because of engagement risk. Proponents contend that it is appropriate for auditors to accumulate additional evidence, assign more experienced personnel, and review the audit more thoroughly on audits where legal exposure is high or other potential adverse actions affecting the auditor exist, as long as the assurance level is not decreased below a reasonably high level when low engagement risk exists.

Factors Affecting Acceptable Audit Risk

When auditors modify evidence for engagement risk, it is done by control of acceptable audit risk. We believe that a reasonably low acceptable audit risk is always desirable, but in some circumstances an even lower risk is needed because of engagement risk factors. Research points to several factors affecting engagement risk and, therefore, acceptable audit risk. Only three of those are discussed here: the degree to which external users rely on the statements, the likelihood that a client will have financial difficulties after the audit report is issued, and the integrity of management.

The Degree to Which External Users Rely on the Statements When external users place heavy reliance on the financial statements, it is appropriate to decrease acceptable audit risk. When the statements are heavily relied on, a great social harm can result if a significant misstatement remains undetected in the financial statements. Auditors can more easily justify the cost of additional evidence when the loss to users from material misstatements is substantial. Several factors are good indicators of the degree to which statements are relied on by external users:

- *Client's size.* Generally speaking, the larger a client's operations, the more widely the statements are used. The client's size, measured by total assets or total revenues, will have an effect on acceptable audit risk.
- *Distribution of ownership.* The statements of publicly held corporations are normally relied on by many more users than are those of closely held corporations. For these companies, the interested parties include the SEC, financial analysts, and the general public.
- *Nature and amount of liabilities.* When statements include a large amount of liabilities, they are more likely to be used extensively by actual and potential creditors than when there are few liabilities.

The Likelihood That a Client Will Have Financial Difficulties After the Audit Report Is Issued If a client is forced to file for bankruptcy or suffers a significant loss after completion of the audit, auditors face a greater chance of being required to defend the quality of the audit than if the client were under no financial strain. The natural tendency for those who lose money in a bankruptcy, or because of a stock price reversal, is to file suit against the auditor. This can result both from the honest belief that the auditor failed to conduct an adequate audit and from the users' desire to recover part of their loss regardless of the adequacy of the audit work.

In situations in which the auditor believes the chance of financial failure or loss is high and a corresponding increase in engagement risk occurs, acceptable audit risk should be reduced. If a subsequent challenge occurs, the auditor will thus be in a better position to defend the audit results successfully. Total audit evidence and costs will increase, but this is justifiable because of the additional risk of lawsuits that the auditor faces.

It is difficult for an auditor to predict financial failure before it occurs, but certain factors are good indicators of its increased probability:

- *Liquidity position.* If a client is constantly short of cash and working capital, it indicates a future problem in paying bills. The auditor must assess the likelihood and significance of a steadily declining liquidity position.
- *Profits (losses) in previous years.* When a company has rapidly declining profits or increasing losses for several years, the auditor should recognize the future solvency problems that the client is likely to encounter. It is also important to consider the changing profits relative to the balance remaining in retained earnings.
- *Method of financing growth.* The more a client relies on debt as a means of financing, the greater the risk of financial difficulty if the client's operating success declines. Auditors should evaluate whether fixed assets are being financed with short- or long-term loans, as large amounts of required cash outflows during a short time can force a company into bankruptcy.
- *Nature of the client's operations.* Certain types of businesses are inherently riskier than others. For example, other things being equal, a start-up technology company dependent on one product is much more likely to go bankrupt than a diversified food manufacturer.
- *Competence of management.* Competent management is constantly alert for potential financial difficulties and modifies its operating methods to minimize the effects of short-run problems. Auditors must assess the ability of management as a part of the evaluation of the likelihood of bankruptcy.

The Auditor's Evaluation of Management's Integrity As we discussed in Chapter 8, as a part of new client investigation and continuing client evaluation, if a client has questionable integrity, the auditor is likely to assess a lower acceptable audit risk. Companies with low integrity often conduct their business affairs in a manner that results in conflicts with their stockholders, regulators, and customers. In turn, these conflicts often reflect on the users' perceived quality of the audit and can result in lawsuits and other disagreements. A prior criminal conviction of key management personnel is an obvious example of questionable management

GROUPON: A LIGHTNING-ROD CLIENT

Groupon, Inc., started in 2008, is an Internet-based local marketplace that connects merchants to consumers by offering goods and services at a discount. The company has grown rapidly since its formation in October 2008. However, when the company was going public in 2011, it would have been classified as an audit client with high inherent risk: an Internet-based business model, an upcoming initial public offering (IPO), top management turnover, low working capital, and aggressive accounting practices, just to mention a few of the indicators.

Groupon offers deep-discount deals online for local and national retailers. When a customer purchases a deal, Groupon keeps a portion of the proceeds and forwards the remainder on to the retailer. Prior to going public, Groupon recorded revenue for the entire amount of proceeds received despite owing a portion to the retailer, an aggressive practice that was deemed acceptable by their auditors, but ultimately found not acceptable by the SEC. The SEC forced Groupon to amend its registration statement prior to their IPO and reduce sales revenue by approximately 50 percent. In fact, Groupon had to amend its registration statement eight times before it eventually went public in November 2011. The SEC also disagreed with the Company's inclusion of a non-GAAP income measure in their registration statement. Groupon touted "adjusted consolidated segment operating income," which was essentially income before selling, general and administrative expenses, which the SEC understandably argued was misleading to potential investors.

Their financial reporting troubles did not end with the IPO. The company had to revise its fourth-quarter 2011 earnings release prior to issuing audited results for the year because they failed to sufficiently reserve for customer refunds on higher-priced items. Company management also reported a material weakness in internal control in their 2011 financial statements. All of this led to an investor lawsuit against Groupon, and a drop in stock price, in April 2012. The news headline that followed was appropriate: "GRPN is Now Half Price Without a Groupon."

Sources: 1. Francine McKenna, "Groupon: Ernst & Young's Accounting Challenged Client," *Forbes* (April 23, 2012); 2. Joan Lappin, "GRPN is Now Half Price Without a Groupon," *Forbes.com* (April 23, 2012).

integrity. Other examples of questionable integrity might include frequent disagreements with previous auditors, the Internal Revenue Service, and the SEC. Frequent turnover of key financial and internal audit personnel and ongoing conflicts with labor unions and employees may also indicate integrity problems.

Making the Acceptable Audit Risk Decision

To assess acceptable audit risk, the auditor must first assess each of the factors affecting acceptable audit risk. Table 9-2 illustrates the methods used by auditors to assess each of the three factors already discussed. After examining Table 9-2, it is easy to observe that the assessment of each of the factors is highly subjective, meaning overall assessment of acceptable audit risk is also highly subjective. A typical evaluation of acceptable audit risk is high, medium, or low, where a low acceptable audit risk assessment means a "risky" client requiring more extensive evidence, assignment of more experienced personnel, and/or a more extensive review of audit documentation. As the engagement progresses, auditors obtain additional information about the client, and acceptable audit risk may be modified.

TABLE 9-2 Methods Practitioners Use to Assess Acceptable Audit Risk

Factors	Methods Used to Assess Acceptable Audit Risk
External users' reliance on financial statements	• Examine the financial statements, including footnotes, such as the Form 10-K for a publicly held company. • Read minutes of board of directors meetings to determine future plans. • Read financial analysts' reports for a publicly held company. • Discuss financing plans with management.
Likelihood of financial difficulties	• Analyze the financial statements for financial difficulties using ratios and other analytical procedures. • Examine historical and projected cash flow statements for the nature of cash inflows and outflows.
Management integrity	• Follow the procedures discussed in Chapter 8 for client acceptance and continuance.

ASSESSING INHERENT RISK

OBJECTIVE 9-7

Consider the impact of several factors on the assessment of inherent risk.

The inclusion of inherent risk in the audit risk model indicates that auditors should attempt to predict where misstatements are most and least likely in the financial statement segments. This information affects the amount of evidence that the auditor needs to accumulate, the assignment of staff, and the review of audit documentation.

Factors Affecting Inherent Risk

The auditor must assess the factors that make up the risk and modify audit evidence to take them into consideration. The auditor should consider several major factors when assessing inherent risk:

- Nature of the client's business
- Results of previous audits
- Initial versus repeat engagement
- Related parties
- Complex or nonroutine transactions
- Judgment required to correctly record account balances and transactions
- Makeup of the population
- Factors related to fraudulent financial reporting
- Factors related to misappropriation of assets

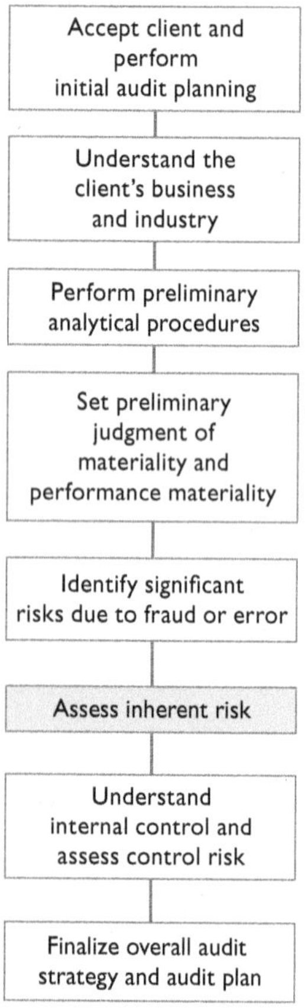

Accept client and perform initial audit planning

Understand the client's business and industry

Perform preliminary analytical procedures

Set preliminary judgment of materiality and performance materiality

Identify significant risks due to fraud or error

Assess inherent risk

Understand internal control and assess control risk

Finalize overall audit strategy and audit plan

Nature of the Client's Business Inherent risk for certain audit objectives is affected by the nature of the client's business. For example, an electronics manufacturer faces a greater likelihood of obsolete inventory than a steel fabricator does. Inherent risk is most likely to vary from business to business for accounts such as inventory, accounts and loans receivable, investments, and property, plant, and equipment. The nature of the client's business should have little or no effect on inherent risk for accounts such as cash, notes, and mortgages payable. Information gained while obtaining knowledge about the client's business and industry and assessing client business risk, as discussed in Chapter 8, is useful for assessing this factor.

Results of Previous Audits Misstatements found in the previous year's audit have a high likelihood of occurring again in the current year's audit, because many types of misstatements are systemic in nature, and organizations are often slow in making changes to eliminate them. Therefore, an auditor is negligent if the results of the preceding year's audit are ignored during the development of the current year's audit program. For example, if the auditor found significant inventory valuation misstatements in last year's audit, the auditor will likely assess inherent risk as high in the current year's audit, and extensive testing will have to be done as a means of determining whether the deficiency in the client's system has been corrected. If, however, the auditor found no misstatements for the past several years in conducting tests of an audit area, the auditor is justified in reducing inherent risk, provided that changes in relevant circumstances have not occurred.

Initial Versus Repeat Engagement Auditors gain experience and knowledge about the likelihood of misstatements after auditing a client for several years. The lack of previous years' audit results causes most auditors to assess a higher inherent risk for initial audits than for repeat engagements in which no material misstatements were previously found. Most auditors set a higher inherent risk in the first year of an audit and reduce it in subsequent years as they gain more knowledge about the client.

Related Parties Transactions between parent and subsidiary companies, and those between management and the corporate entity, are examples of related party transactions as defined by accounting standards. Because these transactions do not occur between two independent parties dealing at "arm's length," a greater likelihood exists that they might be misstated or inadequately disclosed, causing an increase in inherent risk. We discussed related party transactions in Chapter 8.

Complex or Nonroutine Transactions Transactions that are unusual for a client, or involve lengthy or complex contracts, are more likely to be incorrectly recorded than routine transactions because the client often lacks experience recording them. Examples include fire losses, major property acquisitions, purchase of complex investments, and restructuring changes resulting from discontinued operations. By knowing the client's business and reviewing minutes of meetings, the auditor can assess the consequences of complex or nonroutine transactions.

Judgment Required to Correctly Record Account Balances and Transactions Many account balances such as certain investments recorded at fair value, allowances for uncollectible accounts receivable, obsolete inventory, asset impairments, liability for warranty payments, major repairs versus partial replacement of assets, and bank loan loss reserves require estimates and a great deal of management judgment related to valuation. Because they require considerable judgment, the likelihood of misstatements increases, and as a result the auditor should increase inherent risk.

Makeup of the Population Often, individual items making up the total population also affect the auditor's expectation of material misstatement. Most auditors use a higher inherent risk for valuation of accounts receivable where most accounts are significantly overdue than where most accounts are current. Examples of items requiring a higher inherent risk include transactions with affiliated companies, amounts due from officers, cash disbursements made payable to cash, and accounts receivable outstanding for several months. These situations require greater investigation because of a greater likelihood of misstatement than occurs with more typical transactions.

Factors Related to Fraudulent Financial Reporting and Misappropriation of Assets In Chapter 6, we discussed the auditor's responsibilities to assess the risk of fraudulent financial reporting and misappropriation of assets. It is difficult in concept and practice to separate fraud risk factors into acceptable audit risk, inherent risk, and control risk. For example, management that lacks integrity and is motivated to misstate financial statements is one of the factors in acceptable audit risk, but it may also affect control risk. Similarly, several of the other risk factors influencing management characteristics are a part of the control environment, as we'll discuss in Chapter 11. These include the attitude, actions, and policies that reflect the overall attitudes of top management about integrity, ethical values, and commitment to competence.

To satisfy the requirements of auditing standards, it is more important for the auditor to assess the risks and to respond to them than it is to categorize them into a risk type. For this reason, many audit firms perform additional procedures to assess fraud risk beyond assessing the risk of material misstatements in relevant audit objectives.

The risk of fraud should be assessed for the entire audit as well as by cycle, account, and objective. For example, a strong incentive for management to meet unduly aggressive earnings expectations may affect the entire audit, while the susceptibility of inventory to theft may affect only the inventory account. For both the risk of fraudulent financial reporting and the risk of misappropriation of assets, auditors focus on specific areas of increased fraud risk and designing audit procedures or changing the overall conduct of the audit to respond to those risks. The specific response to an identified risk of fraud can include revising assessments of acceptable audit risk, inherent risk, and control risk. Assessing fraud risk will be the focus of Chapter 10.

Making the Inherent Risk Decision

The auditor must evaluate the information affecting inherent risk to assess the risk of material misstatements at the audit objective level for cycles, balances, and disclosures. Some factors, such as an initial versus repeat engagement, will affect many or perhaps all cycles, whereas others, such as nonroutine transactions, will affect only specific accounts or audit objectives. Although the profession has not established standards or guidelines for setting inherent risk, we believe that auditors are generally conservative in making such assessments. Assume that in the audit of inventory the auditor notes that (1) a large number of misstatements were found in the previous year and (2) inventory turnover has slowed in the current year. Auditors will likely set inherent risk at a relatively high level (some will use 100 percent) for each audit objective for inventory in this situation.

Obtain Information to Assess Inherent Risk

Auditors begin their assessments of inherent risk during the planning phase and update the assessments throughout the audit. Chapter 8 discussed how auditors gather information relevant to inherent risk assessment during the planning phase. For example, to obtain knowledge of the client's business and industry, auditors may tour the client's plant and offices and identify related parties. This and other information about the entity and its environment discussed in Chapter 8 pertain directly to assessing inherent risk. Also, several of the items discussed earlier under factors affecting inherent risk, such as the results of previous audits and nonroutine transactions, are evaluated separately to help assess inherent risk. As audit tests are performed during an audit, the auditor may obtain additional information that affects the original assessment.

RELATIONSHIP OF RISKS TO EVIDENCE AND FACTORS INFLUENCING RISKS

OBJECTIVE 9-8

Discuss the relationship of risks to audit evidence.

Figure 9-3 summarizes factors that determine each of the risks, the effect of the three component risks on the determination of planned detection risk, and the relationship of all four risks to planned audit evidence. "D" in the figure indicates a direct relationship between a component risk and planned detection risk or planned evidence. "I" indicates an inverse relationship. For example, an increase in acceptable audit risk results in an increase in planned detection risk (D) and a decrease in planned audit evidence (I). Compare Figure 9-3 to Table 9-1 (p. 270) and observe that these two illustrations include the same concepts.

Auditors respond to risk primarily by changing the extent of testing and types of audit procedures, including incorporating unpredictability in the audit procedures used. In addition to modifying audit evidence, there are two other ways that auditors can change the audit to respond to risks:

1. *The engagement may require more experienced staff.* CPA firms should staff all engagements with qualified staff. For low acceptable audit risk clients, special care is appropriate in staffing, and the importance of professional skepticism should be emphasized. Similarly, if an audit area such as inventory has a high inherent risk, it is important to assign that area to someone with experience in auditing inventory.
2. *The engagement will be reviewed more carefully than usual.* CPA firms need to ensure adequate review of the audit files that document the auditor's planning, evidence accumulation and conclusions, and other matters in the audit. When acceptable audit risk is low, more extensive review is often warranted, including a review by personnel who were not assigned to the engagement. If the risk of material misstatements (the combination of inherent risk and control risk) is high for certain audit objectives for an account, the reviewer will likely spend more time making sure the evidence was appropriate and correctly evaluated.

Audit Risk for Segments

The risk of material misstatements, control risk, and inherent risk are assessed for each audit objective in each segment of the audit. The assessments are likely to vary on the same audit from cycle to cycle, account to account, and objective to objective. For example, internal controls may be more effective for the existence of cash than for

FIGURE 9-3 Factors Influencing Risks and Relationship of Risks to Planned Evidence

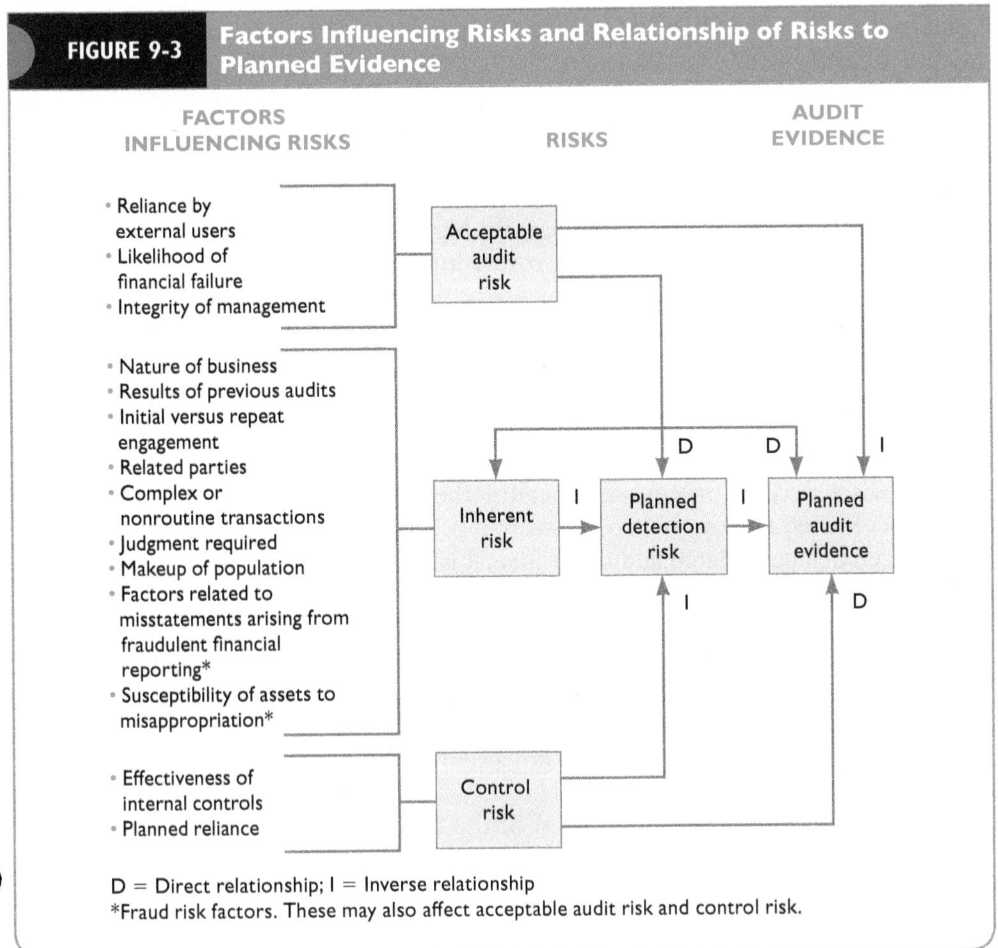

those related to fixed asset accuracy or net realizable value audit objectives. Control risk will therefore be lower for the existence of cash than for fixed asset valuation. Factors affecting inherent risk, such as susceptibility to misappropriation of assets and routineness of the transactions, are also likely to differ from account to account or among audit objectives for a single account. For that reason, it is normal to have inherent risk vary for different accounts in the same audit.

Acceptable audit risk is ordinarily assessed by the auditor during planning and held constant for each major cycle and account. Auditors normally use the same acceptable audit risk for each segment because the factors affecting acceptable audit risk are related to the entire audit, not individual accounts. For example, the extent to which external users' decisions rely upon financial statements is usually related to the overall financial statements, not just one or two accounts.

In some cases, however, a *lower* acceptable audit risk may be more appropriate for one account than for others. If an auditor decided to use a medium acceptable audit risk for the audit as a whole, the auditor might decide to reduce acceptable audit risk to low for inventory if inventory is used as collateral for a short-term loan.

Some auditors use the same acceptable audit risk for all segments based on their belief that at the end of the audit, financial statement users should have the same level of assurance for every segment of the financial statements. Other auditors use a different level of assurance for different segments based on their belief that financial statement users may be more concerned about certain account balances relative to other accounts in a given audit. For illustrations in this and subsequent chapters, we use the same acceptable audit risk for all segments in the audit. Note, however, that changing the risk for different segments is also acceptable.

Like control risk and inherent risk, planned detection risk and required audit evidence will vary from cycle to cycle, account to account, or audit objective to audit objective. This conclusion should not be surprising. As the circumstances of each engagement differ, the extent and nature of evidence needed will depend on the unique circumstances. For example, inventory might require extensive testing on an engagement because of deficient internal controls and the auditor's concerns about obsolescence resulting from technological changes in the industry. On the same engagement, accounts receivable may require little testing because of effective internal controls, fast collection of receivables, excellent relationships between the client and customers, and good audit results in previous years. Similarly, for a given audit of inventory, an auditor may assess a higher inherent risk of a realizable value misstatement because of the higher potential for obsolescence but a low inherent risk of a classification misstatement because there is only purchased inventory.

Relating Performance Materiality and Risks to Balance-Related Audit Objectives

Chapter 8 discussed the process of allocating the preliminary judgment about materiality to segments. Although it is common in practice to assess inherent and control risks for each balance-related audit objective, it is not common to allocate materiality to those objectives. Auditors are able to effectively associate most risks with different objectives, and it is reasonably easy to determine the relationship between a risk and one or two objectives. For example, obsolescence in inventory is unlikely to affect any objective other than realizable value. It is more difficult to decide how much of the materiality allocated to a given account should in turn be allocated to one or two objectives. Therefore, most auditors do not attempt to do so.

Measurement Limitations

One major limitation in the application of the audit risk model is the difficulty of measuring the components of the model. Despite the auditor's best efforts in planning, the assessments of acceptable audit risk, inherent risk, and control risk, and therefore planned detection risk, are highly subjective and are only approximations of reality. Imagine, for example, attempting to precisely assess inherent risk by determining the impact of factors such as the misstatements discovered in prior years' audits and technology changes in the client's industry.

To offset this measurement problem, many auditors use broad and subjective measurement terms, such as *low, medium,* and *high.* As Table 9-3 shows, auditors can use this information to decide on the appropriate amount and types of evidence to accumulate. For example, in situation 1, the auditor has decided on a high acceptable audit risk for an account or objective. The auditor has concluded a low risk of misstatement in the financial statements exists and that internal controls are effective. Therefore, a high planned detection risk is appropriate. As a result, a low level of evidence is needed. Situation 3 is at the opposite extreme. If both inherent and control risks are high and the auditor wants a low acceptable audit risk, considerable evidence is required. The other three situations fall between these two extremes.

It is equally difficult to measure the amount of evidence implied by a given planned detection risk. A typical audit program intended to reduce detection risk to the planned level is a combination of several audit procedures, each using a different type of evidence that is applied to different audit objectives. Auditors' measurement methods are too imprecise to permit an accurate quantitative measure of the combined evidence. Instead, auditors subjectively evaluate whether sufficient appropriate evidence has been planned to satisfy a planned detection risk of low, medium, or high. Presumably, measurement methods are sufficient to permit an auditor to determine whether more or different types of evidence are needed to satisfy a low planned detection risk than for medium or high. Considerable professional judgment is needed to decide how much more.

In applying the audit risk model, auditors are concerned about both over-auditing and under-auditing. Most auditors are more concerned about the latter, as

TABLE 9-3	Relationships of Risk to Evidence				
Situation	**Acceptable Audit Risk**	**Inherent Risk**	**Control Risk**	**Planned Detection Risk**	**Amount of Evidence Required**
1	High	Low	Low	High	Low
2	Low	Low	Low	Medium	Medium
3	Low	High	High	Low	High
4	Medium	Medium	Medium	Medium	Medium
5	High	Low	Medium	Medium	Medium

under-auditing exposes the CPA firm to legal liability and loss of professional reputation. Because of the concern to avoid under-auditing, auditors typically assess risks conservatively. For example, an auditor might not assess either control risk or inherent risk below .5 even when the likelihood of misstatement is low. In these audits, a low risk might be .5, medium .8, and high 1.0, if the risks are quantified.

Tests of Details of Balances Evidence-Planning Worksheet

Auditors develop various types of decision aids to help link judgments affecting audit evidence with the appropriate evidence to accumulate. One such worksheet is included in Figure 9-4 (p. 282) for the audit of accounts receivable for Hillsburg Hardware Co. The eight balance-related audit objectives introduced in Chapter 6 are included in the columns at the top of the worksheet to help ensure the auditor considers risks related to all the relevant balance-related assertions. Rows one and two are acceptable audit risk and inherent risk. Performance materiality for accounts receivable is included at the bottom of the worksheet. The engagement in-charge, Fran Moore, made the following decisions in the audit of Hillsburg Hardware Co.:

- *Performance materiality.* The preliminary judgment about materiality for the financial statements as a whole was set at $442,000 (approximately 6 percent of earnings from operations of $7,370,000). She allocated $265,000 to the audit of accounts receivable (see Figure 8-7 on page 240).
- *Acceptable audit risk.* Moore assessed acceptable audit risk as medium because the company is publicly traded, but is in good financial condition, and has high management integrity. Although Hillsburg is a publicly traded company, its stock is not widely held or extensively followed by financial analysts.
- *Inherent risk.* Moore assessed inherent risk as medium for existence and cutoff because of concerns over revenue recognition. Moore also assessed inherent risk as medium for realizable value. In past years, audit adjustments to the allowance for uncollectible accounts were made because it was found to be understated. Inherent risk was assessed as low for all other objectives.

Planned detection risk would be approximately the same for each balance-related audit objective in the audit of accounts receivable for Hillsburg Hardware Co. if the only three factors the auditor needed to consider were acceptable audit risk, inherent risk, and performance materiality. The evidence-planning worksheet shows that other factors must also be considered before making the final evidence decisions. (These are studied in subsequent chapters and will be integrated into the evidence-planning worksheet at that time.)

Revising Risks and Evidence

The audit risk model is primarily a planning model and is, therefore, of limited use in evaluating results. No difficulties occur when the auditor accumulates planned evidence and concludes that the assessment of each of the risks was reasonable or better than originally thought. The auditor will conclude that sufficient appropriate evidence has been collected for the audit objectives related to that account or cycle.

FIGURE 9-4 Evidence-Planning Worksheet to Decide Tests of Details of Balances for Hillsburg Hardware Co.—Accounts Receivable

	Detail tie-in	Existence	Completeness	Accuracy	Classification	Cutoff	Realizable value	Rights
Acceptable audit risk	Medium	Medium	Medium	Medium	Medium	Medium	Medium	Medium
Inherent risk	Low	Medium	Low	Low	Low	Medium	Medium	Low
Control risk—Sales								
Control risk—Cash receipts								
Control risk—Additional controls								
Substantive tests of transactions—Sales								
Substantive tests of transactions—Cash receipts								
Substantive analytical procedures								
Planned detection risk for tests of details of balances								
Planned audit evidence for tests of details of balances								

Performance materiality $265,000

However, special care must be exercised when the auditor decides, on the basis of accumulated evidence, that the original assessment of control risk or inherent risk was understated or acceptable audit risk was overstated. In such a circumstance, the auditor should follow a two-step approach.

1. The auditor must revise the original assessment of the appropriate risk. It violates due care to leave the original assessment unchanged if the auditor knows it is inappropriate.
2. The auditor should consider the effect of the revision on evidence requirements, *without use of the audit risk model*. If a revised risk is used in the audit risk model to determine a revised planned detection risk, there is a danger of not increasing the evidence sufficiently. Instead, the auditor should carefully evaluate the implications of the revision of the risk and modify evidence appropriately, outside of the audit risk model.

For example, assume that the auditor confirms accounts receivable and, based on the misstatements found, concludes that the original control risk assessment as low was inappropriate. The auditor should revise the estimate of control risk upward and carefully consider the effect of the revision on the additional evidence needed in the audit of receivables and the sales and collection cycle. Based on the results of the additional tests performed, the auditor should carefully evaluate whether sufficient appropriate evidence has been gathered in the circumstances to reduce audit risk to an acceptable level.

RELATIONSHIP OF RISK AND MATERIALITY TO AUDIT EVIDENCE

OBJECTIVE 9-9

Discuss how materiality and risk are related and integrated into the audit process.

The concepts of materiality and risk in auditing are closely related and inseparable. Risk is a measure of uncertainty, whereas materiality is a measure of magnitude or size. Taken together, they measure the uncertainty of amounts of a given magnitude. For example, the statement that the auditor plans to accumulate evidence such that there is only a 5 percent risk (acceptable audit risk) of failing to uncover misstatements exceeding performance materiality of $265,000 is a precise and meaningful statement. If the statement eliminates either the risk or materiality portion, it is meaningless. A 5 percent risk without a specific materiality measure could imply that a $100 or $1 million misstatement is acceptable. A $265,000 overstatement without a specific risk could imply that a 1 percent or 80 percent risk is acceptable.

The relationships among performance materiality and the four risks to planned audit evidence are shown in Figure 9-5. This figure expands Figure 9-4 by including performance materiality. Observe that performance materiality does not affect any of the four risks, and the risks have no effect on performance materiality, but together they determine planned evidence. Stated differently, performance materiality is not a part of the audit risk model, but the combination of performance materiality and the audit risk model factors determines planned audit evidence.

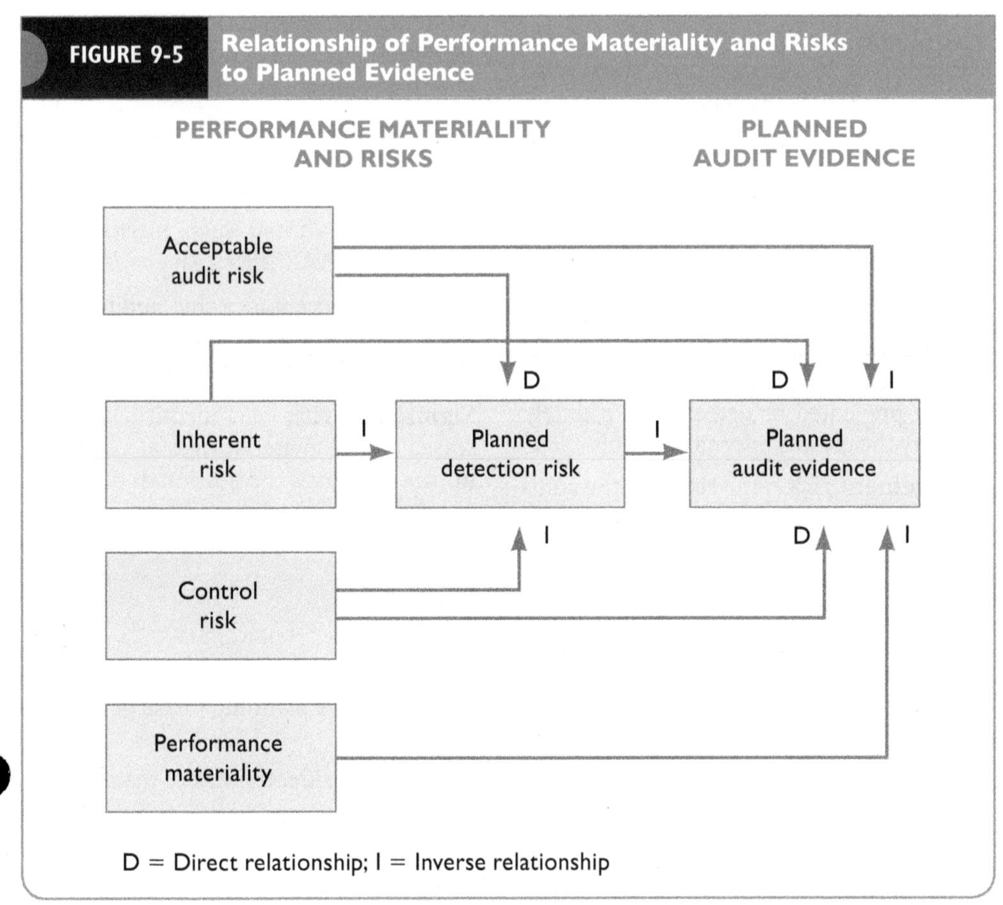

CONCEPT CHECK

1. Define the audit risk model and explain each term in the model.
2. Explain the causes of an increased or decreased planned detection risk.

SUMMARY

Because the auditor's opinion addresses whether the financial statements are free of material misstatements, audit planning hinges on effective assessments of the risk of material misstatements at both the overall financial statement level and at the assertion level. While auditors accept some level of uncertainty in performing the audit function, the consideration of risk as defined by the audit risk model is necessary for the auditor to effectively address those risks in the most appropriate manner. Using the audit risk model and performance materiality for each audit objective, the auditor determines the audit evidence needed to achieve an acceptable level of audit risk for the financial statements as a whole.

ESSENTIAL TERMS

Acceptable audit risk—a measure of how willing the auditor is to accept that the financial statements may be materially misstated after the audit is completed and an unmodified audit opinion has been issued; see also *audit assurance*

Audit assurance—a complement to acceptable audit risk; an acceptable audit risk of two percent is the same as audit assurance of 98 percent; also called *overall assurance* and *level of assurance*

Audit risk model—a formal model reflecting the relationships between acceptable audit risk (*AAR*), inherent risk (*IR*), control risk (*CR*), and planned detection risk (*PDR*); $PDR = AAR/(IR \times CR)$

Control risk—a measure of the auditor's assessment of the risk that a material misstatement could occur in an assertion and not be prevented or detected on a timely basis by the client's internal controls

Engagement risk—the risk that the auditor or audit firm will suffer harm because of a client relationship, even though the audit report rendered for the client was correct

Inherent risk—a measure of the auditor's assessment of the susceptibility of an assertion to material misstatement before considering the effectiveness of internal control

Nonroutine transaction—a transaction that is unusual, either due to size or nature, and that is infrequent in occurrence

Planned detection risk—a measure of the risk that audit evidence for a segment will fail to detect misstatements that could be material, should such misstatements exist; $PDR = AAR/(IR \times CR)$

Risk—the acceptance by auditors that there is some level of uncertainty in performing the audit function

Significant risk—an identified and assessed risk of material misstatement that, in the auditor's professional judgment, requires special audit consideration

REVIEW QUESTIONS

9-1 (OBJECTIVE 9-1) Chapter 8 introduced the eight parts of the planning phase of an audit. Which parts involve the evaluation of risk?

9-2 (OBJECTIVE 9-1) Why is it important for the auditor to consider the risk of material misstatement at the overall financial statement level?

9-3 (OBJECTIVE 9-1) Provide two examples of factors that might increase the risk of material misstatement at the overall financial statement level.

9-4 **(OBJECTIVE 9-1)** Assume that you are concerned that your client has recorded revenues that did not occur. What audit objective would you assess as having a high risk of material misstatement?

9-5 **(OBJECTIVE 9-2)** Describe the types of procedures auditors perform as part of their risk assessment procedures.

9-6 **(OBJECTIVE 9-2)** In addition to inquiring of individuals among management who are involved in financial reporting positions, such as the CFO and controller, which additional individuals should you consider making inquiries of as part of your risk assessment procedures? Be sure to describe how those individuals might be helpful to you in assessing risks of material misstatement.

9-7 **(OBJECTIVE 9-2)** Auditing standards require that the engagement team members engage in discussion about the risk of material misstatement. Describe the nature of this required discussion and who should be involved.

9-8 **(OBJECTIVE 9-2)** Auditing standards require that the engagement team members engage in discussion about the susceptibility of the financial statements to the risk of fraud. How does this discussion relate to the required discussion about the risk of material misstatement?

9-9 **(OBJECTIVE 9-3)** Why is it important to distinguish the auditor's assessment of the risk of material misstatement due to fraud from the assessment of the risk of material misstatement due to error?

9-10 **(OBJECTIVE 9-3)** How should the auditor consider risks related to revenue recognition when assessing the risk of material misstatement due to fraud?

9-11 **(OBJECTIVE 9-3)** What types of inquiries should the auditor make when considering the risk of material misstatement due to fraud?

9-12 **(OBJECTIVE 9-4)** What constitutes a significant risk?

9-13 **(OBJECTIVE 9-4)** Describe examples of characteristics of transactions and balances that might cause an auditor to determine that a risk of material misstatement is a significant risk.

9-14 **(OBJECTIVE 9-5)** Describe which two factors of the audit risk model relate to the risk of material misstatement at the assertion level.

9-15 **(OBJECTIVE 9-5)** Explain the causes of an increased or decreased planned detection risk.

9-16 **(OBJECTIVES 9-5, 9-7)** Define what is meant by inherent risk. Identify four factors that are associated with higher inherent risk in audits.

9-17 **(OBJECTIVE 9-7)** Explain why inherent risk is set for audit objectives for segments (classes of transactions, balances, and presentation and disclosure) rather than for the overall audit. What is the effect on the amount of evidence the auditor must accumulate when inherent risk is increased from medium to high for an audit objective?

9-18 **(OBJECTIVE 9-7)** Explain the effect of extensive misstatements found in the prior year's audit on inherent risk, planned detection risk, and planned audit evidence.

9-19 **(OBJECTIVES 9-5, 9-6)** Explain what is meant by the term *acceptable audit risk*. What is its relevance to evidence accumulation?

9-20 **(OBJECTIVE 9-6)** Explain the relationship between acceptable audit risk and the legal liability of auditors.

9-21 **(OBJECTIVE 9-5)** Explain why there is an inverse relationship between planned detection risk and the amount of evidence an auditor collects for a specific audit objective.

9-22 **(OBJECTIVE 9-8)** Auditors have not been successful in measuring the components of the audit risk model. How is it possible to use the model in a meaningful way without a precise way of measuring the risk?

9-23 **(OBJECTIVE 9-9)** Explain the circumstances when the auditor should revise the components of the audit risk model and the effect of the revisions on planned detection risk and planned evidence.

9-24 **(OBJECTIVE 9-9)** Explain how audit risk and materiality are related and why they need to be considered together in planning an audit.

MULTIPLE CHOICE QUESTIONS FROM CPA EXAMINATIONS

9-25 (OBJECTIVES 9-1, 9-3, 9-4) The following questions concern the assessment of the risk of material misstatements. Choose the best response.

a. Which of the following circumstances most likely would cause the auditor to suspect that there are material misstatements in the entity's financial statements?
   (1) The entity's management places no emphasis on meeting publicized earnings projections.
   (2) Significant differences between the physical inventory count and the accounting records are not investigated.
   (3) Monthly bank reconciliations ordinarily include several large outstanding checks.
   (4) Cash transactions are electronically processed and recorded, leaving no paper audit trail.

b. Which of the following statements describes why a properly designed and executed audit may not detect a material misstatement in the financial statements resulting from fraud?
   (1) Audit procedures that are effective for detecting an unintentional misstatement may be ineffective for an intentional misstatement that is concealed through collusion.
   (2) An audit is designed to provide reasonable assurance of detecting material errors, but there is no similar responsibility concerning fraud.
   (3) The factors considered in assessing control risk indicated an increased risk of intentional misstatements, but only a low risk of unintentional errors in the financial statements.
   (4) The auditor did not consider factors influencing audit risk for account balances that have effects pervasive to the financial statements as a whole.

c. Prior to, or in conjunction with, the information-gathering procedures for an audit, audit team members should discuss the potential for material misstatement due to fraud. Which of the following best characterizes the mindset that the audit team should maintain during this discussion?
   (1) Presumptive
   (2) Judgmental
   (3) Criticizing
   (4) Questioning

9-26 (OBJECTIVES 9-5, 9-7) The following questions concern the audit risk model. Choose the best response.

a. Some account balances, such as those for pensions and leases, are the result of complex calculations. The susceptibility to material misstatements in these types of accounts is defined as
   (1) audit risk.
   (2) detection risk.
   (3) inherent risk.
   (4) sampling risk.

b. As the acceptable level of detection risk decreases, the auditor may do one or more of the following except change the
   (1) nature of audit procedures to more effective procedures.
   (2) timing of audit procedures, by perhaps performing them at year-end rather than an interim date.
   (3) extent of audit procedures, by perhaps using larger sample sizes.
   (4) assurances provided by audit procedures to a lower level.

c. Inherent risk and control risk differ from planned detection risk in that they
   (1) arise from the misapplication of auditing procedures.

(2) may be assessed in either quantitative or nonquantitative terms.
(3) exist independently of the financial statement audit.
(4) can be changed at the auditor's discretion.

9-27 (OBJECTIVE 9-8) The following questions deal with audit risk and evidence. Choose the best response.

a. Which of the following does not increase the need for sufficient appropriate audit evidence?
   (1) A lower acceptable level of detection risk
   (2) An increase in the assessed control risk
   (3) A lower acceptable audit risk
   (4) A decrease in the assessed inherent risk
b. As lower acceptable levels of both audit risk and materiality are established, the auditor should plan more work on individual accounts to
   (1) find smaller misstatements.
   (2) find larger misstatements.
   (3) increase the performance materiality in the accounts.
   (4) increase inherent risk in the accounts.
c. Based on evidence gathered and evaluated, an auditor decides to increase the assessed level of control risk from that originally planned. To achieve an overall audit risk level that is substantially the same as the planned audit risk level, the auditor could
   (1) decrease detection risk.
   (2) increase materiality levels.
   (3) decrease substantive testing.
   (4) increase inherent risk.

MULTIPLE CHOICE QUESTIONS FROM BECKER CPA EXAM REVIEW

9-28 (OBJECTIVES 9-1, 9-2, 9-5, 9-6, 9-8) The following questions concern auditor responsibilities related to the assessment of risks of material misstatement. Choose the best response.

a. Which of the following procedures would a CPA most likely perform during the planning stage of the audit?
   (1) Evaluate the reasonableness of management's allowance for doubtful accounts.
   (2) Determine areas where there is a higher risk of material misstatement.
   (3) Evaluate the significance of uncorrected misstatements.
   (4) Confirm a sample of accounts receivable.
b. Dan, CPA, has been engaged to audit Modern Home, a manufacturing company that specializes in furniture. Which of the following matters related to the year under audit would most likely result in an increase of inherent risk?
   (1) The furniture industry has experienced an overall increase in demand.
   (2) Modern Home recently engaged in a complex derivative transaction.
   (3) Modern Home experienced an increase in working capital.
   (4) Modern Home purchased expensive new equipment in the current year.
c. After making a preliminary assessment of the risk of material misstatement during planning and beginning to apply audit procedures, an auditor determines that this risk is actually higher than anticipated. Which would be the most likely effect of this finding on the auditor's desired level of detection risk and the overall level of audit risk, as compared to the levels originally planned?

	Auditor's Desired Level of Detection Risk	Overall Level of Audit Risk
(1)	Decrease	Same
(2)	Increase	Same
(3)	Same	Higher
(4)	Decrease	Lower

DISCUSSION QUESTIONS AND PROBLEMS

9-29 **(OBJECTIVES 9-1, 9-2, 9-3, 9-6, 9-7, 9-9)** The following are concepts discussed in Chapter 8 and this chapter:

1. Preliminary judgment about materiality
2. Control risk
3. Risk of fraud
4. Inherent risk
5. Risk of material misstatements
6. Known misstatement
7. Estimated total misstatement in a segment
8. Planned detection risk
9. Estimate of the combined misstatement
10. Significant risk
11. Acceptable audit risk
12. Performance materiality

Required

a. Identify which items are *audit planning decisions* requiring professional judgment.
b. Identify which items are *audit conclusions* resulting from application of audit procedures and requiring professional judgment.
c. Under what circumstances is it acceptable to change those items in part a. after the audit is started? Which items can be changed after the audit is 95% completed?

9-30 **(OBJECTIVES 9-1, 9-2)** This problem requires you to access PCAOB Auditing Standard No. 12, *Identifying and Assessing Risks of Material Misstatements* (pcaobus.org). Use this standard to answer each of the questions below. For each answer, document the paragraph(s) in AS No. 12 supporting your answer.

Required

a. What types of information does AS No. 12 suggest the auditor should consider when obtaining an understanding of the company and its environment?
b. What types of performance measurements might affect the risk of material misstatement?
c. What specific issues should be included in the discussion among engagement team members regarding the risk of material misstatement?
d. What factors should the auditor consider to determine if a risk is a "significant risk"?
e. What guidance is provided about revising the risk assessment as the audit continues?

9-31 **(OBJECTIVES 9-1, 9-2)** Moranda and Sills, LLP, has served for over 10 years as the auditor of the financial statements of Highland Bank and Trust. The firm is conducting its audit planning for the current fiscal year and is in the process of performing risk assessment procedures. Based on inquiries and other information obtained, the auditors learned that the bank is finalizing an acquisition of a smaller community bank located in another region of the state. Management anticipates that the transaction will close in the third quarter, and, while there will be some challenges in integrating the IT systems of the acquired bank with Highland systems, the bank should realize a number of operational cost savings over the long-term.

During the past year, the bank has expanded its online service options for customers, who can now remotely deposit funds into and withdraw funds from checking and savings accounts. The system has been well received by customers and the bank hopes to continue expanding those services. The challenge for Highland is that they are struggling to retain IT personnel given the strong job market for individuals with those skills.

Credit risk management continues to be a challenge for all banks, including Highland, and regulators continue to spend a lot of time on credit evaluation issues. The bank has a dedicated underwriting staff that continually evaluates the collectibility of loans outstanding. Unfortunately, some of the credit review staff recently left the bank to work for a competitor. Competition in the community banking space is tough, especially given the slow loan demand in the marketplace.

The bank has expanded its investment portfolio into a number of new types of instruments subject to fair value accounting. Management has engaged an outside valuation expert to ensure that the valuations are properly measured and reported.

Fortunately, the bank's capital position is strong and it far exceeds regulatory minimums. Capital is available to support growth goals in the bank's three-year strategic plan.

Required

a. Describe any risks of material misstatement at the financial statement level.
b. Describe any risks of material misstatement at the assertion level.
c. Which, if any, risks would be considered a significant risk?

9-32 **(OBJECTIVES 9-5, 9-6)** Describe what is meant by acceptable audit risk. Explain why each of the following statements is true:

a. A CPA firm should attempt to achieve the same audit risk for all audit clients when circumstances are similar.
b. A CPA firm should decrease acceptable audit risk for audit clients when external users rely heavily on the statements.
c. A CPA firm should decrease acceptable audit risk for audit clients when engagement risk is high.
d. Different CPA firms should attempt to achieve reasonably similar audit risks for clients with similar circumstances.

9-33 **(OBJECTIVE 9-6)** Bohrer, CPA, is considering the following factors in assessing audit risk at the financial statement level in planning the audit of Waste Remediation Services (WRS), Inc.'s financial statements for the year ended December 31, 2016. WRS is a privately held company that contracts with municipal governments to close landfills. Audit risk at the financial statement level is influenced by the risk of material misstatements, which may be indicated by factors related to the entity, management, and the industry environment.

1. This was the first year WRS operated at a profit since 2011 because the municipalities received increased federal and state funding for environmental purposes.
2. WRS's Board of Directors is controlled by Tucker, the majority shareholder, who also acts as the chief executive officer.
3. The internal auditor reports to the controller and the controller reports to Tucker.
4. The accounting department has experienced a high rate of turnover of key personnel.
5. WRS's bank has a loan officer who meets regularly with WRS's CEO and controller to monitor WRS's financial performance.
6. WRS's employees are paid bi-weekly.
7. Bohrer has audited WRS for five years.
8. During 2016, WRS changed its method of preparing its financial statements from the cash basis to generally accepted accounting principles.
9. During 2016, WRS sold one half of its controlling interest in Sanitation Equipment Leasing Co. (SEL). WRS retained a significant interest in SEL.
10. During 2016, litigation filed against WRS in 2003 alleging that WRS discharged pollutants into state waterways was dropped by the state. Loss contingency disclosures that WRS included in prior years' financial statements are being removed for the 2016 financial statements.
11. During December 2016, WRS signed a contract to lease disposal equipment from an entity owned by Tucker's parents. This related party transaction is not disclosed in WRS's notes to its 2016 financial statements.
12. During December 2016, WRS increased its casualty insurance coverage on several pieces of sophisticated machinery from historical cost to replacement cost.

13. WRS recorded a substantial increase in revenue in the fourth quarter of 2016. Inquiries indicated that WRS initiated a new policy and guaranteed several municipalities that it would refund state and federal funding paid to WRS on behalf of the municipality if it failed a federal or state site inspection in 2017.
14. An initial public offering of WRS stock is planned in 2017.

Required For each of the 14 factors listed above, indicate whether the item would likely increase audit risk, decrease audit risk, or have no effect on audit risk.*

9-34 **(OBJECTIVES 9-5, 9-8)** Following are six situations that involve the audit risk model as it is used for planning audit evidence requirements in the audit of inventory.

	Situation					
Risk	**1**	**2**	**3**	**4**	**5**	**6**
Acceptable audit risk	High	High	Low	Low	High	Medium
Inherent risk	Low	High	High	Low	Medium	Medium
Control risk	Low	Low	High	High	Medium	Medium
Planned detection risk	—	—	—	—	—	—
Planned evidence	—	—	—	—	—	—

Required

a. Explain what *low, medium,* and *high* mean for each of the four risks and planned evidence.
b. Fill in the blanks for planned detection risk and planned evidence using the terms low, medium, or high.
c. Using your knowledge of the relationships among the foregoing factors, state the effect on planned evidence (increase or decrease) of changing each of the following five factors, while the other three remain constant:
   (1) A decrease in acceptable audit risk
   (2) A decrease in control risk
   (3) A decrease in planned detection risk
   (4) A decrease in inherent risk
   (5) A decrease in inherent risk and an increase in control risk of the same amount

9-35 **(OBJECTIVES 9-5, 9-7, 9-8)** Mark Hopper is planning the audit of the investments account for audit client Garden Supply Co. (GSC). GSC invests excess cash at the end of the summer sales season through an investment manager who invests in equity and debt securities for GSC's account. Hopper has assessed the following risks as low, medium, or high for the relevant balance-related audit objectives in the investment account.

		Risk of Material Misstatements		
Balance-Related Audit Objectives	**Acceptable Audit Risk**	**Inherent Risk**	**Control Risk**	**Planned Detection Risk**
Existence	Medium	Medium	Medium	
Completeness	Medium	Low	Medium	
Accuracy	Low	High	Medium	
Classification	Medium	Low	Low	
Cutoff	Medium	Medium	Low	
Detail tie-in	Low	Medium	Low	
Realizable value	Low	High	Medium	
Rights and obligations	Medium	Medium	Low	

Required

a. Describe each of the four identified risks in the columns of the table above.
b. Fill in the blank for planned detection risk for each balance-related audit objective using the terms low, medium, or high.
c. Which audit objectives require the greatest amount of evidence and which require the least?
d. Through audit testing, Hopper finds the investment manager's controls over recording purchases and sales of securities are not as effective as originally assessed. What should Hopper do?

*Based on AICPA question paper, American Institute of Certified Public Accountants.

9-36 **(OBJECTIVE 9-5)** Below are ten independent risk factors:

1. The client lacks sufficient working capital to continue operations.
2. The client fails to detect employee theft of inventory from the warehouse because there are no restrictions on warehouse access and the client does not reconcile inventory on hand to recorded amounts on a timely basis.
3. The company is publicly traded.
4. The auditor has identified numerous material misstatements during prior year audit engagements.
5. The assigned staff on the audit engagement lack the necessary skills to identify actual errors in an account balance when examining audit evidence accumulated.
6. The client is one of the industry's largest based on its size and market share.
7. The client engages in several material transactions with entities owned by family members of several of the client's senior executives.
8. The allowance for doubtful accounts is based on significant assumptions made by management.
9. The audit program omits several necessary audit procedures.
10. The client fails to reconcile bank accounts to recorded cash balances.

Required

Identify which of the following audit risk model components relates most directly to each of the ten risk factors:

- Acceptable audit risk
- Control risk
- Inherent risk
- Planned detection risk

9-37 **(OBJECTIVES 9-5, 9-9)** Using the audit risk model, state the effect on control risk, inherent risk, acceptable audit risk, and planned evidence for each of the following independent events. In each of the events a. through j., circle one letter for each of the three independent variables and planned evidence: I = increase, D = decrease, N = no effect, and C = cannot determine from the information provided.

a. The client's management materially decreased long-term contractual debt:

Control risk	I D N C	Acceptable audit risk	I D N C
Inherent risk	I D N C	Planned evidence	I D N C

b. The client changed from a privately held company to a publicly held company:

Control risk	I D N C	Acceptable audit risk	I D N C
Inherent risk	I D N C	Planned evidence	I D N C

c. The auditor decided to set assessed control risk at the maximum (it was previously assessed below the maximum):

Control risk	I D N C	Acceptable audit risk	I D N C
Inherent risk	I D N C	Planned evidence	I D N C

d. The client acquired a new subsidiary located in Italy:

Control risk	I D N C	Acceptable audit risk	I D N C
Inherent risk	I D N C	Planned evidence	I D N C

e. The account balance increased materially from the preceding year without apparent reason:

Control risk	I D N C	Acceptable audit risk	I D N C
Inherent risk	I D N C	Planned evidence	I D N C

f. You determined through the planning phase that working capital, debt-to-equity ratio, and other indicators of financial condition improved during the past year:

Control risk	I D N C	Acceptable audit risk	I D N C
Inherent risk	I D N C	Planned evidence	I D N C

g. This is the second year of the engagement, and there were few misstatements found in the previous year's audit. The auditor also decided to increase reliance on internal control:

Control risk	I D N C	Acceptable audit risk	I D N C
Inherent risk	I D N C	Planned evidence	I D N C

h. The client began selling products online to customers through its Web page during the year under audit. The online customer ordering process is not integrated with the company's accounting system. Client sales staff print out customer order information and enter that data into the sales accounting system:

Control risk	I D N C	Acceptable audit risk	I D N C
Inherent risk	I D N C	Planned evidence	I D N C

i. There has been a change in several key management personnel. You believe that management is somewhat lacking in personal integrity compared with the previous management. You believe it is still appropriate to do the audit:

Control risk	I D N C	Acceptable audit risk	I D N C
Inherent risk	I D N C	Planned evidence	I D N C

j. In discussions with management, you conclude that management is planning to sell the business in the next few months. Because of the planned changes, several key accounting personnel quit several months ago for alternative employment. You also observe that the gross margin percent has significantly increased compared with that of the preceding year:

Control risk	I D N C	Acceptable audit risk	I D N C
Inherent risk	I D N C	Planned evidence	I D N C

CASES

9-38 **(OBJECTIVES 9-5, 9-6, 9-7)** Whitehead, CPA, is planning the audit of a newly obtained client, Henderson Energy Corporation, for the year ended December 31, 2016. Henderson Energy is regulated by the state utility commission, and because it is a publicly traded company the audited financial statements must be filed with the Securities and Exchange Commission (SEC).

Henderson Energy is considerably more profitable than many of its competitors, largely due to its extensive investment in information technologies used in its energy distribution and other key business processes. Recent growth into rural markets, however, has placed some strain on 2016 operations. Additionally, Henderson Energy expanded its investments into speculative markets and is also making greater use of derivative and hedging transactions to mitigate some of its investment risks. Because of the complexities of the underlying accounting associated with these activities, Henderson Energy added several highly experienced accountants within its financial reporting team. Internal audit, which has direct reporting responsibility to the audit committee, is also actively involved in reviewing key accounting assumptions and estimates on a quarterly basis.

Whitehead's discussions with the predecessor auditor revealed that the client has experienced some difficulty in correctly tracking existing property, plant, and equipment items. This largely involves equipment located at its multiple energy production facilities. During the recent year, Henderson acquired a regional electric company, which expanded the number of energy production facilities.

Whitehead plans to staff the audit engagement with several members of the firm who have experience in auditing energy and public companies. The extent of partner review of key accounts will be extensive.

Required Based on the above information, identify factors that affect the risk of material misstatements in the December 31, 2016, financial statements of Henderson Energy. Indicate whether the factor increases or decreases the risk of material misstatements. Also, identify which audit risk model component is affected by the factor. Use the format below:

Factor	Effect on the Risk of Material Misstatement	Audit Risk Model Component
Henderson is a new client	Increases	Inherent risk

FIGURE 9-6 Stanton Enterprises Summary Financial Statements

Balance Sheet

	Preliminary 12-31-16	Audited 12-31-15
Cash	$ 243,689	$ 133,981
Trade accounts receivable	3,544,009	2,224,921
Allowance for uncollectible accounts	(120,000)	(215,000)
Inventories	4,520,902	3,888,400
Prepaid expenses	29,500	24,700
Total current assets	8,218,100	6,057,002
Property, plant, and equipment:		
At cost	12,945,255	9,922,534
Less accumulated depreciation	(4,382,990)	(3,775,911)
Total prop., plant, and equipment	8,562,265	6,146,623
Goodwill	1,200,000	345,000
Total assets	$17,980,365	$12,548,625
Accounts payable	$ 2,141,552	$ 2,526,789
Bank loan payable	150,000	—
Accrued liabilities	723,600	598,020
Federal income taxes payable	1,200,000	1,759,000
Current portion of long-term debt	240,000	240,000
Total current liabilities	4,455,152	5,123,809
Long-term debt	960,000	1,200,000
Stockholders' equity:		
Common stock	1,250,000	1,000,000
Additional paid-in capital	2,469,921	1,333,801
Retained earnings	8,845,292	3,891,015
Total stockholders' equity	12,565,213	6,224,816
Total liabilities and stockholders' equity	$17,980,365	$12,548,625

Combined Statement of Income and Retained Earnings

	Preliminary 12-31-16	Audited 12-31-15
Sales	$43,994,931	$32,258,015
Cost of goods sold	24,197,212	19,032,229
Gross profit	19,797,719	13,225,786
Selling, general, and administrative expenses	10,592,221	8,900,432
Pension cost	1,117,845	865,030
Interest expense	83,376	104,220
Total operating expenses	11,793,442	9,869,682
Income before taxes	8,004,277	3,356,104
Income tax expense	1,800,000	1,141,000
Net income	6,204,277	2,215,104
Beginning retained earnings	3,891,015	2,675,911
	10,095,292	4,891,015
Dividends declared	(1,250,000)	(1,000,000)
Ending retained earnings	$ 8,845,292	$ 3,891,015

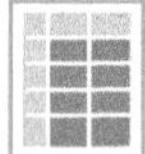

9-39 **(OBJECTIVES 9-5, 9-6, 9-7, 9-9)** Pamela Albright is the manager of the audit of Stanton Enterprises, a public company that manufactures formed steel subassemblies for other manufacturers. Albright is planning the 2016 audit and is considering an appropriate amount for overall financial statement materiality, what performance materiality should be set for the financial statement accounts, and the appropriate inherent risks. Summary financial statement information is shown in Figure 9-6 (p. 293). Additional relevant planning information is summarized next.

1. Stanton has been a client for 4 years, and Albright's firm has always had a good relationship with the company. Management and the accounting people have always been cooperative, honest, and positive about the audit and financial reporting. No material misstatements were found in the prior years' audits. Albright's firm has monitored the relationship carefully, because when the audit was obtained, Leonard Stanton, the CEO, had the reputation of being a "high-flyer" and had been through bankruptcy at an earlier time in his career.
2. Stanton runs the company in an autocratic way, primarily because of a somewhat controlling personality. He believes that it is his job to make all the tough decisions. He delegates responsibility to others but is not always willing to delegate a commensurate amount of authority.
3. The industry in which Stanton participates has been in a favorable cycle the past few years, and that trend is continuing in the current year. Industry profits are reasonably favorable, and there are no competitive or other apparent threats on the horizon.
4. Internal controls for Stanton are evaluated as reasonably effective for all cycles but not unusually strong. Although Stanton supports the idea of control, Albright has been disappointed that management has continually rejected Albright's recommendation to improve its internal audit function.
5. Stanton has a contract with its employees that if earnings before taxes, interest expense, and pension cost exceed $7.8 million for the year, an additional contribution must be made to the pension fund equal to 5% of the excess.

Required

a. You are to play the role of Pamela Albright in the 12-31-16 audit of Stanton Enterprises. Make a preliminary judgment of materiality and determine performance materiality for the financial statement accounts. Prepare an audit schedule showing your calculations. (Instructor option: prepare the schedule using an electronic spreadsheet.)
b. Make an acceptable audit risk decision for the current year as high, medium, or low, and support your answer.
c. Perform analytical procedures for Stanton Enterprises that will help you identify accounts that may require additional evidence in the current year's audit. Document the analytical procedures you perform and your conclusions. (Instructor option: use an electronic spreadsheet to calculate analytical procedures.)
d. The evidence-planning worksheet to decide tests of details of balances for Stanton's accounts receivable is shown in Figure 9-7. Use the information in the case and your conclusions in parts a. through c. to complete the following rows of the evidence-planning worksheet: Acceptable audit risk, Inherent risk, and Substantive analytical procedures. Also fill in performance materiality for accounts receivable at the bottom of the worksheet. Make any assumptions you believe are reasonable and appropriate and document them.

INTEGRATED CASE APPLICATION—PINNACLE MANUFACTURING: PART II

9-40 **(OBJECTIVES 9-6, 9-7)** In Part I of the case, you performed preliminary analytical procedures for Pinnacle (pp. 257–259). The purpose of Part II is to identify factors influencing risks and the relationship of risks to audit evidence.

FIGURE 9-7 **Stanton Enterprises Evidence-Planning Worksheet to Decide Tests of Details of Balances for Accounts Receivable**

	Detail tie-in	Existence	Completeness	Accuracy	Classification	Cutoff	Realizable value	Rights
Acceptable audit risk								
Inherent risk								
Control risk—Sales								
Control risk—Cash receipts								
Control risk—Additional controls								
Substantive tests of transactions—Sales								
Substantive tests of transactions—Cash receipts								
Substantive analytical procedures								
Planned detection risk for tests of details of balances								
Planned audit evidence for tests of details of balances								

Performance materiality ______

During the planning phase of the audit, you meet with Pinnacle's management team and perform other planning activities. You encounter the following situations that you believe may be relevant to the audit:

1. Your firm has an employee who reads and saves articles about issues that may affect key clients. You read an article in the file titled, "EPA Regulations Encouraging Solar-Powered Engines Postponed?" After reading the article, you realize that the regulations management is relying upon to increase sales of the Solar-Electro division might not go into effect for at least ten years. A second article is titled, "Stick to Diesel, Pinnacle!" The article claims that although Pinnacle has proven itself within the diesel engine industry, they lack the knowledge and people necessary to perform well in the solar-powered engine industry.
2. You ask management for a tour of the Solar-Electro facilities. While touring the warehouse, you notice a section of solar-powered engines that do not look like the ones advertised on Pinnacle's Web site. You ask the warehouse manager when those items were first manufactured. He responds by telling you, "I'm not sure. I've been here a year and they were here when I first arrived."

3. You also observe that new computerized manufacturing equipment has been installed at Solar-Electro. The machines have been stamped with the words, "Product of Welburn Manufacturing, Detroit, Michigan."
4. During discussions with the Pinnacle controller, you learn that Pinnacle employees did a significant amount of the construction work for a building addition because of employee idle time and to save costs. The controller stated that the work was carefully coordinated with the construction company responsible for the addition.
5. While reading the footnotes of the previous year's financial statements, you note that one customer, Auto-Electro, accounts for nearly 15% of the company's accounts receivable balance. You investigate this receivable and learn the customer has not made any payments for several months.
6. During a meeting with the facilities director, you learn that the board of directors has decided to raise a significant amount of debt to finance the construction of a new manufacturing plant for the Solar-Electro division. The company also plans to make a considerable investment in modifications to the property on which the plant will be built.
7. While standing in line at a vending machine, you see a Pinnacle vice president wearing a golf shirt with the words "Todd-Machinery." You are familiar with the company and noticed some of its repairmen working in the plant earlier. You tell the man you like the shirt and he responds by saying, "Thank you. My wife and I own the company, but we hire people to manage it."
8. After inquiry of the internal audit team, you realize there is significant turnover in the internal audit department. You conclude the turnover is only present at the higher-level positions.
9. While reviewing Pinnacle's long-term debt agreements, you identify several restrictive covenants. Two requirements are to keep the current ratio above 2.0 and debt-to-equity below 1.0 at all times.
10. The engagement partner from your CPA firm called today notifying you that Brian Sioux, an industry specialist and senior tax manager from the firm's Ontario office, will be coming on-site to Pinnacle's facilities to investigate an ongoing dispute between the Internal Revenue Service and Pinnacle.
11. A member of your CPA firm, who is currently on-site in Detroit at the Welburn division, calls you to see how everything is going while you are visiting Solar-Electro in Texas. During your conversation, he asks if you know anything about the recent intercompany loan from Welburn to Solar-Electro.

Required

a. Review Part I of the case and the situations in Part II and identify information that affects your assessment of acceptable audit risk. Note that only some of the situations in Part II will relate to acceptable audit risk. Classify the information based on the three factors that affect acceptable audit risk.

   External users' reliance on financial statements
   Likelihood of financial difficulties
   Management integrity

b. Assess acceptable audit risk as high, medium, or low considering the items you identified in requirement a. (A risky client will be assessed as a low acceptable audit risk.) Justify your response.

c. Identify inherent risks for the audit of Pinnacle using the information from Parts I and II. For each inherent risk, identify the account or accounts and the relevant audit objectives that may be affected.

Inherent Risk	Account or Accounts Affected	Relevant Audit Objectives

ASSESSING AND RESPONDING TO FRAUD RISKS

CHAPTER 10

Accounting Scandal Rocks Public Trust

The accounting profession was under fire. Throughout the long, hot summer, newspapers were filled with new details of a corporate accounting scandal. One of the largest, most respected companies in the United States had been caught inflating earnings and assets through blatant manipulation of the accounting rules. Thousands of investors and employees had suffered. Congressional hearings were called to examine and understand the fraud, and everyone asked, "Where were the auditors?" The accounting profession was under immense political pressure from reform-minded lawmakers, and the negative publicity surrounding the perceived audit failure cast all CPAs in the most unfavorable light.

The year was 1938. The corporate accounting scandal was McKesson-Robbins, and it arguably had a greater impact on the way audits are performed than any subsequent scandal, including Enron and WorldCom.

In 1924, Philip Musica, a high-school dropout with fraud convictions and a prison record, reinvented himself as F. Donald Coster and awarded himself a medical degree. "Dr. Coster" took control of McKesson-Robbins and embarked on a massive fraud to inflate its share price. McKesson-Robbins inflated assets and earnings by $19 million through the reporting of nonexistent inventory and fictitious sales. Coster duped McKesson's auditors, and the investing public, into believing that the company had a huge drug inventory, worth multimillions of dollars, that didn't exist. Coster created phony purchase orders, sales invoices, and other documents, all of which McKesson's auditors dutifully reviewed as evidence of the imaginary inventory. The fraud succeeded because the auditing standards of the day permitted auditors to confine themselves to reviewing documents and talking to management. They were not required to physically examine and verify inventories.

During an emergency board meeting, hastily called after the fraud came to light, word was received that Coster had committed suicide. An investment bank partner who served as a McKesson outside director, concerned about his responsibilities, responded to the news by exclaiming, "Let's fire him anyway!"

Sources: 1. Michael Ramos, *Fraud Detection in a GAAS Audit: SAS No. 99 Implementation Guide*, AICPA (2003), p. ix; 2. Presentation by PCAOB Board Member Daniel L. Goelzer at Investment Company Institute's 2003 Tax & Accounting Conference, September 15, 2003 (pcaobus.org).

LEARNING OBJECTIVES

After studying this chapter, you should be able to

10-1 Define fraud and distinguish between fraudulent financial reporting and misappropriation of assets.

10-2 Describe the fraud triangle and identify conditions for fraud.

10-3 Understand the auditor's responsibility for assessing the risk of fraud and detecting material misstatements due to fraud.

10-4 Identify corporate governance and other control environment factors that reduce fraud risks.

10-5 Develop responses to identified fraud risks.

10-6 Recognize specific fraud risk areas and develop procedures to detect fraud.

10-7 Understand interview techniques and other activities after fraud is suspected.

10-8 Describe information about the fraud risk assessment that must be documented in the working papers.

The classic fraud at McKesson-Robbins illustrates that financial statement fraud is not just a recent occurrence. In the wake of that scandal, the auditing profession responded by setting the first formal standards for auditing procedures. Those standards required confirmation of receivables and observation of physical inventory, procedures that are standard today, plus guidance on the auditor's responsibilities for detecting fraud.

In response to more recent frauds, Congress passed the Sarbanes–Oxley Act in 2002 and the AICPA developed specific auditing standards to deal with fraud risk assessment and detection. In this chapter we will discuss the auditor's responsibility to assess the risk of fraud and detect material misstatements due to fraud and describe major areas of fraud risk, as well as controls to prevent fraud and audit procedures to detect fraud.

TYPES OF FRAUD

OBJECTIVE 10-1

Define fraud and distinguish between fraudulent financial reporting and misappropriation of assets.

As a broad legal concept, fraud describes any intentional deceit meant to deprive another person or party of their property or rights. In the context of auditing financial statements, fraud is defined as an intentional misstatement of financial statements. The two main categories are fraudulent financial reporting and misappropriation of assets, which we introduced when defining the auditor's responsibilities for detecting material misstatements in Chapter 6.

Fraudulent Financial Reporting

Fraudulent financial reporting is an intentional misstatement or omission of amounts or disclosures with the intent to deceive users. Most cases involve the intentional misstatement of amounts, rather than disclosures. For example, WorldCom capitalized as fixed assets billions of dollars that should have been expensed. Omissions of amounts are less common, but a company can overstate income by omitting accounts payable and other liabilities.

While most cases of fraudulent financial reporting involve an attempt to overstate income—either by overstatement of assets and income or by omission of liabilities and expenses—companies also deliberately understate income. At privately held companies, this may be done in an attempt to reduce income taxes. Companies may also intentionally understate income when earnings are high to create a reserve of earnings or "cookie jar reserves" that may be used to increase earnings in future periods. Such practices are called income smoothing and earnings management. **Earnings management** involves deliberate actions taken by management to meet earnings objectives. **Income smoothing** is a form of earnings management in which revenues and expenses are shifted between periods to reduce fluctuations in earnings. One technique to smooth income is to reduce the value of inventory and other assets of an acquired company at the time of acquisition, resulting in higher earnings when the assets are later sold. Companies may also deliberately overstate inventory obsolescence reserves and allowances for doubtful accounts to counter higher earnings.

Although less frequent, several notable cases of fraudulent financial reporting involved inadequate disclosure. For example, a central issue in the Enron case was whether the company adequately disclosed obligations to affiliates known as special-purpose entities. E. F. Hutton, a now defunct brokerage firm, was charged with intentionally overdrawing accounts at various banks to increase interest earnings. These overdrafts were included as liabilities on the balance sheet, but the balance sheet description of the obligations did not clearly state the nature of the liabilities.

Misappropriation of Assets

Misappropriation of assets is fraud that involves theft of an entity's assets. In many cases, but not all, the amounts involved are not material to the financial statements. However, the theft of company assets is often a management concern, regardless of the materiality of the amounts involved, because small thefts can easily increase in size over time and they often lead to significant reputational harm once discovered and disclosed.

The term misappropriation of assets is normally used to refer to theft involving employees and others internal to the organization. According to estimates of the Association of Certified Fraud Examiners, the average company loses five percent of its revenues to fraud, although much of this fraud involves external parties, such as shoplifting by customers and cheating by suppliers.

Misappropriation of assets is normally perpetrated at lower levels of the organization hierarchy. In some notable cases, however, top management is involved in the theft of company assets. Because of management's greater authority and control over organization assets, embezzlements involving top management can involve significant amounts. In one extreme example, the former CEO of Tyco International was charged by the SEC with stealing over $100 million in assets. A fraud survey conducted by the Association of Certified Fraud Examiners found that asset misappropriations are the most common fraud scheme, although the size of the fraud is much greater for fraudulent financial reporting.

CONDITIONS FOR FRAUD

OBJECTIVE 10-2

Describe the fraud triangle and identify conditions for fraud.

Three conditions for fraud arising from fraudulent financial reporting and misappropriations of assets are described in the auditing standards. As shown in Figure 10-1, these three conditions are referred to as the **fraud triangle**.

1. *Incentives/Pressures.* Management or other employees have incentives or pressures to commit fraud.
2. *Opportunities.* Circumstances provide opportunities for management or employees to commit fraud.
3. *Attitudes/Rationalization.* An attitude, character, or set of ethical values exists that allows management or employees to commit a dishonest act, or they are in an environment that imposes sufficient pressure that causes them to rationalize committing a dishonest act.

Risk Factors for Fraudulent Financial Reporting

An essential consideration by the auditor in uncovering fraud is identifying factors that increase the risk of fraud. Table 10-1 (p. 300) provides examples of these **fraud risk factors** for each of the three conditions of fraud for fraudulent financial reporting. In the fraud triangle, fraudulent financial reporting and misappropriation of assets share the same three conditions, but the risk factors differ. We'll first address the risk factors for fraudulent financial reporting, and then discuss those for misappropriation of assets. Later in the chapter, the auditor's use of the risk factors in uncovering fraud is discussed.

Incentives/Pressures A common incentive for companies to manipulate financial statements is a decline in the company's financial prospects. For example, a decline in earnings may threaten the company's ability to obtain financing. Companies may also manipulate earnings to meet analysts' forecasts or benchmarks such as prior-year earnings, to meet debt covenant restrictions, to achieve a bonus target based

FIGURE 10-1 The Fraud Triangle

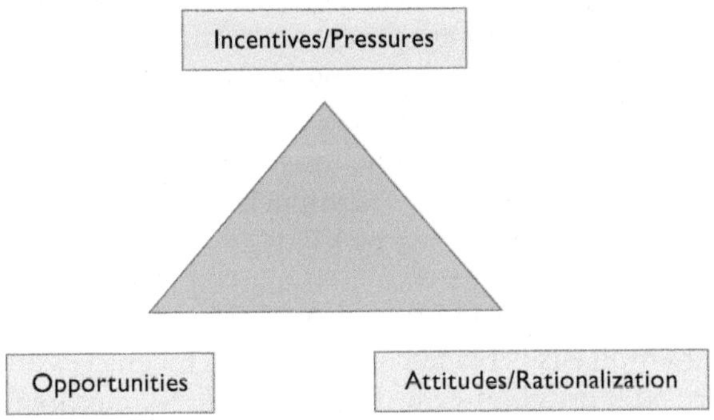

Incentives/Pressures

Opportunities

Attitudes/Rationalization

TABLE 10-1 Examples of Risk Factors for Fraudulent Financial Reporting

Three Conditions of Fraud		
Incentives/Pressures	**Opportunities**	**Attitudes/Rationalization**
Management or other employees have incentives or pressures to materially misstate financial statements.	Circumstances provide an opportunity for management or employees to misstate financial statements.	An attitude, character, or set of ethical values exists that allows management or employees to intentionally commit a dishonest act, or they are in an environment that imposes sufficient pressure that causes them to rationalize committing a dishonest act.
Examples of Risk Factors	**Examples of Risk Factors**	**Examples of Risk Factors**
Financial stability or profitability is threatened by economic, industry, or entity operating conditions. Examples include significant declines in customer demand and increasing business failures in either the industry or overall economy. Excessive pressure for management to meet debt repayment or other debt covenant requirements. Management or the board of directors' personal net worth is materially threatened by the entity's financial performance.	Significant accounting estimates involve subjective judgments or uncertainties that are difficult to verify. Ineffective board of director or audit committee oversight over financial reporting. High turnover or ineffective accounting, internal audit, or information technology staff. Deficient internal controls. Significant related-party transactions.	Inappropriate or ineffective communication and support of the entity's values. Known history of violations of securities laws or other laws and regulations. Management's practice of making overly aggressive or unrealistic forecasts to analysts, creditors, and other third parties.

on earnings, or to artificially inflate stock prices. In some cases, management may manipulate earnings just to preserve their reputation. Figure 10-2 highlights KPMG's survey finding that personal financial incentives, especially a desire to fund an extravagant lifestyle, and the need to meet pre-specified business performance targets are often cited as primary incentives to engage in fraudulent actions.

Opportunities Although the financial statements of all companies are potentially subject to manipulation, the risk is greater for companies in industries where significant judgments and estimates are involved. For example, valuation of inventories is subject to greater risk of misstatement for companies with diverse inventories in many locations. The risk of misstatement of inventories is further increased if those inventories are at risk for obsolescence.

Turnover in accounting personnel or other deficiencies in accounting and information processes can create an opportunity for misstatement. Many cases of fraudulent financial reporting went undetected by ineffective audit committee and board of director oversight of financial reporting. Weak internal controls was the most often cited opportunity, as shown in Figure 10-2.

Attitudes/Rationalization The attitude of top management toward financial reporting is a critical risk factor in assessing the likelihood of fraudulent financial statements, as illustrated by Figure 10-2. If the CEO or other top managers display a significant disregard for the financial reporting process, such as consistently issuing overly optimistic forecasts, or they are overly concerned about meeting analysts' earnings forecasts, fraudulent financial reporting is more likely. Management's character or set of ethical values also may make it easier for them to rationalize a fraudulent act. A sense of superiority by executives is the most commonly cited condition related to attitude and rationalization. Figure 10-3 summarizes the profile of the fraud perpetrators in 348 actual fraud cases examined by KPMG.

Risk Factors for Misappropriation of Assets

The same three conditions apply to misappropriation of assets. However, in assessing risk factors, greater emphasis is placed on individual incentives and opportunities for theft. Table 10-2 (p. 302) provides examples of fraud risk factors for each of the three conditions of fraud for misappropriation of assets.

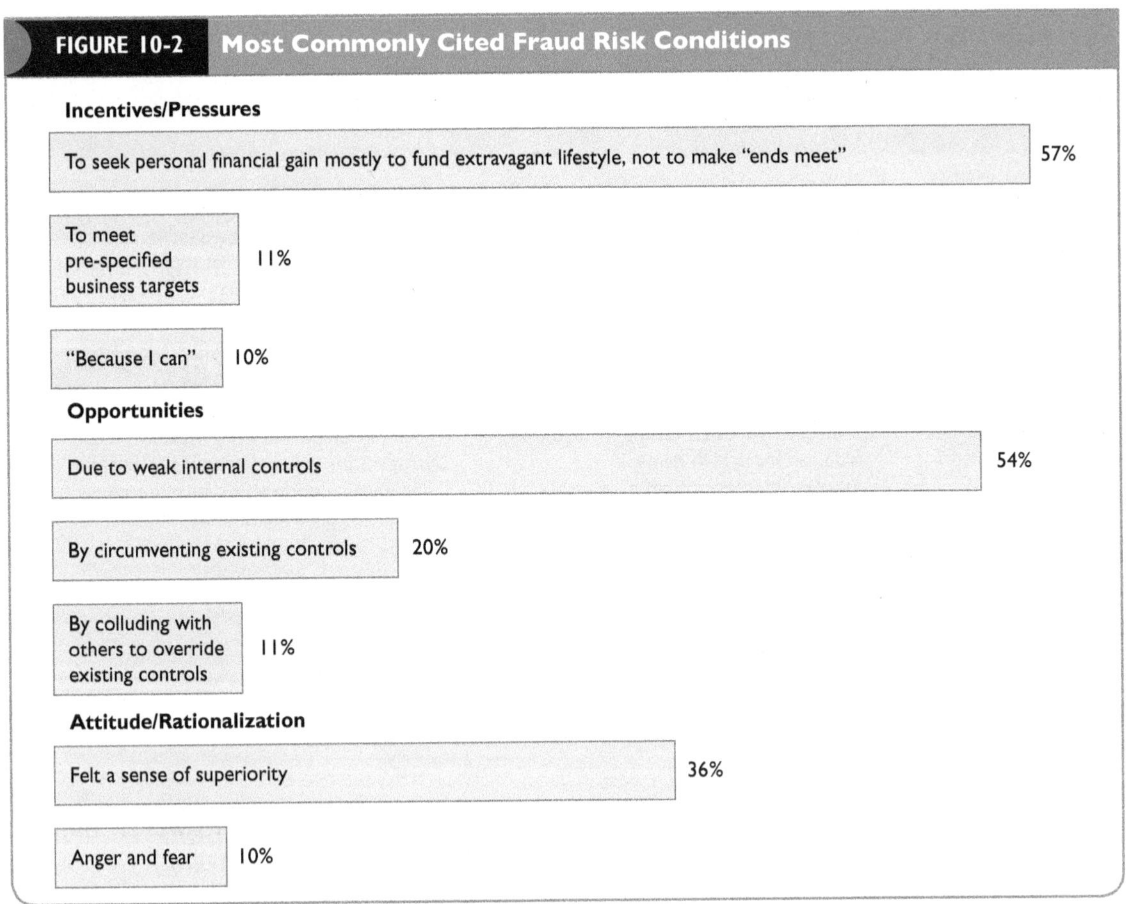

FIGURE 10-2 Most Commonly Cited Fraud Risk Conditions

Source: *Global Profiles of the Fraudster*, KPMG, 2013.

Incentives/Pressures Financial pressures are a common incentive for employees who misappropriate assets. Employees with excessive financial obligations, or those with drug abuse or gambling problems, may steal to meet their personal needs. In other cases, dissatisfied employees may steal from a sense of entitlement or as a form of attack against their employers.

FIGURE 10-3 Characteristics of Fraud Perpetrators

Age of Fraudster (in years)	Percentage	Time at Organization	Percentage	Fraud Committed	Percentage
36-45	41%	3–5 years	29%	In collusion with others	61%
46-55	35%	6–10 years	27%	Acting alone	39%
Other	24%	Over 10 years	33%		
		Other	11%		

Gender		Rank in Organization		Where Perpetrator Works	
Male	87%	Senior management	35%	Finance	32%
Female	13%	Management	29%	CEO	26%
		Other	36%	Operations/Sales	25%
				Other	17%
Employed by Organization Defrauded	90%				

Source: *Who is the Typical Fraudster?* KPMG, 2011.

TABLE 10-2 Examples of Risk Factors for Misappropriation of Assets

Three Conditions of Fraud		
Incentives/Pressures	**Opportunities**	**Attitudes/Rationalization**
Management or other employees have incentives or pressures to misappropriate material assets.	Circumstances provide an opportunity for management or employees to misappropriate assets.	An attitude, character, or set of ethical values exists that allows management or employees to intentionally commit a dishonest act, or they are in an environment that imposes sufficient pressure that causes them to rationalize committing a dishonest act.
Examples of Risk Factors	**Examples of Risk Factors**	**Examples of Risk Factors**
Personal financial obligations create pressure for those with access to cash or other assets susceptible to theft to misappropriate those assets. Adverse relationships between management and employees with access to assets susceptible to theft motivate employees to misappropriate those assets. Examples include the following: • Known or expected employee layoffs. • Promotions, compensation, or other rewards inconsistent with expectations.	Presence of large amounts of cash on hand or inventory items that are small, of high value, or are in high demand. Inadequate internal control over assets due to lack of the following: • Appropriate segregation of duties or independent checks. • An approved vendor list to detect unauthorized or fictitious vendors. • Job applicant screening for employees with access to assets. • Mandatory vacations for employees with access to assets.	Disregard for the need to monitor or reduce risk of misappropriating assets. Disregard for internal controls by overriding existing controls or failing to correct known internal control deficiencies.

Opportunities Opportunities for theft exist in all companies. However, opportunities are greater in companies with accessible cash or with inventory or other valuable assets, especially if the assets are small or easily removed. For example, casinos handle extensive amounts of cash with little formal records of cash received. Similarly, thefts of laptop computers are much more frequent than thefts of desktop systems.

Weak internal controls create opportunities for theft. Inadequate separation of duties is practically a license for employees to steal. Whenever employees have custody or even temporary access to assets and maintain the accounting records for those assets, the potential for theft exists. For example, if inventory storeroom

MADOFF CONVICTED IN LARGEST INVESTOR FRAUD

On March 12, 2009, Bernie Madoff pled guilty to the largest investor fraud ever, in a Ponzi scheme with losses estimated at almost $21 billion. By way of comparison, the massive fraud at WorldCom was approximately $11 billion. Madoff was sentenced to a prison term of 150 years.

In a Ponzi scheme, people are enticed to invest by above-market returns that are paid from the investments of additional investors, rather than actual profits on investments. The scheme usually collapses under its own weight because it depends on a continuing supply of new investors. The scheme is named after Charles Ponzi, who used the scheme in the early 1920s. Although he did not invent the Ponzi scheme, it has become associated with his name because of the scale of his operation. Madoff's scandal lasted a long time, particularly for such a large scheme. Investigators believe the fraud may have begun in the 1970s, although Madoff maintains that his fraudulent activities began in the 1990s. Madoff mainly managed money for charities, many of them private foundations. Private foundations are required by IRS regulations to pay out 5% of their funds each year, and Madoff could easily meet these required payouts using investments into the fund.

Madoff was secretive about his trading practices and marketed his funds to an exclusive clientele. Although concerns were raised over the years about the consistency of the returns generated, and the SEC investigated Madoff several times, his scheme was not revealed until the market plunge in 2008 triggered investor withdrawals from the firm. The market downturn revealed what several critics had alleged, that Madoff was running an elaborate Ponzi scheme.

Sources: 1. Robert Frank, Amir Efrati, Aaron Luchetti, and Chad Bray, "Madoff Jailed After Admitting Epic Scam," *The Wall Street Journal* (March 13, 2009); 2. Securities and Exchange Commission Litigation Complaint, December 11, 2008 (www.sec.gov/litigation).

employees also maintain inventory records, they can easily take inventory items and cover the theft by adjusting the accounting records. A lack of controls over payments to vendors, or payroll systems, can allow employees to create fictitious vendors or employees and bill the company for services or time.

Fraud is more prevalent in smaller businesses and not-for-profit organizations because it is sometimes more difficult for these entities to maintain adequate separation of duties. However, even large organizations may fail to maintain adequate separation in critical areas. Barings Bank collapsed after incurring losses in excess of $1 billion from the activities of one trader because of inadequate separation of duties.

Attitudes/Rationalization Management's attitude toward controls and ethical conduct may allow employees and managers to rationalize the theft of assets. If management cheats customers through overcharging for goods or engaging in high-pressure sales tactics, employees may feel that it is acceptable for them to behave in the same fashion by cheating on expense or time reports.

ASSESSING THE RISK OF FRAUD

OBJECTIVE 10-3

Understand the auditor's responsibility for assessing the risk of fraud and detecting material misstatements due to fraud.

Auditing standards require the auditor to assess the risk of material misstatement due to fraud, and those standards provide guidance to assist the auditor in making that assessment. Auditors must maintain a level of professional skepticism as they consider a broad set of information, including fraud risk factors, to identify and respond to fraud risk. As we discussed in Chapter 6, the auditor has a responsibility to respond to fraud risk by planning and performing the audit to obtain reasonable assurance that material misstatements, whether due to fraud or errors, are detected.

Professional Skepticism

As we discussed in Chapter 6, auditing standards require that the audit be planned and performed with an *attitude of professional skepticism* in all aspects of the engagement, recognizing the possibility that a material misstatement could exist regardless of the auditor's prior experience with the integrity and honesty of client management and those charged with governance. In practice, maintaining this attitude of professional skepticism can be difficult because, despite some recent high-profile examples of fraudulent financial statements, material frauds are infrequent compared to the number of audits of financial statements conducted annually. Most auditors will never encounter a material fraud during their careers. Also, through client acceptance and continuance evaluation procedures, auditors reject most potential clients perceived as lacking honesty and integrity.

Questioning Mind Auditing standards emphasize consideration of a client's susceptibility to fraud, regardless of the auditor's beliefs about the likelihood of fraud and management's honesty and integrity. During audit planning for every audit, the engagement team must discuss the need to maintain a questioning mind throughout the audit to identify fraud risks and critically evaluate audit evidence. There is always a risk that even an honest person can rationalize fraudulent actions when incentives or pressures become extreme.

Critical Evaluation of Audit Evidence Upon discovering information or other conditions that indicate a material misstatement due to fraud may have occurred, auditors should thoroughly probe the issues, acquire additional evidence as needed, and consult with other team members. Auditors must be careful not to rationalize or assume a misstatement is an isolated incident. For example, say an auditor uncovers a current-year sale that should properly be reflected as a sale in the following year. The auditor should evaluate the reasons for the misstatement, determine whether it was intentional or a fraud, and consider whether other such misstatements are likely to have occurred.

FIGURE 10-4 Sources of Information Gathered to Assess Fraud Risks

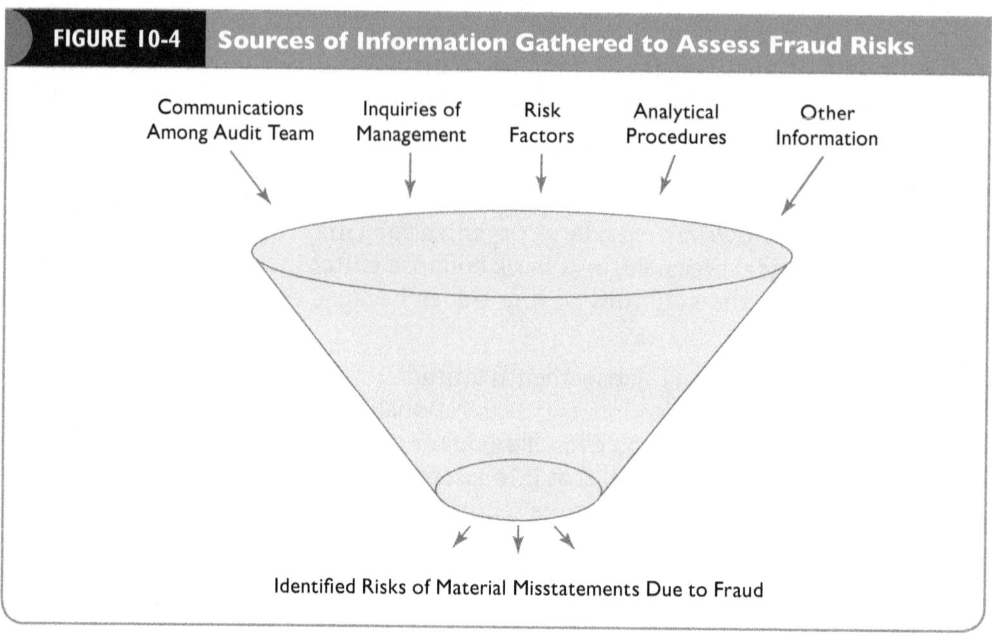

Sources of Information to Assess Fraud Risks

Figure 10-4 summarizes the information used to assess fraud risk. The five sources of information to assess these fraud risks on the top of the figure are discussed further in this section.

Communications Among Audit Team Auditing standards require the audit team, including the engagement partner and key engagement team members, conduct discussions to share insights from more experienced audit team members and to "brainstorm" ideas that address the following:

1. How and where they believe the entity's financial statements might be susceptible to material misstatement due to fraud. This should include consideration of known external and internal factors affecting the entity that might:
   - create an incentive or pressure for management to commit fraud.
   - provide the opportunity for fraud to be perpetrated, including the risk of management override of internal controls.
   - indicate a culture or environment that enables management to rationalize fraudulent acts.
2. How management could perpetrate and conceal fraudulent financial reporting.
3. How anyone might misappropriate assets of the entity.
4. How the auditor might respond to the susceptibility of material misstatements due to fraud.

These discussions about fraud risks will likely take place at the same time as discussions about the susceptibility of the entity's financial statements to other types of material misstatement, which were addressed in Chapter 9. When engaging in these discussions, the engagement team should set aside beliefs about the honesty and integrity of management and those charged with governance, and the team should be reminded of the importance of maintaining professional skepticism regarding the potential for material misstatement due to fraud throughout the audit.

Inquiries of Management Auditing standards require the auditor to make specific inquiries about fraud in every audit. Inquiries of management and others within the company provide employees with an opportunity to tell the auditor information that otherwise might not be communicated. Moreover, their responses to the auditor's questions often reveal information on the likelihood of fraud.

The auditor's inquiries of management should address whether management has knowledge of any fraud or suspected fraud within the company. Auditors should also

IT PAYS TO BLOW THE WHISTLE ON FRAUD

In an effort to combat fraud, Congress included a monetary reward for being a whistleblower in the Dodd-Frank Wall Street Reform and Consumer Protection Act. The whistleblower program is overseen by the SEC and provides a monetary reward to anyone providing information about a violation of a federal securities law that leads to a successful enforcement action resulting in at least $1 million in sanctions. The reward is between 10% and 30% of the amount recovered by the SEC. Tips can be anonymous and do not even have to be from a direct observation of the fraudulent activity. In addition, the new provisions strengthen anti-retaliation rules so that penalizing a whistleblower constitutes a violation of the securities laws.

In fiscal 2014, the SEC whistleblower office received over 3,600 tips, or an average of 10 per day, which was an increase from the approximately 3,200 tips received in 2013. The most common allegations relate to financial statements and disclosures, securities offering fraud, and manipulating the stock market. The program has paid out nearly $50 million to a total of seventeen whistleblowers as of the first quarter of 2015. Three individuals have received more than $1 million and the largest payout to date is over $30 million.

Source: Mary Jo White, "The SEC as the Whistleblower's Advocate" (April 30, 2015) (www.sec.gov).

inquire about management's process of assessing fraud risks, the nature of fraud risks identified by management, any internal controls implemented to address those risks, and any information about fraud risks and related controls that management has reported to the audit committee or others charged with governance.

The audit committee often assumes an active role in overseeing management's fraud risk assessment and response processes. The auditor must inquire of the audit committee or others charged with governance about their views of the risks of fraud and whether they have knowledge of any fraud or suspected fraud. For entities with an internal audit function, the auditor should inquire about internal audit's views of fraud risks, whether they have performed any procedures to identify or detect fraud during the year, and whether they have any knowledge of any actual fraud.

Auditing standards also require the auditor to make inquiries of others within the entity whose duties lie outside the normal financial reporting lines of responsibility. When coming into contact with company personnel, such as the inventory warehouse manager or purchasing agents, the auditor may inquire about the existence or suspicion of fraud. Throughout the audit, inquiries of executives and a wide variety of other employees provide opportunities for the auditor to learn about risks of fraud. When responses are inconsistent, the auditor should obtain additional audit evidence to resolve the inconsistency and to support or refute the original risk assessment.

Risk Factors Auditing standards require the auditor to evaluate whether fraud risk factors indicate incentives or pressures to perpetrate fraud, opportunities to carry out fraud, or attitudes or rationalizations used to justify a fraudulent action. Tables 10-1 (p. 300) and 10-2 (p. 302) outline examples of the fraud risk factors auditors consider. The existence of fraud risk factors does not mean fraud exists, but that the likelihood of fraud is higher. Auditors should consider these factors along with any other information used to assess the risks of fraud.

Analytical Procedures As we discussed in Chapter 7, auditors must perform analytical procedures during the planning and completion phases of the audit to help identify unusual transactions or events that might indicate the presence of material misstatements in the financial statements. When results from analytical procedures differ from the auditor's expectations, the auditor evaluates those results in light of other information obtained about the likelihood of fraud to determine if fraud risk is heightened.

In addition to the ratio analysis performed as part of preliminary analytical procedures described in Chapter 8, the auditor may perform horizontal and vertical analysis of the financial statements. In **horizontal analysis**, the account balance is compared to the previous period, and the percentage change in the account balances for the period is calculated. Figure 10-5 (p. 306) is an example of horizontal analysis applied to the condensed income statement for Hillsburg Hardware. For example, sales increased $11,860 (in 000's) from the prior year, which represents a 9.0% increase ($11,860/$131,226). In

FIGURE 10-5 Horizontal Analysis of Income Statement

Hillsburg Hardware Company Horizontal Analysis of Income Statement (in thousands)	Year Ended December 31			
	2016	2015	Change	% Change
Net sales	$143,086	$131,226	$11,860	9.0%
Cost of sales	103,241	94,876	8,365	8.8%
Gross profit	39,845	36,350	3,495	9.6%
Selling, general, and administrative expenses	32,475	29,656	2,819	9.5%
Operating income	7,370	6,694	676	10.1%
Other income and expense				
Interest expense	2,409	2,035	374	18.4%
Gain on sale of assets	(720)	—	(720)	N/A
Total other income/expense (net)	1,689	2,035	(346)	−17.0%
Earnings before income taxes	5,681	4,659	1,022	21.9%
Provision for income taxes	1,747	1,465	282	19.2%
Net income	$ 3,934	$ 3,194	$ 740	23.2%

vertical analysis, the financial statement numbers are converted to percentages. The common-size financial statement in Figure 8-4 on page 233 is an example of vertical analysis applied to the detailed income statement for Hillsburg Hardware, with each income statement amount calculated as a percentage of sales. In vertical analysis of the balance sheet, balances are calculated as a percentage of total assets.

Because occurrences of fraudulent financial reporting often involve manipulation of revenue, auditing standards require the auditor to perform analytical procedures on revenue accounts. The objective is to identify unusual or unexpected relationships involving revenue accounts that may indicate fraudulent financial reporting. By comparing the sales volume based on recorded revenue with actual production capacity, for example, the auditor can reveal revenues beyond the entity's production capabilities. The auditor may review monthly sales in the general ledger and may also review quarterly or monthly sales by product line. By reviewing sales trends, the auditor may identify unusual sales activity. For example, at one company the reversals of improperly recorded sales resulted in negative sales for a month.

Other Information Auditors should consider all information they have obtained in any phase or part of the audit as they assess the risk of fraud. Many of the risk assessment procedures that the auditor performs during planning to assess the risk of material misstatement may indicate a heightened risk of fraud. For example, information about management's integrity and honesty obtained during client acceptance procedures, inquiries and analytical procedures done in connection with the auditor's review of the client's quarterly financial statements, and information considered in assessing inherent and control risks may lead to auditor concerns about the likelihood of misstatements due to fraud.

Identified Risks of Material Misstatement Due to Fraud

As illustrated by Figure 10-4 (p. 304), auditors evaluate all the sources of information gathered to assess the risk of material misstatement due to fraud as part of audit planning. Auditors assess fraud risk at both the overall financial statement level and at the assertion level for classes of transactions, account balances, and presentation and disclosure. While the assessment of fraud is conducted as part of audit planning, the auditor's assessment of fraud risk should be ongoing throughout the audit, given the auditor may learn new information when performing further audit procedures that provide new insights about the risk of material misstatement.

As discussed in Chapter 9, auditing standards require that the auditor presume that there is a risk of fraud in revenue recognition, given that fraudulently misstated financial statements often include misstated revenue amounts due to the premature recognition of revenue transactions or the recording of fictitious revenues. In light of this presumption, auditors should evaluate the types of revenue and revenue transactions, and the assertions related to these transactions, which may increase fraud risk. The auditor may conclude that the presumption that revenue recognition represents a fraud risk is not applicable for a particular client. If so, the auditor must document that conclusion in the working papers.

When the auditor concludes that there is a risk of material misstatement due to fraud, auditing standards require the auditor to treat those risks as significant risks. For significant risks, including fraud risks, the auditor should obtain an understanding of internal control related to such risks, including an evaluation of whether the controls are suitably designed and implemented. Corporate governance and other control factors that reduce fraud risks are discussed in the next section.

CORPORATE GOVERNANCE OVERSIGHT TO REDUCE FRAUD RISKS

OBJECTIVE 10-4

Identify corporate governance and other control environment factors that reduce fraud risks.

Management is responsible for implementing corporate governance and control procedures to minimize the risk of fraud, which can be reduced through a combination of prevention, deterrence, and detection measures. Because collusion and false documentation make detection of fraud a challenge, it is often more effective and economical for companies to focus on fraud prevention and deterrence. By implementing antifraud programs and controls, management can prevent fraud by reducing opportunity. By communicating fraud detection and punishment policies, management can deter employees from committing fraud.

Guidance developed by the AICPA identifies three elements to prevent, deter, and detect fraud:

1. Culture of honesty and high ethics
2. Management's responsibility to evaluate risks of fraud
3. Audit committee oversight

Let's examine these elements closely, as auditors should have a thorough understanding of each to assess the extent to which clients have implemented fraud-reducing activities.

Culture of Honesty and High Ethics

Research indicates that the most effective way to prevent and deter fraud is to implement antifraud programs and controls that are based on core values embraced by the company. Such values create an environment that reinforces acceptable behavior and expectations that employees can use to guide their actions. These values help create a culture of honesty and ethics that provides the foundation for employees' job responsibilities. Creating a culture of honesty and high ethics includes six elements.

Setting the Tone at the Top Management and the board of directors are responsible for setting the "tone at the top" for ethical behavior in the company. Honesty and integrity by management reinforces honesty and integrity to employees throughout the organization. Management cannot act one way and expect others in the company to behave differently. Through its actions and communications, management can show that dishonest and unethical behaviors are not tolerated, even if the results benefit the company.

A "tone at the top" based on honesty and integrity provides the foundation upon which a more detailed code of conduct can be developed to provide more specific guidance about permitted and prohibited behavior. Table 10-3 (p. 308) provides an example of the key contents of an effective code of conduct.

TABLE 10-3 Example Elements of a Code of Conduct

Code of Conduct Element	Description
Organizational Code of Conduct	The organization and its employees must at all times comply with all applicable laws and regulations, with all business conduct well above the minimum standards required by law.
General Employee Conduct	The organization expects its employees to conduct themselves in a businesslike manner and prohibits unprofessional activities, such as drinking, gambling, fighting, and swearing, while on the job.
Conflicts of Interest	The organization expects that employees will perform their duties conscientiously, honestly, and in accordance with the best interests of the organization and will not use their positions or knowledge gained for private or personal advantage.
Outside Activities, Employment, and Directorships	All employees share a responsibility for the organization's good public relations. Employees should avoid activities outside the organization that create an excessive demand on their time or create a conflict of interest.
Relationships with Clients and Suppliers	Employees should avoid investing in or acquiring a financial interest in any business organization that has a contractual relationship with the organization.
Gifts, Entertainment, and Favors	Employees must not accept entertainment, gifts, or personal favors that could influence or appear to influence business decisions in favor of any person with whom the organization has business dealings.
Kickbacks and Secret Commissions	Employees may not receive payment or compensation of any kind, except as authorized under organizational remuneration policies.
Organization Funds and Other Assets	Employees who have access to organization funds must follow prescribed procedures for recording, handling, and protecting money.
Organization Records and Communications	Employees responsible for accounting and record keeping must not make or engage in any false record or communication of any kind, whether external or internal.
Dealing with Outside People and Organizations	Employees must take care to separate their personal roles from their organizational positions when communicating on matters not involving the organization's business.
Prompt Communications	All employees must make every effort to achieve complete, accurate, and timely communications in all matters relevant to customers, suppliers, government authorities, the public, and others within the organization.
Privacy and Confidentiality	When handling financial and personal information about customers and others with whom the organization has dealings, employees should collect, use, and retain only the information necessary for the organization's business; internal access to information should be limited to those with a legitimate business reason for seeking that information.

Source: AICPA, "*CPA's Handbook of Fraud and Commercial Crime Prevention.*"

Creating a Positive Workplace Environment Research shows that wrongdoing occurs less frequently when employees have positive feelings about their employer than when they feel abused, threatened, or ignored. A positive workplace can generate improved employee morale, which may reduce employees' likelihood of committing fraud against the company.

Employees should also have the ability to obtain advice internally before making decisions that appear to have legal or ethical implications. Many organizations, including all U.S. public companies, have a whistleblowing process for employees to report actual or suspected wrongdoing or potential violations of the code of conduct or ethics policy. Whistleblower hotlines are often directed to or monitored by an ethics officer or other trusted individual responsible for investigating and reporting fraud or illegal acts.

Hiring and Promoting Appropriate Employees To be successful in preventing fraud, well-run companies implement effective screening policies to reduce the likelihood of hiring and promoting individuals with low levels of honesty, especially those who hold positions of trust. Such policies may include background checks on individuals being considered for employment or for promotion to positions of trust. Background checks verify a candidate's education, employment history, and personal references, including references about character and integrity. After an employee is hired, continuous evaluation of employee compliance with the company's values and code of conduct also reduces the likelihood of fraud.

Training All new employees should be trained about the company's expectations of employees' ethical conduct. Employees should be told of their duty to communicate actual or suspected fraud and the appropriate way to do so. In addition, fraud awareness training should be tailored to employees' specific job responsibilities with, for example, different training for purchasing agents and sales agents.

Confirmation Most companies require employees to periodically confirm their responsibilities for complying with the code of conduct. Employees are asked to state that they understand the company's expectations and have complied with the code, and that they are unaware of any violations. These confirmations help reinforce the code of conduct policies and also help deter employees from committing fraud or other ethics violations. By following up on disclosures and non-replies, internal auditors or others may uncover significant issues.

Discipline Employees must know that they will be held accountable for failing to follow the company's code of conduct. Enforcement of violations of the code, regardless of the level of the employee committing the act, sends clear messages to all employees that compliance with the code of conduct and other ethical standards is important and expected. Thorough investigation of all violations and appropriate and consistent responses can be effective deterrents to fraud.

Management's Responsibility to Evaluate Risks of Fraud

Fraud cannot occur without a perceived opportunity to commit and conceal the act. Management is responsible for identifying and measuring fraud risks, taking steps to mitigate identified risks, and monitoring internal controls that prevent and detect fraud.

Identifying and Measuring Fraud Risks Effective fraud oversight begins with management's recognition that fraud is possible and that almost any employee is capable of committing a dishonest act under the right circumstances. This recognition increases the likelihood that effective fraud prevention, deterrence, and detection programs and controls are implemented. *The Report to the Nations on Occupational Fraud and Abuse* issued by the Association of Certified Fraud Examiners highlights the impact of the presence of 18 common internal controls on the median losses suffered by organizations for all types of fraud and the impact of those controls on the duration of the fraud scheme before it was detected. The report compares the size and duration of loss due to fraud for organizations where that control was present to organizations where the control was absent and finds that frauds perpetrated in organizations with any of the 18 common controls resulted in significantly lower losses as compared to the losses in organizations that lacked these controls. Figure 10-6 (p. 310) reflects the percentage of reduction in losses from, and duration of, frauds that occurred as a result of these antifraud controls.

Mitigating Fraud Risks Management is responsible for designing and implementing programs and controls to mitigate fraud risks, and it can change business activities and processes prone to fraud to reduce incentives and opportunities for fraud. For example, management can outsource certain operations, such as transferring cash collections from company personnel to a bank lockbox system. Other programs and controls may be implemented at a company-wide level, such as the training of all employees about fraud risks and strengthening employment and promotion policies.

Monitoring Fraud Prevention Programs and Controls For high fraud risk areas, management should periodically evaluate whether appropriate antifraud programs and controls have been implemented and are operating effectively. For example, management's review and evaluation of results for operating units or subsidiaries increases the likelihood that manipulated results will be detected.

Internal audit plays a key role in monitoring activities to ensure that antifraud programs and controls are operating effectively. Internal audit activities can both deter and detect fraud. Internal auditors assist in deterring fraud by examining and evaluating internal controls that reduce fraud risk. They assist in fraud detection by performing audit procedures that may uncover fraudulent financial reporting and misappropriation of assets.

FIGURE 10-6 Impact of Antifraud Controls on Fraud Deterrence		
Control	**Percent Reduction in Median Loss from Fraud**	**Percent Reduction in Median Duration of Fraud**
Antifraud policy	35.5%	50.0%
Code of conduct	50.0%	33.3%
Dedicated fraud department, function or team	39.0%	50.0%
Employee support programs	55.0%	22.2%
External audit of financial statements	32.8%	25.0%
External audit of internal control over financial reporting	42.8%	37.5%
Formal fraud risk assessments	44.0%	47.9%
Fraud training for employees	39.0%	50.0%
Fraud training for managers/ executives	40.5%	38.1%
Hotline	40.5%	50.0%
Independent audit committee	20.0%	41.7%
Internal audit department	44.4%	41.7%
Job rotation/mandatory vacation	33.3%	40.0%
Management review	51.9%	45.8%
Management certification of financial statements	34.8%	37.5%
Proactive data monitoring/ analysis	59.7%	50.0%
Rewards for whistleblowers	25.9%	33.3%
Surprise audits	43.3%	50.0%

Sources: 1. *The Fraud Resistant Organization: Tools and Techniques to Deter and Detect Financial Reporting Fraud*, The Center for Audit Quality, 2014; 2. *Report to the Nations on Occupational Fraud and Abuse*, Association of Certified Fraud Examiners, 2014. Provided courtesy of The Center for Audit Quality.

Audit Committee Oversight

The audit committee has primary responsibility to oversee the organization's financial reporting and internal control processes. In fulfilling this responsibility, the audit committee considers the potential for management override of internal controls and oversees management's fraud risk assessment process, as well as antifraud programs and controls. The audit committee also assists in creating an effective "tone at the top" about the importance of honesty and ethical behavior by reinforcing management's zero tolerance for fraud. As a subcommittee of the board of directors, the audit committee is ultimately accountable for mitigating the risk of fraud, as illustrated by Figure 10-7.

Audit committee oversight also serves as a deterrent to fraud by senior management. For example, to increase the likelihood that any attempt by senior management to involve employees in committing or concealing fraud is promptly disclosed, oversight may include:

- Direct reporting of key findings by internal auditors to the audit committee
- Periodic reports by ethics officers about whistleblowing
- Other reports about lack of ethical behavior or suspected fraud

Because the audit committee plays an important role in establishing a proper tone at the top and in overseeing the actions of management, PCAOB auditing standards require the auditor of a public company to evaluate the effectiveness of the board and audit committee as part of the auditor's evaluation of the operating effectiveness of internal control over financial reporting. As part of the evaluation, the auditor might consider the audit committee's independence from management and the level of understanding between management and the audit committee regarding the latter's

FIGURE 10-7 Responsibility for Mitigating Fraud Risk

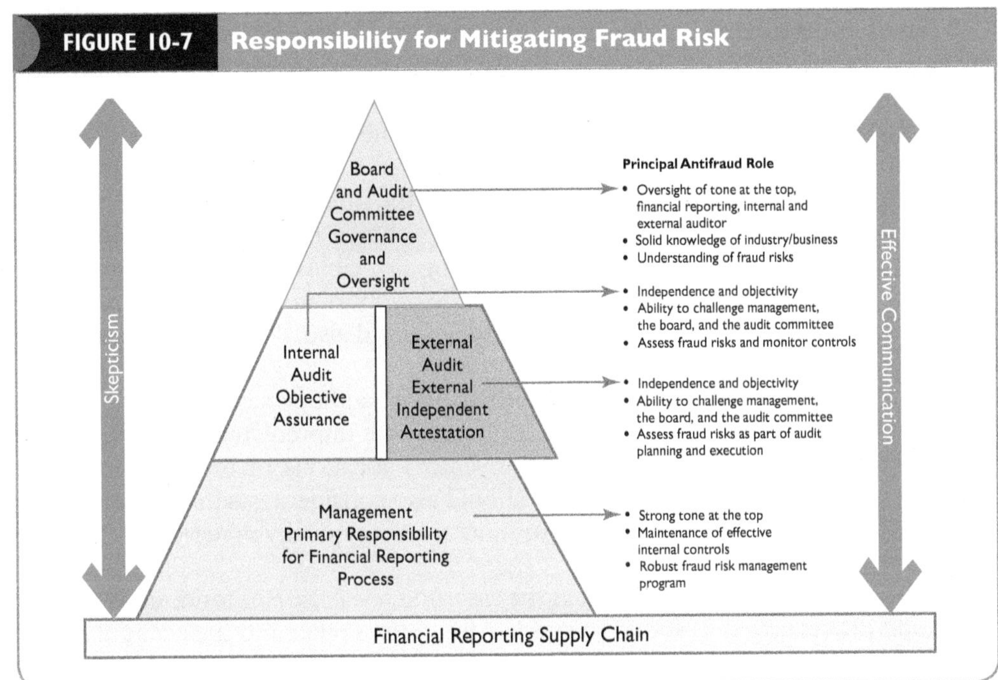

Source: Deterring and Detecting Financial Reporting Fraud: A Platform for Action, provided courtesy of The Center for Audit Quality, 2010. Reprinted with permission.

responsibilities. An external auditor may gather insights by observing interactions between the audit team, the audit committee, and internal audit regarding the level of audit committee commitment to overseeing the financial reporting process. PCAOB auditing standards note that ineffective oversight by the audit committee may be a strong indicator of a material weakness in internal control over financial reporting.

CONCEPT CHECK

1. What are the three conditions of fraud often referred to as "the fraud triangle"?
2. What sources are used by the auditor to gather information to assess fraud risk?

RESPONDING TO THE RISK OF FRAUD

OBJECTIVE 10-5

Develop responses to identified fraud risks.

When the auditor identifies risks of material misstatements due to fraud, auditing standards require the auditor to develop responses to those risks at three levels: overall responses, responses at the assertion level, and responses related to management override. Some responses to fraud risks relate to overall engagement management, such as the types of personnel assigned to the engagement, while other responses are specific to assertions, such as procedures to evaluate the timing of the recording of a revenue transaction. Responses are also needed to address the risk of management override given it is present in all organizations.

Overall Responses to Fraud Risks

Auditors can choose among several overall responses to an increased fraud risk. The auditor should first discuss the auditor's findings about fraud risk with management and obtain management's views of the potential for fraud and existing controls designed to prevent or detect misstatements. As described in the previous section, management may have programs designed to prevent, deter, and detect fraud, as well as controls designed to mitigate specific risks of fraud. Auditors should then consider whether such antifraud programs and controls mitigate the identified risks of material misstatements due to fraud or whether control deficiencies increase the risk of fraud.

If the risk of misstatement due to fraud is increased, more experienced personnel may be assigned to the audit. In some cases, a fraud specialist may be assigned to the audit team. Greater emphasis should also be placed on the importance of increased professional skepticism, such as greater sensitivity in the selection and extent of documentation examined in support of transactions and more corroboration of management explanations about unusual matters affecting the financial statements.

Auditors should also consider management's choice of accounting principles. Careful attention should be placed on accounting principles that involve subjective measurements or complex transactions. Because auditors are required to presume fraud risk is present in revenue recognition, they should also evaluate the company's revenue recognition policies.

Fraud perpetrators are often knowledgeable about audit procedures. For this reason, auditing standards require auditors to incorporate unpredictability in the audit strategy. For example, auditors may visit inventory locations or test accounts that were not tested in prior periods. Auditors should also consider tests that address misappropriation of assets, even when the amounts are not typically material.

Responses to Fraud Risk at the Assertion Level

When the auditor identifies fraud risk at the assertion level, the auditor designs appropriate audit procedures to respond to specific fraud risks related to the account being audited and type of fraud risk identified. For example, if concerns are raised about revenue recognition because of cutoff or channel stuffing, the auditor may review the sales journal for unusual activity near the end of the period and review the terms of sales.

The auditor's response to fraud risk at the assertion level may involve changing the nature, timing, and extent of audit procedures. The nature of the procedures may need to be modified to obtain audit evidence that is more reliable and relevant. For example, the auditor may decide to physically examine certain assets rather than rely on inspection of documentation related to those assets. The timing of procedures may also need to be modified. For example, the auditor may choose to conduct substantive testing at the end of the period rather than performing those procedures based on interim data. The extent of procedures may also be changed to obtain more evidence in response to fraud risk at the assertion level. For example, the auditor may increase sample sizes when testing revenue transactions. Later in this chapter, procedures for specific fraud risk areas are discussed.

Responses to Address Management Override of Controls

The risk of management override of controls exists in almost all audits. Because management is in a unique position to perpetrate fraud by overriding controls that are otherwise operating effectively, auditors must perform procedures in every audit to address the risk of management override. Three procedures must be performed in every audit.

Examine Journal Entries and Other Adjustments for Evidence of Possible Misstatements Due to Fraud Fraud often results from adjustments to amounts reported in the financial statements, even when effective internal controls exist over the rest of the recording processes. The auditor should first obtain an understanding of the entity's financial reporting process, as well as controls over journal entries and other adjustments, and inquire of employees involved in the financial reporting process about inappropriate or unusual activity in processing journal entries and other adjustments. In some organizations, management uses spreadsheet software to make adjustments to financial information generated by the accounting system. These "top-side adjustments" have been used to manipulate financial statements. Auditing standards require testing of journal entries and other financial statement adjustments. The extent of testing is affected by the effectiveness of controls and results of the inquiries.

Review Accounting Estimates for Biases Fraudulent financial reporting is often accomplished through intentional misstatement of accounting estimates. Auditing standards require the auditor to consider the potential for management bias when reviewing current-year estimates. The auditor is required to "look back" at significant prior-year estimates to identify any changes in the company's processes or management's judgments and assumptions that might indicate a potential bias. For example, management's estimates may have been clustered at the high end of the range of acceptable amounts in the prior year and at the low end in the current year.

Accounting standards increasingly require that assets be recorded at fair value. Although market value is readily determinable for some assets, determining fair value often depends on estimates and judgment, creating opportunities for manipulation.

Evaluate the Business Rationale for Significant Unusual Transactions Auditing standards emphasize understanding the underlying business rationale for significant unusual transactions that might be outside the normal course of business for the company. The auditor should gain an understanding of the purposes of significant transactions to assess whether transactions have been entered into to engage in fraudulent financial reporting. For example, the company may engage in financing transactions to avoid reporting liabilities on the balance sheet. The auditor should determine whether the accounting treatment for any unusual transaction is appropriate in the circumstances, and whether information about the transaction is adequately disclosed in the financial statements.

Update Risk Assessment Process

The auditor's assessment of the risks of material misstatement due to fraud should be ongoing throughout the audit and coordinated with the auditor's other risk assessment procedures. Auditors should be alert for the following conditions when doing the audit:

- Discrepancies in the accounting records
- Conflicting or missing audit evidence
- Problematic or unusual relationships between the auditor and management
- Results from substantive or final review stage analytical procedures that indicate a previously unrecognized fraud risk
- Responses to inquiries made throughout the audit that are vague or implausible or that produce evidence that is inconsistent with other information

SPECIFIC FRAUD RISK AREAS

OBJECTIVE 10-6

Recognize specific fraud risk areas and develop procedures to detect fraud.

Depending on the client's industry, certain accounts are especially susceptible to manipulation or theft. Specific high-risk accounts are discussed next, including warning signs of fraud. But even when auditors are armed with knowledge of common fraud symptoms, fraud remains extremely difficult to detect. However, an awareness of common fraud conditions and other fraud detection techniques increases an auditor's likelihood of identifying misstatements due to fraud.

Revenue and Accounts Receivable Fraud Risks

Revenue and related accounts receivable and cash accounts are especially susceptible to manipulation and theft. A study sponsored by the Committee of Sponsoring Organizations (COSO) found that more than half of financial statement frauds involve revenues and accounts receivable. Similarly, because sales are often made for cash or are quickly converted to cash, cash is also highly susceptible to theft.

Fraudulent Financial Reporting Risk for Revenue As a result of the frequency of financial reporting frauds involving revenue recognition, the AICPA and SEC issued guidance dealing with revenue recognition. Auditing standards specifically require auditors to identify revenue recognition as a fraud risk in most audits.

Several reasons make revenue susceptible to manipulation. Most important, revenue is almost always the largest account on the income statement; therefore a misstatement only representing a small percentage of revenues can still have a large effect on income. An overstatement of revenues often increases net income by an

ASSET MISAPPROPRIATION AND COLLUSION AT KOSS CORPORATION

Fraud is more difficult to uncover and often goes undetected for a longer period of time when there is collusion among the perpetrators. Koss Corporation, a manufacturer of headphones located in Milwaukee, and their auditors found this out the hard way when the company was notified by American Express that their principal accounting officer, who also served as vice president of finance and secretary, had been wiring funds from Koss Corporation's account into her personal American Express account to fund her lavish lifestyle. Over a five-year period, she embezzled more than $31 million, which she used to purchase personal items such as cars, fur coats, and expensive jewelry, and to fund travel to exotic locations and extensive home improvements.

The principal accounting officer colluded with two other accounting personnel in order to conceal the fraud. The three together overrode existing internal controls over the processing of payments, and concealed the fraud from management and the auditors. The embezzlement was hidden in the financial statements by overstating assets, expenses, and cost of sales, and understating liabilities and sales. When Koss Corp. ultimately restated their financial statements, their gross profit was actually higher than originally reported.

The principal accounting officer pled guilty to six counts of wire fraud, was sentenced to 11 years in prison, and was required to pay $34 million in restitution. It was a classic case where a trusted, long-time employee was able to commit and conceal fraud for an extended period of time.

Because of the size of the company's market capitalization, Koss was not subject to the Sarbanes–Oxley (SOX) Section 404(b) requirement to obtain their auditor's opinion on the effectiveness of internal control over financial reporting. Some may argue that this is a prime example of why SOX 404(b) audits of internal controls over financial reporting should also be required for non-accelerated filers. If Koss had been subject to an integrated audit, the fraud may have been prevented or at least detected sooner.

Source: Based on Bill Singer, "Sachdeva fraud: Another lost soul without a Wales," *Forbes.com* (January 14, 2011).

equal amount, because related costs of sales are usually not recognized on fictitious or prematurely recognized revenues. Revenue growth is often a key performance indicator for analysts and investors, providing an even greater incentive to inflate revenue. Another reason revenue is susceptible to manipulation is the difficulty of determining the appropriate timing of revenue recognition in many situations.

Three main types of revenue manipulations are:

1. Fictitious revenues
2. Premature revenue recognition
3. Manipulation of adjustments to revenues

Fictitious Revenues The most egregious forms of revenue fraud involve creating fictitious revenues. You may be aware of several recent cases involving fictitious revenues, but this type of fraud is not new. The 1931 *Ultramares* case described in Chapter 5 (p. 122) involved fictitious revenue entries in the general ledger.

Fraud perpetrators often go to great lengths to support fictitious revenue. Fraudulent activity at Equity Funding Corp. of America, which involved issuing fictitious insurance policies, lasted nearly a decade (from 1964 to 1973) and involved dozens of company employees. The perpetrators held file-stuffing parties to create the fictitious policies.

Premature Revenue Recognition Companies often accelerate the timing of revenue recognition to meet earnings or sales forecasts. **Premature revenue recognition**, the recognition of revenue before accounting standards requirements for recording revenue have been met, should be distinguished from cutoff errors, in which transactions are inadvertently recorded in the incorrect period. In the simplest form of accelerated revenue recognition, sales that should have been recorded in the subsequent period are recorded as current period sales.

One method of fraudulently accelerating revenue is through violating accounting rules related to "bill-and-hold" sales. Sales are normally recognized at the time goods are shipped, but in a bill-and-hold sale, the goods are invoiced before they are shipped. These types of sales can be legitimate depending on the contract terms, but can violate accounting standards if the required terms are not met. Another method involves issuing side agreements that modify the terms of the sales transaction. For example, revenue recognition is likely to be inappropriate if a major customer agrees to "buy" a significant amount of inventory at year-end, but a side agreement provides for more favorable pricing and unrestricted return of the goods if not sold by the customer. In some cases, as a result of the terms of the side agreement, the transaction does not qualify as a sale under accounting standards.

Two notable examples of premature revenue recognition involve Bausch and Lomb and Xerox Corporation. In the Bausch and Lomb case, items were shipped that were not ordered by customers, with unrestricted right of return and promises that the goods did not have to be paid for until sold. The revenue recognition issues at Xerox were more complex. Capital equipment leases include sales, financing, and service components. Because the sales component is recognized immediately, Xerox attempted to maximize the amount allocated to this aspect of the transaction.

Manipulation of Adjustments to Revenues The most common adjustment to revenue involves sales returns and allowances. A company may hide sales returns from the auditor to overstate net sales and income. If the returned goods are counted as part of physical inventory, the return may increase reported income. In this case, an asset increase is recognized through the counting of physical inventory, but the reduction in the related accounts receivable balance is not made.

Companies may also understate bad debt expense, in part because significant judgment is required to determine the correct amount. Companies may attempt to reduce bad debt expense by understating the allowance for doubtful accounts. Because the required allowance depends on the age and quality of accounts receivable, some companies have altered the aging of accounts receivable to make them appear more current.

Warning Signs of Revenue Fraud Many potential warning signals or symptoms indicate revenue fraud. Two of the most useful are analytical procedures and documentary discrepancies.

Analytical Procedures Analytical procedures often signal revenue frauds, especially gross margin percentage and accounts receivable turnover. Fictitious revenue overstates the gross margin percentage, and premature revenue recognition also overstates gross margin if the related cost of sales is not recognized. Fictitious revenues also lower accounts receivable turnover, because the fictitious revenues are also included in uncollected receivables. Table 10-4 includes comparative sales, cost of sales, and accounts receivable data for Regina Vacuum, including the year before the fraud and the two fraud years. Notice how both a higher gross profit percentage and lower accounts receivable turnover ratio in the most recent two years that include the fraud helped signal fictitious accounts receivable.

TABLE 10-4 Example of the Effect of Fictitious Receivables on Accounting Ratios Based on Regina Vacuum Company

	Year Ended June 30		
	1988	1987	1986
Sales	$181,123	$126,234	$76,144
Cost of sales	(94,934)	(70,756)	(46,213)
Gross profit	86,189	55,478	29,931
Gross profit percentage	47.6%	43.9%	39.3%
Year-end accounts receivable	51,076	27,801	14,402
Accounts receivable turnover[a]	3.55	4.54	5.29

[a] Accounts receivable turnover calculated as Sales/Ending accounts receivable

POCKETING PARKING CASH

Sam Ralston was in charge of a university parking lot. He was supposed to place a parking receipt on the dash of the car when he received cash from the driver, but he would often collect the cash and wave the driver in without a receipt, particularly for sporting events. The university considered it too expensive to have two employees handle parking, and it was difficult to count the paid vehicles in a lot because some cars were parked by university employees with passes.

After several years, the university rotated Sam to another lot. An astute employee in the accounting office noticed that revenues collected from the lot seemed to increase after Sam's departure. Further investigation revealed that average revenues declined at the new lot to which Sam had been assigned. Confronted with the evidence, Sam confessed and was terminated from employment.

In some frauds, management generated fictitious revenues to make analytical procedures results, such as gross margin, similar to the prior year's. In frauds like this, analytical procedures are typically not useful to signal the fraud, although the manipulation may affect related ratios such as accounts receivable turnover.

Documentary Discrepancies Despite the best efforts of fraud perpetrators, fictitious transactions rarely have the same level of documentary evidence as legitimate transactions. For example, in the well-known fraud at ZZZZ Best, insurance restoration contracts worth millions of dollars were supported by one- or two-page agreements and lacked many of the supporting details and evidence, such as permits, that are normally associated with these types of contracts.

Auditors should be aware of unusual markings and alterations on documents, and they should rely on original rather than duplicate copies of documents. Because fraud perpetrators attempt to conceal fraud, even one unusual transaction in a sample should be considered a potential indicator of fraud that should be investigated.

Misappropriation of Receipts Involving Revenue Although misappropriation of cash receipts is rarely as material as fraudulent reporting of revenues, such frauds can be costly to the organization because of the direct loss of assets. A typical misappropriation of cash involves failure to record a sale or an adjustment to customer accounts receivable to hide the theft.

Failure to Record a Sale One of the most difficult frauds to detect is when a sale is not recorded and the cash from the sale is stolen. Such frauds are easier to detect when goods are shipped on credit to customers. Tracing shipping documents to sales entries in the sales journal and accounting for all shipping documents can be used to verify that all sales have been recorded.

It is much more difficult to verify that all cash sales have been recorded, especially if no shipping documents exist to verify the completeness of sales, and no customer account receivable records support the sale. In such cases, other documentary evidence is necessary to verify that all sales are recorded. For example, a retail establishment may require that all sales be recorded on a cash register. Recorded sales can then be compared to the total amount of sales on the cash register tape. If the sale is not included in the cash register, it is almost impossible to detect the fraud.

Theft of Cash Receipts After a Sale Is Recorded It is much more difficult to hide the theft of cash receipts after a sale is recorded. If a customer's payment is stolen, regular billing of unpaid accounts will quickly uncover the fraud. As a result, to hide the theft, the fraud perpetrator must reduce the customer's account in one of three ways:

1. Record a sales return or allowance
2. Write off the customer's account
3. Apply the payment from another customer to the customer's account, which is also known as lapping

Warning Signs of Misappropriation of Revenues and Cash Receipts Relatively small thefts of sales and related cash receipts are best prevented and detected by internal controls designed to minimize the opportunity for fraud. For detecting larger frauds, analytical procedures and other comparisons may be useful.

Inventory Fraud Risks

Inventory is often the largest account on many companies' balance sheets, and auditors often find it difficult to verify the existence and valuation of inventories. As a result, inventory is susceptible to manipulation by managers who want to achieve certain financial reporting objectives. Because it is also usually readily saleable, inventory is also susceptible to misappropriation.

Fraudulent Financial Reporting Risk for Inventory Fictitious inventory has been at the center of several major cases of fraudulent financial reporting. Many large companies have varied and extensive inventory in multiple locations, making it relatively easy for the company to add fictitious inventory to accounting records.

While auditors are required to verify the existence of physical inventories, audit testing is done on a sample basis, and not all locations with inventory are typically tested. In some cases involving fictitious inventories, auditors informed the client in advance which inventory locations were to be tested. As a result, it was relatively easy for the client to transfer inventories to the locations being tested.

Warning Signs of Inventory Fraud Similar to deceptions involving accounts receivable, many potential warning signals or symptoms point to inventory fraud. Analytical procedures are one useful technique for detecting inventory fraud.

Analytical Procedures Analytical procedures, especially gross margin percentage and inventory turnover, often help uncover inventory fraud. Fictitious inventory understates cost of goods sold and overstates the gross margin percentage. Fictitious inventory also lowers inventory turnover. Table 10-5 is an example of the effects of fictitious inventory on inventory turnover based on the Crazy Eddie fraud. Note that the gross profit percentage did not signal the existence of fictitious inventories, but the significant decrease in inventory turnover was a sign of fictitious inventories.

Purchases and Accounts Payable Fraud Risks

Cases of fraudulent financial reporting involving accounts payable are relatively common although less frequent than frauds involving inventory or accounts receivable. The deliberate understatement of accounts payable generally results in an understatement of purchases and cost of goods sold and an overstatement of net income. Significant misappropriations involving purchases can also occur in the form of payments to fictitious vendors, as well as kickbacks and other illegal arrangements with suppliers.

Fraudulent Financial Reporting Risk for Accounts Payable Companies may engage in deliberate attempts to understate accounts payable and overstate income. This can

TABLE 10-5 Example of the Effect of Fictitious Inventory on Inventory Turnover Based on Crazy Eddie, Inc.

	Year Ended March 1, 1987	Year Ended March 2, 1986	9 Months Ended March 3, 1985
Sales	$352,523	$262,268	$136,319
Cost of sales	(272,255)	(194,371)	(103,421)
Gross profit	80,268	67,897	32,898
Gross profit percentage	22.8%	25.9%	24.1%
Year-end inventories	109,072	59,864	26,543
Inventory turnover[a]	2.50	3.20	5.20[b]

[a] Inventory turnover calculated as Cost of sales/Ending inventory.
[b] Inventory turnover calculated based on annualized Cost of sales.

be accomplished by not recording accounts payable until the subsequent period or by recording fictitious reductions to accounts payable.

All purchases received before the end of the year should be recorded as liabilities. This is relatively easy to verify if the company accounts for prenumbered receiving reports. However, if the receiving reports are not prenumbered or the company deliberately omits receiving reports from the accounting records, it may be difficult for the auditor to verify whether all liabilities have been recorded. In such cases, analytical evidence, such as unusual changes in ratios, may signal that accounts payable are understated.

Companies often have complex arrangements with suppliers that result in reductions to accounts payable for advertising credits and other allowances. These arrangements are often not as well documented as acquisition transactions. Some companies have used fictitious reductions to accounts payable to overstate net income. Therefore, auditors should read agreements with suppliers when amounts are material and make sure the financial statements reflect the substance of the agreements.

Misappropriations in the Acquisition and Payment Cycle The most common fraud in the acquisitions area is for the perpetrator to issue payments to fictitious vendors and deposit the cash in a fictitious account. These frauds can be prevented by allowing payments to be made only to approved vendors and by carefully scrutinizing documentation supporting the acquisitions by authorized personnel before payments are made. In other misappropriation cases, the accounts payable clerk or other employee steals a check to a legitimate vendor. Documentation related to the purchase is then resubmitted for payment to the vendor. Such fraud can be prevented by canceling supporting documents to prevent their use as support for multiple payments.

Other Areas of Fraud Risk

Although some accounts are more susceptible than others, almost every account is subject to manipulation. Let's examine some other accounts with specific risks of fraudulent financial reporting or misappropriation.

Fixed Assets Fixed assets, a large balance sheet account for many companies, are often based on subjectively determined valuations. As a result, fixed assets may be a target for manipulation, especially for companies without material receivables or inventories. For example, companies may capitalize repairs or other operating expenses as fixed assets. Such frauds are relatively easy to detect if the auditor examines evidence supporting fixed asset additions. Nevertheless, prior cases of fraudulent financial reporting, such as WorldCom, have involved improper capitalization of assets.

Because of their value and salability, fixed assets are also targets for theft. This is especially true for fixed assets that are readily portable, such as laptop computers. To reduce the potential for theft, fixed assets should be physically protected whenever possible, engraved, or otherwise permanently labeled, and should be periodically inventoried.

Intangible Assets Intangible assets, such as goodwill, patents, and copyrights, are based mostly on accounting estimates dependent on subjective assumptions about their future benefits to the organization. As a result, their valuations may be subject to manipulation by management. For example, valuation of goodwill is dependent on key assumptions made by management about any potential impairment. To address fraud risks related to intangible assets, auditors often involve specialists, such as a business valuation expert, to assist them in the evaluation of audit evidence related to management's recorded amounts.

Payroll Expenses Payroll is rarely a significant risk area for fraudulent financial reporting. However, companies may overstate inventories and net income by recording excess labor costs in inventory. Company employees are sometimes used to construct fixed assets. Excess labor cost may also be capitalized as fixed assets in these circumstances. Material fringe benefits, such as retirement benefits, are also subject to manipulation.

Payroll fraud involving misappropriation of assets is fairly common, but the amounts involved are often immaterial. The two most common areas of fraud are the creation of fictitious employees and overstatement of individual payroll hours. The existence of fictitious employees can usually be prevented by separation of the human resource and payroll functions. Overstatement of hours is typically prevented by use of time clocks or approval of payroll hours.

RESPONSIBILITIES WHEN FRAUD IS SUSPECTED

OBJECTIVE 10-7

Understand interview techniques and other activities after fraud is suspected.

Frauds are often detected through the receipt of an anonymous tip, by management review, by internal audit, or by accident. Figure 10-8 highlights the most common detection methods, with tips being the most frequent method of fraud detection. External auditors detect a relatively small percentage of frauds, but are more likely to detect fraud when it materially impacts the financial statements.

Responding to Misstatements That May Be the Result of Fraud

Throughout an audit, the auditor continually evaluates whether evidence gathered and other observations made indicate material misstatement due to fraud. All misstatements the auditor finds during the audit should be evaluated for any indication of fraud. When fraud is suspected, the auditor gathers additional information to determine whether fraud actually exists. Often, the auditor begins by making additional inquiries of management and others.

Use of Inquiry Inquiry can be an effective audit evidence gathering technique, as we discussed in Chapter 7, and specific inquiries about the risk of fraud are required by

FIGURE 10-8 Fraud Detection Methods

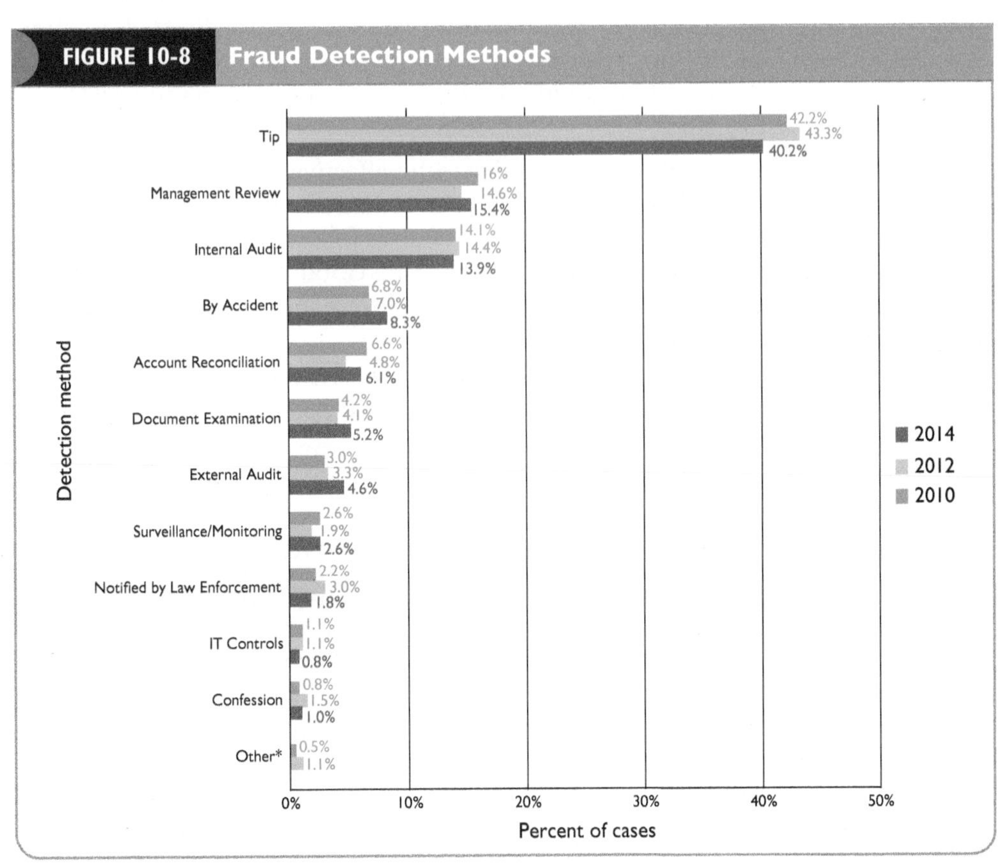

* "Other" category was not included in the 2010 report.

Source: Report to the Nations on Occupational Fraud and Abuse, Association of Certified Fraud Examiners, 2014.

auditing standards. Interviewing allows the auditor to clarify unobservable issues and observe the respondent's verbal and nonverbal responses. Interviewing can also help identify issues omitted from documentation or confirmations. The auditor can also modify questions during the interview based on the interviewee's responses.

Inquiry as an audit evidence technique should be tailored to the purpose for which it is being used. Depending on the purpose, the auditor may ask different types of questions and change the tone of the interview. Additionally, auditors should also apply professional skepticism as they consider how management responds to the auditor's inquiries. One or more of three categories of inquiry can be used, depending on the auditor's objectives.

Categories of Inquiry An auditor uses **informational inquiry** to obtain information about facts and details that the auditor does not have, usually about past or current events or processes. Auditors often use informational inquiry when gathering follow-up evidence about programs and controls or other evidence involving a misstatement or suspected fraud uncovered during the audit. Auditors can most effectively use informational inquiry by posing open-ended questions about details of events, processes, or circumstances.

An auditor uses **assessment inquiry** to corroborate or contradict prior information. The auditor often starts assessment inquiry with broad, open-ended questions that allow the interviewee to provide detailed responses that can later be followed up with more specific questions. One common use of assessment inquiry is to corroborate management responses to earlier inquiries by asking questions of other employees.

Interrogative inquiry is often used to determine if the individual is being deceptive or purposefully omitting disclosure of key knowledge of facts, events, or circumstances. Often, interrogative inquiry is confrontational, given that subjects may be defensive, as they cover up their knowledge of specific facts, events, or circumstances. When using interrogative inquiry, the auditor often asks specific directed questions that seek either a "yes" or "no" response. Interrogative interviewing should typically be done by senior members of the audit team who are experienced and knowledgeable about the client's affairs.

Evaluating Responses to Inquiry For inquiry to be effective, an auditor needs to be skilled at listening and evaluating responses to questions. Typically, the interviewee's initial response will omit useful information. Effective follow-up questions often lead to better information to assess whether fraud exists. Good listening techniques and observation of behavioral cues strengthen the auditor's inquiry techniques, and it helps the auditor apply professional skepticism.

Listening Techniques It is critical for the auditor to use effective listening skills throughout the inquiry process to maintain a questioning mindset. The auditor should stay attentive by maintaining eye contact, nodding in agreement, or demonstrating other signs of comprehension. Auditors should also attempt to avoid preconceived ideas about the information being provided. Good listeners also take advantage of silence to think about the information provided and to prioritize and review information heard.

Observing Behavioral Cues An auditor who is skilled in using inquiry evaluates verbal and nonverbal cues when listening to the interviewee. Verbal cues, such as those outlined in Table 10-6, may indicate the responder's nervousness, lack of knowledge, or even deceit. In addition to observing verbal cues, the use of inquiry allows the auditor to observe nonverbal behaviors. Expert investigators note that subjects who are uncomfortable providing a response to an inquiry often exhibit many of the nonverbal behaviors shown in Table 10-7.

Of course, not everyone who exhibits these behaviors is uncomfortable responding to the auditor's inquiry. The key is to identify when the individual's behavior begins to change from his or her normal behavior. Less-experienced auditors should

TABLE 10-6 Observing Verbal Cues During Inquiry

Verbal Cue Examples	Implications
Extensive use of modifiers, such as "generally," "usually," "often," "normally," etc.	Auditors should probe further to determine whether the use of the modifier indicates that there are exceptions to the processes or circumstances being examined.
Frequent rephrasing by the interviewee of the auditor's question.	Skilled auditors recognize that rephrasing often indicates that the interviewee is uncertain about his or her response or is attempting to stall for time.
Filler terms, such as "um," "well," "to tell you the truth," etc.	Auditors should be alert for filler terms, given that they often suggest that the interviewee is hesitant or unable to respond to the inquiry.
Forgetfulness and acknowledgments of nervousness, such as "I'm a bit nervous" or "I just can't remember."	When this continues to occur, auditors should be concerned about the possibility of deception.
Tolerant attitudes, such as "it depends on the circumstances," and overqualified responses, such as "to the best of my memory."	Dishonest people are often tolerant toward someone who may have committed fraud.
Reluctance to end an interview.	Someone who has been honest generally is ready to terminate an interview. Those trying to deceive may try to continue the inquiry process to convince the auditor that they are telling the truth.

Source: Based on "Association of Certified Fraud Examiners (ACFE) Fraud Manual," The Association of Certified Fraud Examiners (www.acfe.org). Reprinted by permission of The Association of Certified Fraud Examiners.

be cautious when they start to observe unusual behaviors, and they should discuss their concerns with senior members of the audit team before doing anything in response to those behaviors.

Other Responsibilities When Fraud Is Suspected When the auditor suspects that fraud may be present, auditing standards require the auditor to obtain additional evidence to determine whether material fraud has occurred. Auditors often use inquiry, as previously discussed, as part of that information-gathering process.

Audit Software Analysis Auditors often use audit software such as ACL or IDEA to determine whether fraud may exist. For example, software tools can be used to search for fictitious revenue transactions by searching for duplicate sales invoice numbers, or by reconciling databases of sales invoices to databases of shipping records to ensure that all sales are supported by evidence of shipping. Similarly, these tools provide efficient searches for breaks in document sequences, which may indicate misstatements related to the completeness objective for liabilities and expense accounts. Auditors use audit software, including basic spreadsheet tools such as Excel, to sort transactions or account balances into subcategories for further audit testing. For example, an auditor

TABLE 10-7 Observing Nonverbal Cues During Inquiry

Nonverbal Cue Examples	Implications
Physical Barriers—Interviewees may • Block their mouth with their hands, pens, pencils, papers, etc. • Cross their arms or legs. • Use distracting noises, such as finger tapping or drumming. • Lean away from the auditor, usually toward the door or window, in an effort to create spatial distance.	When the interviewee feels uncomfortable with a specific inquiry, he or she may put up nonverbal barriers to try to keep the auditor at a comfortable distance.
Signs of Stress—Interviewees under stress may • Show signs of having a dry mouth. • Lick lips, swallow, or clear their throats frequently. • Fidget, tap their foot, or shake a leg. • Sweat or become flushed in the face. • Avoid eye contact.	In most people, lying will produce stress, which can manifest itself physically.

Source: Based on Sawyer's Internal Auditing, 5th Edition, copyright 2003.

may use spreadsheet options to sort transactions exceeding a certain size or consisting of other unusual characteristics such as nonstandard account numbers or unusual dollar balances (for example, transactions with rounded dollar amounts may be unusual for certain industries).

Auditors also use basic spreadsheet tools, such as Excel, to perform analytical procedures at disaggregated levels. For example, sales can be sorted to disaggregate the data by location, by product type, and across time (monthly) for further analytical procedure analysis. Unusual trends not observable at the aggregate level may be detected when the data is analyzed in greater detail.

Expanded Substantive Testing Auditors may also expand other substantive procedures to address heightened risks of fraud. For example, when there is a risk that sales terms may have been altered to prematurely record revenues, the auditor may modify the accounts receivable confirmation requests to obtain more detailed responses from customers about specific terms of the transactions, such as payment, transfer of custody, and return policy terms. In some instances, the auditor may confirm individual transactions rather than entire account balances, particularly for large transactions recorded close to year-end.

Often the risk of fraud is high for accounts that are based on management's subjective estimation. To respond to heightened risks that management used inappropriate assumptions to estimate account balances, such as the allowance for inventory obsolescence, the auditor may use specialists to assist in evaluating the accuracy and reasonableness of key assumptions. For example, auditors may rely on inventory specialists to assess the obsolescence of electronic parts inventories and business valuation experts to assess the reasonableness of market value assumptions made for certain investments.

Other Audit Implications Auditing standards require the auditor to consider the implications for other aspects of the audit. For example, fraud involving the misappropriation of cash from a small petty cash fund normally is of little significance to the auditor, unless the matter involves higher-level management, which may indicate a more pervasive problem involving management's integrity. This may indicate to the auditor a need to reevaluate the fraud risk assessment and the impact on the nature, timing, and extent of audit evidence.

When the auditor determines that fraud may be present, auditing standards require the auditor to discuss the matter and audit approach for further investigation with an appropriate level of management, even if the matter might be considered inconsequential. The appropriate level of management should be at least one level above those involved, as well as senior management and the audit committee. If the auditor believes that senior management may be involved in the fraud, the auditor should discuss the matter directly with the audit committee.

The discovery that fraud exists also has implications for the public company auditor's report on internal control over financial reporting. PCAOB auditing standards state that fraud of any magnitude by senior management may have important implications for the auditor's opinion on internal control over financial reporting, which is discussed in Chapter 12. This includes fraud by senior management that results in even immaterial misstatements. If the fraud by senior management is a material weakness, the auditor's report on internal control over financial reporting will contain an adverse opinion.

Sometimes, auditors identify risks of material misstatements due to fraud that have internal control implications. In some cases, the auditor's consideration of management's antifraud programs and controls identifies deficiencies that fail to mitigate these risks of fraud. When auditing the financial statements of a public company, the auditor should consider those deficiencies when auditing internal controls over financial reporting, which is described in Chapter 12.

The disclosure of possible fraud to parties other than the client's senior management and its audit committee ordinarily is not part of the auditor's responsibility. As described in Chapter 4, such disclosure is prevented by the auditor's professional code of conduct and may violate legal obligations of confidentiality.

The results of the auditor's procedures may indicate such a significant risk of material misstatement due to fraud that the auditor should consider withdrawing from the audit. Withdrawal may depend on management's integrity and the diligence and cooperation of management and the board of directors in investigating the potential fraud and taking appropriate action.

DOCUMENTING THE FRAUD ASSESSMENT

OBJECTIVE 10-8

Describe information about the fraud risk assessment that must be documented in the working papers.

Auditing standards require that auditors document the following matters related to the auditor's consideration of material misstatements due to fraud:

- Significant decisions made during the discussion among engagement team personnel in planning the audit about the susceptibility of the entity's financial statements to material fraud, including how and when the discussion occurred and who participated.
- Procedures performed to obtain information necessary to identify and assess the risks of material fraud.
- Specific risks of material fraud that were identified at both the overall financial statement level and the assertion level and a description of the auditor's responses to those risks.
- Reasons supporting a conclusion that there is not a significant risk of material improper revenue recognition.
- Results of the procedures performed to address the risk of management override of controls.
- Other conditions and analytical relationships indicating that additional auditing procedures or other responses were required, and the actions taken by the auditor in response.
- The nature of communications about fraud made to management, the audit committee, or others.

CONCEPT CHECK

1. What are the three ways auditors respond to fraud risks?
2. Describe the three main techniques used to manipulate revenue.

SUMMARY

This chapter examined the two types of fraud considered by auditors when auditing financial statements: fraudulent financial reporting and misappropriations of assets. Auditors are responsible for obtaining reasonable assurance that material misstatements are detected, whether due to fraud or error. The chapter described the way auditors gather information to assess fraud risk in every audit and develop appropriate responses to identified fraud risks, after considering the effectiveness of management's antifraud programs and controls. Several illustrations of typical fraud techniques highlighted areas subject to greater fraud risk and provided examples of effective audit procedures to address those risk areas.

Once auditors suspect fraud, they gather additional evidence, often through inquiry, and are responsible for making certain communications about suspected or detected fraud to senior management and the audit committee. Auditors of large public companies must consider the implications of their fraud risk assessments, including any suspected fraud, when arriving at their opinion on the operating effectiveness of internal control over financial reporting.

ESSENTIAL TERMS

Assessment inquiry—inquiry to corroborate or contradict prior information obtained

Earnings management—deliberate actions taken by management to meet earnings objectives

Fraud risk factors—entity factors that increase the risk of fraud

Fraud triangle—represents the three conditions of fraud: incentives/pressures, opportunities, and attitudes/rationalization

Horizontal analysis—analysis of percentage changes in financial statement numbers compared to the previous period

Income smoothing—form of earnings management in which revenues and expenses are shifted between periods to reduce fluctuations in earnings

Informational inquiry—inquiry to obtain information about facts and details the auditor does not have

Interrogative inquiry—inquiry used to determine if the interviewee is being deceptive or purposefully omitting disclosure of key knowledge of facts, events, or circumstances

Premature revenue recognition—recognition of revenue before accounting standards requirements for recording revenue have been met

Vertical analysis—analysis in which financial statement numbers are converted to percentages of a base; also called common-size financial statements

REVIEW QUESTIONS

10-1 (OBJECTIVE 10-1) Define fraudulent financial reporting and give two examples that illustrate fraudulent financial reporting.

10-2 (OBJECTIVE 10-1) Define misappropriation of assets and give two examples of misappropriation of assets.

10-3 (OBJECTIVE 10-2) Give examples of risk factors for fraudulent financial reporting for each of the three fraud conditions: incentives/pressures, opportunities, and attitudes/rationalization.

10-4 (OBJECTIVE 10-2) Give examples of risk factors for misappropriation of assets for each of the three fraud conditions: incentives/pressures, opportunities, and attitudes/rationalization.

10-5 (OBJECTIVE 10-3) What should the audit team consider in its planning discussion about fraud risks?

10-6 (OBJECTIVE 10-3) Auditors are required to make inquiries of individuals in the company when gathering information to assess fraud risk. Identify those with whom the auditor must make inquiries.

10-7 (OBJECTIVE 10-3) The two components of professional skepticism are a questioning mind and a critical assessment of the audit evidence. How do these components help an auditor distinguish an unintentional misstatement from an intentional (fraudulent) misstatement?

10-8 (OBJECTIVE 10-4) Describe the purpose of corporate codes of conduct and identify three examples of items addressed in a typical code of conduct.

10-9 (OBJECTIVE 10-4) Discuss the importance of the control environment, or "setting the tone at the top," in establishing a culture of honesty and integrity in a company.

10-10 (OBJECTIVE 10-4) Distinguish management's responsibility from the audit committee's responsibility for designing and implementing antifraud programs and controls within a company.

10-11 (OBJECTIVE 10-5) Describe the types of overall responses by auditors to address fraud risk.

10-12 (OBJECTIVE 10-5) What three auditor actions are required to address the potential for management override of controls?

10-13 **(OBJECTIVES 10-3, 10-6)** What do auditing standards require the auditor to consider when assessing the risk of material misstatements in revenue?

10-14 **(OBJECTIVE 10-6)** You go through the drive-through window of a fast food restaurant and notice a sign that reads, "Your meal is free if we fail to give you a receipt." Why would the restaurant post this sign?

10-15 **(OBJECTIVE 10-7)** Name the three categories of inquiry and describe the purpose of each when used by an auditor to obtain additional information about a suspected fraud.

10-16 **(OBJECTIVE 10-7)** Identify three verbal and three nonverbal cues that may be observed when making inquiries of an individual who is being deceitful.

10-17 **(OBJECTIVE 10-7)** You have identified a suspected fraud involving the company's controller. What must you do in response to this discovery? How might this discovery affect your report on internal control when auditing a public company?

10-18 **(OBJECTIVE 10-8)** Describe the types of information that should be included in the auditor's working papers as evidence of the auditor's fraud assessment procedures.

MULTIPLE CHOICE QUESTIONS FROM CPA EXAMINATIONS

10-19 **(OBJECTIVES 10-2, 10-3)** The following questions address fraud risk factors and the assessment of fraud risk.

a. Which of the following characteristics is most likely to heighten an auditor's concern about the risk of material misstatements due to fraud in an entity's financial statements?
   (1) The entity's industry is experiencing declining customer demand.
   (2) Employees who handle cash receipts are not bonded.
   (3) Internal auditors have direct access to the board of directors and the entity's management.
   (4) The board of directors is active in overseeing the entity's financial reporting policies.

b. Which of the following circumstances is most likely to cause an auditor to increase the assessment of the risk of material misstatement of the financial statements due to fraud?
   (1) Property and equipment are usually sold at a loss before being fully depreciated.
   (2) Unusual discrepancies exist between the entity's records and confirmation replies.
   (3) Monthly bank reconciliations usually include several in-transit items.
   (4) Clerical errors are listed on a computer-generated exception report.

c. Which of the following statements reflects an auditor's responsibility for detecting fraud?
   (1) An auditor is responsible for detecting employee errors and simple fraud, but not for discovering fraudulent acts involving employee collusion or management override.
   (2) An auditor should plan the audit to detect fraud caused by departures from GAAP.
   (3) An auditor is not responsible for detecting fraud unless the application of auditing standards would result in such detection.
   (4) An auditor should design the audit to provide reasonable assurance of detecting errors and fraud that are material to the financial statements.

10-20 **(OBJECTIVES 10-5, 10-7)** The following questions concern the auditor's responses to the possibility of fraud.

a. When fraud risk factors are identified during an audit, the auditor's documentation should include

	The Risk Factors Identified	The Auditor's Response to The Risk Factors Identified
(1)	Yes	Yes
(2)	Yes	No
(3)	No	Yes
(4)	No	No

b. If an independent audit leading to an opinion on financial statements causes the auditor to believe that a material misstatement due to fraud exists, the auditor should first
   (1) request that management investigate to determine whether fraud has actually occurred.
   (2) make the investigation necessary to determine whether fraud has actually occurred.
   (3) consider the implications for other aspects of the audit and discuss the matter with the appropriate levels of management.
   (4) consider whether fraud was the result of a failure by employees to comply with existing controls.

c. Which of the following is least likely to suggest to an auditor that the client's management may have overridden internal control?
   (1) There are numerous delays in preparing timely internal financial reports.
   (2) Management does not correct internal control weaknesses that it knows about.
   (3) Differences are always disclosed on a computer exception report.
   (4) There have been two new controllers this year.

10-21 **(OBJECTIVE 10-6)** The following questions address fraud risks in specific audit areas and accounts.

a. Cash receipts from sales on account have been misappropriated. Which of the following acts will conceal this embezzlement and be least likely to be detected by the auditor?
   (1) Understating the sales journal
   (2) Overstating the accounts receivable control account
   (3) Overstating the accounts receivable subsidiary records
   (4) Understating the cash receipts journal

b. An auditor discovers that a client's accounts receivable turnover is substantially lower for the current year than for the prior year. This trend may indicate that
   (1) the client recently tightened its credit-granting policies.
   (2) employees have stolen inventory just before year-end.
   (3) fictitious credit sales have been recorded during the year.
   (4) an employee has been lapping receivables in both years.

c. Which of the following internal controls will best detect the theft of valuable items from an inventory that consists of hundreds of different items selling for $1 to $10 and a few items selling for hundreds of dollars?
   (1) Maintain a perpetual inventory of only the more valuable items, with frequent periodic verification of the validity of the perpetual inventory records.
   (2) Have an independent auditing firm examine and report on management's assertion about the design and operating effectiveness of the control activities relevant to inventory.
   (3) Have separate warehouse space for the more valuable items, with sequentially numbered tags.
   (4) Require an authorized officer's signature on all requisitions for the more valuable items.

MULTIPLE CHOICE QUESTIONS FROM BECKER CPA EXAM REVIEW

10-22 **(OBJECTIVES 10-2, 10-3)** The following questions concern auditor responsibilities related to the identification and assessment of fraud risk. Choose the best response.

a. While performing a preliminary assessment for a new client audit, the auditor determines that the client has had excessive growth over the past several years due to

recent acquisitions and internal expansion. Through discussions with management, the auditor concludes that the company's operational staff is too lean and that internal controls in several operational functions may be currently insufficient to accommodate this rapid growth. About which of the following fraud risk factors related to the client would the auditor have the greatest concern?
(1) Rationalization/attitude
(2) Inadequate organizational structure
(3) Opportunity
(4) Incentives/pressures

b. Which one of the following is a true statement about the required fraud risk assessment discussion?
(1) The discussion about the susceptibility of the entity's financial statements to material misstatement must be held separately from the discussion about the susceptibility of the entity's financial statements to fraud.
(2) The discussion should involve all members who participate on the audit team, including the engagement partner.
(3) The discussion should include consideration of the risk of management override of controls.
(4) The fraud risk assessment discussion should occur during the overall review stage of the audit.

c. Which of the following circumstances would most likely cause an auditor to suspect that there are material misstatements in an entity's financial statements?
(1) The entity's management strictly enforces its integrity and ethical values.
(2) Monthly bank reconciliations ordinarily include several outstanding checks.
(3) Management outsources the internal audit function to another CPA firm.
(4) The auditor identifies an inappropriate valuation method that is widely applied by the entity.

DISCUSSION QUESTIONS AND PROBLEMS

10-23 (OBJECTIVE 10-2) During audit planning, an auditor obtained the following information:

1. Significant operations are located and conducted across international borders in jurisdictions where differing business environments and cultures exist.
2. There are recurring attempts by management to justify marginal or inappropriate accounting on the basis of materiality.
3. The company's controller works very hard, including evenings and weekends, and has not taken a vacation in two years.
4. The company's board of directors includes a majority of directors who are independent of management.
5. Assets and revenues are based on significant estimates that involve subjective judgments and uncertainties that are hard to corroborate.
6. The company is marginally able to meet exchange listing and debt covenant requirements.
7. The company's financial performance is threatened by a high degree of competition and market saturation.
8. New accounting pronouncements have resulted in explanatory paragraphs for consistency for the company and other firms in the industry.
9. The company has experienced low turnover in management and its internal audit function.

Required

a. Indicate whether the information indicates an increased risk for fraud.
b. If the information indicates an increased risk of fraud, indicate which fraud condition (incentives/pressures, opportunities, or attitudes/rationalization) is indicated.

10-24 **(OBJECTIVES 10-1, 10-2, 10-3, 10-8)** Assessing the risk of fraud in a financial statement audit is a difficult audit judgment. Auditing standards require the auditor to perform several audit procedures to accumulate information to assess the risk of fraud. You are the in-charge auditor responsible for planning the financial statement audit of Spencer, Inc. Two new staff auditors are assisting you with the initial audit planning and have asked you the following questions.

Required Briefly summarize your response to these staff auditor questions:

a. What is the purpose of the audit team's brainstorming session?
b. Who should attend the brainstorming session and when should the session be held?
c. What is the role of the two staff auditors in the brainstorming session?
d. What is the auditor's responsibility under auditing standards for detecting fraud?
e. What must the auditor document in the working papers related to this brainstorming session?

10-25 **(OBJECTIVES 10-2, 10-6)** The Art Appreciation Society operates a museum for the benefit and enjoyment of the community.

When the museum is open to the public, two clerks who are positioned at the entrance collect a $5.00 admission fee from each nonmember patron. Members of the Art Appreciation Society are permitted to enter free of charge upon presentation of their membership cards.

At the end of each day, one of the clerks delivers the proceeds to the treasurer. The treasurer counts the cash in the presence of the clerk and places it in a safe. Each Friday afternoon, the treasurer and one of the clerks deliver all cash held in the safe to the bank and receive an authenticated deposit slip that provides the basis for the weekly entry in the accounting records.

The Art Appreciation Society board of directors has identified a need to improve its internal controls over cash admission fees. The board has determined that the cost of installing turnstiles, sales booths, or otherwise altering the physical layout of the museum will greatly exceed any benefits. However, the board has agreed that the sale of admission tickets must be an integral part of its improvement efforts.

Smith has been asked by the board of directors of the Art Appreciation Society to review the internal control over cash admission fees and provide suggestions for improvements.

Required a. Indicate weaknesses in their processes over cash admission fees that Smith should identify, and recommend one improvement for each of the weaknesses identified. Organize the answer as indicated in the following illustrative example.*

Weaknesses in Processes	Recommendations
1. There is no basis for establishing the number of paying patrons.	1. Prenumbered admission tickets should be issued upon payment of the admission fee.

b. Indicate which of the weaknesses, if any, increase the likelihood of misappropriation of assets.
c. Indicate which of the weaknesses, if any, increase the likelihood of fraudulent financial reporting.

10-26 **(OBJECTIVES 10-1, 10-2, 10-3, 10-4)** The chapter vignette "Asset Misappropriation and Collusion at Koss Corporation" on page 314 highlights the fraud at Koss Corporation, where the principal accounting officer, Sujata ("Sue") Sachdeva, embezzled approximately $31 million over 5 years to fund her lavish lifestyle. This was a material amount in relation to Koss Corporation's reported net income ($1,976,668 for 2009 and $4,494,289 for 2008). The fraud was not detected by the external auditors. Ms. Sachdeva used wire transfers from the company's account to her American Express account, cashier's checks, manual checks, and traveler's checks drawn on the company's account to fund her purchases.

*Based on AICPA question paper, American Institute of Certified Public Accountants.

The embezzlement was concealed by overstating assets, expenses, and cost of sales and understating liabilities and sales, through the collusion of two employees in the accounting department. At the time Ms. Sachdeva was arrested, more than 22,000 items were confiscated from her home that had been purchased using Koss Corporation funds. Below are just a few examples taken from the court complaint filed against her of purchases Ms. Sachdeva made on her American Express charge card that were later paid for by wire-transferring money from Koss Corp. to American Express as payment:

1. $127,400 from A.C. Zuckennan Jewelers;
2. $670,000 from Au Courant, a women's clothing store;
3. $12,500 from Channel BTQ #16;
4. $14,000 from Georgio-Armani;
5. $40,000 from Holzman's Furs;
6. $255,000 from Karat 22 Jewelers;
7. $1,358,322 from Valentina Boutique, a women's clothing store.

Required

a. Is this fraud an example of asset misappropriation or fraudulent financial reporting?
b. Ms. Sachdeva came from a wealthy family, so the theft was not necessary for her to live comfortably. What incentive and attitude/rationalization do you believe drove Ms. Sachdeva to embezzle? Would there have been behavioral red flags that should have alerted auditors to the fraud?
c. Koss Corporation designs, manufactures, and sells stereo headphones and related accessories. Do you think it would be normal for a manufacturing company to have recurring disbursements to American Express or more than 100 cashier's checks written per year? How could auditors have used audit software to detect these disbursements?
d. What internal controls could Koss Corporation have had in place to prevent employee collusion in the first place or detect the fraud after it began?
e. Ms. Sachdeva avoided using wire transfers during the month of June because she knew this was the month the auditors would review the bank records. What could the auditors have done differently to detect the fraud?
f. Do you believe auditors should be held liable for not detecting fraud when management attempts to hide the fraud and there is employee collusion? Does it matter whether the amounts are material or immaterial to the financial statements?

10-27 **(OBJECTIVES 10-1, 10-4, 10-6)** The following misstatements are included in the accounting records of the Joyce Manufacturing Company:

1. A material sale was recorded on the last day of the year even though the goods were not shipped until three days later.
2. Merchandise was shipped to a customer, but no bill of lading was prepared. Because billings are prepared from bills of lading, the customer was not billed.
3. The controller approved a payment to a consulting firm owned by his sister. The consulting firm did not actually perform any services for the company.
4. The shipping clerk included several additional valuable items in a shipment that were not included in the customer's order and were not invoiced to the customer. The shipping clerk has an arrangement with the customer to share the proceeds from sales of the additional items shipped.
5. Cash paid on accounts receivable was stolen by the mail clerk when the mail was opened.
6. A sales invoice was miscalculated by $1,000 as a result of a key-entry mistake.
7. Cash paid on accounts receivable that had been prelisted by a secretary was stolen by the bookkeeper, who records cash receipts and accounts receivable. He failed to record the transactions.

Required

a. Identify whether each misstatement is an error or fraud.
b. For each misstatement, list one or more procedures that could be implemented to prevent it from occurring on a continuing basis.
c. For each misstatement, identify evidence the auditor can use to uncover it.

10-28 **(OBJECTIVES 10-2, 10-4, 10-6)** Appliances Repair and Service Company bills all customers rather than collecting in cash when services are provided. All mail is opened by

Tom Gyders, treasurer. Gyders, a CPA, is the most qualified person in the company who is in the office daily. Therefore, he can solve problems and respond to customers' needs quickly. Upon receipt of cash, he immediately prepares a listing of the cash and a duplicate deposit slip. Cash is deposited daily. Gyders uses the listing to enter the financial transactions in the computerized accounting records. He also contacts customers about uncollected accounts receivable. Because he is so knowledgeable about the business and each customer, he grants credit, authorizes all sales allowances, and charges off uncollectible accounts. The owner is extremely pleased with the efficiency of the company. He can run the business without spending much time there because of Gyders' effectiveness.

Imagine the owner's surprise when he discovers that Gyders has committed a major theft of the company's cash receipts. He did so by not recording sales, recording improper credits to recorded accounts receivable, and overstating receivables.

Required

a. What weaknesses in the company's processes might have permitted the fraud?
b. What suggestions do you have for changing the process to reduce the future potential for fraud?

10-29 **(OBJECTIVES 10-2, 10-4, 10-6)** The Kowal Manufacturing Company employs about 50 production workers and has the following payroll procedures.

The factory foreman interviews applicants and on the basis of the interview either hires or rejects them. When applicants are hired, they prepare a W-4 form (Employee's Withholding Exemption Certificate) and give it to the foreman. The foreman writes the hourly rate of pay for the new employee in the corner of the W-4 form and then gives the form to a payroll clerk as notice that the worker has been employed. The foreman verbally advises the payroll department of rate adjustments.

A supply of blank time cards is kept in a box near the time clock at the entrance to the factory. Each worker takes a time card on Monday morning, fills in his or her name, and punches the time clock upon their daily arrival and departure. At the end of the week, the workers drop the time cards in a box near the door to the factory.

On Monday morning, the completed time cards are taken from the box by a payroll clerk. One of the payroll clerks then enters the payroll transactions into the computer, which records all information for the payroll journal that was calculated by the clerk and automatically updates the employees' earnings records and general ledger. Employees are automatically removed from the payroll when they fail to turn in a time card.

The payroll checks that are not directly deposited into employees' bank accounts are manually signed by the chief accountant and given to the foreman. The foreman distributes the checks to the workers in the factory and arranges for the delivery of the checks to the workers who are absent. The payroll bank account is reconciled by the chief accountant, who also prepares the various quarterly and annual payroll tax reports.

Required

a. List the most important weaknesses in their processes and state the misstatements that are likely to result from the weakness.
b. For each weakness that increases the likelihood of fraud, identify whether the likely fraud is misappropriation of assets or fraudulent financial reporting.*

10-30 **(OBJECTIVES 10-2, 10-5, 10-8)** This problem requires you to access PCAOB Auditing Standards (pcaobus.org) to answer each of the following questions. You can access those standards by viewing content found under the link "Standards." For each answer, document the paragraph(s) in the relevant standard supporting your answer. Review PCAOB auditing standards related to the auditor's consideration of fraud in a financial statement audit, to answer questions in parts a. through d. Review PCAOB Auditing Standard No. 12, *Identifying and Assessing Risks of Material Misstatement*, to answer parts e. and f.

Required

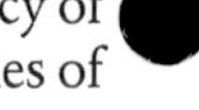

a. You have determined that there is a fraud risk related to the existence and accuracy of inventory. Review the guidance in PCAOB auditing standards to provide examples of

*Based on AICPA question paper, American Institute of Certified Public Accountants.

auditor responses involving changes to the nature, timing, and extent of audit procedures related to this assessed fraud risk for inventory.

b. What do PCAOB auditing standards say about how the auditor should assess risk related to revenue recognition?
c. What examples of auditor responses to fraud risk related to revenue recognition are provided in PCAOB auditing standards?
d. What kind of documentation is required for the auditor's consideration of fraud?
e. What kinds of inquiries about fraud risks are required by PCAOB Standard No. 12?
f. How does PCAOB Standard No. 12 define "fraud risk factors"? Do all conditions have to be present for fraud risk to exist?

10-31 **(OBJECTIVE 10-5)** The following audit procedures are included in the audit program of Harris Manufacturing, Inc.

1. Use audit software to examine journal entries in the sales, cash receipts, purchases, cash disbursements, payroll, and general journals for any amounts exceeding $1 million and for any entries with unusual account codings. Review related supporting documentation for reasonableness.
2. Examine the estimate for the Allowance for Doubtful Accounts recorded in the prior year audited financial statements. Obtain information about receivable writeoffs recorded during the current fiscal year for receivables included in the prior year audited financial statements and obtain other information to perform a hindsight evaluation of the reasonableness of the allowance account included in the prior year audited financial statements.
3. Continue to observe inventories at Harris' two main distribution centers, but for this year examine inventories at its two smaller warehouses not examined in prior years. Management does not expect you to examine those additional warehouses.
4. During the current year, Harris has entered into a joint venture partnership with a company that serves similar customers, but makes an entirely different product than Harris. Inquire of management about the business rationale for this transaction.
5. Review for reasonableness any manual journal entries made by management to adjust the computer-generated accounting records.

Required

a. What is the overarching purpose for performing all of these procedures?
b. How might each audit procedure in 1 through 5 help the auditor identify fraud risk?

10-32 **(OBJECTIVES 10-2, 10-3, 10-4, 10-6)** Each year near the balance sheet date, when the president of Bargon Construction, Inc., takes a 3-week vacation to Hawaii, she signs several checks to pay major bills during the period she is absent. Jack Morgan, head bookkeeper for the company, uses this practice to his advantage. Morgan makes out a check to himself for the amount of a large vendor's invoice and, because there is no acquisitions journal, he records the amount in the cash disbursements journal as an acquisition from the supplier listed on the invoice. He holds the check until several weeks into the subsequent period to make sure that the auditors do not get an opportunity to examine an electronic copy of the cancelled check. Shortly after the first of the year when the president returns, Morgan resubmits the invoice for payment and again records the check in the cash disbursements journal. At that point, he marks the invoice "paid" and files it with all other paid invoices. Morgan has been following this practice successfully for several years and feels confident that he has developed a foolproof method.

Required

a. What is the auditor's responsibility for discovering this type of embezzlement?
b. What weaknesses in Bargon's processes exist?
c. What evidence can the auditor use to uncover the fraud?

10-33 **(OBJECTIVES 10-5, 10-6)** The following are various potential frauds in the sales and collection cycle:

1. The company engaged in channel stuffing by shipping goods to customers that had not been ordered.
2. The allowance for doubtful accounts was understated because the company altered the aging of accounts receivable to reduce the number of days outstanding for delinquent receivables.

3. The accounts receivable clerk stole checks received in the mail and deposited them in an account that he controlled. He issued credit memos to the customers in the amount of the diverted cash receipts.
4. The company contacted a major customer and asked them to accept a major shipment of goods before year-end. The customer was told that they could return the goods without penalty if they were unable to sell the goods.
5. A cashier stole cash receipts that had been recorded in the cash register.
6. The company recorded "bill-and-hold sales" at year-end. Although the invoices were recorded as sales before year-end, the goods were stored in the warehouse and shipped after year-end.
7. The company did not record credit memos for returns received in the last month of the year. The goods received were counted as part of the company's year-end physical inventory procedures.
8. A cashier stole cash receipts by failing to record the sales in the cash register.
9. The CFO recorded fictitious credit sales at the end of the year without recording the associated cost of sales and reduction in inventory.

Required

a. Indicate whether the fraud involves misappropriation of assets or fraudulent financial reporting.
b. For those frauds that involve misappropriation of assets, state a control that would be effective in preventing or detecting the misappropriation.
c. For those frauds that involve fraudulent financial reporting, state an audit procedure that would be effective in detecting the fraud.

10-34 (OBJECTIVES 10-6, 10-7) The following audit procedures are included in the audit program because of heightened risks of material misstatements due to fraud.

1. Use audit software to search cash disbursement master files for missing check numbers.
2. Search the accounts receivable master file for account balances with missing or unusual customer numbers (e.g., "99999").
3. Use audit software to create a list of all credits to the repair and maintenance expense account for follow-up testing.
4. Engage an actuarial specialist to examine management's assumptions about average length of employment and average life expectancy of retirees used in pension accounting decisions.
5. Send confirmations to customers for large sales transactions made in the fourth quarter of the year to obtain customer responses about terms related to the transfer of title and ability to return merchandise.
6. Use audit software to search purchase transactions to identify any with nonstandard vendor numbers or with vendor names reflecting related parties.
7. Search sales databases for missing bill of lading numbers.
8. Use audit software to search for journal entries posted to the sales revenue account from a nonstandard source (other than the daily sales journal).

Required

For each audit procedure:

a. Describe the type of fraud risk that is likely associated with the need for this audit procedure.
b. Identify the related accounts likely affected by the potential fraud misstatement.
c. Identify the related audit objective(s) that this procedure addresses.

CASE

10-35 (OBJECTIVES 10-2, 10-3, 10-4) Kent, CPA, is the engagement partner on the financial statement audit of Super Computer Services Co. (SCS) for the year ended April 30, 2016. On May 6, 2016, Smith, the senior auditor assigned to the engagement, had the following conversation with Kent concerning the planning phase of the audit:*

*Based on AICPA question paper, American Institute of Certified Public Accountants.

KENT: Do you have all the audit programs updated yet for the SCS engagement?

SMITH: Mostly. I still have work to do on the fraud risk assessment.

KENT: Why? Our "errors and irregularities" program from last year is still OK. It has passed peer review several times. Besides, we don't have specific duties regarding fraud. If we find it, we'll deal with it then.

SMITH: I don't think so. That new CEO, Mint, has almost no salary, mostly bonuses and stock options. Doesn't that concern you?

KENT: No. Mint's employment contract was approved by the board of directors just three months ago. It was passed unanimously.

SMITH: I guess so, but Mint told those stock analysts that SCS's earnings would increase 30 percent next year. Can Mint deliver numbers like that?

KENT: Who knows? We're auditing the 2016 financial statements, not 2017. Mint will probably amend that forecast every month between now and next May.

SMITH: Sure, but all this may change our other audit programs.

KENT: No, it won't. The programs are fine as is. If you find fraud in any of your tests, just let me know. Maybe we'll have to extend the tests. Or maybe we'll just report it to the audit committee.

SMITH: What would they do? Green is the audit committee's chair, and remember, Green hired Mint. They've been best friends for years. Besides, Mint is calling all the shots now. Brown, the old CEO, is still on the board, but Brown's never around. Brown's even been skipping the board meetings. Nobody in management or on the board would stand up to Mint.

KENT: That's nothing new. Brown was like that years ago. Brown caused frequent disputes with Jones, CPA, the predecessor auditor. Three years ago, Jones told Brown how ineffective the internal audit department was then. Next thing you know, Jones is out and I'm in. Why bother? I'm just as happy that those understaffed internal auditors don't get in our way. Just remember, the bottom line is... are the financial statements fairly presented? And they always have been. We don't provide any assurances about fraud. That's management's job.

SMITH: But what about the lack of segregation of duties in the cash disbursements department? That clerk could write a check for anything.

KENT: Sure. That's a material weakness every year and probably will be again this year. But we're talking cost-effectiveness here, not fraud. We just have to do lots of testing on cash disbursements and report it again.

SMITH: What about the big layoffs coming up next month? It's more than a rumor. Even the employees know it's going to happen, and they're real uptight about it.

KENT: I know, it's the worst kept secret at SCS, but we don't have to consider that now. Even if it happens, it will only improve next year's financial results. Brown should have let these people go years ago. Let's face it, how else can Mint even come close to the 30 percent earnings increase next year?

Required

a. Describe the fraud risk factors that are indicated in the dialogue.
b. Describe Kent's misconceptions regarding the consideration of fraud in the audit of SCS's financial statements that are contained in the dialogue, and explain why each is a misconception.
c. Describe an auditor's audit documentation requirements regarding the assessment of the risk of material misstatement due to fraud.

INTEGRATED CASE APPLICATION—PINNACLE MANUFACTURING: PART III

10-36 **(OBJECTIVES 10-2, 10-3)** In Parts I (pp. 257–259) and II (pp. 294–296) of this case, you performed preliminary analytical procedures and assessed acceptable audit risk and inherent risk for Pinnacle Manufacturing.

The auditor also assesses fraud risk as part of risk assessment procedures performed during audit planning. You have been invited by the audit partner on the Pinnacle engagement to participate in the fraud brainstorming session conducted as part of audit planning. The purpose of Part III is to identify fraud risks and the response to these fraud risks in the audit of Pinnacle Manufacturing.

Required

a. Use the fraud triangle and information from Parts I and II of this case to identify incentives/pressures, opportunities, and attitudes/rationalizations for Pinnacle to engage in fraudulent financial reporting.
b. Identify one or more fraud risks that you believe exist due to the nature of Pinnacle's industry. Indicate the accounts most likely to be affected by the identified fraud risks.
c. Auditors must generally identify a fraud risk for revenue recognition. Indicate at least two ways that Pinnacle might engage in revenue recognition fraud. Identify the specific nature of the potential fraud and an audit procedure that you would perform to determine whether fraud is occurring.
d. In Part I of this case you performed preliminary analytical procedures on Pinnacle's financial statements. Identify changes in account balances or ratios that you believe indicate the potential for fraud, and describe the nature of the potential fraud.
e. Part II of the case includes 11 situations that you encountered in audit planning. For each situation, describe whether it indicates a potential fraud risk. For each potential fraud risk, identify the related fraud risk triangle element(s).

ACL PROBLEM

10-37 **(OBJECTIVE 10-6)** This problem requires the use of ACL software, which can be accessed through the textbook Web site. Information about downloading and using ACL and the commands used in this problem can also be found on the textbook Web site. You should read all of the reference material preceding the instructions about "Quick Sort" before locating the appropriate command to answer parts a. through e. For this problem, use the file labeled "Pcard Transactions" in the ACL_Cypress_Pcards Project. (Pcards, or purchasing cards, are issued to certain employees to allow them to make purchases on behalf of the company.) The suggested command or other source of information needed to solve the problem requirement is included at the end of each question.

Required

a. Compute the total of the Amount column for comparison to the total Pcard purchases amount as recorded by the client. (Total)
b. Pcard purchases over $1,000 are required to be reviewed by a supervisor. Print any purchases for subsequent follow-up where the total exceeded that amount. (Filter)
c. Identify the three vendors from which the largest total Pcard purchases were made. You will need to save the summary by vendor as a file, by clicking on "Output" within the Summarize command, in order to sort the data. (Summarize and Quick Sort)
d. For the vendor with the largest total amount identified in part c., identify and print out any transactions that exceeded $1,000 for subsequent follow-up. (Filter and Quick Sort)
e. You are concerned that some employees may be structuring transactions to keep them below the $1,000 threshold for approval. Identify transactions that are between $990.00 and $999.99. (Filter)

INTERNAL CONTROL AND COSO FRAMEWORK

CHAPTER 11

LEARNING OBJECTIVES

After studying this chapter, you should be able to

11-1 Describe the three primary objectives of effective internal control.

11-2 Contrast management's responsibilities for maintaining internal control with the auditor's responsibilities for evaluating and reporting on internal control.

11-3 Explain the five components of the COSO internal control framework.

11-4 Explain how general controls and application controls reduce information technology risks.

11-5 Identify types of information technology systems and their impact on internal controls.

Cyberattacks: A New Reality

When Michael Lynton, Chief Executive Officer of Sony Pictures, answered his phone at 6:00 a.m. on a late November 2014 morning, he had no idea of the magnitude of the crisis that was developing. Mr. Lynton was informed that Sony's computer system had been hacked, but the extent of the damage was still unclear. Ultimately, Sony would realize they underestimated the magnitude of the cyberattack at this early stage, but it became all too clear as events unfolded.

Sony had to shut down all of their computer systems in the California offices of Sony Pictures, as well as overseas locations. The company had to resort to manual systems, and had lost the ability to communicate via e-mail or voice mail. According to a New York Times article, it became clear that "mountains of documents had been stolen, internal data centers had been wiped clean, and 75 percent of the servers had been destroyed." The hackers began releasing information to the Internet, including films that had not yet been released, and thousands of e-mails from Mr. Lynton's account.

The company's financial reporting systems were compromised as well. On January 23, 2015, Sony Corp. reported that they would be unable to meet the stock-market deadline for reporting their third-quarter earnings because of the November cyberattack. They anticipated that a portion of the Sony Pictures computer systems would still be offline until at least February, which meant the accountants could not finalize the financial results for one of their subsidiaries.

The Federal Bureau of Investigation was involved in the investigation and ultimately, U.S. authorities concluded the North Korean government was involved in the cyberattack in an effort to stop the film "The Interview" from being released to the public. This was a wake-up call for companies around the world about the reality and extent of cybersecurity threats.

Sources: 1. Michael Cieply and Brooks Barnes, "Sony Cyberattack, First a Nuisance, Swiftly Grew Into a Firestorm," *The New York Times* (December 30, 2014) (www.nytimes.com); 2. Takashi Mochizuki and Megumi Fujikawa, "Sony Hacking Attacks Delay Earnings Report," *The Wall Street Journal* (January 23, 2015) (www.wsj.com).

The opening story involving Sony demonstrates the importance of internal controls and understanding potential threats. Deficiencies in internal control can cause significant losses, can delay financial reporting, or can result in material misstatements in financial statements. Financial reporting problems at companies such as Enron and WorldCom also exposed serious deficiencies in internal control. To address these concerns, Section 404 of the Sarbanes–Oxley Act requires management of U.S. public companies to assess and report on the effectiveness of their internal control over financial reporting, and auditor reports on the effectiveness of internal control are required for larger public companies. Similar legislation has arisen around the world, such as Japan's "J-SOX," which also mandates management and auditor reporting on internal controls for Japanese companies.

In this chapter and the next, we continue our discussion of planning the audit by focusing on the role of internal controls. We first discuss an internal control framework as well as controls unique to computer-based information systems. In the next chapter, we discuss how effective internal controls can reduce planned audit evidence in the audit of financial statements. To support the assessment of the control risk component of the audit risk model, auditors must obtain an understanding of internal control and gather evidence to support that assessment. The chart in the margin shows where these tasks fit into planning the audit.

INTERNAL CONTROL OBJECTIVES

OBJECTIVE 11-1

Describe the three primary objectives of effective internal control.

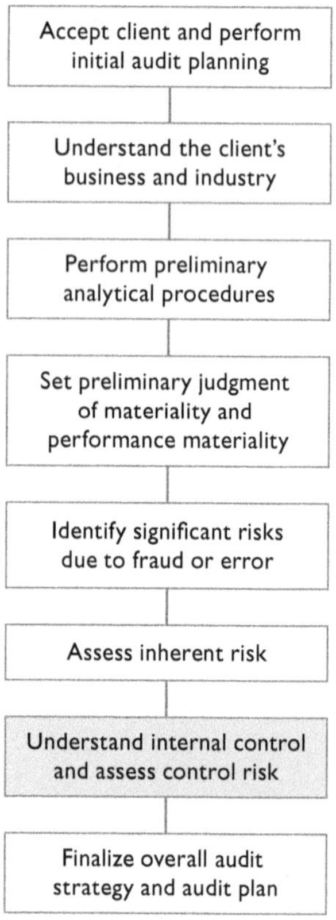

A system of internal control consists of policies and procedures designed to provide management with reasonable assurance that the company achieves its objectives and goals. These policies and procedures are often called controls, and collectively, they make up the entity's **internal control**. Management typically has three broad objectives in designing an effective internal control system:

1. *Reliability of reporting.* This objective relates to internal and external financial reporting as well as nonfinancial reporting; however, in this chapter we focus our discussion on the reliability of external financial reporting. As we discussed in Chapter 6, management is responsible for preparing financial statements for investors, creditors, and other users. Management has both a legal and professional responsibility to be sure that the information is fairly presented in accordance with reporting requirements of accounting frameworks such as U.S. GAAP and IFRS. The objective of effective internal control over financial reporting is to fulfill these financial reporting responsibilities.
2. *Efficiency and effectiveness of operations.* Controls within a company encourage efficient and effective use of its resources to optimize the company's goals. An important objective of these controls is accurate financial and nonfinancial information about the company's operations for decision making.
3. *Compliance with laws and regulations.* Section 404 requires management of all public companies to issue a report about the operating effectiveness of internal control over financial reporting. In addition to the legal provisions of Section 404, public, nonpublic, and not-for-profit organizations are required to follow many laws and regulations. Some relate to accounting only indirectly, such as environmental protection and civil rights laws. Others are closely related to accounting, such as income tax regulations and anti-fraud legal provisions.

Management designs systems of internal control to accomplish all three objectives. The auditor's focus in both the audit of financial statements and the audit of internal controls is on controls over the reliability of financial reporting plus those controls over operations and compliance with laws and regulations that could materially affect financial reporting.

Accept client and perform initial audit planning

Understand the client's business and industry

Perform preliminary analytical procedures

Set preliminary judgment of materiality and performance materiality

Identify significant risks due to fraud or error

Assess inherent risk

Understand internal control and assess control risk

Finalize overall audit strategy and audit plan

MANAGEMENT AND AUDITOR RESPONSIBILITIES FOR INTERNAL CONTROL

OBJECTIVE 11-2

Contrast management's responsibilities for maintaining internal control with the auditor's responsibilities for evaluating and reporting on internal control.

Responsibilities for internal controls differ between management and the auditor. Management is responsible for establishing and maintaining the entity's internal controls. Management is also required by Section 404 to publicly report on the operating effectiveness of those controls. In contrast, the auditor's responsibilities include understanding and testing internal control over financial reporting. Auditors of larger public companies are required by the SEC to annually issue an audit report on the operating effectiveness of those controls.

Management's Responsibilities for Establishing Internal Control

Management, not the auditor, must establish and maintain the entity's internal controls. This concept is consistent with the requirement that management, not the auditor, is responsible for the preparation of financial statements in accordance with applicable accounting frameworks such as GAAP or IFRS. Two key concepts underlie management's design and implementation of internal control—reasonable assurance and inherent limitations.

Reasonable Assurance A company should develop internal controls that provide reasonable, but not absolute, assurance that the financial statements are fairly stated. Internal controls are developed by management after considering both the costs and benefits of the controls. Reasonable assurance is a high level of assurance that allows for only a low likelihood that material misstatements will not be prevented or detected on a timely basis by internal control.

Inherent Limitations Internal controls can never be completely effective, regardless of the care followed in their design and implementation. Even if management can design an ideal system, its effectiveness depends on the competency and dependability of the people using it. Assume, for example, that a carefully developed procedure for counting inventory requires two employees to count independently. If neither of the employees understands the instructions or if both are careless in doing the counts, the inventory count is likely to be wrong. Even if the count is correct, management might override the procedure and instruct an employee to increase the count to improve reported earnings. Similarly, the employees might decide to overstate the counts to intentionally cover up a theft of inventory by one or both of them. An act of two or more employees who conspire to steal assets or misstate records is called **collusion**.

Management's Section 404 Reporting Responsibilities

Section 404(a) of the Sarbanes–Oxley Act requires management of all public companies to issue an internal control report that includes the following:

- A statement that management is responsible for establishing and maintaining an adequate internal control structure and procedures for financial reporting
- An assessment of the effectiveness of the internal control structure and procedures for financial reporting as of the end of the company's fiscal year

Management must also identify the framework used to evaluate the effectiveness of internal control. The internal control framework used by most U.S. companies is the Committee of Sponsoring Organizations of the Treadway Commission (COSO) *Internal Control—Integrated Framework*, which was originally published in 1992 and updated in 2013. Other internal control frameworks exist around the world, such as the Financial Reporting Council of the United Kingdom's *Guidance on Risk Management, Internal Control and Related Financial and Business Reporting*, and Canada's *Guidance on Assessing Control* (known as "CoCo").

Management's assessment of internal control over financial reporting consists of two key aspects. First, management must evaluate the *design* of internal control over financial reporting. Second, management must test the *operating effectiveness* of those controls.

FIGURE 11-1 Example Section 404 Management Report on Internal Control Over Financial Reporting

> The management of Marble Corporation is responsible for establishing and maintaining adequate internal control over financial reporting. Marble's internal control system was designed to provide reasonable assurance to the company's management and board of directors regarding the preparation and fair presentation of published financial statements.
>
> Marble management assessed the effectiveness of the company's internal control over financial reporting as of December 31, 2016. In making this assessment, it used the criteria set forth by the Committee of Sponsoring Organizations of the Treadway Commission (COSO) in *Internal Control—Integrated Framework*. Based on our assessment, we believe that, as of December 31, 2016, the company's internal control over financial reporting is effective based on those criteria.
>
> Marble's independent auditors have issued an audit report on our assessment of the company's internal control over financial reporting. This report appears on the following page.
>
> February 15, 2017
>
> Fred Narsky, President   Karen Wilson, Chief Financial Officer

Design of Internal Control Management must evaluate whether the controls are designed and put in place to prevent or detect material misstatements in the financial statements. Management's focus is on controls that address risks related to all relevant assertions for all significant accounts and disclosures in the financial statements. This includes evaluating how significant transactions are initiated, authorized, recorded, processed, and reported to identify points in the flow of transactions where material misstatements due to error or fraud could occur.

Operating Effectiveness of Controls In addition, management must test the operating effectiveness of controls. The testing objective is to determine whether the controls are operating as designed and whether the person performing the control possesses the necessary authority and qualifications to perform the control effectively. Management's test results, which must also be documented, form the basis for management's assertion at the end of the fiscal year about the controls' operating effectiveness. Management must disclose any material weakness in internal control. Even if only one material weakness is present, management must conclude that the company's internal control over financial reporting is not effective.

The SEC requires management to include its report on internal control in its annual Form 10-K report filed with the SEC. Figure 11-1 includes an example of management's report on internal control that complies with Section 404 requirements and related SEC rules.

Auditor Responsibilities for Understanding Internal Control

One of the principles in the preface to the clarified AICPA auditing standards is that the auditor "identifies and assesses risks of material misstatement, whether due to fraud or error, based on an understanding of the entity and its environment, including the entity's internal control."[1] Auditing standards require the auditor to obtain an understanding of internal control relevant to the audit on every audit engagement. Auditors are primarily concerned about controls over the reliability of financial reporting and controls over classes of transactions. We briefly discuss auditor responsibilities below but provide a more extensive discussion in the next chapter.

Controls Over the Reliability of Financial Reporting Auditors focus primarily on controls related to the first of management's internal control concerns: reliability of financial reporting. Financial statements are not likely to correctly reflect GAAP or IFRS if internal controls over financial reporting are inadequate. Unlike the client, the

[1] Copyright by American Institute of CPAs. All rights reserved. Used with permission.

auditor is less concerned with controls that affect the efficiency and effectiveness of company operations, because such controls may not influence the fair presentation of financial statements. Auditors should not, however, ignore controls affecting internal management information, such as budgets and internal performance reports. These types of information are often important sources used by management to run the business and can be important sources of evidence that help the auditor decide whether the financial statements are fairly presented. If the controls over these internal reports are inadequate, the value of the reports as evidence diminishes.

Controls Over Classes of Transactions Auditors emphasize internal control over classes of transactions rather than account balances because the accuracy of accounting system outputs (account balances) depends heavily on the accuracy of inputs and processing (transactions). For example, if products sold, units shipped, or unit selling prices are wrong in billing customers for sales, both sales and accounts receivable will be misstated. On the other hand, if controls are adequate to ensure correct billings, cash receipts, sales returns and allowances, and write-offs, the ending balance in accounts receivable is likely to be correct. Because of the emphasis on classes of transactions, auditors are primarily concerned with the transaction-related audit objectives discussed in Chapter 6 when assessing internal controls over financial reporting.

Even though auditors emphasize transaction-related controls, the auditor must also gain an understanding of controls over ending account balance and presentation and disclosure objectives. For example, transaction-related audit objectives typically have no effect on two balance-related audit objectives: realizable value and rights and obligations. They also are unlikely to have an effect on the four presentation and disclosure objectives. The auditor is likely to evaluate separately whether management has implemented internal control for each of these two account balance objectives and the four presentation and disclosure objectives.

Auditor Responsibilities for Reporting on Internal Control

Section 404(b) of the Sarbanes–Oxley Act requires that the auditor report on the effectiveness of internal control over financial reporting. As discussed in Chapter 1, as a result of the Dodd–Frank federal financial reform legislation passed by Congress in July 2010, only larger public companies (accelerated filers) are required to obtain an audit report on internal control over financial reporting.

To express an opinion on these controls, the auditor obtains an understanding of and performs tests of controls for all significant account balances, classes of transactions, and disclosures and related assertions in the financial statements. We will discuss tests of controls in Chapter 12 and in considerable detail in several other chapters throughout the text. Auditor reporting on internal control is also discussed in Chapter 12.

CONCEPT CHECK

1. Describe the three broad objectives management has when designing effective internal control.
2. Section 404(a) of the Sarbanes–Oxley Act requires management to issue a report on internal control over financial reporting. Identify the specific Section 404(a) reporting requirements for management.

COSO COMPONENTS OF INTERNAL CONTROL

OBJECTIVE 11-3

Explain the five components of the COSO internal control framework.

COSO's *Internal Control—Integrated Framework* was first developed in 1992 and has become the most widely accepted internal control framework in the United States and the world. Since the original development of the Framework, business and operating environments have become more global, complex, and technologically driven. Stakeholders have become more engaged, seeking greater transparency and accountability for the integrity

FIGURE 11-2 COSO Internal Control Objectives and Components

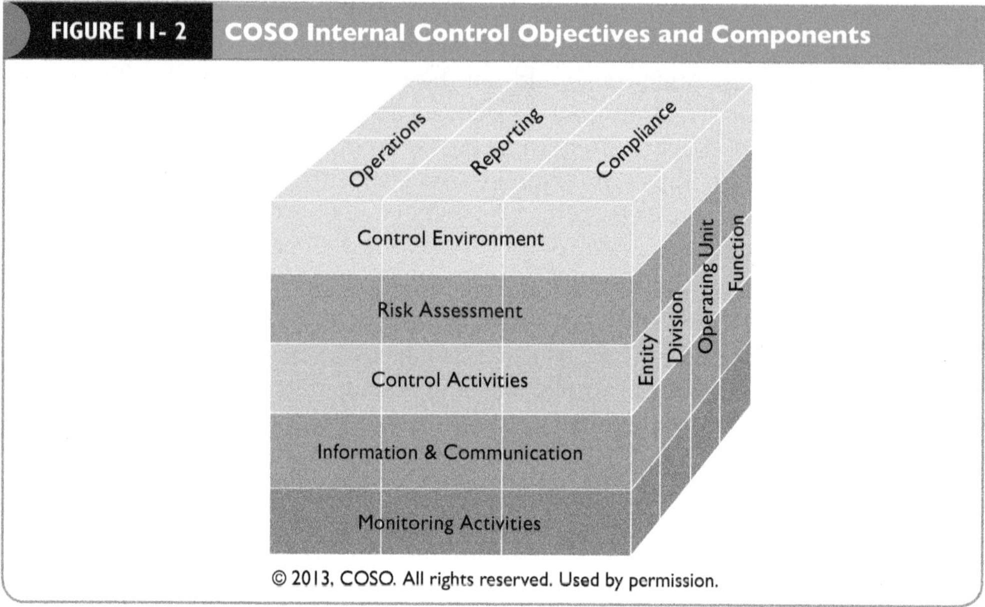

of systems of internal control, including controls related to reporting objectives beyond financial reporting, such as corporate responsibility and sustainability. COSO updated the Framework in 2013 to make it more relevant in the current business environment. The general structure of the Framework remains unchanged, but the updated Framework provides a principles-based approach that provides additional guidance on designing and implementing effective systems of internal control.

The COSO Framework describes five components of internal control that management designs and implements to provide reasonable assurance that its control objectives will be met. Each component contains many controls, but auditors concentrate on those designed to prevent or detect material misstatements in the financial statements. The COSO internal control components include the following:

1. Control environment
2. Risk assessment
3. Control activities
4. Information and communication
5. Monitoring

As illustrated in Figure 11-2, COSO represents the direct relationship between the three internal control objectives, the five components of internal control, and the organizational structure in the form of a cube.

Within each of the COSO components, the updated Framework includes a total of seventeen broad principles that provide more guidance to support the respective component. The **COSO principles** apply across all types of entities and to each of the internal control objectives: reporting, operations, and compliance. All of the seventeen principles must be present and functioning for internal controls to be effective. We introduce these principles as we discuss each of the five components in greater detail.

The Control Environment

The **control environment** consists of the actions, policies, and procedures that reflect the overall attitudes of top management, directors, and owners of an entity about internal control and its importance to the entity. As shown in Figure 11-3, the control environment serves as the umbrella for the other four components. Without an effective control environment, the other four components are unlikely to result in effective internal control, regardless of their quality. The essence of an effectively controlled organization lies in the attitude of its board of directors and senior management. If top management believes that control is important, others in the organization will sense this commitment and respond by conscientiously observing the controls established. If members of the organization believe that control is not an important concern to top management, it is almost certain that management's control objectives will not be effectively achieved.

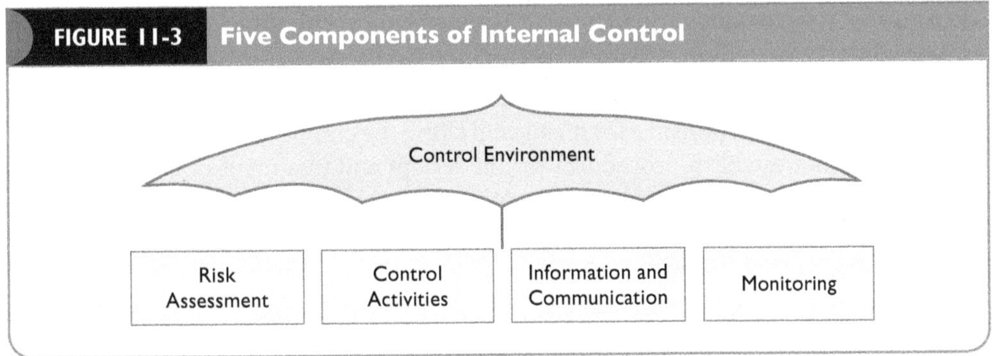

FIGURE 11-3 Five Components of Internal Control

The five underlying principles related to the control environment include a commitment to integrity and ethical values; an independent board of directors that is responsible for oversight of internal controls; establishing appropriate structures and reporting lines; a commitment to attracting, developing, and retaining competent personnel; and holding individuals accountable for internal control responsibilities. To understand and assess the control environment, auditors should consider these important control subcomponents.

Integrity and Ethical Values Integrity and ethical values are the product of the entity's ethical and behavioral standards, as well as how they are communicated and reinforced in practice. They include management's actions to remove or reduce incentives and temptations that might prompt personnel to engage in dishonest, illegal, or unethical acts. They also include the communication of entity values and behavioral standards to personnel through policy statements, codes of conduct, and by example.

Management, through its activities, provides clear signals to employees about the importance of internal control. For example, does management take significant risks or is it risk averse? Are sales and earnings targets unrealistic, and are employees encouraged to take aggressive actions to meet those targets? Can management be described as "fat and bureaucratic"; "lean and mean" (dominated by one or a few individuals, resulting in an imbalance of power); or "just right"? Understanding these and similar aspects of management's philosophy and operating style gives the auditor a sense of management's attitude about internal control.

Board of Director or Audit Committee Participation The board of directors is essential for effective corporate governance because it has ultimate responsibility to make sure management implements proper internal control and financial reporting processes. An effective board of directors is independent of management, and its members stay involved in and scrutinize management's activities. Although the board delegates responsibility for internal control to management, the board must exercise oversight of the design and performance of controls. In addition, an active and objective board can reduce the likelihood that management overrides existing controls.

To assist the board in its oversight, the board creates an audit committee that is charged with oversight responsibility for financial reporting. The audit committee is also responsible for maintaining ongoing communication with both external and internal auditors, including the approval of audit and nonaudit services done by auditors for public companies. This allows the auditors and directors to discuss matters that might relate to such things as management integrity or the appropriateness of actions taken by management.

The audit committee's independence from management and knowledge of financial reporting issues are important determinants of its ability to effectively evaluate internal controls and financial statements prepared by management. The Sarbanes–Oxley Act directed the SEC to require the national stock exchanges (NYSE and NASDAQ) to strengthen audit committee requirements for public companies listing securities on the exchanges. In response, the exchanges will not list any security from a company with an audit committee that:

1. Is not comprised solely of independent directors
2. Is not solely responsible for hiring and firing the company's auditors
3. Does not establish procedures for the receipt and treatment of complaints (e.g., "whistleblowing") regarding accounting, internal control, or auditing matters
4. Does not have the ability to engage its own counsel and other advisors
5. Is inadequately funded

Similar provisions exist outside the U.S., such as the European Commission's 8th Directive, which requires each public-interest entity to have an audit committee with at least one member who is independent and who has competence in accounting or auditing. PCAOB auditing standards require the auditor to evaluate the effectiveness of the audit committee's oversight of the company's external financial reporting and internal control over financial reporting.

Many privately held companies also create an effective audit committee. For other privately held companies, governance may be provided by owners, partners, trustees, or a committee of management, such as a finance or budget committee. Individuals responsible for overseeing the strategic direction of the entity and the accountability of the entity, including financial reporting and disclosure, are called **those charged with governance** by auditing standards.

Organizational Structure The entity's organizational structure defines the existing lines of responsibility and authority. As shown in the COSO cube in Figure 11-2 (p. 340), the organizational structure can consist of the entity level, divisions, operating units, and functions within those units, and controls operate at each of these levels. By understanding the client's organizational structure, the auditor can learn the management and functional elements of the business and perceive how controls are implemented.

Commitment to Competence Competence is the knowledge and skills necessary to accomplish tasks that define an individual's job. Commitment to competence includes management's consideration of the competence levels for specific jobs and how those levels translate into requisite skills and knowledge. If employees are competent and trustworthy, other controls can be absent, and reliable financial statements will still result. Incompetent or dishonest people can reduce the system to a shambles—even if there are numerous controls in place. Honest, efficient people are able to perform at a high level even when there are few other controls to support them. However, even competent and trustworthy people can have shortcomings. For example, they can become bored or dissatisfied, personal problems can disrupt their performance, or their goals may change. Because of the importance of competent, trustworthy personnel in providing effective control, the methods by which persons are hired, evaluated, trained, promoted, and compensated are an important part of internal control.

Accountability Management and the board of directors are responsible for communicating expectations and holding individuals accountable for internal control duties. The effectiveness of this process depends on the other subcomponents discussed above. For example, management must set the appropriate tone and put in place appropriate structures and reporting lines in order to hold individuals accountable. Incentives should be provided for employees to fulfill their internal control duties.

Risk Assessment

Risk assessment involves a process for identifying and analyzing risks that may prevent the organization from achieving its objectives. The four underlying principles related to risk assessment are that the organization should have clear objectives in order to be able to identify and assess the risks relating to those objectives; should determine how the risks should be managed; should consider the potential for fraudulent behavior; and should monitor changes that could impact internal controls. Specific risks related to

USING KEY RISK INDICATORS FOR RISK AWARENESS

COSO has issued thought guidance to assist management and the board in the development of key risk indicators (KRIs) to provide early signals of increasing risk exposures. KRIs help management and the board be prepared for and better manage risk events that may arise in the future.

KRIs should be distinguished from key performance indicators (KPIs). KPIs are metrics that provide a high-level overview of past performance. Such measures may not provide a warning of developing risks because they focus on results that have already occurred. In contrast, KRIs are leading indicators of emerging risks. For example, data about recent write-offs of accounts receivable is a key performance indicator for accounts receivable collection. In contrast, analysis of financial results of major customers could be used as a key risk indicator of future collection concerns.

KRIs can provide timely and relevant information for effective risk oversight. Ideally, these indicators should be developed by teams that include risk management staff and business unit managers, and developed in conjunction with strategic plans for business units. Developing KRIs can result in improved performance by reducing losses and identifying risks that can be strategically exploited to the company's benefit. Use of KRIs can improve processes by reducing the risk of service disruptions and episodes of crisis management. Well-developed KRIs reduce surprises by placing management and boards in a proactive, rather than a reactive stance.

Source: Mark Beasley, Bruce Branson, and Bonnie Hancock, "Developing Key Risk Indicators to Strengthen Enterprise Risk Management," COSO, December 2010 (www.coso.org).

information technology (IT) should be considered, as these risks can lead to substantial losses if ignored, as demonstrated in the opening vignette related to the cyberattack on Sony Pictures. If IT systems fail, organizations can be paralyzed by the inability to retrieve information or by the use of unreliable information caused by processing errors. Given the significance of IT risks, we discuss these in more detail later in the chapter.

Risk assessment specifically related to financial reporting involves management's identification and analysis of risks relevant to the preparation of financial statements in conformity with appropriate accounting standards. For example, if a company frequently sells products at a price below inventory cost because of rapid technology changes, it is essential for the company to incorporate adequate controls to address the risk of overstating inventory. Similarly, failure to meet prior objectives, quality of personnel, geographic dispersion of company operations, significance and complexity of core business processes, introduction of new information technologies, economic downturns, and entrance of new competitors are examples of factors that may lead to increased risk. Once management identifies a risk, it estimates the significance of that risk, assesses the likelihood of the risk occurring, and develops specific actions that need to be taken to reduce the risk to an acceptable level.

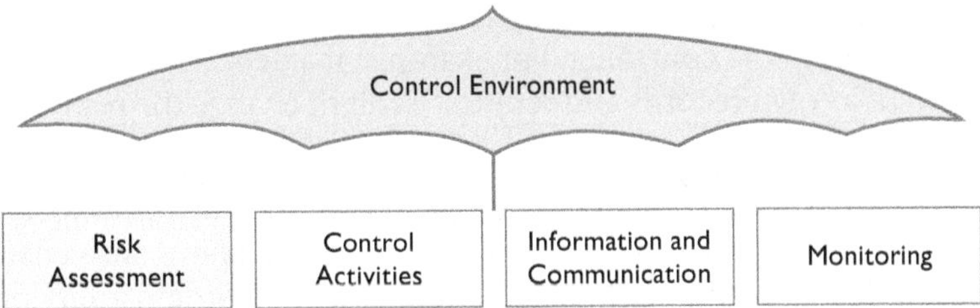

Management's risk assessment differs from but is closely related to the auditor's risk assessment discussed in Chapter 9. While management assesses risks as a part of designing and operating internal controls to minimize errors and fraud, auditors assess risks to decide the evidence needed in the audit. If management effectively assesses and responds to risks, the auditor will typically accumulate less evidence than when management fails to identify or respond to significant risks.

Control Activities

Control activities are the policies and procedures, in addition to those included in the other four control components, that help ensure that necessary actions are taken to address risks to the achievement of the entity's objectives. There are three underlying principles related to control activities: developing control activities that mitigate risks to an acceptable level, developing general controls over technology, and establishing appropriate policies, procedures, and expectations. There are potentially many such control activities in any entity, including controls performed manually and controls built into a computer-based system (automated controls). The control activities generally fall into the following five types, which are discussed next:

1. Adequate separation of duties
2. Proper authorization of transactions and activities
3. Adequate documents and records
4. Physical control over assets and records
5. Independent checks on performance

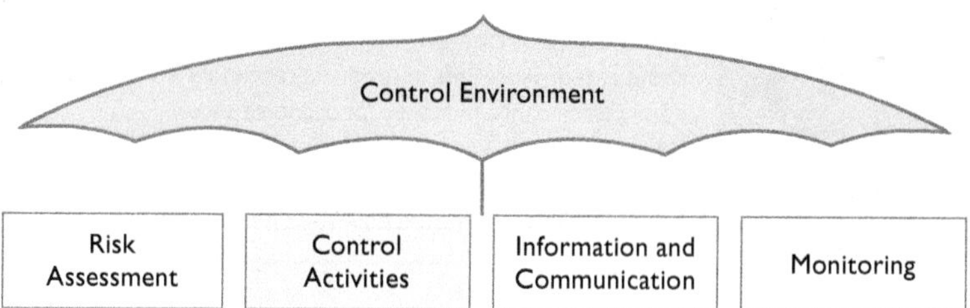

Adequate Separation of Duties Four general guidelines for adequate **separation of duties** to prevent both fraud and errors are especially significant for auditors.

Separation of the Custody of Assets from Accounting To protect a company from embezzlement, a person who has temporary or permanent custody of an asset should not account for that asset. Allowing one person to perform both functions increases the risk of that person disposing of the asset for personal gain and adjusting the records to cover up the theft. If the cashier, for example, receives cash and is responsible for data entry for cash receipts and sales, that person could pocket the cash received and adjust the customer's account by failing to record a sale or by recording a fictitious credit to the account.

Separation of the Authorization of Transactions from the Custody of Related Assets It is desirable to prevent persons who authorize transactions from having control over the related asset, to reduce the likelihood of embezzlement. For example, the same person should not authorize the payment of a vendor's invoice and also approve the disbursement of funds to pay the bill.

Separation of Operational Responsibility from Record-Keeping Responsibility To ensure unbiased information, record keeping is typically the responsibility of a separate department reporting to the controller. For example, if a department or division oversees the creation of its own records and reports, it might change the results to improve its reported performance.

Separation of IT Duties from User Departments As the level of complexity of IT systems increases, the separation of authorization, record keeping, and custody often becomes blurred. For example, sales agents may enter customer orders online. The computer authorizes those sales based on its comparison of customer credit limits to the master file and posts all approved sales in the sales cycle journals. Therefore, the computer plays a significant role in the authorization and record keeping of sales transactions. To compensate for these potential overlaps of duties, it is important for companies to separate major IT-related functions from key user department functions. In this example, responsibility for designing and controlling accounting software programs that contain the sales authorization and posting controls should be under the authority of IT, whereas the ability to update information in the master file of customer credit limits should reside in the company's credit department outside the IT function.

Proper Authorization of Transactions and Activities Every transaction must be properly authorized if controls are to be satisfactory. If any person in an organization could acquire or expend assets at will, complete chaos would result. Authorization can be either general or specific. Under **general authorization**, management establishes policies and subordinates are instructed to implement these general authorizations by approving all transactions within the limits set by the policy. General authorization decisions include the issuance of fixed price lists for the sale of products, credit limits for customers, and fixed reorder points for making acquisitions.

Specific authorization applies to individual transactions. For certain transactions, management prefers to authorize each transaction. An example is the authorization of a sales transaction by the sales manager for a used-car company.

The distinction between authorization and approval is also important. Authorization is a policy decision for either a general class of transactions or specific transactions. Approval is the implementation of management's general authorization decisions. An example of a general authorization is management setting a policy authorizing the ordering of inventory when less than a three-week supply is on hand. When a department orders inventory, the clerk responsible for maintaining the perpetual record approves the order to indicate that the authorization policy has been met. In other cases, the computer approves the transactions by comparing quantities of inventory on hand to a master file of reorder points and automatically submits purchase orders to authorized suppliers in the vendor master file. In this case, the computer is performing the approval function using preauthorized information contained in the master files.

Adequate Documents and Records Documents and records are the records upon which transactions are entered and summarized. They include such diverse items as sales invoices, purchase orders, subsidiary records, sales journals, and employee time reports. Many of these documents and records are maintained in electronic rather than paper formats. Adequate documents are essential for correct recording of transactions and control of assets. For example, if the receiving department completes an electronic receiving report when material is received, the accounts payable computer application can verify the quantity and description on the vendor's invoice by comparing them with the information on the receiving report, with exceptions resolved by the accounts payable department.

Certain principles dictate the proper design and use of documents and records. Documents and records should be:

- Prenumbered consecutively to facilitate control over missing documents and records and as an aid in locating them when they are needed at a later date. Prenumbered documents and records are important for the completeness assertion.
- Prepared at the time a transaction takes place, or as soon as possible thereafter, to minimize timing errors.
- Designed for multiple use, when possible, to minimize the number of different forms. For example, a properly designed electronic shipping record can be the basis for releasing goods from storage to the shipping department, informing billing of the quantity of goods to bill to the customer and the appropriate billing date, and updating the perpetual inventory records.
- Constructed in a manner that encourages correct preparation. This can be done by providing internal checks within the form or record. For example, computer screen prompts may force online data entry of critical information before the record is electronically routed for authorizations and approvals. Similarly, screen controls can validate the information entered, such as when an invalid general ledger account number is automatically rejected because the account number does not match the chart of accounts master file.

ROGUE TRADER CIRCUMVENTS CONTROLS CAUSING $7 BILLION IN LOSSES

The size of the trading losses at French bank Société Générale were staggering. Jérôme Kerviel, a junior trader with a modest base salary of around $70,000, had gambled more than the bank's entire net worth in high-risk bets involving unauthorized trades related to European stock index funds. Kerviel's role was to make trades that bet whether European stock markets would rise or fall. Each bet was supposed to be offset by a trade in the opposite direction to keep risk at a minimum, with the bank making a profit or loss based on the difference between the parallel bets. However, within months of joining the trading desk, he began placing his bets all in one direction, rather than hedging the trades as he was expected to do. One bet paid off handsomely after an attack on the London transport system sent European markets into a dive. "Bingo, 500,000 euros," Kerviel said in an interview with investigators. This success led him to make even bolder bets.

Société Générale played up their use of computer systems to ward off risk. The bank's equity-derivatives unit had not experienced a major incident in 15 years. "We didn't think it was possible," said one Société Générale executive discussing the losses. Unfortunately, Kerviel knew how to hide his trades to avoid detection, but keeping the trades hidden required constant vigilance. He needed to continue to delete and re-enter fake trades to avoid detection. As a result, Kerviel regularly skipped holidays and rarely took vacation. "It is one of the rules of controls: a trader who doesn't take holidays is a trader who doesn't want his books to be seen by others," Kerviel stated to investigators.

Finally, a fictitious trade made in the name of a German brokerage house triggered an alarm in Société Générale's systems. Under repeated questioning, Kerviel revealed that his bets had over 50 billion euros (€) at risk for the bank. By the time the French bank unwound the bets, it had lost €4.9 billion (about $7.4 billion), nearly destroying the 145-year-old bank. At Kerviel's trial, one of the bank's former executives admitted that the bank had failed by creating an environment where there was "too much trust." And, Kerviel's former boss commented, "If you're not looking for anything, you don't find anything."

Sources: 1. Nicola Clark and Katrin Behnhold, "A Société Générale Trader Remains a Mystery as His Criminal Trial Ends," *The New York Times* (June 25, 2010); 2. David Gauthier-Villars and Carrick Mollenkamp, "Portrait Emerges of Rogue Trader at French Bank," *The Wall Street Journal* (February 2–3, 2008), p. A1.

A control closely related to documents and records is the **chart of accounts**, which classifies transactions into individual balance sheet and income statement accounts. The chart of accounts is helpful in preventing classification errors if it accurately describes which type of transactions should be in each account.

Physical Control Over Assets and Records To maintain adequate internal control, assets and records must be protected. If assets are left unprotected, they can be stolen. If records are not adequately protected, they can be stolen, damaged, altered, or lost, which can seriously disrupt the accounting process and business operations. When a company is highly computerized, its computer equipment, programs, and data files that represent the records of the company must be protected, given they could be costly or even impossible to reconstruct.

The most important type of protective measure for safeguarding assets and records is the use of physical precautions. An example is the use of storerooms for inventory to guard against theft. When the storeroom is under the control of a competent employee, there is further assurance that theft is minimized. Fireproof safes and safety deposit vaults for the protection of assets such as currency and securities are other important physical safeguards in addition to off-site backup of computer software and data files.

Independent Checks on Performance The last category of control activities is the careful and continuous review of the other four, often called **independent checks** or internal verification. The need for independent checks arises because internal controls tend to change over time, unless there is frequent review. Personnel are likely to forget or intentionally fail to follow procedures, or they may become careless unless someone observes and evaluates their performance. Regardless of the quality of the controls, personnel can make errors or commit fraud.

Personnel responsible for performing internal verification procedures must be independent of those originally responsible for preparing the data. The least expensive means of internal verification is the separation of duties in the manner previously discussed. For example, when the bank reconciliation is done by a person independent of the accounting records and handling of cash, there is an opportunity for verification without incurring significant additional costs.

Most accounting systems involve technologies where many internal verification procedures are automated as part of the system. For example, the computer can prevent processing payment on a vendor invoice if there is no matching purchase order number or receiving report number for that invoice included in the system. With the extensive reliance on the use of technology to perform a number of control activities, there are a number of risks related to the overall security and functionality of IT-based services that must be managed at a system-wide or enterprise-wide level. Organizations implement IT general controls to address those risks, as described later in this chapter.

Information and Communication

The purpose of an entity's accounting **information and communication** system is to initiate, record, process, and report the entity's transactions and to maintain accountability for the related assets. The underlying principles related to information and communication stress the importance of using relevant, quality information that is communicated both internally and externally as necessary to support the proper functioning of internal controls. An accounting information and communication system has several subcomponents, typically made up of classes of transactions such as sales, sales returns, cash receipts, acquisitions, and so on. For each class of transactions, the accounting system must satisfy all of the transaction-related management assertions identified in Chapter 6. For example, the sales accounting system should be designed to ensure that all shipments of goods are correctly recorded as sales (completeness and accuracy assertions) and are reflected in the financial statements in the proper period (cutoff assertion). The system must also avoid duplicate recording of sales and recording a sale if a shipment did not occur (occurrence assertion).

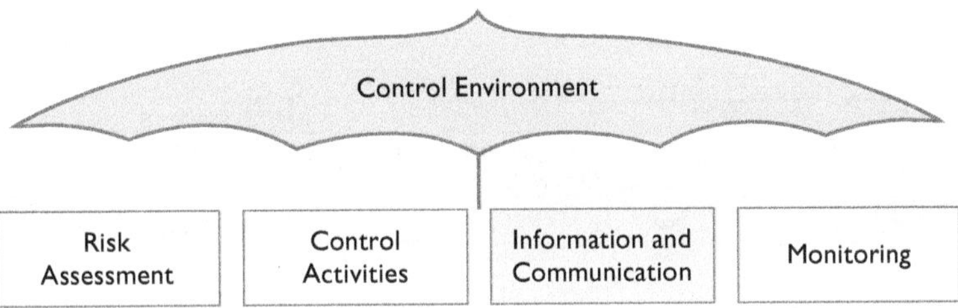

Monitoring

Monitoring activities deal with ongoing or periodic assessment of the quality of internal control by management to determine that controls are operating as intended and that they are modified as appropriate for changes in conditions. The underlying principles related to monitoring include performing periodic evaluations and communicating any identified deficiencies to the appropriate parties responsible for taking actions to remediate the deficiencies. The information being assessed comes from a variety of sources, including studies of existing internal controls, internal auditor reports, exception reporting on control activities, reports by regulators such as bank regulatory agencies, feedback from operating personnel, and complaints from customers about billing charges.

For many companies, especially larger ones, an internal audit department is essential for effective monitoring of the operating performance of internal controls. To be effective, the internal audit function must be performed by staff who are independent of both the operating and accounting departments and who report directly to a high level of authority within the organization, either top management or the audit committee of the board of directors.

In addition to its role in monitoring an entity's internal control, an adequate internal audit staff can reduce external audit costs by providing direct assistance to the external auditor. PCAOB auditing standards define the extent that auditors can use the work done by internal auditors when reporting on internal control under Section 404. Auditing standards provide guidance to help the external auditor obtain evidence that supports the competence, integrity, and objectivity of internal auditors, which allows the external auditor to rely on the internal auditor's work in a number of ways.

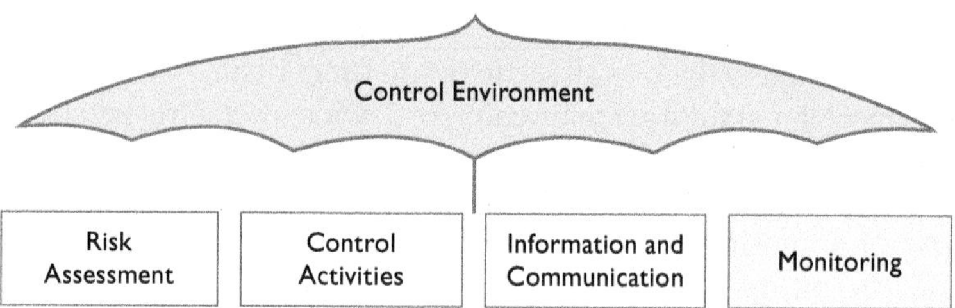

COSO's five components of internal control discussed in the preceding sections, and the related principles, are summarized in Table 11-1. Certain control elements within the five COSO control components have a pervasive effect on the entity's system of internal control and are referred to as **entity-level controls** in auditing standards. Examples include the board and audit committee element of the control environment, the entity's risk assessment process, and internal audit's role in monitoring controls.

CONCEPT CHECK

1. What are the five components of internal control in the COSO internal control framework? What is the relationship among these five components?
2. How do the COSO principles help an organization assess whether internal controls are designed and operating effectively?

TABLE 11-1 COSO Components of Internal Control and Underlying Principles

INTERNAL CONTROL		
Component	**Description of Component**	**Principles**
Control environment	Actions, policies, and procedures that reflect the overall attitude of top management, directors, and owners of an entity about internal control and its importance	• Integrity and ethical values • Board of director and audit committee participation • Organizational structure • Commitment to competence • Accountability
Risk assessment	Management's identification and analysis of risks relevant to the preparation of financial statements in accordance with appropriate accounting frameworks such as GAAP or IFRS	• Have clear objectives in order to identify risks related to those objectives • Determine how risks should be managed • Consider the potential for fraud • Monitor changes
Control activities	Policies and procedures that management has established to meet its objectives for financial reporting	• Develop control activities that mitigate risks to an acceptable level • Develop general controls over technology • Establish appropriate policies, procedures, and expectations
Information and communication	Methods used to initiate, record, process, and report an entity's transactions and to maintain accountability for related assets	• Use relevant, quality information to support the functioning of internal controls • Communicate information internally, including objectives and responsibilities for internal control • Communicate with external parties relevant information related to internal controls
Monitoring	Management's ongoing and periodic assessment of the quality of internal control performance to determine whether controls are operating as intended and are modified when needed	• Perform periodic evaluations • Communicate identified deficiencies to those who can remediate

INTERNAL CONTROLS SPECIFIC TO INFORMATION TECHNOLOGY

OBJECTIVE 11-4

Explain how general controls and application controls reduce information technology risks.

Technology can strengthen a company's system of internal control but can also provide challenges. To address risks associated with reliance on technology, organizations often implement specific IT controls. Auditing standards describe two categories of controls for IT systems: general controls and application controls.

General controls apply to all aspects of the IT function, including IT administration; separation of IT duties; systems development; physical and online security over access to hardware, software, and related data; backup and contingency planning in the event of unexpected emergencies; and hardware controls. Because general controls often apply on an entity-wide basis and affect many different software applications, auditors evaluate general controls for the company as a whole.

Application controls typically operate at the business process level and apply to processing transactions, such as controls over the processing of sales or cash receipts. Auditors must evaluate application controls for every class of transactions or account in which the auditor plans to reduce assessed control risk, because IT controls will be different across classes of transactions and accounts. Application controls are likely to be effective only when general controls are effective.

Figure 11-4 illustrates the relationship between general controls and application controls. The oval represents the general controls that provide assurance that all application controls are effective. Effective general controls reduce the types of risks identified in the boxes outside the general controls oval in Figure 11-4.

Table 11-2 (p. 350) describes six categories of general controls and three categories of application controls, with specific examples for each category. Let's examine these categories of general and application controls in more detail.

FIGURE 11-4 **Relationship Between General and Application Controls**

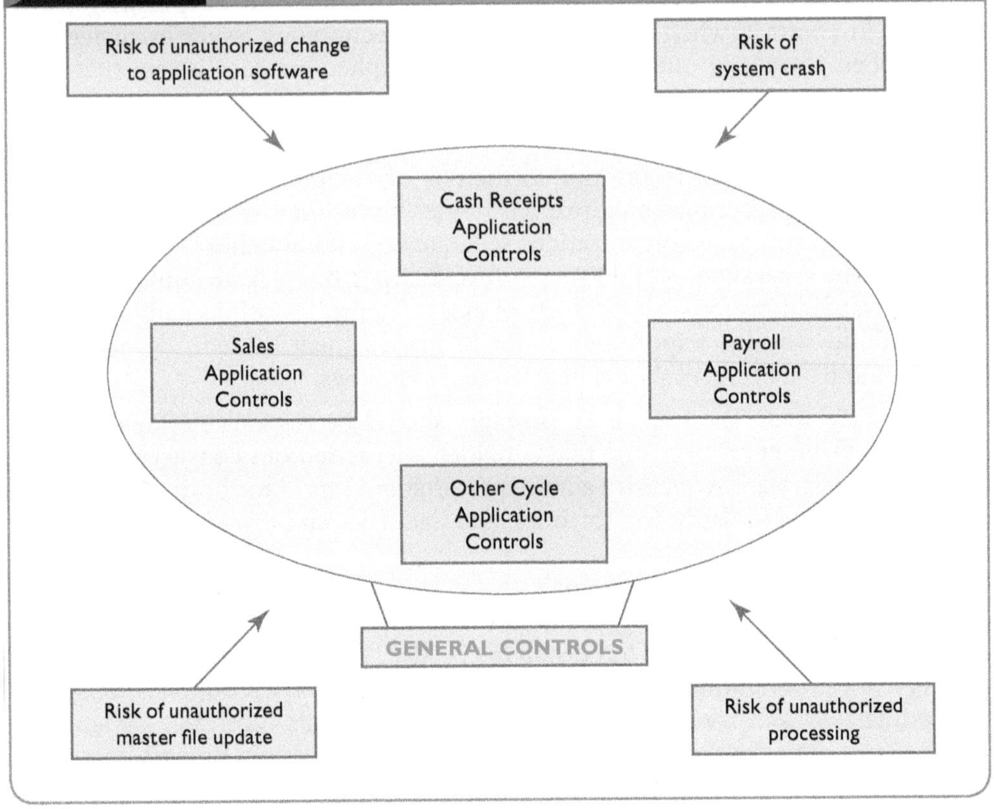

TABLE 11-2 Categories of General and Application Controls

Control Type	Category of Control	Example of Control
General controls	Administration of the IT function	Chief information officer or IT manager reports to senior management and board.
	Separation of IT duties	Responsibilities for programming, operations, and data control are separated.
	Systems development	Teams of users, systems analysts, and programmers develop and thoroughly test software.
	Physical and online security	Access to hardware is restricted, passwords and user IDs limit access to software and data files, and encryption and firewalls protect data and programs from external parties.
	Backup and contingency planning	Written backup plans are prepared and tested regularly throughout the year.
	Hardware controls	Memory failure or hard drive failure causes error messages on the monitor.
Application controls	Input controls	Preformatted screens prompt data input personnel for information to be entered.
	Processing controls	Reasonableness tests review unit-selling prices used to process a sale.
	Output controls	The sales department does postprocessing review of sales transactions.

General Controls

Similar to the effect that the control environment has on other components of internal control, the six categories of general controls have an entity-wide effect on all IT functions. Auditors typically evaluate general controls early in the audit because of their impact on application controls.

Administration of the IT Function The board of directors' and senior management's attitude about IT affect the perceived importance of IT within an organization. Their oversight, resource allocation, and involvement in key IT decisions each signal the importance of IT to the organization. In complex environments, management may establish IT steering committees to help monitor the organization's technology needs. In less complex organizations, the board may rely on regular reporting by a chief information officer (CIO) or other senior IT manager to keep management informed. In contrast, when management assigns technology issues exclusively to lower-level employees or outside consultants, an implied message is sent that IT is not a high priority. The result is often an understaffed, underfunded, and poorly controlled IT function.

Separation of IT Duties To respond to the risk of combining traditional custody, authorization, and record-keeping responsibilities by having the computer perform those tasks, well-controlled organizations separate key duties within IT. For example, there should be separation of IT duties to prevent IT personnel from authorizing and recording transactions to cover the theft of assets. Figure 11-5 shows an ideal separation of duties. Ideally, responsibilities for IT management, systems development, operations, and data control should be separated as follows:

- *IT management.* The CIO or IT manager should be responsible for oversight of the IT function to ensure that activities are carried out consistent with the IT strategic plan. A security administrator should monitor both physical and online access to hardware, software, and data files and investigate all security breaches.
- *Systems development.* Systems analysts are not only responsible for the overall design of each application system, but they also coordinate the development, acquisition, and changes to IT systems by the IT personnel (who are responsible for programming the application or acquiring software applications) and primary system users outside of IT (such as accounts receivable personnel). Programmers develop flowcharts for each new application, prepare computer instructions, test the programs, and document the results.

Programmers should not have access to input data or computer operations to avoid using their knowledge of the system for personal benefit. They should be allowed to work only with test copies of programs and data so they can only make software changes after proper authorization.

- *Operations.* Computer operators are responsible for the day-to-day operations of the computer, following the schedule established by the CIO. They also monitor computer consoles for messages about computer efficiency and malfunctions.

  A librarian is responsible for controlling the use of computer programs, transaction files, and other computer records and documentation. The librarian releases them to operators only when authorized. For example, programs and transaction files are released to operators only when a job is scheduled to be processed. Similarly, the librarian releases a test copy to programmers only on approval by senior management. Network administrators also affect IT operations because they are responsible for planning, implementing, and maintaining operations of the network of servers that link users to various applications and data files.
- *Data control.* Data input/output control personnel independently verify the quality of input and the reasonableness of output. For organizations that use databases to store information shared by accounting and other functions, database administrators are responsible for the operation and access security of shared databases.

Naturally, the extent of separation of duties depends on the organization's size and complexity. In many small companies, it is not practical to segregate the duties to the extent illustrated in Figure 11-5. For example, some entities acquire accounting systems from third-party vendors or they access applications through the Internet. As a result, they may have few staff dedicated to systems development or the librarian function.

Systems Development Systems development includes:

- Purchasing software or developing in-house software that meets the organization's needs. A key to implementing the right software is to involve a team of both IT and non-IT personnel, including key users of the software and internal auditors. This combination increases the likelihood that information needs, as well as software design and implementation concerns, are properly addressed. Involving users also results in better acceptance by key users.
- Testing all software to ensure that the new software is compatible with existing hardware and software and determining whether the hardware and software can handle the needed volume of transactions. Whether software is purchased or developed internally, extensive testing of all software with realistic data is

FIGURE 11-5 Segregation of IT Duties

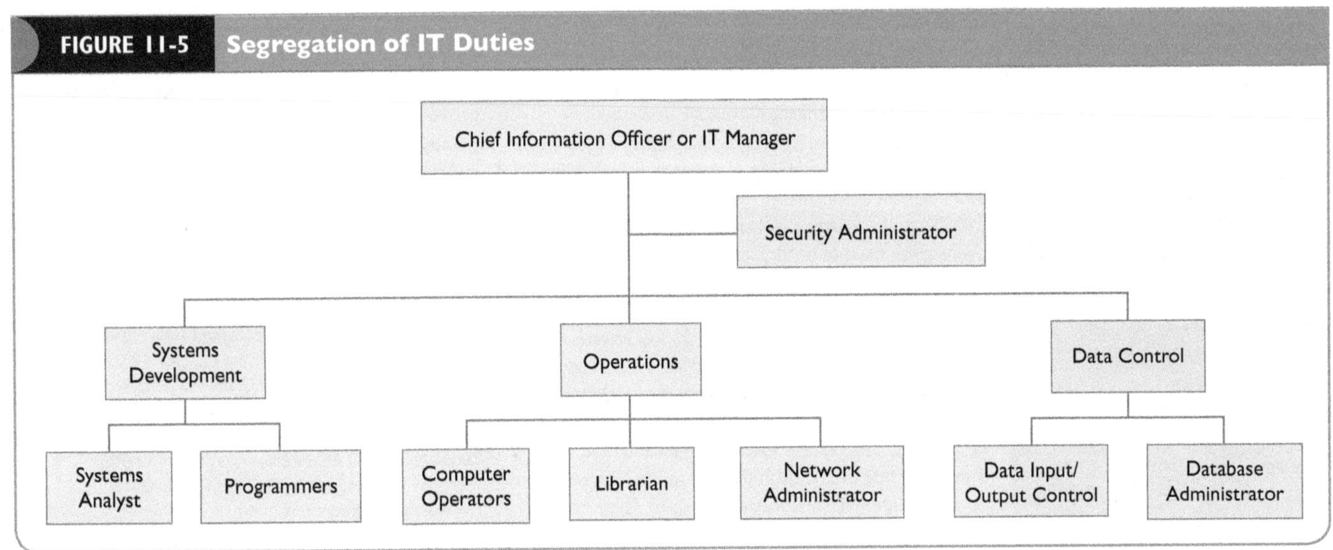

critical. Companies typically use one or a combination of the following two test approaches:

1. **Pilot testing**: A new system is implemented in one part of the organization while other locations continue to rely on the old system.
2. **Parallel testing**: The old and new systems operate simultaneously in all locations.

Proper documentation of the system is required for all new and modified software. After the software has been successfully tested and documented, it is transferred to the librarian in a controlled manner to ensure only authorized software is ultimately accepted as the authorized version.

Physical and Online Security Physical controls over computers and restrictions to online software and related data files decrease the risk of unauthorized changes to programs and improper use of programs and data files. The information technology and internal control processes an organization has in place to protect computers, networks, programs, and data from unauthorized access is often referred to as **cybersecurity**. Security plans should be in writing and monitored. Security controls include both physical controls and online access controls.

- *Physical controls.* Proper physical controls over computer equipment restrict access to hardware, software, and backup data files. Common examples to physically restrict unauthorized use include keypad entrances, badge-entry systems, security cameras, and security personnel. More sophisticated controls only allow physical and online access after employee fingerprints are read or employee retinas are scanned and matched with an approved database. Other physical controls include monitoring of cooling and humidity to ensure that the equipment functions properly and installing fire-extinguishing equipment to reduce fire damage.
- *Online access controls.* Proper user IDs and passwords control access to software and related data files, reducing the likelihood that unauthorized changes are made to software applications and data files. Separate add-on security software packages, such as firewall and encryption programs, can be installed to improve a system's security. (See later in this chapter on p. 356 for a description of firewall and encryption programs.)

As noted in the opening vignette related to Sony Pictures, cybersecurity is becoming an increasing focus of management and boards of directors due to the potentially severe damage that can occur to an organization in a cyberattack.

Backup and Contingency Planning Power failures, fire, excessive heat or humidity, water damage, or even sabotage can have serious consequences to businesses using IT. To prevent data loss during power outages, many companies rely on battery backups

TECHNOLOGY GLITCHES BUNGLE FACEBOOK'S IPO

The buildup surrounding Facebook, Inc.'s May 18, 2012, initial public offering set expectations high; however, the opening days of trading led quickly to disappointment. Just days before its debut, the company's CFO decided to boost the number of shares to be offered by 25 percent and increased the opening offer price to $38 per share, believing demand would be high. On opening day, massive demand for the social network's initial offering actually led to a 30-minute delay in the start of trading of the stock on the NASDAQ Stock Market. The technology glitch left individual investors puzzled about whether their buy and sell orders had actually been executed, when normally those acknowledgments are instantaneous. When U.S. regulators, including the SEC, initially examined the disruption, they noted that even though the mishap was blamed on a computer malfunction, the underlying cause may have been programmer failure in designing the systems to be robust enough to handle the volume of orders. In May 2013, NASDAQ agreed to pay a $10 million penalty to the SEC related to the Facebook IPO, and in April 2015, NASDAQ agreed to a settlement of $26.5 million for a class action lawsuit filed by retail investors who suffered damages in the IPO.

Sources: 1. Jacob Blunge, "Regulators Probe Role of 'Glitches' in Market Upheavals," NASDAQ News (June 27, 2012) (www.nasdaq.com); 2. John McCrank, "Nasdaq to settle Facebook IPO lawsuit for $26.5 million" (April 23, 2015) (www.reuters.com); 3. John McCrank and Jonathan Spicer, "Facebook Investors Left Guessing after NASDAQ Glitch," Reuters (May 21, 2012) (www.reuters.com); 4. Andrew Tangel, "NASDAQ Offers Brokerages $40 Million for Facebook Glitches," *Los Angeles Times* (June 6, 2012) (www.articles.latimes.com).

or on-site generators. For more serious disasters, organizations need detailed backup and contingency plans such as off-site storage of critical software and data files or outsourcing to firms that specialize in secure data storage.

Backup and contingency plans should also identify alternative hardware that can be used to process company data. Companies with small IT systems can purchase replacement computers in an emergency and reprocess their accounting records by using backup copies of software and data files. Larger companies often contract with IT data centers that specialize in providing access to off-site computers and data storage and other IT services for use in the event of an IT disaster.

Hardware Controls **Hardware controls** are built into computer equipment by manufacturers to detect and report equipment failures. Auditors are more concerned with how the client handles errors identified by the hardware controls than with their adequacy. Regardless of the quality of hardware controls, output will be corrected only if the client has provided for handling machine errors.

Application Controls

Application controls are designed for each software application and are intended to help a company satisfy the transaction-related management assertions discussed in previous chapters. Although some application controls affect one or only a few transaction-related assertions, most controls prevent or detect several types of misstatements. Other application controls concern account balance and presentation and disclosure assertions.

Application controls may be done by computers or client personnel. When they are done by client personnel, they are called **manual controls**. The effectiveness of manual controls depends on both the competence of the people performing the controls and the care they exercise when doing them. For example, when credit department personnel review exception reports that identify credit sales exceeding a customer's authorized credit limit, the auditor may need to evaluate the person's ability to make the assessment and test the accuracy of the exception report. When controls are done by computers, they are called **automated controls**. Because of the nature of computer processing, automated controls, if properly designed, lead to consistent operation of the controls.

Application controls fall into three categories: input, processing, and output. Although the objectives for each category are the same, the procedures for meeting the objectives vary considerably. Let's examine each more closely.

Input Controls **Input controls** are designed to ensure that the information entered into the computer is authorized, accurate, and complete. They are critical because a large portion of errors in IT systems result from data entry errors and, of course, regardless of the quality of information processing, input errors result in output errors. Typical controls developed for manual systems are still important in IT systems, such as:

- Management's authorization of transactions
- Adequate preparation of input source documents
- Competent personnel

Controls specific to IT include:

- Adequately designed input screens with preformatted prompts for transaction information
- Pull-down menu lists of available software options
- Computer-performed validation tests of input accuracy, such as the validation of customer numbers against customer master files
- Online-based input controls for e-commerce applications where external parties, such as customers and suppliers, perform the initial part of the transaction inputting
- Immediate error correction procedures, to provide for early detection and correction of input errors
- Accumulation of errors in an error file for subsequent follow-up by data input personnel

TABLE 11-3	Batch Input Controls	
Control	**Definition**	**Examples**
Financial total	Summary total of field amounts for all records in a batch that represent a meaningful total such as dollars or amounts	The total of dollars of all vendor invoices to be paid
Hash total	Summary total of codes from all records in a batch that do not represent a meaningful total	The total of all vendor account numbers for vendor invoices to be paid
Record count	Summary total of physical records in a batch	The total number of vendor invoices to be processed

For IT systems that group similar transactions together into batches, the use of financial batch totals, hash totals, and record count totals helps increase the accuracy and completeness of input. Batch input controls are described in Table 11-3. For example, the comparison of a record count calculated before data entry of the number of vendor invoices to be entered and the number of vendor invoices processed by the system would help determine if any invoices were omitted or entered more than once during data entry.

Processing Controls **Processing controls** prevent and detect errors while transaction data are processed. General controls, especially controls related to systems development and security, provide essential control for minimizing processing errors. Specific application processing controls are often programmed into software to prevent, detect, and correct processing errors. Examples of processing controls are illustrated in Table 11-4.

Output Controls **Output controls** focus on detecting errors after processing is completed, rather than on preventing errors. The most important output control is review of the data for reasonableness by someone knowledgeable about the output. Users can often identify errors because they know the approximate correct amounts. Several common controls for detecting errors in outputs include:

- Reconcile computer-produced output to manual control totals
- Compare the number of units processed to the number of units submitted for processing
- Compare a sample of transaction output to input source documents
- Verify dates and times of processing to identify any out-of-sequence processing

For sensitive computer output, such as payroll checks, control can be improved by requiring employees to present employee identification before they receive their checks or by requiring the use of direct deposit into the employees' pre-approved bank accounts. Also, access to sensitive output stored in electronic files or transmitted across networks, including the Internet, is often restricted by requiring passwords, user IDs, and encryption techniques.

TABLE 11-4	Processing Controls	
Type of Processing Control	**Description**	**Example**
Validation test	Ensures that a particular type of transaction is appropriate for processing	Does the transaction code for the processing of a recent purchase match predetermined inventory codes?
Sequence test	Determines that data submitted for processing are in the correct order	Has the file of payroll input transactions been sorted in departmental order before processing?
Arithmetic accuracy test	Checks the accuracy of processed data	Does the sum of net pay plus withholdings equal gross pay for the entire payroll?
Data reasonableness test	Determines whether data exceed prespecified amounts	Does employee's gross pay exceed 60 hours or $1,999 for the week?
Completeness test	Determines that every field in a record has been completed	Are employee number, name, number of regular hours, number of overtime hours, department number, etc., included for each employee?

CONCEPT CHECK

1. Distinguish between general controls and application controls and give two examples of each.
2. Identify the typical duties within an IT function and describe how those duties should be segregated among IT personnel.

IMPACT OF IT INFRASTUCTURE ON INTERNAL CONTROL

OBJECTIVE 11-5

Identify types of information technology systems and their impact on internal controls.

Virtually all entities, including small, family-owned businesses, rely on IT to record and process business transactions. As a result of advancements in IT, even relatively small businesses use personal computers with commercial accounting software for their accounting. As businesses grow and have increased information needs, they typically upgrade their IT systems. The accounting function's use of complex IT networks, databases, the Internet (including cloud computing), and centralized IT functions is now commonplace. The types of internal controls will vary based on the type and complexity of the IT system, and we briefly discuss a few of these systems below.

The use of networks that link equipment such as desktops, midrange computers, mainframes, workstations, servers, and printers is common for most businesses. **Local area networks (LANs)** link equipment within a single or small cluster of buildings and are used only within a company. LANs are often used to transfer data and programs from one computer or workstation using network system software that allows all of the devices to function together. **Wide area networks (WANs)** link equipment in larger geographic regions, including global operations.

In networks, application software and data files used to process transactions are included on several computers that are linked together. Access to the application from desktop computers or workstations is managed by network server software or other interfaces with cloud computing technology. Even small companies can have several computer servers linked together on a network, while larger companies may have hundreds of servers in dozens of locations networked together. It is common for networks to consist of various combinations of equipment and procedures, which may not have standard security options. Lack of equipment compatibility across a network may occur when responsibility for purchasing equipment and software, maintenance, administration, and physical security resides with key user groups rather than with a centralized IT function. Sometimes network security may be compromised when networks consist of equipment with incompatible security features.

Database management systems allow clients to create databases that include information that can be shared across multiple applications. In nondatabase systems, each application has its own data file, whereas in database management systems, many applications share files. Clients implement database management systems to reduce data redundancy, improve control over data, and provide better information for decision making by integrating information throughout functions and departments. For example, customer data, such as the customer's name and address, can be shared in the sales, credit, accounting, marketing, and shipping functions, resulting in consistent information for all users and significant cost reductions. Companies often integrate database management systems within the entire organization using **enterprise resource planning (ERP) systems** that integrate numerous aspects of an organization's activities into one accounting information system. ERP systems share data across accounting and nonaccounting business functions of the organization. For example, customer order data may be used by accounting to record a sale, by production to meet increased production demand, by purchasing to order additional raw materials, and by human resources to arrange labor schedules.

Controls often improve when data are centralized in a database management system by eliminating duplicate data files. However, database management systems also can create internal control risks. Risks increase when multiple users, including individuals outside of accounting, can access and update data files. To counter the risks of unauthorized, inaccurate, and incomplete data files, companies must implement proper database administration and access controls. With the centralization of data in a single system, they must also ensure proper backup of data on a regular basis.

Companies using e-commerce systems to transact business electronically link their internal accounting systems to external parties' systems, such as customers and suppliers. As a result, a company's risks depend in part on how well its e-commerce partners identify and manage risks in their own IT systems. To manage these interdependency risks, companies must ensure that their business partners manage IT system risks before conducting business with them electronically. Some of the assurance services discussed in Chapter 1 provide objective information about the reliability of a business partner's IT system. The use of e-commerce systems also exposes sensitive company data, programs, and hardware to potential interception or sabotage by external parties. To limit these exposures, companies use firewalls, encryption techniques, and digital signatures.

A **firewall** protects data, programs, and other IT resources from unauthorized external users accessing the system through networks, such as the Internet. A firewall is a system of hardware and software that monitors and controls the flow of e-commerce communications by channeling all network connections through controls that verify external users, grant access to authorized users, deny access to unauthorized users, and direct authorized users to requested programs or data. Firewalls are becoming increasingly sophisticated as the frequency and severity of cyberattacks grow.

Encryption techniques protect the security of electronic communication when information is transmitted and when it is stored. Computerized encryption changes a standard message or data file into one that is coded (encrypted), requiring the receiver of the electronic message or user of the encrypted data file to use a decryption program to decode the message or data. A public key encryption technique is often used, where one key (the public key) is used for encoding the message and another key (the private key) is used to decode the message. The public key is distributed to all approved users of the e-commerce system. The private key is distributed only to internal users with the authority to decode the message.

To authenticate the validity of a trading partner conducting business electronically, companies may rely on external certification authorities, who verify the source of the public key by using **digital signatures**. A trusted certification authority issues a digital certificate to individuals and companies engaging in e-commerce. The digital signature contains the holder's name and its public key. It also contains the name of the certification authority and the certificate's expiration date and other specified information. To guarantee integrity and authenticity, each signature is digitally signed by the private key maintained by the certification authority.

Many clients outsource some or all of their IT needs to an independent organization commonly referred to as a computer **service center**, including **application service providers (ASPs)** and **cloud computing environments**, rather than maintain an internal IT center. Cloud computing is a computer resource deployment and procurement model that enables an organization to obtain IT resources and applications from any location via an Internet connection. Depending on the arrangement, all or parts of an entity's IT hardware, software, and data might reside in an IT service center shared with other organizations and managed by a third-party vendor. The name cloud computing comes from the use of a cloud-shaped symbol in systems diagrams to represent complex IT infrastructures.

Smaller companies often outsource their payroll function because payroll is reasonably standard from company to company, and many reliable providers of payroll services are available. Companies also outsource their e-commerce systems to external Web site service providers, including those that offer cloud computing services as described above. Like all outsourcing decisions, companies decide whether to outsource IT on a cost-benefit basis.

When outsourcing to a computer service center, the client submits input data, which the service center processes for a fee and then returns the agreed-upon output and the original input. For payroll, the company submits data from time records, pay rates, and W-4s to the service center. The service center returns payroll checks, journals, and input data each week and W-2s at the end of each year. The service center is responsible for designing the computer system and providing adequate controls to ensure that the processing is reliable.

Outsourcing can provide challenges from an internal control perspective. Management is responsible for the design and operating effectiveness of internal controls, and this includes controls that are outsourced to a service provider. The ethics and integrity of service providers, as well as the design and functioning of their internal controls, need to be considered by management when selecting a service provider, and evaluated regularly.

SUMMARY

This chapter focused on internal controls, including internal controls related to computer-based information systems, and the COSO Framework. We use this framework as a basis for discussing the auditor's responsibilities related to internal controls in the next chapter. To rely on a client's internal controls to report on internal control over financial reporting and to reduce planned audit evidence for audits of financial statements, the auditor must first obtain an understanding of each of the five components of internal control. Knowledge about the design of the client's control environment, risk assessment, control activities, information and communication, and monitoring activities and information about whether internal control components have been implemented assist the auditor in assessing control risk for each transaction-related audit objective.

ESSENTIAL TERMS

Application controls—controls typically at the business process level that apply to processing transactions, such as the inputting, processing, and outputting of sales or cash receipts

Application service providers (ASPs)—third-party entities that manage and supply software applications or software-related services to customers through the Internet

Automated controls—application controls done by the computer

Chart of accounts—a listing of all the entity's accounts that classifies transactions into individual balance sheet and income statement accounts

Cloud computing environments—a computer resource deployment and procurement model that enables an organization to obtain IT resources and applications at an IT service center shared with other organizations from any location via an Internet connection

Collusion—an act of two or more employees who conspire to steal assets or misstate records

Control activities—policies and procedures, in addition to those included in the other four components of internal control, that help ensure that necessary actions are taken to address risks in the achievement of the entity's objectives; they typically include the following five specific control activities: (1) adequate separation of duties, (2) proper authorization of transactions and activities, (3) adequate documents and records, (4) physical control over assets and records, and (5) independent checks on performance

Control environment—the actions, policies, and procedures that reflect the overall attitudes of top management, directors, and owners of an entity about internal control and its importance to the entity

COSO principles—represent the fundamental concepts related to each of the five components of internal control; all principles must be functioning for controls to be effective

Cybersecurity—the information technology and internal control processes an organization has in place to protect computers, networks, programs, and data from unauthorized access

Database management systems—hardware and software systems that allow clients to establish and maintain databases shared by multiple applications

Digital signatures—electronic certificates that are used to authenticate the validity of individuals and companies conducting business electronically

Encryption techniques—computer programs that change a standard message or data file into one that is coded, then decoded using a decryption program

Enterprise resource planning (ERP) systems—systems that integrate numerous aspects of an organization's activities into one accounting information system

Entity-level controls—controls that have a pervasive effect on the entity's system of internal control; also referred to as company-level controls

Firewall—a system of hardware and software that monitors and controls the flow of e-commerce communications by channeling all network connections through a control gateway

General authorization—companywide policies for the approval of all transactions within stated limits

General controls— controls that relate to all parts of the IT function and affect many different software applications

Hardware controls—controls built into the computer equipment by the manufacturer to detect and report equipment failure

Independent checks—internal control activities designed for the continuous internal verification of other controls

Information and communication—the set of manual and/or computerized procedures that initiate, record, process, and report an entity's transactions and maintain accountability for the related assets

Input controls—controls designed by an organization to ensure that the information to be processed by the computer is authorized, accurate, and complete

Internal control—a process designed to provide reasonable assurance regarding the achievement of management's objectives in the following categories: (1) reliability of reporting, (2) effectiveness and efficiency of operations, and (3) compliance with applicable laws and regulations

Local area networks (LANs)—networks that connect computer equipment, data files, software, and peripheral equipment within a local area, such as a single building or a small cluster of buildings, for intracompany use

Manual controls—application controls done by people

Monitoring—management's ongoing and periodic assessment of the quality of internal control performance to determine that controls are operating as intended and are modified when needed

Output controls—controls designed to ensure that computer-generated data are valid, accurate, complete, and distributed only to authorized people

Parallel testing—a company's computer testing approach that involves operating the old and new systems simultaneously

Pilot testing—a company's computer testing approach that involves implementing a new system in just one part of the organization while maintaining the old system at other locations

Processing controls—controls designed to ensure that data input into the system are accurately and completely processed

Risk assessment—management's identification and analysis of risks relevant to the preparation of financial statements in accordance with an applicable accounting framework

Separation of duties—separation of the following activities in an organization: (1) custody of assets from accounting, (2) authorization from custody of assets, (3) operational responsibility from record keeping, and (4) IT duties from outside users of IT

Service center—an organization that provides IT services for companies on an outsourcing basis

Specific authorization—case-by-case approval of transactions not covered by companywide policies

Those charged with governance—the person(s) with responsibility for overseeing the strategic direction of the entity and its obligations related to the accountability of the entity, including overseeing the financial reporting and disclosure process

Wide area networks (WANs)—networks that connect computer equipment, databases, software, and peripheral equipment that reside in many geographic locations, such as client offices located around the world

REVIEW QUESTIONS

11-1 (OBJECTIVE 11-1) Describe which of the three categories of broad objectives for internal controls are considered by the auditor in an audit of both the financial statements and internal control over financial reporting.

11-2 (OBJECTIVE 11-2) What two aspects of internal control must management assess when reporting on internal control to comply with Section 404 of the Sarbanes–Oxley Act?

11-3 (OBJECTIVE 11-2) Chapter 8 introduced the eight parts of the planning phase of audits. Which part is understanding internal control and assessing control risk? What parts precede and follow that understanding and assessing control risk?

11-4 (OBJECTIVE 11-2) When performing an integrated audit of a public company, what are the auditor's responsibilities related to internal control as required by PCAOB standards?

11-5 (OBJECTIVE 11-2) What two aspects of internal control must the auditor assess when performing procedures to obtain an understanding of internal control?

11-6 (OBJECTIVES 11-2, 11-3) Management must identify the framework used to evaluate the effectiveness of internal control over financial reporting. What framework is used by most U.S. public companies?

11-7 (OBJECTIVE 11-3) What is meant by the control environment? What is the relationship between the control environment and the other four components of internal control?

11-8 (OBJECTIVE 11-3) List the types of specific control activities and provide one specific illustration of a control in the sales area for each control activity.

11-9 (OBJECTIVE 11-3) The separation of operational responsibility from record keeping is meant to prevent different types of misstatements than the separation of the custody of assets from accounting. Explain the difference in the purposes of these two types of separation of duties.

11-10 (OBJECTIVE 11-3) For each of the following, give an example of a physical control the client can use to protect the asset or record:

1. Computers
2. Cash received by retail clerks
3. Accounts receivable records
4. Raw material inventory
5. Perishable tools
6. Manufacturing equipment
7. Marketable securities

11-11 (OBJECTIVE 11-3) Explain what is meant by independent checks on performance and give five specific examples.

11-12 (OBJECTIVE 11-3) Frank James, a highly competent employee of Brinkwater Sales Corporation, had been responsible for accounting-related matters for two decades. His devotion to the firm and his duties had always been exceptional, and over the years, he had been given increased responsibility. Both the president of Brinkwater and the partner of an independent CPA firm in charge of the audit were shocked and dismayed to discover that James had embezzled more than $500,000 over a 10-year period by not recording billings in the sales journal and subsequently diverting the cash receipts. What major factors permitted the embezzlement to take place?

11-13 (OBJECTIVE 11-3) Describe why auditors generally evaluate entity-level controls before evaluating transaction-level controls.

11-14 (OBJECTIVE 11-4) Explain how client internal controls can be improved through the proper installation of IT.

11-15 **(OBJECTIVE 11-4)** Identify risks for extensive IT-based accounting systems.

11-16 **(OBJECTIVE 11-4)** Identify the traditionally segregated duties in IT systems.

11-17 **(OBJECTIVE 11-4)** Explain how the effectiveness of general controls impacts the effectiveness of automated application controls.

11-18 **(OBJECTIVE 11-5)** Compare the risks associated with network systems and database systems to those associated with centralized IT functions.

11-19 **(OBJECTIVE 11-5)** An audit client is creating an online, Web-based sales ordering system for customers to purchase products using personal credit cards for payment. Identify three risks related to an online sales system that management should consider. For each risk, identify an internal control that could be implemented to reduce that risk.

MULTIPLE CHOICE QUESTIONS FROM CPA EXAMINATIONS

11-20 **(OBJECTIVES 11-1, 11-2, 11-3)** The following are general questions about internal control. Choose the best response.

a. Which of the following would not be considered an inherent limitation of the potential effectiveness of an entity's internal control structure?
   (1) Incompatible duties
   (2) Management override
   (3) Mistakes in judgment
   (4) Collusion among employees

b. Actions, policies, and procedures that reflect the overall attitude of management, directors, and owners of the entity about internal control relate to which of the following internal control components?
   (1) Control environment
   (2) Information and communication
   (3) Risk assessment
   (4) Monitoring

c. Vendor account reconciliations are performed by three clerks in the accounts payable department on Friday of each week. The accounts payable supervisor reviews the completed reconciliations the following Monday to ensure they have been completed. The work performed by the supervisor is an example of which COSO component?
   (1) Control activities
   (2) Information and communication
   (3) Risk assessment
   (4) Monitoring

11-21 **(OBJECTIVES 11-4, 11-5)** The following questions concern the characteristics of IT systems and their impact on internal controls. Choose the best response.

a. Which of the following is an advantage of a computer-based system for transaction processing over a manual system? A computer-based system
   (1) does not require as stringent a set of internal controls.
   (2) will produce a more accurate set of financial statements.
   (3) will be more efficient in generating financial statements.
   (4) eliminates the need to reconcile control accounts and subsidiary ledgers.

b. Which of the following is an example of an application control?
   (1) The client uses access security software to limit access to each of the accounting applications.
   (2) Employees are assigned a user ID and password that must be changed every quarter.
   (3) The sales system automatically computes the total sale amount and posts the total to the sales journal master file.
   (4) Systems programmers are restricted from doing applications programming functions.

c. Which of the following is generally *not* considered a category of IT general controls?
   (1) Controls that determine whether a vendor number matches the pre-approved vendors in the vendor master file
   (2) Controls that restrict system-wide access to programs and data
   (3) Controls that oversee the acquisition of application software
   (4) Controls that oversee the day-to-day operation of IT applications

MULTIPLE CHOICE QUESTIONS FROM BECKER CPA EXAM REVIEW

11-22 **(OBJECTIVES 11-1, 11-2, 11-3)** The following are general questions about internal control. Choose the best response.

a. Which of the following correctly describes an internal control component?
   (1) *Control activities* set the tone of the organization.
   (2) *Information and communication systems* have to do with management's analysis of risk.
   (3) *Risk assessment* relates to assessing the quality of the internal control structure over time.
   (4) *Monitoring* relates to ongoing assessment by management to determine whether controls are operating as intended.

b. Which of the following situations is *not* an example of an inherent limitation of internal control?
   (1) A programming error in the design of an automated control allows an employee to give himself an unauthorized pay increase.
   (2) Management's failure to enforce control policies surrounding access to inventory allows employees to steal assets.
   (3) A lack of physical controls over the safeguarding of assets allows an employee to steal company assets.
   (4) A fraud scheme whereby an employee orders personal goods and his supervisor, who is in on the scheme, signs the checks to pay for those goods.

c. Which of the following factors are included in an entity's control environment?

	Participation of Those Charged With Governance	Integrity and Ethical Values	Organizational Structure
(1)	Yes	Yes	No
(2)	Yes	Yes	Yes
(3)	No	Yes	Yes
(4)	Yes	No	Yes

DISCUSSION QUESTIONS AND PROBLEMS

11-23 **(OBJECTIVES 11-3, 11-4)** Following are descriptions of ten internal controls.

1. The company's computer systems track individual transactions and automatically accumulate transactions to create a trial balance.
2. On a monthly basis, department heads compare a budget to actual performance report and investigate unusual differences.
3. The company must receive university transcripts documenting all college degrees earned before an individual can begin his or her first day of employment with the company.
4. Senior management obtains data about external events that might affect the entity and evaluates the impact of that information on its existing accounting processes.
5. Each quarter, department managers are required to perform a self-assessment of the department's compliance with company policies. Reports summarizing the results are to be submitted to the senior executive overseeing that department.
6. Before a cash disbursement can be processed, all payee information must be verified by matching the payee to the company's approved vendor listing.
7. The system automatically reconciles the detailed accounts receivable subsidiary ledger to the accounts receivable general ledger account on a daily basis.

8. The company has developed a detailed series of accounting policy and procedures manuals to help provide detailed instructions to employees about how controls are to be performed.
9. The company has an organizational chart that establishes the formal lines of reporting and authorization protocols.
10. The compensation committee reviews compensation plans for senior executives to determine if those plans create unintended pressures that might lead to distorted financial statements.

Required Indicate which of the five COSO internal control components is best represented by each internal control.

a. Control environment
b. Risk assessment
c. Control activities
d. Information and communication
e. Monitoring

11-24 **(OBJECTIVES 11-3, 11-4)** The following are internal controls related to various cycles.

1. Sales invoices are matched with shipping documents by the computer system and an exception report is generated.
2. Receiving reports are prenumbered and accounted for on a daily basis.
3. Sales invoices are independently verified before being sent to customers.
4. Payments by check are received in the mail by the receptionist, who lists the checks and restrictively endorses them.
5. Labor hours for payroll are reviewed for reasonableness by the computer system.
6. Checks are signed by the company president, who compares the checks with the underlying supporting documents.
7. Unmatched shipping documents are accounted for on a daily basis.
8. The computer system verifies that all payroll payments have a valid employee identification number assigned by the human resources department at the time of hiring.
9. The accounts receivable master file is reconciled to the general ledger on a monthly basis.

Required

a. For each internal control, identify the type(s) of specific control activity (or activities) to which it applies (such as proper authorization and adequate documents and records).
b. For each internal control, identify the transaction-related management assertion(s) to which it applies.

11-25 **(OBJECTIVE 11-3)** The following are misstatements that have occurred in Fresh Foods Grocery Store, a retail and wholesale grocery company:

1. On the last day of the year, a truckload of beef was set aside for shipment but was not shipped. Because it was still on hand, the inventory was counted. The shipping document was dated the last day of the year, so it was also included as a current-year sale.
2. The incorrect price was used on sales invoices for billing shipments to customers because the wrong price was entered into the computer master file of prices.
3. A vendor invoice was paid even though no merchandise was ever received. The accounts payable software application does not require the input of a valid receiving report number before payment can be made.
4. Employees in the receiving department took sides of beef for their personal use. When a shipment of meat was received, the receiving department filled out a receiving report and forwarded it to the accounting department for the amount of goods actually received. At that time, two sides of beef were put in an employee's pickup truck rather than in the storage freezer.
5. An accounts payable clerk processed payments to himself by adding a fictitious vendor address to the approved vendor master file.
6. During the physical count of inventory of the retail grocery, one counter wrote down the wrong description of several products and miscounted the quantity.
7. A salesperson sold an entire carload of lamb at a price below cost because she did not know the cost of lamb had increased in the past week.

8. A vendor's invoice was paid twice for the same shipment. The second payment arose because the vendor sent a duplicate copy of the original 2 weeks after the payment was due.

Required

a. For each misstatement, identify one or more types of controls that were absent.
b. For each misstatement, identify the transaction-related management assertions that have not been met.
c. For each misstatement, suggest a control that may have prevented or detected the misstatement.

11-26 **(OBJECTIVE 11-3)** The division of the following duties is meant to provide the best possible controls for the Meridian Paint Company, a small wholesale store:

†1. Approve credit for customers included in the customer credit master file.
†2. Input shipping and billing information to bill customers, record invoices in the sales journal, and update the accounts receivable master file.
†3. Open the mail and prepare a prelisting of cash receipts.
†4. Enter cash receipts data to prepare the cash receipts journal and update the accounts receivable master file.
†5. Prepare daily cash deposits.
†6. Deliver daily cash deposits to the bank.
†7. Assemble the payroll time cards and input the data to prepare payroll checks and update the payroll journal and payroll master files.
†8. Sign payroll checks.
†9. Assemble supporting documents for general and payroll cash disbursements.
†10. Sign general cash disbursement checks.
†11. Input information to prepare checks for signature, record checks in the cash disbursements journal, and update the appropriate master files.
†12. Mail checks to suppliers and deliver checks to employees.
13. Cancel supporting documents to prevent their reuse.
14. Update the general ledger at the end of each month and review all accounts for unexpected balances.
15. Reconcile the accounts receivable master file with the control account and review accounts outstanding more than 90 days.
16. Prepare monthly statements for customers by printing the accounts receivable master file; then mail the statements to customers.
17. Reconcile the monthly statements from vendors with the accounts payable master file.
18. Reconcile the bank account.

Required

You are to divide the accounting-related duties 1 through 18 among Robert Smith, James Cooper, and Mohini Singh. All of the responsibilities marked with a dagger (†) are assumed to take about the same amount of time and must be divided equally between Smith and Cooper. Both employees are equally competent. Singh, who is president of the company, is not willing to perform any functions designated by a dagger and will perform only a maximum of two of the other functions.*

11-27 **(OBJECTIVES 11-3, 11-4)** The following are misstatements that can occur in the sales and collection cycle:

1. A customer number on a sales invoice was transposed and, as a result, charged to the wrong customer. By the time the error was found, the original customer was no longer in business.
2. A former computer operator, who is now a programmer, entered information for a fictitious sales return and ran it through the computer system at night. When the money came in, he took it and deposited it in his own account.
3. A nonexistent part number was included in the description of goods on a shipping document. Therefore, no charge was made for those goods.

* Based on AICPA question paper, American Institute of Certified Public Accountants.

4. A customer order was filled and shipped to a former customer, which had already filed for bankruptcy.
5. The sales manager approved the price of goods ordered by a customer, but he wrote down the wrong price.
6. A computer operator picked up a computer-based data file for sales of the wrong week and processed them through the system a second time.
7. For a sale, a data entry operator erroneously failed to enter the information for the salesman's department. As a result, the salesman received no commission for that sale.
8. Several remittance advices were batched together for inputting. The cash receipts clerk stopped for coffee, set them on a box, and failed to deliver them to the data input personnel.

Required

a. Identify the transaction-related management assertion(s) to which the misstatement pertains.
b. Identify one automated control that would have likely prevented each misstatement.

11-28 **(OBJECTIVES 11-3, 11-4)** You are doing the audit of Phelps College, a private school with approximately 2,500 students. With your firm's consultation, they have instituted an IT system that separates the responsibilities of the computer operator, systems analyst, librarian, programmer, and data control group by having a different person do each function. Now, a budget reduction is necessary and one of the five people must be laid off. You are requested to give the college advice as to how the five functions could be done with reduced personnel and minimal negative effects on internal control. The amount of time the functions take is not relevant because all five people also do nonaccounting functions.

Required

a. Divide the five functions among four people in such a way as to maintain the best possible control system.
b. Assume that economic times become worse for Phelps College and it must terminate employment of another person. Divide the five functions among three people in such a way as to maintain the best possible internal control. Again, the amount of time each function takes should not be a consideration in your decision.
c. Assume that economic times become so severe for Phelps College that only two people can be employed to do IT functions. Divide the five functions between two people in such a way as to maintain the best possible control system.
d. If the five functions were done by one person, will internal controls be so inadequate that an audit cannot be done? Discuss.

11-29 **(OBJECTIVE 11-4)** During your audit of Wilcoxon Sports, Inc., a retail chain of stores, you learn that a programmer made an unauthorized change to the sales application program even though no work on that application had been approved by IT management. In order for the sales application program to work, the programmer had to make modifications to the operating software security features. The unauthorized change forced the sales program to calculate an automatic discount for a customer who happens to be the brother-in-law of the programmer. The customer and programmer split the savings from the unauthorized discount. The programmer modified the program and returned it to the librarian, who placed it into the files for live production use. No other information was forwarded to the librarian.

Required

1. What recommendation do you have for management of Wilcoxon Sports, Inc., to prevent this from recurring?
2. Explain why you believe the suggested internal control improvements will prevent problems in the future.

11-30 **(OBJECTIVES 11-3, 11-4)** Your new audit client, Hardwood Lumber Company, has a computerized accounting system for all financial statement cycles. During planning, you visited with the information systems vice president and learned that personnel in information systems are assigned to one of four departments: systems programming, applications programming, operations, or data control. Job tasks are specific to the individual and no responsibilities overlap with other departments. Hardwood Lumber relies on the operating system software to restrict online access to individuals. The operating system allows an employee with "READ" capabilities to only view the contents of the program or file. "CHANGE" allows the employee to update the contents of the program or file. "RUN" allows the employee to use a program to process data. Programmers, both systems and applications, are restricted to a READ-only access to all live application software program files but have READ and CHANGE capabilities for test copies of those software program files. Operators have READ and RUN capabilities for live application programs. Data control clerks have CHANGE access to data files only and no access to software program files. The person in charge of operations maintains access to the operating software security features and is responsible for assigning access rights to individuals. The computer room is locked and requires a card-key to access the room. Only operations staff have a card-key to access the room, and security cameras monitor access. A TV screen is in the information systems vice president's office to allow periodic monitoring of access. The TV presents the live picture and no record is maintained. The librarian, who is in the operations department, is responsible for maintaining the library of program files. The librarian has READ and CHANGE access rights to program files. Backup copies of program files are stored on an external drive, and data files are maintained on a backup server. The external drive and backup server are located in a room adjacent to the computer room.

Required

a. Identify the strengths of Hardwood Lumber Company's computerized accounting system.
b. What recommendations for change can you suggest to improve Hardwood's information systems function?

11-31 **(OBJECTIVES 11-3, 11-4)** A growing number of organizations have been the target of hacking attacks, or cyberattacks, in recent years. High-profile examples in the U.S. include Target Corp., Home Depot Inc., the Internal Revenue Service, and other government agencies such as the Office of Personnel Management. Companies and governments need to consider the risks of a cyberattack, and consider backup plans in the event a cyberattack results in a loss of hardware, software, or data. The Committee of Sponsoring Organizations of the Treadway Commission (COSO) issued a thought paper, *COSO in the Cyber Age*, to help organizations assess and mitigate risks associated with cybersecurity through the existing COSO Framework. Visit the COSO Web site (www.coso.org), and refer to the "Guidance" tab. Read the thought paper to answer the following questions:

Required

a. The COSO guidance acknowledges that "cyber risk is not something that can be avoided; instead it must be managed." Why is cyber risk unavoidable? Does this acknowledgement make it more or less difficult to address and mitigate cyber risk?
b. At the control environment level (the first of the five components of internal control), what should organizations do to address cyber risk?
c. The paper identifies five broad categories of cyberattack perpetrators and motivations. Briefly describe each group of perpetrators and their motivation.
d. What types of control activities are recommended to address cyber risks?

CASE

11-32 **(OBJECTIVE 11-3)** The following is the description of sales and cash receipts for the Lady's Fashion Fair, a retail store dealing in expensive women's clothing. Sales are for cash or credit, using the store's own billing rather than credit cards.

Each salesclerk has her own sales book with prenumbered, three-copy, multicolored sales slips attached, but perforated. Only a central cash register is used. It is operated by the store supervisor, who has been employed for 10 years by Alice Olson, the store owner. The cash register is at the store entrance to control theft of clothes.

Salesclerks prepare the sales invoices in triplicate. The original and the second copy are given to the cashier. The third copy is retained by the salesclerk in the sales book. When the sale is for cash, the customer pays the salesclerk, who marks all three copies "paid" and presents the money to the cashier with the invoice copies.

All clothing is put into boxes or packages by the supervisor after comparing the clothing to the description on the invoice and the price on the sales tag. She also rechecks the clerk's calculations. Any corrections are approved by the salesclerk. The clerk changes her sales book at that time.

A credit sale is approved by the supervisor from an approved credit list after the salesclerk prepares the three-part invoice. Next, the supervisor enters the sale in her cash register as a credit or cash sale. The second copy of the invoice, which has been validated by the cash register, is given to the customer.

At the end of the day, the supervisor recaps the sales and cash and compares the totals to the cash register tape. The supervisor deposits the cash at the end of each day in the bank's deposit box. The cashier's copies of the invoices are sent to the accounts receivable clerk along with a summary of the day's receipts. The bank mails the deposit slip directly to the accounts receivable clerk.

Each clerk summarizes her sales each day on a daily summary form, which is used in part to calculate employees' sales commissions. Marge, the accountant, who is prohibited from handling cash, receives the supervisor's summary and the clerk's daily summary form. Daily, she puts all sales invoice information into the firm's computer, which provides a complete printout of all input and summaries. The accounting summary includes sales by salesclerk, cash sales, credit sales, and total sales. Marge compares this output with the supervisor's and salesclerks' summaries and reconciles all differences.

The computer updates accounts receivable, inventory, and general ledger master files. After the update procedure has been run on the computer, Marge's assistant files all sales invoices by customer number. A list of the invoice numbers in numerical sequence is included in the sales printout.

The mail is opened each morning by a secretary in the owner's office. All correspondence and complaints are given to the owner. The secretary prepares a prelist of cash receipts. He totals the list, prepares a deposit slip, and deposits the cash daily. A copy of the prelist, the deposit slip, and all remittances returned with the cash receipts are given to Marge. She uses this list and the remittances to record cash receipts and update accounts receivable, again by computer. She reconciles the total receipts on the prelist to the deposit slip and to her printout. At the same time, she compares the deposit slip received from the bank for cash sales to the cash receipts journal.

A weekly aged trial balance of accounts receivable is automatically generated by the computer. A separate listing of all unpaid bills over 60 days is also automatically prepared. These are given to Mrs. Olson, who acts as her own credit collector. She also approves all write-offs of uncollectible items and forwards the list to Marge, who writes them off.

Each month Marge mails statements generated by the computer to customers. Complaints and disagreements from customers are directed to Mrs. Olson, who resolves them and informs Marge in writing of any write-downs or misstatements that require correction.

The computer system also automatically totals the journals and posts the totals to the general ledger. A general ledger trial balance is printed out, from which Marge prepares financial statements. Marge also prepares a monthly bank reconciliation and reconciles the general ledger to the aged accounts receivable trial balance.

Because of the importance of inventory control, Marge prints out the inventory perpetual totals monthly, on the last day of each month. Salesclerks count all inventory after store hours on the last day of each month for comparison with the perpetuals. An inventory shortages report is provided to Mrs. Olson. The perpetuals are adjusted by Marge after Mrs. Olson has approved the adjustments.

Required

a. For each sales transaction-related management assertion, identify one or more existing controls.
b. For each cash receipts transaction-related management assertion, identify one or more existing controls.
c. Identify deficiencies in internal control for sales and cash receipts.

ASSESSING CONTROL RISK AND REPORTING ON INTERNAL CONTROLS

CHAPTER 12

Just Because the Computer Did the Work Doesn't Mean It's Right

Foster Wellman's audit client, Manion's Department Stores, Inc., installed a software program that processed and aged customer accounts receivable. The aging, which indicated how long the customers' accounts were outstanding, was useful to Wellman when evaluating the collectibility of those accounts.

Because Wellman didn't know whether the aging totals were computed correctly, he decided to test Manion's aging by using his own firm's audit software to recalculate the aging, using an electronic copy of Manion's accounts receivable data file. He reasoned that if the aging produced by his audit software was in reasonable agreement with Manion's aging, he would have evidence that Manion's aging was correct.

Wellman was shocked when he found a material difference between his and Manion's calculated aging. Rudy Rose, the manager of Manion's information technology (IT) function, investigated the discrepancy and discovered that programmer errors had resulted in design flaws in Manion's software used to calculate the aging. This outcome caused Wellman to substantially increase the amount of his testing of the year-end balance of the allowance for uncollectible accounts, and it resulted in a significant audit adjustment to Manion's allowance account.

LEARNING OBJECTIVES

After studying this chapter, you should be able to

12-1 Obtain and document an understanding of internal control.

12-2 Assess control risk by linking key controls and control deficiencies to transaction-related audit objectives.

12-3 Describe the process of designing and performing tests of controls.

12-4 Understand how control risk impacts detection risk and the design of substantive tests.

12-5 Understand requirements for auditor reporting on internal control.

12-6 Describe the differences in evaluating, reporting, and testing internal control for nonpublic and smaller public companies.

12-7 Describe how the complexity of the IT environment impacts control risk assessment and testing.

OBTAIN AND DOCUMENT UNDERSTANDING OF INTERNAL CONTROL

OBJECTIVE 12-1

Obtain and document an understanding of internal control.

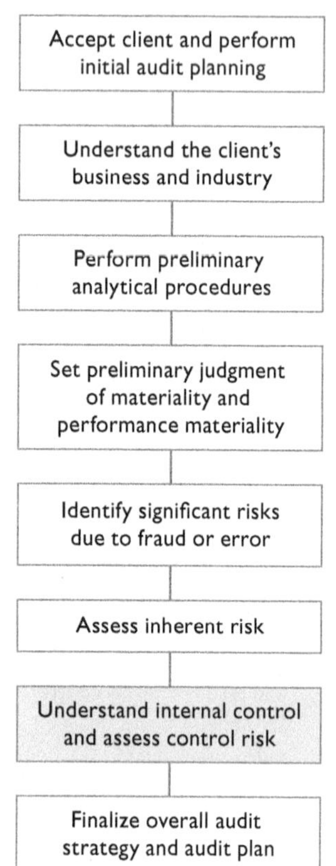

In the previous chapter, we discussed the components of the COSO internal control framework and how companies integrate technology into their system of internal controls. In this chapter, we discuss how auditors obtain and document their understanding of internal controls and assess control risk as part of the audit planning process. The opening story about Manion's overreliance on the accuracy of the computer-produced accounts receivable aging illustrates the importance of testing controls and also the efficiency and effectiveness of using audit software. People often assume "the information is correct because the computer produced it." Unfortunately, auditors sometimes depend on the untested accuracy of computer-generated output because they forget that computers perform only as well as they are programmed. Before concluding that information is reliable, auditors must understand and test computer-based controls in the same way they need to understand and test manual controls.

For financial statement audits, auditors need to understand controls that are relevant to the audit in order to identify and assess the risks of material misstatements. For integrated audits of large, publicly traded companies, the level of understanding of internal control and the extent of testing need to be sufficient to issue an opinion on the effectiveness of internal control over financial reporting in addition to assessing the risks of material misstatement as part of the audit planning process. Thus, the level of understanding required for the audit of internal control exceeds what is required for an audit of only the financial statements.

Figure 12-1 provides an overview of the process of understanding internal control and assessing control risk. The figure shows that there are four steps in the process. Each of these four steps is discussed in this chapter.

FIGURE 12-1 Process for Understanding Internal Control and Assessing Control Risk

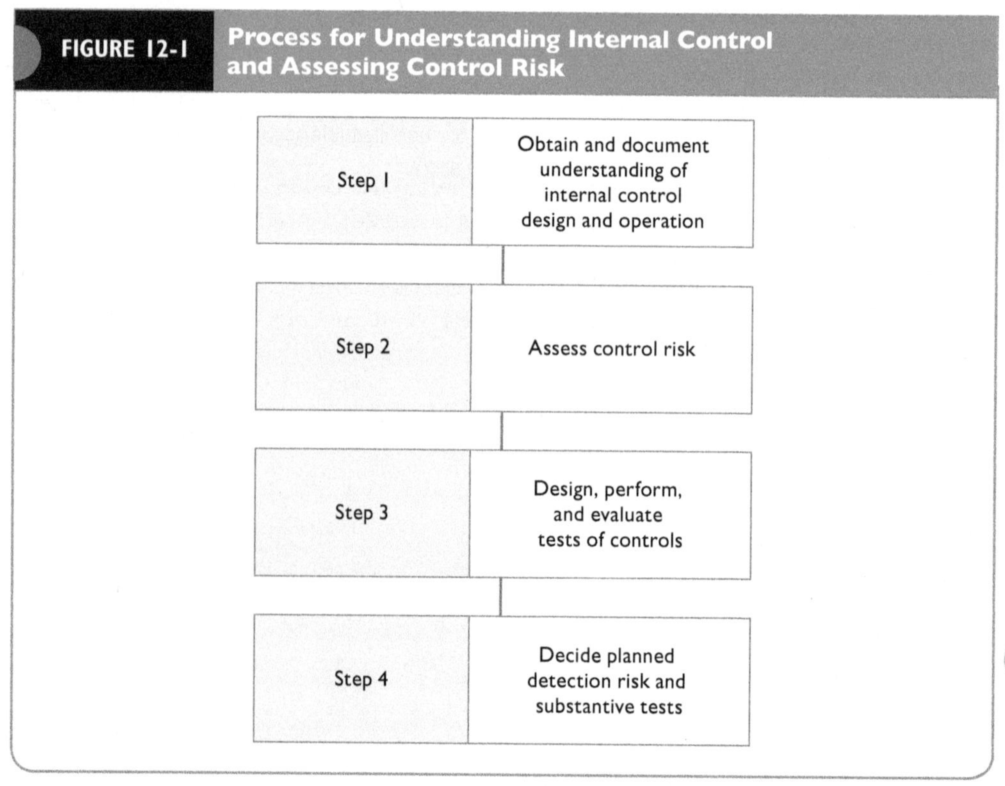

Obtain and Document Understanding of Internal Control

Auditing standards require auditors to obtain and document their understanding of internal control for every audit. This understanding is necessary for both the audit of internal controls over financial reporting and the audit of financial statements. Management's documentation is a major source of information in gaining this understanding.

As part of the auditor's risk assessment procedures, the auditor uses **procedures to obtain an understanding**, which involve gathering evidence about the design of internal controls and whether they have been implemented, and then using that information as a basis for assessing control risk and for the integrated audit. The auditor generally uses four of the eight types of evidence described in Chapter 7 to obtain an understanding of the design and implementation of controls: inspection, inquiry of entity personnel, observation of employees performing control processes, and reperformance by tracing one or a few transactions through the accounting system from start to finish.

Auditors commonly use three types of documents to obtain and document their understanding of the design of internal control: narratives, flowcharts, and internal control questionnaires. Because Section 404 of the Sarbanes–Oxley Act requires management to assess and document the design effectiveness of internal control over financial reporting, they have usually already prepared this documentation. Narratives, flowcharts, and internal control questionnaires, used by the auditor separately or in combination to document internal control, are discussed next.

Narrative A **narrative** is a written description of a client's internal controls. A proper narrative of an accounting system and related controls describes four things:

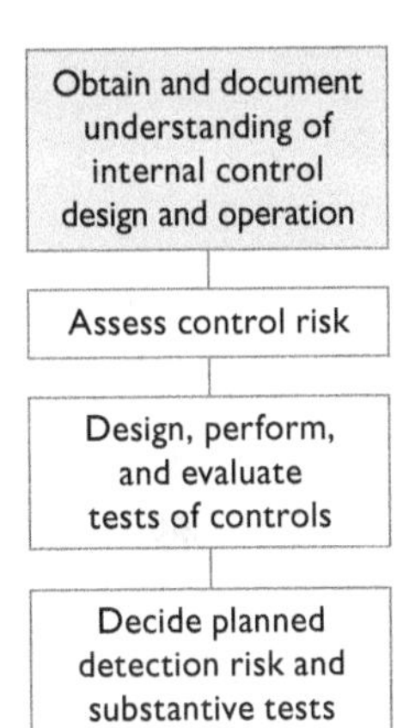

1. *The origin of every document and record in the system.* For example, the description should state where customer orders come from and how sales invoices are generated.
2. *All processing that takes place.* For example, if sales amounts are determined by a computer program that multiplies quantities shipped by standard prices contained in price master files, that process should be described.
3. *The disposition of every document and record in the system.* The filing or electronic archiving of documents, sending them to customers, or destroying them should be described.
4. *An indication of the controls relevant to the assessment of control risk.* These typically include separation of duties (such as separating recording cash from handling cash), authorizations and approvals (such as credit approvals), and internal verification (such as comparison of unit selling prices to sales contracts).

Flowchart An internal control **flowchart** is a diagram of the client's documents and their sequential flow in the organization. An adequate flowchart includes the same four characteristics identified for narratives.

Well-prepared flowcharts are advantageous primarily because they provide a concise overview of the client's system, including separation of duties, which helps auditors identify controls and deficiencies in the client's system. Flowcharts have two advantages over narratives: typically they are easier to read and easier to update. It is unusual to use both a narrative and a flowchart to describe the same system because both present the same information.

Internal Control Questionnaire An **internal control questionnaire** asks a series of questions about the controls in each audit area as a means of identifying internal control deficiencies. Most questionnaires require a "yes" or a "no" response, with "no" responses indicating potential internal control deficiencies. By using a questionnaire, auditors cover each audit area reasonably quickly. The two main disadvantages of questionnaires are their inability to provide an overview of the system and their inapplicability for some audits, especially smaller ones.

Figure 12-2 (p. 370) illustrates part of an internal control questionnaire for the sales and collection cycle of Hillsburg Hardware Co. Notice how the questionnaire incorporates the six transaction-related audit objectives A through F as each applies to sales transactions (see shaded portions). The same is true for all other audit areas.

These methods are also used to obtain an understanding of IT general controls. The auditor interviews IT personnel and key users; examines system documentation such as flowcharts, user manuals, program change requests, and system testing results; and reviews detailed questionnaires completed by IT staff. In most cases,

FIGURE 12-2 Partial Internal Control Questionnaire for Sales

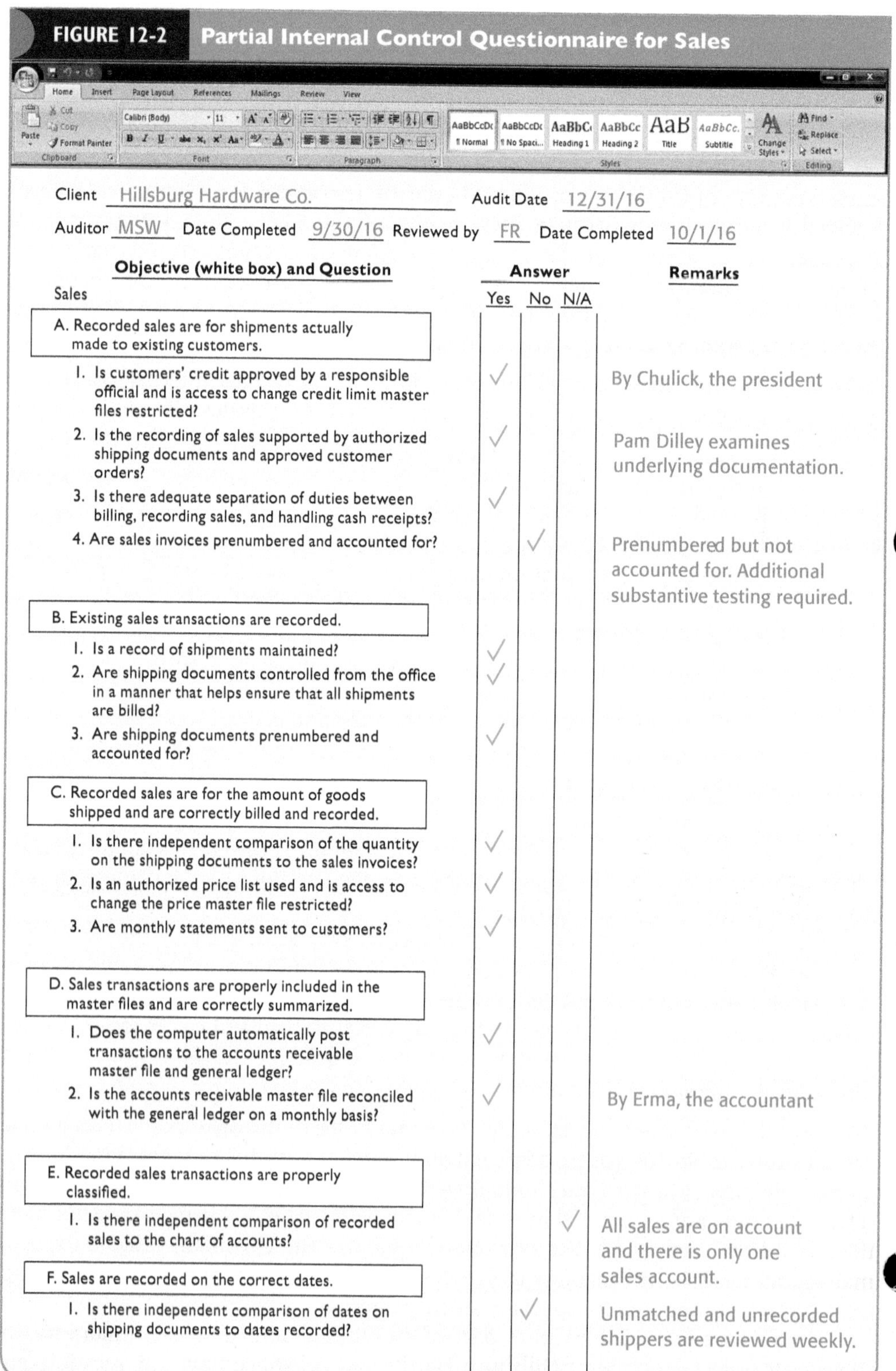

Client Hillsburg Hardware Co. Audit Date 12/31/16

Auditor MSW Date Completed 9/30/16 Reviewed by FR Date Completed 10/1/16

Objective (white box) and Question	Yes	No	N/A	Remarks
Sales				
A. Recorded sales are for shipments actually made to existing customers.				
1. Is customers' credit approved by a responsible official and is access to change credit limit master files restricted?	✓			By Chulick, the president
2. Is the recording of sales supported by authorized shipping documents and approved customer orders?	✓			Pam Dilley examines underlying documentation.
3. Is there adequate separation of duties between billing, recording sales, and handling cash receipts?	✓			
4. Are sales invoices prenumbered and accounted for?		✓		Prenumbered but not accounted for. Additional substantive testing required.
B. Existing sales transactions are recorded.				
1. Is a record of shipments maintained?	✓			
2. Are shipping documents controlled from the office in a manner that helps ensure that all shipments are billed?	✓			
3. Are shipping documents prenumbered and accounted for?	✓			
C. Recorded sales are for the amount of goods shipped and are correctly billed and recorded.				
1. Is there independent comparison of the quantity on the shipping documents to the sales invoices?	✓			
2. Is an authorized price list used and is access to change the price master file restricted?	✓			
3. Are monthly statements sent to customers?	✓			
D. Sales transactions are properly included in the master files and are correctly summarized.				
1. Does the computer automatically post transactions to the accounts receivable master file and general ledger?	✓			
2. Is the accounts receivable master file reconciled with the general ledger on a monthly basis?	✓			By Erma, the accountant
E. Recorded sales transactions are properly classified.				
1. Is there independent comparison of recorded sales to the chart of accounts?			✓	All sales are on account and there is only one sales account.
F. Sales are recorded on the correct dates.				
1. Is there independent comparison of dates on shipping documents to dates recorded?		✓		Unmatched and unrecorded shippers are reviewed weekly.

auditors should use several of these approaches in understanding general controls because each offers different information. For example, interviews with the chief information officer and systems analysts provide useful information about the operation of the entire IT function, the extent of software development and hardware changes made to accounting application software, and an overview of any planned changes. Reviews of program change requests and system test results are useful to identify program changes in application software. Questionnaires help auditors identify specific internal controls.

The use of questionnaires and flowcharts together is useful for understanding the client's internal control design and identifying internal controls and deficiencies. Flowcharts provide an overview of the system, while questionnaires offer useful checklists to remind the auditor of many different types of internal controls that should exist.

Evaluating Internal Control Implementation

In addition to understanding the design of the internal controls, the auditor must also evaluate whether the designed controls are implemented. In practice, the understanding of the design and the implementation are often done simultaneously. Following are common methods.

Update and Evaluate Auditor's Previous Experience with the Entity Most audits of a company are done annually by the same CPA firm. After the first year's audit, the auditor begins with a great deal of information from prior years about the client's internal control. It is especially useful to determine whether controls that were not previously operating effectively have been improved.

Make Inquiries of Client Personnel Auditors should ask management and other personnel to explain their duties. Careful questioning of appropriate personnel helps auditors evaluate whether employees understand their duties and do what is described in the client's control documentation.

Examine Documents and Records The five components of internal control all involve the creation of many documents and records. By examining completed documents, records, and computer files, the auditor can evaluate whether information described in flowcharts, narratives, and questionnaires has been implemented.

Observe Entity Activities and Operations When auditors observe client personnel carrying out their normal accounting and control activities, including their preparation of documents and records, it further improves the auditors' understanding and knowledge that controls have been implemented.

Perform Walkthroughs of the Accounting System In a **walkthrough**, the auditor selects one or a few documents of a transaction type and traces them from initiation through the entire accounting process. At each stage of processing, the auditor makes inquiries, observes activities, and examines completed documents and records. Walkthroughs conveniently combine observation, inspection, and inquiry to assure that the controls designed by management have been implemented.

ASSESS CONTROL RISK

OBJECTIVE 12-2

Assess control risk by linking key controls and control deficiencies to transaction-related audit objectives.

The auditor obtains an understanding of the design and implementation of internal control to make a preliminary assessment of control risk as part of the auditor's overall assessment of the risk of material misstatements. As described in Chapter 9, the auditor uses this preliminary assessment of control risk to plan the audit for each material class of transactions. However, in some instances the auditor may learn that the control deficiencies are significant such that the client's financial statements may not be auditable. For example, if management lacks integrity or the accounting records are deficient, most auditors will not accept the engagement.

Determine Assessed Control Risk Supported by the Understanding Obtained

After obtaining an understanding of internal control, the auditor makes a preliminary **assessment of control risk** as part of the auditor's overall assessment of the risk of material misstatement. This assessment is a measure of the auditor's expectation that internal controls will prevent material misstatements from occurring or detect and correct them if they have occurred.

The starting point for most auditors is the assessment of entity-level controls. By their nature, entity-level controls, such as many of the elements contained in the control environment, risk assessment, and monitoring components, have an overarching impact on most major types of transactions in each transaction cycle. For example, an ineffective board of directors or management's failure to have any process to identify, assess, or manage key risks has the potential to undermine controls for most of the transaction-related audit objectives (for an example, see the vignette below related to Livent, Inc.). Thus, auditors generally assess entity-level controls before assessing transaction-specific controls.

Similarly, auditors should evaluate the effectiveness of IT general controls before evaluating automated application controls or manual controls dependent on IT output. Ineffective general controls create the potential for material misstatements across all system applications, regardless of the quality of individual application controls. For example, if the auditor observes that data files are inadequately safeguarded, the auditor may conclude that there is a significant risk of loss of data for every class of transaction that relies on that data to conduct application controls. On the other hand, if general controls are effective, the auditor may be able to place greater reliance on application controls whose functionality is dependent on IT.

Once auditors determine that entity-level controls, including general controls, are designed and placed in operation, they next make a preliminary assessment for each transaction-related audit objective for each major type of transaction in each transaction cycle. For example, in the sales and collection cycle, the types of transactions usually involve sales, sales returns and allowances, cash receipts, and the provision for and write-off of uncollectible accounts. The auditor also makes the preliminary assessment for controls affecting audit objectives for balance sheet accounts and presentations and disclosures in each cycle.

Use of a Control Risk Matrix to Assess Control Risk

Many auditors use a **control risk matrix** to assist in the control risk assessment process at the transaction level. The purpose is to provide a convenient way to organize assessing control risk for each audit objective. Figure 12-3 illustrates the use of a control risk matrix for sales transaction audit objectives of Hillsburg Hardware Co. While Figure 12-3 only illustrates the control risk matrix for transaction-related audit

PHANTOM BOOKS

Senior executives at Livent, Inc., the Toronto theater owner and producer of Broadway-style shows including Show Boat, Ragtime, and Phantom of the Opera, took their theatrics to a new level when they allegedly engaged in a pervasive fraud to materially distort their financial statements over an eight-year period. According to charges filed by the Securities and Exchange Commission, the former chairman and CEO and the former president together coaxed several of their longtime company associates, including the CFO and IT manager, to participate in a multifaceted scheme to manipulate profits.

In addition to orchestrating vendor kickback schemes to siphon off millions of dollars and numerous customer side-agreements to falsify revenues, senior management manipulated the accounting records to shift costs of shows to fixed assets from expenses. Their techniques included alteration of computer programs to lower expenses without a trace in order to hide the fraud from Livent auditors. In addition, they created "phantom" accounting records showing the adjustments so senior management could track the fraudulent entries and know the company's true financial condition. Ultimately, their distortions were revealed, and the executives faced charges both in the United States and Canada. Livent filed for bankruptcy and was subsequently sold to a team headed by a former Walt Disney Company executive.

Sources: 1. Securities and Exchange Commission, *Litigation Release No. 16022*, Washington, DC, January 1999; 2. Canadian Broadcasting Company, "Livent Founders Charged with Fraud," *Arts Now*, Toronto, October 10, 2002.

FIGURE 12-3 **Control Risk Matrix for Hillsburg Hardware Co.—Sales**

	INTERNAL CONTROL	SALES TRANSACTION-RELATED AUDIT OBJECTIVES: Recorded sales are for shipments actually made to nonfictitious customers (occurrence).	Existing sales transactions are recorded (completeness).	Recorded sales are for the amount of goods shipped and are correctly billed and recorded (accuracy).	Sales transactions are correctly included in the accounts receivable master file and are correctly summarized (posting and summarization).	Sales transactions are correctly classified (classification).	Sales are recorded on the correct dates (timing).
CONTROLS	Credit is approved automatically by computer by comparison to authorized credit limits (C1).	C					
CONTROLS	Recorded sales are supported by authorized shipping documents and approved customers orders (C2).	C		C			
CONTROLS	Separation of duties exists among billing, recording of sales, and handling of cash receipts (C3).	C	C		C		
CONTROLS	Shipping documents are forwarded to billing daily and are billed the subsequent day (C4).	C					C
CONTROLS	Shipping documents are prenumbered and accounted for weekly (C5).		C				C
CONTROLS	Batch totals of quantities shipped are compared with quantities billed (C6).	C	C	C			
CONTROLS	Unit selling prices are obtained from the price list master file of approved prices (C7).			C			
CONTROLS	Sales transactions are internally verified (C8).					C	
CONTROLS	Statements are mailed to customers each month (C9).	C		C	C		
CONTROLS	Computer automatically posts transactions to the accounts receivable subsidiary records and to the general ledger (C10).				C		
CONTROLS	Accounts receivable master file is reconciled to the general ledger on a monthly basis (C11).				C		
DEFICIENCIES	There is a lack of internal verification for the possibility of sales invoices being recorded more than once (D1).	D					
DEFICIENCIES	There is a lack of control to test for timely recording (D2).						D
	Assessed control risk	Med.	Low	Low	Low	Low	Med.

*Because there are no cash sales, classification is not a problem.
C = Control; D = Control Deficiency.

Note: This matrix was developed using an internal control questionnaire, part of which is included in Figure 12-2 (p. 370), as well as flowcharts and other documentation of the auditor's understanding of internal control.

objectives, auditors use a similar control risk matrix format to assess control risk for balance-related and presentation and disclosure-related audit objectives. The control risk matrix can include both manual and automated application controls. We now discuss the preparation of the matrix.

Identify Audit Objectives The first step in the assessment is to identify the audit objectives for classes of transactions, account balances, and presentation and disclosure to which the assessment applies. For example, this is done for classes of transactions by applying the specific transaction-related audit objectives introduced earlier, which were stated in general form, to each major type of transaction for the entity. For example, the auditor makes an assessment of the occurrence objective for sales and a separate assessment of the completeness objective. Transaction-related audit objectives are shown for sales transactions for Hillsburg Hardware at the top of Figure 12-3 (p. 373).

Identify Existing Controls Next, the auditor uses the information discussed in the previous section on obtaining and documenting an understanding of internal control to identify the controls that contribute to accomplishing transaction-related audit objectives. One way for the auditor to do this is to identify controls to satisfy each objective. For example, the auditor can use knowledge of the client's system to identify controls that are likely to prevent errors or fraud in the occurrence transaction-related audit objective. The same thing can be done for all other objectives. It is also helpful for the auditor to use the five control activities (separation of duties, proper authorization, adequate documents and records, physical control over assets and records, and independent checks on performance) as reminders of controls. For example: Is there adequate separation of duties and how is it achieved? Are transactions properly authorized? Are prenumbered documents properly accounted for? Are key master files properly restricted from unauthorized access? Is an independent verification of processes performed?

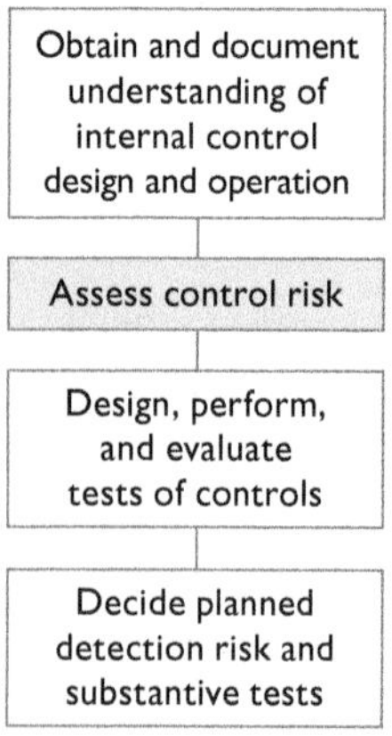

Obtain and document understanding of internal control design and operation

Assess control risk

Design, perform, and evaluate tests of controls

Decide planned detection risk and substantive tests

The auditor should identify and include only those controls that are expected to have the greatest effect on meeting the transaction-related audit objectives. These are often called **key controls**. The reason for including only key controls is that they will be sufficient to achieve the transaction-related audit objectives and also provide audit efficiency. Examples of key controls for Hillsburg Hardware are shown in Figure 12-3.

Associate Controls with Related Audit Objectives Each control satisfies one or more related audit objectives. This can be seen in Figure 12-3 for transaction-related audit objectives. The body of the matrix is used to show how each control contributes to the accomplishment of one or more transaction-related audit objectives. In this illustration, a C was entered in each cell where a control partially or fully satisfied an objective. A similar control risk matrix would be completed for balance-related and presentation and disclosure-related audit objectives. For example, the mailing of statements to customers satisfies three objectives in the audit of Hillsburg Hardware, which is indicated by the placement of a C on the row in Figure 12-3 describing that control.

Identify and Evaluate Control Deficiencies, Significant Deficiencies, and Material Weaknesses Auditors must evaluate whether key controls are absent in the design of internal control over financial reporting as a part of evaluating control risk and the likelihood of financial statement misstatements. Auditing standards define three levels of the absence of internal controls:

1. *Control deficiency.* A **control deficiency** exists if the design and implementation or operation of controls does not permit company personnel to prevent or detect misstatements on a timely basis in the normal course of performing their assigned functions. A *design deficiency* exists if a necessary control is missing, is not properly designed, or is not properly implemented. An *operation deficiency* exists if a well-designed control does not operate as designed or if the person performing the control is insufficiently qualified or authorized.

2. *Significant deficiency.* A **significant deficiency** exists if one or more control deficiencies exist that are less severe than a material weakness (defined next), but are important enough to merit attention by those responsible for oversight of the company's financial reporting.
3. *Material weakness.* A **material weakness** exists if a significant deficiency, by itself or in combination with other significant deficiencies, results in a reasonable possibility that internal control will not prevent or detect material financial statement misstatements on a timely basis.

   To determine if a significant internal control deficiency or deficiencies are a material weakness, they must be evaluated along two dimensions: likelihood and significance. The horizontal line in Figure 12-4 depicts the likelihood of a misstatement resulting from the significant deficiency, while the vertical line depicts its significance. If there is more than a reasonable possibility (likelihood) that a material misstatement (significance) could result from the significant deficiency or deficiencies, then it is considered a material weakness.

Identify Deficiencies, Significant Deficiencies, and Material Weaknesses

A five-step approach can be used to identify deficiencies, significant deficiencies, and material weaknesses:

1. *Identify existing controls.* Because deficiencies and material weaknesses are the absence of adequate controls, the auditor must first know which controls exist. The methods for identifying controls have already been discussed.
2. *Identify the absence of key controls.* Internal control questionnaires, flowcharts, and walkthroughs are useful tools to identify where controls are lacking and the likelihood of misstatement is therefore increased. It is also useful to examine the control risk matrix, such as the one in Figure 12-3, to look for objectives where there are no or only a few controls to prevent or detect misstatements.
3. *Consider the possibility of compensating controls.* A **compensating control** is one elsewhere in the system that offsets the absence of a key control. A common example in a small business is the active involvement of the owner. When a compensating control exists, there is no longer a significant deficiency or material weakness.
4. *Decide whether there is a significant deficiency or material weakness.* The likelihood of misstatements and their potential materiality are used to evaluate if there are significant deficiencies or material weaknesses.
5. *Determine potential misstatements that could result.* This step is intended to identify specific misstatements that are likely to result because of the significant deficiency or material weakness. The importance of a significant deficiency or material weakness is directly related to the likelihood and materiality of potential misstatements.

FIGURE 12-4 Evaluating Significant Control Deficiencies

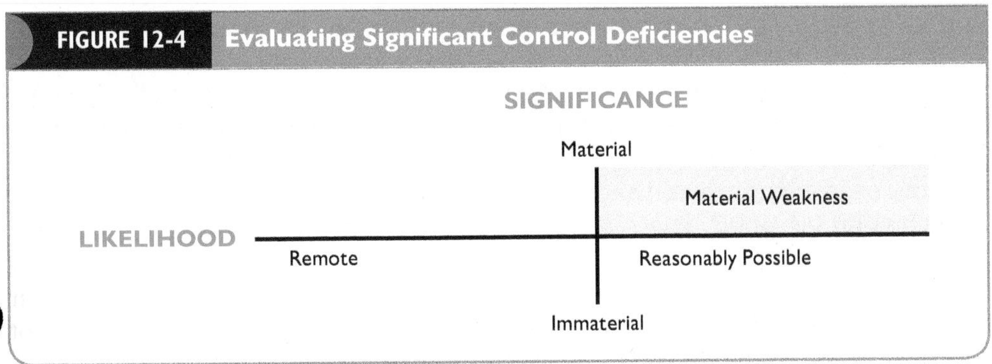

Source: Michael Ramos, "Section 404 Compliance in the Annual Report," *Journal of Accountancy*, October 2004, pp. 43–48.

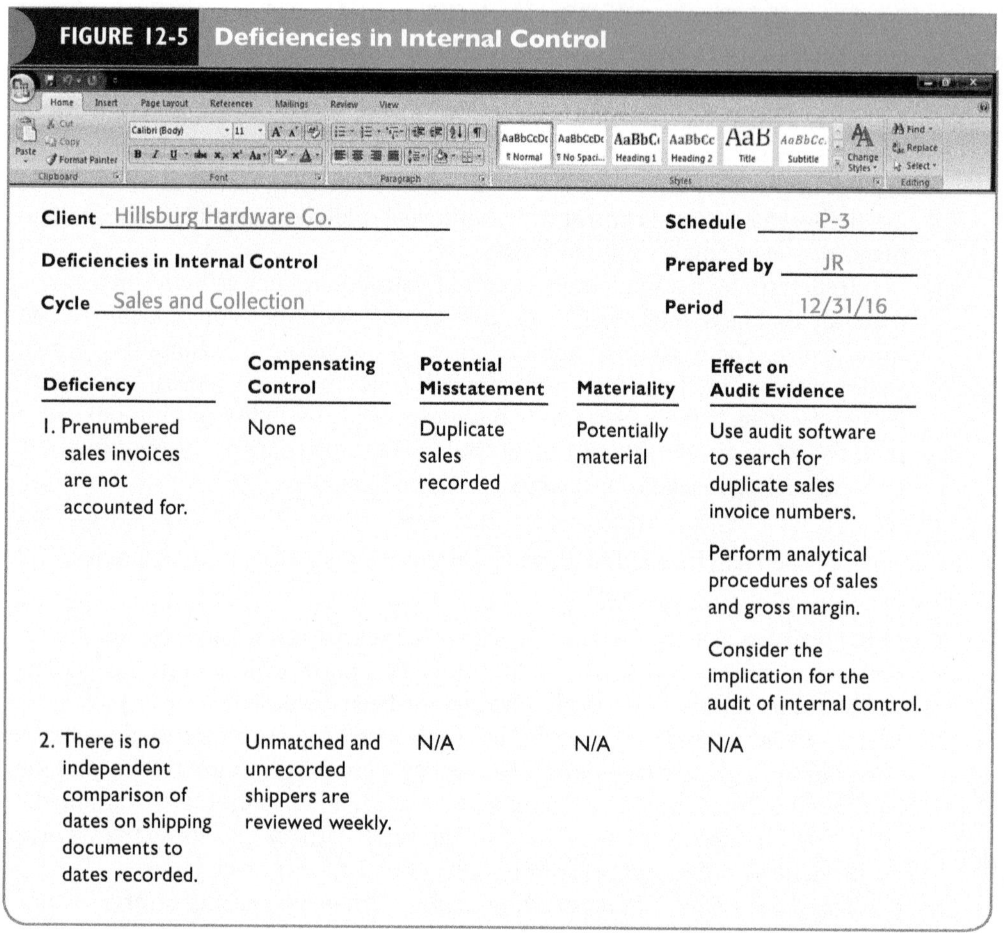

FIGURE 12-5 **Deficiencies in Internal Control**

Client Hillsburg Hardware Co. **Schedule** P-3

Deficiencies in Internal Control **Prepared by** JR

Cycle Sales and Collection **Period** 12/31/16

Deficiency	Compensating Control	Potential Misstatement	Materiality	Effect on Audit Evidence
1. Prenumbered sales invoices are not accounted for.	None	Duplicate sales recorded	Potentially material	Use audit software to search for duplicate sales invoice numbers. Perform analytical procedures of sales and gross margin. Consider the implication for the audit of internal control.
2. There is no independent comparison of dates on shipping documents to dates recorded.	Unmatched and unrecorded shippers are reviewed weekly.	N/A	N/A	N/A

Figure 12-5 for Hillsburg Hardware includes two control deficiencies. Neither deficiency was considered a material weakness; the first weakness, which is related to prenumbered sales invoices, was considered a significant deficiency.

Associate Control Deficiencies with Related Audit Objectives The same as for controls, each significant deficiency or material weakness can apply to one or more related audit objectives. In the case of Hillsburg Hardware in Figure 12-3 (p. 373), there are two control deficiencies, and each applies to only one transaction-related objective. The control deficiencies are indicated in the body of the figure by a D in the appropriate objective column.

Assess Control Risk for Each Related Audit Objective After controls and control deficiencies are identified and associated with transaction-related audit objectives, the auditor can assess control risk for transaction-related audit objectives. This is the critical decision in the evaluation of internal control. The auditor uses all of the information discussed previously to make a subjective control risk assessment for each objective. There are different ways to express this assessment. Some auditors use a subjective expression such as high, moderate, or low. Others use numerical probabilities such as 1.0, 0.6, or 0.2.

Again, the control risk matrix is a useful tool for making the assessment. Referring to Figure 12-3, the auditor assessed control risk for each objective for Hillsburg's sales by reviewing each column for pertinent controls and control deficiencies and asking, "What is the likelihood that a material misstatement would not be prevented or detected, or corrected if it occurred, by these controls, and what is the effect of the deficiencies or weaknesses?" If the likelihood is low, then control risk is low, and so forth. Figure 12-3 for Hillsburg Hardware shows that all objectives are assessed as low except occurrence and timing, which are medium.

This assessment is not the final one. Before making the final assessment at the end of an audit, the auditor will test controls and perform substantive tests. These procedures can either support the preliminary assessment or cause the auditor to make changes. In some cases, management can correct deficiencies and material weaknesses before the auditor does significant testing, which may permit a reduction in control risk.

After a preliminary assessment of control risk is made for sales and cash receipts, the auditor can complete the three control-risk rows of the evidence-planning worksheet that was introduced in Chapter 9 on page 282. If tests of controls results do not support the preliminary assessment of control risk, the auditor must modify the worksheet later. Alternatively, the auditor can wait until tests of controls are done to complete the three control-risk rows of the worksheet. An evidence-planning worksheet for Hillsburg Hardware with the three rows for control risk completed is illustrated in Figure 15-6 on page 504.

TESTS OF CONTROLS

OBJECTIVE 12-3

Describe the process of designing and performing tests of controls.

We've examined how auditors link controls and control deficiencies to related audit objectives to assess control risk for each objective. Now we'll address how auditors test those controls that are used to support a control risk assessment. For example, each key control in Figure 12-3 that the auditor intends to rely on to support a control risk below the maximum must be supported by sufficient tests of controls. We will deal with tests of controls for both audits of internal control for financial reporting and audits of financial statements.

Purpose of Tests of Controls

Assessing control risk requires the auditor to consider the design, implementation, and operation of controls to evaluate whether they will likely be effective in meeting related audit objectives. During the understanding phase, the auditor will have already gathered some evidence in support of both the design of the controls and their implementation by using procedures to obtain an understanding (see pages 368–371). In most cases, the auditor *will not* have gathered enough evidence to reduce assessed control risk to a sufficiently low level. The auditor must therefore obtain additional evidence about the operating effectiveness of controls throughout all, or at least most, of the period under audit. The procedures to test effectiveness of controls in support of a reduced assessed control risk are called **tests of controls**.

If the results of tests of controls support the design and operation of controls as expected, the auditor uses the same assessed control risk as the preliminary assessment. If, however, the tests of controls indicate that the controls did not operate effectively, the assessed control risk must be reconsidered. For example, the tests may indicate that the application of a control was curtailed midway through the year or that the person applying it made frequent misstatements. In such situations, the auditor uses a higher assessed control risk, unless compensating controls for the same related audit objectives are identified and found to be effective. For integrated audits, the auditor must also consider the impact of those controls that are not operating effectively on the auditor's report on internal control.

Procedures for Tests of Controls

The auditor is likely to use four types of procedures to support the operating effectiveness of internal controls. Management's testing of internal control will likely include the same types of procedures. The four types of procedures are as follows:

1. *Make inquiries of appropriate client personnel.* Although inquiry is not a highly reliable source of evidence about the effective operation of controls, it is still

appropriate. For example, to determine that unauthorized personnel are denied access to computer files, the auditor may make inquiries of the person who controls the computer library and of the person who controls online-access security-password assignments.

2. *Examine documents, records, and reports.* Many controls leave a clear trail of documentary evidence (both electronic and paper) that can be used to test controls. Suppose, for example, that when a customer order is received, it is used to create a customer sales order, which is approved for credit. (See the first and second key controls in Figure 12-3 on page 373.) Then the customer order is attached to the sales order as authorization for further processing. The auditor can test the control by examining the documents to make sure that they are complete and properly matched and that required signatures or initials are present.

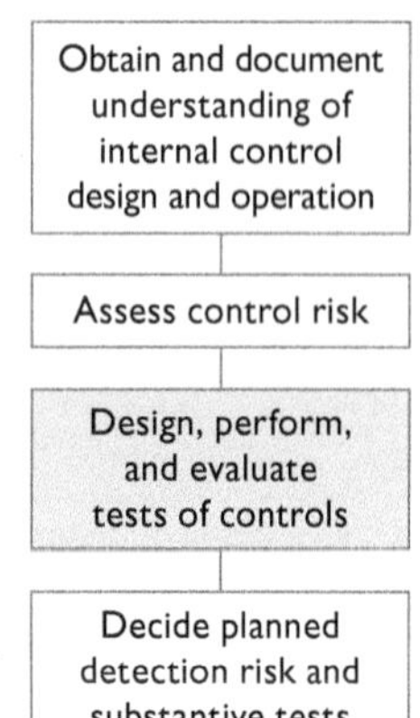

3. *Observe control-related activities.* Some controls do not leave an evidence trail, which means that it is not possible at a later date to examine evidence that the control was executed. For example, separation of duties relies on specific persons performing specific tasks, and there is typically no documentation of the separate performance. (See the third key control in Figure 12-3.) For controls that leave no documentary evidence, the auditor generally observes them being applied at various points during the year.
4. *Reperform client procedures.* There are also control-related activities for which there are related documents and records, but their content is insufficient for the auditor's purpose of assessing whether controls are operating effectively. For example, assume that prices on sales invoices are obtained from the master price list, but no indication of the control is documented on the sales invoices. (See the seventh key control in Figure 12-3.) In these cases, it is common for the auditor to reperform the control activity to see whether the proper results were obtained. For this example, the auditor can reperform the procedure by tracing the sales prices to the authorized price list in effect at the date of the transaction. If no misstatements are found, the auditor can conclude that the procedure is operating as intended.

Extent of Procedures

The extent to which tests of controls are applied depends on the preliminary assessed control risk. If the auditor wants a lower assessed control risk, more extensive tests of controls are applied, both in terms of the number of controls tested and the extent of the tests for each control. For example, if the auditor wants to use a low assessed control risk, a larger sample size for inspection, observation, and reperformance procedures should be applied.

The extent of testing also depends on the frequency of the operation of the controls, and whether it is manual or automated. For example, some financial reporting controls only operate at the end of the fiscal year, or quarterly, as opposed to operating on a daily basis. The auditor will test year-end controls, but will also test a sample of controls that operate quarterly or monthly. For manual controls, the auditor will select a sample of transactions and test whether the control is operating effectively. As an example, if the client manually compares a purchase order, receiving report, and vendor's invoice before approving payment to a vendor, an auditor may select a sample of recorded purchases throughout the year and verify the documents were properly matched and approved for payment. Because manual controls are performed by people, they are always subject to random error or manipulation. For automated controls, as long as the computer is programmed accurately and that program remains unchanged, automated controls will consistently perform as programmed until the software application is changed. Using the purchases example, the matching of the purchase order, receiving report, and vendor's invoice can be automated and the computer can generate a list of exceptions, rather than an employee manually comparing. As a result, when there are effective general controls and an automated application control, the auditor may be able to justify testing only one transaction and may not need to select a sample of transactions to verify. Therefore, the extent of testing will vary. The auditor will use one of several approaches to determine whether the design and implementation of automated controls are appropriate and that they are operating effectively. These approaches are discussed further later in the chapter when we discuss controls in more complex IT environments.

Reliance on Evidence from the Prior Year's Audit When auditors plan to use evidence about the operating effectiveness of internal control obtained in prior audits, auditing standards require tests of the controls' effectiveness at least every third year. If auditors determine that a key control has been changed since it was last tested, they should test it in the current year. This applies to both manual and automated controls. When there are a number of controls tested in prior audits that have not been changed, auditing standards require auditors to test some of those controls each year to ensure there is a rotation of controls testing throughout the three-year period.

Testing of Controls Related to Significant Risks As described in Chapter 9, significant risks are those risks that the auditor believes require special audit consideration. When the auditor's risk assessment procedures identify significant risks, the auditor is required to test the operating effectiveness of controls that mitigate these risks in the current year audit, if the auditor plans to rely on those controls to support a control risk assessment below 100%. The greater the risk, the more audit evidence the auditor should obtain that controls are operating effectively.

Testing Less Than the Entire Audit Period Recall that management's report on internal control deals with the effectiveness of internal controls as of the end of the fiscal year. PCAOB auditing standards require the auditor to perform tests of controls that are adequate to determine whether controls are operating effectively at year-end. The timing of the auditor's tests of controls will therefore depend on the nature of the controls and when the company uses them. For controls that are applied throughout the accounting period, it is usually practical to test them at an interim date. The auditor will then determine later if changes in controls occurred in the period not tested and decide the implication of any change. Controls dealing with financial statement preparation occur only quarterly or at year-end and must therefore also be tested at quarter-end and year-end.

Relationship Between Tests of Controls and Procedures to Obtain an Understanding

There is a significant overlap between tests of controls and procedures to obtain an understanding. Both include inquiry, inspection, and observation. There are two primary differences in the application of these common procedures.

1. In obtaining an understanding of internal control, the procedures to obtain an understanding are applied to all controls identified during that phase. Tests of controls, on the other hand, are applied only when the assessed control risk has not been satisfied by the procedures to obtain an understanding.
2. Procedures to obtain an understanding are performed only on one or a few transactions or, in the case of observations, at a single point in time. Tests of controls are performed on larger samples of transactions (perhaps 20 to 100), and often, observations are made at more than one point in time.

For key controls, tests of controls other than reperformance are essentially an extension of procedures to obtain an understanding. Therefore, assuming the auditors plan to obtain a low assessed control risk from the beginning of the audit, they will likely combine both types of procedures and perform them simultaneously. Table 12-1 (p. 380) illustrates this concept in more detail. One option is to perform the audit procedures separately, as shown in Table 12-1, where minimum procedures to obtain an understanding of design and operation are performed, followed by additional tests of controls. An alternative is to combine both columns and do them simultaneously. The same amount of evidence is accumulated in the second approach, but more efficiently.

TABLE 12-1	Relationship of Assessed Control Risk and Extent of Procedures	
	Assessed Control Risk	
Type of Procedure	**High Level: Procedures to Obtain an Understanding**	**Lower Level: Tests of Controls***
Inquiry	Yes—extensive	Yes—some
Inspection	Yes—with transaction walkthrough	Yes—using sampling
Observation	Yes—with transaction walkthrough	Yes—at multiple times
Reperformance	No	Yes—using sampling or audit software

**Note*: In an integrated audit for a public company, the auditor will likely combine procedures to obtain an understanding with tests of controls and perform them simultaneously.

The determination of the appropriate sample size for tests of controls is an important audit decision. That topic is covered in Chapter 15.

Understanding Internal Controls in Outsourced Systems When clients use a service center for processing transactions, such as a payroll service provider or a broker for processing investment transactions, the auditor faces a difficulty when obtaining an understanding of the client's internal controls for these transaction areas. Many of the controls reside at the service center, and the auditor cannot assume that the controls are adequate simply because it is an independent enterprise. Auditing standards require the auditor to consider the need to obtain an understanding and test the service center's controls if the service center application involves processing significant financial data. For example, many of the controls for payroll transaction-related audit objectives reside within the software program maintained and supported by the payroll services company, not the audit client.

When obtaining an understanding of and testing the service center's controls, the auditor should use the same criteria that was used in evaluating a client's internal controls. The depth of the auditor's understanding depends on the complexity of the system and the extent to which the control is relied upon to reduce control risk. The depth of understanding also depends on the extent to which key controls over transaction-related audit objectives reside at the service center for audits of internal control for public companies. If the auditor concludes that active involvement at the service center is the only way to conduct the audit, it may be necessary to obtain an understanding of internal controls at the service center and test controls using test data and other tests of controls.

Reliance on Service Center Auditors In recent years, it has become increasingly common for service centers to engage a CPA firm to obtain an understanding and test internal controls of the service center (often referred to as "service organization controls" or "SOC") and issue a SOC report for use by all customers and their independent auditors. The purpose of this independent assessment is to provide service center customers reasonable assurance about the adequacy of the service center's general and application controls and to eliminate the need for redundant audits by customers' auditors. If the service center has many customers and each requires an understanding of the service center's internal control by its own independent auditor, the inconvenience and cost to the service center can be substantial.

Attestation standards provide guidance to auditors who issue reports on the internal control of service organizations (*service auditors*), while auditing standards provide guidance to auditors of user organizations (*user auditors*) that rely on the service auditor's report. Service auditors may issue two types of reports:

- Report on management's description of a service organization's system and the suitability of the design of controls (referred to as a Type 1 report)

- Report on management's description of a service organization's system and the suitability of the design and operating effectiveness of controls (referred to as a Type 2 report)

A Type 1 report helps auditors obtain an understanding of internal control to plan the audit. However, auditors also require evidence about the operating effectiveness of controls to assess control risk, especially when auditing internal control over financial reporting for public companies. This evidence can:

- Be based on the service auditor's Type 2 report, which includes tests of the operating effectiveness of controls
- Come from tests of the user organization's controls over the activities of the service organization
- Be created when the user auditor does appropriate tests at the service organization

If the user auditor decides to rely on the service auditor's report, appropriate inquiries should be made about the service auditor's reputation. Auditing standards state that the user auditor should not make reference to the report of the service auditor in the opinion on the user organization's financial statements.

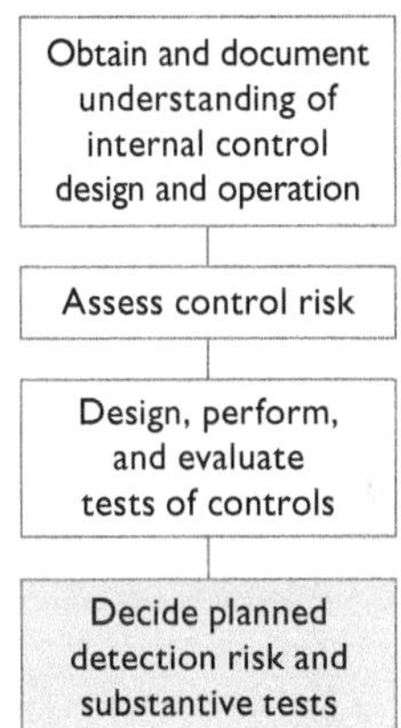

CONCEPT CHECK

1. Describe the four steps performed by the auditor when obtaining an understanding of internal control and assessing control risk.
2. What is the purpose of a control risk matrix?
3. What four types of procedures are used by auditors to test whether internal controls are operating effectively?

DECIDE PLANNED DETECTION RISK AND DESIGN SUBSTANTIVE TESTS

OBJECTIVE 12-4

Understand how control risk impacts detection risk and the design of substantive tests.

We've focused on how auditors assess control risk for each related audit objective and support control risk assessments with tests of controls. The completion of these activities is sufficient for the audit of internal control over financial reporting, even though the report will not be finalized until the auditor completes the audit of financial statements.

The auditor uses the control risk assessment and results of tests of controls to determine planned detection risk and related substantive tests for the audit of

PCAOB IDENTIFIES DEFICIENCIES IN AUDITS OF INTERNAL CONTROL OVER FINANCIAL REPORTING

The PCAOB frequently issues practice alerts to highlight new or noteworthy circumstances or to summarize findings from their inspection process. In October 2013, the PCAOB issued Staff Audit Practice Alert No. 11, titled "Considerations for Audits of Internal Control over Financial Reporting." This practice alert discusses common themes identified during inspections of integrated audit engagements. The most common audit deficiencies related to audits of internal controls include a failure in identification and testing of controls intended to address the risk of material misstatement; improperly assessing management review controls; a failure to properly update interim testing of controls; insufficient testing of controls over system-generated data; a failure to perform the appropriate tests when relying on the work of others; and a failure to properly assess the severity of identified control deficiencies. In many cases, the PCAOB concluded that insufficient evidence was obtained to form an opinion on the effectiveness of internal controls over financial reporting. The PCAOB also points out that a failure to properly assess control risk will often result in a failure to collect sufficient appropriate evidence for the financial statement audit.

Audit practice alerts typically result in a national-level response by the audit firms. Audit firms, particularly the largest firms, will increase their internal training related to the matters identified by the PCAOB, increase their level of testing on all integrated audits, and increase documentation in the audit workpapers to demonstrate to the PCAOB that they are striving to improve audit quality.

Source: PCAOB Audit Practice Alert No. 11, "Considerations for Audits of Internal Control over Financial Reporting," October 24, 2013 (pcaobus.org).

financial statements. The auditor does this by linking the control risk assessments to the balance-related audit objectives for the accounts affected by the major transaction types and to the four presentation and disclosure audit objectives. The appropriate level of detection risk for each balance-related audit objective is then decided using the audit risk model. The relationship of transaction-related audit objectives to balance-related audit objectives and the selection and design of audit procedures for substantive tests of financial statement balances are discussed and illustrated in Chapter 13.

AUDITOR REPORTING ON INTERNAL CONTROL

OBJECTIVE 12-5

Understand requirements for auditor reporting on internal control.

As part of understanding internal control and assessing control risk, the auditor is required to communicate certain matters to those charged with governance. This information and other recommendations about controls are also often communicated to management.

Communications to Those Charged with Governance and Management Letters

Communications to Those Charged with Governance The auditor must communicate significant deficiencies and material weaknesses in writing to those charged with governance as soon as the auditor becomes aware of their existence. The communication is usually addressed to the audit committee and to management. Timely communications may provide management an opportunity to address control deficiencies before management's report on internal control must be issued. In some instances, deficiencies can be corrected sufficiently early such that both management and the auditor can conclude that controls are operating effectively as of the balance sheet date. Regardless, these communications must be made no later than 60 days following the audit report release. An example of a report used in the audit of a nonpublic company is provided in Figure 12-6.

Management Letters In addition to these matters, auditors often identify less significant internal control–related issues, as well as opportunities for the client to make operational improvements. These should also be communicated to the client. The form of communication is often a separate letter for that purpose, called a **management letter**. Although management letters are not required by auditing standards, auditors generally prepare them as a value-added service of the audit.

Section 404 Reporting Requirements

Based on the auditor's assessment and testing of internal control, the auditor is required to prepare an audit report on internal control over financial reporting for accelerated filer public companies subject to Section 404(b) reporting requirements. As described in Chapter 3, the auditor may issue separate or combined audit reports on the financial statements and on internal control over financial reporting. An example of a separate report is illustrated in Figure 3-4 on page 53.

The scope of the auditor's report on internal control is limited to obtaining reasonable assurance that material weaknesses in internal control are identified. Thus, the audit is not designed to detect deficiencies in internal control that individually, or in the aggregate, are less severe than a material weakness. The distinction between deficiencies, significant deficiencies, and material weaknesses was discussed earlier.

Types of Opinions

Unqualified Opinion The auditor will issue an unqualified opinion on internal control over financial reporting when two conditions exist:

- There are no identified material weaknesses as of the end of the fiscal year.
- There have been no restrictions on the scope of the auditor's work.

Adverse Opinion When one or more material weaknesses exist, the auditor must express an adverse opinion on the effectiveness of internal control. The most common cause of an adverse opinion in the auditor's report on internal control is when management identified a material weakness in its report.

FIGURE 12-6 Letter Regarding Significant Deficiencies in Internal Control

JOHNSON AND SEYGROVES
Certified Public Accountants
2016 Village Boulevard
Troy, Michigan 48801

February 12, 2017

Audit Committee
Airtight Machine Company
1729 Athens Street
Troy, MI 48801

In planning and performing our audit of the financial statements of Airtight Machine Company as of and for the year ended December 31, 2016, in accordance with auditing standards generally accepted in the United States of America, we considered Airtight Machine Company's internal control over financial reporting (internal control) as a basis for designing audit procedures that are appropriate in the circumstances for the purpose of expressing our opinion on the financial statements, but not for the purpose of expressing an opinion on the effectiveness of Airtight Machine Company's internal control. Accordingly, we do not express an opinion on the effectiveness of the company's internal control.

Our consideration of internal control was for the limited purpose described in the preceding paragraph and was not designed to identify all deficiencies in internal control that might be significant deficiencies or material weaknesses. However, as discussed below, we identified certain deficiencies in internal control that we consider to be significant deficiencies.

A deficiency in internal control exists when the design or operation of a control does not allow management or employees, in the normal course of performing their assigned functions, to prevent, or detect and correct, misstatements on a timely basis. A significant deficiency is a control deficiency, or combination of control deficiencies, that adversely affects the entity's ability to initiate, authorize, record, process, or report financial data reliably in accordance with generally accepted accounting principles that is less severe than a material weakness, yet important enough to merit attention by those charged with governance. We consider the following deficiency to be a significant deficiency in internal control:

> There is a lack of independent verification of the key entry of the customer's name, product number, quantity shipped, prices used, and the related mathematical extensions on sales invoices and credit memos. As a consequence, errors in these activities could occur and remain uncorrected, adversely affecting both recorded net sales and accounts receivable. This deficiency is significant because of the large size of the average sale at Airtight Machine Company.

This communication is intended solely for the information and use of management and the board of directors and is not intended to be and should not be used by anyone other than these specified parties.

Very truly yours,

Johnson and Seygroves, CPAs

Johnson and Seygroves

Qualified or Disclaimer of Opinion A scope limitation requires the auditor to express a qualified opinion or a disclaimer of opinion on internal control over financial reporting. This type of opinion is issued when the auditor is unable to determine if there are material weaknesses, due to a restriction on the scope of the audit of internal control over financial reporting or other circumstances where the auditor is unable to obtain sufficient appropriate evidence.

The auditor's opinion on the effectiveness of internal controls is as of the end of the fiscal year. The auditor is attesting to the effectiveness of internal controls as of that date rather than attesting to the effectiveness of controls throughout the fiscal year. If a material weakness is identified prior to the end of the fiscal year, the auditor can still issue an unqualified opinion if the material weakness has been remediated and the revised control has been tested to ensure it is designed, implemented, and operating effectively.

Because the audit of the financial statements and the audit of internal control over financial reporting are integrated, the auditor must consider the results of audit procedures performed to issue the audit report on the financial statements when issuing the audit report on internal control. For example, assume the auditor identifies a material misstatement in the financial statements that was not initially identified by the company's internal controls. The following four responses to this finding are likely:

1. Because there is a material error in the financial statements, the auditor should consider whether the misstatement indicates the existence of a material weakness. Determining if the misstatement is in fact a material weakness or a significant deficiency involves judgment and depends on the nature and size of the misstatement.
2. The auditor can issue an unqualified opinion on the financial statements if the client adjusts the statements to correct the misstatement prior to issuance.
3. Management is likely to change its report on internal control to assert that the controls are not operating effectively.
4. The auditor must issue an adverse opinion on internal control over financial reporting if the deficiency is considered a material weakness.

Figure 12-7 illustrates the definition of material weakness and opinion paragraphs from an auditor's separate report on internal control when the auditor expresses an adverse opinion on the effectiveness of internal control over financial reporting because of the existence of a material weakness. If the material weakness has not been included in management's assessment, the report should note that a material weakness has been identified but not included in management's assessment.

FIGURE 12-7 Partial Section 404 Auditor Report on Internal Control when Material Weaknesses Exist (bold added)*

REPORT OF INDEPENDENT REGISTERED PUBLIC ACCOUNTING FIRM

[*Definition of material weakness paragraph*]

A **material weakness** is a deficiency, or combination of deficiencies, in internal control over financial reporting, such that there is a **reasonable possibility** that a material misstatement of the company's interim or annual financial statements will not be prevented or detected on a timely basis.

[*Opinion paragraph*]

In our opinion, because of the effect of the material weakness described above on the achievement of the objectives of the control criteria, Kincannon Company has not maintained effective internal control over financial reporting as of December 31, 2016, based on criteria established in *Internal Control—Integrated Framework* issued by the Committee of Sponsoring Organizations of the Treadway Commission (2013 Framework).

Kellum & Kellum, LLP
Brentwood, Tennessee

February 2, 2017

*The introductory, scope, definition of internal control, inherent limitations of internal control, and reference to the opinion on the financial statements paragraphs use standard wording and are not included. The explanatory paragraph describing the nature of the weakness is also not included.

EVALUATING, REPORTING, AND TESTING INTERNAL CONTROL FOR NONPUBLIC AND SMALLER PUBLIC COMPANIES

OBJECTIVE 12-6

Describe the differences in evaluating, reporting, and testing internal control for nonpublic and smaller public companies.

Most of the concepts in this chapter apply equally to audits of large public companies (accelerated filers), smaller public companies, and nonpublic companies. The following identifies and discusses the most important differences in evaluating, reporting, and testing internal control for nonpublic companies and smaller public companies that are not subject to Section 404(b) audits of internal control.

1. *Reporting requirements.* In audits of nonpublic companies and non-accelerated filers, there is no requirement for an audit of internal control over financial reporting. The auditor, therefore, focuses on internal control only to the extent needed to assess the risks of material misstatements and do a quality audit of financial statements. The AICPA Auditing Standards Board recently moved the guidance from the attestation standards to auditing standards that applies when nonpublic entities engage the auditor to conduct an examination of the design and operating effectiveness of internal controls over financial reporting that is integrated with the audit of the financial statements. The approach for an integrated audit of a nonpublic company under the attestation standards is consistent with the approach to an integrated audit of a public company under PCAOB auditing standards.
2. *Extent of required internal controls.* A company's size has a significant effect on the nature of internal control and the specific controls that are implemented. Obviously, it is more difficult to establish adequate separation of duties in a small company. It is also unreasonable to expect a small firm to have internal auditors. However, if the various components of internal control are examined, it becomes apparent that most are applicable to both large and small companies. Even though it may not be common to formalize policies in manuals, it is certainly possible for a small company to have (1) competent, trustworthy personnel with clear lines of authority; (2) proper procedures for authorization, execution, and recording of transactions; (3) adequate documents, records, and reports; (4) physical controls over assets and records; and, (5) to a limited degree, independent checks on performance.
3. *Extent of understanding needed.* Auditing standards require that the auditor obtain a sufficient understanding of internal control to assess the risk of material misstatement at the overall financial statement level and at the relevant assertion level. These risks are assessed in order to design effective audit procedures. In practice, the procedures to gain an understanding of internal control vary considerably from client to client. For smaller companies, if the auditor determines that controls are not designed or implemented properly, or not operating effectively, the auditor assesses control risk at maximum and designs and performs detailed substantive procedures. For larger nonpublic clients, the understanding of controls can be the same as that for public companies.
4. *Assessing control risk.* The most important difference in a nonpublic company in assessing control risk is the assessment of control risk at maximum for any or all control-related objectives when internal controls for the objective or objectives are nonexistent or ineffective. Because of the expectation that public companies should have effective internal controls for all significant transactions and accounts, there is an initial presumption that control risk is low in the audit of public company financial statements. Thus, it is unlikely that a public company auditor will make a preliminary assessment of control risk at maximum.

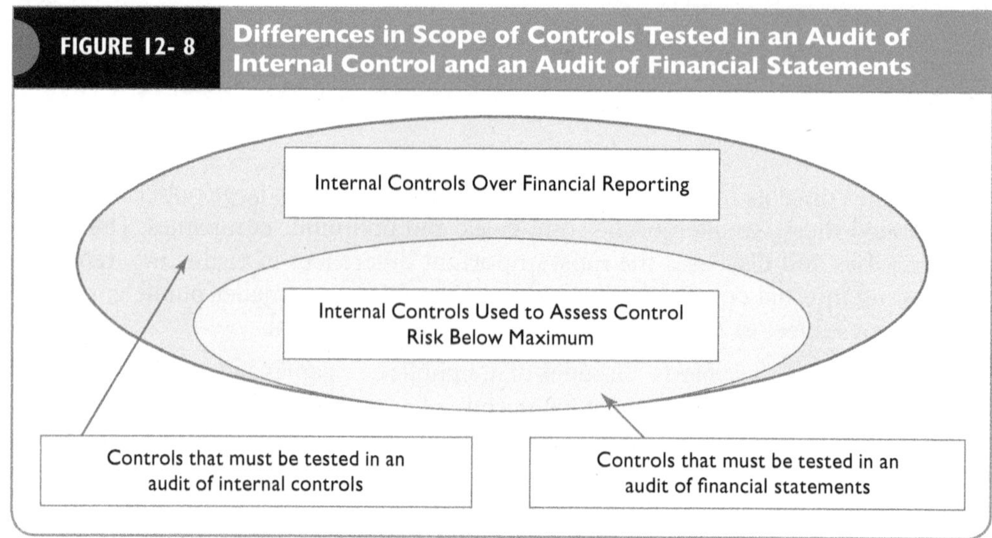

FIGURE 12-8 Differences in Scope of Controls Tested in an Audit of Internal Control and an Audit of Financial Statements

5. *Extent of tests of controls needed.* The auditor will not perform tests of controls when the auditor assesses control risk at maximum, either because of inadequate controls, or because the audit can be completed more efficiently by not relying on and testing controls. When control risk is assessed below the maximum, the auditor designs and performs a combination of tests of controls and substantive procedures to obtain reasonable assurance that the financial statements are fairly stated. The difference in the extent of testing is displayed graphically in Figure 12-8.

CONCEPT CHECK

1. Why are the financial statement audit findings relevant to the auditor's opinion on the effectiveness of internal controls over financial reporting?
2. Explain the difference in the requirements for reporting on the effectiveness of internal controls over financial reporting for integrated audits versus financial statement–only audits.

IMPACT OF IT ENVIRONMENT ON CONTROL RISK ASSESSMENT AND TESTING

OBJECTIVE 12-7

Describe how the complexity of the IT environment impacts control risk assessment and testing.

The impact of general controls and application controls on audits is likely to vary depending on the level of complexity in the IT environment. Even in a less complex IT environment, the auditor is still responsible for obtaining an understanding of general and application computer controls because such knowledge is useful in identifying risks that may affect the financial statements. However, the extent of testing will depend on the assessment of control risk, as discussed earlier. In this section, we discuss auditing in a more complex IT environment and the opportunities and challenges this provides for auditors.

Auditing in More Complex IT Environments

As organizations expand their use of IT, internal controls are often embedded in applications that are available only electronically. When traditional source documents such as invoices, purchase orders, billing records, and accounting records such as sales journals, inventory listings, and accounts receivable subsidiary records exist only electronically, auditors must change their approach to auditing. This approach is often called **auditing through the computer**. Auditors use three approaches to test the effectiveness of automated controls when auditing through the computer: test data approach, parallel simulation, and embedded audit module approach.

Test Data Approach In the **test data approach**, auditors process their own test data using the client's computer system and application program to determine whether the automated controls correctly process the test data. Auditors design the test data to include transactions that the client's system should either accept or reject. After the test data are processed on the client's system, auditors compare the actual output to the expected output to assess the effectiveness of the application program's automated controls. Figure 12-9 illustrates the use of the test data approach.

When using the test data approach, auditors have three main considerations:

1. *Test data should include all relevant conditions that the auditor wants tested.* Auditors should design test data to test all key computer-based controls and include realistic data that are likely to be a part of the client's normal processing, including both valid and invalid transactions. For example, assume the client's payroll application contains a limit check that disallows a payroll transaction that exceeds 80 hours per week. To test this control, the auditor can prepare payroll transactions with 79, 80, and 81 hours for each sampled week and process them through the client's system in a manner shown in Figure 12-9. If the limit check control is operating effectively, the client's system should reject the transaction for 81 hours, and the client's error listing should report the 81-hour transaction error.

FIGURE 12-9 Test Data Approach

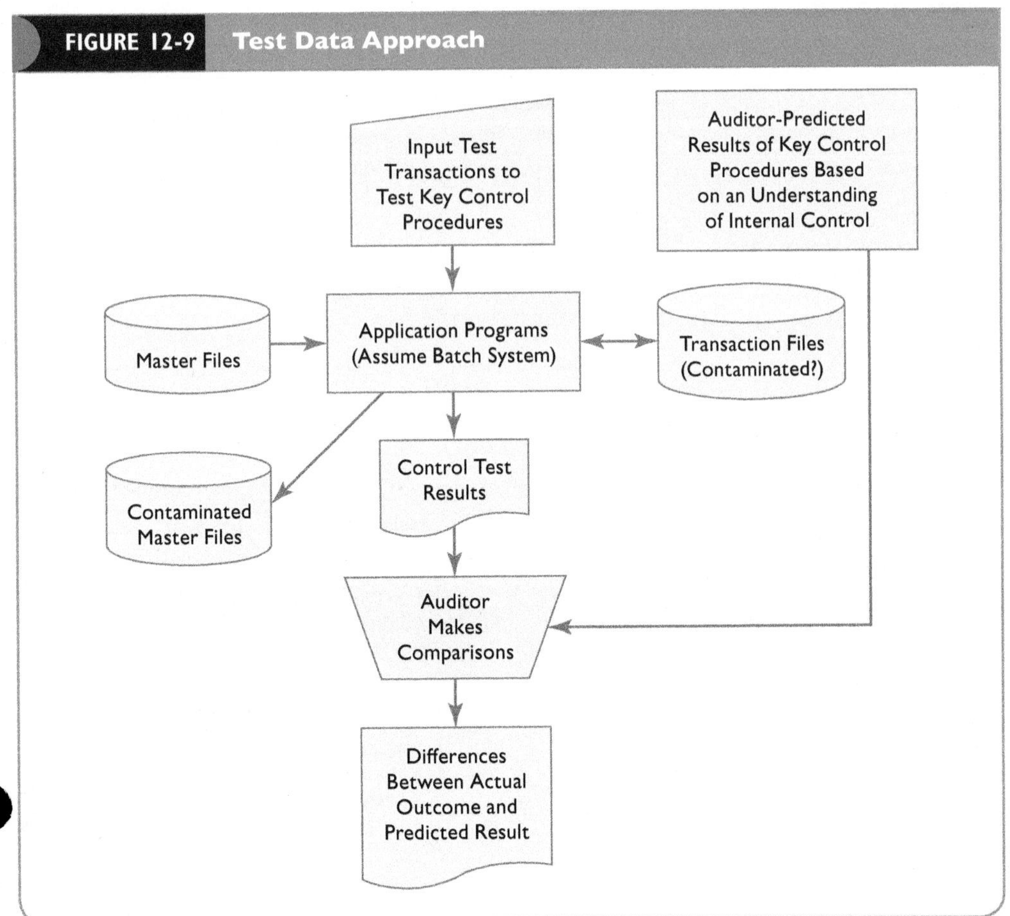

2. *Application programs tested by auditors' test data must be the same as those the client used throughout the year.* One approach is to run the test data on a surprise basis, possibly at random times throughout the year, even though doing so is costly and time consuming. Another method is to rely on the client's general controls in the librarian and systems development functions to ensure that the program tested is the one used in normal processing.
3. *Test data must be eliminated from the client's records.* If auditors process test data while the client is processing its own transactions, auditors must eliminate the test data in the client's master files after the tests are completed to prevent master files and transaction files from being permanently contaminated by the auditor's testing. Auditors can do this by developing and processing data that reverses the effect of the test data.

Because of the complexities of many clients' application software programs, auditors who use the test data approach often obtain assistance from a computer audit specialist. Many larger CPA firms have staff dedicated to assisting in testing client automated application controls.

Parallel Simulation Auditors often use auditor-controlled software to do the same operations that the client's software does, using the same data files. The purpose is to determine the effectiveness of automated controls and to obtain evidence about electronic account balances. This testing approach is called **parallel simulation testing**. Figure 12-10 shows a typical parallel simulation. Whether testing controls or ending balances, the auditor compares the output from the auditor's software to output from the client's system to test the effectiveness of the client's software and

FIGURE 12-10 Parallel Simulation

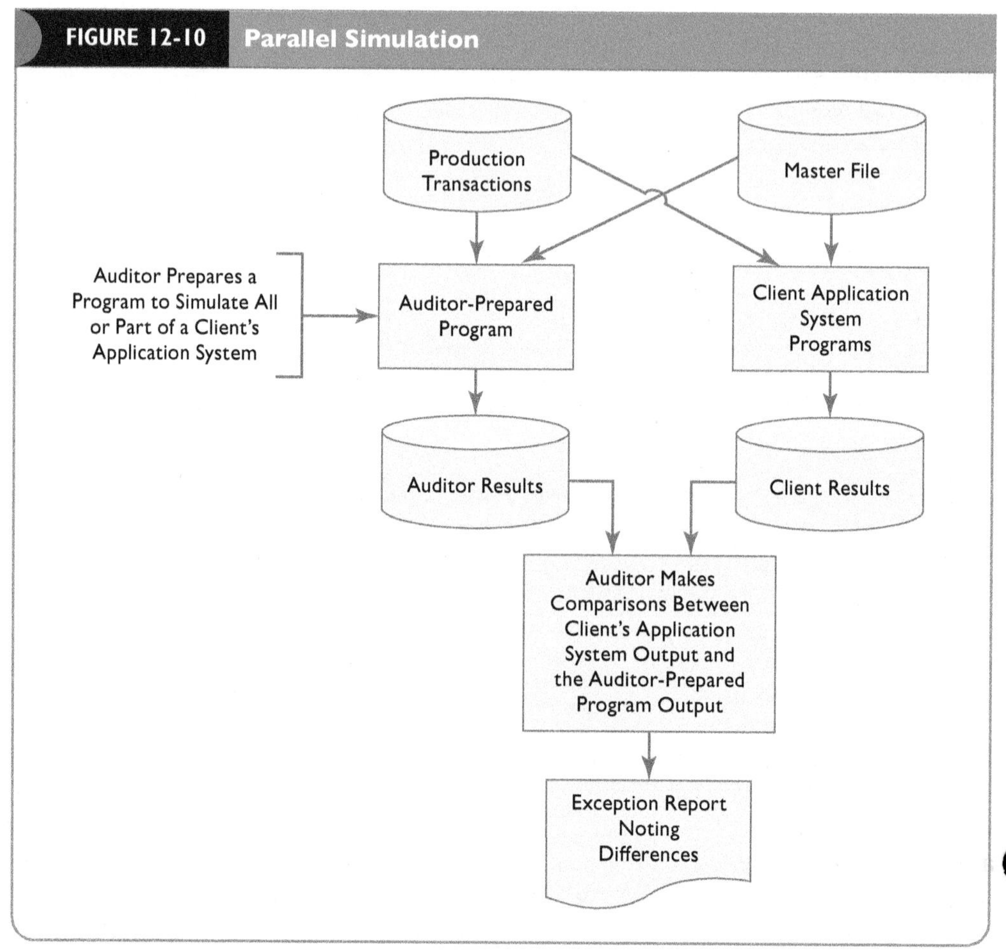

TABLE 12-2 Common Uses of Generalized Audit Software

Uses	Description	Examples
Verify extensions and footings	Verify the accuracy of the client's computations by calculating information independently	Foot accounts receivable trial balance
Examine records for quality, completeness, consistency, and correctness	Scan all records using specified criteria	Review payroll files for terminated employees
Compare data on separate files	Determine that information in two or more data files agrees	Compare changes in accounts receivable balances between two dates using sales and cash receipts in transaction files
Summarize or resequence data and do analyses	Change or aggregate data	Resequence inventory items by location to facilitate physical observation
Select audit samples	Select samples from machine-readable data	Randomly select accounts receivable for confirmation
Print confirmation requests	Print data for sample items selected for confirmation testing	Print customer name, address, and account balance information from master files
Compare data obtained through other audit procedures with company records	Compare machine-readable data with audit evidence gathered manually, which is converted to machine-readable form	Compare confirmation responses with accounts receivable master files

to determine if the client's balance is correct. A variety of software is available to assist auditors.

Auditors commonly do parallel simulation testing using **generalized audit software (GAS)**, which is programs designed specifically for auditing purposes. Commercially available audit software, such as ACL and IDEA, can be easily operated on auditors' desktop or laptop computers. Auditors obtain copies of machine-readable client databases or master files and use the generalized audit software to do a variety of tests of the client's electronic data. Instead of GAS, some auditors use spreadsheet software to do simple parallel simulation tests. Others develop their own customized audit software.

Generalized audit software provides three advantages: it is relatively easy to train audit staff in its use, even if they have had little audit-related IT training; the software can be applied to a wide variety of clients with minimal customization; and it has the ability to do audit tests much faster and in more detail than using traditional manual procedures. Table 12-2 includes some of the common uses of generalized audit software. Two are examined in detail:

1. *Generalized audit software is used to test automated controls.* An auditor obtains copies of a client's customer credit limit master file and a customer order file, and then instructs the auditor's computer to list transactions that exceed the customer's authorized credit limit. The auditor then compares the audit output to the client's list of customer orders that were rejected for exceeding authorized credit limits.
2. *Generalized audit software is used to verify the client's account balances.* An auditor can use the software to sum the master file of customer accounts receivable to determine whether the total agrees with the general ledger balance.

Embedded Audit Module Approach When using the **embedded audit module approach**, auditors insert an audit module into the client's application system to identify specific types of transactions. For example, auditors might use an embedded module to identify all purchases exceeding $25,000 for follow-up with more detailed examination for the occurrence and accuracy transaction-related audit objectives. In some cases, auditors later copy the identified transactions to a separate data file and then process those transactions using parallel simulation to duplicate the function done by the client's system. The auditor then compares the client's output with the auditor's output. Discrepancies are printed on an exception report for auditor follow-up.

The embedded audit module approach allows auditors to continuously audit transactions by identifying actual transactions processed by the client, as compared to test data and parallel simulation approaches, which only allow intermittent testing. Internal audit may also find this technique useful.

Although auditors may use one or any combination of testing approaches, they typically use:

- Test data to do tests of controls and substantive tests of transactions
- Parallel simulation for substantive testing, such as recalculating transaction amounts and footing master file subsidiary records of account balances
- Embedded audit modules to identify unusual transactions for substantive testing

SUMMARY

This chapter focused on the auditor's responsibility for understanding, evaluating, and testing internal control, including integrated audits of financial statements and internal control over financial reporting under Section 404 of the Sarbanes–Oxley Act and PCAOB requirements. To rely on a client's internal controls to report on internal control over financial reporting and to reduce planned audit evidence for audits of financial statements, the auditor must first obtain an understanding of each of the five components of internal control. Knowledge about the design of the client's control environment, risk assessment, control activities, information and communication, and monitoring activities and information about whether internal control components have been implemented assist the auditor in assessing control risk for each audit objective.

The chapter also included a discussion of the differences in the audit of nonpublic and smaller public companies because they are not subject to Section 404(b) and PCAOB requirements to report on internal control over financial reporting. For nonpublic companies, auditors have the option of assessing a higher level of control risk, depending on the quality of the client's internal controls and cost–benefit considerations.

The chapter ended with a discussion of the impact of a more complex information technology environment on control risk assessment and testing. Knowledge about general controls provides a basis for the auditor to rely on automated application controls and may reduce the extent of tests of key automated controls in audits of financial statements and internal controls. Some of the auditor's tests of controls can be done by the computer, often as a way to achieve more effective and efficient audits.

The process followed by auditors in assessing control risk for integrated audits of financial statements and internal control over financial reporting and audits of the financial statements only is summarized in Figure 12-11.

ESSENTIAL TERMS

Assessment of control risk—a measure of the auditor's expectation that internal controls will neither prevent material misstatements from occurring nor detect and correct them if they have occurred

Auditing through the computer—auditing by testing automated internal controls and account balances electronically, generally because effective general controls exist

FIGURE 12-11 Summary of Understanding Internal Control and Assessing Control Risk

Financial Statement Audit		Integrated Audit of Financial Statements and Internal Control over Financial Reporting	
Sufficient to audit financial statements	Obtain an understanding of internal control design and operation	Sufficient to audit internal control over financial reporting	STEP 1
Varies depending on extent and effectiveness of controls and the auditor's planned reliance on controls	Decide control risk at the objective level for each transaction type Three alternatives Maximum / Intermediate / Low	Decide low for all objectives unless there are significant deficiencies or material weaknesses	STEP 2
Varies depending on assessed level of control risk	Plan and perform tests of controls and evaluate results	Extensive tests for all objectives	STEP 3
Revise for tests of controls results	Revise assessed control risk if appropriate	Revise for tests of controls results	
Likely to be more reliance on substantive tests, depending on assessed control risk option selected	Plan detection risk and perform substantive tests considering control risk and other audit risk model factors	Likely to be less reliance on substantive tests due to extensive tests of controls	STEP 4
Must communicate in writing to those charged with governance describing significant deficiencies or material weaknesses.	Issue internal control report or letter	Must issue report on internal control over financial reporting and issue a written communication to audit committee describing significant deficiencies or material weaknesses	

Compensating control—a control elsewhere in the system that offsets the absence of a key control

Control deficiency—a deficiency in the design or operation of controls that does not permit company personnel to prevent or detect and correct misstatements on a timely basis

Control risk matrix—a methodology used to help the auditor assess control risk by matching key internal controls and internal control deficiencies with transaction-related audit objectives

Embedded audit module approach—a method of auditing transactions processed by IT whereby the auditor embeds a module in the client's application software to identify transactions with characteristics that are of interest to the auditor; the auditor is then able to analyze these transactions on a real-time, continuous basis as client transactions are processed

Flowchart—a diagrammatic representation of the client's documents and records and the sequence in which they are processed

Generalized audit software (GAS)—computer programs used by auditors that provide data retrieval, data manipulation, and reporting capabilities specifically oriented to the needs of auditors

Internal control questionnaire—a series of questions about the controls in each audit area used as a means of indicating to the auditor aspects of internal control that may be inadequate

Key controls—controls that are expected to have the greatest effect on meeting audit objectives

Management letter—an optional letter written by the auditor to a client's management containing the auditor's recommendations for improving any aspect of the client's business

Material weakness—a significant deficiency in internal control that, by itself or in combination with other significant deficiencies, results in a reasonable possibility that a material misstatement of the financial statements will not be prevented or detected

Narrative—a written description of a client's internal controls, including the origin, processing, and disposition of documents and records, and the relevant control procedures

Parallel simulation testing—an audit testing approach that involves the auditor's use of audit software, either purchased or programmed by the auditor, to replicate some part of a client's application system

Procedures to obtain an understanding—procedures used by the auditor to gather evidence about the design and implementation of specific controls

Significant deficiency—a control deficiency, or a combination of control deficiencies, that is less severe than a material weakness, but important enough to merit attention by those responsible for oversight of the company's financial reporting

Test data approach—a method of auditing an IT system that uses the auditor's test data to determine whether the client's computer program correctly processes valid and invalid transactions

Tests of controls—audit procedures to test the operating effectiveness of controls in support of reduced assessed control risk

Walkthrough—the tracing of selected transactions through the accounting system to determine that controls are in place

REVIEW QUESTIONS

12-1 (OBJECTIVES 12-1, 12-6) What is the auditor's responsibility for obtaining an understanding of internal control? How does that responsibility differ for audits of public and nonpublic companies?

12-2 (OBJECTIVE 12-1) Jeanne Maier, CPA, believes that it is appropriate to obtain an understanding of internal control about halfway through the audit, after she is familiar with the client's operations and the way the system actually works. She has found through experience that filling out internal control questionnaires and flowcharts early in the engagement is not beneficial because the system rarely functions the way it is supposed to. Later in the engagement, the auditor can prepare flowcharts and questionnaires with relative ease because of the knowledge already obtained on the audit. Evaluate her approach.

12-3 (OBJECTIVE 12-1) What is a walkthrough of internal control? What is its purpose?

12-4 (OBJECTIVE 12-2) Describe how the nature of evidence used to evaluate the control environment differs from the nature of evidence used to evaluate control activities.

12-5 (OBJECTIVES 12-2, 12-5) Distinguish a significant deficiency in internal control from a material weakness in internal control. How will the presence of one significant deficiency affect an auditor's report on internal control under PCAOB standards? How will the presence of one material weakness affect an auditor's report on internal control under PCAOB standards?

12-6 **(OBJECTIVES 12-3, 12-6)** Distinguish the auditor's responsibility for testing controls in an integrated audit of a public company from the responsibility to test controls in an audit of a nonpublic company.

12-7 **(OBJECTIVE 12-3)** During the prior-year audits of McKimmon, Inc., a private company, the auditor did tests of controls for all relevant financial statement assertions. Some of the related controls are manual while others are automated. Describe the extent to which the auditor can rely on tests of controls performed in prior years.

12-8 **(OBJECTIVES 12-2, 12-3)** The auditor's risk assessment procedures identified several risks that the auditor deems to be significant risks. Several internal controls exist that are designed to mitigate the risks identified. Describe the auditor's responsibilities for considering those controls in the current audit.

12-9 **(OBJECTIVE 12-3)** Your client has outsourced the majority of the accounting information system to a third-party data center. What impact does that have on your audit of the financial statements?

12-10 **(OBJECTIVE 12-4)** How does the auditor use information obtained from the control risk assessment and testing of controls to plan audit procedures?

12-11 **(OBJECTIVE 12-4)** If the auditor assesses control risk as high for a transaction-related audit objective, what does that imply for detection risk and the level of substantive testing?

12-12 **(OBJECTIVE 12-5)** What two conditions must be present for the auditor to issue an unqualified opinion on internal control over financial reporting? What type of condition will cause the auditor to issue a qualified or disclaimer of opinion on internal control over financial reporting?

12-13 **(OBJECTIVE 12-6)** Explain how control risk assessment differs for an integrated audit versus a financial statement-only audit.

12-14 **(OBJECTIVE 12-7)** Explain what is meant by auditing through the computer, and describe the challenges and benefits of this approach in an audit of a client that uses IT extensively to process accounting information.

12-15 **(OBJECTIVE 12-7)** Explain what is meant by the test data approach. What are the major difficulties with using this approach? Define parallel simulation with audit software and provide an example of how it can be used to test a client's payroll system.

MULTIPLE CHOICE QUESTIONS FROM CPA EXAMINATIONS

12-16 **(OBJECTIVES 12-2, 12-5)** The following questions deal with deficiencies in internal control. Choose the best response.

a. Which of the following is an example of an operation deficiency in internal control?
   (1) The company does not have a code of conduct for employees to consider.
   (2) The cashier has online ability to post write-offs to accounts receivable accounts.
   (3) Clerks who conduct monthly reconciliation of intercompany accounts do not understand the nature of misstatements that could occur in those accounts.
   (4) Management does not have a process to identify and assess risks on a recurring basis.

b. A material weakness in internal control represents a control deficiency that
   (1) more than remotely adversely affects a company's ability to initiate, authorize, record, process, or report external financial statements reliably.
   (2) results in a reasonable possibility that internal control will not prevent or detect material financial statement misstatements.
   (3) exists because a necessary control is missing or not properly designed.
   (4) reduces the efficiency and effectiveness of the entity's operations.

c. An auditor of a large public company identifies a material weakness in internal control. The auditor
   (1) will be unable to issue an unqualified opinion on the financial statements.
   (2) must issue a qualified or disclaimer of opinion on internal control over financial reporting.
   (3) may still be able to issue an unqualified opinion on internal control over financial reporting.
   (4) must issue an adverse opinion on internal control over financial reporting.

12-17 **(OBJECTIVES 12-2, 12-4)** The following questions deal with assessing control risk in a financial statement audit. Choose the best response.

a. The auditor's tests of controls revealed that required approvals of cash disbursements were absent for a large number of sample transactions examined. Which of the following is least likely to be the appropriate auditor response?
   (1) The auditor will communicate the deficiency to those charged with governance.
   (2) The auditor will increase the planned detection risk.
   (3) The auditor will not select more sample items to audit.
   (4) The auditor will perform more extensive substantive tests surrounding cash disbursements.

b. An auditor uses assessed control risk to
   (1) evaluate the effectiveness of the entity's internal controls.
   (2) identify transactions and account balances where inherent risk is at the maximum.
   (3) indicate whether materiality thresholds for planning and evaluation purposes are sufficiently high.
   (4) determine the acceptable level of detection risk for financial statement assertions.

c. On the basis of audit evidence gathered and evaluated, an auditor decides to increase assessed control risk from that originally planned. To achieve an audit risk level (AcAR) that is substantially the same as the planned audit risk level (AAR), the auditor will
   (1) increase inherent risk.
   (2) increase materiality levels.
   (3) decrease substantive testing.
   (4) decrease planned detection risk.

12-18 **(OBJECTIVE 12-7)** The following questions concern auditing complex IT systems. Choose the best response.

a. As general IT controls weaken, the auditor is most likely to
   (1) reduce testing of automated application controls done by the computer.
   (2) increase testing of general IT controls to conclude whether they are operating effectively.
   (3) expand testing of automated application controls used to reduce control risk to cover greater portions of the fiscal year under audit.
   (4) ignore obtaining knowledge about the design of general IT controls and whether they have been implemented.

b. Before processing, the system validates the sequence of items to identify any breaks in sequence of input documents. This automated control is primarily designed to ensure the
   (1) accuracy of input.
   (2) authorization of data entry.
   (3) completeness of input.
   (4) restriction of duplicate entries.

c. An auditor will use the test data approach to obtain certain assurances with respect to the
   (1) input data.
   (2) machine capacity.
   (3) procedures contained within the program.
   (4) degree of data entry accuracy.

MULTIPLE CHOICE QUESTIONS FROM BECKER CPA EXAM REVIEW

12-19 **(OBJECTIVES 12-2, 12-3, 12-4, 12-5)** The following are general questions about assessing control risk, testing controls, and reporting on internal controls. Choose the best response.

a. During the planning stage of an audit, the auditor initially assessed both inherent risk and control risk at a high level. Further testing of the client's internal controls led the auditor to reduce the assessment of control risk. Which of the following will most likely occur as a result?
   (1) The auditor may reduce the assessment of inherent risk to match the control risk, since they were assessed at the same level during the initial planning.
   (2) The auditor may decrease the allowed level of detection risk.
   (3) The auditor may rely solely on analytical procedures, with no substantive procedures performed.
   (4) The auditor may reduce the amount of substantive procedures performed.

b. In which of the following scenarios would an auditor most likely increase tests of controls?
   (1) When the client's IT system is extensively integrated throughout the company's accounting system
   (2) When the client's accounting system is largely based on manual processes
   (3) When the auditor has decided not to rely on internal controls and instead elects to increase substantive testing
   (4) When the auditor's assessment of inherent risk is low

c. Jefferson, CPA, has identified five significant deficiencies in internal control during the audit of Portico Industries, a nonpublic company. Two of these conditions are considered to be material weaknesses. Which best describes Jefferson's communication requirements?
   (1) Communicate the two material weaknesses to Portico's management and those charged with governance, but not the three significant deficiencies that are not material weaknesses.
   (2) Communicate all five significant deficiencies to Portico's management and those charged with governance, distinguishing between material weaknesses and significant deficiencies.
   (3) Communicate all five significant deficiencies to Portico's management and those charged with governance, but only require a management response with respect to the two material weaknesses.
   (4) Communicate all five significant deficiencies to Portico's management and those charged with governance, without distinction among the deficiencies.

DISCUSSION QUESTIONS AND PROBLEMS

12-20 **(OBJECTIVES 12-2, 12-3, 12-4)** Each of the following internal controls has been taken from a standard internal control questionnaire used by a CPA firm for assessing control risk in the payroll and personnel cycle.

1. Approval of department head or foreman on time records is required before preparing payroll.
2. All prenumbered time records are accounted for before beginning data entry for preparation of payroll.

3. The computer calculates gross and net pay based on hours inputted and information in employee master files, and payroll accounting personnel double-check the mathematical accuracy on a test basis.
4. All voided and spoiled payroll checks are properly mutilated and retained.
5. Human resource policies require an investigation of an employment application from new employees. Investigation includes checking the employee's background, former employers, and references.
6. The payroll accounting software application will not accept data input for an employee number not contained in the employee master file.
7. Persons preparing the payroll do not perform other payroll duties (e.g., timekeeping or distribution of checks) nor do they have access to payroll data master files or cash.
8. Written termination notices, with properly documented reasons for termination, and approval by an appropriate official are required.
9. All checks and notices of electronic payments not distributed to employees are returned to the treasurer for safekeeping and follow-up.
10. Online ability to add employees or change pay rates to the payroll master file is restricted via passwords to authorized human resource personnel.

Required

a. For each internal control, identify the type(s) of specific control activity (or activities) to which it applies (such as adequate documents and records or physical control over assets and records).
b. For each internal control, identify the transaction-related audit objective(s) to which it applies.
c. For each internal control, identify a specific misstatement that is likely to be prevented if the control exists and is effective.
d. For each control, list a specific misstatement that could result from the absence of the control.
e. For each control, identify one audit test that the auditor could use to uncover misstatements resulting from the absence of the control.

12-21 **(OBJECTIVES 12-1, 12-2, 12-3, 12-6)** Lew Pherson and Vera Collier are friends who are employed by different CPA firms. One day during lunch they are discussing the importance of internal control in determining the amount of audit evidence required for an engagement. Pherson expresses the view that internal control must be evaluated carefully in all companies, regardless of their size or whether they are publicly held, in a similar manner. His CPA firm requires a standard internal control questionnaire on every audit as well as a flowchart of every transaction area. In addition, he says the firm requires a careful evaluation of the system and a modification in the evidence accumulated based on the controls and deficiencies in the system.

Collier responds by saying she believes that internal control cannot be adequate in many of the small companies she audits; therefore, she simply ignores internal control and acts under the assumption of inadequate controls. She goes on to say, "Why should I spend a lot of time obtaining an understanding of internal control and assessing control risk when I know it has all kinds of weaknesses before I start? I would rather spend the time it takes to fill out all those forms in testing whether the statements are correct."

Required

a. Express in general terms the most important difference between the nature of the potential controls available for large and small companies.
b. Criticize the positions taken by Pherson and Collier, and express your own opinion about the similarities and differences that should exist in understanding internal control and assessing control risk for different-sized companies.
c. Discuss whether Collier's approach is acceptable under existing auditing standards for either public or nonpublic companies.
d. Describe what additional procedures Pherson must perform if auditing the financial statements of a large public company.

12-22 **(OBJECTIVE 12-2)** The following are partial descriptions of internal controls for companies engaged in the manufacturing business:

1. When Mr. Clark orders materials, an electronic copy of the purchase order is sent to the receiving department. During the delivery of materials, Mr. Smith, the receiving clerk, records the receipt of shipment on this purchase order and then sends the purchase order to the accounting department, where it is used to record materials purchased and accounts payable. The materials are transported to the storage area by forklifts. The additional purchased quantities are recorded on storage records.
2. Every day, hundreds of employees clock in using their employee identification cards at Generous Motors Corporation. The data on these time records is used in the preparation of the labor cost distribution records, the payroll journal, and the electronic payments and payroll checks. The treasurer, Angela Lee, compares the payroll journal with the payroll records, signs the checks, and returns the payroll notifications and checks to Charles Strode, the supervisor of the computer department. The payroll checks and payment notices are distributed to the employees by Strode.
3. The smallest branch of Connor Cosmetics employs Mary Cooper, the branch manager, and her sales assistant, Janet Hendrix. The branch uses a bank account to pay expenses. The account is kept in the name of "Connor Cosmetics—Special Account." To pay expenses, checks must be signed by Cooper or by the treasurer, John Winters. Cooper receives the cancelled checks and bank statements. She reconciles the branch account herself and files cancelled checks and bank statements in her records. She also periodically prepares reports of cash disbursements and sends them to the home office.

Required

a. List the deficiencies in internal control for each of these situations. To identify the deficiencies, use the methodology that was discussed in this chapter.
b. For each deficiency, state the type(s) of misstatement(s) that is (are) likely to result. Be as specific as possible.
c. How would you improve internal controls for each of the three companies?*

12-23 **(OBJECTIVE 12-3)** Internal controls 1 through 5 were tested in prior audits. Evaluate each internal control independently and determine which controls must be tested in the current year's audit of the December 31, 2016, financial statements. Be sure to explain why testing is or is not required in the current year.

1. The general ledger accounting software system automatically reconciles totals in each of the subsidiary master files for accounts receivable, accounts payable, and inventory accounts to the respective general ledger accounts. This control was most recently tested in the prior year. No changes to the software have been made since testing and there are effective controls over IT security and software program changes.
2. The accounts payable clerk matches vendor invoices with related purchase orders and receiving reports and investigates any differences noted. This control was tested in the 2015 fiscal year-end audit. No changes to this control or personnel involved have occurred since testing was performed.
3. The sales system automatically determines whether a customer's purchase order and related accounts receivable balance are within the customer's credit limit. The risk of shipping goods to customers who exceed their credit limit is deemed to be a significant risk. This control was last tested in the December 31, 2014, financial statement audit.
4. The perpetual inventory system automatically extends the unit price times quantity for inventory on hand. This control was last tested in the audit of December 31, 2014, financial statements. During 2016, the client made changes to this software system.
5. The client's purchase accounting system was acquired from a reputable software vendor several years ago. This system contains numerous automated controls. The auditor tested those controls most recently in the 2015 audit. No changes have been made to any of these controls since testing and the client's controls over IT security and software program changes are excellent.

*Based on AICPA question paper, American Institute of Certified Public Accountants.

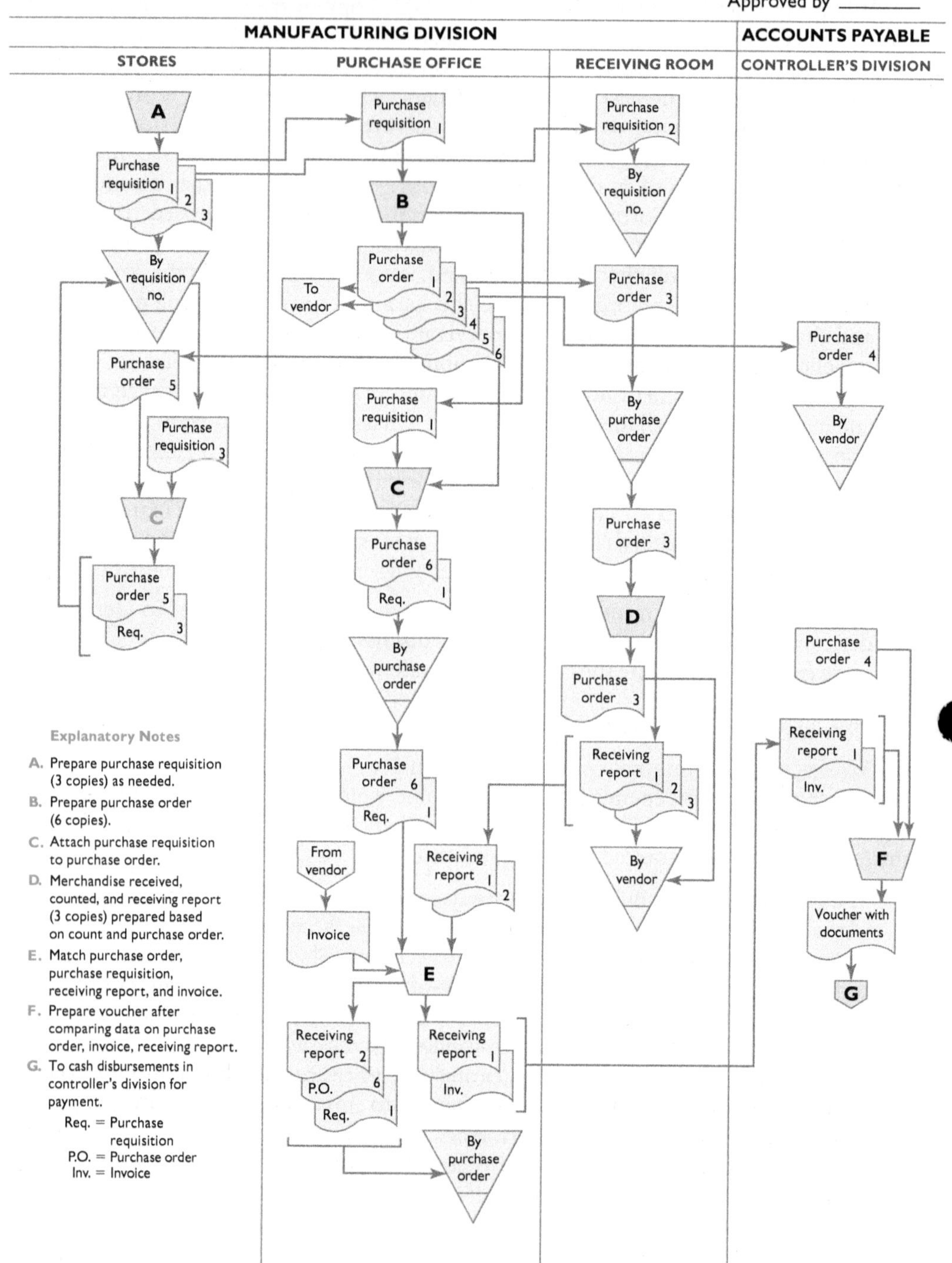

12-24 **(OBJECTIVES 12-1, 12-2)** Anthony Liu, CPA, prepared the flowchart above that portrays the raw materials purchasing function of one of Anthony's clients, Medium-Sized Manufacturing Company, from the preparation of initial documents through the vouching of invoices for payment in accounts payable. Assume that all documents are prenumbered.

Required Identify the deficiencies in internal control that can be determined from the flowchart. Use the methodology discussed in this chapter. Include internal control deficiencies resulting from activities performed or not performed.*

*Based on AICPA question paper, American Institute of Certified Public Accountants.

12-25 **(OBJECTIVE 12-5)** The following are independent situations for which you will recommend an appropriate audit report on internal control over financial reporting as required by PCAOB auditing standards:

1. The auditor identified a material misstatement in the financial statements that was not detected by management of the company.
2. The auditor was unable to obtain any evidence about the operating effectiveness of internal control over financial reporting.
3. The auditor identified several significant deficiencies in internal control. Because of these significant deficiencies, the auditor believes that there is a reasonable possibility that internal control will not prevent or detect material misstatements on a timely basis.
4. The auditor determined that a deficiency in internal control exists that will not prevent or detect a material misstatement in the financial statements.
5. During interim testing, the auditor identified and communicated to management a significant control deficiency. Management immediately corrected the deficiency and the auditor was able to sufficiently test the newly instituted internal control before the end of the fiscal period.
6. As a result of performing tests of controls, the auditor identified a significant deficiency in internal control over financial reporting; however, the auditor does not believe that it represents a material weakness in internal control.

Required

For each situation, state the appropriate audit report from the following alternatives:

- Unqualified opinion on internal control over financial reporting
- Qualified or disclaimer of opinion on internal control over financial reporting
- Adverse opinion on internal control over financial reporting

12-26 **(OBJECTIVES 12-2, 12-3)** The Meyers Pharmaceutical Company has the following system for billing and recording accounts receivable:

1. An incoming customer's purchase order is received in the order department by a clerk, who prepares a prenumbered company sales order on which the pertinent information, such as the customer's name and address, customer's account number, and items and quantities ordered, is inserted. After the sales order has been prepared, the customer's purchase order is stapled to it.
2. The sales order is then passed to the credit department for credit approval. Rough approximations of the billing values of the orders are made in the credit department for those accounts on which credit limitations are imposed. After investigation, approval of credit is noted on the sales order.
3. Next, the sales order is passed to the billing department, where a clerk key-enters the sales order information into a data file, including unit sales prices obtained from an approved price list. The data file is used to prepare sales invoices.

   The billing application automatically accumulates daily totals of customer account numbers and invoice amounts to provide "hash" totals and control amounts. These totals, which are inserted in a daily record book, serve as predetermined batch totals for verification of computer inputs. The billing is done on prenumbered, continuous, multicopy forms that have the following designations:
   (a) Customer copy
   (b) Sales department copy, for information purposes
   (c) File copy
   (d) Shipping department copy, which serves as a shipping order

   Bills of lading are also prepared as by-products of the invoicing procedure.
4. The shipping department copy of the invoice and the bills of lading are then sent to the shipping department. After the order has been shipped, copies of the bill of lading are returned to the billing department. The shipping department copy of the invoice is filed in the shipping department.
5. In the billing department, one copy of the bill of lading is attached to the customer's copy of the invoice and both are mailed to the customer. The other copy of the bill of lading, together with the sales order, is then stapled to the invoice file copy and filed in invoice numerical order.

6. The data file is updated for shipments that are different from those billed earlier. After these changes are made, the file is used to prepare a sales journal in sales invoice order and to update the accounts receivable master file. Daily totals are printed to match the control totals prepared earlier. These totals are compared with the "hash" and control totals by an independent person.

Required

a. Identify the important controls and related sales transaction-related audit objectives.
b. List the procedures that a CPA will use in an audit of sales transactions to test the identified controls and the substantive aspects of the sales transactions.

12-27 (OBJECTIVES 12-2, 12-7) Most grocery stores use bar code scanning technologies that interface with cash registers used to process customer purchases. Cashiers use the scanners to read bar code labels attached to each product, which the system then uses to obtain unit prices, calculate transaction totals, including sales taxes, and update perpetual inventory databases. Similarly, cashiers scan bar codes on coupons or member discount cards presented by the customer to process discounts. Along with the scanning technologies, groceries use point-of-sale technologies that allow customers to swipe debit and credit cards for payment, while still maintaining the ability for customers to pay with cash.

Required

a. Which financial statement accounts are impacted by the use of these technologies in a typical grocery store?
b. Identify risks inherent to this business process in a grocery store that might affect the financial statement accounts identified in part a. For each risk, describe how these technologies help reduce the inherent risk.
c. How might an auditor use technology to test the operating effectiveness of a bar code scanner–based check-out system?

12-28 (OBJECTIVES 12-3, 12-7) A CPA's client, Boos & Baumkirchner, Inc., is a medium-size manufacturer of products for the leisure-time activities market (camping equipment, scuba gear, bows and arrows, and so forth). During the past year, a computer system was installed and inventory records of finished goods and parts were converted to computer processing. The inventory master file is maintained electronically. Each record of the file contains the following information:

- Item or part number
- Description
- Size
- Unit-of-measure code
- Quantity on hand
- Cost per unit
- Total value of inventory on hand at cost
- Date of last sale or usage
- Quantity used or sold this year
- Economic order quantity
- Code number of major vendor
- Code number of secondary vendor

In preparation for year-end inventory, the client has two identical sets of preprinted inventory count cards. One set is for the client's inventory counts, and the other is for the CPA's use to make audit test counts. The following information is on each card:

- Item or part number
- Description
- Size
- Unit-of-measure code

In taking the year-end inventory, the client's personnel will write the actual counted quantity on the face of each card. When all counts are complete, the counted quantity will be entered into the system. The cards will be processed against the inventory database, and quantity-on-hand figures will be adjusted to reflect the actual count. A computer-generated edit listing will be prepared to show any missing inventory count cards and all quantity adjustments of more than $100 in value. These items will be investigated by client personnel, and all required adjustments will be made. When adjustments have been completed, the final year-end balances will be computed and posted to the general ledger.

The CPA has available generalized audit software that will run on the client's computer and can process the client's electronic records.

Required

a. In general and without regard to the facts in this case, discuss the nature of generalized audit software and list the various types and uses.
b. List and describe at least five ways generalized audit software can be used to assist in all aspects of the audit of the inventory of Boos & Baumkirchner, Inc. (For example,

the software can be used to read the inventory master file and list items and parts with a high unit cost or total value. Such items can be included in the test counts to increase the dollar coverage of the audit verification.)*

12-29 **(OBJECTIVES 12-2, 12-3)** Following are 10 key internal controls in the payroll cycle for Gilman Stores, Inc.

Key Controls

1. To input hours worked, payroll accounting personnel input the employee's Social Security number. The system does not allow input of hours worked for invalid employee numbers.
2. The payroll application is programmed so that only human resource personnel are able to add employee names to the employee master files.
3. Input menus distinguish executive payroll, administrative payroll, and factory payroll.
4. The system automatically computes pay at time and a half once hours worked exceed 80 in a 2-week pay period.
5. The system accumulates totals each pay period of employee checks processed and debits the payroll expense general ledger account for the total amount.
6. Each pay period, payroll accounting clerks count the number of time sheets submitted by department heads for processing and compare that total with the number of checks printed by the system to ensure that each time sheet has a check.
7. For factory personnel, the payroll system matches employee ID numbers with ID numbers listed on job costing tickets as direct labor per the cost accounting system. The purpose of the reconciliation is to verify that the amount paid to each employee matches the amount charged to production during the time period.
8. The system generates a listing by employee name of checks processed. Department heads review these listings to ensure that each employee actually worked during the pay period.
9. On a test basis, payroll accounting personnel obtain a listing of pay rates and withholding information for a sample of employees from human resources to recalculate gross and net pay.
10. The system automatically rejects processing an employee's pay if inputted hours exceed 160 hours for a 2-week pay period.

Required

For each control:

a. Identify whether the control is an automated application control (AC) or a manual control done by Gilman employees (MC).
b. Identify the transaction-related audit objective that is affected by the control.
c. Identify which controls, if tested within the last two prior year audits, would not have to be retested in the current year, assuming there are effective IT general controls and no changes to the noted control have been made since auditor testing was completed.

12-30 **(OBJECTIVES 12-2, 12-4, 12-7)** Parts for Wheels, Inc., has historically sold auto parts directly to consumers through its retail stores. Due to competitive pressure, Parts for Wheels installed an Internet-based sales system that allows customers to place orders through the company's Web site. The company hired an outside Web site design consultant to create the sales system because the company's IT personnel lack the necessary experience.

Customers use the link to the inventory parts listing on the Web site to view product descriptions and prices. The inventory parts listing is updated weekly. To get the system online quickly, management decided not to link the order system to the sales and inventory accounting systems. Customers submit orders for products through the online system and provide credit card information for payment. Each day, accounting department clerks print submitted orders from the online system. After credit authorization is verified with the credit card agency, the accounting department enters the sale into the sales journal. The accounting department then sends a copy of the order to warehouse personnel, who process the shipment. The inventory system is updated based on bills of lading information forwarded to accounting after shipment.

*Based on AICPA question paper, American Institute of Certified Public Accountants.

Customers may return parts for full refund if returned within 30 days of submitting the order online. The company agrees to refund shipping costs incurred by the customer for returned goods.

Required

a. Describe deficiencies in Parts for Wheels' online sales system that may lead to material misstatements in the financial statements.
b. Identify changes in manual procedures that could be made to minimize risks, without having to reprogram the current online system.
c. What transaction-related and balance-related audit objectives would the auditors be most concerned about based on the process currently in place?
d. Explain how auditors might use generalized audit software to address the concerns identified in part c.

12-31 **(OBJECTIVE 12-3)** Based on a cost-benefit analysis, management at First Community Bank decided to contract with Technology Solutions, a local data center operator, to host all of the bank's financial reporting applications. To avoid the significant costs of developing and maintaining its own data center, First Community contracts with Technology Solutions to provide IT server access in a highly secure, environmentally controlled data center facility owned by Technology Solutions. Similar to First Community, other businesses also contract with Technology Solutions to host applications at the same data center.

The bank is directly linked through highly secure telecommunication lines to the data center, which allows bank personnel to transmit data to and from the data center as if the data center was owned by First Community. For a monthly fee, Technology Solutions supports the server hardware in an environment with numerous backup controls in the event power is lost or other hardware failures occur. Bank personnel are responsible for selecting and maintaining all application software loaded on Technology Solutions servers, and selected bank personnel have access to those servers located at the Technology Solutions data center. Bank personnel enter all data, run applications hosted at Technology Solutions, and retrieve reports summarizing the processing of all bank transactions.

Required

a. What risks might First Community assume with this approach to IT system support?
b. How does the use of Technology Solutions impact First Community's internal controls?
c. What impact, if any, does reliance on Technology Solutions as the data center provider have on the audit of First Community's financial statements?

12-32 **(OBJECTIVE 12-3)** Beds and Spreads, Inc., specializes in bed and bath furnishings. Its inventory system is linked through the Internet to key suppliers. The auditor identified the following internal controls in the inventory cycle:

1. The computer initiates an order only when perpetual inventory levels fall below prespecified inventory levels in the inventory master file.
2. The sales and purchasing department managers review inventory reorder points on a monthly basis for reasonableness. Approved changes to reorder points are entered into the master file by the purchasing department manager and an updated printout is generated for final review. Both managers verify that all changes were entered correctly and initial the final printout, indicating final approval. These printouts are maintained in the purchasing department.
3. The computer will initiate a purchase order only for inventory product numbers maintained in the inventory master file.
4. The purchasing department manager reviews a computer-generated exception report that highlights weekly purchases that exceed $10,000 per vendor.
5. Sales clerks send damaged merchandise on the store shelves to the back storage room. The sales department manager examines the damaged merchandise each month and prepares a listing showing the estimated salvage value by product number. The accounting department uses the listing to prepare a monthly adjustment to recorded inventory values.

Required

a. Consider each of the preceding controls separately. Identify whether the control is a(n)
   (1) automated control embedded in computer software.
   (2) manual control with effectiveness based significantly on IT-generated information.

(3) manual control with effectiveness not significantly reliant on IT-generated information.

b. Describe how the extent of testing of each control will be affected in subsequent years if general controls are effective, particularly controls over program and master file changes.

12-33 **(OBJECTIVE 12-5)** PCAOB Auditing Standard No. 5, titled "An Audit of Internal Control Over Financial Reporting That Is Integrated with An Audit of Financial Statements," provides guidance for auditors when performing integrated audits. Visit the PCAOB Web site (pcaobus.org) and refer to the "Standards" tab. Read the auditing standard to answer the following questions.

Required

a. In what situations does the integrated audit standard apply?
b. According to the standard, what is the objective of an audit of internal control over financial reporting? What is the objective of an audit of the financial statements?
c. What is the role of risk assessment as it relates to the audit of internal control over financial reporting?
d. How should the auditor determine which controls to test?
e. How might the auditor use evidence obtained in the audit of the financial statements when concluding on the effectiveness of internal control over financial reporting?

12-34 **(OBJECTIVE 12-5)** Section 404(a) of the Sarbanes–Oxley Act requires management of a public company to issue a report on internal control over financial reporting (ICOFR) as of the end of the company's fiscal year. Many companies have reported that their ICOFR was operating effectively, while others have reported that such controls were not effective in design or operation.

Required

1. Visit the SEC Web site (www.sec.gov) and search for the Form 10-K filing for Bob Evans Farms, Inc., for the fiscal year ended April 25, 2014.
2. Locate Management's Annual Report on Internal Control Over Financial Reporting to answer the following questions:
   (a) Who is responsible for establishing and implementing effective internal controls?
   (b) What type of internal controls is the report addressing?
   (c) What framework did management use to evaluate its internal control?
   (d) What was management's conclusion about the operating effectiveness of internal control?
   (e) What information is provided to help readers understand why management arrived at that conclusion?
   (f) What changes, if any, has management made to improve internal controls?
3. Locate the report of the independent registered public accounting firm. What information, if any, does the audit firm provide about its evaluation of internal controls over financial reporting?

CASE

12-35 **(OBJECTIVES 12-2, 12-3)** The information technology (IT) department at Jacobsons, Inc., consists of eight employees, including the IT Manager, Melinda Cullen. Cullen is responsible for the day-to-day oversight of the IT function and reports to Jacobsons' chief operating officer (COO). The COO is a senior vice president responsible for the overall retail operations who reports directly to the president and chief executive officer. The COO attends board of director meetings to provide an update of key operating performance issues. Because Cullen takes an active role in managing the IT department, the COO rarely discusses IT issues with the board or CEO. Cullen and the COO identify hardware and software needs and are authorized to approve those purchases.

In addition to Cullen, the IT department is composed of seven other individuals: three programmers, three operators, and one data control clerk. Cullen has been employed by Jacobsons for 12 years, working her way up through various positions in the department. Fortunately, she has been able to retain a fairly stable staff and has experienced minimal turnover. All IT personnel have been employed in their current positions since mid-2009.

When hiring personnel, Cullen does extensive background checks on prospective employees, including reference, credit, and criminal checks. Cullen has developed a trust with each employee and, as a result, delegates extensively to each individual. This is especially beneficial because Cullen spends most of her time working with user departments in a systems analyst role, identifying changes needed to existing applications. She conducts weekly IT departmental meetings on Tuesday mornings. Each staff member attends, including night operators, to discuss issues affecting the performance of the department.

The three programmers are responsible for maintaining and updating systems and application software. The lead programmer is responsible for assigning duties among the programming staff. All three programmers have extensive experience with the operating, utility, security, and library software as well as all of Jacobsons' application software packages. Programming assignments are made based on who is least busy among the programming staff at the time. This method of management keeps all programmers familiar with most software packages in use at Jacobsons and keeps programmers excited about the job tasks because of the variety of assignments they receive. Cullen encourages each programmer to take continuing education courses to keep current with the latest technical developments. In addition to programming responsibilities, the programming staff maintains the library of programs and data tapes, which is located in a locked room nearby. The programming staff maintains extensive logs of tape use and of changes made to program files.

The three operators consist of a day operator and two night operators. Most of the applications are based on online inputting from various user departments for batch processing overnight. Thus, the heaviest volume of processing occurs during the night shift, although there is some daytime processing of payroll and general ledger applications. All operators are responsible for monitoring the operation of the equipment and correcting system-caused errors. In addition, they do routine monthly backup procedures. The computer operators have programming experience with the program language used in application programs. Occasionally, when a small change is identified for an application program, Cullen asks the day shift operator to implement that change to avoid overburdening the programming staff.

Operators follow the production schedule prepared by Cullen, who consults with user departments to develop the schedule. The day shift operator reviews the job processed log (which chronologically details the jobs processed) generated at the end of the previous night shift for deviations from the schedule, and the lead night shift operator reviews the job processed log generated at the end of the previous day shift for deviations from the schedule. If jobs processed reconcile to the job schedule, the job processed log is discarded. When there are deviations, the operator doing the review leaves a copy for Cullen, highlighting the deviation. Before doing batch processing jobs, the operators generate an input listing report that summarizes the number of online input entries submitted during the day for processing. This number is recorded and then later compared by the operators with the computer output generated after batch processing and file updating occur. This provides a check figure of the number of transactions processed. When the numbers agree, the output is submitted to the data control clerk. When the numbers disagree, the operators identify the error and resubmit the application for processing.

The data control clerk collates all computer output, including output reports and exception listings. The data control clerk reviews exception reports and prepares correction forms for reprocessing. Examples of changes that the data control clerk might make include correcting inputting errors (for example, amounts accidentally transposed) and preparing change request forms for changes to existing master files (examples include revising sales price lists and inventory product numbers in the sales master file and adding new employee names, addresses, and Social Security numbers to the payroll master file). After all corrections are made, the data control clerk distributes all computer output to the various user departments. User departments have high regard for the IT staff. Output reports are reconciled to input reports by users on a test basis quarterly.

Required You are the senior auditor assigned to the audit of Jacobsons. The audit partner has asked you to assist in doing the IT general controls review. The partner has asked you to review this narrative information and respond to the following questions:

1. What controls and deficiencies exist in the lines of reporting from IT to senior management? If you note any deficiencies, provide recommendations that can be included in the management letter.
2. What is your assessment of how Melinda Cullen fulfills her IT management responsibilities? Identify tasks that she does that strengthen the department. Which of her tasks cause you concern? What changes in her day-to-day responsibilities would you make?
3. What is your assessment of the programming function at Jacobsons? What are the strengths? What are the deficiencies? Make recommendations for improvement.
4. What is your assessment of the IT operations function at Jacobsons? What are the strengths? What are the deficiencies? Make recommendations for improvement.
5. What is your assessment of the data control function at Jacobsons? What are the strengths? What are the deficiencies? Make recommendations for improvement.
6. Make recommendations for improving controls over the involvement of users.

ACL PROBLEM

ACL

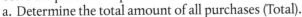

12-36 **(OBJECTIVE 12-7)** This problem requires the use of ACL software, which can be accessed through the textbook Web site. Information about downloading and using ACL and the commands used in this problem can also be found on the textbook Web site. You should read all of the reference material preceding the instructions about "Quick Sort" before locating the appropriate command to answer parts a. through f. For this problem, use the file labeled "Purchase_Orders" in the "Acquisitions_Payment" subfolder of the ACL_Rockwood project. The suggested command or other source of information needed to solve the problem requirement is included at the end of each question.

a. Determine the total amount of all purchases (Total).
b. To better understand the purchasing activity, stratify and print the purchases by purchase amount. Use $100 as the minimum value and $100,000 as the maximum value, and create 10 strata. Which stratum accounts for the greatest number of purchases? (Stratify)
c. Determine if there are any duplicates or missing purchase order numbers in the file. State your audit concerns with any gaps or duplicates. Provide a possible explanation for any gaps or duplicates that you find. (Gaps and Duplicates)
d. How many purchase orders relate to purchases that did not have a requisition (based on the Requisition Number column)? What is the total dollar amount of purchases made without a requisition? (Summarize). State your audit concerns related to purchases without a requisition.
e. Determine and print the percent of total purchases by vendor number. Do any vendors account for more than 5% of total purchases? (Classify and Quick Sort).
f. Rockwood requires a second approval for all purchases exceeding $100,000. Select all purchases greater than $100,000 and print the list for follow-up testing of proper approval. (Filter)

INTEGRATED CASE APPLICATION—PINNACLE MANUFACTURING: PART IV

12-37 **(OBJECTIVES 12-1, 12-2)** In Parts I and II of this case, you performed preliminary analytical procedures and assessed acceptable audit risk and inherent risk for Pinnacle Manufacturing. In Part III, you considered fraud risks. Your team has been assigned the responsibility of auditing the acquisition and payment cycle and one related balance sheet account, accounts payable. The general approach to be taken will be to reduce assessed control risk to a low level, if possible, for the two main types of transactions affecting accounts payable: acquisitions and cash disbursements. The following are furnished as background information:

- A summary of key information from the audit of the acquisition and payment cycle and accounts payable in the prior year, which was extracted from the previous audit firm's audit files (Figure 12-12, p. 406)

FIGURE 12-12 Information for Audit of Accounts Payable—Previous Year	
Accounts payable, 12-31-15	
Number of accounts	452
Total accounts payable	$9,460,776
Range of individual balances	$33.27–$677,632.97
Performance materiality for accounts payable	$230,000
Transactions, 2015	
Acquisitions:	
Number of acquisitions	16,243
Total acquisitions	$92,883,712
Cash disbursements:	
Number of disbursements	23,661
Total cash disbursements	$87,280,031
Results of audit procedures—tests of controls and substantive tests of transactions for acquisitions (sample size of 100):	
Purchase order not approved	1
Purchase quantities, prices, and/or extensions not correct	1
Transactions charged to wrong general ledger account	2
Transactions recorded in wrong period	1
No other exceptions	
Results of audit procedures—cash disbursements (sample size of 100):	
Cash disbursement recorded in wrong period	2
No other exceptions	
Results of audit procedures—accounts payable: (50% of vendors' balances were verified; combined net understatement amounts were projected to the population as follows):	
Three cutoff misstatements	$52,349
One difference in amounts due to disputes and discounts	$9,552
No adjustment was necessary because the total projected misstatement was not material.	

- A flowchart description of the accounting system and internal controls for the acquisition and payment cycle (Figure 12-13)—the flowchart shows that although each of the company's three divisions has its own receiving department, the purchasing and accounts payable functions are centralized

The purpose of Part IV is to obtain an understanding of internal control and assess control risk for Pinnacle Manufacturing's acquisition and cash disbursement transactions.

a. Familiarize yourself with the internal control system for acquisitions and cash disbursements by studying the information in Figure 12-12 and Figure 12-13.
b. Prepare a control risk matrix for acquisitions and a separate one for cash disbursements using Figure 12-3 on page 373 as a guide. A formatted control risk matrix is available online. The objectives should be specific transaction-related audit objectives for acquisitions for the first matrix and cash disbursements for the second matrix. See pages 611–615 in Chapter 18 for transaction-related audit objectives for acquisitions and cash disbursements. In doing Part IV, the following steps are recommended:
   (1) *Controls*
      a. Identify key controls for acquisitions and for cash disbursements. After you decide on the key controls, include each control in one of the two matrices.
      b. Include a "C" in the matrix in each column for the objective(s) to which each control applies. Several of the controls should satisfy multiple objectives.

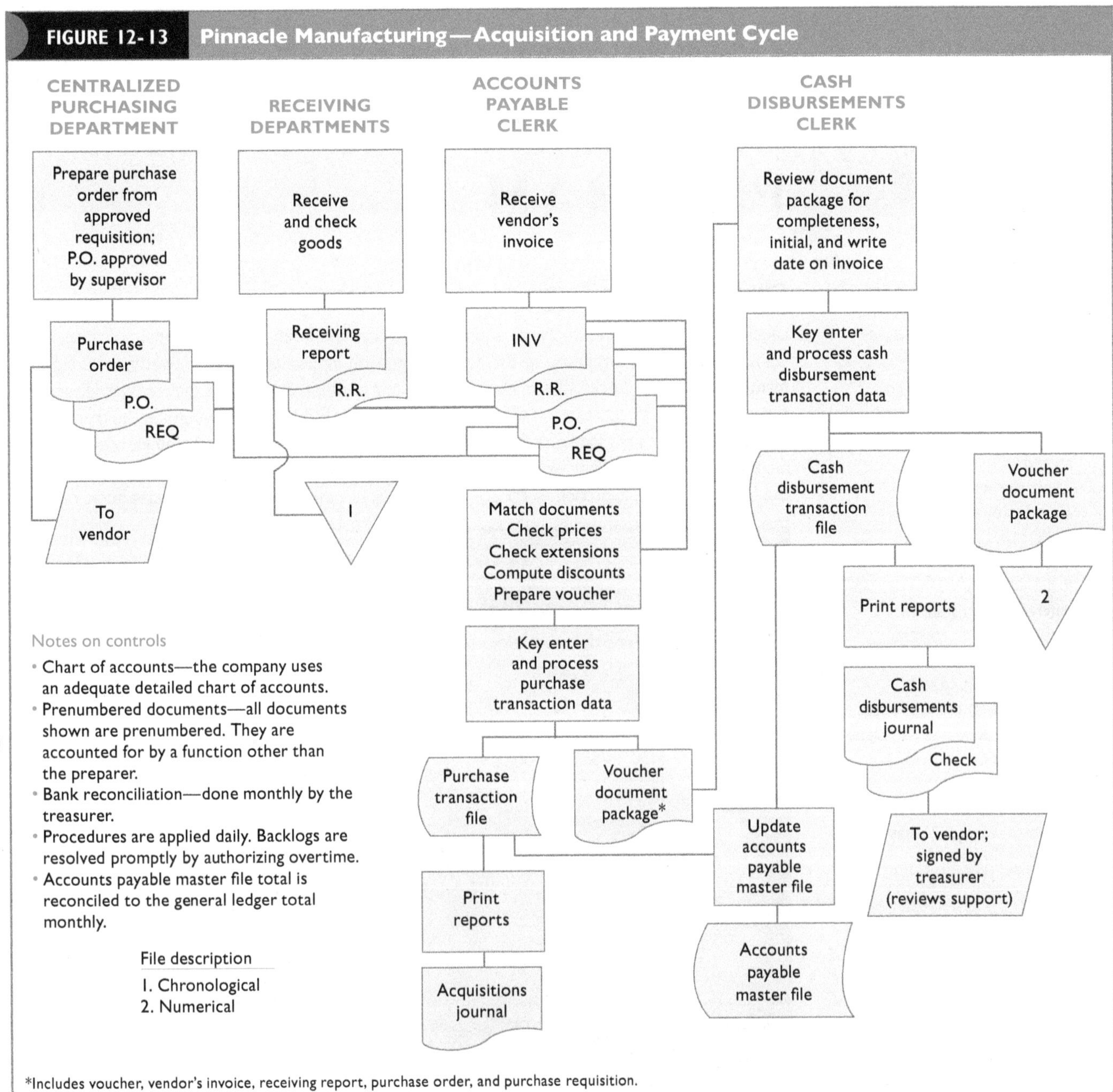

(2) *Deficiencies*
   a. Identify key deficiencies for acquisitions and for cash disbursements. After you decide on the deficiencies, include each deficiency in the bottom portion of one of the two matrices.
   b. Include a "D" in the matrix in each column for the objective(s) to which each control deficiency applies.

(3) Assess control risk as high, medium, or low for each objective using your best judgment. Do this for both the acquisitions and cash disbursements matrices.

CHAPTER

13

OVERALL AUDIT STRATEGY AND AUDIT PROGRAM

LEARNING OBJECTIVES

After studying this chapter, you should be able to

13-1 Use the five types of audit tests to determine whether financial statements are fairly stated.

13-2 Select the appropriate types of audit tests.

13-3 Understand the concept of evidence mix and how it should be varied in different circumstances.

13-4 Design an audit program.

13-5 Compare and contrast transaction-related audit objectives with balance-related and presentation and disclosure-related audit objectives.

13-6 Understand key evidence-related terms.

13-7 Integrate the four phases of the audit process.

Change in Audit Strategy Pays Dividends

Lakeisha Jackson was the in-charge auditor at Probert and Reed, a large regional public accounting firm. As she was wrapping up the audit of Simpson Industries, a large, privately held clothing manufacturer, Jason Locke, the manager on the engagement, announced that he was leaving the firm. Susan Reed, the partner on the engagement, told Jackson that she would be the manager on the following year's engagement. Reed further told her, "I'd like you to do some early planning for next year's audit. The client would like us to keep any fee increase minimal. I'd like to see how we can adjust our audit approach to reduce audit hours, but maintain or even increase audit quality."

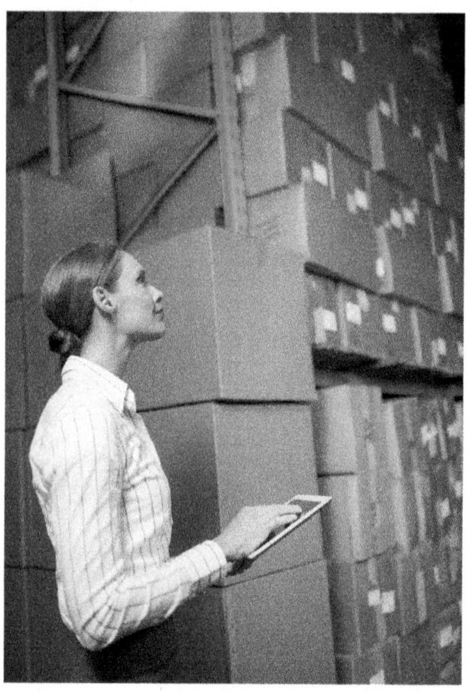

Jackson spent several hours reviewing the audit files and time budget. "I wonder how Susan is going to feel about changing our audit approach when she sees these hours charged to the client," she thought. Still, she had some ideas. Most of the hours on the engagement were spent on inventory and accounts receivable. In addition, because Simpson had extensive fixed assets, considerable hours were also spent testing fixed assets. Simpson had excellent controls, and had recently invested in their inventory accounting system, including new hand-held scanners that made it easy to track inventory. They had begun using cycle counts of inventory, but still took complete year-end physical counts of inventory at several locations. Although Probert and Reed had gained an understanding of internal control at Simpson, as required by auditing standards, they had done minimal testing of controls and had taken a substantive approach to the audit. Jackson summarized her proposed changes in a memo, but waited a day to reevaluate her suggestions before sending them to Reed.

When Reed received the memo, she was initially taken aback. Jackson's ideas did not involve tinkering at the edges and adjusting a few samples sizes. But the more Reed thought about it, the more the changes made sense. First, Jackson recommended greater reliance on controls over inventory and sales. Most of the controls were automated, and the firm's information risk specialists could assist with the testing. Jackson also recommended elimination of year-end physical counts of inventory, and reliance on cycle counts. Additionally, she recommended that Simpson rely solely on cycle counts to test the accuracy of their inventory accounting records. For receivables, Jackson proposed testing controls over sales and performing substantive analytical procedures. As a result, the sample size for accounts less than performance materiality could be dramatically reduced. Finally, Jackson recommended that detail tests of depreciation be replaced by substantive analytical procedures.

As Reed reviewed the files at the completion of the following year's engagement, a smile crossed her face. Simpson had always been a good audit client, but the change in auditing strategy made her even more confident that the financial statements were fairly stated, and even with additional planning hours, total time on the engagement had been significantly reduced. More importantly, client management was also very satisfied. Reed met with Chris Palmer, Simpson's Chief Financial Officer, toward the end of the engagement. "We did not think we were ready to use only cycle counts," said Palmer, "but your suggestion encouraged us that we were ready." He further noted, "This was the smoothest year-end close and audit we've had."

Reed met with Jackson at the conclusion of the engagement. "You know, I was a little nervous adopting all the recommendations you made last year, but they all worked out great." Jackson smiled, thinking she had been a little nervous herself. "Oh, I almost forgot to tell you," Reed added. "The partners just voted to promote you, effective July 1." Jackson thought back to her initial planning for the engagement, and was glad that she had not recommended a same-as-last-year audit approach.

This chapter deals with the eighth and last step in the planning phase of an audit. This critical step finalizes the audit strategy and entire audit program the auditor plans to follow, including all audit procedures, sample sizes, items to select, and timing. The chapter-opening vignette deals with the importance of the decisions involving the overall audit strategy and audit plan and program, considering both audit effectiveness and efficiency.

First, the overall audit strategy is discussed, which means selecting a mix of five types of tests that will result in an effective and efficient audit. This topic includes discussion of the trade-offs among the types of tests, including consideration of the cost of each type. After deciding on the most cost-effective mix of the types of tests, the auditor designs a detailed audit program. Later in the chapter, we'll address how phase I, which includes all of the audit planning steps, relates to the other three phases of the audit.

TYPES OF TESTS

OBJECTIVE 13-1

Use the five types of audit tests to determine whether financial statements are fairly stated.

In developing an overall audit strategy, auditors use five **types of tests** to determine whether financial statements are fairly stated. Auditors use risk assessment procedures to identify significant risks due to fraud or error, and design tests that address those risks. Auditors also assess the risk of material misstatement, represented by the combination of inherent risk and control risk as described in Chapter 9. The other four types of tests represent **further audit procedures** performed in response to the risks identified. Each audit procedure falls into one, and sometimes more than one, of these five categories.

Figure 13-1 (p. 410) shows the relationship of the four types of further audit procedures to the audit risk model. As Figure 13-1 illustrates, tests of controls are performed to support a reduced assessment of control risk, while auditors use substantive analytical procedures and tests of details of balances to satisfy planned detection risk. Substantive tests of transactions affect both control risk and planned detection risk, because they test the effectiveness of internal controls and the dollar amounts of transactions.

Risk Assessment Procedures

Auditing standards require the auditor to obtain an understanding of the entity and its environment, including its internal control, to assess the risk of material misstatement in the client's financial statements. Chapter 8 described how the auditor performs procedures to understand the client's business and industry to assess the risk of material misstatement. Chapters 9 and 10 further described how auditors perform procedures to identify significant risks and assess inherent risk and control risk, while Chapter 12 illustrated how auditors perform procedures to obtain an understanding of internal control to assess control risk. Collectively, procedures performed to obtain an understanding of the entity and its environment, including internal controls, represent the auditor's risk assessment procedures.

Risk assessment procedures are performed to assess the risk of material misstatement in the financial statements. The auditor performs tests of controls, substantive tests of transactions, substantive analytical procedures, and tests of details of balances in response to the auditor's assessment of the risk of material misstatements. The combination of these four types of further audit procedures provides the basis for the auditor's opinion, as illustrated by Figure 13-1.

FIGURE 13-1 Further Audit Procedures and the Audit Risk Model

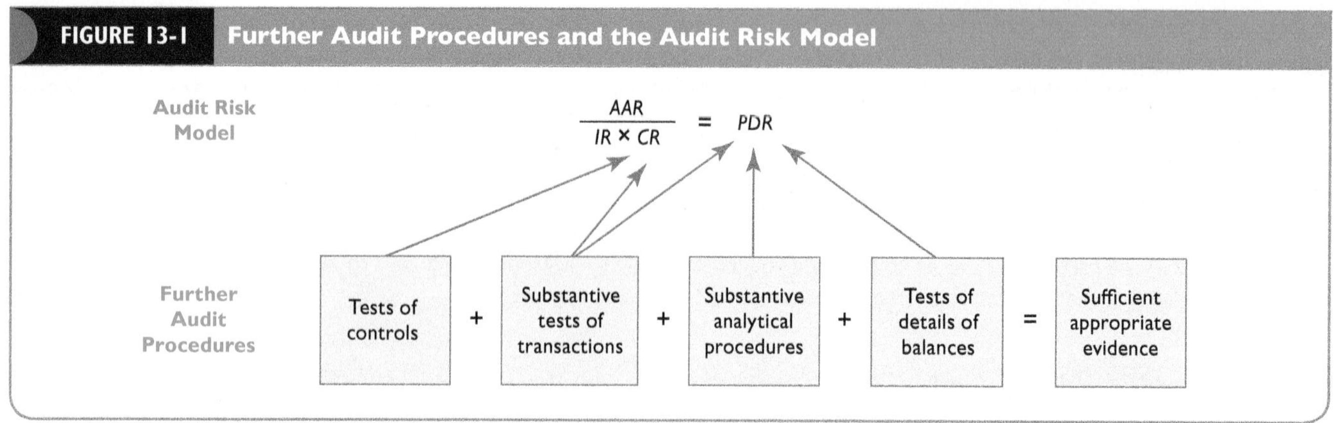

A major part of the auditor's risk assessment procedures is done to obtain an understanding of internal control. **Procedures to obtain an understanding of internal control**, which were studied in Chapter 12, focus on both the *design* and *implementation* of internal control and are used to assess control risk for each transaction-related audit objective.

Tests of Controls

The auditor's understanding of internal control is used to assess control risk for each transaction-related audit objective. Examples are assessing the accuracy objective for sales transactions as low and the occurrence objective as moderate. When control policies and procedures are believed to be effectively designed and implemented, the auditor assesses control risk at a level that reflects the relative effectiveness of those controls. To obtain sufficient appropriate evidence to support that assessment, the auditor performs **tests of controls.**

Tests of controls, either manual or automated, may include the following types of evidence. (Note that the first three procedures are the same as those used to obtain an understanding of internal control.)

- Make inquiries of appropriate client personnel
- Examine documents, records, and reports
- Observe control-related activities
- Reperform client procedures

Auditors perform a system walkthrough as part of procedures to obtain an understanding to help them determine whether controls have been appropriately implemented. The walkthrough is normally applied to one or a few transactions and follows that transaction through the entire process. For example, the auditor may select one sales transaction for a system walkthrough of the credit approval process, then follow the credit approval process from initiation of the sales transaction through the granting of credit.

Procedures to obtain an understanding of internal control generally do not provide sufficient appropriate evidence that a control is operating effectively. Tests of controls are used to determine whether these controls are effective, and manual controls usually involve testing a sample of transactions. As a test of the operating effectiveness of the credit approval process, for example, the auditor might examine a sample of 50 sales transactions from throughout the year to determine whether credit was granted before the shipment of goods.

For automated controls, the auditor's procedures to determine whether the automated control has been implemented may also serve as the test of that control, if the auditor determines that general controls are effective and there is minimal risk that the automated control has been changed since the understanding was obtained. Then, no additional tests of controls would be required.

FIGURE 13-2 Role of Audit Tests in the Audit of the Sales and Collection Cycle

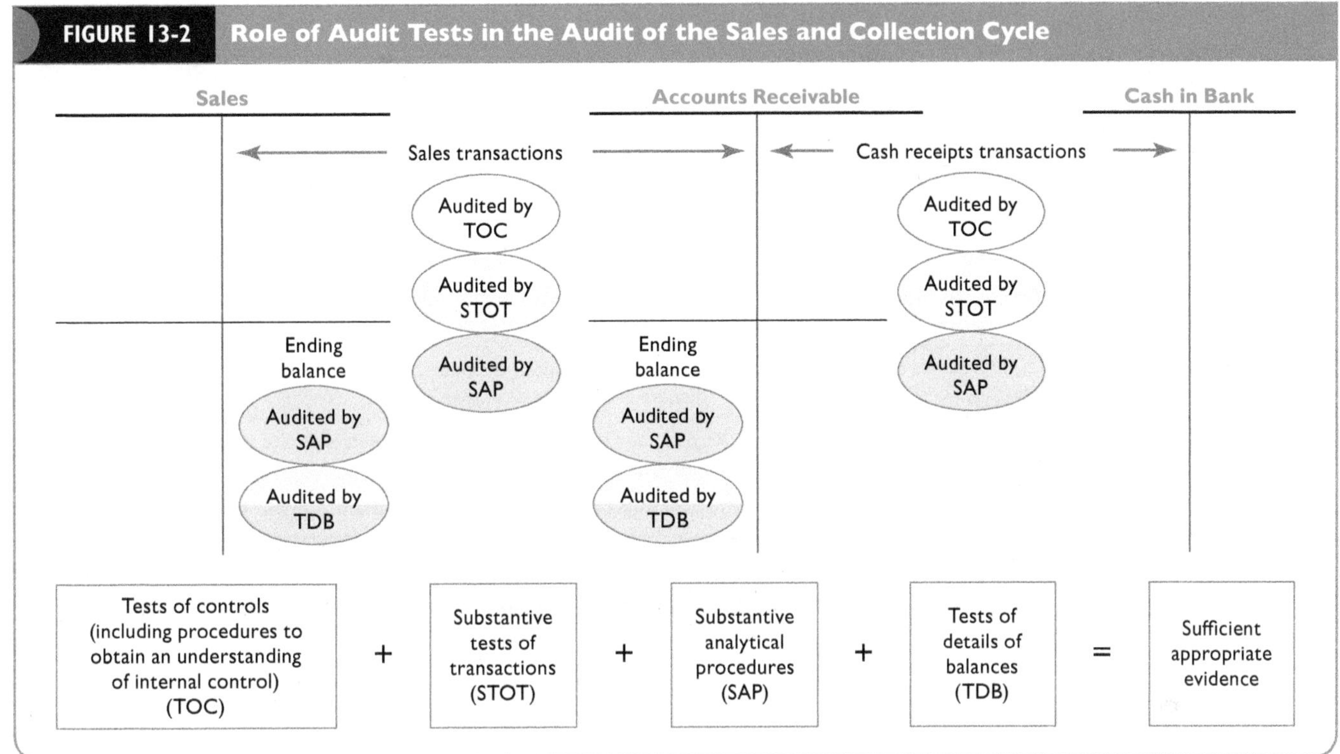

The amount of additional evidence required for tests of controls depends on two things:

1. The extent of evidence obtained in gaining the understanding of internal control
2. The planned reduction in control risk

Figure 13-2 shows the role of tests of controls in the audit of the sales and collection cycle relative to other tests performed to provide sufficient appropriate evidence for the auditor's opinion. Note the unshaded ovals with the words "Audited by TOC." For simplicity, we make two assumptions: Only sales and cash receipts transactions and three general ledger balances make up the sales and collection cycle and the beginning balances in cash and accounts receivable were audited in the previous year and are considered correct.

If auditors verify that sales and cash receipts transactions are correctly recorded in the accounting records and posted to the general ledger, they can conclude that the ending balances in accounts receivable and sales are correct. (Cash disbursements transactions will have to be audited before the auditor can reach a conclusion about the ending balance in the cash account.) One way the auditor can verify recording of transactions is to perform tests of controls. If controls are in place over sales and cash receipts transactions, the auditor can perform tests of controls to determine whether the six transaction-related audit objectives are being met for that cycle. Substantive tests of transactions, which we will examine in the next section, also affect audit assurance for sales and cash receipts transactions.

To illustrate typical tests of controls, let's return to the control risk matrix for Hillsburg Hardware Co. in Figure 12-3 (p. 373). For each of the 11 controls included in Figure 12-3, Table 13-1 (p. 412) identifies a test of control that might be performed to test its effectiveness.

Substantive Tests of Transactions

Substantive tests are procedures designed to test for dollar misstatements (often called *monetary misstatements*) that directly affect the correctness of financial statement balances. Auditors rely on three types of substantive tests: substantive tests of transactions, substantive analytical procedures, and tests of details of balances.

TABLE 13-1 Illustration of Tests of Controls	
Illustrative Key Controls	**Typical Tests of Controls**
Credit is approved automatically by the computer by comparison to authorized credit limits (C1).	Use test data to determine if the computer system automatically approves transactions below authorized credit limits and rejects transactions above authorized credit limits (reperformance).
Recorded sales are supported by authorized shipping documents and approved customer orders (C2).	Examine a sample of duplicate sales invoices to determine that each one is supported by an authorized shipping document and approved customer order (inspection).
Separation of duties exists among billing, recording of sales, and handling of cash receipts (C3).	Observe whether personnel responsible for handling cash have no accounting responsibilities and inquire as to their duties (observation and inquiry).
Shipping documents are electronically forwarded to billing daily and are billed the subsequent day (C4).	Observe whether shipping documents are forwarded daily to billing and observe when they are billed (observation).
Shipping documents are prenumbered and accounted for weekly (C5).	Account for a sequence of shipping documents and trace each to the sales journal (inspection and reperformance).
Batch totals of quantities shipped are compared with quantities billed (C6).	Examine a sample of daily batches, recalculate the shipping quantities, and trace totals to reconciliation with input reports (reperformance).
Unit selling prices are obtained from the price list master file of approved prices (C7).	Examine a sample of sales invoices and agree prices to authorized computer price list. Review changes to price file throughout the year for proper approval (reperformance and inspection).
Sales transactions are internally verified (C8).	Examine documents for internal verification (inspection).
Statements are mailed to customers each month (C9).	Observe whether statements are mailed for one month and inquire about who is responsible for mailing the statements (observation and inquiry).
Computer automatically posts transactions to the accounts receivable subsidiary records and to the general ledger (C10).	Use audit software to trace postings from the batch of sales transactions to the subsidiary records and general ledger (reperformance).
Accounts receivable master file is reconciled to the general ledger on a monthly basis (C11).	Examine evidence of reconciliation for test month, and test accuracy of reconciliation (inspection and reperformance).

Substantive tests of transactions are used to determine whether all six transaction-related audit objectives have been satisfied for each class of transactions. Two of those objectives for sales transactions are recorded sales transactions exist (occurrence objective) and existing sales transactions are recorded (completeness objective). See Chapter 6, pages 161–162, for the six transaction-related audit objectives.

When auditors are confident that all transactions were correctly recorded in the journals and correctly posted, considering all six transaction-related audit objectives, they can be confident that general ledger totals are correct.

Figure 13-2 (p. 411) illustrates the role of substantive tests of transactions in the audit of the sales and collection cycle by lightly shaded ovals with the words "Audited by STOT." Observe that both tests of controls and substantive tests of transactions are performed for transactions in the cycle, not on the ending account balances. The auditor verifies the recording and summarizing of sales and cash receipts transactions by performing substantive tests of transactions. Figure 13-2 shows one set of tests for sales and another for cash receipts.

Auditors can perform tests of controls separately from all other tests, but it's often more efficient to do them at the same time as substantive tests of transactions. For example, auditors can usually apply tests of controls involving inspection and reperformance to the same transactions tested for monetary misstatements. (Reperformance simultaneously provides evidence about both controls and monetary correctness.) In the rest of this book, we will assume that tests of controls and substantive tests of transactions are done at the same time.

Substantive Analytical Procedures

As we first discussed in Chapter 7, **analytical procedures** involve comparisons of recorded amounts to expectations developed by the auditor. Auditing standards require that these comparisons be done during planning and completing the audit.

Although not required, analytical procedures may also be performed to audit an account balance. The two most important purposes of **substantive analytical procedures** in the audit of account balances are to:

1. Indicate possible misstatements in the financial statements
2. Provide substantive evidence

Analytical procedures done during planning typically differ from those done in the testing phase. Even if, for example, auditors calculate the gross margin during planning, they probably do it using interim data. Later, during the tests of the ending balances, they will recalculate the ratio using full-year data. If auditors believe that analytical procedures indicate a reasonable possibility of misstatement, they may perform additional analytical procedures or decide to modify tests of details of balances.

When the auditor develops expectations using substantive analytical procedures and concludes that the client's ending balances in certain accounts appear reasonable, certain tests of details of balances may be eliminated or sample sizes reduced. Auditing standards state that substantive analytical procedures are a type of substantive test, when they are performed to provide evidence about an account balance. The extent to which auditors may be willing to rely on substantive analytical procedures in support of an account balance depends on several factors, including the precision of the expectation developed by the auditor, materiality, and the risk of material misstatement.

Figure 13-2 (p. 411) illustrates the role of substantive analytical procedures in the audit of the sales and collection cycle by the dark shaded ovals with the words "Audited by SAP." Observe that the auditor performs substantive analytical procedures on sales and cash receipts transactions, as well as on the ending balances of the accounts in the cycle.

Tests of Details of Balances

Tests of details of balances focus on the ending general ledger balances for both balance sheet and income statement accounts. The primary emphasis in most tests of details of balances is on the balance sheet. Examples include confirmation of customer balances for accounts receivable, physical examination of inventory, and examination of vendors' statements for accounts payable. Tests of ending balances are essential because the evidence is usually obtained from a source independent of the client, which is considered highly reliable. Much like for transactions, the auditor's tests of details of balances must satisfy all balance-related audit objectives for each significant balance sheet account. These objectives were introduced in Chapter 6 and are shown on pages 163–165.

Figure 13-2 illustrates the role of tests of details of balances by the ovals with half-dark and half-light shading and the words "Audited by TDB." Auditors perform detailed tests of the ending balances for sales and accounts receivable, including procedures such as confirmation of account receivable balances and sales cutoff tests. The extent of these tests depends on the results of tests of controls, substantive tests of transactions, and substantive analytical procedures for these accounts.

Tests of details of balances help establish the monetary correctness of the accounts they relate to and therefore are substantive tests. For example, confirmations test for monetary misstatements in accounts receivable and are therefore substantive tests. Similarly, counts of inventory and marketable securities are also substantive tests.

Summary of Types of Tests

Figure 13-2 summarizes how auditors respond to the risks of material misstatements identified through risk assessment procedures by using the four types of further audit procedures to obtain audit assurance in the audit of the sales and collection cycle. Tests of controls help auditors evaluate whether controls over transactions in the cycle are sufficiently effective to support the reduced assessment of control risk, and thereby allow reduced substantive testing. Tests of controls also form the basis for the auditor's report on internal control over financial reporting for larger public companies. Substantive tests of transactions are used to verify transactions recorded in the journals and posted in the general ledger. Substantive analytical procedures emphasize the overall reasonableness of transactions and the general ledger balances. Tests of details of balances emphasize the ending balances in the general ledger.

By combining the types of audit tests shown in Figure 13-2, the auditor obtains a higher overall assurance for transactions and accounts in the sales and collection cycle than the assurance obtained from any one test. To increase overall assurance for the cycle, the auditor can increase the assurance obtained from any one of the tests.

SELECTING WHICH TYPES OF TESTS TO PERFORM

OBJECTIVE 13-2

Select the appropriate types of audit tests.

Typically, auditors use all five types of tests when performing an audit of the financial statements, but certain types may be emphasized, depending on the circumstances. Recall that risk assessment procedures are required in all audits to assess the risk of material misstatement while the other four types of tests are performed in response to the risks identified to provide the basis for the auditor's opinion. Note also that only risk assessment procedures, especially procedures to obtain an understanding of controls, and tests of controls are performed in an audit of internal control over financial reporting.

Several factors influence the auditor's choice of the types of tests to select, including the availability of the eight types of evidence, the relative costs of each type of test, the effectiveness of internal controls, and inherent risks. Only the first two are discussed further because the last two were discussed in earlier chapters.

Availability of Types of Evidence for Further Audit Procedures

Each of the four types of further audit procedures involves only certain types of evidence (confirmation, inspection, and so forth). Table 13-2 summarizes the relationship between further audit procedures and types of evidence. We can make several observations about the table:

- More types of evidence, six in total, are used for tests of details of balances than for any other type of test.
- Only tests of details of balances involve physical examination and confirmation.
- Inquiries of the client are made for every type of test.

TABLE 13-2 Relationship Between Further Audit Procedures and Evidence

	Type of Evidence							
Further Audit Procedures	Physical Examination	Confirmation	Inspection	Observation	Inquiries of the Client	Reperformance	Analytical Procedures	Recalculation
Tests of controls (including procedures to obtain an understanding of internal control)			√	√	√	√		
Substantive tests of transactions			√		√	√		√
Substantive analytical procedures					√		√	
Tests of details of balances	√	√	√		√	√		√

- Inspection is used in every type of test except substantive analytical procedures.
- Reperformance is used in every type of test except substantive analytical procedures. Auditors may reperform a control as part of a transaction walk-through or to test a control that is not supported by sufficient documentary evidence.
- Recalculation is used to verify the mathematical accuracy of transactions when performing substantive tests of transactions and account balances when performing tests of details of balances.

Relative Costs

When auditors must decide which type of test to select for obtaining sufficient appropriate evidence, the cost of the evidence is an important consideration. The types of tests are listed below in order of increasing cost:

- Substantive analytical procedures
- Risk assessment procedures, including procedures to obtain an understanding of internal control
- Tests of controls
- Substantive tests of transactions
- Tests of details of balances

Substantive analytical procedures are the least costly because of the relative ease of making calculations and comparisons. Often, considerable information about potential misstatements can be obtained by simply comparing two or three numbers. However, when substantive analytical procedures are the primary evidence for an account balance, or are used to reduce tests of details of balances, the auditor must develop a sufficiently precise expectation to support the account balance. This may involve more complex calculations and obtaining evidence to support the expectation.

Risk assessment procedures, including procedures to obtain an understanding of internal control, are not as costly as other audit tests because auditors can easily make inquiries and observations and perform planning analytical procedures. Also, examining such things as documents summarizing the client's business operations and processes and management and governance structure are relatively cheaper than other audit tests.

Because tests of controls also involve inquiry, observation, and inspection, their relative costs are also low compared to substantive tests. However, tests of controls are more costly relative to the auditor's risk assessment procedures due to the greater extent of testing required to obtain evidence that a control is operating effectively, especially when those tests of controls involve reperformance. Often, auditors can perform a large number of tests of controls quickly using audit software. Such software can test controls in clients' computerized accounting systems, such as in computerized accounts receivable systems that automatically authorize sales to existing customers by comparing the proposed sales amount and existing accounts receivable balance with each customer's credit limit.

Substantive tests of transactions cost more than tests of controls that do not include reperformance because the former often require recalculations and tracings. In a computerized environment, however, the auditor can often perform substantive tests of transactions quickly for a large sample of transactions.

Tests of details of balances almost always cost considerably more than any of the other types of procedures because of the cost of procedures such as sending confirmations and counting inventories. Because of the high cost of tests of details of balances, auditors usually try to plan the audit to minimize their use.

Naturally, the cost of each type of evidence varies in different situations. For example, the cost of an auditor's test-counting inventory (a substantive test of the details of the inventory balance) often depends on the type and dollar value of the inventory, its location, and the number of different items, as well as the effectiveness of the client's controls over inventory.

Relationship Between Tests of Controls and Substantive Tests

To better understand tests of controls and substantive tests, let's examine how they differ. An exception in a test of control only *indicates* the likelihood of misstatements affecting the dollar value of the financial statements, whereas an exception in a substantive test of transactions or a test of details of balances is a financial statement misstatement. Exceptions in tests of controls are called *control test deviations.*

From Chapter 12, you may recall the three levels of control deficiencies: deficiencies, significant deficiencies, and material weaknesses. Auditors are most likely to believe material dollar misstatements exist in the financial statements when control test deviations are considered to be significant deficiencies or material weaknesses. Auditors should then perform substantive tests of transactions or tests of details of balances to determine whether material dollar misstatements have actually occurred.

Assume that the client's controls require an independent clerk to verify the quantity, price, and extension of each sales invoice, after which the clerk must initial the duplicate invoice to indicate performance. A test of control audit procedure is to inspect a sample of duplicate sales invoices for the initials of the person who verified the information. If a significant number of documents lack initials, the auditor should consider implications for the audit of internal control over financial reporting and follow up with substantive tests for the financial statement audit. This can be done by extending tests of duplicate sales invoices to include verifying prices, extensions, and footings (substantive tests of transactions) or by increasing the sample size for the confirmation of accounts receivable (substantive test of details of balances). Even though the control is not operating effectively, the invoices may still be correct, especially if the person originally preparing the sales invoices did a conscientious and competent job.

On the other hand, if no documents or only a few of them are missing initials, the control will be considered effective and the auditor can therefore reduce substantive tests of transactions and tests of details of balances. However, some reperformance and recalculation substantive tests are still necessary to provide the auditor assurance that the clerk did not initial documents without actually performing the control procedure or performed it carelessly. Because of the need to complete some reperformance and recalculation tests, many auditors perform them as a part of the original tests of controls. Others wait until they know the results of the tests of controls and then determine the total sample size needed.

Relationship Between Substantive Analytical Procedures and Other Substantive Tests

Like tests of controls, analytical procedures only *indicate* the likelihood of misstatements affecting the dollar value of the financial statements. Unusual fluctuations in the relationships of an account to other accounts, or to nonfinancial information, may indicate an increased likelihood that material misstatements exist without necessarily providing direct evidence of a material misstatement. When analytical procedures identify unusual fluctuations, auditors should perform substantive tests of transactions or tests of details of balances to determine whether dollar misstatements have actually occurred. If the auditor performs substantive analytical procedures and believes that the likelihood of material misstatement is low, other substantive tests can be reduced. For accounts with small balances and only minimal potential for material misstatements, such as many supplies and prepaid expense accounts, auditors often limit their tests to substantive analytical procedures if they conclude the accounts are reasonably stated.

Trade-Off Between Tests of Controls and Substantive Tests

There is a trade-off between tests of controls and substantive tests. During planning, auditors decide whether to assess control risk below the maximum. When they do, they must then perform tests of controls to determine whether the assessed level of control risk is supported. (They must always perform tests of controls in an audit of internal control over financial reporting.) If tests of controls support the control risk

FIGURE 13-3 Audit Assurance from Substantive Tests and Tests of Controls at Different Levels of Internal Control Effectiveness

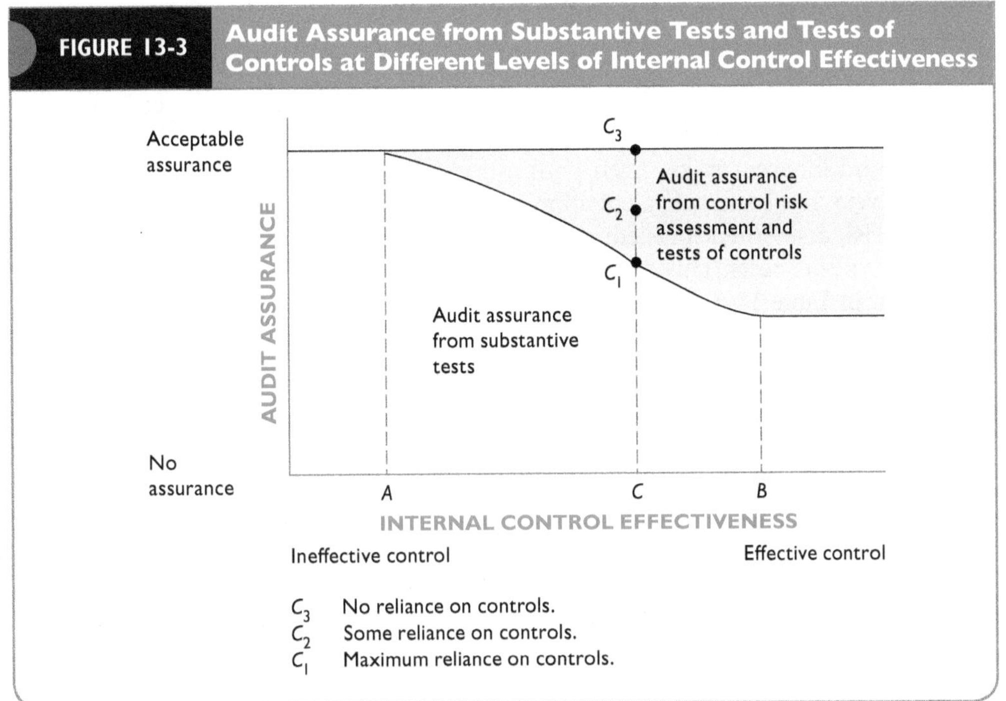

assessment, planned detection risk in the audit risk model is increased, and planned substantive tests can therefore be reduced. Figure 13-3 shows the relationship between substantive tests and control risk assessment (including tests of controls) at differing levels of internal control effectiveness.

The shaded area in Figure 13-3 is the maximum assurance obtainable from control risk assessment and tests of controls. At any point to the left of point A, assessed control risk is 1.0 because the auditor initially evaluated internal controls as ineffective based on the performance of risk assessment procedures. Notice in Figure 13-3 that any point to the right of point B results in no further reduction of control risk because even with maximum reliance on controls, some substantive procedures are still required in an audit of financial statements. Because the audit of financial statements and the audit of internal control over financial reporting are integrated, accelerated filer public company audits will most likely be represented by point B.

The auditor's understanding of internal control performed as part of risk assessment procedures provides the basis for the auditor's initial assessment of control risk. Assuming that the auditor determines that the design of internal control is effective and the controls are implemented, the auditor selects a point within the shaded area of Figure 13-3 that is consistent with the assessed control risk the auditor decides to support with tests of controls. Assume the auditor contends that internal control effectiveness is at point C. Tests of controls at the C_1 level will be extensive to support the low assessment of control risk. The auditor may then determine through the performance of tests of controls that the initial low assessment of control risk at point C is not supported and that internal control is not operating effectively. Then, the auditor's revised control risk assessment would be at the maximum (point C_3) and audit assurance will be obtained from substantive tests. Any point between the two, such as C_2, represents situations where the audit assurance obtained from tests of controls is less than the maximum level of assurance represented by point C_1. If C_2 is selected, the audit assurance from tests of controls is $C_3 - C_2$ and from substantive tests is $C - C_2$. The auditor will likely select C_1, C_2, or C_3 based on the relative cost of tests of controls and substantive tests.

EVIDENCE MIX

OBJECTIVE 13-3

Understand the concept of evidence mix and how it should be varied in different circumstances.

The choice of which types of tests to use and how extensively they need to be performed can vary widely among audits for differing levels of internal control effectiveness and inherent risks. Even within a given audit, variations may occur from cycle to cycle. To obtain sufficient appropriate evidence in response to risks identified through risk assessment procedures, auditors employ a combination of the four remaining types of tests. This combination is often called the **evidence mix**, which is illustrated in Table 13-3 for four different audits. In each case, assume that sufficient appropriate evidence was accumulated. In each audit, you should be able to determine the description of the client from the evidence mix in Table 13-3.

Analysis of Audit 1 This client is a large company with sophisticated internal controls and low inherent risk. Therefore, the auditor performs extensive tests of controls and relies heavily on the client's internal controls to reduce substantive tests. Extensive substantive analytical procedures are also performed to reduce other substantive tests. Substantive tests of transactions and tests of details of balances are therefore minimized. Because of the emphasis on tests of controls and substantive analytical procedures, this audit can be done relatively inexpensively. This audit likely represents the mix of evidence used in the integrated audit of a public company's financial statements and internal control over financial reporting.

Analysis of Audit 2 This company is medium sized, with some controls and a few inherent risks. The auditor has decided to do a medium amount of testing for all types of tests except substantive analytical procedures, which will be done extensively. More extensive testing will be required if specific inherent risks are discovered.

Analysis of Audit 3 This company is medium sized but has few effective controls and significant inherent risks. Perhaps management has decided that better internal controls are not cost effective. Because of the lack of effective internal control, we can assume this company is probably a nonpublic company. No tests of controls are done because reliance on internal controls is inappropriate when controls are insufficient for a nonpublic company. The auditor emphasizes tests of details of balances and substantive tests of transactions, but some substantive analytical procedures are also done. Substantive analytical procedures are usually performed to reduce other substantive tests because they provide evidence about the likelihood of material misstatements. If the auditor already expects to find material misstatements in the account balances, additional analytical procedures are not cost effective. The cost of the audit is likely to be relatively high because of the amount of detailed substantive testing.

Analysis of Audit 4 The original plan on this audit was to follow the approach used in Audit 2. However, the auditor likely found extensive control test deviations and significant misstatements while performing substantive tests of transactions and

TABLE 13-3 Variations in Evidence Mix

	Tests of Controls	Substantive Tests of Transactions	Substantive Analytical Procedures	Tests of Details of Balances
Audit 1	E	S	E	S
Audit 2	M	M	E	M
Audit 3	N	E	M	E
Audit 4	M	E	E	E

E = Extensive amount of testing; M = Medium amount of testing; S = Small amount of testing; N = No testing.

substantive analytical procedures. Therefore, the auditor concluded that the internal controls were not effective. Extensive tests of details of balances are performed to offset the unacceptable results of the other tests. The cost of this audit is higher because tests of controls and substantive tests of transactions were performed but cannot be used to reduce tests of details of balances.

CONCEPT CHECK

1. What are the five types of tests auditors use to determine whether financial statements are fairly stated? Identify which tests are performed to reduce control risk and which tests are performed to reduce planned detection risk.
2. In Figure 13-3 (p. 417), explain the differences among C_3, C_2, and C_1. Explain the circumstances under which it would be a good decision to obtain audit assurance from substantive tests at point C_1. Do the same for points C_2 and C_3.

DESIGN OF THE AUDIT PROGRAM

OBJECTIVE 13-4

Design an audit program.

After the auditor uses risk assessment procedures to determine the appropriate emphasis on each of the other four types of tests, the specific audit procedures for each type of test must be designed. These audit procedures are then combined to form the audit program. In most audits, the engagement in-charge auditor recommends the evidence mix to the engagement manager. After the evidence mix is approved, the in-charge prepares the audit program or modifies an existing program to satisfy all audit objectives, considering such things as materiality, evidence mix, inherent risk, control risk, and any identified significant risks, as well as the need for an integrated audit for larger public companies. The in-charge is also likely to get approval from the manager before performing the audit procedures or delegating their performance to an assistant.

Let's focus on designing audit programs to satisfy transaction-related and balance-related audit objectives. Keep in mind the auditor will also design audit programs to satisfy presentation and disclosure-related audit objectives. In addition to the section of the audit program that contains the risk assessment procedures performed in planning, the audit program for most audits is designed in three additional parts: tests of controls and substantive tests of transactions, substantive analytical procedures, and tests of details of balances.

SOLE PRACTITIONER SANCTIONED FOR INSUFFICENT AUDIT EVIDENCE AND DOCUMENTATION

John Kinross-Kennedy was a sole practitioner CPA with six public company audit clients that were traded on the over-the-counter (OTC) market and OTC bulletin board, and at times was the independent accountant for as many as 23 public companies. PCAOB audit standards require that audit documentation contain sufficient information to enable an experienced auditor with no previous connection to the engagement to (a) understand the nature, timing, extent, and results of the procedures performed, evidence obtained, and conclusions reached, and (b) determine who performed the work and the date such work was completed as well as the person who reviewed the work and the date of the review.

Kinross-Kennedy did not include written audit programs or document his conclusions for most audit areas. He frequently did not sign or initial and date the audit workpapers that he prepared. He engaged Wilfred Hanson to perform an engagement quality review for five of the 40 audit reports he issued for fiscal years after 2009, but he did not obtain any reviews for the remaining 35 engagements, and he did not verify whether Hanson was qualified to perform the reviews. For one of the engagements, Kinross-Kennedy failed to adequately test revenues and cost of goods sold, and also relied upon documents he could not read, either because they were written in Chinese or illegible. Other SEC findings included failures in the confirmation process, failure to adequately evaluate related party transactions, and inadequate evaluation of audit differences identified during testing. Kinross-Kennedy was barred from practicing before the SEC for five years.

Source: Securities and Exchange Commission Accounting and Auditing Enforcement Release No. 3502, September 30, 2013 (www.sec.gov).

Each transaction cycle will likely be evaluated using a separate set of sub-audit programs. In the sales and collection cycle, for example, the auditor might use:

- A test of controls and substantive tests of transactions audit program for sales and cash receipts
- A substantive analytical procedures audit program for the entire cycle
- Tests of details of balances audit programs for cash, accounts receivable, bad debt expense, allowance for uncollectible accounts, and miscellaneous accounts receivable

Tests of Controls and Substantive Tests of Transactions

The tests of controls and substantive tests of transactions audit program normally includes a descriptive section documenting the understanding of internal control obtained during the performance of risk assessment procedures. The program is also likely to include a description of the procedures performed to obtain an understanding of internal control and a description of the assessed level of control risk. The auditor uses this information to develop the tests of controls and substantive tests of transactions audit program. Figure 13-4 illustrates the methodology used to design these tests. (We previously discussed the steps in the first three boxes of Figure 13-4 on pages 368–381 of Chapter 12.) The audit procedures include both tests of controls and substantive tests of transactions, which vary depending on assessed control risk. When controls are effective and control risk is assessed as low, auditors put heavy emphasis on tests of controls. Some substantive tests of transactions will also be included. If control risk is assessed at maximum, only substantive tests of transactions will be used, assuming the audit is of a smaller public company or a nonpublic company.

Audit Procedures When designing tests of controls and substantive tests of transactions, auditors emphasize satisfying the transaction-related audit objectives developed in Chapter 6. Auditors follow a four-step approach to reduce assessed control risk.

1. Apply the transaction-related audit objectives to the class of transactions being tested, such as sales.

FIGURE 13-4 Methodology for Designing Tests of Controls and Substantive Tests of Transactions

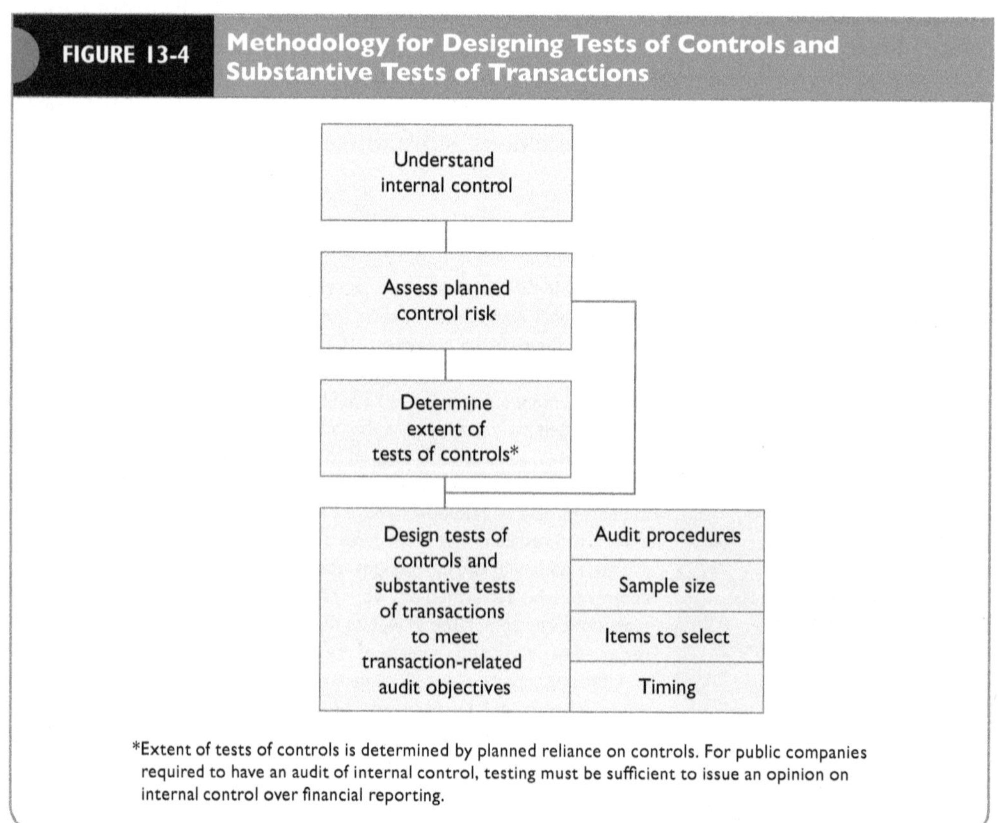

*Extent of tests of controls is determined by planned reliance on controls. For public companies required to have an audit of internal control, testing must be sufficient to issue an opinion on internal control over financial reporting.

2. Identify key controls that should reduce control risk for each transaction-related audit objective.
3. Develop appropriate tests of controls for all internal controls that are used to reduce the preliminary assessment of control risk below maximum (key controls).
4. For potential types of misstatements related to each transaction-related audit objective, design appropriate substantive tests of transactions, considering deficiencies in internal control and expected results of the tests of controls in step 3.

Figure 13-5 summarizes this four-step approach to designing tests of controls and substantive tests of transactions.

Substantive Analytical Procedures

Because substantive analytical procedures are relatively inexpensive, many auditors perform them on all audits. Analytical procedures performed during substantive testing, such as for the audit of accounts receivable, are typically more focused and more extensive than those done as part of planning. The auditor is likely to use disaggregated data to increase the precision of the auditor's expectations. During planning, the auditor might calculate the gross margin percentage for total sales, while during substantive testing of accounts receivable, the auditor might calculate gross margin percentage by month or by line of business, or possibly both. Analytical procedures calculated using monthly amounts will typically be more effective in detecting misstatements than those calculated using annual amounts, and comparisons by line of business will usually be more effective than companywide comparisons.

If sales and accounts receivable are based on predictable relationships with nonfinancial data, the auditor often uses that information for analytical procedures. For example, if revenue billings are based on the number of hours professionals charge to clients, such as in law firms and other organizations that provide services, the auditor can estimate total revenue by multiplying hours billed by the average billing rate.

FIGURE 13-5 Four-Step Approach to Designing Tests of Controls and Substantive Tests of Transactions

Apply transaction-related audit objectives to a class of transactions (step 1)

Identify key controls and make a preliminary assessment of control risk (step 2)

Design tests of controls (step 3)
- Audit procedures
- Sample size
- Items to select
- Timing

Design substantive tests of transactions (step 4)
- Audit procedures
- Sample size
- Items to select
- Timing

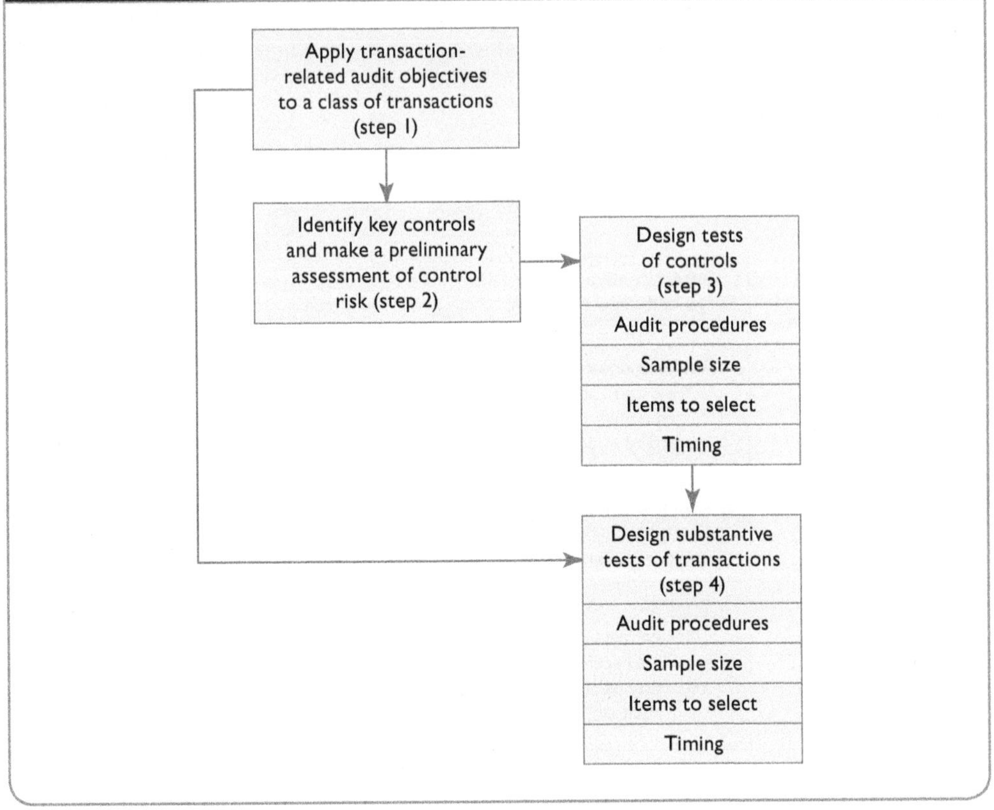

When the auditor plans to use analytical procedures to provide substantive assurance about an account balance, the data used in the calculations must be considered sufficiently reliable. This is true for all data, especially nonfinancial data. For example, if auditors estimate total revenue using hours billed and the average billing rate, they must be confident that both numbers are reasonably reliable.

Tests of Details of Balances

To design tests of details of balances audit procedures, auditors use a methodology oriented to the balance-related audit objectives we covered in Chapter 6 (pp. 163–165). If the auditor is verifying accounts receivable, for example, the planned audit procedures must be sufficient to satisfy each of the balance-related audit objectives. In planning tests of details of balances audit procedures to satisfy these objectives, many auditors follow a methodology such as the one shown in Figure 13-6 for accounts receivable. The design of these procedures is normally the most difficult part of the entire planning process because it is subjective and requires considerable professional judgment.

Let's discuss the key decisions in designing tests of details of balances audit procedures as shown in Figure 13-6.

Identify Significant Risks and Assess Risk of Material Misstatement for Accounts Receivable As part of gaining an understanding of the client's business and industry, the auditor identifies and evaluates significant client business risks to determine whether they result in a significant risk or increased risk of material misstatements in the financial statements. If the auditor identifies a significant risk due to either fraud or error, the auditor should identify client controls to mitigate the risk, and design substantive procedures to determine whether material misstatements occurred due to the significant risk. An increased risk of material misstatement should be incorporated in the auditor's evaluation of inherent risk or control risk, which will then affect the appropriate extent of evidence.

FIGURE 13-6 Methodology for Designing Tests of Details of Balances—Accounts Receivable

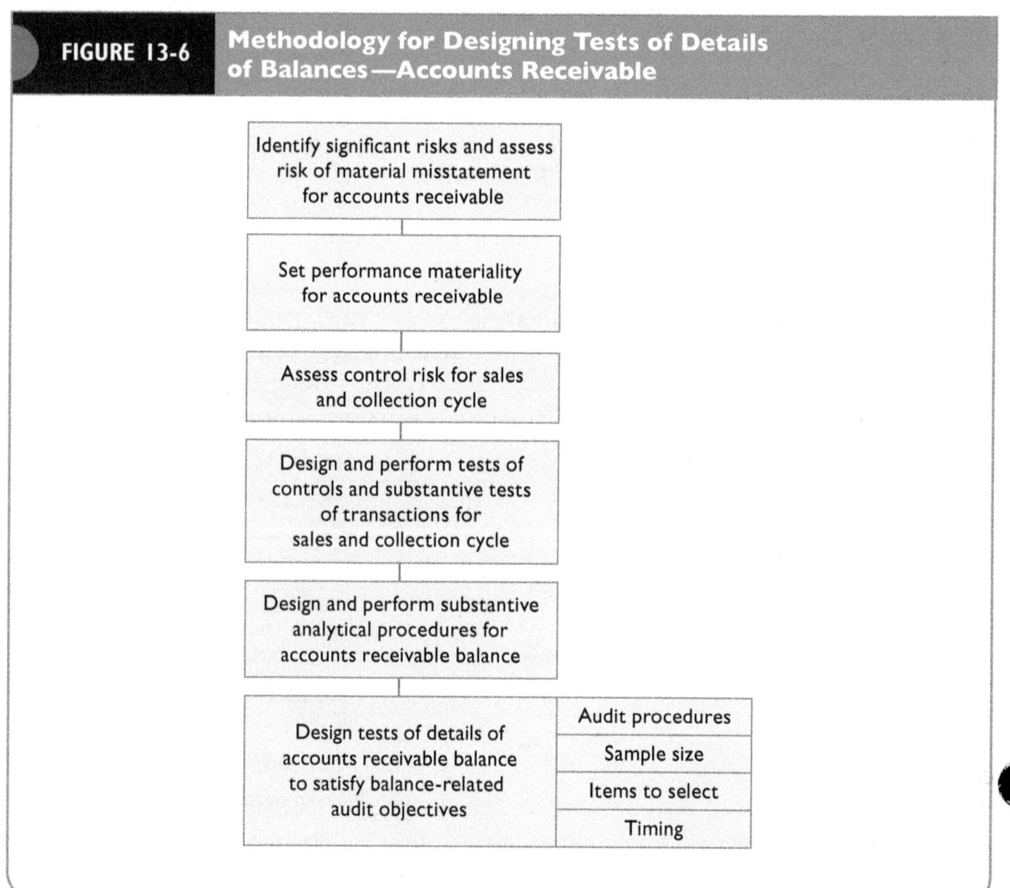
Identify significant risks and assess risk of material misstatement for accounts receivable
Set performance materiality for accounts receivable
Assess control risk for sales and collection cycle
Design and perform tests of controls and substantive tests of transactions for sales and collection cycle
Design and perform substantive analytical procedures for accounts receivable balance
Design tests of details of accounts receivable balance to satisfy balance-related audit objectives
Audit procedures
Sample size
Items to select
Timing

PEER REVIEW DATA IMPROVES AUDITS

To help improve audit practices, the AICPA Peer Review Team has been collecting data on "Matters for Further Consideration (MFCs)." Matters identified during peer reviews are retained electronically using an MFC form to identify problem areas. Audit firms can use this information to identify areas where they can improve audit quality.

The most common audit-related matters identified include:

- Failure to update the report to conform to audit standards.
- Failure to appropriately document planning procedures, including risk assessment and linkage of risks to procedures performed, planning analytics, and control testing.
- Client representation letters that were dated incorrectly, did not cover the appropriate periods, or were missing required representations.
- Failure to communicate and/or document required communications with those charged with governance.
- Insufficient appropriate evidence in audit documentation to support the firm's opinion on the financial statements.

In addition to findings related to audit standards, the Peer Review Team also reports findings related to compliance with GAAP, accounting and review services, service organization reports, governmental audits, and other areas. The listing of findings will be updated quarterly to provide auditors with current information on matters most frequently found in peer reviews.

Source: Adapted from Ken Tysiac, "Learn from Data to Improve Audits," *Journal of Accountancy* (September 2014), pp. 34–37.

Inherent risk is assessed by identifying any aspect of the client's history, environment, or operations that indicates a high likelihood of misstatement in the current year's financial statements. Considerations affecting inherent risk that may apply to accounts receivable include makeup of accounts receivable, nature of the client's business, initial engagement, and other inherent risk factors discussed in Chapter 9. An account balance for which inherent risk has been assessed as high will result in more evidence accumulation than for an account with low inherent risk.

Inherent risk also can be extended to individual balance-related audit objectives. For example, adverse economic conditions in the client's industry may make the auditor conclude that a high risk of uncollectible accounts receivable (realizable value objective) exists. Inherent risk can still be low for all other objectives.

Set Performance Materiality Auditors must decide the preliminary judgment about materiality for the audit as a whole and then allocate the total to account balances, to establish performance materiality for each significant balance. For a lower materiality level, more testing of details is required, and vice versa. Some auditors allocate performance materiality to individual balance-related audit objectives, but most do not.

Assess Control Risk for the Sales and Collection Cycle The methodology for evaluating control risk will be applied to both sales and cash receipts in the audit of accounts receivable. Effective controls will reduce control risk and, along with it, the amount of evidence required for substantive tests of transactions and tests of details of balances. Inadequate controls will increase the substantive evidence needed.

Design and Perform Tests of Controls and Substantive Tests of Transactions for the Sales and Collection Cycle Tests of controls and substantive tests of transactions are designed with the expectation that certain results will be obtained. These predicted results affect the design of tests of details of balances. For example, the auditor usually plans to do extensive tests of controls when control risk is assessed as low. This will permit less extensive substantive testing of accounts receivable balances.

Design and Perform Substantive Analytical Procedures for Accounts Receivable Balance Auditors perform substantive analytical procedures for an account such as accounts receivable for two purposes: to identify possible misstatements in the account balance and to reduce detailed audit tests. The results of substantive analytical procedures directly affect the extent of tests of details of balances.

Design Tests of Details of Accounts Receivable Balance to Satisfy Balance-Related Audit Objectives The planned tests of details of balances include audit procedures, sample size, items to select, and timing. Procedures must be selected and designed for each account and each balance-related audit objective within each account.

A difficulty auditors face in designing tests of details of balances is the need to predict the outcome of the tests of controls, substantive tests of transactions, and substantive analytical procedures before they are performed. This is necessary because the auditor should design tests of details of balances during the planning phase, but the appropriate design depends on the outcome of the other tests. In planning tests of details of balances, the auditor usually predicts few or no exceptions will occur in tests of controls, substantive tests of transactions, and substantive analytical procedures. If the results of the tests of controls, substantive tests of transactions, and substantive analytical procedures are *not* consistent with the predictions, auditors will need to change the tests of details of balances as the audit progresses.

Figure 13-7 summarizes the discussion about the approach to designing tests of details of balances applied to accounts receivable. The light shaded boxes on the left side of the figure correspond to the design of tests of controls and substantive tests of transactions, as presented in Figure 13-5 (p. 421). Figure 13-7 builds on Figure 13-5 by also showing how tests of controls and substantive tests of transactions affect the design of the tests of details of balances. Other factors affecting that decision are shown in the darker shaded boxes on the right side of the figure.

One of the most challenging parts of auditing is properly applying the factors that affect tests of details of balances. Each of the factors is subjective. Moreover, the impact of each factor on tests of details of balances is equally subjective. For example,

FIGURE 13-7 Approach to Designing Tests of Details of Balances

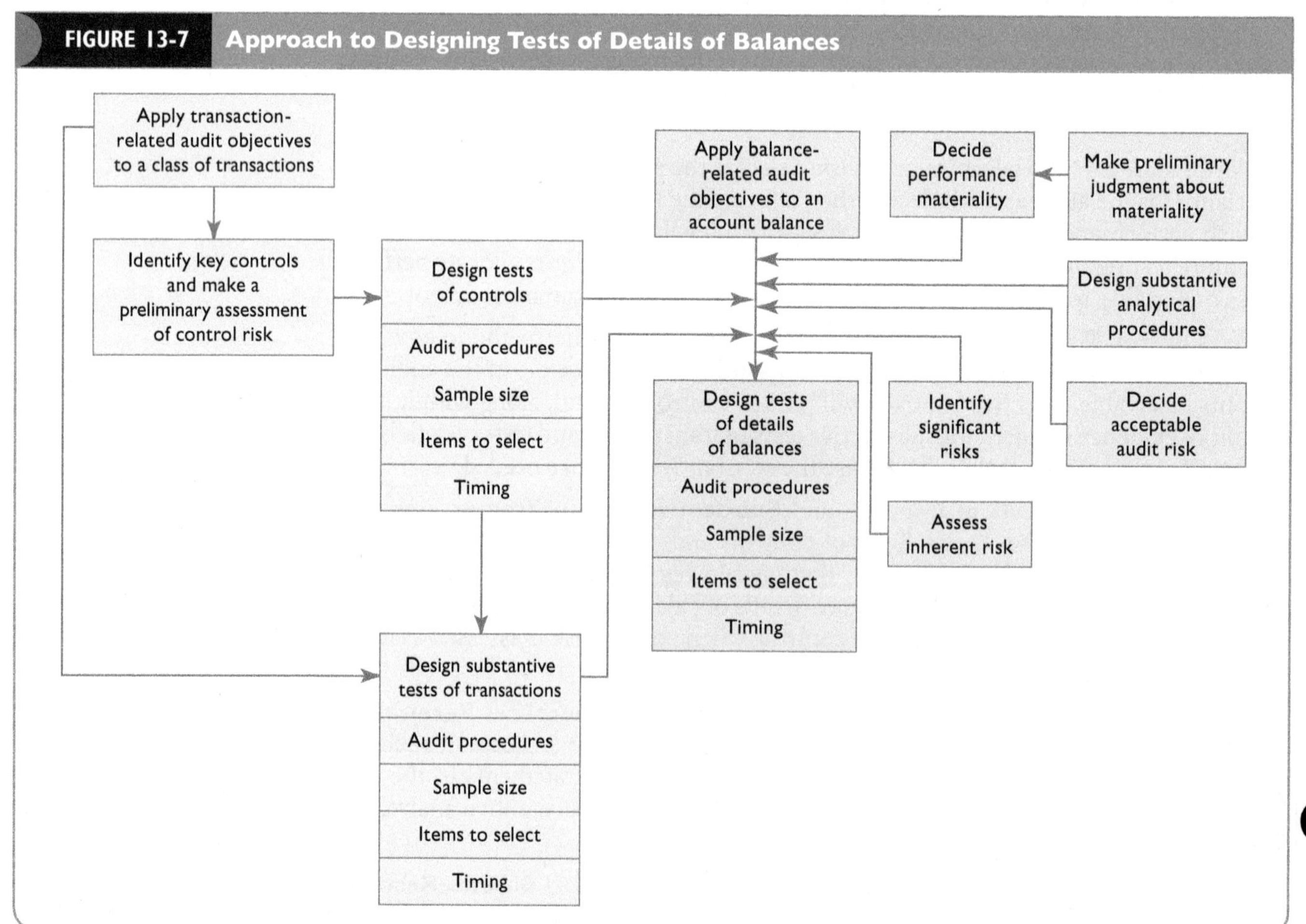

if inherent risk is reduced from medium to low, there is agreement that tests of details of balances can be reduced. Auditors need to use considerable professional judgment to decide the specific effects of such a change on audit procedures, sample size, items to select, and timing.

Level of Disaggregation of Planning Activities

The various planning activities we have discussed in Chapters 6 through 13 are applied at different levels of disaggregation, depending on the nature of the activity. Figure 13-8 shows the primary planning activities and the levels of disaggregation normally applied. These levels of disaggregation range from the overall audit to the balance-related audit objective for each account. For example, risk assessment

FIGURE 13-8 Disaggregation Level to Which Planning Activities Are Applied

	LEVEL OF DISAGGREGATION				
PLANNING ACTIVITY	Overall Audit	Cycle	Account	Transaction-Related Audit Objective	Balance-Related Audit Objective
Accept client and perform initial planning	P				
Understand client's business and industry	P				
Identify significant risks	P				
Set preliminary judgment about materiality	P				
Set performance materiality			P		
Understand internal control:					
Control environment	P				
Risk assessment		P			
Control activities		P			
Information and communication		P			
Monitoring		P			
Identify key internal controls				P	
Identify internal control deficiencies				P	
Design tests of controls				P	
Design substantive tests of transactions				P	
Assess control risk				P	
Assess inherent risk			P		P
Assess acceptable audit risk	P				
Design substantive analytical procedures			P		P
Design tests of details of balances					P

P = Primary level to which planning activity is applied

procedures related to obtaining background information about the client's business and industry pertain to the overall audit. Auditors will first use that information in assessing acceptable audit risk for the engagement as whole. They will then use information about the client and industry obtained through risk assessment procedures to assess risk of material misstatement for specific audit objectives, including any significant risks whether due to fraud or error. As the audit progresses, they will likely use that information when making decisions about tests of details of balances. Similarly, the auditor will first assess the risk of fraud for the overall audit, and later consider whether any fraud risks exist that may affect fraud risk assessments for specific accounts and the audit procedures and sample sizes for tests of details of balances for accounts that are affected.

Illustrative Audit Program

Auditing standards require the auditor to use a written audit program. Table 13-4 shows the tests of details of balances segment of an audit program for accounts receivable. The format used relates the audit procedures to the balance-related audit objectives. Notice that most procedures satisfy more than one objective, and that more than one audit procedure is used for each objective. Audit software helps auditors select appropriate audit procedures and organize them into an audit program, considering significant risk, inherent risk, control risk, and other planning considerations. Audit procedures can be added or deleted as the auditor deems necessary. For most audit procedures, sample size, items to select, and timing can also be changed.

The audit program in Table 13-4 was developed after consideration of all factors affecting tests of details of balances and is based on several assumptions about inherent risk, control risk, and the results of tests of controls, substantive tests of transactions, and substantive analytical procedures. As indicated, if those assumptions are materially incorrect, the planned audit program will likely need revision. For example, analytical procedures performed near the end of the audit can indicate potential misstatements for several balance-related audit objectives, requiring a revision of the audit plan to gather additional evidence.

Relationship of Transaction-Related Audit Objectives to Balance-Related and Presentation and Disclosure-Related Audit Objectives

OBJECTIVE 13-5

Compare and contrast transaction-related audit objectives with balance-related and presentation and disclosure-related audit objectives.

We discussed earlier that tests of details of balances must be designed to satisfy balance-related audit objectives for each account and the extent of these tests can be reduced when transaction-related audit objectives have been satisfied by tests of controls or substantive tests of transactions. You also need to understand how each transaction-related audit objective relates to each balance-related audit objective. Table 13-5 (p. 428) gives a general presentation of these relationships and illustrates that, even when all transaction-related audit objectives are met, the auditor will still rely primarily on substantive tests of balances to meet the following balance-related audit objectives:

- Realizable value
- Rights and obligations

Additional substantive tests of balances are also likely for the other balance-related audit objectives, depending on the results of the tests of controls and substantive tests of transactions.

This chapter emphasizes the relationship between audit procedures performed to satisfy transaction-related audit objectives and balance-related audit objectives. The auditor also performs audit procedures to obtain assurance about the four presentation and disclosure-related audit objectives described in Chapter 6. The auditor's approach to obtaining evidence related to presentation and disclosure-related audit objectives is consistent with the approach described in this chapter. The auditor performs tests of controls and substantive procedures to obtain assurance that all audit objectives are achieved for information and amounts included in those disclosures.

TABLE 13-4 Tests of Details of Balances Audit Program for Accounts Receivable

Tests of Details of Balances Audit Procedures	Sample Size for Each Audit Procedure	Items to Select from the Population	Timing of the Test	Accounts Receivable Balance-Related Audit Objectives							
				Detail tie-in	Existence	Completeness	Accuracy	Classification	Cutoff	Realizable value	Rights
1. Obtain an aged list of receivables: trace accounts to the master file, foot schedule, and trace to general ledger	Trace 20 items; foot two pages and all subtotals	Random	I	X							
2. Obtain an analysis of the allowance for doubtful accounts and bad debt expense: test accuracy, examine authorization for write-offs, and trace to general ledger.	All	All	Y	X	X	X	X			X	
3. Obtain direct confirmation of accounts receivable and perform alternative procedures for nonresponses.	50	10 largest 40 random	I*		X		X	X	X		X
4. Review accounts receivable control account for the period. Investigate the nature of and review support for any large or unusual entries or any entries not arising from normal journal sources. Also investigate any significant increases or decreases in sales toward year-end.	NA	NA	Y		X		X	X	X		X
5. Review receivables for any that have been assigned or discounted.	All	All	Y								X
6. Investigate collectibility of account balances.	NA	NA	Y							X	
7. Review lists of balances for amounts due from related parties or employees, credit balances, and unusual items, as well as notes receivable due after one year.	All	All	Y		X			X			
8. Determine that proper cutoff procedures were applied at the balance sheet date to ensure that sales, cash receipts, and credit memos have been recorded in the correct period.	20 transactions for sales and cash receipts; 10 for credit memos	50% before and 50% after year-end	Y						X		

I = Interim; Y = Year-end; NA = Not applicable.
*Confirmations sent as of October 31.

SUMMARY OF KEY EVIDENCE-RELATED TERMS

OBJECTIVE 13-6

Understand key evidence-related terms.

Several evidence-related terms have been used in the past several chapters. To help you distinguish and understand each of these terms, we summarize them in Table 13-6 (p. 429), and comment briefly on each term.

Phases of the Audit Process The four **phases of the audit process** in the first column are the primary way that audits are organized, as described in Chapter 6. Figure 13-9 (p. 430) shows the key components of these four phases of the audit process.

TABLE 13-5 Relationship of Transaction-Related Audit Objectives to Balance-Related Audit Objectives

Transaction-Related Audit Objective	Balance-Related Audit Objective	Nature of Relationship	Explanation
Occurrence	Existence or completeness	Direct	There is a direct relationship of the occurrence transaction-related audit objective to the existence balance-related audit objective if a class of transactions increases the related account balance (e.g., sales transactions increase accounts receivable). There is a direct relationship of the occurrence transaction-related audit objective to the completeness balance-related audit objective if a class of transactions decreases the related account balance (e.g., cash receipts transactions decrease accounts receivable).
Completeness	Completeness or existence	Direct	See comments for existence objective.
Accuracy	Accuracy	Direct	—
Posting and summarization	Detail tie-in	Direct	—
Classification	Classification	Direct	—
Timing	Cutoff	Direct	—
	Realizable value	None	Few internal controls over realizable value are related to classes of transactions, but the credit approval process affects the extent of tests.
	Rights and obligations	None	Few internal controls over rights and obligations are related to classes of transactions.

Audit Objectives These are the objectives of an audit that must be met before the auditor can conclude that any given class of transactions or account balance is fairly stated. There are six transaction-related, eight balance-related, and four presentation and disclosure-related audit objectives, all of which are listed in Table 13-6. Observe that transaction-related audit objectives are primarily addressed in phase II, balance-related audit objectives in phase III, and presentation and disclosure-related audit objectives in phase IV.

Types of Tests The five types of audit tests discussed earlier in the chapter that auditors use to determine whether financial statements are fairly stated are included in the third column in Table 13-6. Observe that analytical procedures are used in Phase III and Phase IV. Keep in mind that analytical procedures are required as part of the planning risk assessment procedures in Phase I. Recall that analytical procedures are also required at the completion of the audit, which is why they are included in Phase IV. It may appear unusual to have tests of details of balances included in Phase IV. We will explain the nature of the procedures auditors use during completing the audit in Chapter 24, including meeting the presentation and disclosure-related objectives.

Evidence Decisions The four subcategories of decisions the auditor makes in accumulating audit evidence are included in the fourth column in Table 13-6. Except for substantive analytical procedures and risk assessment procedures, all four evidence decisions apply to each type of test.

Types of Evidence The eight broad categories of evidence auditors accumulate are included in the last column of Table 13-6. The relationship of types of evidence to types of tests was summarized in Table 13-2 on page 414.

CONCEPT CHECK

1. State the four-step approach to designing tests of controls and substantive tests of transactions.
2. Explain the relationship of performance materiality, inherent risk, and control risk to planned tests of details of balances.

TABLE 13-6 Relationship Among Five Key Evidence-Related Terms

Phases of the Audit Process	Audit Objectives	Types of Tests	Evidence Decisions	Types of Evidence
Plan and Design an Audit Approach (Phase I)		Risk assessment procedures • Procedures to understand client's business and industry • Procedures to understand internal control • Planning analytical procedures	• Audit procedures • Timing	Inspection Inquiries of client Analytical procedures
Perform Tests of Controls and Substantive Tests of Transactions (Phase II)	Transaction-related audit objectives • Occurrence • Completeness • Accuracy • Posting and summarization • Classification • Timing	Procedures to obtain an understanding and tests of controls Substantive tests of transactions	• Audit procedures • Sample size • Items to select • Timing • Audit procedures • Sample size • Items to select • Timing	Inspection Observation Inquiries of client Reperformance Recalculation
Perform Substantive Analytical Procedures and Tests of Details of Balances (Phase III)	Balance-related audit objectives • Existence • Completeness • Accuracy • Classification • Cutoff • Detail tie-in • Realizable value • Rights and obligations	Substantive analytical procedures Tests of details of balances	• Audit procedures • Timing • Audit procedures • Sample size • Items to select • Timing	Physical examination Confirmation Inspection Inquiries of client Reperformance Analytical procedures Recalculation
Complete the Audit and Issue an Audit Report (Phase IV)	Presentation and disclosure-related audit objectives • Occurrence and rights and obligations • Completeness • Accuracy and valuation • Classification and understandability	Analytical procedures Tests of details of balances	• Audit procedures • Timing • Audit procedures • Sample size • Items to select • Timing	Analytical procedures Inspection Inquiries of client

SUMMARY OF THE AUDIT PROCESS

OBJECTIVE 13-7

Integrate the four phases of the audit process.

Figure 13-9 (p. 430) shows the four phases for the entire audit process, and Table 13-7 (p. 431) shows the timing of the tests in each phase for an audit with a December 31 balance sheet date.

Phase I: Plan and Design an Audit Approach

Auditors use information obtained from risk assessment procedures related to client acceptance and initial planning, understanding the client's business and industry, and performing preliminary analytical procedures (first three boxes in Figure 13-9) primarily to assess acceptable audit risk and identify significant risks. Auditors use assessments of materiality, acceptable audit risk, inherent risk, control risk, and any identified significant risks due to fraud or errors to develop an overall audit strategy and audit program.

At the end of phase I, the auditor should have a well-defined audit strategy and plan and a specific audit program for the entire audit.

Phase II: Perform Tests of Controls and Substantive Tests of Transactions

Auditors perform tests of controls and substantive tests of transactions during this phase. The objectives of phase II are to:

1. Obtain evidence in support of the specific controls that contribute to the auditor's assessed control risk (that is, where it is reduced below the maximum), including integrated audits of internal control over financial reporting.
2. Obtain evidence in support of the monetary correctness of transactions.

FIGURE 13-9 Summary of the Audit Process

PHASE I
Plan and design an audit approach

- Accept client and perform initial audit planning
- Understand the client's business and industry
- Perform preliminary analytical procedures
- Set preliminary judgment of materiality and performance materiality
- Identify significant risks due to fraud or error
- Assess inherent risk
- Understand internal control and assess control risk
- Finalize overall audit strategy and audit plan

PHASE II
Perform tests of controls and substantive tests of transactions

- Plan to reduce assessed level of control risk?
  - Yes → Perform tests of controls*
  - No → Perform substantive tests of transactions
- Perform substantive tests of transactions
- Assess likelihood of misstatements in financial statements

PHASE III
Perform substantive analytical procedures and tests of details of balances

- Low / Medium / High or unknown
- Perform substantive analytical procedures
- Perform tests of key items
- Perform additional tests of details of balances

PHASE IV
Complete the audit and issue an audit report

- Perform additional tests for presentation and disclosure
- Accumulate final evidence
- Evaluate results
- Issue audit report
- Communicate with audit committee and management

*The extent of tests of controls is determined by planned reliance on controls. For public companies required to have an audit of internal control, testing must be sufficient to issue an opinion on internal control over financial reporting.

TABLE 13-7	Timing of Tests		
Phase I	Plan and design audit approach. Update understanding of internal control. Update audit program. Perform preliminary analytical procedures.	8-31-16	
Phase II	Perform tests of controls and substantive tests of transactions for first nine months of the year.	9-30-16	
Phase III	Confirm accounts receivable. Observe inventory.	10-31-16	
	Perform cutoff tests. Request various other confirmations.	12-31-16	Balance sheet date
	Perform substantive analytical procedures, complete tests of controls and substantive tests of transactions, and complete most tests of details of balances.	1-7-17	Books closed
Phase IV	Perform procedures to support presentation and disclosure-related audit objectives, summarize results, accumulate final evidence (including analytical procedures), and finalize audit.	2-15-17	Date of audit report
	Issue audit report.	2-25-17	

The first objective is met by performing tests of controls, and the second by performing substantive tests of transactions. Frequently both types of tests are done simultaneously on the same transactions. When controls are not considered effective or when the auditor finds deviations, substantive tests can be expanded in this phase or in phase III, along with considering the implications for the auditor's report on internal control over financial reporting in an integrated audit.

Because the results of tests of controls and substantive tests of transactions are a major determinant of the extent of tests of details of balances, they are often done two or three months before the balance sheet date. This helps the auditor revise the tests of details of balance audit program for unexpected results in the earlier tests and to complete the audit as soon as possible after the balance sheet date. This approach is also used in an integrated audit to allow management an opportunity to correct control deficiencies in time to allow auditor testing of the newly implemented controls before year-end. Auditors update their testing of internal controls near year-end to verify that the controls continue to operate effectively.

For clients with highly sophisticated computerized accounting systems, auditors often perform tests of controls and substantive tests of transactions throughout the year to identify significant or unusual transactions and determine whether any changes have been made to the client's computer programs. This approach is often called continuous auditing and is frequently used in integrated audits of financial statements and internal control for public companies.

Phase III: Perform Substantive Analytical Procedures and Tests of Details of Balances

The objective of phase III is to obtain sufficient additional evidence to determine whether the ending balances and footnotes in financial statements are fairly stated. The nature and extent of the work will depend heavily on the findings of the two previous phases.

The two general categories of phase III procedures are:

1. Substantive analytical procedures that assess the overall reasonableness of transactions and balances.
2. Tests of details of balances, which are audit procedures to test for monetary misstatements in the balances in the financial statements.

Table 13-7 shows analytical procedures are performed before and after the balance sheet date. Because of their low cost, analytical procedures are commonly used whenever they are relevant. They are often performed early, using preliminary data before year-end, as a means of planning and directing other audit tests to specific areas. But the greatest benefit from calculating ratios and making comparisons occurs after the client has finished preparing its financial statements. Ideally, substantive analytical procedures are done before tests of details of balances so they can then be used to determine how extensively to test balances. Analytical procedures are also used as a part of performing tests of balances and during the completion phase of the audit.

Table 13-7 also shows that tests of details of balances are normally done last. On some audits, all are done after the balance sheet date. When clients want to issue statements soon after the balance sheet date, the more time-consuming tests of details of balances are done at interim dates before year-end with additional work being done to roll-forward the audited interim-date balances to year-end. Substantive tests of balances performed before year-end provide less assurance and are normally only done when internal controls are effective.

Phase IV: Complete the Audit and Issue an Audit Report

After the first three phases are completed, auditors must accumulate additional evidence related to presentation and disclosure-related objectives, summarize the results, issue the audit report, and perform other forms of communication. As shown in Figure 13-9 (p. 430), this phase has several parts.

Perform Additional Tests for Presentation and Disclosure Recall from Chapter 6 that auditors accumulate evidence related to presentation and disclosure-related audit objectives. The procedures auditors perform to support the four presentation and disclosure-related objectives are similar to audit procedures performed to support both transaction- and balance-related audit objectives. For example, management implements internal controls to ensure that all required footnote disclosures are included and that amounts and other information disclosed are accurate. Auditor tests of those controls provide evidence supporting the *completeness* and *accuracy* presentation and disclosure-related audit objectives. Auditors also perform substantive tests to obtain sufficient appropriate evidence that information disclosed in the footnotes reflects actual transactions and balances that have occurred and that represent obligations of the client to support the *occurrence and rights and obligation* objectives. A considerable portion of the auditor's testing related to presentation and disclosure-related objectives is done during the first three phases, but additional testing is done in phase IV.

During this last phase of the audit, auditors perform audit procedures related to contingent liabilities and subsequent events. Contingent liabilities are potential liabilities that must be disclosed in the client's footnotes. Auditors must make sure that the disclosure is complete and accurate. Subsequent events represent events that occasionally occur after the balance sheet date, but before the issuance of the financial statements and auditor's report, that have an effect on the financial statements. Specific review procedures are designed to bring to the auditor's attention any subsequent events that affect the financial statements. Both contingent liabilities and subsequent events are studied in Chapter 24.

Accumulate Final Evidence In addition to the evidence obtained for each cycle during phases I and II, and for each account during phase III, auditors must gather the following evidence for the financial statements as a whole during the completion phase:

- Perform final analytical procedures
- Evaluate the going-concern assumption
- Obtain a client representation letter
- Read information in the annual report to make sure that it is consistent with the financial statements

Issue Audit Report The type of audit report issued depends on the evidence accumulated and the audit findings. The appropriate reports for differing circumstances were studied in Chapter 3.

Communicate with Audit Committee and Management The auditor is required to communicate significant deficiencies in internal control to the audit committee or senior management. Auditing standards also require the auditor to communicate certain other matters to those charged with governance, such as the audit committee or a similarly designated body, upon completion of the audit, if not sooner. Although not required, auditors often also make suggestions to management to improve business performance.

SUMMARY

This chapter concludes our discussion of the audit planning process. In earlier chapters, we discussed how the auditor performs risk assessment procedures to understand the client's business and industry, and to assess the risks of material misstatement, including fraud risks and other significant risks. The auditor also gains an understanding of internal control to assess control risk. The auditor uses the information obtained from the risk assessment procedures to design further audit procedures, which consist of tests of controls, substantive tests of transactions, substantive analytical procedures, and tests of details of balances. The evidence mix reflects the emphasis placed on the various types of tests, and depends on the auditor's assessment of risks and the relative costs of each type of test. The auditor's objective in choosing the evidence mix is to obtain sufficient appropriate evidence while minimizing costs. The auditor then selects the specific procedures to be performed, which are combined into the audit program, which contains the detailed instructions for the gathering of audit evidence to support the auditor's opinion.

ESSENTIAL TERMS

Analytical procedures—evaluations of financial information through analysis of plausible relationships among financial and nonfinancial data

Evidence mix—the combination of the types of tests to obtain sufficient appropriate evidence for a cycle; there are likely to be variations in the mix from cycle to cycle depending on the circumstances of the audit

Further audit procedures—combination of tests of controls, substantive tests of transactions, substantive analytical procedures, and tests of details of balances performed in response to risks of material misstatement identified by the auditor's risk assessment procedures

Phases of the audit process—the four aspects of a complete audit: (1) plan and design an audit approach, (2) perform tests of controls and substantive tests of transactions, (3) perform substantive analytical procedures and tests of details of balances, and (4) complete the audit and issue an audit report

Procedures to obtain an understanding of internal control—procedures used by the auditor to gather evidence about the design and implementation of specific controls

Substantive analytical procedure—an analytical procedure in which the auditor develops an expectation of recorded amounts or ratios to provide evidence supporting an account balance

Substantive tests—audit procedures designed to test for dollar (monetary) misstatements of financial statement balances

Substantive tests of transactions—audit procedures testing for monetary misstatements to determine whether the six transaction-related audit objectives have been satisfied for each class of transactions

Tests of controls—audit procedures to test the effectiveness of controls in support of a reduced assessed control risk

Tests of details of balances—audit procedures testing for monetary misstatements to determine whether the eight balance-related audit objectives have been satisfied for each significant account balance

Types of tests—the five categories of audit tests auditors use to determine whether financial statements are fairly stated: risk assessment procedures, tests of controls, substantive tests of transactions, substantive analytical procedures, and tests of details of balances

REVIEW QUESTIONS

13-1 **(OBJECTIVE 13-1)** What is the purpose of risk assessment procedures and how do they differ from the four other types of audit tests?

13-2 **(OBJECTIVE 13-1)** What is the purpose of tests of controls? Identify specific accounts on the financial statements that are affected by performing tests of controls for the acquisition and payment cycle.

13-3 **(OBJECTIVE 13-1)** Distinguish between a test of control and a substantive test of transactions. Give two examples of each.

13-4 **(OBJECTIVES 13-1, 13-3)** State a test of control audit procedure to test the effectiveness of the following control: Approved wage rates are used in calculating employees' earnings. State a substantive test of transactions audit procedure to determine whether approved wage rates are actually used in calculating employees' earnings.

13-5 **(OBJECTIVE 13-1)** A considerable portion of the tests of controls and substantive tests of transactions are performed simultaneously as a matter of audit convenience. But the substantive tests of transactions procedures and sample size, in part, depend on the results of the tests of controls. How can the auditor resolve this apparent inconsistency?

13-6 **(OBJECTIVE 13-1)** Distinguish between substantive tests of transactions and tests of details of balances. Give one example of each for the acquisition and payment cycle.

13-7 **(OBJECTIVES 13-1, 13-2)** Explain how the calculation and comparison to previous years of the gross margin percentage and the ratio of accounts receivable to sales are related to the confirmation of accounts receivable and other tests of the accuracy of accounts receivable.

13-8 **(OBJECTIVES 13-2, 13-4)** Evaluate the following statement: "Tests of sales and cash receipts transactions are such an essential part of every audit that I like to perform them as near the end of the audit as possible. By that time I have a fairly good understanding of the client's business and its internal controls because confirmations, cutoff tests, and other procedures have already been completed."

13-9 **(OBJECTIVE 13-2)** The auditor of Ferguson's, Inc., identified two internal controls in the sales and collection cycle for testing. In the first control, the computer verifies that a planned sale on account will not exceed the customer's credit limit entered in the accounts receivable master file. In the second control, the accounts receivable clerk matches bills of lading, sales invoices, and customer orders before recording in the sales journal. Describe how the presence of general controls over software programs and master file changes affects the extent of audit testing of each of these two internal controls.

13-10 **(OBJECTIVE 13-2)** For each of the eight types of evidence discussed in Chapter 7, identify whether it is applicable for risk assessment procedures, tests of controls, substantive tests of transactions, substantive analytical procedures, and tests of details of balances.

13-11 **(OBJECTIVE 13-2)** Rank the following types of tests from most costly to least costly: substantive analytical procedures, tests of details of balances, risk assessment procedures, tests of controls, and substantive tests of transactions.

13-12 **(OBJECTIVE 13-3)** Assume that the client's internal controls over the recording and classifying of fixed asset additions are considered deficient because the individual responsible for recording new acquisitions has inadequate technical training and limited experience in accounting. How will this situation affect the evidence you should accumulate in auditing fixed assets as compared with another audit in which the controls are excellent? Be as specific as possible.

13-13 **(OBJECTIVE 13-3)** Table 13-3 (p. 418) illustrates variations in the emphasis on different types of audit tests. What are the benefits to the auditor of identifying the best mix of tests?

13-14 **(OBJECTIVE 13-4)** Explain the relationship between the methodology for designing tests of controls and substantive tests of transactions in Figure 13-4 (p. 420) and the methodology for designing tests of details of balances in Figure 13-6 (p. 422).

13-15 **(OBJECTIVE 13-4)** Why is it desirable to design tests of details of balances before performing tests of controls and substantive tests of transactions? State the assumptions that the auditor must make in doing so. What does the auditor do if the assumptions are wrong?

13-16 **(OBJECTIVE 13-4)** List the eight balance-related audit objectives in the verification of the ending balance in inventory and provide one useful audit procedure for each of the objectives.

13-17 **(OBJECTIVE 13-5)** Explain the relationship between the occurrence transaction-related audit objective and the existence and completeness balance-related audit objectives.

13-18 **(OBJECTIVE 13-6)** Indicate the four phases of the audit process. In which phase does the auditor perform tests of controls?

13-19 **(OBJECTIVE 13-7)** Why do auditors often consider it desirable to perform audit tests throughout the year rather than wait until year-end? List several examples of evidence that can be accumulated before year-end.

MULTIPLE CHOICE QUESTIONS FROM CPA EXAMINATIONS

13-20 **(OBJECTIVES 13-1, 13-5, 13-7)** The following questions concern types of audit tests. Choose the best response.

a. An auditor's decision either to apply analytical procedures as substantive tests or to perform substantive tests of transactions and account balances usually is determined by the
   (1) availability of data aggregated at a high level.
   (2) relative effectiveness and efficiency of the tests.
   (3) timing of tests performed after the balance sheet date.
   (4) auditor's familiarity with industry trends.

b. The auditor faces a risk that the audit will not detect material misstatements that occur in the accounting process. To minimize this risk, the auditor relies primarily on
   (1) substantive tests.
   (2) tests of controls.
   (3) internal control.
   (4) statistical analysis.

c. A conceptually logical approach to the auditor's evaluation of internal control consists of the following four steps:
   I. Determining the internal controls that should prevent or detect errors and fraud.
   II. Identifying control deficiencies to determine their effect on the nature, timing, or extent of auditing procedures to be applied and suggestions to be made to the client.
   III. Determining whether the necessary internal control procedures are prescribed and are being followed satisfactorily.
   IV. Considering the types of errors and fraud that can occur.

   What should be the order in which these four steps are performed?
   (1) I, II, III, and IV
   (2) I, III, IV, and II
   (3) III, IV, I, and II
   (4) IV, I, III, and II

13-21 **(OBJECTIVE 13-1)** The following questions deal with tests of controls. Choose the best response.

a. To support the auditor's initial assessment of control risk below maximum, the auditor performs procedures to determine that internal controls are operating effectively. Which of the following audit procedures is the auditor performing?
   (1) Tests of details of balances
   (2) Substantive tests of transactions
   (3) Tests of controls
   (4) Tests of trends and ratios

b. The primary objective of performing tests of controls is to obtain
   (1) a reasonable degree of assurance that the client's internal controls are operating effectively on a consistent basis throughout the year.
   (2) sufficient appropriate audit evidence to afford a reasonable basis for the auditor's opinion, without the need for additional evidence.
   (3) assurances that informative disclosures in the financial statements are reasonably adequate.
   (4) knowledge and understanding of the client's prescribed procedures and methods.

c. Tests of controls are most likely to be omitted when
   (1) an account balance reflects many transactions.
   (2) control risk is assessed at less than the maximum.
   (3) the understanding of internal control indicates that evaluating the effectiveness of control policies and procedures is likely to be inefficient.
   (4) the auditor wishes to increase the acceptable level of detection risk.

MULTIPLE CHOICE QUESTIONS FROM BECKER CPA EXAM REVIEW

13-22 (OBJECTIVES 13-1, 13-3, 13-4) The following questions concern the overall audit strategy and audit program, including selection of the type of test to perform. Choose the best response.

a. In the financial statement audit of a nonpublic company, the auditor decides to perform tests of the controls related to the occurrence of sales transactions. Which of the following best explains why the auditor decided to test these controls?
   (1) In a nonissuer financial statement audit, the auditor is required to test the operating effectiveness of internal controls.
   (2) The auditor wants to obtain an understanding of the design of the internal controls.
   (3) Control risk is assessed at below the maximum.
   (4) The auditor wants to obtain an understanding of the implementation of the internal controls.

b. Substantive analytical procedures are most likely to be used to test which of the following accounts?
   (1) Interest income
   (2) Cash
   (3) Accounts payable
   (4) Treasury stock

c. Which of the following is the auditor least likely to consider when developing the overall audit strategy?
   (1) Complexity of the company's operations
   (2) Evaluation of accounts receivable confirmations
   (3) Preliminary judgment about materiality
   (4) The economic conditions affecting the industry in which the company operates

DISCUSSION QUESTIONS AND PROBLEMS

13-23 (OBJECTIVES 13-1, 13-2) The following are 11 audit procedures taken from an audit program:

1. Discuss the duties of the cash disbursements clerk with him and observe whether he has responsibility for handling cash or preparing the bank reconciliation.

2. Examine vendors' invoices and other supporting documents to determine whether large amounts in the repair and maintenance account should be capitalized.
3. Inquire about the accounts payable supervisor's monthly review of a computer-generated exception report of receiving reports and purchase orders that have not been matched with a vendor invoice.
4. Foot the accounts payable trial balance and compare the total with the general ledger.
5. Confirm accounts payable balances directly with vendors.
6. Account for a sequence of checks in the cash disbursements journal to determine whether any have been omitted.
7. Examine vendors' invoices to verify the ending balance in accounts payable.
8. Compare the balance in payroll tax expense with previous years. The comparison takes the increase in payroll tax rates into account.
9. Examine the internal auditor's initials on monthly bank reconciliations as an indication of whether they have been reviewed.
10. Examine vendors' invoices and other documentation in support of recorded transactions in the acquisitions journal.
11. Multiply the commission rate by total sales and compare the result with commission expense.

Required

a. Indicate whether each procedure is a test of control, substantive test of transactions, substantive analytical procedure, or a test of details of balances.
b. Identify the type of evidence for each procedure.

13-24 **(OBJECTIVES 13-1, 13-2)** The following are audit procedures from different transaction cycles:

1. Trace a sample of shipping documents to entry in the sales journal.
2. Examine a sample of warehouse removal slips for signature of authorized official.
3. Examine duplicate copy of shipping documents for evidence that quantities were verified before shipment.
4. Select a sample of payroll checks and agree hours to employee time records.
5. Use audit software to foot and cross-foot the sales journal and trace the balance to the general ledger.
6. Examine voucher packages and related vendor invoices for evidence of approval of account classification.
7. Select a sample of sales invoices and agree prices to the approved price list.
8. Select a sample of entries in the cash receipts journal and trace to posting in individual customer accounts receivable records.

Required

a. For each audit procedure, identify whether it is a test of control or a substantive test of transactions.
b. For each audit procedure, identify the transaction-related audit objective or objectives being satisfied.

13-25 **(OBJECTIVES 13-1, 13-2, 13-5)** The following are audit procedures from different transaction cycles:

1. Examine sales invoices for evidence of internal verification of prices, quantities, and extensions.
2. Select items from the client's perpetual inventory records and examine the items in the company's warehouse.
3. Use audit software to foot and cross-foot the cash disbursements journal and trace the balance to the general ledger.
4. Select a sample of entries in the acquisitions journal and trace each one to a related vendor's invoice to determine whether one exists.
5. Examine documentation for acquisition transactions before and after the balance sheet date to determine whether they are recorded in the proper period.
6. Inquire of the credit manager whether each account receivable on the aged trial balance is collectible.
7. Compute inventory turnover for each major product and compare with previous years.
8. Confirm a sample of notes payable balances, interest rates, and collateral with lenders.

9. Use audit software to foot the accounts receivable trial balance and compare the balance with the general ledger.

Required

a. For each audit procedure, identify the transaction cycle being audited.
b. For each audit procedure, identify the type of evidence.
c. For each audit procedure, identify whether it is a test of control or a substantive test.
d. For each substantive audit procedure, identify whether it is a substantive test of transactions, a test of details of balances, or a substantive analytical procedure.
e. For each test of control or substantive test of transactions procedure, identify the transaction-related audit objective or objectives being satisfied.
f. For each substantive analytical procedure or test of details of balances procedure, identify the balance-related audit objective or objectives being satisfied.

13-26 **(OBJECTIVES 13-1, 13-4, 13-5)** The following are independent internal controls commonly found in the acquisition and payment cycle. Each control is to be considered independently.

1. Before a check is prepared to pay for acquisitions by the accounts payable department, the related purchase order and receiving report are attached to the vendor's invoice being paid. A clerk compares the quantity on the invoice with the receiving report and purchase order, compares the price with the purchase order, recomputes the extensions, re-adds the total, and examines the account number indicated on the invoice to determine whether it is correctly classified. He indicates his performance of these procedures by initialing the invoice.
2. At the end of each month, an accounting clerk accounts for all prenumbered receiving reports (documents evidencing the receipt of goods) issued during the month and traces each one to the related vendor's invoice and acquisitions journal entry. The clerk's tests do not include testing the quantity or description of the merchandise received.
3. The cash disbursements clerk is prohibited from handling cash. The bank account is reconciled by another person even though the clerk has sufficient expertise and time to do it.
4. Before a check is signed by the controller, she examines the supporting documentation accompanying the check. At that time, she initials each vendor's invoice to indicate her approval.
5. After the controller signs the checks, her secretary writes the check number and the date the check was issued on each of the supporting documents to prevent their reuse.

Required

a. For each of the internal controls, state the transaction-related audit objective(s) the control is meant to fulfill.
b. For each control, list one test of control the auditor could perform to test the effectiveness of the control.
c. For each control, list one substantive test the auditor could perform to determine whether financial misstatements are actually taking place.

13-27 **(OBJECTIVES 13-1, 13-4, 13-5)** The following internal controls for the acquisition and payment cycle were selected from a standard internal control questionnaire.

1. Approved purchase orders are required for all acquisitions of goods.
2. Prenumbered receiving reports are prepared as support for acquisitions and numerically accounted for.
3. Dates on receiving reports are compared with vendors' invoices before entry into the acquisitions journal.
4. Account classifications are reviewed by someone other than the preparer.
5. All supporting documents are cancelled after checks are signed or electronic funds transfers are approved.
6. The authorized signer compares data on supporting documents with checks and electronic funds transfer authorizations.
7. Vendors' invoices are recalculated before payment.
8. All checks are signed by the owner or manager.
9. Checks are mailed by the owner or manager or a person under her supervision after signing.

10. The accounts payable master file is updated, balanced, and reconciled to the general ledger monthly.

Required

a. For each control, identify which element of the five categories of control activities is applicable (separation of duties, proper authorization, adequate documents or records, physical control over assets and records, or independent checks on performance).
b. For each control, state which transaction-related audit objective(s) is (are) applicable.
c. For each control, write an audit procedure that could be used to test the control for effectiveness.
d. For each control, identify a likely misstatement, assuming that the control does not exist or is not functioning.
e. For each likely misstatement, identify a substantive audit procedure to determine whether the misstatement exists.

13-28 **(OBJECTIVES 13-4, 13-7)** Following are evidence decisions for the three audits described in Figure 13-3 on page 417:

Audit A Ineffective client internal controls
Audit B Very effective client internal controls
Audit C Somewhat effective client internal controls

Evidence Decisions

1. The auditor decided it was possible to assess control risk below the maximum.
2. The auditor identified effective controls and also identified some deficiencies in controls.
3. The auditor performed extensive positive confirmations at the balance sheet date.
4. The auditor performed tests of controls.
5. The auditor performed extensive tests of controls and minimal substantive tests.
6. The auditor performed substantive tests.
7. This audit was likely the least expensive to conduct.
8. The auditor confirmed receivables at an interim date.

Required

a. Explain why Audit B represents the maximum amount of reliance that can be placed on internal control. Why can't all the audit assurance be obtained by tests of controls?
b. Explain why the auditor may not place the maximum extent of reliance on controls in Audit B and Audit C.
c. For each of the eight evidence decisions, indicate whether the evidence decision relates to each of the audits described above. Every evidence decision relates to at least one of the audits, and some may relate to two or all three audits.

13-29 **(OBJECTIVES 13-3, 13-4)** Following are several decisions that the auditor must make in an audit of a nonpublic company. Letters indicate alternative conclusions that could be made.

Decisions	Alternative Conclusions
1. Determine whether it is cost effective to perform tests of controls.	A. It is cost effective B. It is not cost effective
2. Perform substantive tests of details of balances.	C. Perform reduced tests D. Perform expanded tests
3. Complete initial assessment of control risk.	E. Controls are effective F. Controls are ineffective
4. Perform tests of controls.	G. Controls are effective H. Controls are ineffective

Required

a. Identify the sequence in which the auditor should make decisions 1 to 4.
b. For the audit of the sales and collection cycle and accounts receivable, an auditor reached the following conclusions: A, D, E, H. Put the letters in the appropriate sequence and evaluate whether the auditor's logic was reasonable. Explain your answer.

c. For the audit of inventory and related inventory cost records, an auditor reached the following conclusions: B, C, E, G. Put the letters in the appropriate sequence and evaluate whether the auditor used good professional judgment. Explain your answer.

d. For the audit of property, plant, and equipment and related acquisition records, an auditor reached the following conclusions: A, C, F, G. Put the letters in the appropriate sequence and evaluate whether the auditor used good professional judgment. Explain your answer.

e. For the audit of payroll expenses and related liabilities, an auditor recorded the following conclusions: D, F. Put the letters in the appropriate sequence and evaluate whether the auditor used good professional judgment. Explain your answer.

13-30 **(OBJECTIVE 13-3)** The following are three situations, all involving nonpublic companies, in which the auditor is required to develop an audit strategy:

1. The client has inventory at approximately 50 locations in a three-state region. The inventory is difficult to count and can be observed only by traveling by automobile. The internal controls over acquisitions, cash disbursements, and perpetual records are considered effective. This is the fifth year that you have done the audit, and audit results in past years have always been excellent. The client is in excellent financial condition.
2. This is the first year of an audit of a medium-sized company that is considering selling its business because of severe underfinancing. A review of the acquisition and payment cycle indicates that controls over cash disbursements are excellent but controls over acquisitions cannot be considered effective. The client lacks receiving reports and a policy as to the proper timing to record acquisitions. When you review the general ledger, you observe that there are many large adjusting entries to correct accounts payable.
3. You are doing the audit of a small loan company with extensive receivables from customers. Controls over granting loans, collections, and loans outstanding are considered effective, and there is extensive follow-up of all outstanding loans weekly. You have recommended a new computer system for the past two years, but management believes the cost is too great, given their low profitability. Collections are an ongoing problem because many of the customers have severe financial problems. Because of adverse economic conditions, loans receivable have significantly increased and collections are less than normal. In previous years, you have had relatively few adjusting entries.

Required

a. For audit 1, recommend an evidence mix for the five types of tests for the audit of inventory and cost of goods sold. Justify your answer. Include in your recommendations both tests of controls and substantive tests.

b. For audit 2, recommend an evidence mix for the audit of the acquisition and payment cycle, including accounts payable. Justify your answer.

c. For audit 3, recommend an evidence mix for the audit of outstanding loans. Justify your answer.

13-31 **(OBJECTIVE 13-3)** Angela Walsh is a new staff auditor. On her first three engagements, she was assigned to perform tests of controls for acquisitions and payments and test of details of balances for accounts payable. The approach taken in each audit is briefly described below:

Audit 1– The client is a medium-sized company. Extensive tests of controls were performed for acquisitions and payments. Fairly extensive substantive analytical procedures were also performed. The tests of details of balances of the year-end accounts payable balance were minimal, and no confirmations were sent (confirmations are not required for testing accounts payable).

Audit 2– This company is also medium-sized. Extensive tests of controls were also performed, but after these tests were completed, additional substantive tests of transactions were performed. Extensive tests of the year-end accounts payable balance were performed, although no confirmations were sent.

Audit 3– Although the auditors gained an understanding of internal control, no tests of controls were performed over acquisitions and payments. However, extensive substantive tests of transactions were performed, and confirmations were sent as part of the extensive testing of year-end accounts payable. Although this company was smaller than the first two companies, the total audit time spent testing accounts payable was greater than for the first two audits.

Angela is confused by the apparent inconsistency in the audit approach on the three audits, and concludes that the audit approach and amount of audit evidence to collect depends on the audit partner in charge of the engagement.

Required

a. Match each engagement with one of the following descriptions:
   (1) Extensive reliance on controls was planned for this audit engagement, but control risk was increased after tests of controls.
   (2) This audit is likely for a public company, and is also the most efficient audit.
   (3) This company has ineffective controls, and may also have fraud risks present.
b. What other factors likely explain the different approaches to the audit of acquisitions and payments and accounts payable for these three engagements?
c. What could Angela's supervisors have done to improve her understanding of the audit strategy for each engagement?

13-32 (OBJECTIVES 13-4, 13-6, 13-7) The following are parts of a typical audit for a company with a fiscal year-end of July 31.

1. Understand internal control and assess control risk.
2. Perform substantive analytical procedures for accounts payable.
3. Confirm accounts payable.
4. Perform tests of controls and substantive tests of transactions for the acquisition and payment and payroll and personnel cycles.
5. Perform other tests of details of balances for accounts payable.
6. Perform tests for review of subsequent events.
7. Accept the client.
8. Issue the audit report.
9. Set acceptable audit risk and decide preliminary judgment about materiality and performance materiality.

Required

a. Identify the phase of the audit in which each activity occurs.
b. Put parts 1 through 9 of the audit in the sequential order in which you would expect them to be performed in a typical audit.
c. Identify those parts that will frequently be done before July 31.

13-33 (OBJECTIVES 13-2, 13-3) Auditors develop overall audit plans to ensure that they obtain sufficient appropriate audit evidence. The timing and extent of audit procedures auditors use is a matter of professional judgment, which depends upon a number of factors. Decisions about the mix of audit procedures and the timing of procedures significantly impact the date on which the audit report is issued. Visit the company Web sites for Google, Inc. (www.google.com), Boeing (www.boeing.com), and Microsoft (www.microsoft.com). Search under "Investor Relations" for the most recent annual report and locate the independent auditor's report.

Required

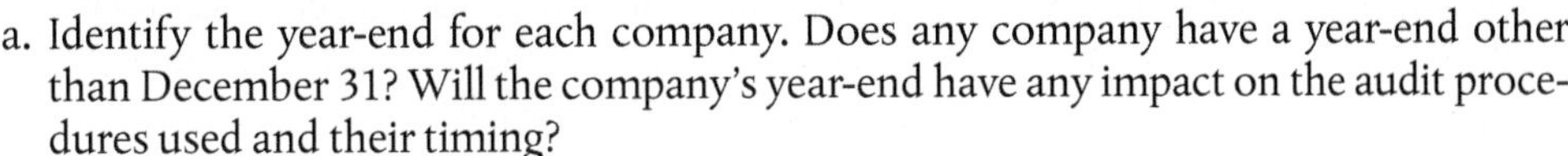

a. Identify the year-end for each company. Does any company have a year-end other than December 31? Will the company's year-end have any impact on the audit procedures used and their timing?
b. Indicate the number of days between each company's year-end and the date of the audit report. What factors may impact the number of days to issue the audit report?
c. Based on the number of days between each company's year-end and the date of the audit report, and your knowledge of each company's operations, on which audit do you think the auditors place the greatest reliance on substantive tests of details of balances? Explain.

CASES

13-34 **(OBJECTIVES 13-3, 13-4)** Gale Brewer, CPA, has been the partner in charge of the audit of Merkle Manufacturing Company, a nonpublic company, for 13 years. Merkle has had excellent growth and profits in the past decade, primarily as a result of the excellent leadership provided by Bill Merkle and other competent executives. Brewer has always enjoyed a close relationship with the company and prides himself on having made several constructive comments over the years that have aided in the success of the firm. Several times in the past few years, Brewer's CPA firm has considered rotating a different audit team on the engagement, but this has been strongly resisted by both Brewer and Merkle.

For the first few years of the audit, internal controls were inadequate and the accounting personnel had inadequate qualifications for their responsibilities. Extensive audit evidence was required during the audit, and numerous adjusting entries were necessary. However, because of Brewer's constant prodding, internal controls improved gradually and competent personnel were hired. In recent years, there were normally no audit adjustments required, and the extent of the evidence accumulation was gradually reduced. During the past three years, Brewer was able to devote less time to the audit because of the relative ease of conducting the audit and the cooperation obtained throughout the engagement.

In the current year's audit, Brewer decided that the total time budget for the engagement should be kept approximately the same as in recent years. The senior in charge of the audit, Phil Warren, was new on the job and highly competent, and he had the reputation of being able to cut time off the budget. The fact that Merkle had recently acquired a new division through merger would probably add to the time, but Warren's efficiency would probably compensate for it.

The interim tests of controls took somewhat longer than expected because of the use of several new assistants, a change in the accounting system programs for inventory and other accounting records, a change in accounting personnel, and the existence of a few more errors in the tests of the system. Neither Brewer nor Warren was concerned about the budget deficit, however, because they could easily make up the difference at year-end.

At year-end, Warren assigned the responsibility for inventory to an assistant who also had not been on the audit before but was competent and extremely fast at his work. Even though the total value of inventory had increased, he reduced the size of the sample from that of other years because there had been few errors in the preceding year. He found several items in the sample that were overstated as a result of errors in pricing and obsolescence, but the combination of all of the errors in the sample was immaterial. He completed the tests in 25% less time than the preceding year. The entire audit was completed on schedule and in slightly less time than the preceding year. There were only a few adjusting entries for the year, and only two of them were material. Brewer was extremely pleased with the results and sent an e-mail message to Warren and the inventory assistant complimenting them on the audit.

Six months later, Brewer received a telephone call from Merkle and was informed that the company was in serious financial trouble. Subsequent investigation revealed that the inventory had been significantly overstated. The major cause of the misstatement was the inclusion of obsolete items in inventory (especially in the new division), errors in pricing as a result of the new computer system, and the inclusion of nonexistent inventory in the final inventory listing. The new controller had intentionally overstated the inventory to compensate for the reduction in sales volume from the preceding year.

Required

a. List the major deficiencies in the audit and state why they took place.
b. What things should have been apparent to Brewer in the conduct of the audit?
c. If Brewer's firm is sued by creditors, what is the likely outcome?

13-35 **(OBJECTIVES 13-3, 13-4)** McClain Plastics has been an audit client of Belcor, Rich, Smith & Barnes, CPAs (BRS&B), for several years. McClain Plastics was started by Evers McClain, who owns 51% of the company's stock. The balance is owned by about 20 stockholders, who are investors with no operational responsibilities. McClain Plastics makes products that have plastic as their primary material. Some are made to order, but most products are made for inventory. An example of a McClain-manufactured product is a plastic chair pad that is used in a carpeted office. Another is a plastic bushing that is used with certain fastener systems.

McClain has grown from a small, two-product company, when they first engaged BRS&B, to a successful, diverse company. At the time Randall Sessions of BRS&B became manager of the audit, annual sales had grown to $200 million and profits to $10.9 million. Historically, the company presented no unusual audit problems, and BRS&B had issued an unmodified opinion every year.

The audit approach BRS&B always used on the audit of McClain Plastics was a "substantive" audit approach. Under this approach, the in-charge auditor obtained an understanding of internal control as part of the risk assessment procedures, but control risk was assessed at the maximum (100%). Extensive analytical procedures were done on the income statement, and unusual fluctuations were investigated. Detailed audit procedures emphasized balance sheet accounts. The theory was that if the balance sheet accounts were correct at year-end and had been audited as of the beginning of the year, then retained earnings and the income statement must be correct.

Part I

In evaluating the audit approach for McClain for the current year's audit, Sessions believed that a substantive approach was really only appropriate for the audits of small nonpublic companies. In his judgment, McClain Plastics, with sales of $200 million and 146 employees, had reached the size where it was not economical, and probably not wise, to concentrate all the tests on the balance sheet. Furthermore, although McClain is not a public company, Sessions recognized that similar public companies are required by Section 404 of the Sarbanes–Oxley Act and related PCAOB standards to have an integrated audit of the financial statements and internal control over financial reporting. Therefore, he designed an audit program that emphasized identifying internal controls in all major transaction cycles and included tests of controls. The intended economic benefit of this "reducing control risk" approach was that the time spent testing controls would be more than offset by reduced tests of details of the balance sheet accounts.

In planning tests of inventories, Sessions used the audit risk model included in auditing standards to determine the number of inventory items BRS&B would test at year-end. Because of the number of different products, features, sizes, and colors, McClain's inventory consisted of 2,450 different items. These were maintained on a perpetual inventory management system that used a relational database.

In using the audit risk model for inventories, Sessions believed that an audit risk of 5% was acceptable. He assessed inherent risk as high (100%) because inventory, by its nature, is subject to many types of misstatements. Based on his understanding of the relevant transaction cycles, Sessions believed that internal controls were effective. He therefore assessed control risk as low (50%) before performing tests of controls. Sessions also planned to use substantive analytical procedures for tests of inventory. These planned tests included comparing gross profit margins by month and reviewing for slow-moving items. Sessions believed that these tests would provide assurance of 40%. Substantive tests of details would include tests of inventory quantities, costs, and net realizable values at an interim date two months before year-end. Cutoff tests would be done at year-end. Inquiries and substantive analytical procedures would be relied on for assurance about events between the interim audit date and fiscal year-end.

Required

a. Decide which of the following will likely be done under both a reducing control risk approach and a substantive approach:
   (1) Assess inherent risk.
   (2) Obtain an understanding of internal control.
   (3) Perform tests of controls.
   (4) Perform substantive analytical procedures.
   (5) Assess planned detection risk.

b. What advantages does the reducing control risk approach Sessions planned to use have over the substantive approach previously used in the audit of McClain Plastics?
c. What advantages did the substantive approach have over the reducing control risk approach?

Part II

The engagement partner agreed with Sessions's recommended approach. In planning the audit evidence for detailed inventory tests, the audit risk model was applied with the following results:

$$PDR = \frac{AAR}{IR \times CR \times APR}$$

where:

PDR = Planned detection risk

AAR = acceptable audit risk

IR = inherent risk

CR = control risk

APR = analytical procedures risk

Therefore, using Sessions's assessments and judgments as described previously,

$$PDR = \frac{.05}{1.0 \times .5 \times .6}$$

$$PDR = .17$$

Required

a. Explain what .17 means in this audit.
b. Calculate *PDR* assuming that Sessions had assessed control risk at 100% and all other risks as they are stated.
c. Explain the effect of your answer in requirement b. on the planned audit procedures and sample size in the audit of inventory compared with the .17 calculated by Sessions.

Part III

Although the planning went well, the actual testing yielded some surprises. When conducting tests of controls over acquisitions and additions to the perpetual inventory, the staff person performing the tests found that the deviation rates for several key controls were significantly higher than expected. As a result, the staff person considered internal control to be operating less effectively, supporting an 80% control risk rather than the 50% level used. Accordingly, the staff person "reworked" the audit risk model as follows:

$$PDR = \frac{.05}{1.0 \times .8 \times .6}$$

$$PDR = .10$$

A 10% test of details risk still seemed to the staff person to be in the "moderate" range, so he recommended no increase in planned sample size for substantive tests.

Required

Do you agree with the staff person's revised judgments about the effect of tests of controls on planned substantive tests? Explain the nature and basis of any disagreement. If BRS&B was also issuing a report on internal control over financial reporting, describe the implications of these results on the auditor's internal control report.

APPLICATION OF THE AUDIT PROCESS TO THE SALES AND COLLECTION CYCLE

CHAPTERS 14–17

The four chapters of **PART 3** apply the concepts you learned in Part 2 to the audit of sales, cash receipts, and the related income statement and balance sheet accounts in the cycle.

For you to appreciate how auditing is done in practice, you need to understand how auditing concepts are applied to specific auditing areas. We'll first look at one important part of every audit, the sales and collection cycle, to examine the practical application of auditing concepts.

- **Chapter 14** will help you learn the methodology for designing tests of controls and substantive tests of transactions audit procedures for sales, cash receipts, and the other classes of transactions in the sales and collection cycle.
- **Chapter 15** deals with nonstatistical and statistical sampling methods for tests of controls and substantive tests of transactions.
- **Chapter 16** presents the methodology for designing audit procedures for the audit of accounts receivable and other account balances in the sales and collection cycle.
- **Chapter 17** covers audit sampling for tests of details of balances.

CHAPTER

14

AUDIT OF THE SALES AND COLLECTION CYCLE: TESTS OF CONTROLS AND SUBSTANTIVE TESTS OF TRANSACTIONS

LEARNING OBJECTIVES

After studying this chapter, you should be able to

14-1 Identify the accounts and the classes of transactions in the sales and collection cycle.

14-2 Describe the business functions and the related documents and records in the sales and collection cycle.

14-3 Understand internal control, and design and perform tests of controls and substantive tests of transactions for sales.

14-4 Apply the methodology for controls over sales transactions to controls over sales returns and allowances.

14-5 Understand internal control, and design and perform tests of controls and substantive tests of transactions for cash receipts.

14-6 Apply the methodology for controls over the sales and collection cycle to controls related to uncollectible accounts receivable.

14-7 Understand the effect of tests of controls and substantive tests of transactions on substantive tests of details of balances.

The Choice Is Simple—Rely on Internal Control

City Finance is the largest client managed out of the Pittsburgh office of a Big Four firm. It is a financial services conglomerate with almost 1,000 offices in the United States and Canada, as well as correspondent offices overseas. The company's records contain more than a million accounts receivable and it processes millions of sales and other transactions annually.

The company's computer data center is in a large, environmentally controlled room that contains several large computer servers and a great deal of ancillary equipment. There are two complete online systems, one serving as a backup for the other, as systems failure would preclude operations in all of the company's branches.

The company has an unusual system of checks and balances in which branch office transaction records are reconciled to data processing controls daily, which, in turn, are reconciled to outside bank account records monthly. Whenever this reconciliation process indicates a significant out-of-balance condition, procedures are initiated to resolve the problem as quickly as possible. A large internal audit staff oversees any special investigative efforts.

Because City Finance is a large public company, it must file its annual financial report including management's report on internal control over financial reporting on Form 10-K with the Securities and Exchange Commission within 60 days after its fiscal year-end. In addition, the company likes to announce annual earnings and issue its annual report as soon after year-end as reasonably feasible. Under these circumstances, there is always a great deal of pressure on the CPA firm to complete the audit quickly.

The CPA firm must conduct an integrated audit of the financial statements and internal control over financial reporting in accordance with PCAOB Standard 5. In the case of City Finance, there is no question that the auditor must rely extensively on internal control in the integrated audit and extensively test internal control over financial reporting. Even if the auditing standards requirements did not exist, it would be difficult to complete the audit within the reporting deadlines without extensively relying on key controls. In all honesty, if City Finance did not have excellent internal controls, the CPA firm admits that an audit of the financial statements just could not be done.

The circumstances of City Finance in the opening story illustrate an audit in which extensive reliance on internal controls in the sales and collection cycle will likely require the auditor to do extensive tests of controls and substantive tests of transactions. In other situations not involving the audit of an accelerated filer public company, the auditor may rely far less on internal controls but, as was shown in Chapter 12, will still need to understand the internal controls over sales and cash receipts. Auditors need to know when they should rely extensively on internal controls and when they should place less reliance on controls. This chapter studies assessing control risk and designing tests of controls and substantive tests of transactions for each of the classes of transactions in the sales and collection cycle.

Before we study assessing control risk and designing tests of controls and substantive tests of transactions for each class of transactions in detail, we will cover two related topics.

1. You need to know the sales and collection cycle classes of transactions and account balances in a typical company. We discussed these earlier, but we review them again here.
2. Because a considerable portion of the audit of transactions in the sales and collection cycle involves documents and records, it is essential to understand the typical documents and records used in the cycle.

ACCOUNTS AND CLASSES OF TRANSACTIONS IN THE SALES AND COLLECTION CYCLE

OBJECTIVE 14-1

Identify the accounts and the classes of transactions in the sales and collection cycle.

The overall objective in the audit of the sales and collection cycle is to evaluate whether the account balances affected by the cycle are fairly presented in accordance with accounting standards. Figure 14-1 shows typical accounts included in the sales and collection cycle using T accounts. The nature of the accounts may vary, of course, depending on the industry and client involved. There are differences in the nature and account titles for a service industry, a retail company, and an insurance company, but the key concepts remain the same. To provide a frame of reference for understanding the material in this chapter, let's assume we're dealing with a wholesale merchandising company.

Figure 14-1 shows the way accounting information flows through the various accounts in the sales and collection cycle. This figure shows that there are five **classes of transactions in the sales and collection cycle**:

FIGURE 14-1 Accounts in the Sales and Collection Cycle

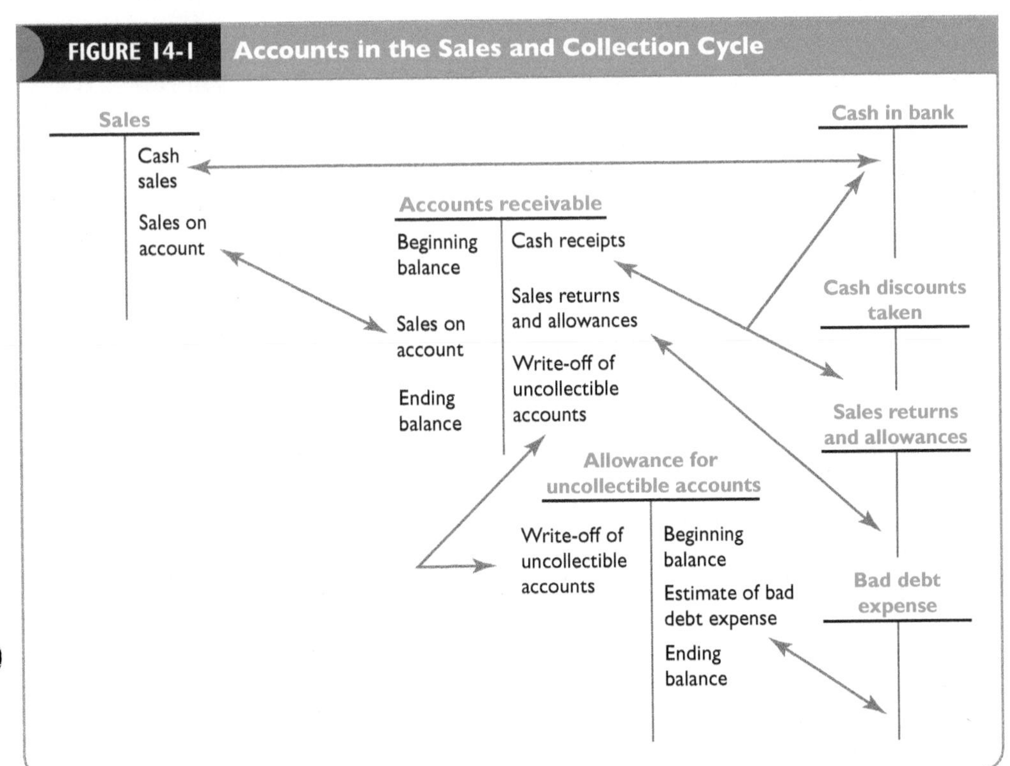

1. Sales (cash and sales on account)
2. Cash receipts
3. Sales returns and allowances
4. Write-off of uncollectible accounts
5. Estimate of bad debt expense

Figure 14-1 also shows that, with the exception of cash sales, every transaction and amount is ultimately included in one of two balance sheet accounts, accounts receivable or allowance for uncollectible accounts. For simplicity, we assume that the same internal controls exist for both cash and credit sales.

BUSINESS FUNCTIONS IN THE CYCLE AND RELATED DOCUMENTS AND RECORDS

OBJECTIVE 14-2

Describe the business functions and the related documents and records in the sales and collection cycle.

The **sales and collection cycle** involves the decisions and processes necessary for the transfer of the ownership of goods and services to customers after they are made available for sale. It begins with a request by a customer and ends with the conversion of material or service into an account receivable, and ultimately into cash.

The eight **business functions for the sales and collection cycle** are shown in the third column of Table 14-1. They occur in every business in the recording of the five classes of transactions in the sales and collection cycle. Under "Business Functions," observe that the first four processes are for recording sales, while every other class of transactions includes only one business function. In this section, we'll explain each of the eight business functions and describe typical documents and records for each function, which appear in the fourth column of Table 14-1. Before auditors can assess control risk and design tests of controls and substantive tests of transactions, they need to understand the business functions and documents and records in a business.

TABLE 14-1 Classes of Transactions, Accounts, Business Functions, and Related Documents and Records for the Sales and Collection Cycle

Classes of Transactions	Accounts	Business Functions	Documents and Records
Sales	Sales Accounts receivable	Processing customer orders Granting credit Shipping goods Billing customers and recording sales	Customer order Sales order Customer order or sales order Shipping document Sales invoice Sales transaction file Sales journal or listing Accounts receivable master file Accounts receivable trial balance Monthly statement
Cash receipts	Cash in bank (debits from cash receipts) Accounts receivable	Processing and recording cash receipts	Remittance advice Prelisting of cash receipts Cash receipts transaction file Cash receipts journal or listing
Sales returns and allowances	Sales returns and allowances Accounts receivable	Processing and recording sales returns and allowances	Credit memo Sales returns and allowances journal
Write-off of uncollectible accounts	Accounts receivable Allowance for uncollectible accounts	Writing off uncollectible accounts receivable	Uncollectible account authorization form General journal
Bad debt expense	Bad debt expense Allowance for uncollectible accounts	Providing for bad debts	General journal

Processing Customer Orders

A customer's request for goods initiates the entire cycle. Legally, it is an offer to buy goods under specified terms. The receipt of a customer order often results in the immediate creation of a sales order.

Customer Order A customer order is a request for merchandise by a customer. It may be received by telephone, letter, a printed form that has been sent to prospective and existing customers, through salespeople, electronic submission of the customer order through the Internet, or other network linkage between the supplier and the customer.

Sales Order A sales order is a document for communicating the description, quantity, and related information for goods ordered by a customer. This is often used to indicate credit approval and authorization for shipment.

Granting Credit

Before goods are shipped, a properly authorized person must *approve credit* to the customer for sales on account. Weak practices in credit approval often result in excessive bad debts and accounts receivable that may be uncollectible. An indication of credit approval on the sales order often serves as the approval to ship the goods. In many companies, the computer automatically approves a credit sale based on preapproved credit limits maintained in a customer master file. The computer allows the sale to proceed only when the proposed sales order total plus the existing customer balance is less than the credit limit in the master file.

Shipping Goods

This critical function is the first point in the cycle at which the company transfers ownership of assets. Most companies recognize sales when goods are shipped. A shipping document is prepared at the time of shipment, which can be done automatically by computer, based on sales order information. The shipping document, which is often a multicopy bill of lading, is essential to the proper billing of shipments to customers. Companies that maintain perpetual inventory records also update them based on shipping records.

Shipping Document A shipping document is prepared to initiate shipment of the goods, indicating the description of the merchandise, the quantity shipped, and other relevant data. The company sends the original to the customer and retains one or more copies. The shipping document serves as a signal to bill the customer and may be in electronic or paper form.

One type of shipping document is a bill of lading, which is a written contract between the carrier and the seller of the receipt and shipment of goods. Often, bills of lading include only the number of boxes or pounds shipped, rather than complete details of quantity and description. (For the purpose of this textbook chapter, however, we will assume that complete details are included on bills of lading.)

The bill of lading is often transmitted electronically, once goods have been shipped, and automatically generates the related sales invoice as well as the entry in the sales journal. Many companies use bar codes and handheld computers to record removal of inventory from the warehouse. This information is used to update the perpetual inventory records.

Billing Customers and Recording Sales

Because billing customers is the means by which the customer is informed of the amount due for the goods, it must be done correctly and on a timely basis. The most important aspects of billing are:

- All shipments made have been billed (completeness)
- No shipment has been billed more than once (occurrence)
- Each one is billed for the proper amount (accuracy)

Billing the proper amount is dependent on charging the customer for the quantity shipped at the authorized price, which includes consideration for freight charges, insurance, and terms of payment.

COMPANY CHARGED FOR PREMATURE REVENUE RECOGNITION FOR SALES ON HOME SHOPPING NETWORK

Intercontinental Commercial Television, Inc. (ICTV), is a marketer of "fountain of youth" beauty products. Its best-selling product is the Derma Wand, a skin care appliance used to reduce lines and wrinkles and improve overall skin appearance. The company sells directly to users through infomercials produced by the company and through third-party distributors for sale to end users. In 2007, ICTV entered into a contract to sell through Home Shopping Network (HSN). HSN ordered product that would be sold on the air to customers. The contract was a "drop-ship" arrangement in which HSN did not purchase the product, but facilitated the sales to end users. ICTV retained title to the product until sold on-air and shipped to customers. Further, HSN could return any product from its customers for 60 days after delivery.

Despite these contract terms, ICTV recognized revenue upon receipt of an order from HSN. In some cases, it also recognized revenue without a request for product from HSN. In these cases, ICTV recognized revenue based on alleged confirmation from a third-party fulfillment warehouse that products had been segregated for HSN's use. ICTV recorded seven sales through HSN totaling $2.8 million. Although the company's auditors understood that the sales through HSN presented potential revenue recognition issues, they did not research the issue and failed to obtain copies of the agreements with HSN. In addition, they did not confirm ICTV's accounts receivable or inventory held in outside warehouses, and they did not perform adequate alternative procedures to test these balances. ICTV had previously reported almost $1.475 million in net income for 2007. When ICTV restated its 2007 financial statements, it reflected a loss of over $1 million.

Source: Securities and Exchange Commission Accounting and Auditing Enforcement Release No. 3232, January 20, 2011 (www.sec.gov).

In most systems, billing of the customer includes preparation of an electronic record or a multicopy sales invoice and real-time updating of the sales transactions file, accounts receivable master file, and general ledger master file for sales and accounts receivable. The accounting system uses this information to generate the sales journal and, along with cash receipts and miscellaneous credits, to prepare the accounts receivable trial balance.

Sales Invoice A sales invoice is a document or electronic record indicating the description and quantity of goods sold, the price, freight charges, insurance, terms, and other relevant data. The sales invoice is the method of indicating to the customer the amount of a sale and the payment due date. Companies send the original to the customer, and retain one or more copies. Typically, the computer automatically prepares the sales invoice after the customer number, quantity, destination of goods shipped, and sales terms are entered. The computer calculates the invoice extensions and total sales amount using the information entered, along with prices in the inventory master file.

Sales Transaction File This is a computer-generated file that includes all sales transactions processed by the accounting system for a period, which could be a day, week, or month. It includes all information entered into the system and information for each transaction, such as customer name, date, amount, account classification or classifications, salesperson, and commission rate. The file can also include returns and allowances, or there can be a separate file for those transactions.

The information in the sales transaction file is used for a variety of records, listings, or reports, depending on the company's needs. These may include a sales journal, accounts receivable master file, and transactions for a certain account balance or division.

Sales Journal or Listing This is a listing or report generated from the sales transaction file that typically includes the customer name, date, amount, and account classification or classifications for each transaction, such as division or product line. It also identifies whether the sale was for cash or accounts receivable. The journal or listing is usually for a month but can cover any period of time. Typically, the journal or listing includes totals of every account number for the time period. The same transactions included in the journal or listing are also posted simultaneously to the general ledger and, if they are on account, to the accounts receivable master file. The journal or listing can also include returns and allowances or there can be a separate journal or listing of those transactions.

Accounts Receivable Master File This is a computer file used to record individual sales, cash receipts, and sales returns and allowances for each customer and to maintain customer account balances. The master file is updated from the sales, sales returns and allowances, and cash receipts computer transaction files. The total of the individual account balances in the master file equals the total balance of accounts receivable in the general ledger. A printout of the accounts receivable master file shows, by customer, the beginning balance in accounts receivable, each sales transaction, sales returns and allowances, cash receipts, and the ending balance.

In this book, we use the term *master file* to refer to either the computer file or a printout of that file, but it is sometimes called the accounts receivable subsidiary ledger or subledger.

Accounts Receivable Trial Balance This list or report shows the amount receivable from each customer at a point in time. It is prepared directly from the accounts receivable master file and is usually an *aged* trial balance that includes the total balance outstanding and the number of days the receivable has been outstanding, grouped by category of days (such as less than 30 days, 31 to 60 days, and so on).

Monthly Statement This is a document sent by mail or electronically to each customer, indicating the beginning balance of their accounts receivable, the amount and date of each sale, payments received, credit memos issued, and the ending balance due. It is, in essence, a copy of the customer's portion of the accounts receivable master file.

Processing and Recording Cash Receipts

The four sales transaction functions are necessary for getting the goods into the hands of customers, correctly billing them, and reflecting the information in the accounting records. The remaining four functions involve the collection and recording of cash, sales returns and allowances, write-off of uncollectible accounts, and providing for bad debt expense.

Processing and recording cash receipts includes receiving, depositing, and recording cash. Cash includes currency, checks, and electronic funds transfers. The most important concern is the possibility of theft. Theft can occur before receipts are entered in the records or later. It is important that all cash receipts are deposited in the bank at the proper amount on a timely basis and recorded in the cash receipts transaction file. This file is used to prepare the cash receipts journal and update the accounts receivable and general ledger master files.

Remittance Advice A remittance advice is a document mailed to the customer and typically returned to the seller with the customer's payment. It indicates the customer name, the sales invoice number, and the amount of the invoice. A remittance advice is used as a record of the payment received to permit the immediate deposit of checks received and to improve control over the custody of assets. If the customer fails to include the remittance advice with the payment, it is common for the person opening the mail to prepare one at that time.

Prelisting of Cash Receipts This is a list prepared when cash is received by someone who has no responsibility for recording sales, accounts receivable, or cash and who has no access to accounting records. It is used to verify whether cash received was recorded and deposited at the correct amounts and on a timely basis.

Many companies use a bank to process cash receipts from customers. Some companies use a lockbox system in which customers mail payments directly to an address maintained by the bank. The bank is responsible for opening all receipts, maintaining records of all customer payments received at the lockbox address, and depositing receipts into the company's bank account on a timely basis. In other cases, receipts are submitted electronically from a customer's bank account to a company bank account through the use of electronic funds transfer (EFT). When customers purchase goods by credit card, the issuer of the credit card uses EFT to transfer funds into the company's bank account. For both lockbox systems and EFT transactions, the bank provides information to the company to prepare the cash receipt entries in the accounting records.

Cash Receipts Transaction File This is a computer-generated file that includes all cash receipts transactions processed by the accounting system for a period such as a day, week, or month. It includes the same type of information as the sales transaction file.

Cash Receipts Journal or Listing This listing or report is generated from the cash receipts transaction file and includes all transactions for a time period. The same transactions, including all relevant information, are included in the accounts receivable master file and general ledger.

Processing and Recording Sales Returns and Allowances

When a customer is dissatisfied with the goods, the seller often accepts the return of the goods or grants a reduction in the charges. The company prepares a receiving report for returned goods and returns them to storage. Returns and allowances are recorded in the sales returns and allowances transaction file, as well as the accounts receivable master file. Credit memos are issued for returns and allowances to aid in maintaining control and to facilitate record keeping.

Credit Memo A credit memo indicates a reduction in the amount due from a customer because of returned goods or an allowance. It often takes the same general form as a sales invoice, but it supports reductions in accounts receivable rather than increases.

Sales Returns and Allowances Journal This is the journal used to record sales returns and allowances. It performs the same function as the sales journal. Many companies record these transactions in the sales journal rather than in a separate journal.

Writing Off Uncollectible Accounts Receivable

Regardless of the diligence of credit departments, some customers do not pay their bills. After concluding that an amount cannot be collected, the company must write it off. Typically, this occurs after a customer files for bankruptcy or the account is turned over to a collection agency. Proper accounting requires an adjustment for these uncollectible accounts.

Uncollectible Account Authorization Form This is a document used internally to indicate authority to write an account receivable off as uncollectible.

Providing for Bad Debts

Because companies cannot expect to collect on 100% of their sales, accounting principles require them to record bad debt expense for the amount they do not expect to collect. Most companies record this transaction at the end of each month or quarter.

CONCEPT CHECK

1. Describe the nature of the following documents and records and explain their use in the sales and collection cycle: customer order, sales invoice, prelisting of cash receipts, and monthly statement to customers.
2. What is the role of the shipping document in invoicing customers? What are the most important management assertions related to customer billing?

METHODOLOGY FOR DESIGNING TESTS OF CONTROLS AND SUBSTANTIVE TESTS OF TRANSACTIONS FOR SALES

OBJECTIVE 14-3

Understand internal control, and design and perform tests of controls and substantive tests of transactions for sales.

In this chapter, we've discussed account balances, classes of transactions, business functions, and related documents and records for the sales and collection cycle. Now, we will study the design of tests of controls and substantive tests of transactions for each of the five classes of transactions in the cycle. Although our focus in this chapter is on controls over transactions, the auditor must also understand controls over balances and presentation and disclosure, particularly in an integrated audit of the financial statements and internal control over financial reporting.

FIGURE 14-2 **Methodology for Designing Tests of Controls and Substantive Tests of Transactions for Sales**

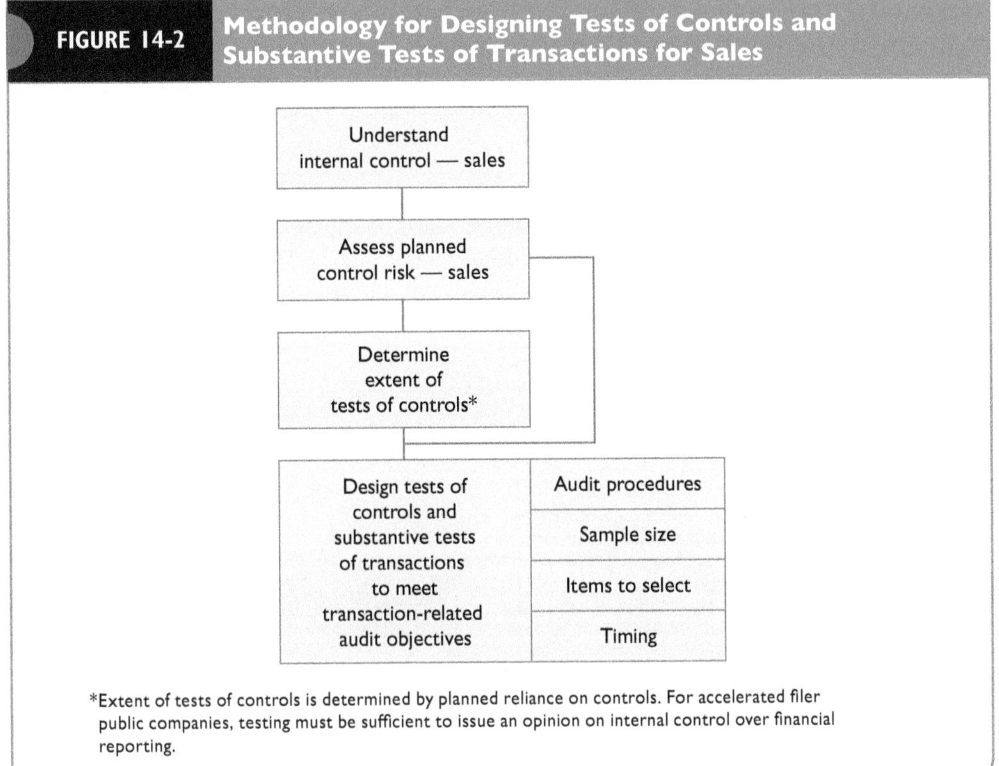
Understand internal control — sales
Assess planned control risk — sales
Determine extent of tests of controls*
Design tests of controls and substantive tests of transactions to meet transaction-related audit objectives
Audit procedures
Sample size
Items to select
Timing
*Extent of tests of controls is determined by planned reliance on controls. For accelerated filer public companies, testing must be sufficient to issue an opinion on internal control over financial reporting.

Figure 14-2 illustrates the methodology for obtaining an understanding of internal control and designing tests of controls and substantive tests of transactions for sales. The content of the figure was introduced and explained in Chapter 13. We will organize the following discussion around this illustration and apply it to sales and cash receipts for Hillsburg Hardware Co.

Understand Internal Control—Sales

As discussed in Chapter 12, to obtain an understanding of internal control for sales, auditors study the client's flowcharts or other control documentation, make inquiries of the client using an internal control questionnaire, and perform walkthrough tests of sales. We will examine the flowchart of the sales and cash receipts function for Hillsburg Hardware Co. in Figure 14-3 (p. 454) to demonstrate the design of tests of controls and substantive tests of transactions audit procedures.

Assess Planned Control Risk—Sales

The auditor uses the information obtained in understanding internal control to assess control risk. Four steps are essential to this assessment.

1. The auditor needs a framework for assessing control risk. The six transaction-related audit objectives provide this framework. These are shown for sales for Hillsburg Hardware in Figure 12-3 (p. 373). These six objectives are the same for every audit of sales.
2. The auditor must identify the key internal controls and deficiencies for sales, also shown in Figure 12-3. These will differ for every audit because every client has different internal controls. The controls and deficiencies for Hillsburg Hardware Co. were identified from the flowchart in Figure 14-3 and the internal control checklist in Figure 12-2 (p. 370).
3. After identifying the controls and deficiencies, the auditor associates them with the objectives, as shown with C's and D's in appropriate columns in Figure 12-3.
4. The auditor assesses control risk for each objective by evaluating the controls and deficiencies for each objective. This step is critical because it affects the auditor's decisions about both tests of controls and substantive tests. It is a highly subjective decision. The bottom row of Figure 12-3 labeled "Assessed control risk" shows the auditor's conclusions about assessed control risk for Hillsburg Hardware.

FIGURE 14-3 Hillsburg Hardware—Flowchart of Sales and Cash Receipts

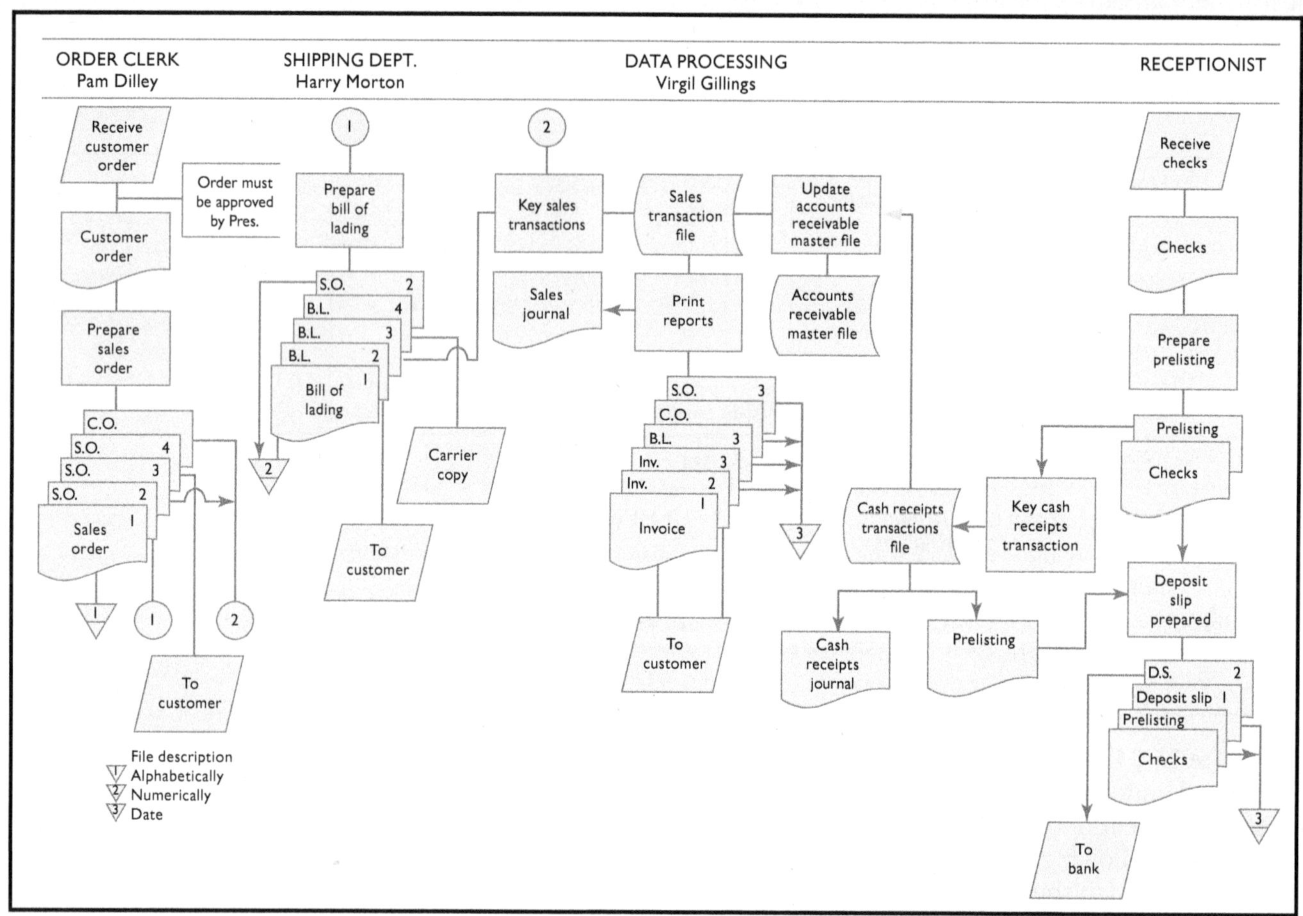

NOTES

1. All correspondence is sent to the president.
2. All sales order numbers are accounted for weekly by the controller.
3. All bills of lading numbers are accounted for weekly by the controller.
4. Sales amount recorded on sales invoice is based on standard price list. The price list is stored in the inventory master file and can be changed only with authorization of the vice president of sales.
5. Duplicate sales invoice is compared with bill of lading daily by Pam Dilley for descriptions and quantities and the sales invoice is reviewed for reasonableness of the extensions and footing. She initials a copy of the invoice before the original is mailed to the customer.
6. Sales are batched daily by Pam Dilley. The batch totals are compared with the sales journal weekly.
7. Statements are sent to customers monthly.
8. Accounts receivable master file total is compared with general ledger by the controller on a monthly basis.
9. Unpaid invoices are filed separately from paid invoices.
10. The receptionist stamps incoming checks with a restrictive endorsement immediately upon receipt.
11. There are no cash sales.
12. Deposits are made daily.
13. Cash receipts are batched daily by the receptionist. The batch totals are compared with the cash receipts journal weekly.
14. The bank account is reconciled by the controller on a monthly basis.
15. All bad debt expense and write-off of bad debts are approved by the president after being initiated by the controller.
16. Financial statements are printed monthly by the controller and reviewed by the president.
17. All errors are reviewed daily by the controller immediately after the updating run. Corrections are made the same day.

We next examine key control activities for sales. Knowledge of these control activities assists in identifying the key controls and deficiencies for sales.

Adequate Separation of Duties Proper separation of duties helps prevent various types of misstatements due to both errors and fraud. To prevent fraud, management should deny cash access to anyone responsible for entering sales and cash receipts transaction information into the computer. The credit-granting function should be separated from the sales function, because credit checks are intended to offset the natural tendency of sales personnel to optimize volume even at the expense of high bad debt write-offs. Personnel responsible for doing internal comparisons should be independent of those entering the original data. For example, comparison of batch control totals with summary reports and comparison of accounts receivable master file totals with the general ledger balance should be done by someone independent of those who input sales and cash receipt transactions.

Proper Authorization The auditor is concerned about authorization at *three key points*:

1. Credit must be properly authorized before a sale takes place.
2. Goods should be shipped only after proper authorization.
3. Prices, including basic terms, freight, and discounts, must be authorized.

The first two controls are meant to prevent the loss of company assets by shipping to fictitious customers or those who will fail to pay for the goods. Price authorization is meant to ensure that the sale is billed at the price set by company policy. Authorization may be done for each individual transaction or general authorization may be given for specific classes of transactions. General authorizations are often done automatically by computer.

Adequate Documents and Records Because each company has a unique system of originating, processing, and recording transactions, auditors may find it difficult to evaluate whether each client's procedures are designed for maximum control. Nevertheless, adequate record-keeping procedures must exist before most of the transaction-related assertions can be met. Some companies, for example, automatically prepare a multicopy prenumbered sales invoice at the time a customer order is received. Copies of this document are used to approve credit, authorize shipment, record the number of units shipped, and bill customers. This system greatly reduces the chance of the failure to bill a customer if all invoices are accounted for periodically, but controls have to exist to ensure the sale isn't recorded until shipment occurs. Under a system in which the sales invoice is prepared only after a shipment has been made, the likelihood of failure to bill a customer is high unless some compensating control exists. In many organizations, all sales documents are electronic and no paper documents are prepared.

Prenumbered Documents Prenumbering is meant to prevent both the *failure* to bill or record sales and the occurrence of *duplicate* billings and recordings. Of course, it does not do much good to have prenumbered documents unless they are properly accounted for. To use this control effectively, a billing clerk will file a copy of all shipping documents in sequential order after each shipment is billed, while someone else will periodically account for all numbers and investigate the reason for any missing documents.

Monthly Statements Sending monthly statements is a useful control because it encourages customers to respond if the balance is incorrectly stated. These statements should be controlled by persons who have no responsibility for handling cash or recording sales or accounts receivable to avoid the intentional failure to send the statements. For maximum effectiveness, all disagreements about the account balance should be directed to a designated person who has no responsibility for handling cash or recording sales or accounts receivable.

Internal Verification Procedures Computer programs or independent personnel should check that the processing and recording of sales transactions fulfill each of the six transaction-related audit objectives. Examples include accounting for the numerical sequence of prenumbered documents, checking the accuracy of document preparation, and reviewing reports for unusual or incorrect items.

Determine Extent of Tests of Controls

After auditors identify the key internal controls and control deficiencies, they assess control risk, often using a matrix format similar to Figure 12-3 on page 373. For audits of accelerated filer public companies, the auditor must perform extensive tests of key controls and evaluate the impact of the deficiencies on the auditor's report on internal control over financial reporting. The extent of tests of controls in audits of non-accelerated filers and nonpublic companies depends on the effectiveness of the controls and the extent to which the auditor believes they can be relied on to reduce control risk. In determining the extent of reliance to place on controls, the auditor also considers the cost of the increased tests of controls compared to the potential reduction in substantive tests. A lower assessed level of control risk will result in increased testing of controls to support the lower control risk, with a corresponding increase in detection risk and decrease in the amount of substantive tests.

Recall from Chapters 9 and 10 that auditing standards require the auditor to presume that a fraud risk exists for revenue recognition. Any identified fraud risk is considered to be a significant risk, and auditing standards require the auditor to obtain an understanding of internal controls related to all significant risks. If the auditor plans to rely on controls over a significant risk, the auditor should test the operating effectiveness of those controls.

Design Tests of Controls for Sales

For each key control, one or more tests of controls must be designed to verify its effectiveness. In most audits, it is relatively easy to determine the nature of the test of the control from the nature of the control. For example, if the internal control is to initial customer orders after they have been approved for credit, the test of control is to examine the customer order for proper initials.

The first three columns of Table 14-2 illustrate the design of tests of controls for sales for Hillsburg Hardware Co. Column 3 shows one test of control for each key internal control in column 2. Observe that this table is organized by transaction-related audit objective. For example, the second key internal control for the occurrence objective is "sales are supported by authorized shipping documents and approved customer orders." The test of control is to "examine sales invoice for supporting bill of lading and customer order." For this test, the auditor should start with sales invoices and examine documents in support of the sales invoices rather than going in the opposite direction. If the auditor traced from shipping documents to sales invoices, it is a test of completeness. (Direction of tests is discussed later in this chapter on p. 459.)

As shown in the third column of Table 14-2 for the completeness objective, a common test of control for sales is to account for a sequence of various types of documents. For example, accounting for a sequence of shipping documents and tracing each one to the duplicate sales invoice and recording in the sales journal provides evidence of completeness.

To simultaneously provide evidence of both the occurrence and completeness objectives, an auditor can check the sequence of sales invoices selected from the sales journal and watch for duplicate and omitted numbers or invoices outside the normal sequence. Assume the auditor selects sales invoices #18100 to #18199. The completeness objective for this procedure will be satisfied if all 100 sales invoices are recorded. The occurrence objective will be satisfied if there is no duplicate recording of any of the invoice numbers. As indicated in Table 14-2, the lack of verification to prevent the possibility of duplicate recording of sales invoices is a deficiency at Hillsburg Hardware Co.

The appropriate tests of controls for separation of duties are ordinarily restricted to the auditor's observations of activities and discussions with personnel. For example, it is possible to observe whether the billing clerk has access to cash receipts when incoming mail is opened or cash is deposited. It is usually also necessary to ask personnel what their responsibilities are and if there are any circumstances where their responsibilities are different from the normal policy. For example, the employee responsible for billing customers may state that he or she does not have access to cash. Further discussion may reveal that he or she actually takes over the cashier's duties when the cashier is on vacation.

Several of the tests of controls in Table 14-2 can be performed using the computer. For example, the auditor can test whether credit is properly authorized by the computer by attempting to initiate transactions that exceed a customer's credit limit. If the control is working effectively, the proposed sales order should be rejected.

TABLE 14-2 Transaction-Related Audit Objectives, Key Existing Controls, Tests of Controls, Deficiencies, and Substantive Tests of Transactions for Sales—Hillsburg Hardware Co.

Transaction-Related Audit Objective	Key Existing Controls*	Test of Controls†	Deficiencies*	Substantive Tests of Transactions†
Recorded sales are for shipments actually made to nonfictitious customers (occurrence).	Credit is approved automatically by computer by comparison to authorized credit limits (C1). Sales are supported by authorized shipping documents and approved customer orders (C2). Batch totals of quantities shipped are compared with quantities billed (C6). Statements are sent to customers each month (C9).	Examine customer order for evidence of credit approval (13e). Examine sales invoice for supporting bill of lading and customer order (13b). Examine file of batch totals for initials of data control clerk (8). Observe whether monthly statements are sent (6).	There is a lack of internal verification for the possibility of sales invoices being recorded more than once (D1).	Review sales journal and master file for unusual transactions and amounts (1). Account for a sequence of sales invoices (12). Trace sales journal entries to supporting documents, including duplicate sales invoice, bill of lading, sales order, and customer order (14).
Existing sales transactions are recorded (completeness).	Shipping documents are prenumbered and accounted for weekly (C5). Batch totals of quantities shipped are compared with quantities billed (C6).	Account for a sequence of shipping documents (10). Examine file of batch totals for initials of data control clerk (8).		Trace selected shipping documents to the sales journal to be sure that each one is included (11).
Recorded sales are for the amount of goods shipped and are correctly billed and recorded (accuracy).	Sales are supported by authorized shipping documents and approved customer orders (C2). Batch totals of quantities shipped are compared with quantities billed (C6). Unit selling prices are obtained from the price list master file of approved prices (C7). Statements are sent to customers each month (C9).	Examine sales invoice for supporting documents (13b). Examine file of batch totals for initials of data control clerk (8). Examine the approved price list for accuracy and proper authorization (9). Observe whether monthly statements are sent (6).		Trace entries in sales journal to sales invoices (13b). Recompute prices and extensions on sales invoices (13b). Trace details on sales invoices to • shipping documents (13c) • sales order (13d) • customer order (13e)
Sales transactions are correctly included in the accounts receivable master file and are correctly summarized (posting and summarization).	Computer automatically posts transactions to the accounts receivable master file and general ledger (C10). Accounts receivable master file is reconciled to the general ledger on a monthly basis (C11). Statements are sent to customers each month (C9).	Examine evidence that accounts receivable master file is reconciled to the general ledger (7). Examine evidence that accounts receivable master file is reconciled to the general ledger (7). Observe whether monthly statements are sent (6).		Trace selected sales invoices from the sales journal to the accounts receivable master file and test for amount, date, and invoice number (13a). Use audit software to foot and cross-foot the sales journal and trace totals to the general ledger (2).
Sales transactions are correctly classified (classification).	Account classifications are internally verified (C8).	Examine document package for internal verification (13b).		Examine duplicate sales invoice for proper account classification (13b).
Sales are recorded on the correct dates (timing).	Shipping documents are prenumbered and accounted for weekly by the accountant (C5).	Account for a sequence of shipping documents (10).	There is a lack of control to test for timely recording (D2).	Compare date of recording of sale in sales journal with duplicate sales invoice and bill of lading (13b and 13c).

* Controls (C) and Deficiencies (D) are from the control matrix for sales in Figure 12-3 (p. 373). Controls C3 and C4 from the control matrix are not included here.
† The number in parentheses after each test of control and substantive test of transaction refers to an audit procedure in the performance format audit program in Figure 14-6 (p. 467).

The occurrence of sales can be similarly tested by attempting to input nonexistent customer numbers, which should be rejected by the computer. This key control will reduce the likelihood of fictitious sales.

Design Substantive Tests of Transactions for Sales In deciding substantive tests of transactions, auditors commonly use some procedures on every audit regardless of the circumstances, whereas others are dependent on the adequacy of the controls and the results of the tests of controls. In the fifth column of Table 14-2, the substantive tests of transactions are related to the transaction-related audit objectives in the first column and are designed to determine whether any monetary misstatements for that objective exist in the transaction. The audit procedures used are affected by the internal controls and tests of controls for that objective. Performance materiality, results of the prior year, and the risk of material misstatement also influence the procedures used.

Determining the proper substantive tests of transactions procedures for sales is relatively difficult because they vary considerably depending on the circumstances. Table 14-2 addresses the substantive tests of transactions procedures in the order of the sales transaction-related audit objectives. Note that some audit procedures fulfill more than one transaction-related audit objective [for example, audit procedure (13b) is included for three objectives].

Auditing standards indicate that if the auditor identifies a significant risk at the assertion level, the auditor should perform substantive procedures that are responsive to that risk. If the approach to a significant risk consists only of substantive procedures, the procedures should include tests of details. As a result, to address the presumption of a fraud risk over revenue recognition, many auditors perform substantive tests of transactions to test recorded revenue transactions. Many auditors also perform substantive analytical procedures to test the reasonableness of recorded revenue. Note, however, that substantive analytical procedures cannot be the only substantive evidence to address a significant risk related to revenue, unless the auditor has tested the operating effectiveness of controls that mitigate the risk.

The following paragraphs discuss substantive tests of transaction audit procedures that may be performed for each transaction-related balance objective, depending on the effectiveness of controls and whether any significant risks have been identified.

Recorded Sales Occurred For this objective, the auditor is concerned with the possibility of *three types of misstatements*:

1. Sales included in the journals for which no shipment was made
2. Sales recorded more than once
3. Shipments made to nonexistent customers and recorded as sales

The first two types of misstatements can be due to an error or fraud. The last type is always a fraud. The potential consequences of all three are significant because they lead to an overstatement of assets and income.

Unintentional overstatements of sales are typically more easily discovered than fraudulent overstatements. An unintentional overstatement normally also results in an overstatement of accounts receivable, which the client can detect by sending monthly statements to customers. Unintentional misstatements at year-end can often be easily found by the auditor through confirmation procedures. With fraudulent overstatements, the perpetrator will attempt to conceal the overstatement, making it more difficult for auditors to find. Substantive tests of transactions may be necessary to discover overstated sales in these circumstances.

The appropriate substantive tests of transactions for testing the occurrence objective depend on where the auditor believes misstatements are likely. Therefore, the nature of the tests depends on the nature of the potential misstatement as follows:

Recorded Sale for Which There Was No Shipment The auditor can vouch selected entries in the sales journal to related copies of shipping and other supporting documents to make sure they occurred. If the auditor is concerned about the possibility of a fictitious duplicate copy of a shipping document, it may be necessary to trace the amounts to the perpetual inventory records as a test of whether inventory was reduced.

Sale Recorded More Than Once Duplicate sales can be determined by reviewing a numerically sorted list of recorded sales transactions for duplicate numbers. The auditor can also test for the proper cancellation of shipping documents. Proper cancellation decreases the likelihood that a shipping document will be used to record another sale.

Shipment Made to Nonexistent Customers This type of fraud normally occurs only when the person recording sales is also in a position to authorize shipments. Deficient internal controls make it difficult to detect fictitious shipments, such as shipments to other locations of the company. To test for nonexistent customers, the auditor can trace customer information on the sales invoice to the customer master file. These revenue frauds are often referred to as "sham sales."

Another effective approach to detecting the three types of misstatements of sales transactions just discussed is to trace the *credit* in the accounts receivable master file to its source. If the receivable was actually collected in cash or the goods were returned, the original sale likely occurred, unless the auditor has reason to believe that the payment or return of goods was also fraudulent. If the credit was for a bad debt write-off or a credit memo, or if the account was still unpaid at the time of the audit, this could indicate an inappropriately recorded sales transaction. The auditor must examine shipping and customer order documents to determine if there is adequate support that a sales transaction actually occurred.

Existing Sales Transactions Are Recorded In many audits, no substantive tests of transactions are done for the completeness objective. This is because overstatements of assets and income from sales transactions are more likely than understatements, and overstatements also represent a greater source of audit risk. As a result, auditors often rely on substantive analytical procedures to test the completeness of revenue. If controls are inadequate, which is likely if the client does no independent internal tracing from shipping documents to the sales journal, substantive tests are likely necessary.

To test for unbilled shipments, auditors can trace selected shipping documents from a file in the shipping department to related duplicate sales invoices and the sales journal. To conduct a meaningful test using this procedure, the auditor must be confident that all shipping documents are included in the file. This can be done by accounting for a numerical sequence of the documents. Generalized audit software tools, such as ACL or IDEA, can be used to efficiently identify duplicates and gaps in the numerical sequence of electronic records.

Direction of Tests Auditors need to understand the difference between tracing from source documents to the journals and vouching from the journals back to source documents. The former tests for *omitted transactions* (completeness objective); the latter tests for *nonexistent transactions* (occurrence objective).

To test for the occurrence objective, the auditor starts by selecting a sample of invoice numbers *from* the journal and vouches them *to* duplicate sales invoices, shipping documents, and customer orders, as illustrated in Figure 14-4 (p. 460). In testing for the completeness objective, the auditor typically starts by selecting a sample of shipping documents and traces them *to* duplicate sales invoices and the sales journal as a test of omissions.

When designing audit procedures for the occurrence and completeness objectives, the starting point for the test is essential. This is called the **direction of tests** and is illustrated in Figure 14-4. For example, if the auditor is concerned about the occurrence objective but tests in the wrong direction (from shipping documents to the journals), a serious audit deficiency exists. In testing for the other four transaction-related audit objectives, the direction of tests is usually not relevant. For example, the accuracy of sales transactions can be examined by testing from a duplicate sales invoice to a shipping document or vice versa.

FIGURE 14-4 Direction of Tests for Sales

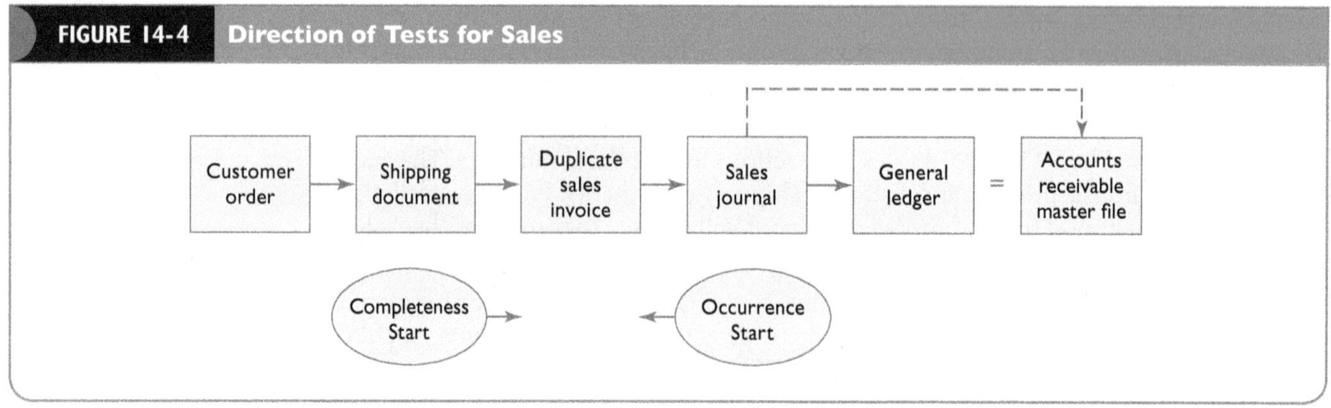

Sales Are Accurately Recorded The accurate recording of sales transactions concerns:

- Shipping the amount of goods ordered
- Accurately billing for the amount of goods shipped
- Accurately recording the amount billed in the accounting records

Auditors typically do substantive tests of transactions in every audit to ensure that each of these three aspects of accuracy are done correctly by recalculating

PCAOB FOCUSES ON AUDITING REVENUE

The PCAOB issues audit practice alerts to highlight new, emerging, or otherwise noteworthy circumstances. Revenue is the largest account in the financial statements for many companies, and many fraudulent financial reporting cases have involved the intentional overstatement of revenue. For these reasons, the audit of revenue is often a significant focus of PCAOB inspections of registered firms. PCAOB Staff Audit Practice Alert No. 12 highlights several matters related to auditing revenue identified through inspections, including:

- *Revenue from contractual arrangements.* In cases of construction-type or production-type contracts, auditors failed to perform procedures to (1) test management's estimated cost to complete projects; (2) test the progress of the construction or production contracts; or (3) evaluate the company's approach for applying the percentage-of-completion method.
- *Multiple-element revenue arrangements.* In some instances, auditors failed to evaluate the recognition of revenue from transactions with multiple elements, such as a transaction involving an initial sale and ongoing service commitment.
- *Testing whether revenue was recognized in the correct period.* PCAOB staff noted cases of failure to perform cutoff procedures to address the risk of material misstatement, and failures to obtain evidence about whether the delivery of goods had occurred to allow the company to recognize revenue.
- *Responding to fraud risks associated with revenue.* Deficiencies included a failure to identify and respond to the presumed fraud risk related to improper revenue recognition, including not changing the nature of the audit procedures.
- *Testing and evaluating controls over revenue.* Auditors relied on controls over revenue to reduce substantive testing, but this reliance was not supported because the testing of the controls was insufficient, or testing identified control deficiencies.
- *Substantive analytical procedures over revenue.* When properly applied under appropriate conditions, substantive analytical procedures can potentially identify a material misstatement in revenue. Deficiencies identified included (1) using expectations that were not sufficiently precise, including evaluating whether there was a plausible and predictable relationship among the data; (2) failure to investigate significant differences and to corroborate management's responses regarding these differences; and (3) failure to test the completeness and accuracy of the information obtained from the client that was used in performing the analytical procedure.
- *Testing revenue in companies with multiple locations.* In some cases, auditors did not test, or test sufficiently, revenues at locations that had specific risks, including fraud risks.

The Financial Accounting Standards Board and International Accounting Standards Board have jointly adopted a converged standard on revenue recognition. The PCAOB notes that the auditing matters they have identified in the audit practice alert will continue to be relevant under the new accounting standard for revenue recognition.

Source: Public Company Accounting Oversight Board Staff Audit Practice Alert No. 12, *Matters Related to Auditing Revenue in an Audit of Financial Statements*, September 9, 2014 (pcaobus.org).

information in the accounting records and comparing information on different documents. Auditors commonly compare prices on duplicate sales invoices with an approved price list, recalculate extensions and footings, and compare the details on the invoices with shipping records for description, quantity, and customer identification. Often, auditors also examine customer orders and sales orders for the same information. In a *three-way match* test, the auditor compares the quantity and description of items billed to the same information on the shipping document and customer order to determine whether they are in agreement.

The comparison of tests of controls and substantive tests of transactions for the accuracy objective is a good example of how audit time can be saved when effective internal controls exist. Obviously, the test of control for this objective takes almost no time because it involves examining only initials or other evidence of internal verification. If the controls over verification of invoice quantities, prices, and extensions are automated, tests can be further reduced, assuming general IT controls are effective. If controls are effective, the sample size for substantive tests of transactions can be reduced, yielding significant savings.

Sales Transactions Are Correctly Included in the Master File and Correctly Summarized The proper inclusion of all sales transactions in the accounts receivable master file is essential because the accuracy of these records affects the client's ability to collect outstanding receivables. Similarly, the sales journal must be correctly totaled and posted to the general ledger if the financial statements are to be correct. In most engagements, auditors perform some clerical accuracy tests, such as footing the journals and tracing the totals and details to the general ledger and the master file, to check whether there are errors or fraud in the processing of sales transactions. The extent to which such tests are needed is determined by the quality of internal controls. Generalized audit software allows for efficient testing of the accuracy of electronic journals and records.

Tracing from the sales journal to the master file is typically done as a part of fulfilling other transaction-related audit objectives, but footing the sales journal and tracing the totals to the general ledger are done as separate procedures.

Posting and summarization tests differ from those for other transaction-related audit objectives because they include footing journals, master file records, and ledgers, and tracing from one to the other among these three.

When footing and comparisons are restricted to these three records, the transaction-related audit objective is posting and summarization. When the journals, master files, or ledgers are traced to or from a document, the objective is one of the other five objectives, depending on what is being verified. To illustrate, when an auditor compares an amount on a duplicate sales invoice with either the sales journal or master file entry, it is an accuracy audit objective procedure. When an auditor traces an entry from the sales journal to the master file, it is a posting and summarization procedure.

Recorded Sales Are Correctly Classified Although it is less of a problem in sales than in some transaction cycles, auditors must still be concerned that transactions are charged to the correct general ledger account. With cash and credit sales, company personnel should not debit accounts receivable for a cash sale or credit sales for collection of a receivable. They should also not classify sales of operating assets, such as buildings, as sales. For those companies using more than one sales classification, such as companies issuing segmented earnings statements, proper classification is essential.

Auditors commonly test sales for proper classification as part of testing for accuracy. They examine supporting documents to determine the proper classification of a given transaction and compare this with the actual account to which it is charged.

Sales Are Recorded on the Correct Dates Sales should be billed and recorded as soon after shipment takes place as possible to prevent the unintentional omission of transactions from the records and to make sure that sales are recorded in the proper period. Timely recorded transactions are also less likely to contain misstatements. When auditors do substantive tests of transactions procedures for accuracy, they commonly compare the date on selected bills of lading or other shipping documents with the date on related duplicate sales invoices, the sales journal, and the accounts receivable master file. Significant differences indicate potential cutoff problems in the test of year-end balances.

Summary of Methodology for Sales

Figure 14-2 (p. 453) is an overview of how auditors design tests of controls and substantive tests of transactions for sales. Table 14-2 (p. 457) is a matrix that shows how auditors decide tests of controls and substantive tests of transactions for sales after controls and control deficiencies have been identified. The following is a discussion of Table 14-2.

Transaction-Related Audit Objectives (Column 1) The transaction-related audit objectives for sales in Table 14-2 are derived from the framework presented in earlier chapters. Although certain internal controls satisfy more than one objective, auditors should consider each objective separately to facilitate a better assessment of control risk.

Key Existing Controls (Column 2) Management designs the internal controls for sales to achieve the six transaction-related audit objectives. If the controls necessary to satisfy any one of the objectives are inadequate, the likelihood of misstatements related to that objective is increased, regardless of the controls for the other objectives. (The methodology for determining existing controls was addressed on page 374 in Chapter 12.)

The controls in column 2 were identified by the auditor earlier in the audit and come from the auditor's control risk matrix, such as the one illustrated in Figure 12-3 (p. 373). A control is included in more than one row in Table 14-2 if there is more than one C for that control on the control risk matrix.

Tests of Controls (Column 3) For each internal control in column 2, the auditor designs a test of control to verify its effectiveness. Observe that the tests of controls in Table 14-2 relate directly to the internal controls. For each control, there should be at least one test of control, but there can be more than one.

Deficiencies (Column 4) Deficiencies identified by the auditor indicate the absence of effective controls. The auditor should evaluate control deficiencies by considering potential misstatements that could occur and any compensating controls. An auditor can respond to a deficiency in internal control in a financial statement audit by expanding substantive tests of transactions to determine whether the deficiency resulted in a significant number of misstatements.

Substantive Tests of Transactions (Column 5) These tests help auditors determine whether monetary misstatements exist in sales transactions. In Table 14-2, the substantive tests of transactions directly relate to the objectives in the first column.

It is essential for auditors to understand the relationships among the columns in Table 14-2.

- The first column includes the six transaction-related audit objectives. The general objectives are the same for any class of transactions, but the specific objectives vary for sales, cash receipts, or any other classes of transactions.
- Column 2 lists one or more illustrative internal controls *for each transaction-related audit objective*. Each control must be related to one or more audit objectives.
- Column 3 includes one test of control that tests the *internal control in column 2*. A test of control has no meaning unless it tests a specific control. The table contains one test of control in column 3 for each internal control in column 2, but the auditor can decide to use more than one test of control for a given control.
- Column 4 includes internal control deficiencies. They represent a lack of effective internal controls and are determined using the same approach used for identifying controls.
- The last column includes common substantive tests of transactions that support *a specific transaction-related audit objective* in column 1. The substantive tests

of transactions are not directly related to the key control or test of control columns, but the extent of substantive tests of transactions depends, in part, on which key controls exist, the results of the tests of controls, and any internal control deficiencies for the transaction-related audit objective.

Design and Performance Format Audit Procedures

The information presented in Table 14-2 is intended to help auditors design audit programs that satisfy the transaction-related audit objectives in a given set of circumstances. This methodology helps the auditor design an effective and efficient audit program that responds to the unique risks of material misstatements at each client.

After the appropriate audit procedures for a given set of circumstances have been designed, they must, of course, be performed. However, it is likely to be inefficient to do the audit procedures as they are stated in the design format of Table 14-2. In converting from a **design format audit program** to a **performance format audit program**, procedures are combined. This achieves the following:

- Eliminates duplicate procedures.
- Makes sure that when a given document is examined, all procedures to be performed on that document are done at that time.
- Enables the auditor to do the procedures in the most effective order. For example, by footing the journal and reviewing the journal for unusual items first, the auditor gains a better perspective in doing the detailed tests.

Figure 14-6 (p. 467) illustrates a performance format audit program for sales and cash receipts for Hillsburg Hardware. It is a summary of the audit procedures in Tables 14-2 and 14-3 (p. 465). The numbers for the audit procedures in Figure 14-6 correspond to the numbers at the end of the tests of control and substantive audit procedures in Tables 14-2 and 14-3. These numbers are included to help you see the relationship between the two tables and Figure 14-6.

CONCEPT CHECK

1. What three types of authorizations are commonly used as internal controls for sales? Explain the importance of each.
2. List the transaction-related audit objectives for the audit of sales transactions. For each objective, state one internal control that the client can use to reduce the likelihood of misstatements.

SALES RETURNS AND ALLOWANCES

OBJECTIVE 14-4

Apply the methodology for controls over sales transactions to controls over sales returns and allowances.

The transaction-related audit objectives and the client's methods of controlling misstatements are essentially the same for processing credit memos as those described for sales, with two differences. The first is *materiality*. In many instances, sales returns and allowances are so immaterial the auditor can ignore them.

The second difference is *emphasis on the occurrence objective*. For sales returns and allowances, auditors usually emphasize testing recorded transactions to uncover any theft of cash from the collection of accounts receivable that was covered up by a fictitious sales return or allowance. (Although auditors usually emphasize the occurrence objective for sales returns and allowances transactions, the *completeness* objective is especially important in tests of account balances to determine if sales and returns are understated at year-end.)

Naturally, other objectives should not be ignored. But because the objectives and methodology for auditing sales returns and allowances are essentially the same as for sales, we do not include a detailed study of them. If you need to audit sales returns and allowances, you should be able to apply the same logic to arrive at suitable controls, tests of controls, and substantive tests of transactions to verify the amounts.

METHODOLOGY FOR DESIGNING TESTS OF CONTROLS AND SUBSTANTIVE TESTS OF TRANSACTIONS FOR CASH RECEIPTS

OBJECTIVE 14-5

Understand internal control, and design and perform tests of controls and substantive tests of transactions for cash receipts.

Auditors use the same methodology for designing tests of controls and substantive tests of transactions for cash receipts as they use for sales. Cash receipts tests of controls and substantive tests of transactions audit procedures are developed around the same framework used for sales, but of course the specific objectives are applied to cash receipts. Given the transaction-related audit objectives, the auditor follows this process:

- Determine key internal controls for each audit objective
- Design tests of control for each control used to support a reduced control risk
- Design substantive tests of transactions to test for monetary misstatements for each objective

As in all other audit areas, the tests of controls depend on the controls the auditor identifies, the extent they will be relied on to reduce assessed control risk, and whether the company being audited is publicly traded.

Figure 14-5 (p. 466) presents the control risk matrix for cash receipts for Hillsburg Hardware. It is based on the information in the sales and cash receipts flowchart in Figure 14-3 (p. 454).

Table 14-3 lists key internal controls, common tests of controls, and common substantive tests of transactions to satisfy each of the transaction-related audit objectives for cash receipts for Hillsburg Hardware Co. Table 14-3 follows the same format used for sales as shown in Table 14-2 (p. 457). The tests of controls and substantive tests of transactions for cash receipts are combined with those for sales in the performance format audit program in Figure 14-6 (p. 467).

Because the methodology for cash receipts is similar to that for sales, our discussion is not as detailed as our discussion of the internal controls, tests of controls, and substantive tests of transactions for the audit of sales. Instead, we focus on the substantive audit procedures that are most likely to be misunderstood.

An essential part of the auditor's responsibility in auditing cash receipts is to identify deficiencies in internal control that increase the likelihood of fraud. To expand on Table 14-3, we emphasize those audit procedures that are designed primarily for the discovery of fraud. We omit discussion of some procedures only because their purpose and the methodology for applying them should be apparent from the description provided in Table 14-3.

Determine Whether Cash Received Was Recorded

The most difficult type of cash embezzlement for auditors to detect is when it occurs *before the cash is recorded* in the cash receipts journal or other cash listing, especially if the sale and cash receipt are recorded simultaneously. For example, if a grocery store clerk takes cash and intentionally fails to record the sale and receipt of cash on the cash register, it is extremely difficult to discover the theft. To prevent this type of fraud, internal controls such as those included in the second objective in Table 14-3 are implemented by many companies. The type of control will, of course, depend on the type of business. For example, the controls for a retail store in which the cash is received by the same person who sells the merchandise and enters cash receipts in a cash register should be different from the controls for a company in which all receipts are received through the mail several weeks after the sales have taken place.

It is normal practice to trace from prenumbered remittance advices or prelists of cash receipts to the cash receipts journal and subsidiary accounts receivable records as a substantive test of the recording of actual cash received. This test will be effective only if a prelisting or other record of payments was prepared at the time payments were received.

Prepare Proof of Cash Receipts

A useful audit procedure to test whether all recorded cash receipts have been deposited in the bank account is a **proof of cash receipts**. In this test, the total cash receipts recorded in the cash receipts journal for a given period, such as a month, are reconciled

TABLE 14-3 Transaction-Related Audit Objectives, Key Existing Controls, Tests of Controls, Deficiencies, and Substantive Tests of Transactions for Cash Receipts—Hillsburg Hardware Co.

Transaction-Related Audit Objective	Key Existing Controls*	Test of Controls†	Deficiencies*	Substantive Tests of Transactions†
Recorded cash receipts are for funds actually received by the company (occurrence).	Accountant independently reconciles bank account (C1). Batch totals of cash receipts are compared with computer summary reports (C4).	Observe whether accountant reconciles bank account (3). Examine file of batch totals for initials of data control clerk (8).		Review cash receipts journal and master file for unusual transactions and amounts (1). Trace cash receipts entries from the cash receipts journal entries to the bank statement (19). Prepare a proof of cash receipts (18).
Cash received is recorded in the cash receipts journal (completeness).	Prelisting of cash receipts is prepared (C2). Checks are restrictively endorsed (C3). Batch totals of cash receipts are compared with computer summary reports (C4). Statements are sent to customers each month (C5).	Observe prelisting of cash receipts (4). Observe endorsement of incoming checks (5). Examine file of batch totals for initials of data control clerk (8). Observe whether monthly statements are sent (6).	Prelisting of cash is not used to verify recorded cash receipts (D1).	Obtain prelisting of cash receipts and trace amounts to the cash receipts journal, testing for names, amounts, and dates (15). Compare the prelisting with the duplicate deposit slip (16).
Cash receipts are deposited and recorded at the amounts received (accuracy).	Accountant independently reconciles bank account (C1). Batch totals of cash receipts are compared with computer summary reports (C4). Statements are sent to customers each month (C5).	Observe whether accountant reconciles bank account (3). Examine file of batch totals for initials of data control clerk (8). Observe whether monthly statements are sent (6).		Obtain prelisting of cash receipts and trace amounts to the cash receipts journal, testing for names, amounts, and dates (15). Prepare proof of cash receipts (18).
Cash receipts are correctly included in the accounts receivable master file and are correctly summarized (posting and summarization).	Computer automatically posts transactions to the accounts receivable master file and general ledger (C8). Accounts receivable master file is reconciled to the general ledger on a monthly basis (C9). Statements are sent to customers each month (C5).	Examine evidence that accounts receivable master file is reconciled to general ledger (7). Examine evidence that accounts receivable master file is reconciled to general ledger (7). Observe whether monthly statements are sent (6).		Trace selected entries from the cash receipts journal to the accounts receivable master file and test for dates and amounts (20). Trace selected credits from the accounts receivable master file to the cash receipts journal and test for dates and amounts (21). Use audit software to foot and cross-foot the sales journal and trace totals to the general ledger (2).
Cash receipts transactions are correctly classified (classification).	Cash receipts transactions are internally verified (C6).	Examine evidence of internal verification (15).		Examine prelisting for proper account classification (17).
Cash receipts are recorded on the correct dates (timing).	Procedures require recording of cash on a daily basis (C7).	Observe unrecorded cash at a point in time (4).		Compare date of deposit per bank statement to the dates in the cash receipts journal and prelisting of cash receipts (16).

* Controls (C) and Deficiencies (D) are from control matrix for cash receipts in Figure 14-5 (p. 466).
† The number in parentheses after each test of control and substantive test of transaction refers to an audit procedure in the performance format audit program in Figure 14-6 (p. 467).

with the actual deposits made to the bank during the same period. A difference in the two may be the result of deposits in transit and other items, but the amounts can be reconciled and compared. This procedure is not useful in discovering cash receipts that have not been recorded in the journals or time lags in making deposits, but it can help

FIGURE 14-5 **Control Risk Matrix for Hillsburg Hardware Co.—Cash Receipts**

	Internal Control	Recorded cash receipts are for funds actually received by the company (occurrence).	Cash received is recorded in the cash receipts journal (completeness).	Cash receipts are deposited and recorded at the amounts received (accuracy).	Cash receipts are correctly included in the accounts receivable master file and are correctly summarized (posting and summarization).	Cash receipts transactions are correctly classified (classification).	Cash receipts are recorded on the correct dates (timing).
		Cash Receipts Transaction-Related Audit Objectives					
CONTROLS	Accountant independently reconciles bank account (C1).	C		C			
	Prelisting of cash receipts is prepared (C2).		C				
	Checks are restrictively endorsed (C3).		C				
	Batch totals of cash receipts are compared with computer summary reports (C4).	C	C	C			
	Statements are sent to customers each month (C5).		C	C	C		
	Cash receipts transactions are internally verified (C6).					C	
	Procedures require recording of cash on a daily basis (C7).						C
	Computer automatically posts transactions to the accounts receivable master file and to the general ledger (C8).				C		
	Accounts receivable master file is reconciled to the general ledger on a monthly basis (C9).				C		
DEFICIENCY	Prelisting of cash is not used to verify recorded cash receipts (D1).		D				
	Assessed control risk	Low	Medium	Low	Low	Low	Low

C = Control; D = Significant deficiency or material weakness

uncover recorded cash receipts that have not been deposited, unrecorded deposits, unrecorded loans, bank loans deposited directly into the bank account, and similar misstatements. Ordinarily, this somewhat time-consuming procedure is used only when the controls are deficient. In rare instances, when controls are extremely weak, the period covered by the proof of cash receipts may cover the entire year.

Test to Discover Lapping of Accounts Receivable

Lapping of accounts receivable is the postponement of entries for the collection of receivables to *conceal an existing cash shortage*. The embezzlement is perpetrated by a person who handles cash receipts and then enters them into the computer system. He or she defers recording the cash receipts from one customer and covers the shortages with receipts of another. These in turn are covered from the receipts of a third customer

FIGURE 14-6 **Audit Program for Tests of Controls and Substantive Tests of Transactions for Sales and Cash Receipts for Hillsburg Hardware Co. (Performance Format)**

Hillsburg Hardware Co.

Tests of Controls and Substantive Tests of Transactions Audit Procedures for Sales and Cash Receipts

(Sample size and the items in the sample are not included.)

General

1. Review journals and master file for unusual transactions and amounts.
2. Use audit software to foot and cross-foot the sales and cash receipts journals and trace the totals to the general ledger.
3. Observe whether accountant reconciles the bank account.
4. Observe whether cash is prelisted and the existence of any unrecorded cash.
5. Observe whether restrictive endorsement is used on cash receipts.
6. Observe whether monthly statements are sent.
7. Observe whether accountant compares master file total with general ledger account.
8. Examine file of batch totals for initials of data control clerk.
9. Examine the approved price list in the inventory master file for accuracy and proper authorization.

Shipment of Goods

10. Account for a sequence of shipping documents.
11. Trace selected shipping documents to the sales journal to be sure that each one has been included.

Billing of Customers and Recording the Sales in the Records

12. Account for a sequence of sales invoices in the sales journal.
13. Trace selected sales invoice numbers from the sales journal to
    a. accounts receivable master file and test for amount, date, and invoice number.
    b. duplicate sales invoice and check for the total amount recorded in the journal, date, customer name, and account classification. Check the pricing, extensions, and footings. Examine underlying documents for indication of internal verification.
    c. bill of lading and test for customer name, product description, quantity, and date.
    d. duplicate sales order and test for customer name, product description, quantity, date, and indication of internal verification.
    e. customer order and test for customer name, product description, quantity, date, and credit approval.
14. Trace recorded sales from the sales journal to the file of supporting documents, which includes a duplicate sales invoice, bill of lading, sales order, and customer order.

Processing Cash Receipts and Recording the Amounts in the Records

15. Obtain the prelisting of cash receipts and trace amounts to the cash receipts journal, testing for names, amounts, dates, and internal verification.
16. Compare the prelisting of cash receipts with the duplicate deposit slip, testing for names, amounts, and dates. Trace the total from the cash receipts journal to the bank statement, testing for a delay in deposit.
17. Examine prelisting for proper account classification.
18. Prepare a proof of cash receipts.
19. Trace cash receipt entries from the cash receipts journal to the bank statement, testing for dates and amounts of deposits.
20. Trace selected entries from the cash receipts journal to entries in the accounts receivable master file and test for dates and amounts.
21. Trace selected credits from the accounts receivable master file to the cash receipts journal and test for dates and amounts.

WHY THE DELAY?

Ann Mundy was an internal auditor for Speedtrack Convenience Stores. Each store was responsible for making daily deposits into a local bank account and providing a daily sales report to the central office. While reviewing monthly bank reconciliations, she observed that all the deposits in transit at month-end cleared the next day, except for the deposit at one store, which cleared a day later. She did not think this was unusual and did not investigate further.

The following month, Ann was performing the same procedure and obtained the same results. All the deposits cleared the next day, except for the deposit for one store, which cleared a day later. The delayed deposit was for the same store that had had a delayed deposit the previous month. Upon investigation, Ann discovered that the store manager had stolen the receipts for one day. Because stores had to report daily sales, the manager reported the sales for the next day as having occurred the previous day. The manager had to repeat this process every day to hide the theft, which made it appear that there was an extra-day delay in the deposit clearing the bank. The manager was immediately fired, and Speedtrack instituted new procedures that required same-day reporting of sales and procedures to investigate immediately any delay in cleared deposits.

a few days later. The employee must continue to cover the shortage through repeated lapping, replace the stolen money, or find another way to conceal the shortage.

This embezzlement can be easily prevented by separation of duties and a mandatory vacation policy for employees who both handle cash and enter cash receipts into the system. It can be detected by comparing the name, amount, and dates shown on remittance advices with cash receipts journal entries and related duplicate deposit slips. Because this procedure is relatively time-consuming, it is ordinarily performed only when specific concerns with embezzlement exist because of a deficiency in internal control.

AUDIT TESTS FOR UNCOLLECTIBLE ACCOUNTS

OBJECTIVE 14-6

Apply the methodology for controls over the sales and collection cycle to controls related to uncollectible accounts receivable.

The same as for sales returns and allowances, the auditor's primary concern in the audit of the write-off of uncollectible accounts receivable is the possibility of client personnel covering up an embezzlement by writing off accounts receivable that have already been collected (the occurrence transaction-related audit objective). The major control for preventing this fraud is proper authorization of the write-off of uncollectible accounts by a designated level of management only after a thorough investigation of the reason the customer has not paid.

Normally, verification of the accounts written off takes relatively little time. Typically, the auditor examines approvals by the appropriate persons. For a sample of accounts written off, it is also usually necessary for the auditor to examine correspondence in the client's files establishing their uncollectibility. In some cases, the auditor also examines credit reports such as those provided by Dun & Bradstreet. After the auditor has concluded that the accounts written off by general journal entries are proper, selected items should be traced to the accounts receivable master file to test whether the write-off was properly recorded.

Realizable value is an essential balance-related audit objective for accounts receivable because collectibility of receivables is often a significant concern. Ideally, clients establish several controls to reduce the likelihood of uncollectible accounts. We've already discussed credit approval by an appropriate person. Two other controls are:

- The preparation of a periodic aged accounts receivable trial balance for review and follow-up by appropriate management personnel.
- A policy of writing off uncollectible accounts when they are no longer likely to be collected.

The estimation of bad debt expense, which is the fifth class of transactions in the sales and collection cycle, obviously relates to realizable value and the write-off of uncollectible accounts. However, because the estimation of bad debts is based on the year-end accounts receivable balances, the auditor evaluates the estimate for uncollectible accounts and related controls as part of the tests of details of ending accounts receivable balances, which we discuss in Chapter 16.

EFFECT OF RESULTS OF TESTS OF CONTROLS AND SUBSTANTIVE TESTS OF TRANSACTIONS

OBJECTIVE 14-7

Understand the effect of tests of controls and substantive tests of transactions on substantive tests of details of balances.

The results of the tests of controls and substantive tests of transactions have a significant effect on the remainder of the audit, especially on substantive tests of details of balances. The parts of the audit most affected by the tests of controls and substantive tests of transactions for the sales and collection cycle are the balances in accounts receivable, cash, bad debt expense, and allowance for doubtful accounts.

Furthermore, if the test results are unsatisfactory, it is necessary to do additional substantive testing of sales, sales returns and allowances, write-off of uncollectible accounts, and processing cash receipts. Auditors of accelerated filer public companies

FIGURE 14-7 Types of Audit Tests for the Sales and Collection Cycle (see Figure 14-1 on p. 447 for accounts)

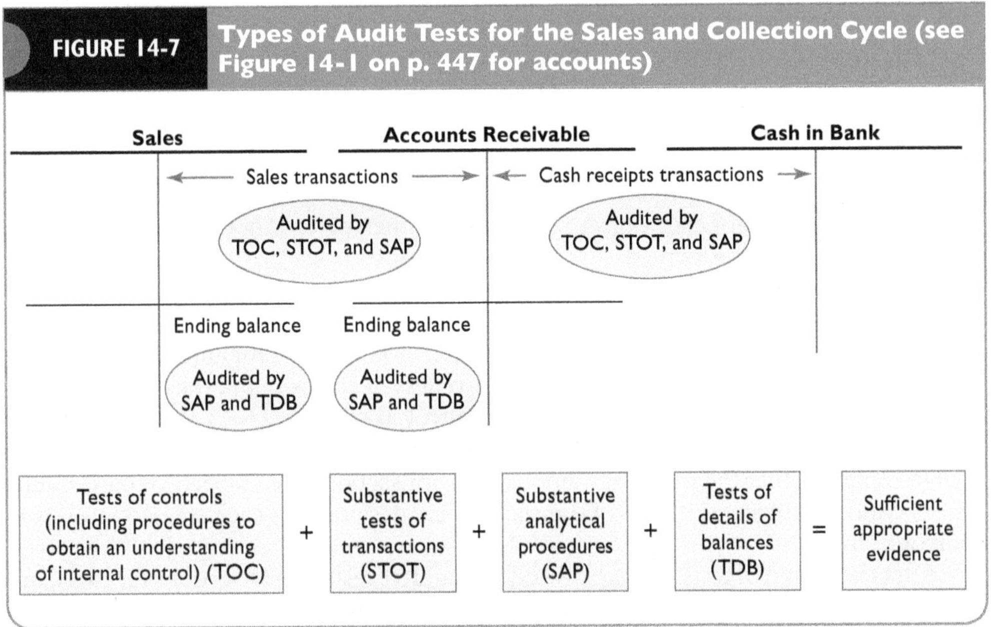

must also consider the impact of the unsatisfactory test results on the audit of internal control over financial reporting.

At the completion of the tests of controls and substantive tests of transactions, auditors must analyze each exception, for both public and nonpublic company audits, to determine its cause and the implication of the exception on assessed control risk, which may affect the supported detection risk and related remaining substantive tests. The methodology and implications of exceptions analysis are explained more fully in the next chapter.

The most significant effect of the results of the tests of controls and substantive tests of transactions in the sales and collection cycle is on the confirmation of accounts receivable. The type of confirmation, the size of the sample, and the timing of the test are all affected. The effect of the tests on accounts receivable, bad debt expense, and allowance for uncollectible accounts is considered in Chapter 16.

Figure 14-7 illustrates the major accounts in the sales and collection cycle and the types of audit tests used to audit these accounts. This figure was introduced in the preceding chapter (p. 411) and is presented here for further review.

CONCEPT CHECK

1. Describe whether the auditor is more concerned about the occurrence or completeness objective related to cash receipts.
2. How might the write-off of accounts receivable increase the risk of fraud related to cash receipts?

SUMMARY

This chapter deals with designing tests of controls and substantive tests of transactions for each of the five classes of transactions in the sales and collection cycle, including sales, cash receipts, sales returns and allowances, write-off of uncollectible accounts receivable, and bad debt expense.

The methodology for designing tests of controls and substantive tests of transactions is, in concept, the same for each of the five classes of transactions and includes the following steps:

- Understand internal control
- Assess planned control risk

- Determine the extent of tests of controls
- Design tests of controls and substantive tests of transactions to meet transaction-related audit objectives

In designing tests of controls for each class of transactions, auditors focus on testing internal controls that they intend to rely upon to reduce control risk. First, the auditor identifies internal controls, if any exist, for each transaction-related audit objective. After assessing control risk for each objective, the auditor then determines the extent of tests of controls that must be performed.

If the auditor is reporting on the effectiveness of internal control over financial reporting, extensive tests of controls must be performed to provide the basis for the auditor's report. For audits of non-accelerated filers and nonpublic companies, the decision to perform tests of controls is based on the effectiveness of controls and the extent to which the auditor intends to rely on them to reduce control risk.

The auditor also designs substantive tests of transactions for each class of transactions to determine whether the monetary amounts of transactions are correctly recorded. Like tests of controls, substantive tests of transactions are designed for each transaction-related audit objective.

After the design of tests of controls and substantive tests of transactions for each audit objective and each class of transactions is completed, the auditor organizes the audit procedures into a performance format audit program. The purpose of this audit program is to help the auditor complete the audit tests efficiently.

ESSENTIAL TERMS

Business functions for the sales and collection cycle—the key activities that an organization must complete to execute and record business transactions for sales, cash receipts, sales returns and allowances, write-off of uncollectible accounts, and bad debt expense

Classes of transactions in the sales and collection cycle—the categories of transactions for the sales and collection cycle in a typical company: sales, cash receipts, sales returns and allowances, write-off of uncollectible accounts, and bad debt expense

Design format audit program—the audit procedures resulting from the auditor's decisions about the appropriate audit procedures for each audit objective; this audit program is used to prepare a performance format audit program

Direction of tests—the starting point for testing the occurrence and completeness transaction-related audit objectives; vouching from journals to source documents tests for occurrence and tracing from source documents to journals tests for completeness

Lapping of accounts receivable—the postponement of entries for the collection of receivables to conceal an existing cash shortage

Performance format audit program—the audit procedures for a class of transactions organized in the format in which they will be performed; this audit program is prepared from a design format audit program

Proof of cash receipts—an audit procedure to test whether all recorded cash receipts have been deposited in the bank account by reconciling the total cash receipts recorded in the cash receipts journal for a given period with the actual deposits made to the bank

Sales and collection cycle—involves the decisions and processes necessary for the transfer of the ownership of goods and services to customers after they are made available for sale; it begins with a request by a customer and ends with the conversion of material or service into an account receivable, and ultimately into cash

REVIEW QUESTIONS

14-1 (OBJECTIVE 14-2) Describe the following documents and records and explain their use in the sales and collection cycle: bill of lading, credit memo, remittance advice, and accounts receivable trial balance.

14-2 (OBJECTIVE 14-2) Explain the importance of proper credit approval for sales. What effect do adequate controls in the credit function have on the auditor's evidence accumulation?

14-3 (OBJECTIVE 14-2) Distinguish between the sales journal and the accounts receivable master file. What type of information is recorded in each and how do these accounting records relate?

14-4 (OBJECTIVE 14-2) BestSellers.com sells fiction and nonfiction books and e-books to customers through the company's Web site. Customers place orders for books via the Web site by providing their name, address, credit card number, and expiration date. What internal controls could BestSellers.com implement to ensure that shipments of books occur only for customers who have the ability to pay for those books? At what point will BestSellers.com be able to record the sale as revenue?

14-5 (OBJECTIVE 14-3) State one test of control and one substantive test of transactions that the auditor can use to verify the following sales transaction-related audit objective: Recorded sales are stated at the proper amounts.

14-6 (OBJECTIVE 14-3) List the most important duties that should be segregated in the sales and collection cycle. Explain why it is desirable that each duty be segregated.

14-7 (OBJECTIVE 14-3) Explain how prenumbered shipping documents and sales invoices can be useful controls for preventing misstatements in sales.

14-8 (OBJECTIVE 14-3) Explain the purpose of footing and cross-footing the sales journal and tracing the totals to the general ledger.

14-9 (OBJECTIVE 14-4) What is the difference between the auditor's approach in verifying sales returns and allowances and that for sales? Explain the reasons for the difference.

14-10 (OBJECTIVE 14-5) Explain why auditors usually emphasize the detection of fraud in the audit of cash receipts. Is this consistent or inconsistent with the auditor's responsibility in the audit? Explain.

14-11 (OBJECTIVE 14-5) List the transaction-related audit objectives for the verification of cash receipts. For each objective, state one internal control that the client can use to reduce the likelihood of misstatements.

14-12 (OBJECTIVE 14-5) List several audit procedures that the auditor can use to determine whether all cash received was recorded.

14-13 (OBJECTIVE 14-5) Explain what is meant by a proof of cash receipts and state its purpose.

14-14 (OBJECTIVE 14-5) Explain what is meant by lapping and discuss how the auditor can uncover it. Under what circumstances should the auditor make a special effort to uncover lapping?

14-15 (OBJECTIVE 14-6) What audit procedures are most likely to be used to verify accounts receivable written off as uncollectible? State the purpose of each of these procedures.

14-16 (OBJECTIVES 14-3, 14-5) Under what circumstances is it acceptable to perform tests of controls and substantive tests of transactions for sales and cash receipts at an interim date?

14-17 (OBJECTIVES 14-3, 14-5, 14-7) State the relationship between the confirmation of accounts receivable and the results of the tests of controls and substantive tests of transactions.

14-18 (OBJECTIVE 14-7) Diane Smith, CPA, performed tests of controls and substantive tests of transactions for sales for the month of March in an audit of the financial statements for the year ended December 31, 2016. Based on the excellent results of both the tests of controls and the substantive tests of transactions, she decided to significantly reduce her substantive tests of details of balances at year-end. Evaluate this decision.

MULTIPLE CHOICE QUESTIONS FROM CPA EXAMINATIONS

14-19 **(OBJECTIVES 14-3, 14-5)** The following questions deal with internal controls in the sales and collection cycle. Choose the best response.

a. The accounting system will not post a sales transaction to the sales journal without a valid bill of lading number. This control is most relevant to which transaction-related objective for sales?

(1) Accuracy
(2) Occurrence
(3) Completeness
(4) Posting and summarization

b. The accounting system automatically obtains the unit price based on scans of bar codes for merchandise sold. This control is most relevant to which transaction-related objective for sales?

(1) Accuracy
(2) Occurrence
(3) Completeness
(4) Posting and summarization

c. Which of the following controls would be most effective in detecting a failure to record cash received from customers paying on their accounts?

(1) A person in accounting reconciles the bank deposit to the cash receipts journal.
(2) Transactions recorded in the cash receipts journal are posted on a real-time basis to the accounts receivable master file.
(3) Monthly statements are sent to customers and any discrepancies are resolved by someone independent of cash handling and accounting.
(4) Deposits of cash received are made daily.

14-20 **(OBJECTIVES 14-3, 14-6)** For each of the following types of misstatements (parts a. through c.), select the control that should have prevented the misstatement:

a. Which of the following controls most likely will be effective in offsetting the tendency of sales personnel to maximize sales volume at the expense of high bad debt write-offs?

(1) Employees responsible for authorizing sales and bad debt write-offs are denied access to cash.
(2) Employees involved in the credit-granting function are separated from the sales function.
(3) Shipping documents and sales invoices are matched by an employee who does not have the authority to write off bad debts.
(4) Subsidiary accounts receivable records are reconciled to the control account by an employee independent of the authorization of credit.

b. A sales invoice for $5,200 was computed correctly but, by mistake, was entered as $2,500 to the sales journal and posted to the accounts receivable master file. The customer remitted only $2,500, the amount on his monthly statement.

(1) Sales invoice numbers, prices, discounts, extensions, and footings are independently checked.
(2) The customers' monthly statements are verified and mailed by a responsible person other than the bookkeeper who prepared them.
(3) Prelistings and predetermined totals are used to control postings.
(4) Unauthorized remittance deductions made by customers or other matters in dispute are investigated promptly by a person independent of the accounts receivable function.

c. Shipments occurring in December 2016 did not get recorded until the first few days of January 2017.

(1) The system automatically assigns bill of lading numbers and ensures no duplicates are issued.
(2) As goods leave the shipping dock, the system generates a bill of lading and associated sales invoice, which is automatically recorded in the sales journal.

(3) The accounting system requires entry of a valid bill of lading number provided by the shipping department before a sales transaction is accepted for entry.
(4) The system prevents the creation of a bill of lading without a customer order dated prior to the shipping date.

14-21 **(OBJECTIVES 14-2, 14-3)** The following questions deal with audit evidence for the sales and collection cycle. Choose the best response.

a. An auditor is performing substantive tests of transactions for sales. One step is to trace a sample of debit entries from the accounts receivable master file back to the supporting duplicate sales invoices. What will the auditor intend to establish by this step?
   (1) Sales invoices represent existing sales.
   (2) All sales have been recorded.
   (3) All sales invoices have been correctly posted to customer accounts.
   (4) Debit entries in the accounts receivable master file are correctly supported by sales invoices.

b. Which audit procedure is most effective in testing credit sales for overstatement?
   (1) Trace a sample of postings from the sales journal to the sales account in the general ledger.
   (2) Vouch a sample of recorded sales from the sales journal to shipping documents.
   (3) Prepare an aging of accounts receivable.
   (4) Trace a sample of initial sales orders to sales recorded in the sales journal.

c. To determine whether internal control relative to the revenue cycle of a wholesaling entity is operating effectively in minimizing the failure to prepare sales invoices, an auditor would most likely select a sample of transactions from the population represented by the
   (1) sales order file.
   (2) customer order file.
   (3) shipping document file.
   (4) sales invoice file.

MULTIPLE CHOICE QUESTIONS FROM BECKER CPA EXAM REVIEW

14-22 **(OBJECTIVES 14-2, 14-3)** The following questions deal with internal control and audit evidence in the sales and collection cycle. Choose the best response.

a. Tracing shipping documents to sales invoices provides evidence that
   (1) sales billed to customers were actually shipped.
   (2) shipments to customers were properly invoiced.
   (3) shipments to customers were recorded as sales.
   (4) all goods ordered by customers were shipped.

b. Which of the following procedures most likely represents an internal control designed to reduce the risk of errors in the billing process?
   (1) Comparing control totals for shipping documents with corresponding totals for sales invoices.
   (2) Matching receiving documents with approved sales orders before invoice preparation.
   (3) Reconciling the control totals for sales invoices with the accounts receivable subsidiary ledger.
   (4) Requiring customers that purchase on account to be approved by the credit department.

c. An auditor wishes to test the completeness assertion for sales. Which of the following audit tests would most likely accomplish this objective?
   (1) Select a sample of shipments occurring during the year and trace each one to inclusion in the sales journal.

(2) Compare accounts receivable turnover (net credit sales/average gross receivables) in the current year to that achieved in the prior year.
(3) Use common size analysis to compare recorded sales to sales recorded by other companies in the same industry.
(4) Select large individual sales recorded during the year and review supporting documentation.

DISCUSSION QUESTIONS AND PROBLEMS

14-23 **(OBJECTIVES 14-2, 14-3, 14-4, 14-5)** Items 1 through 9 are selected questions of the type generally found in internal control questionnaires used by auditors to obtain an understanding of internal control in the sales and collection cycle. In using the questionnaire for a client, a "yes" response to a question indicates a possible internal control, whereas a "no" indicates a potential deficiency.

1. Are customer orders evaluated for credit approval by someone independent of sales?
2. Is the bill of lading information forwarded in a timely fashion to accounting to ensure recording in the sales journal?
3. Is the numerical sequence of bills of ladings accounted for to identify duplicates or missing documents?
4. Are online sales automatically recorded in the sales system?
5. Are unit prices obtained from a preapproved and restricted master file of unit prices?
6. Are sales invoice amounts independently verified for correctness?
7. Are entries in the sales journal restricted to those that are supported by a valid bill of lading?
8. Are entries in the sales journal timely recorded in the accounts receivable master file?
9. Are individuals responsible for handling cash collections independent of accounting and shipping functions?

Required

a. For each of the preceding questions, state the transaction-related audit objectives being fulfilled if the control is in effect.
b. For each control, list a test of control to test its effectiveness.
c. For each of the preceding questions, identify the nature of the potential financial misstatements.
d. For each of the potential misstatements in part c., list a substantive audit procedure to determine whether a material misstatement exists.

14-24 **(OBJECTIVES 14-2, 14-3)** Auditing standards require the auditor to obtain an understanding of the entity and its environment as a basis for assessing the risks of material misstatements. Business models differ across organizations and industries, leading to unique business processes needed to account for transactions. While the core business functions for the sales and collection cycle discussed in this chapter are generally relevant to all organizations, the underlying business processes and related documents and records are often unique to each organization. Below are four descriptions of different businesses.

1. The Starbucks Coffee Company sells regular and specialty coffees and teas in over 20,000 stores spanning more than 60 countries. Customers use cash, debit or credit cards, pre-paid Starbucks cards, or mobile payment apps to purchase individual drinks that are served to them within minutes.
2. Amazon.com is one of the world's largest online retailers of all kinds of products. While consumers can find a wide variety of products available at Amazon.com, the company is known for its huge selection of new and used books that can be purchased on its Web site.
3. Most people have a personal physician who provides medical care when needed, including annual physicals and other medical services. Patients make appointments to be seen by their physician, who examines the patient and prescribes treatments and medications when needed. Insured patients often pay a co-payment, with the balance paid by the insurance company.

4. The majority of universities generate a significant portion of their revenue from tuition. Universities bill students in advance for classes that will be taken in an upcoming term. For full-time students, most universities charge a set tuition amount after students enroll in a minimum number of courses per term.

Required

Analyze each of the above independent business scenarios to answer each of the following questions:

a. Using the eight business functions for the sales and collection cycle illustrated in Table 14-1 on page 448 as a guide, briefly describe the underlying business processes related to each of the eight functions for the sales and cash collections for the above independent scenarios.
b. What documents or other source evidence would you use to test the occurrence transaction-related audit objective for sales for each of the four scenarios?
c. For which of the four scenarios would the sales returns and allowances business function not be applicable?
d. For which of the four scenarios would the write-off of uncollectible accounts and bad debt expense business functions not be applicable?

14-25 **(OBJECTIVES 14-3, 14-4, 14-5)** The following are commonly performed tests of controls and substantive tests of transactions audit procedures in the sales and collection cycle:

1. Review the prelisting of cash receipts to determine whether cash is prelisted daily.
2. Reconcile the recorded cash receipts on the prelisting with the cash receipts journal and the bank statement for a one-month period.
3. Account for a sequence of shipping documents and examine each one to make sure that a duplicate sales invoice is attached.
4. Account for a sequence of sales invoices and examine each one to make sure that a duplicate copy of the shipping document is attached.
5. Compare the quantity and description of items on shipping documents with the related duplicate sales invoices.
6. Trace recorded sales in the sales journal to the related accounts receivable master file and compare the customer name, date, and amount for each one.
7. Examine sales returns for approval by an authorized official.

Required

a. Identify whether each audit procedure is a test of control or a substantive test of transactions.
b. State which of the six transaction-related audit objectives each of the audit procedures fulfills.
c. Identify the type of evidence used for each audit procedure, such as inspection and observation.

14-26 **(OBJECTIVES 14-3, 14-4)** The following is a list of possible errors or fraud (1 through 8) involving sales and controls (a. through k.) that may prevent or detect the errors or fraud:

Possible Errors or Fraud

1. Goods are removed from inventory for unauthorized orders.
2. Credit sales are made to customers with unsatisfactory credit ratings.
3. Invoices are sent to co-participants in a fraudulent scheme, and sales are recorded for fictitious transactions.
4. Goods shipped to customers do not agree with goods ordered by customers.
5. Invoices are sent for shipped goods, but are not recorded in the sales journal.
6. Invoices are sent for shipped goods, and are recorded in the sales journal, but are not posted to any customer accounts.
7. Invoices for goods sold are posted to incorrect customer accounts.
8. Invalid transactions granting credit for sales returns are recorded.

Internal Controls

a. Customer orders are compared with an approved customer list.
b. Sales orders are prepared for each customer order.

c. Shipping clerks compare goods received from warehouse with details on shipping documents.
d. Prenumbered credit memos are used for granting credit for goods returned.
e. Goods returned for credit are approved by the supervisor of the sales department.
f. Approved sales orders are required for goods to be released from the warehouse.
g. Monthly statements are mailed to customers with outstanding balances.
h. Shipping clerks compare goods received from warehouse with approved sales orders.
i. Sales invoices are compared with shipping documents and approved customer orders before invoices are mailed.
j. Control amounts posted to the accounts receivable ledger are compared with the control totals of invoices.
k. Daily sales summaries are compared with control total of invoices.

Required For each error or fraud, select one internal control that if properly designed and implemented, most likely would be effective in preventing or detecting the errors and fraud. Each response in the list of controls may be used once, more than once, or not at all.*

14-27 (OBJECTIVES 14-2, 14-3) The following sales procedures were encountered during the annual audit of Marvel Wholesale Distributing Company:

Customer orders are received by the sales order department. A clerk computes the approximate dollar amount of the order and sends it to the credit department for approval. Credit approval is stamped on the order and sent to the accounting department. A computer is then used to generate two copies of a sales invoice. The order is filed in the customer order file.

The customer copy of the sales invoice is held in a pending file awaiting notification that the order was shipped. The shipping copy of the sales invoice is routed through the warehouse, and the shipping department has authority for the respective departments to release and ship the merchandise. Shipping department personnel pack the order and manually prepare a three-copy bill of lading: The original copy is sent to the customer, the second copy is sent with the shipment, and the other is filed in sequence in the bill of lading file. The sales invoice shipping copy is sent to the accounting department with any changes resulting from lack of available merchandise.

A clerk in accounting matches the received sales invoice shipping copy with the sales invoice customer copy from the pending file. Quantities on the two invoices are compared and prices are compared to an approved price list. The customer copy is then mailed to the customer, and the shipping copy is sent to the data processing department.

The data processing clerk in accounting enters the sales invoice data into the computer, which is used to prepare the sales journal and update the accounts receivable master file. She files the shipping copy in the sales invoice file in numerical sequence.

Required

a. To determine whether the internal controls operated effectively to minimize instances of failure to invoice a shipment, the auditor would select a sample of transactions from the population represented by the
   (1) customer order file.
   (2) bill of lading file.
   (3) customers' accounts receivable master file.
   (4) sales invoice file.

b. To gather audit evidence that uncollected items in customers' accounts represented existing trade receivables, the auditor would select a sample of items from the population represented by the
   (1) customer order file.
   (2) bill of lading file.
   (3) customers' accounts receivable master file.
   (4) sales invoice file.

c. To determine whether the internal controls operated effectively to minimize instances of failure to post invoices to customers' accounts receivable master file, the auditor would select a sample of transactions from the population represented by the

*Based on AICPA question paper, American Institute of Certified Public Accountants.

(1) customer order file.
(2) bill of lading file.
(3) customers' accounts receivable master file.
(4) sales invoice file.*

14-28 (OBJECTIVE 14-3) The Committee of Sponsoring Organizations of the Treadway Commission (COSO) issued a report called *Fraudulent Financial Reporting: 1998-2007, An Analysis of Public Companies.* Download the report at www.coso.org to answer the following questions (information on fraud techniques can be found on pp. 17–18 of the report):

Required

a. How many fraud companies were included in the report? What percentage of the frauds involved improper revenue recognition?
b. What are the two broad categories of improper revenue recognition included in Table 9 of the report? What is the difference between the two types of improper revenue recognition?
c. Review the specific techniques used to overstate revenue. Describe a conditional sale and a bill and hold sale.

14-29 (OBJECTIVES 14-3, 14-5) The following are common audit procedures for tests of sales and cash receipts:

1. Examine the sales journal for related-party transactions, notes receivable, and other unusual items.
2. Select a sample of customer orders and trace the document to related shipping documents, sales invoices, and the accounts receivable master file for comparison of name, date, and amount.
3. Examine duplicate sales invoices for an indication that unit selling prices were compared to the approved price list.
4. Examine duplicate sales invoices to determine whether the account classification for sales has been included on the document.
5. Compare the quantity and description of items on duplicate sales invoices with related shipping documents.
6. Perform a proof of cash receipts.
7. Examine a sample of remittance advices for approval of cash discounts.
8. Account for a numerical sequence of remittance advices and determine whether there is a cross-reference mark for each one, indicating that it has been recorded in the cash receipts journal.
9. Trace recorded cash receipts in the accounts receivable master file to the cash receipts journal and compare the customer name, date, and amount of each one.

Required

a. Identify whether each audit procedure is a test of control or a substantive test of transactions.
b. State which transaction-related audit objective(s) each of the audit procedures fulfills.
c. For each test of control in part a., state a substantive test that could be used to determine whether there was a monetary misstatement.

14-30 (OBJECTIVE 14-5) The following is a list of possible errors or fraud (1 through 5) involving cash receipts and controls (a. through g.) that may prevent or detect the errors or fraud:

Possible Errors or Fraud

1. Customer checks are properly credited to customer accounts and are properly deposited, but errors are made in recording receipts in the cash receipts journal.
2. Customer checks are misappropriated before being forwarded to the cashier for deposit.
3. Customer checks are received for less than the customers' full account balances, but the customers' full account balances are credited.
4. Customer checks are credited to incorrect customer accounts.
5. Different customer accounts are each credited for the same cash receipt.

*Based on AICPA question paper, American Institute of Certified Public Accountants.

Internal Controls

a. Customer orders are compared with an approved customer list.
b. Prenumbered credit memos are used for granting credit for returned goods.
c. Remittance advices are separated from the checks in the mailroom and forwarded to the accounting department.
d. The cashier examines each check for proper endorsement.
e. Total amounts posted to the accounts receivable subsidiary records from remittance advices are compared with the validated bank deposit slip.
f. Monthly statements are mailed to customers with outstanding balances.
g. An employee, other than the bookkeeper, periodically prepares a bank reconciliation.

Required For each error or fraud, select one internal control that if properly designed and implemented, most likely would be effective in preventing or detecting the errors and fraud. Each response in the list of controls may be used once, more than once, or not at all.*

14-31 **(OBJECTIVE 14-5)** You have been asked by the board of trustees of a local church to review its accounting procedures. As part of this review you have prepared the following comments about the collections made at weekly services and record keeping for members' pledges and contributions:

1. The church's board of trustees has delegated responsibility for financial management and audit of the financial records to the finance committee. This group prepares the annual budget and approves major cash disbursements, but is not involved in collections or record keeping. No audit has been considered necessary in recent years because the same trusted employee has kept church records and served as financial secretary for 15 years.
2. The collection at the weekly service is taken by a team of ushers. The head usher counts the collection in the church office after each service. She then places the collection and a notation of the amount in the church safe. The next morning, the financial secretary opens the safe and recounts the collection. He withholds about $100 to meet cash expenditures during the coming week and deposits the remainder intact. To facilitate the deposit, members who contribute by check are asked to enter "Cash" on the payee line.
3. At their request, a few members are furnished prenumbered, predated envelopes in which to insert their weekly contributions. The head usher removes the cash from the envelopes to be counted with the loose cash included in the collection and discards the envelopes. No record is maintained of issuance or return of the envelopes, and the envelope system is not encouraged.
4. Each member is asked to prepare a contribution pledge card annually. The pledge is regarded as a moral commitment by the member to contribute a stated weekly amount. Some members have inquired about having weekly contributions automatically withdrawn from their bank account or charged to their credit card, but the church has not established procedures that would allow payments other than by cash or check at weekly services. Based on the amounts shown on the pledge cards, the financial secretary furnishes a letter to members, upon request, to support the tax deductibility of their contributions.

Required Identify the deficiencies and recommend improvements in procedures for collection made at weekly services and record keeping for members' pledges and contributions. Use the methodology for identifying deficiencies discussed in Chapter 12. Organize your answer sheets as follows:*

Deficiency	Recommended Improvement

14-32 **(OBJECTIVES 14-3, 14-5)** Items 1 through 10 present various internal control strengths or internal control deficiencies.

1. Credit is granted by a credit department.
2. Once shipment occurs and is recorded in the sales journal, all shipping documents are marked "recorded" by the accounting staff.
3. Sales returns are presented to a sales department clerk, who prepares a written, prenumbered receiving report.

*Based on AICPA question paper, American Institute of Certified Public Accountants.

4. Cash receipts received in the mail are received by a secretary with no record-keeping responsibility.
5. Cash receipts received in the mail are forwarded unopened with remittance advices to accounting.
6. The cash receipts journal is prepared by the treasurer's department.
7. Cash is deposited weekly.
8. Statements are sent monthly to customers.
9. Write-offs of accounts receivable are approved by the controller.
10. The bank reconciliation is prepared by individuals independent of cash receipts record keeping.

Required

a. For each of the preceding 1–10 items, indicate whether the item represents an:
   A. Internal control strength for the sales and collection cycle.
   B. Internal control deficiency for the sales and collection cycle.
b. For each item that you answered (A), indicate the transaction-related audit objective(s) to which the control relates.
c. For each item that you answered (B), indicate the nature of the deficiency.*

14-33 **(OBJECTIVE 14-3)** YourTeam.com is an online retailer of college and professional sports team memorabilia, such as hats, shirts, pennants, and other sports logo products. Consumers select the college or professional team from a pull-down menu on the company's Web site. For each listed team, the Web site provides a product description, picture, and price for all products sold online. Customers click on the product number of the items they wish to purchase. The following are internal controls YourTeam.com has established for its online sales:

1. Only products shown on the Web site can be purchased online. Other company products not shown on the Web site listing are unavailable for online sale.
2. The online sales system is linked to the perpetual inventory system, which verifies quantities on hand before processing the sale.
3. Before the sale is authorized, YourTeam.com obtains credit card authorization codes electronically from the credit card agency.
4. Online sales are rejected if the customer's shipping address does not match the credit card's billing address.
5. Before the sale is finalized, the online screen shows the product name, description, unit price, and total sales price for the online transaction. Customers must click on the Accept or Reject sales button to indicate approval or rejection of the online sale.
6. Once customers approve the online sale, the online sales system generates a Pending Sales file, which is an online data file that is used by warehouse personnel to process shipments. Online sales are not recorded in the sales journal until warehouse personnel enter the bill of lading number and date of shipment into the Pending Sales data file.

Required

a. For each control, identify the transaction-related audit objective(s) being fulfilled if each control is in effect.
b. For each control, describe potential financial misstatements that could occur if the control was not present.

CASE

14-34 **(OBJECTIVE 14-4)** The Meyers Pharmaceutical Company, a drug manufacturer, has the following internal controls for billing and recording accounts receivable:

1. An incoming customer's purchase order is received in the order department by a clerk who prepares a prenumbered company sales order form on which is inserted the pertinent information, such as the customer's name and address, customer's account number, quantity, and items ordered. After the sales order form has been prepared, the customer's purchase order is attached to it.
2. The sales order form is then passed to the credit department for credit approval. Rough approximations of the billing values of the orders are made in the credit

*Based on AICPA question paper, American Institute of Certified Public Accountants.

department for those accounts on which credit limitations are imposed. After investigation, approval of credit is noted on the form.

3. Next, the sales order form is passed to the billing department, where a clerk uses a computer to generate the customer's invoice. It automatically multiplies the number of items times the unit price and adds the extended amounts for the total amount of the invoice. The billing clerk determines the unit prices for the items from a list of billing prices. The invoice copies are designated as follows:
   (a) Customer's copy.
   (b) Sales department copy, for information purposes.
   (c) File copy.
   (d) Shipping department copy, which serves as a shipping order. Bills of lading are also prepared as carbon copy by-products of the invoicing procedure.
4. The shipping department copy of the invoice and the bills of lading are then sent to the shipping department. After the order has been shipped, copies of the bill of lading are returned to the billing department. The shipping department copy of the invoice is filed in the shipping department.
5. In the billing department, one copy of the bill of lading is attached to the customer's copy of the invoice and both are mailed to the customer. The other copy of the bill of lading, together with the sales order form, is then attached to the invoice file copy and filed in invoice numerical order.
6. As the computer generates invoices, it also stores the transactions in an electronic file that is used to update the accounting records daily. A summary report is generated and all journals and ledgers are printed for a hardcopy of the records.
7. Periodically, an internal auditor traces a sample of sales orders all the way through the system to the journals and ledgers, testing both the procedures and dollar amounts. The procedures include comparing control totals with output, recalculating invoices and refooting journals, and tracing totals to the master file and general ledger.

Required

a. Flowchart the billing function as a means of understanding the system.
b. List the internal controls over sales for each of the six transaction-related audit objectives.
c. For each control, list a useful test of control to verify the effectiveness of the control.
d. For each transaction-related audit objective for sales, list appropriate substantive tests of transactions audit procedures, considering internal controls.
e. Combine the audit procedures from parts c. and d. into an efficient audit program for sales.

INTEGRATED CASE APPLICATION— PINNACLE MANUFACTURING: PART V

14-35 (OBJECTIVES 14-3, 14-5) In Part IV of this case study, you obtained an understanding of internal control and made an initial assessment of control risk for each transaction-related audit objective for acquisition and cash disbursement transactions. The purpose of Part V is to continue the assessment of control risk by determining the appropriate tests of controls and substantive tests of transactions. In order to do this, you must complete the steps needed to prepare a high-quality performance format audit program for tests of controls and substantive tests of transactions for acquisitions and cash disbursements.

Assume in Part IV that you identified the following as the key controls you want to rely on (even though your answers were likely different from these):

1. Segregation of the purchasing, receiving, and cash disbursements functions
2. Use of prenumbered voucher packages, properly accounted for
3. Use of prenumbered checks, properly accounted for
4. Use of prenumbered receiving reports, properly accounted for
5. Internal verification of document package before check preparation
6. Review of supporting documents and signing of checks by an independent, authorized person
7. Cancellation of documents prior to signing of the check
8. Monthly reconciliation of the accounts payable master file with the general ledger

9. Independent reconciliation of the monthly bank statements

Required

a. Prepare an audit file listing the nine controls or get them online.
b. After each control, identify the transaction-related audit objective(s) that it partially or fully satisfies.
c. Immediately below the control, list one audit procedure to test the control. Use the most reliable test of control evidence that you can think of. Write the audit procedure in good form.
d. Immediately below the test of control, list one substantive test of transactions audit procedure to test whether the control failed to be effective. Use the most reliable substantive tests of transactions evidence that you can think of.
e. Create a separate audit schedule labeled "Acquisitions Substantive Tests of Transactions." Decide and write one substantive test of transactions audit procedure for each transaction-related audit objective for acquisitions. The audit procedures must be different from the ones in requirement d. The schedule should be designed as follows:

Acquisitions Substantive Tests of Transactions	
Occurrence	Write the substantive audit procedure
Completeness	Write the substantive audit procedure
Etc.	

f. Using a separate heading labeled "Cash Disbursements Substantive Tests of Transactions," decide and write one substantive test of transactions audit procedure for each transaction-related audit objective for cash disbursements. The audit procedures must be different from the ones in requirements d. and e. The audit schedule should be designed the same as the one in requirement e.
g. Prepare a performance audit program for acquisitions and cash disbursements using all audit procedures in requirements c. through f. See Figure 14-6 (p. 467) for a format. To the extent possible, follow the approach in procedure 13 a. through e. in Figure 14-6 of having "one starting point" procedure followed by other related procedures. Do this for both acquisitions and cash disbursements. Be sure to eliminate any duplicate audit procedures.

ACL PROBLEM

14-36 (OBJECTIVES 14-3) This problem requires the use of ACL software, which can be accessed through the textbook Web site. Information about downloading and using ACL and the commands used in this problem can also be found on the textbook Web site. You should read all of the reference material preceding the instructions for "Quick Sort" before locating the appropriate command to answer questions a. through f. For this problem use the file labeled "Shipments" in the "Sales_and_collection" subfolder of the ACL_Rockwood project. This file includes all shipments recorded as sales in 2014. The suggested command or other source of information needed to solve the problem requirement is included at the end of each question.

Required

a. Determine the total number of shipments recorded as sales in calendar year 2014 as listed at the bottom of the worksheet.
b. Sort the ship_date column in both ascending and descending order. What concerns do you have about shipments recorded as sales in 2014, if any? (Quick Sort)
c. Are there any gaps or duplicates in Shipping Numbers? What might be a plausible explanation for gaps or duplicates observed? (Gaps and Duplicates)
d. Create a new file of shipments summarized by customer. Which customer accounts for the most sales activity by total number of shipments? Which customer accounts for the most sales activity by the total number of items shipped? Are these amounts significant relative to total shipments? (Summarize and Quick Sort)
e. Using the file of shipments by customer created in part d. above, sort by customer number. Do you have any concerns based on this information? (Quick Sort)
f. To help decide the number of shipments to select for testing, you decide to stratify on the number of items shipped after excluding all shipments with fewer than 100 items. Print the output. (Filter and Stratify)

CHAPTER

15

AUDIT SAMPLING FOR TESTS OF CONTROLS AND SUBSTANTIVE TESTS OF TRANSACTIONS

LEARNING OBJECTIVES

After studying this chapter, you should be able to

15-1 Explain the concept of representative sampling.

15-2 Distinguish between statistical and nonstatistical sampling and between probabilistic and nonprobabilistic sample selection.

15-3 Select samples using probabilistic and nonprobabilistic methods.

15-4 Define and describe audit sampling for exception rates.

15-5 Use nonstatistical sampling in tests of controls and substantive tests of transactions.

15-6 Define and describe attributes sampling and a sampling distribution.

15-7 Use attributes sampling in tests of controls and substantive tests of transactions.

Sometimes an Isolated Exception Is the Tip of the Iceberg

David Chen was an experienced assistant on the audit of Sol Systems, a manufacturer of solar panels. While performing tests of controls over sales transactions, he discovered that one of the sales transactions selected for testing was missing shipping information. When asked about the missing documentation, the controller suggested this was an isolated clerical mistake. An hour later, he provided Chen with the shipping document, which appeared to be valid. Since this was the only one in the sample with a problem, Chen thought that the results of the test would be considered acceptable under the sampling plan his firm had established, even if the transaction was considered an exception. Still, the transaction was for a fairly large amount, and Chen was concerned that the documentation was not initially available.

Chen consulted with Cindy Hubbard, the experienced senior on the engagement. Her initial reaction was to accept the documentation so Chen could move on to other testing. But after considering it for a few minutes, she asked Chen to look further into the transaction. Chen discovered that the receivable had not been paid. Instead, a journal entry had been recorded to credit the receivable from the sale. Through a series of journal entries, the receivable ultimately ended up recorded as an asset in a long-term asset account. He examined additional transactions involving this customer and found that they had been handled the same way.

Hubbard escalated the findings to the engagement partner. The firm's forensic auditors discovered that Sol was engaged in a large-scale fraud to overstate sales and earnings. The firm resigned from the engagement and reported their findings to the SEC. Chen was promoted to audit senior a year earlier than normal for assistants.

Chapter 14 dealt with designing tests of controls and substantive tests of transactions for the sales and collection cycle. Many of these procedures involve the use of sampling. As demonstrated by the story about David Chen and the audit of Sol Systems, appropriately applying audit sampling is a challenging part of the audit. This chapter discusses nonstatistical and statistical sampling for tests of controls and substantive tests of transactions. The discussion is based on the sales and collection cycle, but the sampling concepts apply equally to all other cycles.

The clarified audit standards define **audit sampling** as:

> The selection and evaluation of less than 100 percent of the population of audit relevance such that the auditor expects the items selected to be representative of the population and, thus, likely to provide a reasonable basis for conclusions about the population.

We begin by discussing representative samples and the risks associated with sampling.

REPRESENTATIVE SAMPLES

OBJECTIVE 15-1

Explain the concept of representative sampling.

When selecting a sample from a population, the auditor strives to obtain a representative sample. A **representative sample** is one in which the characteristics in the sample are approximately the same as those of the population. This means that the sampled items are similar to the items not sampled. Assume a client's internal controls require a clerk to attach a shipping document to every duplicate sales invoice, but the clerk fails to follow the procedure exactly 3 percent of the time. If the auditor selects a sample of 100 duplicate sales invoices and finds three are missing attached shipping documents, the sample is highly representative. If two or four such items are found in the sample, the sample is reasonably representative. If no or many missing items are found, the sample is nonrepresentative.

In practice, auditors never know whether a sample is representative, even after all testing is complete. (The only way to know if a sample is representative is to subsequently audit the entire population.) However, auditors can increase the likelihood of a sample being representative by using care in designing the sampling process, sample selection, and evaluation of sample results. A sample result can lead to an incorrect conclusion due to sampling error or nonsampling error. The risk of these two types of errors occurring is called sampling risk and nonsampling risk.

Sampling risk is the risk that an auditor reaches an incorrect conclusion because the sample is not representative of the population. Sampling risk is an inherent part of sampling that results from testing less than the entire population. For example, assume the auditor decided that a control is not effective if there is a population exception rate of 6 percent. Assume the auditor accepts the control as effective based on tests of the control with a sample of 100 items that had two exceptions. If the population actually has an 8 percent exception rate, the auditor incorrectly accepted the population because the sample was not sufficiently representative of the population.

Auditors have two ways to control sampling risk:

1. Adjust sample size
2. Use an appropriate method of selecting sample items from the population

Increasing sample size reduces sampling risk, and vice versa. At one extreme, a sample of all the items of a population has a zero sampling risk. At the other extreme, a sample of one or two items has an extremely high sampling risk.

Using an appropriate sample selection method increases the likelihood of representativeness. This does not eliminate or even reduce sampling risk, but it does allow the auditor to measure the risk associated with a given sample size if statistical methods of sample selection and evaluation are used.

Nonsampling risk is the risk that the auditor reaches an incorrect conclusion for any reason not related to sampling risk. The two causes of nonsampling risk are the auditor's failure to recognize exceptions and inappropriate or ineffective audit procedures.

An auditor might fail to recognize an exception because of exhaustion, boredom, or lack of understanding of what might constitute an exception. In the preceding example, assume three shipping documents were not attached to duplicate sales invoices in a sample of 100. If the auditor concluded that no exceptions existed, that is a nonsampling error. An ineffective audit procedure for detecting the exceptions in question would be to examine a sample of shipping documents and determine whether each is attached to a duplicate sales invoice, rather than to examine a sample of duplicate sales invoices to determine if shipping documents are attached. In this case, the auditor has done the test in the wrong direction by starting with the shipping document instead of the duplicate sales invoice. Careful design of audit procedures, proper instruction, supervision, and review are ways to control nonsampling risk.

STATISTICAL VERSUS NONSTATISTICAL SAMPLING AND PROBABILISTIC VERSUS NONPROBABILISTIC SAMPLE SELECTION

Before discussing the methods of sample selection to obtain representative samples, it is useful to make distinctions between statistical versus nonstatistical sampling, and between probabilistic versus nonprobabilistic sample selection.

Statistical Versus Nonstatistical Sampling

OBJECTIVE 15-2

Distinguish between statistical and nonstatistical sampling and between probabilistic and non-probabilistic sample selection.

Audit sampling methods can be divided into two broad categories: statistical sampling and nonstatistical sampling. These categories are similar in that they both involve three phases:

1. Plan the sample
2. Select the sample and perform the tests
3. Evaluate the results

The purpose of planning the sample is to make sure that the audit tests are performed in a manner that provides the desired sampling risk and minimizes the likelihood of nonsampling error. Selecting the sample involves deciding how a sample is selected from the population. The auditor can perform the audit tests only after the sample items are selected. Evaluating the results is the drawing of conclusions based on the audit tests.

Assume that an auditor selects a sample of 100 duplicate sales invoices from a population, tests each to determine whether a shipping document is attached, and determines that there are three exceptions. Let's look at those actions step-by-step:

Action	Step
• Decide that a sample size of 100 is needed.	1. Plan the sample.
• Decide which 100 items to select from the population. • Perform the audit procedure for each of the 100 items and determine that three exceptions exist.	2. Select the sample and perform the tests.
• Reach conclusions about the likely exception rate in the total population when the sample exception rate equals 3 percent.	3. Evaluate the results.

Statistical sampling differs from nonstatistical sampling in that, by applying mathematical rules, auditors can quantify (measure) sampling risk in planning the sample (step 1) and in evaluating the results (step 3). (You may remember calculating a statistical result at a 95 percent confidence level in a statistics course. A 95 percent confidence level provides a 5 percent sampling risk.)

In **nonstatistical sampling**, auditors do not quantify sampling risk. However, a properly designed nonstatistical sample that considers the same factors as a properly designed statistical sample can provide results that are as effective as a properly designed statistical sample.

Probabilistic Versus Nonprobabilistic Sample Selection

Both probabilistic and nonprobabilistic sample selection fall under step 2. When using **probabilistic sample selection**, the auditor randomly selects items such that each population item has a known probability of being included in the sample. This process requires great care and uses one of several methods discussed shortly. In **nonprobabilistic sample selection**, the auditor selects sample items using nonprobabilistic methods that approximate a random sampling approach. Auditors can use one of several nonprobabilistic sample selection methods.

Applying Statistical and Nonstatistical Sampling in Practice and Sample Selection Methods

Auditing standards permit auditors to use either statistical or nonstatistical sampling methods. However, it is essential that either method be applied with due care. All steps of the process must be followed carefully. When statistical sampling is used, the sample *must be a probabilistic one* and appropriate statistical evaluation methods must be used with the sample results to make the sampling risk computations. Auditors may make nonstatistical evaluations when using probabilistic selection, but it is never acceptable to evaluate a nonprobabilistic sample using statistical methods. We will now discuss different selection methods.

SAMPLE SELECTION METHODS

OBJECTIVE 15-3

Select samples using probabilistic and nonprobabilistic methods.

There are a number of techniques that auditors can use to select a sample. However, only probabilistic techniques are applicable when using statistical sampling. Probabilistic sample selection methods include the following:

1. Simple random sample selection
2. Systematic sample selection
3. Probability proportional to size sample selection

Nonprobabilistic sample selection methods include:

1. Haphazard sample selection
2. Block sample selection

Auditors can also use probabilistic methods even when using nonstatistical sampling. We will discuss each of these techniques, beginning with probabilistic sample selection methods.

Probabilistic Sample Selection Methods

Statistical sampling requires a probabilistic sample to measure sampling risk. For probabilistic samples, the auditor uses no judgment about which sample items are selected, except in choosing which probabilistic selection method to use.

Simple Random Sample Selection In a simple **random sample**, every possible combination of population items has an equal chance of being included in the sample. Auditors use simple random sampling to sample populations when there is no need to emphasize one or more types of population items. Say, for example, auditors want to sample a client's cash disbursements for the year. They might select a simple random sample of 60 items from the cash disbursements journal, apply appropriate auditing procedures to the 60 items selected, and draw conclusions about all recorded cash disbursement transactions.

When auditors obtain a simple random sample, they must use a method that ensures all items in the population have an equal chance of selection. Suppose an auditor decides to select a sample from a total of 12,000 cash disbursement transactions for the year. A simple random sample of one transaction will be such that each of

FIGURE 15-1 Computer Generation of Random Numbers—Hillsburg Hardware Co.

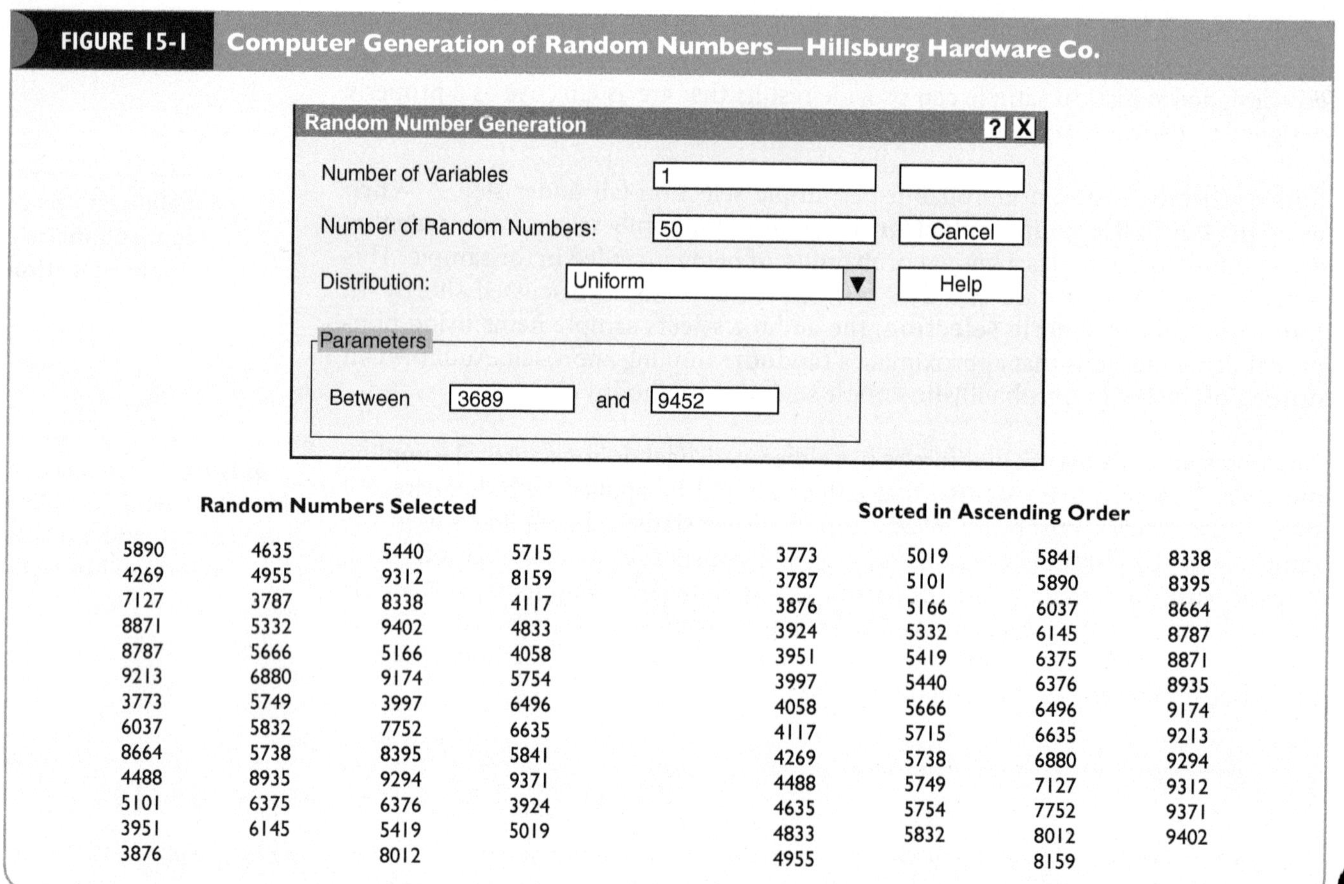

Random Numbers Selected

5890	4635	5440	5715
4269	4955	9312	8159
7127	3787	8338	4117
8871	5332	9402	4833
8787	5666	5166	4058
9213	6880	9174	5754
3773	5749	3997	6496
6037	5832	7752	6635
8664	5738	8395	5841
4488	8935	9294	9371
5101	6375	6376	3924
3951	6145	5419	5019
3876		8012	

Sorted in Ascending Order

3773	5019	5841	8338
3787	5101	5890	8395
3876	5166	6037	8664
3924	5332	6145	8787
3951	5419	6375	8871
3997	5440	6376	8935
4058	5666	6496	9174
4117	5715	6635	9213
4269	5738	6880	9294
4488	5749	7127	9312
4635	5754	7752	9371
4833	5832	8012	9402
4955		8159	

the 12,000 transactions has an equal chance of being selected. The auditor will select one random number between 1 and 12,000. Assume that number is 3,895. The auditor will select and test only the 3,895th cash disbursement transaction. For a random sample of 100, each population item also has an equal chance of being selected.

Auditors most often generate random numbers by using one of three computer sample selection techniques: electronic spreadsheets, random number generators, and generalized audit software. Figure 15-1 shows the random selection of sales invoices for the audit of Hillsburg Hardware Co. using an electronic spreadsheet program. In the example, the auditor wants 50 sample items from a population of sales invoices numbered from 3689 to 9452. The program requires only input parameters to create a sample for the auditor to select. Such programs possess great flexibility, are able to generate random dates or ranges of sets of numbers (such as page and line numbers or sales invoice numbers for multiple divisions), and provide output in either sorted or selection order.

Random numbers may be obtained with or without replacement. With replacement means an element in the population can be included in the sample more than once. In selection without replacement, an item can be included only once. Although both selection approaches are consistent with sound statistical theory, auditors rarely use replacement sampling.

Systematic Sample Selection In **systematic sample selection** (also called systematic sampling), the auditor calculates an interval and then selects the items for the sample based on the size of the interval. The interval is determined by dividing the population size by the desired sample size. In a population of sales invoices ranging from 652 to 3,151, with a desired sample size of 125, the interval is 20 [(3,151 − 651)/125]. The auditor first selects a random number between 0 and 19 (the interval size) to determine the starting point for the sample. If the randomly selected number is 9, the first item in the sample will be invoice number 661 (652 + 9). The remaining 124 items will be 681 (661 + 20), 701 (681 + 20), and so on through item 3,141.

The advantage of systematic selection is its ease of use. In most populations, a systematic sample can be drawn quickly and the approach automatically puts the numbers in sequence, making it easy to develop the appropriate documentation.

A concern with systematic selection is the possibility of bias. Because of the way systematic selection is done, once the first item in the sample is selected, all other items are chosen automatically. This causes no problem if the characteristic of interest, such as a possible control deviation, is distributed randomly throughout the population, but this may not always be the case. For example, if a control deviation occurred at a certain time of the month or only with certain types of documents, a systematic sample can have a higher likelihood of failing to be representative than a simple random sample. Therefore, when auditors use systematic selection, they must consider possible patterns in the population data that can cause sample bias.

Probability Proportional to Size and Stratified Sample Selection In many auditing situations, it is advantageous to select samples that emphasize population items with larger recorded amounts. There are two ways to obtain such samples:

1. Take a sample in which the probability of selecting any individual population item is proportional to its recorded amount. This method is called sampling with probability proportional to size (PPS), and it is evaluated using nonstatistical sampling or monetary unit statistical sampling.
2. Divide the population into subpopulations, usually by dollar size, and take larger samples from the subpopulations with larger sizes. This is called stratified sampling, and it is evaluated using nonstatistical sampling or variables statistical sampling.

These selection methods and their related evaluation methods are discussed in more detail in Chapter 17.

Nonprobabilistic Sample Selection Methods

Nonprobabilistic sample selection methods are those that do not meet the technical requirements for probabilistic sample selection. Because these methods are not based on mathematical probabilities, the representativeness of the sample may be difficult to determine.

Haphazard Sample Selection **Haphazard sample selection** is the selection of items without any conscious bias by the auditor. In such cases, the auditor selects population items without regard to their size, source, or other distinguishing characteristics.

The most serious shortcoming of haphazard sample selection is the difficulty of remaining completely unbiased in the selection. Because of the auditor's training and unintentional bias, certain population items are more likely than others to be included in the sample.

Block Sample Selection In **block sample selection** auditors select the first item in a block, and the remainder of the block is chosen in sequence. For example, assume the block sample will be a sequence of 100 sales transactions from the sales journal for the third week of March. Auditors can select the total sample of 100 by taking 5 blocks of 20 items, 10 blocks of 10, 50 blocks of 2, or one block of 100.

It is ordinarily acceptable to use block samples only if a reasonable number of blocks is used. If few blocks are used, the probability of obtaining a nonrepresentative sample is too great, considering the possibility of employee turnover, changes in the accounting system, and the seasonal nature of many businesses. For example, in the previous example, sampling 10 blocks of 10 from the third week of March is far less appropriate than selecting 10 blocks of 10 from 10 different months.

Although haphazard and block sample selection appear to be less logical than other sample selection methods, they are often useful in situations where the nature of the data makes it more difficult to use a probabilistic method. For example, assume that the auditor wants to trace credits from the accounts receivable master files to the cash receipts journal and other authorized sources as a test for fictitious credits in the master files, but the credits are not numbered in a way that a random sample can be easily selected. In this situation, many auditors use a haphazard or block approach, because it is simpler than other selection methods. However, for many nonstatistical sampling applications involving tests of controls and substantive tests of transactions, auditors prefer to use a probabilistic sample selection method to increase the likelihood of selecting a representative sample.

SAMPLING FOR EXCEPTION RATES

OBJECTIVE 15-4

Define and describe audit sampling for exception rates.

Auditors use sampling for tests of controls and substantive tests of transactions to determine whether controls are operating effectively and whether the rate of monetary errors is below tolerable limits. To do this, auditors estimate the percent of items in a population containing a characteristic or **attribute** of interest. This percent is called the **occurrence rate** or **exception rate**. For example, if an auditor determines that the exception rate for the internal verification of sales invoices is approximately 3 percent, then on average 3 of every 100 invoices are not properly verified.

Auditors are interested in the following types of exceptions in populations of accounting data:

1. Deviations from the client's established controls
2. Monetary misstatements in populations of transaction data
3. Monetary misstatements in populations of account balance details

Knowing the exception rate is particularly helpful for the first two types of exceptions, which involve transactions. Therefore, auditors make extensive use of audit sampling that measures the exception rate in doing tests of controls and substantive tests of transactions. With the third type of exception, auditors usually need to estimate the total dollar amount of the exceptions because they must decide whether the misstatements are material. When auditors want to know the total amount of a misstatement, they use methods that measure dollars, not the exception rate.

The exception rate in a sample is used to estimate the exception rate in the entire population, meaning it is the auditor's "best estimate" of the population exception rate. The term *exception* should be understood to refer to both deviations from the client's control procedures and amounts that are not monetarily correct, whether because of an unintentional accounting error or any other cause. The term *deviation* refers specifically to a departure from prescribed controls.

Assume, for example, that the auditor wants to determine the percentage of duplicate sales invoices that do not have shipping documents attached. Because the auditor cannot check every invoice, the actual percentage of missing shipping documents remains unknown. The auditor obtains a sample of duplicate sales invoices and determines the percentage of the invoices that do not have shipping documents attached. The auditor then concludes that the sample exception rate is the best estimate of the population exception rate.

Because the exception rate is based on a sample, there is a significant likelihood that the sample exception rate differs from the actual population exception rate. This difference is called the *sampling error*. The auditor is concerned with both the estimate of the sampling error and the reliability of that estimate, called *sampling risk*. Assume the auditor determines a 3 percent sample exception rate, and a sampling error of 1 percent, with a sampling risk of 10 percent. The auditor can state that the interval estimate of the population exception rate is between 2 percent and

4 percent (3 percent ± 1) with a 10 percent risk of being wrong (and a 90 percent chance of being right).

In using audit sampling for exception rates, the auditor wants to know the *most* the exception rate is likely to be, rather than the width of the confidence interval. So, the auditor focuses on the upper limit of the interval estimate, which is called the estimated or **computed upper exception rate (CUER)** in tests of controls and substantive tests of transactions. Using figures from the preceding example, an auditor might conclude that the CUER for missing shipping documents is 4 percent at a 5 percent sampling risk, meaning the auditor concludes that the exception rate in the population is no greater than 4 percent with a 5 percent risk of the exception rate exceeding 4 percent. Once it is calculated, the auditor can consider CUER in the context of specific audit objectives. If testing for missing shipping documents, for example, the auditor must determine whether a 4 percent exception rate indicates an acceptable control risk for the occurrence objective.

CONCEPT CHECK

1. State what is meant by a representative sample and explain its importance in sampling audit populations.
2. Explain the major difference between statistical and nonstatistical sampling. Are both methods acceptable according to auditing standards?

APPLICATION OF NONSTATISTICAL AUDIT SAMPLING

OBJECTIVE 15-5

Use nonstatistical sampling in tests of controls and substantive tests of transactions.

We will now examine the application of nonstatistical audit sampling in testing transactions for control deviations and monetary misstatements. Statistical sampling is examined later in this chapter. Before doing so, key terminology are defined and summarized in Table 15-1. The same terminology is used for statistical sampling.

The auditor first determines whether to apply nonstatistical sampling to those attributes where sampling applies. As previously discussed, there are three phases when sampling for tests of controls and substantive tests of transactions. The auditor must (1) plan the sample; (2) select the sample and perform the audit procedures; and (3) evaluate

TABLE 15-1 Terms Used in Audit Sampling

Term	Definition
Terms Related to Planning	
Characteristic or attribute	The characteristic being tested in the application
Acceptable risk of overreliance (ARO)	The risk that the auditor is willing to take of accepting a control as effective or a rate of monetary misstatements as tolerable, when the true population exception rate is greater than the tolerable exception rate
Tolerable exception rate (TER)	Exception rate that the auditor will permit in the population and still be willing to conclude the control is operating effectively and/or the amount of monetary misstatements in the transactions established during planning is acceptable
Estimated population exception rate (EPER)	Exception rate that the auditor expects to find in the population before testing begins
Initial sample size	Sample size decided after considering the above factors in planning
Terms Related to Evaluating Results	
Exception	Exception from the attribute in a sample item
Sample exception rate (SER)	Number of exceptions in the sample divided by the sample size
Computed upper exception rate (CUER)	The highest estimated exception rate in the population at a given ARO

the results to conclude on the acceptability of the population. These three phases involve 14 well-defined steps. Auditors should follow these steps carefully to ensure proper application of both the auditing and sampling requirements. We use the example audit of Hillsburg Hardware Co. to illustrate the steps in the following discussion.

Plan the Sample

1. State the objectives of the audit test.
2. Decide whether audit sampling applies.
3. Define attributes and exception conditions.
4. Define the population.
5. Define the sampling unit.
6. Specify the tolerable exception rate.
7. Specify acceptable risk of overreliance.
8. Estimate the population deviation or exception rate.
9. Determine the initial sample size.

Select the Sample and Perform the Audit Procedures

10. Select the sample.
11. Perform the audit procedures.

Evaluate the Results

12. Generalize from the sample to the population.
13. Analyze exceptions.
14. Decide the acceptability of the population.

State the Objectives of the Audit Test

The objectives of the test must be stated in terms of the transaction cycle being tested. Typically, auditors define the objectives of tests of controls and substantive tests of transactions as follows:

- Test the operating effectiveness of controls
- Determine whether the transactions contain monetary misstatements

The objectives of these tests in the sales and collection cycle are usually to test the effectiveness of internal controls over sales and cash receipts and to determine whether sales and cash receipts transactions contain monetary misstatements. Auditors normally define these objectives as a part of designing the audit program, which was discussed for the sales and collection cycle in Chapter 14. You can find the audit program for the sales and collection cycle for Hillsburg Hardware in Figure 14-6 (p. 467).

Decide Whether Audit Sampling Applies

Audit sampling applies whenever the auditor plans to reach conclusions about a population based on a sample. The auditor should examine the audit program and select those audit procedures where audit sampling applies. To illustrate, assume the following partial audit program:

1. Review sales transactions for large and unusual amounts (analytical procedure).
2. Observe whether the duties of the accounts receivable clerk are separate from handling cash (test of control).
3. Examine a sample of duplicate sales invoices for
   a. credit approval by the credit manager (test of control).
   b. existence of an attached shipping document (test of control).
   c. inclusion of a chart of accounts number (test of control).
4. Select a sample of shipping documents and trace each to related duplicate sales invoices (test of control).
5. Compare the quantity on each duplicate sales invoice with the quantity on related shipping documents (substantive test of transactions).

Audit sampling does not apply for the first two procedures in this audit program. The first is an analytical procedure for which sampling is inappropriate. The second is an observation procedure for which no documentation exists to perform audit

TABLE 15-2 Audit Procedures—Hillsburg Hardware Co.

Procedure	Comment
Shipment of Goods	
10. Account for a sequence of shipping documents.	It is possible to do this by selecting a random sample and accounting for all shipping documents selected. This requires a separate set of random numbers because the sampling unit is different from that used for the other tests.
11. Trace selected shipping documents to the sales journal to be sure that each one has been included.	No exceptions are expected, and a 6 percent TER is considered acceptable at an ARO of 10 percent. A sample size of 40 is selected. The shipping documents are traced to the sales journal. This is done for all 40 items. There are no exceptions for either test. The results are considered acceptable. There is no further information about this portion of the tests in this illustration.
Billing of Customers and Recording the Sales in the Records	
12. Account for a sequence of sales invoices in the sales journal.	The audit procedures for billing and recording sales (procedures 12 to 14) are the only ones included for illustration throughout this chapter.
13. Trace selected sales invoice numbers from the sales journal to a. accounts receivable master file and test for amount, date, and invoice number. b. duplicate sales invoice and check for the total amount recorded in the journal, date, customer name, and account classification. Check the pricing, extensions, and footings. Examine underlying documents for indication of internal verification. c. bill of lading and test for customer name, product description, quantity, and date. d. duplicate sales order and test for customer name, product description, quantity, date, and indication of internal verification. e. customer order and test for customer name, product description, quantity, date, and credit approval.	
14. Trace recorded sales from the sales journal to the file of supporting documents, which includes a duplicate sales invoice, bill of lading, sales order, and customer order.	

Note: Random selection and statistical sampling are not applicable for the nine general audit procedures in Figure 14-6 (p. 467). Advanced statistical techniques, such as regression analysis, can be applicable for analysis of the results of analytical procedures. Except for audit procedure 18, random selection may be possible for cash receipt procedures 15 through 21. Random selection can also be used for procedure 2.

sampling. Audit sampling can be used for the remaining three procedures. Audit sampling generally applies to manual controls. Automated controls can be tested using the computer assisted auditing techniques described in Chapter 12. Table 15-2 indicates the audit procedures for the sales cycle for Hillsburg Hardware Co. where audit sampling is appropriate.

Define Attributes and Exception Conditions

When audit sampling is used, auditors must carefully define the characteristics (attributes) being tested and the exception conditions. Unless each attribute is carefully defined in advance, the staff person who performs the audit procedures will have no guidelines to identify exceptions.

Attributes of interest and exception conditions for audit sampling are taken directly from the auditor's audit procedures. Table 15-3 (p. 492) shows nine attributes of interest and exception conditions taken from audit procedures 12 through 14 in the audit of Hillsburg's billing function. Samples of sales invoices will be used to verify these attributes. The absence of the attribute for any sample item will be an exception for that attribute. Both missing documents and immaterial misstatements result in exceptions unless the auditor specifically states otherwise in the exception conditions.

Define the Population

The population is those items about which the auditor wishes to generalize. Auditors can define the population to include any items they want, but when they select the

TABLE 15-3	Attributes Defined—Tests of Hillsburg Hardware Co.'s Billing Function
Attribute	**Exception Condition**
1. Existence of the sales invoice number in the sales journal (procedure 12).	No record of sales invoice number in the sales journal.
2. Amount and other data in the master file agree with sales journal entry (procedure 13a).	The amount recorded in the master file differs from the amount recorded in the sales journal.
3. Amount and other data on the duplicate sales invoice agree with the sales journal entry (procedure 13b).	Customer name and account number on the invoice differ from the information recorded in the sales journal.
4. Evidence that pricing, extensions, and footings are checked (initials and correct amounts) (procedure 13b).	Lack of initials indicating verification of pricing, extensions, and footings.
5. Quantity and other data on the bill of lading agree with the duplicate sales invoice and sales journal (procedure 13c).	Quantity of goods shipped differs from quantity on the duplicate sales invoice.
6. Quantity and other data on the sales order agree with the duplicate sales invoice (procedure 13d).	Quantity on the sales order differs from the quantity on the duplicate sales invoice.
7. Quantity and other data on the customer order agree with the duplicate sales invoice (procedure 13e).	Product number and description on the customer order differ from information on the duplicate sales invoice.
8. Credit is approved (procedure 13e).	Lack of initials indicating credit approval.
9. For recorded sales in the sales journal, the file of supporting documents includes a duplicate sales invoice, bill of lading, sales order, and customer order (procedure 14).	Bill of lading is not attached to the duplicate sales invoice and the customer order.

sample, it must be selected from the entire population as it has been defined. The auditor should test the population for completeness and detail tie-in before a sample is selected to ensure that all population items are subjected to sample selection.

The auditor may generalize *only* about that population that has been sampled. For example, when performing tests of controls and substantive tests of sales transactions, the auditor generally defines the population as all recorded sales invoices for the year. If the auditor samples from only one month's transactions, it is invalid to draw conclusions about the invoices for the entire year.

The auditor must carefully define the population in advance, consistent with the objectives of the audit tests. In some cases, it may be necessary to define separate populations for different audit procedures. For example, in the audit of the sales and collection cycle for Hillsburg Hardware Co., the direction of testing in audit procedures 12 through 14 in Table 15-2 (p. 491) proceeds from sales invoices in the sales journal to source documentation. In contrast, the direction of testing for audit procedures 10 and 11 proceeds from the shipping documents to the sales journal. Thus, the auditor defines two populations—a population of sales invoices in the sales journal and a population of shipping documents.

Define the Sampling Unit

The sampling unit is defined by the auditor based on the definition of the population and objective of the audit test. The sampling unit is the physical unit that corresponds to the random numbers the auditor generates. It is often helpful to think of the sampling unit as the starting point for doing the audit tests. For the sales and collection cycle, the sampling unit is typically a sales invoice or shipping document number. For example, if the auditor wants to test the occurrence of sales, the appropriate sampling unit is sales invoices recorded in the sales journal. If the objective is to determine whether the quantity of the goods described on the customer's order is accurately shipped and billed, the auditor can define the sampling unit as the customer's order, the shipping document, or the duplicate sales invoice, because the direction of the audit test doesn't matter for this audit procedure.

Audit procedure 14 in Table 15-2 is a test for the occurrence of recorded sales. What is the appropriate sampling unit? It is the duplicate sales invoice. Is the appropriate sampling unit for audit procedure 11 the shipping document? Yes, because this tests that existing sales are recorded (completeness). Either the duplicate sales invoice or the shipping document is appropriate for audit procedures 13a through 13e because these are all nondirectional tests.

To perform audit procedures 12 through 14, the auditor will define the sampling unit as the duplicate sales invoice. Audit procedures 10 and 11 will have to be tested separately using a sample of shipping documents.

Specify the Tolerable Exception Rate

Establishing the **tolerable exception rate (TER)** for each attribute requires an auditor's professional judgment. TER represents the highest exception rate the auditor will permit in the control being tested and still be willing to conclude the control is operating effectively (and/or the rate of monetary misstatements in the transactions is acceptable). For example, assume that the auditor decides that TER for attribute 8 in Table 15-3 is 9 percent. That means that the auditor has decided that even if 9 percent of the duplicate sales invoices are not approved for credit, the credit approval control is still effective in terms of the assessed control risk included in the audit plan.

When determining TER, the auditor considers the degree of reliance to be placed on the control and the significance of the control to the audit. If only one internal control is used to support a low control risk assessment for an objective, TER will be lower for the attribute than if multiple controls are used to support a low control risk assessment for the same objective. Control deviations increase the risk of material misstatements in the accounting records, but do not necessarily result in misstatements. For example, a disbursement that does not have evidence of proper approval may have been properly authorized and recorded. For this reason, the tolerable rate of deviation for tests of controls is normally higher than the comparable tolerable rate of exception for monetary misstatements.

TER can have a significant impact on sample size. A larger sample size is needed for a low TER than for a high TER. For example, a larger sample size is needed for the test of credit approval (attribute 8) if the TER is decreased from 9 percent to 6 percent. Since a lower TER is used for significant account balances, the auditor requires a larger sample size to gather sufficient evidence about the effectiveness of the control or absence of monetary misstatements.

Most auditors use some type of template to document each sampling application. Figure 15-2 (p. 494) shows one example of a commonly used form. Notice that the top part of the form includes a definition of the objective, the population, and the sampling unit.

Auditors determine the TER for each attribute being tested in audit procedures 12 through 14 in Table 15-3 by deciding what exception rate is material. As Figure 15-2, indicates:

- For attribute 1, the failure to record a sales invoice would be highly significant, so the lowest TER (4 percent) is chosen.
- For attributes 2-5, the incorrect billing to a customer and recording the transaction is potentially significant, but no misstatement is likely to be for the full amount of the invoice. As a result, the auditor chose a 5 percent TER for each of these attributes.
- Attributes 6-9 have higher TERs because they are of less importance in the audit.

FIGURE 15-2 **Sampling Data Sheet: Tests of Hillsburg Hardware Co.'s Billing Function**

Client: Hillsburg Hardware **Year-end:** 12/31/16
Audit Area: Tests of Controls and Substantive Tests of Transactions— Billing Function **Pop. size:** 5,764

Define the objective(s): Examine duplicate sales invoices and related documents to determine whether the system has functioned as intended and as described in the audit program.

Define the population precisely (including stratification, if any): Sales invoices for the period 1/1/16 to 10/31/16. First invoice number = 3689. Last invoice number = 9452.

Define the sampling unit, organization of population items, and random selection procedures: Sales invoice number, recorded in the sales journal sequentially; computer generation of random numbers.

	Planned Audit				Actual Results			
Description of Attributes	EPER	TER	ARO	Initial sample size	Sample size	Number of exceptions	Sample exception rate	Calculated Allowance for Sampling Risk (TER–SER)
1. Existence of the sales invoice number in the sales journal (procedure 12).	0	4	Low	75				
2. Amount and other data in the master file agree with sales journal entry (procedure 13a).	1	5	Low	100				
3. Amount and other data on the duplicate sales invoice agree with the sales journal entry (procedure 13b).	1	5	Low	100				
4. Evidence that pricing, extensions, and footings are checked (initials and correct amounts) (procedure 13b).	1	5	Low	100				
5. Quantity and other data on the bill of lading agree with the duplicate sales invoice and sales journal (procedure 13c).	1	5	Low	100				
6. Quantity and other data on the sales order agree with the duplicate sales invoice (procedure 13d).	1	7	Low	65				
7. Quantity and other data on the customer order agree with the duplicate sales invoice (procedure 13e).	1.5	9	Low	50				
8. Credit is approved (procedure 13e).	1.5	9	Low	50				
9. For recorded sales in the sales journal, the file of supporting documents includes a duplicate sales invoice, bill of lading, sales order, and customer order (procedure 14).	1	7	Low	65				

Intended use of sampling results:

1. Effect on Audit Plan:

2. Recommendations to Management:

Specify Acceptable Risk of Overreliance

Whenever auditors take a sample, they risk making incorrect conclusions about the population. The risk that the auditor concludes that controls are more effective than they actually are is the risk of overreliance. The risk of underreliance is the risk that the auditor will erroneously conclude that the controls are less effective than they actually are. Underreliance affects the efficiency of the audit. The incorrect conclusion that a control is ineffective may lead to an unnecessary increase in assessed control risk and substantive tests. In contrast, overreliance on a control impacts the effectiveness of the audit, because reliance on an ineffective control leads to an inappropriate reduction in substantive tests.

Auditors are normally more concerned with the risk of overreliance because it impacts the effectiveness of the audit. The **acceptable risk of overreliance (ARO)** measures the risk the auditor is willing to take of accepting a control as effective (or a rate of misstatements as tolerable) when the true population exception rate is greater than TER.

ARO represents the auditor's measure of sampling risk. Assume that TER is 6 percent, ARO is high, and the true population exception rate is 8 percent. The control in this case is not acceptable because the true exception rate of 8 percent exceeds TER. The auditor, of course, does not know the true population exception rate. The ARO of high means that the auditor is willing to take a fairly substantial risk of concluding that the control is effective after all testing is completed, even when it is ineffective. If the control were found to be effective in this illustration, the auditor would have overrelied on the system of internal control (used a lower assessed control risk than was justified).

In choosing the appropriate ARO for each attribute, auditors must use their best judgment. Their main consideration is the extent to which they plan to reduce assessed control risk as a basis for the extent of tests of details of balances. Auditors normally assess ARO at a lower level when auditing an accelerated filer public company because the auditor needs greater assurance that the internal controls are effective to support the opinion on internal control over financial reporting. In audits of non-accelerated filers and private companies, the appropriate ARO and extent of tests of controls depend on assessed control risk. For audits where there is extensive reliance on internal control, control risk will be assessed as low and therefore ARO will also be assessed as low. Conversely, if the auditor plans to rely on internal controls only to a limited extent, control risk will be assessed as high and so will ARO.

For nonstatistical sampling, it is common for auditors to use ARO of high, medium, or low instead of a percentage. For statistical sampling, it is common for auditors to use a percent, such as 5% or 10%. A low ARO implies that the tests of controls are important and will correspond to a low assessed control risk and reduced substantive tests of details of balances. As summarized in Figure 15-2, ARO for the audit of the billing function at Hillsburg Hardware Co. is assessed as low for all attributes, because it is an accelerated filer public company and the auditor's tests of controls must provide a basis for the opinion on internal control over financial reporting. As a result, the auditor requires a low risk of overrelying on controls. Stated another way, the auditor needs greater assurance and therefore a larger sample size to support the lower risk of overreliance.

Like for TER, there is an inverse relationship between ARO and planned sample size. If the auditor reduces ARO from high to low, planned sample size must be increased. ARO represents the auditor's risk of incorrectly accepting the control as effective, and a larger sample size is required to lower this risk.

The auditor can establish different TER and ARO levels for different attributes of an audit test, depending on the importance of the attribute and related control. For example, auditors commonly use higher TER and ARO levels for tests of credit approval than for tests of the occurrence of duplicate sales invoices and bills of lading. This makes sense because the exceptions for the latter are likely to have a more direct impact on the correctness of the financial statements than the former.

Tables 15-4 and 15-5 on the following page present illustrative guidelines for establishing TER and ARO. The guidelines should not be interpreted as representing broad professional standards. However, they are typical of the types of guidelines CPA firms issue to their staff.

Estimate the Population Exception Rate

Auditors should make an advance estimate of the population exception rate to plan the appropriate sample size. If the **estimated population exception rate (EPER)** is low, a relatively small sample size will satisfy the auditor's tolerable exception rate, because a less precise estimate is required.

Auditors often use the preceding year's audit results to estimate EPER. If prior-year results are not available, or if they are considered unreliable, the auditor can take a small preliminary sample of the current year's population for this purpose. It is not critical that the estimate be precise because the current year's sample exception rate

TABLE 15-4 Guidelines for ARO and TER for Nonstatistical Sampling: Tests of Controls

Planned Reduction in Substantive Tests of Details of Balances	Judgment	Guideline
Assessed control risk. Consider: Need to issue a separate report on internal control over financial reporting for accelerated filer public companies Nature, extent, and timing of substantive tests (extensive planned substantive tests relate to higher assessed control risk and vice versa) Quality of evidence available for tests of controls (a lower quality of evidence available results in a higher assessed control risk and vice versa)	• Lowest assessed control risk • Moderate assessed control risk • Higher assessed control risk • 100% assessed control risk	• ARO of low • ARO of medium • ARO of high • ARO is not applicable
Significance of the transactions and related account balances that the internal controls are intended to affect	• Highly significant balances • Significant balances • Less significant balances	• TER of 4% • TER of 5% • TER of 6%

Note: The guidelines should recognize that there may be variations in AROs based on audit considerations. The guidelines above are the most conservative that should be followed.

TABLE 15-5 Guidelines for ARO and TER for Nonstatistical Sampling: Substantive Tests of Transactions

Planned Reduction in Substantive Tests of Details of Balances	Results of Understanding Internal Control and Tests of Controls	ARO for Substantive Tests of Transactions	TER for Substantive Tests of Transactions
Large	Excellent[1] Good Not good	High Medium Low	Percent or amount based on materiality considerations for related accounts
Moderate	Excellent[1] Good Not good	High Medium Medium-low	Percent or amount based on materiality considerations for related accounts
Small[2]	Excellent[1] Good Not good	High Medium-high Medium	Percent or amount based on materiality considerations for related accounts

Note: The guidelines should also recognize that there may be variations in AROs based on audit considerations. The guidelines above are the most conservative that should be followed.

[1]In this situation, both internal control and evidence about it are good. Substantive tests of transactions are least likely to be performed in this situation.

[2]In this situation, little emphasis is being placed on internal controls. Neither tests of controls nor substantive tests of transactions are likely in this situation.

is ultimately used to estimate the population characteristics. If a preliminary sample is used, it can be included in the total sample, as long as appropriate sample selection procedures are followed. In the Hillsburg Hardware Co. audit, the estimated population exception rates for the attributes in Figure 15-2 (p. 494) are based on the previous year's results, modified slightly to account for the change in personnel.

Determine the Initial Sample Size

Four factors determine the **initial sample size** for audit sampling: population size, TER, ARO, and EPER. Population size is not a significant factor and typically can be ignored, especially for large populations. Auditors using nonstatistical sampling decide the sample size using professional judgment rather than using a statistical formula. Once the three major factors affecting sample size have been determined, the auditor can decide an initial sample size. It is called an initial sample size because the exceptions in the actual sample must be evaluated before auditors can decide whether the sample is sufficiently large to achieve the objectives of the tests.

Sensitivity of Sample Size to a Change in the Factors To understand the concepts underlying sampling in auditing, you need to understand the effect of increasing or decreasing any of the four factors that determine sample size, while the other factors are held constant. Table 15-6 shows the effect on sample size of independently increasing each factor. The opposite effect will occur for decreasing each factor.

A combination of two factors has the greatest effect on sample size: TER minus EPER. The difference between the two factors is the *precision* of the initial sample

TABLE 15-6 Effect on Sample Size of Changing Factors

Type of Change	Effect on Initial Sample Size
Increase acceptable risk of overreliance	Decrease
Increase tolerable exception rate	Decrease
Increase estimated population exception rate	Increase
Increase population size	Increase (minor effect)

estimate. A smaller precision, which is called a more precise estimate, requires a larger sample. At one extreme, assume TER is 4% and EPER is 3%. In this case, precision is 1%, which will result in a large sample size. Now assume TER is 8% and EPER is zero, for an 8% precision. In this case the sample size can be small and still give the auditor confidence that the actual exception rate is less than 8%, assuming no exceptions are found when auditing the sample.

Figure 15-2 summarizes the different sample sizes selected for testing attributes 1 through 9 for the Hillsburg audit. The largest sample (a size of 100) is selected for tests of attributes 2 through 5, because of the degree of precision required. For those attributes, the difference between TER and EPER is smallest, thus requiring a larger sample size than attributes 6 through 9. Although the difference between TER and EPER for attribute 1 is the same as that for attributes 2 through 5, the estimated population exception rate of zero justifies a smaller sample of 75 items. Because a less precise estimate is needed (TER minus EPER is larger) for attributes 7 and 8, a sample size of only 50 items is needed.

Select the Sample

After auditors determine the initial sample size for the audit sampling application, they must choose the items in the population to include in the sample. Auditors can choose the sample using any of the probabilistic or nonprobabilistic methods we discussed earlier in this chapter. To minimize the possibility of the client altering the sample items, the auditor should not inform the client too far in advance of the sample items selected. The auditor should also control the sample after the client provides the documents. Several additional sample items may be selected as extras to replace any voided items in the original sample.

The random selection for the Hillsburg audit procedures is straightforward except for the different sample sizes needed for different attributes. To overcome this problem, auditors can select a random sample of 50 for use on all nine attributes, followed by another sample of 15 for all attributes except attributes 7 and 8, an additional 10 for attributes 1 through 5, and 25 more for attributes 2 through 5.

SAMPLE SIZES FOR SMALL POPULATIONS AND INFREQUENTLY OPERATING CONTROLS

Many important controls, such as controls over the year-end closing process, may be performed only once a year. Other controls, such as reconciliations and exception reports, may operate on a weekly or monthly basis. The AICPA *Audit Sampling* Audit Guide provides guidance for testing the operating effectiveness of small populations.

Control Frequency and Population Size	Items to Test
Quarterly (4)	2
Monthly (12)	2–4
Semimonthly (24)	3–8
Weekly (52)	5–9

Sample sizes near the low end of the range are appropriate for control reliance in normal financial statement audit situations. Sample sizes near or above the upper range are appropriate where other sources of evidence are less persuasive, where there are concerns about the operations of the control, when controls have changed, or where deficiencies have been experienced in the past. Auditors can use sampling parameters such as risk and the tolerable exception rate to determine sample sizes when the test is the sole source of evidence about the effectiveness of the control and a high level of audit evidence is desired.

Source: Based on *Audit Sampling* Audit Guide, American Institute of Certified Public Accountants, 2014.

As Figure 15-4 (p. 500) illustrates, in the Hillsburg audit, the results for attributes 2, 4, 5, and 8 were unacceptable. Because the sales transactions tested at Hillsburg represented transactions recorded only through October 31, 2016, timely communication of these deficiencies may allow Hillsburg management to correct the noted deficiencies in time for the auditor to test the corrected controls before year-end for purposes of auditing internal control over financial reporting.

In Figure 15-5 (p. 501), the last column summarizes the follow-up actions the auditor plans to do regardless of whether the control deficiencies were corrected. No follow-up actions are required to address the exception noted for attribute 6, given the large difference between SER and TER. The conclusions reached about each attribute are also documented at the bottom of Figure 15-4.

Documentation and Evidence Planning

The auditor needs to retain adequate records of the procedures performed, the methods used to select the sample and perform the tests, the results found in the tests, and the conclusions reached. Documentation is needed for both statistical and nonstatistical sampling to evaluate the combined results of all tests and to defend the audit if the need arises. Figures 15-2 through 15-6 illustrate the type of documentation commonly found in practice.

Figure 15-6 (p. 504) illustrates the evidence-planning worksheet used in the audit of Hillsburg Hardware to decide the tests of balances for accounts receivable. After completing tests of controls and substantive tests of transactions, the auditor should complete rows 3 through 7 of the worksheet. (You may recall that rows 1 and 2 were completed in Chapter 9.) Rows 3 through 5 document control risk for sales, cash receipts, and additional controls. The control risk assessments in Figure 15-6 are the same as the preliminary assessments in the control risk matrices for Hillsburg Hardware in earlier chapters on pages 373 and 466, with the following modifications:

- Control risk is high for the accuracy objective for sales because of the unsatisfactory results for attribute 4 (procedure 13b).
- Control risk is high for the realizable value objective for accounts receivable based on the results for attribute 8 related to credit approval for sales transactions (procedure 13e).
- The occurrence (completeness) objective for cash receipts relates to the completeness (existence) objective for accounts receivable.

Finally, note in Figure 15-6 that all substantive tests of transactions results were satisfactory except for the accuracy and cutoff objectives for sales. Refer back to Figure 15-5 and you can see that:

- Substantive tests of transactions results for the accuracy objective were only fair because of exceptions found for attribute 2 (procedure 13a).
- Results were unacceptable for the cutoff objective because of unsatisfactory results for attribute 5 (procedure 13c).

All of the steps involved in nonstatistical sampling are summarized in Figure 15-7 (p. 505). Although this figure deals with nonstatistical sampling, the 14 steps in the figure also apply to statistical sampling, which is covered next.

STATISTICAL AUDIT SAMPLING

OBJECTIVE 15-6

Define and describe attributes sampling and a sampling distribution.

The statistical sampling method most commonly used for tests of controls and substantive tests of transactions is **attributes sampling**. (When the term *attributes sampling* is used in this text, it refers to attributes statistical sampling. Nonstatistical sampling also has attributes, which are the characteristics being tested for in the population, but attributes sampling is a statistical method.)

FIGURE 15-6 Evidence-Planning Worksheet to Decide Tests of Details of Balances for Hillsburg Hardware Co.—Accounts Receivable

	Detail tie-in	Existence	Completeness	Accuracy	Classification	Cutoff	Realizable value	Rights
Acceptable audit risk	Medium	Medium	Medium	Medium	Medium	Medium	Medium	Medium
Inherent risk	Low	Medium	Low	Low	Low	Medium	Medium	Low
Control risk—Sales	Low	Medium	Low	High	Low	Medium	High	Not applicable
Control risk—Cash receipts	Low	Medium	Low	Low	Low	Low	Not applicable	Not applicable
Control risk—Additional controls	None	None	None	None	None	None	None	Low
Substantive tests of transactions—Sales	Good results	Good results	Good results	Fair results	Good results	Unacceptable results	Not applicable	Not applicable
Substantive tests of transactions—Cash receipts	Good results	Good results	Good results	Good results	Good results	Good results	Not applicable	Not applicable
Substantive analytical procedures								
Planned detection risk for tests of details of balances								
Planned audit evidence for tests of details of balances								

Performance materiality $265,000

Differences Between Attributes Sampling and Nonstatistical Sampling

The application of attributes sampling for tests of controls and substantive tests of transactions has far more similarities to nonstatistical sampling than differences. The same 14 steps are used for both approaches, and the terminology is essentially the same. The main differences are (1) the calculation of initial sample sizes developed from statistical probability distributions using tables or audit software and (2) the calculation of estimated upper exception rates using audit software or tables similar to those for calculating sample sizes.

Sampling Distribution

Auditors base their statistical inferences on sampling distributions. A **sampling distribution** is a frequency distribution of the results of all possible samples of a

FIGURE 15-7 Summary of Audit Sampling Steps

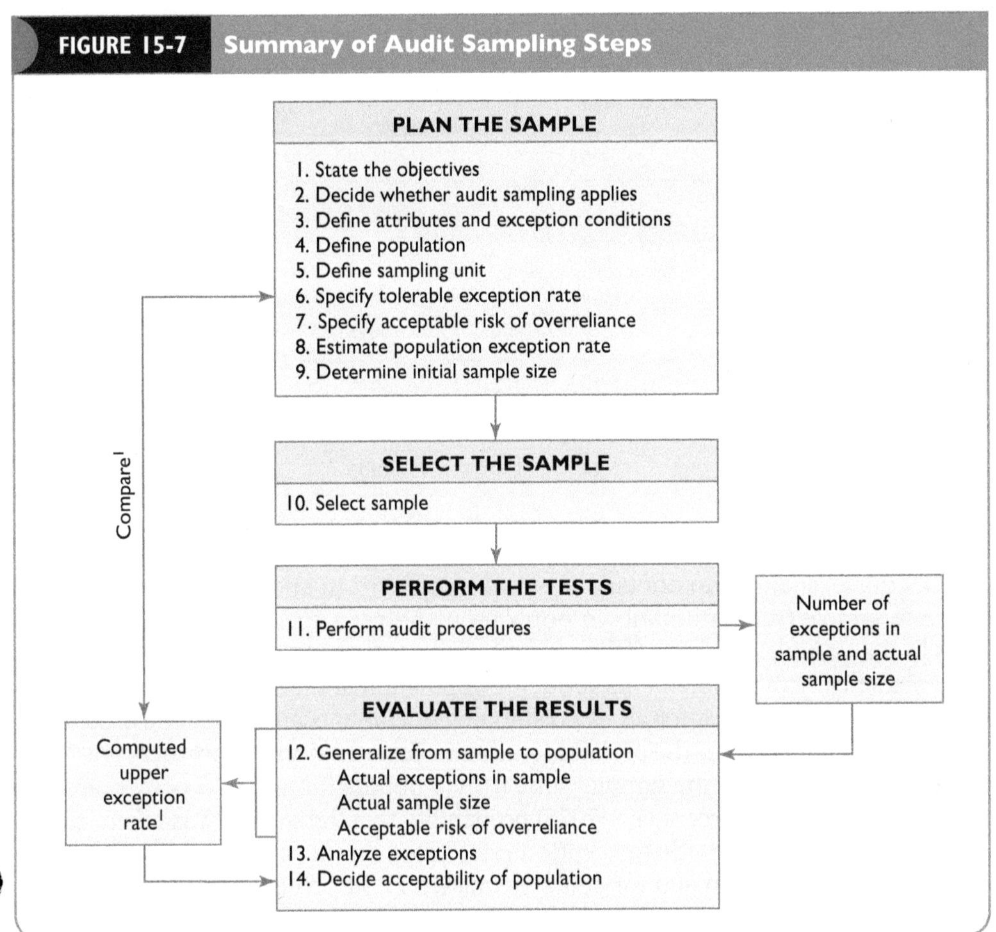

[1]Many auditors using nonstatistical methods calculate tolerable exception rate minus sample exception rate and evaluate whether the difference is sufficiently large.

specified size that could be obtained from a population containing some specific characteristics. Sampling distributions allow the auditor to make probability statements about the likely representativeness of any sample that is in the distribution. Attributes sampling is based on the binomial distribution, in which each possible sample in the population has one of two possible values, such as yes/no, black/white, or control deviation/no control deviation.

Assume that in a population of sales invoices, 5 percent have no shipping documents attached as required by the client's internal controls. If the auditor takes a sample of 50 sales invoices, how many will be found that have no shipping documents? Simple multiplication would estimate 2.5 exceptions (5% of 50), but that number is impossible because there is no such thing as half an exception. In reality, the sample could contain no exceptions or even more than ten. A binomial-based sampling distribution tells us the probability of each possible number of exceptions occurring. Table 15-7 illustrates the sampling distribution for the example population with a sample of 50 items from a very large population and an exception rate of 5 percent. To calculate the probability of obtaining a sample with at least one exception, subtract the probability of no exceptions occurring from 1 (100 percent). By doing so, we find the likelihood of finding a sample with at least one exception is 1 – .0769, or 92.31 percent.

Each population exception rate and sample size has a unique sampling distribution. The distribution for a sample size of 100 from a population with a 5 percent exception rate differs from the previous example, as will the distribution for a sample of 50 from a population with a 3 percent exception rate.

TABLE 15-7	Probability of Each Exception Rate—5 Percent Population Exception Rate and Sample Size of 50		
Number of Exceptions	**Percentage of Exception**	**Probability**	**Cumulative Probability**
0	0	.0769	.0769
1	2	.2025	.2794
2	4	.2611	.5405
3	6	.2199	.7604
4	8	.1360	.8964
5	10	.0656	.9620
6	12	.0260	.9880
7	14	.0120	1.0000

Of course, auditors do not take repeated samples from known populations. They take one sample from an unknown population and get a specific number of exceptions in that sample. But knowledge about sampling distributions enables auditors to make statistically valid statements about the population. If the auditor selects a sample of 50 sales invoices to test for attached shipping documents and finds one exception, the auditor could examine the probability table in Table 15-7 and know there is a 20.25 percent probability that the sample came from a population with a 5 percent exception rate, and a 79.75 percent (1 – .2025) probability that the sample was taken from a population having some other exception rate. Based on the cumulative probabilities column in Table 15-7, an auditor could estimate a 27.94 percent probability that the sample came from a population with more than a 5 percent exception rate and a 72.06 percent (1 – .2794) probability that the sample was taken from a population having an exception rate of 5 percent or less. Because it is also possible to calculate the probability distributions for other population exception rates, auditors use these to draw statistical conclusions about the unknown population being sampled. These sampling distributions are the basis for the tables and sampling software used by auditors for attributes sampling.

APPLICATION OF ATTRIBUTES SAMPLING

OBJECTIVE 15-7

Use attributes sampling in tests of controls and substantive tests of transactions.

The steps discussed for nonstatistical sampling are equally applicable to attributes sampling. In this section, we'll focus on the differences between the two sampling methods.

Plan the Sample

1. *State the objectives of the audit test.* Same for attributes and nonstatistical sampling.
2. *Decide whether audit sampling applies.* Same for attributes and nonstatistical sampling.
3. *Define attributes and exception conditions.* Same for attributes and nonstatistical sampling.
4. *Define the population.* Same for attributes and nonstatistical sampling.
5. *Define the sampling unit.* Same for attributes and nonstatistical sampling.
6. *Specify the tolerable exception rate.* Same for attributes and nonstatistical sampling.
7. *Specify acceptable risk of overreliance.* The concepts of specifying this risk are the same for both statistical and nonstatistical sampling, but the method of quantification is usually different. For nonstatistical sampling, most auditors use low, medium, or high acceptable risk, whereas auditors using attributes sampling assign a

specific amount, such as 10 percent or 5 percent risk. The methods differ because auditors need to evaluate results statistically.

8. *Estimate the population exception rate.* Same for attributes and nonstatistical sampling.
9. *Determine the initial sample size.* Four factors determine the initial sample size for both statistical and nonstatistical sampling: population size, TER, ARO, and EPER. In attributes sampling, auditors determine sample size by using audit software with a sampling module or tables developed from statistical formulas.

If auditors use audit software to determine sample size, they enter values for population size, TER, ARO, and EPER and the software returns the appropriate sample size based on sampling distributions as discussed above. Alternatively, auditors can use tables such as those shown in Table 15-8 (p. 508), which come from the AICPA *Audit Sampling* Audit Guide. The top one shows sample sizes for a 5 percent ARO, while the bottom one is for a 10 percent ARO.

Use of the Tables When auditors use the tables to determine initial sample size, they follow these four steps:

i. Select the table corresponding to the ARO.
ii. Locate the TER at the top of the table.
iii. Locate the EPER in the far left column.
iv. Read down the appropriate TER column until it intersects with the appropriate EPER row. The number at the intersection is the initial sample size.

Using the Hillsburg Hardware Co. example, assume that an auditor is willing to reduce assessed control risk for the agreement between sales orders and invoices if the number of exceptions in the population (attribute 6 in Table 15-3 on p. 492) does not exceed 7 percent (TER), at a 5 percent ARO. On the basis of past experience, the auditor sets EPER at 1 percent. On the 5 percent ARO table, locate the 7 percent TER column, and read down the column until it intersects with the 1 percent EPER row. The initial sample size is 66.

Is 66 a large enough sample size for this audit? It is not possible to decide until after the tests have been performed. If the actual exception rate in the sample turns out to be greater than 1 percent, the auditor will be unsure of the effectiveness of the control. The reasons will become apparent in the following sections.

Effect of Population Size In the preceding discussion, auditors ignored the size of the population in determining the initial sample size. Statistical theory shows that in populations where attributes sampling applies, population size is a minor consideration in determining sample size. Because most auditors use attributes sampling for reasonably large populations, the reduction of sample size for smaller populations is ignored here.

Select the Sample and Perform the Audit Procedures

10. *Select the sample.* The only difference in sample selection for statistical and nonstatistical sampling is the requirement that probabilistic methods must be used for statistical sampling. Either simple random or systematic sampling is used for attributes sampling. Audit or spreadsheet software can generate a sample using either of these probabilistic methods.
11. *Perform the audit procedures.* Same for attributes and nonstatistical sampling.

Evaluate the Results

12. *Generalize from the sample to the population.* For attributes sampling, the auditor calculates the computed upper exception rate (CUER, also referred to as upper precision limit) at a specified ARO, again using special computer programs or tables developed from statistical formulas. The calculations are illustrated in tables like Table 15-9 (p. 509). These are "one-sided tables," meaning they represent the upper exception rate for a given ARO.

TABLE 15-8 Determining Sample Size for Attributes Sampling*

5 PERCENT RISK OF OVERRELIANCE

Estimated Population Exception Rate (in Percent)	Tolerable Exception Rate (in Percent)										
	2	3	4	5	6	7	8	9	10	15	20
0.00	149	99	74	59	49	42	36	32	29	19	14
0.25	236	157	117	93	78	66	58	51	46	30	22
0.50	313	157	117	93	78	66	58	51	46	30	22
0.75	386	208	117	93	78	66	58	51	46	30	22
1.00		257	156	93	78	66	58	51	46	30	22
1.25		303	156	124	78	66	58	51	46	30	22
1.50		392	192	124	103	66	58	51	46	30	22
1.75			227	153	103	88	77	51	46	30	22
2.00			294	181	127	88	77	68	46	30	22
2.25			390	208	127	88	77	68	61	30	22
2.50				234	150	109	77	68	61	30	22
2.75				286	173	109	95	68	61	30	22
3.00				361	195	129	95	84	61	30	22
3.25				458	238	148	112	84	61	30	22
3.50					280	167	112	84	76	40	22
3.75					341	185	129	100	76	40	22
4.00					421	221	146	100	89	40	22
5.00						478	240	158	116	40	30
6.00								266	179	50	30
7.00									298	68	37

10 PERCENT RISK OF OVERRELIANCE

Estimated Population Exception Rate (in Percent)	Tolerable Exception Rate (in Percent)										
	2	3	4	5	6	7	8	9	10	15	20
0.00	114	76	57	45	38	32	28	25	22	15	11
0.25	194	129	96	77	64	55	48	42	38	25	18
0.50	194	129	96	77	64	55	48	42	38	25	18
0.75	265	129	96	77	64	55	48	42	38	25	18
1.00	398	176	96	77	64	55	48	42	38	25	18
1.25		221	132	77	64	55	48	42	38	25	18
1.50		265	132	105	64	55	48	42	38	25	18
1.75		390	166	105	88	55	48	42	38	25	18
2.00			198	132	88	75	48	42	38	25	18
2.25			262	132	88	75	65	42	38	25	18
2.50			353	158	110	75	65	58	38	25	18
2.75			471	209	132	94	65	58	52	25	18
3.00				258	132	94	65	58	52	25	18
3.25				306	153	113	82	58	52	25	18
3.50				400	194	113	82	73	52	25	18
3.75					235	131	98	73	52	25	18
4.00					274	149	98	73	65	25	18
5.00						318	160	115	78	34	18
6.00							349	182	116	43	25
7.00								385	199	52	25
8.00									424	60	25

Notes: 1. This table assumes a large population. 2. Tables do not include higher estimated population exception rates, and sample sizes over 500 are not reported. 3. Sample sizes are the same in certain columns even when estimated population exception rates differ because of the method of constructing the tables. Sample sizes are calculated for attributes sampling by using the expected number of exceptions in the population, but auditors can deal more conveniently with estimated population exception rates. For example, in the 15 percent column for tolerable exception rate, at an ARO of 5 percent, the initial sample size for most EPERs is 30. One exception, divided by a sample size of 30, is 3.3 percent. Therefore, for all EPERs greater than zero but less than 3.3 percent, the initial sample size is the same.

*Source: Data from AICPA *Audit Sampling* Audit Guide, March 1, 2014 (www.aicpa.org).

TABLE 15-9 Evaluating Sample Results Using Attributes Sampling*

5 PERCENT RISK OF OVERRELIANCE											
	Actual Number of Exceptions Found										
Sample Size	0	1	2	3	4	5	6	7	8	9	10
20	14.0	21.7	28.3	34.4	40.2	45.6	50.8	55.9	60.7	65.4	69.9
25	11.3	17.7	23.2	28.2	33.0	37.6	42.0	46.3	50.4	54.4	58.4
30	9.6	14.9	19.6	23.9	28.0	31.9	35.8	39.4	43.0	46.6	50.0
35	8.3	12.9	17.0	20.7	24.3	27.8	31.1	34.4	37.5	40.6	43.7
40	7.3	11.4	15.0	18.3	21.5	24.6	27.5	30.4	33.3	36.0	38.8
45	6.5	10.2	13.4	16.4	19.2	22.0	24.7	27.3	29.8	32.4	34.8
50	5.9	9.2	12.1	14.8	17.4	19.9	22.4	24.7	27.1	29.4	31.6
55	5.4	8.4	11.1	13.5	15.9	18.2	20.5	22.6	24.8	26.9	28.9
60	4.9	7.7	10.2	12.5	14.7	16.8	18.8	20.8	22.8	24.8	26.7
65	4.6	7.1	9.4	11.5	13.6	15.5	17.5	19.3	21.2	23.0	24.7
70	4.2	6.6	8.8	10.8	12.7	14.5	16.3	18.0	19.7	21.4	23.1
75	4.0	6.2	8.2	10.1	11.8	13.6	15.2	16.9	18.5	20.1	21.6
80	3.7	5.8	7.7	9.5	11.1	12.7	14.3	15.9	17.4	18.9	20.3
90	3.3	5.2	6.9	8.4	9.9	11.4	12.8	14.2	15.5	16.9	18.2
100	3.0	4.7	6.2	7.6	9.0	10.3	11.5	12.8	14.0	15.2	16.4
125	2.4	3.8	5.0	6.1	7.2	8.3	9.3	10.3	11.3	12.3	13.2
150	2.0	3.2	4.2	5.1	6.0	6.9	7.8	8.6	9.5	10.3	11.1
200	1.5	2.4	3.2	3.9	4.6	5.2	5.9	6.5	7.2	7.8	8.4
10 PERCENT RISK OF OVERRELIANCE											
	Actual Number of Exceptions Found										
Sample Size	0	1	2	3	4	5	6	7	8	9	10
20	10.9	18.1	24.5	30.5	36.1	41.5	46.8	51.9	56.8	61.6	66.2
25	8.8	14.7	20.0	24.9	29.5	34.0	38.4	42.6	46.8	50.8	54.8
30	7.4	12.4	16.8	21.0	24.9	28.8	32.5	36.2	39.7	43.2	46.7
35	6.4	10.7	14.5	18.2	21.6	24.9	28.2	31.4	34.5	37.6	40.6
40	5.6	9.4	12.8	16.0	19.0	22.0	24.9	27.7	30.5	33.2	35.9
45	5.0	8.4	11.4	14.3	17.0	19.7	22.3	24.8	27.3	29.8	32.2
50	4.6	7.6	10.3	12.9	15.4	17.8	20.2	22.5	24.7	27.0	29.2
55	4.2	6.9	9.4	11.8	14.1	16.3	18.4	20.5	22.6	24.6	26.7
60	3.8	6.4	8.7	10.8	12.9	15.0	16.9	18.9	20.8	22.7	24.6
65	3.5	5.9	8.0	10.0	12.0	13.9	15.7	17.5	19.3	21.0	22.8
70	3.3	5.5	7.5	9.3	11.1	12.9	14.6	16.3	18.0	19.6	21.2
75	3.1	5.1	7.0	8.7	10.4	12.1	13.7	15.2	16.8	18.3	19.8
80	2.9	4.8	6.6	8.2	9.8	11.3	12.8	14.3	15.8	17.2	18.7
90	2.6	4.3	5.9	7.3	8.7	10.1	11.5	12.8	14.1	15.4	16.7
100	2.3	3.9	5.3	6.6	7.9	9.1	10.3	11.5	12.7	13.9	15.0
125	1.9	3.1	4.3	5.3	6.3	7.3	8.3	9.3	10.2	11.2	12.1
150	1.6	2.6	3.6	4.4	5.3	6.1	7.0	7.8	8.6	9.4	10.1
200	1.2	2.0	2.7	3.4	4.0	4.6	5.3	5.9	6.5	7.1	7.6

Note: This table presents computed upper exception rates as percentages. Table assumes a large population. Sample sizes greater than 200 not shown.
*Source: Data from AICPA *Audit Sampling* Audit Guide, March 1, 2014 (www.aicpa.org).

Use of the Tables Use of tables to compute CUER involves four steps:

i. Select the table corresponding to the auditor's ARO. This ARO should be the same as the ARO used for determining the initial sample size.
ii. Locate the actual number of exceptions found in the audit tests at the top of the table.
iii. Locate the actual sample size in the far left column.
iv. Read down the appropriate actual number of exceptions column until it intersects with the appropriate sample size row. The number at the intersection is the CUER.

To use the evaluation table for Hillsburg Hardware, assume an actual sample size of 70 and one exception in attribute 6. Using an ARO of 5 percent, CUER equals 6.6 percent. In other words, the CUER for attribute 6 is 6.6 percent at a 5 percent ARO. Does this mean that if 100 percent of the population were tested, the true exception rate would be 6.6 percent? No, the true exception rate remains unknown. What this result means is this: if the auditor concludes that the true exception rate does not exceed 6.6 percent, there is a 95 percent probability that the conclusion is right and a 5 percent chance that it is wrong.

It is possible to have a sample size that is not equal to those provided for in the attributes sampling evaluation tables. When this occurs, it is common for auditors to interpolate to estimate the data points that fall between those listed in the table.

These tables assume a very large (infinite) population size, which results in a more conservative CUER than for smaller populations. As with sample size, the effect of population size on CUER is typically very small, so it is ignored.

13. *Analyze exceptions.* Same for attributes and nonstatistical sampling.
14. *Decide the acceptability of the population.* The methodology for deciding the acceptability of the population is similar for attributes and nonstatistical sampling. Because attributes sampling is a statistical sampling approach, it allows the auditor to quantify the allowance for sampling risk and the upper exception rate. For attributes sampling, the auditor compares CUER with TER for each attribute. Before the population can be considered acceptable, the CUER determined on the basis of the actual sample results must be *less than or equal to* TER when both are based on the same ARO. In our example, when the auditor specified a TER of 7 percent at a 5 percent ARO and the CUER was 6.6 percent, the requirements of the sample have been met. In this case, the control being tested can be used to reduce assessed control risk as planned, provided a careful analysis of the cause of exceptions does not indicate the possibility of a significant problem in an aspect of the control not previously considered. Recall that with nonstatistical sampling, the auditor cannot calculate CUER but instead compares TER with the sample exception rate (SER) and uses his or her judgment to decide whether the difference is sufficiently large.

    When the CUER is greater than the TER, it is necessary to take specific action. The four courses of action discussed for nonstatistical sampling are equally applicable to attributes sampling.

Figure 15-8 illustrates the sampling documentation completed for the tests of attributes 1 through 9 in Table 15-3 for Hillsburg Hardware Co. using attributes sampling. Notice that much of the information in Figure 15-8 is consistent with information presented in the nonstatistical sampling example illustrated in Figure 15-4 (p. 500). The key differences between Figures 15-4 and 15-8 are the auditor's judgment about ARO and the initial sample size determined when planning the audit, and the calculation of CUER using the actual test results. Notice that the ARO judgment is numerical (5 percent) in the attributes sampling application (Figure 15-8). The numerical judgment about ARO is considered along with the assessments of EPER and TER to determine the initial sample sizes for each attribute using Table 15-8 (p. 508). The CUER in Figure 15-8 is determined using Table 15-9 (p. 509) based on the sample exceptions identified and the actual sample size tested.

Need for Professional Judgment

A criticism occasionally leveled against statistical sampling is that it reduces the auditor's use of professional judgment. A comparison of the 14 steps discussed in this chapter for nonstatistical and attributes sampling shows that this criticism is unwarranted. For proper application, attributes sampling requires auditors to use professional judgment in most of the steps. To select the initial sample size, auditors depend primarily on TER and ARO, which require a high level of professional judgment, as well as EPER, which requires a careful estimate. Similarly, the final evaluation of the adequacy of the entire application of attributes sampling, including the adequacy of the sample size, must also be based on high-level professional judgment.

FIGURE 15-8 Attributes Sampling Data Sheet: Tests of Hillsburg Hardware Co.'s Billing Function

Client: Hillsburg Hardware
Audit Area: Tests of Controls and Substantive Tests of Transactions—Billing Function

Year-end: 12/31/16
Pop. size: 5,764

Define the objective(s): Examine duplicate sales invoices and related documents to determine whether the system has functioned as intended and as described in the audit program.

Define the population precisely (including stratification, if any): Sales invoices for the period 1/1/16 to 10/31/16. First invoice number = 3689. Last invoice number = 9452.

Define the sampling unit, organization of population items, and random selection procedures: Sales invoice number, recorded in the sales journal sequentially; computer generation of random numbers.

	Planned Audit				Actual Results			
Description of Attributes	EPER	TER	ARO	Initial sample size	Sample size	Number of exceptions	Sample exception rate	CUER
1. Existence of the sales invoice number in the sales journal (procedure 12).	0	4	5	74	75	0	0	4.0
2. Amount and other data in the master file agree with sales journal entry (procedure 13a).	1	5	5	93	100	2	2	6.2
3. Amount and other data on the duplicate sales invoice agree with the sales journal entry (procedure 13b).	1	5	5	93	100	0	0	3.0
4. Evidence that pricing, extensions, and footings are checked (initials and correct amounts) (procedure 13b).	1	5	5	93	100	10	10	16.4
5. Quantity and other data on the bill of lading agree with the duplicate sales invoice and sales journal (procedure 13c).	1	5	5	93	100	4	4	9.0
6. Quantity and other data on the sales order agree with the duplicate sales invoice (procedure 13d).	1	7	5	66	70	1	1.5	6.6
7. Quantity and other data on the customer order agree with the duplicate sales invoice (procedure 13e).	1.5	9	5	51	50	0	0	5.9
8. Credit is approved (procedure 13e).	1.5	9	5	51	50	10	20	31.6
9. For recorded sales in the sales journal, the file of supporting documents includes a duplicate sales invoice, bill of lading, sales order, and customer order (procedure 14).	1	7	5	66	65	0	0	4.6

Intended use of sampling results:

1. Effect on Audit Plan: Controls tested through attributes 1, 3, 6, 7, and 9 can be viewed as operating effectively given that TER equals or exceeds CUER. Additional emphasis is needed in confirmation, allowance for uncollectible accounts, cutoff tests, and price tests for the financial statement audit due to results of tests for attributes 2, 4, 5, and 8.

2. Effect on Report on Internal Control: CUER exceeds TER for attributes 2, 4, 5, and 8. These findings have been communicated to management to allow an opportunity for correction of the control deficiency to be made before year-end. If timely correction is made by management, the corrected controls will be tested before year-end for purposes of reporting on internal control over financial reporting.

3. Recommendations to Management: Each of the exceptions should be discussed with management. Specific recommendations are needed to correct the internal verification of sales invoices and to improve the approach to credit approvals.

CONCEPT CHECK

1. Explain what is meant by analysis of exceptions and explain its importance.
2. What are the steps of the audit sampling process that differ across statistical and nonstatistical sampling approaches? In what ways do they differ?

SUMMARY

In this chapter we described representative samples and discussed the differences between statistical and nonstatistical sampling and probabilistic and nonprobabilistic sample selection. We also described the 14 steps in sampling for exception rates used in tests of controls and substantive tests of transactions. Nonstatistical and statistical attributes sampling for exception rates were illustrated for the Hillsburg Hardware Co.

ESSENTIAL TERMS

Acceptable risk of overreliance (ARO)—the risk that the auditor is willing to take of accepting a control as effective or a rate of monetary misstatements as tolerable when the true population exception rate is greater than the tolerable exception rate

Attribute—the characteristic being tested for in the population

Attributes sampling—a statistical, probabilistic method of sample evaluation that results in an estimate of the proportion of items in a population containing a characteristic or attribute of interest

Audit sampling—testing less than 100 percent of a population for the purpose of making inferences about that population

Block sample selection—a nonprobabilistic method of sample selection in which items are selected in measured sequences

Computed upper exception rate (CUER)—the upper limit of the probable population exception rate; the highest exception rate in the population at a given ARO

Estimated population exception rate (EPER)—exception rate the auditor expects to find in the population before testing begins

Exception rate—the percent of items in a population that include deviations in prescribed controls or exceptions in monetary correctness

Haphazard sample selection—a nonprobabilistic method of sample selection in which items are chosen without regard to their size, source, or other distinguishing characteristics

Initial sample size—sample size determined by professional judgment (nonstatistical sampling) or by statistical tables (attributes sampling)

Nonprobabilistic sample selection—a method of sample selection in which the auditor uses professional judgment to select items from the population

Nonsampling risk—the risk that the auditor fails to identify existing exceptions in the sample; nonsampling risk (nonsampling error) is caused by failure to recognize exceptions and by inappropriate or ineffective audit procedures

Nonstatistical sampling—a sampling procedure that does not permit the numerical measurement of the sampling risk

Occurrence rate—see exception rate

Probabilistic sample selection—a method of selecting a sample such that each population item has a known probability of being included in the sample and the sample is selected by a random process

Random sample—a sample in which every possible combination of elements in the population has an equal chance of constituting the sample

Representative sample—a sample with characteristics the same as those of the population

Sample exception rate (SER)—number of exceptions in the sample divided by the sample size

Sampling distribution—a frequency distribution of the results of all possible samples of a specified size that could be obtained from a population containing some specific parameters

Sampling risk—risk of reaching an incorrect conclusion inherent in tests of less than the entire population because the sample is not representative of the population; sampling risk may be reduced by using an increased sample size and an appropriate method of selecting sample items from the population

Statistical sampling—the use of mathematical measurement techniques to calculate formal statistical results and quantify sampling risk

Systematic sample selection—a probabilistic method of sampling in which the auditor calculates an interval (the population size divided by the number of sample items desired) and selects the items for the sample based on the size of the interval and a randomly selected starting point between zero and the length of the interval

Tolerable exception rate (TER)—the exception rate that the auditor will permit in the population and still be willing to conclude the control is operating effectively and/or the amount of monetary misstatements in the transactions established during planning is acceptable

REVIEW QUESTIONS

15-1 (OBJECTIVE 15-1) Distinguish between sampling risk and nonsampling risk. How can each be reduced?

15-2 (OBJECTIVE 15-2) What are the three main phases of audit sampling? Are these phases the same for statistical and nonstatistical sampling methods?

15-3 (OBJECTIVE 15-2) Explain the difference between probabilistic and nonprobabilistic sample selection.

15-4 (OBJECTIVE 15-2) Explain what is meant by block sample selection and describe how an auditor can obtain five blocks of 20 sales invoices from a sales journal.

15-5 (OBJECTIVE 15-3) Explain the difference between replacement sampling and nonreplacement sampling. Which method do auditors usually follow? Why?

15-6 (OBJECTIVE 15-3) What are the two types of simple random sample selection methods? Which of the two methods is used most often by auditors and why?

15-7 (OBJECTIVE 15-3) Describe systematic sample selection and explain how an auditor will select 40 numbers from a population of 2,800 items using this approach. What are the advantages and disadvantages of systematic sample selection?

15-8 (OBJECTIVE 15-3) Distinguish between probabilistic selection and statistical measurement. State the circumstances under which one can be used without the other.

15-9 (OBJECTIVE 15-4) What is the purpose of using nonstatistical sampling for tests of controls and substantive tests of transactions?

15-10 (OBJECTIVE 15-4) What is meant by an attribute in sampling for tests of controls and substantive tests of transactions? What is the source of the attributes that the auditor selects?

15-11 (OBJECTIVE 15-4) Explain the difference between an attribute and an exception condition. State the exception condition for the audit procedure: The duplicate sales invoice has been initialed, indicating the performance of internal verification.

15-12 (OBJECTIVE 15-5) Define each of the following terms:

a. Acceptable risk of overreliance (ARO)
b. Computed upper exception rate (CUER)
c. Estimated population exception rate (EPER)
d. Sample exception rate (SER)
e. Tolerable exception rate (TER)

15-13 (OBJECTIVE 15-5) Describe what is meant by a sampling unit. Explain why the sampling unit for verifying the occurrence of recorded sales differs from the sampling unit for testing for the possibility of omitted sales.

15-14 (OBJECTIVE 15-5) Distinguish between the TER and the CUER. How is each determined?

15-15 (OBJECTIVE 15-5) Identify the factors an auditor uses to decide the appropriate TER. Compare the sample size for a TER of 7% with that of 4%, all other factors being equal.

15-16 **(OBJECTIVE 15-5)** Identify the factors an auditor uses to decide the appropriate ARO. Compare the sample size for an ARO of 10% with that of 5%, all other factors being equal.

15-17 **(OBJECTIVE 15-5)** State the relationship between the following:

a. ARO and sample size
b. Population size and sample size
c. TER and sample size
d. EPER and sample size

15-18 **(OBJECTIVE 15-5)** When the CUER exceeds the TER, what courses of action are available to the auditor? Under what circumstances should each of these be followed?

15-19 **(OBJECTIVE 15-6)** Define attributes sampling. For which types of tests do auditors use attributes sampling?

15-20 **(OBJECTIVE 15-7)** Assume that the auditor has selected 100 sales invoices from a population of 100,000 to test for an indication of internal verification of pricing and extensions. Determine the CUER at a 10% ARO if four exceptions are found in the sample using attributes sampling. Explain the meaning of the statistical results in auditing terms.

15-21 **(OBJECTIVE 15-7)** List the major decisions that the auditor must make in using attributes sampling. State the most important considerations involved in making each decision.

MULTIPLE CHOICE QUESTIONS FROM CPA EXAMINATIONS

15-22 **(OBJECTIVES 15-5, 15-7)** The following items apply to determining sample sizes using random sampling from large populations for attributes sampling. Select the most appropriate response for each question.

a. If all other factors specified in a sampling plan remain constant, changing the ARO from 5% to 10% will cause the required sample size to
   (1) increase.
   (2) remain the same.
   (3) decrease.
   (4) become indeterminate.

b. Of the four factors that determine the initial sample size in attributes sampling (population size, tolerable exception rate, acceptable risk of overreliance, and expected population exception rate), which factor has the least effect on sample size?
   (1) Population size
   (2) Expected population exception rate
   (3) Tolerable exception rate
   (4) Acceptable risk of overreliance

c. The sample size of a test of controls varies inversely with:

	Expected population exception rate	Tolerable exception rate
(1)	No	Yes
(2)	Yes	No
(3)	No	No
(4)	Yes	Yes

15-23 **(OBJECTIVES 15-5, 15-7)** The following items concern determining exception rates using random sampling from large populations using attributes sampling. Select the best response.

a. The upper precision limit (CUER) in statistical sampling is
   (1) the percentage of items in a sample that possess a particular attribute.
   (2) the percentage of items in a population that possess a particular attribute.
   (3) a statistical measure, at a specified confidence level, of the maximum rate of occurrence of an attribute.
   (4) the maximum rate of exception that the auditor would be willing to accept in the population without altering the planned reliance on the attribute.

b. In addition to evaluating the frequency of deviations in tests of controls, an auditor should also consider certain qualitative aspects of the deviations. The auditor most likely would give additional consideration to the implications of a deviation if it was
   (1) the only deviation discovered in the sample.
   (2) identical to a deviation discovered during the prior year's audit.
   (3) caused by an employee's misunderstanding of instructions.
   (4) initially concealed by a forged document.

c. An auditor who uses statistical sampling for attributes in testing internal controls should reduce the planned reliance on a prescribed control when the
   (1) sample exception rate plus the allowance for sampling risk equals the tolerable rate.
   (2) sample exception rate is less than the expected rate of exception used in planning the sample.
   (3) tolerable rate less the allowance for sampling risk exceeds the sample exception rate.
   (4) sample exception rate plus the allowance for sampling risk exceeds the tolerable rate.

15-24 **(OBJECTIVES 15-1, 15-2, 15-6)** The following questions concern audit sampling. Choose the best response.

a. An advantage of statistical sampling over nonstatistical sampling is that statistical sampling helps an auditor
   (1) minimize the failure to detect errors and fraud.
   (2) eliminate the risk of nonsampling errors.
   (3) design more effective audit procedures.
   (4) measure the sufficiency of the audit evidence by quantifying sampling risk.

b. Which of the following best illustrates the concept of sampling risk?
   (1) The documents related to the chosen sample may not be available to the auditor for inspection.
   (2) An auditor may fail to recognize errors in the documents from the sample.
   (3) A randomly chosen sample may not be representative of the population as a whole for the characteristic of interest.
   (4) An auditor may select audit procedures that are not appropriate to achieve the specific objective.

c. For which of the following tests would an auditor most likely use attributes sampling?
   (1) Selecting accounts receivable for confirmation of account balances.
   (2) Inspecting employee time cards for proper approval by supervisors.
   (3) Making an independent estimate of the amount of a LIFO inventory.
   (4) Examining invoices in support of the valuation of fixed asset additions.

MULTIPLE CHOICE QUESTIONS FROM BECKER CPA EXAM REVIEW

15-25 **(OBJECTIVES 15-2, 15-5, 15-7)** The following questions concern audit sampling. Choose the best response.

a. As compared to a nonstatistical sampling plan, a statistical sampling plan
   (1) eliminates the need to apply professional judgment in determining sample size.
   (2) provides a more representative sample from the population.
   (3) makes greater use of mathematical methods in determining an appropriate sample size.
   (4) emphasizes qualitative evaluation of results as opposed to quantitative evaluations.

b. The diagram below depicts an auditor's computed upper exception rate (CUER) compared with the tolerable exception rate (TER), and also depicts the true population exception rate compared with the TER.

	True state of population	
Auditor's estimate based on sample results	**True exception rate is less than TER**	**True exception rate exceeds TER**
CUER is less than TER	I	III
CUER exceeds TER	II	IV

As a result of tests of controls, the auditor assesses control risk too low and thereby decreases substantive testing. This is illustrated by which situation?
(1) I
(2) II
(3) III
(4) IV

c. In assessing sampling risk, the risk of underreliance (i.e. the risk of assessing control risk too high) relates to the
(1) efficiency of the audit.
(2) effectiveness of the audit.
(3) selection of the items in the sample.
(4) audit quality controls.

DISCUSSION QUESTIONS AND PROBLEMS

15-26 **(OBJECTIVES 15-1, 15-2, 15-5)** Auditing standards provide general guidance to auditors regarding audit sampling but do not require statistical versus nonstatistical sampling or specify which sampling method auditors should use. Search the Internet for "PCAOB Audit Sampling" or go to pcaobus.org to locate the PCAOB's auditing standard related to sampling (AU Section 350) and refer to the standard to answer the following questions.

Required

a. What are the costs and benefits of using statistical sampling versus nonstatistical sampling?
b. What is the relationship among audit risk, sampling risk, and nonsampling risk?
c. When is sampling not an appropriate method of performing tests of controls (refer to paragraph 32 of AU Section 350)?
d. Define the risk of assessing control risk too low and the risk of assessing control risk too high. How do these risks impact the efficiency and effectiveness of the audit?

15-27 **(OBJECTIVE 15-3)**

Required

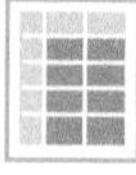

a. As a staff auditor, you need to develop a sampling plan and select an unbiased random sample for each of the three independent scenarios listed below. The in-charge on the audit engagement has instructed you to use the Excel RANDBETWEEN function to select the sample items. For each scenario, develop a sampling plan that includes defining the sampling unit, establishing a numbering system for the population, and determining how to use the Excel RANDBETWEEN function to select the sample. After the plan has been designed, select the sample items according to the plan. Assume that the sample size is 75 for each of (1) through (3).
(1) Prenumbered sales invoices in a sales journal where the lowest invoice number is 1 and the highest is 8274.
(2) Prenumbered bills of lading where the lowest document number is 18221 and the highest is 29427.
(3) Accounts receivable on 20 pages with 50 lines per page except the last page, which has only 29 full lines. Each line has a customer name and an amount receivable.

b. As an alternative to using a random number generator, an auditor can use systematic sampling to select an unbiased sample. Using systematic sampling, select the first five sample items for populations (1) through (3) from part a., using the random starting points shown. Recall that the sample size is 75 in each case.
   (1) Invoice #39
   (2) Bill of lading #18259
   (3) Page 1, line #11

15-28 **(OBJECTIVES 15-3, 15-5, 15-7)** Lenter Supply Company is a medium-sized distributor of wholesale hardware supplies in the central Ohio area. It has been a client of yours for several years and has instituted excellent internal controls for sales at your recommendation.

In providing control over shipments, the client has prenumbered "warehouse removal slips" that are used for every sale. It is company policy never to remove goods from the warehouse without an authorized warehouse removal slip. After shipment, two copies of the warehouse removal slip are sent to billing for the computerized preparation of a sales invoice. One copy is stapled to the duplicate copy of a prenumbered sales invoice, and the other copy is filed numerically. In some cases, more than one warehouse removal slip is used for billing one sales invoice. The smallest warehouse removal slip number for the year is 11741 and the largest is 34687. The smallest sales invoice number is 45302 and the largest is 65747.

In the audit of sales, one of the major concerns is the effectiveness of the controls in ensuring that all shipments are billed. You have decided to use audit sampling in testing internal controls.

Required

a. State an effective audit procedure for testing whether shipments have been billed. What is the sampling unit for the audit procedure?
b. Assume that you expect no exceptions in the sample but are willing to accept a TER of 4%. At a 5% ARO, what is the appropriate sample size for the audit test? You may complete this requirement using attributes sampling.
c. Design a random selection plan for selecting the sample from the population, using either systematic sampling or computer generation of random numbers. Use the sample size determined in part b. If you use systematic sampling, use a random starting point of 11878.
d. Your supervisor suggests the possibility of performing other sales tests with the same sample as a means of efficiently using your audit time. List two other audit procedures that can conveniently be performed using the same sample, and state the purpose of each of the procedures.
e. Is it desirable to test the occurrence of sales with the random sample you have designed in part c.? Why or why not?

15-29 **(OBJECTIVE 15-7)** The following is a partial audit program for the audit of sales transactions.

1. Foot the sales journal for one month and trace the postings to the general ledger.
2. Review the sales journal for any large or unusual transactions.
3. Examine sales order for evidence of credit approval prior to shipment.
4. Vouch entries in sales journal to sales invoice and shipping document.
5. Examine evidence on sales invoice that the prices were agreed to the approved price list.
6. Recompute extensions of price and quantities on the sales invoice.
7. Trace entries in sales journal to entry in accounts receivable master file.

Required

a. Identify which audit procedures can be tested by using attributes sampling.
b. What is the appropriate sampling unit for the tests in part a.?
c. List the attributes for testing in part a.
d. Assume an ARO of 5% and a TER of 6% for tests of controls and 5% for substantive tests of transactions. The EPER for tests of controls is 1.0%, and for substantive tests of transactions it is 0.5%. What is the initial sample size for each attribute?

15-30 **(OBJECTIVES 15-5, 15-7)** The following questions concern the determination of the proper sample size in audit sampling using the following table:

	1	2	3	4	5	6	7
ARO (in percent)	10	5	5	5	10	10	5
TER	6	6	5	6	20	20	2
EPER (in percent)	2	2	2	2	8	2	0
Population size	1,000	100,000	6,000	1,000	500	500	1,000,000

Required

a. Assume that the initial sample size for column 1 using nonstatistical sampling is 90 items. For each of columns 2 through 7, use your judgment to decide the appropriate nonstatistical sample size. In deciding each sample size, consider the effects of changes in each of the four factors (ARO, TER, EPER, and population size) compared with column 1.

b. For each of the columns numbered 1 through 7, determine the initial sample size needed to satisfy the auditor's requirements using attributes sampling from the appropriate part of Table 15-8 (p. 508).

c. Using your understanding of the relationship between the following factors and sample size, state the effect on the initial sample size (increase or decrease) of changing each of the following factors while the other three are held constant:
(1) An increase in ARO
(2) An increase in the TER
(3) An increase in the EPER
(4) An increase in the population size

d. Explain why there is such a large difference in the sample sizes for columns 3 and 6.

e. Compare your answers in part c. with the results you determined in part a. (nonstatistical sampling) or part b. (attributes sampling). Which of the four factors appears to have the greatest effect on the initial sample size? Which one appears to have the least effect?

f. Why is the sample size called the initial sample size?

15-31 **(OBJECTIVES 15-5, 15-7)** The questions below relate to determining the CUER in audit sampling for tests of controls, using the following table:

	1	2	3	4	5	6	7	8
ARO (in percent)	5	5	10	5	5	5	5	5
Population size	50,000	500	5,000	5,000	5,000	900	5,000	500
Sample size	200	100	200	200	50	100	100	25
Number of exceptions	4	2	4	4	1	10	0	0

Required

a. Using nonstatistical sampling, calculate TER – SER for each of columns 1 through 8 and evaluate whether or not the calculated allowance for sampling risk is large enough to accept the population. Assume that TER is 5% for each column.

b. For each of columns 1 through 8, determine CUER using attributes sampling from the appropriate part of Table 15-9 (p. 509).

c. Using your understanding of the relationship between the four preceding factors and the CUER, state the effect on the CUER (increase or decrease) of changing each of the following factors while the other three are held constant:
(1) A decrease in the ARO
(2) A decrease in the population size
(3) A decrease in the sample size
(4) A decrease in the number of exceptions in the sample

d. Compare your answers in part c. with the results you determined in part a. (nonstatistical sampling) or part b. (attributes sampling). Which of the factors appears to have the greatest effect on the CUER? Which one appears to have the least effect?

e. Why is it necessary to compare the CUER with the TER?

15-32 **(OBJECTIVE 15-7)** The following are auditor judgments and attributes sampling results for six populations. Assume large population sizes.

	1	2	3	4	5	6
EPER (in percent)	2	1	1	0	3	8
TER (in percent)	6	5	20	3	8	15
ARO (in percent)	5	5	10	5	10	10
Actual sample size	100	100	20	100	60	60
Actual number of exceptions in the sample	2	4	1	0	1	8

Required

a. For each population, did the auditor select a smaller sample size than is indicated by using the attributes sampling tables in Table 15-8 (p. 508) for determining sample size? What are the implications of selecting either a larger or smaller sample size than those determined using the tables?

b. Calculate the SER and CUER for each population.

c. For which of the six populations should the sample results be considered unacceptable? What options are available to the auditor?

d. Why is analysis of the exceptions necessary even when the populations are considered acceptable?

e. For the following terms, identify which is an audit decision, a nonstatistical estimate made by the auditor, a sample result, and a statistical conclusion about the population:
   (1) EPER
   (2) TER
   (3) ARO
   (4) Actual sample size
   (5) Actual number of exceptions in the sample
   (6) SER
   (7) CUER

15-33 **(OBJECTIVES 15-5, 15-7)** Annie Zhao is using attributes sampling in testing controls over sales transactions. She is testing five attributes related to sales invoices using an ARO of 5% (confidence level of 95%), and zero expected deviations for each attribute based on prior experience with the client. Annie has determined that the tolerable exception rate for each attribute is 5%. Using her firm's audit software, she entered the population size (number of invoices), desired confidence level, TER, and EPER, and determined a sample size of 60 invoices. She used the audit software to select a random sample of invoices and performed the control tests. She found zero deviations for four of the five attributes and concluded that the control can be relied upon for each of those attributes. For the remaining attribute, she found one control deviation. In projecting the sample results to the population for the attribute with one control deviation identified, Annie entered the confidence level, sample size, and one deviation into the audit software sampling module and determined that the computed upper exception rate for the attribute is 7.92%.

Required

a. Explain how Annie should interpret the CUER of 7.92%.

b. What should Annie conclude about the effectiveness of the control attribute with one identified deviation?

c. What are the alternatives for Annie if she concludes the control cannot be relied upon?

d. Assume Annie discusses the deviation with the controller and learns this deviation occurred while a temporary employee was covering for the regular clerk, who was on vacation. Would this information be relevant in determining which of the alternatives in answer c. would be the most appropriate response? What testing and documentation would be needed to conclude this control can be relied upon?

15-34 **(OBJECTIVE 15-5)** For the audit of the financial statements of Mercury Fifo Company, Stella Mason, CPA, has decided to apply nonstatistical audit sampling in

the tests of controls and substantive tests of transactions for sales transactions [see Figure 15-2 (p. 494) for examples of the types of attributes tested]. Based on her knowledge of Mercury's operations in the area of sales, she decides that the EPER is likely to be 3% and that she is willing to accept a 5% risk that the true population exception rate is not greater than 6%. Given this information, Mason selects a random sample of 150 sales invoices from the 5,000 generated during the year and examines them for exceptions. She notes the following exceptions in her audit schedules. There is no other documentation.

Invoice No.	Comment
5028	Sales invoice was originally footed incorrectly but was corrected by client before the bill was sent out.
6791	Voided sales invoice examined by auditor.
6810	Shipping document for a sale of merchandise could not be located.
7364	Sales invoice for $2,875 has not been collected and is 6 months past due.
7625	Client unable to locate the duplicate sales invoice.
8431	Invoice was dated 3 days later than the date entered in the sales journal.
8528	Customer order is not attached to the duplicate sales invoice.
8566	Billing is for $100 less than it should be due to an unintentional pricing error. No indication of internal verification is included on the invoice.
8780	Client unable to locate the duplicate sales invoice.
9169	Credit not authorized, but the sale was for only $7.65.
9974	Lack of indication of internal verification of price extensions and postings of sales invoice.

Required

a. Which of the preceding should be defined as an exception?

b. Explain why it is inappropriate to set a single acceptable TER and EPER for the combined exceptions.

c. Calculate SER for each attribute tested in the population. (You must decide which attributes should be combined, which should be kept separate, and which exceptions are actual exceptions before you can calculate SER.)

d. Calculate TER – SER for each attribute and evaluate whether the calculated allowance for sampling risk is sufficiently large given the 5% ARO. Assume TER is 6% for each attribute.

e. State the appropriate analysis of exceptions for each of the exceptions in the sample, including additional procedures to be performed.

15-35 **(OBJECTIVES 15-6, 15-7)** The sampling data sheet below is missing selected information for six attributes involving tests of transactions for the sales and collection cycle.

	Planned Audit				Actual Results		
Attributes	EPER	TER	ARO	Initial Sample Size	Sample Size	Number of Exceptions	CUER
Attribute 1	0%	6%	5%	49	50	1	____
Attribute 2	0.50%	5%	10%	____	80	0	2.9%
Attribute 3	1%	____	10%	55	55	1	6.9%
Attribute 4	1%	6%	5%	78	80	____	5.8%
Attribute 5	0%	4%	____	74	80	0	3.7%
Attribute 6	0.50%	6%	10%	64	____	2	7.5%

a. Use Table 15-8 (p. 508) and Table 15-9 (p. 509) to complete the missing information for each attribute. **Required**
b. For which attributes are the sample results unacceptable?
c. Compare attributes 1 and 3. Why does attribute 1 have the smaller sample size?
d. Compare attributes 2 and 5. Why is CUER higher for attribute 5?

CASE

15-36 **(OBJECTIVES 15-4, 15-5, 15-7)** For the audit of Carbald Supply Company, Carole Wever, CPA, is conducting a test of sales for nine months of the year ended December 31, 2016. Included among her audit procedures are the following:

1. Foot and cross-foot the sales journal and trace the balance to the general ledger.
2. Review all sales transactions for reasonableness.
3. Select a sample of recorded sales from the sales journal and trace the customer name and amounts to duplicate sales invoices and the related shipping document.
4. Select a sample of shipping document numbers and perform the following tests:
   (a) Trace the shipping document to the related duplicate sales invoice.
   (b) Examine the duplicate sales invoice to determine whether copies of the shipping document, shipping order, and customer order are attached.
   (c) Examine the shipping order for an authorized credit approval.
   (d) Examine the duplicate sales invoice for an indication of internal verification of quantity, price, extensions, and footings, and trace the balance to the accounts receivable master file.
   (e) Compare the price on the duplicate sales invoice with the approved price list and the quantity with the shipping document.
   (f) Trace the balance in the duplicate sales invoice to the sales journal and accounts receivable master file for customer name, amount, and date.

a. For which of these procedures can audit sampling for exceptions be conveniently used? **Required**
b. Considering the audit procedures Wever developed, what is the most appropriate sampling unit for conducting most of the audit sampling tests?
c. Set up a sampling data sheet following the format in Figure 15-2 (p. 494) using attributes or nonstatistical sampling. For all tests of controls, assume a TER rate of 5% and an EPER of 1%. For all substantive tests of transactions, use a 4% TER and a 0% EPER. Use a 10% ARO for all tests. Determine the sample size for each attribute.

INTEGRATED CASE APPLICATION— PINNACLE MANUFACTURING: PART VI

15-37 **(OBJECTIVES 15-3, 15-5, 15-7)** In Part V of the Pinnacle Manufacturing case, you prepared a performance format audit program. In Part VI , sample sizes will be determined by using nonstatistical or attributes sampling, and the results of the tests will be evaluated. You should use nonstatistical sampling unless your professor tells you to use statistical sampling.

After reviewing the audit program you created in Part V, the audit manager decided to make some modifications. You agreed with her changes. The modified program is included in Figure 15-9 (p. 522).

The audit manager has decided that the tests should be performed for the first 10 months including the month ended 10/31/16. You determine that document numbers are as follows:

Document	First number	Last number
Voucher	6734	33722
Receiving report	9315	23108
Check	12376	37318
Purchase order	3162	17200

Required

a. Using the audit program in Figure 15-9, prepare a nonstatistical sampling data sheet for acquisitions following the format in Figure 15-2 (p. 494). Prepare all parts of the sampling data sheet except those that are blank in Figure 15-2. A formatted sampling data sheet is available online. Use the following guidelines:
   (1) Use only one sampling data sheet.
   (2) Select the sampling unit that will permit you to perform the most acquisition audit procedures on the audit program.
   (3) Include all audit procedures on the audit program that are consistent with the sampling unit you selected.
   (4) Decide EPER, TER, and ARO for each attribute. Consider prior-year results for EPER. (See Figure 12-12 on p. 406 in Part IV.) Use your judgment for the other two factors.
   (5) Decide the sample size for each attribute.

b. Do the same thing for cash disbursements that you did in requirement a. for acquisitions. You will not complete the actual results portion of the cash disbursements sampling data sheet.

c. For acquisitions only, use an Excel spreadsheet to select random numbers for the largest sample size in the acquisitions sampling data sheet. Include the numbers in both random order and sorted numbers, from low to high. Document how you selected the numbers.

d. Assume that you performed all audit procedures included in Figure 15-9 using the sample sizes in part (5) of requirement a. The only exceptions found when you

FIGURE 15-9 Audit Program for Acquisitions and Cash Disbursements

General

1. Discuss the following items with client personnel and observe activities:
   a. Segregation of duties
   b. Use of an adequate chart of accounts
   c. Monthly reconciliation of accounts payable master file with the general ledger
2. Foot acquisitions and cash disbursements journals for a test month and trace postings to the general ledger.
3. Examine file of completed bank reconciliations.
4. Account for a sequence of cancelled checks.
5. Reconcile recorded cash disbursements with cash disbursements on the bank statement for a test month.

Acquisitions

6. Trace entries in the acquisitions journal to related vendors' invoices, receiving reports, and purchase orders.
   a. Examine indication of internal verification of dates, unit costs, prices, extensions and footings, account classifications, recording in the journal, and posting and summarization.
   b. Examine supporting documents for propriety.
   c. Compare prices on vendors' invoices with approved price limits established by management.
   d. Recompute information on vendors' invoices.
   e. Examine vendors' invoices for proper account classification.
   f. Compare dates of recorded acquisitions with dates on receiving reports.
   g. Examine voucher document package for indication of internal verification.
7. Account for a sequence of purchase orders and voucher document packages.
8. Trace a sample of receiving reports to the acquisitions journal.

Cash Disbursements

9. Select a sample of cancelled checks.
   a. Trace cancelled check to the related cash disbursements journal entry and date.
   b. Examine check for signature, proper endorsement, and cancellation by the bank.
   c. Compare date on cancelled check with bank cancellation date.
   d. Recompute cash discounts.

performed the tests include the following: two missing indications of internal verification on a vendor's invoice, one acquisition of inventory transaction recorded for $2,000 more than the amount stated on the vendor's invoice (the vendor was also overpaid by $2,000), and two vendors' invoices recorded as acquisitions several days after the receipt of the goods. Complete the sampling data sheet prepared in requirement a. Use Figure 15-4 (p. 500) as a frame of reference for completing the sampling data sheet.

ACL PROBLEM

15-38 **(OBJECTIVE 15-7)** This problem requires the use of ACL software, which can be accessed through the textbook Web site. Information about downloading and using ACL and the commands used in this problem can also be found on the textbook Web site. You should read all of the reference material, especially the material on sampling, to answer questions a. through f. For this problem, use the "Invoices" file in the "Sales and Collection" subfolder under tables in the ACL_Rockwood project. This file contains information on sales invoices generated during calendar year 2014, including those that have been paid versus those still outstanding. Suggested commands, where applicable, are indicated at the end of the problem requirements.

Required

a. How many records are included in the Invoices file as noted at the bottom of the screen?

b. Using the Invoices file, calculate the sample size and sampling interval for a record sample to be used for tests of transactions. Use a confidence level of 90%, upper error limit of 6% (tolerable error rate or precision), and expected error rate of zero. (Sampling/Calculate Sample Size; select "Record" radio button.)

c. What is the sample size if you increase the confidence level to 95% and do not change the other sampling parameters? What is the sample size if you increase the upper error limit to 8%, with a confidence level of 90% and expected error rate of zero?

d. Select the sample based on the sample size determined in part b. (Sampling /Sample; select the "Record" radio button under "Sample type." For "Sample Parameters" select the "Random" radio button and sample size you determined in part b., use a seed of 5.) Save the file using a naming convention such as invoice_sample.

e. What is the invoice number of the largest invoice selected for testing? Does your sampling plan consider invoice amount? (Quick Sort)

f. Assume you found one error in the sample. Without using ACL, will your results be acceptable? Explain. Now use ACL to calculate the upper error limit frequency. (Sampling/Evaluate Error; input the confidence level, sample size, and one error.)

CHAPTER

16

COMPLETING THE TESTS IN THE SALES AND COLLECTION CYCLE: ACCOUNTS RECEIVABLE

LEARNING OBJECTIVES

After studying this chapter, you should be able to

16-1 Describe the methodology for designing tests of details of balances using the audit risk model.

16-2 Design and perform substantive analytical procedures for accounts in the sales and collection cycle.

16-3 Design and perform tests of details of balances for accounts receivable.

16-4 Obtain and evaluate accounts receivable confirmations.

16-5 Design audit procedures for the audit of accounts receivable, using an evidence-planning worksheet as a guide.

When More Isn't Better

On Susan Jackson's first audit assignment, she was asked to handle the confirmation of accounts receivable of a retailer with a large number of customer accounts. She was excited because accounts receivable was one of the areas in her auditing class that she was confident she understood. In previous years, Jackson's firm confirmed these accounts using negative confirmations, requesting customers to respond only if the balance information was incorrect. Last year, 200 negative confirmations were sent one month before year-end. Those that were returned showed only timing differences; none represented a misstatement in the client's books.

The tentative audit plan for the current year did not differ from the prior year. When Jackson obtained an understanding of internal controls over sales and cash receipts transactions, she discovered that a new real-time system for processing sales transactions had been implemented. The client was having considerable problems getting the system to work properly, and a significant number of misstatements occurred in recording sales during the past few months. Jackson's tests of controls and substantive tests of sales transactions also identified similar misstatements.

Before sending confirmation requests for the current year, Jackson took her findings to her supervisor and asked him what to do. He responded, "No problem, Susan. Just send 300 confirmation requests instead of the usual 200. And be sure you get a good random sample so we can get a good projection of the results." Jackson was seriously bothered by this instruction. She recalled from her auditing class that negative confirmation requests aren't considered satisfactory evidence when controls are weak. Because customers are asked to respond only when differences occur, the auditor cannot be confident of the correct value for each misstatement in the sample. If this is so, then the results of using negative confirmations will be misleading even if a request is sent to every account. Jackson concluded that expanding the sample size was the wrong solution. When Jackson talked with her supervisor about her point of view, this time he responded, "You are absolutely right. I spoke too quickly. We need to sit down and think about a better strategy to find out if accounts receivable is materially misstated."

In the preceding two chapters, we examined tests of controls and substantive tests of transactions for the sales and collection cycle. Both types of tests are part of phase II of the audit process. We now move to phase III and turn our attention to substantive analytical procedures and tests of details of balances for the sales and collection cycle.

This chapter shows that it is essential for auditors to select the appropriate evidence to verify the account balances in the sales and collection cycle, after considering performance materiality, identifying significant risks, performing risk assessment procedures to assess inherent and control risks, and performing tests of controls and substantive tests of transactions. This chapter examines designing substantive analytical procedures and tests of details of balances for the two key balance sheet accounts in the cycle: accounts receivable and the allowance for uncollectible accounts.

METHODOLOGY FOR DESIGNING TESTS OF DETAILS OF BALANCES

OBJECTIVE 16-1

Describe the methodology for designing tests of details of balances using the audit risk model.

Figure 16-1 shows the methodology auditors follow in designing the appropriate tests of details of balances for accounts receivable. This methodology was introduced in Chapter 13 and is now applied to the audit of accounts receivable.

The methodology shown in Figure 16-1 relates directly to the evidence-planning worksheet first introduced in Chapter 9. The worksheet was partially completed on page 282 in that chapter for materiality and risk considerations (part of phase I) and was further completed as a part of the study of tests of controls and substantive tests of transactions on page 504 in Chapter 15 (phase II). We will continue to complete the worksheet as we proceed through phase III in this chapter. For now, you might want to look at the example of a completed worksheet in Figure 16-7 on page 544 to see what the completed worksheet looks like, to provide you an overview of the focus of this chapter.

FIGURE 16-1 Methodology for Designing Tests of Details of Balances for Accounts Receivable

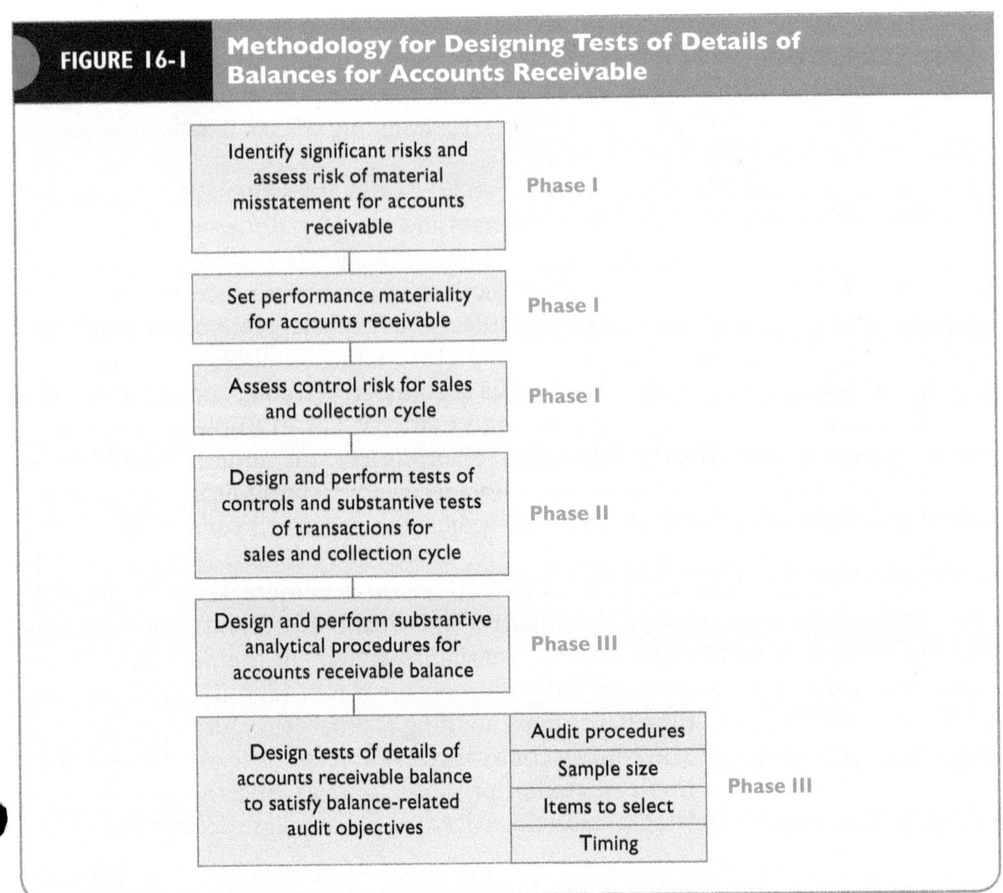

Identify significant risks and assess risk of material misstatement for accounts receivable
Phase I
Set performance materiality for accounts receivable
Phase I
Assess control risk for sales and collection cycle
Phase I
Design and perform tests of controls and substantive tests of transactions for sales and collection cycle
Phase II
Design and perform substantive analytical procedures for accounts receivable balance
Phase III
Design tests of details of accounts receivable balance to satisfy balance-related audit objectives
Audit procedures
Sample size
Items to select
Timing
Phase III

The appropriate evidence to be obtained from tests of details of balances must be decided on an objective-by-objective basis. Because several interactions affect the need for evidence from tests of details of balances, this audit decision can be complex. For example, the auditor must evaluate the potential for fraud and also consider inherent risk, which may vary by objective, as well as the results of tests of controls and the related control risk assessment, which also may vary by objective. The auditor must also consider the results of substantive tests of sales and cash receipts.

In designing tests of details of balances for accounts receivable, auditors must satisfy each of the eight balance-related audit objectives first discussed on pages 162–165 in Chapter 6. These eight general objectives are the same for all accounts. Specifically applied to accounts receivable, they are called **accounts receivable balance-related audit objectives** and are as follows:[1]

1. Accounts receivable in the aged trial balance agree with related master file amounts, and the total is correctly added and agrees with the general ledger. (Detail tie-in)
2. Recorded accounts receivable exist. (Existence)
3. Existing accounts receivable are included. (Completeness)
4. Accounts receivable are accurate. (Accuracy)
5. Accounts receivable are correctly classified. (Classification)
6. Cutoff for accounts receivable is correct. (Cutoff)
7. Accounts receivable is stated at realizable value. (Realizable value)
8. The client has rights to accounts receivable. (Rights)

The columns in the evidence-planning worksheet in Figure 16-7 (p. 544) include the balance-related audit objectives. The auditor uses the factors in the rows to aid in assessing planned detection risk for accounts receivable, by objective.

Students of auditing need to understand the entire methodology for designing tests of details of balances for accounts receivable and all other accounts. The following overview explains the methodology. Portions of the discussion are a review of information studied in earlier chapters, but they are intended to aid in understanding the relationship of each part of Figure 16-1 (p. 525) to designing tests of details of balances.

Identify Significant Risks and Assess the Risk of Material Misstatement for Accounts Receivable (Phase I)

Tests of accounts receivable are based on the auditor's risk assessment procedures that provide an understanding of the client's business and industry, discussed in Chapter 8. As part of this understanding, the auditor studies the client's industry and external environment and evaluates management objectives and business processes to identify significant client business risks that could affect the financial statements, including accounts receivable. As part of gaining this understanding, auditors assess inherent risk for each objective for an account, such as accounts receivable, considering client business risk and the nature of the client and industry. For example, as a result of adverse changes in the industry's economic environment, the auditor may increase inherent risk for net realizable value of accounts receivable. The auditor also performs preliminary analytical procedures that may indicate increased risk of misstatements in accounts receivable.

As part of the assessment of the risk of material misstatement, the auditor determines whether any of the risks identified are a significant risk. Significant risks represent an identified and assessed risk of material misstatement that, in the auditor's professional judgment, requires special audit consideration. Identifying significant risks as part of planning is important, given auditing standards require the auditor to obtain an understanding of the entity's controls relevant to significant risks in order to evaluate the design and implementation of those controls, and the auditor must perform substantive tests related to assertions deemed to have significant risks.

[1] Detail tie-in is included as the first objective here, compared with being objective 6 in Chapter 6, because tests for detail tie-in are normally done first.

For most audits, revenue recognition is considered to be a significant risk because auditing standards require the auditor to presume that revenue recognition is a specific fraud risk. When sales are made on account, the double-entry nature of accounting means this presumption typically also affects the auditor's assessment of inherent risk for the following accounts receivable balance-related objectives: existence, sales cutoff, and sales returns and allowances cutoff. It is common for clients to misstate cutoff either by error or through fraud. It is also common for clients to unintentionally or fraudulently misstate the allowance for uncollectible accounts (realizable value) because of the difficulty in determining the correct balance. Thus, the auditor may also identify the risk of misstatement related to the realizable value balance-related objective for accounts receivable as a significant risk.

Set Performance Materiality for Accounts Receivable (Phase I)

As studied in Chapter 8, the auditor first decides the preliminary judgment about materiality for the entire financial statements, and then allocates the preliminary judgment amount to each significant balance sheet account, including accounts receivable. This allocation is called *setting performance materiality*. Accounts receivable is typically one of the most material accounts in the financial statements for companies that sell on credit. For even small accounts receivable balances, the transactions in the sales and collection cycle that affect the balance in accounts receivable are almost certain to be highly significant.

Assess Control Risk for the Sales and Collection Cycle (Phase I)

Internal controls over sales and cash receipts and the related accounts receivable are at least reasonably effective for most companies because management is concerned with keeping accurate records to maintain good relations with customers. Auditors are especially concerned with three aspects of internal controls:

1. Controls that prevent or detect embezzlements
2. Controls over cutoff
3. Controls related to the allowance for uncollectible accounts

Earlier, we studied transaction-related audit objectives in the sales and collection cycle (see Chapter 14). The auditor must relate control risk for transaction-related audit objectives to balance-related audit objectives in deciding planned detection risk and planned evidence for tests of details of balances. For the most part, this relationship is straightforward. Figure 16-2 (p. 528) shows the relationship for the two primary classes of transactions in the sales and collection cycle. For example, assume the auditor concluded that control risk for both sales and cash receipts transactions is low for the accuracy transaction-related audit objective. The auditor can therefore conclude that controls for the accuracy balance-related audit objective for accounts receivable are effective because the only transactions that affect accounts receivable are sales and cash receipts. Of course, if sales returns and allowances and write-off of uncollectible accounts receivable are significant, assessed control risk must also be considered for these two classes of transactions.

Two aspects of the relationships in Figure 16-2 deserve special mention:

1. For sales, the occurrence transaction-related audit objective affects the existence balance-related audit objective. For cash receipts, however, the occurrence transaction-related audit objective affects the completeness balance-related audit objective. A similar relationship exists for the completeness transaction-related audit objective. The reason for this somewhat surprising conclusion is that an increase in sales increases accounts receivable, but an increase in cash receipts decreases accounts receivable. For example, recording a sale that did not occur violates the occurrence transaction-related audit objective and existence balance-related audit objective (both overstatements). Recording a cash receipt that did not occur violates the occurrence transaction-related audit objective for cash receipts, but it also violates the completeness balance-related audit objective for accounts receivable because a receivable that is still outstanding is no longer included in the records.

2. The realizable value and rights accounts receivable balance-related audit objectives, as well as the presentation and disclosure-related objectives, are not affected by assessed control risk for classes of transactions. To assess control risk below the maximum for these objectives, the auditor must identify and test separate controls that support those objectives.

Figure 16-7 (p. 544) includes three rows for assessed control risk: one for sales, one for cash receipts, and one for additional controls related to the accounts receivable balance. The source of each control risk for sales and cash receipts is the control risk matrix assuming that the tests of controls results supported the original assessment. The auditor makes a separate assessment of control risk for objectives that are related only to the accounts receivable balance or to presentation and disclosure audit objectives.

Design and Perform Tests of Controls and Substantive Tests of Transactions (Phase II)

Chapters 14 and 15 covered designing audit procedures for tests of controls and substantive tests of transactions, deciding sample size, and evaluating the results of those tests. The results of the tests of controls determine whether assessed control risk for sales and cash receipts needs to be revised. Auditors use the results of the substantive tests of transactions to determine the extent to which planned detection risk is satisfied for each accounts receivable balance-related audit objective. The evidence-planning worksheet in Figure 16-7 shows three rows for control risk and two for substantive tests of transactions, one for sales, and the other for cash receipts.

FIGURE 16-2 Relationship Between Transaction-Related Audit Objectives for the Sales and Collection Cycle and Balance-Related Audit Objectives for Accounts Receivable

		ACCOUNTS RECEIVABLE BALANCE-RELATED AUDIT OBJECTIVES							
CLASS OF TRANSACTIONS	TRANSACTION-RELATED AUDIT OBJECTIVES	Detail tie-in	Existence	Completeness	Accuracy	Classification	Cutoff	Realizable value	Rights
Sales	Occurrence		X						
	Completeness			X					
	Accuracy				X				
	Posting and summarization	X							
	Classification					X			
	Timing						X		
Cash receipts	Occurrence			X					
	Completeness		X						
	Accuracy				X				
	Posting and summarization	X							
	Classification					X			
	Timing						X		

Design and Perform Substantive Analytical Procedures (Phase III)

OBJECTIVE 16-2

Design and perform substantive analytical procedures for accounts in the sales and collection cycle.

As discussed in Chapter 7, analytical procedures are often done during three phases of the audit: during planning, when performing detailed tests, and as a part of completing the audit. This chapter covers planning analytical procedures and substantive analytical procedures done when performing detailed tests for accounts in the sales and collection cycle.

Most substantive analytical procedures performed during the detailed testing phase are done after the balance sheet date but before tests of details of balances. It makes little sense to perform extensive substantive analytical procedures before the client has recorded all transactions for the year and finalized the financial statements.

Auditors perform both planning and substantive analytical procedures for the entire sales and collection cycle, not just accounts receivable. This is necessary because of the close relationship between income statement and balance sheet accounts. If the auditor identifies a possible misstatement in sales or sales returns and allowances using analytical procedures, accounts receivable will likely be the offsetting misstatement.

Table 16-1 presents examples of ratios and comparisons for the sales and collection cycle and potential misstatements that analytical procedures may uncover. Although Table 16-1 focuses on the comparison of current year results with previous years, auditors also consider current year results compared to budgets and industry trends. Observe in the "possible misstatement" column how both balance sheet and income statement accounts are affected. For example, when the auditor performs analytical procedures for sales, evidence is being obtained about both sales and accounts receivable. Auditors may use the same types of ratios and comparisons shown in Table 16-1 as planning analytical procedures or as substantive analytical procedures. However, while planning analytical procedures might be based on interim data or aggregate data, such as company-wide sales for the first six months of the fiscal period, substantive analytical procedures will likely use disaggregate data, such as sales amounts by month and product based on data for the full year under audit.

In addition to the analytical procedures in Table 16-1, auditors should also review accounts receivable for large and unusual amounts, such as large balances; accounts

TABLE 16-1 Analytical Procedures for the Sales and Collection Cycle

Analytical Procedure	Possible Misstatement
Compare gross margin percentage with previous years (by product line).	Overstatement or understatement of sales and accounts receivable.
Compare sales by month (by product line) over time.	Overstatement or understatement of sales and accounts receivable.
Compare sales returns and allowances as a percentage of gross sales with previous years (by product line).	Overstatement or understatement of sales returns and allowances and accounts receivable.
Compare individual customer balances over a stated amount with previous years.	Misstatements in accounts receivable and related income statement accounts.
Compare bad debt expense as a percentage of gross sales with previous years.	Uncollectible accounts receivable that have not been provided for.
Compare number of days that accounts receivable are outstanding with previous years and related turnover of accounts receivable.	Overstatement or understatement of allowance for uncollectible accounts and bad debt expense; also may indicate fictitious accounts receivable.
Compare aging categories as a percentage of accounts receivable with previous years.	Overstatement or understatement of allowance for uncollectible accounts and bad debt expense.
Compare allowance for uncollectible accounts as a percentage of accounts receivable with previous years.	Overstatement or understatement of allowance for uncollectible accounts and bad debt expense.
Compare write-off of uncollectible accounts as a percentage of total accounts receivable with previous years.	Overstatement or understatement of allowance for uncollectible accounts and bad debt expense.

TABLE 16-2 Comparative Information for Hillsburg Hardware Co.—Sales and Collection Cycle

	Amount				
	12-31-16 (in Thousands)	Percent Change 2015–2016	12-31-15 (in Thousands)	Percent Change 2014–2015	12-31-14 (in Thousands)
Sales	$144,328	9.0%	$132,421	7.0%	$123,737
Sales returns and allowances	1,242	3.9	1,195	13.6	1,052
Gross margin	39,845	9.6	36,350	7.0	33,961
Accounts receivable	20,197	15.3	17,521	3.3	16,961
Allowance for uncollectible accounts	1,240	(5.4)	1,311	21.5	1,079
Bad debt expense	3,323	(2.1)	3,394	7.3	3,162
Total current assets	51,027	2.3	49,895	1.5	49,157
Total assets	61,367	0.9	60,791	1.8	59,696
Net earnings before taxes	5,681	21.9	4,659	39.0	3,351
Number of accounts receivable	258	16.7	221	5.7	209
Number of accounts receivable with balances over $100,000	37	15.6	32	6.7	30

that have been outstanding for a long time; receivables from affiliated companies, officers, directors, and other related parties; and credit balances. To identify these amounts, the auditor should review the listing of accounts (aged trial balance) at the balance sheet date, or use audit software, to determine which accounts should be investigated further.

To illustrate the use of substantive analytical procedures during the detailed testing phase, Table 16-2 presents comparative trial balance information for the sales and collection cycle information for Hillsburg Hardware Co. Building on that information, Table 16-3 demonstrates several substantive analytical procedures. The only potential misstatement indicated in these two tables is in the allowance for uncollectible accounts. This is indicated by the ratio of the allowance to accounts receivable, as explained at the bottom of Table 16-3.

The auditor's conclusions about substantive analytical procedures for the sales and collection cycle are incorporated in the evidence-planning worksheet in Figure 16-7 (p. 544) in the third row from the bottom. Because analytical procedures

TABLE 16-3 Substantive Analytical Procedures for Hillsburg Hardware Co.—Sales and Collection Cycle

	12-31-16	12-31-15	12-31-14
Gross margin/net sales	27.85%	27.70%	27.68%
Sales returns and allowances/gross sales	0.9%	0.9%	0.9%
Bad debt expense/net sales	2.3%	2.6%	2.6%
Allowance for uncollectible accounts/accounts receivable	6.1%	7.5%	6.4%
Number of days receivables outstanding*	48.09	47.96	49.32
Net accounts receivable/total current assets	37.2%	32.5%	32.3%

*Based on year-end accounts receivable only.

Comment: Allowance as a percentage of accounts receivable has declined from 6.4% to 6.1%. Number of days receivables outstanding and economic conditions do not justify this change. Potential misstatement is approximately $60,000 ($20,197,000 × [.064 − .061]).

are substantive tests, they reduce the extent to which the auditor needs to perform detailed tests of balances, if the analytical procedure results are favorable.

When substantive analytical procedures in the sales and collection cycle uncover unusual fluctuations, however, the auditor should make additional inquiries of management. Management's responses should be critically evaluated to determine whether they adequately explain the unusual fluctuations and whether they are supported by corroborating evidence.

Design and Perform Tests of Details of Accounts Receivable Balance (Phase III)

The appropriate tests of details of balances depend on the factors listed in the evidence-planning worksheet in Figure 16-7 (p. 544). Planned detection risk for each accounts receivable balance-related audit objective is shown in the second row from the bottom. It is a subjective decision made by auditors after they have combined the conclusions reached about each of the factors listed above that row.

The task of combining the factors that determine planned detection risk is complex because the measurement for each factor is imprecise and the appropriate weight given to each factor is highly subjective. Conversely, the relationship between each factor and planned detection risk is well established. For example, auditors know that a high inherent risk or control risk decreases planned detection risk and increases planned substantive tests, whereas good results of substantive tests of transactions increase planned detection risk and decrease other planned substantive tests.

The bottom row in Figure 16-7 shows the planned audit evidence for tests of details of balances for accounts receivable by objective. As we've discussed, planned audit evidence is the inverse of planned detection risk. After deciding whether planned audit evidence for a given objective is high, medium, or low, the auditor must then decide on the appropriate audit procedures, sample size, items to select, and timing.

For the remainder of this chapter, we will discuss how auditors decide on the specific audit procedures and their timing for auditing accounts receivable. In Chapter 17, we'll address sample size and selecting items from the population for testing.

DESIGNING TESTS OF DETAILS OF BALANCES

OBJECTIVE 16-3

Design and perform tests of details of balances for accounts receivable.

Even though auditors emphasize balance sheet accounts in tests of details of balances, they are not ignoring income statement accounts because the income statement accounts are tested as a by-product of the balance sheet tests. For example, if the auditor confirms accounts receivable balances and finds overstatements caused by mistakes in billing customers, then both accounts receivable and sales are overstated.

Confirmation of accounts receivable is the most important test of details of accounts receivable. We will discuss confirmation briefly as we study the appropriate tests for each of the balance-related audit objectives. We'll examine it in more detail later in this chapter.

For our discussion of tests of details of balances for accounts receivable, we will focus on balance-related audit objectives. We will also assume two things:

1. Auditors have completed an evidence-planning worksheet similar to the one in Figure 16-7.
2. They have decided planned detection risk for tests of details for each balance-related audit objective.

The audit procedures selected and their sample size will depend heavily on whether planned evidence for a given objective is low, medium, or high.

The Summation of Accounts Receivable Agrees with the Master File and the General Ledger

Most tests of accounts receivable and the allowance for uncollectible accounts are based on the aged trial balance. An **aged trial balance** lists the balances in the accounts receivable master file at the balance sheet date, including individual customer balances outstanding and a breakdown of each balance by the time passed between

FIGURE 16-3 Aged Trial Balance for Hillsburg Hardware Co.

PBC

Hillsburg Hardware Co.
Accounts Receivable
Aged Trial Balance
12/31/16

Schedule
Prepared by Client
Approved by

Date
1/5/17

Account Number	Customer	Balance 12/31/16	Aging, Based on Invoice Date 0–30 days	31–60 days	61–90 days	91–120 days	over 120 days
01011	Adams Supply	146,589	90,220	56,369			
01044	Argonaut, Inc.	30,842	30,842				
01100	Atwater Brothers	210,389	210,389				
01191	Beekman Bearings	83,526	73,526		10,000		
01270	Brown and Phillips	60,000				60,000	
01301	Christopher Plumbing	15,789					15,789
09733	Travelers Equipment	59,576	59,576				
09742	Underhill Parts and Maintenance	179,263	179,263				
09810	UJW Co.	102,211	34,911	34,700	32,600		
09907	Zephyr Plastics	286,300	186,000	100,300			
		$20,196,800	$14,217,156	$2,869,366	$1,408,642	$1,038,926	$662,710

the date of sale and the balance sheet date. Figure 16-3 illustrates a typical aged trial balance, based on the Hillsburg Hardware example. Notice that the total is the same as accounts receivable on the general ledger trial balance in Figure 6-5 on page 154.

Ordinarily, auditors test the information on the aged trial balance for detail tie-in before any other tests to verify that the population being tested agrees with the general ledger and accounts receivable master file. The total column and the columns depicting the aging must be test-footed and the total on the trial balance compared with the general ledger. In addition, auditors should trace a sample of individual balances to supporting documents such as duplicate sales invoices to verify the customer's name, balance, and proper aging. The extent of the testing for detail tie-in depends on the number of accounts involved, the degree to which the master file has been tested as a part of tests of controls and substantive tests of transactions, and the extent to which the schedule has been verified by an internal auditor or other independent person before it is given to the auditor. Auditors often use audit software to foot and cross-foot the aged trial balance and to recalculate the aging.

Recorded Accounts Receivable Exist

Confirmation of customers' balances is the most important test of details of balances for determining the existence of recorded accounts receivable. When customers do not respond to confirmations, auditors also examine supporting documents to verify the shipment of goods and evidence of subsequent cash receipts to determine whether the accounts were collected. Normally, auditors do not examine shipping documents or evidence of subsequent cash receipts for any account in the sample that is confirmed, but they may use these documents extensively as alternative evidence for nonresponses.

Existing Accounts Receivable Are Included

It is difficult for auditors to test for account balances omitted from the aged trial balance except by relying on the self-balancing nature of the accounts receivable master file. For example, if the client accidentally excluded an account receivable from the trial balance, the only likely way it will be discovered is for the auditor to foot the accounts receivable trial balance and reconcile the balance with the control account in the general ledger.

If all sales to a customer are omitted from the sales journal, the understatement of accounts receivable is almost impossible to uncover by tests of details of balances. For example, auditors rarely send accounts receivable confirmations to customers with zero balances, in part because research shows that customers are less likely to respond to requests that indicate their balances are understated. In addition, unrecorded sales to a new customer are difficult to identify for confirmation because that customer is not included in the accounts receivable master file. The understatement of sales and accounts receivable is best uncovered by substantive tests of transactions for shipments made but not recorded (completeness objective for tests of sales transactions) and by substantive analytical procedures.

Accounts Receivable Are Accurate

Confirmation of accounts selected from the trial balance is the most common test of details of balances for the accuracy of accounts receivable. When customers do not respond to confirmation requests, auditors examine supporting documents in the same way as described for the existence objective. Auditors perform tests of the debits and credits to individual customers' balances by examining supporting documentation for shipments and cash receipts.

Accounts Receivable Are Properly Classified

Normally, auditors can evaluate the classification of accounts receivable relatively easily, by reviewing the aged trial balance for material receivables from affiliates, officers, directors, or other related parties. Auditors should verify that notes receivable or accounts that should be classified as noncurrent assets are separated from regular accounts, and significant credit balances in accounts receivable are reclassified as accounts payable.

There is a close relationship between the classification balance-related objective and the related classification and understandability presentation and disclosure objective. To satisfy the classification balance-related audit objective, the auditor must determine whether the client has correctly separated different classifications of accounts receivable. For example, the auditor will determine whether receivables from related parties have been separated on the aged trial balance. To satisfy the objective for presentation and disclosure, the auditor must make sure that the classifications are properly presented by determining whether related party transactions are correctly shown in the financial statements during the completion phase of the audit.

Cutoff for Accounts Receivable Is Correct

Cutoff misstatements exist when current period transactions are recorded in the subsequent period or vice versa. The objective of cutoff tests, regardless of the type of transaction, is to verify whether transactions near the end of the accounting period are recorded in the proper period. The cutoff objective is one of the most important in the cycle because misstatements in cutoff can significantly affect current period income. For example, the intentional or unintentional inclusion of several large, subsequent period sales in the current period — or the exclusion of several current period sales returns and allowances — can materially overstate net earnings.

Cutoff misstatements can occur for *sales, sales returns and allowances,* and *cash receipts.* For each one, auditors require a threefold approach to determine the reasonableness of cutoff:

1. Decide on the appropriate *criteria for cutoff.*
2. Evaluate whether the client has established *adequate procedures* to ensure a reasonable cutoff.
3. *Test* whether the cutoff was correct.

Sales Cutoff Most merchandising and manufacturing clients record a sale based on *shipment of goods* criterion. However, some companies record invoices at the time title passes, which can occur before shipment (as in the case of custom-manufactured goods), at the time of shipment, or subsequent to shipment. For the correct measurement of current period income, the method must be in accordance with accounting standards and consistently applied.

The most important part of evaluating the client's method of obtaining a reliable cutoff is to determine the procedures in use. When a client issues prenumbered

EARLY REVENUE RECOGNITION BOOSTS PROFITS

Faced with declining sales for its traditional product lines, Xerox prematurely recognized revenues to meet market expectations, according to charges filed by the SEC. The SEC stated that Xerox accelerated the recognition of equipment revenue to increase revenues by over $3 billion and pre-tax earnings by approximately $1.5 billion over the period 1997 through 2000. The early revenue recognition and other actions to increase earnings were significant, representing 37 percent of reported pre-tax earnings for the fourth quarters of 1997 and 1998. Without these actions to increase earnings, the SEC charged that Xerox would have fallen short of market earnings expectations for almost every reporting period from 1997 through 1999.

A primary issue was how Xerox accounted for lease revenue. The revenue in Xerox's leasing arrangements represented three components: the value of the equipment, servicing over the life of the lease, and financing. The revenue from the equipment was recorded at the beginning of the lease, but revenues from servicing and financing were recognized over the life of the lease contract. According to the SEC complaint, Xerox took a number of actions to shift servicing and financing revenue to the value of the equipment, so that more of the revenue could be recognized immediately.

The SEC alleged that these actions were set by the "tone at the top" and ordered six senior executives to pay over $22 million in penalties and disgorgement of profits from their actions. Without admitting or denying the allegations made in the SEC complaint, Xerox agreed to pay a $10 million fine, at that time the largest ever for a public company.

Sources: 1. Securities and Exchange Commission Accounting and Auditing Enforcement Release No. 1542 (April 11, 2002); 2. Securities and Exchange Commission Press Release 2003-70 (June 5, 2003) (www.sec.gov).

shipping documents sequentially, it is usually a simple matter to evaluate and test cutoff. Moreover, the segregation of duties between the shipping and the billing function also enhances the likelihood of recording transactions in the proper period. However, if shipments are made by company truck, if the shipping records are unnumbered, and if shipping and billing department personnel are not independent of each other, it may be difficult, if not impossible, to be assured of an accurate cutoff.

When the client's internal controls are effective, auditors can usually verify the cutoff by obtaining the shipping document number for the last shipment made at the end of the period and comparing this number with current and subsequent period recorded sales. As an illustration, assume the shipping document number for the last shipment in the current period is 1489. All recorded sales before the end of the period should bear a shipping document number preceding number 1490, and no sales recorded and shipped in the subsequent period should have a bill of lading numbered 1489 or lower. An auditor can easily test this by comparing recorded sales with the related shipping documents for the last few days of the current period and the first few days of the subsequent period.

Sales Returns and Allowances Cutoff Accounting standards require that sales returns and allowances be *matched with related sales* if the amounts are material. For example, if current period shipments are returned in the subsequent period, the sales return should appear in the current period. (The returned goods should be treated as current period inventory.) For most companies, however, sales returns and allowances are recorded in the *accounting period in which they occur,* under the assumption of approximately equal, offsetting amounts at the beginning and end of each accounting period. This approach is acceptable as long as the amounts are not material. Some companies establish a reserve, similar to the allowance for uncollectible accounts, for the expected amount of returns in the subsequent period.

When the auditor is confident that the client records all sales returns and allowances promptly, the cutoff tests are simple and straightforward. The auditor can examine supporting documentation for a sample of sales returns and allowances recorded during several weeks subsequent to the closing date to determine the date of the original sale. If auditors discover that the amounts recorded in the subsequent period are significantly different from unrecorded returns and allowances at the beginning of the period under audit, they must consider an adjustment. For example, a company may experience an increase in sales returns when it launches a new product. In addition, if the internal controls for recording sales returns and allowances are evaluated as ineffective, a larger sample is needed to verify cutoff.

Cash Receipts Cutoff For most audits, a proper cash receipts cutoff is *less important* than either the sales or the sales returns and allowances cutoff because the improper cutoff of cash affects only the cash and the accounts receivable balances, not earnings. Nevertheless, if the misstatement is material, it can affect the fair presentation of these accounts, especially when cash is a small or negative balance.

It is easy to test for a cash receipts cutoff misstatement (often called *holding the cash receipts book open*) by tracing recorded cash receipts to subsequent period bank deposits on the bank statement. A delay of several days could indicate a cutoff misstatement.

To some degree, auditors may also rely on the confirmation of accounts receivable to uncover cutoff misstatements for sales, sales returns and allowances, and cash receipts. However, it is often difficult to distinguish a cutoff misstatement from a normal **timing difference** due to shipments and payments in transit at year end. For example, if a customer mails and records a check to a client for payment of an unpaid account on December 30 and the client receives and records the amount on January 2, the records of the two organizations will be different on December 31. This is not a cutoff misstatement, but a timing difference due to the delivery time. It may be difficult for the auditor to evaluate whether a cutoff misstatement or a timing difference occurred when a confirmation reply is the source of information. This type of situation requires additional investigation, such as inspection of supporting documents.

Accounts Receivable Is Stated at Realizable Value

Accounting standards require that companies state accounts receivable at the amount that will ultimately be collected. The **realizable value of accounts receivable** equals gross accounts receivable less the *allowance for uncollectible accounts.* To calculate the allowance, the client estimates the total amount of accounts receivable that it expects to be uncollectible. Obviously, clients cannot predict the future precisely, but it is necessary for the auditor to evaluate whether the client's allowance is reasonable, considering all available facts. To assist with this evaluation, the auditor often prepares an audit schedule that analyzes the allowance for uncollectible accounts, as illustrated in Figure 16-4 (p. 536). In this example, the analysis indicates that the allowance is understated. This can be the result of the client failing to adjust the allowance or economic factors. Note that the potential understatement of the reserve was signaled by the analytical procedures in Table 16-3 (p. 530) for Hillsburg Hardware.

To begin the evaluation of the allowance for uncollectible accounts, the auditor reviews the results of the tests of controls that are concerned with the client's credit policy. If the client's credit policy has remained unchanged and the results of the tests of credit policy and credit approval are consistent with those of the preceding year, the change in the balance in the allowance for uncollectible accounts should reflect only changes in economic conditions and sales volume. However, if the client's credit policy or the degree to which it correctly functions has significantly changed, auditors must take great care to consider the effects of these changes as well.

Auditors often evaluate the adequacy of the allowance by carefully examining the noncurrent accounts on the aged trial balance to determine which ones have not been paid subsequent to the balance sheet date. The size and age of unpaid balances can then be compared with similar information from previous years to evaluate whether the amount of noncurrent receivables is increasing or decreasing over time. Auditors also gain insights into the collectibility of the accounts by examining credit files, discussions with the credit manager, and review of the client's correspondence file. These procedures are especially important if a few large balances are noncurrent and are not being paid on a regular basis.

Auditors face two shortcomings in evaluating the allowance by reviewing individual noncurrent balances on the aged trial balance. First, the current accounts are ignored in establishing the adequacy of the allowance, even though some of these amounts will undoubtedly become uncollectible. Second, it is difficult to compare the results of the current year with those of previous years on such an unstructured

FIGURE 16-4 **Analysis of Allowance for Uncollectible Accounts for Hillsburg Hardware Co.**

Hillsburg Hardware Co. Analysis of Allowance for Uncollectible Accounts 12/31/16			Schedule B-4 Prepared by TW Approved by SB	Date 1/8/17 1/10/17
A/R Category	**A/R Balance 12/31/16**	**Estimated Allowance Percentage**	**Estimated Required Allowance**	
0–30 days	$ 14,217,156 ✓	3% ×	$ 426,515	
31–60 days	2,869,366 ✓	6% ×	172,162	
61–90 days	1,408,642 ✓	15% ×	211,296	
91–120 days	1,038,926 ✓	25% ×	259,732	
Over 120	662,710 ✓	40% ×	265,084	
Total	$ 20,196,800		$ 1,334,789	
Recorded Allowance			$ 1,240,000	TB
Difference			$ 94,789	

✓ — Traced to aged accounts receivable trial balance.
× — Allowance percentages are consistent with prior year and appear reasonable based on historical loss percentages documented in permanent file.
TB — Agreed to trial balance.

Conclusion: Recorded allowance appears understated based on aging analysis. Approximate amount of $95,000 not considered material. Include on Summary of Possible Misstatements schedule on A-3. (See Figure 24-6 on p. 785.)

basis. If the accounts are becoming progressively uncollectible over several years, this fact can be overlooked. To avoid these two shortcomings, clients can establish a history of bad debt write-offs over a period of time as a frame of reference for evaluating the current year's allowance. For example, a client might calculate that 2 percent of current accounts, 10 percent of 30- to 90-day accounts, and 35 percent of all balances over 90 days ultimately become uncollectible. Auditors can apply these percentages to the current year's aged trial balance totals and compare the result with the balance in the allowance account. Of course, the auditor has to verify the appropriateness of the percentages used and be careful to modify the calculations for changed conditions.

Bad Debt Expense After the auditor is satisfied with the allowance for uncollectible accounts, it is easy to verify bad debt expense. Assume that:

- The beginning balance in the allowance account was verified as a part of the previous audit.
- The uncollectible accounts written off were verified as a part of the substantive tests of transactions.
- The ending balance in the allowance account has been verified by various means.

Bad debt expense is then simply a residual balance that can be verified by recalculation.

The Client Has Rights to Accounts Receivable

The client's rights to accounts receivable ordinarily cause no audit problems because the receivables usually belong to the client. In some cases, however, a portion of the receivables may have been pledged as collateral, assigned to someone else, factored, or sold at discount. Normally, the client's customers are not aware of the existence of such matters, so the confirmation of receivables will not bring them to light. To uncover instances in which the client has limited rights to receivables, the auditor may review the minutes, discuss with the client, confirm with banks, examine debt contracts for evidence of accounts receivable pledged as collateral, and examine correspondence files.

Accounts Receivable Presentation and Disclosure

Tests of the four presentation and disclosure-related audit objectives are generally done as part of the completion phase of the audit. However, some tests of presentation and disclosure are often done with tests to meet the balance-related audit objectives. For example, when testing sales and accounts receivable, the auditor must understand and evaluate the appropriateness of the client's revenue recognition policy to determine whether it is properly disclosed in the financial statements. The auditor must also decide whether the client has properly combined amounts and disclosed related party information in the statements. To evaluate the adequacy of the presentation and disclosure, the auditor must have a thorough understanding of accounting standards and presentation and disclosure requirements.

An important part of the evaluation involves deciding whether the client has separated material amounts requiring separate disclosure in the statements. For example, receivables from officers and affiliated companies must be segregated from accounts receivable from customers if the amounts are material. Similarly, under SEC requirements, companies must disclose sales and assets for different business segments separately. The proper aggregation of general ledger balances in the financial statements also requires combining account balances that are not relevant for external users of the statements. If all accounts included in the general ledger were disclosed separately on the statements, most statement users would be more confused than enlightened.

CONCEPT CHECK

1. Describe two types of substantive analytical procedures often performed in the audit of the sales and collection cycle and describe how they might indicate a possible misstatement in the financial statements.
2. Which of the eight accounts receivable balance-related audit objectives can be partially satisfied by confirmations with customers?

CONFIRMATION OF ACCOUNTS RECEIVABLE

OBJECTIVE 16-4

Obtain and evaluate accounts receivable confirmations.

Confirmation of accounts receivable was a recurring concept in our discussion about designing tests of details of balances for accounts receivable. The primary purpose of accounts receivable confirmation is to satisfy the *existence, accuracy*, and *cutoff* objectives.

Confirmations are one of the eight types of audit evidence introduced in Chapter 7. Most typically, a confirmation is a direct written response from a third party in paper or electronic form, but it may also include information the auditor is able to obtain through direct access provided by a third party to information that is held by the third party, such as direct access to a supplier's vendor management system. Confirmations are considered to be highly reliable evidence because they are received directly from third parties. Although an oral response provides audit evidence, it is not considered a confirmation.

Auditing Standards Requirements

U.S. auditing standards indicate that auditors should use external confirmations for accounts receivable. Confirmation may not be appropriate in the following circumstances:

1. *The overall accounts receivable balance is immaterial.* Some clients, such as fast-food restaurants, may generate sales mostly on a cash basis, resulting in a negligible accounts receivable balance.

2. *The auditor considers confirmations ineffective evidence because response rates will likely be inadequate or unreliable.* In certain industries, such as hospitals, response rates to confirmations are very low.
3. *The auditor's assessed level of the risk of material misstatement (represented by the combined level of inherent risk and control risk) is low and other substantive evidence can be accumulated to provide sufficient evidence.* If a client has effective internal controls and low inherent risk for the sales and collection cycle, the auditor should often be able to satisfy the evidence requirements by tests of controls, substantive tests of transactions, and substantive analytical procedures.

If the auditor decides not to confirm accounts receivable that are material, the justification for doing so must be documented in the audit files. While U.S. auditing standards require the use of confirmations for accounts receivable in most circumstances, international auditing standards suggest but do not require their use. This is one of the few notable differences between requirements of U.S. and international auditing standards. The PCAOB is also considering changes to its Auditing Standards that might expand the use of confirmations by potentially eliminating the exceptions noted above and by expanding the types of receivables that should be confirmed.

Types of Confirmation

In performing confirmation procedures, the auditor must first decide the type of confirmation to use.

Positive Confirmation A **positive confirmation** is a communication addressed to the debtor requesting the recipient to confirm directly whether the balance as stated on the confirmation request is correct or incorrect. Figure 16-5 illustrates a positive confirmation in the audit of Hillsburg Hardware Co. Notice that this confirmation is for one of the largest accounts on the aged trial balance in Figure 16-3 (p. 532).

A **blank confirmation form** is a type of positive confirmation that does not state the amount on the confirmation but requests the recipient to fill in the balance or furnish other information. Because blank forms require the recipient to determine the information requested, they are considered more reliable than confirmations that include balance information. Blank forms are rarely used in practice because they often result in lower response rates.

An **invoice confirmation** is another type of positive confirmation in which an individual invoice is confirmed, rather than the customer's entire accounts receivable balance. Many customers use voucher systems that allow them to confirm individual invoices but not balance information. As a result, the use of invoice confirmations may improve confirmation response rates. Invoice confirmations also result in

REVENUES AND MARGINS TOO GOOD TO BE TRUE

Channel-stuffing is a form of aggressive revenue recognition that can sometimes cross the line to fraudulent reporting and that is often carried out by enticing or pressuring customers to accept additional products through pricing or other incentives. That was the case with Bristol-Myers Squibb and their largest pharmaceutical wholesalers such as D&K Healthcare Resources, Inc. Top executives at Bristol-Myers Squibb were found guilty of fraudulent channel-stuffing practices in which they encouraged wholesalers to accept inventory products above and beyond what they would normally purchase, by offering pricing discounts and by helping to cover inventory carrying costs, effectively making the sale a consignment arrangement. This practice overstated revenue by $2.5 billion over a three-year period. The channel-stuffing and side agreements had a ripple effect on wholesalers by inflating their gross margins as a result of the "purchasing incentives." When Bristol-Myers was investigated by the SEC and forced to stop their channel-stuffing practices, both Bristol Myers and D&K restated previously reported results and were named as defendants in class action lawsuits. Incidences of channel-stuffing like this illustrate why an auditor should consider confirming sales transaction terms, such as right of return or side agreements, in addition to the balance owed by the customer.

Sources: 1. SEC 2004-105. Bristol-Myers Squibb Company Agrees to Pay $150 Million to Settle Fraud Charges, August 4, 2004 (www.sec.gov); 2. Gary Dutton vs. D&K Healthcare Resources, Class Action Litigation Complaint (www.securities.stanford.edu).

FIGURE 16-5 Positive Confirmation

HILLSBURG HARDWARE CO.
Gary, Indiana

January 5, 2017

Atwater Brothers
19 South Main Street
Middleton, Ohio 36947

To Whom It May Concern:

In connection with an audit of our financial statements, please confirm directly to our auditors

BERGER & ANTHONY, CPAs
Gary, Indiana

the correctness of the balance of your account with us as of December 31, 2016, as shown below.

This is not a request for payment; please do not send your remittance to our auditors. Your prompt attention to this request will be appreciated. An envelope is enclosed for your reply.

Erma Swanson, Controller

BERGER & ANTHONY, CPAs
Gary, Indiana

Erma Swanson

The balance receivable from us of $210,389 as of December 31, 2016, is correct except as noted below:

____
____
____
____

Date ____________ By ________________

fewer timing differences and other reconciling items than balance confirmations. However, invoice confirmations have the disadvantage of not directly confirming ending balances.

Sales to major customers often involve special terms or side-agreements for the return of goods that may affect the amount and timing of revenue to be recognized from the sale. When this has been identified as a significant risk, positive confirmations often request the customer to confirm the existence of any special terms or side-agreements between the client and customer. The vignette on the prior page illustrates the importance of confirming transaction terms.

Negative Confirmation A **negative confirmation** is also addressed to the debtor but requests a response only when the debtor disagrees with the stated amount. Figure 16-6 (p. 540) illustrates a negative confirmation in the audit of Hillsburg Hardware Co. that has been attached to a customer's monthly statement.

A positive confirmation is *more reliable* evidence because the auditor can perform follow-up procedures if a response is not received from the debtor. With a negative confirmation, failure to reply must be regarded as a correct response, even though the debtor may have ignored the confirmation request.

Offsetting the reliability disadvantage, negative confirmations are less expensive to send than positive confirmations, and thus more can be distributed for the same

FIGURE 16-6 Negative Confirmation

AUDITOR'S ACCOUNT CONFIRMATION

Please examine this statement carefully. If it does NOT agree with your records, please report any exceptions directly to our auditors

BERGER & ANTHONY, CPAs
Gary, Indiana

who are conducting an audit of our financial statements as of December 31, 2016. An addressed envelope is enclosed for your convenience in replying.

Do not send your remittance to our auditors.

total cost. Negative confirmations cost less because there are no second requests and no follow-up of nonresponses.

The determination of which type of confirmation to use is an auditor's decision, and it should be based on the facts in the audit. Auditing standards state that it is acceptable to use negative confirmations as the sole substantive audit procedure to address an assessed risk of material misstatement at the assertion level only when *all* of the following circumstances are present:

1. The auditor has assessed the risk of material misstatement as low and has obtained sufficient appropriate evidence regarding the design and operating effectiveness of controls relevant to the assertion being tested by the confirmation procedure.
2. The population of items subject to negative confirmation procedures is made up of a large number of small, homogenous account balances, transactions, or other items.
3. The auditor expects a low exception rate.
4. The auditor reasonably believes that recipients of negative confirmation requests will give the requests adequate consideration. For example, if the response rate to positive confirmations in prior years was extremely high or if there are high response rates on audits of similar clients, it is likely that recipients will give negative confirmations reasonable consideration as well.

Typically, when negative confirmations are used, the auditor puts considerable emphasis on the effectiveness of internal controls, substantive tests of transactions, and substantive analytical procedures as evidence of the fairness of accounts receivable, and assumes that the large majority of the recipients will provide a conscientious reading and response to the confirmation request.

Negative confirmations are often used for audits of hospitals, retail stores, banks, and other industries in which the receivables are due from the general public. Auditors may use a combination of negative and positive confirmations by sending the latter to accounts with large balances and the former to those with small balances.

The auditor's choice of confirmation falls along a continuum, starting with the use of no confirmations in some circumstances, to using only negatives, to using both negatives and positives, to using only positives. The primary factors affecting the auditor's decision are the materiality of total accounts receivable, the number and size of individual accounts, control risk, inherent risk, the effectiveness of confirmations as audit evidence, and the availability of other audit evidence.

Timing

The most reliable evidence from confirmations is obtained when they are sent as close to the balance sheet date as possible. This permits the auditor to directly test the accounts receivable balance on the financial statements without making any inferences about the transactions taking place between the confirmation date and the balance sheet date. However, as a means of completing the audit on a timely basis, it is often necessary to confirm the accounts at an interim date. This is permissible if internal controls are adequate and can provide reasonable assurance that sales, cash receipts, and other credits are properly recorded between the date of the confirmation and the end of the accounting period. The auditor is likely to consider other factors in making the decision, including the materiality of accounts receivable and the auditor's exposure to lawsuits because of the possibility of client bankruptcy and similar risks.

If the decision is made to confirm accounts receivable before year-end, the auditor typically prepares a roll-forward schedule that reconciles the accounts receivable balance at the confirmation date to accounts receivable at the balance sheet date. In addition to performing analytical procedures on the activity during the intervening period, it may be necessary to test the transactions occurring between the confirmation date and the balance sheet date. The auditor can accomplish this by examining internal documents such as duplicate sales invoices, shipping documents, and evidence of cash receipts.

Sampling Decisions

Sample Size The major factors affecting sample size for confirming accounts receivable fall into several categories and include the following:

- Performance materiality
- Inherent risk (relative size of total accounts receivable, number of accounts, prior-year results, and expected misstatements)
- Control risk
- Achieved detection risk from other substantive tests (extent and results of substantive tests of transactions, substantive analytical procedures, and other tests of details)
- Type of confirmation (negatives normally require a larger sample size)

Selection of the Items for Testing Some type of *stratification* is desirable with most confirmations. In a typical approach to stratification for selecting the balances for confirmation, an auditor considers both the dollar size of individual accounts and the length of time an account has been outstanding. In most audits, the emphasis should be on confirming larger and older balances because these are most likely to include a significant misstatement. But it is also important to sample some items from every material segment of the population. In many cases, the auditor selects all accounts above a certain dollar amount and selects a random sample from the remainder.

Management may refuse to allow the auditor to send confirmation requests to certain customers. The auditor must inquire about the reason for the client's request, which is often due to litigation or negotiations between the client and customer. The auditor should obtain evidence to evaluate the reasonableness of the client's request, and evaluate whether the request indicates a potential fraud risk or increased risk of material misstatement.

Verification of Addresses and Maintaining Control

The auditor should perform procedures to verify the addresses or email addresses used for confirmation. For example, auditors should consider performing additional procedures when the address is a post office box or when an email address is inconsistent with the customer's Web site address.

For confirmations sent by mail, the auditor must maintain control of the confirmations until they are returned from the customer. The client may assist with preparing the confirmations, but the auditor must be responsible for mailing the confirmation *outside* the client's office. A return address must be included on all envelopes to make sure that undelivered mail is received by the CPA firm. Similarly, self-addressed return envelopes accompanying the confirmations must be addressed for delivery to the CPA firm's office. These procedures are designed to ensure that responses will be received directly by the auditor.

Follow-Up on Nonresponses

It is inappropriate to regard confirmations mailed but not returned by customers as significant audit evidence. For example, nonresponses to positive confirmations do not provide audit evidence. Similarly, for negative confirmations, the auditor should not conclude that the recipient received the confirmation request and verified the information requested. Negative confirmations do, however, provide some evidence of the existence assertion.

ELECTRONIC CONFIRMATION SERVICES

Given that confirmations are used as audit evidence in most audits, the volume of confirmations processed by entities, including customers, vendors, banks, and debtholders, is staggering. Technologies, including the Internet, have allowed businesses to be created to help streamline the efficiency and effectiveness of the confirmation process. One example is Capital Confirmation's patented Confirmation.com service, which provides secure electronic confirmation services for auditors. Not only does this service help save costs and time related to the audit, it also helps minimize fraud through features that validate the authenticity and authorization of each user. Auditors can use services such as those offered by Capital Confirmation to upload accounts receivable samples in spreadsheet form so that confirmation can be sent electronically to thousands of "in-network" companies that are already validated and ready to respond electronically. For companies that are "out-of-network," confirmation service providers such as Capital Confirmation can assist the auditor with printing and posting confirmations, and with customer responses mailed directly to the auditor or submitted to the auditor through the Confirmation.com platform.

Source: Capital Confirmation (www.confirmation.com).

When positive confirmations are used, auditing standards require follow-up procedures for confirmations not returned by the customer. It is common to send second and sometimes even third requests for confirmations. Even with these efforts, some customers do not return the confirmation, so it is necessary to follow up with **alternative procedures**. The objective of alternative procedures is to determine by a means other than confirmation whether the nonconfirmed account existed and was properly stated at the confirmation date. For any positive confirmation not returned, auditors can examine the following documentation to verify the existence and accuracy of individual sales transactions making up the ending balance in accounts receivable:

Subsequent Cash Receipts Evidence of the receipt of cash subsequent to the confirmation date includes examining remittance advices, entries in the cash receipts records, or perhaps even subsequent credits in the accounts receivable master file. On the one hand, the examination of evidence of subsequent cash receipts is a highly useful alternative procedure because it is reasonable to assume that a customer would not have made a payment unless it was an existing receivable. On the other hand, payment does not establish whether an obligation existed on the date of the confirmation. In addition, auditors should take care to match each unpaid sales transaction with evidence of its subsequent payment as a test for disputes or disagreements over individual outstanding invoices.

Duplicate Sales Invoices These are useful in verifying the actual issuance of a sales invoice and the actual date of the billing.

Shipping Documents These are important in establishing whether the shipment was actually made and as a test of cutoff.

Correspondence with the Client Usually, the auditor does not need to review correspondence as a part of alternative procedures, but correspondence can be used to discover disputed and questionable receivables not uncovered by other means.

The extent and nature of the alternative procedures depend primarily on the materiality of the nonresponses, the types of misstatements discovered in the confirmed responses, the subsequent cash receipts from the nonresponses, and the auditor's conclusions about internal control.

It is normally desirable to account for all unconfirmed balances with alternative procedures even if the amounts are small, as a means of properly generalizing from the sample to the population. Another acceptable approach is to assume that nonresponses are 100 percent overstatement amounts.

Analysis of Differences

When the confirmation requests are returned by the customer, the auditor must determine the reason for any reported differences. In many cases, they are caused by timing differences between the client's and the customer's records. It is important to distinguish between timing differences and *exceptions,* which represent misstatements of the accounts receivable balance. The most commonly reported types of differences in confirmations include:

Payment Has Already Been Made Reported differences typically arise when the customer has made a payment before the confirmation date, but the client has not received the payment in time for recording before the confirmation date. Such instances should be carefully investigated to determine the possibility of a cash receipts cutoff misstatement, lapping, or a theft of cash.

Goods Have Not Been Received These differences typically result because the client records the sale at the date of shipment and the customer records the acquisition when the goods are received. The time that the goods are in transit is often the cause of differences reported on confirmations. These should be investigated to determine the possibility of the customer not receiving the goods at all or the existence of a cutoff misstatement on the client's records.

The Goods Have Been Returned The client's failure to record a credit memo could have resulted from timing differences or the improper recording of sales returns and allowances. Like other differences, these must be investigated.

Clerical Errors and Disputed Amounts The most likely types of reported differences in a client's records are when the customer states that there is an error in the price charged for the goods, the goods are damaged, the proper quantity of goods was not received, and so forth. These differences must be investigated to determine whether the client is in error and the amount of the error.

In most instances, the auditor will ask the client to reconcile the difference and, if necessary, will communicate with the customer to resolve any disagreements. Naturally, the auditor must carefully verify the client's conclusions on each significant difference.

Drawing Conclusions

When all differences have been resolved, including those discovered in performing alternative procedures, the auditor must *reevaluate internal control*. Each client misstatement must be analyzed to determine whether it was consistent or inconsistent with the original assessed level of control risk. If a significant number of misstatements occurred that are inconsistent with the assessment of control risk, it is necessary to revise the assessment and consider the effect of the revision on the audit. Auditors of public companies must also consider implications for the audit of internal control over financial reporting.

It is also necessary to generalize from the sample to the entire population of accounts receivable. Even though the sum of the misstatements in the sample may not significantly affect the financial statements, the auditor must consider whether the population is likely to be materially misstated. Generalizing from the sample to the population can be done using nonstatistical or statistical sampling techniques and is discussed in Chapter 17.

The auditor should always evaluate the qualitative nature of the misstatements found in the sample, regardless of the dollar amount of the estimated population misstatement. Even if the estimated misstatement is less than performance materiality for accounts receivable, the misstatements found in a sample can be symptomatic of a more serious problem.

The final decision about accounts receivable and sales is whether sufficient appropriate evidence has been obtained through tests of controls and substantive tests of transactions, substantive analytical procedures, cutoff procedures, confirmation, and other substantive tests to justify drawing conclusions about the correctness of the stated balance.

DEVELOPING TESTS OF DETAILS AUDIT PROGRAM

OBJECTIVE 16-5

Design audit procedures for the audit of accounts receivable, using an evidence-planning worksheet as a guide.

We use Hillsburg Hardware Co. to illustrate the development of audit program procedures for tests of details in the sales and collection cycle. The determination of these procedures is based on the tests of controls and substantive tests of transactions, as illustrated in Chapters 14 and 15, and the analytical procedures described earlier in this chapter.

FIGURE 16-7 **Evidence-Planning Worksheet to Decide Tests of Details of Balances for Hillsburg Hardware Co.—Accounts Receivable**

	Detail tie-in	Existence	Completeness	Accuracy	Classification	Cutoff	Realizable value	Rights
Acceptable audit risk	Medium	Medium	Medium	Medium	Medium	Medium	Medium	Medium
Inherent risk	Low	Medium	Low	Low	Low	Medium	Medium	Low
Control risk—Sales	Low	Medium	Low	High	Low	Medium	High	Not applicable
Control risk—Cash receipts	Low	Medium	Low	Low	Low	Low	Not applicable	Not applicable
Control risk—Additional controls	None	None	None	None	None	None	None	Low
Substantive tests of transactions—Sales	Good results	Good results	Good results	Fair results	Good results	Unacceptable results	Not applicable	Not applicable
Substantive tests of transactions—Cash receipts	Good results	Good results	Good results	Good results	Good results	Good results	Not applicable	Not applicable
Substantive analytical procedures	Good results	Good results	Good results	Good results	Good results	Good results	Unacceptable results	Not applicable
Planned detection risk for tests of details of balances	High	Medium	High	Medium	High	Low	Low	High
Planned audit evidence for tests of details of balances	Low	Medium	Low	Medium	Low	High	High	Low

Performance materiality $265,000

Fran Moore, the audit senior, prepared the evidence-planning worksheet in Figure 16-7 as an aid to help her decide the extent of planned tests of details of balances. The source of each of the rows is as follows:

- *Performance materiality.* The preliminary judgment of materiality for the financial statements as a whole was set at $442,000 (approximately 6 percent of earnings from operations of $7,370,000). She allocated $265,000 as performance materiality to the audit of accounts receivable (see Figure 8-7 on p. 240).
- *Acceptable audit risk.* Fran assessed acceptable audit risk as medium because the company is publicly traded, but is in good financial condition, and has high management integrity. Although Hillsburg is a publicly traded company, its stock is not widely held or extensively followed by financial analysts.

TABLE 16-4	Balance-Related Audit Objectives and Audit Program for Hillsburg Hardware Co.—Sales and Collection Cycle (Design Format)
Balance-Related Audit Objective	**Audit Procedures**
Accounts receivable in the aged trial balance agree with related master file amounts, and the total is correctly added and agrees with the general ledger (detail tie-in).	Obtain the accounts receivable aged trial balance and trace the balance to the general ledger (1). Use audit software to foot and cross-foot the aged trial balance (2). Trace 10 accounts from the trial balance to accounts on master file (8).
The accounts receivable on the aged trial balance exist (existence).	Confirm accounts receivable, using positive confirmations. Confirm all amounts over $100,000 and a statistical sample of the remainder (10). Perform alternative procedures for all confirmations not returned on the first or second request (11). Review accounts receivable trial balance for large and unusual receivables (3).
Existing accounts receivable are included in the aged trial balance (completeness).	Trace five accounts from the accounts receivable master file to the aged trial balance (9).
Accounts receivable in the trial balance are accurate (accuracy).	Confirm accounts receivable, using positive confirmations. Confirm all amounts over $100,000 and a statistical sample of the remainder (10). Perform alternative procedures for all confirmations not returned on the first or second request (11). Review accounts receivable trial balance for large and unusual receivables (3).
Accounts receivable on the aged trial balance are correctly classified (classification).	Review the receivables listed on the aged trial balance for notes and related party receivables (5). Inquire of management whether there are any related party notes or long-term receivables included in the trial balance (6).
Transactions in the sales and collection cycle are recorded in the proper period (cutoff).	Select the last 20 sales transactions from the current year's sales journal and the first 20 from the subsequent year's and trace each to the related shipping documents, checking for the date of actual shipment and the correct recording (14). Review large sales returns and allowances before and after the balance sheet date to determine whether they are recorded in the correct period (15).
Accounts receivable is stated at realizable value (realizable value).	Trace 10 accounts from the aged trial balance to the accounts receivable master file to test for correctness of aging and the balance (8). Use audit software to foot and cross-foot the aged trial balance (2). Discuss with the credit manager the likelihood of collecting older accounts. Examine subsequent cash receipts and the credit file on all accounts over 90 days and evaluate whether the receivables are collectible (12). Evaluate whether the allowance is adequate after performing other audit procedures for collectibility of receivables (13).
The client has rights to accounts receivable on the trial balance (rights).	Review the minutes of the board of directors meetings for any indication of pledged or factored accounts receivable (7). Inquire of management whether any receivables are pledged or factored (7).

Note: The procedures are summarized into a performance format in Table 16-5 on page 546. The numbers in parentheses after the procedures refer to Table 16-5.

- *Inherent risk.* Fran assessed inherent risk as medium for existence and cutoff because of concerns over revenue recognition identified in auditing standards. Fran also assessed inherent risk as medium for realizable value. In past years, the client made audit adjustments to the allowance for uncollectible accounts because it was found to be understated. Inherent risk was assessed as low for all other objectives.
- *Control risk.* Control risk assessments for each audit objective are the same as those in Figure 15-6 on page 504. (Recall that results of tests of controls and substantive tests of transactions in Chapter 15 were consistent with the auditor's initial control risk assessments, except for the accuracy and realizable value objectives for sales.)

TABLE 16-5	Test of Details of Balances Audit Program for Hillsburg Hardware Co.—Sales and Collection Cycle (Performance Format)
1. Obtain the accounts receivable aged trial balance and trace the balance to the general ledger.	
2. Use audit software to foot and cross-foot the aged trial balance.	
3. Review aged trial balance for large and unusual receivables.	
4. Calculate analytical procedures indicated in carry-forward audit schedules (not included) and follow up on any significant changes from prior years.	
5. Review the receivables listed on the aged trial balance for notes and related party receivables.	
6. Inquire of management whether there are any related party notes or long-term receivables included in the trial balance.	
7. Review the minutes of the board of directors meetings and inquire of management to determine whether any receivables are pledged or factored.	
8. Trace 10 accounts from the aged trial balance to the accounts receivable master file to test for correctness of aging and the balance.	
9. Trace five accounts from the accounts receivable master file to the aged trial balance.	
10. Confirm accounts receivable, using positive confirmations. Confirm all amounts over $100,000 and select a statistical sample using audit software for the remaining accounts.	
11. Perform alternative procedures for all confirmations not returned on the first or second request.	
12. Discuss with the credit manager the likelihood of collecting older accounts. Examine subsequent cash receipts and the credit file on all larger accounts over 90 days and evaluate whether the receivables are collected.	
13. Evaluate whether the allowance is adequate after performing other audit procedures for collectibility of receivables.	
14. Select the last 20 sales transactions from the current year's sales journal and the first 20 from the subsequent year's and trace each to the related shipping documents, checking for the date of actual shipment and the correct recording.	
15. Review large sales returns and allowances before and after the balance sheet date to determine whether they are recorded in the correct period.	

- *Substantive tests of transactions results.* These results were also taken from Figure 15-6. (Recall from Chapter 15 that all results were acceptable except for the accuracy and cutoff objectives for sales.)
- *Substantive analytical procedures.* See Tables 16-2 and 16-3 (both on page 530).
- *Planned detection risk and planned audit evidence.* These two rows are decided for each objective based on the conclusions in the other rows.

Table 16-4 (p. 545) shows the tests of details audit program for accounts receivable, by objective, and for the allowance for uncollectible accounts. The audit program reflects the conclusions for planned audit evidence on the evidence-planning worksheet in Figure 16-7 (p. 544).

Table 16-5 shows the audit program in a performance format. The audit procedures are identical to those in Table 16-4 except for procedure 4, which is a substantive analytical procedure. The numbers in parentheses are a cross reference between the two tables.

CONCEPT CHECK

1. Distinguish between a positive and a negative confirmation and state the circumstances in which each should be used.
2. Define what is meant by alternative procedures in the confirmation of accounts receivable and explain their purpose. Which alternative procedures are the most reliable? Why?

SUMMARY

This chapter completes the overview of the methodology auditors follow in designing the audit of the sales and collection cycle. Chapters 14 and 15 examined tests of controls and substantive tests of transactions for the sales and collection cycle, both of which are part of phase II of the audit process. This chapter examines the design of substantive analytical procedures and tests of details for the two key balance sheet accounts in the cycle: accounts receivable and the allowance for doubtful accounts. Because auditing standards require auditors to confirm material accounts receivable in most audits, this chapter highlighted practices appropriate when using either positive or negative confirmations. We ended the chapter by emphasizing how auditors use evidence accumulated through the performance of a combination of procedures including tests of controls, substantive tests of transactions, substantive analytical procedures, and tests of details to evaluate accounts receivable.

ESSENTIAL TERMS

Accounts receivable balance-related audit objectives—the eight specific audit objectives used by the auditor to decide the appropriate audit evidence for accounts receivable

Aged trial balance—a listing of the balances in the accounts receivable master file at the balance sheet date broken down according to the amount of time passed between the date of sale and the balance sheet date

Alternative procedures—the follow-up of a positive confirmation not returned by the debtor with the use of documentation evidence to determine whether the recorded receivable exists

Blank confirmation form—a letter, addressed to the debtor, requesting the recipient to fill in the amount of the accounts receivable balance; it is considered a positive confirmation

Cutoff misstatements—misstatements that take place as a result of current period transactions being recorded in a subsequent period, or subsequent period transactions being recorded in the current period

Invoice confirmation—a type of positive confirmation in which an individual invoice is confirmed, rather than the customer's entire accounts receivable balance

Negative confirmation—a letter, addressed to the debtor, requesting a response only if the recipient disagrees with the amount of the stated account balance

Positive confirmation—a letter, addressed to the debtor, requesting that the recipient indicate directly on the letter whether the stated account balance is correct or incorrect and, if incorrect, by what amount

Realizable value of accounts receivable—the amount of the outstanding balances in accounts receivable that will ultimately be collected

Timing difference—a reported difference in a confirmation from a debtor that is determined to be a timing difference between the client's and debtor's records and therefore not a misstatement

REVIEW QUESTIONS

16-1 (OBJECTIVE 16-1) Distinguish among tests of details of balances, tests of controls, and substantive tests of transactions for the sales and collection cycle. Explain how the tests of controls and substantive tests of transactions affect the tests of details of balances.

16-2 (OBJECTIVE 16-1) Cynthia Roberts, CPA, expresses the following viewpoint: "I do not believe in performing tests of controls and substantive tests of transactions for the sales and collection cycle. As an alternative, I send a lot of negative confirmations on every audit at an interim date. If I find a lot of misstatements, I analyze them to determine their cause. If internal controls are inadequate, I send positive confirmations at year-end to evaluate the amount of misstatements. If the negative confirmations result in minimal misstatements, which is often the case, I have found that the internal controls are effective without bothering to perform tests of controls and substantive tests of transactions, and the confirmation requirement has been satisfied at the same time. In my opinion, the best test of internal controls is to go directly to third parties." Evaluate her point of view.

16-3 **(OBJECTIVE 16-2)** List five analytical procedures for the sales and collection cycle. For each test, describe a misstatement that could be identified.

16-4 **(OBJECTIVE 16-3)** Explain why you agree or disagree with the following statement: "In most audits, it is more important to test carefully the cutoff for sales than for cash receipts." Describe how you perform each type of test, assuming documents are prenumbered.

16-5 **(OBJECTIVE 16-3)** Identify the eight accounts receivable balance-related audit objectives. For each objective, list one audit procedure.

16-6 **(OBJECTIVE 16-3)** Why does an auditor review sales returns subsequent to year-end? What audit objective does this procedure satisfy?

16-7 **(OBJECTIVE 16-3)** State the purpose of footing the total column in the client's accounts receivable trial balance, tracing individual customer names and amounts to the accounts receivable master file, and tracing the total to the general ledger. Is it necessary to trace each amount to the master file? Why?

16-8 **(OBJECTIVE 16-3)** Distinguish between accuracy tests of gross accounts receivable and tests of the realizable value of receivables.

16-9 **(OBJECTIVE 16-4)** Evaluate the following statement: "In many audits in which accounts receivable is material, the requirement of confirming customer balances is a waste of time and would not be performed by competent auditors if it were not required by auditing standards. When internal controls are excellent and there are a large number of small receivables from customers who do not recognize the function of confirmation, it is a meaningless procedure. Examples include well-run utilities and retail stores. In these situations, tests of controls and substantive tests of transactions are far more effective than confirmations."

16-10 **(OBJECTIVE 16-4)** Why do CPA firms sometimes use a combination of positive and negative confirmations on the same audit?

16-11 **(OBJECTIVE 16-4)** Under what circumstances is it acceptable to confirm accounts receivable before the balance sheet date?

16-12 **(OBJECTIVE 16-4)** State the most important factors affecting the sample size in confirmations of accounts receivable.

16-13 **(OBJECTIVE 16-4)** Discuss whether email responses and oral responses are acceptable confirmation responses. How can an auditor verify the addresses for confirmations sent by mail and confirmations sent electronically?

16-14 **(OBJECTIVE 16-4)** Under what circumstances would an auditor choose to confirm information such as the right of return or special sales terms in addition to the customer balance?

16-15 **(OBJECTIVE 16-4)** Explain why the analysis of differences is important in the confirmation of accounts receivable, even if the misstatements in the sample are not material.

16-16 **(OBJECTIVE 16-4)** State three types of differences that might be observed in the confirmation of accounts receivable that do not constitute misstatements. For each, state an audit procedure that will verify the difference.

16-17 **(OBJECTIVE 16-5)** What is the relationship of each of the following to the sales and collection cycle: flowcharts, assessing control risk, tests of controls, and tests of details of balances?

16-18 **(OBJECTIVE 16-5)** Explain how unacceptable results from tests of controls and substantive tests of transactions might impact the auditor's planned reliance on tests of details of balances.

MULTIPLE CHOICE QUESTIONS FROM CPA EXAMINATIONS

16-19 **(OBJECTIVE 16-2)** The following questions concern analytical procedures in the sales and collection cycle. Choose the best response.

a. As a result of analytical procedures, the auditor determines that the gross profit percentage has declined from 30% in the preceding year to 20% in the current year. The auditor should
   (1) express a qualified opinion due to inability of the client company to continue as a going concern.
   (2) evaluate management's performance in causing this decline.
   (3) require footnote disclosure.
   (4) consider the possibility of a misstatement in the financial statements.

b. An auditor's preliminary analysis of accounts receivable turnover revealed the following rates over these accounting periods:

2016	2015	2014
4.3	6.2	7.3

   Which of the following is the most likely cause of the decrease in accounts receivable turnover?
   (1) Increase in the cash discount offered
   (2) Liberalization of credit policy
   (3) Shortening of due date terms
   (4) Increased cash sales

c. After a CPA has determined that accounts receivable have increased as a result of slow collections in a "tight money" environment, the CPA will be likely to
   (1) increase the balance in the allowance for bad debt account.
   (2) review the going concern ramifications.
   (3) review the credit and collection policy.
   (4) expand tests of collectibility.

16-20 **(OBJECTIVE 16-4)** The following questions deal with confirmation of accounts receivable. Choose the best response.

a. Which of the following procedures will an auditor most likely perform for year-end accounts receivable confirmations when the auditor did not receive replies to second requests?
   (1) Review the cash receipts journal for the month prior to year end.
   (2) Intensify the study of internal control concerning the revenue cycle.
   (3) Inspect the shipping records documenting the merchandise sold to the debtors.
   (4) Increase the assessed level of detection risk for the existence assertion.

b. The negative form of accounts receivable confirmation request is useful *except* when
   (1) internal control surrounding accounts receivable is considered to be effective.
   (2) a large number of small balances are involved.
   (3) the auditor has reason to believe the persons receiving the requests are likely to give them consideration.
   (4) individual account balances are relatively large.

c. The return of a positive confirmation of accounts receivable without an exception attests to the
   (1) collectibility of the receivable balance.
   (2) accuracy of the allowance for uncollectible accounts.
   (3) accuracy of the aging of accounts receivable.
   (4) accuracy of the receivable balance.

16-21 **(OBJECTIVE 16-3)** The following questions concern audit objectives and management assertions for accounts receivable. Choose the best response.

a. Which of the following will likely provide the most assurance concerning the accuracy balance-related objective for accounts receivable?
   (1) Vouch amounts in the subsidiary ledger to details on shipping documents.
   (2) Compare receivable turnover ratios with industry statistics for reasonableness.

(3) Inquire about receivables pledged under loan agreements.
(4) Assess the allowance for uncollectible accounts for reasonableness.

b. Which of the following audit procedures will best uncover an understatement of sales and accounts receivable?
(1) Test a sample of sales transactions, selecting the sample from prenumbered shipping documents.
(2) Test a sample of sales transactions, selecting the sample from sales invoices recorded in the sales journal.
(3) Confirm accounts receivable.
(4) Review the aged accounts receivable trial balance.

c. The confirmation of customers' accounts receivable rarely provides reliable evidence about the completeness assertion because
(1) customers may not be inclined to report understatement errors in their accounts.
(2) recipients usually respond only if they disagree with the information on the request.
(3) many customers merely sign and return the confirmation without verifying details.
(4) there is likely to be reliable third-party evidence available.

MULTIPLE CHOICE QUESTIONS FROM BECKER CPA EXAM REVIEW

16-22 **(OBJECTIVES 16-2, 16-3, 16-4)** The following questions concern auditor responsibilities related to the audit of accounts receivable. Choose the best response.

a. Which of the following is least likely to be a reasonable explanation for an increase in accounts receivable turnover?
(1) Early payment incentives for customers
(2) Tightening of credit policy
(3) Implementation of more aggressive collection policies
(4) Allowance of a new grace period for customer payments

b. An auditor who is auditing accounts receivable would least likely perform which of the following tests?
(1) Select cash disbursements made shortly after year-end and examine the supporting documentation such as receiving reports and vendor invoices.
(2) Confirm a sample of accounts receivables with the customers that owe the balances.
(3) Vouch cash receipts to the accounts receivables transactions.
(4) Obtain an aged trial balance of accounts receivable and trace the total to the general ledger control account.

c. The auditor sends out positive accounts receivable confirmations for a client. Assuming a second confirmation is sent out to a major customer who still fails to respond, the auditor should:
(1) Consider the nonresponse as a minor audit finding and use responding confirmations as a basis for test results.
(2) Issue a qualified opinion due to the lack of sufficient audit evidence.
(3) Send out a third confirmation request and if no response, perform alternative procedures.
(4) Provide the client a copy of the accounts receivable confirmation and request that they obtain the information from the customer.

DISCUSSION QUESTIONS AND PROBLEMS

16-23 **(OBJECTIVE 16-1)** Because revenue recognition is presumed to be a fraud risk in most audits, generally the double-entry nature of accounting means the existence of accounts receivable is also at risk. In recent years, several high-profile incidents of improper revenue recognition attracted the attention of the business media. The SEC has also expressed concerns about the number of instances of improper revenue recognition identified by SEC staff. One revenue issue involves "bill and hold" sales. Read the SEC guidance on revenue recognition (www.sec.gov/interps/account/sabcodet13.htm) to answer the following questions:

Required

a. What does the SEC indicate are the four basic criteria for determining whether revenue is realized or realizable?
b. What is a "bill and hold" transaction?
c. Why would a bill and hold transaction normally not qualify as a sale? What might justify recording a bill and hold transaction as a sale with a related receivable?
d. A customer of your audit client, Henson, LLC, made a formal, written request to establish a bill and hold arrangement in November 2016, an arrangement that is typical in the industry. The customer's written request outlines a delivery schedule that will begin in February 2017. As of November 2016, the product to be shipped in February is already complete and ready for shipment. Because the sale was completed in 2016, your audit client would like to record the bill and hold transaction described as a sale in 2016. You do not recall noticing any inventory held in a separate area of the client's warehouse during the December 31, 2016, inventory observation. In making your determination regarding the timing of the revenue recognition, what criteria has the SEC determined to be important?

16-24 (OBJECTIVES 16-1, 16-2, 16-4) You are responsible for designing the audit of notes receivable for Hickory Appliance Retailers, which sells appliances and electronics to consumers for their homes or small businesses. Hickory Appliance has eight store locations in different cities located in the upper Midwestern part of the United States. One of Hickory's unique competitive advantages has been its ability to offer more attractive credit terms for appliance purchases for their customers relative to traditional credit cards. Thus, most of their sales involve Hickory-financed purchases by their customers. As part of obtaining an understanding of the client's business and industry, you learned that some of the stores are located in cities that have recently experienced higher rates of unemployment.

Required

a. Which notes receivable balance-related audit objective(s) might have a high risk of material misstatement?
b. What risks, if any, would you consider to be a significant risk related to notes receivable?
c. How might the number of days receivables outstanding in the current year compare to prior years'?
d. Do you plan to send notes receivable confirmations in the current year? Why or why not?
e. To what extent will confirmations of notes receivable help you assess collectibility of the accounts as of year-end?

16-25 (OBJECTIVE 16-3) The following are common tests of details of balances or substantive analytical procedures for the audit of accounts receivable:

1. Select 10 customer accounts from the accounts receivable master file and trace to the aged accounts receivable listing to verify name and amount.
2. Select 10 customer accounts from the aged accounts receivable listing and trace to the accounts receivable master file for name, amount, and aging categories.
3. Obtain a list of aged accounts receivable, foot and cross-foot the list, and trace the total to the general ledger.
4. Compute accounts receivable turnover for the current year and compare to the prior year.
5. Perform alternative procedures on accounts not responding to second requests by examining subsequent cash receipts documentation and shipping reports or sales invoices.
6. Request 30 positive and 50 negative confirmations of accounts receivable.

Required

a. For each audit procedure, identify the balance-related audit objective or objectives it partially or fully satisfies.
b. In which order would the auditor perform the six procedures? Briefly justify your answer.

16-26 (OBJECTIVE 16-3) The following misstatements are sometimes found in the sales and collection cycle's account balances:

1. Several cash receipts were posted to the incorrect customer accounts.
2. A shipment made in the subsequent period is recorded as a current period sale.
3. The allowance for uncollectible accounts is inadequate because of the client's failure to reflect depressed economic conditions in the allowance.
4. Several accounts receivable are in dispute as a result of claims of defective merchandise.
5. The pledging of accounts receivable to the bank for a loan is not disclosed in the financial statements.
6. Goods were returned for credit on the last day of the fiscal year but the sales return was not recorded until the following fiscal year.
7. Several accounts receivable in the accounts receivable master file are not included in the aged trial balance.
8. One account receivable in the accounts receivable master file is included on the aged trial balance twice.
9. Long-term interest-bearing notes receivable from affiliated companies are included in accounts receivable.

Required

a. For each misstatement, identify the balance-related audit objective to which it pertains.
b. For each misstatement, list an internal control that should prevent it.
c. For each misstatement, list one test of details of balances audit procedure that the auditor can use to detect it.

16-27 (OBJECTIVE 16-3) The following are the eight balance-related audit objectives, six tests of details of balances for accounts receivable, and seven tests of controls or substantive tests of transactions for the sales and collection cycle:

Balance-Related Audit Objective

Detail tie-in	Classification
Existence	Cutoff
Completeness	Realizable value
Accuracy	Rights

Test of Details of Balances, Test of Control, or Substantive Test of Transactions Audit Procedure

1. Confirm accounts receivable ending balances and sales terms, such as right of return and consignment arrangements.
2. Review sales returns after the balance sheet date to determine whether any are applicable to the current year.
3. Compare dates on shipping documents with the sales journal throughout the year.
4. Perform alternative procedures for nonresponses to confirmations.
5. Examine sales transactions for related-party or employee sales recorded as regular sales.
6. Examine duplicate sales invoices for consignment sales and other shipments for which title has not passed.
7. Trace a sample of accounts from the accounts receivable master file to the aged trial balance.
8. Trace recorded sales transactions to shipping documents to determine whether a document exists.
9. Examine duplicate sales invoices for initials that indicate internal verification of extensions and footings.
10. Trace a sample of shipping documents to related sales invoice entries in the sales journal.
11. Compare amounts and dates on the aged trial balance with the accounts receivable master file.
12. Trace from the sales journal to the accounts receivable master file to make sure the information is the same.

13. Inquire of management whether there are notes from related parties included with trade receivables.

a. Identify which procedures are tests of details of balances, which are tests of controls, and which are substantive tests of transactions. **Required**
b. For each balance-related audit objective, identify which test of details of balances and test of controls or substantive test of transactions partially satisfy the balance-related objective.

16-28 **(OBJECTIVE 16-3)** Niosoki Auto Parts sells new parts for foreign automobiles to auto dealers. Company policy requires that a prenumbered shipping document be issued for each sale. At the time of pickup or shipment, the shipping clerk writes the date on the shipping document. The last shipment made in the fiscal year ended August 31, 2016, was recorded on document 2167. Shipments are billed in the order that the billing clerk receives the shipping documents.

For late August and early September, shipping documents are billed on sales invoices as follows:

Shipping Document No.	Sales Invoice No.
2163	5437
2164	5431
2165	5432
2166	5435
2167	5436
2168	5433
2169	5434
2170	5438
2171	5440
2172	5439

The August and September sales journals have the following information included:

SALES JOURNAL—AUGUST 2016

Day of Month	Sales Invoice No.	Amount of Sale
30	5431	$ 726.11
30	5434	4,214.30
31	5432	419.83
31	5433	1,620.22
31	5435	47.74

SALES JOURNAL—SEPTEMBER 2016

Day of Month	Sales Invoice No.	Amount of Sale
1	5437	$2,541.31
1	5436	106.39
1	5438	852.06
2	5440	1,250.50
2	5439	646.58

a. What are the accounting requirements for a correct sales cutoff? **Required**
b. Which sales invoices, if any, are recorded in the wrong accounting period? Prepare an adjusting entry to correct the financial statement for the year ended August 31, 2016. Assume that the company uses a periodic inventory system (inventory and cost of sales do not need to be adjusted).

c. Assume that the shipping clerk accidentally wrote "August 31" on shipping documents 2168 through 2172. Explain how that will affect the correctness of the financial statements. How will you, as an auditor, discover that error?
d. Describe, in general terms, the audit procedures you would follow in making sure that cutoff for sales is accurate at the balance sheet date.
e. Identify internal controls that will reduce the likelihood of cutoff misstatements. How would you test each control?

16-29 **(OBJECTIVE 16-3)** The following are audit procedures in the sales and collection cycle:

1. Add the columns on the aged trial balance and compare the total with the general ledger.
2. Examine a sample of shipping documents to determine whether each has a sales invoice number included on it.
3. Discuss with the sales manager whether any sales allowances have been granted after the balance sheet date that may apply to the current period.
4. Observe whether the controller makes an independent comparison of the total in the general ledger with the trial balance of accounts receivable.
5. Compare the date on a sample of shipping documents throughout the year with related duplicate sales invoices and the accounts receivable master file.
6. Examine a sample of customer orders and see if each has a credit authorization.
7. Compare the date on a sample of shipping documents a few days before and after the balance sheet date with related sales journal transactions.
8. Compute the ratio of allowance for uncollectible accounts divided by accounts receivable and compare with previous years.

Required

a. For each procedure, identify the applicable type of audit evidence.
b. For each procedure, identify which of the following it is:
   (1) Substantive analytical procedure
   (2) Test of control
   (3) Substantive test of transactions
   (4) Test of details of balances
c. For those procedures you identified as a test of control or substantive test of transactions, what transaction-related audit objective or objectives are being satisfied?
d. For those procedures you identified as a test of details of balances, what balance-related audit objective or objectives are being satisfied?

16-30 **(OBJECTIVE 16-4)** Dodge, CPA, is auditing the financial statements of a manufacturing company with a significant amount of trade accounts receivable. Dodge is satisfied that the accounts are correctly summarized and classified and that allocations, reclassifications, and valuations are made in accordance with GAAP. Dodge is planning to use accounts receivable confirmation requests to obtain sufficient appropriate evidence as to trade accounts receivable.

Required

a. Identify and describe the two primary forms of accounts receivable confirmation requests and indicate what factors Dodge will consider in determining when to use each.
b. Assume that Dodge has received a satisfactory response to the confirmation requests. Describe how Dodge can evaluate collectibility of the trade accounts receivable.
c. What are the implications to a CPA if, during an audit of accounts receivable, some of a client's trade customers do not respond to a request for positive confirmation of their accounts?
d. What auditing steps should a CPA perform if there is no response to a second request for a positive confirmation?*

16-31 **(OBJECTIVES 16-3, 16-4)** Tim Flynn is the engagement manager for the audit of O'Donnell Enterprises. Tim is currently planning tests of details of balances for accounts receivable and is considering the use of electronic confirmation requests to improve response rates. The historical response rate to written confirmation requests sent to O'Donnell's customers has been below 50% and Tim believes they can increase that to

*Based on AICPA question paper, American Institute of Certified Public Accountants.

over 80% using electronic requests. Tim is considering two different options. The first option is to use email confirmation requests, with requests emailed directly to customers and the customers emailing responses directly to the audit firm. The second option is to use direct access to customers' electronic records through Web site links for O'Donnell's largest customers, and then written requests to the remaining customers.

Required

a. What factors does Tim need to consider in deciding whether to use written confirmation requests, email requests, or direct access to electronic records?
b. How will the audit firm ensure the reliability of the responses? For example, how might they verify the email addresses or the reliability of the electronic records? Who should provide the email addresses for the email confirmations, or the Web site links for direct access to electronic records?

16-32 **(OBJECTIVES 16-2, 16-3)** The Albring Company sells electronics equipment and has grown rapidly in the last year by adding new customers. The audit partner has asked you to evaluate the allowance for doubtful accounts at December 31, 2016. Comparative information on sales and accounts receivable is included next:

	Year Ended 12/31/16	Year Ended 12/31/15
Sales	$12,169,876	$10,452,51[illegible]
Accounts Receivable	1,440,381	1,030,933
Allowance for doubtful accounts	90,000	75,000
Bad debt charge-offs	114,849	103,471
Accounts Receivable:		
0–30 days	$ 897,035	$ 695,041
30–60 days	254,269	160,989
60–90 days	171,846	105,997
Over 90 days	117,231	68,906
TOTAL	$ 1,440,381	$ 1,030,933

Required

a. Identify what tests of controls and substantive tests of transactions you recommend be performed before conducting your analysis of the allowance for doubtful accounts.
b. Perform substantive analytical procedures to evaluate whether the allowance is fairly stated at December 31, 2016. Assume performance materiality for the allowance account is $15,000.

16-33 **(OBJECTIVE 16-4)** You have been assigned to the first audit of the Chicago Company for the year ending March 31, 2016. Accounts receivable were confirmed on December 31, 2015, and at that date the receivables consisted of approximately 200 accounts with balances totaling $956,750. Fifty of these accounts, with balances totaling $650,725, were selected for confirmation. All but 10 of the confirmation requests have been returned; 24 were returned without any exceptions, 6 had minor differences that have been cleared satisfactorily, and 10 confirmations had the following information and comments:

1. We are sorry, but we cannot answer your request for confirmation of our account as the PDQ Company uses an accounts payable voucher system and can only confirm individual invoices.
2. The balance of $1,050 was paid on December 28, 2015.
3. The balance of $7,750 was paid on January 5, 2016.
4. The balance of $2,975 was paid on December 13, 2015.
5. We do not owe you anything at December 31, 2015, as the goods, represented by your invoice dated December 30, 2015, number 25050, in the amount of $11,550, were received on January 5, 2016, on FOB destination terms.
6. An advance payment of $2,500 made by us in November 2015 should cover the two invoices totaling $1,350 shown on the statement attached.

7. This confirmation was returned as undeliverable by the post office.
8. We are contesting the propriety of this $12,525 charge. We think the charge is excessive.
9. We do not owe this balance as our agreement with the company allows us to return any unsold goods without penalty. Amount okay. As the goods have been shipped to us on consignment, we will remit payment upon selling the goods.
10. Your credit memo dated December 5, 2015, in the amount of $440 cancels the balance above.

Required

a. Indicate which of these confirmation responses likely represent timing differences.
b. Which of the 10 confirmation responses likely represent a misstatement? Explain why the response indicates a misstatement.
c. For each of the 10 confirmation responses, indicate the procedures you would perform to determine whether the exception is a misstatement or has been appropriately recorded by the client.*

16-34 **(OBJECTIVES 16-3, 16-5)** The following are various changes in audit circumstances.

Audit Circumstance

1. Substantive analytical procedures indicated a significant slowing in accounts receivable turnover.
2. The client entered into sales contracts with new customers that differ from the client's standard sales contracts.
3. The client had a significant increase in sales near year-end.
4. Accounts receivable confirmations were ineffective due to a very low response rate in the prior year audit.
5. The client began experiencing an increase in returns due to product changes that resulted in increased defects.
6. You found several pricing errors in your substantive tests of transactions for sales.
7. In performing substantive tests of transactions for cash receipts, you found that receipts were promptly recorded in customer accounts, but there were delays in depositing the receipts at the bank.
8. The client entered into a new loan agreement with the bank. Accounts receivable are pledged as collateral for the loan.
9. The client did not reconcile the accounts receivable subsidiary records with the accounts receivable balance in the general ledger on a regular basis.

Required Match each change in audit circumstance with the most likely test of details of balances response. Each response is used once.

a. Expand testing of sales returns after year-end and compare the level of returns with the prior year.
b. Send positive confirmations that include requests for information on side agreements and special terms.
c. Increase the number of accounts traced from the accounts receivable trial balance to the accounts receivable subsidiary records.
d. Expand the review of cash receipts after year-end to evaluate the collectibility of accounts receivable.
e. Increase the sample size for sales cutoff testing for sales recorded before year-end.
f. Send a confirmation to the bank confirming amounts pledged as collateral under loan agreements.
g. Increase the sample size for positive confirmations of accounts receivable.
h. While at the client's premises at year-end, obtain information on the last few cash receipts at year-end for cash receipts cutoff testing.
i. Perform alternative procedures to test the existence and accuracy of accounts receivable instead of sending positive confirmations.

16-35 **(OBJECTIVE 16-4)** In the confirmation of accounts receivable for the Reliable Service Company, 85 positive and no negative confirmations were mailed to customers. This represents 35% of the dollar balance of the total accounts receivable. Second requests were

*Based on AICPA question paper, American Institute of Certified Public Accountants.

sent for all nonresponses, but there were still 10 customers who did not respond. The decision was made to perform alternative procedures on the 10 unanswered confirmation requests. An assistant is requested to conduct the alternative procedures and report to the senior auditor after he has completed his tests on two accounts. He prepared the following information for the audit files:

Required

1. Confirmation request no. 9
   Customer name — Jolene Milling Co.
   Balance — $3,621 at December 31, 2016
   Subsequent cash receipts per the accounts receivable master file: January 15, 2017 — $1,837; January 29, 2017 — $1,263; February 6, 2017 — $1,429
2. Confirmation request no. 26
   Customer name — Rosenthal Repair Service
   Balance — $2,500 at December 31, 2016
   Subsequent cash receipts per the accounts receivable master file: February 9, 2017 — $500
   Sales invoices per the accounts receivable master file (I examined the duplicate invoice): September 1, 2016 — $4,200

Required

a. If you are asked to evaluate the adequacy of the sample size, the type of confirmation used, and the percent of accounts confirmed, what additional information will you need?
b. Discuss the need to send second requests and perform alternative procedures for nonresponses.
c. Evaluate the adequacy of the alternative procedures used for verifying the two nonresponses.

CASE

16-36 (OBJECTIVES 16-1, 16-3, 16-4, 16-5) You are auditing the sales and collection cycle for the Smalltown Regional Hospital, a small not-for-profit hospital. The hospital has a reputation for excellent medical services and deficient record keeping. The medical people have a tradition of doing all aspects of their job correctly, but because of a shortage of accounting personnel, there is not time for internal verification or careful performance. In previous years, your CPA firm has found quite a few misstatements in billings, cash receipts, and accounts receivable. As in all hospitals, the two largest assets are accounts receivable and property, plant, and equipment.

The hospital has several large loans payable to local banks, and the two banks have told management that they are reluctant to extend more credit, especially considering the modern hospital that is being built in a nearby city. In the past, county taxes have made up deficits, but in the past year, the county has also been incurring deficits because of high unemployment.

In previous years, your response from patients to confirmation requests has been frustrating at best. The response rate has been extremely low, and those who did respond did not know the purpose of the confirmations or their correct outstanding balance. You have had the same experience in confirming receivables at other hospitals.

You conclude that control over cash is excellent and the likelihood of fraud is extremely small. You are less confident about unintentional errors in billing, recording sales, cash receipts, accounts receivable, and bad debts.

Required

a. Identify the major factors affecting client business risk and acceptable audit risk for this audit.
b. What inherent risks are you concerned about?
c. What risks would you consider to be significant risks?
d. For each of the following, explain whether you plan to emphasize the tests in the audit of the sales and collection cycle and give reasons:
   (1) Tests of controls
   (2) Substantive tests of transactions
   (3) Substantive analytical procedures
   (4) Tests of details of balances

INTEGRATED CASE APPLICATION—
PINNACLE MANUFACTURING: PART VII

16-37 **(OBJECTIVES 16-2, 16-3, 16-4)** In Parts IV, V, and VI of this case study, you were asked to apply concepts we have discussed in previous chapters related to the sales and collection cycle to the acquisition and cash disbursement cycle. Parts IV, V, and VI dealt with obtaining an understanding of internal control and assessing control risk for transactions affecting accounts payable of Pinnacle Manufacturing. In Part VII, you will design substantive analytical procedures and design and perform tests of details of balances for accounts payable.

Assume that your understanding of internal controls over acquisitions and cash disbursements and the related tests of controls and substantive tests of transactions support an assessment of a low control risk. The listing of the 519 accounts making up the accounts payable balance of $12,969,686 at December 31, 2016, is available online.

Required

a. List those relationships, ratios, and trends that you believe will provide useful information about the overall reasonableness of accounts payable. You should consider income statement accounts that affect accounts payable in selecting the analytical procedures.

b. Study Table 18-5 (p. 620) containing balance-related audit objectives and tests of details of balances for accounts payable to be sure you understand each procedure and its purpose. Prepare an audit program for accounts payable in a performance format, using the audit procedures in Table 18-5. The format of the audit program should be similar to Table 16-5 (p. 546). Be sure to include a sample size for each procedure.

c. Assume for requirement b. that (1) assessed control risk had been high rather than low for each transaction-related audit objective, (2) inherent risk was high for each balance-related audit objective, and (3) analytical procedures indicated a high potential for misstatement. What would the effect have been on the audit procedures and sample sizes for requirement b.?

d. Confirmation requests were sent to a stratified sample of 51 vendors listed in Figure 16-8. Confirmation responses from 45 vendors were returned indicating no difference between the vendor's and the company's records. Figure 16-9 (p. 560) presents the six replies that indicate a difference between the vendor's balance and the company's records. The auditor's follow-up findings are indicated on each reply. Prepare an audit schedule similar to the one illustrated in Figure 16-10 (p. 562) to determine the misstatements, if any, for each difference. The audit schedule format shown in Figure 16-10 is available online. The exception for Fiberchem is analyzed as an illustration. Assume that Pinnacle Manufacturing took a complete physical inventory at December 31, 2016, and the auditor concluded that recorded inventory reflects all inventory on hand at the balance sheet date. Include the balances confirmed without exception as one amount on the schedule for each stratum, and total the schedule columns.

e. Estimate the total misstatement in the income statement, not just the misstatements in the sample, based on the income statement misstatements you identified in requirement d. The total misstatement should include a projected misstatement and an estimated allowance for sampling risk. *Hint:* See pages 241–243 for guidance on calculating the point estimate. Note that the misstatements should be projected separately for each stratum. You will need to determine the size of each stratum using the accounts payable listing. Use your judgment to estimate sampling risk, considering the size of the population and the amounts tested.

f. Estimate the total misstatement in accounts payable in the same way you did for the income statement in requirement e. *Hint:* A misstatement caused by the failure to record an FOB origin purchase is an understatement of accounts payable and inventory and has no effect on income.

FIGURE 16-8 Pinnacle Manufacturing Sample of Accounts Payable Selected for Confirmation—December 31, 2016

High-Volume Items (>$250,000)		
1. American Press	$ 340,767.94	
2. Clean-O-Rama Co.	317,668.63	
3. Fiberchem	793,049.89	
4. Rufus Austin Antiques	400,046.08	
5. Todd Machinery	531,073.93	
6. Welburn Manufacturing	388,836.07	$2,771,442.54
Large Balance Items ($50,001–$250,000)		
1. A & M Sandler, Inc.	$ 81,348.54	
2. American Baby/USTC	75,432.73	
3. Beach & Hoover Refining	76,408.79	
4. Bearing Drives Co.	73,017.24	
5. Burton Martin	78,682.54	
6. Cable Sys./Ind. Traf. Cons.	71,288.95	
7. Eddie Ventura, Inc.	60,255.55	
8. Fiberoptics	60,102.78	
9. Finish Metals, Inc.	60,769.71	
10. Freeman Furniture–Attn A/P	130,493.51	
11. GP Chambers Co.	64,125.44	
12. Godwin Drug Co.	84,331.05	
13. Holy Family Hospital	117,916.83	
14. Las Flores Designs, Inc.	88,644.92	
15. Lean Corp.	67,985.23	
16. MacDonald Svc. Corporation	147,943.95	
17. McCoys, Inc.	67,936.32	
18. Metadyne Corp.	85,432.51	
19. Micron Power Systems	136,071.37	
20. Mobil Oil	93,210.48	
21. National Elevator & Mach. Co.	76,921.40	
22. Norris Industries	88,314.64	
23. R & B Products	80,092.46	
24. Remington Supply	123,411.24	
25. Safety Envelope Co.	223,950.34	
26. Scandec USA, Inc.	65,942.94	
27. The Dutton Company	63,882.02	
28. The Haberdashery Co.	71,869.16	
29. University of California	80,624.95	
30. ZZZZ Bank Adjustments	64,471.21	$2,660,878.80
Items $50,000 and less		
1. Advent Sign Mfg. Co.	$ 51,750.00	
2. B&K Mfg. Co., Inc.	42,668.50	
3. Bellco	42,710.74	
4. Boston Shoecase Co.	52,174.50	
5. Dynamic Metal Products	36,546.05	
6. Everhart Co.	47,519.14	
7. Fuller Travel	32,470.11	
8. Good House Home Video, Inc.	46,472.67	
9. Harrah's Metals, Inc.	51,279.85	
10. J C Licht Co.—Glendale Hts.	53,228.47	
11. Liberty Lighting	46,802.78	
12. Long Beach Lawn Service	48,488.96	
13. Premier Whirlpool Bath	6,550.33	
14. Quaker Transanalysis	50,363.69	
15. Tower International	37,299.55	$ 646,325.34
TOTAL TESTED		$6,078,646.68

FIGURE 16-9 Replies to Requests for Information

STATEMENT FROM FIBERCHEM

Pinnacle Manufacturing
Detroit, MI

Amounts due as of December 31, 2016:

Invoice No.	Date	Amount	Balance Due
8312	11-22-16	$300,000.00	$300,000.00
8469	12-02-16	178,000.00	478,000.00
8819	12-18-16	315,049.89	793,049.89 (1)
9002	12-30-16	32,500.00 (2)	825,549.89

Auditor's notes:
(1) Agrees with accounts payable listing.
(2) Goods shipped FOB Fiberchem's plant on December 31, 2016; arrived at Pinnacle Manufacturing on January 4, 2017.

STATEMENT FROM MOBIL OIL

Pinnacle Manufacturing
Detroit, MI

Amounts due as of December 31, 2016:

Invoice No.	Date	Amount	Balance Due
DX14777	12-23-16	$93,210.48	$ 93,210.48 (1)
DX16908	12-29-16	37,812.00 (2)	131,022.48

Auditor's notes:
(1) Agrees with accounts payable listing.
(2) Goods shipped FOB Pinnacle Manufacturing on December 29, 2016; arrived at Pinnacle Manufacturing on January 3, 2017.

STATEMENT FROM NORRIS INDUSTRIES

Pinnacle Manufacturing
Detroit, MI

Amounts due as of December 31, 2016:

Invoice No.	Date	Amount	Balance Due
14896	12-27-16	$ 88,314.64	$ 88,314.64 (1)
15111	12-28-16	117,296.00 (2)	205,610.64

Auditor's notes:
(1) Agrees with accounts payable listing.
(2) Goods received December 30, 2016; recorded on January 2, 2017.

g. What is your conclusion about the fairness of the recorded balance in accounts payable for Pinnacle Manufacturing as it affects the income statement and balance sheet? How does this affect your assessment of control risk as being low for all transaction-related audit objectives? Assume you decided that performance materiality for accounts payable as it affects the income statement is $250,000.

FIGURE 16-9 Replies to Requests for Information (Cont.)

STATEMENT FROM REMINGTON SUPPLY

Pinnacle Manufacturing
Detroit, MI

Amounts due as of December 31, 2016:

Invoice No.	Date	Amount	Balance Due
141702	11-11-16	$23,067.00	$ 23,067.00
142619	11-19-16	12,000.00	35,067.00
142811	12-04-16	7,100.00	42,167.00
143600	12-21-16	27,715.24	69,882.24
144927	12-29-16 (2)	53,529.00	123,411.24 (1)

Auditor's notes:
(1) Agrees with accounts payable listing.
(2) Goods shipped FOB Pinnacle Manufacturing on December 29, 2016; arrived at Pinnacle Manufacturing on January 4, 2017.

STATEMENT FROM ADVENT SIGN MFG. CO.

Pinnacle Manufacturing
Detroit, MI

Amounts due as of December 31, 2016:

First progress billing per contract	$51,750.00 (1)
Second progress billing per contract	7,500.00 (2)
Total due	$59,250.00

Auditor's notes:
(1) Agrees with accounts payable listing.
(2) Progress payment due as of December 31, 2016, per contract for construction of new custom electric sign; sign installation completed on January 15, 2017.

STATEMENT FROM FULLER TRAVEL

Pinnacle Manufacturing
Detroit, MI

Amounts due as of December 31, 2016:

Invoice No.	Date	Amount	Balance Due
84360110	12-04-16	$9,411.63 (2)	$ 9,411.63
84360181	12-12-16	9,411.63 (2)	18,823.26
84360222	12-21-16	7,100.00 (1)	25,923.26
84360291	12-26-16	13,646.85 (2)	39,570.11

Auditor's notes:
(1) Paid by Pinnacle Manufacturing on December 28, 2016; payment in transit at year-end.
(2) The total of these items of $32,470.11 agrees with accounts payable listing.

FIGURE 16-10 Pinnacle Manufacturing Analysis of Trade Accounts Payable—December 31, 2016

					Misstatement in Related Accounts			
Vendor	Balance per Books	Amount Confirmed by Vendor	Books Over (Under) Amount Confirmed	Timing Difference: No Misstatement	Misstatement in Accounts Payable o/s (u/s)*	Other Balance Sheet Misstatement o/s (u/s)*	Income Statement Misstatement o/s (u/s)*	Brief Explanation
Key Accounts (>$250,000)								
Fiberchem	$793,049.89	$825,549.89	$(32,500.00)		$(32,500.00)	$(32,500.00)		F.O.B. Origin error: Dr. Inv. Cr. A/P
Accounts in stratum $50,001–$250,000								
Accounts in stratum less than or equal to $50,000								

* o/s = overstatement   u/s = understatement

ACL PROBLEM

16-38 **(OBJECTIVE 16-3)** This problem requires the use of ACL software, which can be accessed through the textbook Web site. Information about downloading and using ACL and the commands used in this problem can also be found on the textbook Web site. You should read all of the reference material, especially the material on sampling, to answer questions a. through d. For this problem, use the "Invoices" file in the "Sales and Collection" subfolder under tables in the ACL_Rockwood project. This file contains information on sales invoices generated during calendar year 2014, including those that have been paid versus those still outstanding. The suggested command or other source of information needed to solve the problem requirement is included at the end of each question.

Required

a. Using the Invoices file, filter the file to retain only those invoices that are still outstanding and save this filter as "Accounts_Receivable." (Filter) Determine the number and total dollar amount of the outstanding invoices (Total).
b. Determine accounts receivable outstanding from each customer and total the amount for comparison to part a. (Summarize and Total) Which customer number has the largest balance due?
c. What is the largest and smallest account balance outstanding? (Quick Sort)
d. Using the "Accounts_Receivable" data, age the balances based on invoice date. Use December 31, 2014 as the cutoff date, and enter aging periods of 0, 30, 60, and 90 days. (Age) How many invoices are more than 90 days outstanding? How will the auditors use the aging information in the audit of accounts receivable?

CHAPTER

17

AUDIT SAMPLING FOR TESTS OF DETAILS OF BALANCES

LEARNING OBJECTIVES

After studying this chapter, you should be able to

17-1 Differentiate audit sampling for tests of details of balances and for tests of controls and substantive tests of transactions.

17-2 Apply nonstatistical sampling to tests of details of balances.

17-3 Apply monetary unit sampling.

17-4 Describe variables sampling.

17-5 Use difference estimation in tests of details of balances.

Both Statistical and Nonstatistical Sampling Are Acceptable Under Auditing Standards, But Whichever Is Used, It Must Be Done Right

Bob Lake was the manager on the audit of Images, Inc., a specialty retailer that had shops throughout the Midwest. Images appealed to upscale working women and offered its own credit card. Images' accounting was done centrally. Transactions were captured online and sales and accounts receivable files were maintained on a database.

Bob Lake's firm encouraged the use of statistical sampling in its practice and provided a training program for the development of a statistical coordinator for each office. The coordinator in Lake's office was Barbara Ennis. Lake believed that sales transactions and accounts receivable confirmation tests should be done using statistical sampling and he asked Ennis to help design and oversee the statistical aspects of this testing.

Ennis developed a program for the design of confirmation audit procedures as part of doing tests of details of balances for accounts receivable. Her work included determining sample sizes. She left the program with Lake to carry out and said that she would be available to help evaluate the results after the tests were performed.

When all the confirmation replies were received or alternative procedures were completed several weeks later, Lake called Ennis to do the statistical evaluation. Much to his dismay, he found out that Ennis had left the firm, and worse, there was no statistically trained person to take her place. Lake was under a lot of pressure to get the job completed and decided to make the statistical calculations himself. Based on his calculations, he concluded that the potential misstatement was large, but not material, so Lake concluded the objectives of the confirmation tests had been met.

The next year, Images, Inc.'s earnings declined sharply, partially because of large write-offs of accounts receivable. The stock price dropped sharply and a class action suit was filed naming Lake's firm among the defendants. An outside expert was brought in to review the audit documentation. The expert redid all of Lake's work and found errors in the statistical calculations. The expert calculated that the misstatement in accounts receivable, based on the auditor's sample, was significantly more than a material amount. Lake's firm settled the suit for $3.5 million.

In Chapter 16, we moved into phase III of the audit process by examining substantive analytical procedures and tests of details of balances for accounts receivable. We will now continue with phase III by discussing sampling for accounts receivable, including determining sample size, selecting items to test from the population, and evaluating sample results. Although the concepts in this chapter deal with accounts receivable, they apply to the audit of many other account balances.

As the story about the audit of Images, Inc., demonstrates, auditors must correctly use sampling to avoid making incorrect conclusions about a population. While both statistical and nonstatistical audit sampling methods are used extensively for tests of details of balances, auditors must decide which method to use, depending on their preference, experience, and knowledge about statistical sampling. This chapter should help you make correct inferences about populations using either statistical or nonstatistical methods.

Before starting the study of this chapter, we suggest you refer to Figure 13-9 on page 430 to be sure you understand where we are in the audit process. At this stage, all items in phases I and II will have been completed before auditors determine sample size and items to select from the population. Also, the auditor will have completed substantive analytical procedures and designed audit procedures for tests of details of balances, as covered in Chapter 16 (part of phase III). The auditor considers risk assessments, materiality, and the results of tests of controls, substantive tests of transactions, and substantive analytical procedures in deciding the sampling approach and extent of sampling for tests of details.

COMPARISONS OF AUDIT SAMPLING FOR TESTS OF DETAILS OF BALANCES AND FOR TESTS OF CONTROLS AND SUBSTANTIVE TESTS OF TRANSACTIONS

OBJECTIVE 17-1

Differentiate audit sampling for tests of details of balances and for tests of controls and substantive tests of transactions.

Most of the sampling concepts for tests of controls and substantive tests of transactions, which were discussed in Chapter 15, apply equally to sampling for tests of details of balances. In both cases, an auditor wants to make inferences about the entire population based on a sample. Both sampling and nonsampling risks are therefore important for tests of controls, substantive tests of transactions, and tests of details of balances. To address sampling risk, auditors can use either nonstatistical or statistical methods for all three types of tests.

The main differences among tests of controls, substantive tests of transactions, and tests of details of balances are in what the auditor wants to measure.

Type of Test	What It Measures
Tests of controls	• The operating effectiveness of internal controls
Substantive tests of transactions	• The operating effectiveness of internal controls • The monetary correctness of transactions in the accounting system
Tests of details of balances	• Whether the dollar amounts of account balances are materially misstated

Auditors perform tests of controls and substantive tests of transactions:

- To determine whether the exception rate in the population is sufficiently low
- To reduce assessed control risk and thereby reduce tests of details of balances
- For larger public companies, to conclude that the control is operating effectively for purposes of auditing internal control over financial reporting

Unlike for tests of controls and substantive tests of transactions, auditors rarely use rate of occurrence tests in tests of details of balances. Instead, auditors use sampling methods that provide results in *dollar* terms. There are three primary types of sampling methods used for calculating dollar misstatements in account balances addressed in this chapter: nonstatistical sampling, monetary unit sampling, and variables sampling.

NONSTATISTICAL SAMPLING

OBJECTIVE 17-2

Apply nonstatistical sampling to tests of details of balances.

Audit sampling for tests of details of balances is similar to audit sampling for tests of controls and substantive tests of transactions, although the objectives differ. The steps involved parallel those used for sampling for tests of controls and substantive tests of transactions. The primary differences in applying audit sampling for tests of details of balances are indicated in italics.

Steps—Audit Sampling for Tests of Details of Balances	Steps—Audit Sampling for Tests of Controls and Substantive Tests of Transactions (see p. 490)
Plan the Sample	***Plan the Sample***
1. State the objectives of the audit test.	1. State the objectives of the audit test.
2. Decide whether audit sampling applies.	2. Decide whether audit sampling applies.
3. *Define a misstatement.*	3. Define attributes and exception conditions.
4. Define the population.	4. Define the population.
5. Define the sampling unit.	5. Define the sampling unit.
6. *Specify tolerable misstatement.*	6. Specify the tolerable exception rate.
7. *Specify acceptable risk of incorrect acceptance.*	7. Specify acceptable risk of overreliance.
8. *Estimate misstatements in the population.*	8. Estimate the population exception rate.
9. Determine the initial sample size.	9. Determine the initial sample size.
Select the Sample and Perform the Audit Procedures	***Select the Sample and Perform the Audit Procedures***
10. Select the sample.	10. Select the sample.
11. Perform the audit procedures.	11. Perform the audit procedures.
Evaluate the Results	***Evaluate the Results***
12. Generalize from the sample to the population.	12. Generalize from the sample to the population.
13. *Analyze the misstatements.*	13. Analyze the exceptions.
14. Decide the acceptability of the population.	14. Decide the acceptability of the population.

State the Objectives of the Audit Test

Auditors sample for tests of details of balances to determine whether the account balance being audited is fairly stated. The population of 40 accounts receivable in Table 17-1, totaling $207,295, illustrates the application of nonstatistical sampling. An auditor will do tests of details of balances to determine whether the balance of $207,295 is materially misstated.

Decide Whether Audit Sampling Applies

As stated in Chapter 15, "Audit sampling applies whenever the auditor plans to reach conclusions about a population based on a sample." Although auditors commonly sample in many accounts, in some situations sampling does not apply. For the population in Table 17-1, the auditor may decide to audit only items over $5,000 and ignore all others because the total of the smaller items is immaterial. Similarly, if the auditor is verifying fixed asset additions and finds many small additions and one extremely large purchase of a building, the auditor may decide to ignore the small items entirely. In either case, the auditor has not sampled.

Define a Misstatement

Because audit sampling for tests of details of balances measures monetary misstatements, a misstatement exists whenever a sample item is misstated. In auditing

TABLE 17-1	Illustrative Accounts Receivable Population		
Population Item	**Recorded Amount**	**Population Item (cont.)**	**Recorded Amount (cont.)**
1	$ 1,410	21	$ 4,865
2	9,130	22	770
3	660	23	2,305
4	3,355	24	2,665
5	5,725	25	1,000
6	8,210	26	6,225
7	580	27	3,675
8	44,110	28	6,250
9	825	29	1,890
10	1,155	30	27,705
11	2,270	31	935
12	50	32	5,595
13	5,785	33	930
14	940	34	4,045
15	1,820	35	9,480
16	3,380	36	360
17	530	37	1,145
18	955	38	6,400
19	4,490	39	100
20	17,140	40	8,435
			$207,295

accounts receivable, any client misstatement in a customer balance included in the auditor's sample is a misstatement. As discussed in Chapter 16, the auditor must distinguish misstatements from differences such as timing differences in the recording of transactions that do not represent misstatements.

Define the Population

In tests of details of balances, the population is defined as the items making up the *recorded dollar population.* The recorded population of accounts receivable in Table 17-1 consists of 40 accounts totaling $207,295. Most accounting populations that auditors sample will, of course, include far more items totaling a much larger dollar amount. The auditor will evaluate whether the recorded population is overstated or understated.

Stratified Sampling For many populations, auditors separate the population into two or more subpopulations before applying audit sampling. This is called **stratified sampling**, where each subpopulation is a called a stratum. Stratification enables the auditor to emphasize certain population items and deemphasize others. In most audit sampling situations, including confirming accounts receivable, auditors want to emphasize the larger recorded dollar values, so they define each stratum on the basis of the size of recorded dollar values.

By examining the population in Table 17-1, you can see that there are different ways to stratify the population. Assume that the auditor decided to stratify as follows:

Stratum	Stratum Criteria	No. in Population	Dollars in Population
1	>$15,000	3	$ 88,955
2	$5,000–$15,000	10	71,235
3	<$5,000	27	47,105
		40	$207,295

There are many alternative ways to stratify this population. One example is to have four strata (make stratum 3 items between $2,000 and $5,000, and add a fourth stratum for items less than $2,000).

Define the Sampling Unit

For nonstatistical audit sampling in tests of details of balances, the sampling unit is almost always the items making up the account balance. For example, for the accounts receivable in Table 17-1, the sampling unit will be the customer number. Auditors can use the items making up the recorded population as the sampling unit for testing all audit objectives except completeness. If auditors are concerned about the completeness objective, they should select the sample from a different source, such as customers with zero balances. Accordingly, the sampling unit for a completeness test will be customers with zero balances.

Specify Tolerable Misstatement

Tolerable misstatement is the application of performance materiality to a particular sampling procedure. Performance materiality was defined in Chapter 8 and is an amount set less than materiality for the financial statements as a whole and applied to audit segments to reduce to an appropriately low level the probability that the aggregate of uncorrected and undetected misstatements exceeds materiality for the financial statements as a whole. Tolerable misstatement may be the same amount as performance materiality, or may be lower if the population from which the sample is selected is smaller than the account balance. Auditors seek an appropriate level of assurance that the actual misstatements in the population do not exceed tolerable misstatement. The required sample size increases as tolerable misstatement decreases for the sampling procedure.

Specify Acceptable Risk of Incorrect Acceptance

For all statistical and nonstatistical sampling applications, auditors risk making incorrect quantitative conclusions about the population. This is always true unless the auditor tests 100 percent of the population.

Acceptable risk of incorrect acceptance (ARIA) is the risk that the sample supports the conclusion that the recorded account balance is not materially misstated when it is materially misstated. ARIA measures the auditor's desired assurance for an account balance. For greater assurance in auditing a balance, auditors will set ARIA lower. Note that ARIA is the equivalent term to ARO (acceptable risk of overreliance) for tests of controls and substantive tests of transactions. Like for ARO, ARIA can be set quantitatively (such as 5% or 10%), or qualitatively (such as low, medium, or high).

There is an inverse relationship between ARIA and required sample size. If, for example, an auditor decides to reduce ARIA from 10 percent to 5 percent, the required sample size will increase. Stated differently, if the auditor is less willing to take risk, a larger sample size is needed.

An important factor affecting the auditor's decision about ARIA is assessed control risk, which, along with inherent risk, is part of the assessed risk of material misstatement. When internal controls are effective, control risk can be reduced, permitting the auditor to increase ARIA. This, in turn, reduces the sample size required for the test of details of the related account balance.

You need to understand how ARO and ARIA interact to affect evidence accumulation. You already know from earlier chapters that tests of details of balances for monetary misstatements can be reduced if auditors find internal controls effective after assessing control risk and performing tests of controls. The effects of ARO and ARIA are consistent with that conclusion. If the auditor concludes that internal controls are likely to be effective, preliminary control risk can be reduced. A lower control risk requires a lower ARO in testing the controls, which requires a larger sample size.

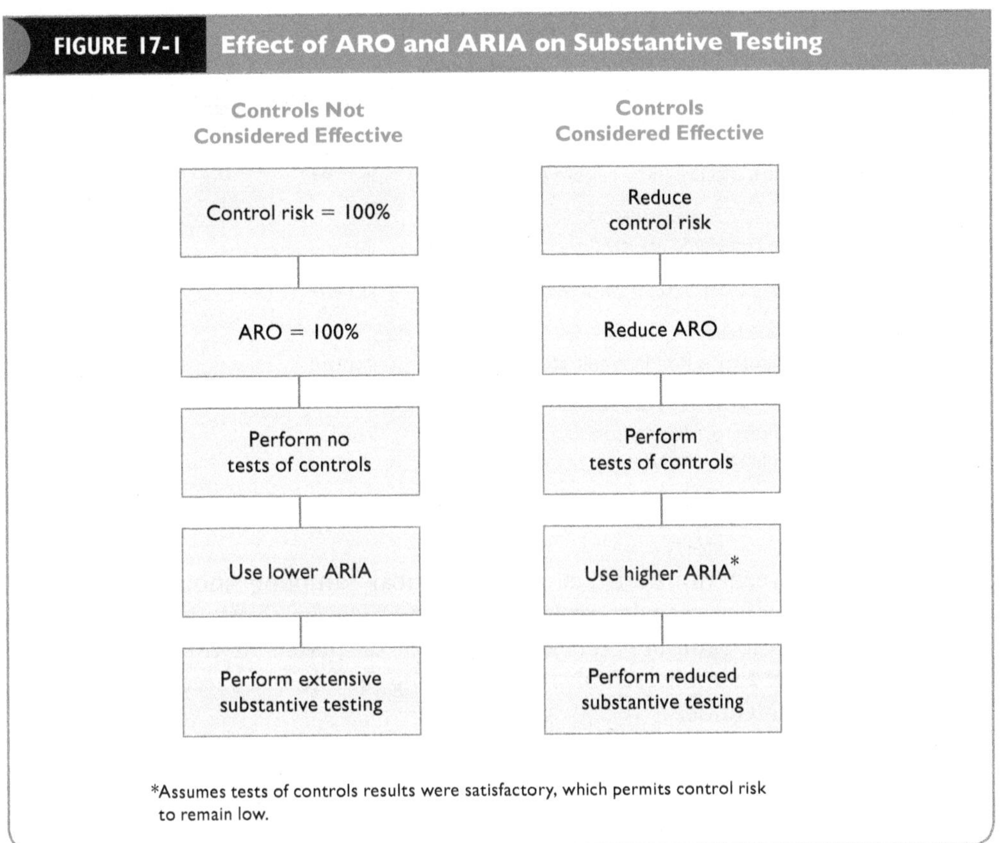
FIGURE 17-1 Effect of ARO and ARIA on Substantive Testing
Controls Not Considered Effective
Controls Considered Effective
Control risk = 100%
Reduce control risk
ARO = 100%
Reduce ARO
Perform no tests of controls
Perform tests of controls
Use lower ARIA
Use higher ARIA*
Perform extensive substantive testing
Perform reduced substantive testing
*Assumes tests of controls results were satisfactory, which permits control risk to remain low.

If controls are found to be effective, control risk can remain low, which permits the auditor to increase ARIA (through use of the audit risk model), thereby requiring a smaller sample size in the related substantive tests of details of balances. Figure 17-1 shows the effect of ARO and ARIA on substantive testing when controls are not considered effective and when they are considered effective.

In addition to control risk, ARIA is directly affected by acceptable audit risk and inversely affected by other substantive tests already performed (or planned) for the account balance. If auditors reduce acceptable audit risk, they should also reduce ARIA. If substantive analytical procedures indicate that the account balance is likely to be fairly stated, ARIA can be increased. In other words, substantive analytical procedures are evidence supporting the account balance, meaning auditors require smaller sample sizes in tests of details of balances to achieve the desired acceptable audit risk. The same conclusion is appropriate for the relationship among substantive tests of transactions, ARIA, and sample size for tests of details of balances. The various relationships affecting ARIA are summarized in Table 17-2 on the following page.

Estimate Misstatements in the Population

The auditor typically makes this estimate based on prior experience with the client and by assessing inherent risk, considering the results of tests of controls, substantive tests of transactions, and analytical procedures already performed. The planned sample size increases as the amount of misstatements expected in the population approaches tolerable misstatement.

Determine the Initial Sample Size

When using nonstatistical sampling, auditors determine the initial sample size by considering the factors we've discussed so far. Table 17-3 (p. 570) summarizes these factors, including the effect of changing each factor on sample size. It shouldn't be surprising that considering all of these factors requires considerable judgment.

TABLE 17-2 Relationship Among Factors Affecting ARIA, Effect on ARIA, and Required Sample Size for Audit Sampling

Factor Affecting ARIA	Example	Effect on ARIA	Effect on Sample Size
Effectiveness of internal controls (control risk)	Internal controls are effective (reduced control risk).	Increase	Decrease
Likelihood of misstatements (inherent risk)	Misstatements are considered unlikely (lower inherent risk).	Increase	Decrease
Substantive tests of transactions	No exceptions were found in substantive tests of transactions.	Increase	Decrease
Acceptable audit risk	Likelihood of bankruptcy is low (increased acceptable audit risk).	Increase	Decrease
Substantive analytical procedures	Substantive analytical procedures are performed with no indications of likely misstatements.	Increase	Decrease

Sample sizes between nonstatistical and statistical sampling should be similar. Accordingly, the auditor may determine the sample size for nonstatistical sampling using monetary unit sampling tables, which are discussed in the next section. Figure 17-2 presents a simple formula for computing sample size based on the AICPA *Audit Sampling* Audit Guide.

Assume an auditor applied this formula to the population in Table 17-1 (p. 567) and that tolerable misstatement is \$15,000. The auditor decided to eliminate from the recorded population the three items making up the first stratum because they exceed tolerable misstatement. These three individually material accounts will be tested separately. The remaining population to be sampled is \$118,340, which is the combined amount of stratum 2 and 3. Further, assume that the combined assessed inherent and control risk is moderate and that there is a moderate risk that substantive tests of transactions and substantive analytical procedures will not detect a material misstatement. Considering these factors, the auditor determined that a 14% risk of incorrect acceptance (86% assurance) was appropriate. Using the table in Figure 17-2, the auditor applied a confidence factor of 2, and the computed sample size is 16 $[(\$118,340/\$15,000) \times 2 = 15.8]$.

TABLE 17-3 Factors Influencing Sample Sizes for Tests of Details of Balances

Factor	Conditions Leading to Smaller Sample Size	Conditions Leading to Larger Sample Size
Inherent risk—Affects acceptable risk of incorrect acceptance	Low inherent risk	High inherent risk
Control risk (ARO)—Affects acceptable risk of incorrect acceptance	Low control risk	High control risk
Results of other substantive procedures related to the same assertion (including substantive analytical procedures and other relevant substantive tests)—Affect acceptable risk of incorrect acceptance	Satisfactory results in other related substantive procedures	Unsatisfactory results in other related substantive procedures
Tolerable misstatement for a specific account	Larger tolerable misstatement	Smaller tolerable misstatement
Expected size and frequency of misstatements—Affect estimated misstatements in the population	Smaller misstatements or lower frequency	Larger misstatements or higher frequency
Dollar amount of population	Smaller account balance	Larger account balance
Number of items in the population	Almost no effect on sample size unless population is very small	Almost no effect on sample size unless population is very small

FIGURE 17-2 **Formula for Computing Nonstatistical Tests of Details of Balances Sample Size Based on AICPA Audit Sampling Formula**

$$\text{Sample size} = \frac{\text{Population Recorded Amount}^* \times \text{Confidence Factor}}{\text{Tolerable misstatement}}$$

Risk of Incorrect Acceptance	Confidence of Sample	Confidence Factor
37%	63%	1
14%	86%	2
5%	95%	3

*High risk items and individual items exceeding tolerable misstatement are often removed from the population and selected for 100 percent examination.

When auditors use stratified sampling, they must allocate sample size among the strata, typically allocating a higher portion of the sample items to larger population items. In the example from Table 17-1, the auditor must test all items in stratum 1, which is not audit sampling. They decided to allocate the sample size of 16 to nine from stratum 2 and seven from stratum 3.

Select the Sample

For nonstatistical sampling, auditing standards permit the auditor to use any of the selection methods discussed in Chapter 15. The auditor will make the decision after considering the advantages and disadvantages of each method, including cost considerations.

For stratified sampling, the auditor selects samples independently from each stratum. In our example from Table 17-1 (p. 567), the auditor will select nine sample items from the 10 population items in stratum 2 and seven of the 27 items in stratum 3.

Perform the Audit Procedures

To perform the audit procedures, the auditor applies the appropriate audit procedures to each item in the sample to determine whether it contains a misstatement. In the confirmation of accounts receivable, auditors send the sample of positive confirmations in the manner described in Chapter 16 and determine the amount of misstatement in each account confirmed. For nonresponses, they use alternative procedures to determine the misstatements.

Referring to our example from Table 17-1 again, assume an auditor sends first and second requests for confirmations and performs alternative procedures. Also assume the auditor reaches the following conclusions about the sample after reconciling all timing differences:

		Dollars Audited		
Stratum	**Sample Size**	**Recorded Value**	**Audited Value**	**Client Misstatement**
1	3	$ 88,955	$ 91,695	$ (2,740)
2	9	43,995	43,024	971
3	7	13,105	10,947	2,158
Total	19	$ 146,055	$ 145,666	$ 389

Generalize from the Sample to the Population and Decide the Acceptability of the Population

Auditing standards indicate the auditor should generalize from the sample to the population by (1) projecting misstatements from the sample results to the population and (2) considering sampling risk (ARIA). In our example, will the auditor conclude that accounts receivable is overstated by $389? No, the auditor is interested in the *population* results, not those of the sample. It is therefore necessary to project from the sample to the population to estimate the population misstatement.

The first step is to calculate a **point estimate**. The point estimate can be calculated in different ways, but a common approach is to assume that misstatements in the unaudited population are proportional to the misstatements in the sample. That calculation must be done for each stratum and then totaled, rather than combining the total misstatements in the sample. In our example, the point estimate of the misstatement is calculated by using a weighted-average method, as shown next.

Stratum	Client Misstatement ÷ Recorded Value of the Sample	×	Recorded Book Value for the Stratum	=	Point Estimate of Misstatement
1	$(2,740)/$88,955		$88,955		$(2,740)
2	$ 971 /$43,995		71,235		1,572
3	$ 2,158 /$13,105		47,105		7,757
Total					$ 6,589

The point estimate of the misstatement in the population is $6,589, indicating an overstatement. The point estimate, by itself, is not an adequate measure of the population misstatement, however, because of sampling risk. In other words, because the estimate is based on a sample, it will be close to the true population misstatement, but it is unlikely to be exactly the same. Whenever the point estimate ($6,589 in the example) is less than tolerable misstatement ($15,000 in the example), the auditor must consider the possibility that the true population misstatement is greater than the amount of misstatement that is tolerable in the circumstances. This must be done for both statistical and nonstatistical samples.

An auditor using nonstatistical sampling cannot formally measure sampling risk and therefore must subjectively consider the possibility that the true population misstatement exceeds a tolerable amount. Auditors do this by considering:

1. The difference between the point estimate and tolerable misstatement (this is called calculated sampling risk)
2. The extent to which items in the population have been audited 100 percent
3. Whether misstatements tend to be offsetting or in only one direction
4. The amounts of individual misstatements
5. The sample size

In our example, suppose that tolerable misstatement is $40,000. In that case, the auditor may conclude it is unlikely, given the point estimate of $6,589, that the true population misstatement exceeds the tolerable amount (calculated allowance for sampling risk is $33,411).

Suppose that tolerable misstatement is $15,000 (as it was in the example), only $8,411 greater than the point estimate. In that case, the auditor will consider other factors. If the larger items in the population were audited 100 percent (as was done here), any unidentified misstatements will be restricted to smaller items. If the misstatements tend to be offsetting and are relatively small in size, the auditor may conclude that the true population misstatement is likely to be less than the tolerable amount. Also, the larger the sample size, the more confident the auditor can be that the point estimate is close to the true population value. In this example, when sample size is considered large, auditors will be more willing to accept that the true population misstatement is less than tolerable misstatement. However, if one or more of these other conditions differs, auditors may judge the chance of a misstatement in excess of the tolerable amount to be high and the recorded population unacceptable.

Even if the amount of likely misstatement is not considered material, the auditor must wait to make a final evaluation until the entire audit is completed. The estimated total misstatement and estimated sampling risk in accounts receivable must be combined with estimates of misstatements in all other parts of the audit to evaluate the effect of all misstatements on the financial statements as a whole. However, regardless of whether the sample results support the conclusion that the account is not materially misstated, the auditor should request that the client record an adjustment for the factual misstatements, unless they are clearly trivial.

Analyze the Misstatements

It is essential for auditors to evaluate the nature and cause of each misstatement found in tests of details of balances. For example, suppose that when the auditor confirmed accounts receivable, all misstatements resulted from the client's failure to record returned goods. The auditor will determine why that type of misstatement occurred so often, the implications of the misstatements on other audit areas, the potential impact on the financial statements, and its effect on company operations. The same approach is followed for all misstatements.

The auditor must do misstatement analysis to decide whether any modification of the audit risk model is needed. In the preceding paragraph, if the auditor concluded that the failure to record the returns resulted from a breakdown of internal controls, it might be necessary to reassess control risk. That in turn will probably cause the auditor to reduce ARIA, which will increase planned sample size. As we discussed in Chapter 9, revisions of the audit risk model must be done with extreme care because the model is intended primarily for planning, not evaluating results.

Action When a Population Is Rejected

When the auditor concludes that the misstatement in a population may be larger than tolerable misstatement after considering sampling risk, the population is not considered acceptable. At that point, an auditor has several possible courses of action.

Take No Action Until Tests of Other Audit Areas Are Completed Ultimately, the auditor must evaluate whether the financial statements taken as a whole are materially misstated. If offsetting misstatements are found in other parts of the audit, such as in inventory, the auditor may conclude that the estimated misstatements in accounts receivable are acceptable. Of course, before the audit is finalized, the auditor must evaluate whether a misstatement in one account may make the financial statements misleading even if there are offsetting misstatements.

Perform Expanded Audit Tests in Specific Areas If the analysis indicates an individual error is unique or most of the misstatements are of a specific type, it may be appropriate to restrict the additional audit effort to the problem area. For example, if an analysis of the misstatements in confirmations indicates that most of the misstatements result from failure to record sales returns, the auditor can make an extended search of returned goods to make sure that they have been recorded. However, care must be taken to evaluate the

MORTGAGE LENDER CHARGED FOR IGNORING SAMPLE RESULTS ON QUALITY OF MORTGAGE-BACKED SECURITIES

IndyMac Bank was a bank that primarily made, purchased, and sold residential mortgage loans. The SEC charged S. Blair Anthony, the former executive vice president and chief financial officer of IndyMac, with making false and misleading statements in connection with six offerings of residential mortgage-backed securities (RMBS) totaling $2.5 billion dollars in 2007. RMBS investors receive payments out of the principal and interest payments made by residential loan borrowers on the underlying loan. A number of these loans contained misrepresentations, which were not adequately disclosed in the RMBS offering documents. The six RMBS offerings experienced significant loan delinquencies and rating downgrades. The Federal Deposit Insurance Corporation (FDIC) placed IndyMac under receivership in July 2008, and the bank was sold to OneWest Bank in March 2009.

IndyMac's post-production quality control unit performed monthly quality control audits of IndyMac's loan production. Each month, the quality control unit selected a statistically valid random sample of the bank's loan production and, for each loan selected for testing, assessed whether the borrower or a third party (such as a mortgage broker or appraiser) misrepresented information in obtaining the loan. Misrepresentations involved things such as whether the home was a primary residence; the appraised value; and the loan applicant's employment, income, assets, and credit. The quality control audits indicated that 12% to 18% of the loans contained misrepresentations.

The prospectus supplements for the registration statements for the RMBS offerings were based on the original information on the loans, and IndyMac indicated that it would not include a loan in the offering if anything came to the bank's attention that showed the loan contained a misrepresentation. This statement was false because the bank knew, based on its audits, that 12% to 18% of the loans contained misrepresentations. Anthony was ordered to disgorge gains resulting from his misconduct and to pay a civil penalty.

Source: Securities and Exchange Commission Litigation Complaint No. 21853, February 11, 2011 (www.sec.gov).

cause of all misstatements in the sample before a conclusion is reached about the proper emphasis in the expanded tests. Problems may exist in more than one area.

When auditors analyze a problem area and correct it by proposing an adjustment to the client's records, the sample items that led to isolating the problem area can then be shown as "correct." The point estimate can now be recalculated without the misstatements that have been "corrected." However, this is only true when the error can be isolated to a specific area. U.S. auditing standards indicate that misstatements should be projected to the population being sampled, even if the client adjusts for the misstatement. International auditing standards indicate that an error could be an anomaly, and the AICPA *Audit Sampling* Audit Guide indicates that in limited circumstances, it may be appropriate to not project a misstatement to the population. As this discussion indicates, auditors should be cautious in reaching the conclusion to not project a misstatement, and should clearly document the reasons and evidence that support this conclusion.

Increase the Sample Size If the original sample is considered representative, the rate of misstatements in the expanded sample will be similar to the original sample. As a result, an increase in sample size would normally not be expected to significantly change the point estimate of likely misstatement in the population. However, when the auditor increases the sample size, sampling risk is reduced if the rate of misstatements in the expanded sample, their dollar amounts, and their direction are similar to those in the original sample. Therefore, increasing the sample size may allow the auditor to conclude that the true population misstatement is unlikely to exceed tolerable misstatement.

Increasing the sample size sufficiently to conclude that the population is fairly stated is often costly, especially when the difference between tolerable misstatement and projected misstatement is small. Moreover, an increased sample size does not guarantee a satisfactory result. If the number, amount, and direction of the misstatements in the extended sample are proportionately greater or more variable than in the original sample, the results are still likely to be unacceptable.

For tests such as accounts receivable confirmation and inventory observation, it is often difficult to increase the sample size because of the practical problem of "reopening" those procedures once the initial work is done. By the time the auditor discovers that the sample was not large enough, several weeks have usually passed.

Despite these difficulties, sometimes the auditor must increase the sample size after the original testing is completed. It is much more common to increase sample size in audit areas other than confirmations and inventory observation, but it is occasionally necessary to do so even for these two areas. When stratified sampling is used, increased samples usually focus on the strata containing larger amounts, unless misstatements appear to be concentrated in some other strata.

Adjust the Account Balance When the auditor concludes that an account balance is materially misstated, the client may be willing to adjust the book value based on the sample results. In the preceding example, assume the client is willing to reduce book value by the amount of the point estimate ($6,589) to adjust for the estimate of the misstatement. The auditor's estimate of the misstatement is now zero, but it is still necessary to consider sampling risk. Again, assuming a tolerable misstatement of $15,000, the auditor must now assess whether sampling risk exceeds $15,000, not the $8,411 originally considered. If the auditor believes sampling risk is $15,000 or less, accounts receivable is acceptable after the adjustment. If the auditor believes it is more than $15,000, adjusting the account balance is not a practical option. Clients are often unwilling to record adjustments for estimated misstatements based on a sample. However, as previously noted, the client is encouraged to record an adjustment for the factual misstatements, which will reduce the estimate of the misstatement and increase the actual allowance for sampling risk by the amount of the adjustment for the factual errors.

Request the Client to Correct the Population In some cases, the client's records are so inadequate that a correction of the entire population is required before the audit can be completed. For example, in accounts receivable, the client may be asked to correct the accounts receivable records and prepare the accounts receivable listing again if the auditor concludes that it has significant misstatements. When the client changes the valuation of some items in the population, the results must be audited again.

Refuse to Give an Unmodified Opinion If the auditor believes that the recorded amount in an account is not fairly stated, it is necessary to follow at least one of the preceding alternatives or to modify the audit report in an appropriate manner. If the auditor believes that there is a reasonable chance that the financial statements are materially misstated, it would be a serious breach of auditing standards to issue an unmodified opinion. For purposes of reporting on internal control, the material misstatement should be considered a potential indicator of a material weakness in internal control over financial reporting.

CONCEPT CHECK

1. What are the major differences in the 14 steps used in nonstatistical sampling for tests of details of balances versus the steps for tests of controls and substantive tests of transactions?
2. What alternative courses of action are appropriate when a population is rejected using nonstatistical sampling for tests of details of balances? When should each option be followed?

MONETARY UNIT SAMPLING

OBJECTIVE 17-3

Apply monetary unit sampling.

Now that we have discussed nonstatistical sampling, we will move on to statistical sampling, starting with monetary unit sampling, which is a statistical sampling methodology developed specifically for use by auditors. **Monetary unit sampling (MUS)** is the most commonly used statistical method of sampling for tests of details of balances because it has the statistical simplicity of attributes sampling yet provides a statistical result expressed in dollars (or another appropriate currency). MUS is also called dollar unit sampling, cumulative monetary amount sampling, and sampling with probability proportional to size.

Differences Between MUS and Nonstatistical Sampling

MUS is similar to using nonstatistical sampling. All 14 of the steps must also be performed for MUS, although some are done differently. Understanding those differences is the key to understanding MUS. Let's examine these differences in detail.

The Definition of the Sampling Unit Is an Individual Dollar A critical feature of MUS is the definition of the sampling unit as an individual dollar in an account balance. The name of the statistical method, monetary unit sampling, results from this distinctive feature. For example, in the population in Table 17-1 (p. 567), the sampling unit is 1 dollar and the population size is 207,295 dollars, not the 40 physical units discussed earlier. (A physical unit is an accounts receivable customer balance, an inventory item in an inventory listing, and other such identifiable units in a listing.)

By focusing on the individual dollar as the sampling unit, MUS automatically emphasizes physical units with larger recorded balances. Because the sample is selected on the basis of individual dollars, an account with a large balance has a greater chance of being included than an account with a small balance. For example, in accounts receivable confirmation, an account with a $5,000 balance has a 10 times greater probability of selection than one with a $500 balance, as it contains 10 times as many dollar units. As a result, stratified sampling is unnecessary with MUS. Stratification occurs automatically.

The Population Size Is the Recorded Dollar Population For example, the population of accounts receivable in Table 17-1 consists of 207,295 dollars, which is the

TABLE 17-4 Accounts Receivable Population		
Population Item (Physical Unit)	**Recorded Amount**	**Cumulative Total (Dollar Unit)**
1	$ 357	$ 357
2	1,281	1,638
3	60	1,698
4	573	2,271
5	691	2,962
6	143	3,105
7	2,125	5,230
8	278	5,508
9	242	5,750
10	826	6,576
11	404	6,980
12	396	7,376

population size, not the 40 accounts receivable balances. This is the recorded dollar amount of accounts receivable.

Because of the method of sample selection in MUS, which is discussed later, it is not possible to evaluate the likelihood of unrecorded items in the population. Assume, for example, that MUS is used to evaluate whether inventory is fairly stated. MUS cannot be used to evaluate whether certain inventory items exist but have not been counted. If the completeness objective is important in the audit test, and it usually is, that objective must be satisfied separately from the MUS tests.

Sample Size Is Determined Using a Formula We illustrate the calculation of sample sizes after we have discussed the 14 sampling steps for MUS.

Sample Selection Is Done Using PPS Monetary unit samples are selected with **probability proportional to size sample selection (PPS)**. PPS samples can be obtained by using computer software or systematic sampling techniques. Table 17-4 provides an illustration of an accounts receivable population, including cumulative totals that will be used to demonstrate selecting a sample.

Assume that the auditor wants to select a PPS sample of four accounts from the population in Table 17-4. Because the sampling unit is defined as an individual dollar, the population size is 7,376. Auditors often use fixed interval systematic sampling because all items greater than the sampling interval will be automatically selected for testing. However, as discussed earlier in the section on nonstatistical sampling, the auditor may choose to examine all the individually material times that are greater than tolerable misstatement, and sample the remaining items.

Using systematic selection, the sampling interval is 1,844 (7,376 ÷ 4) and the auditor then chooses a random start between 1 and 1,844 (the length of the sampling interval). Assume the auditor randomly selects a start of 822. The sample dollars selected for testing are 822; 2,666 (822 + 1,844); 4,510 (2,666 + 1,844); and 6,354 (4,510 + 1,844).

The population physical unit items that contain these random dollars are determined by reference to the cumulative total column. Looking again at Table 17-4, the items selected are items 2 (containing dollars 358 through 1,638), 5 (dollars 2,272 through 2,962), 7 (dollars 3,106 through 5,230), and 10 (dollars 5,751 through 6,576). Note that item 7 is larger than the sampling interval and will therefore always be included in the sample using systematic selection. If a population item is several times larger than the sampling interval, it may be included in the sample more than once. Therefore, the actual number of units selected for testing may be less than the computed sample size.

The auditor may also use random selection of dollars, rather than systematic selection. Assume the auditor uses a computer program to generate four random numbers from between 1 and 7,376 to generate the sample and generates numbers 6,586; 1,756; 850; and 6,599. Referring again to Table 17-4, the items selected are items 11 (containing dollars 6,577 through 6,980), 4 (dollars 1,699 through 2,271), 2 (dollars 358 through 1,638), and 11 (dollars 6,577 through 6,980). These accounts will be audited because the cumulative total associated with these accounts includes the random dollars selected. Item 11 was treated as two sample items because it was randomly selected twice, even though the recorded balance of the account of $404 is much smaller than the sampling interval using systematic selection.

One problem using PPS selection is that population items with a zero recorded balance have no chance of being selected with PPS sample selection, even though they may be misstated. Similarly, small balances that are significantly understated have little chance of being included in the sample. This problem can be overcome by doing specific audit tests for zero- and small-balance items, assuming that they are of concern.

Another problem with PPS is its inability to include negative balances, such as credit balances in accounts receivable, in the PPS (monetary unit) sample. It is possible to ignore negative balances for PPS selection and test those amounts by some other means. An alternative is to treat them as positive balances and add them to the total number of monetary units being tested. However, this complicates the evaluation process.

The Auditor Generalizes from the Sample to the Population Using MUS Techniques Regardless of the sampling method selected, the auditor must generalize from the sample to the population by (1) projecting misstatements from the sample results to the population and (2) determining the related sampling risk. The statistical result when MUS is used is called a **misstatement bound**. The misstatement bound is an estimate of the likely maximum overstatement at a given ARIA. The discussion and example that follow are limited to overstatements because MUS is designed primarily to test for overstatements. Calculation of misstatement bounds is usually done using audit software or computer templates. We illustrate the calculation of the projected misstatement and misstatement bound in the next section after we discuss the 14 sampling steps for MUS.

Decide the Acceptability of the Population Using MUS

The auditor compares the calculated misstatement bound to tolerable misstatement. If the bound exceeds tolerable misstatement, the population is not considered acceptable. The options available to the auditor when the population is rejected are the same ones already discussed for nonstatistical sampling on pages 573–575.

Now that we have discussed the differences between MUS and nonstatistical sampling for tests of details of balances, we examine the determination of sample sizes and calculation of misstatement bounds in further detail.

Determining Sample Sizes Using MUS

We illustrate the formula for computing sample sizes using MUS based on the AICPA *Audit Sampling* Audit Guide. We first discuss the factors used in computing sample size.

Acceptable Risk of Incorrect Acceptance ARIA is an auditor judgment of the level of assurance required for the sampling application. As illustrated in Figure 17-1 (p. 569) and Table 17-2 (p. 570), ARIA depends on audit risk model factors and the amount of assurance provided by substantive analytical procedures and other substantive tests. For this example, we will assume that the auditor concluded an ARIA of 10 percent was appropriate.

Recorded Population Value The dollar value of the population is taken from the client's records. For this example, it is $5 million.

Tolerable Misstatement Tolerable misstatement is generally the same as performance materiality, but the auditor may decrease the amount of tolerable misstatement if less than 100 percent of the population is tested. For this example, tolerable misstatement is $150,000.

TABLE 17-5	Confidence Factors for Monetary Unit Sample Size Design*							
	Risk of Incorrect Acceptance							
Ratio of Expected to Tolerable Misstatement	5%	10%	15%	20%	25%	30%	35%	50%
0.00	3.00	2.31	1.90	1.61	1.39	1.21	1.05	0.70
0.05	3.31	2.52	2.06	1.74	1.49	1.29	1.12	0.73
0.10	3.68	2.77	2.25	1.89	1.61	1.39	1.20	0.77
0.15	4.11	3.07	2.47	2.06	1.74	1.49	1.28	0.82
0.20	4.63	3.41	2.73	2.26	1.90	1.62	1.38	0.87
0.25	5.24	3.83	3.04	2.49	2.09	1.76	1.50	0.92
0.30	6.00	4.33	3.41	2.77	2.30	1.93	1.63	0.99
0.35	6.92	4.95	3.86	3.12	2.57	2.14	1.79	1.06
0.40	8.09	5.72	4.42	3.54	2.89	2.39	1.99	1.14
0.45	9.59	6.71	5.13	4.07	3.29	2.70	2.22	1.25
0.50	11.54	7.99	6.04	4.75	3.80	3.08	2.51	1.37
0.55	14.18	9.70	7.26	5.64	4.47	3.58	2.89	1.52
0.60	17.85	12.07	8.93	6.86	5.37	4.25	3.38	1.70

*Source: Data from AICPA *Audit Sampling* Audit Guide, March 1, 2014 (www.aicpa.org).

Tolerable Misstatement as a Percentage of Population Value The auditor computes tolerable misstatement as a percentage of the population recorded value. This equals .03 ($150,000 ÷ $5,000,000) based on the example tolerable misstatement and population value.

Estimated Population Misstatement MUS is most often used when no or few misstatements are expected. The estimated population misstatement is usually based on the sample results for the prior year, although some auditors calculate the estimated misstatement as a percentage of tolerable misstatement or performance materiality. For this example, a $15,000 overstatement is expected.

Ratio of Estimated Population Misstatement to Tolerable Misstatement The auditor computes the ratio of estimated misstatement to tolerable misstatement. The ratio equals .10 ($15,000 ÷ $150,000) for this example.

Confidence Factor The auditor uses Table 17-5 to determine an appropriate confidence factor based on the auditor's judgment of ARIA and the ratio of expected misstatement to tolerable misstatement. Based on an ARIA of 10 percent and a ratio of expected to tolerable misstatement of .10, the appropriate confidence factor is 2.77.

Sample Size The appropriate sample size is then calculated as the confidence factor divided by the tolerable misstatement as a percentage of the population value.

$$\text{Sample Size} = \frac{\text{Confidence Factor (2.77)}}{\text{Tolerable Misstatement as Percentage of Population Value (.03)}} = 93 \text{ (rounded up)}$$

Sampling Interval The appropriate sampling interval can now be computed as the population recorded amount of $5 million divided by the sample size of 93.

$$\text{Sampling Interval} = \$5{,}000{,}000 \div 93 = \$53{,}763$$

TABLE 17-6	Summary of Steps to Calculate Sample Size in MUS	
Steps to Calculate Sample Size	**Amount**	**Source or Calculation**
1. Determine ARIA	10%	Determined based on factors in Table 17-2 (p. 570)
2. Population recorded value	$5,000,000	—
3. Tolerable misstatement	$150,000	—
4. Tolerable misstatement as percentage of population value	3%	$150,000 ÷ $5,000,000
5. Estimated population misstatement	$15,000	Based on prior year results
6. Ratio of estimated population misstatement to tolerable misstatement	.10	$15,000 ÷ $150,000
7. Confidence factor	2.77	Table 17-5 based on ARIA of 10% and ratio of expected to tolerable misstatement of .10
8. Calculate sample size	93	2.77 ÷ .03 (confidence factor divided by tolerable misstatement as a percentage of population value)
9. Calculate sampling interval	$53,763	$5,000,000 ÷ 93

The steps involved in calculating the sample size are illustrated in Table 17-6. The formula method is just one method of determining sample size using MUS. The *Audit Sampling* Audit Guide also provides tables to determine sample size based on ARIA, the tolerable misstatement as a percentage of the population, and ratio of expected to tolerable misstatement. Because MUS is based on attribute theory, the attribute sampling tables in Table 15-8 (p. 508) can also be used. ARIA is used instead of ARO, the tolerable misstatement as a percentage of the population value is used for the tolerable exception rate, and the ratio of estimated population misstatement to tolerable misstatement is used for the estimated population exception rate. Most auditors use audit software to calculate sample size and evaluate sample results using MUS.

Generalizing from the Sample to the Population When No Misstatements Are Found Using MUS

After performing tests on the sample items, the auditor projects the sample misstatements to the population and calculates an allowance for sampling risk when using MUS. If the entire sample is audited and no misstatements are found in the sample, the auditor may conclude without making additional calculations that the recorded amount of the population is not overstated by more than tolerable misstatement at the specified risk of incorrect acceptance. The upper limit when no misstatements are found is the confidence factor for no misstatements multiplied by the length of the sampling interval.

Suppose that the auditor is confirming a population of accounts receivable for monetary correctness. The population totals $1,200,000, and a sample of 100 confirmations is obtained. Upon audit, no misstatements are uncovered in the sample. Assuming an ARIA of 5%, the confidence factor from Table 17-7 (p. 580) is 3.0. Applied to a sampling interval of $12,000 (population of $1,200,000 ÷ 100 sample items = $12,000 sampling interval), the upper misstatement bound is calculated as:

$$\text{Upper misstatement bound} = \$12{,}000 \times 3.0 = \$36{,}000$$

The upper limit when no misstatements are found is also referred to as **basic precision**, and represents the minimum allowance for sampling risk inherent in the sample. For this example, because no misstatements were found, the projected misstatement is zero, and the allowance for sampling risk equals the upper limit on misstatement of $36,000.

TABLE 17-7 **Confidence Factors for Monetary Unit Sample Size Evaluation***

Number of Overstatement Misstatements	Risk of Incorrect Acceptance							
	5%	10%	15%	20%	25%	30%	35%	50%
0	3.00	2.31	1.90	1.61	1.39	1.21	1.05	0.70
1	4.75	3.89	3.38	3.00	2.70	2.44	2.22	1.68
2	6.30	5.33	4.73	4.28	3.93	3.62	3.35	2.68
3	7.76	6.69	6.02	5.52	5.11	4.77	4.46	3.68
4	9.16	8.00	7.27	6.73	6.28	5.90	5.55	4.68
5	10.52	9.28	8.50	7.91	7.43	7.01	6.64	5.68
6	11.85	10.54	9.71	9.08	8.56	8.12	7.72	6.67
7	13.15	11.78	10.90	10.24	9.69	9.21	8.79	7.67
8	14.44	13.00	12.08	11.38	10.81	10.31	9.85	8.67
9	15.71	14.21	13.25	12.52	11.92	11.39	10.92	9.67
10	16.97	15.41	14.42	13.66	13.02	12.47	11.98	10.67

*Source: Data from AICPA *Audit Sampling* Audit Guide, March 1, 2014 (www.aicpa.org). Misstatements greater than 10 not illustrated.

Generalizing from the Sample to the Population When Misstatements Are Found Using MUS

Assume that the auditor tested the sample and found the three overstatements included in Table 17-8. Calculating the upper misstatement bound involves three steps.

1. Calculate the percentage misstatement for each misstatement.
2. Project the sample misstatements by multiplying the percentage misstatement by the length of the sampling interval.
3. Add an allowance for sampling risk based on the confidence factors for the actual number of misstatements and acceptable risk of incorrect acceptance.

Calculate Percentage Misstatement Assumption (Tainting) When misstatements are found, the auditor calculates a projected misstatement and an allowance for sampling risk. The percent of misstatement in the sampling unit represents the percentage of misstatement or tainting for the entire sampling interval, which is calculated by dividing the misstatement by the recorded amount. Table 17-8 indicates the percentage misstatement for the three misstatements found in the sample. The misstatements are ranked by percentage size for calculation of the allowance for sampling risk.

Project Sample Misstatements The projected misstatement is the percentage misstatement times the sampling interval, since the percentage of misstatement is for the whole sampling interval. For example, if the sampling interval is $10,000 and a

TABLE 17-8 **Percent of Misstatement**

Customer No.	Recorded Accounts Receivable Amount	Audited Accounts Receivable Amount	Factual Misstatement	Percentage Misstatement = Misstatement ÷ Recorded Amount
2073	$ 6,200	$ 6,100	$ 100	.016
5111	12,910	12,000	910	N/A(1)
9816	8,947	2,947	$6,000	.671

(1) Percentage misstatement is N/A because recorded amount is greater than the sampling interval. In this situation, the projected misstatement equals the actual misstatement.

TABLE 17-9 Calculation of Projected Misstatement and Allowance for Sampling Risk							
A	B	C	D	E	F	G	H
Recorded Amount	Audit Amount	Factual Misstatement (A - B)	Percentage Misstatement (C ÷ A)	Sampling Interval	Projected Misstatement (D × E)	(see Table 17-10) Incremental Change in Confidence Factor	Projected Misstatement Plus Incremental Allowance for Sampling Risk (F × G)
$12,910	$12,000	$ 910	N/A(1)	N/A(1)	$ 910	N/A	$ 910
8,947	2,947	6,000	67.1%	12,000	8,052	1.75	14,091
6,200	6,100	100	1.6%	12,000	192	1.55	298
Totals		$7,010			$9,154		$15,299
Add basic precision							36,000
Upper misstatement bound							$51,299

(1) Percentage misstatement is N/A because recorded amount is greater than the sampling interval. In this situation, the projected misstatement equals the actual misstatement.

recorded amount of $100 has an audited value of $75, the projected misstatement is $2,500 ($25 misstatement is 25% of the recorded amount × $10,000 sampling interval). If the recorded amount of the sample item is greater than the sampling interval, then the projected misstatement equals the actual sample misstatement. Table 17-9 indicates the calculation of projected misstatement for the three actual sample misstatements.

Calculate the Allowance for Sampling Risk The projected misstatement is increased by the allowance for sampling risk, which is calculated as basic precision plus an incremental allowance for sampling risk for each misstatement found in sampling units that are smaller than the sampling interval. There is no incremental allowance for sampling risk in sampling units that are greater than the sampling interval since all of the monetary units in the sampling interval were examined.

A conservative approach is to rank the misstatements by the percentage misstatement. The misstatements are then multiplied by the incremental change in the confidence factor to compute the projected misstatement plus the incremental allowance for sampling risk. Table 17-10 provides an example of the incremental changes in the confidence factor for five misstatements and a 5% ARIA.

The last two columns of Table 17-9 show the incremental changes in the confidence factor, and projected misstatement plus the incremental allowance for sampling risk. Including the basic precision of $36,000, the upper misstatement bound is $51,299. Therefore, based on an ARIA of 5%, the auditor can state that there is a 5 percent risk that the recorded amount is overstated by more than $51,299.

TABLE 17-10 Incremental Changes in Confidence Factor—Five Percent Risk of Incorrect Acceptance		
Number of Overstatements	Confidence Factor	Incremental Changes in Factor
0	3.00	—
1	4.75	1.75
2	6.30	1.55
3	7.76	1.46
4	9.16	1.40
5	10.52	1.36

The sample results can be summarized as follows:

- The sample contains factual misstatements of $7,010.
- The total factual and projected misstatement is $9,154.
- The upper misstatement bound representing the total factual and projected misstatement plus an allowance for sampling risk is $51,299.
- The allowance for sampling risk representing basic precision and the incremental allowance for sampling risk is $42,145 [$36,000 basic precision + $6,145 incremental allowance for sampling risk ($15,299 – $9,154)].

The results are considered acceptable if the upper misstatement bound of $51,299 is less than tolerable misstatement. If the upper misstatement bound exceeds tolerable misstatement, the population is not acceptable based on the results of the sample, and the auditor will take one or more of the actions discussed in the "Action When a Population Is Rejected" section on pages 573–575.

Relationship of the Audit Risk Model to Sample Size for MUS The audit risk model for planning was introduced in Chapter 9 and covered in subsequent chapters as:

$$PDR = \frac{AAR}{IR \times CR}$$

(See pp. 271–273 for description of the terms.)

Chapter 16 discussed how the auditor reduces detection risk to the planned level by performing substantive tests of transactions, substantive analytical procedures, and tests of details of balances. MUS is used in performing tests of details of balances. Therefore, auditors need to understand the relationship of the three independent factors in the audit risk model, plus substantive analytical procedures and substantive tests of transactions, to sample size for tests of details of balances.

Table 17-2 on page 570 shows that four of these five factors (control risk, substantive tests of transactions, acceptable audit risk, and substantive analytical procedures) affect ARIA. ARIA in turn determines the planned sample size. The other factor, inherent risk, is also considered in determining ARIA, and directly affects sample size through the estimated population misstatement.

Audit Uses of Monetary Unit Sampling

MUS appeals to auditors for at least four reasons:

1. MUS automatically increases the likelihood of selecting high dollar items from the population being audited. Auditors make a practice of concentrating on these items because they generally represent the greatest risk of material misstatements. Stratified sampling can also be used for this purpose, but MUS is often easier to apply.
2. MUS often reduces the cost of doing the audit testing because several sample items are tested at once. For example, if one large item makes up 10 percent of the total recorded dollar value of the population and the sample size is 100, the PPS sample selection method is likely to result in approximately 10 percent of the sample items from that one large population item. Naturally, that item needs to be audited only once, but it counts as a sample of 10. If the item is misstated, it is also counted as 10 misstatements. Larger population items may be eliminated from the sampled population by auditing them 100 percent and evaluating them separately, if the auditor so desires.
3. MUS is easy to apply. Monetary unit samples can be evaluated by the application of simple tables. It is easy to teach and to supervise the use of MUS techniques. Firms that utilize MUS extensively use audit software or other computer programs that streamline sample size determination and evaluation even further than shown in this chapter.
4. MUS provides a statistical conclusion rather than a nonstatistical one. Many auditors believe that statistical sampling aids them in making better and more defensible conclusions.

There are two main disadvantages of MUS.

1. The total misstatement bounds resulting when misstatements are found may be too high to be useful to the auditor. This is because these evaluation methods are inherently conservative when misstatements are found and often produce bounds far in excess of materiality. To overcome this problem, larger samples may be required.
2. It may be cumbersome to select PPS samples from large populations without computer assistance.

For all these reasons, auditors commonly use MUS when zero or few misstatements are expected, a dollar result is desired, and the population data are accessible in electronic format.

CONCEPT CHECK

1. Define the sampling interval when using MUS sampling. How is it calculated?
2. Assume that the auditor tested an account receivable with a balance of $3,000 and determined that the audited value was $2,700. That is, the auditor determined the receivable was overstated by $300. What is the projected misstatement (excluding the incremental allowance for sampling risk) if the sampling interval is $15,000?

VARIABLES SAMPLING

OBJECTIVE 17-4

Describe variables sampling.

Variables sampling, like MUS, is a statistical method that auditors use. Variables sampling and nonstatistical sampling for tests of details of balances have the same objective—to measure the misstatement in an account balance. As with nonstatistical sampling, when auditors determine that the misstatement amount exceeds the tolerable amount, they reject the population and take additional actions.

Several sampling techniques make up the general class of methods called variables sampling: difference estimation, ratio estimation, and mean-per-unit estimation. These are discussed later.

Differences Between Variables and Nonstatistical Sampling

The use of variables methods shares many similarities with nonstatistical sampling. All 14 steps we discussed for nonstatistical sampling must be performed for variables methods, and most are identical. Some of the differences between variables and nonstatistical sampling are examined after we discuss sampling distributions.

Sampling Distributions

To understand why and how auditors use variables sampling methods in auditing, it is useful to understand sampling distributions and how they affect auditors' statistical conclusions. The auditor does not know the mean value (average) of misstatements in the population, the distribution of the misstatement amounts, or the audited values. These population characteristics must be *estimated* from samples, which, of course, is the purpose of the audit test.

Assume that an auditor, as an experiment, took thousands of repeated samples of equal size from a population of accounting data having a mean value of $\overline{X}$. For each sample, the auditor calculates the mean value of the items in the sample as follows:

$$\bar{x} = \frac{\Sigma x_j}{n}$$

where

$\bar{x}$ = mean value of the sample items

x_j = value of each individual sample item

n = sample size

FIGURE 17-3 Frequency Distribution of Sample Means

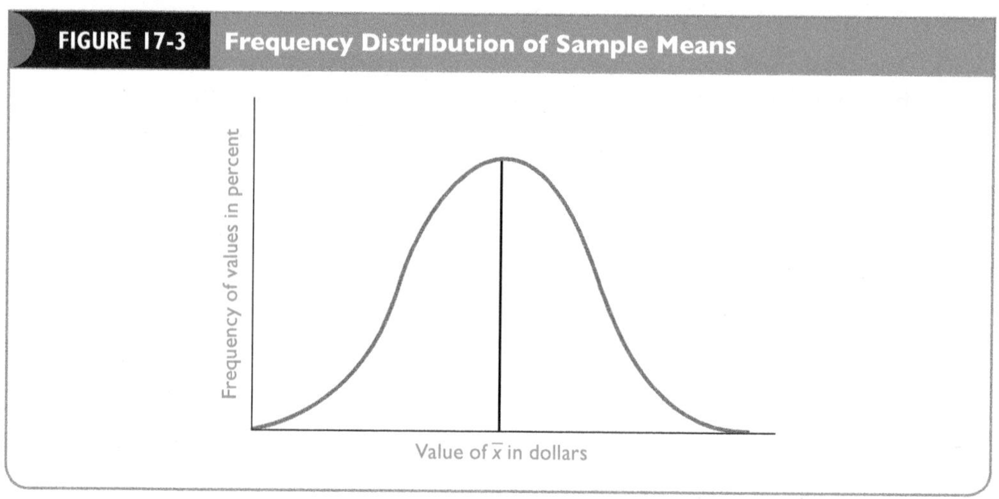

After calculating ($\bar{x}$) for each sample, the auditor plots them into a frequency distribution. As long as the sample size is sufficient, the frequency distribution of the sample means will appear much like that shown in Figure 17-3.

A distribution of the sample means such as this is normal and has all the characteristics of the normal curve: (1) the curve is symmetrical, and (2) the sample means fall within known portions of the sampling distribution around the average or mean of those means, measured by the distance along the horizontal axis in terms of standard deviations.

Furthermore, the mean of the sample means (the midpoint of the sampling distribution) is equal to the population mean, and the standard deviation of the sampling distribution is equal to $SD/\sqrt{n}$, where SD is the population standard deviation and n is the sample size.

To illustrate, assume a population with a mean of \$40 and a standard deviation of \$15 ($\bar{X}$ = \$40 and SD = \$15), from which we elected to take many random samples of 100 items each. The standard deviation of our sampling distribution is \$1.50 ($SD/\sqrt{n} = 15/\sqrt{100} = 1.50$). The reference to "standard deviation" of the population and to "standard deviation" of the sampling distribution is often confusing. To avoid confusion, remember that the standard deviation of the distribution of the sample means is often called the standard error of the mean (SE). With this information, auditors can make the tabulation of the sampling distribution, as shown in Table 17-11.

To summarize, three things shape the results of the experiment of taking a large number of samples from a known population:

1. The mean value of all the sample means is equal to the population mean ($\bar{X}$). A corollary is that the sample mean value ($\bar{x}$) with the highest frequency of occurrence is also equal to the population mean.

TABLE 17-11 Calculated Sampling Distribution from a Population with a Known Mean and Standard Deviation

(1) Number of Standard Errors of the Mean (Confidence Coefficient)	(2) Value [(1) × \$1.50]	(3) Range Around $\bar{X}$ [\$40 +/− (2)]	(4) Percent of Sample Means Included in Range
1	\$1.50	\$38.50 − \$41.50	68.2
2	\$3.00	\$37.00 − \$43.00	95.4
3	\$4.50	\$35.50 − \$44.50	99.7
			(taken from table for normal curve)

FIGURE 17-4 Sampling Distribution for a Population Distribution

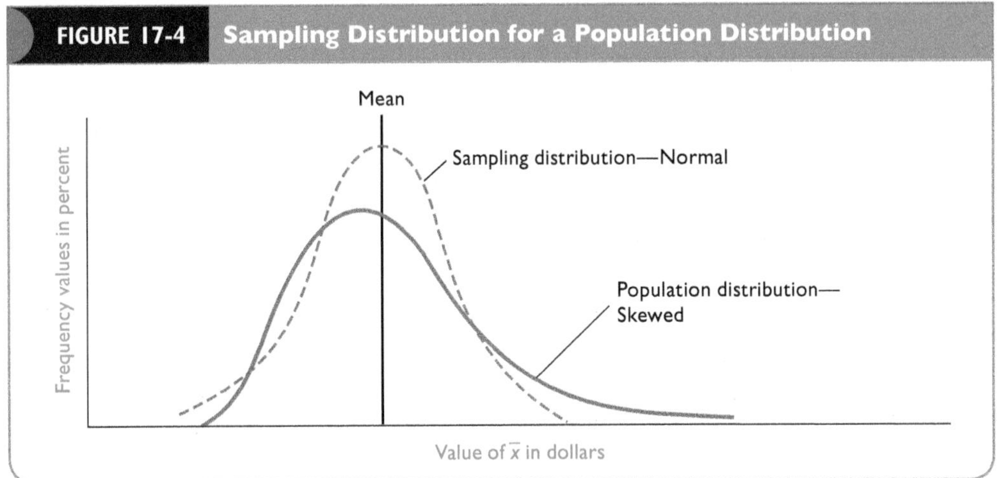

2. The shape of the frequency distribution of the sample means is that of a normal distribution (curve), as long as the sample size is sufficiently large, *regardless of the distribution of the population*, as illustrated in Figure 17-4.
3. The percentage of sample means between any two values of the sampling distribution is measurable. The percentage can be calculated by determining the number of standard errors between any two values and determining the percentage of sample means represented from a table for normal curves.

Statistical Inference

Naturally, when samples are taken from a population in an actual audit situation, the auditor does not know the population's characteristics and, ordinarily, only one sample is taken from the population. But the *knowledge of sampling distributions* enables auditors to draw statistical conclusions, or **statistical inferences**, about the population. For example, assume that the auditor takes a sample from a population and calculates ($\bar{x}$) as \$46 and SE at \$9. (We'll explain how SE is calculated later.) We can now calculate a confidence interval of the population mean using the logic gained from the study of sampling distributions. It is as follows:

$$CI_{\bar{x}} = \hat{X} \pm Z \cdot SE$$

where:

$$CI_{\bar{x}} = \text{confidence interval for the population mean}$$

$$\hat{X} = \text{point estimate of the population mean}$$

$$Z = \text{confidence coefficient} \begin{cases} 1 = 68.2\% \text{ confidence level} \\ 2 = 95.4\% \text{ confidence level} \\ 3 = 99.7\% \text{ confidence level} \end{cases}$$

$$SE = \text{standard error of the mean}$$

$$Z \cdot SE = \text{precision interval}$$

For the example:

$$CI_{\bar{x}} = \$46 \pm 1(\$9) = \$46 \pm \$9 \text{ at a } 68.2\% \text{ confidence level}$$

$$CI_{\bar{x}} = \$46 \pm 2(\$9) = \$46 \pm \$18 \text{ at a } 95.4\% \text{ confidence level}$$

$$CI_{\bar{x}} = \$46 \pm 3(\$9) = \$46 \pm \$27 \text{ at a } 99.7\% \text{ confidence level}$$

The results can also be stated in terms of confidence limits ($CI_{\bar{x}}$). The upper confidence limit ($UCL_{\bar{x}}$) is $\hat{X} + Z \cdot SE$ (\$46 + \$18 = \$64 at a 95 percent confidence level) and a lower confidence limit ($LCL_{\bar{x}}$) is $\hat{\bar{X}} - Z \cdot SE$ ($46 − $18 = $28 at a 95 percent confidence level). Graphically, the results are as follows:

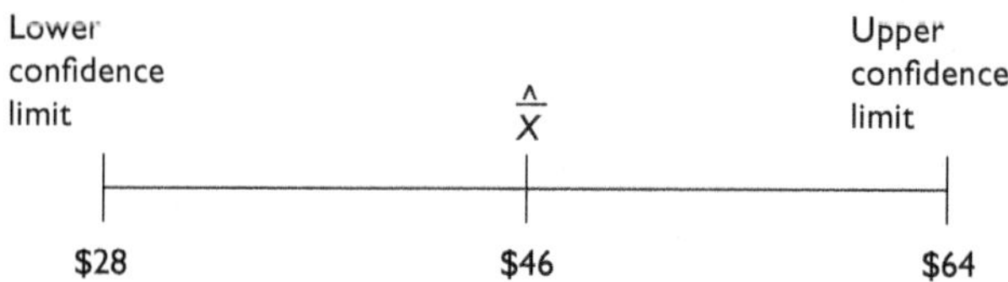

Auditors can state the conclusions drawn from a confidence interval using statistical inference in different ways. However, they must take care to avoid incorrect conclusions, remembering that the true population value is always unknown. There is always a possibility that the sample is not sufficiently representative of the population to provide a sample mean and/or standard deviation reasonably close to those of the population. The auditor can say, however, that the procedure used to obtain the sample and compute the confidence interval will provide an interval that will contain the true population mean value a given percent of the time. In short, the auditor knows the reliability of the statistical inference process that is used to draw conclusions.

Variables Methods

Auditors use the preceding statistical inference process for all the variables sampling methods. Each method is distinguished by what is being measured. Let's examine the three variables methods individually.

Difference Estimation Auditors use **difference estimation** to measure the estimated total misstatement amount in a population when both a recorded value and an audited value exist for each item in the sample, which is almost always the case in audits. For example, an auditor might confirm a sample of accounts receivable and determine the difference (misstatement) between the client's recorded amount and the amount the auditor considers correct for each selected account. The auditor makes an estimate of the population misstatement based on the number of misstatements in the sample, average misstatement size, individual misstatements in the sample, and sample size. The result is stated as a point estimate of the population misstatement plus or minus a computed precision interval at a stated confidence level. Referring back to the discussion of sampling distributions, assume the auditor confirmed a random sample of 100 from a population of 1,000 accounts receivable and concluded that the confidence limits of the mean of the misstatement for accounts receivable were between $28 and $64 at a 95 percent confidence level. The estimate of the total population misstatement can also be easily calculated as being between $28,000 and $64,000 at a 95 percent confidence level (1,000 × $28 and 1,000 × $64). If the auditor's tolerable misstatement is $100,000, the population is clearly acceptable. If tolerable misstatement is $40,000, the population is not acceptable. An illustration using difference estimation is shown at the end of this chapter on pages 588–591.

Difference estimation frequently results in smaller sample sizes than any other method, and it is relatively easy to use. For that reason, difference estimation is often the preferred variables method.

Ratio Estimation **Ratio estimation** is similar to difference estimation except the auditor calculates the ratio between the misstatements and their recorded value and projects this to the population to estimate the total population misstatement. For example, assume that an auditor finds misstatements totaling $12,000 in a sample with a recorded value of $208,000. The misstatement ratio is .06 ($12,000/$208,000). If the total recorded value of the population is $1,040,000, the projected misstatement in the population is $62,400 ($1,040,000 × .06). The auditor can then calculate confidence limits of the total misstatement for ratio estimation with a calculation similar to the one shown for difference estimation. Ratio estimation can result in sample sizes even smaller than difference estimation if the size of the misstatements in the population is proportionate to the recorded value of the population items. If the size of the individual misstatements is independent of the recorded value, difference estimation results in smaller sample sizes. Most auditors prefer difference estimation because it is somewhat simpler to calculate confidence intervals.

Mean-per-Unit Estimation In **mean-per-unit estimation**, the auditor focuses on the audited value rather than the misstatement amount of each item in the sample. Except for the definition of what is being measured, the mean-per-unit estimate is calculated in exactly the same manner as the difference estimate. The point estimate of the audited value equals the average audited value of items in the sample times the population size. The computed precision interval is calculated on the basis of the audited value of the sample items rather than the misstatements. When auditors have computed the upper and lower confidence limits, they decide the acceptability of the population by comparing these amounts with the recorded book value. For example, assume the auditor takes a sample of 100 items from an inventory listing containing 3,000 items and a recorded value $265,000. If the mean value of the items sampled is $85, the estimated value of the inventory is $255,000 ($85 × 3,000). If the recorded value of $265,000 is within the upper confidence limit, the auditor would accept the population balance. Mean-per-unit estimation is rarely used in practice because sample sizes are typically much larger than for the two previous methods.

Stratified Statistical Methods

As we discussed earlier in this chapter, stratified sampling is a method of sampling in which all the elements in the total population are divided into two or more subpopulations. Each subpopulation is then independently tested. The calculations are made for each stratum and then combined into one overall population estimate for a confidence interval of the entire population. The results are measured statistically. Stratification is applicable to difference, ratio, and mean-per-unit estimation, but is most commonly used with mean-per-unit estimation.

Sampling Risks

We have discussed acceptable risk of incorrect acceptance (ARIA) for nonstatistical and MUS sampling. For variables sampling, auditors use ARIA as well as acceptable risk of incorrect rejection (ARIR). It is important to understand the distinctions between and uses of the two risks.

ARIA After auditors perform an audit test and calculate statistical results, they must conclude either that the population is or is not materially misstated. ARIA is the statistical risk that the auditor has accepted a population that is, in fact, materially misstated. ARIA is a serious concern to auditors because of the potential legal implications of concluding that an account balance is fairly stated when it is misstated by a material amount.

An account balance can be either overstated or understated, but not both; therefore, ARIA is a one-tailed statistical test. The confidence coefficients for ARIA are therefore different from the confidence level. (Confidence level = 1 – 2 × ARIA. So, if ARIA equals 10 percent, the confidence level is 80 percent.) The confidence coefficients for various ARIAs are shown in Table 17-12 (p. 588) together with confidence coefficients for the confidence level and ARIR.

ARIR **Acceptable risk of incorrect rejection (ARIR)** is the statistical risk that the auditor has concluded that a population is materially misstated when it is not. ARIR affects auditors' actions only when they conclude that a population is not fairly stated. When auditors find a balance not fairly stated, they typically increase the sample size or perform other tests. An increased sample size will usually lead the auditor to conclude that the balance is fairly stated if the account is, in fact, not materially misstated. While ARIA is always important, ARIR is important only when there is a high cost to increasing the sample size or performing other tests. Confidence coefficients for ARIR are also shown in Table 17-12.

TABLE 17-12 Confidence Coefficient for Confidence Levels, ARIAs, and ARIRs

Confidence Level (%)	ARIA (%)	ARIR (%)	Confidence Coefficient
99	.5	1	2.58
95	2.5	5	1.96
90	5	10	1.64
80	10	20	1.28
75	12.5	25	1.15
70	15	30	1.04
60	20	40	.84
50	25	50	.67
40	30	60	.52
30	35	70	.39
20	40	80	.25
10	45	90	.13
0	50	100	.0

TABLE 17-13 ARIA and ARIR

	Actual State of the Population	
Actual Audit Decision	**Materially Misstated**	**Not Materially Misstated**
Conclude that the population is materially misstated	Correct conclusion—no risk	Incorrect conclusion—risk is ARIR
Conclude that the population is not materially misstated	Incorrect conclusion—risk is ARIA	Correct conclusion—no risk

As you examine the summary of ARIA and ARIR in Table 17-13, you might conclude that auditors should attempt to minimize ARIA and ARIR. To accomplish that, auditors have to increase the sample size, thus minimizing the risks. However, the cost of that approach makes having reasonable ARIA and ARIR a more desirable goal.

CONCEPT CHECK

1. Distinguish among difference estimation, ratio estimation, mean-per-unit estimation, and stratified mean-per-unit estimation. Give one example in which each can be used.
2. An essential step in difference estimation is the comparison of each computed confidence limit with tolerable misstatement. Why is this step so important, and what should the auditor do if one of the confidence limits is larger than the tolerable misstatement?

ILLUSTRATION USING DIFFERENCE ESTIMATION

OBJECTIVE 17-5

Use difference estimation in tests of details of balances.

We illustrate the use of difference estimation in the audit of accounts receivable for Hart Lumber Company. Accounts receivable consists of 4,000 accounts listed on the aged trial balance with a recorded value of $600,000. Tolerable misstatement has been set at $21,000.

Plan the Sample and Calculate the Sample Size Using Difference Estimation

Specify Acceptable Risk The auditor specifies two risks:

1. *Acceptable risk of incorrect acceptance (ARIA).* It is the risk of accepting accounts receivable as correct if it is actually misstated by more than $21,000. ARIA is affected by acceptable audit risk, results of tests of controls and substantive tests of transactions, substantive analytical procedures, and the relative significance of

accounts receivable in the financial statements. For the Hart Lumber audit, assume an ARIA of 10 percent.

2. *Acceptable risk of incorrect rejection (ARIR).* It is the risk of rejecting accounts receivable as incorrect if it is not actually misstated by a material amount. ARIR is affected by the additional cost of resampling. Because it is fairly costly to confirm receivables a second time, assume an ARIR of 25 percent.

Estimate Misstatements in the Population This estimate has two parts:

1. *Estimate an expected point estimate.* Auditors need an advance estimate of the population point estimate for difference estimation, much as they need an estimated population exception rate for attributes sampling. The advance estimate is $1,500 (overstatement) for Hart Lumber, based on the previous year's audit tests.
2. *Make an advance population standard deviation estimate—variability of the population.* To determine the initial sample size, auditors need an advance estimate of the variation in the misstatements in the population as measured by the population standard deviation. (The calculation of the standard deviation is explained later, when audit results are evaluated.) For Hart Lumber, it is estimated to be $20 based on the previous year's audit tests.

Calculate the Initial Sample Size The initial sample size for Hart Lumber can be now calculated using the following formula:

$$n = \left[\frac{SD^*(Z_A + Z_R)N}{TM - E^*}\right]^2$$

where:

n = initial sample size

SD^* = advance estimate of the standard deviation

Z_A = confidence coefficient for ARIA (see Table 17-12)

Z_R = confidence coefficient for ARIR (see Table 17-12)

N = population size

TM = tolerable misstatement for the population (materiality)

E^* = estimated point estimate of the population misstatement

Applied to Hart Lumber, this equation yields:

$$n = \left[\frac{20(1.28 + 1.15)4{,}000}{21{,}000 - 1{,}500}\right]^2 = (9.97)^2 = 100$$

Evaluate the Results

Generalize from the Sample to the Population The auditor selects the sample, performs the testing, and identifies sample misstatements. The misstatements for Hart Lumber are shown in Table 17-14. The following four steps describe the calculation of the confidence limits for Hart Lumber Company. (The calculations are illustrated in Table 17-14, Steps 3 through 6.)

1. *Compute the point estimate of the total misstatement.* The point estimate is a direct extrapolation from the misstatements in the sample to the misstatements in the population. The calculation of the point estimate for Hart Lumber is shown in Table 17-14, step 3.
2. *Compute an estimate of the population standard deviation.* The population standard deviation is a statistical measure of the variability in the values of the individual items in the population. If there is a large amount of variation in the values of population items, the standard deviation will be larger than when the variation is small.

The standard deviation has a significant effect on the computed precision interval. The auditor can compute a reasonable estimate of the value of the population standard deviation by using the standard statistical formula shown in Table 17-14, step 4.

3. *Compute the precision interval.* The precision interval is calculated by a statistical formula. For the computed precision interval to have any meaning, it must be associated with ARIA. The formula to calculate the precision interval is shown in Table 17-14, step 5.

TABLE 17-14 Calculation of Confidence Limits

Step	Statistical Formula	Illustration for Hart Lumber
1. Take a random sample of size n.	n = sample size	100 accounts receivable are selected randomly from the aged trial balance containing 4,000 accounts.
2. Determine the value of each misstatement in the sample.		75 accounts are confirmed by customers, and 25 accounts are verified by alternative procedures. After reconciling timing differences and customer errors, the following 12 items were determined to be client errors (understatements) stated in dollars: 1. $12.75 7. (.87) 2. (69.46) 8. 24.32 3. 85.28 9. 36.59 4. 100.00 10. (102.16) 5. (27.30) 11. 54.71 6. 41.06 12. 71.56 Sum = $226.48
3. Compute the point estimate of the total misstatement.	$\bar{e} = \frac{\Sigma e_j}{n}$ $\hat{E} = N\bar{e}$ or $N\frac{\Sigma e_j}{n}$ where: $\bar{e}$ = average misstatement in the sample Σ = summation e_j = an individual misstatement in the sample n = sample size $\hat{E}$ = point estimate of the total misstatement N = population size	$\bar{e} = \frac{\$226.48}{100} = \$2.26$ $\hat{E} = 4{,}000\ (\$2.26) = \$9{,}040$ or $\hat{E} = 4{,}000 \left(\frac{\$226.48}{100}\right) = \$9{,}040$
4. Compute the population standard deviation of the misstatements from the sample.	$SD = \sqrt{\frac{\Sigma(e_j)^2 - n(\bar{e})^2}{n-1}}$ where: SD = standard deviation e_j = an individual misstatement in the sample n = sample size $\bar{e}$ = average misstatement in sample	(rounded to nearest dollar) e_j $(e_j)^2$ 1. $13 $ 169 2. (69) 4,761 3. 85 7,225 4. 100 10,000 5. (27) 729 6. 41 1,681 7. (1) 1 8. 24 576 9. 37 1,369 10. (102) 10,404 11. 55 3,025 12. 72 5,184 $228 $45,124 $SD = \sqrt{\frac{\$45{,}124 - 100\ (\$2.26)^2}{99}}$ SD = $21.2

TABLE 17-14 Calculation of Confidence Limits (Cont.)

Step	Statistical Formula	Illustration for Hart Lumber
5. Compute the precision interval for the estimate of the total population misstatement at the desired confidence level.	$CPI = NZ_A \frac{SD}{\sqrt{n}} \sqrt{\frac{N-n}{N}}$ where: CPI = computed precision interval N = population size Z_A = confidence coefficient for ARIA (see Table 17-12) SD = population standard deviation n = sample size $\sqrt{\frac{N-n}{N}}$ = finite correction factor	$CPI = 4{,}000 \cdot 1.28 \cdot \frac{\$21.2}{\sqrt{100}} \sqrt{\frac{4{,}000 - 100}{4{,}000}}$ $= 4{,}000 \cdot 1.28 \cdot \frac{\$21.2}{10} \cdot .99$ $= 4{,}000 \cdot 1.28 \cdot \$2.12 \cdot .99$ = $10,800 (rounded)
6. Compute the confidence limits at the CL desired.	$UCL = \hat{E} + CPI$ $LCL = \hat{E} - CPI$ where: UCL = computed upper confidence limit LCL = computed lower confidence limit $\hat{E}$ = point estimate of the total misstatement CPI = computed precision interval at desired CL	UCL = $9,040 + $10,800 = $19,840 LCL = $9,040 − $10,800 = $(1,760)

4. *Compute the confidence limits.* Auditors calculate the confidence limits, which define the confidence interval, by combining the point estimate of the total misstatements and the computed precision interval at the desired confidence level (point estimate ± computed precision interval). The formula to calculate the confidence limits is shown in Table 17-14, step 6.

The lower and upper confidence limits for Hart Lumber are ($1,760) and $19,840, respectively. There is a 10 percent statistical risk that the population is understated by more than $1,760, and the same risk that it is overstated by more than $19,840. (Remember, an ARIA of 10 percent is equivalent to a confidence level of 80 percent.) Since the confidence limits are less than tolerable misstatement, the auditor concludes that the population is not materially misstated.

SUMMARY

This chapter discussed nonstatistical and statistical audit sampling methods for tests of details of balances. In sampling for tests of balances, the auditor determines whether the dollar amount of an account balance is materially misstated. We then discussed the 14 steps in nonstatistical sampling for tests of balances. When performing nonstatistical audit sampling, the auditor uses judgment in generalizing from the sample to the population to determine whether it is acceptable. Monetary unit sampling is the most common statistical method for tests of balances. This method defines the sampling unit as individual dollars in the recorded account balance, and as a result, larger accounts are more likely to be included in the sample. Variables statistical sampling methods include difference estimation, ratio estimation, and mean-per-unit estimation. These methods compare audited sample values to recorded values to develop an estimate of the misstatement in the account value. Use of variables sampling was illustrated using difference estimation.

ESSENTIAL TERMS

Acceptable risk of incorrect acceptance (ARIA)—the risk that the auditor is willing to take of accepting a balance as correct when the true misstatement in the balance exceeds tolerable misstatement

Acceptable risk of incorrect rejection (ARIR)—the risk that the auditor is willing to take of rejecting a balance as incorrect when it is not misstated by a material amount

Basic precision—the minimum allowance for sampling risk inherent in the sample for MUS; it is equal to the allowance for sampling risk when no misstatements are found in the sample

Difference estimation—a method of variables sampling in which the auditor estimates the population misstatement by multiplying the average misstatement in the sample by the total number of population items and also calculates sampling risk

Mean-per-unit estimation—a method of variables sampling in which the auditor estimates the audited value of a population by multiplying the average audited value of the sample by the population size and also calculates sampling risk

Misstatement bound—an estimate of the largest likely overstatement in a population at a given ARIA, using monetary unit sampling

Monetary unit sampling (MUS)—a statistical sampling method that provides misstatement bounds expressed in monetary amounts; also referred to as dollar unit sampling, cumulative monetary amount sampling, and sampling with probability proportional to size

Point estimate—a method of projecting from the sample to the population to estimate the population misstatement, commonly by assuming that misstatements in the unaudited population are proportional to the misstatements found in the sample

Probability proportional to size sample selection (PPS)—sample selection of individual dollars in a population by the use of random or systematic sample selection

Ratio estimation—a method of variables sampling in which the auditor estimates the population misstatement by multiplying the portion of sample dollars misstated by the total recorded population book value and also calculates sampling risk

Statistical inferences—conclusions that the auditor draws from sample results based on knowledge of sampling distributions

Stratified sampling—a method of sampling in which all the elements in the total population are divided into two or more subpopulations that are independently tested and evaluated

Tolerable misstatement—the application of performance materiality to a particular sampling procedure

Variables sampling—sampling techniques for tests of details of balances that use the statistical inference process

REVIEW QUESTIONS

17-1 (OBJECTIVE 17-1) What major difference between (a) tests of controls and substantive tests of transactions and (b) tests of details of balances makes attributes sampling inappropriate for tests of details of balances?

17-2 (OBJECTIVE 17-2) Define stratified sampling and explain its importance in auditing. How can an auditor obtain a stratified sample of 30 items from each of three strata in the confirmation of accounts receivable?

17-3 (OBJECTIVE 17-2) What is the relationship between ARIA for tests of details of balances and ARO for tests of controls?

17-4 (OBJECTIVE 17-2) Distinguish between the point estimate of the total misstatements and the true value of the misstatements in the population. How can each be determined?

17-5 (OBJECTIVE 17-2) Evaluate the following statement made by an auditor: "On every aspect of the audit where it is possible, I calculate the point estimate of the misstatements and evaluate whether the amount is material. If it is, I investigate the cause and continue to test the population until I determine whether there is a serious problem. The use of statistical sampling in this manner is a valuable audit tool."

17-6 **(OBJECTIVE 17-3)** Define monetary unit sampling and explain its importance in auditing. How does it combine the features of attributes and variables sampling?

17-7 **(OBJECTIVES 17-1, 17-2, 17-3, 17-4)** Define what is meant by sampling risk. Does sampling risk apply to nonstatistical sampling, MUS, attributes sampling, and variables sampling? Explain.

17-8 **(OBJECTIVE 17-3)** An auditor is determining the appropriate sample size for testing inventory valuation using MUS. The population has 2,620 inventory items valued at $12,625,000. The tolerable misstatement is $500,000 at a 10% ARIA. No misstatements are expected in the population. Calculate the preliminary sample size.

17-9 **(OBJECTIVE 17-3)** The 2,620 inventory items described in Question 17-8 are listed on 44 inventory pages with 60 lines per page. There is a total for each page. The client's data are not in machine-readable form. Describe how a monetary unit sample can be selected in this situation.

17-10 **(OBJECTIVE 17-2)** Explain what is meant by acceptable risk of incorrect acceptance. What are the major audit factors affecting ARIA?

17-11 **(OBJECTIVE 17-4)** Evaluate the following statement made by an auditor: "I took a random sample and derived a 90 percent confidence interval of $800,000 to $900,000. That means that the true population value will be between $800,000 and $900,000, 90 percent of the time."

17-12 **(OBJECTIVE 17-3)** Explain what is meant by basic precision. How is it determined?

17-13 **(OBJECTIVE 17-3)** Assume that a sample of 100 units was obtained in sampling the inventory in Question 17-8. Assume further that the following three misstatements were found:

Misstatement	Recorded Value	Audited Value
1	$ 897.16	$ 609.16
2	47.02	0
3	1,621.68	1,522.68

Calculate the overstatement bound for the population. Draw audit conclusions based on the results.

17-14 **(OBJECTIVE 17-3)** Why is it difficult to determine the appropriate sample size for MUS? How should the auditor determine the proper sample size?

17-15 **(OBJECTIVE 17-4)** Define what is meant by the population standard deviation and explain its importance in variables sampling. What is the relationship between the population standard deviation and the required sample size?

17-16 **(OBJECTIVE 17-5)** In using difference estimation, an auditor took a random sample of 100 inventory items from a large population to test for proper pricing. Several of the inventory items were misstated, but the combined net amount of the sample misstatement was not material. In addition, a review of the individual misstatements indicated that no misstatement was by itself material. As a result, the auditor did not investigate the misstatements or make a statistical evaluation. Explain why this practice is improper.

17-17 **(OBJECTIVE 17-4)** Explain why difference estimation is commonly used by auditors.

17-18 **(OBJECTIVES 17-3, 17-4)** Give an example of the use of attributes sampling, MUS, and variables sampling in the form of an audit conclusion.

MULTIPLE CHOICE QUESTIONS FROM CPA AND CIA EXAMINATIONS

17-19 **(OBJECTIVE 17-2)** The following questions relate to determining sample size in tests of details of balances. For each one, select the best response.

a. Mr. Murray decides to use stratified sampling. The reason for using stratified sampling rather than unrestricted random sampling is to
   (1) reduce as much as possible the degree of variability in the overall population.
   (2) give every element in the population an equal chance of being included in the sample.

(3) allow the person selecting the sample to use personal judgment in deciding which elements should be included in the sample.
(4) allow the auditor to emphasize larger items from the population.

b. Which of the following sample planning factors will influence the sample size for a test of details of balances for a specific account?

	Expected Amount of Misstatements	Measure of Tolerable Misstatement
(1)	No	No
(2)	Yes	Yes
(3)	No	Yes
(4)	Yes	No

c. How would increases in tolerable misstatement and assessed level of control risk affect the sample size in substantive tests of details?

	Increase in Tolerable Misstatement	Increase in Assessed Level of Control Risk
(1)	Increase sample size	Increase sample size
(2)	Increase sample size	Decrease sample size
(3)	Decrease sample size	Increase sample size
(4)	Decrease sample size	Decrease sample size

17-20 **(OBJECTIVES 17-2, 17-3, 17-4)** The following apply to evaluating results of audit sampling for tests of details of balances. For each one, select the best response.

a. While performing a substantive test of details during an audit, the auditor determined that the sample results supported the conclusion that the recorded account balance was materially misstated. It was, in fact, not materially misstated. This situation illustrates the risk of
(1) assessing control risk too high.
(2) assessing control risk too low.
(3) incorrect rejection.
(4) incorrect acceptance.

b. In an MUS sample with a sampling interval of $5,000, an auditor discovered that a selected accounts receivable with a recorded amount of $10,000 had an audit value of $8,000. If this is the only error discovered by the auditor, the projected error of the sample would be
(1) $1,000.
(2) $2,000.
(3) $4,000.
(4) $5,000.

c. The accounting department reports the accounts receivable balance as $175,000. You are willing to accept that balance if it is within $15,000 of the actual balance. Using a variables sampling plan, you compute a 95% confidence interval of $173,000 to $187,000. You would therefore
(1) find it impossible to determine the acceptability of the balance.
(2) accept the balance but with a lower level of confidence.
(3) take a larger sample before rejecting the sample and requiring adjustments.
(4) accept the $175,000 balance because the confidence interval is within the materiality limits.

17-21 **(OBJECTIVES 17-3, 17-4, 17-5)** The following relate to the use of statistical sampling for tests of details of balances. For each one, select the best response.

a. When the auditor uses monetary unit statistical sampling to examine the total dollar value of invoices, each invoice
(1) has an equal probability of being selected.
(2) can be represented by no more than one monetary unit.
(3) has an unknown probability of being selected.
(4) has a probability proportional to its dollar value of being selected.

b. Which of the following would be an advantage of using variables sampling rather than probability-proportional-to-size (PPS) sampling?
   (1) An estimate of the standard deviation of the population's recorded amount is not required.
   (2) The auditor rarely needs the assistance of a computer program to design an efficient sample.
   (3) The inclusion of zero and negative balances usually does not require special design considerations.
   (4) Any amount that is individually significant is automatically identified and selected.

c. In applying variables sampling, an auditor attempts to
   (1) estimate a qualitative characteristic of interest.
   (2) determine various rates of occurrence for specified attributes.
   (3) discover at least one instance of a critical deviation.
   (4) predict a monetary population value within a range of precision.

MULTIPLE CHOICE QUESTIONS FROM BECKER CPA EXAM REVIEW

17-22 **(OBJECTIVES 17-2, 17-3)** The following questions relate to nonstatistical and monetary unit sampling. Choose the best response.

a. A number of factors influence the sample size for a substantive test of details of an account balance. All other factors being equal, which of the following would lead to a larger sample size?
   (1) Greater reliance on internal control
   (2) Greater reliance on substantive analytical procedures
   (3) Smaller expected frequency of errors
   (4) Smaller measure of tolerable misstatement

b. The risk of incorrect acceptance relates to
   (1) substantive tests and affects audit efficiency.
   (2) substantive tests and affects audit effectiveness.
   (3) tests of controls and affects audit efficiency.
   (4) tests of controls and affects audit effectiveness.

c. In a probability-proportional-to-size sample with a sampling interval of $3,000, which of the following is true?
   I. An overstatement error of $200 in an item recorded at $300 will result in a projected error of $2,000.
   II. An overstatement error of $700 in an item recorded at $3,500 will result in a projected error of $600.
      (1) I only
      (2) II only
      (3) Both I and II
      (4) Neither I nor II

DISCUSSION QUESTIONS AND PROBLEMS

17-23 **(OBJECTIVE 17-2)** You are planning to use nonstatistical sampling to evaluate the results of accounts receivable confirmation for the Meridian Company. You have already performed tests of controls for sales, sales returns and allowances, and cash receipts, and they are considered excellent. Because of the quality of the controls, you decide to use an acceptable risk of incorrect acceptance of 10%, rather than a lower percentage. There are

3,000 accounts receivable with a gross value of $6,900,000. The accounts are similar in size and will be treated as a single stratum. Tolerable misstatement for this test of accounts receivable confirmations is $150,000.

Required

a. Calculate the required sample size. Assume your firm uses the following nonstatistical formula to determine sample size:

$$\text{Sample size} = \frac{\text{Population Recorded Amount} \times \text{Confidence Factor}}{\text{Tolerable Misstatement}}$$

A confidence factor of 2 is used for a 10% ARIA.

b. Assume that instead of good results, poor results were obtained for tests of controls and substantive tests of transactions for sales, sales returns and allowances, and cash receipts. How will this affect your required sample size? How will you use this information in your sample size determination?

c. Regardless of your answer to part a., assume you decide to select a sample of 100 accounts for testing. Indicate how you will select the accounts for testing using systematic selection.

d. Assume a total book value of $230,000 for the 100 accounts selected for testing. You uncover three overstatements totaling $1,500 in the sample. Evaluate whether the population is fairly stated.

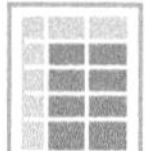

17-24 (OBJECTIVE 17-2) You are evaluating the results of a nonstatistical sample of 85 accounts receivable confirmations for the Bohrer Company. Information on the sample and population are included below. Tolerable misstatement for accounts receivable confirmation sampling is $100,000.

		Sample		Population	
Stratum		**# of Accounts**	**Recorded Value**	**# of Accounts**	**Recorded Value**
1	>$75,000	8	$1,287,643	8	$1,287,643
2	$10,000–$74,999	40	1,349,678	257	4,348,268
3	<$10,000	25	94,637	712	947,682
		73	$2,731,958	977	$6,583,593

The confirmation responses were received without exception, other than the following items:

Acct. No.	Recorded Value	Confirmation Response	Auditor Follow-up
147	$ 24,692	$ 22,486	Customer was charged the wrong price.
228	183,219	157,216	$26,003 shipment recorded on December 30th; goods were not shipped until January 3rd.
278	7,546	5,546	Customer sent $2,000 payment on December 29th; received on January 2nd.
497	15,319	0	$17,443 shipment made on December 30th; goods were received by the customer on January 2nd.
564	8,397	7,858	Customer received less than the full quantity ordered.
653	32,687	19,328	$13,359 shipment recorded on December 30th; goods were not shipped until January 2nd.
830	5,286	0	$5,286 shipment recorded on December 30th; goods were not shipped until January 3rd.

a. Evaluate each of the confirmation exceptions to determine whether they represent misstatements. **Required**
b. Estimate the total amount of misstatement in the accounts receivable population. Ignore sampling risk in the calculation.
c. Is the population acceptable? If not, indicate what follow-up action(s) you consider appropriate in the circumstances.

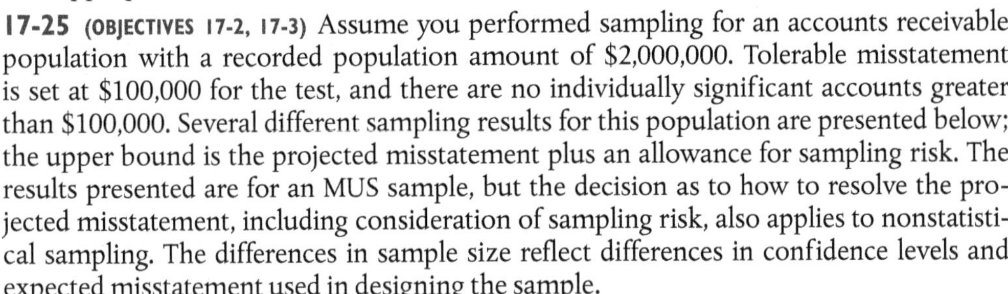

17-25 **(OBJECTIVES 17-2, 17-3)** Assume you performed sampling for an accounts receivable population with a recorded population amount of $2,000,000. Tolerable misstatement is set at $100,000 for the test, and there are no individually significant accounts greater than $100,000. Several different sampling results for this population are presented below; the upper bound is the projected misstatement plus an allowance for sampling risk. The results presented are for an MUS sample, but the decision as to how to resolve the projected misstatement, including consideration of sampling risk, also applies to nonstatistical sampling. The differences in sample size reflect differences in confidence levels and expected misstatement used in designing the sample.

You are to make a recommendation as to the appropriate action to take given the sample results. Assume that the client is willing to record an audit adjustment for actual misstatements detected in your testing, but is unwilling to record an adjustment for projected errors. Issuing a qualified or adverse opinion is not included as an option. Because the audited financial statements are required under the terms of a loan agreement, the client will agree to additional testing or will correct the population if needed to receive an unmodified opinion.

	Sample Size	Interval	Number of Misstatements	Dollar Amount of Actual Misstatements	Projected Misstatement	Upper Bound	Nature of Misstatements
1.	54	36,450	1	20,000	20,000	104,200	Improper contract price applied
2.	46	43,290	3	425	4,731	106,979	Various pricing and quantity errors
3.	54	36,450	8	20,400	110,568	241,468	Incorrect shipments, cutoff errors, and pricing errors
4.	33	60,385	1	4,000	12,077	114,007	Incorrect currency translation on foreign shipment
5.	72	27,500	1	400	7,333	95,333	Incorrect product shipped
6.	44	44,845	2	2,500	29,897	112,934	Duplicate shipment, incorrect price

For each of the sampling results 1 through 6, recommend the appropriate response(s) from the options listed below. Explain the reason for your decision. **Required**

a. Accept the population as fairly stated.
b. Request the client to record an adjustment for the actual misstatements.
c. Expand the sample size.
d. Request the client to fix the population, which will then be reaudited.
e. Treat the misstatement as an anomaly that is an isolated occurrence that should not be projected to the population.

17-26 **(OBJECTIVE 17-3)** The accounts receivable population for Jake's Bookbinding Company follows. This table is the same as Table 17-1 on page 567, except that cumulative amounts are included to assist you in completing the problem. The population is smaller than is ordinarily the case for statistical sampling, but an entire population is useful to show how to select PPS samples.

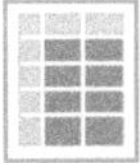

a. Select a random PPS sample of 10 items, using computer software. **Required**
b. Select a sample of 10 items using systematic PPS sampling. Use a starting point of 1857. Identify the physical units associated with the sample dollars.

c. Which sample items will always be included in the systematic PPS sample regardless of the starting point? Will that also be true of random PPS sampling?
d. Which method is preferable in terms of ease of selection in this case?
e. Why will an auditor use MUS?

Population Item	Recorded Amount	Cumulative Amount	Population Item (cont.)	Recorded Amount (cont.)	Cumulative Amount (cont.)
1	$ 1,410	$ 1,410	21	$ 4,865	$117,385
2	9,130	10,540	22	770	118,155
3	660	11,200	23	2,305	120,460
4	3,355	14,555	24	2,665	123,125
5	5,725	20,280	25	1,000	124,125
6	8,210	28,490	26	6,225	130,350
7	580	29,070	27	3,675	134,025
8	44,110	73,180	28	6,250	140,275
9	825	74,005	29	1,890	142,165
10	1,155	75,160	30	27,705	169,870
11	2,270	77,430	31	935	170,805
12	50	77,480	32	5,595	176,400
13	5,785	83,265	33	930	177,330
14	940	84,205	34	4,045	181,375
15	1,820	86,025	35	9,480	190,855
16	3,380	89,405	36	360	191,215
17	530	89,935	37	1,145	192,360
18	955	90,890	38	6,400	198,760
19	4,490	95,380	39	100	198,860
20	17,140	112,520	40	8,435	207,295

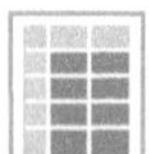

17-27 (OBJECTIVE 17-3) In the audit of Price Seed Company for the year ended September 30, the auditor set a tolerable misstatement of $50,000 at an ARIA of 10%. A PPS sample of 100 was selected from an accounts receivable population that had a recorded balance of $1,975,000. The following table shows the differences uncovered in the confirmation process:

Accounts Receivable per Records	Accounts Receivable per Confirmation	Follow-up Comments by Auditor
1. $2,728.00	$2,498.00	Pricing error on two invoices.
2. $5,125.00	-0-	Customer mailed check 9/26; company received check 10/3.
3. $3,890.00	$1,190.00	Merchandise returned 9/30 and counted in inventory; credit was issued 10/6.
4. $ 815.00	$ 785.00	Footing error on an invoice.
5. $ 548.00	-0-	Goods were shipped 9/28; customer received goods on 10/2; sale was recorded on 9/28.
6. $3,215.00	$3,190.00	Pricing error on a credit memorandum.
7. $1,540.00	-0-	Goods were shipped on 9/29; customer received goods 10/3; sale was recorded on 9/30.

Required

a. Calculate the upper misstatement bound on the basis of the client misstatements in the sample.
b. Is the population acceptable as stated? If not, what options are available to the auditor at this point? Which option should the auditor select? Explain.

17-28 **(OBJECTIVE 17-3)** You intend to use MUS as a part of the audit of several accounts for Roynpower Manufacturing Company. You have done the audit for the past several years, and there has rarely been an adjusting entry of any kind. Your audit tests of all tests of controls and substantive tests of transactions cycles were completed at an interim date, and control risk has been assessed as low. You therefore decide to use an ARIA of 10% and a ratio of expected misstatement to tolerable misstatement of 0% for all tests of details of balances.

You intend to use MUS in the audit of the three most material asset balance sheet account balances: accounts receivable, inventory, and marketable securities. You feel justified in using the same ARIA for each audit area because of the low assessed control risk.

The recorded balances and related information for the three accounts are as follows:

	Recorded Value
Accounts receivable	$3,600,000
Inventory	4,800,000
Marketable securities	1,600,000
	$10,000,000

Net earnings before taxes for Roynpower are $2,000,000. You decide that a combined misstatement of $100,000 is allowable for the client.

The audit approach to be followed will be to determine the total sample size needed for all three accounts. A sample will be selected from all $10 million, and the appropriate testing for a sample item will depend on whether the item is a receivable, inventory, or marketable security. The audit conclusions will pertain to the entire $10 million, and no conclusion will be made about the three individual accounts unless significant misstatements are found in the sample.

Required

a. Evaluate the audit approach of testing all three account balances in one sample.
b. Calculate the required sample size for a combined sample of all three accounts. Use $100,000 as the measure of tolerable misstatement for the combined test.
c. Calculate the required sample size for each of the three accounts, assuming you decide that the tolerable misstatement in each account is $100,000.
d. Assume that you select the random sample using computer software. How will you identify which sample item in the population to audit for the number 4,627,871? What audit procedures will be performed?
e. Assume that you select a sample of 200 sample items for testing and you find one misstatement in inventory. The recorded value is $987.12 and the audit value is $887.12. Calculate the misstatement bounds for the three combined accounts and reach appropriate audit conclusions.

17-29 **(OBJECTIVES 17-2, 17-3, 17-4)** An audit partner is developing an office training program to familiarize her professional staff with audit sampling decision models applicable to the audit of dollar-value balances. She wishes to demonstrate the relationship of sample sizes to population size and estimated population misstatement rate and the auditor's specifications as to tolerable misstatement and ARIA. The partner prepared the following table to show comparative population characteristics and audit specifications of the two populations:

	Characteristics of Population 1 Relative to Population 2		Audit Specifications as to a Sample from Population 1 Relative to a Sample from Population 2	
	Size	**Estimated Population Misstatement Rate**	**Tolerable Misstatement**	**ARIA**
Case 1	Equal	Equal	Equal	Lower
Case 2	Larger	Equal	Smaller	Higher
Case 3	Smaller	Smaller	Equal	Higher
Case 4	Larger	Equal	Equal	Lower
Case 5	Equal	Larger	Larger	Equal

Required In items (1) through (5) you are to indicate for the specific case from the table the required sample size to be selected from population 1 relative to the sample from population 2.

(1) In case 1, the required sample size from population 1 is ____.
(2) In case 2, the required sample size from population 1 is ____.
(3) In case 3, the required sample size from population 1 is ____.
(4) In case 4, the required sample size from population 1 is ____.
(5) In case 5, the required sample size from population 1 is ____.

Your answer choice should be selected from the following responses:

a. Larger than the required sample size from population 2.
b. Equal to the required sample size from population 2.
c. Smaller than the required sample size from population 2.
d. Indeterminate relative to the required sample size from population 2.*

17-30 (OBJECTIVE 17-5) In auditing the valuation of inventory, the auditor, Claire Butler, decided to use difference estimation. She decided to select an unrestricted random sample of 80 inventory items from a population of 1,840 that had a book value of $175,820. Butler decided in advance that she was willing to accept a maximum misstatement in the population of $6,000 at an ARIA of 5 percent. There were eight misstatements in the sample, which were as follows:

	Audit Value	Book Value	Sample Misstatements
	$ 812.50	$ 740.50	$(72.00)
	12.50	78.20	65.70
	10.00	51.10	41.10
	25.40	61.50	36.10
	600.10	651.90	51.80
	.12	0	(.12)
	51.06	81.06	30.00
	83.11	104.22	21.11
Total	$1,594.79	$1,768.48	$173.69

Required

a. Calculate the point estimate, the computed precision interval, the confidence interval, and the confidence limits for the population. Label each calculation.
b. Should Butler accept the book value of the population? Explain.
c. What options are available to her at this point?

CASES

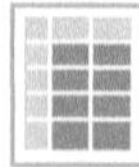

17-31 (OBJECTIVE 17-3) You are performing the audit of Peckinpah Tire and Parts, a wholesale auto parts company. You have decided to use monetary unit sampling (MUS) for the audit of accounts receivable and inventory. The following are the recorded balances:

Accounts receivable	$12,000,000
Inventory	$23,000,000

You have already made the following judgments:

Performance materiality	$800,000
Acceptable audit risk	5%
Inherent risk:	
Accounts receivable	80%
Inventory	100%

*Based on AICPA question paper, American Institute of Certified Public Accountants.

Assessed control risk:	
Accounts receivable	50%
Inventory	80%

Substantive analytical procedures have been planned for inventory, but not for accounts receivable. The substantive analytical procedures for inventory are expected to have a 60% chance of detecting a material misstatement should one exist. Performance materiality will be used as the measure of tolerable misstatement for each test and for the combined sample.

You have concluded that it will be difficult to alter sample size for accounts receivable confirmation once confirmations are sent and replies are received. However, inventory tests can be reopened without great difficulty.

After discussions with the client, you believe that the accounts are in about the same condition this year as they were last year. Last year, no misstatements were found in the confirmation of accounts receivable. Inventory tests revealed an overstatement amount of about 1%.

For requirements a. through c., make any assumptions necessary in deciding the factors affecting sample size. If no table is available for the ARIA chosen, estimate sample size judgmentally.

Required

a. Plan the sample size for the confirmation of accounts receivable using MUS.
b. Plan the sample size for the test of pricing of inventories using MUS.
c. Plan the combined sample size for both the confirmation of accounts receivable and the price tests of inventory using MUS.
d. Using an electronic spreadsheet, generate a list of random dollars in generation order and in ascending order for the sample of accounts receivable items determined in part a.

17-32 (OBJECTIVES 17-2, 17-3) You have just completed the accounts receivable confirmation process in the audit of Danforth Paper Company, a paper supplier to retail shops and commercial users. Following are the data related to this process:

Accounts receivable recorded balance	$ 2,760,000
Number of accounts	7,320
A nonstatistical sample was taken as follows:	
All accounts over $10,000 (23 accounts)	$ 465,000
77 accounts under $10,000	$ 81,500
Tolerable misstatement for the confirmation test	$ 100,000
Inherent and control risk are both high	
No relevant substantive analytical procedures were performed	

The following are the results of the confirmation procedures:

	Recorded Value	Audited Value
Items over $10,000	$ 465,000	$ 432,000
Items under $10,000	81,500	77,150
Individual misstatements for items under $10,000:		
Item 12	5,120	4,820
Item 19	485	385
Item 33	1,250	250
Item 35	3,975	3,875
Item 51	1,850	1,825
Item 59	4,200	3,780
Item 74	2,405	0

Required

a. Evaluate the results of the nonstatistical sample. Consider both the direct implications of the misstatements found and the effect of using a sample.
b. Assume that the sample was a PPS sample. Evaluate the results using monetary unit sampling.

ACL PROBLEM

17-33 (OBJECTIVE 17-3) This problem requires the use of ACL software, which can be accessed through the textbook Web site. Information about downloading and using ACL and the commands used in this problem can also be found on the textbook Web site. You should read all of the reference material, especially the material on sampling, to answer questions a. through e. For this problem, use the "Invoices" file in the "Sales and Collection" subfolder under tables in the ACL_Rockwood project. This file contains information on sales invoices generated during calendar year 2014, including those that have been paid versus those still outstanding. Suggested commands, where applicable, are indicated at the end of the problem requirements.

Required

a. Using the Invoices file, filter the file to retain only those invoices that are still outstanding and save this filter as "Accounts_Receivable." (Filter) Determine the total dollar amount of the outstanding invoices (Total). Using the "Accounts_Receivable" data, calculate the sample size and sampling interval for an MUS sample based on total Invoice Amount. Use a confidence level of 90%, materiality of $50,000, and expected errors of $2,500. (Sampling/Calculate Sample Size; select "monetary" radio button)
b. What is the sampling size and sampling interval if you increase materiality to $60,000 and decrease expected errors to $1,000?
c. Select the sample based on the sampling interval determined in part a. (Sampling / Sample; select "Sample type" as MUS. For "Sample Parameters" select fixed interval and enter the interval from part a.; use a random start of 3179.)
d. How many items were selected for testing? Why is the number selected for testing less than the sample size determined in part a.?
e. What is the largest item selected for testing? How many sample items are larger than the sampling interval? How many items are larger than the sampling interval in the population?

APPLICATION OF THE AUDIT PROCESS TO OTHER CYCLES

CHAPTERS 18–23

Each chapter in **PART 4** demonstrates the relationship of internal controls, substantive tests of transactions, and substantive analytical procedures to the related balance sheet and income statement accounts in the cycle and to test of details of balances.

- **Chapters 18 and 19** address the audit of the acquisition and payment cycle, including the audit of accounts payable and other liability accounts.
- **Chapter 20** covers the audit of the payroll and personnel cycle.
- **Chapter 21** addresses the audit of the inventory and warehousing cycle, including physical observation tests and the relationship of the inventory and warehousing cycle to other cycles.
- **Chapter 22** includes the audit of the capital acquisition and repayment cycle.
- **Chapter 23** is the audit of cash and investment balances, which is covered last because cash is affected by the transactions in other cycles.

CHAPTER

18

AUDIT OF THE ACQUISITION AND PAYMENT CYCLE: TESTS OF CONTROLS, SUBSTANTIVE TESTS OF TRANSACTIONS, AND ACCOUNTS PAYABLE

LEARNING OBJECTIVES

After studying this chapter, you should be able to

18-1 Identify the accounts and the classes of transactions in the acquisition and payment cycle.

18-2 Describe the business functions and the related documents and records in the acquisition and payment cycle.

18-3 Understand internal control, and design and perform tests of controls and substantive tests of transactions for the acquisition and payment cycle.

18-4 Describe the methodology for designing tests of details of balances for accounts payable using the audit risk model.

18-5 Design and perform substantive analytical procedures for accounts payable.

18-6 Design and perform tests of details of balances for accounts payable, including out-of-period liability tests.

18-7 Distinguish the reliability of vendors' invoices, vendors' statements, and confirmations of accounts payable as audit evidence.

False Purchases Camouflage Overstated Profits

Comptronix Corporation announced that senior members of its management team overstated profits, and there would be material adjustments to the prior years' audited financial statements. Central to the fraud was the use of fictitious purchases of large equipment items to overstate fixed assets and hide fictitious sales.

The senior executives circumvented Comptronix's existing internal controls by bypassing the purchasing and receiving departments so that no one at Comptronix could discover the scheme. Comptronix employees usually created a fairly extensive paper trail for equipment purchases. Company internal controls over acquisition and cash disbursement transactions typically required a purchase order, receiving report, and vendor invoice before payment could be authorized by the chief operating officer or the controller/treasurer, who were both participants in the fraud. As a result, the executives were able to bypass controls over cash disbursements and authorize payment for nonexistent purchases without creating any documents for the fictitious transactions.

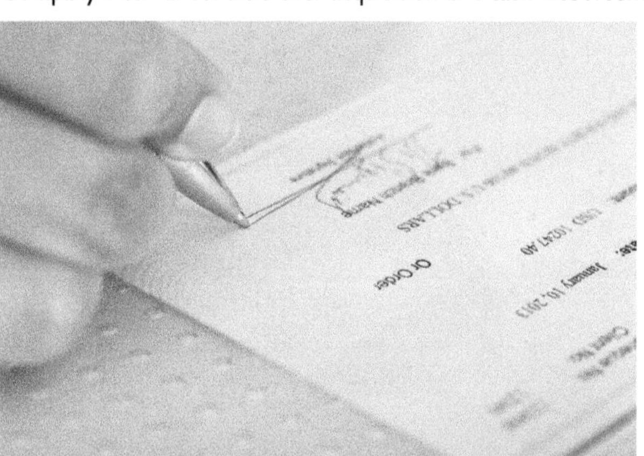

The company also created fictitious sales and related receivables. The company issued checks to pay for the false purchase transactions. The checks were then redeposited into the company's bank account and recorded as collections on the fictitious receivables. As a result, it appeared that the fictitious sales were collected, and that payments were made to support the false fixed asset purchases.

The fraud scheme grossly exaggerated the company's performance by reporting profits when the company was actually incurring losses. On the day that the public announcement of the fraud was made, Comptronix's common stock price declined abruptly by 72 percent! The SEC ultimately charged the executives with violating the antifraud provisions of the Securities Act of 1933 and the Securities Exchange Act of 1934. The SEC permanently barred the executives from serving as officers or directors of any public company, ordered them to repay bonuses and trading losses avoided, and imposed civil monetary penalties against them.

Source: Based on *Accounting and Auditing Enforcement Release No. 543*, Commerce Clearing House, Inc., Chicago.

We'll now discuss the **acquisition and payment cycle**. The acquisition of goods and services includes the acquisition of such things as raw materials, equipment, supplies, utilities, repairs and maintenance, and research and development. In the first part of the chapter, we'll examine assessing control risk and designing tests of controls and substantive tests of transactions for the classes of transactions in the acquisition and payment cycle. Then, we'll cover performing tests of details of balances for accounts payable.

As with the sales and collection cycle, auditors need to understand the business functions and documents and records in a company before they can assess control risk and design tests of controls and substantive tests of transactions. We first examine two related topics:

1. The acquisition and payment cycle classes of transactions and account balances in a typical company
2. Typical documents and records used in the acquisition and payment cycle

ACCOUNTS AND CLASSES OF TRANSACTIONS IN THE ACQUISITION AND PAYMENT CYCLE

OBJECTIVE 18-1

Identify the accounts and the classes of transactions in the acquisition and payment cycle.

The objective in the audit of the acquisition and payment cycle is to evaluate whether the accounts affected by the acquisitions of goods and services and the cash disbursements for those acquisitions are fairly presented in accordance with accounting standards. Figure 18-1 shows the way accounting information flows through the various accounts in the acquisition and payment cycle.

There are three classes of transactions included in the cycle:

1. Acquisitions of goods and services
2. Cash disbursements
3. Purchase returns and allowances and purchase discounts

FIGURE 18-1 Accounts in the Acquisition and Payment Cycle

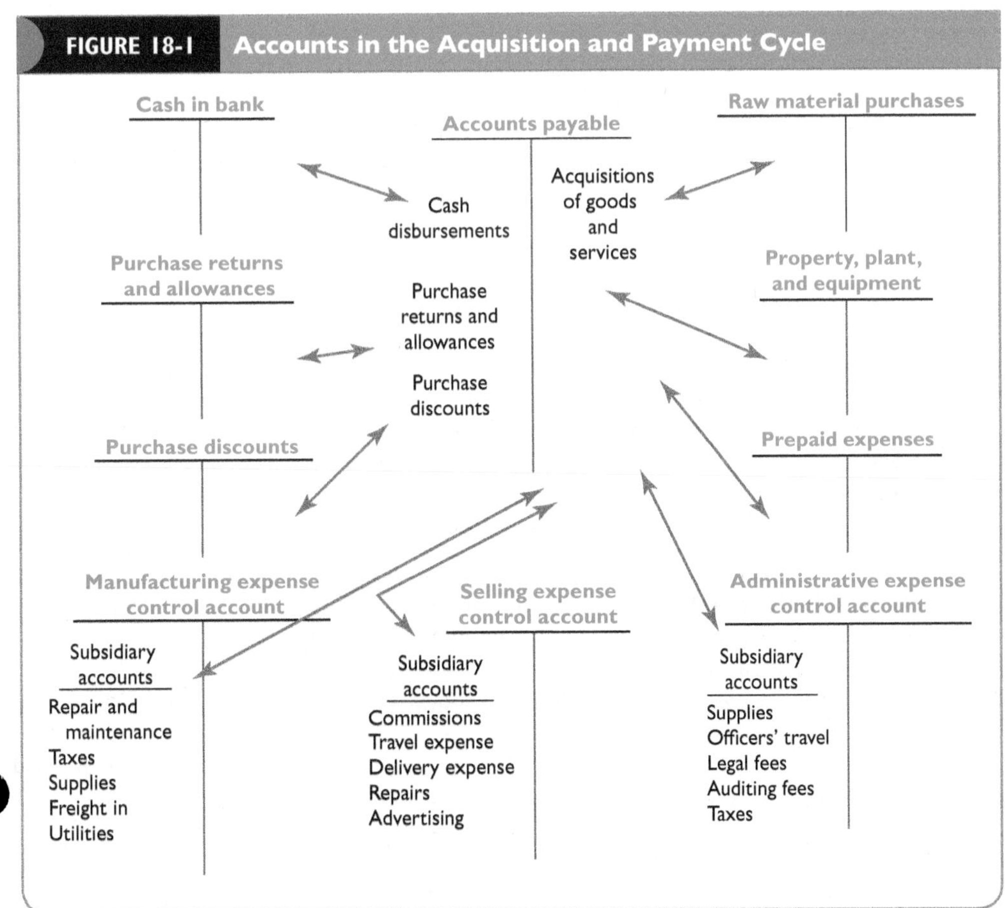

Ten typical accounts involved in the acquisition and payment cycle are shown by T accounts in Figure 18-1. For simplicity, we show only the control accounts for the three major categories of expenses used by most companies. For each control account, examples of the subsidiary expense accounts are also given. Note the large number of accounts affected by this cycle. It is therefore not surprising that auditing the acquisition and payment cycle often takes more time than auditing any other cycle.

Figure 18-1 shows that every transaction is either debited or credited to accounts payable. Because some companies make acquisitions directly by check or electronic transfer or with cash on hand, the figure is an oversimplification. We assume that acquisitions made for cash are processed in the same manner as those made by accounts payable.

BUSINESS FUNCTIONS IN THE CYCLE AND RELATED DOCUMENTS AND RECORDS

OBJECTIVE 18-2

Describe the business functions and the related documents and records in the acquisition and payment cycle.

The acquisition and payment cycle involves the decisions and processes necessary for obtaining the goods and services for operating a business. The cycle typically begins with the initiation of a purchase requisition by an authorized employee who needs the goods or services, and it ends with payment on accounts payable. In the following discussion, the example of a small manufacturing company that makes tangible products for sale to third parties is used, but the principles covered here also apply to service companies, government entities, and other types of organizations.

The third column of Table 18-1 lists four business functions that occur in every business in recording the three classes of transactions in the acquisition and payment cycle. The first three functions are for recording the acquisition of goods and services on account, and the fourth function is for recording cash disbursements for payments to vendors. For simplicity, our illustration does not show processing purchase returns and allowances and purchase discounts. Although purchase returns and allowances and purchase discounts business functions also occur in this cycle, we omit them here because the amounts are not significant for most companies.

Next, we examine in more detail each of the four business functions, paying particular attention to the typical documents and records used. These are listed in the fourth column of Table 18-1.

Processing Purchase Orders

The request for goods or services by the client's personnel is the starting point for the cycle. The exact form of the request and the required approval depend on the nature of the goods and services and company policy. Common documents include:

Purchase Requisition A **purchase requisition** is used to request goods and services by an authorized employee. This may take the form of a request for such acquisitions as materials by production staff or the storeroom supervisor, outside repairs by office or plant personnel, or insurance by the vice president in charge of property and equipment. Companies often rely on pre-specified reorder points used by the computer to initiate inventory purchase requisitions automatically.

Purchase Order A **purchase order** is a document used to order goods and services from vendors. It includes the description, quantity, and related information for goods and services the company intends to purchase and is often used to indicate authorization of the acquisition. Companies often submit purchase orders electronically to vendors who have made arrangements for electronic data interchange (EDI).

Receiving Goods and Services

The receipt by the company of goods or services from the vendor is a critical point in the cycle because it is when most companies first recognize the acquisition and related liability on their records. When goods are received, adequate control requires examination for description, quantity, timely arrival, and condition. A **receiving report** is a paper or electronic document prepared at the time goods are received. It

TABLE 18-1	Classes of Transactions, Accounts, Business Functions, and Related Documents and Records for the Acquisition and Payment Cycle		
Classes of Transactions	**Accounts**	**Business Functions**	**Documents and Records**
Acquisitions	Inventory Property, plant, and equipment Prepaid expenses Leasehold improvements Accounts payable Manufacturing expenses Selling expenses Administrative expenses	Processing purchase orders	Purchase requisition Purchase order
		Receiving goods and services	Receiving report
		Recognizing the liability	Vendor's invoice Debit memo Voucher Acquisitions transaction file Acquisitions journal or listing Accounts payable master file Accounts payable trial balance Vendor's statement
Cash disbursements	Cash in bank Accounts payable Purchase discounts	Processing and recording cash disbursements	Check or electronic payment Cash disbursements transaction file Cash disbursements journal or listing

includes a description of the goods, the quantity received, the date received, and other relevant data.

Recognizing the Liability

The proper recognition of the liability for the receipt of goods and services requires *prompt and accurate* recording. The initial recording affects the financial statements and the actual cash disbursement; therefore, companies must take care to include all acquisition transactions, only acquisitions that occurred, and at the correct amounts. Common documents and records include:

Vendor's Invoice A **vendor's invoice** is a document received from the vendor and shows the amount owed for an acquisition. It indicates the description and quantity of goods and services received, price (including freight), cash discount terms, date of the billing, and total amount. The vendor's invoice is important because it indicates the amount recorded in the acquisition transaction file. For companies using EDI, the vendor's invoice is transmitted electronically, which affects how the auditor evaluates evidence.

Debit Memo A **debit memo** is also a document received from the vendor and indicates a reduction in the amount owed to a vendor because of returned goods or an allowance granted. It often takes the same form as a vendor's invoice, but it supports reductions in accounts payable rather than increases.

Voucher A **voucher** is commonly used by organizations to establish a formal means of recording and controlling acquisitions, primarily by enabling each acquisition transaction to be sequentially numbered. Vouchers include a cover sheet or folder for containing documents and a package of relevant documents such as the purchase order, copy of the packing slip, receiving report, and vendor's invoice. After payment, a copy of the check or electronic funds transfer is added to the voucher package.

Acquisitions Transaction File This is a computer-generated file that includes all acquisition transactions processed by the accounting system for a period, such as a day, week, or month. It contains all information entered into the system and includes information for each transaction, such as vendor name, date, amount, account classification or classifications, and description and quantity of goods and services purchased. The file can also include purchase returns and allowances or there can be a separate file for those transactions. Depending on the company's needs, the information in the acquisitions transaction file is used for a variety of records, listings, or reports, such as an acquisitions journal, accounts payable master file, and transactions for a certain account balance or division.

Acquisitions Journal or Listing The **acquisitions journal** or listing, often referred to as the purchases journal, is generated from the acquisitions transaction file and typically includes the vendor name, date, amount, and account classification or classifications for each transaction, such as repair and maintenance, inventory, or utilities. It also identifies whether the acquisition was for cash or accounts payable. The journal or listing can cover any time period, typically a month. The journal or listing includes totals of every account number included for the time period. The same transactions included in the journal or listing are also posted simultaneously to the general ledger and, if they are on account, to the accounts payable master file.

Accounts Payable Master File An **accounts payable master file** records acquisitions, cash disbursements, and acquisition returns and allowances transactions for each vendor. The master file is updated from the acquisition, returns and allowances, and cash disbursement computer transaction files. The total of the individual account balances in the master file equals the total balance of accounts payable in the general ledger. A printout of the accounts payable master file shows, by vendor, the beginning balance in accounts payable, each acquisition, acquisition return and allowance, cash disbursement, and the ending balance. Many companies do not maintain an accounts payable master file by vendor. These companies pay on the basis of individual vendor's invoices. Therefore, the total of unpaid vendors' invoices in the master file equals total accounts payable.

Accounts Payable Trial Balance An **accounts payable trial balance** listing includes the amount owed to each vendor or for each invoice or voucher at a point in time. It is prepared directly from the accounts payable master file.

Vendor's Statement A **vendor's statement** is a document prepared monthly by the vendor that indicates the beginning balance, acquisitions, returns and allowances, payments to the vendor, and ending balance. These balances and activities are the vendor's representations of the transactions for the period, not the client's. Except for disputed amounts and timing differences, the client's accounts payable master file should be the same as the vendor's statement.

Processing and Recording Cash Disbursements

The payment for goods and services represents a significant activity for all entities. This activity directly reduces balances in liability accounts, particularly accounts payable. Documents associated with the disbursement process that auditors examine include:

Check This document is commonly used to pay for the acquisition when payment is due. Most companies use computer-prepared checks based on information included in the acquisition transactions file at the time goods and services are received. Checks are typically prepared in a multi-copy format, with the original going to the payee, one copy filed with the vendor's invoice and other supporting documents, and another filed numerically. In most cases, individual checks are recorded in a cash disbursements transaction file.

After a check includes the signature of an authorized person, it is an asset. Therefore, signed checks should be mailed by the signer or a person under the signer's control. When cashed by the vendor and cleared by the client's bank, it is called a cancelled check. At that point it is no longer an asset, but now is a document. In many EDI arrangements, the company submits payments to the vendor electronically through an electronic funds transfer (EFT) between the company's bank and the vendor's bank.

Cash Disbursements Transaction File This is a computer-generated file that includes all cash disbursements transactions processed by the accounting system for a period, such as a day, week, or month. It includes the same type of information discussed for the acquisitions transaction file.

Cash Disbursements Journal or Listing This is a listing or report generated from the cash disbursements transaction file that includes all transactions for any time period. The same transactions, including all relevant information, are included in the accounts payable master file and general ledger.

METHODOLOGY FOR DESIGNING TESTS OF CONTROLS AND SUBSTANTIVE TESTS OF TRANSACTIONS

OBJECTIVE 18-3

Understand internal control, and design and perform tests of controls and substantive tests of transactions for the acquisition and payment cycle.

In a typical audit, the most time-consuming accounts to verify by substantive tests of details of balances are accounts receivable, inventory, fixed assets, accounts payable, and expense accounts. Notice that four of these five are directly related to the acquisition and payment cycle. If the auditor can reduce tests of details of the account balances by using tests of controls and substantive tests of transactions to verify the effectiveness of internal controls for acquisitions and cash disbursements, the net time saved can be dramatic. Tests of controls and substantive tests of transactions for the acquisition and payment cycle receive a considerable amount of attention, especially when the client has effective internal controls.

Tests of controls and substantive tests of transactions for the acquisition and payment cycle are divided into two broad areas:

1. Tests of acquisitions, which concern three of the four business functions discussed earlier in this chapter: processing purchase orders, receiving goods and services, and recognizing the liability
2. Tests of payments, which concern the fourth function, processing and recording cash disbursements

Figure 18-2 (p. 610) illustrates the methodology for designing tests of controls and substantive tests of transactions for the acquisition and payment cycle. It is the same methodology used in earlier chapters. Next, let's examine each part of Figure 18-2, starting with understanding internal control.

Understand Internal Control

The auditor gains an understanding of internal control for the acquisition and payment cycle as part of performing risk assessment procedures by studying the client's flowcharts, reviewing internal control questionnaires, and performing walkthrough tests for acquisition and cash disbursement transactions. The procedures for understanding internal control in the acquisition and payment cycle are similar to the procedures performed in other transaction cycles, as discussed in earlier chapters.

Assess Planned Control Risk

Next, the key internal controls for each of the business functions described earlier in this chapter are examined. These are authorization of purchases, separation of the custody of the received goods from other functions, timely recording and independent review of transactions, and authorization of payments to vendors.

Authorization of Purchases Proper authorization for acquisitions ensures that the goods and services acquired are for authorized company purposes, and it avoids the acquisition of excessive or unnecessary items. Most companies require different levels of authorization for different types of acquisitions or dollar amounts. For example, acquisitions of fixed assets in excess of a specified dollar limit require approval by the board of directors; items acquired relatively infrequently, such as insurance policies and long-term service contracts, are approved by certain officers; supplies and services costing less than a designated amount are approved by supervisors and department heads; and some types of raw materials and supplies are reordered automatically when they fall below a predetermined level, often by direct communication with vendors' computers.

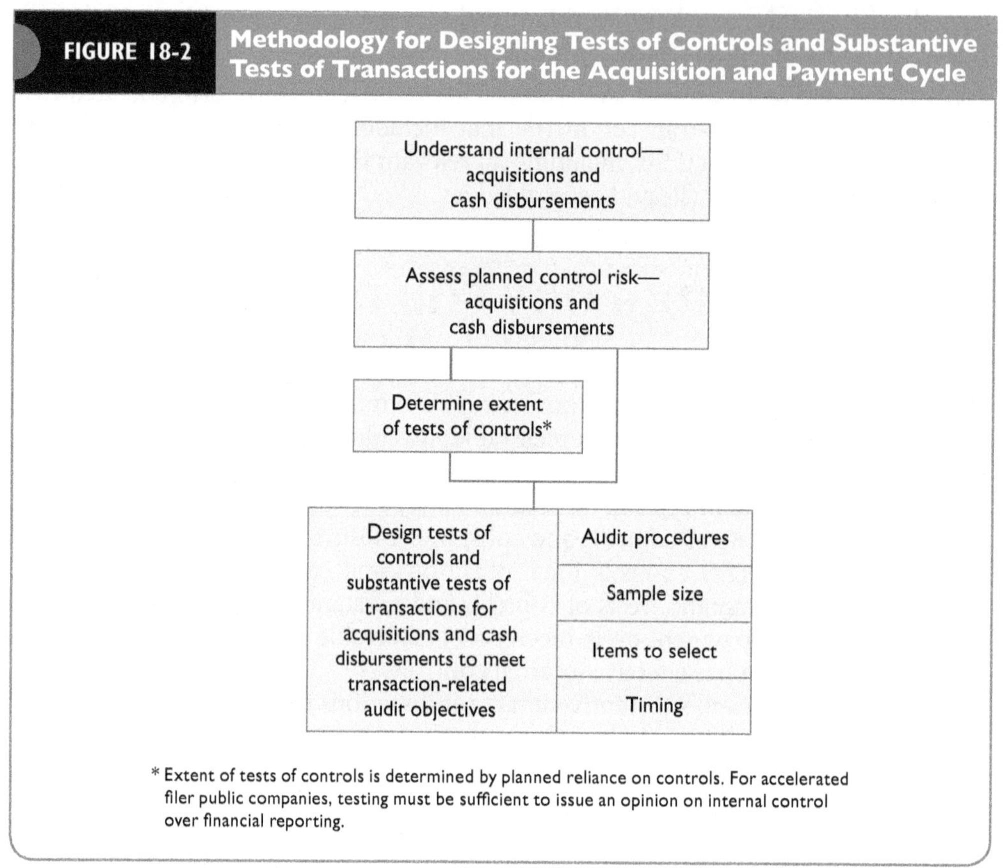
Understand internal control—acquisitions and cash disbursements
Assess planned control risk—acquisitions and cash disbursements
Determine extent of tests of controls*
Design tests of controls and substantive tests of transactions for acquisitions and cash disbursements to meet transaction-related audit objectives
Audit procedures
Sample size
Items to select
Timing
* Extent of tests of controls is determined by planned reliance on controls. For accelerated filer public companies, testing must be sufficient to issue an opinion on internal control over financial reporting.
FIGURE 18-2 Methodology for Designing Tests of Controls and Substantive Tests of Transactions for the Acquisition and Payment Cycle

After the purchase requisition for an acquisition has been approved, a purchase order to acquire the goods or services must be initiated. A purchase order is issued to a vendor for a specified item at a certain price to be delivered at or by a designated time. The purchase order, issued either in written or electronic form, is generally viewed as a legal document, and represents an offer to buy the goods or services.

Companies commonly establish purchasing departments to ensure an adequate quality of goods and services at a minimum price. For effective internal control, the purchasing department should be separate from those who authorize the acquisition or receive the goods. All purchase orders should be prenumbered to permit easier accounting for all outstanding purchase orders and should be designed to minimize the likelihood of unintentional omissions on the form when goods are ordered.

Separation of Asset Custody from Other Functions Most companies have the receiving department initiate a receiving report as evidence of the receipt and examination of goods. One copy is normally sent to the raw materials storeroom and another to the accounts payable department for their information needs. To prevent theft and misuse, the goods should be *physically controlled* from the time of their receipt until their use or disposal. The personnel in the receiving department should be independent of the storeroom personnel and the accounting department. Finally, the accounting records should transfer responsibility for the goods each time they are moved, from receiving to storage, from storage to manufacturing, etc.

Timely Recording and Independent Review of Transactions In some companies, the recording of the liability for acquisitions is made on the basis of the receipt of goods and services. In others, recording is deferred until the vendor's invoice is received. In either case, the accounts payable department typically has responsibility for verifying the appropriateness of acquisitions. This is done by comparing the details on the purchase order, the receiving report, and the vendor's invoice to determine that the descriptions, prices, quantities, terms, and freight on the vendor's invoice are correct. Typically, the accounts payable department also verifies extensions, footings, and account distributions. In some cases, computer software matches documents and verifies invoice accuracy automatically. The accounts payable department should also account for all receiving reports to assure that the completeness objective is satisfied.

An important control in the accounts payable and information technology departments is the requirement that personnel who record acquisitions do not have access to cash, marketable securities, and other assets. Adequate documents and records, proper procedures for record keeping, and independent checks on performance are also necessary controls in the accounts payable function.

Authorization of Payments The most important controls over cash disbursements include:

- The signing of checks by an individual with proper authority
- Separation of responsibilities for signing checks and performing the accounts payable function
- Careful examination of supporting documents by the check signer at the time the check is signed

The checks should be prenumbered to make it easier to account for all checks and printed on special paper that makes it difficult to alter the payee or amount. Companies should take care to provide physical control over blank, voided, and signed checks. They should also have a method of canceling supporting documents to prevent their reuse as support for another check at a later time. A common method is to document the check number on the supporting documents. A number of organizations issue payment electronically using EDI technologies that disburse funds from the organization's bank accounts to the vendors' accounts. Controls over authorization of electronic payments are just as important as controls over printed checks. Restrictions should be in place that allow only authorized individuals to issue an electronic payment, and those individuals should be separate from the accounts payable function.

Determine Extent of Tests of Controls

After auditors identify key internal controls and deficiencies, they assess control risk. When an auditor intends to rely on controls to support a preliminary control risk assessment below maximum, the auditor performs tests of controls to obtain evidence that controls are operating effectively. As the operating effectiveness of controls improves and is supported by additional tests of controls, the auditor is able to reduce substantive testing. Of course, if the client is an accelerated filer public company, the auditor must document and test controls sufficiently to issue an opinion on internal control over financial reporting.

Design Tests of Controls and Substantive Tests of Transactions for Acquisitions

Table 18-2 (p. 612) summarizes key internal controls, common tests of controls, and common substantive tests of transactions for each transaction-related audit objective. We assume the existence of a separate acquisitions journal or listing for recording all acquisitions.

As you examine Table 18-2, you should:

- Relate each of the internal controls to transaction-related audit objectives
- Relate tests of controls to internal controls
- Relate substantive tests of transactions to transaction-related audit objectives after considering controls and deficiencies in the system

The audit evidence for an audit engagement will vary with the internal controls and other circumstances. Significant audit efficiencies can be achieved on many audits when controls are operating effectively.

TABLE 18-2 Summary of Transaction-Related Audit Objectives, Key Controls, Tests of Controls, and Substantive Tests of Transactions for Acquisitions

Transaction-Related Audit Objectives	Key Internal Controls	Common Tests of Controls	Common Substantive Tests of Transactions
Recorded acquisitions are for goods and services received, consistent with the best interests of the client (occurrence).	Purchase requisition, purchase order, receiving report, and vendor's invoice are attached to the voucher.* Acquisitions are approved at the proper level. Computer accepts entry of purchases only from authorized vendors in the vendor master file. Documents are cancelled to prevent their reuse. Vendors' invoices, receiving reports, purchase orders, and purchase requisitions are internally verified.*	Examine documents in voucher package for existence. Examine indication of approval. Attempt to input transactions with valid and invalid vendors. Examine indication of cancellation. Examine indication of internal verification.	Review the acquisitions journal, general ledger, and accounts payable master file for large or unusual amounts.† Examine underlying documents for reasonableness and authenticity (vendors' invoices, receiving reports, purchase orders, and purchase requisitions).* Examine vendor master file for unusual vendors. Trace inventory acquisitions to inventory master file. Examine fixed assets acquired.
Existing acquisition transactions are recorded (completeness).	Purchase orders are prenumbered and accounted for. Receiving reports are prenumbered and accounted for.* Vouchers are prenumbered and accounted for.	Account for a sequence of purchase orders. Account for a sequence of receiving reports. Account for a sequence of vouchers.	Trace from a file of receiving reports to the acquisitions journal.* Trace from a file of vendors' invoices to the acquisitions journal.
Recorded acquisition transactions are accurate (accuracy).	Calculations and amounts are internally verified. Batch totals are compared with computer summary reports. Acquisitions are approved for prices and discounts.	Examine indication of internal verification. Examine file of batch totals for initials of data control clerk; compare totals to summary reports. Examine indication of approval.	Compare recorded transactions in the acquisitions journal with the vendor's invoice, receiving report, and other supporting documentation.* Recompute the clerical accuracy on the vendor's invoice, including discounts and freight.
Acquisition transactions are correctly included in the accounts payable and inventory master files and are correctly summarized (posting and summarization).	Accounts payable master file contents are internally verified. Accounts payable master file or trial balance totals are compared with general ledger balances.	Examine indication of internal verification. Examine initials on general ledger accounts indicating comparison.	Test clerical accuracy by footing the journals and tracing postings to general ledger and accounts payable and inventory master files.
Acquisition transactions are correctly classified (classification).	An adequate chart of accounts is used. Account classifications are internally verified.	Examine procedures manual and chart of accounts. Examine indication of internal verification.	Compare classification with chart of accounts by referring to vendors' invoices.
Acquisition transactions are recorded on the correct dates (timing).	Procedures require recording transactions as soon as possible after the goods and services have been received. Dates are internally verified.	Examine procedures manual and observe whether unrecorded vendors' invoices exist. Examine indication of internal verification.	Compare dates of receiving reports and vendors' invoices with dates in the acquisition journal.*

*Receiving reports are used only for tangible goods and are therefore not used for services, such as utilities and repairs and maintenance. Often, vendors' invoices are the only documentation available.

†This analytical procedure can also apply to other objectives, including completeness, accuracy, and timing.

APPLE MANAGER ACCUSED OF RECEIVING KICKBACKS RELATED TO IPHONE AND IPOD

An Apple Computer manager was accused of receiving over $1 million in kickbacks from Asian suppliers of iPhone and iPod accessories. The manager transmitted confidential information to the suppliers that allowed them to negotiate favorable contracts with Apple.

The alleged scheme involved a chain of U.S. and foreign bank accounts, as well as a front company to receive payments. The manager reportedly opened bank accounts in several countries in Asia to receive the kickbacks, and also received payments directly when traveling to Asia. The payments were referred to by code words such as "sample" to avoid detection by coworkers.

Source: Based on Pete Carey, "Apple Manager Indicted in Kickback Scheme," *San Jose Mercury News*, August 13, 2010 (www.mercurynews.com).

Four of the six transaction-related audit objectives for acquisitions deserve special attention and are therefore examined more closely. The correctness of many asset, liability, and expense accounts depends on the correct recording of transactions in the acquisitions journal, especially related to these four objectives.

1. *Recorded Acquisitions Are for Goods and Services Received, Consistent with the Best Interests of the Client (Occurrence).* If the auditor is satisfied that the controls are adequate for this objective, tests for improper transactions and recorded transactions that did not occur can be greatly reduced. Adequate controls prevent the unintentional recording of acquisitions that did not occur, especially recording duplicate acquisitions. Adequate controls are also likely to prevent the client from including as a business expense or asset fraudulent transactions or those that primarily benefit management or other employees rather than the entity being audited. In some instances, improper transactions are obvious, such as the acquisition of unauthorized personal items by employees. In other instances, the appropriateness of a transaction is more difficult to evaluate, such as the payment of officers' memberships to country clubs or expense-paid vacations to foreign countries for management and their families. If the controls over improper transactions or transactions that did not occur are inadequate, more extensive examination of supporting documentation is necessary.
2. *Existing Acquisitions Are Recorded (Completeness).* Failure to record the acquisition of goods and services received understates accounts payable and may result in an overstatement of net income and owners' equity. Therefore, auditors consider this an essential objective for acquisitions. It may be difficult in some audits to perform tests of details of balances to determine whether unrecorded transactions exist, so the auditor must rely on controls and substantive tests of transactions for this purpose. In addition, because the audit of accounts payable usually takes considerable time, effective internal controls, properly tested, can significantly reduce audit costs.
3. *Acquisitions Are Accurately Recorded (Accuracy).* The extent of tests of details of many balance sheet and expense accounts depends on the auditor's evaluation of the effectiveness of the internal controls over the accuracy of recorded acquisition transactions. For example, if the auditor believes that the fixed asset transactions are correctly recorded in the acquisitions journal, it is acceptable to vouch fewer current period acquisitions during tests of details of balances than if the controls are inadequate.

   When a client uses perpetual inventory records, tests of details of inventory can also be significantly reduced if the auditor believes the perpetual records are accurate. The controls over acquisitions included in the perpetual records are normally tested as a part of the tests of controls and substantive tests of transactions for acquisitions.
4. *Acquisitions Are Correctly Classified (Classification).* Tests of details of certain individual accounts can be reduced if the auditor believes that internal controls are adequate to provide reasonable assurance of correct classification in the acquisitions journal. Although all accounts are affected to some degree by effective controls over classification, the two areas most affected are current period acquisitions of fixed assets, and all expense accounts, such as repairs and maintenance, utilities, and advertising.

DEFICIENT INTERNAL CONTROL OVER DISBURSEMENTS LEADS TO $8 MILLION EMBEZZLEMENT

When Nathan Mueller, an employee of ING, first learned that he was able to both initiate a check request and subsequently approve the disbursement, he managed to resist the temptation. Ultimately, though, when he and his wife were having financial difficulties, he headed down the slippery slope that would end with his embezzling over $8 million. Mueller was part of a team that implemented an enterprise resource planning system at ING. He and a coworker were accidentally given the authority to approve check requests over $250,000. That responsibility, coupled with a loose control environment in the small accounting department, where coworkers regularly logged in for each other in order to process transactions when others were away from the office, allowed Mueller to log into a coworker's account to request checks, and then log into his own account to approve them. Mueller's accounting responsibilities also allowed him to enter the account codes for the other side of the transaction and successfully hide the disbursements.

Initially, Mueller requested a check made out to one of his credit card companies, which happened to have a name that was very similar to a vendor frequently used by ING. Based on his success with that transaction, he opened an account and created a legal entity that also had a name similar to an ING vendor, and then wrote several checks to the account for over $1 million each. Several red flags were missed or ignored by other ING workers, including a check to his credit card company that was returned to ING, and obvious clues that Mueller was living beyond his means. After four years of requesting and approving checks, Mueller was caught by a coworker who became suspicious and began investigating after Mueller's then ex-wife disclosed that she did not believe Mueller was simply lucky at gambling, which had been his cover for his extravagant lifestyle. Mueller was sentenced to 97 months in prison and is slowly repaying the funds he embezzled.

Source: M.J. Nigrini and N.J. Mueller. "Lessons from an $8 million fraud," *Journal of Accountancy* (August 1, 2014) (www.journalofaccountancy.com).

It is relatively time-consuming for auditors to perform documentation tests of current period fixed asset acquisitions and expense accounts for accuracy and classification. Therefore, time savings can be significant when controls are effective.

Design Tests of Controls and Substantive Tests of Transactions for Cash Disbursements

Table 18-3 for cash disbursements uses the same format as Table 18-2 (p. 612) for acquisitions. We assume for these controls and audit procedures that separate cash disbursements and acquisitions journals exist. Our comments about the methodology and process for developing audit procedures for acquisitions apply equally to cash disbursements.

Auditors typically perform the acquisitions and cash disbursements tests at the same time. For a transaction selected for examination from the acquisitions journal, the vendor's invoice, receiving report, and other acquisition documentation are examined at the same time as the related cancelled check. Thus, the verification is done efficiently without reducing the effectiveness of the tests.

Attributes Sampling for Tests of Controls and Substantive Tests of Transactions

Because of the importance of tests of controls and substantive tests of transactions for acquisitions and cash disbursements, the use of attributes sampling is common. The approach is similar to that used for the tests of controls and substantive tests of transactions for sales discussed in the "Statistical Audit Sampling" section on pages 503–506 of Chapter 15.

There are three important differences in acquisitions and payments compared to other cycles.

1. As discussed in the beginning of the chapter, there are a larger number of accounts involved in this cycle, including both income statement and balance sheet accounts. The effect is an increased potential for classification misstatements, some of which are likely to affect income. An example is a misclassification between repair and maintenance expenses and fixed assets. As a result, auditors often reduce the tolerable exception rate, especially for the classification attribute.
2. It is more common in this cycle for transactions to require significant judgment, such as for leases and construction costs. These judgment requirements result in an increased likelihood of misstatements. As a result, auditors often reduce the tolerable exception rate for the accuracy attribute.
3. The dollar amounts of individual transactions in the cycle cover a wide range. As a result, auditors commonly segregate large and unusual items and test them on a 100 percent basis.

TABLE 18-3 **Summary of Transaction-Related Audit Objectives, Key Controls, Tests of Controls, and Substantive Tests of Transactions for Cash Disbursements**

Transaction-Related Audit Objectives	Key Internal Controls	Common Tests of Controls	Common Substantive Tests of Transactions
Recorded cash disbursements are for goods and services actually received (occurrence).	There is adequate segregation of duties between accounts payable and custody of signed checks or authority to disburse funds electronically. Supporting documentation is examined before signing of checks or electronic disbursement of funds by an authorized person. Approval of payment on supporting documents is given at the time checks are signed.	Discuss with personnel and observe activities. Discuss with personnel and observe activities. Examine indication of approval.	Review the cash disbursements journal, general ledger, and accounts payable master file for large or unusual amounts.* Trace the cancelled check or electronic bank records of disbursements to the related acquisitions journal entry and examine for payee name and amount. Examine cancelled check for authorized signature, proper endorsement, and cancellation by the bank or use bank records to verify payee for electronic payments. Examine supporting documents as part of the tests of acquisitions.
Existing cash disbursement transactions are recorded (completeness).	Checks are prenumbered and accounted for. The bank reconciliation is prepared monthly by an employee independent of recording cash disbursements or custody of assets.	Account for a sequence of checks. Examine bank reconciliations and observe their preparation.	Reconcile recorded cash disbursements with the cash disbursements on the bank statement (proof of cash disbursements).
Recorded cash disbursement transactions are accurate (accuracy).	Calculations and amounts are internally verified. The bank reconciliation is prepared monthly by an independent person.	Examine indication of internal verification. Examine bank reconciliations and observe their preparation.	Compare cancelled checks and electronic bank records of disbursements with the related acquisitions journal and cash disbursements journal entries. Recompute cash discounts. Prepare a proof of cash disbursements.
Cash disbursement transactions are correctly included in the accounts payable master file and are correctly summarized (posting and summarization).	Accounts payable master file contents are internally verified. Accounts payable master file or trial balance totals are compared with general ledger balances.	Examine indication of internal verification. Examine initials on general ledger accounts indicating comparison.	Test clerical accuracy by footing journals and tracing postings to general ledger and accounts payable master file.
Cash disbursement transactions are correctly classified (classification).	An adequate chart of accounts is used. Account classifications are internally verified.	Examine procedures manual and chart of accounts. Examine indication of internal verification.	Compare classification with chart of accounts by referring to vendors' invoices and acquisitions journal.
Cash disbursement transactions are recorded on the correct dates (timing).	Procedures require recording of transactions as soon as possible after the check has been signed or electronically submitted for bank processing. Dates are internally verified.	Examine procedures manual and observe whether unrecorded checks exist. Examine indication of internal verification.	Compare dates on cancelled checks or electronic bank records with the cash disbursements journal. Compare dates on cancelled checks or electronic bank records with the bank cancellation date.

*This analytical procedure can also apply to other objectives, including completeness, accuracy, and timing.

CONCEPT CHECK

1. What are the most significant balance sheet and income statement accounts related to the acquisition and payment cycle?
2. What is meant by a voucher? Explain how its use can improve an organization's internal controls.
3. Explain why most auditors consider the receipt of goods and services the most important point in the acquisition and payment cycle.

METHODOLOGY FOR DESIGNING TESTS OF DETAILS OF BALANCES FOR ACCOUNTS PAYABLE

OBJECTIVE 18-4

Describe the methodology for designing tests of details of balances for accounts payable using the audit risk model.

Because all acquisition and payment cycle transactions typically flow through accounts payable, this account is critical to any audit of the acquisition and payment cycle. Accounts payable are *unpaid obligations* for goods and services received in the ordinary course of business. Accounts payable includes obligations for the acquisition of raw materials, equipment, utilities, repairs, and many other types of goods and services that were received before the end of the year. Most accounts payable can also be identified by the existence of vendors' invoices for the obligation.

Accounts payable should be distinguished from accrued liabilities and interest-bearing obligations. A liability is an account payable only if the total amount of the obligation is *known and owed at the balance sheet date.* If the obligation includes the payment of interest, it should be recorded as a note payable, contract payable, mortgage payable, or bond payable.

Figure 18-3 summarizes the methodology for designing tests of details for accounts payable. This methodology is the same as that used for accounts receivable in Chapter 16 (see Figure 16-1 on p. 525).

If tests of controls and related substantive tests of transactions show that controls are operating effectively, and if substantive analytical procedures results are satisfactory, the auditor is likely to reduce tests of details of balances for accounts payable. However, because accounts payable tend to be material for most companies, auditors almost always perform some tests of details of balances.

Identify Significant Risks and Assess the Risk of Material Misstatement for Accounts Payable (Phase I)

Like accounts receivable, a large number of transactions can affect accounts payable. The balance is often significant and made up of a large number of vendor balances, and it is relatively expensive to audit the account. For these reasons, auditors often assess inherent risk as medium or high. They are especially concerned about the completeness and cutoff balance-related audit objectives because of the potential for understatements in the account balance.

As part of the process of identifying significant risks and assessing the risk of material misstatement in accounts payable, the auditor considers any recent changes in the acquisition and payment cycle. The focus by many companies on improving their supply-chain management activities has led to numerous changes in the design of systems used to initiate and record acquisition and payment activities. Efforts to streamline the purchasing of goods and services, including increased sharing of information with suppliers and the use of technology and e-commerce to transact business, are changing all aspects of the acquisition and payment cycle for many companies. These arrangements and systems can be complex.

Significant client business risks may arise from these changes. For example, suppliers may have greater access to accounts payable records, allowing them to continually monitor the status of payable balances and to perform detailed reconciliations of transactions. Access by external parties, such as suppliers, to accounting records

FIGURE 18-3 Methodology for Designing Tests of Details of Balances for Accounts Payable

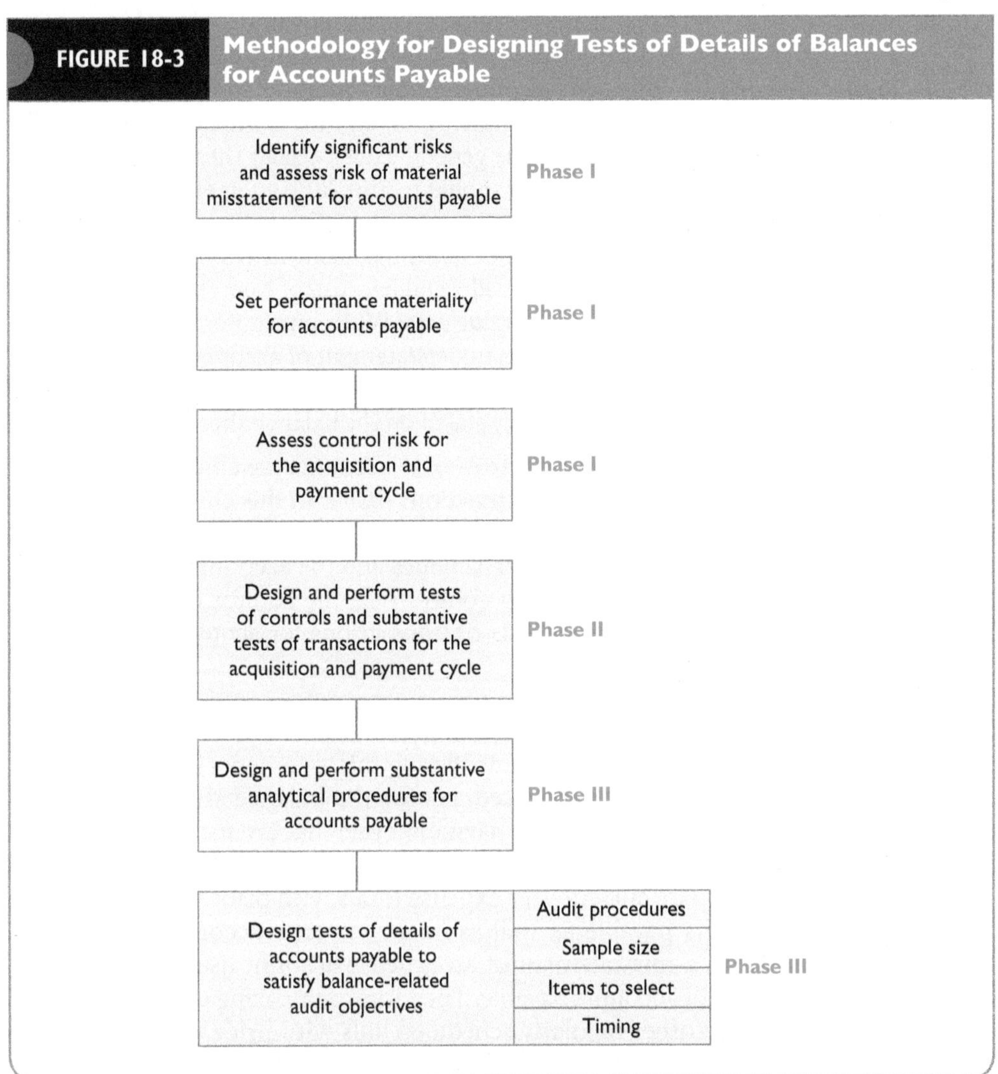

Identify significant risks and assess risk of material misstatement for accounts payable
Phase I
Set performance materiality for accounts payable
Phase I
Assess control risk for the acquisition and payment cycle
Phase I
Design and perform tests of controls and substantive tests of transactions for the acquisition and payment cycle
Phase II
Design and perform substantive analytical procedures for accounts payable
Phase III
Design tests of details of accounts payable to satisfy balance-related audit objectives
Audit procedures
Sample size
Items to select
Timing
Phase III

threatens the likelihood of misstatement if that access is not properly controlled. Also, increased focus on improving the logistics of physically moving inventory throughout a company's distribution chain may increase the difficulty of establishing effective cutoff of accounts payable balances at year-end.

Set Performance Materiality (Phase I)

Because a large number of transactions affect accounts payable, its balance is often significant and made up of multiple vendor balances, and it is relatively expensive to audit, auditors typically set performance materiality for accounts payable relatively high. These are the same reasons that result in a higher assessed inherent risk.

Assess Control Risk and Design and Perform Tests of Controls and Substantive Tests of Transactions (Phases I and II)

As shown in Figure 18-3, after auditors set performance materiality and assess risk of material misstatement for accounts payable, they assess control risk based on an understanding of internal control. The auditor's ultimate substantive tests depend on the relative effectiveness of internal controls related to accounts payable. Therefore, auditors must have a thorough understanding of how these controls relate to accounts payable.

The effects of the client's internal controls on accounts payable tests can be illustrated by two examples:

1. Assume that the client has highly effective internal controls over recording and paying for acquisitions. The receipt of goods is promptly documented by prenumbered receiving reports; prenumbered vouchers are promptly and efficiently prepared and recorded in the acquisition transactions file and the accounts

payable master file. Cash disbursements are made promptly when due and immediately recorded in the cash disbursements transactions file and the accounts payable master file. Individual accounts payable balances in the master file are reconciled monthly with vendors' statements, and the computer automatically reconciles the master file total to the general ledger. Under these circumstances, the verification of accounts payable should require little audit effort once the auditor concludes that internal controls are operating effectively.

2. Assume that receiving reports are not used, the client defers recording acquisitions until cash disbursements are made, and because of cash shortages, bills are often paid several months after their due date. When an auditor faces such a situation, there is a high likelihood of an understatement of accounts payable; therefore, extensive tests of details of accounts payable are necessary to determine whether accounts payable is correctly stated on the balance sheet date.

We discussed the most important controls over accounts payable and the related tests of controls and substantive tests of transactions earlier in this chapter. In addition to those controls, each month an independent person or computer program should reconcile vendors' statements with recorded liabilities and the accounts payable master file with the general ledger. After assessing control risk, the auditor designs and performs tests of controls and substantive tests of transactions for acquisitions and cash disbursements.

Design and Perform Substantive Analytical Procedures (Phase III)

OBJECTIVE 18-5

Design and perform substantive analytical procedures for accounts payable.

The use of analytical procedures is as important in the acquisition and payment cycle as it is in every other cycle, especially for uncovering misstatements in accounts payable. Table 18-4 illustrates analytical procedures for the balance sheet and income statement accounts in the acquisition and payment cycle that are useful for uncovering areas in which additional investigation is desirable.

Auditors should compare current year expense totals with prior years to uncover misstatements of accounts payable as well as in the expense accounts. Because of double-entry accounting, a misstatement of an expense account usually also results in an equal misstatement of accounts payable. Therefore, comparing current expenses such as rent, utilities, and other regularly scheduled bills with prior years is an effective procedure for analyzing accounts payable when expenses from year to year are expected to be relatively stable.

Design and Perform Tests of Details of Accounts Payable Balance (Phase III)

OBJECTIVE 18-6

Design and perform tests of details of balances for accounts payable, including out-of-period liability tests.

The overall objective in the audit of accounts payable is to determine whether the accounts payable balance is fairly stated and properly disclosed. Seven of the eight balance-related audit objectives discussed in Chapter 6 (pp. 162–164) are applicable to accounts payable: existence, completeness, accuracy, classification, cutoff, detail tie-in, and rights and obligations. Realizable value is not applicable to liabilities.

TABLE 18-4 Substantive Analytical Procedures for the Acquisition and Payment Cycle

Substantive Analytical Procedure	Possible Misstatement
Compare acquisition-related expense account balances with prior years.	Misstatement of accounts payable and expenses.
Review list of accounts payable for unusual, nonvendor, and interest-bearing payables.	Classification misstatement for nontrade liabilities.
Compare individual accounts payable with previous years.	Unrecorded or nonexistent accounts, or misstatements.
Calculate ratios, such as purchases divided by accounts payable, and accounts payable divided by current liabilities.	Unrecorded or nonexistent accounts, or misstatements.

There is an important difference in emphasis in the audit of liabilities and assets. When auditors verify assets, they emphasize overstatements through verification by confirmation, physical examination, and examination of supporting documents. The opposite approach is taken in verifying liability balances; that is, the main focus is on understated or omitted liabilities.

The difference in emphasis in auditing assets and liabilities results directly from the *legal liability of CPAs*. If equity investors, creditors, and other users determine subsequent to the issuance of the audited financial statements that earnings and owners' equity were materially overstated, a lawsuit against the CPA firm is fairly likely. Because an overstatement of owners' equity can arise either from an overstatement of assets or an understatement of liabilities, it is natural for CPAs to emphasize those two types of misstatements. Auditors should not ignore the possibility that assets are understated or liabilities are overstated, and should design tests to detect material understatements of earnings and owners' equity, including those arising from material overstatements of accounts payable.

We will use the same balance-related audit objectives from Chapter 16 that we applied to verifying accounts receivable, as they also apply to liabilities, with three minor modifications:

1. The realizable value objective is not applicable to liabilities. Realizable value applies only to assets.
2. The rights aspect of the rights and obligations objective is not applicable to liabilities. For assets, the auditor is concerned with the client's rights to the use and disposal of the assets. For liabilities, the auditor is concerned with the client's obligations for the payment of the liability. If the client has no obligation to pay a liability, it should not be included as a liability.
3. For liabilities, there is emphasis on the search for understatements rather than for overstatements, as we just discussed.

Table 18-5 (p. 620) includes the balance-related audit objectives and common tests of details of balances procedures for accounts payable. The auditor's actual audit procedures vary considerably depending on the nature of the entity, the materiality of accounts payable, the nature and effectiveness of internal controls, and inherent risk. As auditors perform tests of details of balances for accounts payable and other liability accounts, they may also gather evidence about the four presentation and disclosure objectives, especially when performing completeness objective tests. Other procedures related to presentation and disclosure objectives are done as part of procedures to complete the audit, which we will discuss in Chapter 24.

Out-of-Period Liability Tests Because of the emphasis on understatements in liability accounts, *out-of-period liability tests* are important for accounts payable. The extent of tests to uncover unrecorded accounts payable, often called the *search for unrecorded accounts payable*, depends heavily on assessed control risk and the materiality of the potential balance in the account. The same audit procedures used to uncover unrecorded payables are applicable to the accuracy objective. The following are typical audit procedures:

Examine Underlying Documentation for Subsequent Cash Disbursements Auditors examine supporting documentation for cash disbursements subsequent to the balance sheet date to determine whether a cash disbursement was for a current period liability. If it is a current period liability, the auditor should trace it to the accounts payable trial balance to make sure it is included. The receiving report indicates the date inventory was received and is therefore an especially useful document. Similarly, the vendor's invoice usually indicates the date services were provided. Auditors often examine documentation for cash disbursements made in the subsequent period for several weeks after the balance sheet date, especially when the client does not pay bills on a timely basis.

TABLE 18-5 Balance-Related Audit Objectives and Tests of Details of Balances for Accounts Payable

Balance-Related Audit Objective	Common Tests of Details of Balances Procedures	Comments
Accounts payable in the accounts payable list agree with related master file, and the total is correctly added and agrees with the general ledger (detail tie-in).	Re-add or use the computer to total the accounts payable list. Trace the total to the general ledger. Trace individual vendor's invoices to master file for names and amounts.	All pages need not ordinarily be footed if footing manually. Unless controls are deficient, tracing to master file should be limited.
Accounts payable in the accounts payable list exist (existence).	Trace from accounts payable list to vendors' invoices and statements. Confirm accounts payable, emphasizing large and unusual amounts.	Ordinarily receives little attention because the primary concern is with understatements.
Existing accounts payable are included in the accounts payable list (completeness).	Perform out-of-period liability tests (see discussion).	These are essential audit tests for accounts payable.
Accounts payable in the accounts payable list are accurate (accuracy).	Perform same procedures as those used for existence objective and out-of-period liability tests.	Ordinarily, the emphasis in these procedures for accuracy is understatement rather than omission.
Accounts payable in the accounts payable list are correctly classified (classification).	Review the list and master file for related parties, notes or other interest-bearing liabilities, long-term payables, and debit balances.	Knowledge of the client's business is essential for these tests.
Transactions in the acquisition and payment cycle are recorded in the proper period (cutoff).	Perform out-of-period liability tests (see discussion). Perform detailed tests as part of physical observation of inventory (see discussion). Test for inventory in transit (see discussion).	These are essential audit tests for accounts payable. These are called *cutoff tests.*
The company has an obligation to pay the liabilities included in accounts payable (obligations).	Examine vendors' statements and confirm accounts payable.	Normally not a concern in the audit of accounts payable because all accounts payable are obligations.

Examine Underlying Documentation for Bills Not Paid Several Weeks After the Year-End Auditors carry out this procedure in the same manner as the preceding one and for the same purpose. This procedure differs in that it is done for unpaid obligations near the end of the audit rather than for obligations that have already been paid.

For example, in an audit with a March 31 year-end, assume the auditor examines the supporting documentation for checks paid through June 28. Bills that are still unpaid on June 28 should be examined to determine whether they are obligations at March 31.

Trace Receiving Reports Issued Before Year-End to Related Vendors' Invoices All merchandise received before the year-end of the accounting period should be included as accounts payable. By tracing receiving reports issued up to year-end to vendors' invoices and making sure that they are included in accounts payable, the auditor is testing for unrecorded obligations.

Trace Vendors' Statements That Show a Balance Due to the Accounts Payable Trial Balance If the client maintains a file of vendors' statements, auditors can trace any statement that has a balance due at the balance sheet date to the listing to make sure it is included as an account payable.

Send Confirmations to Vendors with Which the Client Does Business Although the use of confirmations for accounts payable is less common than for accounts receivable, auditors use them occasionally to test for vendors omitted from the accounts payable list, omitted transactions, and misstated account balances. Sending confirmations to active vendors for which a balance has not been included in the accounts payable list is a useful means of searching for omitted amounts. This type of confirmation is commonly called a zero balance confirmation. Additional discussion of confirmation of accounts payable is deferred until the end of this chapter.

Cutoff Tests Accounts payable **cutoff tests** are done to determine whether transactions recorded a few days before and after the balance sheet date are included in the correct period. The five out-of-period liability audit tests we just discussed are all cutoff tests for acquisitions, but they emphasize understatements. For the first three procedures, it is also appropriate to examine supporting documentation as a test of overstatement of accounts payable. For example, the third procedure tests for understatements (unrecorded accounts payable) by tracing receiving reports issued before year-end to related vendors' invoices. To test for overstatement cutoff amounts, the auditor should trace receiving reports issued *after* year-end to related invoices to make sure that they are not recorded as accounts payable (unless they are inventory in transit, which is discussed shortly).

We've already discussed most cutoff tests in the preceding section, but we will focus on two aspects here: the relationship of cutoff to physical observation of inventory and the determination of the amount of inventory in transit.

Relationship of Cutoff to Physical Observation of Inventory In determining that the accounts payable cutoff is correct, *it is essential that the cutoff tests be coordinated with the physical observation of inventory*. For example, assume that an inventory acquisition for $400,000 is received late in the afternoon of December 31, after the physical inventory is completed. If the acquisition is included in accounts payable and purchases but excluded from ending inventory, the result is an understatement of net earnings of $400,000. Conversely, if the acquisition is excluded from both inventory and accounts payable, there is a misstatement in the balance sheet, but the income statement is correct. The only way the auditor will know which type of misstatement has occurred is to coordinate cutoff tests with the observation of inventory.

The cutoff information for acquisitions should be obtained *during the physical observation* of inventory. At that time, the auditor should review the procedures in the receiving department to determine that all inventory received was counted, and the auditor should record in the audit documentation the last receiving report number of inventory included in the physical count. Subsequent to the physical count date, the auditor should then test the accounting records for cutoff. The auditor should trace the previously documented receiving report numbers to the accounts payable records to verify that they are correctly included or excluded. For example, assume that the last receiving report number representing inventory included in the physical count was 3167. The auditor should record this document number and subsequently trace it and several preceding numbers to their related vendors' invoices and to the accounts payable list or the accounts payable master file to determine that they are all included. Similarly, accounts payable for acquisitions recorded on receiving reports with numbers larger than 3167 should be excluded from accounts payable.

When the client's physical inventory takes place before the last day of the year, the auditor must still perform an accounts payable cutoff at the time of the physical count in the manner described in the preceding paragraph. In addition, the auditor must verify whether all acquisitions that took place between the physical count and the end of the year were added to the physical inventory and accounts payable.

Inventory in Transit In accounts payable, auditors must distinguish between acquisitions of inventory that are on an **FOB destination** basis and those that are made **FOB origin**. For FOB destination, title passes to the buyer when the inventory is received, so only inventory received on or before the balance sheet date should be included in inventory and accounts payable at year-end. When an acquisition is FOB origin, the company must record the inventory and related accounts payable in the current period if shipment occurred on or before the balance sheet date.

Auditors can determine whether inventory has been acquired FOB destination or origin by examining vendors' invoices. Auditors should examine invoices for merchandise received shortly after year-end to determine whether they were on an FOB origin basis. For those that were, and when the shipment dates were on or before the balance sheet date, the inventory and related accounts payable must be recorded in the current period if the amounts are material.

Reliability of Evidence

OBJECTIVE 18-7

Distinguish the reliability of vendors' invoices, vendors' statements, and confirmations of accounts payable as audit evidence.

Auditors need to understand the relative reliability of the three primary types of evidence ordinarily used for verifying accounts payable: vendors' invoices, vendors' statements, and confirmations.

Distinction Between Vendors' Invoices and Vendors' Statements Auditors should distinguish between vendors' invoices and vendors' statements in verifying the amount due to a vendor. Auditors get highly reliable *evidence about individual transactions* when they examine vendors' invoices and related supporting documents, such as receiving reports and purchase orders. A vendor's statement is not as desirable as invoices for verifying individual transactions because a statement includes only the total amount of the transaction. The units acquired, price, freight, and other data are not included.

Which of these two documents is better for verifying the correct balance in accounts payable? *The vendor's statement is superior for verifying accounts payable* because it includes the ending balance. The auditor can compare existing vendors' invoices with the client's list and still not uncover missing ones, which is the primary concern in accounts payable.

Which of these two documents is better for testing acquisitions in tests of controls and substantive tests of transactions? *The vendor's invoice is superior for verifying transactions* because the auditor is verifying individual transactions and the invoice shows the details of the acquisitions.

Difference Between Vendors' Statements and Confirmations The most important distinction between a vendor's statement and a confirmation of accounts payable is the source of the information. A vendor's statement has been prepared by the vendor (an independent third party) but is in the hands of the client at the time the auditor examines it. This provides the client with an opportunity to alter a vendor's statement or to withhold certain statements from the auditor.

A response to a confirmation request for accounts payable is normally an itemized statement sent directly to the CPA's office by the vendor. It provides the same information as a vendor's statement but is more reliable. In addition, confirmations of accounts payable often include a request for information about notes and acceptances payable as well as consigned inventory owned by the vendor but stored on the client's premises. An illustration of a typical accounts payable confirmation request is given in Figure 18-4.

Due to the availability of vendors' statements and vendors' invoices, which are both relatively reliable evidence because they originate from a third party, confirmation of accounts payable is less common than confirmation of accounts receivable. If the client has adequate internal controls and vendors' statements are available for examination, confirmations are normally not sent. However, when the client's internal controls are deficient, when statements are not available, or when the auditor questions the client's integrity, it is desirable to send confirmation requests to vendors. Because of the emphasis on understatements of liability accounts, the accounts confirmed should include large, active, zero balance accounts and a representative sample of all others.

When auditors examine vendors' statements or receive confirmations, there must be a reconciliation of the statement or confirmation with the accounts payable list. Differences are often caused by inventory in transit, checks mailed by the client but not received by the vendor at the statement date, and delays in processing accounting

FIGURE 18-4 Accounts Payable Confirmation Request

January 15, 2017

ROGER MEAD, INC.
Jones Sales, Inc.
2116 Stewart Street
Wayneville, Kentucky 36021

To Whom It May Concern:

Our auditors, Murray and Rogers, CPAs, are conducting an audit of our financial statements. For this purpose, please furnish them with the following information as of December 31, 2016.

(1) Itemized statements of our accounts payable to you showing all unpaid items;
(2) A complete list of any notes and acceptances payable to you (including any which have been discounted) showing the original date, dates due, original amount, unpaid balance, collateral, and endorsers; and
(3) An itemized list of your merchandise consigned to us.

Your prompt attention to this request will be appreciated. An envelope is enclosed for your reply.

Yours truly,

Phil Geriovini

Phil Geriovini, President

records. The reconciliation is of the same general nature as that discussed in Chapter 16 for accounts receivable. The documents typically used to reconcile the balances on the accounts payable list with the confirmations or vendors' statements include receiving reports, vendors' invoices, and cancelled checks.

Sample Size

Our discussion of tests of details of the accounts payable balance has focused heavily on the typical audit procedures performed, the documents and records examined, and the timing of the tests. The auditor must also consider sample sizes in the audit of accounts payable. Sample sizes for accounts payable tests vary considerably, depending on such factors as the materiality of accounts payable, the number of accounts outstanding, assessed control risk, and the results of the prior year.

Statistical sampling is less commonly used for the audit of accounts payable than for accounts receivable. Defining the population and determining the population size is more difficult for accounts payable. Because the emphasis is on omitted accounts payable, auditors must try to ensure that the population includes all potential payables.

CONCEPT CHECK

1. Explain the relationship between tests of the acquisition and payment cycle and tests of accounts payable. Give specific examples of how these two types of tests affect each other.
2. In testing the cutoff of accounts payable at the balance sheet date, explain why it is important that auditors coordinate their tests with the physical observation of inventory. What can the auditor do during the physical inventory to enhance the likelihood of an accurate cutoff?
3. What is the primary audit procedure the auditor performs to test the completeness of accounts payable?

SUMMARY

Figure 18-5 summarizes how the four types of audit procedures are used to obtain audit assurance for transactions and accounts in the acquisition and payment cycle. After using procedures to obtain an understanding of internal control and tests of controls, auditors can evaluate whether controls over transactions in the cycle are operating effectively. When control risk is assessed as low, the auditor can reduce substantive testing of ending balances in the related accounts. On the other hand, a higher assessed control risk results in the need for more substantive testing in related accounts. In this chapter, the ending balance we focused on was accounts payable.

By combining all types of audit tests shown in Figure 18-5, the auditor can obtain a higher overall assurance for transactions and accounts in the acquisition and payment cycle than the assurance obtained from any one test. The auditor can increase the assurance obtained from any one of the tests, and thereby increase the overall assurance for the cycle.

FIGURE 18-5 **Types of Audit Tests for the Acquisition and Payment Cycle (see Figure 18-1 on p. 605 for accounts)**

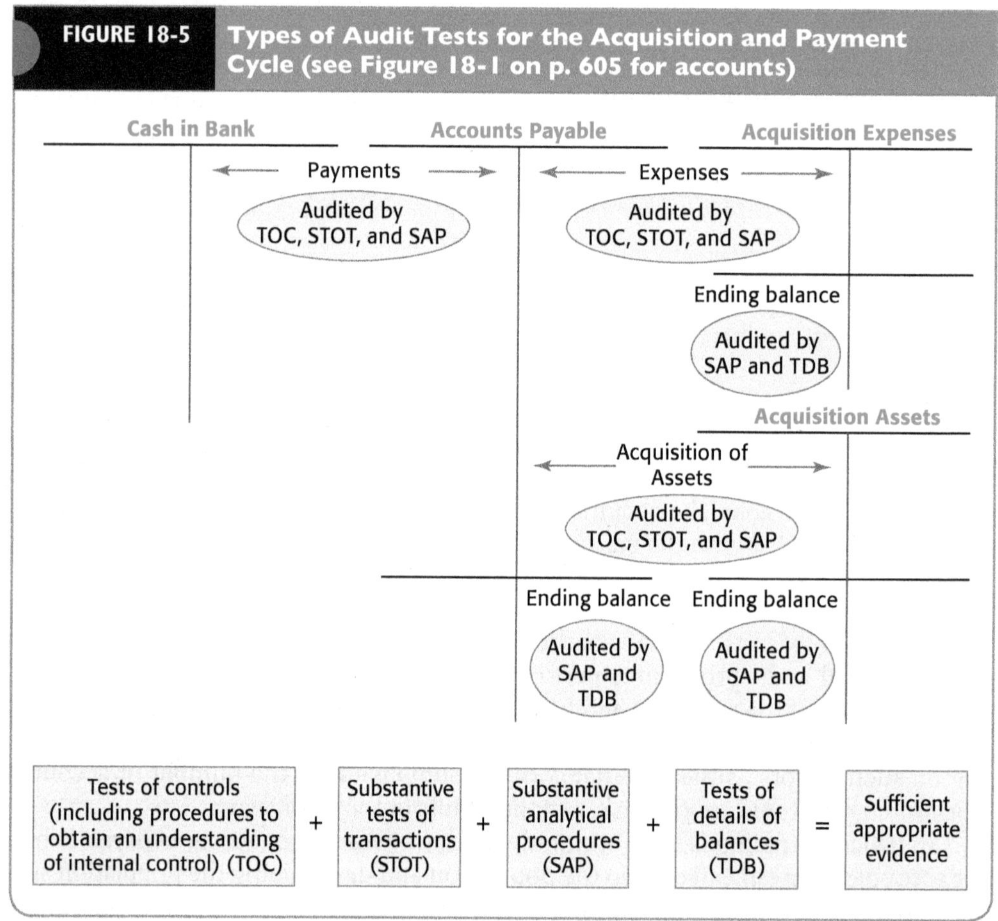

ESSENTIAL TERMS

Accounts payable master file—a computer file for maintaining a record for each vendor of individual acquisitions, cash disbursements, acquisition returns and allowances, and vendor balances

Accounts payable trial balance—a listing of the amount owed to each vendor at a point in time; prepared directly from the accounts payable master file

Acquisition and payment cycle—the transaction cycle that includes the acquisition of and payment for goods and services from suppliers outside the organization

Acquisitions journal—a journal or listing generated from the acquisitions transaction file that typically includes information such as vendor name, date, amount, and account classification for each transaction

Cutoff tests—tests to determine whether transactions recorded a few days before and after the balance sheet date are included in the correct period

Debit memo—a document indicating a reduction in the amount owed to a vendor because of returned goods or an allowance granted

FOB destination—shipping contract in which title to the goods passes to the buyer when the goods are received

FOB origin—shipping contract in which title to the goods passes to the buyer at the time that the goods are shipped

Purchase order—a document prepared or electronically issued by the purchasing department indicating the description, quantity, and related information for goods and services that the company intends to purchase

Purchase requisition—request by an authorized employee to the purchasing department to place an order for inventory and other items used by an entity

Receiving report—a document prepared by the receiving department at the time tangible goods are received, indicating the description of the goods, the quantity received, the date received, and other relevant data; it is part of the documentation necessary for payment to be made

Vendor's invoice—a document or record that specifies the details of an acquisition transaction and amount of money owed to the vendor for an acquisition

Vendor's statement—a statement prepared monthly by the vendor that indicates the customer's beginning balance, acquisitions, payments, and ending balance

Voucher—a document used to establish a formal means of recording and controlling acquisitions, primarily by enabling each acquisition transaction to be sequentially numbered

REVIEW QUESTIONS

18-1 **(OBJECTIVE 18-1)** List five asset accounts, three liability accounts, and five expense accounts included in the acquisition and payment cycle for a typical manufacturing company.

18-2 **(OBJECTIVES 18-2, 18-7)** Distinguish between a vendor's invoice and a vendor's statement. Which document should ideally be used as evidence in auditing acquisition transactions and which is best when verifying accounts payable balances? Why?

18-3 **(OBJECTIVES 18-2, 18-3)** If an audit client does not have prenumbered checks, what type of misstatement has a greater chance of occurring? Under the circumstances, what audit procedure can the auditor use to compensate for the deficiency?

18-4 **(OBJECTIVE 18-3)** List one possible internal control for each of the six transaction-related audit objectives for cash disbursements. For each control, list a test of control to test its effectiveness.

18-5 **(OBJECTIVE 18-3)** List one possible control for each of the six transaction-related audit objectives for acquisitions. For each control, list a test of control to test its effectiveness.

18-6 **(OBJECTIVE 18-3)** Evaluate the following statement by an auditor concerning tests of acquisitions and cash disbursements: "In selecting the acquisitions and cash disbursements sample for testing, the best approach is to select a random month and test every transaction for the period. Using this approach enables me to thoroughly understand internal control because I have examined everything that happened during the period. As a part of the monthly test, I also test the beginning and ending bank reconciliations and prepare a proof of cash for the month. At the completion of these tests I feel I can evaluate the effectiveness of internal control."

18-7 **(OBJECTIVE 18-3)** What is the importance of cash discounts to the client and how can the auditor verify whether they are being taken in accordance with company policy?

18-8 **(OBJECTIVE 18-3)** What are the similarities and differences in the objectives of the following two procedures? (1) Select a random sample of receiving reports and trace them to related vendors' invoices and acquisitions journal entries, comparing the vendor's name, type of material and quantity acquired, and total amount of the acquisition. (2) Select a random sample of acquisitions journal entries and trace them to related vendors' invoices and receiving reports, comparing the vendor's name, type of material and quantity acquired, and total amount of the acquisition.

18-9 **(OBJECTIVES 18-3, 18-6)** Explain the relationship between tests of the acquisition and payment cycle and tests of inventory. Give specific examples of how these two types of tests affect each other.

18-10 **(OBJECTIVE 18-4)** Describe two major changes a client may make to its supply-chain management system and discuss how those changes might increase or decrease the risk of material misstatement in specific accounts.

18-11 **(OBJECTIVE 18-5)** Identify two types of substantive analytical procedures an auditor may perform in testing purchases.

18-12 **(OBJECTIVE 18-6)** The CPA examines all unrecorded invoices on hand as of February 28, 2017, the last day of the audit. Which of the following misstatements is most likely to be uncovered by this procedure? Explain.

a. Accounts payable are overstated at December 31, 2016.

b. Accounts payable are understated at December 31, 2016.

c. Operating expenses are overstated for the 12 months ended December 31, 2016.

d. Operating expenses are overstated for the two months ended February 28, 2017.*

18-13 **(OBJECTIVE 18-7)** Explain why it is common for auditors to send confirmation requests to vendors with "zero balances" on the client's accounts payable listing but uncommon to follow the same approach in verifying accounts receivable.

18-14 **(OBJECTIVE 18-7)** It is less common to confirm accounts payable at an interim date than accounts receivable. Explain why.

18-15 **(OBJECTIVE 18-6)** Distinguish between FOB destination and FOB origin. What procedures should the auditor follow concerning acquisitions of inventory on an FOB origin basis near year-end?

MULTIPLE CHOICE QUESTIONS FROM CPA EXAMINATIONS

18-16 **(OBJECTIVE 18-3)** The following questions concern internal controls in the acquisition and payment cycle. Choose the best response.

a. Which of the following is an internal control that will prevent paid cash disbursement documents from being presented for payment a second time?
   (1) The date on cash disbursement documents must be within a few days of the date that the document is presented for payment.
   (2) The official signing the check compares the check with the documents and should deface the documents.
   (3) Unsigned checks are prepared by individuals who are responsible for signing checks.
   (4) Cash disbursement documents are approved by at least two responsible management officials.

b. Which of the following questions would be best to include in an internal control questionnaire concerning the completeness assertion for purchases?
   (1) Is an authorized purchase order required before the receiving department can accept a shipment or the vouchers payable department can record a voucher?
   (2) Are purchase requisitions prenumbered and independently matched with vendor invoices?
   (3) Is the unpaid voucher file periodically reconciled with inventory records by an employee who does not have access to purchase requisitions?
   (4) Are purchase orders, receiving reports, and vouchers prenumbered and periodically accounted for?

c. The authority to accept incoming goods in receiving should be based on a(n)
   (1) vendor's invoice.
   (2) purchase requisition.
   (3) bill of lading.
   (4) approved purchase order.

* Based on AICPA question paper, American Institute of Certified Public Accountants.

18-17 **(OBJECTIVES 18-6, 18-7)** The following questions concern accumulating evidence in the acquisition and payment cycle. Choose the best response.

a. In auditing accounts payable, an auditor's procedures most likely will focus primarily on management's assertion of

(1) existence.
(2) realizable value.
(3) completeness.
(4) valuation and allocation.

b. Which of the following audit procedures is best for identifying unrecorded trade accounts payable?

(1) Examining unusual relationships between monthly accounts payable balances and recorded cash payments
(2) Reconciling vendors' statements to the file of receiving reports to identify items received just prior to the balance sheet date
(3) Reviewing cash disbursements recorded subsequent to the balance sheet date to determine whether the related payables apply to the prior period
(4) Investigating payables recorded just prior to and just subsequent to the balance sheet date to determine whether they are supported by receiving reports

c. An auditor traced a sample of purchase orders and the related receiving reports to the acquisitions journal and cash disbursements journal. The purpose of this substantive test of transactions most likely was to

(1) identify unusually large purchases that should be investigated further.
(2) verify that cash disbursements were for goods actually received.
(3) determine that purchases were properly recorded.
(4) test whether payments were for goods actually ordered.

d. When using confirmations to provide evidence about the completeness assertion for accounts payable, the appropriate population most likely is

(1) vendors with whom the entity has previously done business.
(2) amounts recorded in the accounts payable subsidiary ledger.
(3) payees of checks drawn in the month after year-end.
(4) invoices filed in the entity's open invoice file.

MULTIPLE CHOICE QUESTIONS FROM BECKER CPA EXAM REVIEW

18-18 **(OBJECTIVES 18-3, 18-6, 18-7)** The following questions concern internal controls and accumulating evidence in the acquisition and payment cycle. Choose the best answer.

a. In assessing control risk for purchases, an auditor vouches a sample of entries in the voucher register to the supporting documents. Which assertion would this test of controls most likely support?

(1) Completeness
(2) Occurrence
(3) Valuation and allocation
(4) Rights and obligations

b. Which of the following tests would an auditor be least likely to perform during an audit of accounts payable?

(1) Examine open vouchers, receiving reports, and vendor invoices shortly after the year-end.
(2) Trace a sample of vouchers to the purchase journal.
(3) Send out accounts payable confirmations.
(4) Select cash disbursements made shortly after year-end and examine supporting documentation such as receiving reports and vendor invoices.

c. While auditing a client's purchase transactions, an auditor selects a sample of vouchers and then compares the dates on the vouchers to the dates on which the corresponding transactions were actually recorded in the client's purchase journal. The audit procedure is most likely designed to test the
   (1) occurrence assertion.
   (2) completeness assertion.
   (3) accuracy assertion.
   (4) cutoff assertion.

DISCUSSION QUESTIONS AND PROBLEMS

18-19 **(OBJECTIVE 18-3)** Questions 1 through 8 are typically found in questionnaires used by auditors to obtain an understanding of internal control in the acquisition and payment cycle. In using the questionnaire for a client, a "yes" response to a question indicates a possible internal control, whereas a "no" indicates a potential deficiency.

1. Is the purchasing function performed by personnel who are independent of the receiving and shipping functions and the payables and disbursing functions?
2. Are all receiving reports prenumbered and the numerical sequence checked by a person independent of check preparation?
3. Are all vendors' invoices routed directly to accounting from the mailroom?
4. Does a responsible employee review and approve the invoice account distribution before the transaction is entered in the computer?
5. Are all extensions, footings, discounts, and freight terms on vendors' invoices checked for accuracy?
6. Are checks automatically posted in the cash disbursements journal as they are prepared?
7. Are all supporting documents properly cancelled at the time the checks are signed?
8. Is the custody of checks after signature and before mailing handled by an employee independent of all payable, disbursing, cash, and general ledger functions?

Required

a. For each of the preceding questions, state the transaction-related audit objective(s) being fulfilled if the control is in effect.
b. For each internal control, list a test of control to test its effectiveness.
c. For each of the preceding questions, identify the nature of the potential financial misstatement(s) if the control is not in effect.
d. For each of the potential misstatements in part c., list a substantive audit procedure that can be used to determine whether a material misstatement exists.

18-20 **(OBJECTIVE 18-3)** The following audit procedures are included in the audit program for the audit of the financial statements of Golden State Overnight Express:

1. Select a sample of acquisitions from the acquisitions journal and perform the following:
   a. Vouch the transaction to the voucher package that includes the matched receiving report, purchase order, and vendor invoice.
   b. Verify that the purchase order was approved by an authorized purchasing agent.
   c. Verify that the initials of an accounts payable clerk are present, indicating that the documents have been appropriately matched and that amounts on the vendor invoice were verified.
   d. Recalculate the invoice amount and compare the dollar amounts per the invoice to the amount recorded in the acquisitions journal.
   e. Examine whether the transaction was recorded to the correct vendor in the accounts payable master file.
   f. Determine if the transaction was recorded in the correct month, based on when the goods were received and the terms of the transaction.
   g. Review the chart of accounts to determine if the transaction was charged to the appropriate general ledger account.
2. Discuss with the accounts payable personnel the nature of procedures they perform when matching acquisitions documentation and discuss the types of discrepancies they typically find and how those are resolved.

3. Scan the acquisitions journal for any unusual entries and investigate those noted.
4. Foot the acquisitions journal for two months of the year and determine that amounts were correctly recorded in the general ledger accounts.
5. Trace a sample of voucher packages to the acquisitions journal throughout the year to determine that the transaction is included in the acquisitions journal.

Required

For each of the above procedures (consider 1.a. through 1.g. as separate procedures), perform the following:

a. Identify the type of audit evidence used for each procedure.
b. Identify the transaction-related audit objective(s) satisfied by each procedure.
c. Identify whether the procedure is a test of control or substantive test of transaction.

18-21 **(OBJECTIVE 18-3)** Donnen Designs, Inc., is a small manufacturer of women's casual-wear jewelry, including bracelets, necklaces, earrings, and other moderately priced accessory items. Most of their products are made from silver, various low-cost stones, beads, and other decorative jewelry pieces. Donnen Designs is not involved in the manufacturing of high-end jewelry items, such as those made of gold and semiprecious or precious stones.

Personnel responsible for purchasing raw material jewelry items for Donnen Designs would like to place orders directly with suppliers who offer their products for sale through Internet Web sites. Most suppliers provide pictures of all jewelry components on their Web sites, along with pricing and other sales-term information. Customers who have valid business licenses are able to purchase the products at wholesale, rather than retail prices. Customers can place orders online and pay for those goods immediately by using a valid credit card. Purchases made by credit card are shipped by the suppliers after the credit approval is received from the credit card agency, which usually occurs the same day. Customers can also place orders online with payment being made later by check. However, in that event, purchases are not shipped until the check is received and cashed by the supplier. Some of the suppliers allow a 30-day, full-payment refund policy, whereas other suppliers accept returns but only grant credit toward future purchases from that supplier.

Required

a. Identify advantages for Donnen Designs if management allows purchasing personnel to order goods online through supplier Web sites.
b. Identify potential risks associated with Donnen Designs' purchase of jewelry pieces through supplier Internet Web sites.
c. Describe advantages of allowing purchasing agents to purchase products online using a Donnen Designs credit card.
d. Describe advantages of allowing purchasing agents to purchase products online with payment made only by check.
e. What internal controls can be implemented to ensure that
   (1) purchasing agents do not use Donnen credit cards to purchase nonjewelry items for their own purposes, if Donnen allows purchasing agents to purchase jewelry using Donnen credit cards?
   (2) purchasing agents do not order jewelry items from the suppliers and ship those items to addresses other than Donnen addresses?
   (3) Donnen does not end up with unused credits with jewelry suppliers as a result of returning unacceptable jewelry items to suppliers who only grant credit toward future purchases?

18-22 **(OBJECTIVES 18-2, 18-3, 18-5)** Data analytics is a powerful tool in fraud detection and is often used to search for signs of fraud in the purchasing function. To learn more about data analytics as a fraud detection tool in purchasing, visit the *Fraud Magazine* Web site (www.fraud-magazine.com) and search for the January 2013 article "Devil in the details: anti-fraud data analytics."

Required

a. The article discusses a purchasing fraud that occurred in a state government agency. What was the nature of the internal controls over the purchasing function in the agency that provided the opportunity for fraud to occur? What were the incentives of the purchasing department to commit the fraud?
b. How can data analytics tools be used to detect fraud in the purchasing function?

c. Describe three analyses a fraud examiner could perform to detect fraud related to a particular vendor (e.g., calculate year-to-year percentage changes in total purchases from each vendor).

18-23 (OBJECTIVES 18-3, 18-4) In testing cash disbursements for the Jay Klein Company, you obtained an understanding of internal control. The controls are reasonably good, and no unusual audit problems arose in previous years.

Although there are not many individuals in the accounting department, there is a reasonable separation of duties in the organization. There is a separate purchasing agent who is responsible for ordering goods and a separate receiving department that counts the goods when they are received and prepares receiving reports. There is a separation of duties between recording acquisitions and cash disbursements, and all information is recorded in the two journals independently. The controller reviews all supporting documents before signing the checks, and he immediately mails the checks to the vendors. Check copies are used for subsequent recording.

All aspects of internal control seem satisfactory to you, and you perform minimum tests of 25 transactions as a means of assessing control risk. In your tests, you discover the following exceptions:

1. One check amount in the cash disbursements journal was for $100 less than the amount stated on the vendor's invoice.
2. One voided check was missing.
3. One invoice was paid twice. The second payment was supported by a duplicate copy of the invoice. Both copies of the invoice were marked "paid."
4. Two items in the acquisitions journal were misclassified.
5. Three invoices were not initialed by the controller, but there were no dollar misstatements evident in the transactions.
6. Five receiving reports were recorded in the acquisitions journal at least two weeks later than their date on the receiving report.
7. Two receiving reports for vendors' invoices were missing from the transaction packets. One vendor's invoice had an extension error, and the invoice was initialed that the amount had been checked.

Required

a. Identify whether each of 1 through 7 is a control test deviation, a monetary misstatement, or both.
b. For each exception, identify which transaction-related audit objective was not met.
c. What is the audit importance of each of these exceptions?
d. What follow-up procedures would you use to determine more about the nature of each exception?
e. How would each of these exceptions affect the rest of your audit? Be specific.
f. Identify internal controls that should have prevented each misstatement.

18-24 (OBJECTIVES 18-3, 18-6) The following misstatements are included in the accounting records of Westgate Manufacturing Company.

1. The accounts payable clerk intentionally excluded from the cash disbursements journal seven large checks written and mailed on December 26 to prevent cash in the bank from having a negative balance on the general ledger. They were recorded on January 2 of the subsequent year.
2. Acquisitions of raw materials are often not recorded until several weeks after the goods are received because receiving personnel fail to forward receiving reports to accounting. When pressure from a vendor's credit department is put on Westgate's accounting department, it searches for the receiving report, records the transactions in the acquisitions journal, and pays the bill.
3. Each month, a fraudulent receiving report is submitted to accounting by an employee in the receiving department. A few days later, he sends Westgate an invoice for the quantity of goods ordered from a small company he owns and operates in the evening. A check is prepared, and the amount is paid when the receiving report and the vendor's invoice are matched by the accounts payable clerk.
4. Telephone expense (account 2112) was unintentionally charged to repairs and maintenance (account 2121).

5. The accounts payable clerk prepares a monthly check to Story Supply Company for the amount of an invoice owed and submits the unsigned check to the treasurer for payment along with related supporting documents that have already been approved. When she receives the signed check from the treasurer, she records it as a debit to accounts payable and deposits the check in a personal bank account for a company named Story Company. A few days later, she records the invoice in the acquisitions journal again, resubmits the documents and a new check to the treasurer, and sends the check to the vendor after it has been signed.
6. The amount of a check in the cash disbursements journal is recorded as $4,612.87 instead of $6,412.87.

Required

a. For each misstatement, identify the transaction-related audit objective that was not met.
b. For each misstatement, state a control that should have prevented it from occurring on a continuing basis.
c. For each misstatement, state a substantive audit procedure that could uncover it.

18-25 (OBJECTIVES 18-5, 18-6, 18-7) The following auditing procedures were performed in the audit of accounts payable:

1. Obtain a list of accounts payable. Re-add and compare with the general ledger.
2. Trace from the general ledger trial balance and supporting documentation to determine whether accounts payable, related parties, and other related assets and liabilities are properly included on the financial statements.
3. Calculate the ratio of purchases to accounts payable and compare to the same ratio from the prior year.
4. For liabilities that are payable in a foreign currency, determine the exchange rate and check calculations.
5. Discuss with the bookkeeper whether any amounts included on the accounts payable list are due to related parties, debit balances, or notes payable.
6. Obtain vendors' statements from the controller and reconcile them to the listing of accounts payable.
7. Obtain vendors' statements directly from vendors and reconcile them to the listing of accounts payable.
8. Examine supporting documents for cash disbursements several days before and after year-end.
9. Examine the acquisitions and cash disbursements journals for the last few days of the current period and first few days of the succeeding period, looking for large or unusual transactions.

Required

a. For each procedure, identify the type of audit evidence used.
b. For each procedure, identify which balance-related audit objective(s) was/were satisfied.
c. Evaluate the need to have certain objectives satisfied by more than one audit procedure.

18-26 (OBJECTIVES 18-3, 18-6) The Broughton Cap Company requires that prenumbered receiving reports be completed when purchased inventory items arrive in the receiving department. At the time of receipt, the receiving clerk writes the date of receipt on the receiving document. The last receipt in the fiscal year ended June 30, 2016, was recorded on receiving report 7279. The accounts payable department prepares prenumbered voucher packages as receiving reports are received from the receiving department. Entries in the acquisitions journal are prepared using information contained in the voucher package.

For late June 2016 and early July 2016, receipts of goods are included in voucher packages as follows:

Receiving Report No.	Voucher No.
7276	2532
7277	2526
7278	2527
7279	2530
7280	2531

Receiving Report No.	Voucher No.
7281	2528
7282	2529

The June 2016 and July 2016 acquisitions journals included the following information:

Acquisitions Journal–June 2016

Day of Month	Voucher No.	Amount of Purchase
29	2526	$7,256.22
29	2528	$3,466.10
30	2531	$8,221.89
30	2532	$1,980.44

Acquisitions Journal–July 2016

Day of Month	Voucher No.	Amount of Purchase
1	2527	$5,001.99
1	2529	$4,888.33
2	2530	$1,933.74

Required

a. Which voucher packages, if any, are recorded in the wrong accounting period? Prepare an adjusting entry to correct the financial statements for the year ended June 30, 2016. Assume Broughton uses a perpetual inventory system and all purchases are inventory items.

b. Assume the receiving clerk accidentally wrote June 30 on receiving reports 7280 through 7282. Explain how that will affect the correctness of the financial statements. How will you, as an auditor, discover that error?

c. Describe, in general terms, the audit procedures you would follow in making sure that cutoff for purchases is accurate at the balance sheet date.

d. Identify internal controls that will reduce the likelihood of cutoff misstatements related to purchases.

18-27 **(OBJECTIVE 18-6)** You were in the final stages of your audit of the financial statements of Ozine Corporation for the year ended December 31, 2016, when you were consulted by the corporation's president, who believes there is no point to your examining the year 2017 acquisitions journal and testing data in support of year 2017 entries. He stated that (a) bills pertaining to 2016 that were received too late to be included in the December acquisitions journal were recorded as of the year-end by the corporation by journal entry, (b) the internal auditor made tests after the year-end, and (c) he will furnish you with a letter certifying that there were no unrecorded liabilities.

Required

a. Should a CPA's test for unrecorded liabilities be affected by the fact that the client made a journal entry to record 2016 bills that were received late? Explain.

b. Should a CPA's test for unrecorded liabilities be eliminated or reduced because of the internal audit tests? Explain.

c. Should a CPA's test for unrecorded liabilities be affected by the fact that a letter is obtained in which a responsible management official certifies that to the best of his or her knowledge, all liabilities have been recorded? Explain.

d. Assume that the corporation, which handled some government contracts, had no internal auditor but that an auditor for a federal agency spent three weeks auditing the records and was just completing his work at this time. How will the CPA's unrecorded liability test be affected by the work of the auditor for a federal agency?

e. What sources in addition to the year 2017 acquisitions journal should the CPA consider to locate possible unrecorded liabilities?*

18-28 **(OBJECTIVE 18-3)** Even though Bergeron Wholesale Company is privately held, management has decided that it is worthwhile to have effective internal controls to the extent

* Based on AICPA question paper, American Institute of Certified Public Accountants.

it is practical in a small company, as a way to reduce the likelihood of error and fraud. They have implemented the following system for acquisitions and payments.

Prenumbered purchase orders are approved and initialed by the vice president of finance for all purchases, including both tangible and service acquisitions. When goods are received, the goods are counted and a prenumbered receiving report is prepared with a copy sent to accounting. The goods are stored in the warehouse under the control of the shipping manager. The receiving report is used to update the perpetual records, which include only quantities and are used to determine the need to reorder goods and for control over the physical quantities of inventory. When a vendor's invoice is received, the chief accountant compares it to the purchase order and, for tangible goods, the receiving report, for both accuracy and appropriateness of the expenditure, and then staples the documents and initials each vendor's invoice. She then records the transaction in the purchases journal and related records using small business accounting software. Password protection is used for all records to prevent unauthorized access.

The chief accountant prepares the checks and updates the cash disbursements journal using the same accounting software and submits the checks to Bergeron's president for signature along with all supporting documentation. The president reviews and initials all support before signing checks and mails them to vendors on his way home from work. The controller receives the monthly bank reconciliation directly from the bank and does a detailed reconciliation, including examining cancelled checks and supporting documentation for larger and unusual amounts. The controller also receives the monthly accounts payable listing from the chief accountant, compares the total to the general ledger, initials the listing, and files it. Once each quarter the inventory is counted and compared to the perpetual records, both as a check on record keeping and to determine if there are inventory losses. Differences are listed, used for discussion with the controller and shipping manager, and filed.

Required

a. List at least ten internal controls in the Bergeron acquisition and payment cycle. Be as specific as possible.
b. For each control, identify the transaction-related audit objective(s) to which the control relates.
c. For each control, list one test of control that is useful to test the effectiveness of the control. Be as specific as possible.

18-29 **(OBJECTIVE 18-7)** As part of the June 30, 2016, audit of accounts payable of Milner Products Company, the auditor sent 22 confirmations of accounts payable to vendors in the form of requests for statements. Four of the statements were not returned by the vendors, and five vendors reported balances different from the amounts recorded in Milner's accounts payable master file. The auditor made duplicate copies of the five vendors' statements to maintain control of the independent information and turned the originals over to the client's accounts payable clerk to reconcile the differences. Two days later, the clerk returned the five statements to the auditor with the information on the audit schedule following part c.

Required

a. Evaluate the acceptability of having the client perform the reconciliations, assuming that the auditor intends to perform adequate additional tests.
b. Describe the additional tests that should be performed for each of the five statements that included differences.
c. What audit procedures should be performed for the nonresponses to the confirmation requests?

Statement 1	Balance per vendor's statement	$ 6,618.01
	Payment by Milner on June 30, 2016	(4,601.01)
	Balance per master file	$ 2,017.00
Statement 2	Balance per vendor's statement	$26,251.80
	Balance per master file	(20,516.11)
	Difference cannot be located because the vendor failed to provide details of its account balance	$ 5,735.69
Statement 3	Balance per vendor's statement	$ 6,170.15
	Credit memo issued by vendor on July 15, 2016	(2,360.15)
	Balance per master file	$ 3,810.00

Statement 4	Balance per vendor's statement	$ 8,619.21
	Payment by Milner on July 3, 2016	(3,000.00)
	Unlocated difference not followed up because of minor amount	215.06
	Balance per master file	$ 5,834.27
Statement 5	Balance per vendor's statement	$ 9,618.93
	Invoices not received by Milner	(2,733.18)
	Payment by Milner on June 15, 2016	(1,000.00)
	Balance per master file	$ 5,885.75

CASE

18-30 **(OBJECTIVES 18-2, 18-3, 18-4, 18-6)** The following tests of controls and substantive tests of transactions audit procedures for acquisitions and cash disbursements are to be used in the audit of Ward Publishing Company. You concluded that internal control appears effective and a reduced assessed control risk is likely to be cost beneficial. Ward's active involvement in the business, good separation of duties, and a competent controller and other employees are factors affecting your opinion.

Ward Publishing Company—Part I
(See p. 635 for Part II, and Case 19-26 on p. 659 for Part III)

Tests of Controls and Substantive Tests of Transactions Audit Procedures for Acquisitions and Cash Disbursements

1. Foot and cross-foot the acquisitions and cash disbursements journals for two months and trace totals to postings in the general ledger.
2. Scan the acquisitions and cash disbursements journals for all months and investigate any unusual entries.
3. Reconcile cash disbursements per books to cash disbursements per bank statement for one month.
4. Examine evidence that the bank reconciliation is prepared by the controller.
5. Inquire and observe whether the accounts payable master file balances are periodically reconciled to vendors' statements by the controller.
6. Examine evidence that the numerical sequence of checks is accounted for by someone independent of the preparation function.
7. Inquire and observe that checks are mailed by D. Ward or someone under his supervision after he signs checks.
8. Examine initials indicating that the controller balances the accounts payable master file to the general ledger monthly.
9. Select a sample of entries in the cash disbursements journal, and
   a. obtain related cancelled checks and compare with entry for payee, date, and amount and examine signature endorsement.
   b. obtain vendors' invoices, receiving reports, and purchase orders, and
      (1) determine that supporting documents are attached to vendors' invoices.
      (2) determine that documents agree with the cash disbursements journal.
      (3) compare vendors' names, amounts, and dates with entries.
      (4) determine whether a discount was taken when appropriate.
      (5) examine vendors' invoices for initials indicating an independent review of chart of account codings.
      (6) examine reasonableness of cash disbursements and account codings.
      (7) review invoices for approval of acquisitions by Ward.
      (8) review purchase orders and/or purchase requisitions for proper approval.
      (9) verify prices and recalculate footings and extensions on invoices.
      (10) compare quantities and descriptions on purchase orders, receiving reports, and vendors' invoices to the extent applicable.
      (11) examine vendors' invoices and receiving reports to determine that the check numbers are included and the documents are marked "paid" at the time of check signing.
   c. Trace postings to the accounts payable master file for name, amount, and date.

10. Select a sample of receiving reports issued during the year and trace to vendors' invoices and entries in the acquisitions journal.
    a. Compare type of merchandise, name of vendor, date received, quantities, and amounts.
    b. If the transaction is indicated in the acquisitions journal as paid, trace the check number to the entry in the cash disbursements journal. If unpaid, investigate reasons.
    c. Trace transactions to accounts payable master file, comparing name, amount, and date.

Required

Prepare all parts of a sampling data sheet (such as the one in Figure 15-2 on p. 494) through the planned sample size for the preceding audit program, assuming that a line item in the cash disbursements journal is used for the sampling unit. Use either nonstatistical or attributes sampling. For all procedures for which the line item in the cash disbursements journal is not an appropriate sampling unit, assume that audit procedures were performed on a nonsampling basis. For all tests of controls, use a tolerable exception rate of 5%, and for all substantive tests of transactions, use a rate of 6%. Use an ARO of 10%, which is considered medium. Plan for an estimated population exception rate of 1% for tests of controls and 0% for substantive tests of transactions.

Prepare the data sheet using the computer (instructor option—also applies to Part II).

Part II

Assume a sample size of 50 for all procedures, regardless of your answers in Part I. For other procedures, assume that an adequate sample size for the circumstance was selected. The only exceptions in your audit tests for all tests of controls and substantive tests of transactions audit procedures are as follows:

1. Procedure 2—Two large transactions were identified as being unusual. Investigation determined that they were authorized acquisitions of fixed assets. They were both correctly recorded.
2. Procedure 9b(1)—A purchase order was not attached to a vendor's invoice. The purchase order was found in a separate file and determined to be approved and appropriate.
3. Procedure 9b(5)—Six vendors' invoices were not initialed as being internally verified. Three actual misclassifications existed. The controller explained that he often did not review codings because of the competence of the accounting clerk doing the coding and was surprised at the mistakes.

Required

a. Complete the sampling data sheet from Part I using either nonstatistical or attributes sampling.
b. Explain the effect of the exceptions on tests of details of accounts payable. Which balance-related audit objectives are affected, and how do those objectives, in turn, affect the audit of accounts payable?
c. Given your tests of controls and substantive tests of transactions results, write an audit program for tests of details of balances for accounts payable. Assume:
    (1) The client provided a list of accounts payable, prepared from the master file.
    (2) Acceptable audit risk for accounts payable is high.
    (3) Inherent risk for accounts payable is low.
    (4) Substantive analytical procedure results were excellent.

CHAPTER

19

COMPLETING THE TESTS IN THE ACQUISITION AND PAYMENT CYCLE: VERIFICATION OF SELECTED ACCOUNTS

LEARNING OBJECTIVES

After studying this chapter, you should be able to

19-1 Recognize the many accounts in the acquisition and payment cycle.

19-2 Design and perform audit tests of property, plant, and equipment and related accounts.

19-3 Design and perform audit tests of prepaid expenses.

19-4 Design and perform audit tests of accrued liabilities.

19-5 Design and perform audit tests of income and expense accounts.

Incorrect Classifications Hide a Greater Net Loss

TV Communications Network (TVCN), a Denver-based wireless cable television company, materially understated losses in its financial statements by improperly recording $2.5 million of expenses as a direct decrease in stockholders' equity. The misstatement took the company from an actual net loss of $4.7 million to a reported loss of only $2.2 million.

According to the investigation by the SEC, the expenses charged to equity were from disbursements for the development and distribution of brochures promoting the company's business prospects. The payments should have been expensed and reflected in the income statement as advertising expenses.

The internal controls associated with the advertising expenses were clearly inadequate. TVCN typically did not have invoices or other documentation available when payments were made by the company's president, who controlled the bank account. Because of the lack of adequate documentation, when the financial statements were prepared, TVCN employees responsible for recording the expenses did not have sufficient information to properly classify the disbursements. The SEC found that even when documentation was available, the accounts where the transactions were recorded conflicted with the supporting documentation.

Unfortunately, TVCN's auditor relied on inquiry of the company president as the primary evidence about the nature of the advertising payments. In substantive testing of transactions exceeding $10,000, the auditor relied on the company controller to identify all transactions meeting the criteria for review. Needless to say, the controller did not present all transactions meeting the $10,000 scope. As you might expect, the SEC brought charges against the auditor for failing to comply with auditing standards.

Source: Based on *Accounting and Auditing Enforcement Release No. 534*, Commerce Clearing House, Inc., Chicago.

In Chapter 18, we noted that transactions in the acquisition and payment cycle affect several asset accounts: supplies, property, plant and equipment, and prepaid expenses accounts, to name a few. Payments made for services also affect many expense accounts. To continue our discussion of the acquisition and payment cycle, this chapter examines audit issues related to other accounts commonly found in the acquisition and payment cycles of most businesses.

The story about TVCN highlights the importance of understanding the nature of acquisition and payment cycle transactions. Because transactions in this cycle affect numerous accounts in both the balance sheet and the income statement, incorrectly classified transactions may significantly affect reported results, as they did for TVCN. Auditors need to understand the nature of transactions flowing through the acquisition and payment cycle so that they can effectively assess the risk of material misstatement and perform further audit procedures to evaluate accounts in the cycle.

TYPES OF OTHER ACCOUNTS IN THE ACQUISITION AND PAYMENT CYCLE

OBJECTIVE 19-1

Recognize the many accounts in the acquisition and payment cycle.

Table 19-1 highlights many of the typical accounts associated with transactions in the acquisition and payment cycle. The types of assets, expenses, and liabilities will differ for many companies, especially those in industries other than retail, wholesale, and manufacturing.

The methodology associated with auditing these accounts is similar to the audits of other accounts discussed in earlier chapters. The methodology is the same as Figure 18-3 on page 617 for accounts payable, except for the name of the account being audited.

The previous chapter presented an overview of typical tests of controls and substantive tests of transactions for acquisition and payment cycle transactions, as well as commonly used analytical procedures and tests of details of balances for accounts payable. In this chapter, the issues for some of the other key accounts in this cycle are examined, namely the audit of:

- Property, plant, and equipment
- Prepaid expenses
- Other liabilities
- Income and expense accounts

AUDIT OF PROPERTY, PLANT, AND EQUIPMENT

OBJECTIVE 19-2

Design and perform audit tests of property, plant, and equipment and related accounts.

Property, plant, and equipment are assets that have expected lives of more than one year, are used in the business, and are not acquired for resale. The intent to use the assets as part of the operation of the client's business and their expected lives of more than one year are the significant characteristics that distinguish these assets from inventory, prepaid expenses, and investments. Table 19-2 on the next page shows

TABLE 19-1 Accounts Typically Associated with Acquisition and Payment Cycle Transactions

Assets	Expenses	Liabilities
Cash	Cost of goods sold	Accounts payable
Inventory	Rent expense	Rent payable
Supplies	Property taxes	Accrued professional fees
Property, plant, and equipment	Income tax expense	Accrued property taxes
Patents, trademarks, and copyrights	Insurance expense	Other accrued expenses
Prepaid rent	Professional fees	Income taxes payable
Prepaid taxes	Retirement benefits	
Prepaid insurance	Utilities	

TABLE 19-2 Classifications of Property, Plant, and Equipment Accounts
Land and land improvements
Buildings and building improvements
Equipment
Furniture, computers, and fixtures
Autos and trucks
Leasehold improvements
Construction-in-process for property, plant, and equipment

examples of some of the typical classifications of property, plant, and equipment accounts. The acquisition of property, plant, and equipment occurs through the acquisition and payment cycle.

Because the audits of property, plant, and equipment accounts are similar, one example (equipment) is used to illustrate an approach to auditing all three types of accounts. Significant differences in the verification of the other two types of accounts are discussed as they arise.

Overview of Equipment-Related Accounts

The accounts commonly used for equipment are illustrated in Figure 19-1. Notice that the debits to equipment arise from the acquisition and payment cycle. Because the source of debits in the asset account is the acquisitions journal, the accounting system has normally already been tested for recording current period additions to equipment as part of the tests of the acquisition and payment cycle (which we studied in the previous chapter). However, because equipment additions are infrequent, often for large amounts, and subject to special controls, such as board of directors' approval, the auditor may decide not to rely heavily on these tests as evidence supporting fixed asset additions.

The primary accounting record for equipment and other property, plant, and equipment accounts is generally a **fixed asset master file**. The master file includes a detailed record for each piece of equipment and other types of property owned. Each record in the file includes a description of the asset, date of acquisition, original cost, current year depreciation, and accumulated depreciation for the property.

The totals for all records in the master file equal the general ledger balances for the related accounts: equipment, depreciation expense, and accumulated depreciation. The master file also contains information about property acquired and disposed of during the year.

FIGURE 19-1 Equipment and Related Accounts

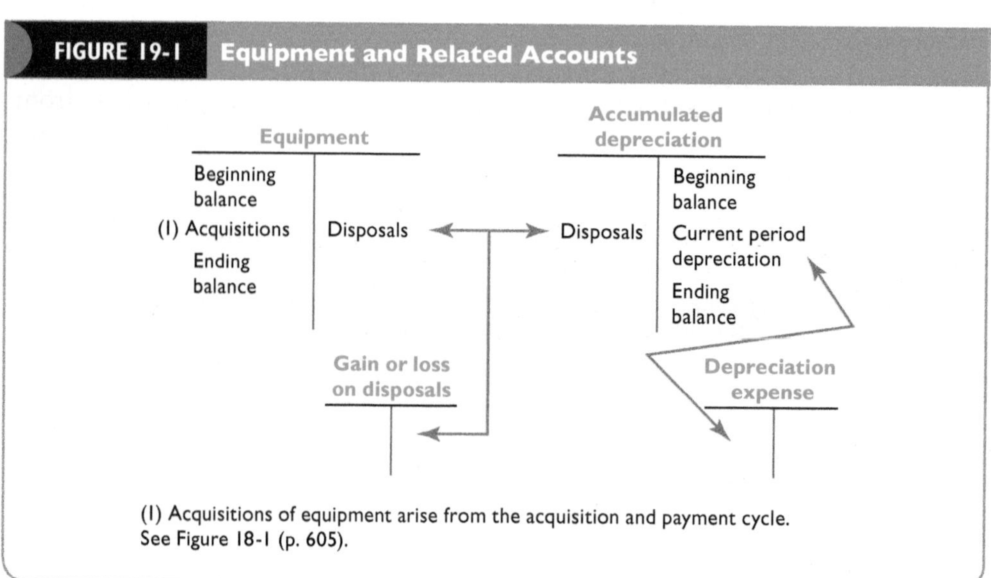

Auditors verify equipment differently from current asset accounts for three reasons:

1. There are usually fewer current period acquisitions of equipment, especially large equipment used in manufacturing.
2. The amount of any given acquisition is often material.
3. The equipment is likely to be kept and maintained in the accounting records for several years.

Because of these differences, the auditing of equipment emphasizes the verification of current period acquisitions rather than the balance in the account carried forward from the preceding year. In addition, the expected life of assets over one year requires depreciation expense and accumulated depreciation accounts, as shown in Figure 19-1, which are verified as part of the audit of the assets. Finally, equipment may be sold or disposed of, triggering a gain or loss entry that the auditor may need to verify.

Although the approach to verifying equipment differs from that used for current assets, several other asset accounts are verified in much the same manner. These include patents, copyrights, catalog costs, and all property, plant, and equipment accounts.

In the audit of equipment and related accounts, it is helpful to separate the tests into the following categories:

- Perform substantive analytical procedures
- Verify current year acquisitions
- Verify current year disposals
- Verify the ending balance in the asset account
- Verify depreciation expense
- Verify the ending balance in accumulated depreciation

Next, let's examine the use of these categories of tests in the audit of equipment, depreciation expense, accumulated depreciation, and gain or loss on disposal accounts.

Perform Substantive Analytical Procedures

As in all audit areas, the type of analytical procedures depends on the nature of the client's operations. Table 19-3 illustrates substantive analytical procedures often performed for equipment.

As you can see, most of the typical substantive analytical procedures are used to assess the likelihood of material misstatements in depreciation expense and accumulated depreciation. Later in the chapter, the substantive procedures auditors often use to test these accounts are discussed. The auditor may use substantive analytical procedures, tests of details of balances, or a combination of both types of tests to verify depreciation expense and accumulated depreciation.

Verify Current Year Acquisitions

Companies must correctly record current year additions because the assets have long-term effects on the financial statements. The failure to capitalize a fixed asset, or the recording of an acquisition at the incorrect amount, affects the balance sheet until the

TABLE 19-3 Substantive Analytical Procedures for Equipment

Substantive Analytical Procedure	Possible Misstatement
Compare depreciation expense divided by gross equipment cost with previous years.	Misstatement in depreciation expense and accumulated depreciation
Compare accumulated depreciation divided by gross equipment cost with previous years.	Misstatement in accumulated depreciation.
Compare monthly or annual repairs and maintenance, supplies expense, small tools expense, and similar accounts with previous years.	Expensing amounts that should be capitalized.
Compare gross manufacturing cost divided by some measure of production with previous years.	Idle equipment or equipment that was disposed of but not written off.

company disposes of the asset. The income statement is affected until the asset is fully depreciated.

Because of the importance of current period acquisitions in the audit of equipment, auditors use seven of the eight balance-related audit objectives as a frame of reference for tests of details of balances: existence, completeness, accuracy, classification, cutoff, detail tie-in, and rights and obligations. (Realizable value is discussed in connection with verifying ending balances.) The balance-related audit objectives and common audit tests are shown in Table 19-4. Existence, completeness, accuracy, classification, and rights are usually the major objectives for this part of the audit.

As in all other audit areas, the actual audit tests and sample size depend heavily on performance materiality, inherent risk, and assessed control risk. Performance materiality is important for verifying current year additions because these transactions vary from immaterial amounts in some years to a large number of significant acquisitions in others.

TABLE 19-4 Balance-Related Audit Objectives and Tests of Details of Balances for Equipment Additions

Balance-Related Audit Objective	Common Tests of Details of Balances Procedures	Comments
Current year acquisitions in the acquisitions schedule agree with related master file amounts, and the total agrees with the general ledger (detail tie-in).	Foot the acquisitions schedule. Trace the individual acquisitions to the master file for amounts and descriptions. Trace the total to the general ledger.	Footing the acquisitions schedule and tracing individual acquisitions should be limited unless controls are deficient. All increases in the general ledger balance for the year should reconcile to the schedule.
Current year acquisitions as listed exist (existence).	Examine vendors' invoices and receiving reports. Physically examine assets.	This objective is one of the most important for equipment. It is uncommon to physically examine assets acquired unless controls are deficient or amounts are material.
Existing acquisitions are recorded (completeness).	Examine vendors' invoices of closely related accounts such as repairs and maintenance to uncover items that should be recorded as equipment. Review lease and rental agreements.	This objective is important if there are significant repairs that may extend the life of assets, or if there have been trade-ins or disposals of assets.
Current year acquisitions as listed are accurate (accuracy).	Examine vendors' invoices.	Extent depends on inherent risk and effectiveness of internal controls.
Current year acquisitions as listed are correctly classified (classification).	Examine vendors' invoices in various equipment accounts to uncover items that should be classified as manufacturing or office equipment, part of the buildings, or repairs. Examine vendors' invoices of closely related accounts such as repairs to uncover items that should be recorded as equipment. Examine rent and lease expense for capitalizable leases.	The objective is closely related to tests for completeness. It is done in conjunction with that objective and tests for accuracy.
Current year acquisitions are recorded in the correct period (cutoff).	Review transactions near the balance sheet date for correct period.	Usually done as part of accounts payable cutoff tests.
The client has rights to current year acquisitions (rights).	Examine vendors' invoices.	Ordinarily the main concern is whether equipment is owned or leased. Purchase or lease contracts are examined for equipment; property deeds, abstracts, and tax bills are frequently examined for land or major buildings.

The starting point for the verification of current year acquisitions is normally a schedule obtained from the client of all acquisitions recorded in the general ledger property, plant, and equipment accounts during the year. The client obtains this information from the property master file. A typical schedule lists each addition separately and includes the date of the acquisition, vendor, description, notation of whether it is new or used, life of the asset for depreciation purposes, depreciation method, and cost.

As you study Table 19-4, notice that the most common audit test to verify additions is to examine vendors' invoices. Additional testing, beyond that which is done as part of the tests of controls and substantive tests of transactions, is often necessary because of the complexity of many equipment transactions and the materiality of the amounts. It is normal for auditors to verify large and unusual transactions for the entire year as well as a representative sample of typical additions. The extent of testing depends on the auditor's assessed control risk for acquisitions and the materiality of the additions.

In testing acquisitions, the auditor must understand accounting standards to make certain the client follows the related requirements. For example, the auditor needs to be alert for the possibility of the client's failure to include material transportation and installation costs as part of the asset's acquisition cost and the failure to properly record the trade-in of existing equipment. The auditor also needs to know the client's capitalization policies to determine whether acquisitions are treated consistently with those of the preceding year. For example, if the client's policy is to automatically expense acquisitions that are less than a certain amount, such as $1,000, the auditor should verify that the policy is followed in the current year.

Auditors should also verify recorded transactions for correct classification among various equipment accounts. In some cases, amounts recorded as manufacturing equipment should be classified as office equipment or as a part of the building. It is also possible the client has incorrectly capitalized repairs, rents, or similar expenses. Poor internal controls over document preparation, as illustrated by the chapter-opening story about TVCN, can result in significant misclassifications of disbursement transactions.

Clients commonly include transactions that should be recorded as assets in repairs and maintenance expense, lease expense, supplies, small tools, and similar accounts. The misstatement may result from a lack of understanding of accounting standards or from clients' desires to avoid income taxes. If auditors conclude that this type of material misstatement is likely, they may need to vouch larger amounts debited to the expense accounts. It is a common practice to do so as part of the audit of the property, plant, and equipment accounts.

Auditors also need to examine whether the client has a right to record equipment as an asset. Some large manufacturing equipment and other types of machinery, such as sophisticated medical equipment or computer data center equipment, may be under an operating lease. Auditors frequently examine purchase or lease contracts to determine whether capitalization of the equipment is appropriate.

Verify Current Year Disposals

Transactions involving the disposal of equipment are often misstated when company internal controls lack a formal method to inform management of the sale, trade-in, abandonment, or theft of recorded machinery and equipment. If the client fails to record disposals, the original cost of the equipment account will be overstated indefinitely, and net book value will be overstated until the asset is fully depreciated. Formal methods of tracking disposals and provisions for proper authorization of the sale or other disposal of equipment help reduce the risk of misstatement. There should also be adequate internal verification of recorded disposals to make sure that assets are correctly removed from the accounting records. The client should periodically take an inventory of fixed assets to identify assets that have been lost or stolen.

The auditor's main objectives in the verification of the sale, trade-in, or abandonment of equipment are to gather sufficient appropriate evidence that all disposals are recorded and at the correct amounts. The starting point for verifying disposals is the client's schedule of recorded disposals. The schedule typically includes the date when the asset was disposed of, name of the person or firm acquiring the asset, selling price, original cost, acquisition date, and accumulated depreciation.

Detail tie-in tests of the recorded disposals schedule are necessary, including footing the schedule, tracing the totals on the schedule to the recorded disposals in the general ledger, and tracing the cost and accumulated depreciation of the disposals to the property master file.

Because the failure to record disposals of equipment no longer used in the business can significantly affect the financial statements, *the search for unrecorded disposals is essential*. The nature and adequacy of the controls over disposals affect the extent of the search. The following procedures are often used for verifying disposals:

- Review whether newly acquired assets replace existing assets
- Analyze gains and losses on the disposal of assets and miscellaneous income for receipts from the disposal of assets
- Review plant modifications and changes in product line, and changes in major, costly computer-related equipment; property taxes; or insurance coverage for indications of deletions of equipment
- Make inquiries of management and production personnel about the possibility of the disposal of assets

When an asset is sold or disposed of without having been traded in for a replacement asset, the *accuracy* of the transaction can be verified by examining the related sales invoice and property master file. The auditor should compare the cost and accumulated depreciation in the master file with the recorded entry in the general journal and recompute the gain or loss on the disposal of the asset for comparison with the accounting records. When *trade-in of an asset for a replacement* occurs, the auditor should make sure that the new asset is capitalized and the replaced asset correctly eliminated from the records, considering the book value of the asset traded in and the additional cost of the new asset.

Verify Ending Balance of Asset Account

Two of the auditor's objectives when auditing the ending balance in the equipment accounts include determining that:

1. All recorded equipment physically exists on the balance sheet date (existence)
2. All equipment owned is recorded (completeness)

When designing audit tests to meet these objectives, auditors first consider the nature of internal controls over equipment. Ideally, auditors are able to conclude that controls are sufficiently effective to allow them to rely on balances carried forward from the prior year. Important controls include the use of a master file for individual fixed assets, adequate physical controls over assets that are easily movable (such as computers, tools, and vehicles), assignment of identification numbers to each plant asset, and periodic physical count of fixed assets and their reconciliation by accounting personnel. A formal method of informing the accounting department of all disposals of fixed assets is also an important control over the balance of assets carried forward into the current year.

Typically, the first audit step concerns the detail tie-in objective: Equipment, as listed in the master file, agrees with the general ledger. Examining the master file that totals to the general ledger balance is ordinarily sufficient. The auditor may choose to use audit software to foot an electronic version of the master file or manually test-foot a few pages.

After assessing control risk for the existence objective, the auditor decides whether it is necessary to verify the existence of individual items of equipment included in the master file. If there is a high likelihood of a material amount of missing fixed assets still included in the master file, the auditor can select a sample from the master file and examine the actual assets. Similarly, based on the auditor's assessment of control risk for the completeness objective, the auditor may physically examine a sample of major equipment items and trace them to the master file. In rare cases, the auditor may decide it is necessary for the client to take a complete physical inventory of fixed

ENERGY COMPANY AND ITS AUDITOR CHARGED WITH OVERSTATING FAIR VALUE OF PURCHASED OIL AND GAS PROPERTIES

Miller Energy was founded in 1967 as an oil and gas exploration and production company. It went public in 1996, and for most of the following decade it was a penny stock, trading at less than one dollar per share. Its stock fell as low as $0.04 per share in December 2007. In 2008, the company named a new CEO and began acquiring additional oil and gas properties.

In December 2009, Miller Energy acquired oil and gas properties in Alaska for $2.25 million and assumed $2 million in liabilities. The assets were owned by a California-based energy company that initially abandoned the assets as part of a bankruptcy proceeding after unsuccessfully attempting to sell the properties. In its quarterly report for the third quarter ended January 31, 2010, Miller Energy reported a value of $480 million for the Alaska acquisition, and reported an after-tax "bargain purchase gain" of $277 million. As a result of the transaction, the company reported net income for the quarter of $272 million, compared to the $556,097 loss reported for the third quarter in the prior year. By March 31, 2010, Miller Energy's stock price had increased to $6.60 per share, and it began trading on NASDAQ. A year later, the company moved to the NYSE, and reached an all-time-high price of $8.83 per share in December 2013.

Accounting standards require that acquisitions that involve a "bargain purchase"—that is, entities purchased at fire sale prices in non-orderly transactions—be measured at fair value, and any resulting gain should be recorded on the income statement. Miller Energy valued the oil and gas properties at $368 million using a reserve report prepared by a petroleum engineer. However, this report did not represent an acceptable method of determining fair value. In fact, the reserve report specifically indicated it should not be considered an estimate of fair value. In addition to the overstated petroleum assets, the company valued fixed assets at $110 million based on an "asset replacement cost study" purportedly prepared by an independent insurance broker. However, these assets were essentially double-counted because they were incorporated in the discounted cash flow model used to value the oil and gas properties.

Miller Energy's financial statements were audited by Sherb & Co. LLP. The now defunct CPA firm was suspended by the SEC for improper professional conduct unrelated to the Miller Energy audit. Carlton W. Vogt III was the partner on the Miller Energy audit engagement. The SEC charged that Vogt failed to perform the 2010 Miller Energy audit in accordance with PCAOB Auditing Standards. Deficiencies identified included failure to properly audit the fair value measurements, including failure to perform the necessary procedures to enable use of the findings of the reserve report. Vogt and his audit staff performed a limited evaluation of the petroleum engineer firm's work and its qualifications as a specialist (as a petroleum engineer, not as a fair value appraiser). The reserve report clearly stated that the engineer firm was not engaged to perform a fair value estimate.

Miller Energy has been delisted from the New York Stock Exchange. As it did before the purchase of the Alaska properties, Miller Energy again trades with the penny stocks on the over-the-counter listings.

Sources: 1. Securities and Exchange Commission Accounting and Auditing Enforcement Release No. 3673, August 6, 2015 (www.sec.gov); 2. Michael Cohn, "Miller Energy Execs Charged with Accounting Fraud" (August 6, 2015) (www.accountingtoday.com).

assets to make sure they all exist, and the fixed asset records are complete. If a physical inventory is taken, the auditor normally observes the count.

The auditor normally does not need to test the accuracy or classification of fixed assets recorded in prior periods because, presumably, they were verified in previous audits at the time they were acquired. But the auditor should be aware that companies may occasionally have equipment on hand that is no longer used in operations. If the amounts are material, the auditor should evaluate whether they should be written down to net realizable value (realizable value objective) or at least classified separately as "nonoperating equipment."

In addition to performing procedures to obtain evidence related to balance-related audit objectives for fixed assets, auditors also perform audit procedures related to the four presentation and disclosure objectives for fixed assets. A major consideration in verifying disclosures related to fixed assets is the possibility of *legal encumbrances* arising from use of fixed assets as collateral for a loan. Auditors may use several methods to determine whether equipment is encumbered, including:

- Read the terms of loan and credit agreements
- Send loan confirmation requests to banks and other lending institutions
- Have discussions with the client or send letters to legal counsel

The *proper presentation and disclosure* of equipment in the financial statements must be evaluated carefully to make sure that accounting standards are followed. Equipment should include the gross cost and should ordinarily be separated from other fixed assets. Leased property should also be disclosed separately, and all liens on property must be included in the footnotes. Auditors must perform sufficient tests to verify that all four presentation and disclosure objectives are met.

Verify Depreciation Expense

Depreciation expense is one of the few expense accounts not verified as part of tests of controls and substantive tests of transactions. The recorded amounts are determined by *internal allocations* rather than by exchange transactions with outside parties. When depreciation expense is material, more tests of details of depreciation expense are required than for an account that has already been verified through tests of controls and substantive tests of transactions.

The most important balance-related audit objective for depreciation expense is accuracy. Auditors focus on determining whether the client followed a *consistent depreciation policy* from period to period and whether the client's *calculations are correct.*

In determining the former, auditors must weigh four considerations:

1. The useful life of current period acquisitions
2. The method of depreciation
3. The estimated salvage value
4. The policy of depreciating assets in the year of acquisition and disposition

The client's policies can be determined by discussions with appropriate personnel and comparing their responses with information in the auditor's permanent files. In deciding on the reasonableness of the useful lives assigned to newly acquired assets, the auditor must consider the physical life of the asset, the expected life (taking into account obsolescence or the company's normal policy of upgrading equipment), and established company policies on trading in equipment.

Occasionally, changing circumstances may necessitate a company to reevaluate the useful life of an asset. When this occurs, the revaluation should involve a change in accounting estimate rather than a change in accounting principle. The effect of this on depreciation must be evaluated.

A useful method of auditing depreciation is a substantive analytical procedure performed by multiplying undepreciated fixed assets by the depreciation rate for the year. In making these calculations, the auditor must make adjustments for current year additions and disposals, assets with different lengths of life, and assets with different methods of depreciation. Many CPA firms maintain an electronic spreadsheet in their permanent file that includes a breakdown of the fixed assets by method of depreciation and length of life. If the auditor's expectation for depreciation is reasonably close to the client's totals, considering performance materiality and assessed control risk for depreciation expense, tests of details for depreciation can be eliminated.

When a substantive analytical procedure cannot be effectively performed or indicates a potential misstatement, more detailed tests are usually needed. To do this, auditors recompute depreciation expense for selected assets to determine whether the client is following a proper and consistent depreciation policy. To be relevant, the detailed calculations should be tied in to the total depreciation calculations by footing the depreciation expense on the property master file and reconciling the total with the general ledger. Because accounting standards require footnote disclosures related to fixed asset depreciation, including disclosure of depreciation methods and related useful lives by asset class, auditors perform procedures to obtain evidence that the four presentation and disclosure-related audit objectives for depreciation are satisfied. For example, auditors compare information obtained through audit tests of the depreciation expense accounts to information disclosed in footnotes to ensure the information presented is consistent with the actual method and assumptions used to calculate and record depreciation.

Verify Ending Balance in Accumulated Depreciation

The debits to accumulated depreciation are normally tested as a part of the audit of disposals of assets, while the credits are verified as a part of depreciation expense. If the auditor traces selected transactions to the accumulated depreciation records in the property master file as a part of these tests, then little additional testing should be required for the ending balance in accumulated depreciation.

Two objectives are usually emphasized in the audit of the ending balance in accumulated depreciation:

1. Accumulated depreciation as stated in the property master file agrees with the general ledger. This objective can be satisfied by test-footing the accumulated depreciation in the property master file and tracing the total to the general ledger.
2. Accumulated depreciation in the master file is accurate.

In some cases, the life of equipment may be significantly reduced because of reductions in customer demand for products, unexpected physical deterioration, a modification in operations, or other changes. Because of these possibilities, auditors must consider whether the value of the assets is impaired to make sure that the net book value does not exceed the realizable value of the assets.

CONCEPT CHECK

1. Explain why the emphasis in auditing property, plant, and equipment is on the current period acquisitions and disposals rather than on the balances in the account carried forward from the preceding year.
2. What is the most important balance-related audit objective for depreciation expense? What are the auditor's primary concerns?

AUDIT OF PREPAID EXPENSES

OBJECTIVE 19-3

Design and perform audit tests of prepaid expenses.

Prepaid expenses, deferred charges, and intangibles are assets that vary in life from several months to several years. These include:

- Prepaid rent
- Organization costs
- Prepaid taxes
- Patents
- Prepaid insurance
- Trademarks
- Deferred charges
- Copyrights
- Goodwill

In some cases, these accounts are highly material. However, in a typical audit, the company does not have many of the accounts listed or they are immaterial.

Substantive analytical procedures are often sufficient for prepaid expenses, deferred charges, and intangibles. In certain audits, some of these assets can be significant and involve complex judgment. For example, the audit of intangibles such as goodwill depends heavily on the auditor's knowledge of the nature of the client's business and industry, and requires testing of management's significant assumptions, its valuation model, and underlying data used as inputs to the model. Given the complexities of evaluating intangible assets, auditors frequently involve business valuation specialists who help evaluate whether the value of the intangible asset has been impaired.

In this section, we examine some of the typical internal controls and related audit tests commonly associated with prepaid expenses. In the following discussion, an example of the audit of prepaid insurance is used as an account representative of this group because:

1. Prepaid insurance is found in most audits—virtually every company has some type of insurance.
2. Problems commonly encountered in the audit of prepaid insurance are typical of this class of accounts.
3. The auditor's responsibility for the review of insurance coverage is an additional consideration not found in the other accounts in this category.

Overview of Prepaid Insurance

Figure 19-2 on the next page illustrates the accounts typically used for prepaid insurance and the relationship between prepaid insurance and the acquisition and payment cycle through the debits to the prepaid insurance account. Because the source of the

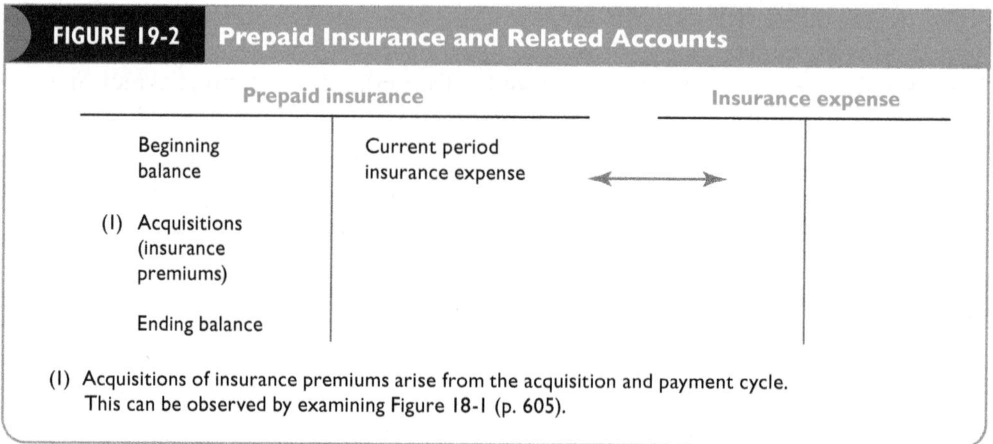

debits in the asset account is the acquisitions journal, the payments of insurance premiums have already been partially tested by means of the tests of controls and substantive tests of acquisition and cash disbursement transactions.

Internal Controls

Internal controls for prepaid insurance and insurance expense can be conveniently divided into three categories: controls over the acquisition and recording of insurance, controls over the insurance register, and controls over the charge-off of insurance expense. Controls over the acquisition and recording of insurance are a part of the acquisition and payment cycle. Consistent with the procedures discussed in that cycle, proper authorization for new insurance policies and payment of insurance premiums are important controls.

An **insurance register** is a record of insurance policies in force and the expiration date of each policy. Auditors use insurance registers to identify policies in force related to prepaid insurance accounts. Payment terms and amounts for the policies in force are contained in the register. Because the terms and amounts provide the basis for determining prepaid insurance amounts, the auditor independently verifies these terms and amounts to the underlying insurance policies or contracts.

Companies often have a standard monthly journal entry to reclassify prepaid insurance as insurance expense. If a significant entry is required to adjust the balance in prepaid insurance at the end of the year, it indicates a potential misstatement in the recording of the acquisition of insurance throughout the year or in the calculation of the year-end balance in prepaid insurance.

Audit Tests

In the audit of prepaid insurance, the auditor obtains a schedule from the client that lists for each policy in force:

- Policy information, including policy number, amount of coverage, and annual premium
- Beginning prepaid insurance balance
- Payment of policy premiums
- Amount charged to insurance expense
- Ending prepaid insurance balance

Throughout the audit of prepaid insurance and insurance expense, the auditor should keep in mind that the amount in insurance expense is a residual. The only tests of the balance in the expense account that are ordinarily necessary include substantive analytical procedures and a test to be sure that all charges to insurance expense arose from credits to prepaid insurance. Because the payments of premiums are tested as part of the tests of controls and substantive tests of transactions and analytical procedures, the emphasis in the tests of details of balances is on prepaid insurance.

The beginning and ending balances in prepaid insurance are frequently *immaterial* and often there are few transactions debited and credited to the balance during the year, most of which are small and simple to understand. Therefore, the auditor can generally spend little time verifying the balance or the transactions. If the auditor decides not to verify the balance in detail, substantive analytical procedures become increasingly important to identify potentially significant misstatements. Auditors commonly perform the following substantive analytical procedures for prepaid insurance and insurance expense:

- Compare total prepaid insurance and insurance expense with previous years.
- Compute the ratio of prepaid insurance to insurance expense and compare it with previous years.
- Compare the individual insurance policy coverage on the schedule of insurance obtained from the client with the preceding year's schedule as a test of the elimination of certain policies or a change in insurance coverage.
- Compare the computed prepaid insurance balance for the current year on a policy-by-policy basis with that of the preceding year as a test of an error in calculation.
- Review the *insurance coverage* listed on the prepaid insurance schedule with an appropriate client official or insurance broker for adequacy of coverage. The auditor cannot be an expert on insurance matters, but the auditor's understanding of accounting and the valuation of assets is necessary to make sure that a company is not underinsured.

For many audits, no additional substantive procedures are needed unless assessed control risk is high or the tests indicate a high likelihood of a significant misstatement. The remaining audit procedures, which are examined next, should be performed only when there is a special reason for doing so. Our discussion of these tests uses the balance-related audit objectives for performing tests of details of asset balances. (Realizable value is not applicable.)

Insurance Policies in the Prepaid Insurance Schedule Exist and Existing Policies Are Listed (Existence and Completeness) Tests for existence and omissions of insurance policies in force can be performed on the client's prepaid insurance schedule in one of two ways:

1. Examine a sample of insurance invoices and policies in force for comparison to the schedule.
2. Obtain a confirmation of insurance information from the company's insurance agent. Auditors typically prefer to send a confirmation to the client's insurance agent, because this approach is usually less time-consuming than vouching tests and it provides third-party verification.

The Client Has Rights to All Insurance Policies in the Prepaid Insurance Schedule (Rights) The party who will receive the benefit if an insurance claim is filed has the rights. Ordinarily, the recipient named in the policy is the client, but when there are mortgages or other liens, the insurance claim may be payable to a creditor. The review of insurance policies for claimants other than the client is an excellent test of unrecorded liabilities and pledged assets.

Prepaid Amounts on the Schedule Are Accurate and the Total Is Correctly Added and Agrees with the General Ledger (Accuracy and Detail Tie-in) Audit tests to verify the accuracy of prepaid insurance involve verifying the amount of the insurance premium, the length of the policy period, and the allocation of the premium to unexpired insurance. The amount of the premium for a given policy and its time period can be verified at the same time by examining the premium invoice or the confirmation from an insurance agent. After these two have been verified, the client's calculations of unexpired insurance can be tested by recalculation. The schedule of prepaid insurance can then be footed and the totals traced to the general ledger to complete the detail tie-in tests.

The Insurance Expense Related to Prepaid Insurance Is Correctly Classified (Classification) The correct classification of debits to different insurance expense accounts should be reviewed as a test of the income statement. In some cases, the appropriate expense account is obvious because of the type of insurance, such as a policy insuring a piece of equipment. In other cases, allocations are necessary. For example, fire insurance on a building may require allocation to several accounts, including manufacturing overhead. Charging the correct accounts and consistency with previous years are the major considerations in evaluating classification.

Insurance Transactions Are Recorded in the Correct Period (Cutoff) Cutoff for acquisitions of insurance is normally not a significant problem because of the small number of policies and the immateriality of the amount. If auditors check cutoff of insurance acquisitions, they do so as part of accounts payable cutoff tests.

AUDIT OF ACCRUED LIABILITIES

OBJECTIVE 19-4

Design and perform audit tests of accrued liabilities.

A third major category of accounts in the acquisition and payment cycle is **accrued liabilities**, which are the estimated unpaid obligations for services or benefits that have been received before the balance sheet date. Many accrued liabilities represent future obligations for unpaid services resulting from the passage of time but are not payable at the balance sheet date. For example, the benefits of property rental accrue throughout the year. Therefore, at the balance sheet date, a certain portion of the total rent cost that has not been paid should be accrued. Other similar liabilities include:

- Accrued payroll
- Accrued payroll taxes
- Accrued officers' bonuses
- Accrued commissions
- Accrued professional fees
- Accrued rent
- Accrued interest

A second type of accrual involves estimates where the amount of the obligation due is uncertain, such as the obligation for federal income taxes when there is a reasonable likelihood that the amount reported on the tax return will be changed after the Internal Revenue Service audits the return. Accrued warranty costs and accrued pension costs are similar accruals.

The verification of accrued expenses varies depending on the nature of the accrual and the circumstances of the client. For most audits, accruals take little audit time. In other instances, certain accounts, such as accrued income taxes, warranty costs, and pension costs, are often material and require considerable audit effort. The following discussion of the audit of accrued property taxes is used as an example of the audit of an accrued liability account.

Auditing Accrued Property Taxes

Figure 19-3 illustrates the accounts typically used by companies for accrued property taxes, showing the relationship between accrued property taxes and the acquisition and

FIGURE 19-3 Accrued Property Taxes and Related Accounts

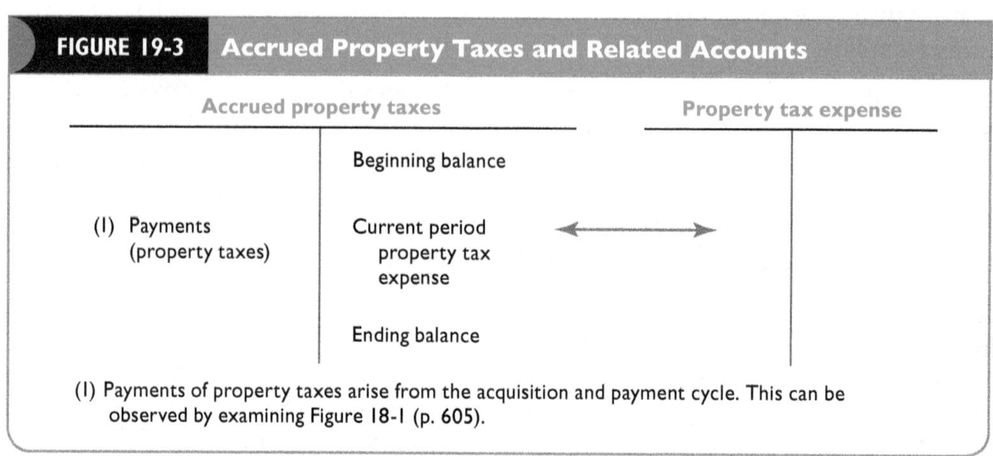

(1) Payments of property taxes arise from the acquisition and payment cycle. This can be observed by examining Figure 18-1 (p. 605).

payment cycle through the debits to the liability account. Because the source of the debits is the cash disbursements journal, the payments of property taxes should have already been partially tested by the tests of the acquisition and payment cycle transactions.

As with insurance expense, the balance in property tax expense is a residual amount that results from the beginning and ending balances in accrued property taxes and the payments of property taxes. Therefore, the emphasis in the tests should be on the ending property tax liability and payments. When auditors verify accrued property taxes, all eight balance-related audit objectives except realizable value are relevant. Two are especially significant:

1. Existing properties for which accrual of taxes is appropriate are on the accrual schedule. The failure to include properties for which taxes should be accrued will understate the property tax liability (completeness). A material misstatement can occur, for example, if taxes on property were not paid before the balance sheet date and not included as accrued property taxes.
2. Accrued property taxes are accurately recorded. The auditor's concern is the consistent treatment of the accrual from year to year (accuracy).

The auditor uses two primary tests for the inclusion of all accruals. Auditors verify the accruals at the same time as the audit of current year property tax payments. In most audits, there are few property tax payments, but each payment is often material, and therefore it is common to verify each one. Auditors also compare the accruals with those of previous years.

The auditor often begins by obtaining a schedule of property tax payments from the client and comparing each payment with the preceding year's schedule to determine whether all payments have been included in the client-prepared schedule. The fixed asset audit schedules also must be examined for major additions and disposals of assets that may affect the property tax accrual. All property affected by local property tax regulations should be included in the schedule, even if the first tax payment has not yet been made.

After auditors are satisfied that all taxable property has been included in the client-prepared schedule, they evaluate the reasonableness of property taxes on each property used by the client to estimate the accrual. In some instances, the total has already been set by the taxing authority and sent to the client, so it is possible to verify the amount by comparing the amount on the schedule with the tax bill. In other cases, the preceding year's total payments must be adjusted for the expected increase in property tax rates.

The auditor can verify the accrued property tax by recalculating the portion of the total tax applicable to the current year for each piece of property. The most important consideration is to use the same portion of each tax payment for the accrual that was used in the preceding year, unless there are justifiable conditions for a change. After the accrual and property tax expense for each piece of property have been recalculated, the totals should be added and compared with the general ledger. In many cases, property taxes are charged to more than one expense account. In that case, the auditor should test for correct classification by evaluating whether the correct amount was charged to each account.

AUDIT OF INCOME AND EXPENSE ACCOUNTS

OBJECTIVE 19-5

Design and perform audit tests of income and expense accounts.

To complete our discussion of key accounts in the acquisition and payment cycle, an overview is provided of procedures auditors typically use to determine whether the income and expense accounts in the financial statements are fairly presented in accordance with accounting standards. The auditor must be satisfied that each of the income and expense totals included in the income statement, as well as net earnings, are not materially misstated.

The auditor needs to be aware that most users of financial statements rely more heavily on the income statement than on the balance sheet for making decisions.

Equity investors, long-term creditors, union representatives, and even short-term creditors are more interested in the ability of a firm to generate profit than in the historical cost or book value of the individual assets.

The following two concepts in the audit of income and expense accounts are essential when considering the purposes of the income statement:

1. The matching of periodic income and expense is necessary for a correct determination of operating results.
2. The consistent application of accounting principles for different periods is necessary for comparability.

Both of these concepts must be applied to the recording of individual transactions and to the combining of accounts in the general ledger for statement presentation.

Approach to Auditing Income and Expense Accounts

The audit of income and expense accounts is directly related to the balance sheet and is not a separate part of the audit process. A misstatement of an income statement account almost always equally affects a balance sheet account, and vice versa. As we have discussed in preceding chapters, the audit of income and expense accounts is intertwined with the other parts of the audit. We provide a brief description of these tests here as a review of material covered in earlier chapters. This review shows the interrelated nature of different parts of the audit with income and expense account testing. The parts of the audit directly affecting these accounts are:

- Substantive analytical procedures
- Tests of controls and substantive tests of transactions
- Tests of details of account balances

Our emphasis here is on income and expense accounts directly related to the acquisition and payment cycle, but the same concepts apply to the income statement accounts in all other cycles.

Substantive Analytical Procedures

Chapter 8 addressed analytical procedures. Subsequent chapters refer back to those procedures as part of specific audit areas. Table 19-5 shows a few substantive analytical procedures and the possible misstatements they may uncover in the audit of income and expense accounts, as well as the related balance sheet accounts.

TABLE 19-5 Substantive Analytical Procedures for Income and Expense Accounts

Substantive Analytical Procedure	Possible Misstatement
Compare individual expenses with previous years.	Overstatement or understatement of a balance in an expense account.
Compare individual asset and liability balances with previous years.	Overstatement or understatement of a balance sheet account that will also affect an income statement account (for example, a misstatement of inventory affects cost of goods sold).
Compare individual expenses with budgets.	Misstatement of expenses and related balance sheet accounts.
Compare gross margin percentage with previous years.	Misstatement of cost of goods sold and inventory.
Compare inventory turnover ratio with previous years.	Misstatement of cost of goods sold and inventory.
Compare prepaid insurance expense with previous years.	Misstatement of insurance expense and prepaid insurance.
Compare commission expense divided by sales with previous years.	Misstatement of commission expense and accrued commissions.
Compare individual manufacturing expenses divided by total manufacturing expenses with previous years.	Misstatement of individual manufacturing expenses and related balance sheet accounts.

Tests of Controls and Substantive Tests of Transactions

Both tests of controls and substantive tests of transactions have the effect of simultaneously verifying balance sheet and income statement accounts. For example, assume an auditor concludes that internal controls are adequate to provide reasonable assurance that transactions in the acquisitions journal occurred and are accurately recorded, correctly classified, and recorded in a timely manner. By doing so, the auditor obtains evidence about the correctness of individual balance sheet accounts, such as accounts payable and fixed assets, and income statement accounts, such as advertising and repairs. Conversely, inadequate controls and misstatements discovered through tests of controls and substantive tests of transactions indicate the likelihood of misstatements in both the income statement and the balance sheet.

The most important means of verifying many of the income statement accounts in each transaction cycle are understanding internal control and performing the related tests of controls and substantive tests of transactions. For example, if the auditor concludes after adequate tests that control risk can be appropriately assessed as low for transactions in the acquisition and payment cycle, the only additional verification of related income statement accounts, such as utilities, advertising, and purchases, will occur through the performance of substantive analytical procedures and cutoff tests. However, certain income and expense accounts are not verified at all by tests of controls and substantive tests of transactions, and others must be tested more extensively by other substantive testing. These are discussed next.

Tests of Details of Account Balances—Expense Analysis

Auditors must analyze the amounts included in certain income statement accounts even though the previously mentioned tests have been performed. Next, we examine the meaning and methodology of analysis of accounts before moving on to a discussion of when expense account analysis is appropriate.

Expense account analysis involves auditor examination of underlying documentation of individual transactions and amounts making up the detail of the total of an expense account. The documents are the same type as those used for examining transactions as part of tests of acquisition transactions, including invoices, receiving reports, purchase orders, and contracts. Figure 19-4 (p. 652) illustrates a typical audit schedule showing expense analysis for legal expenses.

Although the focus of expense account analysis is on transactions, these tests differ from tests of controls and substantive tests of transactions. The tests of controls and substantive tests of transactions are meant to assess control risk. As such, they are tests of classes of transactions, such as acquisitions, and therefore include many different accounts. In the analysis of expense and other income statement accounts, the auditor verifies transactions in specific accounts to determine whether the transactions are appropriate for the client, properly classified, and accurately recorded.

Assuming satisfactory results are found in tests of controls and substantive tests of transactions, auditors normally restrict expense analysis to those accounts with a relatively high likelihood of material misstatement. As examples, auditors often analyze:

- Repairs and maintenance expense accounts to determine whether they erroneously include property, plant, and equipment transactions
- Rent and lease expenses to determine the need to capitalize leases
- Legal expense to determine whether there are potential contingent liabilities, disputes, illegal acts, or other legal issues that may affect the financial statements

Utilities, travel expense, and advertising accounts are rarely analyzed unless substantive analytical procedures indicate high potential for material misstatement.

Auditors often analyze expense account transactions as part of the verification of a related asset. It is common, for example, for auditors to analyze repairs and maintenance as part of verifying fixed assets, and insurance expense as part of testing prepaid insurance.

Tests of Details of Account Balances—Allocation

Several expense accounts result from the **allocation** of accounting data rather than discrete transactions. Such expenses include depreciation, depletion, and the amortization of

FIGURE 19-4 Expense Analysis for Legal Expense

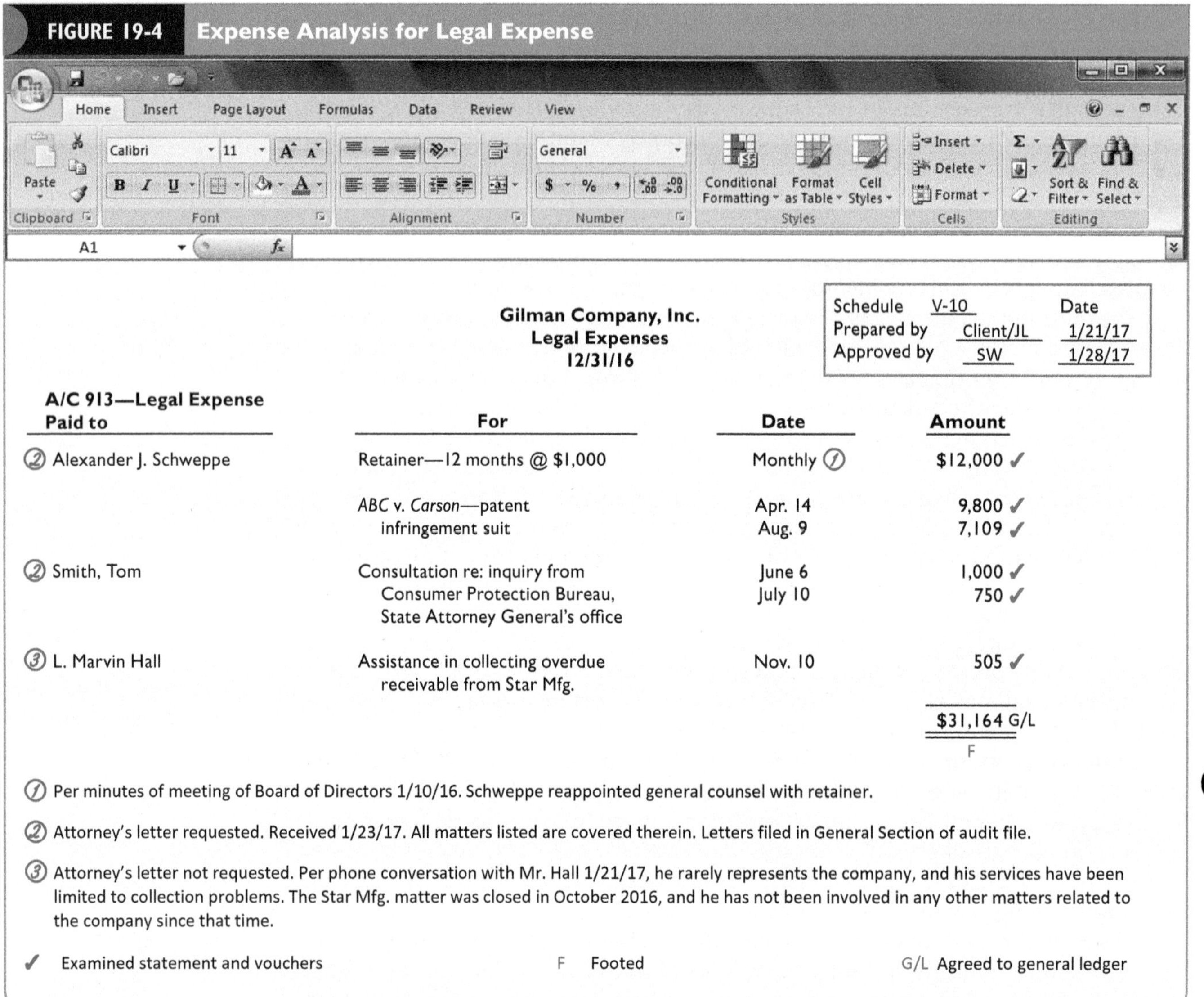

Gilman Company, Inc.
Legal Expenses
12/31/16

Schedule	V-10	Date
Prepared by	Client/JL	1/21/17
Approved by	SW	1/28/17

A/C 913—Legal Expense

Paid to	For	Date	Amount
(2) Alexander J. Schweppe	Retainer—12 months @ $1,000	Monthly (1)	$12,000 ✓
	ABC v. *Carson*—patent infringement suit	Apr. 14 Aug. 9	9,800 ✓ 7,109 ✓
(2) Smith, Tom	Consultation re: inquiry from Consumer Protection Bureau, State Attorney General's office	June 6 July 10	1,000 ✓ 750 ✓
(3) L. Marvin Hall	Assistance in collecting overdue receivable from Star Mfg.	Nov. 10	505 ✓
			$31,164 G/L F

(1) Per minutes of meeting of Board of Directors 1/10/16. Schweppe reappointed general counsel with retainer.

(2) Attorney's letter requested. Received 1/23/17. All matters listed are covered therein. Letters filed in General Section of audit file.

(3) Attorney's letter not requested. Per phone conversation with Mr. Hall 1/21/17, he rarely represents the company, and his services have been limited to collection problems. The Star Mfg. matter was closed in October 2016, and he has not been involved in any other matters related to the company since that time.

✓ Examined statement and vouchers F Footed G/L Agreed to general ledger

copyrights and catalog costs. The allocation of manufacturing overhead between inventory and cost of goods sold is an example of a different type of allocation that affects expenses.

Allocations are important because they determine whether an expenditure is an asset or a current period expense. If the client fails to follow accounting standards or fails to calculate the allocation correctly, the financial statements can be materially misstated. The allocation of expenses such as depreciation of fixed assets and amortization of copyrights is required because the life of the asset is greater than one year. The original cost of the asset is verified at the time of acquisition, but the charge-off takes place over several years.

Other types of allocations directly affecting the financial statements arise because the life of a short-lived asset does not expire on the balance sheet date. These may include prepaid rent and insurance. Finally, accounting standards require the allocation of costs between current period manufacturing expenses and inventory as a means of reflecting all costs of making a product.

In auditing the allocation of expenditures such as prepaid insurance and manufacturing overhead, the two most important considerations are adherence to accounting standards and consistency with the preceding period. The two most important audit procedures for auditing allocations are tests for overall reasonableness using substantive analytical procedures and recalculation of the client's results.

Auditors commonly perform these tests as part of the audit of the related asset or liability accounts. This may include verifying depreciation expense as part of the audit of property, plant, and equipment; testing amortization of patents as part of verifying new patents or the disposal of existing ones; and verifying allocations between inventory and cost of goods sold as part of the audit of inventory.

CONCEPT CHECK

1. Distinguish between the evaluation of the adequacy of insurance coverage and the verification of prepaid insurance. Explain which is more important in a typical audit.
2. In verifying accounts payable, it is common to restrict the audit sample to a small portion of the population items, whereas in auditing accrued property taxes, it is common to verify all transactions for the year. Explain the reason for the difference.
3. What is meant by the analysis of expense accounts? List four expense accounts that are commonly analyzed in audits.

SUMMARY

This chapter concludes our discussion of accounts and transactions in the acquisition and payment cycle. To adequately audit the numerous accounts associated with this cycle, auditors need an understanding of key accounts, classes of transactions, business functions, documents, and records related to acquisition and payment cycle transactions. Many of these accounts—such as accounts payable; property, plant, and equipment; depreciation expense; and prepaid expenses—have unique characteristics that affect how the auditor gathers sufficient appropriate evidence about related account balances. And, finally, interrelationships between different audit tests in the acquisition and payment cycle can provide a basis for the auditor's verification of many financial statement accounts.

ESSENTIAL TERMS

Accrued liabilities—estimated unpaid obligations for services or benefits that have been received prior to the balance sheet date; common accrued liabilities include accrued commissions, accrued income taxes, accrued payroll, and accrued rent

Allocation—the division of certain expenses, such as depreciation and manufacturing overhead, among several expense accounts

Expense account analysis—the examination of underlying documentation of individual transactions and amounts making up the total of an expense account

Fixed asset master file—a computer file containing records for each piece of equipment and other types of property owned; the primary accounting record for manufacturing equipment and other property, plant, and equipment accounts

Insurance register—a record of insurance policies in force, the expiration date of each policy, premium amount and terms, and other policy specifics

REVIEW QUESTIONS

19-1 (OBJECTIVE 19-1) Identify three asset accounts, three expense accounts, and three liability accounts typically associated with acquisition and payment cycle transactions.

19-2 (OBJECTIVE 19-2) Explain the relationship between substantive tests of transactions for the acquisition and payment cycle and tests of details of balances for the verification of property, plant, and equipment. Which aspects of property, plant, and equipment are directly affected by the tests of controls and substantive tests of transactions and which are not?

19-3 (OBJECTIVE 19-2) What is the relationship between the audit of property, plant, and equipment accounts and the audit of repair and maintenance accounts? Explain how the auditor organizes the audit to take this relationship into consideration.

19-4 **(OBJECTIVE 19-2)** List and briefly explain the purpose of all audit procedures that might reasonably be applied by an auditor to determine that all property, plant, and equipment retirements have been recorded in the accounting system.

19-5 **(OBJECTIVE 19-2)** Describe factors the auditor should consider in developing an expectation for depreciation while performing a substantive analytical procedure for depreciation expense.

19-6 **(OBJECTIVE 19-3)** Explain the relationship between substantive tests of transactions for the acquisition and payment cycle and tests of details of balances for the verification of prepaid insurance.

19-7 **(OBJECTIVE 19-3)** Explain why the audit of prepaid insurance should ordinarily take a relatively small amount of audit time if the client's assessed control risk for acquisitions is low.

19-8 **(OBJECTIVE 19-3)** What are the major differences between the audit of prepaid expenses and other asset accounts such as accounts receivable or property, plant, and equipment?

19-9 **(OBJECTIVE 19-4)** Explain the relationship between accrued rent and substantive tests of transactions for the acquisition and payment cycle. Which aspects of accrued rent are not verified as part of the substantive tests of transactions?

19-10 **(OBJECTIVE 19-4)** Which documents will be used to verify accrued property taxes and the related expense accounts?

19-11 **(OBJECTIVE 19-5)** List three expense accounts that are tested as part of the acquisition and payment cycle or the payroll and personnel cycle. List three expense accounts that are not directly verified as part of the cycle.

19-12 **(OBJECTIVE 19-5)** Explain how expense account analysis relates to the tests of controls and substantive tests of transactions that the auditor has already completed for the acquisition and payment cycle.

19-13 **(OBJECTIVES 19-2, 19-5)** How will the approach for verifying repair expense differ from that used to audit depreciation expense? Why will the approach be different?

19-14 **(OBJECTIVE 19-5)** List the factors that should affect the auditor's decision whether to analyze an account balance.

MULTIPLE CHOICE QUESTIONS FROM CPA EXAMINATIONS

19-15 **(OBJECTIVE 19-2)** The following questions concern internal controls in the acquisition and payment cycle. Choose the best response.

a. Which of the following controls will most likely justify a reduced assessed level of control risk for the existence assertion for equipment?
   (1) Internal auditors periodically select equipment items in the fixed assets master file and locate the related equipment on company premises.
   (2) Department heads are asked to provide information to the accounting department each quarter about any equipment no longer in use or somewhat damaged.
   (3) All contracts of equipment purchases are reviewed by both the controller and attorney to verify that legal title transfers to the client and that none represent operating leases.
   (4) As part of quarterly and annual inventory physical counts, factory equipment is listed and subsequently reconciled to the fixed asset master file.

b. Equipment acquisitions that are misclassified as maintenance expense most likely would be detected by an internal control that provides for
   (1) segregation of duties of employees in the accounts payable department.
   (2) authorization by the board of directors of significant equipment acquisitions.
   (3) investigations of variances within a formal budgeting system.
   (4) independent verification of invoices for disbursements recorded as equipment acquisitions.

c. Which of the following questions is an auditor least likely to include on an internal control questionnaire concerning the initiation and execution of equipment transactions?
   (1) Are requests for major repairs approved at a higher level than the department initiating the request?

(2) Are prenumbered purchase orders used for equipment and periodically accounted for?
(3) Are requests for purchases of equipment reviewed for consideration of soliciting competitive bids?
(4) Are procedures in place to monitor and properly restrict access to equipment?

19-16 **(OBJECTIVES 19-2, 19-3)** The following questions concern the audit of asset accounts in the acquisition and payment cycle. Choose the best response.

a. In testing for unrecorded disposals of equipment, an auditor most likely will
   (1) select items of equipment from the accounting records and then locate them during the plant tour.
   (2) compare depreciation journal entries with similar prior-year entries in search of fully depreciated equipment.
   (3) inspect items of equipment observed during the plant tour and then trace them to the equipment master file.
   (4) scan the general journal for unusual equipment additions and excessive debits to repairs and maintenance expense.

b. Which of the following analytical procedure results might suggest that certain repairs and maintenance expenses have been inappropriately capitalized?
   (1) The ratio of additions to equipment divided by the beginning balance in the equipment account is significantly lower than the same ratio from the prior three years.
   (2) The balance in the repairs and maintenance expense account is noticeably lower than amounts recorded in the past several years.
   (3) The balance in the gross equipment account has decreased this year compared to the prior year.
   (4) The ratio of depreciation expense divided by gross equipment is higher in the current year compared to prior years.

c. In connection with the audit of the prepaid insurance account, which of the following procedures is usually not performed by the auditor?
   (1) Recompute the portion of the premium that expired during the year.
   (2) Prepare excerpts of the insurance policies for audit documentation.
   (3) Confirm premium rates with an independent insurance broker.
   (4) Examine support for premium payments.

19-17 **(OBJECTIVES 19-2, 19-5)** The following questions concern the audit of income and expense accounts. Choose the best response.

a. The auditor may note that annual depreciation expense is too low for a class of assets by noting
   (1) insured values greatly in excess of carrying amounts.
   (2) large numbers of fully depreciated assets are still in use.
   (3) continuous trade-ins of relatively new assets.
   (4) excessive recurring losses on assets retired.

b. An auditor's principal objective in analyzing repairs and maintenance expense accounts is to
   (1) determine that all obsolete property, plant, and equipment assets were written off before the year-end.
   (2) verify that all recorded property, plant, and equipment assets actually exist.
   (3) discover expenditures that were expensed but should have been capitalized.
   (4) identify property, plant, and equipment assets that cannot be repaired and should be written off.

c. Which of the following comparisons will be most useful to an auditor in auditing an entity's income and expense accounts?
   (1) Prior year accounts payable to current year accounts payable
   (2) Prior year payroll expense to budgeted current year payroll expense
   (3) Current year revenue to budgeted current year revenue
   (4) Current year warranty expense to current year contingent liabilities

MULTIPLE CHOICE QUESTIONS FROM BECKER CPA EXAM REVIEW

19-18 **(OBJECTIVE 19-2)** The following questions concern internal controls and tests for property, plant, and equipment. Choose the best response.

a. An audit firm performs a preliminary review of the client's internal controls over its property, plant, and equipment cycle. Which of the following would represent a weakness in internal control?
   (1) Each fixed asset has an identification plate that is listed on a control account.
   (2) Assets that are retired are documented on a sequential work order, which includes an authorization signature.
   (3) A subsidiary ledger is used by the client to keep detailed transaction information for each fixed asset.
   (4) The purchasing department generates a special requisition form upon oral or written approval by senior management.

b. In searching for unrecorded retirements, an auditor selects older fixed assets from the subsidiary ledger and then tries to locate those assets. This procedure primarily relates to management's assertion of
   (1) existence.
   (2) completeness.
   (3) rights and obligations.
   (4) understandability and classification.

c. When auditing a client's property, plant, and equipment transactions, which of the following tests of details can be used to support the existence and occurrence assertion?
   (1) Examine a sample of material charges to repairs and maintenance expense to determine if any items should have been capitalized.
   (2) Vouch a sample of purchases to the vendor invoice and receiving report.
   (3) Recalculate any revaluation losses or surplus transactions made to property, plant, and equipment during the year.
   (4) Review fixed asset purchases and dispositions right before and after year-end to determine if recorded in the correct period.

DISCUSSION QUESTIONS AND PROBLEMS

19-19 **(OBJECTIVE 19-2)** For each of the following misstatements in property, plant, and equipment accounts, state an internal control that the client can implement to prevent the misstatement from occurring and a substantive audit procedure that the auditor can use to discover the misstatement:

1. Computer equipment that is abandoned or traded for replacement equipment is not removed from the accounting records.
2. Depreciation expense for manufacturing operations is charged to administrative expenses.
3. The asset lives used to depreciate equipment are less than reasonable, expected useful lives.
4. Capitalizable assets are routinely expensed as repairs and maintenance, perishable tools, or supplies expense.
5. Acquisitions of property are recorded at incorrect amounts.
6. A loan against existing equipment is not recorded in the accounting records. The cash receipts from the loan never reached the company because they were used for the down payment on a piece of equipment now being used as an operating asset. The equipment is also not recorded in the records.
7. Tools necessary for the maintenance of equipment are stolen by company employees for their personal use.

19-20 **(OBJECTIVE 19-2)** The following types of internal controls are commonly used by organizations for property, plant, and equipment:

1. Written policies exist and are known by accounting personnel to differentiate between capitalizable additions, freight, installation costs, replacements, and maintenance expenditures.
2. A fixed asset master file is maintained with a separate record for each fixed asset.
3. Acquisitions of fixed assets in excess of $50,000 are approved by the board of directors.
4. When practical, equipment is labeled with metal tags and is inventoried on a systematic basis.
5. Depreciation charges for individual assets are calculated for each asset; recorded in a fixed asset master file that includes cost, depreciation, and accumulated depreciation for each asset; and verified periodically by an independent clerk.

Required

a. State the purpose of each of the internal controls just listed. Your answer should be in the form of the type of misstatement that is likely to be reduced because of the control.
b. For each internal control, list one test of control the auditor can use to test for its existence.
c. List one substantive procedure for testing whether the control is actually preventing misstatements in property, plant, and equipment.

19-21 **(OBJECTIVES 19-1, 19-2, 19-3, 19-5)** The following audit procedures were planned by Linda King, CPA, in the audit of the acquisition and payment cycle for Cooley Products, Inc.:

1. Review the acquisitions journal for large and unusual transactions.
2. When the check signer's assistant writes "paid" on supporting documents, watch whether she does it after the documents are reviewed and the checks are signed.
3. Examine invoices and related shipping documents included in the client's unpaid invoice file at the audit report date to determine whether they were recorded in the appropriate accounting period and at the correct amounts.
4. For 20 nontangible acquisitions, select a sample of line items from the acquisitions journal and trace each to related vendors' invoices. Examine whether each transaction appears to be a legitimate expenditure for the client and that each was approved and recorded at the correct amount and date in the journal and charged to the correct account per the chart of accounts.
5. Refoot the acquisitions journal for one month and trace all totals to the general ledger.
6. Send letters to several vendors, including a few for which the recorded accounts payable balance is zero, requesting them to inform us of their balance due from Cooley. Ask the controller to sign the letter.
7. Examine a sample of receiving report numbers and determine whether each one has an initial indicating that it was recorded as an account payable.
8. Select a sample of equipment listed on fixed asset master files and inspect the asset to determine that it exists and to determine its condition.
9. Calculate the ratio of equipment repairs and maintenance to total equipment and compare with previous years.
10. Obtain from the client a written statement that all mortgages payable have been included in the current period financial statements and have been accurately recorded and that the collateral for each is included in the footnotes.
11. Select a sample of cancelled checks and trace each one to the cash disbursements journal, comparing the name, date, and amount.
12. Recalculate the portion of insurance premiums on the client's prepaid insurance schedule that is applicable to future periods.

Required

a. For each procedure, identify the type of evidence being used.
b. For each procedure, identify whether it is a substantive analytical procedure, a test of control, a substantive test of transactions, or a test of details of balances.
c. For each test of control or substantive test of transactions, identify the transaction-related audit objective(s) being met.
d. For each test of details of balances, identify the balance-related audit objective(s) being met.

19-22 **(OBJECTIVE 19-2)** Your client, Edgartown Corporation, prepared the following schedule of land, buildings, and equipment for the audit of financial statements for the year ended December 31, 2016:

Account Description	1/1/16 Beginning Balance	Additions	Disposals	12/31/16 Ending Balance
Land	$ 7,500,000	—	—	$ 7,500,000
Building–Office	27,000,000	$250,000	—	27,250,000
Production Equipment	2,345,000	178,223	$ 34,779	2,488,444
Office Equipment	1,765,881	72,517	55,339	1,783,059
IT Hardware	216,542	—	19,098	197,444
Total	$38,827,423	$500,740	$109,216	$39,218,947

Required

a. What type of evidence would you examine to support the beginning balances in the accounts?
b. What types of evidence would you use to support the additions to each account? How might the sources of evidence differ for additions to the building account and the equipment accounts?
c. What types of evidence would you examine to support equipment disposals?
d. What procedures would you perform related to the ending balances in the accounts?
e. In the audit of property, plant, and equipment accounts, auditors should consider whether there are any implications to other accounts in the audit.
   (1) What other accounts might be impacted by the additions of buildings and equipment?
   (2) What other accounts might be impacted by disposals of equipment?

19-23 **(OBJECTIVE 19-4)** The following program has been prepared for the audit of accrued real estate taxes of a client that pays taxes on 25 different pieces of property, some of which have been acquired in the current year:

1. Obtain a schedule of accrued taxes from the client and tie the total to the general ledger.
2. Compare the charges for annual tax payments with property tax assessment bills.
3. Recompute accrued/prepaid amounts for all bills on the basis of the portion of the year expired.

Required

a. State the purpose of each procedure.
b. Evaluate the adequacy of the audit program.

19-24 **(OBJECTIVE 19-4)** As part of the audit of different audit areas, auditors should be alert for the possibility of unrecorded liabilities. For each of the following audit areas or accounts, describe a liability that can be uncovered and the audit procedures that can uncover it:

a. Minutes of the board of directors meetings
b. Land and buildings
c. Rent expense
d. Interest expense
e. Cash surrender value of life insurance
f. Cash in the bank
g. Officers' travel and entertainment expenses

19-25 **(OBJECTIVE 19-5)** You are auditing the financial statements of Austin Software Company, which is a fast-growing software development company. As part of the company's strategy, management has been aggressively pursuing acquisitions of other companies. Some of the prior acquisitions resulted in the recording of goodwill. During your review of income and expense accounts, you noted a material goodwill impairment charge associated with the company's acquisition of Longhorn Software, Inc.

As part of your audit, consider each of the following:

Required

a. What are the underlying accounting standards requirements that are relevant to your evaluation of the company's charge for the impairment of goodwill?
b. What types of evidence would be relevant to your evaluation of whether management's impairment charge is fairly stated?
c. How might the use of a business valuation specialist be helpful in this year's audit?

Ward Publishing Company—Part III (See Case 18-30 for Parts I and II)

19-26 **(OBJECTIVES 19-1, 19-2, 19-5)** Examine the tests of controls and substantive tests of transactions results, including the sampling application in Case 18-30 (pp. 634–635), for Ward Publishing Company. Assume that you have already reached several conclusions.

1. Your tests of details of balances for accounts payable are completed, and you found no exceptions.
2. Acceptable audit risk for property, plant, and equipment and all expenses is high.
3. Inherent risk for property, plant, and equipment is high because in the current year, the client has acquired a material amount of new and used printing equipment and has traded in older equipment. Some of the new equipment was ineffective and returned; an allowance was received on others. Inherent risk for expense accounts is low.
4. New computer equipment and some printing equipment are being leased. The client has never leased equipment before.
5. Substantive analytical procedures for property, plant, and equipment are inconclusive because of the large increases in acquisition and disposal activity.
6. Substantive analytical procedures show that repairs, maintenance, and small tools expenses have increased materially, both in absolute terms and as a percentage of sales. Two other expenses have also materially increased, and one has materially decreased.
7. In examining the sample for tests of controls and substantive tests of transactions, you observe that no sample items included any property, plant, and equipment or lease transactions.

Required

a. Explain the relationship between the tests of controls and substantive tests of transactions results in Case 18-30 and the audit of property, plant, and equipment and leases.

b. How will the tests of controls and substantive tests of transactions results and your conclusions (1 through 7) affect your planned tests of details for property, plant, and equipment and leases? State your conclusions for each balance-related audit objective. Do not write an audit program.

c. Explain the relationship between the tests of controls and substantive tests of transactions results in Case 18-30 and the audit of expenses.

d. How will the tests of controls and substantive tests of transactions results and your conclusions (1 through 7) affect your planned tests of details of balances for expenses? Do not write an audit program.

19-27 **(OBJECTIVE 19-2)** You are doing the audit of the UTE Corporation for the year ended December 31, 2016. The following schedule for the property, plant, and equipment and related allowance for depreciation accounts has been prepared by the client. You have compared the opening balances with the prior year's audit documentation.

UTE Corporation Analysis of Property, Plant, and Equipment and Related Allowance for Depreciation Accounts Year Ended December 31, 2016

Description	Final 12/31/15	Additions	Retirements	Per Books 12/31/16
Assets				
Land	$ 225,000	$50,000		$ 275,000
Buildings	1,200,000	175,000		1,375,000
Machinery and equipment	3,850,000	404,000	260,000	3,994,000
	$ 5,275,000	$ 629,000	$ 260,000	$ 5,644,000
Allowance for Depreciation				
Building	$ 600,000	$ 51,500		$ 651,500
Machinery and equipment	1,732,500	392,200		2,124,700
	$ 2,332,500	$ 443,700		$ 2,776,200

The following information is found during your audit:

1. All equipment is depreciated on the straight-line basis (no salvage value taken into consideration) based on the following estimated lives: buildings, 25 years; all other items, 10 years. The corporation's policy is to take one-half year's depreciation on all asset acquisitions and disposals during the year.
2. On April 1, the corporation entered into a 10-year lease contract for a die-casting machine with annual rentals of $50,000, payable in advance every April 1. The lease is cancelable by either party (60 days' written notice is required), and there is no option to renew the lease or buy the equipment at the end of the lease. The estimated useful life of the machine is 10 years with no salvage value. The corporation recorded the die-casting machine in the machinery and equipment account at $404,000, the present value at the date of the lease, and $20,200, applicable to the machine, has been included in depreciation expense for the year.
3. The corporation completed the construction of a wing on the plant building on June 30. The useful life of the building was not extended by this addition. The lowest construction bid received was $175,000, the amount recorded in the buildings account. Company personnel were used to construct the addition at a cost of $160,000 (materials, $75,000; labor, $55,000; and overhead, $30,000).
4. On August 18, $50,000 was paid for paving and fencing a portion of land owned by the corporation and used as a parking lot for employees. The expenditure was charged to the land account.
5. The amount shown in the machinery and equipment asset retirement column represents cash received on September 5, upon disposal of a machine acquired in July 2012 for $480,000. The bookkeeper recorded depreciation expense of $35,000 on this machine in 2016.
6. Crux City donated land and building appraised at $100,000 and $400,000, respectively, to the UTE Corporation for a plant. On September 1, the corporation began operating the plant. Because no costs were involved, the bookkeeper made no entry for the foregoing transaction.

Required

a. In addition to inquiry of the client, explain how you would have found each of these six items during the audit.

b. Prepare the adjusting journal entries with supporting computations that you would suggest at December 31, 2016, to adjust the accounts for the preceding transactions. Disregard income tax implications.*

19-28 **(OBJECTIVE 19-5)** You are the manager in the audit of Vernal Manufacturing Company and are turning your attention to the income statement accounts. The in-charge auditor assessed control risk for all cycles as low, supported by tests of controls. There are no major inherent risks affecting income and expense accounts. Accordingly, you decide that the major emphasis in auditing the income statement accounts will be to use substantive analytical procedures. The client prepared a schedule of the key income statement accounts that compares the prior-year totals with the current year totals. The in-charge auditor completed the last column of the audit schedule, which includes explanations of variances obtained from discussions with client personnel. The audit schedule is included on the following page.

Required

a. Examine the schedule prepared by the client and your staff and write a memorandum to the in-charge that includes criticisms and concerns about the audit procedures performed and questions for the in-charge auditor to resolve.

b. Evaluate the explanations for variances provided by client personnel. List any alternative explanation to those given.

c. Indicate which variances are of special significance to the audit and how you believe they should be responded to in terms of additional audit procedures.

19-29 **(OBJECTIVE 19-2)** This problem requires you to research the disclosure requirements for fixed assets using the FASB Codification at www.fasb.org. Access to the FASB Codification requires that your educational institution be enrolled in the FASB academic access program, or provides access to the codification through a third-party provider.

*Based on AICPA question paper, American Institute of Certified Public Accountants.

Required

a. Identify the section in the FASB Codification that addresses property, plant, and equipment, and the subsection that provides disclosure requirements.
b. Indicate the disclosures for fixed assets that should be made in the financial statements or footnotes to the statements.
c. The section on disclosure also includes requirements for impairment or disposal of long-lived assets. What is the definition of impairment? (Hover your cursor over the highlighted term to see the glossary definition.)
d. Identify the information that must be disclosed in the notes to the financial statements for the period in which an impairment loss is recognized.

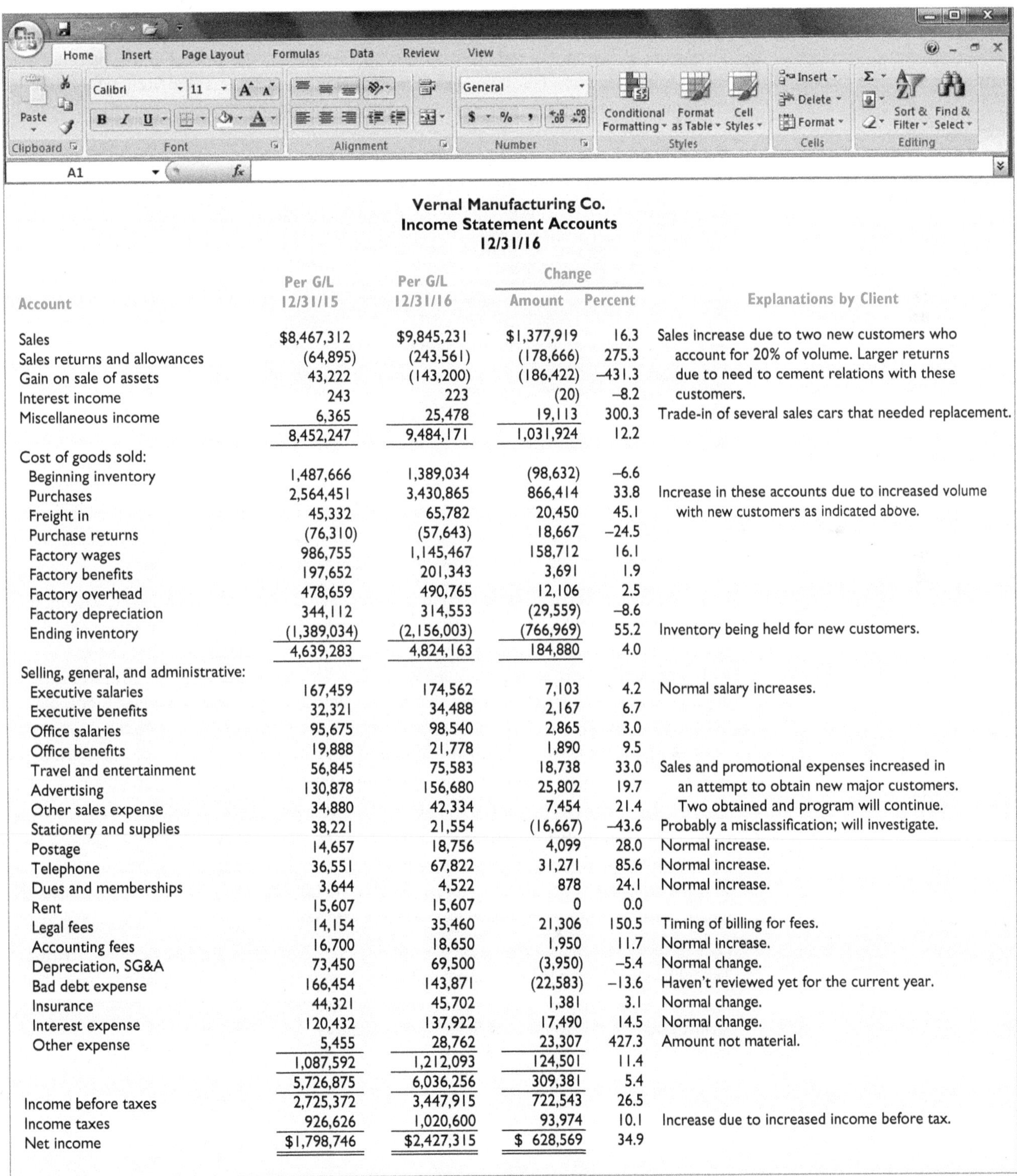

Vernal Manufacturing Co.
Income Statement Accounts
12/31/16

Account	Per G/L 12/31/15	Per G/L 12/31/16	Change Amount	Change Percent	Explanations by Client
Sales	$8,467,312	$9,845,231	$1,377,919	16.3	Sales increase due to two new customers who
Sales returns and allowances	(64,895)	(243,561)	(178,666)	275.3	account for 20% of volume. Larger returns
Gain on sale of assets	43,222	(143,200)	(186,422)	–431.3	due to need to cement relations with these
Interest income	243	223	(20)	–8.2	customers.
Miscellaneous income	6,365	25,478	19,113	300.3	Trade-in of several sales cars that needed replacement.
	8,452,247	9,484,171	1,031,924	12.2	
Cost of goods sold:					
Beginning inventory	1,487,666	1,389,034	(98,632)	–6.6	
Purchases	2,564,451	3,430,865	866,414	33.8	Increase in these accounts due to increased volume
Freight in	45,332	65,782	20,450	45.1	with new customers as indicated above.
Purchase returns	(76,310)	(57,643)	18,667	–24.5	
Factory wages	986,755	1,145,467	158,712	16.1	
Factory benefits	197,652	201,343	3,691	1.9	
Factory overhead	478,659	490,765	12,106	2.5	
Factory depreciation	344,112	314,553	(29,559)	–8.6	
Ending inventory	(1,389,034)	(2,156,003)	(766,969)	55.2	Inventory being held for new customers.
	4,639,283	4,824,163	184,880	4.0	
Selling, general, and administrative:					
Executive salaries	167,459	174,562	7,103	4.2	Normal salary increases.
Executive benefits	32,321	34,488	2,167	6.7	
Office salaries	95,675	98,540	2,865	3.0	
Office benefits	19,888	21,778	1,890	9.5	
Travel and entertainment	56,845	75,583	18,738	33.0	Sales and promotional expenses increased in
Advertising	130,878	156,680	25,802	19.7	an attempt to obtain new major customers.
Other sales expense	34,880	42,334	7,454	21.4	Two obtained and program will continue.
Stationery and supplies	38,221	21,554	(16,667)	–43.6	Probably a misclassification; will investigate.
Postage	14,657	18,756	4,099	28.0	Normal increase.
Telephone	36,551	67,822	31,271	85.6	Normal increase.
Dues and memberships	3,644	4,522	878	24.1	Normal increase.
Rent	15,607	15,607	0	0.0	
Legal fees	14,154	35,460	21,306	150.5	Timing of billing for fees.
Accounting fees	16,700	18,650	1,950	11.7	Normal increase.
Depreciation, SG&A	73,450	69,500	(3,950)	–5.4	Normal change.
Bad debt expense	166,454	143,871	(22,583)	–13.6	Haven't reviewed yet for the current year.
Insurance	44,321	45,702	1,381	3.1	Normal change.
Interest expense	120,432	137,922	17,490	14.5	Normal change.
Other expense	5,455	28,762	23,307	427.3	Amount not material.
	1,087,592	1,212,093	124,501	11.4	
	5,726,875	6,036,256	309,381	5.4	
Income before taxes	2,725,372	3,447,915	722,543	26.5	
Income taxes	926,626	1,020,600	93,974	10.1	Increase due to increased income before tax.
Net income	$1,798,746	$2,427,315	$ 628,569	34.9	

CHAPTER

20 AUDIT OF THE PAYROLL AND PERSONNEL CYCLE

LEARNING OBJECTIVES

After studying this chapter, you should be able to

20-1 Identify the accounts and transactions in the payroll and personnel cycle.

20-2 Describe the business functions and the related documents and records in the payroll and personnel cycle.

20-3 Understand internal control and design and perform tests of controls and substantive tests of transactions for the payroll and personnel cycle.

20-4 Design and perform substantive analytical procedures and tests of details for accounts in the payroll and personnel cycle.

The Staff Auditor Must Never "Simply Follow Orders"

During Leslie Davenport's first "busy season," she worked on the audit of Sysco, Inc., a software development company. Her immediate supervisor on the audit was Bob Stith, who had joined the firm three years earlier and worked on the Sysco audit the previous year.

Stith drafted an audit program for capitalized software development costs, which Davenport was asked to complete. She knew from her coursework that costs cannot be capitalized until technological feasibility has been established, either through detailed program design or product design and the completion of a working model, confirmed by testing.

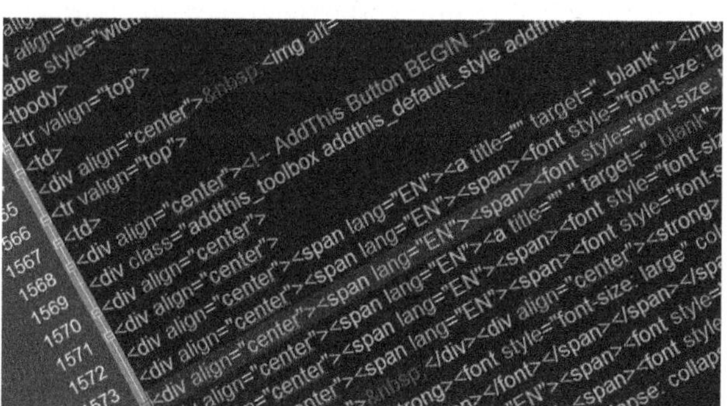

Stith told Davenport to verify the payroll expenses that were a significant part of the development cost and to talk to Jack Smart, Sysco's controller, about whether the projects with capitalized costs had reached the technological feasibility stage. Davenport tested the payroll costs and found no misstatements. She also made inquiries of Smart and was told that the appropriate stage was reached. Davenport documented Smart's representation in the audit files and went on to the next area assigned to her.

Later, Davenport began to have second thoughts. She doubted whether Smart was the most knowledgeable person about the technical status of software projects. Davenport decided to talk to the responsible software engineers about one of the projects. She intended to clear this with Stith, but he was at another client's office, so she proceeded on her own initiative. An engineer on the first project told her that he was almost finished with a working model but had not tested it yet. She inquired about another project and discovered the same thing. Davenport documented these findings, which she discussed with Stith as soon as he returned to the job. Based on her discussion and his review of the documentation, he told her the following:

"Listen, Leslie, I told you to just talk to Jack. You shouldn't do procedures that you're not instructed to do. I want you to destroy this schedule and don't record the wasted time. We're under a lot of time pressure and we can't bill Sysco for procedures that aren't necessary. There's nothing wrong with the capitalized software development costs. The fact that they have working products that they're selling indicates technological feasibility was reached."

Davenport was extremely distressed with this reaction from Stith but followed his instructions. The following fall, the SEC conducted an investigation of Sysco and found, among other things, that they had overstated capitalized software development costs. The SEC brought an action against both the management of Sysco and its auditors.

The **payroll and personnel cycle** involves the employment and payment of all employees. Labor is an important consideration in the valuation of inventory in manufacturing, construction, and other industries. As the story involving Leslie Davenport and the audit of Sysco, Inc., demonstrates, improper valuation and allocation of labor can result in a material misstatement of net income. Payroll is also an area in which company resources can be wasted because of inefficiency or stolen through fraud.

As with the sales and collection and acquisition and payment cycles, the audit of the payroll and personnel cycle includes obtaining an understanding of internal control, assessing control risk, tests of controls and substantive tests of transactions, substantive analytical procedures, and tests of details of balances. In a typical audit, the main differences between the payroll and personnel cycle and other cycles include:

- *There is only one class of transactions for payroll.* Most cycles include at least two classes of transactions. For example, the sales and collection cycle includes both sales and cash receipts transactions, and often includes sales returns and charge-off of uncollectible accounts. Payroll has only one class because the receipt of services from employees and the payment for those services through payroll usually occur within a short time period.
- *Transactions are generally far more significant than related balance sheet accounts.* Payroll-related accounts such as accrued payroll and withheld taxes are usually small compared to the total amount of transactions for the year.
- *Internal controls over payroll are effective for almost all companies, even small ones.* Strict federal and state regulations encourage effective controls for withholding and paying payroll taxes. Also, employee morale problems can occur if employees are not paid or are underpaid.

Because of these three characteristics, auditors typically emphasize tests of controls, substantive tests of transactions, and substantive analytical procedures in the audit of payroll. Tests of details of balances take only a few minutes for most payroll-related accounts. Before we discuss the tests in the cycle, let's review the transactions and account balances, as well as the documents and records used in the payroll and personnel cycle for a typical company.

ACCOUNTS AND TRANSACTIONS IN THE PAYROLL AND PERSONNEL CYCLE

OBJECTIVE 20-1

Identify the accounts and transactions in the payroll and personnel cycle.

The overall objective in the audit of the payroll and personnel cycle is, of course, to evaluate whether the account balances affected by the cycle are fairly stated in accordance with applicable accounting standards.

Typical accounts in the payroll and personnel cycle are shown in Figure 20-1 (p. 664). T accounts are used to illustrate the way in which accounting information flows through the various accounts in the payroll and personnel cycle. In most systems, the accrued wages and salaries account is used only at the end of an accounting period. Throughout the period, expenses are charged when the employees are actually paid rather than when the labor costs are incurred. Accruals for labor are recorded by adjusting entries at the end of the period for any earned-but-unpaid labor costs.

BUSINESS FUNCTIONS IN THE CYCLE AND RELATED DOCUMENTS AND RECORDS

OBJECTIVE 20-2

Describe the business functions and the related documents and records in the payroll and personnel cycle.

The payroll and personnel cycle begins with hiring employees and ends with paying them for the services they performed and the government and other institutions for withheld and accrued payroll taxes and benefits. In between, the cycle involves obtaining services from employees consistent with company objectives, and properly accounting for the services.

Turn to Table 20-1 on page 665. The third column identifies the four business functions in a typical payroll and personnel cycle and illustrates the relationships among the business functions, classes of transactions, accounts, and documents and records. Auditors must understand the business functions and documents and records before they can assess control risk and design tests of controls and substantive tests of transactions.

FIGURE 20-1 Accounts in the Payroll and Personnel Cycle

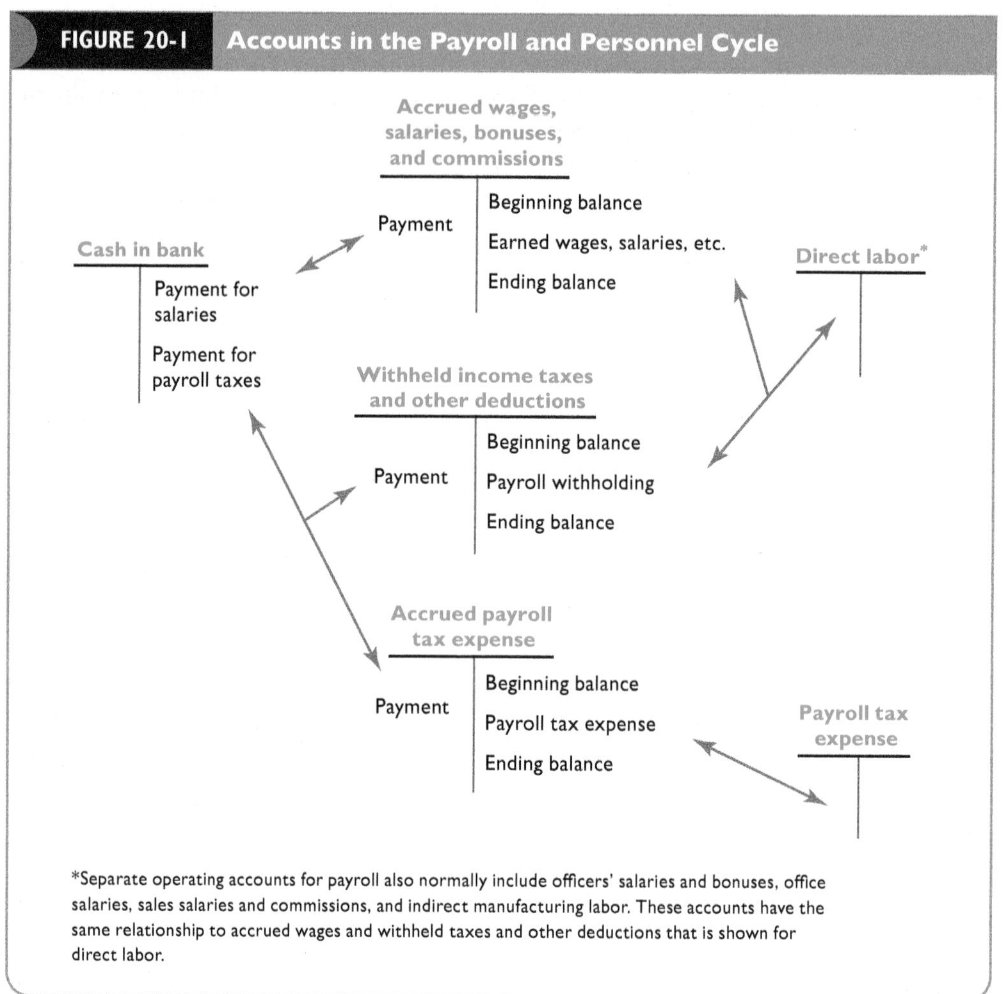

*Separate operating accounts for payroll also normally include officers' salaries and bonuses, office salaries, sales salaries and commissions, and indirect manufacturing labor. These accounts have the same relationship to accrued wages and withheld taxes and other deductions that is shown for direct labor.

Human Resources

The human resources department provides an independent source for interviewing and hiring qualified personnel. The department is also an independent source of records for the internal verification of wage information, including additions and deletions from the payroll and changes in wages and deductions.

Human Resource Records **Human resource records** include such data as the date of employment, personnel investigations, rates of pay, authorized deductions, performance evaluations, and termination of employment.

Deduction Authorization Employees may submit a form or make online selections that authorize payroll deductions, including the number of exemptions for withholding income taxes, 401(K) and other retirement savings plans, health insurance, and union dues.

Rate Authorization A form or other electronic record is used to authorize the rate of pay. The source of the information is a labor contract, authorization by management, or in the case of officers, authorization from the board of directors.

Timekeeping and Payroll Preparation

Timekeeping and payroll preparation are important in the audit of payroll because they directly affect payroll expense for each period. Adequate controls are necessary to prevent misstatements in the following four activities:

- Prepare time records by employees
- Summarize and calculate gross pay, deductions, and net pay
- Payment of payroll
- Prepare payroll records

TABLE 20-1	Classes of Transactions, Accounts, Business Functions, and Related Documents and Records for the Payroll and Personnel Cycle		
Class of Transactions	**Accounts**	**Business Functions**	**Documents and Records**
Payroll	Payroll cash All payroll expense accounts All payroll withholding accounts All payroll accrual accounts	Human resources and employment	Human resource records Deduction authorization form Rate authorization form
		Timekeeping and payroll preparation	Time record Job time ticket Payroll transaction file Payroll journal or listing Payroll master file
		Payment of payroll	Payroll direct deposit or check Payroll bank account reconciliation
		Preparation of payroll tax returns and payment of taxes	W-2 form Payroll tax returns

Time Record The **time record** is a document indicating the time the hourly employee started and stopped working each day and the number of hours the employee worked. Time records may be in paper or electronic form, and they may be prepared automatically by time clocks or identification card readers. In many environments, especially retailers, employees enter arrival and departure times using point-of-sale machines that capture time record information daily. In other environments, time records may be submitted weekly.

Salaried or exempt employees usually do not complete time records. They may be required to complete time reports to be compensated for overtime, vacation, or sick days.

Job Time Ticket The job time ticket is a form indicating which jobs an employee worked on during a given time period. This form is used only when an employee works on different jobs or in different departments. Job time tickets are often done electronically by a time and expense reporting system.

Payroll Transaction File This computer-generated file includes all payroll transactions processed by the accounting system for a period, such as a day, week, or month. The file contains all information entered into the system and information for each transaction, such as employee name and identification number, date, gross and net pay, various withholding amounts, and account classification or classifications. Depending on the company's needs, the information on the payroll transaction file is used for a variety of records, listings, and reports, such as the payroll journal, payroll master file, and payroll bank reconciliation.

Payroll Journal or Listing This report is generated from the payroll transaction file and typically includes the employee name, date, gross and net payroll amounts, withholding amounts, and account classification or classifications for each transaction. The same transactions included in the journal or listing are also posted simultaneously to the general ledger and to the payroll master file.

Payroll Master File The **payroll master file** is a computer file used for recording payroll transactions for each employee and maintaining total employee wages paid for the year to date. The record for each employee includes gross pay for each payroll period, deductions from gross pay, net pay, check number, and date. This master file is updated from payroll transaction files. The total of the individual employee earnings in the master file equals the total balance of gross payroll in various general ledger accounts.

Payment of Payroll

The approval and distribution of payroll must be carefully controlled to prevent theft. To increase control, payroll disbursements are generally processed separately from other disbursements.

Payment of Payroll Payments are issued to employees in exchange for services performed. Payments may be made by check, but are usually deposited directly into employees' individual bank accounts. The amount paid is the gross pay less taxes and other deductions withheld.

Payroll Bank Account Reconciliation An independent bank reconciliation is important for all cash accounts, including payroll, for finding errors and fraud. An **imprest payroll account** is a separate payroll account in which a small balance is maintained. The exact amount of each net payroll is transferred by check or electronic funds transfer from the general account to the imprest account immediately before distribution of the payroll. The imprest account limits the client's exposure to payroll fraud and separates routine payroll expenditures from other expenditures. It also simplifies reconciliation of the payroll bank account.

Preparation of Payroll Tax Returns and Payment of Taxes

Federal and state payroll laws require the timely preparation and submission of payroll tax returns. Most computerized payroll systems prepare payroll tax returns using information on the payroll transaction and master files. To prevent misstatements and potential liability for taxes and penalties, a competent individual must independently verify the output.

W-2 Form This is a form sent to each employee that summarizes the employee's earning for the calendar year, including gross pay, income taxes withheld, and FICA (Social Security) withheld. The same information is also submitted to the Internal Revenue Service and state and local tax commissions when applicable. This information is prepared from the payroll master file and is normally computer generated.

Payroll Tax Returns These are forms submitted to local, state, and federal units of government to show payment of withheld taxes and the employer's tax. The nature and due dates of the forms vary depending on the type of taxes. These forms are prepared from information on the payroll master file and are usually computer generated. Federal withholding and Social Security payments are due semiweekly or monthly, depending on the amount of withholding. Most state unemployment taxes are due quarterly.

CONCEPT CHECK

1. Describe why transactions in the payroll and personnel cycle are generally more significant than payroll-related balance sheet accounts.
2. Explain the differences in the primary roles performed by human resources, the employee's primary supervisor, and those who oversee the creation of a payroll journal or listing and the payroll master file.

METHODOLOGY FOR DESIGNING TESTS OF CONTROLS AND SUBSTANTIVE TESTS OF TRANSACTIONS

OBJECTIVE 20-3

Understand internal control and design and perform tests of controls and substantive tests of transactions for the payroll and personnel cycle.

Now that you are familiar with the business functions and related documents and records in the payroll and personnel cycle, we will discuss understanding internal control, assessing control risk, and designing tests of controls and substantive tests of transactions for the cycle. The methodology for designing tests of controls and substantive tests of transactions for the payroll and personnel cycle is the same as that used in Chapter 14 for the sales and collection cycle and in Chapter 18 for the acquisition and payment cycle: understand internal control, assess planned control risk, determine the extent of testing of controls, and design tests of controls and substantive tests of transactions to meet transaction-related audit objectives.

Understand Internal Control and Assess Control Risk—Payroll and Personnel Cycle

Internal control for payroll is normally highly structured and well controlled to manage cash disbursed, to minimize employee complaints and dissatisfaction, and to minimize payroll fraud. Because of relatively common payroll concerns from company to company, high-quality computerized payroll accounting programs are available.

Because processing payroll is similar for most organizations, and programs need to be modified annually for changes in withholding schedules, companies commonly use an outside payroll service for processing payroll. The auditor can often rely on the internal controls of the service organization if the service organization's auditor issues a report on the service organization's internal control, discussed in Chapter 12 (pp. 380–381).

It is usually not difficult for companies to establish good control in the payroll and personnel cycle. For factory and office employees, there are usually a large number of relatively homogeneous, small-amount transactions. For executives, there are usually fewer payroll transactions, but they are ordinarily consistent in timing and amount. Consequently, auditors seldom expect to find exceptions in testing payroll transactions. Occasionally, control test deviations occur, but most monetary misstatements are corrected by internal verification controls or in response to employee complaints. Even when there are misstatements, they are rarely material. As a result, control risk is often assessed as low for this cycle.

Key controls in the payroll and personnel cycle are summarized in Table 20-2 (p. 668). We take a closer look at these controls as we next describe tests of controls and substantive tests of transactions for the payroll and personnel cycle.

Design Tests of Controls and Substantive Tests of Transactions—Payroll and Personnel Cycle

Tests of controls and substantive tests of transactions procedures are the *most important* means of verifying account balances in the payroll and personnel cycle. These tests are emphasized because of the lack of independent third-party evidence, such as confirmation, for verifying accrued wages, withheld income taxes, accrued payroll taxes, and other balance sheet accounts. Furthermore, in most audits, the amounts in the balance sheet accounts are small and can be verified with relative ease if the auditor is confident that payroll transactions are correctly entered into the computer and payroll tax returns are correctly prepared.

Even though tests of controls and substantive tests of transactions are the most important parts of testing payroll, tests in this area are usually not extensive. Many audits have a minimal risk of material misstatements, even though payroll is often a significant part of total expenses. There are three reasons for this:

1. Employees are likely to complain to management if they are underpaid.
2. All payroll transactions are typically uniform and uncomplicated.
3. Payroll transactions are subject to audit by federal and state governments for income tax withholding, Social Security, and unemployment taxes.

Following the same approach used in Chapter 14 for tests of sales and cash receipts transactions, the internal controls, tests of controls, and substantive tests of transactions for each transaction-related audit objective are summarized in Table 20-2. Again, you should recognize the following:

- Internal controls vary from company to company; therefore, the auditor must identify the controls, significant deficiencies, and material weaknesses for each organization.
- Controls the auditor intends to rely on to reduce assessed control risk must be tested with tests of controls.
- If the auditor is reporting on the effectiveness of internal control over financial reporting, the level of understanding controls and extent of tests of controls must be sufficient to issue an opinion on the effectiveness of internal control over financial reporting.

TABLE 20-2 Summary of Transaction-Related Audit Objectives, Key Controls, Tests of Controls, and Substantive Tests of Transactions for Payroll

Transaction-Related Audit Objectives	Key Internal Controls	Common Tests of Controls	Common Substantive Tests of Transactions
Recorded payroll payments are for work actually performed by existing employees (occurrence).	Time records are approved by supervisor. Time clock is used to record time. Adequate human resource files are maintained. Employment is authorized. There is separation of duties among human resources, timekeeping, and payroll disbursements. Only employees existing in the computer data files are accepted when they are entered. Disbursements are authorized before issuance.	Examine time records for indication of approvals. Examine time records. Review human resource policies. Examine human resource files. Review organization chart, discuss with employees, and observe duties being performed. Examine printouts of transactions rejected by the computer as having nonexistent employee numbers. Examine payroll records for indication of approval.	Review the payroll journal, general ledger, and payroll earnings records for large or unusual transactions or amounts.* Compare cancelled check or direct deposit information with human resource records. Compare cancelled checks with payroll journal for name, amount, and date. Examine cancelled checks for proper endorsement.
Existing payroll transactions are recorded (completeness).	Payroll checks are prenumbered and accounted for. Bank accounts are independently reconciled.	Account for a sequence of payroll checks. Discuss with employees and observe reconciliation.	Reconcile the disbursements in the payroll journal with the disbursements on the payroll bank statement. Prove the bank reconciliation.
Recorded payroll transactions are for the amount of time actually worked and are at the proper pay rates; withholdings are correctly calculated (accuracy).	Calculations and amounts are internally verified. Batch totals are compared with computer summary reports. Wage rate, salary, or commission rate is properly authorized. Withholdings, including amounts for insurance and payroll savings, are properly authorized.	Examine indication of internal verification. Examine file of batch totals for initials of data control clerk; compare totals to summary reports. Examine payroll records for indication of authorization. Examine authorizations in human resource file.	Recompute hours worked from time records. Compare pay rates with union contract, approval by board of directors, or other source. Recompute gross pay. Check withholdings by referring to tax tables and authorization forms in human resource file. Recompute net pay. Compare cancelled check or direct deposit with payroll journal for amount.
Payroll transactions are correctly included in the payroll master file and are correctly summarized (posting and summarization).	Payroll master file contents are internally verified. Payroll master file totals are compared with general ledger totals.	Examine indication of internal verification. Examine initialed summary total reports indicating that comparisons have been made.	Test clerical accuracy by footing the payroll journal and tracing postings to the general ledger and the payroll master file.
Payroll transactions are correctly classified (classification).	An adequate chart of accounts is used. Account classifications are internally verified.	Review chart of accounts. Examine indication of internal verification.	Compare classification with chart of accounts or procedures manual. Review time record for employee department and job ticket for job assignment and trace through to labor distribution.
Payroll transactions are recorded on the correct dates (timing).	Procedures require recording transactions as soon as possible after the payroll is paid. Dates are internally verified.	Examine procedures manual and observe when recording takes place. Examine indication of internal verification.	Compare date of recorded payment in the payroll journal with date on cancelled check or direct deposit and time record. Compare date on check with date the check cleared the bank.

*While this is a type of analytical procedure, it also serves as a substantive test of transaction for the occurrence objective, in addition to other objectives, including completeness, accuracy, and timing.

- Substantive tests of transactions vary depending on the assessed control risk and the other considerations of the audit, such as the effect of payroll on inventory.
- Tests are not actually performed in the order given in Table 20-2. The tests of controls and substantive tests of transactions are combined when appropriate and are performed in as convenient a manner as possible, using a performance format audit program.

The purposes of many internal controls and the nature of the tests of controls and substantive tests of transactions are apparent for most tests from their descriptions in Table 20-2. Next, the key controls for the payroll and personnel cycle for assessing control risk are discussed.

Adequate Separation of Duties Separation of duties is important in the payroll and personnel cycle, especially to prevent overpayments and payments to nonexistent employees. The payroll function should be kept independent of the human resources department, which controls key payroll activities, such as adding and deleting employees. Payroll processing should also be separate from the issuance of payroll disbursements.

Proper Authorization As already noted, only the human resources department should be authorized to add and delete employees from the payroll or change pay rates and deductions. The number of hours worked by each employee, especially overtime, should be authorized by the employee's supervisor. Approval may be indicated electronically or noted on all time records or done on an exception basis only for overtime hours.

Adequate Documents and Records The appropriate documents and records depend on the nature of the payroll system. Time records are necessary for hourly employees but not for salaried employees. For employees compensated based on piece rate or other incentive systems, different records are required. For many companies, time records must be adequate to accumulate payroll costs by job or assignment. Prenumbered documents for recording time are less of a concern for payroll because the completeness objective is normally not a concern.

Physical Control Over Assets and Records Many organizations pay employees through direct deposit. In those situations, access to systems used to authorize payments should be restricted. When payment is made by check, access to unsigned payroll checks should be restricted. Checks should be signed by a responsible employee, and payroll should be distributed by someone independent of the payroll and timekeeping functions. Any unclaimed checks should be returned for redeposit. If checks are signed by a signature machine, access to the machine should be restricted.

Independent Checks on Performance Payroll computations should be independently verified, including comparison of batch totals to summary reports. A member of management or other responsible employee should review the payroll output for any obvious misstatements or unusual amounts. When manufacturing labor affects inventory valuation or when it is necessary to accumulate costs by job, adequate controls are necessary to verify the proper assignment of costs.

Payroll Tax Forms and Payments

Payroll taxes and other withholdings are important in many companies, both because the amounts are often material and because the potential liability for failure to timely file tax forms can be severe.

Preparation of Payroll Tax Forms As a part of understanding internal control, the auditor should review the preparation of at least one of each type of payroll tax form that the client is responsible for filing. The potential for liability for unpaid taxes, penalty, and interest arises if the client fails to prepare the tax forms correctly. The payroll tax forms are for such taxes as federal income and FICA withholding, state and city income withholding, and federal and state unemployment.

A detailed reconciliation of the information on the tax forms and the payroll records may be necessary when the auditor believes the tax returns may be incorrectly prepared. Indications of potential misstatements in the returns include the payment of penalties and interest in the past for improper payments, new personnel in the payroll department who are responsible for the preparation of the returns, the lack of internal verification of the information, and cash flow problems for the client.

Timely Payment of the Payroll Taxes Withheld and Other Withholdings It is desirable to test whether the client has fulfilled its legal obligation in submitting payments for all payroll withholdings as a part of the payroll tests even though the payments are usually made from general cash disbursements. The withholdings of concern in these tests include taxes, 401(K) and other retirement savings, union dues, insurance, and payroll savings.

Auditors must first determine the client's requirements for submitting the payments, which can be determined by referencing such sources as tax laws, union contracts, and agreements with employees. Once auditors know the requirements, they can easily determine whether the client has made timely payments at correct amounts by comparing the subsequent cash disbursement with the payroll records.

Inventory and Fraudulent Payroll Considerations

Auditors often extend their payroll audit procedures if payroll significantly affects the valuation of inventory, or when the auditor is concerned about the possibility of material fraudulent payroll transactions, such as nonexistent employees or fraudulent hours.

Relationship Between Payroll and Inventory Valuation When payroll is a significant portion of inventory, which is common for manufacturing and construction companies, the improper account classification of payroll can materially affect asset valuation for accounts such as work in process, finished goods, or construction in process. For example, the overhead charged to inventory at the balance sheet date can be overstated if the salaries of administrative personnel are inadvertently or intentionally charged to indirect manufacturing overhead. Similarly, the valuation of inventory is affected if the direct labor cost of individual employees is incorrectly charged to the wrong job or process. When jobs are billed on a cost-plus basis, revenue and the valuation of inventory are both affected by charging labor to incorrect jobs.

When labor is a material part of inventory valuation, auditors should emphasize testing internal controls over proper classification of payroll transactions. Consistency from period to period is essential for classification and can be tested by tracing job tickets or other evidence of an employee having worked on a job or process to the accounting records that affect inventory valuation. For example, if employees must account for all of their time each week by assigning it to individual jobs, a useful test is to trace the recorded hours of several employees to the related job-cost records to

CFOs PERSONALLY LIABLE FOR TAXES OF THE ENTITY

Serving as an organization's chief financial officer can be rewarding but challenging. Along with all the responsibilities that come with this role, a detail that may surprise a new CFO is the fact that he or she may be held personally liable if the business fails to pay taxes due, including payroll taxes. State and federal laws include provisions stating that "responsible persons" are personally liable for taxes owed, but not paid, to the government. That would include taxes withheld by the business as wage withholdings from employees and sales taxes collected from customers.

Companies that are struggling financially may be looking for ways to juggle their limited cash flows. In some instances, the company may consider delaying indefinitely the payment of tax obligations with the hope of catching up in the near term. Unfortunately, in those situations companies often fail, and by the time the government begins seeking taxes owed, the company has no way to pay. Responsible person liability laws address that by making individuals, such as CFOs, liable for business taxes due if they fail to ensure that the taxes are submitted. Executives need to implement controls to ensure taxes are properly paid, or they may face a huge personal tax bill.

Sources: 1. Arthur R. Rosen and Matthew C. Boch, "CFOs Face Liability for Business Taxes," *CFO.com* (January 5, 2015) (www.cfo.com); 2. Dennis Brager, "Case Finds CFOs Liable for Payroll Taxes," *CFO.com* (October 4, 2012) (www.cfo.com).

make sure each has been correctly recorded. It may also be desirable to trace from the job-cost records to time records as a test for nonexistent payroll charges being included in inventory.

Tests for Nonexistent Employees Issuing payroll disbursements to individuals who do not work for the company (nonexistent employees) often results from the continuance of an employee on payroll after employment was terminated. Usually, the person committing this type of embezzlement is a payroll clerk, supervisor, fellow employee, or perhaps the former employee. Under some systems, a supervisor can clock in daily for an employee and approve the time card at the end of the time period. If the supervisor also distributes paychecks or if payroll is deposited directly into employees' accounts, considerable opportunity exists for embezzlement.

To detect embezzlement, auditors may compare the names on cancelled checks or the account into which payroll has been deposited with time records and other records for authorized signatures and reasonableness of the endorsements. Audit software can be used to compare all account numbers into which payroll is deposited to search for duplicates. It is also common to scan endorsements on cancelled checks for unusual or recurring second endorsements as an indication of a possible fraudulent check. Examining checks that are recorded as voided is also desirable to make sure that they have not been fraudulently used.

To test for nonexistent employees, auditors can trace selected transactions recorded in the payroll journal to the human resources department to determine whether the employees were actually employed during the payroll period. If paid by check, the endorsement on the cancelled check written out to an employee can be compared with the authorized signature on the employee's withholding authorization forms.

A procedure that tests for proper handling of terminated employees is to select several files from the human resource records for employees who were terminated in the current year to determine whether each received termination pay consistent with company policy. Continuing payments to terminated employees can be tested by using audit software to compare termination dates according to the human resources department to payroll disbursement dates in the payroll journal to verify the employee is no longer being paid. Naturally, this procedure is not effective if the human resources department is not informed of terminations.

In some cases, the auditor may request a surprise payroll payoff. This is a procedure in which all employees must pick up and sign their checks or direct deposit payroll records in the presence of a supervisor and the auditor. Any checks that have not been claimed must be subject to an extensive investigation to determine whether an unclaimed check is fraudulent. Surprise payoff is often expensive, but it may be the only likely means of detecting an embezzlement.

Tests for Fraudulent Hours Fraudulent hours occur when an employee reports more time than was actually worked. Because of the lack of available evidence, it is usually difficult for an auditor to discover fraudulent hours. One procedure is to reconcile the total hours paid according to the payroll records with an independent record of the hours worked, such as those often maintained by production control. Audit software can be used to test the reasonableness of hours worked or total pay for each employee and unusual amounts identified for follow-up testing. Similarly, it may be possible to observe an employee clocking in more than one time card under a buddy approach. However, it is ordinarily easier for the client to prevent this type of embezzlement by adequate controls than for the auditor to detect it.

Fraudulent Expense Reports Reimbursements for travel and entertainment expenses are a part of the acquisition and payment cycle; however, auditors often perform additional procedures as part of payroll and personnel testing. Management falsification of expense reports can be an indicator of disregard for internal controls and the potential for fraud in other areas as well. As a result, auditors should pay particular attention to travel and entertainment expense reports for officers and directors and should perform testing by verifying proper approval and the business purpose of the travel, examining supporting receipts, and determining whether the reimbursements are within company guidelines.

METHODOLOGY FOR DESIGNING SUBSTANTIVE ANALYTICAL PROCEDURES AND TESTS OF DETAILS OF BALANCES

OBJECTIVE 20-4

Design and perform substantive analytical procedures and tests of details for accounts in the payroll and personnel cycle.

During the first two phases of the audit, auditors assess control risk and perform tests of controls and substantive tests of transactions. After completing these tests and assessing the likelihood of misstatement in financial statement accounts in the payroll and personnel cycle, the auditor follows the methodology for designing tests of details of balances.

The methodology for deciding the appropriate tests of details of balances for payroll liability accounts is the same as that followed in Chapter 16 for accounts receivable and Chapters 18 and 19 for acquisition and payment balance sheet accounts. (See Figure 16-1 on p. 525 for the accounts receivable methodology.)

Identify Client Business Risks Affecting Payroll (Phase I)

Significant client business risks affecting payroll are unlikely for most companies. However, client business risk may exist for complex compensation arrangements, including bonus and stock option plans and other deferred compensation arrangements. For example, many technology and other companies provide extensive stock options as part of their compensation packages for key employees that significantly impact compensation expense and shareholders' equity. Examples of other risks include events such as renegotiation of union contracts and discrimination claims. The auditor should understand the likelihood of these events and determine their potential effects on the financial statements, including footnote disclosures.

Set Performance Materiality and Assess Inherent Risk (Phase I)

Most companies have a large number of transactions involving payroll, often with large total amounts. However, balance sheet accounts are normally insignificant, except for labor charged to inventory.

Aside from the potential for fraud, inherent risk is typically low for all balance-related audit objectives. There is inherent risk of payroll fraud because most transactions involve cash. Therefore, auditors often consider the occurrence transaction-related objective important. Also, for manufacturing companies with significant labor charged to inventory, the potential exists for misclassification between payroll expense and inventory, or among categories of inventory. As a part of gaining an understanding of the client, the auditor may identify complex payroll-related issues, such as stock-based compensation plans, that may increase inherent risks related to the accounting and disclosure of those arrangements.

Assess Control Risk and Perform Related Tests (Phases I and II)

Earlier in this chapter, we discussed assessing control risk and the related tests of controls and substantive tests of transactions. Refer to Table 20-2 (p. 668) for a review of these topics.

Perform Substantive Analytical Procedures (Phase III)

The use of substantive analytical procedures is as important in the payroll and personnel cycle as it is in every other cycle. Table 20-3 illustrates substantive analytical procedures for the balance sheet and income statement accounts in the payroll and personnel cycle. Most of the relationships in the first column are predictable and are therefore useful for identifying areas in which additional investigation is desirable.

TABLE 20-3 Substantive Analytical Procedures for the Payroll and Personnel Cycle

Substantive Analytical Procedure	Possible Misstatement
Compare payroll expense account balance with previous years (adjusted for pay rate increases and increases in volume).	Misstatement of payroll expense accounts
Compare direct labor as a percentage of sales with previous years.	Misstatement of direct labor and inventory
Compare commission expense as a percentage of sales with previous years.	Misstatement of commission expense and commission liability
Compare payroll tax expense as a percentage of salaries and wages with previous years (adjusted for changes in the tax rates).	Misstatement of payroll tax expense and payroll tax liability
Compare accrued payroll tax accounts with previous years.	Misstatement of accrued payroll taxes and payroll tax expense

Design and Perform Tests of Details of Balances for Liability and Expense Accounts (Phase III)

The verification of the liability accounts associated with payroll, often termed **accrued payroll expenses**, is ordinarily straightforward if internal controls are operating effectively. When the auditor is satisfied that payroll transactions are being correctly recorded in the payroll journal and the related payroll tax forms are being accurately prepared and taxes promptly paid, the tests of details of balances should not be time consuming.

The two major balance-related audit objectives in testing payroll liabilities are:

1. Accruals in the trial balance are stated at the correct amounts (accuracy).
2. Transactions in the payroll and personnel cycle are recorded in the proper period (cutoff).

The primary concern in both objectives is to make sure that there are no understated or omitted accruals. Next, we examine the major liability accounts in the payroll and personnel cycle.

Amounts Withheld from Employees' Pay Payroll taxes withheld but not yet paid to the government can be tested by comparing the balance with the payroll journal, the payroll tax form prepared in the subsequent period, and the subsequent period cash disbursements. Other withheld items such as retirement savings, union dues, savings bonds, and insurance can be verified in the same manner. If internal controls are operating effectively, cutoff and accuracy can easily be tested at the same time by these procedures.

Accrued Salaries and Wages The accrual for salaries and wages arises whenever employees are not paid for the last few days or hours of earned wages until the subsequent period. Salaried personnel usually receive all of their pay except overtime on the last day of the month, but often, several days of wages for hourly employees are unpaid at the end of the year.

SEC's NEW PAY RATIO DISCLOSURE

The Securities and Exchange Commission (SEC) issued a new rule in August 2015 that requires a public company to disclose the ratio of the compensation of its chief executive officer (CEO) to the median compensation of its employees. This new rule is in response to mandates in the Dodd-Frank Wall Street Reform and Consumer Protection Act. Effective for fiscal years beginning on or after January 1, 2017, public companies will be required to include this disclosure in proxy statements and annual reports that require executive compensation disclosure.

The SEC's rule provides a company flexibility in determining the pay ratio, such as how it selects a methodology for identifying its median employee and that employee's compensation. For example, that methodology might include statistical sampling of the employee population and the rule allows a company to make the median employee determination once every three years. Companies would be required to calculate the annual total compensation for its median employee using the same rules that apply to calculating CEO compensation, and companies must include disclosure that describes the methodology used and any material assumptions, adjustments, or estimates made to identify the median employee or to determine total compensation.

Source: U.S. Securities and Exchange Commission, "Pay Ratio Disclosure," Release Nos. 33-9877; 34-75610; File No. S7-07-13 (August 5, 2015) (www.sec.gov).

The correct cutoff and accuracy of accrued salaries and wages depend on company policy, which should be followed consistently from year to year. Some companies calculate the exact hours of pay that were earned in the current period and paid in the subsequent period, whereas others compute an approximate proportion. For example, if the subsequent payroll results from three days of employment during the current year and two days of employment during the subsequent year, the use of 60 percent of the subsequent period's gross pay as the accrual is an example of an approximation.

After the auditor has determined the company's policy for accruing wages and knows that it is consistent with that of previous years, the appropriate audit procedure to test for cutoff and accuracy is to recalculate the client's accrual. The most likely misstatement of any significance in the balance is the failure to include the proper number of days of earned-but-unpaid wages.

Accrued Commissions The same concepts used in verifying accrued salaries and wages are applicable to accrued commissions, but the accrual is often more difficult to verify because companies often have several different types of agreements with salespeople and other commission employees. For example, some salespeople might be paid a commission every month and earn no salary, whereas others will get a monthly salary plus a commission paid quarterly. In verifying accrued commissions, it is necessary first to determine the nature of the commission agreement and then test the calculations based on the agreement. The auditor should compare the method of accruing commissions with that of previous years for purposes of consistency.

Accrued Bonuses In many companies, the year-end unpaid bonuses to officers and employees are such a major item that the failure to record them will result in a material misstatement. The verification of the recorded accrual can usually be accomplished by comparing it with the amount authorized in the board minutes.

Accrued Vacation Pay, Sick Pay, or Other Benefits The consistent accrual of these liabilities relative to those of the preceding year is the most important consideration in evaluating the fairness of the amounts. The company policy for recording the liability must first be determined, and then the recorded amounts must be recalculated. The company policy should be in accordance with accounting standards for compensated absences.

Accrued Payroll Taxes Payroll taxes, such as FICA and state and federal unemployment taxes, can be verified by examining tax forms prepared in the subsequent period to determine the amount that should have been recorded as a liability at the balance sheet date.

Tests of Details of Balances for Expense Accounts Several accounts on the income statement are affected by payroll transactions. The most important are officers' salaries and bonuses, office salaries, sales salaries and commissions, and direct manufacturing labor. Often, costs may be broken down further by division, product, or branch. Fringe benefits such as medical insurance may also be included in the expenses.

Auditors should need to do relatively little additional testing of the income statement accounts in most audits beyond substantive analytical procedures, tests of controls, substantive tests of transactions, and related tests of liability accounts already discussed. Extensive additional testing should be necessary only when auditors uncover significant deficiencies or material weaknesses in internal control, significant misstatements in the liability tests, or major unexplained variances in the substantive analytical procedures. Nevertheless, some income statement accounts are often tested in the payroll and personnel cycle. These include officers' compensation, commissions, payroll tax expense, total payroll, and contract labor.

Officers' Compensation It is common to verify whether the total compensation of officers is the amount authorized by the board of directors, because their salaries and bonuses must be included in the company's Form 10-K filed with the SEC and federal income tax return. Verification of officers' compensation is also warranted because some individuals may be in a position to pay themselves more than the authorized amount. The usual audit test is to obtain the authorized salary of each officer from the minutes of the board of directors meetings and compare it with the related earnings record.

Commissions Auditors can verify commission expense with relative ease if the commission rate is the same for each type of sale and the necessary sales information is available in the accounting records. The total commission expense can be verified by multiplying the commission rate for each type of sale by the amount of sales in that category. If the desired information is not available, it may be necessary to test the annual or monthly commission payments for selected salespeople and trace those to the total commission payments.

Payroll Tax Expense Payroll tax expense for the year can be tested by first reconciling the total payroll on each payroll tax form with the total payroll for the entire year. Total payroll taxes can then be recomputed by multiplying the appropriate rate by the taxable payroll. The calculation is often time-consuming because the tax is usually applicable on only a portion of the payroll and the rate may change partway through the year if the taxpayer's financial statements are not on a calendar-year basis. On most audits, the calculation is costly and is not necessary unless substantive analytical procedures indicate a problem that cannot be resolved through other procedures. When necessary, the test is ordinarily done in conjunction with tests of payroll tax accruals.

Total Payroll A test closely related to the one for payroll taxes is the reconciliation of total payroll expense in the general ledger with the payroll tax returns and the W-2 forms. The objectives of the test are to determine whether payroll transactions were charged to a non-payroll account or not recorded in the payroll journal at all. Because the payroll tax records and the payroll are both usually prepared directly from the payroll master file, the misstatements, if any, are likely to be in both records. Tests of controls and substantive tests of transactions are a better means of uncovering these two types of misstatements in most audits.

Contract Labor To reduce payroll costs, many organizations contract with outside organizations to provide staffing. The individuals providing the services are employed by the outside organization. For example, companies frequently contract with information technology services firms to handle the company's IT management and staffing functions. The fees paid to the outside organization are tested by comparing the amounts with the signed contract arrangement between the company and the outside services firm.

Presentation and Disclosure Objectives Required disclosures for payroll and personnel cycle transactions and balances are not extensive. However, some complex transactions, such as stock options and other executive officer compensation plans, may require footnote disclosure. Auditors may combine audit procedures related to the four presentation and disclosure objectives with tests of details of balances for liability and expense accounts. Other procedures related to presentation and disclosure objectives are further discussed in Chapter 24.

CONCEPT CHECK

1. List five tests of controls that can be performed for the payroll and personnel cycle and state the purpose of each control tested.
2. Explain the circumstances under which an auditor should perform audit tests primarily designed to uncover fraud in the payroll and personnel cycle.

SUMMARY

This chapter described the audit of the payroll and personnel cycle. Figure 20-2 illustrates the major accounts in the payroll and personnel cycle and the types of audit tests used to audit these accounts. Tests of controls and substantive tests of transactions are emphasized because of the significance of transactions and the high quality of internal controls in most companies. Tests of details of balances are normally limited to substantive analytical procedures and verification of accrued liabilities related to payroll.

FIGURE 20-2 Types of Audit Tests for the Payroll and Personnel Cycle (see Figure 20-1 on p. 664 for accounts)

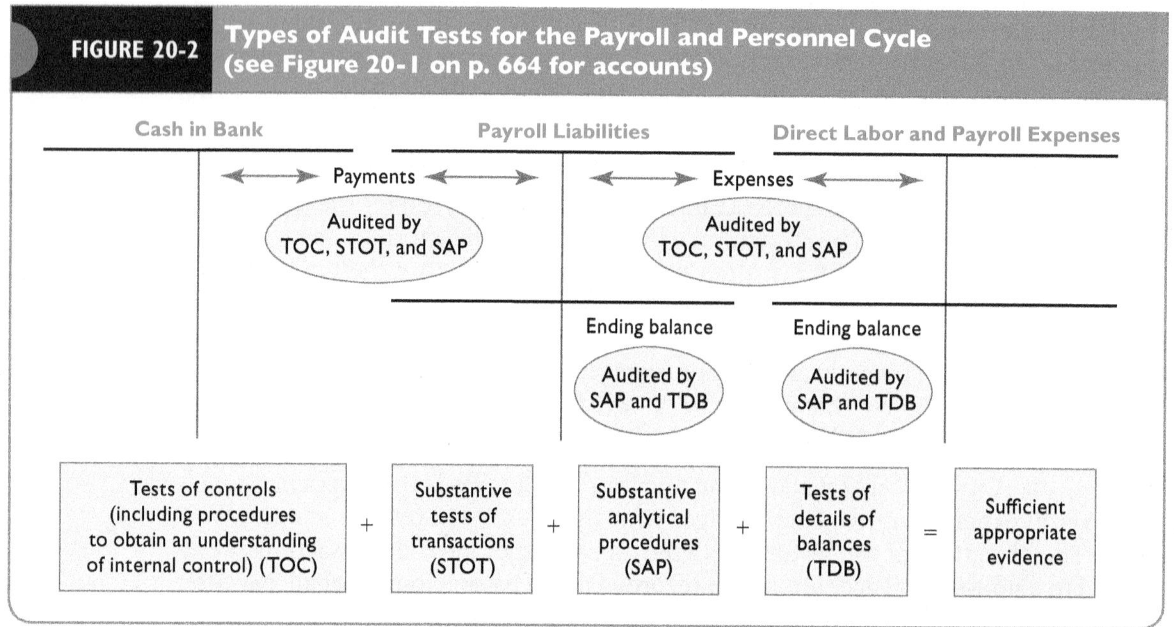

ESSENTIAL TERMS

Accrued payroll expenses—the liability accounts associated with payroll; these include accounts for accrued salaries and wages, accrued commissions, accrued bonuses, accrued benefits, and accrued payroll taxes

Human resource records—records that include such data as the date of employment, personnel investigations, rates of pay, authorized deductions, performance evaluations, and termination of employment

Imprest payroll account—a bank account to which the exact amount of payroll for the pay period is transferred by check or wire transfer from the employer's general cash account

Payroll and personnel cycle—the transaction cycle that begins with the hiring of personnel, includes obtaining and accounting for services from the employees, and ends with payment to the employees for the services performed and to the government and other institutions for withheld and accrued payroll taxes and benefits

Payroll master file—a computer file for recording each payroll transaction for each employee and maintaining total employee wages paid and related data for the year to date

Time record—a document indicating the time that the employee started and stopped working each day and the number of hours worked

REVIEW QUESTIONS

20-1 (OBJECTIVE 20-1) Identify five general ledger accounts that are likely to be affected by the payroll and personnel cycle in most audits.

20-2 (OBJECTIVES 20-1, 20-3) Explain the relationship between the payroll and personnel cycle and inventory valuation.

20-3 **(OBJECTIVE 20-2)** Distinguish among a payroll master file, a W-2 form, and a payroll tax return. Explain the purpose of each.

20-4 **(OBJECTIVE 20-2)** Explain what is meant by an imprest payroll account. What is its purpose as a control over payroll?

20-5 **(OBJECTIVES 20-2, 20-3)** List the supporting documents and records the auditor will examine in a typical payroll audit in which the primary objective is to detect fraud.

20-6 **(OBJECTIVES 20-2, 20-3)** Evaluate the following comment by an auditor: "My job is to determine whether the payroll records are fairly stated in accordance with accounting standards, not to find out whether they are following proper hiring and termination procedures. When I conduct an audit of payroll, I keep out of the human resources department and stick to the time cards, journals, and payroll checks. I don't care whom they hire and whom they fire, as long as they properly pay the employees they have."

20-7 **(OBJECTIVE 20-3)** Distinguish between the following payroll audit procedures and state the purpose of each: (1) trace a random sample of prenumbered time cards to the related payments in the payroll register and compare the hours worked with the hours paid, and (2) trace a random sample of payments from the payroll register to the related time cards and compare the hours worked with the hours paid. Which of these two procedures is typically more important in the audit of payroll? Why?

20-8 **(OBJECTIVE 20-3)** Explain why the percentage of total audit time in the cycle devoted to performing tests of controls and substantive tests of transactions is usually far greater for the payroll and personnel cycle than for the sales and collection cycle.

20-9 **(OBJECTIVE 20-3)** List three audit procedures that are primarily for the detection of fraud and state the type of fraud the procedure is meant to uncover.

20-10 **(OBJECTIVE 20-3)** Identify three tests of controls or substantive tests of transactions in the payroll and personnel cycle that an auditor may perform using audit software.

20-11 **(OBJECTIVE 20-3)** List five types of authorizations in the payroll and personnel cycle and state the type of misstatement that is likely to occur when each authorization is lacking.

20-12 **(OBJECTIVE 20-3)** Explain how audit sampling can be used to test the payroll and personnel cycle.

20-13 **(OBJECTIVE 20-4)** In auditing payroll withholding and payroll tax expense, explain why emphasis should normally be on evaluating the adequacy of the payroll tax return preparation procedures rather than the payroll tax liability. If the preparation procedures are inadequate, explain the effect this will have on the remainder of the audit.

20-14 **(OBJECTIVE 20-4)** List several substantive analytical procedures for the payroll and personnel cycle and explain the type of misstatement that might be indicated when there is a significant difference in the comparison of the current year with previous years' results for each of the tests.

20-15 **(OBJECTIVE 20-4)** Explain why it is common to verify total officers' compensation even when the tests of controls and substantive tests of transactions results in payroll are excellent. What audit procedures can be used to verify officers' compensation?

MULTIPLE CHOICE QUESTIONS FROM CPA EXAMINATIONS

20-16 **(OBJECTIVE 20-3)** The following questions concern internal controls in the payroll and personnel cycle. Choose the best response.

a. Control risk is the risk that a material misstatement in an account will not be prevented or detected on a timely basis by the client's internal controls. The best control to prevent or detect fictitious payroll transactions is to
   (1) use and account for prenumbered payroll checks.
   (2) restrict authorization for hiring, terminating, or changing pay rate or job status to the human resources function.
   (3) verify internally authorized pay rates, computations, and agreement with the payroll register.
   (4) conduct periodic independent bank reconciliations of the payroll bank account.

b. A factory supervisor at Steblecki Corporation discharged an hourly worker but did not notify the human resources department. The supervisor then forged the worker's signature on time cards and work tickets and, when giving out the checks, diverted the payroll checks drawn from the discharged worker to his own use. The most effective procedure for preventing this activity is to
   (1) require written authorization for all employees added to or removed from the payroll.
   (2) have a paymaster who has no other payroll responsibility distribute the payroll checks.
   (3) have someone other than persons who prepare or distribute the payroll obtain custody of unclaimed payroll checks.
   (4) from time to time, rotate persons distributing the payroll.

c. An auditor found that employee time records in one department are not properly approved by the supervisor. Which of the following could result?
   (1) Duplicate paychecks might be issued.
   (2) The wrong hourly rate could be used to calculate gross pay.
   (3) Employees might be paid for hours they did not work.
   (4) Payroll checks might not be distributed to the appropriate employees.

20-17 **(OBJECTIVE 20-3)** The following questions concern audit testing of the payroll and personnel cycle. Choose the best response.

a. A common audit procedure in the audit of payroll transactions involves tracing selected items from the payroll journal to employee time cards that have been approved by supervisory personnel. This procedure is designed to provide evidence in support of the audit proposition that
   (1) only proper employees worked and their pay was correctly computed.
   (2) jobs on which employees worked were charged with the appropriate labor cost.
   (3) internal controls over payroll disbursements are operating effectively.
   (4) all employees worked the number of hours for which their pay was computed.

b. In performing tests concerning the granting of stock options, an auditor should
   (1) confirm the transaction with the Secretary of State in the state of incorporation.
   (2) verify the existence of option holders in the entity's payroll records or stock ledgers.
   (3) determine that sufficient treasury stock is available to cover any new stock issued.
   (4) trace the authorization for the transaction to a vote of the board of directors.

c. An auditor reviews the reconciliation of payroll tax forms that a client is responsible for filing to
   (1) verify that payroll taxes are deducted from employees' gross pay.
   (2) determine whether internal control activities are operating effectively.
   (3) uncover fictitious employees who are receiving payroll checks.
   (4) identify potential liabilities for unpaid payroll taxes.

MULTIPLE CHOICE QUESTIONS FROM BECKER CPA EXAM REVIEW

20-18 **(OBJECTIVES 20-2, 20-3)** The following questions concern auditor responsibilities related to the audit of the payroll and personnel cycle. Choose the best response.

a. In auditing the payroll function of a client, an auditor would least likely
   (1) request specific management representations related to payroll.
   (2) verify proper segregation of duties.
   (3) recalculate year-end payroll accruals.
   (4) apply analytical procedures.

b. An auditor most likely would introduce test data into a computerized payroll system to test internal controls related to the
   (1) existence of unclaimed payroll checks held by supervisors.
   (2) early cashing of payroll checks by employees.
   (3) discovery of invalid employee I.D. numbers.
   (4) proper approval of overtime by supervisors.

c. An auditor is performing a preliminary assessment of a large client's internal controls over payroll. The auditor would identify which of the following as an improper segregation of duties related to the payroll functions?
   (1) Each employee's weekly time card must be approved by the immediate supervisor.
   (2) While the majority of the payroll checks are direct deposits, all manual checks are handed out on a weekly basis by the paymaster.
   (3) All blank checks and the check signature plate are maintained by human resources.
   (4) The payroll department calculates the weekly salary distribution based on information received, and prepares unsigned checks, which are forwarded to the treasurer for approval.

DISCUSSION QUESTIONS AND PROBLEMS

20-19 **(OBJECTIVES 20-2, 20-3)** Items 1 through 8 are selected questions typically found in internal control questionnaires used by auditors to obtain an understanding of internal control in the payroll and personnel cycle. In using the questionnaire for a client, a "yes" response to a question indicates a possible internal control, whereas a "no" indicates a potential deficiency.

1. Does an appropriate official authorize initial rates of pay and any subsequent changes in rates?
2. Are formal records such as time cards used for keeping time?
3. Is approval by a department head or supervisor required for all time cards before they are submitted for payment?
4. Does an adequate process exist to ensure proper coding of time records to specific jobs or products, such as work orders, job numbers, or some similar identification provided to employees?
5. Is the distribution of payments to employees independent of timekeeping?
6. Are employees required to show identification to receive paychecks or are they required to use direct deposit?
7. Are written notices documenting reasons for termination required?
8. Does anyone independently verify the payroll bank account reconciliation?

Required

a. For each of the questions, state the transaction-related audit objective(s) being fulfilled if the control is in effect.
b. For each control, list a test of control to test its effectiveness.
c. For each of the questions, identify the nature of the potential financial misstatement(s) if the control is not in effect.
d. For each of the potential misstatements in part c., list a substantive audit procedure for determining whether a material misstatement exists.

20-20 **(OBJECTIVES 20-2, 20-3)** Following are some of the tests of controls and substantive tests of transactions procedures often performed in the payroll and personnel cycle. (Each procedure is to be done on a sample basis or using audit software.)

1. Reconcile the monthly payroll total for direct manufacturing labor with the labor cost distribution.
2. Examine the time card for the approval of a supervisor.
3. Recompute hours on the time card and compare the total with the total hours for which the employee has been paid.
4. Perform a surprise payroll payoff and observe employees picking up and signing for their checks.

5. Compare the employee name, date, check number, and amounts on cancelled checks with the payroll journal.
6. Trace the hours from the employee time records to job tickets to make sure that the total reconciles, and trace each job ticket to the job-cost record.
7. Use audit software to account for the sequence of payroll checks in the payroll journal.

Required

a. Identify whether each of the procedures is primarily a test of control or a substantive test of transactions.
b. Identify the transaction-related audit objective(s) of each of the procedures.

20-21 (OBJECTIVES 20-2, 20-3) The following misstatements are included in the accounting records of Lathen Manufacturing Company:

1. Joe Block and Frank Demery take turns "punching in" for each other every few days. The absent employee comes in at noon and tells his foreman that he had car trouble or some other problem. The foreman does not know that the employee is getting paid for the time.
2. The foreman submits a fraudulent time card for a former employee each week and delivers the related payroll check to the employee's house on the way home from work. They split the amount of the paycheck.
3. Employees often overlook recording their hours worked on job-cost tickets as required by the system. Many of the client's contracts are on a cost-plus basis.
4. Direct labor was unintentionally charged to job 620 instead of job 602 by the payroll clerk when he key-entered the labor distribution sheets. Job 602 was completed and the costs were expensed in the current year, whereas job 620 was included in work-in-process.
5. The payroll clerk prepares a check to the same nonexistent person every week when he enters payroll transactions in the computer system, which also records the amount in the payroll journal. He submits it along with all other payroll checks for signature. When the checks are returned to him for distribution, he takes the check and deposits it in a special bank account bearing that person's name.
6. In withholding payroll taxes from employees, the computer operator deducts $0.50 extra federal income taxes from several employees each week and credits the amount to his own employee earnings record.
7. The payroll clerk manually prepares payroll checks but often forgets to record one or two checks in the computer-prepared payroll journal.

Required

a. For each misstatement, state a control that should have prevented it from occurring on a continuing basis.
b. For each misstatement, state a substantive audit procedure that could uncover it.

20-22 (OBJECTIVES 20-3, 20-4) The following audit procedures are typical of those found in auditing the payroll and personnel cycle:

1. Obtain a schedule of all payroll liabilities and trace to the general ledger.
2. Discuss with management any payroll liabilities recorded in the prior year that are not provided for in the current period.
3. Scan journals for all periods for unusual transactions to determine whether they are recorded correctly.
4. Select a sample of 40 entries in the payroll journal and trace each to an approved time card.
5. Examine owner approval of rates of pay and withholdings.
6. Examine evidence that payroll hours and wage rates are verified by an independent person.
7. Select a sample of 20 cancelled payroll checks and account for the numerical sequence.
8. Review board of director meeting minutes to verify the salary for the chief executive officer.
9. Compute payroll tax expense as a percentage of total wages, salaries, and commissions.

10. Select a sample of 20 payroll payments and trace to payroll journal entries for name, date, and amounts.

Required

a. Select the type of test for each audit procedure from the following:
   (1) Test of control
   (2) Substantive test of transactions
   (3) Substantive analytical procedure
   (4) Test of details of balances
b. For each test of control or substantive test of transactions, identify the applicable transaction-related audit objective(s).
c. For each test of details of balances, identify the applicable balance-related audit objective(s).

20-23 **(OBJECTIVE 20-4)** Alyssa Ghose is auditing payroll accruals for a manufacturing company. The client has accrued payroll taxes, accrued vacation pay, and accrued bonuses for salespersons as of the end of the fiscal year. Ghose performed the following audit procedures.

1. Compared all accrual balances in the current year to the prior year and noted no significant fluctuations.
2. Traced the subsequent payment of payroll taxes to the cash disbursements journal and the bank statement.
3. Reviewed a sample of contracts with salespersons to verify the bonus formula.
4. Reviewed cancelled checks for a sample of checks disbursed after year end for unused vacation pay.

Required

a. Are the audit procedures performed by Ghose sufficient to test accrued payroll tax, vacation pay, and bonuses? If not, what additional procedures should she perform?
b. For each additional procedure you recommend in part a., identify the related audit objective the procedure would satisfy.

20-24 **(OBJECTIVES 20-3, 20-4)** The following are steps in the methodology for designing tests of controls, substantive tests of transactions, and tests of details of balances for the payroll and personnel cycle:

1. Design tests of details of balances for the payroll and personnel cycle.
2. Evaluate whether control risk can be assessed as low for payroll.
3. Design and perform payroll- and personnel-related substantive analytical procedures.
4. Identify controls and deficiencies in internal control for the payroll and personnel cycle.
5. Obtain an understanding of the payroll and personnel cycle internal controls.
6. Evaluate tests of controls and substantive tests of transactions results.
7. Design payroll and personnel cycle tests of controls and substantive tests of transactions.
8. Assess inherent risk for payroll-related accounts.
9. Evaluate risk and materiality for payroll expense and liability accounts.

Required

a. Identify (1) those steps that are tests of controls or substantive tests of transactions and (2) those that are tests of details of balances.
b. Put steps that are tests of controls and substantive tests of transactions in the order of their performance in most audits.
c. Put the tests of details of balances in their proper order.

20-25 **(OBJECTIVE 20-3)** You are assessing internal control in the audit of the payroll and personnel cycle for Rogers Products Company, a manufacturing company specializing in assembling computer parts. Rogers employs approximately two hundred hourly and thirty salaried employees in three locations. Each location has one foreman who is responsible for overseeing operations. The owner of the company lives in Naples, Florida, and is not actively involved in the business. The two key executives are the vice president of sales and the controller, and both have been employed by the company for more than fifteen years.

New hourly employees are hired by the foremen at each location on an as-needed basis. Each foreman recommends the wage rate for each new employee as well as wage rate increases. The effectiveness of employees varies considerably, and their wages are adjusted accordingly. All wage rates are approved by the controller.

Since each hourly employee works independently, Rogers has a highly flexible work schedule policy, as long as they start after 7:00 a.m. and are finished by 6:00 p.m. Each foreman has a supply of prenumbered time cards that he or she distributes to employees on Monday morning. Because some employees do not start until later in the day, several time cards are kept in a box by the time clock for their use. Hourly employees use time clocks to record when they start and stop working. Each Friday, after the employees complete their work for the week, the foremen account for the time cards they distributed, approve them, and send them by an overnight courier to the main office in Cincinnati.

The payroll clerk receives the time cards on Saturday and enters the information using payroll software that prepares the checks or direct deposit authorizations and the related payroll records. The checks are ready for the controller to sign Monday morning. She compares each check to the payroll transactions list sent by the payroll department and returns the checks using the same courier to each location. The foremen pick up the checks and distribute each check to the appropriate employee. If an employee is not present at the end of the day, the foreman mails it to the employee's address.

Except for the foremen, all salaried employees work in the Cincinnati office. The vice president of sales or the controller hires all salaried employees, depending on their responsibilities, and determines their salaries and salary adjustments. The owner determines the salary of the vice president of sales and the controller. The payroll clerk also processes the payroll transactions for salaried employees using the same payroll software that is used for hourly employees, but all salaried employees use direct deposit so no check is prepared.

The payroll software has access controls that are set by the controller. She is the only person who has access to the salary and wage rate module of the software. She updates the software for new wage rates and salaries and changes of existing ones. The accounting clerk has access to all other payroll modules. The controller's assistant has been taught to reconcile bank accounts and does the reconciliation monthly.

Required

a. Identify the internal control deficiencies in the Rogers Products Company's payroll system.
b. For each deficiency, state the type of misstatement that is likely to result. Be as specific as possible in describing the nature of the misstatement. If the potential misstatement involves fraud, identify who is most likely to perpetuate the fraud.

20-26 **(OBJECTIVE 20-3)** The following are various asset misappropriations involving the payroll and personnel cycle.

1. The payroll clerk increased his salary by $100 each pay period. After a few weeks, he also increased the hourly rate for his friend who works in the shipping department.
2. The payroll clerk submitted payroll information for a fictitious employee and had the funds directly deposited to a bank account that he controlled.
3. An employee adds 10 overtime hours that she did not work to her time record each pay period.
4. Two factory employees have an arrangement that one of them will take each Friday off, and the other employee will record their time worked so that the absent employee will be paid.
5. A supervisor does not notify human resources that an hourly employee has left the company. He continues to submit time records for the employee. The money is directly deposited in the former employee's bank account, and he splits the amount paid with the supervisor.

Required

a. For each misappropriation, indicate the transaction-related audit objective that was not met.
b. Indicate one or more controls that would be most effective in preventing or detecting the misappropriation.
c. Because the controller is concerned about fictitious employees, she has recommended a surprise payroll payoff. Which misappropriations would be detected by the surprise payroll payoff? How is the payoff done if employees do not receive payroll checks because payment is directly deposited into their bank accounts?

20-27 **(OBJECTIVE 20-4)** Archer Uniforms, Inc., is a distributor of professional uniforms to retail stores that sell work clothing to professionals, such as doctors, nurses, security guards, etc. Traditionally, most of the sales are to retail stores throughout the United

States and Canada. Most shipments are processed in bulk for delivery directly to retail stores or to the corporate office warehouse distribution facilities for retail store chains. In early 2016, Archer Uniforms began offering the sale of uniforms directly to professionals through its company Web site. Professionals can access online information about uniform styles, sizes, and prices. Purchases are applied to the customer's personal credit card, and the credit card agencies wire funds to Archer's bank account periodically throughout the month. Management made this decision based on its conclusion that the online sales would tap a new market of professionals who do not have easy access to retail stores. Thus, the volume of shipments to retail stores is expected to remain consistent.

Because Archer's IT staff lacked the necessary experience to create and support the online sales system, management engaged an information technology consulting firm to design and maintain the online sales system.

Required

Before performing substantive analytical procedures related to the payroll and personnel cycle accounts, develop expectations of how these recent events at Archer Uniforms, Inc., will affect payroll expense for the following departments during 2016 compared to prior years. Indicate the degree (extensive, moderate, little) to which you expect the payroll expense account balance to increase or decrease during 2016.

1. Warehouse and Shipping Department
2. IT Department
3. Accounts Receivable Department
4. Accounts Payable Department
5. Receiving Department
6. Executive Management
7. Marketing

20-28 **(OBJECTIVE 20-4)** Chief executive officer compensation can be a material amount and is often scrutinized by regulators, analysts, competitors, and investors. For CEOs of publicly traded companies, compensation can consist of salary, bonus, stock option grants, or other stock awards that can be restricted in terms of how long the officers and directors are required to hold the stock. Publicly traded companies are required by the Securities and Exchange Commission to provide disclosures about the components of executive compensation in the company's annual proxy statement.

Required

a. Visit the SEC's Web site (www.sec.gov) to locate the annual proxy statement (the "DEF 14A" filing) submitted to the SEC on March 20, 2015, for Yum Brands, Inc., which owns Kentucky Fried Chicken, Pizza Hut, and Taco Bell restaurants. Locate the Summary Compensation Table within the annual proxy statement and identify the components of the Chairman and Chief Executive Officer's total compensation for 2014.
b. Provide at least one audit procedure the auditor would perform to test the Chairman and CEO's salary. What audit objective is satisfied with this audit procedure?
c. Provide at least one audit procedure the auditor would perform to test the occurrence objective related to the awarding of the Chairman and CEO's stock awards and stock option/stock appreciation rights (SAR).
d. How would the auditor test the fair value of the stock option/stock appreciation rights (SAR)?
e. Why are the presentation and disclosure-related audit objectives so important for stock-based compensation?

CASE

20-29 **(OBJECTIVE 20-3)** Roost and Briley, CPAs, are doing the audit of Leggert Lumber Co., an international wholesale lumber broker. Because of the nature of their business, payroll and telephone expense are the two largest expenses.

You are the in-charge auditor on the engagement responsible for developing the audit program for the payroll and personnel cycle. Leggert Lumber uses a computer service company to prepare weekly payroll checks, update earnings records, and prepare the weekly payroll journal for its 30 employees. The president maintains all human resource files, knows every employee extremely well, and is a full-time participant in the business.

All employees, except the president, check into the company building daily using a time clock. The president's secretary, Mary Clark, hands out the time cards daily, observes employees clocking in, collects the cards, and immediately returns them to the file. She goes through the same process when employees clock out on their way home.

At the end of each week, employees calculate their own hours. Clark rechecks those hours, and the president approves all time cards. Each Tuesday, Clark submits payroll input to the computer service center. She files a copy of the input data, which includes the following information for each employee:

Information	**Source**
Employee name	Time card
Social Security number	Employee list
Hourly labor rate*	Wage rate list (approved by president)
Regular hours	Time card
Overtime hours	Time card
Special deductions*	Special form (prepared by employee)
W-4 information*	W-4 form
Termination of employment*	President

*Included on input form only for new employees, terminations, and changes.

The service center uses the payroll data to update master files and print out payroll checks and a payroll register. The payroll register has the following headings:

Employee name	Overtime payroll dollars	State taxes withheld
Social Security number	Gross payroll	Other deductions
Regular hours	FICA taxes withheld	Net pay
Overtime hours	Medicare withheld	Check number
Regular payroll dollars	Federal taxes withheld	

A line is prepared for each employee and the journal is totaled.

Payroll checks and the journal are delivered to Clark, who compares the information on the journal with her payroll input and initials the journal. She gives the checks to the president, who signs them and personally delivers them to employees.

Clark re-adds the journal and posts the totals to the ledger. Bank statements with copies of cancelled checks are mailed to the president, and he prepares a monthly bank reconciliation.

Required

a. Is there any loss of documentation because of the computer service center? Explain.
b. For each transaction-related audit objective for the payroll and personnel cycle, write appropriate tests of controls and substantive tests of transactions audit procedures. Consider both controls and deficiencies in writing your program. Label each procedure as either a test of control or a substantive test of transactions.
c. Rearrange your design format audit program in requirement b. into a performance format audit program.
d. Prepare a sampling data sheet using either nonstatistical or attributes sampling, such as the ones shown in Chapter 15, for the audit program in part b. Set ARO and other factors required for sampling as you consider appropriate. Do not assume that you actually performed any tests.

AUDIT OF THE INVENTORY AND WAREHOUSING CYCLE

CHAPTER 21

LEARNING OBJECTIVES

After studying this chapter, you should be able to

21-1 Describe the business functions and the related documents and records in the inventory and warehousing cycle.

21-2 Explain the five parts of the audit of the inventory and warehousing cycle.

21-3 Design and perform audit tests of cost accounting.

21-4 Apply substantive analytical procedures to the accounts in the inventory and warehousing cycle.

21-5 Design and perform physical observation audit tests for inventory.

21-6 Design and perform audit tests of pricing and compilation for inventory.

21-7 Integrate the various parts of the audit of the inventory and warehousing cycle.

Phantom Inventory

Mickey Monus was the local hero in Youngstown, Ohio. He acquired a local drugstore, and within 10 years, added 299 more stores to form the national deep-discount retail chain Phar-Mor, Inc. The company was viewed as the rising star by some retail experts and was considered to be the next Wal-Mart. Even Sam Walton announced that the only company he feared in the expansion of Wal-Mart was Phar-Mor.

Phar-Mor sold a variety of household products and prescription drugs at substantially lower prices than other discount stores. Monus described the company's strategy as "power buying," whereby Phar-Mor loaded up on products when suppliers were selling at rock-bottom prices and passed those savings to cost-conscious customers.

Actually, Phar-Mor's prices were so low that the company was selling goods for less than their cost, causing the company to lose money. Monus continued to argue internally that through Phar-Mor's power buying, it would get so large that it could sell its way out of trouble. Unwilling to allow these shortfalls to damage Phar-Mor's appearance of success, Monus and his team began to engage in creative accounting so that Phar-Mor never reported these losses.

Management dumped the losses into "bucket accounts," only to reallocate those amounts to the company's hundreds of stores in the form of phantom increases in inventory costs. Monus' team issued fake invoices for merchandise purchases, made fraudulent journal entries to increase inventory and decrease cost of goods sold, and overcounted and double-counted inventory items.

Unfortunately, the auditors never uncovered the fraud. They allegedly observed inventory in only four stores out of 300, and they informed Phar-Mor management months in advance about the stores they would visit. Phar-Mor executives fully stocked the four selected stores but allocated the false inventory increases to the other 296 stores.

The fraud was ultimately uncovered when a travel agent received a Phar-Mor check signed by Monus paying for expenses unrelated to Phar-Mor. The agent showed the check to her landlord, who happened to be a Phar-Mor investor, and he contacted Phar-Mor's CEO. Subsequent investigation led to the discovery of the inventory fraud. Monus was eventually convicted and went to jail for 5 years. The audit failure cost the audit firm over $300 million in civil judgments.

Sources: 1. Beasley, Buckless, Glover, and Prawitt, *Auditing Cases: An Interactive Learning Approach*, 6th edition, Pearson Education Inc., 2015, pp. 129–141; 2. Joseph T. Wells, "Ghost Goods: How to Spot Phantom Inventory," *Journal of Accountancy* (June 2001), pp. 33–36.

The **inventory and warehousing cycle** is unique because of its close relationships to other transaction cycles. For a manufacturing company, raw material enters the inventory and warehousing cycle from the acquisition and payment cycle, while direct labor enters it from the payroll and personnel cycle. The inventory and warehousing cycle ends with the sale of goods in the sales and collection cycle.

The audit of inventory, especially tests of the year-end inventory balance, is often the most complex and time-consuming part of the audit. As the audit of Phar-Mor demonstrates, finding misstatements in inventory accounts can be challenging. Factors affecting the complexity of the audit of inventory include:

- Inventory is often the largest account on the balance sheet.
- Inventory is often in different locations, making physical control and counting difficult.
- Diverse inventory items such as jewels, chemicals, and electronic parts are often difficult for auditors to observe and value.
- Inventory valuation is also difficult when estimation of inventory obsolescence is necessary and when manufacturing costs must be allocated to inventory.
- There are several acceptable inventory valuation methods and some organizations may prefer to use different valuation methods for different parts of the inventory, which is acceptable under accounting standards.

BUSINESS FUNCTIONS IN THE CYCLE AND RELATED DOCUMENTS AND RECORDS

OBJECTIVE 21-1

Describe the business functions and the related documents and records in the inventory and warehousing cycle.

Inventory takes many different forms, depending on the nature of the business. For retail or wholesale businesses, the largest account in the financial statements is often merchandise inventory available for sale. To study the inventory and warehousing cycle, we will use the example of a manufacturing company, whose inventory may include raw materials, purchased parts and supplies for use in production, goods in the process of being manufactured, and finished goods available for sale. Still, most of the principles discussed apply to other types of businesses as well.

Figure 21-1 shows the physical flow of goods and the flow of costs in the inventory and warehousing cycle for a typical manufacturing company. Examine the debits to the raw materials, direct labor, and manufacturing overhead T accounts to see how the inventory and warehousing cycle ties in to the acquisition and payment cycle and the payroll and personnel cycle. The direct tie-in to the sales and collection cycle occurs at the point where finished goods are relieved (credited) and a charge is made to cost of goods sold.

FIGURE 21-1 Flow of Inventory and Costs

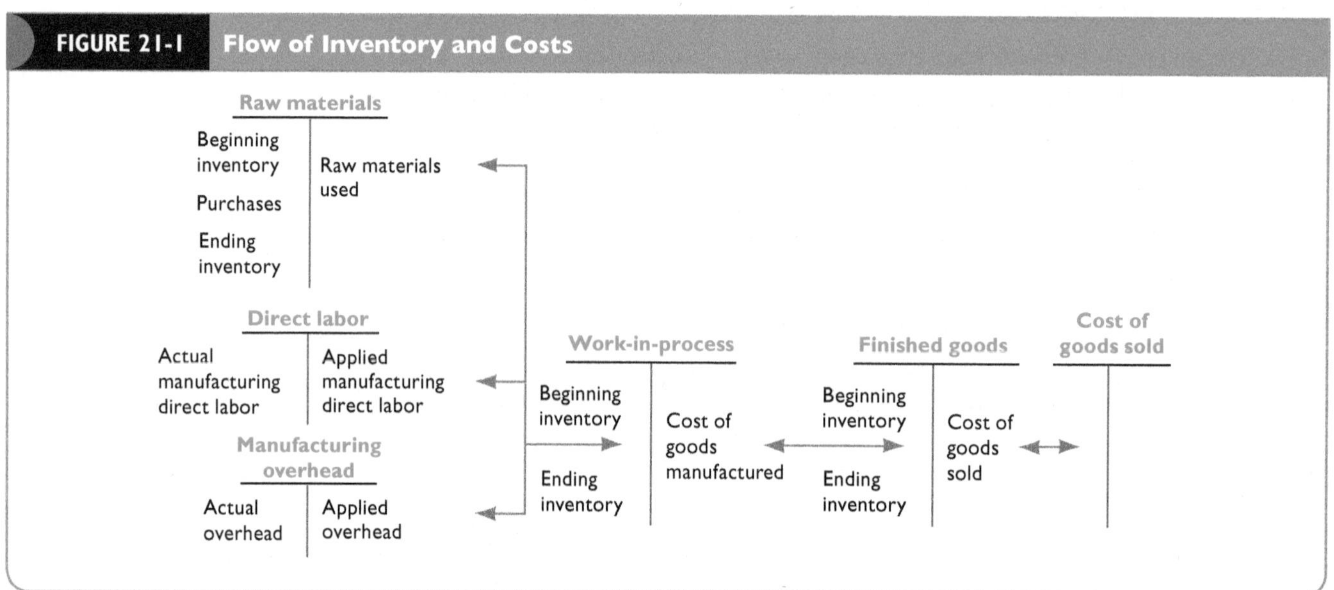

The inventory and warehousing cycle can be thought of as comprising two separate but closely related systems, one involving the *physical flow of goods* and the other the related costs. Six functions make up the inventory and warehousing cycle. Each of these is discussed next.

Process Purchase Orders

The inventory and warehousing cycle begins with the acquisition of raw materials for production. Adequate controls over purchasing must be maintained whether inventory purchases are for raw materials for a manufacturer or finished goods for a retailer. Purchase requisitions are forms used to request the purchasing department to order inventory. These requisitions may be initiated by stockroom personnel as raw materials are needed, by automated computer software when raw materials reach a predetermined level, by orders placed for the materials required to produce a customer order, or by orders initiated on the basis of a periodic raw materials count.

Receive Raw Materials

Receipt of the ordered materials, which is also part of the acquisition and payment cycle, involves the inspection of material received for quantity and quality. The receiving department prepares a receiving report that becomes a part of the documentation before payment is made. After inspection, the material is sent to the storeroom and copies of the receiving documents, or electronic notifications of the receipt of goods, are typically sent to purchasing, the storeroom, and accounts payable. Control and accountability are necessary for all transfers.

Store Raw Materials

Once received, materials are normally stored in a stockroom. When another department needs materials for production, personnel submit a properly approved materials requisition, work order, or similar document or electronic notice that indicates the type and quantity of materials needed. This requisition document is used to update the perpetual inventory master files and record transfers from raw materials to work-in-process accounts. These updates occur automatically in organizations with integrated inventory management and accounting software systems.

Process the Goods

Processing inventory varies greatly from company to company. Companies determine the finished goods items and quantities they will produce based on specific orders from customers, sales forecasts, predetermined finished goods inventory levels, and economical production runs. A separate production control department is often responsible for determining the types and quantities to produce.

An adequate cost accounting system is an important part of the processing of goods function for all manufacturing companies. The system shows the relative profitability of the products for management planning and control and values inventories for preparing financial statements. Two primary types of cost systems exist: job cost systems and process cost systems, but there are many variations and combinations of these systems. In a **job cost system**, costs are accumulated by individual jobs when material is issued and labor costs incurred. In a **process cost system**, they are accumulated by processes, with unit costs for each process assigned to the products passing through the process.

Cost accounting records consist of master files, spreadsheets, and reports that accumulate material, labor, and overhead costs by job or process as those costs are incurred. When jobs or products are completed, the related costs are transferred from work-in-process to finished goods based on production department reports.

Store Finished Goods

When finished goods are completed, they are placed in the stockroom to await shipment. In companies with good internal controls, finished goods are kept under physical control in a separate, limited-access area. The control of finished goods is often considered part of the sales and collection cycle.

Ship Finished Goods

Shipping completed goods is part of the sales and collection cycle. The actual shipment of goods to customers in exchange for cash or other assets, such as accounts receivable, creates the exchange of assets necessary for meeting revenue recognition criteria. For most sales transactions, the actual shipment satisfies the performance obligation and therefore becomes the trigger for recognizing the related accounts receivable and sales in the accounting system. Thus, shipments of finished goods must be authorized by a properly approved shipping document.

Perpetual Inventory Master Files

We have not yet discussed one type of record used for inventory: a **perpetual inventory master file**. With advancements in technologies, separate perpetual records are likely to be kept for raw materials, work-in-process, and finished goods.

Perpetual inventory master files typically include information about the units of inventory acquired, sold, and on hand. In well-designed computerized systems, they also include information about unit costs.

For acquisitions of raw materials, the perpetual inventory master file is updated automatically when acquisitions of inventory are processed as part of recording acquisitions. For example, when the number of units and unit cost for each raw material acquisition are entered in the computer system, this information is used to update perpetual inventory master files along with the acquisitions journal and accounts payable master file.

Transfers of raw material from the storeroom must be separately entered into the computer to update the perpetual records. Typically, only the units transferred need to be entered because the computer determines the unit costs from the master file.

Finished goods perpetual inventory master files include the same type of information as raw materials perpetuals but are considerably more complex if costs are included along with units. Finished goods costs include raw materials, direct labor, and manufacturing overhead, which often requires allocations and detailed record keeping. When finished goods perpetuals include unit costs, the cost accounting records must be integrated into the computer system.

Figure 21-2 summarizes the business functions and the physical flow of inventory from the purchase of raw materials to the shipment of finished goods. It also includes the most common documents and records used to support the functions and physical flows.

CEO AND CFO CHARGED WITH FALSE STATEMENTS ON INTERNAL CONTROLS OVER INVENTORY

Quality Services Group, Inc. (QSGI), was a publicly traded company and as such, its CEO and CFO were responsible for certifying the effectiveness of internal controls over financial reporting under the Sarbanes–Oxley Act. Sherman, CEO, and Cummings, CFO, certified that controls were effective despite being aware of several deficiencies in controls related to inventory. Sherman also certified that he participated in management's assessment of internal controls when in fact he had not. QSGI was a reseller of used computer equipment and also provided maintenance services. In one of the company's two warehouses, employees removed parts from computers sitting in inventory to use in maintenance and repairs of other computers without documenting the removal or notifying accounting. Warehouse personnel received inventory and shipped inventory without recording the transactions. Attempts to strengthen controls were not effective. The CEO and CFO were fully aware that controls in the company's warehouse were ignored. Sherman also circumvented internal controls and frequently accelerated the recording of inventory purchases in order to inflate assets to meet borrowing requirements on a revolving line of credit.

One of the interesting aspects of this case is that no material misstatements of the financial statements were identified when the control deficiencies came to light. But even in the absence of material misstatements, the SEC charged the executives with fraudulent internal control certifications and lying to the auditors by not disclosing in the management representation letter significant deficiencies of which they were aware. This case highlights management's responsibility for understanding internal controls and providing truthful and complete disclosures to auditors.

Source: Securities and Exchange Commission Release No. 2014-152. "SEC Charges Company CEO and Former CFO With Hiding Internal Controls Deficiencies and Violating Sarbanes-Oxley Requirements," July 30, 2014 (www.sec.gov).

PARTS OF THE AUDIT OF INVENTORY

OBJECTIVE 21-2

Explain the five parts of the audit of the inventory and warehousing cycle.

Now that you are familiar with the business functions and the related documents and records in the inventory and warehousing cycle, we turn our attention to the audit of the cycle. The overall objective in the audit of the inventory and warehousing cycle is to provide assurance that the financial statements fairly account for raw materials, work-in-process, finished goods inventory, and cost of goods sold.

The audit of the inventory and warehousing cycle can be divided into five activities within the cycle:

1. Acquire and record raw materials, labor, and overhead
2. Internally transfer assets and costs
3. Ship goods and record revenue and costs
4. Physically observe inventory
5. Price and compile inventory

Acquire and Record Raw Materials, Labor, and Overhead

This part of the audit includes the first three functions in Figure 21-2. These include processing purchase orders, receiving raw materials, and storing raw materials.

The auditor obtains an understanding of internal controls over these three functions and then performs tests of controls and substantive tests of transactions in both the acquisition and payment cycle and the payroll and personnel cycle. These tests should satisfy auditors that controls affecting the acquisitions of raw materials and manufacturing costs are operating effectively and that acquisition transactions are correctly stated. When direct labor is a significant part of manufactured inventory, auditors should verify the proper accounting for these costs in the payroll and personnel cycle.

Transfer Assets and Costs

Internal transfers of inventory include the fourth and fifth functions in Figure 21-2: process the goods and store finished goods. Clients account for these activities in the cost accounting records, which are independent of other cycles and are tested as part of the audit of the inventory and warehousing cycle.

FIGURE 21-2 Functions in the Inventory and Warehousing Cycle

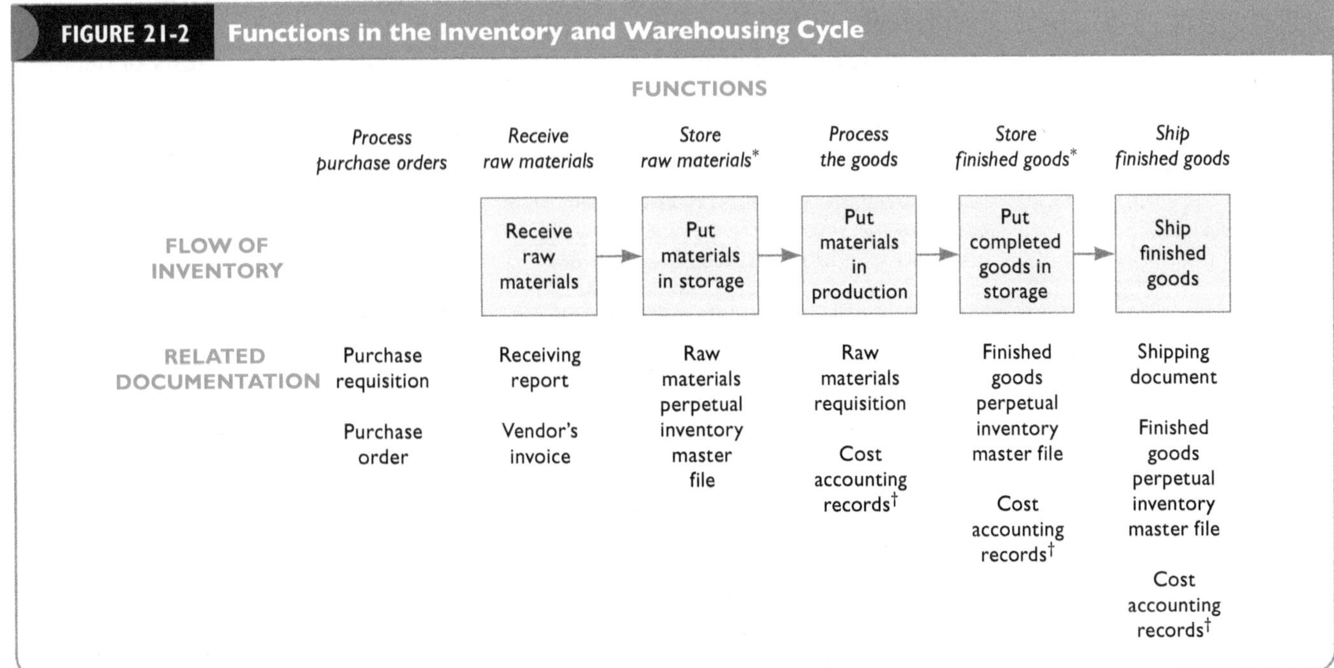

*Inventory counts are taken and compared with perpetual and book amounts at any stage of the cycle. The auditor compares the documentation related to the receipt, movement, and sale of inventory with the physical location of the items to ensure proper cutoff and classification of inventory as raw material, work-in-process, or finished goods. A count must ordinarily be taken once a year. If the perpetual inventory system is operating well, this can be done on a cycle basis throughout the year.
† Includes cost information for materials, direct labor, and overhead.

Ship Goods and Record Revenue and Costs

Recording shipments and related costs is the last function shown in Figure 21-2. Because it is part of the sales and collection cycle, auditors obtain an understanding and test internal controls over recording shipments as a part of auditing that cycle, including procedures to verify the accuracy of the credits to inventory recorded in perpetual inventory master files.

Physically Observe Inventory

Auditors are required by auditing standards to observe the client taking a physical inventory count to determine whether recorded inventory actually exists at the balance sheet date and is correctly counted by the client. Physical examination is an essential type of evidence used to verify the existence and count of inventory. The story at the beginning of this chapter, when auditors failed to uncover Phar-Mor's fraud, demonstrates the importance of physically observing inventories, especially when those inventories are material to the financial statements.

Price and Compile Inventory

Costs used to value inventory must be tested to determine whether the client has correctly followed an inventory method that is both in accordance with accounting standards and consistent with previous years. Audit procedures used to verify these costs are called price tests. In addition, the auditor must perform **inventory compilation tests**, which are tests to verify whether the physical counts were correctly summarized, the inventory quantities and prices were correctly extended, and the extended inventory correctly footed to equal the general ledger inventory balance.

Figure 21-3 summarizes the five parts of the audit of the inventory and warehousing cycle. Because of the interrelationships of the inventory and warehousing cycle with other cycles, some parts of the audit of inventory are most efficiently tested with the audit tests of other cycles. As noted in Figure 21-3, auditors test the acquisition and recording of raw materials, labor, and overhead as part of the audit of the acquisition and payment and payroll and personnel cycles. Also, they test shipment of goods and recording of revenue and related costs in the audit of the sales and collection cycle. Because we have already discussed obtaining an understanding of internal controls and tests of controls and substantive tests of transactions for these other cycles in earlier chapters, they are not repeated here (the first and third boxes in Figure 21-3).

The physical observation of inventory and the pricing and compilation of the inventory are audited using substantive analytical procedures and tests of details of

FIGURE 21-3 Audit of Inventory

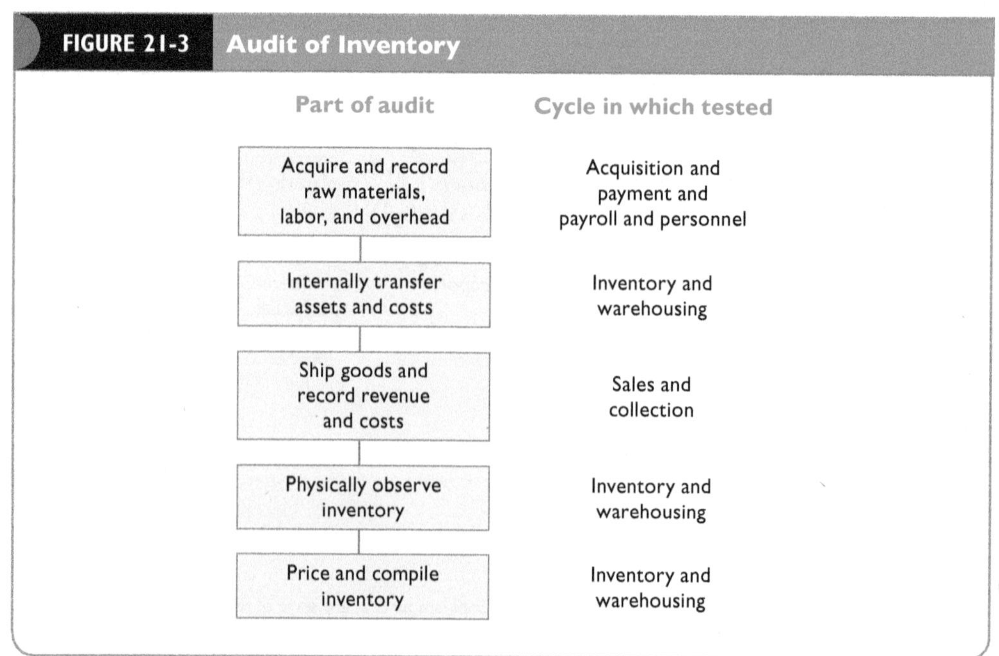

balances (the last two boxes in Figure 21-3). In doing so, the auditor must consider business and inherent risks, set performance materiality for inventory, and evaluate the results of the tests of controls and substantive tests of transactions for the transactions and activities in the first three boxes in Figure 21-3. As part of the risk assessment process, the auditor will consider whether any of the identified risks of material misstatement is considered a significant risk. This is the same methodology that we discussed in Chapters 14–20 for other cycles. The remainder of the chapter deals with the parts of the audit of inventory in Figure 21-3 that are tested as part of the inventory and warehousing cycle, including the use of analytical procedures, tests of the physical inventory observation, and inventory pricing and compilation tests.

AUDIT OF COST ACCOUNTING

OBJECTIVE 21-3

Design and perform audit tests of cost accounting.

Our discussion of the audit of cost accounting begins with the internal transfer of assets from raw materials to work-in-process to finished goods inventory. We also focus on systems and controls related to the transfer of inventory costs, which are accounted for in the cost accounting records.

Cost accounting systems and controls of different companies vary more than most other audit areas because of the wide variety of items of inventory and the level of sophistication desired by management. For example, a company that manufactures farm machines may have completely different cost records and internal controls than a steel fabricating shop that makes and installs custom-made metal cabinets. Of course, small companies with owners actively involved in the manufacturing process need less sophisticated records than large, multiproduct companies.

Cost Accounting Controls

Cost accounting controls are those related to processes affecting physical inventory and the tracking of related costs from the time raw materials are requisitioned to the completion of the manufactured product and its transfer to storage. It is convenient to divide these controls into two broad categories:

1. Physical controls over raw materials, work-in-process, and finished goods inventory
2. Controls over the related costs

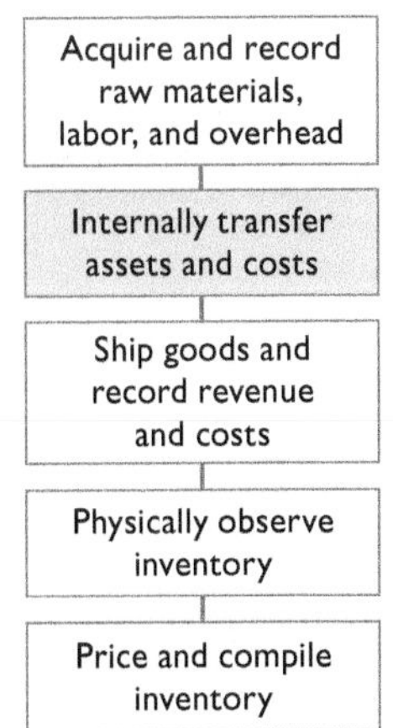

Almost all companies need physical controls over their assets to prevent loss from misuse and theft. To protect assets, most companies physically segregate and restrict access to storage areas for raw material, work-in-process, and finished goods to control the movement of inventory. In some instances, managers assign custody of inventory to specific individuals who are responsible for protecting the inventory. Clients may use approved prenumbered documents for authorizing movement of inventory to protect the assets from improper use. Electronic or paper copies of these documents should be sent directly to accounting by the persons issuing them, bypassing people with custodial responsibilities. An example of an effective document of this type is an approved materials requisition for obtaining raw materials from the storeroom.

Perpetual inventory master files maintained by persons who do not have custody of or access to assets are another useful cost accounting control for a number of reasons:

- They provide a record of inventory on hand, which is used to initiate production or acquisition of additional materials or goods.
- They provide a record of the use of raw materials and the sale of finished goods, which can be reviewed for obsolete or slow-moving items.
- They provide a record to pinpoint responsibility when there are differences between physical counts and the amounts shown on the perpetual listings.

Also, adequate internal controls that integrate production and accounting records to provide accurate costs for all products are important to aid management in pricing finished goods, controlling costs, and costing inventory.

Tests of Cost Accounting

The concepts in auditing inventory cost accounting are no different from those discussed for other transaction cycles: understand internal controls in the cost accounting system, assess planned control risk, determine extent of testing controls, and design tests of controls and substantive tests of transactions to meet transaction-related audit objectives. The auditor is concerned with four aspects of cost accounting:

1. Physical controls over inventory
2. Documents and records for transferring inventory
3. Perpetual inventory master files
4. Unit cost records

Physical Controls Auditor tests of physical controls over raw materials, work-in-process, and finished goods are generally limited to observation and inquiry. Auditors can examine the raw materials storage area to determine whether the inventory is protected from theft and misuse by locks or other security measures, including an inventory custodian. They can ask inventory custodians to explain their duties related to their oversight of inventory monitored by them. If auditors conclude that the physical controls are so inadequate that inventory will be difficult to accurately count, they should expand observation of physical inventory tests to make sure that an adequate count is carried out.

Documents and Records for Transferring Inventory The auditor's primary concerns in verifying the transfer of inventory from one location to another are that recorded transfers exist, all actual transfers are recorded, and the quantity, description, and date of all recorded transfers are accurate. Products labeled with standardized bar codes that can be scanned by laser bar-code readers and other technologies make it easier for clients to track the movement of goods through production.

When auditing inventory transfers, auditors first need to understand the client's internal controls for recording transfers before they can perform relevant tests. After they understand the internal controls, they can easily perform tests of controls or substantive tests of transactions by examining documents and records to test the occurrence and accuracy objectives for the transfer of goods from the raw material storeroom to manufacturing. For example, auditors may account for a sequence of raw material requisitions, examine the requisitions for proper approval, and compare the quantity, description, and date with the information recorded in the raw material perpetual inventory master files to verify that related controls operated effectively and that amounts are correctly recorded. Some of that testing may be done electronically when the related controls are automated. Similarly, the auditor may compare completed production records with perpetual inventory master files to be sure that all manufactured goods were physically delivered to the finished goods storeroom.

Perpetual Inventory Master Files The reliability of perpetual inventory master files affects the *timing* and *extent* of the auditor's physical examination of inventory. When perpetual inventory master files are accurate, auditors can test the physical inventory before the balance sheet date. An interim physical inventory or use of cycle counts throughout the year can result in significant cost savings for both the client and the auditor, and it enables the audit to be completed earlier. The auditor may also reduce tests of physical inventory counts when the client has reliable perpetual inventory records and assessed control risk related to physical observation of inventory is low.

Auditors test perpetual inventory master files by examining documentation that supports additions and reductions of inventory amounts in the master files. For example, as part of the tests of the perpetual records, auditors may examine documents supporting inventory activities including the addition of acquired raw material inventory, the reduction of raw material inventory for use in production, the increase in finished goods inventory when goods have been manufactured, and the decrease when finished goods are sold. Usually, it is relatively easy to test the accuracy of the perpetual inventory master files after the auditor determines the adequacy of the design and implementation of inventory internal controls and the related level of assessed control risk. Auditors test the perpetual records for acquisitions of raw materials in the acquisition and payment cycle, while reductions in finished goods for sale are tested in the sales and collection cycle.

For many companies, traditional documents exist only in electronic form and the perpetual inventory system is integrated with other accounting cycles. As a result, the auditor can test computer controls to support a reduction in control risk, which reduces substantive testing and can result in audit efficiencies.

Unit Cost Records Accurate cost data for raw materials, direct labor, and manufacturing overhead is essential for fairly stated raw materials, work-in-process, and finished goods inventories. To maintain accurate cost data, clients must integrate their cost accounting records with production and other accounting records.

When testing inventory cost records, the auditor must first obtain an understanding of internal control in the cost accounting system. This understanding can be time-consuming because the flow of costs is integrated with accounting records in three other cycles: acquisition and payment, payroll and personnel, and sales and collection.

After auditors understand internal controls affecting cost accounting records, the approach to internal verification of cost accounting records involves the same concepts that were discussed in the verification of acquisition, payroll, and sales transactions. Auditors usually test cost accounting records as a part of the acquisition, payroll, and sales tests to avoid testing the records more than once and to increase audit efficiency. When testing acquisition transactions, auditors should trace the units and unit costs of raw materials to additions recorded in the perpetual inventory master files and the total cost to cost accounting records. Similarly, when clients maintain payroll cost data for different jobs, auditors should trace from the payroll summary directly to job cost records when they audit payroll.

COST OF COFFEE

Keurig Green Mountain, Inc., sells its Keurig single-cup brewers and over 200 varieties of coffee, cocoa, teas, and other beverages for its K-Cup portion packs. In November 2010, the company restated its 2008 and 2009 annual financial statements and its quarterly financial statements for the first three quarters of 2010. The restatements were the result of errors management discovered when preparing its annual report and during the audit of the financial statements for 2010, and as a result of an investigation initiated by the audit committee and inquiry of the Securities and Exchange Commission (SEC).

The restatements, which were triggered by a number of errors, resulted in a cumulative 3 percent overstatement of undistributed earnings for the annual financial statement period and a 6.2 percent overstatement of net income for the first three quarters of 2010. Some of the restatements were linked to the company's accounting for inventory:

- An $8.1 million cumulative overstatement of pre-tax net income over the restatement period was the result of applying incorrect standard costs to intercompany K-Cup portion pack and K-Cup brewer inventory balances, which overstated consolidated inventory and understated cost of sales.
- An additional $1 million cumulative overstatement of pre-tax net income over the restatement period was due to changes in the timing and classification of royalties received from third-party licensed roasters. The company recognized these royalties at the time it purchased K-Cup portion packs from the roasters and classified them as net sales. The royalties should have been recognized as a reduction to the carrying value of the related inventory.

The company's challenges did not end with the restatement of the financial statements, as the filing of a class action lawsuit soon followed. Among allegations in the suit, several confidential witnesses who worked for Keurig Green Mountain alleged that the company moved inventory from location to location without a document trail to overstate inventory counts. Ironically, one of the company's critics was former criminal Sam E. Antar, who helped orchestrate the inventory accounting fraud at Crazy Eddie in the 1980s. Antar's efforts focused on the company's buildup of inventory at rates that were much faster than growth in revenues, alleging that the patterns looked similar to what had happened at Crazy Eddie during its fraud. Management argued that the inventory buildups were in anticipation of the 2012 holiday season. Interestingly, the company began offering $50 rebates for its brewers in September 2012.

Sources: 1. Form 10-K filed by Green Mountain Coffee Roasters, Inc., with the Securities and Exchange Commission, November 26, 2010; 2. Sam E. Antar, "Green Mountain Coffee Roasters' Growing Levels — Is It a Fumble or a Fraud?" Seeking Alpha (seekingalpha.com), September 27, 2012.

Determining the reasonableness of manufacturing overhead costs assigned to work-in-process is challenging for auditors because management must make assumptions that affect overhead allocations that can significantly affect the unit costs of inventory and therefore the fairness of inventory valuation. In evaluating these overhead cost allocations, the auditor must consider the reasonableness of the allocation method, assuming the method complies with accounting standards, and whether it is consistently applied.

Management typically allocates overhead using total direct labor dollars as the basis for allocation. In this case, the overhead rate should approximate total actual manufacturing overhead divided by total actual direct labor dollars. Because auditors test total manufacturing overhead as part of the tests of the acquisition and payment cycle and test direct labor as part of the payroll and personnel cycle, determining the reasonableness of the rate is not difficult. However, if for example, manufacturing overhead is applied on the basis of machine hours, the auditor must verify the reasonableness of the machine hours by separate tests of the client's machine records.

Because internal controls over cost accounting records vary significantly among companies, specific tests of controls are not discussed here. Auditors should design appropriate tests based on their understanding of the cost accounting records and the extent to which they will be relied on to reduce substantive tests.

CONCEPT CHECK

1. Give the reasons why inventory is often the most difficult and time-consuming part of many audits.
2. State what is meant by cost accounting records and explain their importance in the conduct of an audit.

SUBSTANTIVE ANALYTICAL PROCEDURES

OBJECTIVE 21-4

Apply substantive analytical procedures to the accounts in the inventory and warehousing cycle.

Substantive analytical procedures are important in auditing inventory and warehousing, as they are in all other cycles. Table 21-1 shows several common analytical procedures and possible misstatements that may be indicated when fluctuations occur. We've discussed several of those analytical procedures, such as gross margin percentage, in relation to other cycles.

In addition to performing substantive analytical procedures that examine the relationship of inventory account balances with other financial statement accounts

TABLE 21-1 Substantive Analytical Procedures for the Inventory and Warehousing Cycle

Substantive Analytical Procedure	Possible Misstatement
Compare gross margin percentage with that of previous years.	Overstatement or understatement of inventory and cost of goods sold.
Compare inventory turnover (cost of goods sold divided by average inventory) with that of previous years.	Obsolete inventory, which affects inventory and cost of goods sold. Overstatement or understatement of inventory.
Compare unit costs of inventory with those of previous years.	Overstatement or understatement of unit costs, which affect inventory and cost of goods sold.
Compare extended inventory value with that of previous years.	Misstatements in compilation, unit costs, or extensions, which affect inventory and cost of goods sold.
Compare current year manufacturing costs with those of previous years (variable costs should be adjusted for changes in volume).	Misstatements of unit costs of inventory, especially direct labor and manufacturing overhead, which affect inventory and cost of goods sold.

(as shown in Figure 21-1 on page 686), auditors often use nonfinancial information to assess the reasonableness of inventory-related balances. For example, auditors may need knowledge about the size and weight of inventory products, their methods of storage (stacks, tanks, etc.), and the capacity of storage facilities (available square footage) to determine whether recorded inventory is consistent with available inventory storage. After performing the appropriate tests of the cost accounting records and substantive analytical procedures, auditors have a basis for designing and performing tests of details of the ending inventory balance.

PHYSICAL OBSERVATION OF INVENTORY

OBJECTIVE 21-5

Design and perform physical observation audit tests for inventory.

Because inventory varies significantly for different companies, obtaining an understanding of the client's industry and business is more important for both physical inventory observation and inventory pricing and compilation than for most audit areas. Examples of key considerations that auditors should consider include the inventory valuation method selected by management, the potential for inventory obsolescence, and the risk that consignment inventory might be intermingled with owned inventory. Auditors should evaluate whether risks related to inventory qualify as significant risks.

Auditors often first familiarize themselves with the client's inventory by conducting a tour of the client's inventory facilities, including receiving, storage, production, planning, and record-keeping areas. The tour should be led by a supervisor who can answer questions about production, especially about any changes in internal controls and other processes since last year.

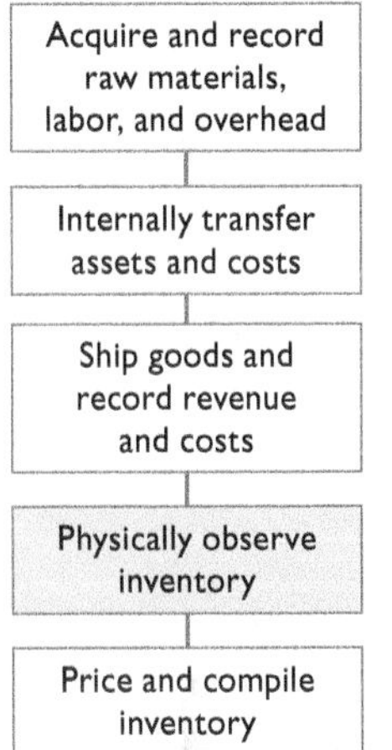

While gaining an understanding of the effect of the client's business and industry on inventory, auditors assess client business risk to determine if those risks increase the likelihood of material misstatements in inventory. Examples of common sources of business risk for inventory include short product cycles, potential obsolescence, use of just-in-time inventory, reliance on a few key suppliers, and use of sophisticated inventory management technology.

After assessing client business risk, the auditor determines performance materiality and assesses inherent risk for inventory, which is typically highly material for manufacturing, wholesale, and retail companies. Auditors often assess a high inherent risk for companies with significant inventory, depending on the circumstances. Auditors often have a greater concern for misstatements when inventory is stored in multiple locations, the costing method is complex, and the potential for inventory obsolescence is great.

When assessing control risk, the auditor is primarily concerned with internal controls over perpetual records, physical controls, inventory counts, and inventory compilation and pricing. The nature and extent of these controls vary widely from company to company.

Inventory Observation Requirements

Auditors have been required to perform physical observation tests of inventory since a major fraud involving the recording of nonexisting inventory was uncovered in 1938 at the McKesson & Robbins Company. The fraud was not discovered because the auditors did not physically observe the inventory, which at the time was not required.

Auditing standards *require* auditors to satisfy themselves about the effectiveness of the client's methods of counting inventory and the reliance they can place on the client's representations about the quantities and physical condition of the inventories. To meet the requirement, auditors must:

- Be present at the time the client counts its inventory for determining year-end balances
- Observe the client's counting procedures
- Make inquiries of client personnel about their counting procedures
- Make their own independent tests of the physical count

An essential point in the auditing standards is the distinction between who observes the physical inventory count and who is responsible for taking the count. The client is responsible for setting up the procedures for taking an accurate physical inventory and actually making and recording the counts. The auditor is responsible for evaluating and observing the client's procedures, including doing test counts of the inventory and drawing conclusions about the adequacy of the physical inventory.

An auditor's physical examination of inventory is not required if inventory is housed in a public warehouse or overseen by outside custodians. In those situations, auditors verify inventory by confirmation with the custodian. However, if inventory stored with outside custodians represents a significant portion of current assets or total assets, the auditor should apply additional procedures, such as investigating the custodian's inventory procedures, obtaining an independent accountant's report on the custodian's control procedures over the custody of goods, or observing the physical count of the goods held by the custodian, if practical.

Controls Over Physical Count

Regardless of the inventory record-keeping method, the client must make a periodic physical count of inventory, but not necessarily every year. The physical count may be performed at or near the balance sheet date, at an interim date, or on a cycle basis throughout the year. The latter two approaches are appropriate only if there are adequate controls over the perpetual inventory master files.

Adequate controls over the client's physical count of inventory include proper client instructions for the physical count, supervision by responsible company personnel, independent internal verification of the counts by other client personnel, independent reconciliations of the physical counts with perpetual inventory master files, and adequate client control over count sheets or tags used to record inventory counts.

Auditors need to understand the client's physical inventory count controls before the count of inventory begins. While this understanding is necessary to evaluate the effectiveness of the client's procedures, it also enables the auditor to make constructive suggestions beforehand. Obviously, if the client's physical inventory count controls are inadequate, the auditor must spend more time making sure that the physical count is accurate.

Audit Decisions

The auditor's decisions in the physical observation of inventory are similar to those made for other audit areas. They include selecting audit procedures, deciding the timing of the procedures, determining sample size, and selecting items for testing. The last three decisions are discussed next, followed by a discussion of the appropriate audit procedures.

Timing The auditor decides whether the physical count can be taken before year-end primarily on the basis of the accuracy of the perpetual inventory master files. When a client does an interim physical count, which the auditor will agree to only when internal controls are effective, the auditor observes the inventory count at that time, and also tests transactions recorded in the perpetual inventory records from the date of the count to year-end. When the perpetual records are accurate and related controls operate effectively, it may be unnecessary for the client to count all the inventory at year-end. Instead, the auditor can compare the perpetuals with the actual inventory on a sample basis at convenient times throughout the year, as long as controls over additions and reductions to the perpetual records are tested and found to operate effectively. When there are no perpetuals and the inventory is material, the client must take a complete physical inventory near the end of the accounting period.

Sample Size The number of inventory items auditors should count is difficult to specify because auditors concentrate on observing the client's procedures rather than on selecting items for testing. For convenience, sample size in physical observation may be considered in terms of the total number of hours spent rather than the number of inventory items counted. The key determinants of the amount of time needed to test inventory are the adequacy of internal controls over the physical counts, accuracy of the perpetual inventory master files, total dollar amount and type of inventory, number of different significant inventory locations, nature and extent of misstatements discovered in previous years, and other inherent risks.

In some situations, inventory is so material that it requires dozens of auditors to observe the physical count. In other situations, one auditor can complete the observation in a short time. Audit planning for inventory count testing and coordination with client personnel is critical. Poor planning may lead to audit difficulties. For example, it is impossible to observe client personnel counting inventory after they have completed their counts and it is difficult to expand sample sizes or reperform tests after the physical inventory has been taken.

Selection of Items When auditors observe the client counting inventory, they should be careful to:

- Observe the counting of the most significant items and a representative sample of typical inventory items
- Inquire about items that are likely to be obsolete or damaged
- Discuss with management the reasons for excluding any material items

Physical Observation Tests

The same balance-related audit objectives discussed in previous sections for tests of details of balances provide a frame of reference for discussing the physical observation tests. However, before discussing those objectives, some overall comments about the client's inventory process are important to consider.

The most important part of the observation of inventory is determining whether the physical count is being taken in accordance with the client's instructions. To do this effectively, it is essential that the auditor be present while the physical count is taking place.

When the client's employees are not following the inventory instructions, the auditor must either contact the supervisor to correct the problem or modify the physical observation procedures. For example, if the procedures require one team to count the inventory and a second team to recount it as a test of accuracy, the auditor should inform management if both teams are observed counting together.

Table 21-2 (p. 698) lists common tests of details of balances audit procedures for physical inventory observation. Detail tie-in is the only balance-related audit objective not included. That balance-related objective is discussed under compilation of inventory. In the discussion that follows, we assume that the client counts inventory on the balance sheet date and records the inventory counts on prenumbered tags. When clients record inventory counts in a different way, audit procedures will vary. In addition to the detailed procedures in Table 21-2, the auditor should also inspect all physical areas where inventory is warehoused to make sure that all inventory has been counted and properly tagged. Boxes or other containers holding inventory should also be opened during test counts to be certain inventory is physically present. As part of their substantive analytical procedures performed after the client has completed the inventory counts, auditors may compare high-dollar-value inventory to counts in the previous year and inventory master files as a test of reasonableness.

AUDIT OF PRICING AND COMPILATION

OBJECTIVE 21-6

Design and perform audit tests of pricing and compilation for inventory.

Auditors must verify that the physical counts or perpetual record quantities are correctly priced and compiled. **Inventory price tests** include all the tests of the client's unit prices to determine whether they are correct. Inventory compilation tests include testing the client's summarization of the inventory counts, recalculating price times quantity, footing the inventory summary, and tracing the totals to the general ledger.

TABLE 21-2 Balance-Related Audit Objectives and Tests of Details of Balances for Physical Inventory Observation

Balance-Related Audit Objective	Common Inventory Observation Procedures	Comments
Inventory as recorded on tags exists (existence).	Select a random sample of tag numbers and identify the tag with that number attached to the actual inventory. Observe whether movement of inventory takes place during the count.	The purpose is to uncover the inclusion of nonexistent items as inventory.
Existing inventory is counted and tagged, and tags are accounted for to make sure none are missing (completeness).	Examine inventory to make sure it is tagged. Observe whether movement of inventory takes place during the count. Inquire as to inventory in other locations. Account for all used and unused tags to make sure none are lost or intentionally omitted. Record the tag numbers for those used and unused for subsequent follow-up.	Special concern should be directed to omission of large sections of inventory. This test should be done at the completion of the physical count. This test should be done at the completion of the physical count.
Inventory is counted accurately (accuracy).	Recount client's counts to make sure the recorded counts are accurate on the tags (also check descriptions and unit of count, such as dozen or gross). Compare physical counts with perpetual inventory master file. Record client's counts for subsequent testing.	Recording client counts in the audit files on inventory count sheets is done for two reasons: to obtain documentation that an adequate physical examination was made and to test for the possibility that the client might change the recorded counts after the auditor leaves the premises.
Inventory is classified correctly on the tags (classification).	Examine inventory descriptions on the tags and compare with the actual inventory for raw material, work-in-process, and finished goods. Evaluate whether the percent of completion recorded on the tags for work-in-process is reasonable.	These tests will be done as a part of the first procedure in the accuracy objective.
Information is obtained to make sure sales and inventory purchases are recorded in the proper period (cutoff).	Record in the audit files for subsequent follow-up the last shipping document number used at year-end. Make sure the inventory for the above item was excluded from the physical count. Review shipping area for inventory set aside for shipment but not counted. Record in the audit files for subsequent follow-up the last receiving report number used at year-end. Make sure the inventory for the above item was included in the physical count. Review receiving area for inventory that should be included in the physical count.	Obtaining proper cutoff information for sales and acquisitions is an essential part of inventory observation. The appropriate tests were discussed for sales in Chapter 16 and for acquisitions in Chapter 18.
Obsolete and unusable inventory items are excluded or noted (realizable value).	Test for obsolete inventory by inquiry of factory employees and management and alertness for items that are damaged, rust- or dust-covered, or located in inappropriate places.	
The client has rights to inventory recorded on tags (rights).	Inquire about consignment or customer inventory included on client's premises. Be alert for inventory that is set aside or specifically marked as indications of non-ownership.	

Pricing and Compilation Controls

Adequate internal controls surrounding the tracking of unit costs that are integrated with production and other accounting records provide assurance that clients use reasonable costs for valuing ending inventory. **Standard cost records** that indicate variances in material, labor, and overhead costs are helpful to evaluate the reasonableness of production records if management has procedures in place to keep the standards updated for changes in production processes and costs. Management should also have someone independent of the department responsible for determining the costs review them for reasonableness.

To prevent including or overstating the value of obsolete inventory, clients should have a formal review and reporting of obsolete, slow-moving, damaged, and overstated inventory items. The review should be done by a knowledgeable employee who reviews perpetual inventory master files for inventory turnover and holds discussions with engineering or production personnel.

Clients need inventory compilation internal controls to ensure that the physical counts are correctly summarized, priced at the same amount as the unit records, correctly extended and totaled, and included in the perpetual inventory master file and related general ledger inventory accounts at the proper amount. The most important internal control for accurate unit costs, extensions, and footings is internal verification by a competent, independent person who relies on adequate documents and records that were used for taking the physical count. If the physical inventory counts are recorded by the client on prenumbered tags and carefully reviewed before the personnel who counted the inventory are released from the physical examination of inventory, there should be little risk of misstatement in summarizing inventory count tags.

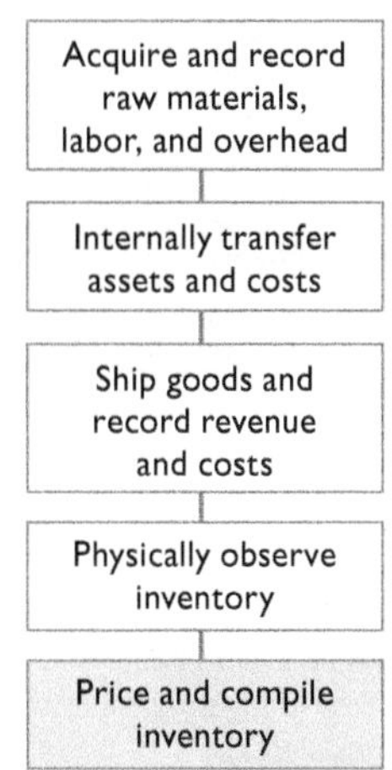

Pricing and Compilation Procedures

Table 21-3 (p. 700) lists the audit objectives and related tests for inventory pricing and compilation, except for the cutoff objective. As we've already discussed, physical observation is a major source of cutoff information for sales and purchases. Tests of the accounting records for cutoff are done as a part of sales (sales and collection cycle) and acquisitions (acquisition and payment cycle).

Auditors can apply the objectives using information obtained from the client as a frame of reference, including each inventory item's description, quantity, unit price, and extended value. We assume the information reflected in the inventory perpetual listing is recorded in inventory item description order, with raw material, work-in-process, and finished goods listed separately. The listing totals should equal the general ledger balance.

Valuation of Inventory

In performing inventory valuation tests (often called price tests), the auditor has three concerns. First, the method must be in accordance with accounting standards. Second, the application of the method must be consistent from year to year. Third, inventory cost versus market value (replacement cost or net realizable value) must be considered. Because the method of verifying the pricing of inventory depends on whether inventory items are acquired or manufactured, these two categories are discussed separately.

Pricing Purchased Inventory The primary types of inventory included in this category are raw materials, purchased parts, and supplies. As a first step in verifying the valuation of purchased inventory, the auditor must determine whether the client uses LIFO, FIFO, weighted average, or some other valuation method. Auditors must also determine which costs should be included in the valuation of an item of inventory. For example, the auditor must find out whether freight, storage, discounts, and other costs are included and the auditor must compare the findings with the preceding year to make sure that the costs are determined consistently.

In selecting specific inventory items for pricing, auditors should focus on larger dollar amounts and on products that are known to have wide fluctuations in price. They should also test a representative sample of all types of inventory and departments. Stratified variables or monetary unit sampling is commonly used for these tests.

The auditor should list the inventory items to be verified for pricing and request the client to locate the appropriate vendors' invoices. The auditor must examine sufficient invoices to account for the entire quantity of inventory for the item being tested, especially for the FIFO valuation method. Assume that the client values an inventory item at $12.00 per unit for 1,000 units, using FIFO. When the auditor examines the most recent invoices for acquisitions of that inventory item, she finds that the most recent acquisition of the inventory item in the year being audited was for 700 units at $12.00 per unit, and the immediately preceding acquisition was for 600 units at $11.30 per unit. Using correct FIFO valuation techniques, the inventory items should be included at $11,790 (700 units at $12 and 300 at $11.30). The client's calculations

TABLE 21-3 **Balance-Related Audit Objectives and Tests of Details of Balances for Inventory Pricing and Compilation**

Balance-Related Audit Objective	Common Inventory Pricing and Compilation Procedures	Comments
Inventory in the inventory listing schedule agrees with the physical inventory counts, the extensions are correct, and the total is correctly added and agrees with the general ledger (detail tie-in).	Perform compilation tests (see existence, completeness, and accuracy objectives). Foot the inventory listing schedules for raw materials, work-in-process, and finished goods. Trace the totals to the general ledger. Extend the quantity times the price on selected items.	Unless controls are deficient, limit extending and footing tests (which are often done using audit software).
Inventory items in the inventory listing schedule exist (existence).	Trace inventory listed in the schedule to inventory tags and auditor's recorded counts for existence and description. Account for unused tag numbers shown in the auditor's documentation to make sure no tags have been added.	The next five objectives are affected by the results of the physical inventory observation. The tag numbers and counts verified as a part of physical inventory observation are traced to the inventory listing schedule as a part of these tests.
Existing inventory items are included in the inventory listing schedule (completeness).	Trace from inventory tags to the inventory listing schedules and make sure inventory on tags is included. Account for tag numbers to make sure none have been deleted.	
Inventory items in the inventory listing schedule are accurate (accuracy).	Trace inventory listed in the schedule to inventory tags and auditor's recorded counts for quantity and description. Perform price tests of inventory. For a discussion of price tests, see the text material throughout this "Audit of Pricing and Compilation" section on pages 697–701.	
Inventory items in the inventory listing schedule are correctly classified (classification).	Verify the classification into raw materials, work-in-process, and finished goods by comparing the descriptions on inventory tags and auditor's recorded test counts with the inventory listing schedule.	
Inventory items in the inventory listing are stated at realizable value (realizable value).	Perform tests of lower of cost or market, selling price, and obsolescence.	
The client has rights to inventory items in the inventory listing schedule (rights).	Trace inventory tags identified as non-owned during the physical observation to the inventory listing schedule to make sure these have not been included. Review contracts with suppliers and customers and inquire of management for the possibility of the inclusion of consigned or other non-owned inventory, or the exclusion of owned inventory.	

overstate inventory by $210.00 ($12,000 – $11,790). Assuming the client makes this same error on many inventory items, the misstatement amount can be material.

When the client has perpetual inventory master files that include unit costs of acquisitions, it is usually much faster to test the pricing by tracing the unit costs to the perpetuals rather than to vendors' invoices. Naturally, when perpetual inventory records are used to verify unit costs, auditors must test the unit costs recorded in the perpetual records to vendors' invoices as a part of the tests of the acquisition and payment cycle transactions.

Pricing Manufactured Inventory In pricing work-in-process and finished goods, the auditor must consider the cost of raw materials, direct labor, and manufacturing overhead. The need to verify each of these makes the audit of work-in-process and finished goods inventory more complex than the audit of purchased inventory. Nevertheless, several considerations that apply to the audit of purchased inventory still apply, such as selecting the items to be tested, testing for whether cost or market value is lower, and evaluating the possibility of obsolescence.

In pricing raw materials in manufactured products, auditors must consider both the unit cost of the raw materials and the number of units required to manufacture a unit of output. The unit cost can be verified in the same manner as that used for other purchased inventory, by examining vendors' invoices or perpetual inventory master files. Auditors must examine engineering specifications, inspect the finished product, or find a similar method to determine the number of units it takes to manufacture a product.

Similarly, while testing direct labor, auditors must verify the hourly costs of direct labor and the number of hours it takes to manufacture a unit of output. Hourly labor costs can be verified by examining labor payroll or union contracts. Auditors can determine the number of hours needed to manufacture the product from engineering specifications or similar sources.

The proper manufacturing overhead in work-in-process and finished goods depends on the approach the client uses to allocate manufacturing overhead. Auditors must evaluate for consistency and reasonableness the method being used and recompute the costs to determine whether the overhead is correct. For example, if the rate is based on direct labor dollars, the auditor can divide the total manufacturing overhead by the total direct labor dollars to determine the actual overhead rate. This rate can then be compared with the overhead rate used by the client to determine unit costs. Testing of pricing for work-in-process and finished goods is often done in conjunction with tests of standard costs. When auditors have tested standard costs with satisfactory results, they can limit testing of the unit costs of ending inventory to tracing the price used to value ending inventory to the standard cost records.

When the client has standard cost records, an efficient and useful method of determining valuation is to review and analyze variances. Small variances in material, labor, and manufacturing overhead are evidence of reliable cost records.

Cost or Market In pricing inventory, auditors must consider whether market value is lower than historical cost. The determination of market value (replacement cost or net realizable value) depends on the costing method used. For purchased finished goods and raw materials, auditors can test for replacement cost by examining vendor invoices of the subsequent period or recent invoices if no purchases of an inventory item were made after year-end. All manufacturing costs must be considered in evaluating realizable value for work-in-process and finished goods for manufactured inventory. Auditors must consider the sales value of inventory items and the possible effect of rapid fluctuation of prices to determine net realizable value.

CONCEPT CHECK

1. Explain why a proper cutoff of purchases and sales is heavily dependent on the physical inventory observation. What information should be obtained during the physical count to ensure that cutoff is accurate?
2. Explain the importance of documenting used, unused, and voided tags at the end of the physical inventory observation. How will the auditor use this information in follow-up inventory testing?
3. A client applies manufacturing overhead to inventory on the basis of $3.47 per direct labor hour. Explain how the auditor will evaluate the reasonableness of total direct labor hours and manufacturing overhead in the ending inventory of finished goods.

INTEGRATION OF THE TESTS

OBJECTIVE 21-7

Integrate the various parts of the audit of the inventory and warehousing cycle.

Figure 21-4 (p. 702) and the discussions that follow summarize and illustrate the audit of the inventory and warehousing cycle as a series of integrated tests.

Tests of the Acquisition and Payment Cycle When auditors verify inventory acquisitions as part of the tests of the acquisition and payment cycle, they are also obtaining evidence about the accuracy of raw materials acquired and all manufacturing

FIGURE 21-4 Interrelationship of Various Audit Tests

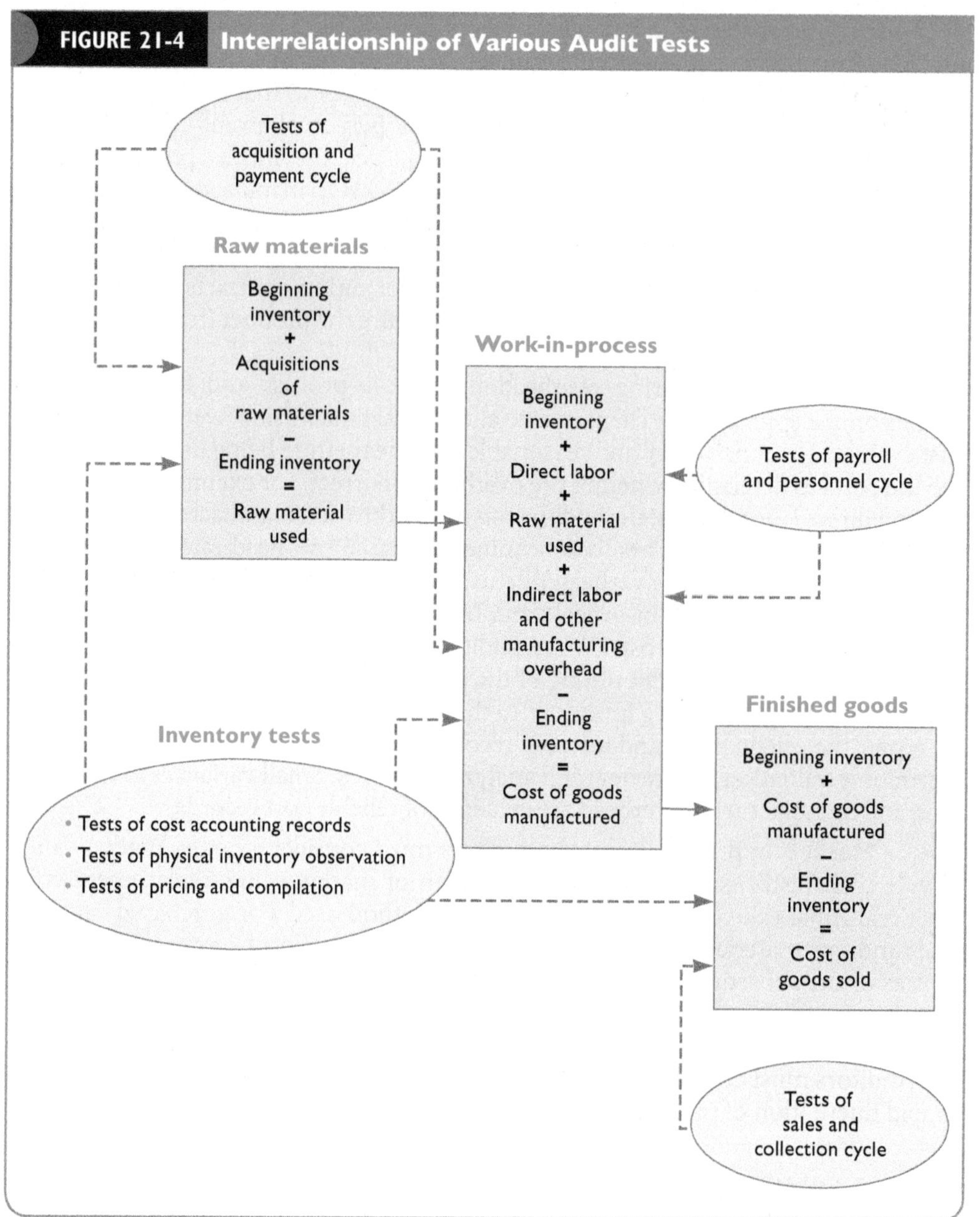

overhead costs incurred except labor. These acquisition costs either flow directly into cost of goods sold or become the largest part of the ending inventory of raw material, work-in-process, and finished goods. In audits where clients have perpetual inventory master files, auditors commonly test these as a part of tests of controls and substantive tests of transactions procedures performed in the acquisition and payment cycle. Similarly, if manufacturing costs are assigned to individual jobs or processes, they are usually tested as a part of the same cycle.

Tests of the Payroll and Personnel Cycle When auditors verify labor costs, the same conditions apply as for acquisitions. In most cases, the cost accounting records for direct and indirect labor costs can be tested as part of the audit of the payroll and personnel cycle.

Tests of the Sales and Collection Cycle The relationship between the sales and collection cycle and the inventory and warehousing cycle is not as interwoven as the two cycles we just discussed. Nonetheless, most of the audit testing in the storage of finished goods, as well as the shipment and recording of sales, takes place when the sales and collection cycle is tested. When the client uses standard cost records, auditors may be able to test the standard cost of goods sold at the same time that sales tests are performed.

Tests of Cost Accounting Tests of cost accounting records are meant to verify the controls affecting inventory that auditors did not verify as part of testing in the preceding three cycles. Auditors test the physical controls, transfers of raw material costs to work-in-process, transfers of costs of completed goods to finished goods, perpetual inventory master files, and unit cost records.

Physical Inventory, Pricing, and Compilation Physical inventory, pricing, and compilation are each equally important in the audit of inventory because a misstatement in any one activity results in misstated inventory and cost of goods sold. In most audits, cost of goods sold is a residual of beginning inventory plus acquisitions of raw materials, direct labor, and other manufacturing costs minus ending inventory. Because cost of goods sold is a residual and often one of the largest accounts on the income statement, the importance of auditing ending inventory becomes obvious.

In testing physical inventory, auditors may rely heavily on the perpetual inventory master files if they have been tested as a part of one or more of the cycles we've discussed and are considered reliable. When that is the case, auditors can observe and test the physical count at a time other than year-end and rely on the perpetuals to keep adequate records of the quantities.

When testing the unit costs, auditors may also rely, to some degree, on the tests of the cost records made during the substantive tests of transactions. Standard cost records are also useful for comparison with the actual unit costs. When standard costs are used to represent historical cost, they must be tested for reliability.

Finally, as auditors test controls and perform substantive tests related to inventory transactions and balances, they also integrate tests related to balance-related audit objectives with tests performed to satisfy the four presentation and disclosure objectives. Accounting standards require disclosure of inventory valuation methods and other relevant inventory information, such as LIFO reserve information, in the footnotes. The auditor should obtain an understanding of client controls related to inventory disclosures and perform tests of those controls and other substantive tests to obtain sufficient appropriate evidence for each of the four presentation and disclosure objectives.

SUMMARY

In this chapter, we discussed the audit of the inventory and warehousing cycle. Because of the difficulties associated with establishing the existence and valuation of inventories, the cycle is often the most time-consuming and complex part of the audit. This cycle is also unique because many of the tests of the inputs to the cycle are tested as part of the audit of other cycles. Tests performed as part of the inventory and warehousing cycle focus on cost accounting records, physical observation, and tests of the pricing and compilation of the ending inventory balance.

ESSENTIAL TERMS

Cost accounting controls—controls over physical inventory and the related costs from the point at which raw materials are requisitioned to the point at which the manufactured product is completed and transferred to storage

Cost accounting records—the accounting records concerned with the manufacturing and processing of the goods and storing of finished goods

Inventory and warehousing cycle—the transaction cycle that involves the physical flow of goods through the organization, as well as related costs

Inventory compilation tests—audit procedures used to verify whether physical counts of inventory are correctly summarized, inventory quantities and prices are correctly extended, and extended inventory is correctly footed

Inventory price tests—audit procedures used to verify the costs used to value physical inventory

Job cost system—system of cost accounting in which costs are accumulated by individual jobs when material is used and labor costs are incurred

Perpetual inventory master file—a continuously updated computerized record of inventory items purchased, used, sold, and on hand for merchandise, raw materials, and finished goods

Process cost system—system of cost accounting in which costs are accumulated for a process, with unit costs for each process assigned to the products passing through the process

Standard cost records—records that indicate variances between projected material, labor, and overhead costs and the actual costs

REVIEW QUESTIONS

21-1 (OBJECTIVES 21-1, 21-2, 21-7) Explain the relationship between the acquisition and payment cycle and the inventory and warehousing cycle in the audit of a manufacturing company. List several audit procedures in the acquisition and payment cycle that support your explanation.

21-2 (OBJECTIVE 21-3) Many auditors assert that certain audit tests can be significantly reduced for clients with adequate perpetual records that include both unit and cost data. What are the most important tests of the perpetual records that the auditor must make before reducing assessed control risk? Assuming the perpetuals are determined to be accurate, which tests can be reduced?

21-3 (OBJECTIVE 21-4) List the major substantive analytical procedures for testing the overall reasonableness of inventory. For each test, explain the type of misstatement that could be identified.

21-4 (OBJECTIVES 21-4, 21-5, 21-6) In the verification of the amount of inventory, one of the auditor's concerns is that slow-moving and obsolete items be identified. List the auditing procedures that can be used to determine whether slow-moving or obsolete items have been included in inventory.

21-5 (OBJECTIVE 21-5) Before the physical examination, the auditor obtains a copy of the client's inventory instructions and reviews them with the controller. In obtaining an understanding of inventory procedures for a small manufacturing company, these deficiencies are identified: Shipping operations will not be completely halted during the physical examination, and there will be no independent verification of the original inventory count by a second counting team. Evaluate the importance of each of these deficiencies and state its effect on the auditor's observation of inventory.

21-6 (OBJECTIVE 21-5) During the taking of physical inventory, the controller intentionally withheld several inventory tags from the employees responsible for the physical count. After the auditor left the client's premises at the completion of the inventory observation, the controller recorded nonexistent inventory on the tags and thereby significantly overstated earnings. How could the auditor have uncovered the misstatement, assuming that there are no perpetual records?

21-7 (OBJECTIVE 21-5) At the completion of an inventory observation, the controller requested the auditor to give him a copy of all recorded test counts to facilitate the correction of all discrepancies between the client's and the auditor's counts. Should the auditor comply with the request? Why?

21-8 (OBJECTIVE 21-5) What major audit procedures are involved in testing for the ownership of inventory during the observation of the physical counts and as a part of subsequent valuation tests?

21-9 (OBJECTIVE 21-5) Assuming that the auditor properly documents receiving report numbers as a part of the physical inventory observation procedures, explain how the proper cutoff of purchases, including tests for the possibility of raw materials in transit, should be verified later in the audit.

21-10 **(OBJECTIVE 21-6)** Define what is meant by compilation tests. List several examples of audit procedures to verify compilation.

21-11 **(OBJECTIVE 21-6)** Included in the December 31, 2016, inventory of the Wholeridge Supply Company are 2,600 deluxe ring binders in the amount of $5,902. An examination of the most recent acquisitions of binders showed the following costs: January 26, 2017, 2,300 at $2.42 each; December 6, 2016, 1,900 at $2.28 each; November 26, 2016, 2,400 at $2.07 each. What is the misstatement in valuation of the December 31, 2016, inventory for deluxe ring binders, assuming FIFO inventory valuation? What would your answer be if the January 26, 2017, acquisition was for 2,300 binders at $2.12 each?

21-12 **(OBJECTIVE 21-7)** Each employee of the Gedding Manufacturing Co., a firm using a job-cost inventory costing method, must reconcile his or her total hours worked with the hours worked on individual jobs using a job time sheet at the time weekly payroll time cards are prepared. The job time sheet is then stapled to the time card. Explain how you could test the direct labor dollars included in inventory as a part of the payroll and personnel tests.

MULTIPLE CHOICE QUESTIONS FROM CPA EXAMINATIONS

21-13 **(OBJECTIVES 21-1, 21-3)** The following questions concern internal controls, and the testing of internal controls, in the inventory and warehousing cycle. Choose the best response.

a. For control purposes, the quantities of materials ordered may be omitted from the copy of the purchase order that is
   (1) returned to the requisitioner.
   (2) forwarded to the receiving department.
   (3) forwarded to the accounting department.
   (4) retained in the purchasing department's files.

b. Which of the following internal control procedures most likely would be used to maintain accurate inventory records?
   (1) Perpetual inventory records are periodically compared with the current cost of individual inventory items.
   (2) A just-in-time inventory ordering system keeps inventory levels to a desired minimum.
   (3) Requisitions, receiving reports, and purchase orders are independently matched before payment is approved.
   (4) Periodic inventory counts are used to adjust the perpetual inventory records.

c. Which of the following sets of duties related to inventory and warehousing causes the greatest concern about inadequate segregation of duties?
   (1) Individuals in charge of approving disbursements related to inventory purchases have "read-only" ability to view the list of vendors in the preapproved vendor master file.
   (2) Purchasing agents who arrange for shipment of raw materials from vendors are responsible for verifying actual receipt of the inventory items at the receiving dock.
   (3) The receiving department has access to copies of the purchase orders that exclude information about quantities ordered.
   (4) Accounts payable personnel have access to receiving reports and purchase orders in addition to vendor invoices for inventory purchases.

21-14 **(OBJECTIVES 21-1, 21-4, 21-5, 21-6)** The following questions deal with tests of details of balances and substantive analytical procedures for inventory. Choose the best response.

a. An auditor selected items for test counts while observing a client's physical inventory. The auditor traced the test counts to the client's inventory listing. This procedure likely obtained evidence about which balance-related audit objective for inventory?
   (1) Existence
   (2) Rights and obligations
   (3) Completeness
   (4) Realizable value

b. Which of the following procedures is the auditor least likely to perform on the actual date the physical inventory count is observed?
   (1) Examine inventory to make sure that it is tagged by client count teams.
   (2) Watch for inventory items that are rust- or dust-covered or otherwise damaged.
   (3) Observe client count teams to determine if they are conducting the physical inventory count in accordance with client policies and procedures.
   (4) Examine documentation supporting the acquisition of highly material inventory items on hand at the count date.

c. An inventory turnover analysis is useful to the auditor because it may detect
   (1) inadequacies in inventory pricing.
   (2) methods of avoiding cyclical holding costs.
   (3) the existence of obsolete merchandise.
   (4) the optimum automatic reorder points.

MULTIPLE CHOICE QUESTIONS FROM BECKER CPA EXAM REVIEW

21-15 **(OBJECTIVES 21-1, 21-3, 21-5, 21-6)** The following questions deal with internal controls in the inventory and warehousing cycle and tests of details of balances for inventory. Choose the best response.

a. As part of the current audit, the auditor begins performing substantive tests on a client's inventory. To test the valuation, allocation, and accuracy assertion, the auditor should perform all of the following procedures except for
   (1) reviewing direct labor rates and testing the computation of the standard overhead rates used.
   (2) performing inventory price tests on a sample of inventory items to ensure the inventory is properly valued.
   (3) testing the mathematical computations of the inventory report and reconciling to the inventory general ledger accounts.
   (4) vouching a sample of items from the client's inventory report sheet to the corresponding prenumbered inventory tags.

b. In auditing a manufacturing entity, which of the following procedures would an auditor most likely perform to determine whether slow-moving, defective, and obsolete items included in inventory are properly identified?
   (1) Test the mathematical accuracy of the inventory report
   (2) Inquire of management about whether inventory has been pledged or assigned
   (3) Tour the manufacturing plant or production facility
   (4) Test the computation of standard overhead rates

c. Alpha Company uses its sales invoices for posting perpetual inventory records. Inadequate controls over the invoicing function allow goods to be shipped that are not invoiced. The inadequate controls could cause an
   (1) understatement of revenues and receivables, and an overstatement of inventory.
   (2) understatement of revenues and receivables, and inventory.
   (3) overstatement of revenues and receivables, and an understatement of inventory.
   (4) overstatement of revenues and receivables, and inventory.

DISCUSSION QUESTIONS AND PROBLEMS

21-16 **(OBJECTIVES 21-1, 21-3, 21-5, 21-6, 21-7)** Items 1 through 8 are selected questions typically found in questionnaires used by auditors to obtain an understanding of internal control in the inventory and warehousing cycle. In using the questionnaire for a client, a

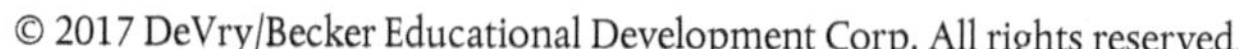

"yes" response to a question indicates a possible internal control, whereas a "no" indicates a potential deficiency.

1. Are all shipments to customers authorized by prenumbered shipping documents?
2. Are standard cost records used for raw materials, direct labor, and manufacturing overhead?
3. Is there a stated policy with specific criteria for writing off obsolete or slow-moving goods?
4. Is a detailed perpetual inventory master file maintained for raw materials inventory?
5. Are physical inventory counts made by someone other than storekeepers and those responsible for maintaining the perpetual inventory master file?
6. Is the clerical accuracy of the final inventory compilation checked by a person independent of those responsible for preparing it?
7. Does the receiving department prepare prenumbered receiving reports and account for the numbers periodically for all inventory received, showing the description and quantity of materials?
8. Is all inventory stored under the control of an inventory custodian in areas where access is limited?

Required

a. For each of the preceding questions, state the purpose of the internal control.
b. For each internal control, list a test of control to test its effectiveness.
c. For each of the preceding questions, identify the nature of the potential financial misstatement(s) if the control is not in effect.
d. For each of the potential misstatements in part c., list a substantive audit procedure to determine whether a material misstatement exists.

21-17 **(OBJECTIVES 21-1, 21-3, 21-5, 21-6, 21-7)** The Frist Corporation has the following internal controls related to inventory:

1. Only authorized inventory and warehousing personnel are allowed in inventory storage areas.
2. All inventory products are stored in warehousing areas that are segregated from other storage areas used to house equipment and supplies.
3. All inventory held on consignment at Frist Corporation is stored in a separate area of the warehouse.
4. The inventory purchasing system only allows purchases from preapproved vendors.
5. The perpetual inventory system tracks the average number of days each inventory product number has been in the warehouse.
6. Microchips are embedded in each product and when inventory items are removed from the warehouse to shipping, radio-frequencies signal a deduction of inventory to the perpetual inventory system.
7. On a weekly basis, inventory accounting personnel take samples of inventory products selected from the perpetual inventory system and verify that the inventory is on hand in the warehouse and that the quantities in the listing are correct.
8. On a weekly basis, inventory accounting personnel select inventory items on hand in the warehouse and verify that the item is included in the perpetual inventory listing at the correct amount.
9. The perpetual inventory system subtotals the quantity of inventory in the system and interfaces with the general ledger system on a daily basis to ensure quantities agree.
10. The perpetual inventory system will not accept inventory additions without the recording on a valid receiving report.

For each of the internal controls:

Required

a. Identify the related transaction-related audit objective(s) affected by the control.
b. Describe risks the control is designed to mitigate.
c. Design a test of control to determine if the control is operating effectively.

21-18 **(OBJECTIVE 21-3)** The cost accounting records are often an essential area to audit in a manufacturing or construction company.

Required

a. Why should the auditor review the cost accounting records and test their accuracy?

b. For the audit of standard cost accounting records in which 35 parts are manufactured, explain how you would determine whether each of the following were reasonable for part no. 21:

(1) Standard direct labor hours
(2) Standard direct labor rate
(3) Standard overhead rate
(4) Standard units of raw materials
(5) Standard cost of a unit of raw materials
(6) Total standard cost

21-19 **(OBJECTIVES 21-1, 21-3, 21-5, 21-6)** Following are audit procedures commonly performed in the inventory and warehousing cycle for a manufacturing company:

1. Read the client's physical inventory instructions and observe whether they are being followed by those responsible for counting the inventory.
2. Use audit software to compute inventory turnover by major product line and compare it to turnover in the prior year.
3. Account for a sequence of inventory tags and trace each tag to the physical inventory to make sure it actually exists.
4. Compare the client's count of physical inventory at an interim date with the perpetual inventory master file.
5. Trace the auditor's test counts recorded in the audit files to the final inventory compilation and compare the tag number, description, and quantity.
6. Compare the unit price on the final inventory summary with vendors' invoices.
7. Account for a sequence of raw material requisitions and examine each requisition for an authorized approval.
8. Trace the recorded additions on the finished goods perpetual inventory master file to the records for completed production.

Required

a. Identify whether each of the procedures is primarily a test of control or a substantive test.

b. State the purpose(s) of each of the procedures.

21-20 **(OBJECTIVES 21-1, 21-5, 21-6)** The following misstatements are included in the inventory and related records of Westbox Manufacturing Company:

1. The clerk in charge of the perpetual inventory master file altered the quantity on an inventory tag to cover up the shortage of inventory caused by its theft during the year.
2. After the auditor left the premises, several inventory tags were lost and were not included in the final inventory summary.
3. When raw material acquisitions were recorded, the improper unit price was included in the perpetual inventory master file. Therefore, the inventory valuation was misstated because the physical inventory was priced by referring to the perpetual records.
4. During the physical count, several obsolete inventory items were included.
5. Because of a significant increase in volume during the current year and excellent control over manufacturing overhead costs, the manufacturing overhead rate applied to inventory was far greater than actual cost.
6. An inventory item was priced at $12 each instead of at the correct cost of $12 per dozen.
7. In taking the physical inventory, the last shipments for the day were excluded from inventory and were not included as a sale until the subsequent year.

Required

a. For each misstatement, state an internal control that should have prevented it from occurring.

b. For each misstatement, state a substantive audit procedure that can be used to uncover it.

21-21 **(OBJECTIVES 21-5, 21-6)** Auditors are required to understand the client's industry and business but may not be experts in identifying the quantity and value of certain inventory items. For example, consider observing a physical inventory and testing inventory valuation for a client who mines rare gems. In such cases, auditors may use a specialist to assist in testing the existence and valuation of inventory. Auditing standards provide guidance on whether and how an auditor can rely on a specialist. Search the PCAOB Web site (pcaobus.org) for PCAOB AU Section 336 guidance on "Using the Work of a Specialist" to answer the following questions.

Required

a. List three examples of inventory items for which an auditor may need to use a specialist for testing existence or valuation, or both. How would the auditor use the specialist in each example?

b. What characteristics should the auditor consider to ensure the specialist is qualified?
c. What level of understanding does the auditor need to have regarding the nature of work performed by the specialist?
d. Does the specialist need to be independent of the client and the auditor?

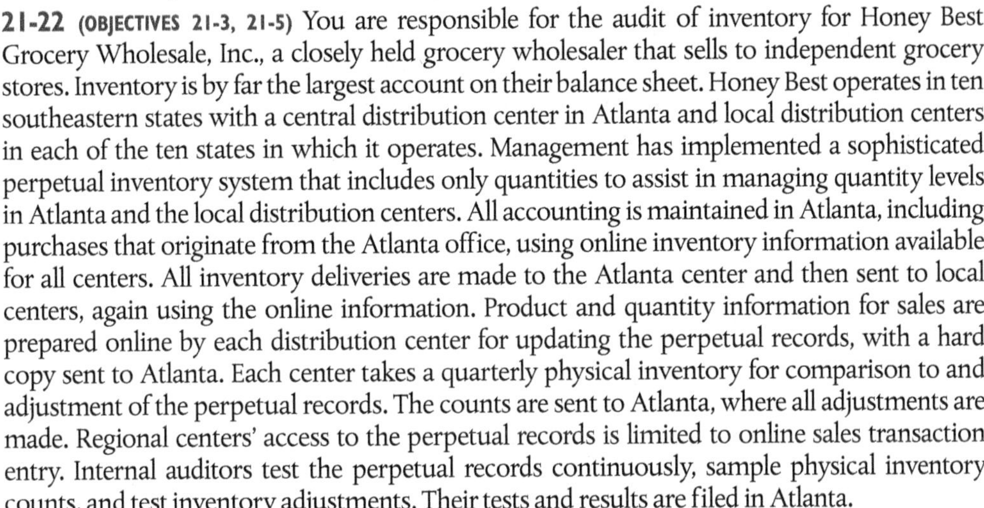

21-22 **(OBJECTIVES 21-3, 21-5)** You are responsible for the audit of inventory for Honey Best Grocery Wholesale, Inc., a closely held grocery wholesaler that sells to independent grocery stores. Inventory is by far the largest account on their balance sheet. Honey Best operates in ten southeastern states with a central distribution center in Atlanta and local distribution centers in each of the ten states in which it operates. Management has implemented a sophisticated perpetual inventory system that includes only quantities to assist in managing quantity levels in Atlanta and the local distribution centers. All accounting is maintained in Atlanta, including purchases that originate from the Atlanta office, using online inventory information available for all centers. All inventory deliveries are made to the Atlanta center and then sent to local centers, again using the online information. Product and quantity information for sales are prepared online by each distribution center for updating the perpetual records, with a hard copy sent to Atlanta. Each center takes a quarterly physical inventory for comparison to and adjustment of the perpetual records. The counts are sent to Atlanta, where all adjustments are made. Regional centers' access to the perpetual records is limited to online sales transaction entry. Internal auditors test the perpetual records continuously, sample physical inventory counts, and test inventory adjustments. Their tests and results are filed in Atlanta.

Required

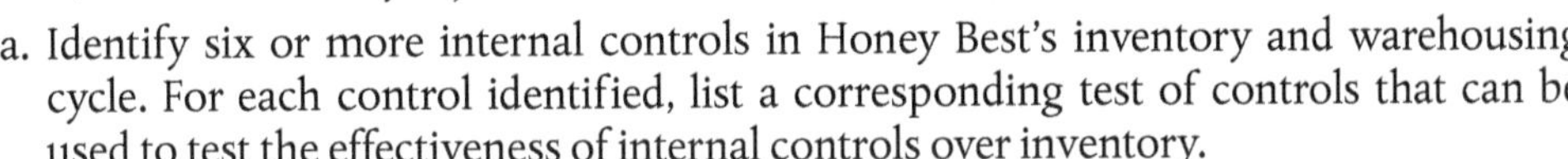

a. Identify six or more internal controls in Honey Best's inventory and warehousing cycle. For each control identified, list a corresponding test of controls that can be used to test the effectiveness of internal controls over inventory.
b. Assuming you determine that internal controls are effective, state how you can reduce or change physical observation tests of inventory. Be specific.

21-23 **(OBJECTIVE 21-4)** Your client, Ridgewood Heating and Cooling, specializes in residential air conditioning and heating installations. The company maintains an inventory of air conditioning units, furnaces, and air handling ductwork. The client has provided the following selected financial statement information for the year ending December 31, 2016:

	12/31/2016	12/31/2015	12/31/2014
Total Sales	$55,443,900	$52,700,440	$50,384,300
Cost of Goods Sold	47,771,880	46,810,900	44,670,400
Ending Inventory	9,582,960	8,100,220	7,730,660

Following is a breakdown of the ending inventory account as of December 31, 2016:

Inventory Description	Quantity	Ending Balance
AC Unit – Model 635	1,240 Units	$ 806,000
AC Unit – Model 770	1,733 Units	1,940,960
Furnace – Model 223	1,992 Furnaces	2,589,600
Furnace – Model 225	2,008 Furnaces	2,761,000
Air Handling Ducts	11,883 Boxes	1,485,400
Total		$9,582,960

Ridgewood stores inventory in a 100,000 square foot warehouse facility at a location different from its corporate office. A single AC unit is stored on a 4 foot by 4 foot pallet. Warehouse storage shelves allow the company to store 1 pallet on the floor while 2 additional pallets are placed on shelves above the first pallet. Furnaces are also stored on similar-sized pallets. Due to the height of the furnaces, only one unit can be stored on a shelf above another pallet that rests on the floor. Air handling ducts are stored in boxes that are 5 foot by 5 foot at the base and 7 feet tall. Three boxes can be stacked on top of the box that sits on the floor.

Required

a. Design substantive analytical procedures to evaluate the reasonableness of the ending inventory account.

b. What concerns, if any, do you have about the ending inventory at Ridgewood Heating and Cooling?

21-24 **(OBJECTIVE 21-5)** You encountered the following situations during the December 31, 2016, physical inventory of Latner Shoe Distributor Company:

Required

a. Latner maintains a large portion of the shoe merchandise in 10 warehouses throughout the eastern United States. This ensures swift delivery service for its chain of stores. You are assigned alone to the Boston warehouse to observe the physical inventory process. During the inventory count, several express trucks pulled in for loading. Although infrequent, express shipments must be attended to immediately. As a result, the employees who were counting the inventory stopped to assist in loading the express trucks. What should you do?

b. (1) In one storeroom of 10,000 items, you have test-counted about 200 items of high value and a few items of low value. You found no misstatements. You also note that the employees are diligently following the inventory instructions. Do you think you have tested enough items? Explain.

(2) What would you do if you test-counted 150 items and found a substantial number of counting errors?

c. In observing an inventory of liquid shoe polish, you note that one lot is five years old. From inspection of some bottles in an open box, you find that the liquid has solidified in most of the bottles. What action should you take?

d. During your observation of the inventory count in the main warehouse, you found that most of the prenumbered tags that had been incorrectly filled out are being destroyed and thrown away. What is the significance of this procedure and what action should you take?

21-25 **(OBJECTIVE 21-5)** Below are four independent client scenarios:

1. Colburn Pharmacy, Inc., has 77 stores located in the New England area. Approximately 60 percent of the inventory recorded on the balance sheet for the consolidated company is located at one of two distribution warehouses, which are in Boston, MA, and Hartford, CT. The remainder of inventory is spread across the 77 stores. The high-dollar-value items in the inventory consist of prescription drugs that are stored in secure areas both in the distribution centers and at the individual stores.
2. Zenith, Inc., manufactures high-end motorcycles in production facilities located in Pennsylvania and Wisconsin. During 2014, the company also opened major production facilities in India and Brazil. Each production facility receives raw materials that are then assembled into motorcycles. Manufactured motorcycles are stored at the production facilities until orders are received from dealers.
3. Texide Electronics manufactures component parts that are used in their customers' computer and other electronic products. Given that customer products differ, each of Texide's products is designed uniquely for each customer's production process. Individual parts are quite small, and the interior components are not visible to the human eye. All inventory items are stored in Texide's only manufacturing plant.
4. Food Giant is a regional grocery store chain located in the Pacific Northwest. Rather than operate a company-owned distribution center, Food Giant uses five different independent storage warehouse companies across the region to store most of its grocery inventory before shipping to the individual stores. Typically, about 75 percent of the inventory is located at the storage warehouses, with the remaining inventory located at one of Food Giant's 42 stores.

Required

a. For each independent client scenario, describe issues the auditor should consider when determining which locations to visit to physically observe the client's inventory count.

b. How would you determine which locations to visit?

c. For each scenario, how does the type of inventory create potential risks of material misstatements in the inventory balances?

d. How might the auditor address the risks noted in part c.?

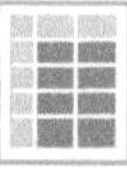

21-26 **(OBJECTIVE 21-4)** The following are sales, cost of sales, and inventory data for Aladdin Products Supply Company, a wholesale distributor of cleaning supplies. Dollar amounts are in millions.

	2016	2015	2014	2013
Sales	$92.8	$86.8	$78.4	$69.6
Cost of sales	68.4	67.2	60.8	54.0
Beginning inventory	9.2	8.4	7.6	6.0
Ending inventory	11.6	9.2	8.4	7.6

Required

a. Calculate the following ratios, using an electronic spreadsheet program (instructor's option):
   (1) Gross margin as a percentage of sales
   (2) Inventory turnover
b. List several logical causes of the changes in the two ratios.
c. Assume that $2,000,000 is considered material for audit planning purposes for 2016. Do any of the fluctuations in the computed ratios indicate a possible material misstatement? Demonstrate this by using the spreadsheet program to perform a sensitivity analysis.
d. What should the auditor do to determine the actual cause of the changes?

21-27 **(OBJECTIVE 21-5)** In an annual audit at December 31, 2016, you find the following transactions near the closing date:

1. Merchandise costing $625 was received on December 28, 2016, and the invoice was not recorded. You located it in the hands of the purchasing agent; it was marked "on consignment."
2. A packing case containing products costing $816 was standing in the shipping room when the physical inventory was taken. It was not included in the inventory because it was marked "Hold for shipping instructions." Your investigation revealed that the customer's order was dated December 18, 2016, but that the case was shipped and the customer billed on January 10, 2017. The product was a stock item of your client.
3. Merchandise received on January 3, 2017, costing $720 was entered in the acquisitions journal on January 4, 2017. The invoice showed shipment was made FOB supplier's warehouse on December 31, 2016. Because it was not on hand December 31, it was not included in inventory.
4. Merchandise costing $1,822 was received on January 3, 2017, and the related acquisition invoice recorded January 5. The invoice showed the shipment was made on December 29, 2016, FOB destination.
5. A special machine, fabricated to order for a customer, was finished and in the shipping room on December 31, 2016. The customer was billed on that date and the machine excluded from inventory, although it was shipped on January 4, 2017.

Assume that each of the amounts is material. **Required**

a. State whether the merchandise should be included in the client's inventory.
b. Give your reason for your decision on each item.*

21-28 **(OBJECTIVE 21-6)** As a part of your clerical tests of inventory for Martin Manufacturing, you have tested about 20% of the dollar items and have found the following exceptions:

1. Extension errors:

Description	Quantity	Price	Extension as Recorded
Wood	920 board feet	$ 0.12/board foot	$ 11.04
Metal-cutting tools	49 units	30.00 each	1,740.00
Cutting fluid	26 barrels	40.00/barrel	240.00
Sandpaper	600 sheets	0.95/hundred	579.00

2. Differences located in comparing last year's costs with the current year's costs on the client's inventory lists:

Description	Quantity	This Year's Cost	Preceding Year's Cost
TA-114 precision-cutting torches	12 units	$800.00 each	Unable to locate
Aluminum scrap	4,500 pounds	8.00/ton	$95.00/ton
Lubricating oil	400 gallons	55.00/gallon	95.00/barrel

*Based on AICPA question paper, American Institute of Certified Public Accountants.

3. Test counts that you were unable to find when tracing from the test counts to the final inventory compilation:

Tag No.	Quantity	Current Year Cost	Description
2958	20 tons	$75.00/ton	Cold-rolled bars
0026	3,000 feet	2.25/foot	4-inch aluminum stripping

4. Page total, footing errors:

Page No.	Client Total	Correct Total
14	$2,375.36	$2,375.30
82	$6,721.18	$6,421.18

Required

a. State the amount of the actual misstatement in each of the four tests. For any item for which the amount of the misstatement cannot be determined from the information given, state the considerations that will affect your estimate of the misstatement.
b. As a result of your findings, what will you do about clerical accuracy tests of the inventory in the current year?
c. What changes, if any, would you suggest in internal controls and procedures for Martin Manufacturing during the compilation of next year's inventory to prevent each type of misstatement?

21-29 **(OBJECTIVE 21-5)** You have been engaged for the audit of the Y Company for the year ended December 31, 2016. The Y Company is in the wholesale chemical business and makes all sales at 25% over cost.

Following are portions of the client's sales and purchases accounts for the calendar year 2016.

SALES

Date	Reference	Amount	Date	Reference	Amount
			Balance Forward		
12-31	Closing entry	$699,860			$658,320
			12-27	†SI#965	5,195
			12-28	SI#966	19,270
			12-28	SI#967	1,302
			12-31	SI#969	5,841
			12-31	SI#970	7,922
			12-31	SI#971	2,010
		$699,860			$699,860

†SI = Sales invoice.

PURCHASES

Date	Reference	Amount	Date	Reference	Amount
Balance Forward					
		$360,300	12-31	Closing entry	$385,346
12-28	‡RR#1059	3,100			
12-30	RR#1061	8,965			
12-31	RR#1062	4,861			
12-31	RR#1063	8,120			
		$385,346			$385,346

‡RR = Receiving report.

You observed the physical inventory of goods in the warehouse on December 31, 2016, and were satisfied that it was properly taken.

When performing a sales and purchases cutoff test, you found that at December 31, 2016, the last receiving report that had been used was no. 1063 and that no shipments have been made on any sales invoices with numbers larger than no. 968. You also obtained the following additional information:

1. Included in the warehouse physical inventory at December 31, 2016, were chemicals that had been acquired and received on receiving report no. 1060 but for which an invoice was not received until the year 2017. Cost was $2,183.
2. In the warehouse at December 31, 2016, were goods that had been sold and paid for by the customer but that were not shipped out until the year 2017. They were all sold on sales invoice no. 965 and were not inventoried.
3. On the evening of December 31, 2016, there were two cars on the Y Company siding:
   a. Car AR38162 was unloaded on January 2, 2017, and received on receiving report no. 1063. The freight was paid by the vendor.
   b. Car BAE74123 was loaded and sealed on December 31, 2016, and was switched off the company's siding on January 2, 2017. The sales price was $12,700 and the freight was paid by the customer. This order was sold on sales invoice no. 968.
4. Temporarily stranded at December 31, 2016, on a railroad siding were two cars of chemicals en route to the Z Pulp and Paper Co. They were sold on sales invoice no. 966, and the terms were FOB destination.
5. En route to the Y Company on December 31, 2016, was a truckload of material that was received on receiving report no. 1064. The material was shipped FOB destination, and freight of $75 was paid by the Y Company. However, the freight was deducted from the purchase price of $975.
6. Included in the physical inventory were chemicals exposed to rain during transit and deemed unsalable. Their invoice cost was $1,250, and freight charges of $350 had been paid on the chemicals.

Required

a. Compute the adjustments that should be made to the client's physical inventory at December 31, 2016.
b. Prepare a worksheet of adjusting entries that are required as of December 31, 2016.*

CASE

21-30 (OBJECTIVE 21-6) You are assigned to the December 31, 2016, audit of Sea Gull Airframes, Inc. The company designs and manufactures aircraft superstructures and airframe components. You observed the physical inventory at December 31 and are satisfied that it was properly taken. The inventory at December 31, 2016, has been priced, extended, and totaled by the client and is made up of about 5,000 inventory items with a total valuation of $8,275,000. In performing inventory price tests, you have decided to stratify your tests and conclude that you should have two strata: items with a value over $5,000 and those with a value of less than $5,000. The book values are as follows:

	No. of Items	Total Value
More than $5,000	500	$4,150,000
Less than $5,000	4,500	4,125,000
	5,000	$8,275,000

In performing pricing and extension tests, you have decided to test about 50 inventory items in detail. You selected 40 of the over $5,000 items and 10 of those under $5,000 at random from the population. You find all items to be correct except for items A through G below, which you believe may be misstated. You have tested the following items, to this point, exclusive of A through G:

	No. of Items	Total Value
More than $5,000	36	$360,000
Less than $5,000	7	2,600

*Based on AICPA question paper, American Institute of Certified Public Accountants.

Sea Gull Airframes uses a periodic inventory system and values its inventory at the lower of FIFO cost or market. You were able to locate all invoices needed for your examination. The seven inventory items in the sample you believe may be misstated, along with the relevant data for determining the proper valuation, are shown next.

INVENTORY ITEMS POSSIBLY MISSTATED

Description	Quantity	Price	Total[1]
A. L37 spars	3,000 meters	$ 8.00/meter	$24,000
B. B68 metal formers	10,000 inches	1.20/foot	12,000
C. R01 metal ribs	1,500 yards	10.00/yard	15,000
D. St26 struts	1,000 feet	8.00/foot	8,000
E. Industrial hand drills	45 units	20.00 each	900
F. L803 steel leaf springs	40 pairs	69.00 each spring	276
G. V16 fasteners	5.50 dozen	10.00/dozen	55

[1]Amounts are as stated on client's inventory.

INFORMATION FOR PRICING FROM INVOICES (SEA GULL AIRFRAMES)

Voucher Number	Voucher Date	Date Paid	Terms	Receiving Report Date	Invoice Description
7-68	8-01-12	8-21-12	Net FOB destination	8-01-12	77 V16 fasteners at $10 per dozen
11-81	10-16-16	11-15-16	Net FOB destination	10-18-16	1,100 yards R01 metal ribs at $9.50 per yard; 2,000 feet St26 struts at $8.20 per foot
12-06	12-08-16	12-30-16	2/10, n/30 FOB S.P.	12-10-16	180 L803 steel leaf springs at $69 each
12-09	12-10-16	12-18-16	Net FOB destination	12-11-16	45 industrial hand drills at $20 each; guaranteed for 4 years
12-18	12-27-16	12-27-16	2/10, n/30 FOB S.P.	12-21-16	4,200 meters L37 spars at $8 per meter
12-23	12-24-16	1-03-17	2/10, n/30 FOB dest.	12-26-16	12,800 inches B68 metal formers at $1.20 per foot
12-61	12-29-16	1-08-17	Net FOB destination	12-29-16	1,000 yards R01 metal ribs at $10 per yard; 800 feet St26 struts at $8 per foot
12-81	12-31-16	1-20-17	Net FOB destination	1-06-17	2,000 meters L37 spars at $7.50 per meter; 2,000 yards R01 metal ribs at $10 per yard

In addition, you noted a freight bill for voucher 12-23 in the amount of $200. This bill was entered in the freight-in account. Virtually all freight was for the metal formers.

Required This is the first time Sea Gull Airframes has been audited by your firm.

a. Review all information and determine the inventory misstatements of the seven items in question. State any assumptions you consider necessary to determine the amount of the misstatements.
b. Prepare an audit schedule to summarize your findings. Use the computer to prepare the schedule (instructor's option).

AUDIT OF THE CAPITAL ACQUISITION AND REPAYMENT CYCLE

CHAPTER

22

LEARNING OBJECTIVES

After studying this chapter, you should be able to

22-1 Identify the accounts and the unique characteristics of the capital acquisition and repayment cycle.

22-2 Design and perform audit tests of notes payable and related accounts and transactions.

22-3 Identify the primary concerns in the audit of owners' equity transactions.

22-4 Design and perform tests of controls, substantive tests of transactions, and tests of details of balances for capital stock and retained earnings.

A Dishonest Client Will Get the Best of the Auditor Almost Every Time

Able Construction Company entered into long-term construction contracts, recognizing income using the percentage of completion method of accounting. To finance its operations, Able borrowed funds from the bank and agreed to comply with restrictive loan covenants dependent on reported income from the long-term contracts. The percentage of completion method of accounting requires, among other things, an agreement with well-defined, enforceable terms; a reliable method of estimating costs to complete the contracts; and recognition of losses at the time they become known. As part of the audit of Able, its auditors read the contracts for all projects in progress, tested costs incurred to date, and assessed the ultimate profitability of the contracts, including discussing them with management. A significant part of verifying income under percentage of completion is auditing costs incurred.

In the current year, management's records and schedules of projects indicate that all projects will result in a profit. For each project, there is a separate schedule showing estimated total revenue from the project, costs incurred in the current period, costs incurred to date, estimated total costs, percentage of completion, and profit recognized in the current period. The auditor discussed each project with management, performed audit tests to support the schedule, and concluded that the revenue, expenses, and profit were reasonably stated. Reported income allowed Able to meet several of the restrictive covenants in its loan agreement with the bank.

In fact, Able had incurred a significant loss on one of its major projects. Able had engaged a subcontractor to do reconstructive work not anticipated in the original contract bid. In awarding the subcontract, Able had entered into an agreement with the subcontractor that the work would not be paid for until after its audit was completed, in an effort to defer recording losses associated with the additional work. Management hid the subcontractor's invoices from the auditors as the invoices were received. During the next year, management recognized this loss but doctored the invoices so that it appeared the "unexpected" additional cost was incurred during that year, and that the previous year's statements were correct and that all loan covenants with the bank were satisfied.

The fraudulent misstatement was discovered several years later when Able went bankrupt and the CPA firm was sued by the bank for performing inadequate audits. The firm was ultimately found not responsible, but only after spending extensive time and large amounts of money defending its audit.

The final transaction cycle we discuss is the **capital acquisition and repayment cycle**, which concerns the acquisition of capital resources through interest-bearing debt and owners' equity and the repayment of capital. This cycle also includes the payment of interest and dividends.

Four characteristics of the capital acquisition and repayment cycle influence the audit of these accounts:

1. *Relatively few transactions affect the account balances, but each transaction is often highly material.* For example, bonds are infrequently issued by companies, but the amount of a bond issue is normally large. Their size makes it common for auditors, as a part of verifying the balance sheet accounts, to verify each transaction taking place in the cycle for the entire year. Audit schedules for most accounts in the cycle include the beginning balance of every account, every transaction that occurred during the year, and the ending balance.
2. *The exclusion or misstatement of a single transaction can be material.* As a result, the auditor's primary emphasis in auditing these accounts is often on the completeness and accuracy balance-related audit objectives.
3. *A legal relationship exists between the client entity and the holder of the stock, bond, or similar ownership document.* As the chapter-opening case of Able Construction Company demonstrates, the auditor must determine whether the client has met the requirements of debt or equity agreements. In the audit of the transactions and amounts in the cycle, the auditor must take great care to make sure the significant legal requirements affecting the financial statements have been met and adequately presented and disclosed in the statements. As a result, the four presentation and disclosure-related audit objectives are also emphasized for the capital acquisition and repayment cycle.
4. *A direct relationship exists between the interest and dividends accounts and debt and equity.* In the audit of interest-bearing debt, auditors should simultaneously verify the related interest expense and interest payable. This is also true for owners' equity, dividends declared, and dividends payable.

Auditors often learn about capital acquisition transactions while gaining an understanding of the client's business and industry, performed as part of the auditor's risk assessment procedures. Also, when public companies issue additional debt and equity securities during the year, SEC rules require auditor consideration of financial information included in the client's new securities offering prospectus. In doing so, auditors frequently identify business risk issues for capital acquisition activities that should be considered in the design of audit procedures for transactions, account balances, and disclosures in the capital acquisition and repayment cycle.

ACCOUNTS IN THE CYCLE

OBJECTIVE 22-1

Identify the accounts and the unique characteristics of the capital acquisition and repayment cycle.

The accounts in a company's capital acquisition and repayment cycle depend on the type of business the company operates and how its operations are financed. All corporations have capital stock and retained earnings, but some may also have preferred stock, additional paid-in capital, and treasury stock. As with other cycles, cash is an important account in the cycle because both the acquisition and repayment of capital affect the cash account. The unique characteristics of the capital acquisition and repayment cycle affect how auditors verify the accounts in the cycle. This cycle often includes these accounts:

- Notes payable
- Contracts payable
- Mortgages payable
- Bonds payable
- Interest expense
- Accrued interest
- Appropriations of retained earnings
- Treasury stock
- Dividends declared
- Cash in the bank
- Capital stock—common
- Capital stock—preferred
- Paid-in capital in excess of par
- Donated capital
- Retained earnings
- Dividends payable
- Proprietorship—capital account
- Partnership—capital account

The methodology for designing tests of details of balances for accounts in the capital acquisition and repayment cycle is the same as that followed for other accounts. (See Figure 16-1 on page 525.) The only difference is the name of the account being audited. For example, in determining the tests of details of balances for notes payable, the auditor considers business risk, performance materiality, inherent risk, control risk, the results of tests of controls and substantive tests of transactions, and the results of substantive analytical procedures.

Auditors often set performance materiality at a low level because it is usually possible to completely audit the account balance and transactions affecting the notes payable account balance. Typically, they also set inherent risk at a low level because the correct account value is usually easy to determine. Auditors are normally most concerned about the completeness objective for notes payable account balances and the completeness objective for notes payable disclosures, such as collateral and covenant restrictions for notes payable. Because the cycle usually contains few transactions, control risk and the results of substantive tests of transactions are normally less important for designing tests of details of balances for accounts such as notes payable.

To best understand the audit procedures for many of the accounts in the capital acquisition and repayment cycle, representative accounts that are significant parts of the cycle for a typical business are included in this chapter. The following sections discuss (1) the audit of notes payable and related interest expense to illustrate interest-bearing capital and (2) the audit of common stock, paid-in capital in excess of par, dividends, and retained earnings to illustrate equity accounts.

NOTES PAYABLE

OBJECTIVE 22-2

Design and perform audit tests of notes payable and related accounts and transactions.

A **note payable** is a legal obligation to a creditor, which may be unsecured or secured by assets, and bears interest. Typically, a note is issued for a period somewhere between one month and one year, but longer-term notes exist. Notes are issued for different purposes, and the property pledged as collateral includes a wide variety of assets, such as securities, accounts receivable, inventory, and fixed assets. The principal and interest payments on the notes must be made in accordance with the terms of the loan agreement. For short-term loans, a principal and interest payment is usually required only when the loan becomes due. For loans over 90 days, the note usually calls for monthly or quarterly interest payments.

Figure 22-1 shows the accounts used for notes payable and related interest. Auditors commonly include tests of principal and interest payments as a part of the audit of the acquisition and payment cycle, because the payments are recorded in the cash disbursements journal. But in many cases, because of their relative infrequency, no capital transactions are included in the auditor's sample for tests of controls and

FIGURE 22-1 Notes Payable and the Related Interest Accounts

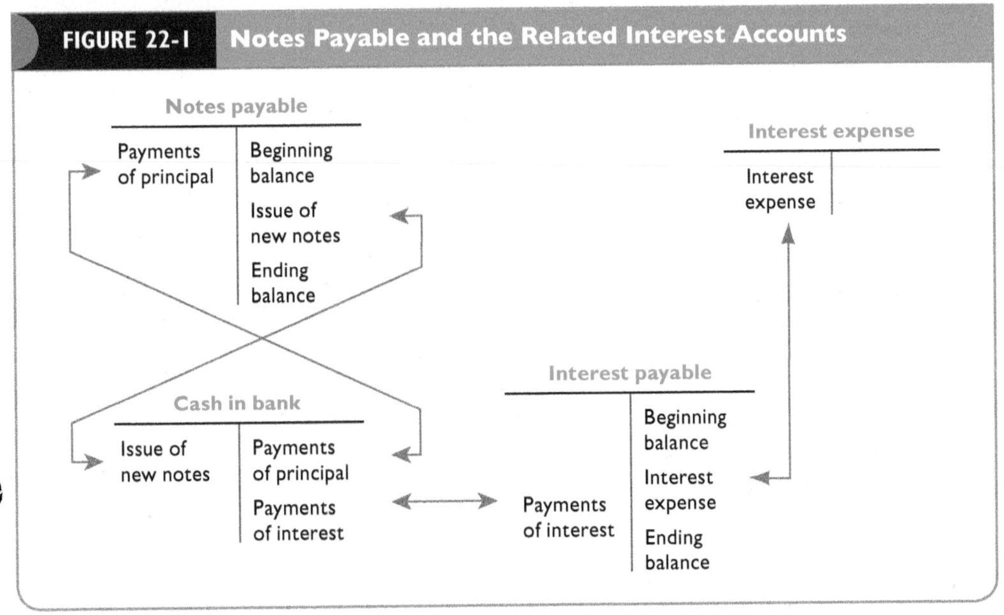

substantive tests of transactions. Therefore, it is also normal to test these transactions as a part of the capital acquisition and repayment cycle.

The objectives of the audit of notes payable are to determine whether:

- Internal controls over notes payable are adequate.
- Transactions for principal and interest involving notes payable are properly authorized and recorded in accordance with the six transaction-related audit objectives.
- The liability for notes payable and the related interest expense and accrued liability are properly stated as defined by seven of the eight balance-related audit objectives. (Realizable value is not applicable to liability accounts.)
- Disclosures related to notes payable and the related interest expense satisfy the four presentation and disclosure audit objectives.

Internal Controls

There are four important controls over notes payable:

1. *Proper authorization for the issue of new notes.* Responsibility for the issuance of new notes should be vested in the board of directors or high-level management personnel. Generally, signatures of multiple properly authorized officials are required for all loan agreements, which usually stipulate the amount of the loan, the interest rate, the repayment terms, and the assets pledged. When notes are renewed, they need to be subject to the same authorization procedures as those for the issuance of new notes.
2. *Adequate controls over the repayment of principal and interest.* The periodic payments of interest and principal should be subject to the controls in the acquisition and payment cycle. At the time the note was issued, the accounting department should have received a copy of the note, much like it receives vendors' invoices and receiving reports. The accounts payable department should automatically issue checks or electronic fund transfers for the notes when they become due, in the same manner in which it prepares payments for acquisitions of goods and services. A copy of the note provides the supporting documentation for payment.
3. *Proper documents and records.* These include subsidiary records and control over blank and paid notes by an authorized person. Paid notes should be cancelled and retained under the custody of an authorized official.
4. *Periodic independent verification.* Periodically, the detailed note records should be reconciled with the general ledger and compared with the note holders' records by an employee who is not responsible for maintaining the detailed records. At the same time, an independent person should recompute the interest expense on notes to test the accuracy of the record keeping.

Tests of Controls and Substantive Tests of Transactions

Tests of notes payable transactions involve the issue of notes and the repayment of principal and interest. These audit tests are a part of tests of controls and substantive tests of transactions for cash receipts (see page 465 in Chapter 14) and cash disbursements (see page 615 in Chapter 18). Additional tests of controls and substantive tests of transactions are often done as a part of tests of details of balances because of the materiality of individual transactions.

Tests of controls for notes payable and related interest should emphasize testing the four internal controls we just discussed. In addition, auditors should verify the accurate recording of receipts from note proceeds and payments of principal and interest.

Substantive Analytical Procedures

Substantive analytical procedures are essential for notes payable because tests of details for interest expense and accrued interest can often be eliminated when results are favorable. Table 22-1 illustrates typical analytical procedures for notes payable and related interest accounts.

The auditor's independent prediction of interest expense, using average notes payable outstanding and average interest rates, helps the auditor evaluate the

TABLE 22-1	Substantive Analytical Procedures for Notes Payable
Substantive Analytical Procedure	**Possible Misstatement**
Recalculate approximate interest expense on the basis of average interest rates and overall monthly notes payable.	Misstatement of interest expense and accrued interest or omission of an outstanding note payable
Compare individual notes outstanding with those of the prior year.	Omission or misstatement of a note payable
Compare total balance in notes payable, interest expense, and accrued interest with prior-year balances.	Misstatement of interest expense and accrued interest or notes payable

reasonableness of interest expense and also tests for omitted notes payable. Turn to page 197 in Chapter 7 and review Figure 7-2 for an illustration of an auditor's schedule where such a substantive analytical procedure has been performed. If actual interest expense is materially larger than the auditor's estimate, one possible cause is recorded interest payments on unrecorded notes payable.

Tests of Details of Balances

The normal starting point for the audit of notes payable is a schedule of notes payable and accrued interest, which the auditor obtains from the client. Figure 22-2 (pp. 720–721) illustrates a typical schedule, including detailed information of all transactions that took place during the entire year for principal and interest, the beginning and ending balances for notes and interest payable, and descriptive information about the notes, such as the due date, the interest rate, and the assets pledged as collateral.

When there are numerous transactions involving notes during the year, it may be impractical for auditors to obtain such a schedule. In those situations, auditors are likely to request the client to prepare a schedule of only those notes with unpaid balances at the end of the year, showing a description of each note, its ending balance, and the interest payable at the end of the year, including the collateral and interest rate.

Table 22-2 (p. 722) summarizes the applicable balance-related audit objectives and common audit procedures as they apply to the schedule of notes payable. Again, the amount of testing depends heavily on the materiality of notes payable and the effectiveness of internal controls.

The two most important balance-related audit objectives in notes payable are:

1. Existing notes payable are included (completeness).
2. Notes payable in the schedule are accurately recorded (accuracy).

DELL GOES PRIVATE

When PC manufacturing giant Dell, Inc., closed its $25 billion leveraged buyout in October 2013, it represented the largest company in terms of revenue to move from being a public company to one that is now privately held. Facing unmet expectations of investors and fending off a number of hostile takeover attempts, Michael Dell, CEO, orchestrated a buyout that allowed him to assume a 75 percent stake in the company he founded in his dorm room.

The decision to take the company private means the company is no longer subject to the regulations required for public companies, allowing Michael Dell and his management team the freedom to make management decisions faster—and with less public scrutiny and oversight. The benefit of speed in decision making and the ability to focus more on long-term versus short-term performance are believed to be key ingredients needed to enable Dell to transform the company from a PC hardware manufacturer to one that is an end-to-end technology solutions provider.

Pursuing the leveraged buyout was a huge, risk-taking venture for Dell, given the company had to take on $17.5 billion in new debt to close the deal. While it no longer has to focus on investor demands, it now has to think about expectations of its debtholders. Attention is now focused on metrics related to cash flow management rather than earnings per share. To address those challenges, the company is already paying down debt as part of its efforts to deleverage its balance sheet over time.

Sources: 1. David McCann, "A Year Later, A New Dell Emerges," *CFO.com* (November 4, 2014) (www.cfo.com); 2. Connie Guglielmo, "Dell Officially Goes Private: Inside the Nastiest Tech Buyout Ever," *Forbes* (November 18, 2013) (www.forbes.com).

FIGURE 22-2 Schedule of Notes Payable and Accrued Interest

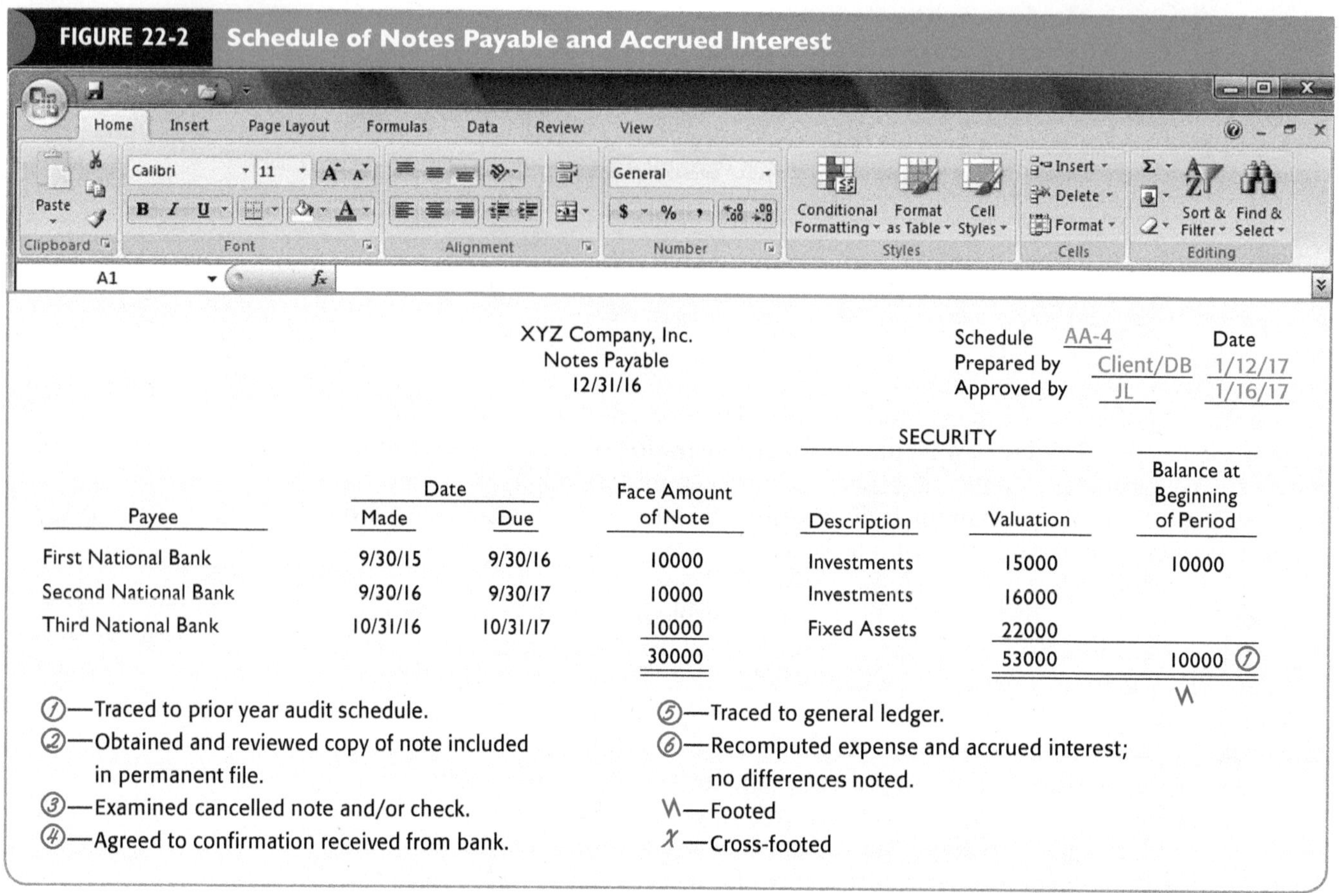

XYZ Company, Inc.
Notes Payable
12/31/16

Schedule AA-4 | Prepared by Client/DB, Date 1/12/17 | Approved by JL, Date 1/16/17

Payee	Date Made	Date Due	Face Amount of Note	Security: Description	Security: Valuation	Balance at Beginning of Period
First National Bank	9/30/15	9/30/16	10000	Investments	15000	10000
Second National Bank	9/30/16	9/30/17	10000	Investments	16000	
Third National Bank	10/31/16	10/31/17	10000	Fixed Assets	22000	
			30000		53000	10000 ① Ʌ

①—Traced to prior year audit schedule.
②—Obtained and reviewed copy of note included in permanent file.
③—Examined cancelled note and/or check.
④—Agreed to confirmation received from bank.
⑤—Traced to general ledger.
⑥—Recomputed expense and accrued interest; no differences noted.
Ʌ—Footed
✗—Cross-footed

(continued on the following page)

These objectives are vital because a misstatement can be material if even one note is omitted or incorrect. Table 22-2 on page 722 shows common procedures to test for the completeness objective for notes payable. When internal controls over notes payable are deficient, auditors may need to perform extended procedures to test for omitted notes payable. For example, the auditor might send confirmations to creditors that have held notes from the client in the past but are not currently included in the notes payable schedule. The auditor might also analyze interest expense for payments to creditors that are not included in the notes payable schedule and review the minutes of the board of directors meetings for authorized but unrecorded notes.

In addition to balance-related objectives, the four presentation and disclosure-related objectives are important for notes payable because accounting standards require that the footnotes adequately describe the terms of notes payable outstanding and the assets pledged as collateral for the loans. If the loans require significant restrictions on the activities of the company, such as compensating balance provisions or restrictions on the payment of dividends, these must also be disclosed in the footnotes. As auditors perform tests of details of balances for balance-related audit objectives, the evidence obtained helps satisfy the notes payable presentation and disclosure objectives.

CONCEPT CHECK

1. Why are liability accounts included in the capital acquisition and repayment cycle audited differently from accounts payable?
2. Which internal controls should the auditor be most concerned about in the audit of notes payable? Explain the importance of each.

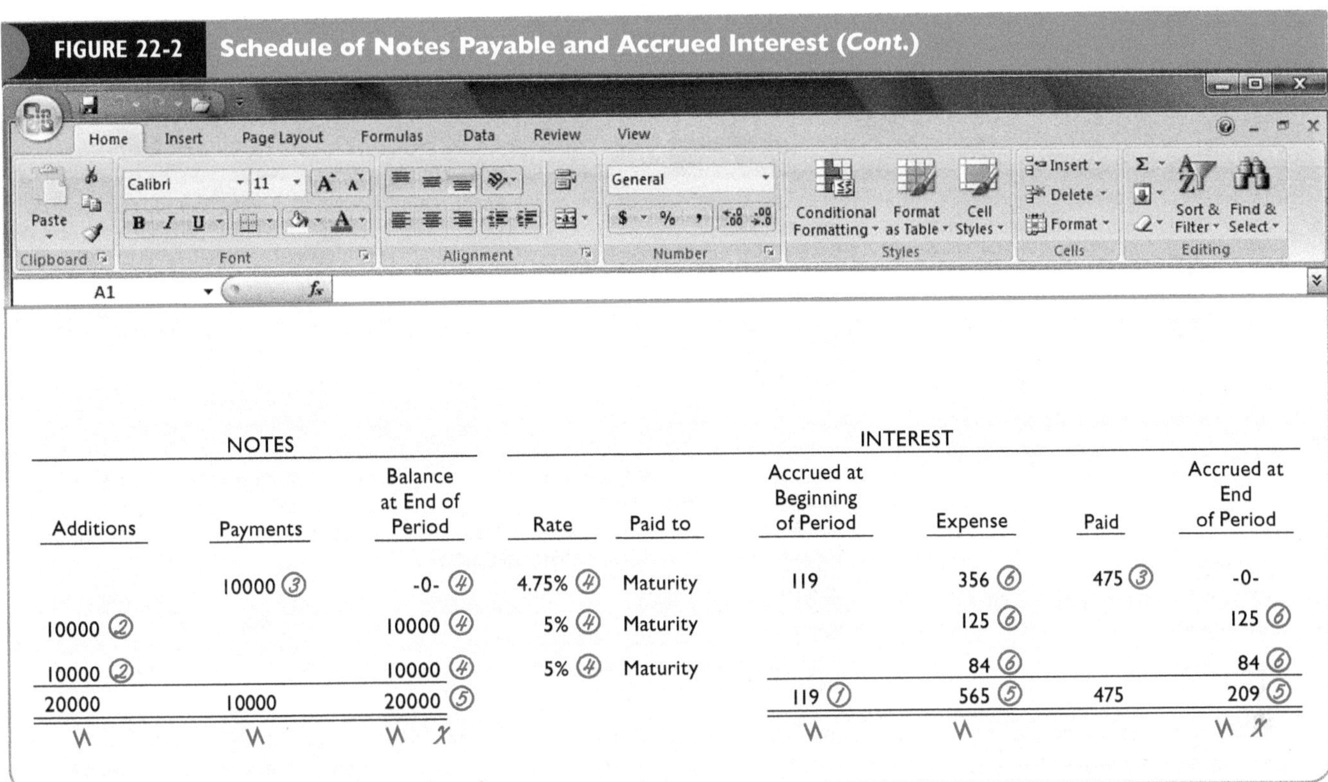

FIGURE 22-2 Schedule of Notes Payable and Accrued Interest (Cont.)

NOTES			INTEREST					
Additions	Payments	Balance at End of Period	Rate	Paid to	Accrued at Beginning of Period	Expense	Paid	Accrued at End of Period
	10000 ③	-0- ④	4.75% ④	Maturity	119	356 ⑥	475 ③	-0-
10000 ②		10000 ④	5% ④	Maturity		125 ⑥		125 ⑥
10000 ②		10000 ④	5% ④	Maturity		84 ⑥		84 ⑥
20000	10000	20000 ⑤			119 ⑦	565 ⑤	475	209 ⑤
W	W	W X			W	W		W X

OWNERS' EQUITY

OBJECTIVE 22-3

Identify the primary concerns in the audit of owners' equity transactions.

There is an important difference in the audit of owners' equity between a **publicly held corporation** and a **closely held corporation**. In most closely held corporations, which typically have few shareholders, occasional, if any, transactions occur during the year for capital stock accounts. The only transactions entered in the owners' equity section are likely to be the change in owners' equity for the annual earnings or loss and the declaration of dividends, if any. Closely held corporations rarely pay dividends, and auditors spend little time verifying owners' equity, even though they must test the corporate records.

For publicly held corporations, however, the verification of owners' equity is more complex because of the larger numbers of shareholders and frequent changes in the individuals holding the stock. The rest of this chapter deals with tests for verifying the major owners' equity accounts in a publicly held corporation, including:

- Capital and common stock
- Paid-in capital in excess of par
- Retained earnings and related dividends

Figure 22-3 (p. 723) provides an overview of the specific owners' equity accounts discussed. The objective for each is to determine whether:

- Internal controls over capital stock and related dividends are adequate
- Owners' equity transactions are correctly recorded, as defined by the six transaction-related audit objectives
- Owners' equity balances are properly recorded, as defined by the eight balance-related audit objectives, and properly presented and disclosed, as defined by the four presentation and disclosure-related audit objectives for owners' equity accounts

Other accounts in owners' equity are verified in much the same way as these.

TABLE 22-2 **Balance-Related Audit Objectives and Tests of Details of Balances for Notes Payable and Interest**

Balance-Related Audit Objective	Common Tests of Details of Balances Procedures	Comments
Notes payable in the notes payable schedule agree with the client's notes payable register or master file, and the total is correctly added and agrees with the general ledger (detail tie-in).	Foot the notes payable list for notes payable and accrued interest. Trace the totals to the general ledger. Trace the individual notes payable to the master file.	These are often done on a 100 percent basis because of the small population size or done by using audit software when there is a large volume of notes.
Notes payable in the schedule exist (existence).	Confirm notes payable. Examine duplicate copies of notes for authorization. Examine corporate minutes for loan approval.	The existence objective is not as important as completeness or accuracy.
Existing notes payable are included in the notes payable schedule (completeness).	Examine notes paid after year-end to determine whether they were liabilities at the balance sheet date. Obtain a *standard bank confirmation* that includes specific reference to the existence of notes payable from all banks with which the client does business. (Bank confirmations are discussed more fully in Chapter 23.) Review the bank reconciliation for new notes credited directly to the bank account by the bank. (Bank reconciliations are also discussed more fully in Chapter 23.)	This objective is important for uncovering both errors and fraud. These three procedures are done on most audits. Additional procedures to search for omitted liabilities may be necessary if internal controls are deficient.
Notes payable and accrued interest on the schedule are accurate (accuracy).	Examine duplicate copies of notes for principal and interest rates. Confirm notes payable, interest rates, and last date for which interest has been paid with holders of notes. Recalculate accrued interest.	In some cases, it may be necessary to calculate, using present-value techniques, the imputed interest rate or the principal amount of the note. An example is when equipment is acquired for a note.
Notes payable in the schedule are correctly classified (classification).	Examine due dates on duplicate copies of notes to determine whether all or part of the notes are a noncurrent liability. Review notes to determine whether any are related party notes or accounts payable.	
Notes payable are included in the proper period (cutoff).	Examine duplicate copies of notes to determine whether notes were dated on or before the balance sheet date.	Notes should be included as current period liabilities when dated on or before the balance sheet date.
The company has an obligation to pay the notes payable (obligations).	Examine notes to determine whether the company has obligations for payment.	

Internal Controls

Several internal controls are important for owners' equity activities. We discuss several of these in the following sections.

Proper Authorization of Transactions Because each owners' equity transaction is typically material, many of these transactions must be approved by the board of directors. The following types of owners' equity transactions usually require specific authorization:

- *Issuance of Capital Stock.* The authorization includes the type of equity to issue (such as preferred or common stock), number of shares to issue, par value of the stock, privileged condition for any stock other than common, and date of the issue.
- *Repurchase of Capital Stock.* The repurchase of common or preferred shares, the timing of the repurchase, and the amount to pay for the shares should all be approved by the board of directors.
- *Declaration of Dividends.* The board of directors must authorize the form of the dividends (such as cash or stock), the amount of the dividend per share, and the record and payment dates of the dividends.

FIGURE 22-3 Owners' Equity and Dividend Accounts

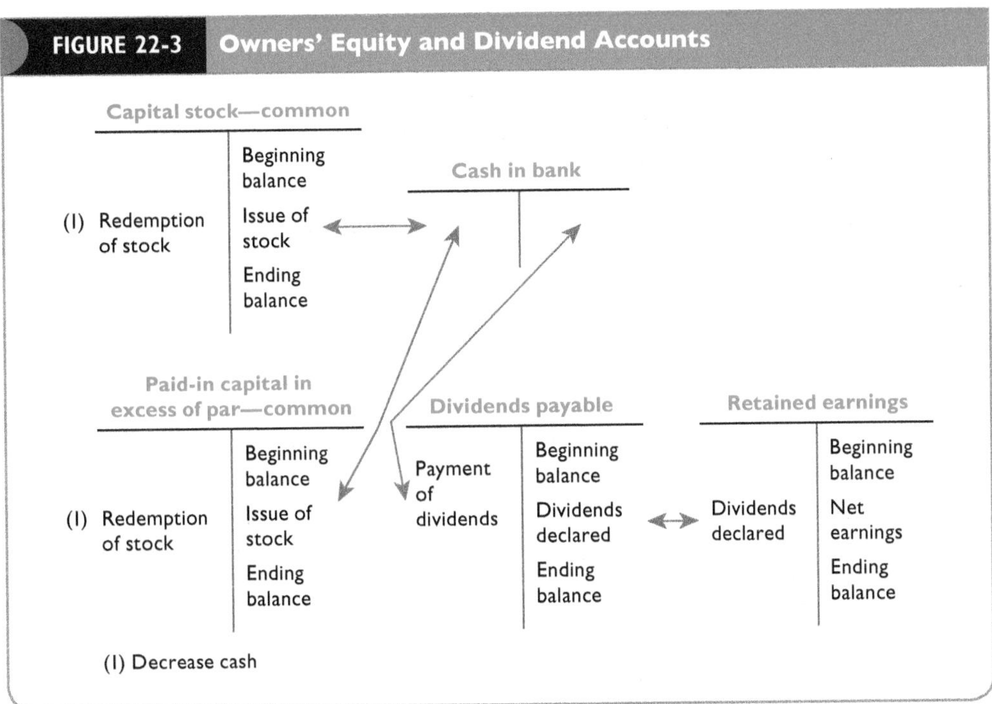

Proper Record Keeping and Segregation of Duties When a company maintains its own records of stock transactions and outstanding stock, the internal controls must be adequate to ensure that:

- Actual owners of the stock are recognized in the corporate records
- The correct amount of dividends is paid to the stockholders owning the stock as of the dividend record date
- The potential for misappropriation of assets is minimized

The proper assignment of personnel, adequate record-keeping procedures, and independent internal verification of information in the records are useful controls for these purposes. The client should also have well-defined policies for preparing stock certificates and for recording capital stock transactions.

When issuing and recording capital stock, the client must comply with both the state laws governing corporations and the requirements in the corporate charter. The par value of the stock, the number of shares the company is authorized to issue, and state taxes on the issue of capital stock all affect issuance and recording.

As a control over capital stock, most companies maintain stock certificate books and a shareholders' capital stock master file. A **capital stock certificate record** records the issuance and repurchase of capital stock for the life of the corporation. The record for a capital stock transaction includes the certificate number, the number of shares issued, the name of the person to whom it was issued, and the issue date. When shares are repurchased, the capital stock certificate book should include the cancelled certificates and the date of their cancellation.

A **shareholders' capital stock master file** is the record of the outstanding shares at any given time. The master file acts as a check on the accuracy of the capital stock certificate record and the common stock balance in the general ledger. It is also used as the basis for the payment of dividends.

The disbursement of cash for the payment of dividends should be controlled in much the same manner as the preparation and payment of payroll, which we described in Chapter 20. Internal controls affecting dividend payments may include:

- Dividend checks are prepared from the capital stock certificate record by someone who is not responsible for maintaining the capital stock records.

- After the checks are prepared, there is independent verification of the stockholders' names and the amounts of the checks and a reconciliation of the total amount of the dividend checks with the total dividends authorized in the minutes.
- A separate *imprest dividend account* is used to prevent the payment of a larger amount of dividends than was authorized.

Independent Registrar and Stock Transfer Agent Any company with stock listed on a securities exchange is required to engage an **independent registrar** as a control to prevent the improper issue of stock certificates. The responsibility of an independent registrar is to make sure that stock is issued by a corporation in accordance with the capital stock provisions in the corporate charter and the authorization of the board of directors. When there is a change in the ownership of the stock, the registrar is responsible for signing all newly issued stock certificates and making sure that old certificates are received and cancelled before a replacement certificate is issued.

Most large corporations also employ the services of a **stock transfer agent** to maintain the stockholder records, including those documenting transfers of stock ownership. The employment of a transfer agent helps strengthen control over the stock records by putting the records in the hands of an independent organization and helps reduce the cost of record keeping by using a specialist. Many companies also have the transfer agent disburse cash dividends to shareholders, further improving internal control.

Audit of Capital Stock and Paid-In Capital

OBJECTIVE 22-4

Design and perform tests of controls, substantive tests of transactions, and tests of details of balances for capital stock and retained earnings.

Auditors have four main concerns in auditing capital stock and paid-in capital in excess of par:

1. Existing capital stock transactions are recorded (completeness transaction-related objective).
2. Recorded capital stock transactions occurred and are accurately recorded (occurrence and accuracy transaction-related objectives).
3. Capital stock is accurately recorded (accuracy balance-related objective).
4. Capital stock is properly presented and disclosed (all four presentation and disclosure objectives).

The first two concerns involve tests of controls and substantive tests of transactions, and the last two involve tests of details of balances and related disclosures.

Existing Capital Stock Transactions Are Recorded This objective is easily satisfied when a registrar or transfer agent is used. The auditor can confirm with that person whether any capital stock transactions occurred and the accuracy of existing transactions, and then determine if all of those transactions have been recorded. To uncover issuances and repurchases of capital stock, auditors also review the minutes of the board of directors meetings, especially near the balance sheet date, and examine client-held stock record books.

Recorded Capital Stock Transactions Occurred and Are Accurately Recorded Extensive auditing is required for transactions involving issuance of capital stock such as the issuance of new capital stock for cash, the merger with another company through an exchange of stock, donated shares, and the purchase of treasury shares. Regardless of the controls, it is normal practice for auditors to verify all capital stock transactions because of their materiality and permanence in the records. The occurrence transaction-related objective can ordinarily be tested by examining the minutes of the board of directors meetings for proper authorization.

Auditors can readily verify accurate recording of capital stock transactions for cash by confirming the amount with the transfer agent and tracing the amount of the recorded capital stock transactions to cash receipts. (In the case of treasury stock, the amounts are traced to the cash disbursements journal.) In addition, the auditor must verify whether the correct amounts were credited to capital stock and paid-in capital in excess of par by referring to the corporate charter to determine the par or stated value of the capital stock.

JUMPSTART OUR BUSINESS STARTUPS (JOBS) ACT OF 2012 SUPPORTS CROWDFUNDING AND LOWERS BARRIERS TO NEW STOCK ISSUES

Critics have long alleged that the Sarbanes–Oxley Act and other regulatory requirements make it difficult for U.S. companies to issue public stock. The Jumpstart Our Business Startups (JOBS) Act of 2012 includes many provisions to make it easier for companies to issue public equity. The Act defines an emerging growth company as a stock issuer that has total annual gross revenue of less than $1 billion.

Companies filing to go public normally must present three years of financial statements in their registration statement; emerging growth companies need only present two years of financial statements. The Act also exempts emerging growth companies for a period of five years from complying with the requirement for auditor attestation on the effectiveness of internal control over financial reporting under Section 404(b) of the Sarbanes–Oxley Act. Note that smaller public companies with a market capitalization of less than $75 million are already exempt from the internal control attestation requirement under the Dodd-Frank Act of 2010. The Act also raises the number of allowable shareholders before a company is required to register with the SEC from 500 shareholders to 2,000 total shareholders.

The Act includes a crowdfunding provision that allows startups and small businesses to raise up to $1 million from small-dollar investments via Web-based platforms that are monitored by the Securities and Exchange Commission. The yearly amount that an individual can invest in such offerings depends on his or her net worth and annual income, up to an annual limit of $10,000.

Source: Based on Amy Wilkinson, "JOBS Act a Win for Startups and Economy," www.cnn.com (April 9, 2012).

Auditing capital stock transactions such as stock dividends, acquisition of property for stock, mergers, or similar noncash transfers is challenging because considerable technical expertise is required and there is often judgment involved to determine proper valuations. For example, in the audit of a major merger transaction, the auditor must often do considerable research to determine the appropriate accounting treatment and proper valuation of the transaction, after considering all the facts in the merger.

Capital Stock Is Accurately Recorded Auditors verify the ending balance in the capital stock account by first determining the number of shares outstanding at the balance sheet date. A confirmation from the transfer agent is the simplest way to obtain this information. When no transfer agent exists, the auditor must rely on examining the stock records and accounting for all shares outstanding in the stock certificate records, examining all cancelled certificates, and accounting for blank certificates.

After the auditor is satisfied that the number of shares outstanding is correct, the recorded par value in the capital account can be verified by multiplying the number of shares by the par value of the stock. The ending balance in the capital in excess of par account is a residual amount. It is audited by verifying the amount of recorded transactions during the year and adding them to or subtracting them from the beginning balance in the account.

A major consideration when auditing the accuracy balance-related objective for capital stock is verifying whether the number of shares used in the calculation of earnings per share is accurate. It is easy to determine the correct number of shares to use in the calculation when there is only one class of stock and a small number of capital stock transactions. The problem becomes much more complex when there are convertible securities, stock options, or stock warrants outstanding. Auditors must have a thorough understanding of requirements of relevant accounting standards before verifying the number of shares for determining basic and diluted earnings per share.

Capital Stock Is Properly Presented and Disclosed The most important sources of information for determining whether all four presentation and disclosure-related objectives for capital stock activities are satisfied are the corporate charter, the minutes of board of directors meetings, and the auditor's analysis of capital stock transactions. The auditor should determine that each class of stock has a proper description, including the number of shares issued and outstanding and any special rights of an individual class. Auditors should also verify the proper presentation and disclosure of stock options, stock warrants, and convertible securities by examining legal documents or other evidence of the provisions of these agreements.

Audit of Dividends

The emphasis in the audit of dividends is on dividend transactions rather than on the ending balance. The exception is when there are dividends payable.

All six transaction-related audit objectives for transactions are relevant for dividends. But typically, transactions related to dividends are audited on a 100 percent basis. The most important objectives, including those concerning dividends payable, are:

1. Recorded dividends occurred (occurrence).
2. Existing dividends are recorded (completeness).
3. Dividends are accurately recorded (accuracy).
4. Dividends are paid to stockholders that exist (occurrence).
5. Dividends payable are recorded (completeness).
6. Dividends payable are accurately recorded (accuracy).

Auditors can verify the occurrence of recorded dividends by examining the minutes of board of directors meetings for authorization of the amount of the dividend per share and the dividend date. When doing so, the auditor should be alert to the possibility of unrecorded dividends declared, particularly shortly before the balance sheet date. A closely related audit procedure is to review the audit permanent file to determine whether restrictions exist on the payment of dividends in bond indenture agreements or preferred stock provisions.

The accuracy of a dividend declaration can be audited by recalculating the amount on the basis of the dividend per share times the number of shares outstanding. If the client uses a transfer agent to disburse dividends, the total can be traced to a cash disbursement entry to the agent and also confirmed.

When a client keeps its own dividend records and pays the dividends itself, the auditor can verify the total amount of the dividend by recalculation and reference to cash disbursed. In addition, auditors must verify whether the payment was made to the stockholders who owned the stock as of the dividend record date. They can test this by selecting a sample of recorded dividend payments and tracing payee information to the records produced by the stock transfer agent or by tracing payee information on the cancelled check to the dividend records. At the same time, auditors can verify the amount and the authenticity of the dividend check.

Tests of dividends payable should be done in conjunction with declared dividends. Any unpaid dividend should be included as a liability.

Audit of Retained Earnings

For most companies, the only transactions involving retained earnings are net earnings for the year and dividends declared. Other changes in retained earnings may include corrections of prior-period earnings, prior-period adjustments charged or credited directly to retained earnings, and the setting up or elimination of appropriations of retained earnings.

To begin the audit of retained earnings, auditors first analyze retained earnings for the entire year. The audit schedule showing the analysis, which is usually a part of the permanent file, includes a description of every transaction affecting the account.

To accomplish the audit of the credit to retained earnings for net income for the year (or the debit for a loss), auditors simply trace the entry in retained earnings to the net earnings figure on the income statement. This procedure must, of course, take place fairly late in the audit after all adjusting entries affecting net earnings have been completed.

In auditing debits and credits to retained earnings, other than net earnings and dividends, auditors must determine whether the transactions should have been included. For example, prior-period adjustments can be included in retained earnings only if they satisfy the requirements of accounting standards.

After the auditor is satisfied that the recorded transactions were correctly classified as retained earnings transactions, the next step is to decide whether they were accurately recorded. The audit evidence necessary to determine accuracy depends on the nature of the transactions. For example, if an appropriation of retained earnings is required for a bond sinking fund, auditors can determine the correct amount of the appropriation by examining the bond indenture agreement. If there is a major loss charged to retained earnings because of a material nonrecurring abandonment of a plant, the evidence needed to determine the amount of the loss can be complex and include examining a large number of documents and records, as well as discussions with management.

Auditors must also evaluate whether any transactions should have been included but were not. For example, if the client declared a stock dividend, the market value of the securities issued should be capitalized by a debit to retained earnings and a credit to capital stock. Similarly, if the financial statements include appropriations of retained earnings, the auditor should evaluate whether it is still necessary to have the appropriation as of the balance sheet date.

Accounting standards require presentation and disclosure of information related to retained earnings. The auditor's primary concern in determining whether presentation and disclosure objectives for retained earnings are satisfied primarily relates to disclosure of any restrictions on the payment of dividends. Often, agreements with bankers, stockholders, and other creditors prohibit or limit the amount of dividends the client can pay. These restrictions must be disclosed in the footnotes to the financial statements.

CONCEPT CHECK

1. What are the primary objectives in the audit of owners' equity accounts?
2. Describe the duties of a stock registrar and a transfer agent. How does the use of their services affect the client's internal controls?

SUMMARY

This chapter discussed the audit of the capital acquisition and repayment cycle, which includes the primary sources of financing for most businesses. The cycle generally involves few transactions, but the individual transactions are often material, which influences the design and performance of tests in the cycle. The approach to auditing this cycle was illustrated for notes payable, for related interest expense and accrued interest, and for owners' equity and related accounts.

ESSENTIAL TERMS

Capital acquisition and repayment cycle—the transaction cycle that involves the acquisition of capital resources in the form of interest-bearing debt and owners' equity, and the repayment of capital

Capital stock certificate record—a record of the issuance and repurchase of capital stock for the life of the corporation

Closely held corporation—corporation with stock that is not publicly traded; typically, there are only a few shareholders and few, if any, capital stock account transactions during the year

Independent registrar—outside entity engaged by a corporation to make sure that its stock is issued in accordance with capital stock provisions in the corporate charter and authorizations by the board of directors; required by the SEC for publicly held corporations

Note payable—a legal obligation to a creditor, which may be unsecured or secured by assets

Publicly held corporation—corporation with stock that is publicly traded; typically, there are many shareholders and frequent changes in the ownership of the stock

Shareholders' capital stock master file—a record of the issuance and repurchase of capital stock for the life of a corporation

Stock transfer agent—outside entity engaged by a corporation to maintain the stockholder records and often to disburse cash dividends

REVIEW QUESTIONS

22-1 (OBJECTIVE 22-1) List four examples of interest-bearing liability accounts commonly found in balance sheets. What characteristics do these liabilities have in common? How do they differ?

22-2 (OBJECTIVE 22-2) It is common practice to audit the balance in notes payable in conjunction with the audit of interest expense and interest payable. Explain the advantages of this approach.

22-3 (OBJECTIVE 22-2) Which analytical procedures are most important in verifying notes payable? Which types of misstatements can the auditor uncover by the use of these tests?

22-4 (OBJECTIVE 22-2) Why is it more important to search for unrecorded notes payable than for unrecorded notes receivable? Suggest audit procedures that the auditor can use to uncover unrecorded notes payable.

22-5 (OBJECTIVE 22-2) What is the primary purpose of analyzing interest expense? Given this purpose, what primary considerations should the auditor keep in mind when doing the analysis?

22-6 (OBJECTIVE 22-2) Distinguish between (a) tests of controls and substantive tests of transactions and (b) tests of details of balances for liability accounts in the capital acquisition and repayment cycle.

22-7 (OBJECTIVE 22-2) List two types of restrictions long-term creditors often put on companies when granting them a loan. How can the auditor find out about these restrictions?

22-8 (OBJECTIVES 22-3, 22-4) Evaluate the following statement: "The corporate charter and the bylaws of a company are legal documents; therefore, they should not be examined by the auditors. If the auditor wants information about these documents, an attorney should be consulted."

22-9 (OBJECTIVE 22-3) What are the major internal controls over owners' equity?

22-10 (OBJECTIVE 22-3) How does the audit of owners' equity for a closely held corporation differ from that for a publicly held corporation? In what respects are there no significant differences?

22-11 (OBJECTIVE 22-4) What kinds of information can be confirmed with a transfer agent?

22-12 (OBJECTIVE 22-4) Evaluate the following statement: "The most important audit procedure to verify dividends for the year is a comparison of a random sample of cancelled dividend checks and electronic payments with a dividend list that has been prepared by management as of the dividend record date."

22-13 (OBJECTIVE 22-4) If a transfer agent disburses dividends for a client, explain how the audit of dividends declared and paid is affected. What audit procedures are necessary to verify dividends paid when a transfer agent is used?

22-14 (OBJECTIVE 22-4) What should be the major emphasis in auditing the retained earnings account? Explain your answer.

22-15 (OBJECTIVES 22-3, 22-4) Explain the relationship between the audit of owners' equity and the calculations of earnings per share. What are the main auditing considerations in verifying the earnings per share figure?

MULTIPLE CHOICE QUESTIONS FROM CPA EXAMINATIONS

22-16 (OBJECTIVE 22-2) The following multiple choice questions concern interest-bearing liabilities. Choose the best response.

a. Which of the following controls will most likely justify a reduced assessed level of control risk for the completeness assertion for notes payable?
   (1) The accounting staff reviews board of director minutes for any indication of any transactions involving outstanding debt to make sure all borrowings are included in the general ledger.

(2) All borrowings that exceed $500,000 require approval from the board of directors before loan contracts can be finalized.
(3) Before approving disbursement of principal payments on notes payable, the treasurer reviews terms in the note.
(4) Accounting maintains a detailed schedule of outstanding notes payable that is reconciled monthly to the general ledger.

b. When an auditor observes that the recorded interest expense seems to be excessive in relation to the balance in the bonds payable account, the auditor might suspect that
(1) discount on bonds payable is understated.
(2) bonds payable are understated.
(3) bonds payable are overstated.
(4) premium on bonds payable is overstated.

c. In the audit of notes payable, which balance-related audit objective is generally one of the most important for the auditor to verify?
(1) Notes payable reflected on the balance sheet at the end of the year exist.
(2) Notes payable due to related parties are properly reflected on the balance sheet.
(3) Existing notes payable are included on the balance sheet as of year end.
(4) Notes payable are reflected at net realizable value as of the balance sheet date.

22-17 **(OBJECTIVES 22-2, 22-3, 22-4)** The following questions concern the audit of accounts in the capital acquisition and repayment cycle. Choose the best response.

a. During an audit of a publicly held company, the auditor should obtain written confirmation regarding debenture transactions from the
(1) debenture holders.
(2) client's attorney.
(3) internal auditors.
(4) trustee.

b. Which of the following internal controls is least likely to reduce risks related to the occurrence transaction-related audit objective for issuances of stock?
(1) The board of directors must approve the distribution of cash dividends.
(2) The issuance of any shares of stock must be preapproved by the board of directors.
(3) The company engages an independent registrar to issue stock certificates.
(4) The company maintains a capital stock certificate record that includes certificate number, number of shares issued, issue date, and name of person to whom certificates are issued.

c. Which of the following audit procedures would be most relevant when examining the completeness transaction-related audit objective for capital stock?
(1) The auditor examines minutes of the board of directors' meetings to identify any actions involving the issuance of capital stock.
(2) The auditor vouches entries in the client's capital stock records to board minutes.
(3) Confirmations of new stock issuances are sent to the client's stock transfer agent.
(4) The auditor traces entries of new stock issuances to the cash receipts journal.

MULTIPLE CHOICE QUESTIONS FROM BECKER CPA EXAM REVIEW

22-18 **(OBJECTIVES 22-2, 22-4)** The following questions concern auditor responsibilities related to the audit of the capital acquisition and repayment cycle. Choose the best response.

a. An auditor is planning the test of details for a client's debt transactions. In order to test the existence and occurrence assertion, the auditor would most likely perform which of the following tests?
(1) Examine the client's bond maturity dates to determine whether the debt should be reflected as a short-term or a long-term liability

(2) Select a sample of debt payments and compare the interest expense to the reported debt balance for reasonableness
(3) Review the board minutes to obtain evidence of new agreements and then follow up by inspecting the new agreements
(4) Review the interest expense account for possible payments to debt holders not included in the debt listing

b. In order to test the valuation assertion related to the client's stockholders' equity transactions, the auditor may complete which of the following substantive procedures?
(1) Analyze the client's retained earnings account by reviewing the propriety of the direct entries to the retained earnings account, starting with the date of the previous audit
(2) Perform inquiries of management regarding any appropriations of retained earnings
(3) Vouch stock transactions recorded in the current period to board minutes
(4) Send third-party confirmations to the stock transfer agent

c. An auditor is in the process of performing substantive procedures on a client's stockholders' equity and vouches stock-related transactions recorded during the year to board minutes. Which of the following assertions is the auditor testing with these procedures?
(1) Valuation
(2) Understandability and classification
(3) Existence and occurrence
(4) Completeness

DISCUSSION QUESTIONS AND PROBLEMS

22-19 **(OBJECTIVE 22-2)** Items 1 through 6 are questions typically found in a standard internal control questionnaire used by auditors to obtain an understanding of internal control for notes payable. In using the questionnaire for a client, a "yes" response indicates a possible internal control, whereas a "no" indicates a potential deficiency.

1. Are liabilities for notes payable incurred only after written authorization by a proper company official?
2. Are paid notes cancelled and retained in the company files?
3. Is a notes payable master file maintained?
4. Is a periodic reconciliation made of the notes payable master file with the actual notes outstanding by an individual who does not maintain the master file?
5. Is the individual who maintains the notes payable master file someone other than the person who approves the issue of new notes or handles cash?
6. Are interest expense and accrued interest recomputed periodically by an individual who does not record interest transactions?

Required

a. For each of the preceding questions, state the purpose of the control.
b. For each of the preceding questions, identify the type of financial statement misstatement that can occur if the control were not in effect.
c. For each of the potential misstatements in part b., list an audit procedure that can be used to determine whether a material misstatement exists.

22-20 **(OBJECTIVE 22-2)** The following are frequently performed audit procedures for the verification of bonds payable issued in previous years:

1. Analyze the general ledger account for bonds payable, interest expense, and unamortized bond discount or premium.
2. Obtain a confirmation from the bondholder.
3. Obtain a copy of the bond indenture agreement and review its important provisions.
4. Determine that each of the bond indenture provisions has been met.
5. Test the client's calculations of interest expense, unamortized bond discount or premium, accrued interest, and bonds payable.

Required

a. State the purpose of each of the five audit procedures listed.
b. List the provisions for which the auditor should be alert in examining the bond indenture agreement.
c. For each provision listed in part b., explain how the auditor can determine whether its terms have been met.
d. Explain how the auditor should verify the unamortized bond discount or premium.
e. List the information that should be requested in the confirmation of bonds payable with the bondholder.

22-21 **(OBJECTIVE 22-2)** The following audit procedures were performed to address presentation and disclosure-related audit objectives related to notes payable.

1. The schedule of notes payable in the footnotes includes all notes outstanding.
2. The footnote identifies which notes are due to related parties.
3. The total of notes payable in the footnotes agrees with the total of notes payable on the balance sheet.
4. The footnote listing of notes payable includes only those obligations that are the responsibility of the company.
5. The footnote clearly describes the assets that are collateral for the note obligations.

Required

Identify the presentation and disclosure-related audit objective(s) for each audit procedure. (Hint: See Table 6-6 on page 165.)

22-22 **(OBJECTIVE 22-2)** Your client, Red Horse, Inc., prepared the following schedule for long-term debt for the audit of financial statements for the year ended December 31, 2016:

Notes Payable Description	Interest Rate	Due Date	1/1/16 Beginning Balance	Additions	Payments	12/31/16 Ending Balance
Mortgage Payable	6.25%	2022	$ 1,125,000	–	$200,000	$ 925,000
Unsecured Notes Payable	6.00%	2024	7,500,000	–	475,000	7,025,000
Secured Bonds	5.75%	2020	2,700,000	$ 1,250,000	300,000	3,650,000
Convertible Debentures	5.25%	2027	—	10,000,000	—	10,000,000
Total			$11,325,000	$11,250,000	$975,000	$21,600,000

Required

a. What type of evidence would you examine to support the beginning balances in the accounts?
b. What types of evidence would you use to support the additions to each account?
c. What types of evidence would you examine to support payments?
d. What procedures would you perform related to the ending balances in the accounts?
e. What evidence would you use to verify interest rates and due dates?
f. How might you use the information presented above to audit interest expense and interest payable accounts?

22-23 **(OBJECTIVE 22-2)** The ending general ledger balance of $186,000 in notes payable for the Sterling Manufacturing Company is made up of 20 notes to eight different payees. The notes vary in duration anywhere from 30 days to two years, and in amounts from $1,000 to $10,000. In some cases, the notes were issued for cash loans; in other cases, the notes were issued directly to vendors for the acquisition of inventory or equipment. The use of relatively short-term financing is necessary because all existing properties are pledged for mortgages. Nevertheless, there is still a serious cash shortage.

Record-keeping procedures for notes payable are not good, considering the large number of loan transactions. There is no notes payable master file or independent verification of ending balances; however, the notes payable records are maintained by a secretary who does not have access to cash.

The audit has been done by the same CPA firm for several years. In the current year, the following procedures were performed to verify notes payable:

1. Obtain a list of notes payable from the client, foot the notes payable balances on the list, and trace the total to the general ledger.
2. Examine duplicate copies of notes for all outstanding notes included on the listing. Compare the name of the lender, amount, and due date on the duplicate copy with the list.
3. Obtain a confirmation from lenders for all listed notes payable. The confirmation should include the due date of the loan, the amount, and interest payable at the balance sheet date.
4. Recompute accrued interest on the list for all notes. The information for determining the correct accrued interest is to be obtained from the duplicate copy of the note. Foot the accrued interest amounts and trace the balance to the general ledger.

Required

a. What should be the emphasis in the verification of notes payable in this situation? Explain.
b. State the purpose of each of the four audit procedures listed.
c. Evaluate whether each of the four audit procedures was necessary. Evaluate the sample size for each procedure.
d. List other audit procedures that should be performed in the audit of notes payable in these circumstances.

22-24 **(OBJECTIVE 22-2)** The following covenants are extracted from the indenture of a bond issue. The indenture provides that failure to comply with its terms in any respect automatically makes the loan immediately due (the regular date is 20 years hence). List any audit steps or reporting requirements you think should be taken or recognized in connection with each one of the following:

a. The debtor company shall endeavor to maintain a working capital ratio of 2-to-1 at all times, and in any fiscal year following a failure to maintain said ratio, the company shall restrict compensation of officers to $100,000 per individual. Officers for this purpose shall include chairman of the board of directors, president, all vice presidents, secretary, and treasurer.
b. The debtor company shall keep all property that is security for this debt insured against loss by fire to the extent of 100% of its actual value. Policies of insurance comprising this protection shall be filed with the trustee.
c. The debtor company shall pay all taxes legally assessed against property that is security for this debt within the time provided by law for payment without penalty and shall deposit receipted tax bills or equally acceptable evidence of payment of same with the trustee.
d. A sinking fund shall be deposited with the trustee by semiannual payments of $300,000, from which the trustee shall, in his discretion, purchase bonds of this issue.*

22-25 **(OBJECTIVE 22-2)** The Redford Corporation took out a 20-year mortgage on June 15, 2016, for $2,600,000 and pledged its only manufacturing building and the land on which the building stands as collateral. Each month subsequent to the issue of the mortgage, a payment of $20,000 was paid to the mortgagor. You are in charge of the current year audit for Redford, which has a balance sheet date of December 31, 2016. The client has been audited previously by your CPA firm, but this is the first time Redford Corporation has had a mortgage.

Required

a. Explain why it is desirable to prepare an audit schedule for the permanent file for the mortgage. What type of information should be included in the schedule?
b. Explain why the audit of mortgage payable, interest expense, and interest payable should all be done together.

*Based on AICPA question paper, American Institute of Certified Public Accountants.

c. List the audit procedures that should ordinarily be performed to verify the issue of the mortgage, the balance in the mortgage and interest payable accounts at December 31, 2016, and the balance in interest expense for the year 2016.
d. Identify the types of information that should be disclosed in the footnotes for this long-term note payable to help the auditor determine whether the completeness presentation and disclosure audit objective is satisfied.

22-26 **(OBJECTIVES 22-3, 22-4)** Items 1 through 6 are common questions found in internal control questionnaires used by auditors to obtain an understanding of internal control for owners' equity. In using the questionnaire for a client, a "yes" response indicates a possible internal control, whereas a "no" indicates a potential deficiency.

1. Are all entries in the owners' equity accounts authorized at the proper level in the organization?
2. Are issues and retirements of stock authorized by the board of directors?
3. Does the company use the services of an independent registrar or transfer agent?
4. If an independent registrar and transfer agent are not used:
   a. Are unissued certificates properly controlled?
   b. Are cancelled certificates mutilated to prevent their reuse?
5. Are common stock master files and stock certificate books periodically reconciled with the general ledger by an independent person?
6. Is an independent transfer agent used for disbursing dividends? If not, is an imprest dividend account maintained?

Required

a. For each of the preceding questions, state the purpose of the control.
b. For each of the preceding questions, identify the type of potential financial statement misstatements if the control is not in effect.
c. For each of the potential misstatements in part b., list an audit procedure that the auditor can use to determine whether a material misstatement exists.

22-27 **(OBJECTIVES 22-3, 22-4)** The table below is an excerpt from Apple Inc.'s Statement of Shareholders' Equity for its fiscal year ended September 27, 2014:

CONSOLIDATED STATEMENTS OF SHAREHOLDERS' EQUITY
(In millions, except number of shares, which are reflected in thousands)

	Common Stock and Additional Paid-In Capital		Retained Earnings	Accumulated Other Comprehensive Income/(Loss)	Total Shareholders' Equity
	Shares	Amount			
Balance as of September 28, 2013	6,294,494	$19,764	$104,256	$(471)	$123,549
Net income			39,510		39,510
Other comprehensive income/(loss)				1,553	1,553
Dividends and dividend equivalents declared			(11,215)		(11,215)
Repurchase of common stock	(488,677)		(45,000)		(45,000)
Share-based compensation		2,863			2,863
Common stock issued, net of shares held for employee taxes	60,344	(49)	(399)		(448)
Tax benefit from equity awards, including transfer price adjustments		735			735
Balance as of September 27, 2014	5,866,161	$23,313	$87,152	$1,082	$111,547

Required

a. How would the auditor verify the balances as of September 28, 2013?
b. What would the auditor do to evaluate the amount shown as Net Income?
c. What sources of evidence might the auditor use to satisfy the occurrence objective for each of the following?
   (1) Repurchase of common stock
   (2) Share-based compensation
   (3) Common shares issued
d. How should the amounts shown as of September 27, 2014, relate to the amounts shown in Apple's balance sheet as of the same date?

22-28 **(OBJECTIVES 22-3, 22-4)** The following audit procedures are commonly performed by auditors in the verification of owners' equity:

1. Review the articles of incorporation and bylaws for provisions about owners' equity.
2. Analyze all owners' equity accounts for the year and document the nature of any recorded change in each account.
3. Account for all certificate numbers in the capital stock book for all shares outstanding.
4. Examine the stock certificate book for any stock that was cancelled.
5. Review the minutes of the board of directors' meetings for the year for approvals related to owners' equity.
6. Recompute earnings per share.
7. Review debt provisions and senior securities with respect to liquidation preferences, dividends in arrears, and restrictions on the payment of dividends or the issue of stock.

Required

a. State the purpose of each of these seven audit procedures.
b. List the type of misstatements the auditors can uncover by the use of each audit procedure.

22-29 **(OBJECTIVE 22-4)** You are a CPA engaged in an audit of the financial statements of Pate Corporation for the year ended December 31, 2016. The financial statements and records of Pate Corporation have not been audited by a CPA in prior years.

The stockholders' equity section of Pate Corporation's balance sheet at December 31, 2016, follows:

Stockholders' Equity	
Capital stock 10,000 shares of $10 par value authorized; 5,000 shares issued and outstanding	$ 50,000
Capital contributed in excess of par value of capital stock	32,580
Retained earnings	47,320
Total stockholders' equity	$129,900

Pate Corporation was founded in 2009. The corporation has 10 stockholders and serves as its own registrar and transfer agent. There are no capital stock subscription contracts in effect.

Required

a. Prepare the detailed audit program for the audit of the three accounts comprising the stockholders' equity section of Pate Corporation's balance sheet. (Do not include in the audit program the verification of the results of the current year's operations.)
b. After every other figure on the balance sheet has been audited, it might appear that the retained earnings figure is a balancing figure and requires no further verification. Why does the CPA verify retained earnings as is done with the other figures on the balance sheet? Discuss.*

22-30 **(OBJECTIVE 22-3)** E-Antiques, Inc., is an Internet-based market for buyers and sellers of antique furniture and jewelry. The company allows sellers of antique items to list descriptions of those items on the E-Antiques Web site. Interested buyers review the Web site for antique items and then enter into negotiations directly with the seller for purchase. E-Antiques receives a commission on each transaction.

*Based on AICPA question paper, American Institute of Certified Public Accountants.

The company, founded in 2012, initially obtained capital through equity funding provided by the founders and through loan proceeds from financial institutions. In early 2015, E-Antiques became a publicly held company when it began selling shares on a national stock exchange. Although the company had never generated profits, the stock offering generated large proceeds based on favorable expectations for the company, and the stock quickly increased to above $100 per share.

Management used the proceeds to pay off loans to financial institutions and to reacquire shares issued to the company founders. Proceeds were also used to fund purchases of hardware and software used to support the online market. The balance of unused proceeds is currently held in the company's bank accounts.

Required

a. Before performing analytical procedures related to the capital acquisition and repayment cycle accounts, consider how the process of becoming publicly held will affect accounts at E-Antiques, Inc. Describe whether each of the following balances would have increased, decreased, or experienced no change between 2014 and 2015 because of the public offering:
   (1) Cash
   (2) Accounts receivable
   (3) Property, plant, and equipment
   (4) Accounts payable
   (5) Long-term debt
   (6) Common stock
   (7) Additional paid-in capital
   (8) Retained earnings
   (9) Treasury stock
   (10) Dividends
   (11) Revenues
b. During 2016, the stock price for E-Antiques plummeted to around $19 per share. No new shares were issued during 2016. Describe the impact of this drop in stock price on the following accounts for the year ended December 31, 2016:
   (1) Common stock
   (2) Additional paid-in capital
   (3) Retained earnings
c. How does the decline in stock price affect your assessment of client business risk and acceptable audit risk?

22-31 (OBJECTIVE 22-3) Before a company can begin trading on an exchange, it must meet certain initial requirements. The exchanges set their own standards for initial listing, which include minimum thresholds for the number of publicly traded shares, total market value, stock price, and number of shareholders.

Required

a. Review the NASDAQ listing requirements and describe the three distinct tiers in the NASDAQ market.[1] Which tier has the most stringent listing requirements?
b. What is the minimum number of shares for the NASDAQ Global Select Market?
c. Companies must meet all of the requirements of one of four standards for the NASDAQ Global Market. What are the four standards? What is the minimum bid price and number of shareholders under the standards?
d. Review the corporate governance requirements. What securities issuances require shareholder approval?

[1]The initial listing requirements for a company to be listed on the NASDAQ can be found on the NASDAQ Web site (https://listingcenter.nasdaqomx.com/assets/initialguide.pdf).

CHAPTER

23

AUDIT OF CASH AND FINANCIAL INSTRUMENTS

LEARNING OBJECTIVES

After studying this chapter, you should be able to

23-1 Identify the major types of cash and financial instruments accounts maintained by business entities.

23-2 Show the relationship of cash in the bank to the various transaction cycles.

23-3 Design and perform audit tests of the general cash account.

23-4 Recognize when to extend audit tests of the general cash account to test further for material fraud.

23-5 Design and perform audit tests of financial instruments accounts.

Fake Bank Confirmation Hides Massive Fraud

Calisto Tanzi formed Parmalat in 1961 at the age of 22 after inheriting a small family-run pasteurization plant in the Italian town of Parma. In 1990, the company went public on the Milan stock exchange. By the end of that decade, Parmalat employed more than 30,000 people in 30 countries, was Italy's eighth largest company, and was a global consumer brand that sought to be the "Coca-Cola of milk."

Parmalat began engaging in fraudulent transactions involving fictitious sales as early as 1993, and investigators indicate that without the fraud, Parmalat would have reported losses every year from 1990 until the fraud was revealed in 2003. During the period, the company took on increasing levels of debt to finance international acquisitions. To raise money and increase sales, Parmalat established three Caribbean shell companies. The shell companies pretended to sell Parmalat products, and Parmalat used credit notes from the shell companies to raise money from banks.

In 1999 the activities of the shell companies were transferred to the Cayman Islands. Two outside auditors allegedly came up with the audacious creation of a bogus milk producer in Singapore that provided 300,000 tons of milk powder to a Cuban importer through the company's Cayman Islands subsidiary. Parmalat claimed that the Cayman Islands subsidiary held €3.95 billion in cash in a New York bank, but the account did not exist. A forged bank confirmation was sent to the subsidiary's auditors to support the fraudulent cash balance.

Parmalat's losses totaled €12 billion, and in 2008, Tanzi was sentenced to 10 years in prison for his role in the fraud. The company restructured and in 2005 was relisted on the Milan stock exchange.

Source: Peter Gumbel, "How It All Went So Sour," *Time* (November 21, 2004) (www.time.com/time/magazine).

Cash is the only account included in every cycle except inventory and warehousing. It makes sense to study this audit area last because the evidence accumulated for cash balances depends heavily on the results of the tests in other cycles. For example, if auditors' understanding of internal control and tests of controls and substantive tests of transactions in the acquisition and payment cycle cause them to believe that it is appropriate to reduce assessed control risk to low, they can reduce detailed tests of the ending balance in cash. If, however, auditors conclude that assessed control risk should be higher, extensive year-end testing may be necessary.

Cash is important because of its susceptibility to theft, and cash can also be significantly misstated, as illustrated in the case of Parmalat. This chapter highlights the linkage of cash in the bank to transaction cycles and describes substantive tests of the cash balance.

Financial instruments, which include investments in debt and equity securities as well as derivative instruments, vary in significance across clients, from a small percentage of assets for a manufacturing firm to a large percentage of assets for a financial institution. Valuation of financial instruments can be complex due to accounting standards and may require the use of specialists. This chapter discusses categories of investments, relevant controls, and audit procedures designed to test the balance of financial instruments.

TYPES OF CASH AND FINANCIAL INSTRUMENTS ACCOUNTS

OBJECTIVE 23-1

Identify the major types of cash and financial instruments accounts maintained by business entities.

We begin by discussing the types of cash and financial instruments accounts commonly used by most companies, because the auditing approach to each varies. Auditors are likely to learn about the various types of cash and financial instruments balances when they obtain an understanding of the client's business. The following are the major types of accounts.

General Cash Account

The **general cash account** is the focal point of cash for most organizations because virtually all cash receipts and disbursements flow through this account. For example, the disbursements for the acquisition and payment cycle are normally paid from this account, while the receipts of cash in the sales and collection cycle are deposited in the account.

Imprest Accounts

As discussed in Chapter 20 (p. 666), many companies establish a separate imprest payroll account to improve internal control over payroll disbursements. A fixed balance, such as $25,000, is maintained in the imprest payroll bank account. Immediately before each pay period, one check or electronic transfer is drawn on the general cash account to deposit the total amount of the net payroll into the payroll account. After all payroll payments have cleared the imprest payroll account, the bank account should have a $25,000 balance. The only deposits into the account are for the weekly and semimonthly payroll, and the only disbursements are payments to employees.

A somewhat different type of imprest account consists of one bank account for receipts and a separate one for disbursements. There may be several of these in a company for different divisions. All receipts are deposited in the imprest account, and the total is transferred to the general account periodically. The disbursement account is set up on an *imprest basis*, but in a different manner than an imprest payroll account. A fixed balance is maintained in the imprest account, and the authorized personnel use these funds for disbursements at their own discretion as long as the payments are consistent with company policy. When the cash balance has been depleted, a reimbursement is made to the imprest disbursement account from the general account after the expenditures have been approved, usually through an online transfer. The use of such an imprest bank account improves controls over receipts and disbursements.

Branch Bank Account

For a company operating in multiple locations, it is often desirable to have a separate bank balance at each location. **Branch bank accounts** are useful for building banking relations in local communities and permitting the centralization of operations at the branch level.

In some companies, the deposits and disbursements for each branch are made to a separate bank account, and the excess cash is periodically transferred electronically to the main office general bank account. The branch account in this instance is much like a general account, but at the branch level.

Imprest Petty Cash Fund

An **imprest petty cash fund** is not a bank account, but it is sufficiently similar to cash in the bank to merit inclusion. A petty cash account is often something as simple as a preset amount of cash set aside in a locked cash drawer or safe for incidental expenses. The use of an imprest petty cash fund is more likely in smaller organizations than larger ones to provide immediate funds for small cash acquisitions that can be paid more conveniently and quickly by cash than by check, or for the convenience of employees in cashing personal or payroll checks. An imprest cash account is set up on the same basis as an imprest branch bank account, but the expenditures are normally for much smaller amounts. Typical expenses include minor office supplies, stamps, and employee meals. A petty cash account usually does not exceed a few hundred dollars and is often reimbursed only once or twice each month. As a result of the immaterial balance, we do not discuss tests of details of balances on petty cash in this chapter. For the organization, the focus is on internal controls.

A growing number of organizations, especially larger organizations, use preapproved purchase cards (known as P-cards) to make miscellaneous purchases instead of maintaining a petty cash fund. These purchase cards function much like a credit card, but contain numerous restrictions on the nature and amount of purchases that can be made.

Cash Equivalents

Companies often invest excess cash accumulated during certain parts of the operating cycle that will be needed in the reasonably near future in short-term, highly liquid **cash equivalents**. These may include time deposits, certificates of deposit, and money market funds. Cash equivalents, which can be highly material, are included in the financial statements as a part of the cash account only if they are short-term investments that are readily convertible to known amounts of cash, and there is insignificant risk of a change of value from interest rate changes.

Figure 23-1 shows the relationship of general cash to the other cash accounts. All cash either originates from or is deposited in general cash. Throughout the chapter, we focus on auditing three types of accounts: the general cash account, imprest payroll bank account, and imprest petty cash. The other accounts are similar enough to these that we need not discuss them separately.

Financial Instruments

Financial instruments accounts include investments in marketable securities such as debt and equity securities, derivative instruments, and hedging activities. Investments

FIGURE 23-1 Relationship of General Cash to Other Cash Accounts

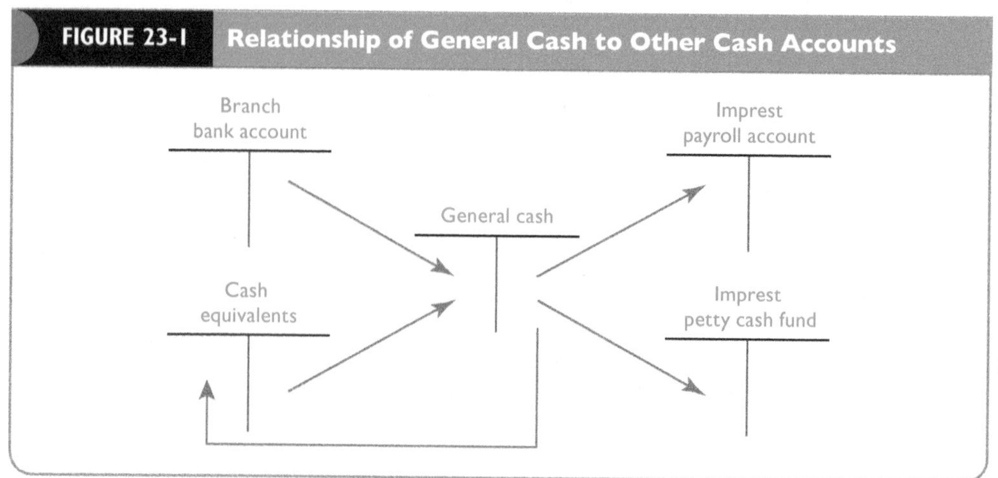

in financial instruments can be classified as trading securities, available-for-sale securities, or held-to-maturity securities, while derivatives can be classified as assets or liabilities, consistent with financial accounting standards. Companies may purchase marketable securities as a way to temporarily invest excess cash or may also invest in derivative financial instruments as a way of hedging. For example, an airline company will invest in fuel hedges as a way to offset increases in operating fuel costs. We discuss internal control and auditing considerations related to financial instruments following our discussion of the cash accounts.

CASH IN THE BANK AND TRANSACTION CYCLES

OBJECTIVE 23-2

Show the relationship of cash in the bank to the various transaction cycles.

A brief discussion of the relationship between cash in the bank and the other transaction cycles serves a dual function:

1. It shows the importance of audit tests of various transaction cycles on the audit of cash.
2. It aids in further understanding the integration of the different transaction cycles.

Figure 23-2 illustrates the relationships of the various transaction cycles, the focal point being the general cash account ("Cash in bank"). By examining Figure 23-2, it is apparent why the general cash account is considered significant in almost all audits, even when the ending balance is immaterial. The amount of cash *flowing* into and out of the cash account is often larger than that for any other account in the financial

FIGURE 23-2 Relationships of Cash in the Bank and Transaction Cycles

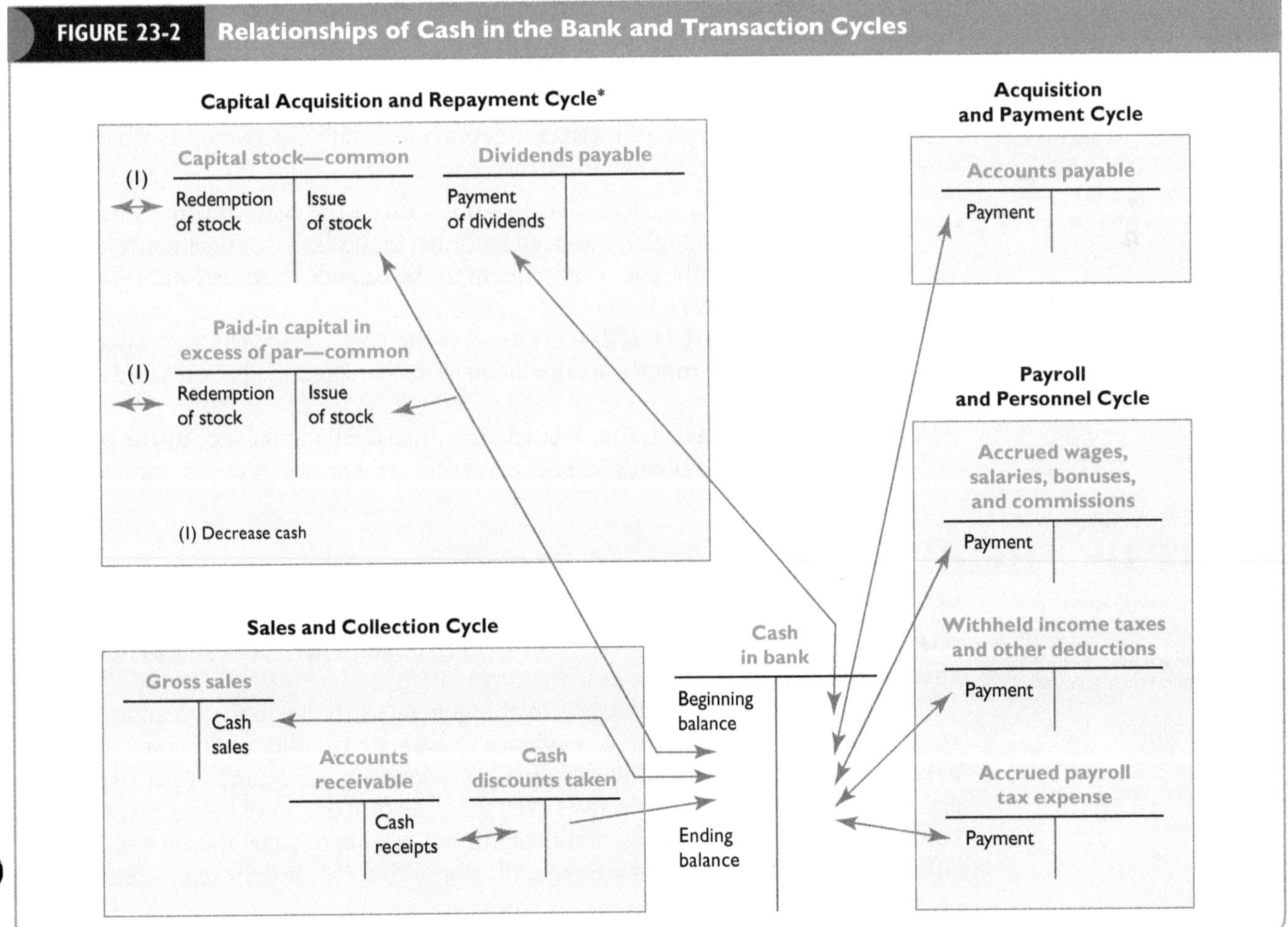

*For simplicity, only owners' equity accounts are shown in this figure. For notes payable accounts, see Figure 22-1 on page 717.

statements. Furthermore, the susceptibility of cash to embezzlement is greater than that for other types of assets because most other assets must be converted to cash to make them usable.

In the audit of cash, auditors must distinguish between verifying the client's reconciliation of the balance on the bank statement to the balance in the general ledger, and verifying whether recorded cash in the general ledger correctly reflects all cash transactions that took place during the year. It is relatively easy to verify the client's reconciliation of the balance in the bank account to the general ledger, but a significant part of the total audit of a company involves verifying whether cash transactions are correctly recorded. For example, each of the following misstatements ultimately results in the improper payment of or the failure to receive cash, but none will normally be discovered as a part of the audit of the bank reconciliation:

- Failure to bill a customer
- An embezzlement of cash by intercepting cash receipts from customers before they are recorded, with the account charged off as a bad debt
- Duplicate payment of a vendor's invoice
- Improper payments of officers' personal expenditures
- Payment for raw materials that were not received
- Payment to an employee for more hours than he or she worked
- Payment of interest to a related party for an amount in excess of the going rate

If these misstatements are to be uncovered in the audit, their discovery must occur through tests of controls and substantive tests of transactions, which we discussed in preceding chapters. The first two misstatements can be discovered as part of the audit of the sales and collection cycle (Chapter 14), the next three in the audit of the acquisition and payment cycle (Chapter 18), and the last two in the tests of the payroll and personnel cycle (Chapter 20) and the capital acquisition and repayment cycle (Chapter 22), respectively.

Entirely different types of misstatements are normally discovered as a part of the tests of the bank reconciliation. These include:

- Failure to include a check that has not cleared the bank on the outstanding check list, even though it has been recorded in the cash disbursements journal
- Cash received by the client subsequent to the balance sheet date but recorded as cash receipts in the current year
- Deposits recorded as cash receipts near the end of the year, deposited in the bank in the same month, and included in the bank reconciliation as a deposit in transit
- Payments on notes payable debited directly to the bank balance by the bank but not entered in the client's records

AUDIT OF THE GENERAL CASH ACCOUNT

OBJECTIVE 23-3

Design and perform audit tests of the general cash account.

The trial balance of Hillsburg Hardware Co. in Figure 6-5 on page 154 includes only one cash account. Notice, however, that all cycles, except inventory and warehousing, affect cash in the bank.

In testing the year-end balance in the general cash account, the auditor must accumulate sufficient appropriate evidence to evaluate whether cash, as stated on the balance sheet, is fairly stated and properly disclosed in accordance with five of the eight balance-related audit objectives used for all tests of details of balances (existence, completeness, accuracy, cutoff, and detail tie-in). Rights to general cash and its classification on the balance sheet are generally not of concern, and the realizable value of cash is not applicable.

The methodology for auditing year-end cash is essentially the same as that for all other balance sheet accounts and is discussed in detail.

Identify Client Business Risks Affecting Cash (Phase I)

Most companies are unlikely to have significant client business risks affecting cash balances. However, client business risk may arise from inappropriate cash management policies or handling of funds held in trust for others.

Client business risk is more likely to arise from cash equivalents and other types of investments. We discuss business risks related to investments in greater detail in the section on auditing financial instruments accounts. The auditor should understand the risks from the client's investment policies and strategies, as well as management controls that mitigate these risks.

Set Performance Materiality and Assess Inherent Risk (Phase I)

The cash balance is not material on many audits, but cash transactions affecting the balance are almost always extremely material. Therefore, the potential often exists for material misstatement of cash.

Because cash is more susceptible to theft than other assets, there is high inherent risk for the existence, completeness, and accuracy objectives. These objectives are usually the focus in auditing cash balances and the auditor may conclude that risks to these objectives are significant risks. Typically, inherent risk is low for all other objectives.

Assess Control Risk (Phase I)

Internal controls over year-end cash balances in the general account can be divided into two categories:

1. *Controls over the transaction cycles* affecting the recording of cash receipts and disbursements
2. *Independent bank reconciliations*

In preceding chapters, we discussed controls affecting the recording of cash transactions, which are essential in assessing control risk for cash. For example, in the acquisition and payment cycle (Chapter 18), major controls include adequate segregation of duties between the check signing and accounts payable functions, signing of checks only by a properly authorized person, use of prenumbered checks printed on special paper, careful review of supporting documentation by the check signer before checks are signed, and adequate internal verification. Similar controls apply to electronic payments. If controls affecting cash-related transactions are operating effectively, control risk is reduced, as are the audit tests for the year-end bank reconciliation.

A monthly **bank reconciliation** of the general bank account on a timely basis by someone independent of the handling or recording of cash receipts and disbursements is an essential control over the ending cash balance. Companies with significant cash balances and large volumes of cash transactions may reconcile cash on a daily basis to online banking records. If a business defers preparing bank reconciliations for long periods, the value of the control is reduced and may affect the auditor's assessment of control risk for cash. The reconciliation ensures that the accounting records reflect the same cash balance as the actual amount of cash in the bank after considering reconciling items. More important, the *independent* reconciliation provides an opportunity for an internal verification of cash receipts and disbursements transactions.

POSITIVE PAY REDUCES CHECK FRAUD

Positive pay is an automated fraud detection tool offered by most banks. A company using positive pay sends a file of issued checks to the bank each day that checks are written. The file sent to the bank includes the check number, account number, issue date, and dollar amount. The positive pay service matches the account number, check number, and dollar amount of each check presented for payment against the list of checks provided by the company. All three components of the check must match exactly for the check to be paid. When a check is presented that does not match, it is reported as an exception and an image of the check is sent to the company. The company reviews the image and instructs the bank to pay or return the check.

Source: Based on "All About Positive Pay" (positivepay.net).

The person performing the bank reconciliation may have read-only access to online bank account information to complete the reconciliation. Alternatively, the individual performing the bank reconciliation may only have access to bank statements mailed by the bank. If bank statements are received unopened by the reconciler, and physical control is maintained over the statements until the reconciliations are complete, copies of cancelled checks, duplicate deposit slips, and other documents included in the statement can be examined without concern for the possibility of alterations, deletions, or additions. A careful bank reconciliation by competent client personnel includes the following actions:

- Compare cancelled checks or electronic bank records of payment with the cash disbursements records for date, payee, and amount
- Examine cancelled checks or electronic bank records of payment for signature, endorsement, and cancellation
- Compare deposits in the bank with recorded cash receipts for date, customer, and amount
- Account for the numerical sequence of checks, and investigate missing ones
- Reconcile all items causing a difference between the book and bank balance and verify their appropriateness for the client's business
- Reconcile total debits on the bank statement with the totals in the cash disbursements records
- Reconcile total credits on the bank statement with the totals in the cash receipts records
- Review month-end interbank transfers for appropriateness and proper recording
- Follow up on outstanding checks and stop-payment notices

Most accounting software packages incorporate bank reconciliation as a part of end-of-month procedures. Even though the software reduces the clerical efforts in performing the bank reconciliation, the preparer still needs to do most of the procedures listed above. The bank reconciliation control is enhanced when a qualified employee reviews the monthly reconciliation as soon as possible after its completion.

Design and Perform Tests of Controls and Substantive Tests of Transactions (Phase II)

Because the cash balance is affected by all other cycles except inventory and warehousing, an extremely large number of transactions affect cash. In several earlier chapters, we discussed in detail the appropriate tests of controls and substantive tests of transactions for the audit of each cycle. For example, controls over cash receipts were studied in Chapter 14, and controls over cash disbursements were studied in Chapter 18. Cash transactions are audited through these transaction cycle tests.

Design and Perform Substantive Analytical Procedures (Phase III)

In many audits, the year-end bank reconciliation is extensively audited. Using substantive analytical procedures to test the reasonableness of the cash balance is therefore less important than it is for most other audit areas.

Auditors commonly compare the ending balance on the bank reconciliation, deposits in transit, outstanding checks, and other reconciling items with the prior-year reconciliation. Similarly, auditors normally compare the ending balance in cash with previous months' balances. These substantive analytical procedures may uncover misstatements in cash.

Design Tests of Details of Cash Balance (Phase III)

The starting point for the verification of the balance in the general bank account is to obtain a bank reconciliation from the client for inclusion in the auditor's documentation. Figure 23-3 shows a bank reconciliation after the client has made adjustments to the account balance. Notice that the bottom figure in the audit schedule is the adjusted balance in the general ledger, which is the balance that should appear on the financial statements. The auditor must determine that the client has made adjustments such as those at the bottom of Figure 23-3, if they are material.

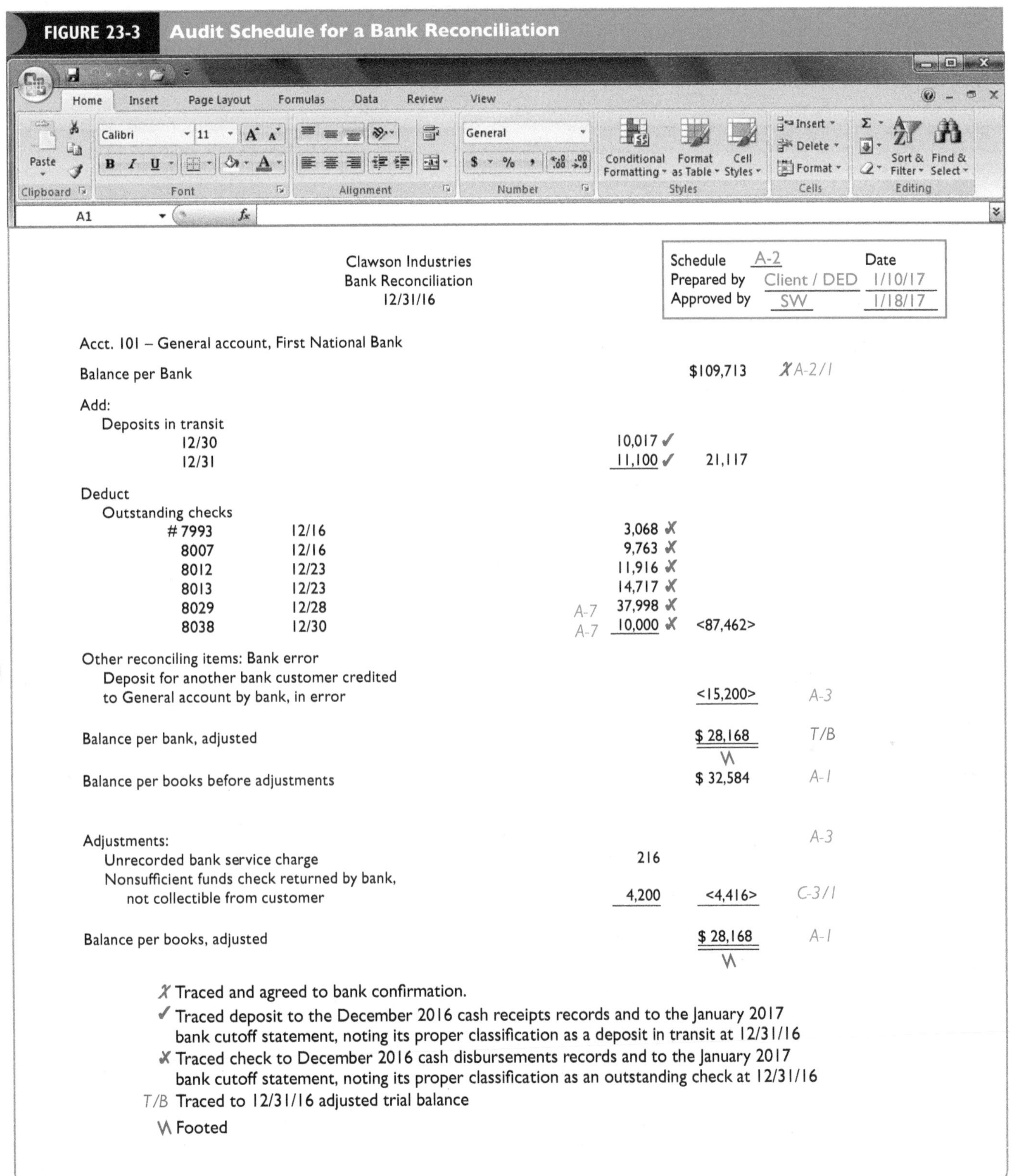

FIGURE 23-3 Audit Schedule for a Bank Reconciliation

Clawson Industries
Bank Reconciliation
12/31/16

Schedule	A-2	Date
Prepared by	Client / DED	1/10/17
Approved by	SW	1/18/17

Acct. 101 – General account, First National Bank

Balance per Bank				$109,713	✗ A-2/1
Add:					
Deposits in transit					
12/30			10,017 ✓		
12/31			11,100 ✓	21,117	
Deduct					
Outstanding checks					
#7993	12/16		3,068 ✘		
8007	12/16		9,763 ✘		
8012	12/23		11,916 ✘		
8013	12/23		14,717 ✘		
8029	12/28	A-7	37,998 ✘		
8038	12/30	A-7	10,000 ✘	<87,462>	
Other reconciling items: Bank error Deposit for another bank customer credited to General account by bank, in error				<15,200>	A-3
Balance per bank, adjusted				$ 28,168 W	T/B
Balance per books before adjustments				$ 32,584	A-1
Adjustments:					A-3
Unrecorded bank service charge			216		
Nonsufficient funds check returned by bank, not collectible from customer			4,200	<4,416>	C-3/1
Balance per books, adjusted				$ 28,168 W	A-1

✗ Traced and agreed to bank confirmation.
✓ Traced deposit to the December 2016 cash receipts records and to the January 2017 bank cutoff statement, noting its proper classification as a deposit in transit at 12/31/16
✘ Traced check to December 2016 cash disbursements records and to the January 2017 bank cutoff statement, noting its proper classification as an outstanding check at 12/31/16
T/B Traced to 12/31/16 adjusted trial balance
W Footed

To audit cash in the bank, the auditor verifies whether the bank reconciliation received from the client is correct. The balance-related audit objectives and common tests of details of balances in the audit of the cash account are shown in Table 23-1. The most important objectives are existence, completeness, and accuracy. Therefore, they receive the greatest attention. In addition to these balance-related objectives, the auditor also performs tests related to the four presentation and disclosure objectives,

TABLE 23-1 Balance-Related Audit Objectives and Tests of Details of Balances for General Cash in the Bank

Balance-Related Audit Objective	Common Tests of Details of Balances Procedures	Comments
Cash in the bank as stated on the reconciliation foots correctly and agrees with the general ledger (detail tie-in).	Foot the outstanding check and electronic payment list and deposits in transit. Prove the bank reconciliation as to additions and subtractions, including all reconciling items. Trace the book balance on the reconciliation to the general ledger.	These tests are done entirely on the bank reconciliation, with no reference to documents or other records except the general ledger.
Cash in the bank as stated on the reconciliation exists (existence). Existing cash in the bank is recorded (completeness). Cash in the bank as stated on the reconciliation is accurate (accuracy).	*(See extended discussion for each of these.)* Receipt and tests of a bank confirmation. Receipt and tests of a cutoff bank statement. Tests of the bank reconciliation. Extended tests of the bank reconciliation. Proof of cash. Tests for kiting.	These are the three most important objectives for cash in the bank. The procedures are combined because of their close interdependence. The last three procedures should be done only when there are internal control deficiencies.
Cash receipts and cash disbursements transactions are recorded in the proper period (cutoff).	*Cash receipts:* Count the cash on hand on the last day of the year and subsequently trace to deposits in transit and the cash receipts journal. Trace deposits in transit to subsequent period bank statement (cutoff bank statement). *Cash disbursements:* Record the last check number used on the last day of the year and subsequently trace to the outstanding checks and the cash disbursements journal. Trace outstanding checks to subsequent period bank statement.	When cash receipts received after year-end are included in the journal, a better cash position than actually exists is shown. It is called "holding open" the cash receipts journal. Holding open the cash disbursements journal reduces accounts payable and usually overstates the current ratio. The first procedure listed for receipts and disbursements cutoff tests requires the auditor's presence on the client's premises at the end of the last day of the year.

such as review of minutes and loan agreements to determine if there are restrictions on cash that must be disclosed. As in all other audit areas, the actual audit procedures depend on materiality and the risks in cash that the auditor has identified in other parts of the audit.

The following three procedures merit additional discussion because of their importance and complexity: receipt of a bank confirmation, receipt of a cutoff bank statement, and tests of the bank reconciliation.

Receipt of a Bank Confirmation Although bank confirmations are not required under auditing standards, auditors usually obtain a direct receipt of a confirmation from every bank or other financial institution with which the client does business, except when there is an unusually large number of inactive accounts. If the bank does not respond to a confirmation request, the auditor should send a second request or ask the client to communicate with the bank to ask it to complete and return the confirmation to the auditor. As a convenience to auditors as well as to bankers who are requested to fill out bank confirmations, the AICPA has approved the use of a **standard bank confirmation form**. Figure 23-4 illustrates a completed standard confirmation, called a "standard form to confirm account balance information with financial institutions." This standard form has been agreed upon by the AICPA and the American Bankers Association. As discussed in the vignette on page 747, bank confirmations are often sent electronically, and some banks will only respond to confirmation requests sent electronically through a designated third-party intermediary.

The importance of bank confirmations in the audit extends beyond the verification of the actual cash balance. Typically, the bank confirms loan information and bank balances on the same form, such as the three outstanding loans in Figure 23-4. Information on liabilities to the bank for notes, mortgages, or other debt typically includes the amount and date of the loan, the loan due date, the interest rate, and the existence of collateral.

Banks are *not responsible* for searching their records for bank balances or loans beyond those included on the form by the CPA firm's client. A statement near the

FIGURE 23-4 Standard Confirmation of Financial Institution Account Balance Information

Clawson Industries
Bank Confirmation
12/31/16

		Date
Schedule	A-2/1	
Prepared by	DED	1/10/17
Approved by	SW	1/18/17

STANDARD FORM TO CONFIRM ACCOUNT
BALANCE INFORMATION WITH FINANCIAL INSTITUTIONS

Clawson Industries
CUSTOMER NAME

Financial Institution's Name and Address

[First National Bank
200 Oak Street
Midvale, Illinois 40093]

We have provided to our accountants the following information as of the close of business on **December 31, 2016,** regarding our deposit and loan balances. Please confirm the accuracy of the information, noting any exceptions to the information provided. If the balances have been left blank, please complete this form by furnishing the balance in the appropriate space below.* Although we do not request nor expect you to conduct a comprehensive, detailed search of your records, if during the process of completing this confirmation additional information about other deposit and loan accounts we may have with you comes to your attention, please include such information below. Please use the enclosed envelope to return the form directly to our accountants.

1. At the close of business on the date listed above, our records indicated the following deposit balance(s):

ACCOUNT NAME	ACCOUNT NUMBER	INTEREST RATE	BALANCE*
General account	19751-974	None	109,713.11 A-2

2. We were directly liable to the financial institution for loans at the close of business on the date listed above as follows:

ACCOUNT NO./ DESCRIPTION	BALANCE*	DATE DUE	INTEREST RATE	DATE THROUGH WHICH INTEREST IS PAID	DESCRIPTION OF COLLATERAL
N/A	50,000.00	1/9/17	4.75%	N/A	General
N/A	90,000.00	1/9/17	4.625%	N/A	Security
N/A	60,000.00	1/23/17	4.75%	N/A	Agreement

A L Moore
(Customer's Authorized Signature)

January 3, 2017
(Date)

The information presented above by the customer is in agreement with our records. Although we have not conducted a comprehensive, detailed search of our records, no other deposit or loan accounts have come to our attention except as noted below.

Margaret Davis
(Financial Institution Authorized Signature)

January 8, 2017
(Date)

Vice President
(Title)

EXCEPTIONS AND/OR COMMENTS

None

Please return this form directly to our accountants:

Jones and Smith CPAs
2111 First Street
Detroit, Michigan 48711

Approved 1990 by American Bankers Association, American Institute of Certified Public Accountants, and Bank Administration Institute. Additional forms available from: AICPA-Order Department, 1-888-777-7077

*Ordinarily, balances are intentionally left blank if they are not available at the time the form is prepared.

bottom of the form obligates banks to inform the CPA firm of any loans not included on the confirmation *about which the bank has knowledge.* The effect of this limited responsibility is to require auditors to satisfy themselves about the completeness objective for unrecorded bank balances and loans from the bank in another manner. Similarly, banks are not expected to inform auditors of such things as open lines of credit, compensating balance requirements, or contingent liabilities for guaranteeing the loans of others. If auditors want confirmation of this type of information, they should obtain a separate confirmation from the financial institution addressing the matters of concern.

After auditors receive the completed bank confirmation, the balance in the bank account confirmed by the bank should be traced to the amount stated on the bank reconciliation. Similarly, all other information on the reconciliation should be traced to the relevant audit schedules. If the bank confirmation does not agree with the audit schedules, auditors must investigate the difference.

Accessing Cutoff Bank Activity after Year-End A **cutoff bank statement** is a partial-period bank statement and the related copies of or digital access to cancelled checks, duplicate deposit slips, and other documents included in bank statements, provided by the bank directly to the CPA firm's office or through online access to the bank's electronic records of the client's bank account information. The purpose of the cutoff bank statement or electronic access to account information on the bank's system is to verify the reconciling items on the client's year-end bank reconciliation with evidence that is maintained by the bank, not the client. To fulfill this purpose, the auditor requests the client to have the bank provide directly to the auditor a partial-period statement, or digital access to the information, for 7 to 10 days subsequent to the balance sheet date.

Alternatively, auditors can wait until the subsequent period bank statement is available to verify reconciling items, if a cutoff statement is not received directly from the bank or online access to client bank account information is not available to the auditor. The purpose is to test whether the client's employees have omitted, added, or altered any of the documents accompanying the statement. Obviously, this tests for intentional misstatements. The auditor performs the following verification in the month subsequent to the balance sheet date:

- Foot the lists of all cancelled checks, debit memos, deposits, and credit memos
- Verify that the bank statement balances when the footed totals are used
- Review the items included in the footings to make sure that they were cancelled by the bank in the proper period and do not include any erasures or alterations

Tests of the Bank Reconciliation A well-prepared independent bank reconciliation is an essential internal control over cash. Auditors test the bank reconciliation to determine whether client personnel have carefully prepared the bank reconciliation and to verify whether the client's recorded bank balance is the same amount as the actual cash in the bank except for deposits in transit, outstanding checks, and other reconciling items.

In verifying the reconciliation, the auditor uses information available to the auditor through online access to client account information provided by the bank or in the cutoff bank statement to verify the appropriateness of reconciling items. The auditor's verification of the reconciliation involves several procedures:

- Verify that the client's bank reconciliation is mathematically accurate.
- Trace the balance on the bank confirmation and/or the beginning balance shown in online client banking records or in the cutoff statement to the balance per bank on the bank reconciliation to ensure they are the same.

ELECTRONIC CONFIRMATIONS OF BANK BALANCES

As illustrated by the Parmalat fraud discussed at the beginning of this chapter, one of the shortcomings of the confirmation process is difficulty authenticating the confirmation respondent. Although auditors generally confirm bank balances because they are considered a highly reliable source of evidence about cash in the bank, obtaining bank confirmations can be a time-consuming process. Organizations may not respond to confirmation requests, and it may take several weeks to receive confirmation responses through the mail.

Automated confirmations using a third-party intermediary can address many of these shortcomings and improve confirmation efficiency and effectiveness. Authentication checks are performed on all parties to the confirmation process (audit firm, client, and financial institution). A secure value-added network with digital signatures and encryption technology is used to allow the client to authorize the confirmation requests and the auditor to communicate directly with the confirming parties.

AICPA auditing standards note that an electronic confirmation system that creates a secure confirmation environment may mitigate the risk of interception or alteration of the confirmation. Those standards also note that when the auditor plans to rely on the controls over such a system or process, an assurance trust services report or another assurance report on the system or process may assist the auditor in assessing the design and operating effectiveness of electronic and manual controls embedded in that system or process.

Sources: 1. George Aldhizer and James Cashell, "Automating the Confirmation Process: How to Enhance Audit Effectiveness and Efficiency," *The CPA Journal* (April 2006) p. 6-10; 2. AICPA *Professional Standards*, AU-C 505, "External Confirmations" (www.aicpa.org).

- Trace checks written and recorded before year-end and included with the cutoff bank statement to the list of outstanding checks on the bank reconciliation and to the cash disbursements journal in the period or periods prior to the balance sheet date. All checks that cleared the bank after the balance sheet date and were included in the cash disbursements journal should also be included on the outstanding check list. If a check was included in the cash disbursements journal, it should be included as an outstanding check if it did not clear before the balance sheet date. Similarly, if a check cleared the bank before the balance sheet date, it should not be on the bank reconciliation.
- Investigate all significant checks included on the outstanding check list that have not cleared the bank on the cutoff statement. The first step in the investigation should be to trace the amount of any items not clearing to the cash disbursements journal. The reason for the check not being cashed should be discussed with the client, and if the auditor is concerned about the possibility of fraud, the vendor's accounts payable balance should be confirmed to determine whether the vendor has recognized the receipt of the cash in its records. In addition, a copy or access to a digital image of the cancelled check should be examined before the last day of the audit if it becomes available.
- Trace deposits in transit to the cutoff bank statement. All cash receipts not deposited in the bank at the end of the year should be traced to the cutoff bank statement to make sure that they were deposited shortly after the beginning of the new year.
- Account for other reconciling items on the bank statement and bank reconciliation. These include such items as bank service charges, bank errors and corrections, and unrecorded transactions debited or credited directly to the bank account by the bank. These reconciling items should be investigated to be sure that they have been treated properly by the client.

Figure 23-5 (p. 748) illustrates how the types of audit tests are used to audit the general cash account. Observe in the figure that tests of controls, substantive tests of transactions, and substantive analytical procedures are done for each transaction cycle involving the cash account.

FIGURE 23-5 Types of Audit Tests Used for General Cash in the Bank

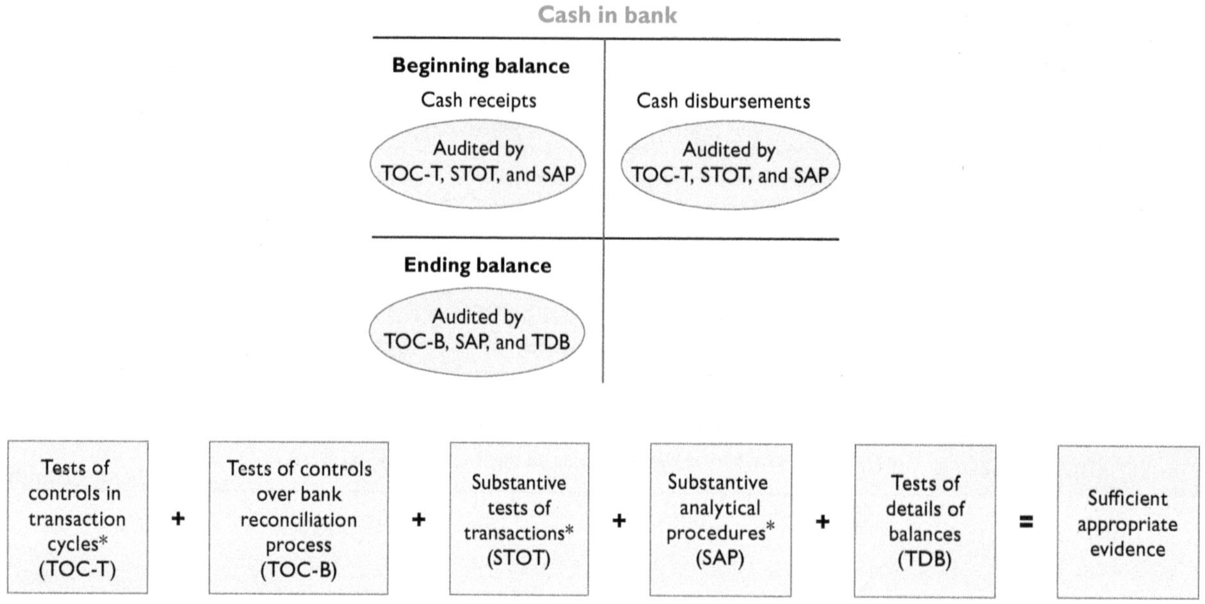

* Tests of controls in transaction cycles, substantive tests of transactions, and substantive analytical procedures are done for the four transaction cycles included in Figure 23-2 (p. 739). The primary tests of the ending cash balance are tests of details of balances.

CONCEPT CHECK

1. Explain the relationships among the initial assessed control risk, tests of controls and substantive tests of transactions for cash disbursements, and the tests of details of cash balances. Give one example in which the conclusions reached about internal controls in cash disbursements will affect the tests of cash balances.
2. Why is the monthly reconciliation of bank accounts by an independent person an important internal control over cash balances? Which individuals will generally not be considered independent for this responsibility?

FRAUD-ORIENTED PROCEDURES

OBJECTIVE 23-4

Recognize when to extend audit tests of the general cash account to test further for material fraud.

A major consideration in the audit of the general cash balance is the possibility of fraud. The auditor must extend the procedures in the audit of year-end cash to determine the possibility of a material fraud when there are inadequate internal controls, especially the improper segregation of duties between the handling of cash and the recording of cash transactions in the accounting records and the lack of an independently prepared monthly bank reconciliation.

In designing procedures for uncovering fraud, auditors should carefully consider the nature of the deficiencies in internal control, the type of fraud that is likely to result from the deficiencies, the potential materiality of the fraud, and the audit procedures that are most effective in uncovering the fraud.

When auditors are specifically testing for fraud, they should keep in mind that audit procedures other than tests of details of cash balances can also be useful. Procedures that may uncover fraud in the cash receipts area include:

- Confirmation of accounts receivable
- Tests performed to detect lapping
- Review of the general ledger entries in the cash account for unusual items

- Comparison of customer orders to sales and subsequent cash receipts
- Examination of approvals and supporting documentation for bad debts and sales returns and allowances

Similar tests can be used for testing for the possibility of fraudulent cash disbursements.

Even with reasonably elaborate fraud-oriented procedures, it is extremely difficult to detect thefts of cash, as well as fraudulent financial reporting involving cash, especially omitted transactions and account balances. If, for example, a company has illegal offshore cash accounts and makes deposits to those accounts from unrecorded sales, it is unlikely that an auditor will uncover the fraud. Nevertheless, auditors are responsible for making a reasonable effort to detect fraud when they have reason to believe it may exist. The following procedures for uncovering fraud are directly related to year-end cash balances: extended tests of the bank reconciliation, proofs of cash, and tests of interbank transfers.

Extended Tests of the Bank Reconciliation

When the auditor believes that the year-end bank reconciliation may be intentionally misstated, it is appropriate to perform extended tests of the year-end bank reconciliation. The extended procedures verify whether all transactions included in the journals for the last month of the year were correctly included in or excluded from the bank reconciliation and verify whether all items in the bank reconciliation were correctly included. Let's assume that there are material internal control weaknesses and the client's year-end is December 31. Using a common approach, auditors:

1. Start with the bank reconciliation for November and compare all reconciling items with cancelled checks and other documents in the December bank statement.
2. Compare all remaining cancelled checks and deposit slips in the December bank statement with the December cash disbursements and receipts journals.
3. Trace all uncleared items in the November bank reconciliation and the December cash disbursements and receipts journals to the client's December 31 bank reconciliation to make sure those items are included.
4. Verify that all reconciling items in the December 31 bank reconciliation represent items from the November bank reconciliation and December's journals that have not yet cleared the bank.

In addition to these four tests, the auditor must carry out procedures subsequent to the end of the year with the use of the bank cutoff statement. These tests are the same as previously discussed.

Proof of Cash

Auditors sometimes prepare a proof of cash when the client has material internal control weaknesses in cash. The auditor uses a proof of cash to determine whether the following were done:

- All recorded cash receipts were deposited
- All deposits in the bank were recorded in the accounting records
- All recorded cash disbursements were paid by the bank
- All amounts that were paid by the bank were recorded

A **proof of cash** includes the following four reconciliation tasks:

1. Reconcile the balance on the bank statement with the general ledger balance at the beginning of the proof-of-cash period.
2. Reconcile cash receipts deposited per the bank with receipts recorded in the cash receipts journal for a given period.
3. Reconcile electronic payments and cancelled checks clearing the bank with those recorded in the cash disbursements journal for a given period.
4. Reconcile the balance on the bank statement with the general ledger balance at the end of the proof-of-cash period.

A proof of cash of this nature is commonly called a four-column proof of cash that contains one column for each of the four types of information listed above. A proof of cash can be performed for one or more interim months, the entire year, or the last month of the year. The concern in an interim-month proof of cash, as shown in Figure 23-6, is not with the ending cash balance. Rather, the auditor's focus is on reconciling the amounts recorded in the books with the amounts included in the bank statement.

When doing a proof of cash, the auditor is combining substantive tests of transactions and tests of details of balances. A proof of cash receipts is a test of recorded transactions, whereas a bank reconciliation is a test of the balance in cash at a point in time. A proof of cash is an excellent method of comparing recorded cash receipts and disbursements with the bank account and with the bank reconciliation. However,

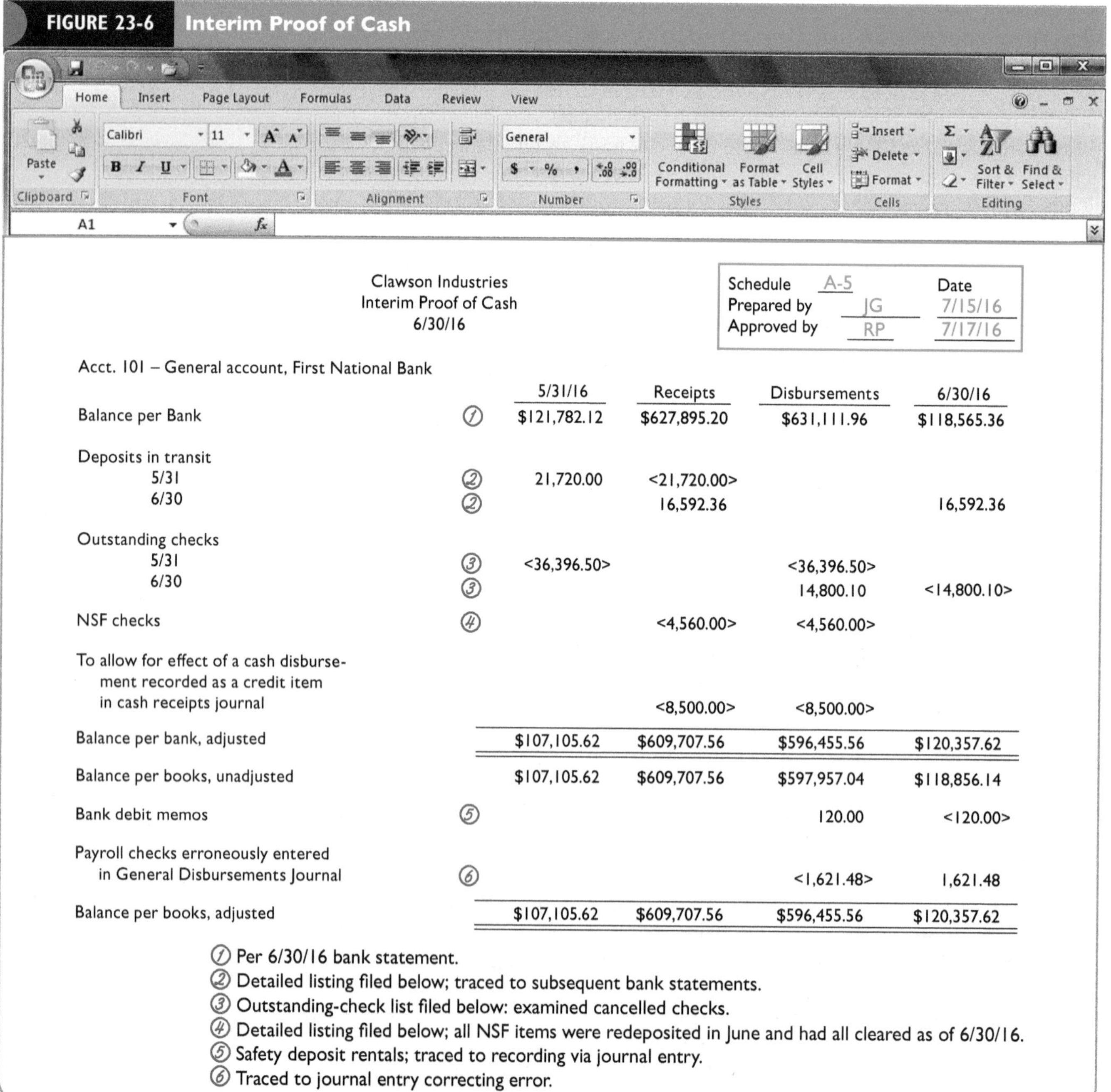

FIGURE 23-6 Interim Proof of Cash

Clawson Industries
Interim Proof of Cash
6/30/16

Schedule A-5 | Date
Prepared by JG | 7/15/16
Approved by RP | 7/17/16

Acct. 101 – General account, First National Bank

		5/31/16	Receipts	Disbursements	6/30/16
Balance per Bank	①	$121,782.12	$627,895.20	$631,111.96	$118,565.36
Deposits in transit					
5/31	②	21,720.00	<21,720.00>		
6/30	②		16,592.36		16,592.36
Outstanding checks					
5/31	③	<36,396.50>		<36,396.50>	
6/30	③			14,800.10	<14,800.10>
NSF checks	④		<4,560.00>	<4,560.00>	
To allow for effect of a cash disbursement recorded as a credit item in cash receipts journal			<8,500.00>	<8,500.00>	
Balance per bank, adjusted		$107,105.62	$609,707.56	$596,455.56	$120,357.62
Balance per books, unadjusted		$107,105.62	$609,707.56	$597,957.04	$118,856.14
Bank debit memos	⑤			120.00	<120.00>
Payroll checks erroneously entered in General Disbursements Journal	⑥			<1,621.48>	1,621.48
Balance per books, adjusted		$107,105.62	$609,707.56	$596,455.56	$120,357.62

① Per 6/30/16 bank statement.
② Detailed listing filed below; traced to subsequent bank statements.
③ Outstanding-check list filed below: examined cancelled checks.
④ Detailed listing filed below; all NSF items were redeposited in June and had all cleared as of 6/30/16.
⑤ Safety deposit rentals; traced to recording via journal entry.
⑥ Traced to journal entry correcting error.

the proof of cash disbursements is not effective for discovering checks written for an improper amount, fraudulent checks, or other misstatements in which the dollar amount appearing on the cash disbursements records is incorrect. Similarly, a proof of cash receipts is not useful for uncovering the theft of cash receipts or the recording and deposit of an improper amount of cash.

Tests of Interbank Transfers

Embezzlers occasionally cover a theft of cash by a practice known as **kiting**: transferring money from one bank to another and incorrectly recording the transaction. Near the balance sheet date, a check is drawn on one bank account and immediately deposited in a second account for credit before the end of the accounting period. In making this transfer, the embezzler is careful to make sure that the check is deposited at a late enough date so that it does not clear the first bank until after the end of the period. If the interbank transfer is not recorded until after the balance sheet date, the amount of the transfer is recorded as an asset in both banks. Although there are other ways to commit this fraud, each involves increasing the bank balance to cover a shortage by the use of interbank transfers.

To test for kiting, as well as for unintentional errors in recording interbank transfers, auditors can list all interbank transfers made a few days before and after the balance sheet date and trace each to the accounting records for proper recording. Figure 23-7 (p. 752) shows an interbank transfer schedule with four interbank transfers made shortly before and after the balance sheet date. There are several things that should be audited on the interbank transfer schedule.

- *The accuracy of the information on the interbank transfer schedule should be verified.* The auditor should compare the disbursement and receipt information on the schedule to the cash disbursements and cash receipts records to make sure that it is accurate. Similarly, the dates on the schedule for transfers that were received and disbursed should be compared with the bank statement. Finally, cash disbursements and receipts records should be examined to make sure that all transfers a few days before and after the balance sheet date have been included on the schedule. (The tick mark explanations on the schedule in Figure 23-7 indicate that these steps have been taken.)
- *The interbank transfers must be recorded in both the receiving and disbursing banks.* If, for example, there was a $10,000 transfer from Bank A to Bank B but only the disbursement was recorded, this is evidence of an attempt to conceal a cash theft.
- *The date of the recording of the disbursements and receipts for each transfer must be in the same fiscal year.* In Figure 23-7, the dates in the two "date recorded in books" columns [(4) and (7)] are in the same period for each transfer; therefore, they are correct. If a cash receipt was recorded in the current fiscal year and the disbursement in the subsequent fiscal year, it may be an attempt to cover a cash shortage.
- *Disbursements on the interbank transfer schedule should be correctly included in or excluded from year-end bank reconciliations as outstanding checks.* In Figure 23-7, the 12-31-16 bank reconciliation for the general cash account should include outstanding checks for the second and third transfers but not the other two. [Compare the dates in columns (4) and (5).] Understatement of outstanding checks on the bank reconciliation indicates the possibility of kiting.
- *Receipts on the interbank transfer schedule should be correctly included in or excluded from year-end bank reconciliations as deposits in transit.* In Figure 23-7, the 12-31-16 bank reconciliations for the savings and payroll accounts should indicate a deposit in transit for the third transfer but not for the other three. (Compare the dates for each transfer in the last two columns.) Overstating deposits in transit on the bank reconciliation indicates the possibility of kiting.

Even though audit tests of interbank transfers are usually fraud oriented, they are often performed on audits in which there are numerous bank transfers, regardless of

FIGURE 23-7 Interbank Transfer Schedule

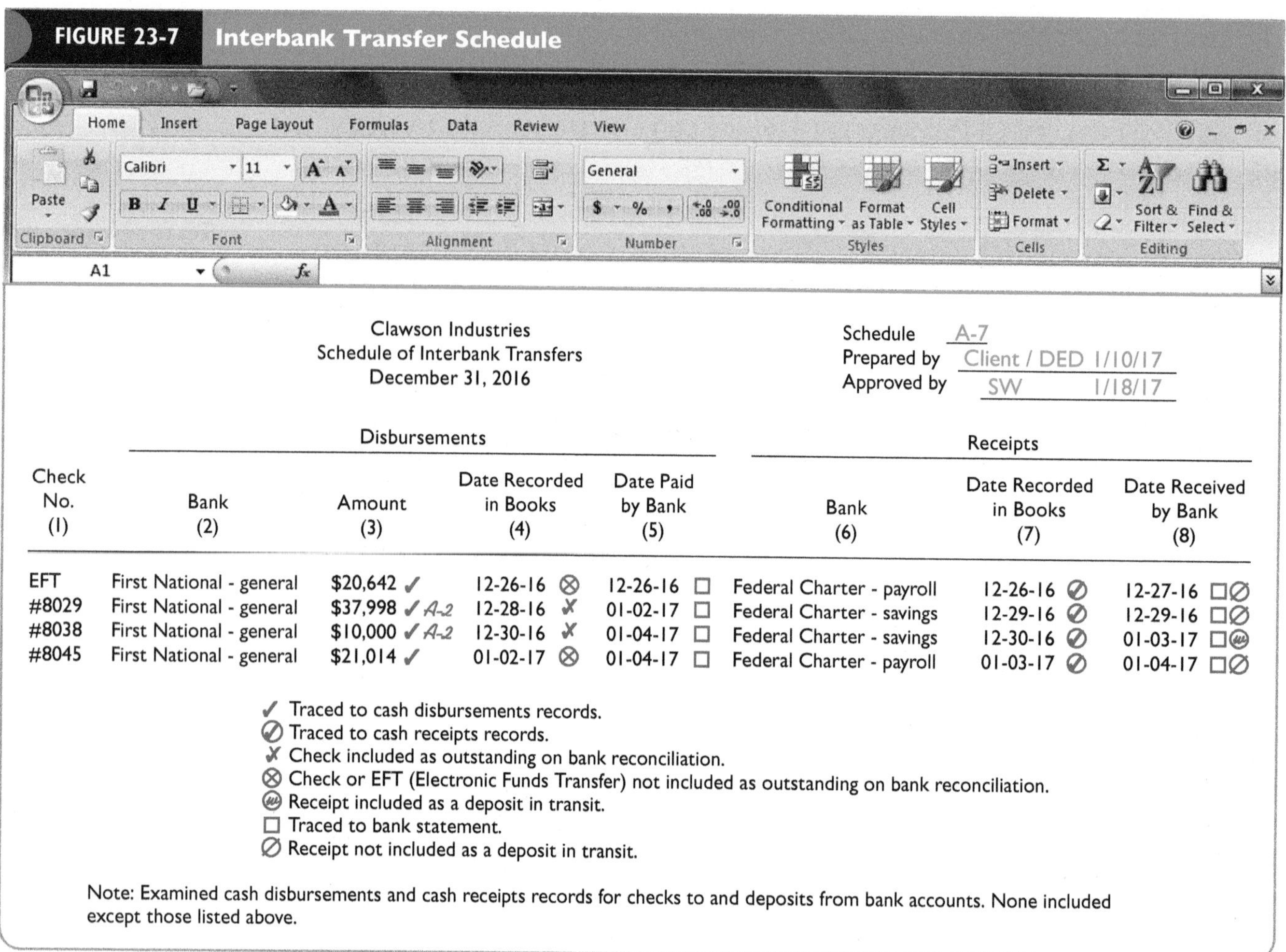

Clawson Industries
Schedule of Interbank Transfers
December 31, 2016

Schedule A-7
Prepared by Client / DED 1/10/17
Approved by SW 1/18/17

	Disbursements				Receipts		
Check No. (1)	Bank (2)	Amount (3)	Date Recorded in Books (4)	Date Paid by Bank (5)	Bank (6)	Date Recorded in Books (7)	Date Received by Bank (8)
EFT	First National - general	$20,642 ✓	12-26-16 ⊗	12-26-16 □	Federal Charter - payroll	12-26-16 ⊘	12-27-16 □∅
#8029	First National - general	$37,998 ✓ A-2	12-28-16 ✗	01-02-17 □	Federal Charter - savings	12-29-16 ⊘	12-29-16 □∅
#8038	First National - general	$10,000 ✓ A-2	12-30-16 ✗	01-04-17 □	Federal Charter - savings	12-30-16 ⊘	01-03-17 □Ⓦ
#8045	First National - general	$21,014 ✓	01-02-17 ⊗	01-04-17 □	Federal Charter - payroll	01-03-17 ⊘	01-04-17 □∅

✓ Traced to cash disbursements records.
⊘ Traced to cash receipts records.
✗ Check included as outstanding on bank reconciliation.
⊗ Check or EFT (Electronic Funds Transfer) not included as outstanding on bank reconciliation.
Ⓦ Receipt included as a deposit in transit.
□ Traced to bank statement.
∅ Receipt not included as a deposit in transit.

Note: Examined cash disbursements and cash receipts records for checks to and deposits from bank accounts. None included except those listed above.

internal controls. In addition to the possibility of kiting, inaccurate handling of transfers can result in a misclassification between cash and accounts payable. The materiality of transfers and the relative ease of performing the tests make many auditors believe they should always be performed.

MASQUERADING FOR CASH

While businesses have always been concerned about someone entering their premises to steal cash on hand, they now have to focus on another type of security threat in which criminals can be in another part of the world but still confiscate an organization's cash. In this new type of fraud, known as "masquerading," fraudsters hack into an organization's email or other communications system and pose as a senior executive, such as the CEO, CFO, or controller, and direct a lower-level employee to urgently execute a financial transaction that involves the disbursement of funds. Money is then wired or transmitted through the banking system to an account controlled by the criminal. In some cases, the fraudsters are so bold that they even pick up the telephone to make the request. While wire transfers can sometimes be cancelled before the transaction is executed, in most cases it is hard to get the money back.

Financial institutions are working hard to raise awareness of masquerading as a fraud technique. Bank of the West offers the following tips:

- Confirm that the request to initiate the wire is from an authorized source within the company
- Double- and triple-check email addresses
- Establish a multi-person approval process for transactions above a certain dollar threshold
- Slow down and be aware that fraud may be present any time wire transfers include tight deadlines
- Be suspicious of confidentiality of the transaction
- Require all wire transfers to be linked to a valid approved purchase or service

Source: David McCann, "Criminals Posing as CFOs to Commit Wire Fraud," August 13, 2014 (www.cfo.com).

AUDIT OF FINANCIAL INSTRUMENTS ACCOUNTS

OBJECTIVE 23-5

Design and perform audit tests of financial instruments accounts.

In testing the year-end balance of financial instruments, the auditor must accumulate sufficient appropriate evidence to evaluate whether the financial instruments accounts, as stated on the balance sheet, are fairly stated and properly disclosed in accordance with all eight balance-related audit objectives used for tests of details of balances (existence, completeness, accuracy, classification, cutoff, detail tie-in, realizable value, and rights), as listed in more detail in Table 23-2 (p. 755). We now discuss the methodology for auditing year-end financial instruments.

Identify Client Business Risks Affecting Financial Instruments (Phase I)

Business risks associated with financial instruments will vary depending on the significance and aggressiveness of a company's investing activity. Risks will be higher for companies investing in less liquid securities or derivative financial instruments, and when investments represent a greater proportion of total assets. Financial services firms are exposed to greater risk due to the sheer volume of activity and types of instruments traded; for example, several firms have suffered large trading losses from the activities of individual "rogue traders" that were hidden by misstating investment and cash balances. In addition, overall market volatility is higher due to increased program trading activity in the markets. The auditor should obtain an understanding of the risks from the client's investment policies and strategies, as well as management controls that mitigate these risks.

Set Performance Materiality and Assess Inherent Risk (Phase I)

The financial instruments account balances may be material depending on the type and frequency of investment activity. Factors that impact inherent risk of financial instruments include management's objectives related to investment activity (e.g., hedging to minimize risk), the complexity of the securities or derivatives, the company's prior experience with certain investments, and whether external factors such as credit risk or interest rate risk impact the relevant assertions. Many of these risks relate to the accuracy, classification, and realizable value audit objectives. An additional factor that increases inherent risk for financial instruments is the complexity of the relevant accounting standards. The majority of financial instruments are valued using **fair value estimates**. Accounting standards distinguish between a level 1 fair value estimate (observable, i.e., quoted, prices in an active market for identical assets or liabilities) and level 2 or level 3 estimates. Level 2 estimates use observable inputs (directly or indirectly) other than quoted prices, such as a price for a similar asset or liability, whereas level 3 estimates use unobservable inputs such as a pricing model or discounted cash flows. These estimates require significant management judgment and the auditor also needs to consider management incentives to classify investments as either fair value level 2 or level 3. All of these risks, combined with recent market volatility and the potential for markets to become illiquid, result in significant potential for misstatements and misclassification of financial instruments balances.

Assess Control Risk (Phase I)

The auditor needs to have an understanding of the design and operating effectiveness of internal controls surrounding the initiation, authorization, processing, fair value measurement, and disclosure of investment activities. Most importantly, management needs to have (1) an investment strategy and an awareness of the level of exposure to various risks; (2) procedures in place to properly classify financial instruments as trading, available-for-sale, or held-to-maturity based on intent; (3) procedures in place to initiate and record transactions; and (4) strong internal controls over determining fair value estimates, such as personnel with appropriate expertise or experience in valuing level 2 or 3 estimates. If a company uses a service organization, such as an investment adviser or manager, to manage its investment activity, the auditor will need to have an understanding of controls for the service organization as well. The auditor can often rely on the internal controls of the service organization if the service organization's auditor issues a report on the service organization's internal control, as discussed in Chapter 12 (pp. 380–381). Otherwise, the auditor may need specialized knowledge or may need to rely on a specialist from within the firm to assist in understanding the relevant information systems.

Design and Perform Tests of Controls and Substantive Tests of Transactions (Phase II)

Unlike some other accounts where an auditor can choose to perform more extensive substantive testing and reduce reliance on controls, assessing internal controls related to financial instruments may be necessary in order to reduce audit risk to an acceptable level, especially for transaction-related audit objectives. Tests of transactions to be performed related to financial instruments include tests of purchases and sales of securities and derivatives or settling of hedging transactions, associated gains or losses, and interest and dividend income. The auditor typically relies on statements and brokers' advices (notifications sent from brokers to a client with details of purchases or sales) from investment managers to test purchases and sales as long as controls are deemed effective, traces payments or proceeds to cash disbursements or receipts, and then tests mathematical accuracy of gains and losses. Interest income can be recomputed, and dividends can be recomputed and compared to a public source such as Standard and Poor's dividend records.

Design and Perform Substantive Analytical Procedures (Phase II)

Substantive analytical procedures are typically not as important in assessing the year-end balance for financial instruments because these balances may fluctuate from year-to-year and are not necessarily linked to other accounts. However, substantive analytical procedures may be used to test the reasonableness of interest and dividend income. Auditors may also compare the relative percentage of investments in each of the three fair value categories (level 1, 2, or 3) from year-to-year to assess changes in investment strategy or portfolio risk.

Design Tests of Details of Financial Instruments Balances (Phase III)

The starting point for testing the ending balance of financial instrument accounts is to obtain a schedule of investment activity for the year. A schedule of investment activity will include beginning balances, purchases and sales of financial instruments as well as the associated gains or losses, and ending balances recorded at fair market value or other value consistent with accounting standards. The schedule will also show dividend and interest income. The balance-related audit objectives and common tests of details of balances in the audit of financial instruments are shown in Table 23-2. The most important objectives are existence, accuracy, and realizable value for investments in securities, while completeness is also important for derivative financial instruments. Presentation and disclosure objectives are also very important given the extensive footnote disclosure requirements related to fair value estimates. In our discussion of detailed tests, we assume the entity is using a service organization as an investment manager and that the auditor has determined that the service organization has effective controls. An investment manager, or investment advisor, typically initiates transactions, holds the securities, and processes and maintains records related to the transactions. We refer to the service organization as the broker-dealer in our discussion of audit procedures.

The auditor requests a confirmation from the broker-dealer to confirm year-end holdings as well as settled and unsettled transactions that occurred during the year. The confirmation provides assurance on existence, completeness, and accuracy. It is important to simultaneously verify the cash, cash equivalents, and financial instruments balances to ensure management is not attempting to cover a cash shortage by double-counting cash. More extensive testing related to completeness is necessary if derivative financial instruments exist, such as examining contracts for embedded derivatives as well as reading minutes from board of directors meetings related to hedging and investment activity.

TABLE 23-2 Balance-Related Audit Objectives and Tests of Details of Balances for Financial Instruments Accounts

Balance-Related Audit Objective	Common Tests of Details of Balances Procedures	Comments
Financial instruments as listed on the schedule of investment activity foot correctly and agree with the general ledger (detail tie-in).	Foot the schedule of investment activity. Prove the schedule of investment activity as to additions and subtractions. Trace the ending balance by category to the general ledger.	Investments will be categorized as trading, available-for-sale, and held-to-maturity. The schedule may include securities valued using level 1, level 2, or level 3 fair value estimates.
Financial instruments as listed on the schedule of investment activity exist (existence). Existing financial instruments are recorded (completeness). Financial instruments as listed on the schedule of investment activity are accurate (accuracy).	Confirmation with the broker-dealer. Physical inspection of the security or derivative contract. Inspection of underlying agreements.	Typically, confirmations provide sufficient evidence without the auditor having to physically inspect the security or contract. Securities and contracts will typically be held by the broker-dealer.
Financial instruments are properly classified in the financial statements (classification).	Test for proper classification as trading, available-for-sale, or held-to-maturity. Verify proper classification in the footnotes as level 1, 2, or 3 fair value estimates.	These classifications are based on management intent and require judgment.
Financial instrument transactions are recorded in the proper period (cutoff).	Examine selected transactions near year-end and related brokers' advices to determine whether they are recorded in the proper period.	Cutoff is more important in testing transactions as a client may want to record a gain or loss on sale at the end of the year.
Financial instruments included in the schedule of investment activity at year-end are stated at appropriate amounts in accordance with accounting standards (realizable value).	Verify quoted market prices. Test management's classifications. Test management's assumptions related to valuation. Consider using a specialist for testing fair value estimates. Consider whether an impairment loss is required.	This is the most difficult objective to test, and procedures will vary depending on the client's investment strategy as well as the types of financial instruments.
The entity has rights to financial instruments included in the schedule of investment activity (rights).	Inspect underlying documents and contracts. Confirm significant terms with the counterparty to a derivative contract. Review minutes of board meetings to determine whether any securities are pledged as collateral.	Rights are tested in conjunction with tests for existence and accuracy when reviewing purchases.

Tests related to realizable value will vary according to the type of security and the associated accounting standards. Accounting standards may require that financial instruments be recorded at cost, fair value, or based on an investee's financial results. Auditing guidance is provided for auditing accounting estimates and specifically for fair value estimates, as considerable auditor judgment is involved. Level 1 fair value estimates (identical assets with quoted market prices) are easier to audit and typically involve observing market prices at the end of the year, which can be done by examining *The Wall Street Journal* or another reputable financial publication. Level 2 and level 3 fair value estimates are more difficult to audit because they involve significant management judgment both in classification (level 2 or 3) and in determining the fair value. The auditor needs to test the reasonableness and appropriateness of assumptions and models used by management to determine fair value estimates. If an auditor chooses to use a specialist to test fair value estimates, auditing standards require the auditor to determine whether the specialist is objective and qualified, and the auditor needs to understand the methods used by the specialist to determine fair values. It is also important for the auditor to consider management's incentives to classify financial instruments as either level 2 or level 3 due to differences in the estimates obtained under the different approaches, as well as the more extensive disclosure requirements related to level 3 fair value estimates.

CONCEPT CHECK

1. Explain why an auditor compares the "date of deposit according to the books" to the "date of disbursement according to the books" on an interbank transfer schedule to detect kiting.
2. Briefly explain why accounting standards related to fair value estimates make the audit of financial instruments more complex.

SUMMARY

In this chapter, we have seen that transactions in most cycles affect the cash account. Because of the relationship between transactions in several cycles and the ending cash account balance, the auditor typically waits to audit the ending cash balance until the results of tests of controls and substantive tests of transactions for all cycles are completed and analyzed. Tests of the cash balance normally include tests of the bank reconciliations of key cash accounts, such as the general cash account, imprest payroll account, and imprest petty cash fund. If auditors assess a high likelihood of fraud in cash, they may perform additional tests such as extended bank reconciliation procedures, a proof of cash, or tests of interbank transfers.

The effort and amount of judgment involved in auditing financial instruments will vary depending on the client's investment strategy and management incentives. Primary tests include confirmation with the broker-dealer as well as testing fair value estimates.

ESSENTIAL TERMS

Bank reconciliation—the monthly reconciliation, usually prepared by client personnel, of the differences between the cash balance recorded in the general ledger and the amount in the bank account

Branch bank accounts—separate bank accounts maintained at local banks by branches of a company

Cash equivalents—excess cash invested in short-term, highly liquid investments such as time deposits, certificates of deposit, and money market funds

Cutoff bank statement—a partial-period bank statement and the related cancelled checks, duplicate deposit slips, and other documents included in bank statements, provided by the bank directly to the auditor; the auditor uses it to verify reconciling items on the client's year-end bank reconciliation

Fair value estimate—the price that would be received to sell an asset or paid to transfer a liability in an orderly transaction between market participants at the measurement date

Financial instruments—a tradable asset of any kind, including cash, equity securities, debt securities, and derivative instruments

General cash account—the primary bank account for most organizations; virtually all cash receipts and disbursements flow through this account at some time

Imprest petty cash fund—a fund of cash maintained within the company for small cash acquisitions or to cash employees' checks; the fund's fixed balance is comparatively small and is periodically reimbursed

Kiting—the transfer of money from one bank to another and improperly recording the transfer so that the amount is recorded as an asset in both accounts; this practice is used by embezzlers to cover a theft of cash

Proof of cash—a four-column audit schedule prepared by the auditor to reconcile the bank's record of the client's beginning balance, cash deposits, cleared checks, and ending balance for the period with the client's records

Standard bank confirmation form—a form approved by the AICPA and American Bankers Association through which the bank responds to the auditor about bank balance and loan information provided on the confirmation

REVIEW QUESTIONS

23-1 **(OBJECTIVES 23-1, 23-2)** Explain the relationships among the initial assessed control risk, tests of controls and substantive tests of transactions for cash receipts, and the tests of details of cash balances.

23-2 **(OBJECTIVE 23-1)** What is meant by an imprest bank account for a branch operation? Explain the purpose of using this type of bank account.

23-3 **(OBJECTIVE 23-3)** Evaluate the effectiveness and state the shortcomings of the preparation of a bank reconciliation by the controller in the manner described in the following statement: "When I reconcile the bank account, the first thing I do is review the sorted list of returned checks and find which numbers are missing. Next I determine the amount of the uncleared checks by referring to the cash disbursements journal. If the bank account reconciles at that point, I am all finished with the reconciliation. If it does not, I search for deposits in transit, checks from the beginning outstanding check list that still have not cleared, other reconciling items, and bank errors until it reconciles. In most instances, I can do the reconciliation in 20 minutes."

23-4 **(OBJECTIVE 23-3)** How do bank confirmations differ from positive confirmations of accounts receivable? Distinguish between them in terms of the nature of the information confirmed, the sample size, and the appropriate action when the confirmation is not returned after the second request. Explain the rationale for the differences between these two types of confirmations.

23-5 **(OBJECTIVE 23-3)** Evaluate the necessity of following the practice described by an auditor: "In confirming bank accounts, I insist upon a response from every bank the client has done business with in the past 2 years, even though the account may be closed at the balance sheet date."

23-6 **(OBJECTIVE 23-3)** Describe what is meant by a cutoff bank statement and state its purpose.

23-7 **(OBJECTIVE 23-3)** Why are auditors usually less concerned about the client's cash receipts cutoff than the cutoff for sales? Explain the procedure involved in testing for the cutoff for cash receipts.

23-8 **(OBJECTIVE 23-3)** Explain why, in verifying bank reconciliations, most auditors emphasize the possibility of a nonexistent deposit in transit being included in the reconciliation and an outstanding check being omitted rather than the omission of a deposit in transit and the inclusion of a nonexistent outstanding check.

23-9 **(OBJECTIVE 23-3)** How will a company's bank reconciliation reflect an electronic deposit of cash received by the bank from credit card agencies making payments on behalf of customers purchasing products from the company's online Web site, but not recorded in the company's records?

23-10 **(OBJECTIVE 23-4)** Explain the purpose of a four-column proof of cash. List two types of misstatements it is meant to uncover.

23-11 **(OBJECTIVE 23-4)** Distinguish between lapping and kiting. Describe audit procedures that can be used to uncover each.

23-12 **(OBJECTIVES 23-3, 23-4)** Why is there a greater emphasis on the detection of fraud in tests of details of cash balances than for other balance sheet accounts? Give two specific examples that demonstrate how this emphasis affects the auditor's evidence accumulation in auditing year-end cash.

23-13 **(OBJECTIVE 23-5)** How would an auditor test the realizable value audit objective for a financial instrument classified as a level 3 fair value estimate?

MULTIPLE CHOICE QUESTIONS FROM CPA EXAMINATIONS

23-14 **(OBJECTIVES 23-3, 23-4, 23-5)** The following questions deal with auditing year-end cash and financial instruments. Choose the best response.

a. A CPA obtains a January 10 cutoff bank statement for a client directly from the bank. Very few of the outstanding checks listed on the client's December 31 bank reconciliation cleared during the cutoff period. A probable cause for this is that the client
   (1) is engaged in kiting.
   (2) is engaged in lapping.
   (3) has overstated its year-end bank balance.
   (4) transmitted the checks to the payees after year-end.

b. In establishing the existence and ownership of an investment held by a corporation in the form of publicly traded stock, an auditor should inspect the securities or
   (1) obtain written representations from management confirming that the securities are properly classified as trading securities.
   (2) inspect the audited financial statements of the investee company.
   (3) confirm the number of shares owned that are held by an independent custodian.
   (4) determine that the investment is carried at the lower of cost or market.

c. The auditor should ordinarily send confirmation requests to all banks with which the client has conducted any business during the year, regardless of the year-end balance, because
   (1) this procedure will detect kiting activities that would otherwise not be detected.
   (2) the confirmation form also seeks information about indebtedness to the bank.
   (3) the sending of confirmation requests to all such banks is required by auditing standards.
   (4) this procedure relieves the auditor of any responsibility with respect to non-detection of forged checks.

23-15 **(OBJECTIVE 23-4)** The following questions deal with discovering fraud in auditing year-end cash. Choose the best response.

a. The auditor should control and verify all liquid assets simultaneously to prevent
   (1) unrecorded disbursements.
   (2) conversion of assets to conceal a shortage.
   (3) unauthorized disbursements.
   (4) embezzlement.

b. Which of the following is one of the better auditing techniques to detect kiting?
   (1) Review composition of authenticated deposit slips
   (2) Review subsequent bank statements and cancelled checks received directly from the banks
   (3) Prepare year-end bank reconciliations
   (4) Prepare a schedule of bank transfers from the client's books

c. Which of the following cash transfers results in a misstatement of cash at December 31, 2016?

BANK TRANSFER SCHEDULE

	Disbursements		Receipt	
Transfer	Recorded in books	Paid by bank	Recorded in books	Received by bank
(1)	12/31/16	1/4/17	12/31/16	12/31/16
(2)	1/4/17	1/5/17	12/31/16	1/4/17
(3)	12/31/16	1/5/17	12/31/16	1/4/17
(4)	1/4/17	1/11/17	1/4/17	1/4/17

MULTIPLE CHOICE QUESTIONS FROM BECKER CPA EXAM REVIEW

23-16 **(OBJECTIVES 23-2, 23-5)** The following questions concern auditing year-end cash and financial instruments. Choose the best response.

a. Which of the following controls would most likely detect a kiting scheme?
   (1) Use of a lockbox system for customer receipts
   (2) Comparison of the details of deposit tickets and recorded remittance advices
   (3) Preparing a bank transfer schedule
   (4) Preparing a bank reconciliation

b. All of the following are effective ways to prevent and/or detect lapping, except for
   (1) comparing the dollar amounts and dates on the bank deposit slips with customer remittance credits entered into the accounts receivable ledger.
   (2) preparing a bank transfer schedule.
   (3) requiring that customers send their payments directly to a lockbox.
   (4) independently comparing the recorded cash receipts with funds actually deposited in the bank.

c. Which of the following discovered by the auditor would be a weakness in the client's internal control over its investments?
   (1) The internal auditor performs a periodic count of the actual securities and reconciles the securities counted to the investment subsidiary ledger.
   (2) Investments not held by an independent third-party custodian are kept in the Treasurer's office.
   (3) A designated accounting individual that has no custody or authorization responsibilities maintains the detailed records of the investment subsidiary ledger.
   (4) The client's board of directors authorizes all purchases and sales of investment securities.

DISCUSSION QUESTIONS AND PROBLEMS

23-17 **(OBJECTIVES 23-3, 23-4)** The following are misstatements that might be found in the client's year-end cash balance (assume that the balance sheet date is June 30):

1. A check that was dated June 26 and disbursed in June was not recorded in the cash disbursements journal, but it was included as an outstanding check on June 30.
2. A check was omitted from the outstanding check list on the bank reconciliation. It cleared the bank September 6.
3. The outstanding checks on the June 30 bank reconciliation were underfooted by $2,000.
4. A loan from the bank on June 26 was credited directly to the client's bank account. The loan was not entered as of June 30.
5. A check was omitted from the outstanding check list on the June 30 bank reconciliation. It cleared the bank July 7.
6. Cash receipts collected on accounts receivable from July 1 to July 5 were included as June 29 and 30 cash receipts.
7. A bank transfer recorded in the accounting records on July 1 was included as a deposit in transit on June 30.

Required

a. Assuming that each of these misstatements was intentional (fraud), state the most likely motivation of the person responsible.
b. What control can be instituted for each fraud to reduce the likelihood of occurrence?
c. List an audit procedure that can be used to discover each fraud.

23-18 **(OBJECTIVES 23-3, 23-4, 23-5)** The following audit procedures are concerned with tests of details of general cash and financial instruments balances:

1. Obtain a standard bank confirmation from each bank with which the client does business.
2. Compare the balance on the bank reconciliation obtained from the client with the bank confirmation.
3. List the check number, payee, and amount of all material checks not returned with the cutoff bank statement.
4. Review minutes of the board of directors meetings, loan agreements, and bank confirmation for interest-bearing deposits, restrictions on the withdrawal of cash, and compensating balance agreements.
5. Prepare a four-column proof of cash.
6. Compare the bank cancellation date with the date on the cancelled check for checks dated on or shortly before the balance sheet date.
7. Trace deposits in transit on the bank reconciliation to the cutoff bank statement and the current year cash receipts journal.
8. Compare the price per share on an equity investment at year-end according to the schedule of investment activity to the quoted market price according to an outside pricing source.
9. Confirm the balance of financial instruments at year-end with the broker-dealer service organization used by the client to manage its investment portfolio.

Required Explain the objective of each audit procedure.

23-19 **(OBJECTIVE 23-3)** You are auditing general cash for the Pittsburgh Supply Company for the fiscal year ended July 31, 2016. The client has not prepared the July 31 bank reconciliation. After a brief discussion with the owner, you agree to prepare the reconciliation, with assistance from one of Pittsburgh Supply's clerks. You obtain the following information:

	General Ledger	Bank Statement
Beginning balance 7/1/16	$ 6,400	$ 8,378
Deposits		25,474
Cash receipts journal	26,874	
Checks cleared		(25,307)
Cash disbursements journal	(23,171)	
July bank service charge		(107)
Note paid directly		(6,400)
NSF check		(516)
Ending balance 7/31/16	$ 10,103	$ 1,522

June 30 Bank Reconciliation

Information in General Ledger and Bank Statement	
Balance per bank	$8,378
Deposits in transit	600
Outstanding checks	2,578
Balance per books	$6,400

Additional information obtained is as follows:

1. Checks clearing that were outstanding on June 30 totaled $2,411.
2. Checks clearing that were recorded in the July disbursements journal totaled $21,120.
3. A check for $1,130 cleared the bank but had not been recorded in the cash disbursements journal. It was for an acquisition of inventory. Pittsburgh Supply uses the periodic-inventory method.
4. A check for $646 was charged to Pittsburgh Supply but had been written on a different company's bank account.
5. Deposits included $600 from June and $24,874 for July.

6. The bank charged Pittsburgh Supply's account for a nonsufficient funds check totaling $516. The credit manager concluded that the customer intentionally closed its account and the owner left the city. The check was turned over to a collection agency.
7. A note for $6,000, plus interest, was paid directly to the bank under an agreement signed four months ago. The note payable was recorded at $6,000 on Pittsburgh Supply's books.

a. Prepare a bank reconciliation that shows both the unadjusted and adjusted balance per books.
b. Prepare all adjusting entries.
c. What audit procedures would you use to verify each item in the bank reconciliation?
d. What is the cash balance that should appear on the July 31, 2016, financial statements?

23-20 **(OBJECTIVES 23-3, 23-4)** In the audit of the Regional Transport Company, a large branch that maintains its own bank account, cash is periodically transferred to the central account in Cedar Rapids. On the branch account's records, bank transfers are recorded as a debit to the home office clearing account and a credit to the branch bank account. Similarly, the home office account is recorded as a debit to the central bank account and a credit to the branch office clearing account. Gordon Light is the head bookkeeper for both the home office and the branch bank accounts. Because he also reconciles the bank account, the senior auditor, Cindy Marintette, is concerned about the internal control deficiency.

As a part of the year-end audit of bank transfers, Marintette asks you to schedule the transfers for the last few days in 2016 and the first few days of 2017. You prepare the following list:

Amount of Transfer	Date Recorded in the Home Office Cash Receipts Journal	Date Recorded in the Branch Office Cash Disbursements Journal	Date Deposited in the Home Office Bank Account	Date Cleared the Branch Bank Account
$17,000	12-27-16	12-29-16	12-26-16	12-27-16
28,000	12-28-16	01-02-17	12-28-16	12-29-16
16,000	01-02-17	12-30-16	12-28-16	12-29-16
10,000	12-26-16	12-26-16	12-28-16	01-03-17
21,000	01-02-17	01-02-17	12-28-16	12-31-16
22,000	01-07-17	01-05-17	12-28-16	01-03-17
39,000	01-04-17	01-06-17	01-03-17	01-05-17

Required

a. In verifying each bank transfer, state the appropriate audit procedures you should perform.
b. Prepare any adjusting entries required in the home office records.
c. Prepare any adjusting entries required in the branch bank records.
d. State how each bank transfer should be included in the December 31, 2016, bank reconciliation for the home office account after your adjustments in part b.
e. State how each bank transfer should be included in the December 31, 2016, bank reconciliation of the branch bank account after your adjustments in part c.

23-21 **(OBJECTIVE 23-4)** The following are various potential misstatements due to errors or fraud (1 through 7), and a list of auditing procedures (a. through h.) the auditor would consider performing to gather evidence to determine whether the error or fraud is present.

Possible Misstatements Due to Errors or Fraud

1. The auditor suspects that a lapping scheme exists because an accounting department employee who has access to cash receipts also maintains the accounts receivable ledger and refuses to take any vacation or sick days.
2. The auditor suspects that the entity is inappropriately increasing the cash reported on its balance sheet by drawing a check on one account and not recording it as an outstanding check on that account and simultaneously recording it as a deposit in a second account.

3. The entity's cash receipts of the first few days of the subsequent year were properly deposited in its general operating account after the year-end. However, the auditor suspects that the entity recorded the cash receipts in its books during the last week of the year under audit.
4. The auditor noticed a significant increase in the number of times that petty cash was reimbursed during the year and suspects that the custodian is stealing from the petty cash fund.
5. The auditor suspects that a kiting scheme exists because an accounting department employee who can issue and record checks seems to be leading an unusually luxurious lifestyle.
6. During tests of the reconciliation of the payroll bank account, the auditor notices that a check to an employee is significantly larger than other payroll checks.
7. The auditor suspects that the controller wrote several checks and recorded the cash disbursements just before year-end but did not mail the checks until after the first week of the subsequent year.

List of Auditing Procedures

a. Compare the details of the cash receipts journal entries with the details of the corresponding daily deposit slips.
b. Count the balance in petty cash at year-end.
c. Agree gross amount on payroll checks to approved hours and pay rates.
d. Obtain the cutoff bank statement and compare the cleared checks to the year-end reconciliation.
e. Examine invoices, receipts, and other documentation supporting reimbursement of petty cash.
f. Send a standard bank confirmation confirming the balance in the bank at year-end.
g. Examine payroll checks clearing after year-end with the payroll journal.
h. Prepare a bank transfer schedule.

Required For each possible misstatement, identify one audit procedure that would be most effective in providing evidence regarding the potential misstatement. Listed auditing procedures may be used once, more than once, or not at all.*

23-22 **(OBJECTIVE 23-4)** You are doing the first-year audit of Sherman School District and have been assigned responsibility for doing a four-column proof of cash for the month of October 2016. You obtain the following information:

1. Balance per books	September 30	$ 10,725
	October 31	5,836
2. Balance per bank	September 30	6,915
	October 31	8,276
3. Outstanding checks	September 30	1,811
	October 31	2,615
4. Cash receipts for October	per bank	28,792
	per books	20,271
5. Deposits in transit	September 30	5,621
	October 31	996

6. Interest on a bank loan for the month of October, charged by the bank but not recorded, was $596.
7. Proceeds on a note of the Jones Company were collected by the bank on October 28 but were not entered on the books:

Principal	$ 2,900
Interest	396
	$ 3,296

*Based on AICPA question paper, American Institute of Certified Public Accountants.

8. On October 26, a $1,144 check of the Billings Company was charged to Sherman School District's account by the bank in error.
9. Dishonored checks are not recorded on the books unless they permanently fail to clear the bank. The bank treats them as disbursements when they are dishonored and as deposits when they are redeposited. Checks totaling $1,335 were dishonored in October; $600 was redeposited in October and $735 in November.

Required

a. Prepare a four-column proof of cash for the month ended October 31. It should show both adjusted and unadjusted cash.
b. Prepare all adjusting entries.

23-23 (OBJECTIVES 23-1, 23-2) The Check Clearing for the 21st Century Act (Check 21 Act) allows recipients of paper checks to create a digital image of the original check, eliminating the need for further handling of the actual check. The Federal Reserve Board has created a consumer guide, Consumer Guide to Check 21 and Substitute Checks, which can be found on the Federal Reserve's Web site (www.federalreserve.gov) by searching the guide's title. Locate the guide to answer questions about Check 21.

Required

a. What is a "substitute check"? Does it constitute a legal copy of the check?
b. How does Check 21 affect the payment of your checks?
c. Do banks have to return actual cancelled checks? Explain.

23-24 (OBJECTIVE 23-5) McNeil Company, a medium-sized manufacturer of microwave ovens, has been an audit client for the past five years. McNeil Co. has been steadily growing and recently hired a new CEO, who has decided to increase the level of investments in financial instruments as a way of generating a profit from excess cash from operations. The new CEO has invested primarily in actively-traded equity securities, but has also invested a portion of the cash in speculative derivative financial instruments. McNeil Co. is using a brokerage firm to execute trades, but the CEO is making the decision as to which securities and derivatives to purchase and sell.

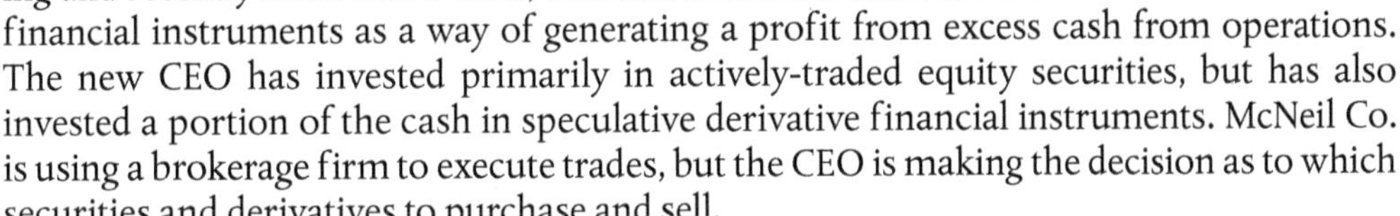

In planning for the current year's audit engagement, you note the following related to the investments in financial instruments:

1. The CEO discusses the investment strategy with the board of directors, but the board is not involved in the purchase and sale decisions and does not approve derivative contracts. The CEO enters into the speculative derivative financial instruments on behalf of McNeil Co.
2. Total investments in financial instruments (trading and available-for-sale securities) at year-end represent approximately 15% of total assets. The majority of investments are classified as trading securities, and many of the equity investments would be considered high-risk stocks.
3. The CEO makes the determination to classify securities as trading or available-for-sale.
4. McNeil Co. has recorded significant gains on sales of financial instruments.
5. The new CEO has an incentive to continue to grow the company and report a profit because he has been given an incentive bonus based on return on assets.

Required

a. Identify the inherent and control risks related to the financial instruments accounts for McNeil Co.
b. Identify at least two audit procedures the auditor would perform to test the existence balance-related audit objective for the trading and available-for-sale securities.
c. How would the auditor test the completeness balance-related audit objective for the speculative derivative financial instruments?
d. Identify at least two audit procedures the auditor would perform to test the realizable value balance-related audit objective for the financial instruments accounts. Assume the investments in stock are all actively-traded in a liquid market, but the derivative financial instruments require a level 3 fair value estimate.
e. In your opinion, would the audit of financial instruments require the use of a valuation specialist? Why or why not?

23-25 **(OBJECTIVE 23-5)** The amount of subjectivity involved in establishing fair value estimates can be complex for management responsible for making the fair value measurements and disclosures contained in financial statements. This is particularly true for fair value measurements for which observable market prices are not available. Auditing standards require auditors to obtain sufficient appropriate audit evidence to provide reasonable assurance that fair value measurements and disclosures are in conformity with accounting standards, and auditing standards provide guidance for auditing those measurements and disclosures contained in financial statements.

Required

a. Visit the PCAOB's Web site (pcaobus.org) to identify where in the PCAOB Auditing Standards guidance is provided for auditing fair value measurements and disclosures.
b. PCAOB auditing standards require the auditor to obtain an understanding of the entity's process for determining fair value measurements and disclosures. Identify five things the auditor should consider when obtaining that understanding.
c. What should the auditor consider when engaging a specialist to perform substantive tests related to fair value assertions?
d. Briefly describe the three types of substantive tests of fair value measurements that the auditor may perform.

COMPLETING THE AUDIT

CHAPTER 24

PART 5 includes only one chapter and covers the fourth and final phase of an audit: completing the audit. Even when auditors perform the other phases of an audit well, if they do a poor job carrying out the completion phase, the quality of the audit will be low. When auditors perform the planning phase (phase I) and the two testing phases (phases II and III) well, the completion phase is typically relatively easy.

CHAPTER

24

COMPLETING THE AUDIT

LEARNING OBJECTIVES

After studying this chapter, you should be able to

24-1 Design and perform audit tests related to presentation and disclosure audit objectives.

24-2 Conduct a review for contingent liabilities and commitments.

24-3 Obtain and evaluate letters from the client's attorneys.

24-4 Conduct a post-balance-sheet review for subsequent events.

24-5 Design and perform the final steps in the evidence-accumulation segment of the audit.

24-6 Integrate the audit evidence gathered and evaluate the overall audit results.

24-7 Communicate effectively with the audit committee and management.

24-8 Identify the auditor's responsibilities when facts affecting the audit report are discovered after its issuance.

Good Review Requires More Than Looking at Audit Files

Larry Lenape, an audit senior at Santro, Best & Harmon, assigned staff assistant Clawson Little the audit of accounts payable for Westside Industries, a large equipment manufacturer. Accounts payable is a major liability account for a manufacturing company, and testing accounts payable cutoff is an important audit area. Testing primarily involves reviewing the liability recorded by the client by examining subsequent payments to suppliers and other creditors to ensure that they were correctly recorded.

Lenape observed that Little was spending a lot of time on the phone, apparently on personal matters. Shortly before the audit was completed, Little announced that he was leaving the firm. Despite Little's distractions due to his personal affairs, he completed the audit work he was assigned within the budgeted time.

Because of Lenape's concern about Little's work habits, he decided to review the audit files with extreme care. Every schedule he reviewed was properly prepared, with tick marks entered and explained by Little, indicating that he had made an extensive examination of underlying data and documents and had found the client's balance to be adequate as stated. Specifically, there were no payments subsequent to year-end for inventory purchases received during the audit period that had not been accrued by the company.

When Lenape finished the audit, he notified Kelsey Mayburn, the engagement audit manager, that the files were ready for her review. She had considerable knowledge about equipment manufacturers and also about Westside Industries. Mayburn reviewed all of the audit files, including substantive analytical procedures performed during the audit. After calculating additional analytical procedures during her review, she contacted Lenape and told him accounts payable did not seem reasonable to her. She asked him to do some additional checking. Lenape went back and looked at all the documents that Little had indicated in the audit files that he had inspected. It was quickly apparent that Little had either not looked at the documents or did not know what he was doing when he inspected them. There were almost $5 million of purchases applicable to the audit period that had not been included as liabilities. Mayburn's review probably saved Santro, Best & Harmon significant embarrassment or worse.

Starting with Chapter 6, the first three phases of the audit process were studied, as outlined by the flowchart in the margin. Attention is now given to the fourth and final phase, which is shaded in the figure: completing the audit. As the chapter-opening case illustrates, the final phase of the audit demands careful and thoughtful review of the audit by an experienced and knowledgeable person. In addition to reviewing the results, several other aspects of completing the audit are critical to the success of an audit. In this chapter, the seven parts of completing the audit outlined by the flowchart in the margin on page 768 are covered.

PERFORM ADDITIONAL TESTS FOR PRESENTATION AND DISCLOSURE

OBJECTIVE 24-1

Design and perform audit tests related to presentation and disclosure audit objectives.

Summary of the Audit Process

PHASE I
Plan and design an audit approach

PHASE II
Perform tests of controls and substantive tests of transactions

PHASE III
Perform substantive analytical procedures and tests of details of balances

PHASE IV
Complete the audit and issue an audit report

Chapter 6 described the need to perform procedures to satisfy the three categories of audit objectives: transaction-related objectives, balance-related objectives, and presentation and disclosure-related objectives. Our discussion of the first three phases of the audit explained how auditors design and perform audit tests to obtain sufficient appropriate evidence to support each of these categories of audit objectives. Our illustrations of transaction cycle testing emphasized performing audit tests to support the six transaction-related and the eight balance-related audit objectives. We've discussed how those procedures also provide evidence about the four presentation and disclosure objectives, which are summarized in the first column of Table 24-1.

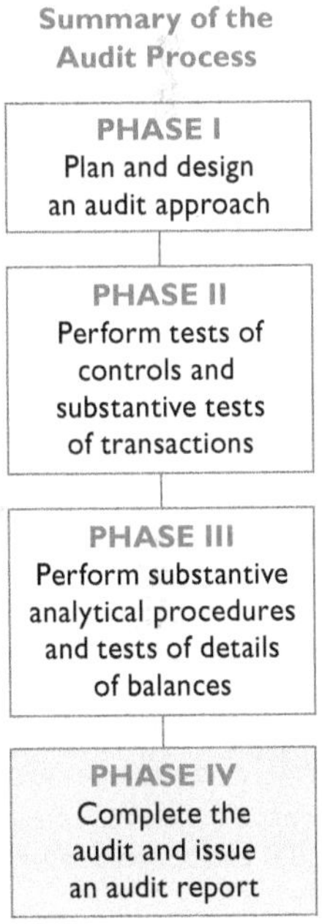

As part of phase IV of the audit, auditors evaluate evidence they obtained during the first three phases of the audit to determine whether they should perform additional procedures for presentation and disclosure-related objectives. Auditors approach obtaining evidence for presentation and disclosure objectives consistent with how they approach obtaining evidence for transaction-related and balance-related objectives.

- Perform procedures to obtain an understanding of controls related to presentation and disclosure objectives as a part of risk assessment procedures.
- Conduct tests of controls related to disclosures when the initial assessment of control risk is below maximum.
- Perform substantive procedures to obtain assurance that all audit objectives are achieved for information and amounts presented and disclosed in the financial statements.

The second column of Table 24-1 includes examples of substantive procedures related to the presentation and disclosure objectives.

Often, procedures for presentation and disclosure-related objectives are integrated with the auditor's tests for transaction-related and balance-related objectives. For

TABLE 24-1 Presentation and Disclosure Audit Objectives

Audit Objectives	Examples of Substantive Procedures
Occurrence and rights and obligations—Disclosed events and transactions have occurred and pertain to the entity.	Review debt contracts to determine that accounts receivable are pledged as collateral.
Completeness—All disclosures that should have been included in the financial statements have been included.	Use a disclosure checklist to determine if the financial statements include all disclosures required by accounting standards.
Classification and understandability—Financial information is appropriately presented and described and disclosures are clearly expressed.	Review financial statements to determine if assets are properly classified between current and noncurrent categories. Read the footnotes for clarity.
Accuracy and valuation—Financial and other information are disclosed fairly and at appropriate amounts.	Reconcile amounts included in the long-term debt footnotes to information examined and supported in the auditor's long-term debt audit files.

example, as part of the audit of accounts receivable, auditors evaluate the need to separate notes receivable and amounts due from affiliates and trade accounts due from customers. They must also determine that current and noncurrent receivables are classified separately and any factoring or discounting of notes receivable is disclosed.

Phase IV—
Completing the Audit

Perform additional tests for presentation and disclosure

Review for contingent liabilities

Review for subsequent events

Accumulate final evidence

Evaluate results

Issue audit report

Communicate with audit committee and management

While much of the information presented and disclosed in the financial statements is audited as part of the auditor's testing in earlier phases of the audit, in phase IV auditors evaluate evidence obtained during the first three phases of the audit to assess whether additional evidence is needed for the presentation and disclosure objectives. In phase IV, auditors also evaluate whether the overall presentation of the financial statements and related footnotes complies with accounting standards. This includes an evaluation of whether individual financial statements reflect the appropriate classification and description of accounts consistent with accounting requirements and that the information is presented in proper form and with the proper terminology required by accounting standards.

One of the auditor's primary concerns related to presentation and disclosure-related objectives is determining whether management has disclosed all required information (completeness objective for presentation and disclosure). To assess risks that the completeness objective for presentation and disclosure is not satisfied, auditors consider information obtained during the first three phases of audit testing to determine if they are aware of facts and circumstances that should be disclosed.

Due to the unique nature of disclosures related to contingent liabilities and subsequent events, auditors often assess the risk as high that all required information may not be completely disclosed in the footnotes. Audit tests performed in earlier audit phases often do not provide sufficient appropriate evidence about contingent liabilities and subsequent events. Therefore, auditors design and perform procedures in every audit to review for contingent liabilities and subsequent events as part of their phase IV testing. These procedures are discussed next.

REVIEW FOR CONTINGENT LIABILITIES AND COMMITMENTS

OBJECTIVE 24-2

Conduct a review for contingent liabilities and commitments.

A **contingent liability** is a potential future obligation to an outside party for an unknown amount resulting from activities that have already taken place. Material contingent liabilities must be disclosed in the footnotes. Three conditions are required for a contingent liability to exist:

1. There is a potential future payment to an outside party or the impairment of an asset that resulted from an existing condition
2. There is uncertainty about the amount of the future payment or impairment
3. The outcome will be resolved by some future event or events

For example, a lawsuit that has been filed but not yet resolved meets all three conditions.

Accounting standards use two primary approaches in dealing with uncertainty in loss contingencies. The first measures the contingency using a fair value approach. The second approach uses a probability threshold. With the probability threshold, the standards describe three levels of likelihood of occurrence (ranging from remote to probable) and the appropriate financial statement treatment for each likelihood. These requirements are summarized in Table 24-2. To evaluate whether the client has applied the appropriate approach and treatment, the auditor must exercise considerable professional judgment.

Contingency footnotes should describe the nature of the contingency to the extent it is known and the opinion of legal counsel or management as to the expected outcome. Figure 24-1 is an illustration of a footnote for pending litigation and

TABLE 24-2 Likelihood of Occurrence and Financial Statement Treatment

Likelihood of Occurrence of Event	Financial Statement Treatment
Remote (slight chance)	No disclosure is necessary.
Reasonably possible (more than remote, but less than probable)	Footnote disclosure is necessary.
Probable (likely to occur)	• If the amount can be reasonably estimated, financial statement accounts are adjusted. • If the amount cannot be reasonably estimated, footnote disclosure is necessary.

company guarantees of debt, which are both accounted for using the probability threshold approach.

Auditors are especially concerned about certain contingent liabilities:

- Pending litigation for patent infringement, product liability, or other actions
- Income tax disputes
- Product warranties
- Notes receivable discounted
- Guarantees of obligations of others
- Unused balances of outstanding letters of credit

Auditing standards make it clear that management, not the auditor, is responsible for identifying and deciding the appropriate accounting treatment for contingent liabilities. In many audits, it is impractical for auditors to uncover contingencies without management's cooperation.

The auditor's primary objectives in verifying contingent liabilities are:

- Evaluate the accounting treatment of known contingent liabilities to determine whether management has properly classified the contingency (classification presentation and disclosure objective).
- Identify to the extent practical any contingencies not already identified by management (completeness presentation and disclosure objective).

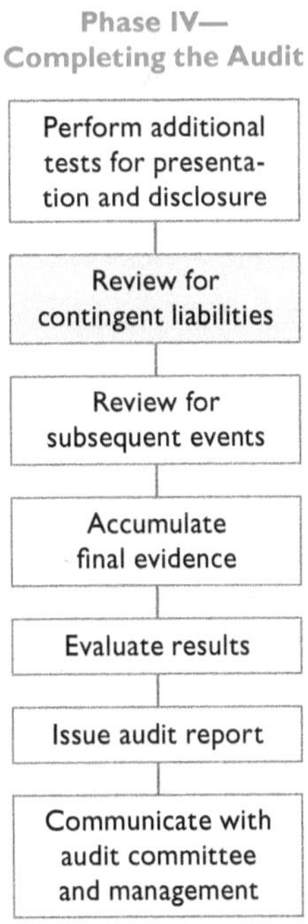

Closely related to contingent liabilities are **commitments**. They include such things as agreements to purchase raw materials or to lease facilities at a certain price and to sell merchandise at a fixed price, as well as bonus plans, profit-sharing and pension plans, and royalty agreements. The most important characteristic of a commitment is the *agreement to commit the firm to a set of fixed conditions* in the future, regardless of what happens to profits or the economy as a whole. Presumably the entity agrees to commitments to better its own interests, but they may turn out to be less or more advantageous than originally anticipated. Companies ordinarily describe all commitments either in a separate footnote or combine them with a footnote related to contingencies.

Phase IV—
Completing the Audit

Perform additional tests for presentation and disclosure

Review for contingent liabilities

Review for subsequent events

Accumulate final evidence

Evaluate results

Issue audit report

Communicate with audit committee and management

FIGURE 24-1 Contingent Liability Footnote

There are various suits and claims pending against the company and its consolidated subsidiaries. It is the opinion of the company's management, based on current available information, that the ultimate liability, if any, resulting from such suits and claims will not materially affect the consolidated financial position or results of operations of the company and its consolidated subsidiaries.

The company has agreed to guarantee the repayment of approximately $14,000,000 loaned by a bank to several affiliated corporations in which the company owns a minority interest.

Audit Procedures for Finding Contingencies

Many of these potential obligations are verified as an integral part of various segments of the audit rather than as a separate activity near the end of the audit. For example, auditors test for unused balances in outstanding letters of credit as a part of confirming bank balances and loans from banks. Similarly, auditors consider the possibility of income tax disputes as a part of analyzing income tax expense, reviewing the general correspondence file, and examining revenue agent reports. Even if contingencies are verified separately, auditors commonly perform the tests well before the last few days of completing the audit to ensure their proper verification. Tests of contingent liabilities near the end of the audit are more of a review than an initial search.

The first step in the audit of contingencies is to *determine whether any contingencies exist* (occurrence presentation and disclosure objective). As you know from studying other audit areas, it is more difficult to discover unrecorded transactions or events than to verify recorded information. Once the auditor knows that contingencies exist, evaluating their materiality and the footnote disclosures can ordinarily be satisfactorily resolved.

The following are some audit procedures commonly used to search for contingent liabilities, but not all are applicable to every audit:

- Inquire of management (orally and in writing) about the possibility of unrecorded contingencies. In these inquiries, the auditor must be specific in describing the different kinds of contingencies that may require disclosure as reminders to management of contingencies they overlooked or do not fully understand. If management overlooked a contingency or does not fully comprehend accounting disclosure requirements, the inquiry can be helpful to identify required disclosures. At the completion of the audit, auditors typically ask management to make a written statement as a part of the letter of representation (discussed later in this chapter) that it is aware of no undisclosed contingent liabilities. Naturally, inquiries of management are not useful in uncovering the intentional failure to disclose contingencies.
- Review current and previous years' internal revenue agent reports for income tax settlements. The reports may indicate areas or years in which there are unsettled disagreements. If a review has been in progress for a long time, there is an increased likelihood of a tax dispute.
- Review the minutes of directors' and stockholders' meetings for indications of lawsuits or other contingencies.
- Analyze legal expense for the period under audit and review invoices and statements from legal counsel for indications of contingent liabilities, especially lawsuits and pending tax assessments.
- Obtain a letter from each major attorney performing legal services for the client as to the status of pending litigation or other contingent liabilities. This procedure is examined in more depth shortly.
- Review audit documentation for any information that may indicate a potential contingency. For example, bank confirmations may indicate notes receivable discounted or guarantees of loans.
- Examine letters of credit in force as of the balance sheet date and obtain a confirmation of the used and unused balances.

Evaluation of Known Contingent Liabilities

If auditors conclude that there are contingent liabilities, they must evaluate the significance of the potential liability and the nature of the disclosure needed in the financial statements to obtain evidence about the occurrence and rights and obligations presentation and disclosure objective. In some instances, the potential liability is sufficiently well known to be included in the statements as an actual liability under the probability threshold approach. In other instances, disclosure may be unnecessary if the contingency is highly remote or immaterial. CPA firms often obtain a separate evaluation of the potential liability from its own legal counsel, especially highly material ones, rather than relying on management or management's attorneys. Because they are advocates for the client, the client's attorneys may lose perspective in evaluating the likelihood of losing the case and the amount of the potential judgment. For those contingencies that require disclosure, the auditor also reviews the draft footnote to ensure that the disclosed information is understandable and fairly states the conditions of the contingency.

Audit Procedures for Finding Commitments

The search for unknown commitments is usually performed as a part of the tests in each audit area. For example, in verifying sales transactions, the auditor should be alert for sales commitments. Similarly, commitments for the purchase of raw materials or equipment can be identified as a part of the audit of each of these accounts. The auditor should also be aware of the possibility of commitments when reading minutes, contracts, and correspondence files.

Inquiry of Client's Attorneys

OBJECTIVE 24-3

Obtain and evaluate letters from the client's attorneys.

Inquiry of the client's attorneys is a major procedure auditors rely on for evaluating known litigation or other claims against the client and identifying additional ones. The auditor relies on the attorney's expertise and knowledge of the client's legal affairs to provide a professional opinion about the expected outcome of existing lawsuits and the likely amount of the liability, including court costs. The attorney is also likely to know of pending litigation and claims that management may have overlooked.

Many CPA firms analyze legal expense for the entire year and have the client send a standard inquiry letter to every attorney the client has been involved with in the current or preceding year, plus any attorney the firm occasionally engages. In some cases, this involves a large number of attorneys, including some who deal in aspects of law that are far removed from potential lawsuits.

The standard inquiry to the client's attorney, prepared on the client's letterhead and signed by one of the company's officials, should include the following:

- *A list including (1) pending threatened litigation and (2) asserted or unasserted claims or assessments with which the attorney has had significant involvement.* This list is typically prepared by management, but management may request that the attorney prepare the list.
- *A request that the attorney furnish information or comment about the progress of each item listed.* The desired information includes the legal action the client intends to take, the likelihood of an unfavorable outcome, and an estimate of the amount or range of the potential loss.
- *A request of the law firm to identify any unlisted pending or threatened legal actions or a statement that the client's list is complete.*
- *A statement informing the attorney of the attorney's responsibility to inform management of legal matters requiring disclosure in the financial statements and to respond directly to the auditor.* If the attorney chooses to limit a response, reasons for doing so are to be included in the letter.

Figure 24-2 provides an example of a typical standard letter sent to the attorney for return directly to the CPA's office. Notice the first paragraph requests that the attorney communicate about contingencies up to approximately *the date of the auditor's report.*

Attorneys in recent years have become reluctant to provide certain information to auditors because of their own exposure to legal liability for providing incorrect or confidential information. The nature of the refusals by attorneys to provide auditors with complete information about contingent liabilities falls into two categories:

1. The attorneys refuse to respond due to a lack of knowledge about matters involving contingent liabilities.
2. The attorneys refuse to disclose information that they consider confidential.

For example, the attorney might be aware of a violation of a patent agreement that could result in a significant loss to the client if it were known (**unasserted claim**).

FIGURE 24-2 Typical Inquiry of Attorney

HILLSBURG HARDWARE CO.
2146 Willow St.
Gary, Indiana 46405

March 1, 2017

Bailwick & Bettle, Attorneys
11216 Michigan Avenue
Chicago, IL 60606

Our auditors, Berger and Anthony, CPAs (P.O. Box 8175, Gary, Indiana 46405), are conducting an audit of our financial statements for the fiscal year ended December 31, 2016. In connection with their audit, we have prepared and furnished to them a description and evaluation of certain contingencies, including those attached, involving matters with respect to which you have been engaged and to which you have devoted substantive attention on behalf of the company in the form of legal consultation or representation. For the purpose of your response to this letter, we believe that as to each contingency an amount in excess of $100,000 would be material, and in total, $700,000. However, determination of materiality with respect to the overall financial statements cannot be made until our auditors complete their audit. Your response should include matters that existed at December 31, 2016, and during the period from that date to the date of the completion of their audit, which is anticipated to be on or about March 15, 2017.

Please provide to our auditors the following information:

(1) Such explanation, if any, that you consider necessary to supplement the listed judgments rendered or settlements made involving the company from the beginning of this fiscal year through the date of your reply.
(2) Such explanation, if any, that you consider necessary to supplement the listing of pending or threatened litigation, including an explanation of those matters as to which your views may differ from those stated and an identification of the omission of any pending or threatened litigation, claim, and assessment or a statement that the list of such matters is complete.
(3) Such explanation, if any, that you consider necessary to supplement the attached information concerning unasserted claims and assessments, including an explanation of those matters as to which your views may differ from those stated.

We understand that whenever, in the course of performing legal services for us with respect to a matter recognized to involve an unasserted possible claim or assessment that may call for financial statement disclosure, you have formed a professional conclusion that we should disclose or consider disclosure concerning such possible claim or assessment, as a matter of professional responsibility to us, you will so advise us and will consult with us concerning the question of such disclosure and the applicable requirements of accounting standards. Please specifically confirm to our auditors that our understanding is correct.

Please specifically identify the nature of and reasons for any limitations in your response.

Yours very truly,
Hillsburg Hardware Co.

RChulick

Rick Chulick, Pres.

Such an instance falls under the second category. The inclusion of the information in a footnote could actually cause the lawsuit and therefore be damaging to the client.

If an attorney refuses to provide the auditor with information about material existing lawsuits (asserted claims) or unasserted claims, *auditors must modify their audit report to reflect the lack of available evidence* (a scope limitation, which requires a qualified

SEC FOCUSES ON LOSS CONTINGENCIES

Disclosure of loss contingencies is a natural source of tension between companies and their auditors. The underlying source of this tension is the culture of transparency in financial reporting, and the adversarial nature of the justice system. While auditors want to learn about pending litigation to meet auditing standards requirements and assess the adequacy of disclosure, companies are concerned that disclosure to the auditor could compromise attorney–client privilege. A framework for communications between auditors and lawyers was developed in a 1975 agreement between the AICPA and the American Bar Association (ABA), "Statement of Policy Regarding Lawyers' Responses to Auditors' Request for Information." Under the FASB Accounting Standards Codification (ASC) Topic 450—Contingencies, a company needs to consider whether a loss from litigation is probable, whether the amount of loss can be reasonably estimated, and whether an estimate of the possible loss or range of loss can be made. The company is likely to discuss these matters with its auditor in making these determinations. The SEC is concerned that the agreement between the AICPA and ABA could limit this discussion, which could impact the adequacy of the company's disclosure.

The FASB had initially proposed a new standard governing contingencies in 2007. The board received 242 comment letters, and many were critical that the new disclosures would require companies to waive client–attorney privilege, and negatively affect a company's ability to defend itself. A revised exposure draft was issued in 2010. Although this proposal limited the required disclosures, the board received 339 comments, and many indicated the disclosures could have a prejudicial effect on pending litigation. Many comments indicated that the problem was a lack of compliance with the existing requirements, rather than a need for additional disclosure. The FASB removed the loss contingencies project from its technical agenda in 2012.

Sources: 1. Kim Nilsen, "Renewed Focus on Loss Contingency Disclosures," *Journal of Accountancy* (April 2011), pp. 37–39; 2. Michael Cohn, "FASB Cancels Loss Contingencies Disclosure Project," *Accounting Today* (July 13, 2012) (www.accountingtoday.com).

or disclaimer of opinion). This requirement in the auditing standards has the effect of requiring management to give its attorneys permission to provide contingent liability information to auditors and to encourage attorneys to cooperate with auditors in obtaining information about contingencies.

As directed by the Sarbanes–Oxley Act, rules require attorneys serving public companies to report material violations of federal securities laws committed by the company. An attorney must report violations to the public company's chief legal counsel or chief executive officer. If the legal officer or CEO fails to appropriately respond, the attorney must report violations to the company's audit committee. Responding to these requirements, the American Bar Association subsequently amended its attorney–client confidentiality rules to permit attorneys to breach confidentiality if a client is committing a crime or fraud.

REVIEW FOR SUBSEQUENT EVENTS

OBJECTIVE 24-4

Conduct a post-balance-sheet review for subsequent events.

The third part of completing the audit is the review for subsequent events. The auditor must review transactions and events that occurred after the balance sheet date to determine whether any of these transactions or events affect the fair presentation or disclosure of the current period statements. The auditing procedures required by auditing standards to verify these transactions and events are commonly called the **review for subsequent events** or *post-balance-sheet review*.

The auditor's responsibility for reviewing subsequent events is normally limited to the period beginning with the balance sheet date and ending with the date of the auditor's report. As a result, the subsequent events review should be completed near the end of the audit.[1] Figure 24-3 shows the period covered by a subsequent events review and the timing of that review.

[1]When the auditor's name is associated with a registration statement under the Securities Act of 1933, the auditor's responsibility for reviewing subsequent events extends beyond the date of the auditor's report to the date the registration becomes effective.

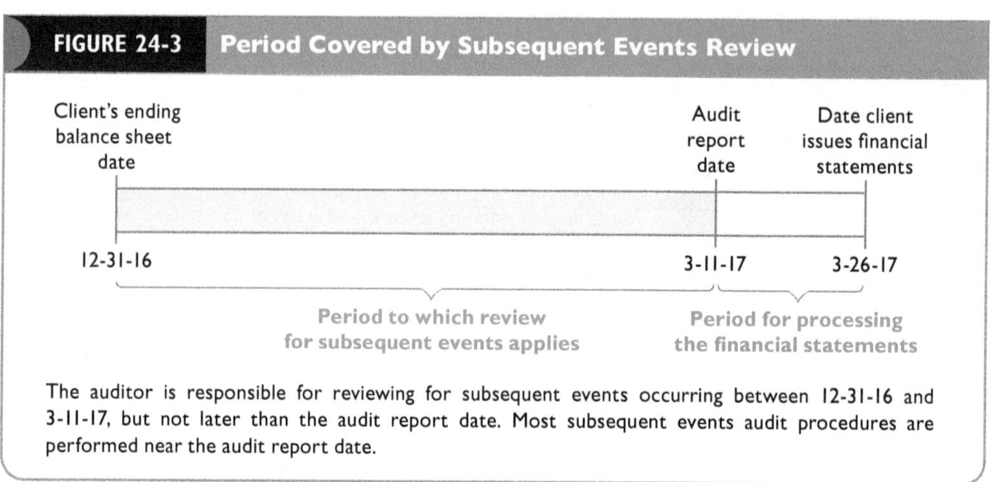

Types of Subsequent Events

Two types of **subsequent events** require consideration by management and evaluation by the auditor: those that have a direct effect on the financial statements and require adjustment of the current year's financial statement amounts and those that have no direct effect on the financial statement amounts but for which disclosure is required.

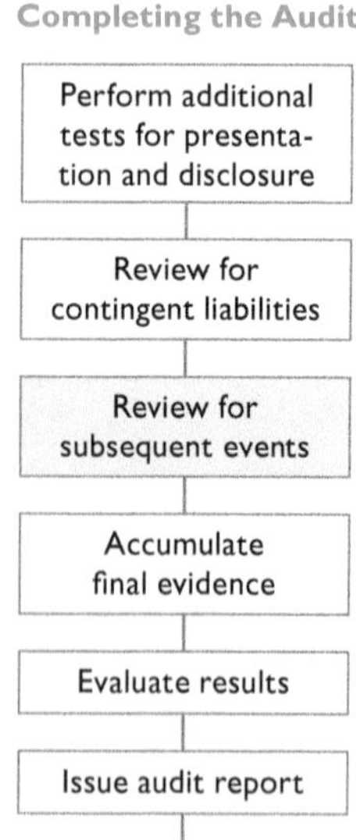

Those That Have a Direct Effect on the Financial Statements and Require Adjustment Some events that occur after the balance sheet date provide additional information to management that helps them determine the fair presentation of account balances as of the balance sheet date. Information about those events helps auditors in verifying the balances. For example, if the auditor is having difficulty determining the correct valuation of inventory because of obsolescence, the sale of raw material inventory as scrap in the subsequent period will indicate the correct value of the inventory as of the balance sheet date.

Subsequent period events, such as the following, require an adjustment of account balances in the current year's financial statements if the amounts are material:

- Declaration of bankruptcy by a customer with an outstanding accounts receivable balance because of the customer's deteriorating financial condition
- Settlement of litigation at an amount different from the amount recorded on the books
- Disposal of equipment not being used in operations at a price below the current book value

When subsequent events are used to evaluate the amounts included in the year-end financial statements, auditors must distinguish between conditions that existed at the balance sheet date and those that came into being after the end of the year. The subsequent information should not be incorporated directly into the statements if the conditions causing the change in valuation took place after year-end. For example, assume one type of a client's inventory suddenly becomes obsolete because of a technology change after the balance sheet date. The sale of the inventory at a loss in the subsequent period is not relevant in the valuation of inventory for obsolescence in this case.

Auditors of accelerated filer public companies must inquire about and consider any information about subsequent events that materially affects the effectiveness of internal control over financial reporting as of the end of the fiscal period. If auditors conclude that the events reflect a material weakness that existed at year-end, they must give an adverse opinion on internal control over financial reporting. If they are unable to determine the effect of the subsequent event on the effectiveness of internal control, they must disclaim their opinion on internal control.

Those That Do Not Have a Direct Effect on the Financial Statements but for Which Disclosure May Be Required Subsequent events of this type are events that provide evidence about conditions that did *not* exist at the date of the balance sheet being reported on but arose after the balance sheet date and may be significant enough to require disclosure. Examples of these types of nonrecognized subsequent events include:

- A decline in the market value of securities held for temporary investment or resale
- The issuance of bonds or equity securities
- A decline in the market value of inventory as a consequence of government action barring further sale of a product
- The uninsured loss of inventories as a result of fire
- A merger or an acquisition

Nonrecognized subsequent events may require disclosure if they are significant and if the financial statements would be misleading without the disclosure. Ordinarily these events can be adequately disclosed by the use of footnotes. Occasionally, an event may be so significant as to require disclosure in *supplemental financial statements,* which include the effect of the event as if it had occurred on the balance sheet date. An example is an extremely material merger.

Auditors of accelerated filer public companies may also identify events related to internal control over financial reporting that arose subsequent to year-end. If the auditor determines that these subsequent events have a material effect on the company's internal control over financial reporting, the auditor's report must include an explanatory paragraph either describing the event and its effect or directing the reader to a disclosure in management's report on internal control of the event and its effect.

Audit Tests

There are two categories of audit procedures for the subsequent events review:

1. Procedures normally integrated as a part of the verification of year-end account balances
2. Procedures performed specifically for the purpose of discovering events or transactions that must be recognized as subsequent events.

The first category includes cutoff and valuation tests done as a part of the tests of details of balances. For example, auditors examine subsequent period sales and acquisition transactions to determine whether the cutoff is accurate. Auditors also test the collectibility of accounts receivable by reviewing subsequent period cash receipts to evaluate the valuation of the allowance for uncollectible accounts. Procedures for cutoff and valuation have been discussed sufficiently in preceding chapters and are not repeated here.

The second category of tests are performed specifically to obtain information to incorporate into the current year's account balances or footnotes as tests of the completeness presentation and disclosure objective. These tests include the following:

Review Records Prepared Subsequent to the Balance Sheet Date Auditors should review journals and ledgers to determine the existence and nature of significant transactions related to the current year. If journals are not kept up-to-date, auditors should review documents that will be used to prepare the journals.

Auditors of public companies that are accelerated filers must inquire about and examine statements issued during the subsequent events review period, such as relevant internal audit reports and regulatory agency reports on the company's internal control over financial reporting.

Review Internal Statements Prepared Subsequent to the Balance Sheet Date In the review, auditors should emphasize changes in the business compared to results for the same period in the year under audit and changes after year-end. They should pay careful attention to major changes in the business or environment in which the client is operating. Auditors should discuss the interim statements with management to determine whether they are prepared on the same basis as the current period statements, and also inquire about significant changes in the operating results.

Examine Minutes Issued Subsequent to the Balance Sheet Date Auditors must examine the minutes of stockholders and directors meetings subsequent to the balance sheet date for subsequent events affecting the current period financial statements.

Correspond with Attorneys As discussed earlier in the chapter, auditors correspond with attorneys as a part of the search for contingent liabilities. Auditors normally request the attorney to date and mail the letter as of the expected audit completion date to fulfill the auditors' responsibility for subsequent events.

Inquire of Management Inquiries vary from client to client, but normally include significant changes in the assets or capital structure of the company after the balance sheet date, the current status of items that were not completely resolved at the balance sheet date, and unusual adjustments made subsequent to the balance sheet date. Public company auditors must also include inquiries of management about any changes in internal control over financial reporting made subsequent to the end of the fiscal period.

Inquiries of management about subsequent events must be done with appropriate client personnel to obtain meaningful answers. For example, it is not useful for the auditor to discuss tax or union matters with an accounts receivable supervisor. Depending on the information desired, auditors usually make inquiries of the controller, vice presidents, and the president.

Obtain a Letter of Representation The letter of representation written by the client's management to the auditor formalizes statements made by management about different matters throughout the audit, including discussions about subsequent events. This letter is mandatory and includes other relevant matters. This letter is discussed in the following section.

Dual Dating

Occasionally, the auditor determines that a subsequent event that affects the current period financial statements occurred after the date of the audit report but *before the audit report was issued*. The source of such information is typically management or the media. For example, what if an audit client acquired another company after the auditor had gathered sufficient appropriate evidence to support the audit opinion? Using the dates in Figure 24-3 on page 774, assume the acquisition occurred on March 23, when the last day of audit testing was March 11. In that situation, auditing standards require the auditor to extend audit tests for the newly discovered subsequent event to make sure that it is correctly disclosed. The auditor has two equally acceptable options for expanding subsequent events tests:

1. Expand all subsequent events tests to the new date
2. Restrict the subsequent events review to matters related to the new subsequent event

For the first option, auditors simply change the audit report date to the new date. For the second option, the auditor issues a **dual-dated audit report**, meaning that the audit report includes two dates: the first date for the completion of audit testing, except for the specific exception, and the second date, which is always later, for the exception. In the example, assume the auditor performs audit tests pertaining only to the acquisition and completes those tests on March 31. The audit report will be dual-dated as follows: March 11, 2017, except for note 17, as to which the date is March 31, 2017.

CONCEPT CHECK

1. Explain the importance of the completeness presentation and disclosure audit objective. What procedures do auditors typically follow to address the completeness of disclosures?
2. Describe a contingency. What conditions are required for a contingent liability to exist?
3. Distinguish between the two general types of subsequent events and explain how they differ. Give two examples of each.

FINAL EVIDENCE ACCUMULATION

OBJECTIVE 24-5

Design and perform the final steps in the evidence-accumulation segment of the audit.

In addition to the review for subsequent events, the auditor has several final evidence-accumulation responsibilities that apply to all cycles. Five types of final evidence accumulation are discussed in this section: perform final analytical procedures, evaluate the going-concern assumption, obtain a management representation letter, consider information accompanying the basic financial statements, and read other information in the annual report. Each of these is done late in the audit.

Perform Final Analytical Procedures

Auditing standards require auditors to perform analytical procedures during the completion of the audit. These procedures are useful as a final review for material misstatements or financial problems not noted during other testing and to help the auditor take a final objective look at the financial statements. It is common for a partner to do the analytical procedures during the final review of audit documentation and financial statements. Typically, a partner has a good understanding of the client and its business because of ongoing relationships. This knowledge combined with effective analytical procedures help the partner identify possible oversights in an audit. The opening story on the audit of Westside Industries illustrates this point.

When performing analytical procedures during the final review stage, the partner generally reads the financial statements, including footnotes, and considers the adequacy of evidence gathered about unusual or unexpected account balances or relationships identified during planning or while conducting the audit. The partner also considers unusual or unexpected account balances or relationships that were not previously identified.

Results from final analytical procedures may indicate that additional audit evidence is necessary. If this is the case, the auditor should perform additional testing to obtain sufficient appropriate evidence that the affected accounts are fairly stated. If the unexpected relationship is due to a client misstatement that is identified in the additional testing, the auditor should propose an adjustment to correct the misstatement if it is material.

Evaluate Going-Concern Assumption

Auditing standards require the auditor to evaluate whether there is a substantial doubt about a client's ability to continue as a going concern for at least one year beyond the balance sheet date. Auditors make that assessment initially as a part of planning but may revise it after obtaining new information. For example, an initial assessment of going concern may need revision if the auditor discovers during the audit that the company has defaulted on a loan, lost its primary customer, or decided to dispose of substantial assets to pay off loans. Auditors use analytical procedures, discussions with management about potential financial difficulties, and their knowledge of the client's business gained throughout the audit to assess the likelihood of financial failure within the next year.

A final assessment of the entity's going-concern status is desirable after all evidence has been accumulated and proposed audit adjustments have been incorporated into the financial statements. When auditors have reservations about the going-concern assumption, they must evaluate management's plans to avoid bankruptcy and the feasibility of achieving these plans. Making the final decision whether to issue a report with a going-concern explanatory paragraph can be time-consuming and difficult, especially during an economic downturn. (For more discussion of going-concern explanatory paragraphs, see page 56 in Chapter 3.)

Obtain Management Representation Letter

Auditing standards require the auditor to obtain written representations from management, usually in a **letter of representation** documenting management's most important oral representations made during the audit. The letter is prepared on the client's letterhead, addressed to the CPA firm, and signed by high-level corporate

FASB ISSUES GUIDANCE ON MANAGEMENT'S RESPONSIBILTY TO EVALUATE GOING CONCERN

Under generally accepted accounting principles (GAAP), financial statements are prepared on the assumption that the entity is a going concern unless liquidation is imminent. If liquidation is imminent, the financial statements should be prepared on the liquidation basis of accounting following the guidance in the FASB Accounting Standards Codification (ASC) under Subtopic 205-30, *Presentation of Financial Statements—Liquidation Basis of Accounting*.

Auditors have long had responsibility to evaluate whether the entity is a going concern, and include information in the auditor's report if there is substantial doubt about the entity's ability to continue as a going concern. However, GAAP did not provide guidance about management's responsibility to evaluate whether there is doubt about the entity's ability to continue as a going concern, and related footnote disclosures. This changed in August 2014 with the FASB's issuance of Accounting Standards Update 2014-15, *Disclosure of Uncertainties about an Entity's Ability to Continue as a Going Concern*, which is effective for annual reporting periods ending after December 15, 2016. The standards update creates a new Subtopic 205-40, *Presentation of Financial Statements—Going Concern*, in the Accounting Standards Codification. If management identifies conditions that raise substantial doubt about the entity's ability to continue as a going concern, they should disclose in the footnotes:

a. The principal conditions or events that raise substantial doubt about the entity's ability to continue as a going concern
b. Management's evaluation of the significance of those conditions or events in relation to the entity's ability to meet its obligations

If management has a plan that alleviates the substantial doubt, then management should also disclose this information. However, if the substantial doubt is not alleviated after considering management's plans, the footnotes should include a statement that there is *substantial doubt about the entity's ability to continue as a going concern* within one year after the financial statements are issued, and should include a discussion of management's plans that are intended to mitigate the conditions or events that raise substantial doubt about the entity's ability to continue as a going concern. The PCAOB is evaluating revisions to the existing PCAOB auditing standard on evaluating going concern in light of the changes to the accounting requirements.

Sources: 1. FASB Accounting Standards Update No. 2014-15, *Disclosure of Uncertainties about an Entity's Ability to Continue as a Going Concern* (August 2014); 2. PCAOB, "Standard Setting Agenda—Office of the Chief Auditor," June 30, 2015 (pcaobus.org).

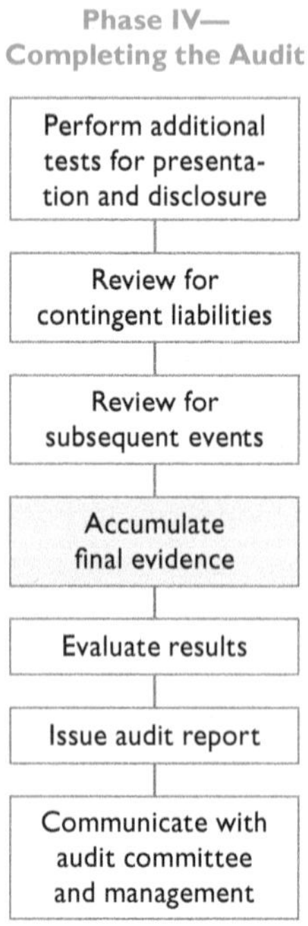

officials, usually the president and chief financial officer. While the letter implies that it has originated with the client, it is common practice for the auditor to prepare the letter and request the client to reproduce it on the company's letterhead and sign it. Refusal by a client to prepare and sign the letter requires a qualified opinion or disclaimer of opinion. The letter should be dated no earlier than the date of the auditor's report to make sure that there are adequate representations about subsequent events.

Phase IV—Completing the Audit

Perform additional tests for presentation and disclosure → Review for contingent liabilities → Review for subsequent events → Accumulate final evidence → Evaluate results → Issue audit report → Communicate with audit committee and management

The three purposes of the client letter of representation are:

1. *To impress upon management its responsibility for the assertions in the financial statements.* It is easy for management to forget that they are responsible, not the auditor, for the fair presentation of financial statements, especially in smaller companies that lack personnel with expertise in accounting.
2. *To remind management of potential misstatements or omissions in the financial statements.* For example, if the letter of representation includes a reference to pledged assets and contingent liabilities, honest management may be reminded of its unintentional failure to disclose the information adequately, which helps satisfy the completeness presentation and disclosure objective. To fulfill this objective, the letter of representation should be sufficiently detailed to act as a reminder to management.
3. *To document the responses from management to inquiries about various aspects of the audit.* This provides written documentation of client representations in the event of disagreement or a lawsuit between the auditor and client. A letter of representation also helps reduce misunderstandings between management and the auditor.

Auditing standards suggest four categories of specific matters that should be included. The four categories, with examples of each, are:

1. *Financial statements*
   - Management's acknowledgment of its responsibility for the fair presentation of the financial statements

- Management's belief that the financial statements are fairly presented in conformity with applicable accounting standards

2. *Completeness of information*
   - Availability of all financial records and related data
   - Completeness and availability of all minutes of meetings of stockholders, directors, and committees of directors
   - Absence of unrecorded transactions

3. *Recognition, measurement, and disclosure*
   - Management's belief that the effects of any uncorrected financial statement misstatements are immaterial to the financial statements (a summary of these items should be included in or attached to the letter)
   - Information concerning fraud involving (a) management, (b) employees who have significant roles in internal control, or (c) others where the fraud could have a material effect on the financial statements
   - Information concerning related party transactions and amounts receivable from or payable to related parties
   - Unasserted claims or assessments that the entity's lawyer has advised are probable of assertion and must be disclosed in accordance with accounting standards

4. *Subsequent events*
   - Bankruptcy of a major customer with an outstanding account receivable at the balance sheet date
   - A merger or acquisition after the balance sheet date

PCAOB auditing standards require the auditor to obtain written representations from management about its responsibility for internal control over financial reporting and management's conclusion about the effectiveness of internal control over financial reporting as of the end of the fiscal period. Auditors of public companies may obtain a combined representation letter for both the audit of the financial statements and the audit of internal control.

A client representation letter is a written statement from a nonindependent source and therefore *cannot be regarded as reliable evidence*. However, the letter does provide documentation that management has been asked certain questions to make sure that management understands its responsibilities and to protect the auditor if management files claims against the auditor.

In some audits, the auditor may find other evidence that contradicts statements in the letter of representation. In such cases, the auditor should investigate the circumstances and consider whether representations in the letter are reliable.

Consider Supplementary Information in Relation to Financial Statements as a Whole

Clients often include additional information beyond the basic financial statements in materials prepared for management or outside users. Auditing standards refer to this additional information as *supplementary information in relation to the financial statements as a whole*. Figure 24-4 (p. 780) illustrates the basic financial statements and additional supplementary information.

Auditing standards intentionally refrain from defining or restricting supplementary information to enable companies to individualize the information to meet the needs of statement users. However, several types of information are commonly included in the additional information section, such as detailed comparative statements supporting the totals on the primary financial statements for accounts such as cost of goods sold and operating expenses.

Auditors must clearly distinguish their audit and reporting responsibility for the primary financial statements and for supplementary information. Usually, the auditor has not performed a sufficiently detailed audit to justify an opinion on the additional information. In some instances, however, the auditor may be engaged by the client to report on the supplementary information accompanying the basic financial

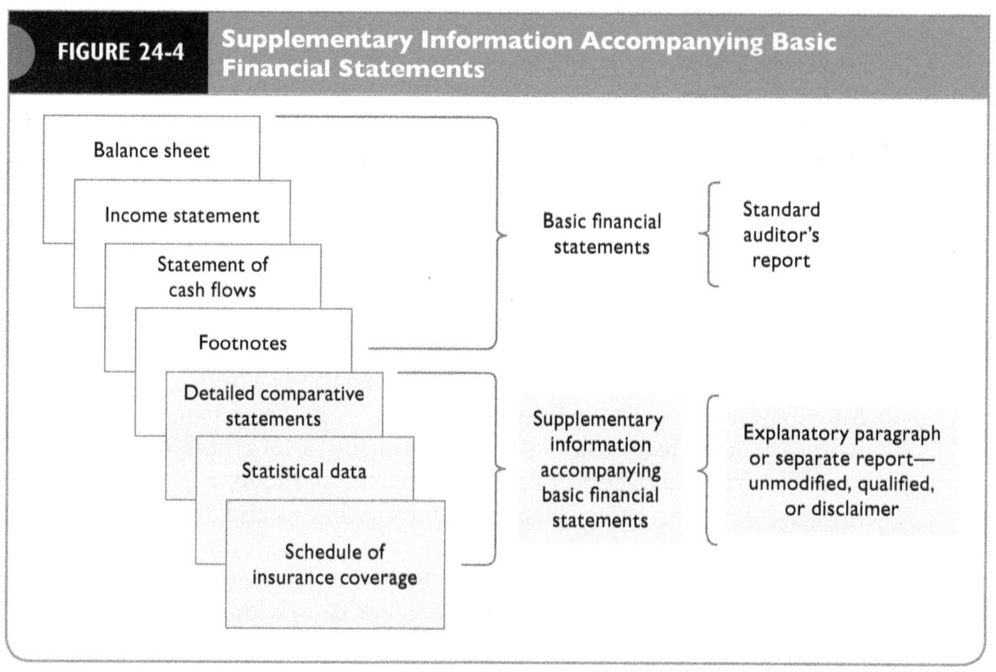

statements. To complete that engagement, the supplementary information must be derived from the accounting records used to generate the basic financial statements and involve the same time period as the basic financial statements. Additionally, the auditor cannot have issued an adverse opinion or disclaimer of opinion on the basic financial statements.

When reporting on supplementary information, the auditor uses the same materiality as that used in forming an opinion on the basic financial statements. As a result, the additional procedures required are less extensive than if the auditor were issuing an opinion on the information taken by itself.

Auditor reporting on supplementary information can be either in an other matter explanatory paragraph following the opinion paragraph in the auditor's report on the financial statements or in a separate report on the supplementary information. The following is an example of an explanatory paragraph reporting on supplementary information in relation to the financial statements as a whole:

> *Our audit was conducted for the purpose of forming an opinion on the financial statements as a whole. The accompanying information on pages x through y is presented for purposes of additional analysis and is not a required part of the financial statements. Such information is the responsibility of management and was derived from and relates directly to the underlying accounting and other records used to prepare the financial statements. The information has been subjected to the auditing procedures applied in the audit of the financial statements and certain additional procedures, including comparing and reconciling such information directly to the underlying accounting and other records used to prepare the financial statements or to the financial statements themselves, and other additional procedures in accordance with auditing standards generally accepted in the United States of America. In our opinion, the information is fairly stated in all material respects in relation to the financial statements as a whole.*

If the auditor concludes that the supplementary information is materially misstated in relation to the financial statements as a whole, the auditor should request management to revise the supplementary information. If management does not make the necessary modifications, the auditor should modify the auditor's opinion on the supplementary information and describe the misstatement in the auditor's report. If a separate report is being issued on the supplementary information, the auditor should withhold the auditor's report on the supplementary information.

Sometimes additional information is required by accounting standards, which auditing standards refer to as *required supplementary information*. Required supplementary information is not part of the basic financial statements; however, a designated accounting standards setter considers the information to be an essential part of financial reporting. When required supplementary information accompanies the basic financial statements, auditing standards require the auditor to perform certain additional procedures that are limited to inquiry of management about the methods of preparing the information and comparison of the information for consistency with management's responses to the auditor's inquiries, the basic financial statements, and to information the auditor obtains during the audit of the basic financial statements. Because these limited procedures do not provide sufficient evidence to provide any assurance about the required supplementary information, the auditor's report on the basic financial statements includes an explanatory paragraph that contains a disclaimer of opinion about the required supplementary information.

Read Other Information in the Annual Report

Auditing standards require the auditor to read **other information included in annual reports** pertaining directly to the financial statements. For example, assume that the president's letter in the annual report refers to an increase in earnings per share from $2.60 to $2.93. The auditor is required to compare that information with the financial statements to make sure it corresponds.

Auditor responsibility to read other information included in annual reports pertains only to information that is not a part of the financial statements but is published with them. Examples are the president's letter and explanations of company activities included in annual reports of nearly all publicly held companies. It usually takes auditors only a few minutes to make sure that the nonfinancial statement information is consistent with the statements. If auditors conclude that a material inconsistency exists, they should request the client to change the information. If the client refuses, which would be unusual, the auditor should include an explanatory paragraph in the audit report or withdraw from the engagement.

EVALUATE RESULTS

OBJECTIVE 24-6

Integrate the audit evidence gathered and evaluate the overall audit results.

After performing all audit procedures in each audit area, including the review for contingencies and subsequent events and accumulating final evidence, the auditor must integrate the results into *one overall conclusion* about the financial statements. Ultimately, the auditor must decide whether sufficient appropriate audit evidence has been accumulated to warrant the conclusion that the financial statements are stated in accordance with the applicable accounting framework. Similarly, when issuing a report on internal control, auditors must also arrive at an overall conclusion about the effectiveness of internal control over financial reporting. The five main aspects of evaluating the results are discussed next.

Sufficient Appropriate Evidence

To make a final evaluation as to whether sufficient appropriate evidence has been accumulated, the auditor reviews the audit documentation for the entire audit to determine whether all material classes of transactions, accounts, and disclosures have been adequately tested, considering all circumstances of the audit. An important part of the review is to make sure that all parts of the audit program have been accurately completed and documented and that all audit objectives have been met. The auditor must decide whether the audit program is adequate, considering problem areas identified as the audit progressed. For example, if misstatements were discovered during tests of sales, the initial plans for tests of details of accounts receivable may have been insufficient.

FIGURE 24-5 Completing the Audit Checklist

	YES	NO
1. Examination of prior year's audit documentation		
a. Were last year's audit files examined for areas of emphasis in the current year audit?	___	___
b. Was the permanent file reviewed for items that affect the current year?	___	___
2. Internal control		
a. Has internal control been adequately understood?	___	___
b. Is the scope of the audit adequate in light of the assessed control risk?	___	___
c. Have all significant deficiencies and material weaknesses been reported in writing to those charged with governance?	___	___
3. General documents		
a. Were all current year minutes and resolutions reviewed, abstracted, and followed up?	___	___
b. Has the permanent file been updated?	___	___
c. Have all major contracts and agreements been reviewed and abstracted, copied, or downloaded to ascertain that the client complies with all existing legal requirements?	___	___

As an aid in deciding whether the audit evidence is adequate, auditors often use a **completing the audit checklist**, which is a reminder of items that may have been overlooked. Figure 24-5 illustrates part of a completing the audit checklist.

If auditors conclude that sufficient evidence has *not* been obtained to decide whether the financial statements are fairly presented, they have two choices: accumulate additional evidence or issue either a qualified opinion or a disclaimer of opinion.

Evidence Supports Auditor's Opinion

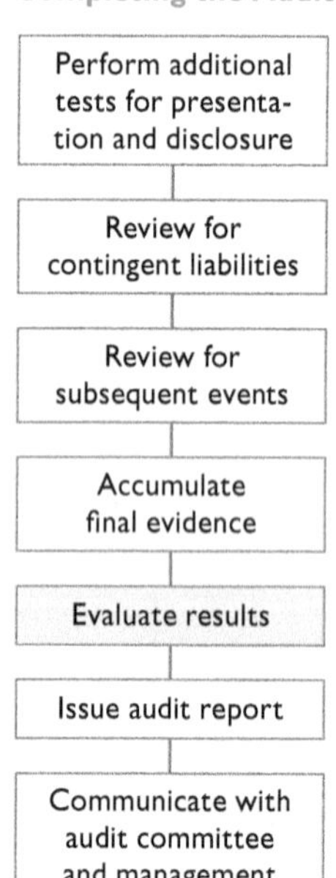

An essential part of evaluating whether the financial statements are fairly stated involves the auditor's review of the summary of misstatements found in the audit. When any one misstatement is material, auditors should propose that the client correct the financial statements. It may be difficult to determine the appropriate amount of adjustment because the exact amount of the misstatement may be unknown if it involves an estimate or includes an estimate for sampling risk. Nevertheless, the auditor must decide on the required adjustment. (In some audits there may be more than one material misstatement.)

In addition to individually material misstatements, there are often several immaterial misstatements that the client did not adjust. Auditors must combine individually immaterial misstatements to evaluate whether the combined amount is material. They can keep a record of these misstatements and combine them in different ways, but many auditors use an **unadjusted misstatement audit schedule** or *summary of possible misstatements.* An example of an unadjusted misstatement worksheet is given in Figure 24-6. Auditors are also required to consider the impact on the current year financial statements of misstatements identified in a prior year that were not corrected.

The schedule in Figure 24-6 includes both known misstatements that the client has decided not to adjust and projected misstatements, including an allowance for sampling risk, and total possible misstatements for several financial statement categories. The bottom left portion of the audit schedule, under the heading "Conclusions," includes a comparison of possible overstatements and understatements to materiality. A summary of this audit schedule should be included with management's representation that the uncorrected misstatements are immaterial.

If auditors believe that there is sufficient evidence but they conclude that the financial statements are not fairly presented, they again have two choices: The statements must be revised to the auditor's satisfaction or either a qualified or an adverse opinion must be issued.

Financial Statement Disclosures

Before completing the audit, auditors must make a final evaluation of whether the disclosures in the financial statements satisfy all presentation and disclosure objectives.

FIGURE 24-6 Unadjusted Misstatement Audit Schedule

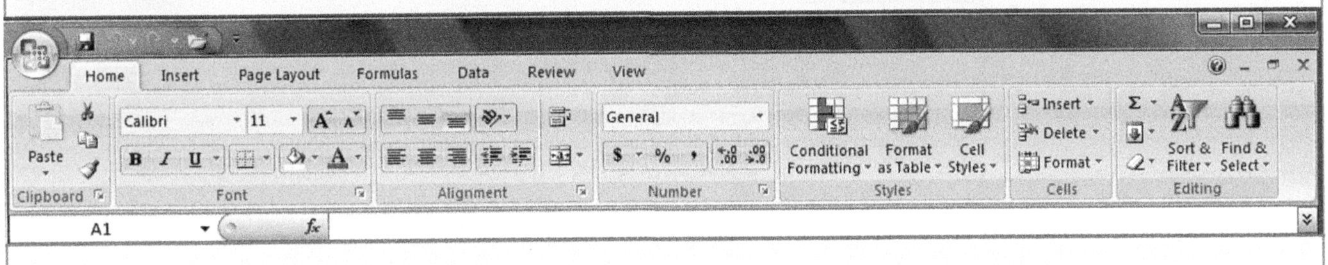

Hillsburg Hardware Co.
Summary of Possible Misstatements
12/31/16

Schedule A-3 Date
Prepared by LF 3/15/17
Approved by JA 3/15/17

Audit File Source		Type of Misstatement	Total Amount	POSSIBLE MISSTATEMENT—OVERSTATEMENT (UNDERSTATEMENT) Current Assets	Noncurrent Assets	Current Liabilities	Income Before Tax
B-4	Understated allowance for uncollectible accounts	[EA]	95,000	95,000			95,000
C-8	Accounts receivable/Sales cutoff misstatements	[P]	60,000	(60,000)			(60,000)
D-2	Difference between physical inventory and book figures	[A]	120,000	(120,000)			(120,000)
H-7/2	Unrecorded liabilities	[P]	285,000	(100,000)	(85,000)	(285,000)	100,000
V-10	Repairs expense items that should have been capitalized	[A]	90,000		(90,000)		(90,000)
Totals				(185,000)	(175,000)	(285,000)	(75,000)

[EA] Estimated based on substantive analytical procedures.
[A] Actual population misstatements.
[P] Estimated population misstatements based on the sample, including allowance for sampling risk.

Conclusions

The net effects of the above items are as follows:

	Net Effects	Materiality
Current assets	(185,000)	1,531,000
Total assets	(360,000)	1,841,000
Income before taxes	(75,000)	442,000

None of these aggregate effects or the individual items has a material effect on the financial statements in total or with respect to the components they pertain to. On this basis, adjustment of any or all of the items is passed.

Leslie Franklin
3/15/17

As part of the final review for financial statement disclosures, many CPA firms require the completion of a **financial statement disclosure checklist** for every audit. These questionnaires are designed to remind the auditor of common disclosure problems in financial statements and to facilitate the final review of the entire audit by an independent partner. Figure 24-7 (p. 784) illustrates a partial financial statement disclosure checklist. Naturally, a checklist is not sufficient to replace the auditor's knowledge of the proper application of accounting standards for the circumstances of the audit.

Audit Documentation Review

There are three reasons why an experienced member of the audit firm must thoroughly review audit documentation at the completion of the audit:

1. *To evaluate the performance of inexperienced personnel.* A considerable portion of most audits is performed by audit personnel with fewer than four or five years of experience. These people may have sufficient technical training to conduct an

FIGURE 24-7 **Financial Statement Disclosure Checklist: Property, Plant, and Equipment**

1. Are the following disclosures included in the financial statements or notes:
   a. Balances of major classes of depreciable assets (land, building, equipment, and so forth) at the balance sheet date?
   b. Allowances for depreciation, by class or in total, at the balance sheet date?
   c. General description of depreciation methods for major classes of PP&E?
   d. Total amount of depreciation charged to expense for each income statement presented?
   e. Basis of evaluation?
2. Are carrying amounts of property mortgaged and encumbered by indebtedness disclosed?
3. Are details of sale and leaseback transactions during the period disclosed?
4. Is the carrying amount of property not a part of operating plant—for example, idle or held for investment or sale—segregated?
5. Has consideration been given to disclosure of fully depreciated capital assets still in use and capital assets not presently in use?

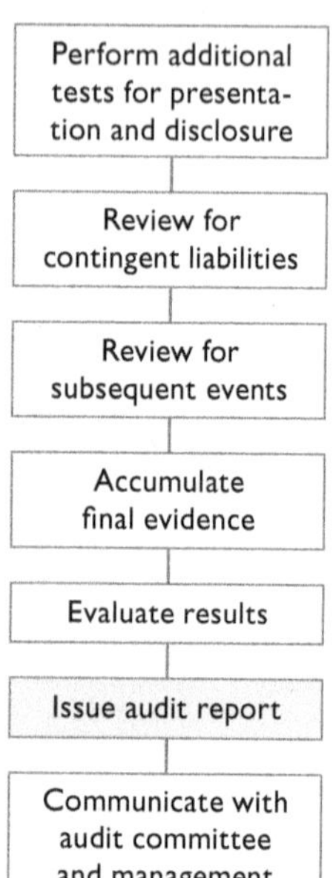
Phase IV—
Completing the Audit
Perform additional tests for presentation and disclosure
Review for contingent liabilities
Review for subsequent events
Accumulate final evidence
Evaluate results
Issue audit report
Communicate with audit committee and management

adequate audit, but their lack of experience affects their ability to make sound professional judgments in complex situations.

2. *To make sure that the audit meets the CPA firm's standard of performance.* Within any CPA firm, the quality of staff performance varies considerably, but careful review by top-level personnel in the firm helps to maintain a uniform quality of auditing.
3. *To counteract the bias that often enters into the auditor's judgment.* Auditors must attempt to remain objective throughout the audit, but they may lose proper perspective on a long audit when complex problems need to be solved.

Except for a final independent review, which is discussed shortly, the **review of audit documentation** should be conducted by someone who is knowledgeable about the client and the circumstances in the audit. Therefore, the auditor's immediate supervisor normally conducts the initial review of audit files prepared by another auditor. For example, the least experienced auditor's work is ordinarily reviewed by the audit senior. The senior's immediate superior, who is normally a supervisor or manager, reviews the senior's work and also reviews, less thoroughly, the schedules of the inexperienced auditor. Finally, the partner assigned to the audit must ultimately review all audit documentation, but the partner reviews those prepared by the supervisor or manager more thoroughly than the others. While performing the review, each reviewer has discussions with the auditor responsible for preparing the audit documentation to learn how significant audit issues were resolved. Except for the final independent review, most audit documentation review is done as each segment of the audit is completed.

Engagement Quality Review

At the completion of larger audits, it is common to have the financial statements and the entire set of audit files reviewed by a completely independent reviewer who has not participated in the audit, but is a member of the audit firm doing the audit. An **engagement quality review**, sometimes referred to as an **independent review**, is required for SEC engagements, including the review of interim financial information and the audit of internal controls. This reviewer often takes an adversarial position to make sure the conduct of the audit was adequate. The audit team must be able to justify the evidence it has accumulated and the conclusions it reached on the basis of the circumstances of the audit.

Summary of Evidence Evaluation

Figure 24-8 summarizes evaluating whether there is sufficient appropriate evidence and whether the evidence supports the opinion on the financial statements. It shows that the auditor evaluates the sufficiency and appropriateness of the evidence by first evaluating achieved audit risk, by account and by cycle, and then making the same

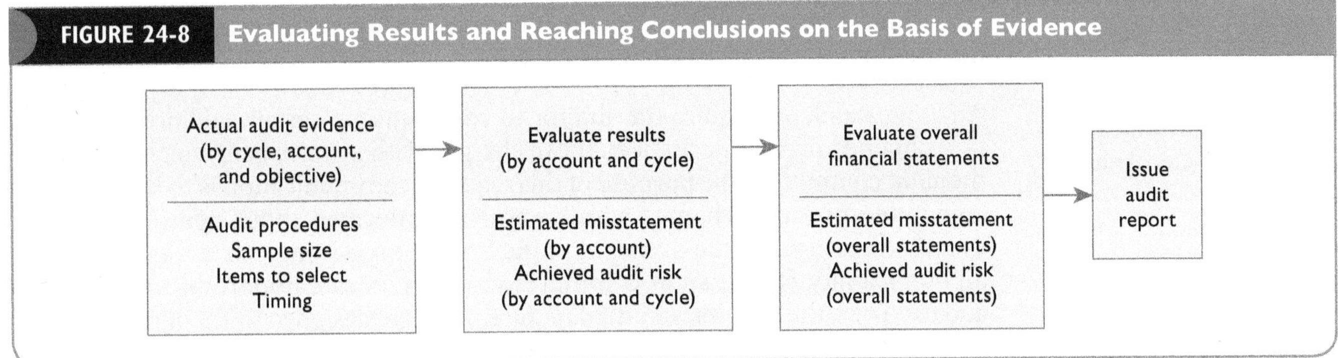

FIGURE 24-8 Evaluating Results and Reaching Conclusions on the Basis of Evidence

evaluation for the overall financial statements. The auditor also evaluates whether the evidence supports the audit opinion by first estimating misstatements in each account and then for the overall financial statements. In practice, the evaluation of achieved audit risk and estimated misstatement are made at the same time. On the basis of these evaluations, the audit report is issued for the financial statements.

ISSUE THE AUDIT REPORT

The auditor should wait to decide the appropriate audit report to issue until all evidence has been accumulated and evaluated, including all steps of completing the audit discussed so far. Because the audit report is the only thing that most users see in the audit process, and the consequences of issuing an inappropriate report can be severe, it is critical that the report be correct.

When a CPA firm decides that a standard unmodified report is inappropriate, there will almost certainly be extensive discussions among technical partners in the CPA firm and often with client personnel. Most CPA firms have comprehensive audit reporting manuals to assist them in selecting the appropriate wording of the report they decide to issue.

COMMUNICATE WITH THE AUDIT COMMITTEE AND MANAGEMENT

OBJECTIVE 24-7

Communicate effectively with the audit committee and management.

After the audit is completed, several potential communications from the auditor may be sent to the audit committee or others charged with governance, including communication of detected fraud and illegal acts, internal control deficiencies, other communications with the audit committee, and a management letter. The first three of these communications are required by auditing standards to make certain that those charged with governance, which is often the audit committee and senior management, are informed of audit findings and auditor recommendations. The fourth item, a management letter, is often communicated to operating management.

Communicate Fraud and Illegal Acts

Auditing standards require the auditor to communicate all fraud and illegal acts to the audit committee or similarly designated group, regardless of materiality. The purpose is to assist the audit committee in performing its supervisory role for reliable financial statements.

Communicate Internal Control Deficiencies

As discussed in Chapter 12, the auditor must also communicate in writing significant internal control deficiencies and material weaknesses in the design or operation of internal control to those charged with governance. In larger companies, this communication is made to the audit committee and in smaller companies, it may be made to the owners or senior management.

Other Communications with Audit Committee

Auditing standards require the auditor to communicate certain additional information obtained during the audit to those charged with governance, which is generally the audit committee. The purpose of this required communication is to keep the audit committee, or others charged with governance, informed about significant and relevant information for the oversight of the financial reporting process and to provide an opportunity for the audit committee to communicate important matters to the auditor. Thus, the auditing standard requirements are designed to encourage two-way communications between the auditor and those charged with governance. There are four principal purposes of this required communication:

1. *To communicate auditor responsibilities in the audit of financial statements.* This communication includes discussion by the auditor that the audit of financial statements is designed to obtain reasonable, rather than absolute, assurance about material misstatements in the financial statements. For audits of financial statements that do not include an audit of internal control over financial reporting, the communication also indicates that the auditor is not providing an opinion on the effectiveness of internal control, in addition to other limitations of an audit of financial statements.
2. *To provide an overview of the scope and timing of the audit.* The purpose of this required communication is to provide a high-level overview, such as the auditor's approach to addressing significant risks and consideration of internal control, and timing of the audit. Details of the nature and timing of audit procedures is not appropriate to avoid compromising the effectiveness and predictability of the audit.
3. *To provide those charged with governance with significant findings arising during the audit.* These communications include discussion of material misstatements detected during the audit that were corrected by the client and uncorrected misstatements that were accumulated by the auditor. The auditor's view of qualitative aspects of significant accounting practices and estimates should also be presented, as well as significant difficulties encountered during the audit, including disagreements with management, among other matters.
4. *To obtain from those charged with governance information relevant to the audit.* The audit committee or others charged with governance, such as the full board of directors, may share strategic decisions that may affect the nature and timing of the auditor's procedures.

Phase IV—Completing the Audit

- Perform additional tests for presentation and disclosure
- Review for contingent liabilities
- Review for subsequent events
- Accumulate final evidence
- Evaluate results
- Issue audit report
- **Communicate with audit committee and management**

Communications about significant findings arising during the audit are normally made in writing. Communications about other matters may be made orally or in writing, with all oral communications documented in the audit files. Communications should be made timely to allow those charged with governance to take appropriate actions. Generally, communications about the auditor's responsibilities and the audit scope and timing occur early in an audit, while communications about significant findings usually occur throughout the entire engagement period.

The Sarbanes–Oxley Act of 2002 includes additional communication requirements for auditors of public companies. For example, auditors must communicate all alternative treatments of financial information within requirements of accounting standards that have been discussed with management, ramifications of the alternative disclosures and treatments, and the treatment preferred by the auditor. As the audit is completed, the auditor should determine that the audit committee is informed about the initial selection of and changes in significant accounting policies or their application during the current audit period, as well as the reasons for any changes. The auditor should also communicate information about methods used to account for any significant unusual transactions and the effect of significant accounting policies in controversial or emerging areas.

Management Letters

A **management letter** is intended to inform client personnel of the CPA's recommendations for improving any part of the client's business. Most recommendations focus on suggestions for more efficient operations. The combination of the auditor's experience in various businesses and a thorough understanding gained in conducting the audit places the auditor in a unique position to provide assistance to management.

Many CPA firms write a management letter for every audit to demonstrate to management that the firm adds value to the business beyond the audit service provided. Their intent is to encourage a better relationship with management and to suggest additional tax and permitted advisory services that the CPA firm can provide.

A management letter differs from a letter reporting significant deficiencies in internal control, which was discussed in Chapter 12. The latter is required when there are significant deficiencies or material weaknesses in internal control, and must follow a prescribed format and be sent in accordance with the requirements of auditing standards. A management letter is optional and is intended to help the client operate its business more effectively.

Each management letter should be developed to meet the style and preferences of the CPA firm and the needs of the client. Some auditors combine the management letter with the letter about significant deficiencies and material weaknesses. On smaller audits, it is common for the auditor to communicate operational suggestions orally rather than by a management letter.

SUBSEQUENT DISCOVERY OF FACTS

OBJECTIVE 24-8

Identify the auditor's responsibilities when facts affecting the audit report are discovered after its issuance.

After the auditor issues the audit report and completes all communications with management and the audit committee, the audit is finished. Usually, the next major contact between the auditor and client occurs when the planning process of the next year's audit begins.

Although it rarely happens, auditors sometimes learn *after the audited financial statements have been issued* that the financial statements are materially misstated. Examples are the inclusion of material nonexistent sales, the failure to write off obsolete inventory, or the omission of an essential footnote. Similarly, following the issuance of a report on internal control over financial reporting as part of an integrated audit, auditors may become aware of conditions that existed at the date of the report that would have changed their opinion had they been aware of those conditions.

When this **subsequent discovery of facts** occurs, the auditor has an obligation to make certain that users who are relying on the financial statements are informed about the misstatements or change in the conclusion on the effectiveness of internal controls. (If the auditor had known about the misstatements before the audit report was issued, the auditor would have insisted that management correct the misstatements or, alternatively, a different audit report would have been issued.) It does not matter whether the failure to discover the misstatement or material weakness was the fault of the auditor or the client. In either case, the auditor's responsibility remains the same. Although subsequent discovery of facts is not part of completing the audit, it is included in this chapter because it is easier to understand in this context.

If the auditor discovers that the statements are misleading after they have been issued, the most desirable action is to request that the client issue an immediate revision of the financial statements that includes an explanation of the reasons for the revision. If a subsequent period's financial statements are completed before the revised statements would be issued, it is acceptable to disclose the misstatements in the subsequent period's statements. When pertinent, the client should inform the

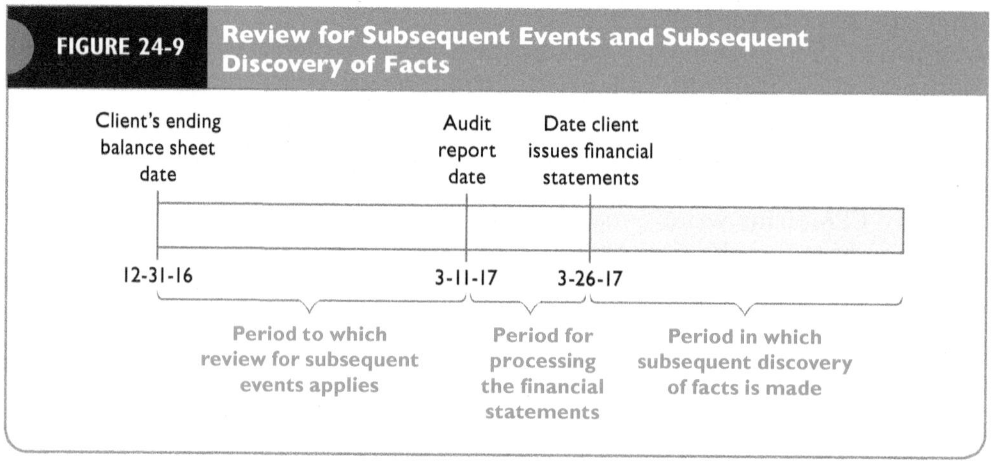

SEC and other regulatory agencies of the misstated financial statements. The auditor is responsible to make certain that the client has taken the appropriate steps to inform users of the misstated statements.

If the client refuses to disclose the misstated statements, the auditor must inform the board of directors. The auditor must also notify regulatory agencies having jurisdiction over the client that the statements are no longer fairly stated and also, when practical, each person who relies on the financial statements. If the stock is publicly held, it is acceptable to request the SEC and the stock exchange to notify stockholders.

The subsequent discovery of facts requiring the recall or reissuance of financial statements *arises only from business events that existed before the date of the auditor's report.* For example, a revision of the financial statements is *not required* if an account receivable is believed to be collectible after an adequate review of the facts at the date of the audit report, but the customer subsequently files bankruptcy. If the customer had filed for bankruptcy before the audit report date, however, there is a subsequent discovery of facts.

The auditor's responsibility for subsequent events review ends on the date of the audit report, when the auditor has gathered sufficient appropriate evidence to form an opinion. Auditors have no responsibility to search for subsequent facts, but if they discover that issued financial statements are incorrectly stated, they must take action to correct them. In most cases, subsequent discovery of facts occurs when auditors discover a material misstatement in issued financial statements during the subsequent year's audit, or when the client reports a misstatement to the auditor.

Figure 24-9 illustrates the periods covered by the review for subsequent events, processing the financial statements, and subsequent discovery of facts after the audit report date. As you review the figure, note that auditors have no responsibility to review subsequent events after the audit report date. If auditors discover subsequent facts after the audit report date (3-11-17), but before the financial statements are issued (3-26-17), they will require that the financial statements be revised before they are issued. Auditors will also follow one of the two options discussed in this chapter's "Dual Dating" section, page 776.

CONCEPT CHECK

1. Explain the purpose of a client letter of representation. What types of information are normally included in the letter?
2. How does an auditor evaluate the unadjusted misstatement schedule (also called summary of possible misstatements) at the end of the audit engagement to assess whether the financial statements are fairly presented?

SUMMARY

The completion phase of the audit is critical to ensuring a quality audit. In this phase, auditors perform additional tests for presentation and disclosure, including reviewing for contingencies and subsequent events. Auditors also review the sufficiency of the audit evidence and the decisions reached to determine whether they support the audit opinion. Auditors then communicate with the audit committee and management about important audit findings and other matters.

ESSENTIAL TERMS

Commitments—agreements that the entity will hold to a fixed set of conditions, such as the purchase or sale of merchandise at a stated price, at a future date, regardless of what happens to profits or to the economy as a whole

Completing the audit checklist—a reminder to the auditor of aspects of the audit that may have been overlooked

Contingent liability—a potential future obligation to an outside party for an unknown amount resulting from activities that have already taken place

Dual-dated audit report—the use of one audit report date for normal subsequent events and a later date for one or more subsequent events that come to the auditor's attention after the date of the audit report

Engagement quality review—a review of the financial statements and the entire set of audit files by a completely independent reviewer to whom the audit team must justify the evidence accumulated and the conclusions reached; also referred to as "independent review"

Financial statement disclosure checklist—a questionnaire that reminds the auditor of disclosure problems commonly encountered in audits and that facilitates final review of the entire audit by an independent partner

Independent review—see "engagement quality review"

Inquiry of the client's attorneys—a letter from the client requesting that legal counsel inform the auditor of pending litigation or any other information involving legal counsel that is relevant to financial statement disclosure

Letter of representation—a written communication from the client to the auditor formalizing statements that the client has made about matters pertinent to the audit

Management letter—an optional letter written by the auditor to a client's management containing the auditor's recommendations for improving any aspect of the client's business

Other information included in annual reports—information that is not a part of the financial statements but is published with them; auditors must read this information for inconsistencies with the financial statements

Review for subsequent events—the auditing procedures performed by auditors to identify and evaluate subsequent events; also known as a *post-balance-sheet review*

Review of audit documentation—a review of the completed audit files by another member of the audit firm to ensure quality and counteract bias

Subsequent discovery of facts—auditor discovery that the financial statements are materially misstated, or that the opinion on internal controls over financial reporting may not have been appropriate, *after* they have been issued

Subsequent events—transactions and other pertinent events that occurred after the balance sheet date that affect the fair presentation or disclosure of the statements being audited

Unadjusted misstatement audit schedule—a summary of immaterial misstatements not adjusted at the time they were found, used to help the auditor assess whether the combined amount is material; also known as a *summary of possible misstatements*

Unasserted claim—a potential legal claim against a client where the condition for a claim exists but no claim has been filed

REVIEW QUESTIONS

24-1 **(OBJECTIVE 24-1)** Identify and describe the four presentation and disclosure audit objectives. Explain how many of the procedures to test presentation and disclosure audit objectives are integrated with tests performed in earlier stages of the audit.

24-2 **(OBJECTIVE 24-2)** Explain why an auditor is interested in a client's future commitments to purchase raw materials at a fixed price.

24-3 **(OBJECTIVE 24-2)** Distinguish between a contingent liability and an actual liability and give three examples of each.

24-4 **(OBJECTIVE 24-2)** In the audit of the James Mobley Company, you are concerned about the possibility of contingent liabilities resulting from a patent dispute. Discuss the procedures you could use for an extensive investigation in this area.

24-5 **(OBJECTIVE 24-3)** Explain why the analysis of legal expense is an essential part of every audit.

24-6 **(OBJECTIVES 24-2, 24-3)** During the audit of the Merrill Manufacturing Company, Ralph Pyson, CPA, has become aware of four lawsuits against the client through discussions with the client, reading corporate minutes, and reviewing correspondence files. How should Pyson determine the materiality of the lawsuits and the proper disclosure in the financial statements?

24-7 **(OBJECTIVE 24-3)** Distinguish between an asserted and an unasserted claim. Explain why a client's attorney may not reveal an unasserted claim.

24-8 **(OBJECTIVE 24-3)** Describe the action that an auditor should take if an attorney refuses to provide information that is within the attorney's jurisdiction and may directly affect the fair presentation of the financial statements.

24-9 **(OBJECTIVE 24-4)** What major considerations should the auditor take into account in determining how extensive the review of subsequent events should be?

24-10 **(OBJECTIVE 24-4)** Identify five audit procedures normally done as a part of the review for subsequent events.

24-11 **(OBJECTIVES 24-4, 24-8)** Five months after issuing an unqualified audit opinion and an unqualified opinion on internal controls for the audit of the year ended December 31, 2016, for a large publicly traded client, the client and the auditor become aware of a material misstatement in sales revenue for the year in question, which was the result of a material weakness in internal controls. Is this a subsequent event or a subsequent discovery of facts? What are the auditor's responsibilities related to the audit opinion and the opinion on internal controls?

24-12 **(OBJECTIVE 24-5)** Miles Lawson, CPA, believes that the final summarization is the easiest part of the audit if careful planning is followed throughout the audit. He makes sure that each segment of the audit is completed before he goes on to the next. When the last segment of the audit is completed, he is finished with the audit. He believes this may cause each part of the audit to take a little longer, but he makes up for it by not having to do the final summarization. Evaluate Lawson's approach.

24-13 **(OBJECTIVES 24-1, 24-5, 24-6)** Compare and contrast the accumulation of audit evidence and the evaluation of the adequacy of the disclosures in the financial statements. Give two examples in which adequate disclosure could depend heavily on the accumulation of evidence and two others in which audit evidence does not normally significantly affect the adequacy of the disclosure.

24-14 **(OBJECTIVES 24-5, 24-7)** Distinguish between a management letter and a letter about significant deficiencies in internal control. Give examples of items that might be included in a management letter.

24-15 **(OBJECTIVE 24-5)** Explain what is meant by information accompanying basic financial statements. Provide two examples of such information. What levels of assurance may the CPA offer for this information?

24-16 **(OBJECTIVE 24-6)** Distinguish between regular audit documentation review and independent review and state the purpose of each. Give two examples of potential findings in each of these two types of review.

24-17 **(OBJECTIVE 24-7)** Describe matters that the auditor must communicate to audit committees of public companies.

MULTIPLE CHOICE QUESTIONS FROM CPA EXAMINATIONS

24-18 **(OBJECTIVES 24-2, 24-4)** The following questions deal with contingent liabilities and the review for subsequent events. Choose the best response.

a. When a contingency is resolved subsequent to the issuance of audited financial statements, which correctly contained disclosure of the contingency in the footnotes based on information available at the date of issuance, the auditor should
   (1) take no action regarding the event.
   (2) insist that the client issue revised financial statements.
   (3) inform the audit committee that the report cannot be relied on.
   (4) inform the appropriate authorities that the report cannot be relied on.

b. Which of the following would be least likely to be included in a standard inquiry to the client's attorney?
   (1) A list provided by the client of pending litigation or asserted or unasserted claims with which the attorney has had some involvement
   (2) A request for the attorney to opine on the correct accounting treatment associated with an outstanding claim or pending lawsuit outcome
   (3) A request that the attorney provide information about the status of pending litigation
   (4) A request for the attorney to identify any pending litigation or threatened legal action not identified on a list provided by the client

c. An audit report was dual-dated for a subsequent event disclosed in the financial statements, which occurred after the completion of the evidence collection process but before the issuance of the financial statements. The auditor's responsibility for events occurring subsequent to the completion of the evidence collection process was
   (1) limited to include only events occurring before the date of the last subsequent event referred to.
   (2) extended to subsequent events occurring through the date of issuance of the financial statements.
   (3) limited to the specific events referred to.
   (4) extended to include all events occurring since the completion of the evidence collection process.

d. An example of an event occurring in the period between the end of the year being audited and the date of the auditor's report that normally will not require disclosure in the financial statements or auditor's report is
   (1) serious damage to the company's plant from a widespread flood.
   (2) issuance of a widely advertised capital stock issue with restrictive covenants.
   (3) settlement of a large liability for considerably less than the amount recorded.
   (4) decreased sales volume resulting from a general business recession.

24-19 **(OBJECTIVES 24-5, 24-7)** The following questions concern communications between management, those charged with governance, and the auditor. Choose the best response.

a. Which of the following is not a required item to be communicated by the auditor to the audit committee or others charged with governance?
   (1) Information about the auditor's responsibility in an audit of financial statements
   (2) Information about the overall scope and timing of the audit
   (3) Recommendations for improving the client's business
   (4) Significant findings arising from the audit

b. Written management representations obtained by the auditor in connection with a financial statement audit should include a
   (1) summary of all corrected misstatements.
   (2) statement of management's belief that any uncorrected misstatements are in fact not misstatements.
   (3) statement of management's belief that the effects of uncorrected misstatements are not material.
   (4) summary of all uncorrected misstatements.

c. A management letter
   (1) is the auditor's report on significant deficiencies and material weaknesses in internal control.
   (2) contains recommendations from the auditor designed to help the client improve the efficiency and effectiveness of its business.
   (3) is mandatory in all audits and must be dated the same date as the audit report.
   (4) contains management's representations to the auditor documenting statements made by management to the auditor during the audit about matters affecting the financial statements.

24-20 **(OBJECTIVE 24-5)** The following questions concern information accompanying basic financial statements. Choose the best response.

a. The Form 10-K filed by management of a public company includes a section on management's discussion and analysis (MD&A) in addition to the annual financial statements. Which of the following best describes the auditor's responsibility for the MD&A information?
   (1) The auditor must perform sufficient appropriate audit procedures to opine on the MD&A information.
   (2) The auditor has no responsibilities related to the MD&A disclosures.
   (3) The auditor must read the MD&A information to determine if there is any material inconsistency with the audited financial statements.
   (4) The auditor must provide a disclaimer of opinion related to the MD&A information.

b. Management of Thurman Corporation included additional supplementary information in documents that include the audited financial statements for the year ended December 31, 2016. Management has asked its audit firm, Wally, CPAs, whether they can report on the supplementary information. Which of the following conditions would preclude Wally, CPAs, from conducting this engagement?
   (1) The supplementary information is derived from the accounting records used to generate the basic financial statements.
   (2) The supplementary information covers the period January 1, 2016, through February 15, 2017.
   (3) Wally's opinion on the basic financial statements was unqualified.
   (4) When evaluating supplementary information, Wally plans to use the same materiality threshold as that used in the audit of the basic financial statements.

c. Investment and property schedules are presented for purposes of additional analysis in a document outside the basic financial statements. The schedules are not required supplementary information. When the auditor is engaged to report on whether the supplementary information is fairly stated in relation to the audited financial statements as a whole, the measurement of materiality is the
   (1) greater of the individual schedule of investments or schedule of property by itself.
   (2) lesser of the individual schedule of investments or schedule of property by itself.
   (3) same as that used in forming an opinion on the basic financial statements as a whole.
   (4) combined total of both the individual schedules of investments and property as a whole.

MULTIPLE CHOICE QUESTIONS FROM BECKER CPA EXAM REVIEW

24-21 **(OBJECTIVES 24-2, 24-5, 24-7)** The following questions concern contingencies, subsequent events, and communications with those charged with governance. Choose the best response.

a. A client acquired 25% of its outstanding capital stock after year-end but prior to the date of the auditor's report. The auditor should
   (1) advise management to adjust the balance sheet to reflect the acquisition.
   (2) issue pro forma financial statements giving effect to the acquisition as if it had occurred at year-end.
   (3) advise management to disclose the acquisition in the notes to the financial statements.
   (4) disclose the acquisition in the opinion paragraph of the auditor's report.

b. Which of the following statements is correct about an auditor's required communication with those charged with governance?
   (1) Any matters communicated with those charged with governance are also required to be communicated to the entity's management.
   (2) The auditor is required to inform those charged with governance about significant misstatements discovered by the auditor and subsequently corrected by management.
   (3) Disagreements with management about the application of accounting principles must be communicated in writing to those charged with governance.
   (4) The auditor should not communicate frequently recurring misstatements unless they are material.

c. In addition to making management inquiries, an auditor should perform the following procedures to identify client contingencies with the exception of
   (1) obtaining a client representation letter.
   (2) reviewing derivative transactions reflected on the quarter-end balance sheet.
   (3) reviewing the status of long-term leases.
   (4) discussing sales contracts with the sales manager.

DISCUSSION QUESTIONS AND PROBLEMS

24-22 **(OBJECTIVES 24-1, 24-2)** Elizabeth Johnson, CPA, has completed the audit of notes payable and other liabilities for Valley River Electrical Services and now plans to audit contingent liabilities and commitments.

Required

a. Distinguish between contingent liabilities and commitments and explain why both are important in an audit.
b. Identify three useful audit procedures for uncovering contingent liabilities that Johnson will likely perform in the normal conduct of the audit, even if she had no responsibility for uncovering contingencies.
c. Identify three other procedures Johnson is likely to perform specifically for the purpose of identifying undisclosed contingencies to help her obtain evidence about the completeness presentation and disclosure objective.
d. Identify three useful audit procedures for uncovering commitments that Johnson will likely perform as part of the audit in other accounts.

24-23 **(OBJECTIVE 24-2)** In an audit of the Marco Corporation as of December 31, 2016, the following situations exist. No entries have been made in the accounting records in relation to these items.

1. During the year 2016, the Marco Corporation was named as a defendant in a suit for damages by the Dalton Company for breach of contract. An adverse decision to the Marco Corporation was rendered and the Dalton Company was awarded $4,000,000 damages. At the time of the audit, the case was under appeal to a higher court.
2. On December 23, 2016, the Marco Corporation declared a common stock dividend of 1,000 shares with a par value of $1,000,000 of its common stock, payable February 2, 2017, to the common stockholders of record December 30, 2016.
3. The Marco Corporation has guaranteed the payment of interest on the 10-year, first mortgage bonds of the Newart Company, an affiliate. Outstanding bonds of the Newart Company amount to $5,500,000 with interest payable at 5% per annum, due June 1 and December 1 of each year. The bonds were issued by the Newart Company on December 1, 2014, and all interest payments have been met by that company with the exception of the payment due December 1, 2016. The Marco Corporation states that it will pay the defaulted interest to the bondholders on January 15, 2017.

Required

a. Define contingent liability.
b. Describe the audit procedures you would use to learn about each of the situations listed.
c. Describe the nature of the adjusting entries or disclosure, if any, you would make for each of these situations.*

24-24 **(OBJECTIVE 24-3)** In analyzing legal expense for the Boastman Bottle Company, Mary Little, CPA, observes that the company has paid legal fees to three different law firms during the current year. In accordance with her CPA firm's normal operating practice, Little requests standard attorney letters as of the balance sheet date from each of the three law firms.

On the last day of field work, Little notes that one of the attorney letters has not yet been received. The second letter contains a statement to the effect that the law firm deals exclusively in registering patents and refuses to comment on any lawsuits or other legal affairs of the client. The third attorney's letter states that there is an outstanding unpaid bill due from the client and recognizes the existence of a potentially material lawsuit against the client but refuses to comment further to protect the legal rights of the client.

Required

a. Evaluate Little's approach to sending the attorney letters and her follow-up on the responses.
b. What should Little do about each of the letters?

24-25 **(OBJECTIVES 24-4, 24-8)** The field work for the June 30, 2016, audit of Tracy Brewing Company was finished August 19, 2016, and the completed financial statements, accompanied by the signed audit reports, were mailed September 6, 2016. In each of the highly material independent events (a. through h.), state the appropriate action (1 through 4) for the situation and justify your response. The alternative actions are as follows:

1. Adjust the June 30, 2016, financial statements.
2. Disclose the information in a footnote in the June 30, 2016, financial statements.
3. Request the client to recall the June 30, 2016, statements for revision.
4. No action is required.

The events are as follows:

a. On August 6, 2016, the auditor discovered that a debtor of Tracy Brewing went bankrupt on July 30, 2016. The cause of the bankruptcy was an unexpected loss of a major lawsuit on July 15, 2016, resulting from a product deficiency suit by a different customer.
b. On December 14, 2016, the auditor discovered that a debtor of Tracy Brewing went bankrupt on July 15, 2016, due to declining financial health. The sale generating the receivable had taken place January 15, 2016.
c. On December 14, 2016, the auditor discovered that a debtor of Tracy Brewing went bankrupt on October 2, 2016. The sale had taken place April 15, 2016, but the amount appeared collectible at June 30, 2016, and August 19, 2016.

*Based on AICPA question paper, American Institute of Certified Public Accountants.

d. On August 15, 2016, the auditor discovered that a debtor of Tracy Brewing went bankrupt on August 1, 2016. The most recent sale had taken place April 2, 2015, and no cash receipts had been received since that date.

e. On July 20, 2016, Tracy Brewing settled a lawsuit out of court that had originated in 2013 and is currently listed as a contingent liability.

f. On September 14, 2016, Tracy Brewing lost a court case that had originated in 2015 for an amount equal to the lawsuit. The June 30, 2016, footnotes state that in the opinion of legal counsel, there will be a favorable settlement.

g. On July 20, 2016, a lawsuit was filed against Tracy Brewing for a patent infringement action that allegedly took place in early 2016. In the opinion of legal counsel, there is a danger of a significant loss to the client.

h. On May 31, 2016, the auditor discovered an uninsured lawsuit against Tracy Brewing that had originated on February 28, 2016.

24-26 **(OBJECTIVE 24-5)** Callie Peters is completing the audit of MakingNewFriends.com for the year ended December 31, 2016. Callie has been the audit manager on this engagement for the past three years. MakingNewFriends.com issued stock two years ago, but has had difficulty establishing a loyal client base and generating advertising revenues. In reviewing results for the current year, Callie noted the client has had operating losses for the past three years, and its working capital ratio has declined from 1.2 in 2015 to 0.9 in 2016. Callie discussed plans for the future with the management of MakingNewFriends.com, and they indicated they are planning on obtaining debt financing in fiscal 2017; however, they have not yet secured the financing with a bank. Management also indicated they are aggressively pursuing new advertising contracts and plan to increase advertising revenues by 20% in 2017.

Required

a. According to auditing standards, what is the auditor's obligation to consider whether the client can continue as a going concern?

b. Over what time period is the auditor required to consider the client's ability to continue as a going concern?

c. What factors discussed above are relevant for a going-concern assessment for MakingNewFriends.com? What additional information might the auditor consider in the going-concern assessment?

d. What responsibility does the auditor have to evaluate whether management's plans will be effective?

24-27 **(OBJECTIVE 24-5)** As a part of the audit of Ren Gold Manufacturing Company, a nonpublic company, management requests basic financial statements and separately, the same basic financial statements accompanied by additional information. Management informs you that the intent is to use the basic financial statements for bankers, other creditors, and the two owners who are not involved in management. The basic financial statements accompanied by the additional information are to be used only by management. Management requests the inclusion of specific information but asks that no audit work be done beyond what is needed for the basic financial statements. The following is requested:

1. A schedule of insurance in force.
2. The auditor's feelings about the adequacy of the insurance coverage.
3. An aged trial balance of accounts receivable and evaluation of the adequacy of the allowance for uncollectible accounts.
4. A summary of fixed asset additions.
5. Material weaknesses in internal control and recommendations to improve internal control.
6. A 5-year summary of the most important company ratios, with the appropriate ratios to be determined at the auditor's discretion.
7. A schedule of notes payable accompanied by interest rates, collateral, and a payment schedule.

Required

a. What is the difference between basic financial statements and additional information?

b. What are the purposes of additional information accompanying basic financial statements?

c. For the previously listed items (1 through 7), state which ones could appropriately be included as additional information. Give reasons for your answer.
d. Assume that an unmodified opinion is appropriate for the basic financial statements report, that no testing was done beyond that required for the basic financial statements report, and that only appropriate information is included in the additional information. Write the proper auditor's report.

24-28 (OBJECTIVE 24-5) Access AICPA Auditing Standard AU-C 450, *Evaluation of Misstatements Identified During the Audit* (www.aicpa.org), to answer the following questions:

Required

a. Describe the three types of misstatements that can be identified by the auditor. What factors may suggest that the misstatement is not an isolated occurrence?
b. What factors should the auditor consider in determining whether uncorrected misstatements are material, either individually or in the aggregate?
c. What documentation is required by AU-C 450?

24-29 (OBJECTIVE 24-6) The following items were discovered during the December 31, 2016, audit of the financial statements of Westmoreland Corporation:

1. The company's financial statements did not include an accrual for bonuses earned by senior management in 2016 but payable in March 2017. The aggregate bonus amount was $125,000.
2. Equipment originally costing $725,000 that was fully depreciated with a remaining residual value of $60,000 was sold for $85,000 on December 29, 2016. The purchaser agreed to pay for the equipment by January 15, 2017.
3. Based on close examination of the client's aged accounts receivable trial balance and correspondence files with customers, the auditor determined that management's allowance for bad debts is overstated by $44,000.
4. Expenses totaling $52,000 associated with the maintenance of equipment were inappropriately debited to the equipment account.
5. Marketing expenses of $43,000 were incorrectly classified as cost of goods sold.
6. The company received new computer equipment on January 3, 2017, that had been ordered and shipped F.O.B. shipping point to Westmoreland on December 27, 2016. No entry has been recorded for this purchase, which was financed by a long-term note payable due in full June 30, 2018.

Required

a. Prepare an Unadjusted Misstatement Audit Schedule using the following format (see Figure 24-6 on page 783 as an example):

	Possible Misstatement – Overstatement (Understatement)				
Total Amount	**Current Assets**	**Noncurrent Assets**	**Current Liabilities**	**Noncurrent Liabilities**	**Income Before Tax**

b. Balance sheet and income statement materiality for the audit of Westmoreland financial statements is $75,000. What is your conclusion about the financial statements if the audit findings are not corrected by Westmoreland management before you issue the audit report?

24-30 (OBJECTIVE 24-7) In a letter to the audit committee of the Cline Wholesale Company, Jerry Schwartz, CPA, informed them of material weaknesses in the controls over inventory. In a separate letter to senior management, he elaborated on how the material weaknesses could result in a significant misstatement of inventory by the failure to recognize the existence of obsolete items. In addition, Schwartz made specific recommendations in the management letter on how to improve internal control and save clerical time by installing a new computer system for the company's perpetual records. Management accepted the recommendations and installed the system under Schwartz's direction. For several months, the system worked beautifully, but unforeseen problems developed when a master file was erased. The cost of reproducing and processing the inventory records to correct the error was significant, and management decided to scrap the entire project. The company sued Schwartz for failure to use adequate professional judgment in making the recommendations.

Required

a. What is Schwartz's legal and professional responsibility in the issuance of management letters?
b. Discuss the major considerations that will determine whether he is liable in this situation.

CASE

24-31 **(OBJECTIVE 24-6)** In your audit of Aviary Industries for calendar year 2016, you found a number of matters that you believe represent possible adjustments to the company's books. These matters are described below. Management's attitude is that "once the books are closed, they're closed," and management does not want to make any adjustments. Planning materiality for the audit was $100,000, determined by computing 5% of expected income before taxes. Actual income before taxes on the financial statements prior to any adjustments is $1,652,867.

Possible adjustments:

1. Several credit memos that were processed and recorded after year-end relate to sales and accounts receivable for 2016. These total $26,451.
2. Inventory cutoff tests indicate that $25,673 of inventory received on December 30, 2016, was recorded as purchases and accounts payable in 2017. These items were included in the inventory count at year-end and therefore were included in ending inventory.
3. Inventory cutoff tests indicate several sales invoices recorded in 2016 for goods that were shipped in early 2017. The goods were included in inventory even though they were set aside in a separate area. The total amount of these shipments was $41,814.
4. The company wrote several checks at the end of 2016 for accounts payable that were held and not mailed until January 15, 2017. These totaled $43,671. Recorded cash and accounts payable at December 31, 2016, are $2,356,553 and $2,666,290, respectively.
5. The company has not established a reserve for obsolescence of inventories. Your tests indicate that such a reserve is appropriate in an amount somewhere between $15,000 and $30,000.
6. Your review of the allowance for uncollectible accounts indicates that it may be understated by between $35,000 and $55,000.

Required

a. Determine the adjustments that you believe must be made for Aviary's financial statements to be fairly presented. Include the amounts and accounts affected by each adjustment.
b. Why may Aviary Industries' management resist making these adjustments?
c. Explain what you consider the most positive way of approaching management personnel to convince them to make your proposed changes.
d. Describe your responsibilities related to unadjusted misstatements that management has determined are immaterial individually and in the aggregate.
e. Assuming Aviary Industries is an accelerated filer public company, describe how the noted adjustments might impact your audit report on internal control over financial reporting.

OTHER ASSURANCE AND NONASSURANCE SERVICES

CHAPTERS 25–26

Chapter 1 introduced assurance and nonassurance services offered by CPA firms and other types of auditors. Assurance services other than audits have become increasingly important to both CPA firms and other auditors. The two chapters in **PART 6** expand on that discussion.

- **Chapter 25** deals with assurance and nonassurance services, both traditional and emerging, that CPA firms offer.
- **Chapter 26** covers services performed most often by governmental and internal auditors, including internal financial auditing, governmental financial auditing, and operational auditing.

OTHER ASSURANCE SERVICES

CHAPTER

25

Skepticism Applies to All Types of Engagements

Barnhart Construction Company was a contractor specializing in apartment complexes in the Southwest. The owner of the construction company, David Barnhart, reached an agreement with a promoter named Alton Leonard to serve as a contractor on three construction projects Leonard was currently marketing. One problem with the agreement was that Barnhart would not receive final payment for the construction work until all the partnership units were sold.

The first partnership offering was completely sold and Barnhart was paid. Unfortunately, the next two partnerships were not completely sold. To solve this problem, Barnhart loaned money to relatives and key employees, who bought the necessary interests for the partnerships to close so that Barnhart would receive the final payment.

Renee Lathrup, CPA, a sole practitioner, was engaged to conduct a review of Barnhart Construction's financial statements. She noticed that the accounting records showed loans receivable from a number of employees and individuals named Barnhart. She also observed that the loans were made just before the second and third partnerships closed and that they were in multiples of $15,000, the cost of a partnership unit. Lathrup asked Barnhart to explain what had happened. Barnhart told Lathrup, "When I received the money from the first partnership escrow, I wanted to do something nice for relatives and employees who had been loyal to me over the years." He told Lathrup, "This is just my way of sharing my good fortune with the ones I love. The equality of the amounts is just a coincidence."

When Lathrup considered the reasonableness of this scenario, she found it hard to believe. First, the timing was odd. Second, the amounts seemed to be an unusual coincidence. Third, if he really had wanted to do something special for these folks, why hadn't he given them something, rather than loaned them money? Lathrup asked that the promoter, Leonard, send her detailed information on the subscriptions for each partnership. Leonard refused, stating that he was under legal obligation to keep all information confidential. When Lathrup pressed Barnhart, he also refused further cooperation, although he did say he would "represent" to Lathrup that the loans had nothing to do with closing the partnerships so that he could get his money. At this point, Lathrup withdrew from the engagement.

LEARNING OBJECTIVES

After studying this chapter, you should be able to

25-1 Understand the level of assurance and evidence requirements for review, compilation, and preparation services.

25-2 Describe special engagements to review interim financial information for public companies.

25-3 Distinguish AICPA attestation standards from auditing standards and know the types of engagements to which they apply.

25-4 Describe engagements to report on internal controls at service organizations (SOC reports).

25-5 Understand special engagements to attest to prospective financial statements.

25-6 Define agreed-upon procedures engagements.

25-7 Describe other audit and limited assurance engagements related to historical financial statements.

Up to this chapter, the book has primarily focused on audits of historical financial statements prepared in accordance with applicable accounting standards. Now, other types of assurance services offered by CPAs involving historical financial statements are discussed, such as reviews of historical financial statements and limited assurance engagements involving historical financial statements to meet specific needs of financial statement users. The chapter also examines assurance services for several types of attestation engagements that do not involve historical financial statements, such as reports on service organizations and reports on forecasted financial statements.

REVIEW, COMPILATION, AND PREPARATION SERVICES

OBJECTIVE 25-1

Understand the level of assurance and evidence requirements for review, compilation, and preparation services.

Many nonpublic companies have their financial statements reviewed, compiled, or prepared by a CPA, instead of having them audited. The opening story about Barnhart Construction Company is an example of a review service. A company's management may believe that an audit is unnecessary because no bank or regulatory agency requires one and management sees no need for audited statements for internal use. Instead, the company may engage the CPA to assist in the preparation of financial statements, either for internal use or to provide to creditors or lenders under loan agreements. Depending on the size of the loan, a lender may require a nonpublic entity to engage a CPA to compile or review financial statements and issue a related report, rather than conduct an audit. A review provides limited assurance on the financial statements, whereas a compilation report provides no expressed assurance. Other nonpublic entities may engage a CPA to prepare the financial statements without having the CPA issue a report.

The standards for preparation, compilation, and review engagements of financial statements, called **Statements on Standards for Accounting and Review Services (SSARS)**, are issued by the Accounting and Review Services Committee of the AICPA. This committee has authority equivalent to the Auditing Standards Board for services involving unaudited financial statements of nonpublic companies. Because they are not doing audits, SSARS refer to CPAs performing review, compilation, and preparation services as accountants, not auditors.

Because the assurance provided in a preparation, compilation, or review engagement is considerably below that of audits, less evidence is required for these services and they can be provided at a lower fee than an audit. Figure 25-1 illustrates the differences in evidence accumulation and level of assurance for audit, review, compilation, and preparation engagements. The amount of evidence and assurance needed for each engagement is not defined by the profession and therefore depends on the accountant's judgment.

FIGURE 25-1 Relationship Between Evidence Accumulation and Assurance Attained

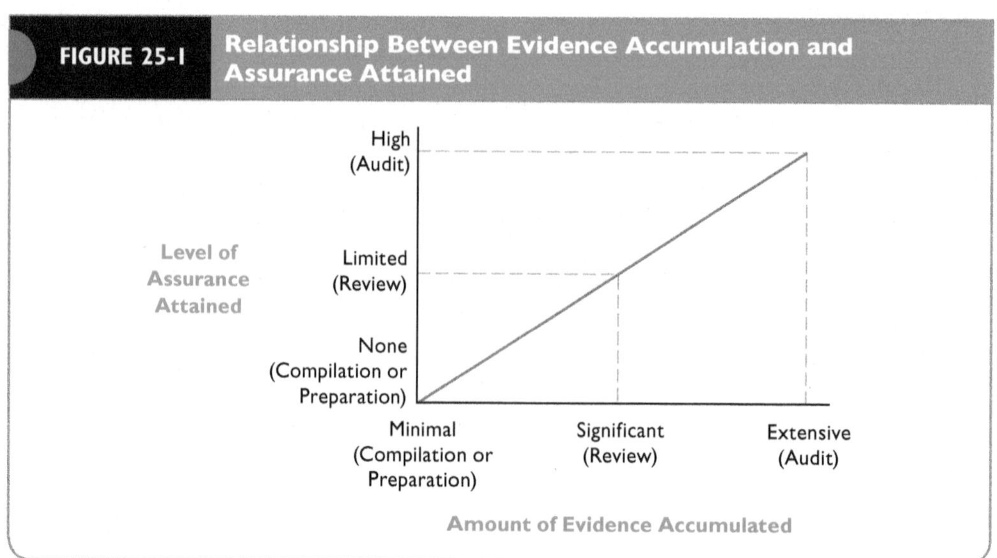

Because review, compilation, and preparation services provide less assurance than audits, the accountant should establish an understanding with the client about the services to be provided through a written engagement letter. The understanding should include a description of the objectives of the engagement, management's responsibilities, the accountant's responsibilities, the type and limitations of the service to be provided, and a description of the type of compilation or review report expected to be issued. As described in the vignette below, the Accounting and Review Services Committee (ARSC) has recently completed a Clarity Project similar to the Auditing Standards Board Clarity Project for auditing standards. The requirements for review, compilation, and preparation services are now discussed in greater detail.

Review Services

A **review service (SSARS review)** engagement allows the accountant to express limited assurance that the financial statements are in accordance with applicable accounting standards, including appropriate informative disclosures, or other comprehensive basis of accounting (OCBOA), such as the cash basis of accounting. CPAs must be independent of the client for review service engagements.

Procedures Suggested for Reviews The evidence for a review engagement consists *primarily of inquiries of management and analytical procedures,* substantially fewer procedures than those required for an audit. For reviews, accountants do not obtain an understanding of internal control, test controls, assess fraud risk, or do substantive tests of transactions or tests of balances, such as confirmation of receivables or physical examination of inventory.

SSARS require the accountant to obtain evidence that consists of the following for a review engagement:

- *Obtain agreement on engagement terms.* The accountant should agree upon the terms of the engagement with management or those charged with governance. SSARS require that the agreement of terms be documented in an engagement letter or other suitable form of written agreement.
- *Obtain knowledge of the accounting principles and practices of the client's industry.* The accountant can study AICPA industry guides or other sources to obtain industry knowledge. The level of knowledge for reviews can be somewhat less than for an audit.
- *Obtain knowledge of the client.* The information should be about the nature of the client's business transactions, its ownership structure, key personnel, accounting records and employees, the accounting principles and practices used by the client, and the content of the financial statements. The level of knowledge can be less than for an audit.

SSARS CLARITY PROJECT

The Accounting and Review Services Committee (ARSC) recently completed its Clarity Project to substantially revise all existing compilation and review standards using drafting provisions similar to those used by the Auditing Standards Board when redrafting auditing standards. However, there was one notable difference in the ARSC drafting conventions. Specifically, ARSC did not use international standards as the base standard when revising the SSARS given unique aspects of the financial reporting environment in the United States. But, similar to the clarified auditing standards, the redrafted SSARS establish objectives for each standard, include definitions, and separate application guidance and other materials from the requirements.

The Clarity Project was completed in October 2014 when ARSC issued SSARS No. 21, *Statement on Standards for Accounting and Review Services: Clarification and Recodification.* That standard superseded all prior SSARS standards except SSARS No. 14, *Compilation of Pro Forma Financial Information,* which is currently being redrafted. SSARS No. 21 also introduced the new preparation engagement service, which is described in more detail later in this chapter. The clarified SSARS are structured as follows:

- Section 60, *General Principles for Engagements Performed in Accordance with Statements on Standards for Accounting and Review Services*
- Section 70, *Preparation of Financial Statements*
- Section 80, *Compilation Engagements*
- Section 90, *Review of Financial Statements*

These sections are codified in the AICPA Professional Standards as AR-C sections.

Source: AICPA *Professional Standards,* Volume 2 (as of June 1, 2015).

- *Make inquiries of management.* Inquiry is the most important review procedure. The objective is to determine whether the financial statements are fairly presented, assuming that management does not intend to deceive the accountant. Inquiries must be made of the appropriate client personnel and typically involve discussions, such as the following illustrative inquiries:

  1. Describe the accounting standards framework used to develop the financial statements, including your procedures for recording, classifying, and summarizing transactions and disclosing information in the statements.
  2. What unusual or significant transactions occurred this year, including important actions taken at meetings of stockholders and the board of directors?
  3. Is each account on the financial statements prepared in conformity with accounting standards and consistently applied?
  4. Do you have knowledge of an actual or suspected fraud, communications from regulatory agencies, subsequent events, or actions taken by those charged with governance that might materially impact the financial statements?

- *Perform analytical procedures.* Based on the accountant's understanding of the industry and knowledge of the client, the accountant designs and performs analytical procedures. These identify relationships and individual items that appear to be unusual. The appropriate analytical procedures are no different from the ones already studied (in Chapters 7 and 8 and in chapters dealing with tests of details of balances). As unusual trends are noted, the accountant engages in further inquiries with client personnel to obtain explanations for any unexpected relationships.
- *Read the financial statements.* The accountant should read the financial statements to determine whether they conform with the financial reporting framework, such as GAAP, IFRS, or OCBOA. The reading of the financial statements may identify items such as headings or section titles in the financial statements that are not consistent with the accounting framework used, arithmetical errors, clerical mistakes, or omitted disclosures.
- *Reconcile the financial statements to underlying accounting records.* The accountant should obtain evidence that the financial statements agree or reconcile with the accounting records.
- *Obtain letter of representation.* The accountant is required to obtain a letter of representation from members of management who are knowledgeable about financial matters.
- *Prepare documentation.* The accountant should prepare documentation that is sufficient in detail to provide a clear understanding of the work performed, the review evidence obtained and its source, and the conclusions reached. Documentation should include the engagement letter, analytical procedures performed, significant matters covered in the inquiries with management, significant findings and issues, communications with management or others regarding possible fraud, and the representation letter.

These procedures ordinarily provide a reasonable basis for obtaining limited assurance. However, in some instances, the accountant may become concerned that information is incorrect, incomplete, or otherwise unsatisfactory. If so, additional procedures should be performed to obtain limited assurance before the accountant issues a standard review services report. And, if the accountant becomes aware that noncompliance with laws or regulations or fraud may have occurred, the accountant should communicate the matter as soon as practicable to the appropriate level of management. When fraud is suspected, the auditor should communicate that to management at least one level above those involved with the suspected fraud. If the fraud involves senior management, the auditor should communicate with those charged with governance, for example, the board of directors.

Form of Report Figure 25-2 provides an example of the review report when the accountant has completed a review engagement and decides that no material changes to the financial statements are needed. In addition to the required report title, the standard review report includes four paragraphs that include the following:

1. An introductory paragraph that identifies the entity and period of financial statements subject to the review and explicitly notes that the accountant has conducted a review. The first paragraph also includes a statement that a review primarily consists of analytical procedures and inquiries and is substantially less in scope than an audit.
2. The second paragraph specifies that management is responsible for the preparation and fairness of the financial statements and for designing, implementing, and maintaining internal controls relevant to financial reporting. The paragraph should include the heading "Management's Responsibility for the Financial Statements."
3. The third paragraph notes that the accountant's responsibility is to conduct a review of management's financial statements in accordance with SSARS and that those standards require the accountant to perform procedures to obtain limited assurance that there are no material modifications that should be made to the financial statements. This paragraph should include the heading "Accountant's Responsibility."
4. The fourth paragraph, which is preceded by the heading "Accountant's Conclusion," expresses limited assurance in the form of negative assurance that "we are not aware of any material modifications that should be made to the accompanying financial statements" in order for them to be in conformity with applicable accounting standards.

The date of the review report should be the date *on which the accountant has accumulated review evidence sufficient to provide a reasonable basis for the report conclusion.* Each page of the financial statements reviewed should include the reference "See independent accountant's review report."

FIGURE 25-2 **Example of Review Report**

Independent Accountant's Review Report

We have reviewed the accompanying financial statements of Archer Technologies, Inc., which comprise the balance sheet as of December 31, 2016, and the related statements of income, changes in stockholders' equity, cash flows for the year then ended, and the related notes to the financial statements. A review includes primarily applying analytical procedures to management's financial data and making inquiries of company management. A review is substantially less in scope than an audit, the objective of which is the expression of an opinion regarding the financial statements as a whole. Accordingly, we do not express such an opinion.

Management's Responsibility for the Financial Statements

Management is responsible for the preparation and fair presentation of these financial statements in accordance with accounting principles generally accepted in the United States of America; this includes the design, implementation, and maintenance of internal control relevant to the preparation and fair presentation of the financial statements that are free from material misstatement, whether due to fraud or error.

Accountant's Responsibility

Our responsibility is to conduct the review engagement in accordance with Statements on Standards for Accounting and Review Services promulgated by the Accounting and Review Services Committee of the AICPA. Those standards require us to perform procedures to obtain limited assurance as a basis for reporting whether we are aware of any material modifications that should be made to the financial statements for them to be in accordance with accounting principles generally accepted in the United States of America. We believe that the results of our procedures provide a reasonable basis for our conclusion.

Accountant's Conclusion

Based on our review, we are not aware of any material modifications that should be made to the accompanying financial statements in order for them to be in accordance with accounting principles generally accepted in the United States of America.

Failure to Follow Applicable Accounting Framework If a client has failed to follow applicable accounting standards in a review engagement, the report must be modified. (Accounting standards are the same for all historical financial statements, including reviews.) The report should disclose the effects of the departure as determined by management or the accountant's review procedures. Even if the effects have not been determined, the disclosure must appear in the report in a *separate paragraph*, under the heading "Known Departures from Accounting Principles Generally Accepted in the United States of America." The following provides an example of suggested wording:

> **Known Departures from Accounting Principles Generally Accepted in the United States of America**
>
> As disclosed in note X to the financial statements, accounting principles generally accepted in the United States of America require that land be stated at cost. Management has informed us that the company has stated its land at appraised value and that, if accounting principles generally accepted in the United States of America had been followed, the land account and stockholders' equity would have been decreased by $500,000.

Compilation Services

A **compilation service** engagement is defined in SSARS as one in which accountants apply accounting and financial reporting expertise to assist management in the preparation of financial statements and issue a report to a client or third party without providing any *CPA assurance about those statements*. Nonpublic entities may engage CPA firms to prepare monthly, quarterly, or annual financial statements and to issue a compilation report that may be provided to external users. The CPA is not required to be independent to perform a compilation and the financial statements can be issued without additional disclosures such as footnotes.

Requirements for Compilation Compilation does not absolve accountants of responsibility, as they are always responsible for exercising due care in performing all duties. In a compilation engagement, an accountant must accomplish the following:

- Establish an understanding with the client in a written engagement letter or other suitable form of written agreement about the objectives of the compilation engagement, type and limitations of the services to be provided including acknowledgement that the accountant does not provide any assurance about the financial statements, and a description of the report, if a report is to be issued. That agreement also should note that management acknowledges its responsibilities for the preparation and fair presentation of the financial statements, including informative disclosures.
- Possess knowledge about the accounting principles and practices of the client's industry.
- Know the client, including a general understanding of the client's organization, the nature of its business transactions, accounting principles and practices used by the client, and content of its financial statements (the knowledge can be less than that for a review).
- Make inquiries to determine whether the client's information is satisfactory.
- Read the compiled financial statements and be alert for any obvious omissions or errors in arithmetic and in the application of accounting standards.
- Request management to provide additional or corrected information if the accountant becomes aware that the records, documents, explanations, or other information, including significant judgments by management, is incomplete, inaccurate, or otherwise unsatisfactory.
- Prepare documentation in sufficient detail to provide a clear understanding of the work performed and any findings or issues that are significant, including any communications with management regarding fraud or illegal acts that came to the accountant's attention.

FIGURE 25-3 Compilation Report with Full Disclosure

Management is responsible for the accompanying financial statements of Williams Company, which comprise the balance sheet as of December 31, 2016, and the related statements of income, changes in stockholders' equity and cash flows for the year then ended, and the related notes to the financial statements in accordance with accounting principles generally accepted in the United States of America. We have performed the compilation engagement in accordance with Statements on Standards for Accounting and Review Services promulgated by the Accounting and Review Services Committee of the AICPA. We did not audit or review the financial statements nor were we required to perform any procedures to verify the accuracy or completeness of the information provided by management. Accordingly, we do not express an opinion, a conclusion, nor provide any form of assurance on these financial statements.

- Request management to revise the financial statements, if the accountant becomes aware of needed revisions to the financial statements required for those statements to be in accordance with the applicable financial reporting framework.

Accountants do not have to make other inquiries or perform other procedures to verify information provided by client personnel. But if they become aware that the statements are not fairly presented, they should obtain additional information. If the client refuses to provide the information, the accountant should withdraw from the compilation engagement.

Form of Report SSARS define three types of compilation reports. The use of each depends on whether management elects to include all the required disclosures with the financial statements and whether the accountant is independent.

1. *Compilation with full disclosure.* A compilation of this type requires disclosures in accordance with accounting standards, the same as for audited financial statements or reviews, as illustrated by Figure 25-3.
2. *Compilation that omits substantially all disclosures.* Figure 25-4 shows the appropriate wording that the accountant adds after the conclusion paragraph of the standard compilation report when the accountant compiles statements without disclosures. This type of compilation is acceptable *if the report indicates the lack of disclosures* and the absence of disclosures *is not,* to the CPA's knowledge, *undertaken with the intent to mislead users.* Typically, this type of statement is used primarily for management purposes.
3. *Compilation without independence.* A CPA firm can issue a compilation report with full or omitted disclosures even if it is not independent of the client, as defined by the AICPA *Code of Professional Conduct.* When the accountant lacks independence, an additional paragraph must be added as the last paragraph of the report that states: "We are not independent with respect to Williams Company."

For all three types of compilation reports, the following elements are also required:

- The date of the accountant's report is the date of completion of the compilation.
- Each page of the financial statements compiled by the accountant should state "See accountant's compilation report."

FIGURE 25-4 Compilation That Omits Substantially All Disclosures

(The first paragraph is the same as the compilation report in Figure 25-3.)

Management has elected to omit substantially all the disclosures ordinarily included in financial statements prepared in accordance with accounting principles generally accepted in the United States of America. If the omitted disclosures were included in the financial statements, they might influence the user's conclusions about the company's financial position, results of operations, and cash flows. Accordingly, the financial statements are not designed for those who are not informed about such matters.

- If the client fails to follow accounting standards, the auditor must include the same modifications in the compilation report that are used in a review report.

Preparation Services

Many entities may want a CPA to assist them in the preparation of monthly, quarterly, or annual financial statements, but they do not want the CPA to provide an accompanying compilation report. As part of the SSARS Clarity Project described in the vignette on p. 801, the Accounting and Review Services Committee created the preparation engagement service as an alternative to the compilation service engagement. In a **preparation service** engagement, the CPA is engaged by the client to prepare or assist in preparing financial statements, but the CPA does not provide any assurance on the financial statements or issue a report, even if the financial statements are expected to be used by, or provided to, a third party. Additionally, because the preparation service is a nonattest service, the CPA does not need to determine whether he or she is independent.

The CPA's responsibilities when performing a preparation service are similar to those performed in a compilation. The key differences are the CPA does not issue a report and the CPA does not need to assess independence. The accountant should ensure that a statement is included on each page of the financial statements indicating, at a minimum, that "no assurance is provided" on the financial statements. If the accountant is prevented from including a statement on each page of the financial statements, he or she should issue a disclaimer that makes clear that no assurance is provided, or the accountant should perform a compilation service engagement, which would include issuance of a compilation report.

REVIEW OF INTERIM FINANCIAL INFORMATION FOR PUBLIC COMPANIES

OBJECTIVE 25-2

Describe special engagements to review interim financial information for public companies.

The SEC requires that quarterly financial statements be reviewed by the company's external auditor prior to the company's filing of the Form 10-Q with the SEC. The SEC also requires a footnote in the annual audited financial statements disclosing quarterly sales, gross profit, income, and earnings per share for the past two years. Typically, the footnote in the annual statements is labeled *unaudited*. At a minimum, the CPA firm must perform review procedures of the footnote information. Because the same CPA firm does both the annual audit and the public company interim financial statement review, they are referred to as auditors, not accountants for the interim review.

Like reviews under SSARS, a **public company interim review** includes five requirements for review service engagements. The auditor must: (1) obtain knowledge of the accounting principles of the client's industry, (2) obtain knowledge of the client, (3) make inquiries of management, (4) perform analytical procedures, and (5) obtain a letter of representation.

Also like SSARS reviews, reviews for public companies do not provide a basis for expressing positive opinion level assurance. Ordinarily, auditors perform no tests of the accounting records, independent confirmations, or physical examinations. However, the two types of reviews differ in several areas. Below are the key differences:

- Because an annual audit is also performed for the public company client, the auditor must obtain sufficient information about the client's internal control for both annual and interim financial information.
- Similarly, because the client is audited annually, the auditor's knowledge of the results of these audit procedures is used in considering the scope and results of the inquiries and analytical procedures for the review.
- Under SSARS, the auditor makes inquiries about actions taken at directors' and stockholders' meetings; for a public company, the auditor reads the minutes of those meetings.

FIGURE 25-5 Example of a Report for Interim Financial Statements for a Public Company

REPORT OF INDEPENDENT REGISTERED PUBLIC ACCOUNTING FIRM

We have reviewed the consolidated balance sheet of Rainer Company and consolidated subsidiaries as of September 30, 2016, and the related statements of earnings, retained earnings, and cash flows for the three-month and nine-month periods then ended. These financial statements are the responsibility of the company's management.

We conducted our review in accordance with the standards of the Public Company Accounting Oversight Board (United States). A review of interim financial information consists principally of applying analytical procedures and making inquiries of persons responsible for financial and accounting matters. It is substantially less in scope than an audit conducted in accordance with the standards of the Public Company Accounting Oversight Board, the objective of which is the expression of an opinion regarding the financial statements taken as a whole. Accordingly, we do not express such an opinion.

Based on our review, we are not aware of any material modifications that should be made to the accompanying interim financial statements for them to be in conformity with accounting principles generally accepted in the United States of America.

- The auditor must also obtain evidence that the interim financial information agrees or reconciles with the accounting records for a public company interim review. For example, the auditor might compare the interim financial information to the general ledger.

A public company interim review is performed following standards of the PCAOB and the review report makes no reference to SSARS. See Figure 25-5 for an example of such a report. Each page of the interim financial information that accompanies the report should be clearly marked as "unaudited."

If the auditor determines the interim statements violate accounting standards, the report should be modified. The language of the modification is similar to that used in a review under SSARS, except that the auditor should state the effect of the departure, if the amount can be determined.

The quarterly data reviewed by the auditor and included as a footnote in the annual audited statements should be labeled "unaudited." However, a separate review report for this information is not required.

CONCEPT CHECK

1. Distinguish among engagements to prepare, compile, and review financial statements. What is the level of assurance for each?
2. What procedures should the auditor use to obtain the information necessary to give the level of assurance required of reviews of financial statements?

ATTESTATION ENGAGEMENTS

OBJECTIVE 25-3

Distinguish AICPA attestation standards from auditing standards and know the types of engagements to which they apply.

Chapter 1 described assurance services as independent professional services that improve the quality of information for decision makers. Individuals who are responsible for making business decisions seek assurance services to help improve the reliability and relevance of the information on which they base their decisions. One category of assurance services provided by CPAs is attestation services.

CPAs have increasingly been asked to perform a variety of audit-like services, known as attest services, for different purposes. In an **attestation engagement**, the CPA reports on the reliability of information or an assertion made by another party. An example is when a bank requests a CPA to report in writing whether an audit client has adhered to all requirements of a loan agreement.

TABLE 25-1 Generally Accepted Attestation Standards

General Standards

1. The practitioner must have adequate technical training and proficiency to perform the attestation engagement.
2. The practitioner must have adequate knowledge of the subject matter.
3. The practitioner must have reason to believe that the subject matter is capable of evaluation against criteria that are suitable and available to users.
4. The practitioner must maintain independence in mental attitude in all matters relating to the engagement.
5. The practitioner must exercise due professional care in the planning and performance of the engagement and the preparation of the report.

Standards of Field Work

1. The practitioner must adequately plan the work and must properly supervise any assistants.
2. The practitioner must obtain sufficient evidence to provide a reasonable basis for the conclusion that is expressed in the report.

Standards of Reporting

1. The practitioner must identify the subject matter or assertion being reported on and state the character of the engagement in the report.
2. The practitioner must state the practitioner's conclusion about the subject matter or the assertion in relation to the criteria against which the subject matter was evaluated in the report.
3. The practitioner must state all of the practitioner's significant reservations about the engagement, the subject matter, and, if applicable, the assertion related thereto in the report.
4. The practitioner must state in the report that the report is intended solely for the information and use of the specified parties under the following circumstances:
   - When the criteria used to evaluate the subject matter are determined by the practitioner to be appropriate only for a limited number of parties who either participated in their establishment or can be presumed to have an adequate understanding of the criteria.
   - When the criteria used to evaluate the subject matter are available only to specified parties.
   - When reporting on subject matter and a written assertion has not been provided by the responsible party.
   - When the report is on an attestation engagement to apply agreed-upon procedures to the subject matter.

Note: The AICPA is in the process of finalizing its clarity project for the attestation standards (see vignette on the next page). When the clarified standards become effective, the 11 attestation standards will not be retained in their current form, but their core aspects will become part of the Preface, which describes the purpose of an attestation engagement along with the accountant's performance and reporting responsibilities.

Attestation Standards

The AICPA has issued 11 attestation standards that are stated in sufficiently general terms to enable CPAs to apply them to any attestation engagement, including new types of engagements that may arise. These standards, which are shown in Table 25-1, closely parallel the principles underlying an audit in accordance with auditing standards.

The most notable differences in the attestation standards and the principles underlying an audit are in general attestation standards 2 and 3. Standard 2 requires that the CPA have adequate knowledge of the subject matter over which there is attestation. For example, for CPAs to attest to a company's compliance with environmental protection laws, they need a thorough knowledge of the laws and methods that companies use to assure compliance. Standard 3 requires that the CPA be able to evaluate the subject matter against criteria that are suitable and available to users. Again, using the example of environmental protection laws, measurement difficulties or the lack of specific criteria may make it difficult for the CPA to conclude whether there is compliance.

To provide additional guidance for doing attestation engagements, the Auditing Standards Board of the AICPA issues **Statements on Standards for Attestation Engagements (SSAE)**. These are normally called attestation standards. The Auditing Standards Board attempts to distinguish between issues that should be addressed by auditing standards and those that should be addressed by attestation standards, even though both are attestations. In general, auditing standards apply to attestations that deal with providing assurance on historical financial statements, including one or more parts of those statements. These may include audits of financial statements prepared in accordance with accounting standards or some other comprehensive basis of accounting, audits of only a balance sheet, and audits of individual accounts.

All other forms of attestation are addressed in the attestation standards (an exception is reviews of historical financial statements of a nonpublic entity, which are addressed in SSARS and were discussed earlier in the chapter). Attestation standards are established by the Auditing Standards Board following the same process used for auditing standards.

CLARITY PROJECT FOR ATTESTATION STANDARDS

Similar to how the AICPA has issued clarified auditing standards and standards for accounting and review services, the Auditing Standards Board has been clarifying the Statements on Standards for Attestation Engagements (SSAEs). As part of the Clarity Project, the ASB is converging SSAEs to those of the International Accounting and Auditing Standards Board (IAASB). The re-drafting of SSAEs is based on similar provisions that include establishing objectives for each standard, including definitions, and separating requirements from application and other explanatory materials. One notable difference is that the revisions restructure the attestation into "chapters" that replace the former sections with the following:

- Chapter 1: Concepts Common to All Attestation Engagements
- Chapter 2: Examination Engagements
- Chapter 3: Review Engagements
- Chapter 4: Agreed-Upon Procedures Engagements
- Chapter 5: Financial Forecasts and Projections
- Chapter 6: Reporting on Pro Forma Financial Information
- Chapter 7: Compliance Attestation
- Chapter 8: Reporting on an Examination of Controls at a Service Organization Relevant to User Entities' Internal Control Over Financial Reporting

As part of the Clarity Project, the ASB has moved the guidance in AT Section 501, *An Examination of an Entity's Internal Control Over Financial Reporting That Is Integrated with an Audit of Its Financial Statements,* from the attestation standards to the auditing standards because it addresses an examination of internal control that is integrated with an audit of financial statements.

The Clarity Project recodifies the AT sections as "AT-C."

Source: AICPA Proposed Statement on Standards for Attestation Engagements *Attestation Standards: Clarification and Recodification* (July 2013); *Subject Matter Specific Attestation Standards: Clarification and Recodification* (January 2014); *Reporting on an Examination of Controls at a Service Organization Relevant to User Entities' Internal Control Over Financial Reporting: Clarification and Recodification* (September 2014).

Types of Attestation Engagements

The Auditing Standards Board decided not to attempt to define the potential boundaries of attestation engagements except in conceptual terms because new services are likely to arise. For example, PricewaterhouseCoopers has been attesting to the balloting for the Miss America contest for decades, but attesting to compliance with environmental protection laws started only in recent years.

The AICPA has developed specific attestation standards to address specific types of engagements. For example, there are standards related to engagements to compile or examine prospective financial statements or to report on internal controls at service organizations. Several of these services are discussed later in this chapter.

Levels of Service

The attestation standards define three levels of engagements and related forms of conclusions:

1. Examinations
2. Reviews
3. Agreed-upon procedures

In addition, compilation engagements are defined for prospective financial statements.

An **examination** results in a *positive* conclusion, which is expressed by the CPA in the form of an opinion. In this type of report, the CPA makes a direct statement about whether the presentation of the assertions, taken as a whole, conforms to the applicable criteria. A report on an examination is unrestricted as to distribution by the client after it is issued. This means that a client can distribute the information widely, including to prospective investors, and for sales and marketing purposes.

Figure 25-6 (p. 810) contains an examination report issued by Deloitte & Touche, LLP, for an engagement to determine if the Statements of Greenhouse Gas Emissions of United Parcel Service, Inc., for the years ended December 31, 2014 and 2013, are presented in accordance with applicable greenhouse reporting standards issued by the World Business Council for Sustainable Development and the World Resources Institute. The second paragraph acknowledges that the firm conducted the examination in accordance with attestation standards established by the AICPA. Because this was an examination-level engagement, the final paragraph contains the firm's opinion.

FIGURE 25-6 Example of an Examination Report Under the Attestation Standards

INDEPENDENT ACCOUNTANT'S EXAMINATION REPORT

We have examined the accompanying Statement of Greenhouse Gas Emissions ("Statement of GHG Emissions") of United Parcel Service, Inc., (the "Company") for the years ended December 31, 2014, and December 31, 2013, and the 2010 base year for Scope 1 and 2 greenhouse gas emissions. The Company's management is responsible for the Statement of GHG Emissions. Our responsibility is to express an opinion based on our examination.

Our examination was conducted in accordance with attestation standards established by the American Institute of Certified Public Accountants and, accordingly, included obtaining an understanding of the nature of the Company's greenhouse gas emissions and its internal control over greenhouse gas emissions information, examining, on a test basis, evidence supporting the Company's Statement of GHG Emissions and performing such other procedures as we considered necessary in the circumstances. We believe that our examination provides a reasonable basis for our opinion.

As described in Note 1, environmental and energy use data are subject to measurement uncertainties resulting from limitations inherent in the nature and the methods used for determining such data. The selection of different but acceptable measurement techniques can result in materially different measurements. The precision of different measurement techniques may also vary.

In our opinion, the Statement of GHG Emissions of the Company for the years ended December 31, 2014, and December 31, 2013, and the 2010 base year for Scope 1 and 2 greenhouse gas emissions and the 2012 base year for Scope 3 greenhouse gas emissions, is presented, in all material respects, in conformity with the Greenhouse Gas Protocol Corporate Accounting and Reporting Standard (Scope 1 and 2) and the Corporate Value Chain (Scope 3) Accounting and Reporting Standard Published by the World Business Council for Sustainable Development and World Resources Institute (collectively, the "GHG Protocol").

Deloitte & Touche, LLP
Stamford, Connecticut
June 26, 2015

In a **review**, the CPA provides a moderate level of assurance that is expressed by the CPA in the form of a *negative assurance* conclusion. For a negative assurance report, the CPA's report states whether any information came to the CPA's attention to indicate that the assertions are not presented in all material respects in conformity with the applicable criteria. A review report is also unrestricted in its distribution. Review engagements are prohibited for most services where specified attestation standards have been issued, such as prospective financial statements, because of the difficulty of setting standards for the limited assurance provided by reviews.

In an **agreed-upon procedures engagement**, all procedures the CPA will perform are agreed upon by the CPA, the responsible party making the assertions, and the specific persons who are the intended users of the CPA's report. The degree of assurance included in such a report varies with the specific procedures agreed to and performed. Accordingly, such reports are limited in their distribution to only the involved parties, who know the procedures the CPA will perform and the level of assurance resulting from them. The report should include a statement of what procedures management and the CPA agreed to and what the CPA found in performing the procedures.

Figure 25-7 summarizes the reporting levels for attestation engagements. Next we discuss three common types of engagements for which detailed attestation standards

FIGURE 25-7 Types of Engagements and Related Reports

Type of Engagement	Amount of Evidence	Level of Assurance	Form of Conclusion	Distribution
Examination	Extensive	High	Positive	General
Review	Significant	Moderate	Negative	General
Agreed-upon procedures	Varying	Varying	Findings	Limited

have been issued: reports on controls at service organizations, prospective financial statements, and agreed-upon procedures.

REPORTS ON CONTROLS AT SERVICE ORGANIZATIONS (SOC REPORTS)

OBJECTIVE 25-4

Describe engagements to report on internal controls at service organizations (SOC reports).

Chapter 12 highlighted that many clients outsource some or all of their IT needs to an independent computer service organization rather than maintain an internal IT function or data center. In those situations, management of those organizations are dependent on the effectiveness of internal controls performed at the service organization. Additionally, their auditors face difficulty when obtaining an understanding of the client's internal control over financial reporting because many of the controls reside at the service organization, and the auditor cannot assume that the controls are adequate because they are provided by an independent IT provider. It has become increasingly common for the service center to engage a CPA firm to obtain an understanding and test internal controls of the service organization and issue a report for use by all customers and their independent auditors. There are three types of **service organization control (SOC) reports**, which are referred to as SOC 1, SOC 2, and SOC 3 reports.

SOC 1 Reports

An SOC 1 report, *Report on Controls at a Service Organization Relevant to User Entities' Internal Control Over Financial Reporting*, is intended to meet the needs of entities (user entities) that use service organizations and their auditors, who are responsible for understanding internal controls over financial reporting at service organizations. SOC 1 reports are used to plan and perform audits of the user entity's financial statements by their auditors, who are referred to as user auditors. The SOC 1 guidance for service auditors is in the attestation standards, while guidance for user auditors is in the auditing standards. The attestation standards provide guidance for service auditors, who are engaged by a service organization to issue one of two types of reports on controls at the service organization relevant to user entities' internal control over financial reporting:

1. Report on management's description of a service organization's system and the suitability of the design of controls (referred to as a Type 1 report).
2. Report on management's description of a service organization's system and the suitability of the design and operating effectiveness of controls (referred to as a Type 2 report).

In a Type 1 report, the service auditor expresses an opinion about the fairness of the description of the service organization's system and an opinion about the suitability of the design of controls in that system. The service auditor obtains and reads the system description prepared by the organization's management and assesses whether the description is fairly presented. In making that assessment, the service auditor evaluates whether management used suitable criteria in preparing and presenting the service organization's system description. For example, the service auditor would evaluate whether the organization's description includes information about procedures by which transactions are initiated, authorized, recorded, processed, corrected, and reported for user entities and the related accounting records prepared to support those processes.

In a Type 1 engagement, the service auditor also performs procedures to obtain sufficient available evidence to obtain reasonable assurance about the suitability of the design of controls. In making that determination, the service auditor evaluates whether controls have been designed to address risks threatening the achievement of control objectives and whether those controls, if operating as described, provide reasonable assurance that those risks would not prevent achievement of control objectives.

In a Type 2 engagement, the service auditor performs tests of the operating effectiveness of the controls at the service organization, in addition to procedures performed in the Type 1 engagement. The service auditor's Type 2 report contains the two opinions about the description and suitability of the design of controls that are provided in a Type 1 report, plus an additional opinion about the operating effectiveness of controls throughout the period.

SOC 2 Reports

Service organizations provide a number of other IT services for entities that may not relate to internal controls over financial reporting. For example, a university that outsources the processing of student applications for admission will likely be subject to laws requiring the university to maintain the privacy of the information included in the application. The university is concerned about the accuracy of that information and is responsible for maintaining the privacy of the information including that residing at the service organization. Management of the university is also concerned about complying with laws or regulations related to processing integrity and privacy and may desire assurance about the service organization's controls relevant to processing integrity and privacy that affect the users' information.

An SOC 2 report, *Report on Controls at a Service Organization Relevant to Security, Availability, Processing Integrity, Confidentiality, or Privacy,* is intended to meet the needs of a broad range of users who need information and assurance about controls at a service organization that affect the security, availability, and processing integrity of the systems the service organization uses to process users' data and the confidentiality and privacy of the information processed by these systems. For example, customers of a service organization may seek an SOC 2 report as part of their vendor risk management considerations.

The service auditor uses the criteria in *Trust Services* Principles for evaluating and reporting on controls related to security, availability, processing integrity, confidentiality, or privacy. The five *Trust Services* principles, which are shown in Table 25-2, represent broad statements of objectives. To provide more specific guidance, there are related *Trust Services* criteria for each of the five principles. The controls that the CPA reports on in these engagements are intended to prevent, or detect and correct, errors or other negative events that affect the service or information provided to user entities as they relate to the principle being reported on.

Similar to SOC 1 reports, there are two types of SOC 2 reports: a type 1 report on management's description of a service organization's system and the suitability of the design of controls and a type 2 report on management's description of a service organization's system and the suitability of the design and operating effectiveness of controls. Use of these reports is generally restricted to specified parties, such as management of user entities, customers of the service organizations, regulators, suppliers, and business partners.

SOC 3 Reports

An SOC 3 report, *Trust Services Report for Service Organizations,* is similar to an SOC 2 report except that the SOC 3 report is intended for wide distribution to current or potential users of the service organization. SOC 3 reports are prepared using the *Trust Services* principles and criteria shown in Table 25-2. While the distribution of an SOC 2 report is generally restricted, an SOC 3 report is a general-use report, which allows the

TABLE 25-2 Five *Trust Services* Principles

Principle	The entity discloses and maintains compliance with its ...
Security	security practices, ensuring that the system is protected against unauthorized access (both physical and logical).
Availability	availability practices, ensuring that the system is available for operation and use as committed or agreed.
Processing Integrity	processing integrity, ensuring that system processing is complete, accurate, timely, and authorized.
Confidentiality	confidentiality practices, ensuring that information designated as confidential is protected as committed or agreed.
Privacy	online privacy practices, ensuring that personal information obtained as a result of e-commerce is collected, used, disclosed, and retained as committed or agreed.

AICPA DISCONTINUES SYSTRUST SERVICES

In October 2014, the AICPA and CPA Canada announced that they had discontinued the *SysTrust* seal program. In a *SysTrust* engagement, the *SysTrust*–licensed CPA evaluated a company's computer system using *Trust Services* principles and criteria and determined whether controls over the system existed. The CPA then performed tests to determine whether those controls were operating effectively during a specified period. If the system met the requirements of the *Trust Services* principles and criteria, an examination-level unqualified attestation report was issued under AICPA attestation standards. Effective immediately, the AICPA and CPA Canada will no longer issue new licenses to practitioners to use the *SysTrust* seal.

While the *WebTrust* seal program continues, the program is being evaluated to determine if the benefits justify the resources necessary to continue the program. In a *WebTrust* attestation engagement, a client engages a CPA to provide reasonable assurance that a company's Web site complies with certain *Trust Services* principles and criteria for one or more aspects of e-commerce activities. A site that meets the *Trust Services* principles is eligible to display the *WebTrust* electronic seal on its transaction or order page, which is intended to give users of the site assurance about the site's credibility. At least once every 12 months, the CPA firm updates its testing of the e-commerce aspects to ensure that the client's site continues to comply with the *Trust Services* principles and criteria. The CPA firm also updates its report. If the site does not comply, the seal can be revoked.

Sources: 1. Brian Loney and Amy Pawlicki, "Letter to SysTrust Licensees" (October 2, 2014) (www.webtrust.org); 2. AICPA and CPA Canada, "Overview of Trust Services" (www.webtrust.org).

service organization to share the report with current or prospective customers or to use it as a marketing tool to demonstrate that they have appropriate controls in place to mitigate risks, such as those related to security or privacy.

PROSPECTIVE FINANCIAL STATEMENTS

OBJECTIVE 25-5

Understand special engagements to attest to prospective financial statements.

As implied by the term, **prospective financial statements** refer to predicted or expected financial statements in some future period (income statement) or at some future date (balance sheet). An example is management's predictions of the income statement and balance sheet one year in the future.

Most CPAs believe there are significant opportunities and potential risks for auditors to provide credibility to prospective financial information. It is widely accepted that users want reliable prospective information to aid their decision making. If auditors can improve the reliability of the information, information risk may be reduced in the same way it is in audits of historical financial statements. The risks arise because the actual results obtained in the future may differ significantly from the results predicted in the prospective financial statements. Regulators, users, and others may criticize and even sue auditors, even if the prospective statements were fairly stated, given the information available when they were prepared.

Forecasts and Projections

AICPA attestation standards define two general types of prospective financial statements:

1. **Forecasts** are prospective financial statements that present an entity's *expected* financial position, results of operations, and cash flows, to the *best* of the responsible party's knowledge and belief. Banks commonly require this information as a part of loan applications.
2. **Projections** are prospective financial statements that present an entity's financial position, results of operations, and cash flows, to the best of the responsible party's knowledge and belief, given one or more *hypothetical assumptions*. For example, projected financial statements might assume the company is able to increase the price of its primary product by 10 percent with no reduction in units sold.

Considerable guidance is provided in the AICPA *Guide for Prospective Financial Statements*, which includes criteria against which an attestation engagement can be compared.

Use of Prospective Financial Statements

Prospective financial statements are prepared for one of two audiences:

1. *General* use statements are prepared for use by any third party, such as the inclusion of a financial forecast in a prospectus for the sale of hospital bonds.

POTENTIAL LEGAL LIABILITY IN PROSPECTIVE FINANCIAL STATEMENTS

A partner in one of the Big Four CPA firms stated that his firm has decided not to do assurance engagements for prospective financial statements because of litigation costs. He reported that his firm calculated their total revenues (not profits) from all prospective financial statement engagements and also calculated all legal costs, including partner and staff time incurred to defend against lawsuits involving these engagements. The firm discovered that legal costs exceeded revenues. The partner said, "You don't have to be a rocket scientist to conclude that if legal costs exceed revenues it's a bad business. Users sue when actual profits are less favorable than those projected regardless of what the CPA firm's report says."

2. *Limited* use statements are prepared solely for third parties with whom the responsible party is dealing directly, such as the inclusion of a financial projection in a bank loan application document.

Forecasts can be provided for both general and limited use. However, projections are restricted to the latter, because limited users are in a better position to understand the prospective statements and related assumptions than other parties. For example, a potential venture capital investor can ask the responsible party about hypothetical assumptions in a projection, whereas a removed user, such as a reader of a company prospectus, cannot. Because general users may have difficulty interpreting hypothetical assumptions without obtaining additional information, the standards prohibit their general use. There is an exception to this rule: a projection may be issued as a supplement to a forecast for general use.

Types of Engagements

AICPA attestation standards prohibit a CPA firm from performing a review of a forecast or projection, because a review service implies the CPA can be "moderately satisfied" about both the computational accuracy of the projections and the assumptions on which the projection is based. To avoid confusion among users, the AICPA created more specific attestation standards, prescribing the following types of engagements for prospective financial statements:

- An examination engagement in which the CPA obtains satisfaction as to the completeness and reasonableness of all the assumptions.
- A compilation engagement in which the CPA is primarily involved with the computational accuracy of the statements, and not the reasonableness of the assumptions.
- An agreed-upon procedures engagement in which the CPA and all users of the statements agree on specific, limited attestation procedures.

Only an examination of prospective statements is included in this chapter.

Examination of Prospective Financial Statements

In an examination level engagement, the CPA:

1. Evaluates the preparation of the prospective financial statements
2. Evaluates the support underlying the assumptions
3. Evaluates the presentation of the prospective financial statements for conformity with AICPA presentation guidelines
4. Issues an examination report

The CPA is not attesting to the accuracy of the prospective financial statements. Instead, the CPA is accumulating evidence about the completeness and reasonableness of the underlying assumptions, as disclosed in the prospective financial statements. To make the evaluation, the CPA needs to become familiar with the client's business and industry, identify the significant matters on which the client's future results are expected to depend ("key factors"), and determine that appropriate assumptions have been included with respect to these key factors.

AGREED-UPON PROCEDURES ENGAGEMENTS

OBJECTIVE 25-6

Define agreed-upon procedures engagements.

When the auditor and management or a third-party user agree that the engagement will be limited to certain specific procedures, it is referred to as an agreed-upon procedures engagement. Many CPAs refer to these as procedures and findings engagements because the resulting reports emphasize the specific procedures performed and the findings of those completed procedures.

Agreed-upon procedures engagements appeal to CPAs because management, or a third-party user, specifies the procedures they want done and then the CPA issues a report describing the procedures agreed upon and the findings resulting from the procedures. Imagine the difficulty a CPA firm faces if it is asked to issue an opinion to a federal agency that a company complied with federal affirmative action laws for a two-year period under compliance attestation standards. Now assume that the federal agency is willing to identify 10 specific procedures the CPA firm will do to satisfy the agency. Obviously, the latter engagement will be much easier to manage. Assuming the CPA firm and federal agency can agree on the procedures, many CPA firms are willing to perform the procedures and issue a report of the related findings. Other agreed-upon procedures engagements might involve a CPA calculating internal rates of return and beta risk for measuring volatility for a mutual fund or gross sales amounts used to compute rent under a store lease for a retail firm.

OTHER AUDITS OR LIMITED ASSURANCE ENGAGEMENTS

OBJECTIVE 25-7

Describe other audit and limited assurance engagements related to historical financial statements.

Now that we have discussed compilation and review services for nonpublic companies, as well as reviews of interim financial information for public companies, we will examine other types of audit and attestation services that fall within the auditing standards but are not audits of historical financial statements in accordance with GAAP or IFRS. Some of these services include: audits of financial statements prepared on another comprehensive basis of accounting (OCBOA); audits of specified elements, accounts, or items; and debt compliance letters.

Other Comprehensive Basis of Accounting

Auditors often audit statements prepared on a basis other than GAAP or IFRS. Auditing standards apply to these audit engagements, but their reporting requirements differ somewhat from those described in Chapter 3. Bases other than GAAP or IFRS for which reports may be issued include:

- *Cash or modified cash basis.* With cash basis accounting, only cash receipts and disbursements are recorded. Under the modified cash basis of accounting, the cash basis is followed except for certain items, such as fixed assets and depreciation. Physicians and attorneys often follow this accounting method.
- *Basis used to comply with the requirements of a regulatory agency.* Common examples include the uniform system of accounts required of railroads, utilities, and some insurance companies.
- *Income tax basis.* The same measurement rules used for filing tax returns are often used for financial statement preparation, even though this is not in accordance with GAAP or IFRS. Many small businesses use this method.
- *Financial Reporting Framework for Small- and Medium-Sized Businesses.* The AICPA has developed this special purpose framework for small- and medium-sized businesses that is a self-contained framework not based on accounting principles generally accepted in the United States of America (GAAP). The framework draws upon a blend of traditional accounting principles and accrual income tax methods of accounting.
- *A definite set of criteria having substantial support.* An example is the price-level basis of accounting. The method of accounting must be applied to all material items in the financial statements.

Auditors usually do these audits in the same way as when clients follow GAAP or IFRS. Naturally, the auditor must fully understand the accounting basis that the client is required to follow. For example, in auditing a railroad, complex accounting requirements require the auditor to have specialized accounting knowledge to conduct the audit.

When clients follow a comprehensive basis other than GAAP or IFRS, the auditor must make sure the statements clearly indicate that they are prepared using another

FIGURE 25-8 Example of a Report on Income Tax Basis

INDEPENDENT AUDITOR'S REPORT

Report on the Financial Statements

We have audited the accompanying financial statements of Triangle Partnership, which comprise the statement of assets, liabilities, and capital–income tax basis as of December 31, 2016, and the related statements of revenue and expenses–income tax basis and of changes in partners' capital accounts–income tax basis for the year then ended, and the related notes to the financial statements.

Management's Responsibility for the Financial Statements

(same paragraph as shown in Figure 3-1 on page 48, except for the need to reference that the income tax basis of accounting has been used)

Auditor's Responsibility

(same three paragraphs as shown in Figure 3-1)

Opinion

In our opinion, the financial statements referred to above present fairly, in all material respects, the assets, liabilities, and capital of Triangle Partnership as of December 31, 2016, and its revenue and expenses and changes in partners' capital accounts for the year then ended in accordance with the basis of accounting Triangle Partnership uses for income tax purposes described in Note X.

Basis of Accounting

We draw attention to Note X of the financial statements, which describes the basis of accounting. The financial statements are prepared on the basis of accounting the Partnership uses for income tax purposes, which is a basis of accounting other than accounting principles generally accepted in the United States of America. Our opinion is not modified with respect to this matter.

basis of accounting. If the statements imply that GAAP is followed, the reporting requirements covered in Chapter 3 apply. Consequently, terms such as *balance sheet* and *statement of operations* must be avoided by the client. Instead, a title such as "Statement of assets and liabilities arising from cash transactions" is appropriate for a cash basis statement. Figure 25-8 illustrates those sections of a report prepared on a partnership following the income tax basis of accounting that differ from the auditor's report on financial statements prepared in accordance with GAAP as illustrated in Figure 3-1 on page 48.

Specified Elements, Accounts, or Items

Auditors are often asked to audit and issue reports on specific aspects of financial statements. A common example is a report on the audit of sales of a retail store in a shopping center to be used as a basis for rental payments. Other common examples include reports on royalties, profit participation, and provision for income taxes. The authority for auditing specified elements, accounts, or items is in the auditing standards.

The audit of specified elements, accounts, or items is much like an ordinary audit of financial statements except it is applied to less than the full financial statements. Materiality is defined in terms of the elements, accounts, or items being audited rather than for the overall statements. The effect is to ordinarily require more evidence than if the item being verified is just one of many parts of the statements. For example, if the sales account is being reported on separately, a smaller misstatement will be considered more material than it is when sales are one of many accounts in a full financial statement audit.

Auditors must extend their audit efforts to include other elements, accounts, or items that are interrelated with those that are being audited. For example, in expressing an opinion on sales, the auditor must also consider the effect of accounts receivable on sales.

Debt Compliance Letters and Similar Reports

Clients occasionally enter into loan agreements that require them to provide the lender with a report from a CPA about the existence or nonexistence of some condition. For example, a bank may require a company to maintain a certain dollar amount of working capital at a specified date and to obtain an audit report that states whether the company complied with the stated working capital requirements.

Auditors may issue reports on debt compliance and similar engagements as separate reports or, by adding a paragraph after the opinion paragraph, as part of a report

FIGURE 25-9 Example of Debt Compliance Report

INDEPENDENT AUDITOR'S REPORT

We have audited, in accordance with auditing standards generally accepted in the United States of America, the financial statements of Bollert Company, which comprise the balance sheet as of December 31, 2016, and the related statements of income, retained earnings, and cash flows for the year then ended, and the related notes to the financial statements, and have issued our report thereon dated February 16, 2017.

In connection with our audit, nothing came to our attention that caused us to believe that the Company failed to comply with the terms, covenants, provisions, or conditions of sections I to IX, inclusive, of the Indenture dated July 21, 2014, with First Bank insofar as they relate to accounting matters. However, our audit was not directed primarily toward obtaining knowledge of such noncompliance. Accordingly, had we performed additional procedures, other matters may have come to our attention regarding the Company's noncompliance with the above-referenced terms, covenants, provisions, or conditions of the Indenture, insofar as they relate to accounting matters.

This report is intended solely for the information and use of the boards of directors and managements of Bollert Company and First Bank and is not intended to be and should not be used by anyone other than these specified parties.

that expresses their opinion on the financial statements. In either case, the auditor must observe the following matters in such engagements:

- Auditors must be qualified to evaluate whether the client has met the provisions in the engagement. In the audit of a debt compliance agreement, auditors are normally qualified to evaluate whether principal and interest payments were made when due; whether the proper limitations were maintained on dividends, working capital, and debt ratios; and whether the accounting records were adequate for conducting an ordinary audit. However, auditors are not qualified to determine whether the client has properly restricted its business activities to the requirements of an agreement or if it has title to pledged property. These are legal questions and the *Code of Professional Conduct* prohibits the auditor from practicing as an attorney in such circumstances.
- The auditor should provide a debt compliance letter only for a client for whom the auditor has done an audit of the overall financial statements. A debt compliance letter on a matter such as the existence of a current ratio of 2.5 or better would be difficult to accomplish without having conducted a complete financial statement audit.
- The auditor's opinion is a *negative assurance*, stating that nothing came to the auditor's attention that would lead the auditor to believe there was noncompliance.

Figure 25-9 provides an example of a separate report on debt compliance. Note that the final paragraph restricts distribution of the report to the directly affected parties.

CONCEPT CHECK

1. Define what is meant by attestation standards. Distinguish between attestation standards and auditing standards.
2. Distinguish the three types of service organization reports.

SUMMARY

This chapter described many of the other assurance services offered by CPAs. The types of services offered continue to grow and expand as society demands assurance on new and different types of information. Depending on the nature of the service, the guidance for performing the service may come from auditing standards, accounting and review services standards, or attestation standards. Table 25-3 (p. 818) provides a summary and examples of the primary categories of services discussed in this chapter.

TABLE 25-3	Primary Categories of Other Assurance Services Engagements	
Type of Engagement	**Example**	**Source of Authoritative Support**
Audits of historical financial statements prepared in accordance with accounting standards	Audit of General Mills' financial statements	Auditing standards
Attestation engagements under the attestation standards	Attestation of General Mills' e-commerce system availability	Attestation standards and *Trust Services* availability principles and criteria
Reviews or compilations of historical financial statements prepared in accordance with accounting standards	Review of Ron's Shoe Store's quarterly financial statements	Accounting and review services standards for nonpublic companies; auditing standards for public companies
Audits or limited assurance engagements other than audits, reviews, or compilations of historical financial statements prepared in accordance with accounting standards	Audit of Ron's Shoe Store's ending balance in inventory	Auditing standards

ESSENTIAL TERMS

Agreed-upon procedures engagement—an engagement in which the procedures to be performed are agreed upon by the CPA, the responsible party making the assertions, and the intended users of the CPA's report; the degree of assurance provided by the CPA will vary based on procedures agreed to and performed

Attestation engagement—a type of assurance service in which the CPA firm issues a report about the reliability of information or an assertion made by another party

Compilation service—a nonaudit engagement in which the accountant is engaged to assist management in the preparation of financial statements and issue a report to a client or third party without providing any CPA assurance about those statements

Examination—an attest engagement that results in positive assurance expressed as an opinion as to whether or not the assertions under examination conform with the applicable criteria

Forecasts—prospective financial statements that present an entity's expected financial position, results of operations, and cash flows for future periods, to the best of the responsible party's knowledge and belief

Preparation service—a nonattest engagement in which the accountant is engaged by the client to prepare or assist in preparing financial statements, but the CPA does not provide any assurance on the financial statements or issue a report, even if the financial statements are expected to be used by, or provided to, a third party

Projections—prospective financial statements that present an entity's financial position and results of operations and cash flows for future periods, to the best of the responsible party's knowledge and belief, given one or more hypothetical assumptions

Prospective financial statements—financial statements that deal with expected future data rather than with historical data

Public company interim review—reviews of interim, unaudited financial information performed to help public companies meet their reporting responsibilities to regulatory agencies

Review—an attestation engagement that provides limited assurance expressed in the form of negative assurance as to the CPA's awareness of any information indicating that the assertions are not presented in conformity with the applicable criteria

Review service (SSARS review)—a review of unaudited financial statements designed to provide limited assurance that no material modifications need be made to the statements in order for them to be in conformity with accounting standards or, if applicable, with another comprehensive basis of accounting

Service organization control (SOC) report—an engagement where a service organization's auditor reports on internal controls at the service organization, with a type 1 report including information about management's description of the service organization's system and the suitability of the design of the organization's controls while the type 2 report also includes information about the operating effectiveness of those controls

Statements on Standards for Accounting and Review Services (SSARS)—standards issued by the AICPA Accounting and Review Services Committee that govern the CPA's association with unaudited financial statements of nonpublic companies

Statements on Standards for Attestation Engagements (SSAE)—statements issued by the AICPA to provide a conceptual framework for various types of attestation services

REVIEW QUESTIONS

25-1 (OBJECTIVE 25-1) What is meant by the term *level of assurance?* How does the level of assurance differ for an audit of historical financial statements, a review, a compilation, and a preparation engagement?

25-2 (OBJECTIVE 25-1) What is negative assurance? Why is it used in a review engagement report?

25-3 (OBJECTIVE 25-1) Distinguish the three forms of compilation reports that a CPA can provide to clients.

25-4 (OBJECTIVE 25-1) List five things that are required of an auditor by SSARS for a compilation.

25-5 (OBJECTIVE 25-1) What steps should auditors take if during a compilation engagement they become aware that the financial statements are misleading?

25-6 (OBJECTIVE 25-1) What are the major differences between a compilation engagement and a preparation engagement?

25-7 (OBJECTIVE 25-1) What should auditors do if during a review of financial statements they discover that applicable accounting standards are not being followed?

25-8 (OBJECTIVES 25-1, 25-2) What are the differences between the review reports for a private company under SSARS and for the interim financial statements of a public company?

25-9 (OBJECTIVE 25-2) Explain why a review of interim financial statements for a public company may provide a greater level of assurance than an SSARS review.

25-10 (OBJECTIVE 25-3) You have been asked to provide assurance on information contained in New Dominion's Corporate Sustainability Report. What standards would you use to perform this engagement?

25-11 (OBJECTIVE 25-4) Describe the five *Trust Services* principles.

25-12 (OBJECTIVE 25-4) Describe the key difference between a type 1 and type 2 SOC 1 report.

25-13 (OBJECTIVE 25-4) What type of report might a service organization use as a marketing tool to provide potential customers information about the internal controls related to security at the service organization?

25-14 (OBJECTIVE 25-4) An audit client has engaged a third-party service organization to host its payroll software package on servers located at the service organization. What options do you have to obtain assurance about the controls embedded in the payroll application?

25-15 (OBJECTIVE 25-5) Explain what is meant by prospective financial statements and distinguish between forecasts and projections. What four things are involved in an examination of prospective financial statements?

25-16 (OBJECTIVE 25-7) The Absco Corporation has requested that Herb Germany, CPA, provide a report to the Northern State Bank as to the existence or nonexistence of certain loan conditions. The conditions to be reported on are the working capital ratio, dividends paid on preferred stock, aging of accounts receivable, and competence of management. This is Herb's first experience with Absco. Should Herb accept this engagement? Substantiate your answer.

MULTIPLE CHOICE QUESTIONS FROM CPA EXAMINATIONS

25-17 (OBJECTIVE 25-1) The following are miscellaneous questions about compilation and review services. Choose the best response.

a. A CPA is performing review services for a small, closely held manufacturing company. As a part of the follow-up of a significant decrease in the gross margin for the current year, the CPA discovers that there are no supporting documents for $40,000 of disbursements. The chief financial officer assures her that the disbursements are proper. What should the CPA do?
   (1) Include the unsupported disbursements without further work in the statements on the grounds that she is not doing an audit.
   (2) Modify the review opinion or withdraw from the engagement unless the unsupported disbursements are satisfactorily explained.
   (3) Exclude the unsupported disbursements from the statements.
   (4) Obtain a written representation from the chief financial officer that the disbursements are proper and should be included in the current financial statements.

b. Which of the following best describes the responsibility of the CPA in performing compilation services for a company?
   (1) The CPA has to satisfy only himself or herself that the financial statements were prepared in conformity with accounting standards.
   (2) The CPA must understand the client's business and accounting methods and read the financial statements for reasonableness.
   (3) The CPA should obtain an understanding of internal control and perform tests of controls.
   (4) The CPA is relieved of any responsibility to third parties.

c. The standard compilation report includes which statement or phrase?
   (1) Management is responsible for the financial statements.
   (2) The accountant does not express an opinion but expresses only limited assurance on the compiled financial statements.
   (3) The objective of a compilation is to assist management in presenting financial information in the form of financial statements.
   (4) The accountant has compiled the financial statements in accordance with standards established by the Auditing Standards Board.

25-18 (OBJECTIVES 25-3, 25-4) The following questions concern attestation engagements. Choose the best response.

a. A Type 1 service auditor's report on internal controls at a service organization
   (1) includes an opinion about the suitability of the design of controls at the service organization.
   (2) is based on the performance of tests of controls and substantive tests of transactions at the service organization.
   (3) contains an opinion about the operating effectiveness of internal controls at the service organization.
   (4) provides an opinion about the fair presentation of the service organization's financial statements in accordance with accounting standards.

b. Which of the following professional services would be considered an attestation engagement?
   (1) Advocating on behalf of a client about trust tax matters under review by the Internal Revenue Service.
   (2) Providing financial analysis, planning, and capital acquisition services as a part-time, in-house controller.
   (3) Advising management in the selection of a computer system to meet business needs.
   (4) Preparing the income statement and balance sheet for one year in the future based on client expectations and predictions.

25-19 **(OBJECTIVE 25-7)** The following questions concern reports issued by auditors, other than those on historical financial statements. Choose the best response.

a. An auditor is reporting on cash basis financial statements. These statements are best referred to in the opinion of the auditor by which of the following descriptions?
   (1) Cash receipts and disbursements and the assets and liabilities arising from cash transactions
   (2) Financial position and results of operations arising from cash transactions
   (3) Balance sheet and income statements resulting from cash transactions
   (4) Cash balance sheet and the source and application of funds

b. When asked to perform an audit to express an opinion on one or more specified elements, accounts, or items of a financial statement, the auditor
   (1) may not describe auditing procedures applied.
   (2) should advise the client that the opinion can be issued only if the financial statements have been audited and found to be fairly presented.
   (3) may assume that the standards of reporting with respect to GAAP do not apply.
   (4) should comply with the request only if they constitute a major portion of the financial statements on which an auditor has disclaimed an opinion based on an audit.

MULTIPLE CHOICE QUESTIONS FROM BECKER CPA EXAM REVIEW

25-20 **(OBJECTIVES 25-1, 25-5)** The following questions concern engagements other than the audit of financial statements performed by accountants. Choose the best response.

a. Which of the following procedures would most likely be performed during an engagement to compile the financial statements of a nonissuer?
   (1) Read the financial statements and consider whether they are appropriate in form and free from obvious material errors
   (2) Perform inquiry and analytical procedures
   (3) Obtain a representation letter from management
   (4) Send accounts receivable confirmations

b. Which of the following procedures would most likely be performed during the engagement to review the annual financial statements of a nonissuer?
   (1) Observation of inventory
   (2) Confirmation of notes receivable
   (3) Communication with the predecessor accountant
   (4) Comparison of the current financial statements with prior period financial statements

c. Which of the following is a prospective financial statement for general use upon which an accountant may appropriately report?
   (1) Financial projection
   (2) Partial presentation
   (3) Pro forma financial statement
   (4) Financial forecast

DISCUSSION QUESTIONS AND PROBLEMS

25-21 **(OBJECTIVE 25-1)** Evaluate the following comments about compiled financial statements: "When CPAs associate their name with compiled financial statements, their only responsibility is to the client and that is limited to the proper summarization and presentation on the financial statements of information provided by the client. The opinion clearly states that the auditor has not conducted an audit and does not express an opinion on this fair presentation. If users rely on compiled financial statements, they do so at their own risk and should never be able to hold the CPA responsible for inadequate performance. Users should interpret the financial statements as if they had been prepared by management."

25-22 **(OBJECTIVE 25-1)** You are doing a review services and related tax work engagement for Murphy Construction Company. You have made extensive inquiries of management about their financial statements and have concluded that management has an excellent understanding of its business and is honest, but lacking in knowledge of technical accounting issues. In doing the review you determine the following:

1. Repairs and maintenance expense has increased significantly compared to the preceding year. The president states that this seems to have been a year with a lot of repairs, in part because their equipment is getting older.
2. Property tax expense is the same as last year even though Murphy purchased a new building, including the land. The president states that there are no real estate taxes on the new building and land until next year.
3. Based on your knowledge of the construction industry, you know that the pipes Murphy uses in construction have had a decrease in selling price to construction companies near the end of the current year. The president states that even though they have a large pipe inventory, it will all be used in the next year or two, so the current price doesn't matter because they won't need to buy any.
4. Accounts receivable has increased almost 25% compared to the previous year, but the allowance for uncollectible accounts has stayed the same. The president states that even though receivables have increased, they still expect uncollectible accounts to be less than the stated allowance.
5. In discussions with the president you determine that there is a material uninsured lawsuit against the company from a former customer. The president believes it is a frivolous lawsuit and will not permit a footnote about it for fear that it will result in similar lawsuits from other customers.

Required

a. Beyond inquiries and analytical procedures, what are the accountant's responsibilities in performing review service engagements?
b. Describe what you should do in each of the preceding situations, assuming each one is material.

25-23 **(OBJECTIVE 25-1)** SSARS contain several procedures that are required when engaged to perform a compilation or review engagement. Below are ten statements that may or may not be relevant to a compilation or review engagement. For each of the ten statements, indicate whether the procedure is to be performed in a compilation or review engagement.

	Required for a	
Description of Procedure	**Compilation Engagement?**	**Review Engagement?**
1. Obtain a written engagement letter.		
2. Understand the client's industry and the nature of the client's business.		
3. Read the financial statements.		
4. Design and perform analytical procedures.		
5. Make inquiries of client management.		
6. Perform tests of controls.		
7. Assess fraud risk.		
8. Obtain a letter of representation from management.		
9. Prepare documentation in sufficient detail to provide a clear understanding of the work performed.		
10. Issue a report that contains limited assurance about whether the accountant is aware of the need for material modification to the financial statements.		

25-24 (OBJECTIVE 25-1) In an engagement to review the financial statements of a nonpublic company, SSARS require the accountant to obtain review evidence that is primarily based on inquiries and analytical procedures. The nature of the accountant's inquiries is a matter of judgment. For example, the accountant may consider the nature and materiality of the items, likelihood of misstatement, how the items may be affected by management's judgment, qualifications of client personnel, among other matters.

Below are several inquiry procedures for the sales and collection cycle:

Revenue

1. Are revenues from the sale of major products and services recognized in the appropriate period?

Receivables

1. Has an adequate allowance been made for doubtful accounts?
2. Have receivables considered uncollectible been written off?
3. If appropriate, has interest been reflected?
4. Has a proper cutoff of sales transactions been made?
5. Are there any receivables from employees and related parties?
6. Are any receivables pledged, discounted, or factored?
7. Have receivables been correctly classified between current and noncurrent?

Required

a. What other information about accounts receivable and revenue, besides the items listed, will the accountant have to obtain?
b. Compare the illustrative procedures for review services and those commonly performed for audits. What are the major differences?
c. Of whom should the accountant make inquiries in a small, closely held company?
d. Under what circumstances will procedures beyond those illustrated likely be performed? Be specific.
e. Compare the levels of achieved assurance for review services and audits. Is the achieved level much higher for audits, somewhat higher, or approximately the same? Give reasons for your answer.

25-25 (OBJECTIVE 25-2) Jennifer Branson is a new staff auditor on the audit engagement of Greenville Light & Sound, which is a publicly traded company with a calendar year-end. The engagement team has completed its review of the third-quarter financial statements, and the firm has been asked to issue a review report on those statements. As the senior auditor on the engagement, you asked Jennifer to draft the firm's report for your review. Here's what she provided you:

> We have examined the accompanying balance sheet of Greenville Light & Sound as of September 30, 2016, and the related statement of operations for the three quarterly periods then ended. A review includes primarily applying analytical procedures to management's financial data, making inquiries of management, and testing internal controls over financial reporting. A review is substantially less in scope than an audit. These financial statements are the responsibility of the company's management.
>
> We conducted our review in accordance with Statements on Standards for Accounting and Review Services issued by the American Institute of Certified Public Accountants. Those standards require us to perform procedures to obtain assurance that there are no misstatements in the financial statements in order to express our opinion on them.
>
> Based on our review, it is our opinion that the financial statements are in accordance with accounting standards generally accepted by the Securities and Exchange Commission for the quarter ended September 30, 2016.

Required

What changes are needed to the report draft provided by Jennifer?

25-26 (OBJECTIVE 25-3) With greater frequency, organizations are issuing sustainability reports that describe how they engage in socially responsible activities. Many believe that users will increasingly want assurances from CPAs about the reliability of the information presented by management in these reports. Visit the Web site for the Home Depot Company (www.homedepot.com) and locate the Company's 2014 Sustainability Report.

Read the report to answer the following:

Required

a. What are the key issues overseen by the company's Sustainability Integration System?
b. What assertions did the company make about the recycling of CFL bulbs and rechargeable batteries, and the water reclamation tanks?
c. To what extent might users of the report demand more assurance about the information contained in the report?
d. What challenges would CPAs face in providing assurance about information contained in this report?

25-27 **(OBJECTIVE 25-4)** With the rapid growth of cloud computing, many organizations are contracting with third-party service providers to process and store all kinds of data off site. In doing so, entities are now dependent on the effectiveness of controls provided by external software providers and data centers that are used to generate and store a huge volume of important information for making critical business decisions.

Required

a. How might the use of an external service provider to process financial statement transactions affect the audit of the entity's financial statements?
b. What options are available to the auditor of the user entity's financial statements to obtain information about the design of internal controls over financial reporting at the service organization?
c. What kind of report could the auditor of the user entity obtain from the service organization, if the user auditor needed information about the operating effectiveness of controls at the service organization?
d. What type of report might the service organization provide to management of an entity that uses the service center to process quality control reports related to the user entity's manufacturing processes?

25-28 **(OBJECTIVE 25-5)** Carl Monson, the owner of Major Products Manufacturing Company, a small, successful, long-time audit client of your firm, has requested you to work with his company in preparing 3-year forecasted information for the year ending December 31, 2017, and two subsequent years. Monson informs you that he intends to use the forecasts, together with the audited financial statements, to seek additional financing to expand the business. Monson has had little experience in formal forecast preparation and counts on you to assist him in any way possible. He wants the most supportive opinion possible from your firm to add to the credibility of the forecast. He informs you that he is willing to do anything necessary to help you prepare the forecast.

First, he wants projections of sales and revenues and earnings from the existing business, which he believes can continue to be financed from existing capital.

Second, he intends to buy a company in a closely related business that is currently operating unsuccessfully. Monson states that he wants to sell some of the operating assets of the business and replace them with others. He believes that the company can then be made highly successful. He has made an offer on the new business, subject to obtaining proper financing. He also informs you that he has received an offer on the assets he intends to sell.

Required

a. Explain circumstances under which it is and is not acceptable to undertake the engagement.
b. Why is it important that Monson understand the nature of your reporting requirements before the engagement proceeds?
c. What information will Monson have to provide to you before you can complete the forecasted statements? Be as specific as possible.
d. Discuss, in as specific terms as possible, the nature of the report you will issue with the forecasts, assuming that you are able to properly complete them.

25-29 **(OBJECTIVE 25-7)** Bengston, CPA, is conducting the audit of Pollution Control Devices, Inc. In addition, a supplemental negative assurance report is required for a major mortgage holder. The supplemental report concerns indenture agreements to keep the client from defaulting on the mortgage. Total assets are $14 million and the mortgage is for $4 million. The major provisions of the indentures are as follows:

1. The current ratio must be maintained above 2.3 to 1.
2. The debt/equity ratio must be maintained below 3.0.
3. Net earnings after taxes must exceed dividends paid by at least $1 million.

a. Write the appropriate supplemental report if all three indenture agreement provisions have been satisfied. **Required**
b. How would the supplemental report change if net earnings after taxes were $1,010,000 and dividends paid were $60,000?
c. Assume the same situation as in part b. and also assume that the client refuses to modify the financial statements or disclose the violation of the indenture agreement provisions on the grounds that the amount is immaterial. What is the nature of the appropriate auditor's report?
d. What is the nature of the appropriate supplemental report if all the indenture agreement provisions have been satisfied but there is a lawsuit against the company that has resulted in disclosure of the lawsuit in a footnote to the financial statements?

25-30 **(OBJECTIVE 25-7)** Jones, CPA, has completed the audit of Sarack Lumber Supply Co. and has issued a standard unmodified report. In addition to a report on the overall financial statements, the company needs a special audited report on three specific accounts: sales, net fixed assets, and inventory valued at FIFO. The report is to be issued to Sarack's lessor, who bases annual rentals on these three accounts. Jones was not aware of the need for the report on the three specific accounts until after the overall audit was completed.

a. Explain why Jones is unlikely to be able to issue the audit report on the three specific accounts without additional audit tests. **Required**
b. What additional tests are likely to be needed before the report on the three specific accounts can be issued?
c. Assuming that Jones is able to satisfy all the requirements needed to issue the report on the three specific accounts, write the report. Make any necessary assumptions.

CHAPTER

26

INTERNAL AND GOVERNMENTAL FINANCIAL AUDITING AND OPERATIONAL AUDITING

LEARNING OBJECTIVES

After studying this chapter, you should be able to

26-1 Explain the role of internal auditors in financial auditing.

26-2 Describe the auditing and reporting requirements under *Government Auditing Standards* and the Single Audit Act.

26-3 Distinguish operational auditing from financial auditing.

26-4 Provide an overview of operational audits.

26-5 Plan and perform an operational audit.

Good Auditing Often Results in Improved Cash Flows

Sandy Previtz is an experienced internal audit staff person with Erhardt Freight Company (EFC), a long-haul trucking company. EFC has been growing rapidly, adding customers and shipping agents daily. Daily volume now exceeds several thousand shipments per day. To address the growing volume of freight bills and related receivables, EFC implemented a new, state-of-the-art computerized information system.

Previtz was assigned to test the accuracy of the aging of the accounts receivable system and the adequacy of the allowance for doubtful accounts. She took an initial sample of 300 freight bills selected at random from a population of 20,000 outstanding freight bills. She used the sample to project an aging and develop an estimate of the required allowance for doubtful accounts. Her tests indicated the allowance could be understated by as much as $1 million.

Previtz informed Martha Harris, the head of internal audit, of the situation. Harris informed the chief financial officer that as long as the tests indicated there could be a material misstatement, EFC must expand the sample until it was clear whether the allowance was materially misstated.

Previtz's second sample increased the total sample to 600 items, with essentially the same results. However, at Harris's request, she analyzed the items from *both* a management standpoint and an accounting standpoint. When Harris and Previtz met with the CFO to discuss the updated information, Harris pointed out that the real problem was not the allowance but that receivables were out of control, and EFC faced a significant loss in cash flows if management didn't act quickly. The CFO agreed and responded by hiring a team of temporary workers to analyze the aging of all 20,000 freight bills and to institute a large-scale collection effort. Not only did the analysis and collection efforts improve cash flows, it also showed that Previtz's estimate was right on target.

The last chapter discussed types of assurance services that external auditors provide. This chapter examines the activities of internal auditors and government auditors, who perform a significant amount of financial auditing similar to that done by external CPA firms. As Sandy Previtz of Erhardt Freight Company demonstrates in the introductory story, internal auditors can have a significant impact on a company's operational efficiency and effectiveness, as well as on earnings and cash flow.

The concepts and methodologies studied in the preceding 25 chapters of this book apply to internal and governmental audits. We begin this chapter by examining the role of internal auditors in financial auditing.

INTERNAL FINANCIAL AUDITING

OBJECTIVE 26-1

Explain the role of internal auditors in financial auditing.

As discussed in Chapter 1, companies employ their own internal auditors to do both financial and operational auditing. During the past two decades, the role of internal auditors has expanded dramatically, primarily because of the increased size and complexity of many corporations. Because internal auditors spend all of their time within one company, they have much greater knowledge about the company's operations and internal controls than external auditors. That kind of knowledge can be critical to effective corporate governance. The New York Stock Exchange requires its registrants to have an internal audit function, and many other public and private companies also have an internal audit function.

The Institute of Internal Auditors Professional Practices Framework provides the following definition of internal auditing:

> Internal auditing is an independent, objective assurance and consulting activity designed to add value and improve an organization's operations. It helps an organization accomplish its objectives by bringing a systematic, disciplined approach to evaluate and improve the effectiveness of risk management, control, and governance processes.

This definition reflects the changing role of internal auditors. They are expected to provide value to the organization through improved operational effectiveness, while also performing traditional responsibilities, such as:

- Reviewing the reliability and integrity of information
- Ensuring compliance with policies and regulations
- Safeguarding assets

The objectives of internal auditors are considerably broader than the objectives of external auditors, providing flexibility for internal auditors to meet their company's needs. At one company, internal auditors may focus exclusively on documenting and testing controls for Sarbanes–Oxley Act Section 404 requirements. At another company, internal auditors may serve primarily as consultants, focusing on recommendations that improve organizational performance. Not only may internal auditors focus on different areas, but the extent of internal auditing may vary from one company to another. Internal audit reports are not standardized because the reporting needs vary for each company and the reports are not relied on by external users.

Institute of Internal Auditors

Professional guidance for internal auditors is provided by the **Institute of Internal Auditors (IIA)**, an organization similar to the AICPA that establishes ethical and practice standards, provides education, and encourages professionalism for its approximately 180,000 worldwide members. The IIA has played a major role in the increasing influence of internal auditing. For example, the IIA has established a highly regarded certification program resulting in the designation of Certified Internal Auditor (CIA) for those who meet specific testing and experience requirements.

The IIA Professional Practice Framework includes a code of ethics and IIA **International Standards for the Professional Practice of Internal Auditing** (known as the "Red Book"). All IIA members and Certified Internal Auditors agree to follow the Institute's Code of Ethics, which requires compliance with the Standards.

FIGURE 26-1 **Institute of Internal Auditors Ethical Principles and Rules of Conduct**

ETHICAL PRINCIPLES

Integrity	The integrity of internal auditors establishes trust and thus provides the basis for reliance on their judgment.
Objectivity	Internal auditors exhibit the highest level of professional objectivity in gathering, evaluating, and communicating information about the activity or process being examined. Internal auditors make a balanced assessment of all the relevant circumstances and are not unduly influenced by their own interests or by others in forming judgments.
Confidentiality	Internal auditors respect the value and ownership of information they receive and do not disclose information without appropriate authority unless there is a legal or professional obligation to do so.
Competency	Internal auditors apply the knowledge, skills, and experience needed in the performance of internal auditing services.

RULES OF CONDUCT

1. Integrity

Internal auditors:

1.1. Shall perform their work with honesty, diligence, and responsibility.
1.2. Shall observe the law and make disclosures expected by the law and the profession.
1.3. Shall not knowingly be a party to any illegal activity or engage in acts that are discreditable to the profession of internal auditing or to the organization.
1.4. Shall respect and contribute to the legitimate and ethical objectives of the organization.

2. Objectvity

Internal auditors:

2.1. Shall not participate in any activity or relationship that may impair or be presumed to impair their unbiased assessment. This participation includes those activities or relationships that may be in conflict with the interests of the organization.
2.2. Shall not accept anything that may impair or be presumed to impair their professional judgment.
2.3. Shall disclose all material facts known to them that, if not disclosed, may distort the reporting of activities under review.

3. Confidentiality

Internal auditors:

3.1. Shall be prudent in the use and protection of information acquired in the course of their duties.
3.2. Shall not use information for any personal gain or in any manner that would be contrary to the law or detrimental to the legitimate and ethical objectives of the organization.

4. Competency

Internal auditors:

4.1. Shall engage only in those services for which they have the necessary knowledge, skills, and experience.
4.2. Shall perform internal auditing services in accordance with the *International Standards for the Professional Practice of Internal Auditing*.
4.3. Shall continually improve their proficiency and the effectiveness and quality of their services.

Source: The Institute of Internal Auditors' Code of Ethics, The Institute of Internal Auditors, Inc., www.theiia.org. Reprinted by permission.

Figure 26-1 outlines the IIA Code of Ethics, which is based on the ethical principles of integrity, objectivity, confidentiality, and competency.

As shown in Figure 26-2, the International Standards for the Professional Practice of Internal Auditing are divided into attribute standards for internal auditors and audit departments, and performance standards for the conduct and reporting of internal audit activities.

The IIA created specific standards within each category. For example, Attribute Standard 1100 on Independence and Objectivity includes individual standards to address organizational independence (1110), individual objectivity (1120), and impairments to independence and objectivity (1130).

In addition, the IIA developed specific implementation standards for assurance and consulting engagements. For example, Implementation Standard 1110.A1 provides guidance for applying Attribute Standard 1110 on organizational independence for assurance engagements, stating that the internal audit activity should be free from interference in determining the scope of internal auditing, performing work, and communicating results.

You may want to compare these standards to the principles of the AICPA auditing standards, as detailed in Figure 2-2 on page 35, to note similarities and differences. **Statements on Internal Auditing Standards (SIASs)** are issued by the Internal Auditing Standards Board to provide authoritative interpretations of the standards.

Relationship of Internal and External Auditors

The responsibilities and conduct of audits by internal and external auditors differ in one important way. Internal auditors are responsible to management and the board,

FIGURE 26-2 **International Standards for the Professional Practice of Internal Auditing**

ATTRIBUTE STANDARDS

1000 Purpose, Authority, and Responsibility. The purpose, authority, and responsibility of the internal audit activity must be formally defined in an internal audit charter, consistent with the Definition of Internal Auditing, the Code of Ethics, and the *Standards*. The chief audit executive must periodically review the internal audit charter and present it to senior management and the board for approval.

1100 Independence and Objectivity. The internal audit activity must be independent, and internal auditors must be objective in performing their work.

1130 Impairment to Independence or Objectivity. If independence or objectivity is impaired in fact or appearance, the details of the impairment must be disclosed to appropriate parties. The nature of the disclosure will depend upon the impairment.

1200 Proficiency and Due Professional Care. Engagements must be performed with proficiency and due professional care.

1300 Quality Assurance and Improvement Program. The chief audit executive must develop and maintain a quality assurance and improvement program that covers all aspects of the internal audit activity.

PERFORMANCE STANDARDS

2000 Managing the Internal Audit Activity. The chief audit executive must effectively manage the internal audit activity to ensure it adds value to the organization.

2100 Nature of Work. The internal audit activity must evaluate and contribute to the improvement of governance, risk management, and control processes using a systematic and disciplined approach.

2200 Engagement Planning. Internal auditors must develop and document a plan for each engagement including the engagement's objectives, scope, timing, and resource allocations.

2300 Performing the Engagement. Internal auditors must identify, analyze, evaluate, and document sufficient information to achieve the engagement's objectives.

2400 Communicating Results. Internal auditors must communicate the results of engagements.

2500 Monitoring Progress. The chief audit executive must establish and maintain a system to monitor the disposition of results communicated to management.

2600 Communicating the Acceptance of Risks. When the chief audit executive concludes that management has accepted a level of risk that may be unacceptable to the organization, the chief audit executive must discuss the matter with senior management. If the chief audit executive determines that the matter has not been resolved, the chief audit executive must communicate the matter to the board.

Source: From *The International Standards for the Professional Practice of Auditing*, Copyright © 2012 by The Institute of Internal Auditors, Inc., 247 Maitland Avenue, Altamonte Springs, FL 32701-4201 (www.theiia.org). Reprinted with permission.

while external auditors are responsible to financial statement users, who rely on the auditor to add credibility to financial statements. Nevertheless, internal and external auditors share many similarities:

- Both must be competent as auditors and remain objective in performing their work and reporting their results.
- Both follow a similar methodology in performing their audits, including planning and performing tests of controls and substantive tests.
- Both consider risk and materiality in deciding the extent of their tests and evaluating results. However, their decisions about materiality and risks may differ because external users may have different needs than management or the board.

External auditors rely on internal auditors when using the audit risk model to assess control risk. If internal auditors are effective, the external auditors can significantly reduce control risk and thereby reduce substantive testing. As a result, external auditors may reduce their fees substantially when the client has a highly regarded internal audit function. External auditors typically consider internal auditors effective if they:

- Are independent of the operating units being evaluated
- Are competent and well trained
- Apply a systematic and disciplined approach, including quality control

The independence and objectivity of the internal audit department depend on the organizational status of the department, for example, the reporting lines, and on whether the auditors can make impartial, unbiased judgments. To determine whether internal auditors are competent and well trained, external auditors consider training of the individuals in the internal audit function, such as their educational backgrounds and certifications. Finally, a systematic and disciplined approach refers

ROLE OF INTERNAL AUDIT IN ERM LEADERSHIP

As expectations continue to grow for boards and senior executives to strengthen their oversight of risks arising across the enterprise, organizations are implementing enterprise risk management (ERM) processes to more robustly identify, assess, and manage all types of risks that might impact value for the organization. Recent research finds that in over 60 percent of organizations surveyed, the board of directors is delegating oversight of management's ERM processes to the audit committee. In about 20 percent of organizations surveyed, the chief internal audit executive is being tasked at the management level with leading the ERM process within those organizations. This approach makes sense given that audit committees and internal auditors already have established lines of reporting and internal audit standards use a risk-based approach to auditing.

While assigning responsibilities for ERM leadership to internal audit may make sense, it does create challenges that might impair internal audit's independence and objectivity from the ERM process. If internal audit assumes too much responsibility for the management of risks, it jeopardizes its ability to provide independent assurance to the audit committee about the effectiveness of ERM processes at the management level.

The Institute of Internal Auditors' Position Paper, "The Role of Internal Auditing in Enterprise-wide Risk Management," highlights various ERM-related activities along a spectrum ranging from those appropriate for internal audit to perform to those deemed not appropriate. The Position Paper categorizes various ERM-related tasks into three categories as follows:

1. Core Internal Audit Roles in Regards to ERM
   - Giving assurance on the risk management processes
   - Giving assurance on whether risks are correctly evaluated
   - Evaluating the reporting of key risks
   - Reviewing the management of key risks
2. Legitimate Internal Audit Roles with Safeguards Needed
   - Facilitating the identification and evaluation of risks
   - Coaching management in responding to risks
   - Coordinating ERM activities
   - Consolidating reporting of risks
   - Maintaining and developing the ERM framework
   - Championing the establishment of ERM
   - Developing the ERM strategy for board approval
3. Roles Internal Audit Should Not Undertake
   - Setting the risk appetite
   - Imposing risk management processes
   - Management assurance on risks
   - Taking decisions on risk responses
   - Implementing risk responses on management's behalf
   - Accountability for risk management

Sources: 1. Mark Beasley, Bruce Branson, and Bonnie Hancock, "Report on the Current State of Enterprise Risk Oversight: Update on Trends and Opportunities," AICPA and NC State University, February 2015 (www.erm.ncsu.edu); 2. "IIA Position Paper: The Role of Internal Auditing in Enterprise-wide Risk Management," The Institute of Internal Auditors, January 2009 (www.theiia.org).

to how the internal audit department plans and performs their engagements and reports outcomes. For example, conducting their audits in accordance with the IIA International Standards for the Professional Practice of Internal Auditing as outlined in Figure 26-2 (p. 829) would be considered a systematic and disciplined approach.

Auditing standards permit the external auditor to use the internal auditor for direct assistance on the audit. By relying on the internal audit staff for performing some of the audit testing, external auditors may be able to complete the audit in less time and at a lower fee. When internal auditors provide direct assistance, the external auditor should assess their competence and objectivity and supervise and evaluate their work.

GOVERNMENTAL FINANCIAL AUDITING

OBJECTIVE 26-2

Describe the auditing and reporting requirements under *Government Auditing Standards* and the Single Audit Act.

Federal and state governments employ their own auditing staffs to perform audits in much the same way as internal auditors. Chapter 1 briefly discussed the United States Government Accountability Office (GAO). All states have their own audit agencies, similar to but smaller than the GAO. In addition, CPA firms do considerable financial auditing of governmental units. For example, some states require that all city and school district financial statements be audited by CPA firms.

The primary source of authoritative literature for doing **government audits** is ***Government Auditing Standards***, which is issued by the GAO. Because of the color of the cover, it is usually referred to as the "**Yellow Book**" rather than by its more formal name. The initial Yellow Book standards were similar to the GAAS standards but have been expanded in subsequent revisions to provide guidance standards for performance audits. These standards are often called generally accepted government auditing standards (**GAGAS**).

Financial auditing under the Yellow Book includes several categories of information to audit, including financial statements of governmental units, government contracts and grants, internal control, fraud, and other noncompliance with laws and regulations. Because governmental units are as concerned with compliance with laws and regulations as they are with the reliability of financial statements, these categories of information are broader than audits under auditing standards and encompass the types of attestation work outlined in Table 25-1 on page 808.

Financial Audit and Reporting Requirements—Yellow Book

The financial auditing standards of the Yellow Book are consistent with the principles of the AICPA auditing standards, and also contain extensive additional guidance, including the following additions and modifications:

- *Materiality and significance.* The Yellow Book recognizes that in government audits the thresholds of acceptable audit risk and materiality may be lower than in an audit of a commercial enterprise. This is because of the sensitivity of government activities and their public accountability.
- *Quality control.* CPA firms and other organizations that audit government entities in compliance with the Yellow Book must have an appropriate system of internal quality control and participate in an external quality control review program. The latter requirement exists for some CPAs, but only as a requirement for membership in the AICPA, and for the audit of public companies.

  Auditors involved in planning, performing, or reporting on audits under GAGAS must complete 80 hours of continuing professional education in each two-year period. At least 24 of these 80 hours of training must be in subjects related to the government environment and government auditing.
- *Compliance auditing.* The audit should be designed to provide reasonable assurance of detecting material misstatements resulting from noncompliance with provisions of contracts or grant agreements that have a material and direct effect on the financial statements.
- *Reporting.* The audit report must state that the audit was made in accordance with generally accepted government auditing standards (GAGAS). In addition, the report on financial statements must describe the scope of the auditors' tests of compliance with laws and regulations and internal controls and present the results of those tests or refer to a separate report that includes the information.

$54 MILLION EMBEZZLED FROM DIXON, IL, CITY GOVERNMENT

The small town of Dixon, Illinois, had a modest annual budget, yet City Treasurer Rita Crundwell embezzled a total of $54 million from the small town over a period of 22 years. The story in Dixon reads like many others where employees take advantage of the trust placed in them to divert funds for their personal use. In this case, Crundwell used the money to fund a lavish lifestyle and equestrian habit. At the time the fraud was detected, she owned approximately 400 horses and had won several national championships.

The fraud began when Crundwell opened up a bank account, presumably on behalf of the city of Dixon, although she was the only authorized check-signer on the account. She then diverted city funds to this account by creating over 180 fake invoices, and writing and signing the checks from the account to fund her lifestyle. In 2013, the bank and the external auditors for the city settled lawsuits filed against them for a total of $40 million. Crundwell, sentenced to 19 years in prison, has helped authorities recover the remainder of the money by selling her personal assets. The details of the case suggest the auditors should have detected the fake invoices. In addition, the external audit firm prepared Crundwell's personal taxes, which should have alerted them to the fact that she was living well beyond the means of her $80,000 annual salary. The city officials, bank officials, and external auditors all share blame in allowing such a massive fraud to continue for decades without being detected.

Source: Melissa Jenco, "Dixon Blames Phony Invoices, Lax Auditors for $54M Fraud," *Chicago Tribune*, September 27, 2013 (www.chicagotribune.com).

Audit and Reporting Requirements—Single Audit Act and OMB Circular A-133

The **Single Audit Act** of 1984 provides for a single coordinated audit to meet the audit requirements of all federal agencies. Entities that receive more than $750,000 in federal funds are subject to a single audit even if more than one agency provided funds. The Single Audit Act applied only to audits of state and local governments, but it was extended in 1990 to higher-education institutions and other not-for-profit organizations by the Office of Management and Budget (OMB) through the issuance of OMB Circular A-133, *Audits of States, Local Governments, and Non-Profit Organizations.* The guidance contained in OMB Circular A-133 is now incorporated into the Code of Federal Regulations in Section 200 (2 CFR part 200 subpart F).

Audit Requirements The Single Audit Act as amended and OMB Circular A-133/2 CFR 200 subpart F (hereafter referred to collectively as the Act) contain requirements for the scope of the audit, including:

- The audit should be in accordance with GAGAS.
- The auditor must obtain an understanding of internal control over federal programs sufficient to support a low assessed level of control risk for major programs.
- The auditor should determine whether the client has complied with laws, regulations, and the provisions of contracts or grant agreements that may have a direct and material effect on each of its major programs.

The OMB regularly provides a *Compliance Supplement* that contains the relevant guidance in one source to help auditors understand the federal program's audit objectives, procedures, and compliance requirements, along with suggested audit procedures that should be considered in every audit. In addition, it lists specific requirements for individual federal programs. The following are examples of specific compliance objectives:

- Whether the amounts reported as expenditures were for allowable services.
- Whether the records show that those who received services or benefits were eligible to receive them.
- Whether matching requirements (where the government unit matches federal funds), levels of effort, and earmarking limitations were met.

Reporting Requirements The following reports are required under OMB Circular A-133/2 CFR 200 subpart F:

- An opinion on whether the financial statements are presented fairly in all material respects in accordance with GAAP.
- An opinion as to whether the schedule of federal awards is presented fairly in all material respects in relation to the financial statements as a whole.
- A report on internal control related to the financial statements and major programs.
- A report on compliance with laws, regulations, and the provisions of contracts or grant agreements, where noncompliance could have a material effect on the financial statements. This report can be combined with the report on internal control.
- A schedule of findings and questioned costs.

AICPA Guidance for Auditors

Auditors doing government auditing often find it complex. The auditor must be familiar with both auditing standards and a series of government audit documents, laws, and regulations. Thus, the first step in preparing for such an engagement is extensive professional development. Two relevant resources are the AICPA audit guide, *Government Auditing Standards and Single Audits,* and the auditing standard, *Compliance Audits.*

CONCEPT CHECK

1. Explain the role of internal auditors for financial auditing. How is it similar to and different from the role of external auditors?
2. Explain how governmental financial auditing is similar to and different from audits of commercial companies. Who does governmental auditing?

OPERATIONAL AUDITING

Beyond financial auditing activities, internal auditors, government auditors, and CPAs also do **operational auditing**, which deals with efficiency and effectiveness of an organization. Other auditors use the terms *management auditing* or *performance auditing* instead of *operational auditing* to refer to these activities, while others do not distinguish among the terms *performance auditing, management auditing*, and *operational auditing* and use them interchangeably.

We prefer to use *operational auditing* broadly, as long as the purpose of the test is to determine the effectiveness or efficiency of any part of an organization. Testing the effectiveness of internal controls by an internal auditor may therefore be considered part of operational auditing—if the purpose is to help an organization operate its business more effectively or efficiently. Similarly, determining whether a company has adequately trained assembly line personnel may also be operational auditing, if the purpose is to determine whether the company is effectively and efficiently producing products.

Differences Between Operational and Financial Auditing

OBJECTIVE 26-3

Distinguish operational auditing from financial auditing.

The three major differences between operational and financial auditing are the purpose of the audit, distribution of the report, and inclusion of nonfinancial areas in operational auditing.

Purpose of the Audit This is the most important difference. Financial auditing emphasizes whether historical information was correctly recorded, while operational auditing emphasizes effectiveness and efficiency. Financial auditing is oriented to the past, while operational auditing focuses on improving future performance. An operational auditor, for example, may evaluate whether a type of new material is being purchased at the lowest cost to save money on future raw material purchases.

Distribution of the Reports Financial auditing reports are typically distributed to external users of financial statements, such as stockholders and bankers, while operational audit reports are intended primarily for management. The widespread distribution of financial auditing reports requires a well-defined structure and wording, as shown in Figure 3-1 on page 48. The limited distribution of operational reports and the diverse nature of audits for efficiency and effectiveness allow operational audit reports to vary considerably from audit to audit.

Inclusion of Nonfinancial Areas Financial audits are limited to matters that directly affect the fairness of financial statement presentation, while operational audits cover any aspect of efficiency and effectiveness in an organization. For example, an operational audit might address the effectiveness of an advertising program or efficiency of factory employees.

Effectiveness Versus Efficiency

OBJECTIVE 26-4

Provide an overview of operational audits.

Before an operational audit can be performed, auditors must define specific criteria for measuring effectiveness and efficiency. In general, **effectiveness** refers to meeting objectives, such as producing parts without defects. Efficiency refers to determining the resources used to achieve those objectives, such as determining whether parts are produced at minimum cost.

Effectiveness In an operational audit for effectiveness, an auditor, for example, might need to assess whether a governmental agency has met its assigned objective of achieving elevator safety in a city. To determine the agency's effectiveness, the auditor must establish specific criteria for elevator safety. For example, is the agency's objective to inspect all elevators in the city at least once a year? Is the objective to ensure that no fatalities occurred as a result of elevator breakdowns, or that no breakdowns occurred?

Efficiency Like effectiveness, there must be defined criteria for what is meant by doing things more efficiently before operational auditing can be meaningful. It is often easier to set efficiency than effectiveness criteria if **efficiency** is defined as reducing cost without reducing effectiveness. For example, if two different production processes manufacture a product of identical quality, the process with the lower cost is considered more efficient. Operational auditing commonly uncovers several types of typical inefficiencies, including:

Types of Inefficiency	*Example*
• Acquisition of goods and services is excessively costly.	• Bids for purchases of materials are not required.
• Raw materials are not available for production when needed.	• An entire assembly line must be shut down because necessary materials were not ordered.
• There is duplication of effort by employees.	• Identical production records are kept by both the accounting and production departments because they are unaware of each other's activities.
• Work is done that serves no purpose.	• Copies of vendors' invoices and receiving reports are sent to the production department, where they are filed without ever being used.
• There are too many employees.	• The office work could be done effectively with one less administrative assistant.

Relationship Between Operational Auditing and Internal Controls

Management establishes internal controls to help meet its goals. As we discussed in Chapter 11, effective internal controls are designed and implemented to help organizations achieve these objectives:

1. Reliability of reporting
2. Efficiency and effectiveness of operations
3. Compliance with applicable laws and regulations

Obviously, the second of these three objectives directly relates to operational auditing, but the other two also affect efficiency and effectiveness. For example, management needs reliable cost accounting information to decide which products to continue producing and the billing price of products. Similarly, failure to comply with a law, such as the Sarbanes–Oxley Act, can result in a large fine to the company.

Two things distinguish internal control evaluation and testing for financial and operational auditing: purpose and scope.

Purpose The purpose of operational auditing of internal control is to evaluate efficiency and effectiveness and to make recommendations to management. In contrast, internal control evaluation for financial auditing has two primary purposes: to determine the extent of substantive audit testing required and, when applicable, to report on the effectiveness of internal control over financial reporting.

For both financial and operational auditing, the auditors may evaluate the control procedures in the same way, but for different purposes. An operational auditor might test whether internal verification procedures for duplicate sales invoices are effective to ensure that the company does not offend customers, but also to collect all receivables. A financial auditor often does the same internal control tests, but the primary purpose is to reduce confirmation of accounts receivable or other substantive tests. (A secondary purpose of many financial audits is also to make operational recommendations to management.)

Scope The scope of operational auditing concerns any control affecting efficiency or effectiveness, while the scope of internal control evaluation for financial audits is restricted to the effectiveness of internal control over financial reporting and its effect on the fair presentation of financial statements. For example, an operational audit can focus on policies and procedures established in the marketing department to determine the effectiveness of catalogs in marketing products.

Types of Operational Audits

Operational audits fall into three broad categories: functional, organizational, and special assignments. In each case, part of the audit is likely to concern evaluating internal controls for efficiency and effectiveness.

Functional Audits Functions are a means of categorizing the activities of a business, such as the billing function or production function. Functions may be categorized and subdivided many different ways. For example, the accounting function may be subdivided into cash disbursement, cash receipt, and payroll disbursement functions. The payroll function may be subdivided into hiring, timekeeping, and payroll disbursement functions. A **functional audit** deals with one or more functions in an organization, concerning, for example, the efficiency and effectiveness of the payroll function for a division or for the company as a whole.

A functional audit has the advantage of permitting specialization by auditors. Certain auditors within an internal audit staff can develop considerable expertise in an area, such as production engineering. They can be more efficient and effective by spending all their time auditing in that area. A disadvantage of functional auditing is the failure to evaluate interrelated functions. For example, the production engineering function interacts with manufacturing and other functions in an organization.

Organizational Audits An operational audit of an organization deals with an entire organizational unit, such as a department, branch, or subsidiary. An **organizational audit** emphasizes how efficiently and effectively functions interact. The plan of organization and the methods to coordinate activities are important in this type of audit.

Special Assignments In operational auditing, **special assignments** arise at the request of management for a wide variety of audits, such as determining the cause of an ineffective IT system, investigating the possibility of fraud in a division, and making recommendations for reducing the cost of a manufactured product.

Who Performs Operational Audits

Operational audits are usually performed by one of three groups: internal auditors, government auditors, or CPA firms.

Internal Auditors Internal auditors are in such a unique position to perform operational audits that some people use the terms *internal auditing* and *operational auditing* interchangeably. It is, however, inappropriate to conclude that all operational auditing is done by internal auditors or that internal auditors do only operational auditing. Many internal audit departments do both operational and financial auditing, often simultaneously. Because they spend all their time working for the company they are auditing, internal auditors have an advantage in doing operational audits. They can develop considerable knowledge about the company and its business, which is essential to effective operational auditing.

To maximize their effectiveness for both financial and operational auditing, the internal audit department should report to the board of directors or president. Internal auditors should also have access to and ongoing communications with the audit committee of the board of directors. This organizational structure helps internal auditors remain independent. If internal auditors report to the controller, it is difficult for them to do independent evaluations and make recommendations to senior management about inefficiencies in the controller's operations.

Government Auditors Different federal and state government auditors perform operational auditing, often as a part of doing financial audits. As already discussed, the most widely recognized government auditor group is the GAO, but many state government auditors are also concerned with financial and operational audits.

The Yellow Book defines and sets standards for performance audits, which are essentially the same as operational audits. Performance audits include the following:

- *Economy and efficiency audits.* The purpose of an **economy and efficiency audit** is to determine:
  1. Whether the entity is acquiring, protecting, and using its resources economically and efficiently
  2. The causes of inefficiencies or uneconomical practices

3. Whether the entity has complied with laws and regulations concerning matters of economy and efficiency

- *Program audits.* The purpose of a **program audit** is to determine:
  1. The extent to which the desired results or benefits established by the legislature or other authorizing body are being achieved
  2. The effectiveness of organizations, programs, activities, or functions
  3. Whether the entity has complied with laws and regulations applicable to the program

The first two objectives of each of these types of performance audits are clearly operational in nature, while the final objective concerns compliance.

To illustrate specific operational activities of a state governmental audit, the 2014 *Operational Audit* report for the City of Hampton, Florida, disclosed 31 key findings in the Executive Summary. Here are three of those findings:

- The city was not able to account for a high rate of water usage, with 46 percent of water pumped unaccounted for, most likely due to leaking pipes, faulty meters, and unmetered users. As a result, the city is unable to ensure whether the appropriate amount of water is being billed.
- The city has not established policies and procedures regarding the assignment of vehicles to employees for 24-hour use. Employees assigned vehicles on a 24-hour basis were not required to maintain usage logs, restricting the ability to determine the extent of personal use of those vehicles.
- The city did not use the adopted budget to control expenditures and the City Council was not provided budget-to-actual comparison reports. The lack of timely budget data resulted in the Council not having information necessary to gain an understanding of the city's financial status.[1]

CPA Firms When a CPA firm does an audit of historical financial statements, part of the audit often consists of identifying operational problems and making recommendations that may benefit the audit client. The recommendations can be made orally, but they are typically included in a management letter. (For coverage of management letters, see page 787 in Chapter 24.)

The background knowledge about a client's business, which an external auditor must obtain while doing an audit, often provides useful information for giving operational recommendations. For example, suppose that the auditor determined that inventory turnover for a client slowed considerably during the current year. The auditor should determine the cause of the slower turnover to evaluate the possibility of obsolete inventory that would misstate the financial statements. In determining the cause of the reduced inventory turnover, the auditor may identify operational causes, such as ineffective inventory acquisition policies, that can be brought to the attention of management. An auditor who has a broad business background and experience with similar businesses is more likely to be effective at providing clients with relevant operational recommendations than a person who lacks those qualities.

A client commonly engages a CPA firm to do operational auditing for one or more specific parts of its business. For example, a company can ask the CPA firm to evaluate the efficiency and effectiveness of its computer systems. Usually, management engages the CPA firm for these audits only when the company does not have an internal audit staff or if the internal audit staff lacks expertise in a certain area. In some cases, management or the board of directors outsources the entire internal audit function to a CPA firm or co-sources select internal audit activities, such as IT operational auditing activities, to be done jointly by a CPA firm and certain members of the company's internal audit staff. In most cases, the CPA firm's management consulting staff

[1]Based on the *City of Hamilton Operational Audit Report* (Report No. 2014-100), issued by the State of Florida Auditor General, David W. Martin (February 2014).

performs these services. Note that CPA firms cannot provide these services to their public company audit clients.

Independence and Competence of Operational Auditors

The two most important qualities for an operational auditor are *independence* and *competence*. The auditor should report to the appropriate level of management to ensure that investigation and recommendations are made without bias. Independence is seldom a problem for CPA firm auditors because they are not employed by the company being audited. The independence of internal auditors is enhanced by having the internal audit department report to the board of directors or president. Similarly, government auditors should report to a level above the operating departments. The GAO, for example, reports directly to Congress as a means of enhancing independence.

The responsibilities of operational auditors can also affect their independence. The auditor should not be responsible for operating functions in a company or for correcting deficiencies when ineffective or inefficient operations are found. For example, it would negatively affect auditors' independence when they audit an IT system for acquisitions if they designed the system or are responsible for correcting deficiencies they found during the audit.

While it is acceptable for auditors to recommend changes in operations, operating personnel must have the authority to accept or reject those recommendations. If auditors had the authority to require implementation of their recommendations, their independence would be reduced.

Competence is, of course, necessary to determine the cause of operational problems and to make appropriate recommendations. When operational auditing deals with wide-ranging operating problems, however, competence can be a major obstacle. For example, imagine the difficulties of finding qualified internal auditors who can evaluate both the effectiveness of an advertising program and the efficiency of a production assembly process. The internal audit staff doing that type of operational auditing will presumably have to include some personnel with backgrounds in marketing and others in production.

Criteria for Evaluating Efficiency and Effectiveness

OBJECTIVE 26-5

Plan and perform an operational audit.

A major challenge of operational auditing is in selecting specific criteria for evaluating whether efficiency and effectiveness have occurred. In auditing historical financial statements, accounting standards provide the broad criteria for evaluating fair presentation, and audit objectives facilitate more specific criteria in deciding whether those standards have been followed. In operational auditing, there are no well-defined criteria.

To establish criteria for operational auditing, auditors could define the objectives as determining whether some aspect of the entity could be made more effective or efficient, and recommending improvements. This approach may be adequate for experienced and well-trained auditors, but it provides little guidance for most auditors.

Specific Criteria More specific criteria are usually desirable before starting an operational audit. For example, suppose that you are doing an operational audit of the equipment layout in plants for a company. Here are some specific criteria, stated as questions, that might be used to evaluate plant layouts:

- Were all plant layouts approved by home office engineering at the time of original design?
- Has home office engineering done a reevaluation study of plant layout in the past five years?
- Is each piece of equipment operating at 60 percent of capacity or more for at least three months each year?
- Does layout facilitate the movement of new materials to the production floor?
- Does layout facilitate the production of finished goods?
- Does layout facilitate the movement of finished goods to distribution centers?
- Does the plant layout effectively use existing equipment?
- Is the safety of employees endangered by the plant layout?

Sources of Criteria To develop specific evaluation criteria, the operational auditor can use several sources, including:

- *Historical performance.* Criteria can be based on actual results from prior periods. By using these criteria, auditors can determine whether things have become "better" or "worse" in comparison. The advantage of this approach is that the criteria are easy to derive. However, they may not provide much insight into how good or bad the results are compared to what they could be.
- *Benchmarking.* Entities within or outside the client's organization may be sufficiently similar to the client's organization to use their operating results as criteria. Auditors should use care in selecting organizations to use as benchmarks. It makes little sense to benchmark with dissimilar organizations or those that perform at a substandard level. For internal comparable entities, the data are often readily available to use as criteria. Outside organizations are often willing to make their operating information available. Also, benchmarking data are often available through industry groups and governmental regulatory agencies.
- *Engineered standards.* It may be possible in some engagements to develop criteria based on engineered standards. For example, auditors can use time and motion studies to determine efficient production output rates. These criteria are often time-consuming and costly to develop because they require considerable expertise, but in some cases it may be worth the cost. Standards can be developed by industry groups for use by all their members, thereby spreading the cost.
- *Discussion and agreement.* Sometimes objective criteria are difficult or costly to obtain and are best developed through discussion and agreement. The parties involved should include management of the entity to be audited, the operational auditor, and the entity or persons to whom the findings will be reported.

Phases in Operational Auditing

The three phases in an operational audit are planning, evidence accumulation and evaluation, and reporting and follow-up.

Planning Planning for operational audits is similar to the planning for audits of historical financial statements that we've discussed in earlier chapters. Like auditors of financial statements, the operational auditor must determine the scope of the engagement and communicate it to the organizational unit. It is also necessary to:

- Staff the engagement properly
- Obtain background information about the organizational unit
- Understand internal control
- Decide on the appropriate evidence to accumulate

The major difference between planning an operational audit and a financial audit is the diversity created by the breadth of operational audits, which often makes it difficult to decide on specific objectives. Auditors select objectives based on the criteria developed for the engagement, depending on the specific circumstances at hand. For example, the objectives for an operational audit of the effectiveness of internal controls over payroll will be dramatically different from those of an operational audit of the efficiency of a research and development department. Yet, these diverse objectives might be part of a single operational audit.

The breadth of operational audits often makes staffing more complicated than in a financial audit. Not only are the areas diverse, such as production control and advertising, but the objectives within those areas often require special technical skills. For example, the auditor may need an engineering background to evaluate performance on a major construction project.

Finally, unlike financial audits, operational audits require auditors to spend more time with the interested parties agreeing on the terms of the engagement and the criteria for evaluation. Regardless of the source of the criteria for evaluation, it is essential that representatives of the entity to be audited, the operational auditor, and the entity or persons to whom the findings will be reported are clear and in agreement on the objectives and criteria involved.

Evidence Accumulation and Evaluation The eight types of evidence—physical examination, confirmation, inspection, analytical procedures, client inquiry, recalculation, reperformance, and observation—introduced in Chapter 7 and discussed throughout this book are equally applicable to operational auditing. Because internal controls and operating procedures are critical parts of operational auditing, it is common to use inspection, client inquiry, analytical procedures, and observation extensively. Confirmation, reperformance, and recalculation are used less extensively for most operational audits than for financial audits because the existence and accuracy objectives are not relevant for most operational audits.

To illustrate evidence accumulation in operational auditing, consider an example of an agency evaluating the safety of elevators in a city. Assume the parties agree that the objective is to determine whether a competent inspector makes an annual inspection of each elevator in the city. To satisfy the completeness objective, auditors might examine blueprints of city buildings and elevator locations and trace them to the agency's list to ensure that all elevators are included in the population. Additional tests on newly constructed buildings will be appropriate to assess the timeliness with which the central listing is updated.

Assuming auditors determine that the agency's list is complete, they can select a sample of elevator locations and collect evidence as to the timing and frequency of inspections. The auditor may want to consider inherent risk by doing greater sampling of older elevators or elevators with previous safety defects. The auditor may also want to examine evidence of the elevator inspectors' competence by reviewing resumes, training programs, competency examinations, and performance reports. It is also likely that the auditor will want to reperform the inspection procedures for a sample of elevators to obtain evidence of inconsistencies in reported and actual conditions.

Just like financial auditors, operational auditors must accumulate sufficient appropriate evidence to provide a basis for a conclusion about the objectives being tested. For an audit of elevator safety, the auditor must accumulate sufficient evidence about elevator safety inspections. After the evidence is accumulated, the auditor must decide whether it is reasonable to conclude that an inspection is made annually of each elevator in the city by a competent inspector.

Reporting and Follow-Up Two major differences in operational and financial auditing reports affect operational auditing reports:

1. In operational audits, the report is usually sent only to management, with a copy to the unit being audited. The lack of third-party users reduces the need for standardized wording in operational auditing reports.
2. The diversity of operational audits requires a tailoring of each report to address the scope of the audit, findings, and recommendations.

Operational auditors often take a significant amount of time to clearly communicate audit findings and recommendations. On performance audits, when reports are being prepared following Yellow Book requirements, specified content must be included, but considerable freedom is permitted in the form of the report. Follow-up is common in operational auditing when auditors make inquiries of management to determine whether the recommended changes were made, and if not, why not.

CONCEPT CHECK

1. Identify the three major differences between financial and operational auditing.
2. Explain what is meant by the criteria for evaluating efficiency and effectiveness. Provide five possible specific criteria for evaluating effectiveness of an IT system for payroll.

Examples of Operational Audit Findings

Governments and governmental agencies often undergo operational audits to examine the efficiency and effectiveness of programs. For example, the *Auditor of State of Ohio—Ohio Performance Team—Annual Report* dated March 30, 2015, provides examples of cost savings resulting from their operational audits. For example, the operational audit of the Ohio Department of Natural Resources resulted in recommendations with projected cost savings of over $12 million in areas such as capital investment management and fishing license pricing. The audit of the Ohio Department of Job and Family Services yielded recommendations resulting in savings of over $45 million by implementing changes in staffing ratios, greater use of electronic portals, and other suggested changes. Recommendations for the Department of Transportation include "right-sizing" various vehicle fleets and closing rest areas near viable alternatives. The annual report suggests that overall, the Ohio Performance Team has saved taxpayers $37 for every dollar spent on the operational audits of the agencies audited to date.

SUMMARY

This chapter discussed the financial auditing activities of internal auditors and the effect of internal auditors on external audits. We also discussed government auditors and the auditing and reporting requirements under *Government Auditing Standards*. Increasingly, internal auditors and government auditors, as well as CPA firms, are also asked to perform operational audits of the efficiency or effectiveness of a company or government unit. In these engagements, the appropriate criteria for evaluating efficiency or effectiveness is essential.

ESSENTIAL TERMS

Economy and efficiency audit—a government audit to determine whether an entity is acquiring, protecting, and using its resources economically and efficiently; the causes of any inefficiencies or uneconomical practices; and whether the entity has complied with laws and regulations concerning matters of economy and efficiency

Effectiveness—the degree to which the organization's objectives are accomplished

Efficiency—the degree to which costs are reduced without reducing effectiveness

Functional audit—an operational audit that deals with one or more specific functions within an organization, such as the payroll function or the production engineering function

***Government Auditing Standards* (GAGAS)**—see Yellow Book

Government audits—financial or operational audits of government agencies or government-funded institutions

Institute of Internal Auditors (IIA)—organization for internal auditors that establishes ethical and practice standards, provides education, and encourages professionalism for its members

International Standards for the Professional Practice of Internal Auditing—guidelines issued by the Institute of Internal Auditors covering the attributes and performance of internal auditors

Operational auditing—the review of an organization for efficiency and effectiveness. The terms *management auditing, performance auditing*, and *operational auditing* are often synonymous terms

Organizational audit—an operational audit that deals with an entire organizational unit, such as a department, branch, or subsidiary, to determine how efficiently and effectively functions interact

Program audit—a government audit to determine the extent to which the desired results or benefits established by the legislature or other authorizing body are being achieved; the effectiveness of organizations, programs, activities, or functions; and whether the entity has complied with laws and regulations applicable to the program

Single Audit Act—federal legislation that provides for a single coordinated audit to satisfy the audit requirements of all federal funding agencies

Special assignments—management requests for an operational audit for a specific purpose, such as investigating the possibility of fraud in a division or making recommendations for reducing the cost of a manufactured product

Statements on Internal Auditing Standards (SIASs)—statements issued by the Internal Auditing Standards Board of the IIA to provide authoritative interpretations of the IIA Practice Standards

Yellow Book—a publication of the GAO that is widely used as a reference by government auditors and CPAs who do governmental audit work; the official title is *Government Auditing Standards*

REVIEW QUESTIONS

26-1 (OBJECTIVE 26-1) What is the nature of the two categories of standards in the IIA International Standards for the Professional Practice of Internal Auditing?

26-2 (OBJECTIVE 26-1) Explain the difference between the independence of internal auditors and external auditors in the audit of historical financial statements. How can internal auditors best achieve independence?

26-3 (OBJECTIVE 26-2) Explain what is meant by the Single Audit Act. What is its purpose?

26-4 (OBJECTIVE 26-2) In what ways is the Yellow Book consistent with the principles in AICPA auditing standards, and what are some additions and modifications?

26-5 (OBJECTIVE 26-2) Identify the primary specific objectives that must be incorporated into the design of audit tests under the Single Audit Act.

26-6 (OBJECTIVE 26-2) Identify the key required reports of the Single Audit Act and OMB Circular A-133.

26-7 (OBJECTIVE 26-3) Describe what is meant by an operational audit.

26-8 (OBJECTIVE 26-4) Distinguish between efficiency and effectiveness in operational audits. State one example of an operational audit examining efficiency and another examining effectiveness.

26-9 (OBJECTIVE 26-4) Distinguish among the following types of operational audits: functional, organizational, and special assignment. State an example of each for a not-for-profit hospital.

26-10 (OBJECTIVE 26-4) Explain why many people think of internal auditors as the primary group responsible for conducting operational audits.

26-11 (OBJECTIVE 26-4) Explain the role of government auditors in operational auditing. How is this similar to and different from the role of internal auditors?

26-12 (OBJECTIVE 26-4) Under what circumstances are external auditors likely to be involved in operational auditing? Give one example of operational auditing by a CPA firm.

26-13 (OBJECTIVE 26-5) Identify the three phases of an operational audit.

26-14 (OBJECTIVE 26-5) Explain how planning for operational auditing is similar to and different from financial auditing.

26-15 (OBJECTIVE 26-5) What are the major differences between reporting for operational and financial auditing?

MULTIPLE CHOICE QUESTIONS FROM CPA, CIA, AND CMA EXAMINATIONS

26-16 (OBJECTIVE 26-1) The following questions deal with internal auditing. Choose the best response.

a. The independence of the internal audit department will most likely be assured if it reports to the
   (1) president.
   (2) controller.
   (3) audit committee of the board of directors.
   (4) vice president of finance.

b. In assessing the competence of internal auditors, an independent CPA most likely would obtain information about the
   (1) influence of management on the scope of the internal auditors' duties.
   (2) policies limiting internal auditors from communicating with the audit committee.
   (3) quality of the internal auditors' working paper documentation.
   (4) entity's ability to continue as a going concern.

c. Which of the following is generally considered to be a major reason for establishing an internal auditing function?
   (1) To relieve overburdened management of the responsibility for establishing effective systems of internal control
   (2) To ensure that operating activities comply with the policies, plans, and procedures established by management
   (3) To ensure the accuracy, reliability, and timeliness of financial and operating data used in management's decision making
   (4) To evaluate and improve the effectiveness of control processes

26-17 **(OBJECTIVE 26-2)** The following questions deal with governmental auditing. Choose the best response.

a. Although the scope of audits of recipients of federal financial assistance in accordance with federal audit regulations varies, these audits generally have which of the following elements in common?
   (1) The auditor is to determine whether the financial assistance has been administered in accordance with applicable laws and regulations.
   (2) The materiality levels are lower and are determined by the governmental entities that provided the federal financial assistance to the recipient.
   (3) The auditor should obtain written management representations that the recipient's internal auditors will report their findings objectively and without fear of political repercussions.
   (4) The auditor is required to express both positive and negative assurance that illegal acts that could have a material effect on the recipient's financial statements are disclosed to the inspector general.

b. A governmental audit may extend beyond an examination leading to the expression of an opinion on the fairness of financial statement presentation to include

	Program Results	Compliance	Economy and Efficiency
(1)	Yes	Yes	No
(2)	Yes	Yes	Yes
(3)	No	Yes	Yes
(4)	Yes	No	Yes

c. Ward is auditing an entity's compliance with requirements governing a major federal financial assistance program in accordance with the Single Audit Act. Ward detected noncompliance with requirements that have a material effect on the program. Ward's report on compliance should express
   (1) no assurance on the compliance tests.
   (2) reasonable assurance on the compliance tests.
   (3) a qualified or adverse opinion.
   (4) an adverse opinion or a disclaimer of opinion.

26-18 **(OBJECTIVES 26-3, 26-4, 26-5)** The following questions deal with operational auditing. Choose the best response.

a. Which of the following best describes the operational audit?
   (1) It requires constant review by internal auditors of the administrative controls as they relate to the operations of the company.
   (2) It concentrates on implementing financial and accounting controls in a newly organized company.

(3) It attempts and is designed to verify the fair presentation of a company's results of operations.
(4) It concentrates on seeking aspects of operations in which waste would be reduced by the introduction of controls.

b. The purpose of governmental effectiveness or program auditing is to determine if the desired results of a program are being achieved. The first step in conducting such an audit is to
(1) evaluate the system used to measure results.
(2) determine the time frame to be audited.
(3) collect quantifiable data on the program's success or failure.
(4) identify the legislative intent of the program being audited.

c. A means of limiting production delays caused by equipment breakdown and repair is to
(1) schedule production based on capacity planning.
(2) plan maintenance activity based on an analysis of equipment repair work orders.
(3) pre-authorize equipment maintenance and overtime pay.
(4) establish a preventive maintenance program for all production equipment.

MULTIPLE CHOICE QUESTIONS FROM BECKER CPA EXAM REVIEW

26-19 **(OBJECTIVES 26-1, 26-2)** The following questions deal with internal and governmental auditing. Choose the best response.

a. In assessing whether the internal audit function applies a systematic and disciplined approach, the independent auditor most likely would consider the
(1) adequacy and use of documented internal audit procedures.
(2) organizational status of the director of internal audit.
(3) entity's ability to continue as a going concern for a reasonable period of time.
(4) internal auditor's assessment of inherent risk and whether it is comparable to the independent auditor's assessment.

b. Which of the following statements regarding the use of internal auditors is correct?
(1) The auditor cannot rely on the work of internal auditors because they are not independent of the client, their employer.
(2) The auditor can rely on the work of internal auditors for any decision because internal auditors are required to report to the audit committee of the board of directors; thus they are independent of the client.
(3) The auditor can rely on the work of internal auditors in limited circumstances, as long as they are not making decisions with a high degree of subjectivity, or decisions that require judgment and assessment.
(4) The use of internal auditors can only be allowed if the audit firm is contracting with and reimbursing the internal auditors.

c. The Lawrence Center for the Performing Arts receives government financial assistance and is subject to *Government Auditing Standards*. The auditor's responsibilities associated with this engagement include all of the following except
(1) assessing whether management has identified laws and regulations that have a direct and material effect on determination of amounts in the financial statements.
(2) obtaining an understanding of the impact of laws and regulations that have a direct and material effect on the determination of financial statement amounts.

(3) communicating to management and the audit committee that an audit performed purely in accordance with generally accepted auditing standards may not be sufficient if there are additional regulatory requirements.
(4) obtaining sufficient evidence to form an opinion on internal control over compliance.

DISCUSSION QUESTIONS AND PROBLEMS

26-20 **(OBJECTIVES 26-1, 26-4)** Lajod Company has an internal audit department consisting of a manager and three staff auditors. The manager of internal audit, in turn, reports to the corporate controller. Copies of audit reports are routinely sent to the audit committee of the board of directors as well as to the corporate controller and the individual responsible for the area or activity being audited.

The manager of internal audit is aware that the external auditors have relied on the internal audit function to a substantial degree in the past. However, recently the external auditors have suggested there may be a problem related to the objectivity of the internal audit function. This objectivity problem may result in more extensive testing and analysis by the external auditors.

The external auditors are concerned about the amount of nonaudit work performed by the internal audit department. The percentage of nonaudit work performed by the internal auditors in recent years has increased to about 25% of their total hours worked. A sample of five recent nonaudit activities are as follows:

1. One of the internal auditors assisted in the preparation of policy statements on internal control. These statements included such things as policies regarding sensitive payments and standards of control for internal controls.
2. The bank statements of the corporation are reconciled each month as a regular assignment for one of the internal auditors. The corporate controller believes this strengthens internal controls because the internal auditor is not involved in the receipt and disbursement of cash.
3. The internal auditors are asked to review the budget data in every area each year for relevance and reasonableness before the budget is approved. In addition, an internal auditor examines the variances each month, along with the associated explanations. These variance analyses are prepared by the corporate controller's staff after consultation with the individuals involved.
4. One of the internal auditors has recently been involved in the design, installation, and initial operation of a new computer system. The auditor was primarily concerned with the design and implementation of internal accounting controls and the computer application controls for the new system. The auditor also conducted the testing of the controls during the test runs.
5. The internal auditors are often asked to make accounting entries for complex transactions before the transactions are recorded. The employees in the accounting department are not adequately trained to handle such transactions. In addition, this serves as a means of maintaining internal control over complex transactions. The manager of internal audit has always made an effort to remain independent of the corporate controller's office and believes that the internal auditors are objective and independent in their audit and nonaudit activities.

Required

a. Define *objectivity* as it relates to the internal audit function.
b. For each of the five situations outlined, explain whether the objectivity of Lajod Company's internal audit department has been materially impaired. Consider each situation independently.
c. The manager of internal audit reports to the corporate controller.
   (1) Does this reporting relationship result in a problem of objectivity? Explain your answer.
   (2) Would your answer to any of the five situations in requirement b. have changed if the manager of internal audit reported to the audit committee of the board of directors? Explain your answer.*

*Based on CMA question paper.

26-21 **(OBJECTIVE 26-1)** The Institute of Internal Auditors (IIA) is an international professional association of more than 180,000 members, with global headquarters in Altamonte Springs, Florida. Throughout the world, the IIA is recognized as the internal audit profession's leader in certification, education, research, and technical guidance. Visit the IIA Web site (www.theiia.org) to answer questions about the IIA and certification of internal auditors.

Required

a. Why should an organization have an internal auditing department? (Hint: Click on the "About Us" link and review the information under the "About the Profession" link.)
b. Visit the link for "Certifications" and identify the six steps to receiving a certification in internal auditing as a Certified Internal Auditor (CIA).
c. What certifications are available to internal auditors?
d. What are the three parts of the CIA exam? How are the requirements for passing the CIA exam similar to and different from those of the CPA exam?

26-22 **(OBJECTIVE 26-2)** The audit firm of Waggoner and Allen, LLP, recently received a request to submit a proposal to audit the financial statements of the Williamson County Public School System. The system is funded mostly through property tax assessments of county residents, but it also receives over $15 million in federal financial funding in addition to private foundation gifts. State law requires all county school systems to engage a CPA to conduct an external audit of the school system's financial statements in accordance with *Government Auditing Standards*. While Waggoner and Allen has never audited a governmental entity, it is seriously considering submitting a proposal to conduct the audit of the school system. The firm asked you to prepare information to help them make a decision about whether to pursue the engagement.

Required

Please respond with your answers to the following questions:

a. Who issues *Government Auditing Standards* and what are the most notable differences between those standards and the AICPA auditing standards?
b. What impact, if any, does the receipt of federal financial assistance have on the audit process?
c. How might the auditor's consideration of materiality and internal control differ from the audit of a commercial enterprise?
d. What types of reports in addition to the report on the audit of the financial statements will Waggoner and Allen need to issue?
e. How might acceptance of this engagement affect training of Waggoner and Allen staff?

26-23 **(OBJECTIVES 26-4, 26-5)** Haskin Company was founded 40 years ago and now has several manufacturing plants in the Northeast and Midwest. The evaluation of proposed capital expenditures became increasingly difficult for management as the company became geographically dispersed and diversified its product line. Thus, the Capital Budgeting Group was organized in 2015 to review all capital expenditure proposals in excess of $100,000.

The Capital Budgeting Group conducts its annual planning and budget meeting each September for the upcoming calendar year. The group establishes a minimum return for investments (hurdle rate) and estimates a target level of capital expenditures for the next year based on the expected available funds. The group then reviews the capital expenditure proposals that have been submitted by the various operating segments. Proposals that meet either the return on investment criterion or a critical need criterion are approved to the extent of available funds.

The Capital Budgeting Group also meets monthly, as necessary, to consider any projects of a critical nature that were not expected or requested in the annual budget review. These monthly meetings allow the Capital Budgeting Group to make adjustments during the year as new developments occur.

Haskin's profits have been decreasing slightly for the past two years despite a small but steady sales growth, a sales growth that is expected to continue through 2017. As a result of the profit stagnation, top management is emphasizing cost control and all aspects of Haskin's operations are being reviewed for cost reduction opportunities.

Haskin's internal audit department has become involved in the companywide cost reduction effort. The department has already identified several areas where cost reductions could be realized and has made recommendations to implement the necessary procedures to effect the cost savings. Tom Watson, internal audit director, is now focusing on the activities of the Capital Budgeting Group in an attempt to determine the efficiency and effectiveness of the capital budgeting process.

In an attempt to gain a better understanding of the capital budgeting process, Watson decided to examine the history of one capital project in detail. A capital expenditure proposal of Haskin's Burlington Plant that was approved by the Capital Budgeting Group in 2016 was selected randomly from a population of all proposals approved by the group at its 2015 and 2016 annual planning and budget meetings.

The Burlington proposal consisted of a request for five new machines to replace equipment that was 20 years old and for which preventive maintenance had become expensive. Four of the machines were for replacement purposes, and the fifth was for planned growth in demand. Each of the four replacement machines was expected to result in annual maintenance cost savings of $20,000. The fifth machine was exactly like the other four and was expected to generate an annual contribution of $30,000 through increased output. Each machine had a cost of $110,000 and an estimated useful life of eight years.

Required

a. Identify and discuss the issues that Haskin Company's internal audit department must address in its examination and evaluation of Burlington Plant's 2016 capital expenditure project.

b. Recommend procedures to be used by Haskin's internal audit department in the audit review of Burlington Plant's 2016 capital expenditure project.*

26-24 **(OBJECTIVES 26-4, 26-5)** Lecimore Company has a centralized purchasing department that is managed by Meg Shen. Shen has established policies and procedures to guide the clerical staff and purchasing agents in the day-to-day operation of the department. She is satisfied that these policies and procedures are in conformity with company objectives and believes there are no major problems in the regular operations of the purchasing department.

Lecimore's internal audit department was assigned to perform an operational audit of the purchasing function. Their first task was to review the specific policies and procedures established by Shen. The policies and procedures are as follows:

- All significant purchases are made on a competitive bid basis. The probability of timely delivery, reliability of vendor, and so forth, are taken into consideration on a subjective basis.
- Detailed specifications of the minimum acceptable quality for all goods purchased are provided to vendors.
- Vendors' adherence to the quality specifications is the responsibility of the materials manager of the inventory control department and not the purchasing department. The materials manager inspects the goods as they arrive to be sure that the quality meets the minimum standards and then sees that the goods are transferred from the receiving dock to the storeroom.
- All purchase requests are prepared by the materials manager based on the production schedule for a four-month period.

The internal audit staff then observed the operations of the purchasing function and gathered the following findings:

- One vendor provides 90% of a critical raw material. This vendor has a good delivery record and is reliable. Furthermore, this vendor has been the low bidder over the past few years.
- As production plans change, rush and expedite orders are made by production directly to the purchasing department. Materials ordered for cancelled production runs are stored for future use. The costs of these special requests are borne by the purchasing department. Shen considers the additional costs associated with these special requests as "costs of being a good member of the corporate team."

*Based on CMA question paper.

- Materials to accomplish engineering changes are ordered by the purchasing department as soon as the changes are made by the engineering department. Shen is proud of the quick response by the purchasing staff to product changes. Materials on hand are not reviewed before any orders are placed.
- Partial shipments and advance shipments (that is, those received before the requested date of delivery) are accepted by the materials manager, who notifies the purchasing department of the receipt. The purchasing department is responsible for follow-up on partial shipments. No action is taken to discourage advance shipments.

Required

Based on the purchasing department's policies and procedures and the findings of Lecimore's internal audit staff:

a. Identify deficiencies and/or inefficiencies in Lecimore Company's purchasing function.

b. Make recommendations for those deficiencies/inefficiencies that you identify.*

Use the following format in preparing your response:

Deficiencies/Inefficiencies	Recommendations
1.	1.

26-25 **(OBJECTIVES 26-4, 26-5)** Superior Co. manufactures automobile parts for sale to the major U.S. automakers. Superior's internal audit staff is to review the internal controls over machinery and equipment and make recommendations for improvements when appropriate. The internal auditors obtained the following information during the assignment:

- Requests for purchase of machinery and equipment are normally initiated by the supervisor in need of the asset. The supervisor discusses the proposed acquisition with the plant manager. A purchase requisition is submitted to the purchasing department when the plant manager is satisfied that the request is reasonable and that there is a remaining balance in the plant's share of the total corporate budget for capital acquisitions.
- Upon receiving a purchase requisition for machinery or equipment, the purchasing department manager looks through the records for an appropriate supplier. A formal purchase order is then completed and mailed. When the machine or equipment is received, it is immediately sent to the user department for installation. This allows the economic benefits from the acquisition to be realized at the earliest possible date.
- The property, plant, and equipment ledger control accounts are supported by computerized depreciation lapse schedules organized by year of acquisition. These lapse schedules are used to compute depreciation as a unit for all assets of a given type that are acquired in the same year. Standard rates, depreciation methods, and salvage values are used for each major type of fixed assets. These rates, methods, and salvage values were set 10 years ago during the company's initial year of operation.
- When machinery or equipment is retired, the plant manager notifies the accounting department so that the appropriate entries can be made in the accounting records.
- There has been no reconciliation since the company began operations between the accounting records and the machinery and equipment on hand.

Required

Identify the internal control deficiencies and recommend improvements that the internal audit staff of Superior Co. should include in its report regarding the internal controls over fixed assets. Use the following format in preparing your answer:*

Deficiencies	Recommendations
1.	1.

*Based on CMA question paper.

INDEX

NOTE: **Essential Terms appear in Boldface**

A

D

E

Q

R

S

T

U

V

W

Y

CREDITS

Chapter 1: p. 3, Naj/Fotolia

Chapter 2: p. 24, adimas/Fotolia

Chapter 3: p. 46, Justaman/Fotolia

Chapter 4: p. 78, Andrew Martin/Fotolia; p. 85 bulleted list, © 2015, AICPA. All rights reserved. Used by permission; p. 87 numbered list, © 2015, AICPA. All rights reserved. Used by permission; pp. 89-102 excerpts, Copyright by American Institute of CPAs. All rights reserved. Used with permission

Chapter 5: p. 114, sergign/Fotolia; p. 117 text excerpt, A Treatise on the Law of Torts: Or the Wrongs which Arise Independent of Contract, by Thomas M. Cooley

Chapter 6: p. 142, Vladimir Wrangel/Fotolia; p. 158 bulleted list, from Auditing Standard No. 15 - Financial Statement Assertions

Chapter 7: p. 179, chatchaiyo/Fotolia

Chapter 8: p. 220, Keith Wood/Corbis

Chapter 9: p. 261, bloomua/Fotolia

Chapter 10: p. 297, Keystone-France\ Gamma-Rapho/Getty Images

Chapter 11: p. 335, Focus Pocus LTD/Fotolia

Chapter 12: p. 367, BillionPhotos.com/ Fotolia

Chapter 13: p. 408, Wavebreak Media Ltd/123RF

Chapter 14: p. 446, boscorelli/Fotolia

Chapter 15: p. 482, acnaleksy/Fotolia

Chapter 16: p. 524, adam121/Fotolia

Chapter 17: p. 564, WavebreakMediaMicro/ Fotolia

Chapter 18: p. 604, Andrey Popov/Fotolia

Chapter 19: p. 636, Vladyslav Danilin/Fotolia

Chapter 20: p. 662, eXpose/Fotolia

Chapter 21: p. 685, Rolandino/Fotolia

Chapter 22: p. 715, frenk58/Fotolia

Chapter 23: p. 736, Niki Love/Fotolia

Chapter 24: p. 766, javiindy/Fotolia

Chapter 25: p. 799, Volodymyr Kyrylyuk/Fotolia

Chapter 26: p. 826, Gary Blakeley/Fotolia

Hillsburg Hardware Insert: p. 1 left to right, Esin Deniz/Fotolia; Mr Twister/Fotolia; markobe/ Fotolia; p. 3, Monkey Business/Fotolia; p. 4 left to right, Michael Levy/Shutterstock; omkar.a.v/ Shutterstock; photocell/Shutterstock; Chad McDermott/Shutterstock; p. 5, BillionPhotos. com/Fotolia; p. 6 bottom left, golubovy/Fotolia: right, top to bottom, ostill/Shutterstock; EDHAR/Shutterstock; Monkey Business/Fotolia; szefei/Shutterstock; Kurhan/Fotolia; Carlos E. Santa Maria/Shutterstock; Kurhan/Fotolia; Steve Cukrov/Shutterstock; p. 7, Sergii Moscaliuk/ Fotolia; p. 9 left to right, Shebeko/Shutterstock; Alex Kuzovlev/Shutterstock; STILLFX/Shutter-stock; Shutterstock; p. 11 left to right, Pi-Lens/ Shutterstock; Andrew Williams/Shutterstock; Melissa King/Shutterstock; sint/Shutterstock; p. 12 left to right, hektoR/Shutterstock; Olegusk/ Shutterstock; Olegusk/Shutterstock; Artography/ Shutterstock; p. 13, francescodemarco/Fotolia

Instructions:

Visit the ACL promo page (https://accounts.aclgrc.com/promo) and enter the promotional code printed below. Each promotional code can only be redeemed once.

An organization account will be created with you as the only member.

You will receive two emails: one describing your software entitlement and the other containing instructions how to activate your user account and set your password.

P6B-2S9-C8W